The
Judicial
Process

The Judicial Process

An Introductory Analysis
of the Courts of the
United States, England,
and France

FIFTH EDITION

Henry J. Abraham
University of Virginia

New York   Oxford
Oxford University Press
1986

Oxford University Press

Oxford   New York   Toronto
Delhi   Bombay   Calcutta   Madras   Karachi
Petaling Jaya   Singapore   Hong Kong   Tokyo
Nairobi   Dar es Salaam   Cape Town
Melbourne   Auckland

and associated companies in
Beirut   Berlin   Ibadan   Nicosia

Library of Congress Cataloging-in-Publication Data
Abraham, Henry Julian, 1921–
    The judicial process.
    Bibliography: p.
    Includes indexes.
    1. Courts—United States.   2. Courts—Great Britain.
3. Courts—France.   4. Judicial process.
I. Title.
K2100.A725   1986   347'.01   85-15261
ISBN 0-19-503713-8   342.71

Printing (last digit):   9   8   7   6   5   4   3   2   1

Printed in the United States of America
on acid-free paper

To
Philip

Preface
to the
Fifth Edition

Initially published in 1962, revised in 1968, 1975, and 1980, *The Judicial Process*'s continued widespread usage at home and abroad has justified a fifth edition. Since the fourth edition appeared, the book has been translated into several languages, including Korean and Chinese, and it has been published under the auspices of Oxford University Press in a number of British, Canadian, and Indian cities. Most gratifying, of course, has been its continued use in the United States by what is now well into a second generation of students.

The latest edition has been thoroughly revised and updated through the 1984–1985 term of the Supreme Court, thus taking cognizance of developments through June–July 1985. Although the work's scope and approach remain those of the original edition, a plethora of changes will be found in its pages—changes on both the domestic and the international frontiers of the judicial process, with approximately one-third of the contents reflecting these changes. Among these are significant new developments in the organization and staffing of courts on all levels, the alterations brought about by the two Reagan Administrations, important changes wrought in the judiciaries of England and Wales and France, and the impact on the judicial branch of new personalities off as well as on the bench. In effect, chapters 2, 3, 4, and 5 have been rewritten; chapter 6 has been accorded a thorough overhaul with the aid of foreign colleagues; and the remaining four chapters have also been carefully restructured to recognize changes and new insights. Close to two dozen tables, charts, and figures are included, as well as two major appendices, three indices, and the four selected bibliographies that now comprise some six thousand listings—the most extensive compilation of its kind extant as an appendix to any current book in the field.

Once again I happily acknowledge my profound debt to a host of colleagues—new as well as old—too numerous to mention, who not only encouraged me to undertake this fifth edition but also generously and readily provided salient assistance. Once again, too, I am especially beholden to my friend Alan H. Bray, M.A. (Oxon.), of Middle Temple Inn, London, Barrister-at-Law, whose unselfish counsel and painstaking reading of the expanded sections on England and Wales were crucial; to my colleagues Paul Shoup at the University of Virginia and Alvin Z. Rubinstein at the University of Pennsylvania, who aided with the data on the Soviet Union; to Professor Giovanni Bognetti of the University of Pavia, who provided much-needed insight on segments pertaining to the special Italian and Austrian tribunals; to my long-time fellow "con law" devotee and colleague, Donald P. Kommers of Notre Dame University, whose expertise on the judiciary of West Germany—and particularly its *Bundesverfassungsgericht*—was indispensable; and to my valued associate in the comparative judicial process, Dr. Margherita Rendel of the Human Rights Division of the University of London's Institute of Education, who did so much to render the materials on France both more current and more comprehensible.

The Mayer and Arlene Mitchell and Abraham A. Mitchell Fund of The Mobile Community Foundation, the Robert W. and Patricia T. Gelfman Fund of The Jewish Communal Fund of New York, and the Earhart Foundation provided deeply appreciated financial research assistance. Susan Rabiner of Oxford University Press was an invaluable editor. Barbara A. Perry, my research assistant, was a veritable tower of strength and gave of her time and intellectual resources far beyond her assignments with unfailing good nature. James S. Todd IV, Linda McClain, and Gregor Baer contributed their talents cheerfully and effectively; and Shirley A. Kohut was a superb typist. My students, of course, were an unceasing source of inspiration and resolve, and my wife, Mildred, and son, Peter, never failed to be supportive as well as constructively critical.

When I wrote the first edition of this book twenty-five years ago, I dedicated it to our older son, Philip, then a four-year-old. Now a college graduate, a member of Governor Robb's 1982–86 administration, married to Janet, and about to enter law school, he remains a staunch fan of *his* book—which is rededicated to him with pride and love.

Charlottesville, Va.   H.J.A.
November 1985

Preface
to the
First Edition

When my *Courts and Judges: An Introduction to the Judicial Process* appeared in 1959, I began its preface by pointing to the general absence of even the most rudimentary knowledge of the judicial process on the part of the vast majority of students of political science entering elementary or even advanced courses and observed that equally striking was the unavailability of accessible materials providing basic data in the field. The measure of success my small book has enjoyed encouraged the writing of the present volume, which is far more ambitious in scope than its predecessor.

This new book is a selective comparative introduction to the judicial process and seeks to analyze and evaluate the main institutions and considerations that affect the administration of justice under law. The rather extensive coverage of certain significant features and elements of comparative judicial processes was prompted not only by several helpful suggestions by users of the earlier book but by the continued neglect of these processes in basic textbooks.

An important segment of this work is thus devoted to the judicial process in England and Wales, France, and—to a necessarily considerably lesser extent in this context—the Soviet Union. Other states are included whenever appropriate, especially in connection with the doctrine and practice of judicial review. Nonetheless, over half of the material deals with the judicial process in the United States.

The detailed Contents obviates capsule explanations of the substance of each chapter in this volume. I have compiled numerous graphs, figures, and charts, all designed to facilitate comprehension. There are two indices—one general and one for cases. And there are four extensive bibliographies dealing with (1) works in general on American constitutional law, (2) biographies and autobiographies of and by Justices of the U.S. Supreme Court, (3) comparative constitutional law, and (4) civil liberties.

Although I have endeavored to be objective in analysis and presentation throughout, in some circumstances it is neither possible nor desirable to shun value judgments; I have thus stated frankly my own opinions where it seemed appropriate to do so.

Once again I express my profound appreciation to the many colleagues who stimulated and urged me on in the writing of this book and whose generous suggestions were so helpful. I am especially grateful to Professors William M. Beaney, David Fellman, Wallace Mendelson, Jewell Cass Phillips, and R. J. Tresolini. Above all, I owe a particular debt of gratitude to Mr. James Wellwood, M.A., of Gray's Inn, Barrister-at-Law, Lecturer in Law at King's College, University of London, for his unselfish counsel and essential criticism on the sections on England and Wales. As they have been throughout my pleasant association with Oxford University Press, Mr. Byron S. Hollinshead, Jr., and Miss Leona Capeless have been delightful and invaluable co-workers. Mrs. Helen White performed the thankless but essential task of typing the entire manuscript cheerfully and efficiently. Whatever errors remain are mine. My wife, Mildred, gave me the kind of constant encouragement and confidence that only a devoted partner can provide.

And the book is happily dedicated to one who also helped in his own way.

Wynnewood, Pa.   H.J.A.
February 1962

Contents

Tables
Charts
and Figures

TABLES

CHARTS

FIGURES

The
Judicial
Process

1

Introduction:
The Law
and the Courts

Respect for the law is one of the select group of principles that we have come to regard as essential to the effective and equitable operation of popular government. As a democratic principle it is recognized as binding on both the governed and those who govern.

In fostering this principle the role of the judiciary is crucial, for, in the words of Mr. Justice Arthur T. Vanderbilt:

> . . . it is in the courts and not in the legislature that our citizens primarily feel the keen, cutting edge of the law. If they have respect for the work of their courts, their respect for law will survive the shortcomings of every other branch of government; but if they lose their respect for the work of the courts, their respect for law and order will vanish with it to the great detriment of society.[1]

This is true whether the judicial branch be technically separated from the other two branches of government, as in the United States, partly fused with them, as in France, or largely fused, as in England. The law will be respected as long as it is interpreted and applied within the structures of justice as accepted by the majority of society—in the long run, if not always in the short. Law is, after all, the expressed will of those who rule society.

But the law, in its procedural as well as its substantive aspects, is essentially made and administered by persons whose views and interpretations are buffeted by the winds of change through the years, so that it has become a "truism that the quality of justice depends more on the quality of the men

---

[1] *The Challenge of Law Reform* (Princeton, NJ: Princeton University Press, 1955), pp. 4–5.

[and women] who administer the law than on the content of the law they administer."[2] Judicial activity, observed Roscoe Pound in one of his lectures, is really the creative element in law. Accordingly, if humankind's great interest on earth is justice, as Daniel Webster put it, then perhaps a more immediate interest is the securing of the most highly qualified individuals to administer justice impartially with a minimum of chicanery and obfuscation. It follows logically that judges must be assured of an optimum degree of independence and relative freedom from prejudicial pressures from forces both inside and outside of government. Moreover, they must be able to function in a hierarchical structure that is effectively conducive to the performance of the basic task at hand—the impartial administration of justice under law.

They pursue this task through the medium of a court, an institution of government. As Carl Brent Swisher noted concisely, along with such other characteristics as it may incidentally possess, a court

> ... determines the facts involved in particular controversies brought before it, relates the facts to the relevant law, settles the controversies in terms of the law, and more or less incidentally makes new law through the process of decision. Over the centuries of Anglo-American history our judiciary has been developed and geared to this process so that it has an integrity or integratedness peculiarly its own. In particular it has a mode of informing the minds of the responsible officers—in this instance the judges—which is unique and which must be kept in sharp focus in any attempt to estimate the capacity of a judiciary to perform competitively in the gray areas which lie between it and institutions which are primarily legislative or executive.[3]

THE NATURE OF LAW

For centuries humankind has discussed the nature of law. In one way or another, it touches every citizen of every nation. The contact may be pleasant or unpleasant, tangible or intangible, direct or indirect, but it is nonetheless a constant force in the lives of people everywhere on the globe. It is essential that we have some understanding of its nature and of the human beings who interpret and administer it.

"What is Law?" has been asked by priests and poets, philosophers and kings, by masses no less than by prophets. A host of answers might be given, yet the answer to the question remains one of the most persistent and elusive problems in the whole range of thought. For one may well view the entire gamut of human life, both in thought and in action, as being comprised

---

[2]Evan Haynes, *The Selection and Tenure of Judges* (Newark, NJ: National Conference of Judicial Councils, 1944), p. 5.

[3]Presidential Address, delivered before the American Political Science Association, New York City, September 8, 1960. (Reprinted in 54 *American Political Science Review* 879–80, December 1960.)

within the concept Law[4] (although a legal system is in fact but part of a larger social order).

It may seem strange that the true essence of such a ubiquitous phenomenon as law should be beyond the grasp of general human understanding. Because law deals with human conduct, to grasp its nature it would appear necessary merely to distinguish it from the other factors relating to that conduct: religion, science, morals, ethics, customs. Yet herein lies the difficulty, so ably stated by James Coolidge Carter more than half a century ago:

> Law, Custom, Conduct, Life—different names for almost the same thing—true names for different aspects of the same thing—are so inseparably blended together that one cannot even be thought of without the other. No improvement can be effected in one without improving the other, and no retrogression can take place in one without a corresponding decline in the other.[5]

There is little doubt that law has much in common with all these other aspects of human conduct, yet it is true that it also possesses at least one characteristic unique to it and lacking in all others: its sanction is applied exclusively by organized political government.

Three Historical Categories. Some kind of law has always existed[6]—however inadequate, or even entirely absent, both legal organization and enforcement machinery may have been. First came *primitive* law, based chiefly on primitive custom and lacking even rudimentary machinery and organization. Still prevailing among some of the aboriginal Indian, Oceanic, and Asiatic tribes, it has always been the law of those "preliterate" peoples who have recognized social rules and have discovered means of coping with social conflict.

Archaic law, featuring some manner of courts and officialdom—institutions that are basic to every legal system—and introducing certain codes of procedure and substance, arrived on the scene during the early days of Rome and among primitive Germanic and African tribes. However, Moses' *Pentateuch,* given in the fifteenth century B.C., may well lay an earlier claim. Certainly the *Great Sanhedrin,* the seventy-one-man supreme council of the Jewish nation in Greco-Roman days, prior to the destruction of the Temple in Jerusalem by Roman forces in A.D. 70, was a judicial body, headed by a chief

---

[4]William A. Robson, *Civilization and the Growth of Law* (New York: Macmillan Co., 1935), p. 3.

[5]*Law: Its Origin, Growth and Function* (New York and London: The Knickerbocker Press, 1907), p. 320.

[6]The earliest known system of written law was the Code of Hammurabi, so named in honor of its founder, a king of Babylonia. It was promulgated about 2050 B.C.—there is considerable disagreement among scholars on the precise decade or even century (estimates vary from 2067 to 1662 B.C.)—and was the embodiment of the existing rules and customs of the land. It presented the idea that justice was humankind's inherent right, derived from supernatural forces rather than being given by royally bestowed favor.

justice, which enacted decrees of religious observance *and* interpreted the law of the Hebrews.

Mature law heralded the professionalization of the law. It fathered the law we know today. As Roman law it existed from the third century B.C. to the fall of Rome. As English law it appeared in the twelfth century.

POSITIVE AND NATURAL LAW

The three kinds of law cited earlier are prongs of *positive law*, the type of law with which we will be concerned throughout this book. It is held to derive from man for the purpose of ruling man; it is a command based on the relationship between ruler and ruled; its primary nature is that it is *man-made*. It springs from no source higher than the human will. This is what John Chipman Gray alluded to when he defined a man's legal rights as

> ... power which he has to make a person or persons do or refrain from doing a certain act or ... acts, as far as the power arises from society.[7]

In other words, according to the tenets of positive law—as defined by John Austin, the English utilitarian jurist (1790–1859) who, inspired by the French social theorist Auguste Comte (1798–1857), became the founder of the analytical school of jurisprudence—law consists of definite rules of human conduct with appropriate sanctions for their enforcement, both of these being prescribed by duly constituted human authority.

Natural Law. But in the eyes of many there is another category of law, *natural law*, known also as "higher law" or "the law of nature." This is law that would be binding on human societies in the absence of, or as a supplement to, positive law. Witness, for example, its impact on the American Declaration of Independence and the Constitution,[8] its citation by conscientious objectors to military conscription, and its invocation by the civil rights movements of the 1950s and 1960s—for instance, by the Reverend Dr. Martin Luther King's exhortations to disobey "unjust" laws. The theory of natural law originated with the Stoics, by whom it was regarded as embodying those rules of justice discernible by right reason. This view was sometimes taken by Roman jurists; thus, the statesman and theorist Cicero (106–43 B.C.), in defining law, was explicit in stating his concept of its essence:

> Law is the highest reason, implanted in Nature, which commands what ought to be done and forbids the opposite ... the origin of justice is to be found in law, for law is its natural force; it is the mind and reason of the intelligent man, the standards by which justice and injustice are measured.

---

[7] *The Nature and Sources of Law* (New York: Columbia University Press, 1916), p. 19.
[8] Its classic exposition in that connection is Edward S. Corwin's superb *The Higher Law Background of American Constitutional Law* (Ithaca, NY: Cornell University Press, 1929), known to every student of constitutional law and the judicial process.

I shall seek the root of justice in nature. . . . [9]

Justinian (483-565) adopted Ulpian's (170-228) definition of natural law as that law which "nature has taught all living beings," thus forecasting the modern bionomic view. The Scholastics generally regarded natural law as that part of the divine law which is not directly revealed but is discernible to reason; and the Rationalists of the eighteenth century derived from their analysis of human societies certain *natural rights* as to life, liberty, and the pursuit of happiness—which they regarded as of prior validity to institutional law.[10] Hence, it is the thread of rationality that holds the system together and gives it a definite order:

> . . . the universe obeys God; seas and lands obey the universe, and human life is subject to the decree of supreme law.[11]

It would seem that natural law thus stands on two assumptions: first, the rationality and intelligence of man; second, the existence of a higher *rational* order of things. Because man is presumed to be intelligent, he can readily "find" the law—that is, understand the higher rational order.

Without endeavoring to prove or disprove this theory and estimate of man, his history at least places the issue in doubt. At best, it appears that man is as capable of capricious action based on passion as he is of rational action based on intelligence. If man's intelligence is placed in doubt, so is his ability to understand a higher rational order. Indeed, it is difficult for man to believe in a higher order or a universal law of justice because of what he sees in real life—as Carneades pointed out so many years ago. Oliver Wendell Holmes, Jr., who rejected natural law with vehemence and sarcasm—for which he was scathingly attacked in word and in print by, among others, prominent Jesuit law professors—regarded it as "mystic overlaw" and the "product of wishful thinking."[12]

Nonetheless, today natural law is identifiable with the abiding sense of justice that pervades the community of man—regardless of its changing substance—a sense of justice based on a body of rules and customs that the general development of mankind shows to be essential to human society. But it is the positive law that finally governs us as law-abiding members of organized society. And, as we shall presently see, although natural law, like equity, has had a marked influence on the English common law, "it is not the same as common law and has never absorbed it."[13]

---

[9]Cicero, "The Laws," in Francis William Coker, *Readings in Political Philosophy*, rev. ed. (New York: The Macmillan Co., 1955), pp. 145-46.

[10]Webster's *New International Dictionary of the English Language*, 3d ed., unabridged (Springfield, MA: G. & C. Merriam Co., 1966).

[11]Cicero, op, cit., p. 151.

[12]See Francis Biddle, *Justice Holmes, Natural Law, and the Supreme Court* (New York: The Macmillan Co., 1961), especially ch. # 2, "The Attack on Justice Holmes."

[13]Ibid., p. 31.

COMMON LAW AND STATUTORY LAW

For our purposes, then, law, broadly speaking, represents the rules of conduct that pertain to a given political order of society, rules that are backed by the organized force of the community. As it has evolved through the centuries, law has been made either by the political representatives of the people— sometimes rather inaccurately styled "bar-made" law—or it has been "bench-made" by judges and justices. The former type is generally known as *statutory law*, the latter as *common law*. Both will bear close examination, but, at the risk of some oversimplification, the crucial distinction between the two is that between codified written law and unwritten law based on custom and tradition. (The terms *bar-made* and *bench-made* are never used in England; there they are called *statutory* and *judge-made*.)

COMMON LAW

Utilized by most English-speaking states, *common law* is variously known also as *English, Anglo-Saxon,* or *Anglo-American law*. Despite its conceptualization by Lord Coke as "the perfection of reason," it is indeed a vast and complex instrument of justice. Although at first glance it may well seem chaotic and abstruse, on closer examination its many diverse components can readily be discerned to be logical, bound into a comprehensive and comprehensible entity.[14]

Common law is judge-made, bench-made law rather than a fixed body of definite rules such as the modern civil law codes. In Roscoe Pound's words, it is a "mode of judicial and juristic thinking, a mode of treating legal problems."[15] He might well have added "a mood." Often based on precedents, common law embodies continuity in that it binds the present with the past. Since it thus necessarily grew, and still grows, by virtue of judicial decisions, it is best to explain and analyze it historically.

Historical Background. With the growth of Christianity and Christian philosophy came the decline and fall of Rome. The concept of the state as the highest form of society began to be questioned with the rise of the Christian Church. With the Norman invasion of the British Isles in 1066, precise and orderly methods were introduced into the government and law of England. Thus began, under the Norman and Angevin monarchs of the eleventh and twelfth centuries, the gradual growth of a central administration and the development of the courts of law. The term *common law* was used for the law developed in the Kings's Courts and was generally employed to distinguish between this law and that of the ecclesiastical courts. In effect, the concept of common law was adopted from the *canon law* of the Christian Church, which was the common law of Christendom. Thus, the common law

---

[14]For an excellent description see F. H. Lawson, *The Rational Strength of English Law* (Stevens, 1951).

[15]Roscoe Pound, *The Spirit of the Common Law* (Boston: Little, Brown and Co., 1921), p.1.

came into use in the reign of Edward I (1272–1307) or just shortly thereafter. It meant "general" as opposed to "special" law; the law common to the whole land; unenacted law as distinguished from statutes and ordinances; the law of the temporal as opposed to the ecclesiastical courts. Later, common law came to be contrasted with equity.[16] The common law of the King's Courts was made by the royal justices from the mass of customary law of the realm and became the common law of England.

There were three great courts of common law: *King's Bench, Exchequer,* and *Common Pleas.* As the routine of these royal courts were firmly established, it became possible to forecast their decisions in terms of similar cases decided by them in the past. However, according to Theodore F. T. Plucknett,[17] the practice of basing decisions on precedent did not come about because it was the best rule to follow in decision making, but because it enabled all existing courts to function with a minimum of trouble.

In at least some respects the common law reflects the feudal structure from which it was derived. Over a period of centuries the law defining the relationship between the Anglo-Norman monarchs and their tenants-in-chief became the law that was applicable to all Englishmen. At first this dealt solely with private law, but it was gradually extended to cover public law as well. The core of the feudal law was the concept of fealty, which long prevailed after the passing of feudalism. Ruler as well as subject was bound—there were well-defined rights and obligations to be adhered to by all parties. Private rights of freemen were not subject to arbitrary change, and the primary task of the monarch was to preserve and protect the law.

But the groups whose rights the monarch had to acknowledge were limited to the nobility, the landed gentry, and some segments of the rising bourgeoisie. Hence it is hardly astonishing that the common law—which was essentially a law of property, in particular landed property—was "regarded by the politically influential class ... as its shield."[18] During the twelfth and thirteenth centuries, however, the practice of issuing *royal writs* was introduced—although they were then practically confined to a few classes of civil cases. But early in the reign of Henry II (1154–89)—often termed the Father of the Common Law, though some would credit Henry I (1100–35) with that title—an ordinance proclaiming that no man could be denied his freehold without a royal writ rendered centralization in a royal court inevitable. This was followed by several writs that continued the trend and culminated in the *Assize of Novel Disseisin of 1166,* ordaining that anyone who was denied his

---

[16]"Equity" is discussed on pp. 14–16, *infra.* For an expert analysis of the genesis and concept of common law, see F. W. Maitland, *The Constitutional History of England,* ed. by H. A. L. Fisher (Cambridge: Cambridge University Press, 1961).

[17]Theodore F. T. Plucknett, *A Concise History of the Common Law,* 5th ed. (Boston: Little, Brown and Co., 1956), p. 342.

[18]Sir Charles Ogilvie, *The King's Government and the Common Law: 1471–1641* (Oxford: Basil Blackwell, 1958), p. 6.

freehold could seek immediate remedy in the King's Court. (The Assize also provided for a jury of one's neighbors in questions of fact.) Thus, by 1166 the King was firmly established as the protector of the freehold.

By 1178 the work of the King's Court had become more than King and Council could handle, and five full-time judges were appointed, some of whom would travel about the countryside, settling disputes in each locality according to prevailing custom. They attended to the bulk of the cases, although the monarch and his Council still disposed of "novel and difficult" matters. This arrangement ultimately led to the schema of legal proceedings based on writs, which were issued in ever-increasing numbers and for a fixed price. Until the middle of the thirteenth century the King issued new writs to deal with a host of new problems. However, the barons became increasingly jealous of his power to make law, and in 1258 the King was forbidden to issue writs without the specific consent of his Council. As a result of that restriction, the thirty or forty writs then extant were often interpreted and stretched to deal with problems they were not designed to cope with.[19]

With the founding of the Inns of Court as legal "guilds" in the latter half of the thirteenth century (see chapter 2), unofficial reports of cases commenced to be published in annual *Year Books*. These books were records of court proceedings dealing mainly with procedural points for the benefit of practitioners rather than full reports of "casebook law" in the modern sense. Nevertheless, they quite naturally came to serve as a source of gradually mounting precedents and were frequently referred to by those practitioners in the courts. *Stare decisis et non quieta movere*—stand by past decisions and do not disturb things at rest—began to have genuine meaning as a judicial policy. According to Charles Ogilvie, the first inkling of the future English system of case law may be found in the *Dialogus de Scaccario*, written by Richard Fitz-Nigel between 1177 and 1179:

> There are cases where the courses of events, and the reasons for decisions are obscure; and in these it is enough to cite precedents.[20]

Thus were laid the bases on which the common law rests. As society became more complex, so did the law. At first it was made by the royal courts, but from the thirteenth century on it was always accepted as the supreme and fundamental law of the land. (The Divine Right of Kings was a sixteenth-century idea, not a medieval one—indeed, the second sentence of the Preface to the *Dialogus* had admonished " . . . there is no power but of God.") Bracton or Henry of Bratton (1216–68), a judge of the King's Bench under Henry III (1207–72)—and without equal as a judicial writer until Blackstone came along five centuries later—stated in his *De Legibus* that the King was "under God and the Law . . . for the Law made the King." He was seconded in 1442 by Sir John Fortescue (1394–1476), Chief Justice of the King's Bench, in his

[19] Ibid., p. 13.
[20] Ibid., p. 17.

remarkable treatise, *De Laudibus Legum Angliae*, and by Sir Edmund Plowden (1518–85), chief builder of Middle Temple Hall, who was probably the foremost common law sage, commentator, and interpreter of his time. And the great Sir Edward (later Lord) Coke (1552–1634)—Attorney General, Member of Parliament, and Chief Justice of the Court of Common Pleas—when called before his King, James I (1603–25), echoed his three famed predecessors in declaring that the monarch should also be bound by law. When the King told him that he could not be subject "to any man," Coke replied that, agreed, the King "is not subject to any man, but to God and the law." It was Lord Coke who, more than any other man of his time, compiled and analyzed precedents of common law and who was largely responsible for the increasingly accepted practice of reporting cases fully. From these he drew a set of maxims and rules, later to be amplified and explained precisely by Sir William Blackstone (1723–80). The latter's monumental four-volume work, *Commentaries on the Law of England* (1765–69) was long the bible of legal training in both England and America. Its basic principles remain useful pillars of English and American law.

Any notion that judges are to serve the popular majority was and is utterly wrong. For while the common law recognized the authority of King and Parliament, it required all men to bow to the law and act within its limits. England's judges have ever abided by their judicial oath to "administer the law without fear or favor." Over the years common law was exported to many countries—among them Canada, Australia, New Zealand, India, Pakistan, Israel, and the thirteen colonies that would become the United States. (Scotland, although itself a member of the United Kingdom, is an interesting exception: its existing legal system was derived from Roman law, as were the Continental systems; but it has been greatly influenced by the common law.) It is, of course, important to recognize that ultimately statutory law is supreme. The judges are bound to give effect to an Act of Parliament. Thus, many statutes have modified the common law (e.g., the doctrine of common employment) or have codified it (e.g., the Sale of Goods Act).

Characteristics. As has already been pointed out, common law is predominantly *judge-made law*. Under it the judge is the creator, interpreter, and modifier of laws. Even when he merely "interprets" law, he may well be creating it. To that extent, statutory law, the law enacted by legislative bodies, is tentative. Discussing the benefits of judge-made law, Justice Cardozo pointed out that the judge can use "free scientific research" when analyzing a problem. By "free" he meant that to a very real extent the common law removes the judge from action by positive authority; by "scientific" he meant that there is an objective element in the judge's decision. Thus, the judge may come closer to the just and the true, for law under the common law system develops by "judicial experience in the decision of cases."[21] For example, in 1972 the U.S. Supreme Court, invoking the ancient common law of

---

[21] Pound, op. cit., p. 216.

nuisance, declared unanimously that federal district courts may order polluters to stop fouling the environment.[22]

Another significant characteristic of common law is the doctrine of *precedent*, under which the judges refer to a previous decision or decisions in order to adjudicate the case at issue. The importance of precedent varies with individual judges, for although common law normally recognizes precedent as binding, judges not only may occasionally depart from precedent when it "appears right to do so," but they may distinguish between various precedents in evolving the new law. Moreover, times and conditions change with changing society, and "every age should be mistress of its own law"—an era should not be hampered by outdated law. "It is revolting," wrote Justice Holmes in characteristically forthright language, "to have no better reason for a rule of law than that it was so laid down in the time of Henry IV [1367–1413]. It is still more revolting if the grounds upon which it was laid down have vanished long since, and the rule simply persists from blind imitation of the past."[23] It is the readiness of the common law judges to discard that which does not serve the public that has contributed to the survival and adoption of common law,[24] wholly or partly, in so many lands. Nevertheless, although Justice Cardozo applauded this, he cautioned that while a judge may discard the old and adopt the new, he must remember that the past is often a reflection of the present and must know and understand it, "for the depths are the foundation of the heights."[25] And although Britain's House of Lords, its highest law court, announced in 1966 that it would henceforth no longer consider itself bound by its own precedents, as it had previously, all judges of first instance are bound by the decisions of higher courts, that is, the Court of Appeal or the House of Lords (and the Court of Appeal is bound by the decisions of the House of Lords).[26]

Because common law as such is uncodified, it is generally described as *unwritten law*. However, case precedents really are not unwritten; they are derived from the principles of law embodied in the judgments of cases that are decided and reported. Presumably most courts keep records, although they are not all required to do so—for example, some Justices of the Peace in certain of the constituent states of the United States who are not regarded as "courts of record."

In summary, the common law appears to have three distinct characteristics that together have enabled the system to develop and expand. First is its *vitality and capability to sustain change*. It does not impress its own pecu-

---

[22] *Illinois v. Milwaukee*, 406 U.S. 91.

[23] From an 1897 address, reprinted in his *Collected Legal Papers* (Boston: A. Harcourt, 1920), p. 187.

[24] See ch. 8, *infra*, pp. 345–48, for a more detailed discussion of precedent.

[25] Margaret E. Hall (ed.), *Selected Writings of Benjamin Nathan Cardozo* (New York: Fallon Law Book Company, 1948), p. 78.

[26] See ch. 6, *infra*, for a description of the British judicial system.

liarities on any other law; it only aids in the systematic development of a richer and presumably more just law. Second is its *practical quality*. It is unwilling to accept anything a priori and follows the notion that ideally all laws ought to be tested in the courts. Thus, rules and regulations are treated as working hypotheses, continually re-tested in what Munroe Smith called "those great laboratories of the law, the courts of justice."[27] Third is its *rendition of law as a moral obligation to be obeyed*. The results of the laboratory tests of the law are accepted as valid and everyone is obliged to obey them. After all, in the famous words of Justice Oliver Wendell Holmes, Jr.:

> The common law is not a brooding omnipresence in the sky, but the articulate voice of some sovereign or quasi-sovereign that can be identified.[28]

And as the great jurist put it so well and so hauntingly in his majestic *The Common Law:*

> The life of the law has not been logic; it has been experience. The felt necessities of the time, the prevalent moral and political theories, intuitions of public policy, avowed or unconscious, even the prejudices which judges share with their fellow-men, have had a good deal more to do than syllogism in determining the rules by which men should be governed. The law embodies the story of a nation's development through many centuries, and it cannot be dealt with as if it contained only the axioms and corollaries of a book of mathematics. In order to know what it is, we must know what it has been, and what it tends to become.... The very considerations which judges most rarely mention, and always with an apology, are the secret root from which the law draws all the juices of life. I mean, of course, considerations of what is expedient for the community concerned.[29]

Some three decades later Holmes emphasized this ever-recurring theme in his opinion for the Supreme Court of the United States in *Gompers v. United States:*

> The provisions of the Constitution are not mathematical formulas having their essence in their form; they are organic living institutions transplanted from English soil. Their significance is vital not formal; it is to be gathered not simply by taking the words and a dictionary, but by considering their origin and the line of their growth.[30]

EQUITY

A branch of Anglo-American jurisprudence, born hundreds of years ago and closely related to the common law, *equity* is actually a supplement to the

---

[27] Quoted by Benjamin N. Cardozo, *The Nature of the Judicial Process* (New Haven, CT: Yale University Press, 1921), p. 23.
[28] *Southern Pacific Co. v. Jensen*, 244 U.S. 205 (1916), at 222.
[29] Oliver Wendell Holmes, Jr., *The Common Law* (Boston: Little, Brown and Co., 1881), pp. 1–2.
[30] 233 U.S. 604 (1914), at 610.

common law. Although the *Court of Chancery* did not appear until the fifteenth century, equity courts arose in England in the fourteenth century—apparently as early as 1340—as a result of a practice that permitted a disappointed litigant at common law to lay his plight before his sovereign. That is, he could petition the King to "do right for the love of God and by way of charity," the King being empowered to mold the law for the sake of "justice," to grant the relief prayed for as an act of grace, when the common law gave no remedy, or no adequate remedy.

Chancellor and Chancery. The monarch, on the other hand, habitually referred these petitions to his Chancellor. This member of his Council, who until the Reformation was always a cleric, became known as the "Keeper of the King's Conscience." He was the Council's most important member and the Keeper of the Great Seal, an office to which considerable powers were attached. It was he who could, for example, issue a writ of *subpoena,* commanding a person to appear before a duly constituted legal authority. From many points of view the Chancellor was second in power only to his monarch. Ultimately, the volume of these petitions brought about the establishment of a separate court, the *Court of Chancery.* This was the early court of equity. It maintained its separate existence until 1875, when it was merged in the *Supreme Court of Judicature* by the Judicature Acts of 1873-75. Today, its jurisdiction is exercised mainly by the Chancery Division of the High Court of Justice. But all courts now administer both common law and equity, with equity prevailing in cases of conflict between them; statutes (acts of Parliament) are supreme, however.

The United States of America never had *separate* courts of equity on the federal level. Yet several states retain such separate courts. In others, the same jurist doubles as law judge and equity judge, sitting one day as the former and one as the latter! In still others, no separate equity courts exist at all—the same courts that decide matters of common and statutory law also administer equity.

Defining Equity. But what is equity? We noted that it is a "supplement" to the common law, thus apparently the "conscience" of the law. It is a supplement to the common law in the sense that the principles of equity—which are now part of the fabric of the common law—were developed by the Court of Chancery as an addition to the principles of the medieval common law. Equity began where the law ended, and it is in that role that we know it today. Thus, it created and continues to create precedents. It takes the form of a *judicial decree*—including, since 1875, the award of damages, if deemed appropriate—not of a judgment of "yes" or "no". Equity leaves the judge reasonably free to order *preventive* measures—and under some circumstances even *remedial* ones—usually in the form of a writ, such as an *injunction,* or restraining order, designed to afford a remedy not otherwise obtainable, and traditionally given upon a showing of peril. The judge in the original Court of Chancery exercised his discretion, since remedies in equity were discretionary—and so they are today.

For instance, in equity an injunction may be issued by a judge to prevent members of a local of the United Steel Workers of America from going out on strike without having banked the furnaces of the Jones and Laughlin Steel Corporation, despite the inapplicability of the permissive injunctive provisions of the Norris-LaGuardia Act in this case, and despite the fact that the union had given due notice to strike in accordance with the requirements of the Taft-Hartley Act. True, the steel firm involved could probably recover monetary compensation for resultant damages from its insurance company, or from the USW if it should be found that a contractual provision had been violated by the action of the workers. However, the company here is not interested in such money; its sole aim is to prevent its furnaces from the certain destruction that would result from a failure to bank them. Hence the demand for an equity decree in the form of an injunction against the union.

Another illustration, although considerably less in the realm of immediate peril, might be John Miller's lovely old copper beech on the edge of his private property, directly in the path of a future highway to be built by the Commonwealth of Pennsylvania. The state has every right to chop down the tree under its power of *eminent domain*, provided only that it does so for a public purpose, which a state public highway certainly is, and that it grant just compensation, which it usually does quite liberally in these circumstances. But Mr. Miller is not interested in financial compensation. He wants to continue to enjoy the beauty and shade of the magnificent tree, and the sentimental attachments that go with it—he proposed to his wife under it; his children and grandchildren climbed it with relish for years. Thus, he, too, may appeal to the courts for equity. His chances for success are undoubtedly considerably less than were those of the steel firm mentioned earlier, but judges are human beings as well.

An interesting and troubling question regarding the contemporarily expansive use of equity by American courts, particularly on the egalitarian front, has become whether equitable relief ought to be confined to *proscription* or may also be *prescriptive*, as it has been judicially applied more and more of late. The issue is a volatile one: in fine, it comes down to the core of the parameters of appropriate judicial power and its exercise.[31]

STATUTORY LAW

Despite the origin of the concept of *statutory law*—variously known as *code*, *written*, *Neo-Roman* or *Roman*, or *civil law*—in ancient Rome, its broad application is essentially a modern one. Whereas the common law has dealt traditionally with matters of a private character, with the relations between

---

[31] For a thoughtful analysis of the problem, see Gary L. McDowell, *Equity and the Constitution: The Supreme Court, Equitable Relief, and Public Policy* (Chicago: University of Chicago Press, (1981).

individuals, statutory law is more frequently concerned with society as a whole. It is law that originates with specifically designated, authoritative law-making bodies—presumably legislatures but also executive-administrative decrees and ordinances, treaties, and protocols, all of which are committed to paper.

Historical Background. Although arguably traceable to the far-distant times of Moses, Manu, and Hammurabi, statutory law as we now conceive of it, developed in and from the homogeneous city-state, exemplified by the Codes of Emperor Justinian I (527–65), the *Corpus Juris Civilis*, which was promulgated about A.D. 535. Hence it is frequently referred to as Roman law and, to confuse teachers and students alike, as *civil* law—which has nothing whatever to do with civil jurisdiction.[32] In contrast to diversified England, with its manifold customs that veritably seemed to cry out for some sort of common law, Rome lent itself ideally to the development of a statutory system, one that could be readily written down or codified. Statutory law had—and has, of course—the advantages of preciseness, simplicity, and clear-cut applicability, although it still remains subject to interpretation by administrators as well as judges.

Enacted by legislative and/or executive-administrative bodies of government, codified and spelled out in writing by the legal profession, clearly and readily available for all to see, statutory law has survived as the generally accepted law for most of the states of continental Europe, Russia, Latin America, and many of the newly emergent African nations. Justinian's Code had been initially introduced into western Europe in 544 when the Eastern Empire reconquered Italy. But it did not assume genuine significance for the West until the systematic study of Roman law was revived at the Italian universities in the twelfth century.[33] One of the most famous codifiers was Emperor Napoleon I (1804–15), whose Civil Code was published in 1804, his Code of Civil Procedure in 1807, and other codes subsequently. Indeed, the *Code Napoleon* has been far more enduring than most of the colorful Emperor's military triumphs. Its first major change did not take place until the Gaullist reforms of 1959 that accorded France's married women increased property rights.

"MIXING" COMMON AND STATUTORY LAW

England and the United States today have legal systems based on the common law that readily and naturally found its way across the Atlantic Ocean from the Mother Country to the Colonies. But although it must be categorized as a common law system, the Anglo-American legal framework in effect now consists of a mixture of common *and* statutory law. A great deal of contemporary law is necessarily statutory; it is coded. However, notwithstanding the great Magna Carta of 1215, this is a relatively recent development, for

---

[32]See p. 21, *infra.*
[33]A. T. von Mehren, *The Civil Law System* (Englewood Cliffs, NJ: Prentice-Hall, 1957), p. 6.

although statutes as a basis of Anglo-American law were not unknown, they played a subsidiary role until the second quarter of the nineteenth century.

The mixture came into its own largely, although certainly not exclusively, as a result of the perpetuating conservatism of the common law, particularly in the realm of the sanctity of private property, based on the overriding concept of economic *laisser faire.* With the advent of a rising spirit of common social consciousness and responsibility, and a gradual movement toward the service or welfare state on both sides of the ocean, legislative bodies everywhere—but considerably more slowly in the United States than in the United Kingdom—commenced to change or even displace the age-old concepts and practices of the common law in favor of what were viewed as primary considerations of necessary public interest.

Nonetheless, common law remained an important basis of legislative motivations and actions, and often an enacted statute would—as indeed it still does today—simply spell out certain aspects of the grand sweep of common law. Furthermore, no legislative body—and sometimes not even the executive—is consistently, or even largely, capable of pinpointing in writing all the aspects and ramifications of a statute or order, nor would that necessarily be desirable even if it were possible. The result is interpretation, usually first by administrative units, then often by the courts, and, as we shall have ample opportunity to observe,[34] when courts interpret, they cause statutes to grow or contract. This interpretation becomes part of the statutes and orders, thus giving them meaning in the spirit and application of the common law. Truly, England and America resort to a framework of law that is a generally wholesome blend of common, statutory, and equity law.

Of course, there are certain areas of statutory law in which little, if any, discretionary elements remain for the judge. The U. S. Criminal Code, for example, represents a compendium of laws that prescribes what shall constitute a crime and what the penalties shall be. A judge may have a modicum of leeway regarding the former, but the sole substantive discretion left to him in the realm of the latter is one reflected in the provision of the code. Thus, a particular law may conceivably permit him to exercise his considered judgment as to the severity of a sentence he is called upon to impose for a given criminal infraction, but this discretion will necessarily be limited by the minimum and maximum penalties as provided in it. Moreover, it may well be limited by the nature of the verdict of the jury. Indeed, *criminal law* is becoming more and more codified everywhere among the common law lands and hence is becoming statutory. The same applies to *public law* generally, although the great bulk of *private law* is still *common law.*

SOME ADDITIONAL LEGAL DEFINITIONS AND CONCEPTS

A few terms and concepts related to notions that play a part in these pages must be elaborated on here, however briefly. A host of others will be treated

---

[34]See chapters 5–9, *infra.*

throughout the book.[35] We begin with a distinction between the two types of law into which *municipal law*—the law that applies within a state—is normally divided, namely, *private* and *public* law.

Private law governs the relationship between private citizens or persons; that is, it regulates the relations of individuals with each other. It is concerned with the definition, regulation, and enforcement of rights in cases in which both the person[36] in whom the right inheres and the person on whom the obligation devolves are private individuals. Obvious examples of private law are the law governing contracts between individuals or corporations and that pertaining to marriage and divorce. In the sense that infractions of the legal obligations inherent in these areas are subject to adjudication by courts, the state is involved, of course, but it is neither the subject of the right nor the object of the duty.

Public law, on the other hand, is a branch or department of law that is very much concerned with the state in its political or sovereign capacities—including the two important subheadings of administrative and constitutional law (to be described presently). Public law deals with the definition, regulation, and enforcement of rights in those cases in which the state *is* viewed as the subject of the right or the object of the duty, including criminal law and criminal procedure. In other words, it is that portion of law which is concerned with political conditions and situations—with the powers, rights, duties, capacities, and incapacities that are characteristic of and peculiar to both supreme and subordinate political authority.

Public law applies to and affects the entire people of a nation or state that adopts or enacts it—in contrast with private law, which affects and applies to only one or a few individuals—for public law regulates both the relations between individuals and the state and the relations between the branches of the government. Thus, the vast majority of legislation enacted by Congress is in the category of public law—and its statutes are codified, preceded by the term "Public Law____ [Number]." Social welfare, defense appropriations, subversive activities control, farm subsidies—all these areas of legislation constitute illustrations of the vast, diversified content of public law.

Administrative law, which has quite naturally achieved ever-increasing prominence over the past few decades, consists of those rules and regulations that are promulgated by the sundry administrative agencies of government that have been empowered to deal with the operation of government under the delegated rule-making authority of the legislative body. That branch of

---

[35] A standard legal dictionary, e.g., *Black's Law Dictionary*, will readily supply answers to any other questions regarding terms that may occur to the inquiring reader. The definitions used in this section are based in part on its 4th ed. (St. Paul: West Publishing Co., 1957), pp. 1394, 1359, 385 and 67.

[36] In 1886 the Supreme Court declared corporations to be legal "persons" under the Constitution. (See p. 364, *infra*.) Yet in 1973 it ruled that human fetuses are *not* "persons" thereunder. (See *Roe v. Wade* and *Doe v. Bolton*, 410 U.S. 113 and 410 U.S. 179, resp.)

public law prescribes in detail the activities of the agencies involved, such as those concerned with the collection of revenue, regulation of competitive practices, coinage, public health, welfare, safety, and morals, sanitation, and regulation of the armed forces. In the United Kingdom, for example, administrative law has developed greatly as a means of controlling, supervising, and sometimes enforcing administrative decisions and actions by the use of prerogative writs.[37]

Constitutional law is the other great branch of public law. It determines the political organization of a state and its powers while also setting certain substantive and procedural limitations on the exercise of governing power. Because of its position and nature it stands legally above all other types of municipal law, public as well as private. In the United States, with its written Constitution, constitutional law consists of the application of fundamental principles of law based on that document, as finally interpreted by its highest judicial organ, the Supreme Court of the United States. A contemporary example is the famous *Steel Seizure case.*[38] Believing himself invested with the power to act in his capacity as Commander in Chief and endowed with what he and his advisers viewed as "inherent authority," President Truman seized the steel mills on April 8, 1952, in order to forestall a nationwide strike in the midst of the Korean War. The owners filed for a writ to enjoin him, charging the absence of both constitutional and legislative authority for his actions. After a series of dramatic skirmishes in the lower federal courts, the U. S. Superme Court received the case for adjudication—clearly a matter in the realm of constitutional law. On June 2, 1952, the Court rendered its decision, featured by seven different opinions! But six of the nine Justices did agree on *one* crucial point: President Truman had violated the Constitution by *usurping legislative power;* therefore, the seizure of the steel mills was hence *ultra vires*—particularly so since Congress had expressly refused to enact a suggested amendment to the Taft-Hartley Act authorizing such governmental seizures in an emergency.[39]

---

[37]"Prerogative writs" include such essential safeguards as the writs of *habeas corpus, certiorari, prohibition mandamus, quo warranto,* and so forth (to be described *infra*).

[38]*Youngstown Sheet and Tube Co.* v. *Sawyer,* 343 U.S. 579 (1952). See the excellent book by Maeva Marcus, *Truman and the Steel Seizure Case: The Limits of Presidential Power* (New York: Columbia University Press, 1977). The dramatic July 1974 decision in *United States v. Nixon,* 417 U.S. 683, is, of course, another pertinent illustration (see pp. 169, 197, 217 *infra*).

[39]Quipped *The Economist* (May 10, 1952) as the case was about to reach the Supreme Court: "At the first sound of a new argument over the United States Constitution and its interpretation, the hearts of Americans leap with a fearful joy. The blood stirs powerfully in their veins and a new lustre brightens their eyes. Like King Harry's men before Harfleur, they stand like greyhounds in the slips, straining upon the start. Last week, the old bugle-note rang out, clear and thrilling, calling Americans to a fresh debate on the Constitution." *The Economist* had an even better time with *United States v. Nixon* in 1974! (January 19 and 26, 1974, pp. 47 and 23, resp.; March 2, 9, and 23, 1974, pp. 49, 58, and 49 resp.; April 20, 1974, p. 63; May 4 and 11, 1974, pp. 53 and 49, resp.; June 15, 1974, p. 49; July 13 and 27, 1974, pp. 45 and 13 resp.; and August 3, 1974, p.11.)

In brief, constitutional law prescribes generally the plan and method under which the public business of the political organ, known as the state, is conducted. And it differs further from the other types of law described in that it is both enacted and changed either in an extraordinary manner by an ordinary legislative body, or by an extraordinary body—such as a constitutional convention—constituted especially for that purpose.

In the United States changes in the letter of the fundamental document are based on the special constitutional amendment provisions of its Article V, which combine extraordinary federal with extraordinary state action. In the United Kingdom, where no formal written constitution and no power of judicial review exist in the sense of striking down legislative or executive action, Parliament is supreme and may effect changes in the constitutional law of the land by ordinary legislation. But, notwithstanding the powerful potential of normally very strict Parliamentary party discipline (used persuasively by the Thatcher government, for one), it is unlikely to tamper with the great cornerstones of its unwritten Constitution—that intriguing British concept consisting of the heritage of the common law, great statutes, important documents, decisions of the courts (other than judicial review), autonomy of local elected authorities, and customs and conventions that combined constitute the very life blood of the realm. The prerogative writs (noted earlier) do provide wide powers of "judicial review," but it is a review quite different from that extant in the United States. In France the written Constitution of the Fifth Republic may be altered only by extraordinary action of Parliament with the cooperation of the President of France, either with or without ratification by a popular referendum, depending on the procedure invoked by the President in the course of the initiating stages. And in Switzerland, not only do constitutional alterations by the government call for mandatory ratification by popular referenda but the Swiss citizens may take the initiative directly by drawing up a proposed constitutional amendment and submitting it for direct popular referendum approval.

CIVIL AND CRIMINAL LAW

Another basic distinction of considerable importance that confronts the observer of the judicial and legal process is that between *civil law* and *criminal law*. (The former is not to be equated with the concept of "civil law" used as a synonym for statutory or Roman law; here the term is used in connection with the *subject matter* governing a particular case.) Whether a particular offense is of a civil or criminal nature determines not only the severity of the legal sanction that may be invoked but frequently the type of tribunal before which the case will be heard. As we shall see in subsequent chapters, some courts are empowered to hear cases involving *both* types of law, as are all three major federal constitutional courts of the United States. But in many instances the judicial hierarchy provides for a separate set of criminal and civil courts, as is the case, to a greater or lesser extent, in both England and France—although many of the English judges are used interchangeably.

Civil Law. A case at *civil law* is normally one between private persons and/or private organizations, for civil law governs the relations between individuals and defines their legal rights. A party bringing suit under it seeks legal redress in a *personal* interest, such as for a breach of contract, a divorce action, a defamation of character, or the use of a copyrighted story without permission. Yet although suits at civil law far more often than not are suits among private persons, the government, too, may conceivably be involved. For example, under the Sherman Anti-Trust Act of 1890, as amended, the federal government of the United States is empowered to bring either civil or criminal action, or both, against an alleged offender. It has much more frequently brought civil than criminal actions under that statute, probably because the former are not as difficult to win and cause less of an uproar in the interested community.

Criminal Law. A case at *criminal law* is invariably brought by and in the name of the legally constituted government, no matter at what level— national, state, or local—it may arise. Almost wholly statutory in the United States, criminal law defines crimes against the public order and provides for appropriate punishment. Prosecution brought under it by the proper governmental authority involves an accusation that the defendant has violated a specific provision of a law, an infraction for which a penalty has normally been provided by statute. Criminal cases comprise such felonies or major crimes as homicide, espionage, sabotage, rape, and perjury, to name but a few. The coverage is as extensive as the lawmakers choose to make it. Because the prosecuting authority in a criminal case is necessarily an agent of the sovereign, the latter's name appears in its title. Hence, assuming one Brown's indictment for murder in Virginia, the case would be docketed for trial as either *The Commonwealth of Virginia v. Brown*, or as *People v. Brown*. Moving to the federal level, one of the cases brought under the Smith Act of 1940 was entitled *United States v. Scales*.[40] However, by far the largest volume of criminal law is still enacted at the state level in the United States and thus is enforced by state officials under state law. Countries with a unitary structure, such as France and the United Kingdom,[41] are not confronted with that jurisdictional problem.

But in all cases and at all levels it is the jurists who render the decisions. Alexis de Tocqueville put it lastingly well when he observed that hardly any question arises in the United States that is not resolved sooner or later into a judicial question. To the jurists, then, their fascinating and significant tasks, and the hierarchical framework in which they perform their duties, we now turn.

---

[40] 367 U.S. 203 (1961).

[41] As noted on p. 11, *supra* (and p. 32, *infra*), Scotland is significantly different from England and Wales because it follows Roman (statutory) law rather than common law. Northern Ireland, too, adheres to a different legal system from that of England and Wales.

2

Staffing
the Courts

SELECTION

What principles should govern the selection of the men and women who
dispense justice? To raise this question brings us face to face with moral as
well as political questions of the greatest importance. However awe-inspiring
their functions may be, our judges are still human beings. As such they make
the ultimate in the judicial process. In essence, there are just two basic methods of selection: *appointment* and *election*—no matter who does the actual
appointing or electing—although, as we shall see, a compromise between the
two modes has been devised and is practiced on certain levels of the judiciary
in a good many jurisdictions. A collateral question is whether judges should
be members of a career service as in France, chosen from a special group of
lawyers as in England (for its above magistrate–level jurists), or selected
through appointments from the legal profession generally as in the United
States. Practices of selection differ in large measure in accordance with the
traditions and needs of the country concerned. A crucial consideration here
is the very position of the judiciary in the framework of government that
provides the rationale for the particular mode adopted and practiced. Under
the Roman law tradition of the Continent, the judiciary is a part of the overall
administrative hierarchy and, as such, represents a position and profession
other than that of the ordinary lawyer. Under the common law system, on
the other hand, the judges are drawn exclusively from the ranks of the legal

profession,[1] except for certain jurists on the state or local level in the United States. Nevertheless, the guiding principles for the selection and tenure of the judiciary in the three nations that concern us most here—England, France, and the United States—display a commonly held ideal: judges are expected to be impartial and hence must be given assurance of independence, security, and dignity of tenure. When these requirements are present, the fact that different techniques govern selection in those lands is hardly of great significance. Nevertheless, the techniques must be studied and understood. The process of selection is assuredly more complicated than might be inferred from the otherwise trenchant observation of W. Curtis Bok's imaginary Judge Ulen, who quipped: "A judge is a member of the bar who once knew a Governor."[2]

THE TWO CHIEF METHODS

The fifty American states (and their local subdivisions) employ at least six diverse types of recruitment systems for their circa 28,000 (1985) judges: partisan election, nonpartisan election, merit selection at one or more levels of the judicial system, gubernatorial appointment, legislative election, and selection by sitting judges. But the *appointive* method is used *exclusively* at the *federal* level of the U.S. government, regardless of whether a tribunal concerned is a constitutional or legislative count (a distinction that will be described in detail in chapter 4). Britain and France use appointment exclusively at all levels.

Appointment. In the *United States* all of the approximately, 1,500 (1985)[3]

---

[1] Justice Black often suggested that at least one non-lawyer be appointed to the U.S. Supreme Court, and other observers of the judiciary—e.g., Arthur Selwyn Miller—have raised the persistent issue of enabling non-lawyers to serve as judges. In 1976 the U.S. Supreme Court in a Kentucky case, *North v. Russell*, 427 U.S. 328, challenging the use of non-lawyer jurists in jail-carrying criminal trials ruled 6:2 that the practice was constitutional, provided the defendant is given the opportunity through an appeal to obtain a second trial, *de novo*, before a judge who *is* legally trained. Kentucky soon adopted a constitutional amendment requiring all judges to be lawyers (except for juvenile court "trial commissioners").

[2] *Backbone of the Herring* (New York: Alfred A. Knopf, 1941), p. 3. H. L. Mencken once observed that "a judge is a law student who marks his own exams" (Press conference, Philadelphia, Pa., July 27, 1948).

[3] This figure does not include the 243 federal "bankruptcy judges" (formerly called "referees") who serve in the ninety-four federal judicial districts. As a result of major revamping legislation enacted in 1984 amidst bitter controversy, they are now appointed for fourteen-year terms by the regional U.S. Courts of Appeals (the law is silent on renewability), are removable by the judicial councils of each circuit, and are paid $66,100 per annum (1984). Nor does the figure 1,500 include the now (1985) approximately 1,200 federal "administrative law judges" (formerly known as "trial examiners") who are appointed directly by the heads of, and serve in, twenty-eight separate federal administrative departments and agencies. These judges dispose of some 150,000 "cases" annually before administrative bodies and can impose penalties of up to $100,000. See the informative article by Thomas O'Toole, "Administrative Law Judge: Opinions Means Dollars," *The Washington Post*, September 13, 1980, p. A3. See also the special issue of of 65 *Judicature* 5 (November 1981), which is devoted exclusively to administrative law judges.

federal judges are appointed by the President, subject to confirmation by simple majority vote of the Senate.[4] Depending on the Chief Executive involved, the President's responsibility (a heavy one) has often been largely delegated to the Attorney General and the Deputy Attorney General. This was noticeably true during the later years of the administration of President Eisenhower, when the selection of members of the federal judiciary was left almost exclusively to Attorney General William P. Rogers and Deputy Attorney General Lawrence E. Walsh. On the other hand, President Lyndon B. Johnson gave Chairman John C. Macy of the U.S. Civil Service Commission, a trusted fellow Texan, *the* crucial role in the judicial selection process in preference to his Justice Department. In the Reagan Administration a formal committee was established under the chairmanship of the President's Counsel, Fred F. Fielding, including the Attorney General plus seven other high officials of the Department of Justice and the White House.[5] That Committee reviews recommendations for vacancies, submits these to checks by the FBI and judgments by the ABA (see later), and then forwards its recommendation to the President. Yet whatever mode is employed, three other crucial factors enter here.

The *first* factor is the obvious need for consultation with the U.S. senator(s) and/or other seats of political power in the home state of the candidate for judicial office, provided these political figures are of the same party as the appointing authority. Thus, care must be taken that the appointee is not "personally obnoxious" to a home-state senator, on pain of having the latter invoke the age-old, almost invariably honored, custom of "senatorial courtesy"[6]—an almost certain death-knell to confirmation by the Senate. The custom is based on the assumption that the President will, as a matter of political patronage, practice, and courtesy, engage in such consultation prior

---

[4]Joe Dolan, Assistant and Deputy Attorney General under Presidents Kennedy and Johnson, told an American Bar Association meeting in 1977 that the Constitution "reads backwards" and that it should say: "The Senators shall nominate and by and with the consent of the President, appoint judges. . . . " (As reported by James Goodman, "The Politics of Picking Federal Judges," *Juris Doctor*, June 1977, p. 20.) The Carter reforms (see pp. 30ff.) and subsequent experiments with merit selection in the states altered that fact of judicio-political life to some extent, but hardly conclusively.

[5]The Deputy Attorney General, the Assistant Attorney General for Legal Policy, the Associate Attorney General, the Chief of Staff for the White House, the Assistant to the President for Congressional Relations, the Assistant to the President for Personnel, and, on some occasions, the Assistant to the President for Political Affairs. See "A Look at Fred F. Fielding," 8 *District Lawyer* 2 (November–December 1983), p. 46.

[6]It dates back to the first years of the Republic, when the Senate recognized the need for solidarity to prevent a President from appointing a senator's political adversary to high office. Actually, it began in the very first session of Congress in 1789, when George Washington nominated Benjamin Fishbourn as a naval officer in the Port of Savannah, Georgia. Although qualified, Fishbourn was opposed by Georgia's two senators, and Washington withdrew his nomination when it was apparent that the Senate would side with its Georgia colleagues. Subsequently, Washington nominated someone favored by the two legislators.

to the nominee's designation—provided that the senator is a member of the President's party. If the President fails to adhere to this custom, the aggrieved senator's colleagues will almost certainly support him or her on the call for the nominee's defeat as a matter of fraternal *quid pro quo* courtesy.

Until the incoming chairman of the Senate Judiciary Committee, Senator Edward M. Kennedy (D.-Mass.), announced early in 1979 that he would not "unilaterally" table a nomination simply because a "blue slip" is not returned by a colleague, the so-called blue slip system had more or less institutionalized senatorial courtesy *cum* patronage. It proceeded as follows: Once the President formally nominated someone, the Senate Judiciary Committee sent to each of the nominee's home-state senators a blue sheet of paper, asking his or her "opinion and information concerning the nomination." In fact, the blue slip asked whether the Chief Executive's formal choice was either the person the senator wanted or someone he or she could agree to. If the senator approved, he or she returned the blue slip: if not, the senator retained the

United States Senate
COMMITTEE ON THE JUDICIARY

——————————, 197—

Dear Senator:

Will you kindly give me, for the use of the Committee, your opinion and information concerning the nomination of

Under a rule of the Committee, unless a reply is received from you within a week from this date, it will be assumed that you have no objection to this nomination.

Respectfully,

Chairman.

To Hon. ————————————
U.S. Senate

REPLY

Figure 1. The Senate's blue slip

slip. If the senator was from the President's own party, a withheld blue slip amounted to a "one-person veto," terminating the nominee's chances. Senator Kennedy's bold effort to end this system met with considerable condemnation by a number of his committee colleagues. When he succeeded to the committee chairmanship in 1981, Senator Strom Thurmond (R.-S.C.) was at first inclined to reinstitute it, but he apparently decided not to do so.[7]

Whatever the future may hold, however, let it be said at once that, as a practical matter of the political process—and regardless of the recent innovations explained later—it is simply not possible for the President to select a candidate for the bench and see that candidate confirmed without at least the grudging approval of his or her home state senators. And some powerful senators of the President's political party will insist not only on the right of prior approval of the presidential choice but also on the right to have particular candidates of their own designated. This recently proved to be the case with Senator Lowell P. Weicker, Jr.'s (R.-Conn.) insistence on the nomination of Connecticut's ex-Governor Thomas J. Meskill to the federal appellate bench in 1974-75, resulting in the latter's ultimate approval by the Senate, 54:36, despite the American Bar Association's unanimous NQ (Not Qualified)[8] rating. On the other hand, following the establishment of President Carter's Circuit Judge Nomination Commission in 1977,[9] and spurred by the President's constant prodding, coupled with his Executive Order 12097 of November 8, 1978, which established guidelines and stipulated standards of candidate qualification, the late 1970s began to witness a burgeoning system of U.S. senator-created merit advisory groups and commissions, charged with recommending nominees for the federal bench to the senators (e.g., Virginia, Pennsylvania, Iowa, Georgia, Florida, Colorado, and New York). By early 1984, fifty senators in thirty-five states had thus agreed to choose federal district judges on a merit basis only, aided by commission recommendations. Others, however, had categorically declined to do so, among them Democrats Adlai E. Stevenson (Illinois), Thomas F. Eagleton (Missouri), Paul S. Sarbanes (Maryland), and Lloyd M. Bentsen (Texas), the latter announcing, "I am the merit commission for Texas."[10]

The *second* factor that has played an increasingly significant role in the appointive process of the federal judiciary in the United States, especially since the latter months of the Truman Administration,[11] is the American Bar

---

[7] For at least some evidence of Thurmond's reluctance, see Sheldon Goldman, "Reagan's Judicial Appointments at Mid-Term: Shaping the Bench in His Own Image," 66 *Judicature* 8 (March 1983), p. 347 and fn. 15.

[8] See p. 29, *infra*.

[9] Ibid.

[10] *The Washington Post*, November 15, 1978, p. 4A. See the article by ex-Senator Joseph W. Tydings, "Merit Selection for Federal Judges," 61 *Judicature* 3 (September 1977).

[11] The groundwork was laid by President Truman's last Deputy Attorney General, Ross B. Malone.

Association's fourteen-member[12] Committee on Federal Judiciary, established in 1946. That Committee was widely utilized thereafter at the preformal nomination stage during President Eisenhower's term of office, a practice continued under all subsequent Presidents, although President Nixon, following the Committee's disapproval of his 1970–71 list of putative candidates, refused to submit names to it until *after* he had already selected and publicized them.[13] The Committee's work has generally produced good results and is understandably popular with the legal profession—although there is no unanimity on that evaluation. There are those who believe deeply that the selection of the members of the judicial branch of the government must rest, in fact as well as in name, with the executive branch, its head being specifically charged to do so under Article III of the Constitution, and that the apparent delegation of important aspects of that authority (i.e., approval of, or at least judgment on, selectees) to a private body, no matter how qualified and how representative—a crucial point—is at best questionable, and at worst a dereliction of duty. Nor is the bar free from political or personal biases, as the contrast between the Committee's handling of the Fortas and the Haynsworth cases in 1969 demonstrated. To cite an earlier case in point, had President Wilson heeded the advice of the ABA, Justice Brandeis would never have been nominated. Furthermore, as an intriguing book-length study of the committee's activities over a period of two decades demonstrated rather convincingly,[14] its membership was initially dominated by the "legal establishment." Until the 1970s, almost all of its members were successful lawyers, older, experienced men, partners in large, big-city firms, and veterans of local bar association politics. Of the relatively few lawyers the Committee had asked to give an evaluation of judicial candidates twenty years ago, 70 percent were officers of local bar associations and 80 percent were senior partners in "respectable" law firms. A genuine and broadly based measure of

---

[12]Initially twelve, it had risen to thirteen as of September 1976, with the addition of the first black ever to be a member of the group in the person of Charles Z. Smith, associate dean of the University of Washington School of Law. It went to fourteen in August 1977 when the large Fifth and Ninth Circuits were assigned two members each (Washington being the Ninth). Each of the other circuits was assigned one member, with a separate slot for a chairman. Members serve for three years, with one possible renewal. In 1980, the Committee, for the first time, named a woman as its head—Brooksley E. Landau Born (of the prestigious Washington law firm of Porter & Arnold, formerly Porter, Fortas, & Arnold). When the 1981–82 circuit court organization acts provided for two new circuits, the Eleventh (created by splitting the fifth) and the Thirteenth— known as the U.S. Court of Appeals for the Federal Circuit—the former but not the latter received a "representative" on the Committee. Thus, the number of members stood at fourteen as of mid-1985,—the Ninth still having two, eleven circuits having one each, and a chairman.

[13]——the A.B.A.!," exclaimed Mr. Nixon, in ordering this future policy of nonsubmittal of Supreme Court nominees *prior* to formal selection in 1971. (As reported by Goodman, op. cit., p. 26.)

[14]Joel B. Grossman, *Lawyers and Judges: The Politics of Judicial Selection* (New York: John Wiley & Sons 1965), especially pp. 87–92.

diversification has demonstrably set in, however,[15] and may confidently be expected to continue.[16]

Whatever the merit of demurrers, the committee has become a powerful and respected vehicle in the vital initial stages of the nominating process— at least below the Supreme Court level.[17] It does *not* generate names for judicial vacancies, but it evaluates the qualifications of actual or potential nominees. After an investigation, customarily lasting from six to eight weeks,[18] it reports to the Justice Department on the qualifications of the prospective nominee and rates him or her in one of four ways: Exceptionally Well Qualified (EWQ), Well Qualified (WQ), Qualified (Q), or Not Qualified (NQ).[19] In a number of cases the consideration of nominees for the federal bench was dropped after the ABA's Committee found them less qualified than others; thus, no NQs were approved between 1965 and 1975 (until the instance of the Meskill nomination approval in the latter year—see footnotes 18 and 22). Moreover, its reports have enabled the Justice Department to rule out certain names recommended by the home-state senator(s)—though "senatorial courtesy" may prevail in the end. It should be noted that the Committee also sends its ratings *independently* to the Senate Judiciary Committee.

To illustrate the Committee's role, in September 1961 the Senate confirmed sixty lower court federal judges nominated by President Kennedy, fifty-two of whom had been rated by the ABA. Nine had been rated Exceptionally Well Qualified, twenty-seven Well Qualified, fourteen Qualified, and two Not Qualified. Yet the two rated Not Qualified—James R. Browning, then the clerk of the U.S. Supreme Court, and Luther Bohanan, an Oklaho-

---

[15] Thus, Professors Richard G. Watson, Rondal G. Downing, and Frederick G. Spiegel, in an article concerned with the members of Missouri's Bar, contend that the notion that the bar is inevitably conservative is *disproved* by the Missouri experience. See "Bar Politics, Judicial Selection and the Representation of Social Interests," 61 *American Political Science Review* 54 (March 1967).

[16] See Elliot E. Slotnick, "The ABA's Standing Committee on Federal Judiciary: A Contemporary Assessment," in 66 *Judicature* 8, 9 (March–April 1983).

[17] For a formal, recently updated description of the Committee's procedures, see *The ABA's Standing Committee on Federal Judiciary: What It is and How It Works* (Chicago: American Bar Association, 1983).

[18] The investigation is based in part on the candidate's responses to a lengthy, detailed questionnaire, one question of which asks about the ten most significant cases the candidate has handled. In his response, former Governor Thomas Meskill (R.-Conn.) included three grotesquely insignificant cases that dealt with civil negligence suits. In its own decision-making process the Senate's Committee on the Judiciary also uses a questionnaire to elicit a candidate's qualifications.

[19] These categories are not applicable to Supreme Court nominees, however, who began to be rated only as of the 1956 Brennan appointment and then simply as Q or NQ to the Senate Judiciary Committee. But after the Haynsworth and Carswell debacles, the Committee, as of the Balckmun nomination, adopted the following Supreme Court rankings: (a) "high standards of integrity, judicial temperament, and professional competence," (b) "not opposed," (c) "not qualified."

man—had sufficiently powerful support to gain confirmation, the latter from that state's powerful Democratic U.S. Senator "Bob" Kerr, the chairman of the Senate Finance Committee. However, a finding of NQ is not necessarily a reflection on a nominee's character or ability. Until 1981 the ABA's Committee would not approve anyone who had reached the age of sixty-four, and no one older than sixty unless he or she was ratable at least WQ. President Kennedy's selection of Sarah T. Hughes of Texas[20] to be a federal district court judge was disapproved on the former ground, but she was confirmed. In the case of a sitting judge the Committee would approve *promotion* up to sixty-eight. The Committee is loath to recommend lawyers without trial experience—which was true of both Browning and Bohanan—and it generally insists on fifteen years of experience in "the rough and tumble of legal practice"[21]—although it adopted a policy of making numerous exceptions on both counts in the instances of women and minorities as of the mid-to-late 1970s.

Considerably more will be said on the point later, but it should be reemphasized here that no alert and prudent Chief Executive of the United States would nowadays attempt to designate members of the judiciary *purely* on the basis of political considerations. Too much is at stake in matters of policy and public awareness, and the American Bar Association is a powerful factor in the selection process. Yet, granted the various needs and drives for appointments on the basis of overall merit and excellence, the political pressures must nevertheless be reckoned with and are disregarded only at the appointing authority's peril.[22] Moreover, a federal judgeship is viewed as a "plum"

---

[20] Judge Hughes swore in Lyndon B. Johnson in the presidential plane "Air Force 1" after President Kennedy's assassination on November 22, 1963. In "age disqualification" characterizations, the ABA Committee used to issue a rating of "Not Qualified by Reason of Age" (NQ-A). But, in response to mounting criticism, it resolved to discontinue this age barrier classification as of January 1, 1981.

[21] Committee member Robert Trescher, personal communication to me, December 9, 1971.

[22] Nixon and then President Ford pushed Senator Lowell P. Weicker, Jr.'s (R.-Conn.) insisted-upon nomination of the professionally potentially unqualified ex-Governor Thomas J. Meskill for a vacancy on the U.S. Court of Appeals for the Second Circuit. Senator Weicker had the crucial support of Connecticut's senior Senator, Democrat Abraham Ribicoff. But it was not until eight months after the Senate received the nomination that it reluctantly confirmed Mr. Meskill by the less than impressive margin of 54:36 in April 1975. (See Jerry Landauer, "How Not to Pick a Judge," The *Wall Street Journal*, April 10, 1975, p. 4.) In late 1978, the Senate confirmed the U.S. District Court nomination of Donald E. O'Brien of Iowa despite the ABA Committee's 14:0 NQ rating. It ought to be noted that Judge Meskill has served ably. Indeed, he received the Association of Trial Lawyers of America's 1983 Outstanding Federal Appellate Judge Award. (*The Washington Post*, July 19, 1983, p. C3.) In 1980, the Senate's Judiciary Committee rejected the U.S. District Court judgeship nomination of Charles H. Winberry, campaign manager of U.S. Senator Robert Morgan (D.-N.C.), after the ABA's Committee had ranked him NQ (having reversed its initial Q verdict). But shortly thereafter that same Committee approved the nomination of U. W. Clemon, a black Alabama legislator, notwithstanding the ABA's NQ rating.

by all concerned, in that it represents a potent patronage-whip in the hands of the executive vis-à-vis state politicians as well as Congress.

Both the continuing problem and its flavor are suggested nicely and candidly by this passage in Senator Joseph S. Clark's newsletter of August 11, 1961, to his constituents in Pennsylvania:

> I have forwarded to the Attorney General recommendations to fill additional Judgeships recently authorized by Congress in the United States District Courts in Pennsylvania, and one vacancy in the Court of Appeals for the Third Circuit. I regret that, by custom, Senators have the obligation of making these recommendations after appropriate consultation with their State political leaders. I believe the selection of judges should be entirely nonpartisan and should be made by the Attorney General and the President without Senatorial intervention [a proposal backed unsuccessfully by Attorney General Elliot L. Richardson during his brief tenure under President Nixon in 1973]. Nevertheless, I must live with the rules as they exist until they are changed. After consultations with [Democratic] Governor Lawrence, Democratic State Chairman Otis Morse II, [Democratic] Congressman William J. Green, Jr., and others, I am satisfied that the recommendations made for existing vacancies are men of ability and integrity. The Attorney General and the President will make the final decisions on these Judgeships of course, and may disregard our recommendations if they wish.

But the very real possibility of a major change, indeed conceivably a revolutionary development, took place on February 14, 1977 when President Carter, having been in office only one month, issued Executive Order 11972 establishing "The United States Circuit Judge Nominating Commission," to make recommendations, based on "merit"—a major 1976 campaign promise—for *all* future judgeship nominations at the level of the U.S. Circuit Courts of Appeals. He noted that he would have preferred to embrace federal district court judgeships under the same order, but, reading the political signs, determined to postpone any such endeavor to a future day. The new commission consists of thirteen separate eleven-member panels—one for each circuit, two each for the big Fifth and Ninth—that under its order's initial terms, were to be composed roughly of one-half lawyers and one-half nonlawyers, and, specifically required the inclusion of both men and women as well as members of minority groups. The panels were designed to be an *ad hoc* nature, with each appointment terminating thirty days after the submittal of each panel's report to the President, unless the latter chose to extend its life. Each panel was expected to forward to the President within sixty days those five names it considered most qualified on the basis of "character, experience, ability, and commitment to equal justice under law" to fill the particular vacancy of which it had been apprised by the Chief Executive (via the Attorney General).

After the first set of President Carter—appointed panels, the sex distribution varied from eight men and three women on the First Circuit's panel to six women and five men on the Western Fifth and Southern Ninth; that of group representation, an overall pattern that continued apace. No judges were among the lawyers that had been appointed to any of the set of 1977, 1978, 1979, and 1980 panels.[23] On May 11, 1978, President Carter promulgated the amendatory Executive Order 12059, that, together with accompanying supplemental instructions, made several important changes in the Commission's composition and procedures. Specifically, panel membership was no longer limited to eleven; there could be more or less. Also, panels were no longer required to be composed of approximately equal numbers of lawyers and non-lawyers. Finally, whereas the 1977 order had required that each state within a panel's circuit be represented by at least one "resident," that of 1978 specified one "lawyer." Moreover, there was now no longer a sixty-day completion-of-operation requirement; the new order neither limited nor required the panel to submit five names, merely calling for a list of " . . . persons . . . best qualified . . . "; and the panel was no longer mandated to report the names of its potential nominees to the President "in confidence."

That the Commission's work and the results thereof had a mixed reception is not surprising, especially since a number of the panels found themselves in heated controversies over charges that in selecting nominees they were more concerned with "group," "sex," and "race" representativeness than with merit. What is clear, however, is that as a result of the new lower federal court staffing policies developed by the Carter Administration, the Circuit and District Court levels witnessed a very marked increase—indeed, a dramatic one—in the number of both women and minority selectees and nominees, with the President and the Department of Justice categorically insisting on that aspect of "affirmative action." By late 1980, with the Carter Administration nearing its end, fully one-half of those chosen under the new system were either female, black, or of Hispanic origin.[24] Questioned by both friendly and inquisitive members of the Senate Judiciary Committee on the matter, Attorney General Griffin Bell had testified earlier that "Mr. Carter was prepared to appoint to the Federal bench a black, Hispanic, or woman lawyer who was found to be *less qualified* than a white male so long as the appointee was found qualified."[25] And in a December 7, 1978, press conference, President Carter had stated: "If I didn't have to get Senate confirmation of appoint-

[23] See Dorothy W. Nelson, "Carter's Merit Plan: A Good First Step," 61 *Judicature* 3 (September 1977); Sheldon Goldman, "A Profile of Carter's Judicial Nominees," 62 *Judicature* (November 1978); Susan Carbon, "The U.S. Circuit Judge Nomination Commission," ibid.; and Elliot E. Slotnick, "What Panelists Are Saying about the Circuit Judge Nomination Commission," ibid. (February 1979).

[24] As of October 1980, President Carter had appointed 45 women and 55 minorities, far more than all his predecessors combined! (When he took office, there were but nineteen blacks, five females, and five Hispanics on the federal benches.)

[25] *The New York Times*, February 13, 1979, p. A16. As of November 1979, President Carter had an option to select a female or a black in 67% of the nomination-suggestions submitted to him. He selected a woman or a black in each instance. (Larry E. Berkson, "Equal Justice Under Law," Paper delivered at the Southern Political Science Association Annual Meeting, Gatlinburg, Tennessee, November 3, 1979.)

ees, I could tell you flatly that 12% of my appointees would be blacks and 3% would be Spanish-speaking and 40% would be women and so forth."[26]

There is a *third* factor: the increasing evidence of the unquestionably significant influence that sitting and retired members of the Court itself, especially the Chief Justice, have on nominations by consulting with and being consulted by the President and the Attorney General in the selection process of a new Supreme Court Justice.[27] Among a good many others, Chief Justices Taft, Hughes, Stone, Vinson, Warren, and Burger, and Associate Justices Harlan I, Miller, Van Devanter, Brandeis, and Frankfurter have thus all been involved—Taft more openly and actively than anyone else on the high bench, followed at some distance by Stone, Hughes, Harlan I, and Miller, in that order.[28] Taft's role in Harding's nomination of Butler is a classic example. In fact, Harding's Attorney General, Harry M. Daugherty, told Henry Taft (William's brother) that "the President would not approve anybody for appointment who was not approved by the Chief Justice."[29] It is entirely possible to make a good case for the practice, but within limits.

In *Britain*—we are here again concerned almost exclusively with England and Wales (for convenience hereafter referred to as England), because Scotland and Northern Ireland, the two other members of the United Kingdom of Great Britain and Northern Ireland, operate separate court systems— judges are designated by the Crown with little direct surrender to politics. Practically speaking, they are the choices of the Lord High Chancellor of Great Britain, the senior law member of the government, who is the Queen's chief adviser on the selection. Because the Lord Chancellor is chosen by the Prime Minister, the latter does have an indirect voice in the selection of judges, however truly small and inaudible that voice is, especially on the middle and higher levels. Among these are the Lords of Appeal in Ordinary (the Law Lords), the Lord Chief Justice, the Master of the Rolls, the President of the Family Division of the High Court of Justice, and the Lord Justices of the Court of Appeal. In the cases of the Lord Chief Justice and the Master of the Rolls, the highest ranking judicial offices, the Prime Minister in effect desig-

---

[26]The White House, Washington, D.C.

[27]See Henry J. Abraham and Bruce A. Murphy, "The Influence of Sitting and Retired Justices on Presidential Supreme Court Nominations," 3 *Hastings Constitutional Law Quarterly* 37 (Winter 1976). The data in the article, plus the subsequent O'Connor appointment, demonstrate that of the 102 individuals who had sat on the Court as of mid-1985, 48 had exerted ascertainable pressure in a total of 95 separate instances involving 44 vacancies.

[28]For a good description of Taft's role in Harding's designation of Pierce Butler, see David Danelski, *A Supreme Court Justice Is Appointed* (New York: Random House, 1964). See also Alpheus T. Mason, *William Howard Taft: Chief Justice* (New York: Simon and Schuster, 1965) and *Harlan Fiske Stone: Pillar of the Law* (New York: Viking Press, 1956). For a full-scale study of *all* nominations and appointments to the Supreme Court through 1984, see my *Justices and Presidents: A Political History of Appointments to the United States Supreme Court*, 2d ed. (New York: Oxford University Press., 1985).

[29]Quoted by Mason, Taft, loc. cit., p. 173.

nates the appointees but acts on the advice of the Lord Chancellor. But it is the Queen who actually issues the commission of appointment.

The Lord Chancellor himself, however, is the politically designated head of the judicial hierarchy of the United Kingdom. In addition, he advises on all appointments to judicial office from the rank of Justice of the Peace to the higher offices of the English Judiciary. As Speaker of the House of Lords he presides from the Woolsack (a bright red padded bench, its name signifying how important the wool trade was to the British economy in earlier centuries); he is a member of the Cabinet; and, as head of the Judiciary, he combines in his person the threefold function of executive, legislator, and jurist— a complete refutation of the principle of separation of powers so dear to Montesquieu. His office, which pays (1984) £25,575 plus £3,375 as Speaker of the House of Lords, for a total of £28,950, is older than that of Prime Minister (whose slaary is the same; high jurists receive more). Because the group of lawyers from whose ranks the Lord Chancellor[30] chooses England's and Wales's approximately five hundred full-time judges (1984) is comparatively small and select, he may know some of them; when members of the Opposition show promise as competent judges, he will certainly not hesitate to cross party lines to make appointments. If he does not personally know, or know of, a candidate, he will probably consult a senior judge or judges and obtain their views—but not their prior approval. Incidentally, barristers must leave the bar when they go on the bench.[31]

No letters of recommendation are accepted, and efforts to put political pressure on the Lord Chancellor are scouted strongly. R. M. Jackson, professor of public law and administration at the University of Cambridge, in his excellent study on the machinery of justice in England,[32] contends—although a good many would voice doubts—that political considerations have hardly entered the process of judicial selection since 1907, while they died a slower death in the selection of Lord Chief Justice; he also insists that, as a consequence, there has been no apparent connection between the "political antecedents" of the judges and their decisions for more than a century. On their resignation, however, members of the House of Commons may be appointed to county court judgeships and also to the High Court.[33]

In France, and in many other countries on the Continent, the trained judges are appointed to, rise in, and are promoted from a type of career serv-

---

[30] On two occasions the title was held by men who were later sainted—Thomas à Becket and Sir Thomas More.

[31] See Shimon Shetreet, Judges on Trial: A Study of the Appointment and Accountability of the English Judiciary (New York: American Elsevier Publishing Co., 1976).

[32] Richard M. Jackson, The Machinery of Justice in England, 7th ed. (Cambridge: Cambridge University Press, 1977), p. 469.

[33] For example, in 1962 two of the members of the High Court were from the House of Commons, and the then new president of its Probate, Divorce, and Admiralty Division (now called the Family Division) was the former Solicitor-General, a member of the House.

ice that is an adjunct of the general civil service. The de Gaulle Constitution of 1958 specifically makes a point of the time-honored concept that an ideal judge is an impartial judge. There is a Ministry of Justice, but the judges of France (numbering circa 5,500 in 1984, one-fourth of them women) do not really feel its authority, although the Minister is part of the appointing process. Political patronage plays only a small role in their selections. They all have either been schooled as judges for a minimum of twenty-eight months by the *École Nationale de la Magistrature* in Bordeaux (established in 1959) or had experience as judges, and they enter the judicial service on the basis of passing competitive examinations.

Theoretically, the President of the Republic, who is charged by the Constitution to be "the guarantor of the independence of judicial authority,"[34] selects the judges; actually, they are chosen either by the eleven-member *Conseil Supérieur de la Magistrature* (High Council of the Judiciary) in the case of the *Cour d'Appel* and the *Cour de Cassation*, or by the Minister of Justice, who may consult with, or receive advice from, the High Council, in the case of the lower courts. The High Council consists of the President of the Republic (as *le président*), the Minister of Justice (as vice-president), and nine persons with legal background chosen by the President for a once-renewable term of four years, partly on the recommendation of the *Cour de Cassation* and the *Conseil d'État*, as follows: one from the latter, three from the former, three from other courts, and two selected for their general legal knowledge and competence. In any event, the selecting authorities have little choice—considerably less than in England and infinitely less, of course, than in the United States.

The assets and liabilities of the appointive versus the elective method are rather obvious. In general the main argument in favor of appointment hinges on the contention that a candidate for a judicial post who is obliged to run on a partisan ballot cannot possibly serve as an *impartial* judge, and that he is selected, as Al Smith once put it, "by an electorate who are not really in a position to pass upon the legal and other abilities of the individual."[35] On the other hand, the champions of election on a partisan ballot argue that appointment by a political executive contains even worse features of political beholdenness than election. As is so often the case, neither side of the argument is *ipso facto* correct on all counts; both contain some merit, and it is easy to oversimplify. Someone, however, has to assume responsibility for staffing the courts; it might as well be the executive, who not only possesses the expertise and has access to all pertinent data but also is fairly well known to the populace at large on almost all levels and, in fact, is usually the sole officer of government with an all-embracing constituency. In a free society, the peo-

---

[34] Title VIII, Article 64.

[35] As quoted by Arthur T. Vanderbilt, "Brief for a Better Court System," *The New York Times Magazine*, May 5, 1957, p. 9.

ple, at least in theory, are always in a position to hold him accountable. Making him responsible for unfortunate judicial appointments is more meaningful and more palatable to the electorate than any arrangement that requires the voters not only to submerge judges into the political arena[36] but also to become intimately familiar with their adjudicatory record. Whatever the ramifications of this balancing of scales, executive appointment of judges—however it may be subject to input and influence by other sources, private as well as public—has proved to be the preferred method of selection in the United States (with notable state-level exceptions), England and Wales, and France. Although compromise arrangements of the type illustrated later may well move onto the scene here and there, there is no chance that election will supplant appointment for the selective process of judges in the vast majority of countries in the free world.[37]

Election. Nevertheless, election of members of that branch of the government is not unknown, even at the national or federal level of governments. In Switzerland, a major exception to the federal appointment principle, judges are elected by the two federal chambers—the Nationalrat and the Ständerat—sitting jointly as the Bundesversammlung (National Assembly) to ensure that German-, French-, and Italian-speaking members are appropriately distributed on the bench. However, re-election is so usual that for all intents and purposes permanent tenure of office is the result. In a drastically different category, the Soviet Union, too, practices the elective method exclusively, but (a) the victorious candidates serve for short terms only and (b) they have been approved by the political hierarchy of the state in advance of their candidacy.

Election of judges, though clearly decreasing, is still widespread in a majority of the states in America, where as recently as 1970 fully 82 percent[38] of the nation's state and local judges ran on various election ballots. Thus, judges may be elected by the electorate (e.g., Arkansas and Alabama) or by the legislature (e.g., South Carolina and Virginia). They may run on partisan tickets (e.g., West Virginia and New Mexico) or on nonpartisan ones (e.g., Wash-

---

[36]For what is almost a textbook illustration of why judges should not run for office in contested elections, see Cynthia Owens Philip, Paul A. Nejelski, and Aric Press, Where Do Judges Come From? (New York: Institute of Judicial Administration, 1977). Their book graphically describes the campaigns for elections to the New York Court of Appeals in 1973 and 1974. (However, the appointive method was adopted for that level of the New York judiciary in 1978.)

[37]In Israel, recommendations for judicial appointments are made to the government by an Appointments Committee, consisting of the President of the Supreme Court, two judges from the court containing the vacancy who are chosen by its members, two Bar Association-selected lawyers, the Minister of Justice, and two members selected by the Knesset (Parliament). Nominees must come from the ranks of experienced judges, advocates, or legal academicians.

[38]Time Magazine, March 30, 1970, p. 48. But real contests are relatively rare, and active politicking by judges is usually, although by no means always, regarded as demeaning.

ington and Michigan) on occasion, but loyal service in partisan politics normally tends to be a prerequisite for nomination—in line with Jacksonian tradition. Also, although the term of office for most elected judges is on the average six to ten years, for some it extends to fifteen years (e.g., in Maryland) and for others to life (e.g., in Rhode Island). In a few states the concept of supporting the sitting judge has been adopted when he or she is up for reelection,[39] but this theoretically laudatory practice has been ignored almost as much as it has been observed. Moreover, the mitigating factors that are inherent in the deviations from the straight, partisan, short-term ballot election are found in but a few states, and even in these they are usually confined to the upper echelon of the judiciary.

Other practices worthy of note in this general consideration of selection are those of at least some judges by gubernatorial appointment subject to legislative consent (e.g., New Jersey and Maine) and appointment of some, either temporary or permanent, by courts (e.g., Alaska and Louisiana). Massachusetts' commission-selected, gubernatorially appointed judges, except justices of the peace, serve for life, "conditioned upon good behavior"; those of New Jersey, strictly gubernatorially selected, serve for seven years and then, if reappointed, for life terms "during good behavior."

A COMPROMISE?

An intriguing attempt at a compromise between the elective and appointive methods of choosing state judges in America has been advanced and popularized in somewhat different versions by a number of states at some or all appellate and/or trial court levels. This is the case (1985) in Georgia, Hawaii, South Dakota, California, Maryland, Idaho, Missouri, Alaska, Kansas, Colorado, Iowa, Arizona, New York, Oklahoma, Indiana, Nebraska, Utah, Florida, Tennessee, Wyoming, Montana, Illinois, and Vermont. This compromise is designed to minimize political influence and provide a degree of security of tenure while retaining an element of popular control. Repeatedly and even enthusiastically supported by leading spokespersons of the legal profession and by knowledgeable laypersons alike, it has been widely adopted; its chief obstacle is powerful political opposition, which views this compromise as a genuine threat to the patronage aspects of judicial selection, as well it might be. California and Missouri, the pioneers in the compromise movement, deserve special discussion.

The California Plan. The first well-known original attempt at a solution to the vexatious problem of judicial selection was the California Plan, adopted

---

[39]Thus, New York State Court of Appeals Associate Judge Stanley H. Fuld, who had demonstrated great talent in twenty years of service on that tribunal, was nominated for the post of Chief Justice on the November 8, 1966, ballot by all four political parties: Republican, Democratic, Liberal, and Conservative. However, as indicated, New York moved to the appointive method for that tribunal as a result of a popular referendum-approved constitutional amendment in 1978.

by a voter initiative and referendum in 1934. Proposed originally in 1912 by the Commonwealth Club of San Francisco, the plan's ratification was assiduously supported by the California State Bar Association, encouraged by its national parent body. The State Bar Association was also closely allied with the California Chamber of Commerce. Both of these powerful state groups had become convinced of the inadequacy of the system under which California then operated—judicial appointment by the governor with subsequent popular approval, which in their eyes constituted little more than public rubber-stamping of the appointing authority's rank political designations.

Under the California Plan, which applies to the judges of the Supreme Court and Courts of Appeal only (trial court appointments are at the governor's discretion), the governor nominates *one* person to the Commission on Judicial Appointments. The latter is composed of the Chief Justice of the State Supreme Court, the Presiding Judge of the Court of Appeals of the area concerned, and the Attorney General.[40] If the commission approves the governor's nominee[41]—and only one has been rejected to date (early 1985)[42]—he or she is deemed appointed *only* until the next general election (but not for less than one year). At the end of that period the nominee stands for popular election for a full twelve-year term of office, his or her name being the only one on the nonpartisan ballot. The sole question appearing on the ballot in connection with the nominee's candidacy is "Shall _____ be elected to the office for the term prescribed by law?" There are no limits on the number of terms to which a successful candidate may aspire. Should the electorate's response to the question on the ballot be in the negative, the governor will designate a successor in the same manner, who ultimately will go before the electorate as well. In any event, the burden of approval is on the people, who must familiarize themselves with the candidate's record—or at least they ought to do so.

The first test of the plan returned the sitting judges by a 2:1 affirmative vote, a margin of approval that has steadily widened since that time. To date

---

[40]Since 1980 all nominees have also been submitted to the California Bar's twenty-five-member Committee on Judicial Nominees Evaluation for a "ranking" (from "excellent" down to "unqualified").

[41]Thus, the first female Chief Justice of the California Supreme Court, Rose Elizabeth Bird, nominated in early 1977 for the post by Governor Edmund G. ("Jerry") Brown, Jr., was approved by the Commission by a 2:1 vote, with Acting Chief Justice Matthew Tobriner casting the decisive vote in her favor. It proved to be a highly controversial choice: in the confirmation election of November 1978, she won by a mere 51.7 percent of the votes cast—the closest margin to date (mid-1985) in the history of California's judicial races. See Preble Stolz, *Judging the Judges: The Investigations of Rose Bird and the California Supreme Court* (New York: The Free Press, 1981).

[42]In 1940, Governor Clubert Olson's nomination of Max Radin, a "liberal" Berkeley professor of law, was defeated by a 2:1 commission vote. From 1934 to 1984 a mere twenty dissenting votes were cast by commission members on some two hundred nominees to the two tiers of appellate courts.

(mid 1985) *no* California jurist running for election under the retention has been rejected by the electorate. Appraisals of the California Plan have generally been favorable, although some have criticized as inadequate what they view as the essentially negative restriction placed on the governor's power by the commission. To refuse to confirm a gubernatorial appointment takes a certain amount of courage, which has not inevitably been demonstrated by the commission. Doubts have also been voiced concerning the wisdom of placing a measure of control over judicial appointments, however negative, into the hands of the chief law officer of the state, the Attorney General. Nonetheless, the plan has worked well and has been favorably received by the vast majority of those concerned.

The Missouri Plan. Desirous of adopting a modified version of the California Plan—a more clearly merit-selected one—and learning a tactical lesson from its defeat in popular referenda in 1938 in both Ohio and Michigan, the supporters of the *Missouri Plan* waged a vigorous and enlightened campaign, headed by both professional and lay groups. The movement for its adoption was spearheaded by the Missouri Institute for the Administration of Justice, an educational corporation composed of one-third lawyers and two-thirds laypersons, who successfully enlisted the active support of civic, labor, farm, and business organizations. They explained to the electorate the true purpose of the plan: to secure an intelligent and impartial selection of personnel for the bench, to eliminate as much as possible the haphazard results of the elective system, and to relieve the judges of the pressures of political campaigning. And the supporters of the plan pointed out shrewdly that neither the California nor the Missouri Plan was designed to supplant entirely the elective method—this was clearly a compromise between appointment and election. Characterized by the American Bar Association as the "most acceptable substitute available for direct election of judges," the plan became law in the form of an amendment to Missouri's Constitution in 1940.

The Missouri Plan is mandatory for the judges of the Missouri Supreme Court, the state's other appellate courts, the circuit and probate courts in St. Louis and in Jackson County, and the St. Louis Court of Corrections. It is optional, subject to popular referenda, in the thirty-eight other circuits of the state. Thus, judges of a number of courts, especially those of the lower levels, may well remain outside the compromise plan, as do the judges in California. Under the Missouri version, nonpartisan nominating boards known as the Missouri Appellate Commissions,[43] operating on different court levels, select *three* candidates for every vacant judgeship. For the Supreme Court and the

---

[43] In December 1974, the "typical commissioner was forty-eight years of age or older, white, male, and either a lawyer, a judge, or a businessman." (James J. Alfini, "Partisan Pressures on the Non-Partisan Plan" 58 *Judicature* 5, p. 221.) But the late 1970s saw a distinct broadening of that base—throughout the land, in fact—to include females and members of minority groups.

appellate courts, the commission consists of the Chief Justice of the State Supreme Court, the chairman; three lawyers, elected by the state bar, one from each of the three courts of appeals; and three citizens who are *not* members of the bar, appointed by the governor, again on the basis of one from each of the three appellate districts. The commissions for the circuit and other lower court judges comprise the presiding judge of the court of appeals district in which the circuit happens to be situated, two members of the bar elected by its own members residing in the circuit involved, and two similarly resident nonbar citizens appointed by the governor. The members of all these nonsalaried commissions are designated for staggered six-year terms of office, with changes taking effect in alternate years. Because the governor has a four-year term and can succeed to the office but once, it is unlikely that he or she would appoint *all* of the lay members. To ensure an additional degree of impartiality, commissioners are permitted to hold neither public office nor an official position in a political party.

The governor of Missouri is obliged to choose *one* of the three individuals selected by the Appellate Commission and appoint him or her until the next general election but not for less than one year, similar to the California Plan. After this probationary period, the appointee must be approved by the electorate for a full twelve-year term in the appellate courts or for a lesser term in the trial courts, running unopposed on a separate, nonpartisan judicial ballot at the time of the general election. The question on the ballot, very similar to that of California, is "Shall Judge _____ of the _____ Court be retained in office? Yes ( ) No ( ) (Scratch one)."

Generally deemed to be the most adult and most attractive system of judicial selection extant in the various states, the Missouri Plan embraces a number of commendable features. It combines the democratic notion of accountability to the electorate with an intelligent method of selecting qualified candidates for judicial office. The necessity of facing the electorate on the record provides the judge with an incentive of judiciousness; and the fact that he or she runs on a personal record rather than against that of an opponent allied with a specific political party goes far toward taking the courts out of the more crass aspects of politics. On the other hand, a case could be made for the contention that the awareness of establishing a "good record" for the electorate's eyes and ears may lead to timid and/or "popular" judgments. The results of the Missouri Plan in action, however, do not generally support that theory.

An examination of the election returns for a number of years demonstrates the over-all acceptance of the plan by Missouri's electorate. In 1942 the state went Republican, but two judges of the Supreme Court, both Democrats, were retained by a favorable vote of 2:1; six circuit court judges in St. Louis were similarly returned for new full terms in that same election. In 1944 Missouri went Democratic, yet two judges of the Supreme Court, one a Republican and one a Democrat, received the same proportion of the popular vote. In 1946 St. Louis went Republican but retained its ten circuit judges, all Democrats, seven of those rolling up 4:1 majorities. In 1948 the state went Democratic, yet of the two judges retained by Kansas City by an identical vote of 5:1, one was a Democrat and one a Republican. In St. Louis, in the same general election, five Democratic circuit judges and one Republican circuit judge were returned for full terms of office, the Republican and two Democrats receiving 4:1 votes and the other three Democrats 3:1 votes.[44]

From 1940 through 1970, 179 judicial elections under the plan were held in Missouri: *only one* of these saw a judge rejected by the vote of the people, and he received 46.4 percent affirmative votes;[45] none has been defeated there since (as of mid-1984). (In marked contrast, six Missouri circuit court judges running on *partisan* ballots were defeated in November 1976!) The political parties have respected the plan and, by and large, have made no effort to influence elections under it. The Missouri Plan has also been strongly defended by the judges, who find themselves in a position to attend to their court dockets free from worries and pressures about forthcoming political campaigns. It is thus not at all astonishing that almost one-half of the states have now (1984) adopted the Missouri Plan or variations thereof,[46] including a number of states that had defeated the California Plan some years earlier. Given such continuing retention statistics as those of 1978, for example, in which only 13 of 486(!) judges on retention ballots were rejected—and 2 of the 13 under extenuating circumstances—it is not astonishing that now the question "Retention Elections: Who Wins When No One Loses?" should be asked more frequently.[47] Indeed, in the first forty-six years of all of the California–Missouri type of retention elections, only 33 judges were not retained![48] Of these, 32 were ousted after 1960.

The two leading plans described represent what is probably a happy com-

---

[44] See Laurence M. Hyde, "Choosing Judges in Missouri," 38 *National Municipal Review* 491 (November 1949).

[45] He was Marian Waltner, a circuit judge, prominently identified with the discredited Pendergast machine. See Richard A. Watson, a leading expert on the Missouri Plan, "Choosing the Judges," 53 *Judicature* 289 (February 1970). In 1976, only 3 of 353 judges on retention ballots throughout the nation were rejected. But California Governor Brown's controversial appointment of Rose Elizabeth Bird as Chief Justice, as noted, survived the 1978 retention test by a mere 51.7 percent of the votes cast. (See fn. 41, *supra*.)

[46] See p. 36, *supra*, for a full list (as of fall 1985). Alaska adopted an interesting variation in 1975, under which the Nominating Commission—called the Judicial Council there—is now required to "conduct an evaluation" of each judge or justice before the retention election and to provide the public with "information about the candidate." In the first "adverse" example of the new system, the individual rated "unqualified" was reelected by the voters with an overwhelming majority!

[47] See the article of that title by William Jenkins, Jr., 61 *Judicature* 2 (August 1977), pp. 79–86. The retention vote percentages averaged 72.1 for all appelate court judges and 74.7 for all trial court judges. Of the thirteen rejectees, one was an appellate judge and twelve were trial judges. For detailed up-to-date statistics, see Kenyon N. Griffin and Michael J. Horan, "Merit Retention Elections: What Influences the Voters?" 63 *Judicature* 78 (August 1979).

[48] Susan B. Carbon, "Judicial Retention Elections: Are They Serving Their Intended Purpose?" 64 *Judicature* 5 (November 1980).

promise between the appointive and elective systems of selection, and they have deservedly engendered considerable support among professionals and laypersons. Yet most students of the political scene are inclined to agree that in a representative democracy the appointive system is the more desirable one for the judiciary, provided it is backed up by long—preferably life—tenure and it possessses a genuine degree of independence.[49] Even when one constructs a pattern based on party allegiance, it becomes evident that *appointed* judges are *much* more willing to "vote" against "their" party on the bench than are elected judges.[50] The appointing authority is not beyond accountability, and there is no meaningful substitute for effectively lodged governmental responsibility in a free society. As has been well said elsewhere, "on balance our judicial system still represents primarily a compromise between representativeness and neutral competence."[51]

TENURE OF OFFICE

Essential to the independence of the judiciary is the security of tenure, particularly in the case of appointed judges—our main concern here. Without a lengthy term of office, preferably life, adequate remuneration, and stringent constitutional and/or statutory safeguards against removal, the concept of judicial independence becomes a mockery. The record of the three major Western democracies in this regard has been laudatory generally; their practices at the level of the national judicial hierarchies are relatively similar.

THE UNITED STATES

At the *federal* level in the United States of America, all judges of the *constitutional* courts—those appointed under the provisions of Article III of the Constitution (the judicial article)—hold their position during "good behavior," which in effect means for life or until they choose to retire. The other federal judges—those of the *legislative* courts, created under the provisions

---

[49]There are notable exceptions: Stuart Nagel, for example, argued in an interesting article, "Political Party Affiliation and Judges' Decisions," 60 *American Political Science Review* 850 (December 1961), that "if judges should have value positions that are representative of the public at large, then is seems arguable that judges (at least on the higher court levels) should be elected, since presumably a judge elected at large will tend to have more representative values than a judge chosen in another manner." Philip L. Dubois, in his *From Ballot to Bench: Elections and the Quest for Accountability* (Austin: University of Texas Press, 1980), argues that, at least on the state appellate level, partisan elections are superior to nonpartisan methods as instruments for obtaining accountability.

[50]Nagel, op. cit., pp. 848–49.

[51]Herbert Kaufman, *Politics and Policies in State and Local Governments* (Englewood Cliffs, N.J.: Prentice-Hall, 1963). p. 60. An intriguing proposal is advanced by Harold W. Chase in his *Federal Judges: The Appointing Process* (Minneapolis: University of Minnesota Press, 1972), pp. 205ff., in which he calls for appointment of all lower federal judges by the nine Justices of the Supreme Court of the United States alone. Alternative suggestions abound, a good many among these propounding the creation of more or less autonomous judicial selection commissions, composed of lay as well as professional members.

of Article I of the Constitution (the legislative article)—occupy their positions for whatever period Congress may have prescribed at the time of its establishment of the court or in subsequent legislation. In some instances this has meant "good behavior" tenure for them too, or, frequently, terms of office ranging between four and fifteen years. The constitutional judges have the additional safeguard, stated in Article III, that their " ... compensation ... shall not be diminished during their continuance in office." Hence, although their salaries may be increased during their incumbency, they may not be lowered, short of constitutional amendment of the section concerned. And were a judge of a constitutional court to be removed from office other than in the manner expressly permitted by the Constitution, his salary would indeed be rather drastically "diminished."[52]

Although far from commensurate with the responsibilities and prestige of their office, and infinitely lower than comparable positions in private enterprise, judicial salaries are adequate. In 1985 the annual salary range on the federal level, as will be discussed in more detail in chapters 4 and 5, was from $76,024 for judges of the U.S. District Court to $104,728 for the Chief Justice of the U.S. Supreme Court, his associates receiving $4,160 less. But it is hardly for financial gain that a person would aspire to high judicial office. (Compared with those of federal judges, the salaries of state judges are suprisingly good, ranging from a 1983–84 average of $58,844 for the highest appellate judge, $58,486 for intermediate, and $50,462 for trial court judges—New York paid as much as $92,500 to the justices in its highest court; Alaska paid $93,084 (up to $86,509 for trial judges!); and California paid $88,818.[53]

Partly to enable aging jurists to step down from the bench with dignity, and concurrently to render their replacement with younger personnel more palatable, Congress enacted a vastly improved retirement statute in 1937. Under its provisions, federal judges may retire—a more accurate description is "enter inactive status," subject to temporary calls to duty at the discretion of the Chief Justice of the United States—on full pay at the age of seventy after having served ten years on the federal bench, or at sixty-five after having

[52]In 1976 a group of 140 federal district and appellate judges entered litigation, alleging that, due to inflation, their constitutional guarantee (Article III, Section 1) against reduction in salary during their tenure of office had been violated. The U.S. Court of Claims, in which the suit was begun, disagreed, 4:2, in *Atkins v. United States*, 556 F.2d 1028 (1977), and the Supreme Court denied review a few months later (429 U.S. 939). But in 1980, following renewed litigation, the latter now ruled 8:0 that two statutes of 1977 and 1980, which had revoked salary increases of 4.8 and 12.9 percent, respectively, in judges compensation *after* those laws had taken effect, constituted a violation of the Compensation Clause of Article III of the Constitution. On the other hand, the Court held that the "Compensation Clause" did *not* apply to the merely *promised*, but not enacted, 1978 and 1979 increases, which Congress had canceled *before* they went into effect. (*United States v. Will*, 499 U.S. 200, Chief Justice Burger writing the opinion for his Court.)

[53]November 30, 1983, figures compiled by the National Center for State Courts, Williamsburg, Va., "Survey of Judicial Salaries," November 1983, as amended in January 1985.

served fifteen years.[54] These requirements are waived in the presence of physical disability, in which case retirement pay is computed in accordance with length of service. Widows and dependents receive an annual purse equivalent to 37.5 percent of the judge's average salary—if the jurists elected to participate in a contributory "judicial survivors annuity plan."

Despite the liberal provisions of the act, the average federal judge—in particular, the average Justice of the Supreme Court (if there is such)—is reluctant to leave active service.[55] More vacancies occur as a result of death in harness, particularly at the higher levels, than in any other way. Of the ninety-six Supreme Court vacancies between 1789 and 1984, death in office was responsible for forty-eight—although, since the passage of the 1937 statute, retirement was responsible for twelve of twenty-two vacancies, resignation or disability for ten. In the entire twentieth century to date only seven Justices have stepped down from the high bench for reasons other than ill health or advanced age: Hughes (to run for President in 1916), Clarke (in 1922, to work for world peace), Byrnes (in 1943, to become F. D. R.'s "Assistant President for Domestic Affairs"), Goldberg (in 1965, to succeed Adlai E. Stevenson at the UN), Tom Clark (in 1967, because his son, Ramsey, had become U.S. Attorney General), Fortas (in 1969, as a result of disclosures of off-Court involvements with financier Louis Wolfson—the first Supreme Court Justice to resign following allegations of misconduct in office), and Potter Stewart (in 1981, simply because he wanted to return to private life). It is human to cling to power and influence, and it is particularly human to enjoy a role of such significance and nationwide esteem.[56]

---

[54]More than half of the Justices have served fifteen years or more on the highest bench. (Indeed, the members of the U.S. Supreme Court have enjoyed significantly greater longevity than men in the general population. See *Statistical Bulletin*, October 1977, p. 3.) An official example of an assignment order directed to a "retired" member of the Court is the following, issued by Chief Justice Warren to retired Associate Justice Stanley Reed. "Assignment Order: An order of the Chief Justice designating and assigning Mr. Justice Reed (retired) to perform judicial duties in the United States Court of Claims beginning November 1, 1965, and ending June 30, 1966, and for such further time as may be required to complete unfinished business, pursuant to 28 U.S.C. Section 294 (A), is ordered entered on the minutes of this court, pursuant to 28 U.S.C. Section 295." (Quoted as it was published in *The New York Times*, October 19, 1965.) A somewhat different order saw Chief Justice Warren assign Justice Tom C. Clark (retired) to service in the U.S. District Court for Northern California in June 1970. Late in 1965 *retired* Justice Charles E. Whittaker submitted his *resignation* in order to accept a legal position with the General Motors Corporation.

[55]When the great Holmes determined to retire at ninety-plus in 1932, he tersely announced: "I won't be down tomorrow."

[56]Thus, Chief Justice Taft: "As long as things continue as they are, and I am able to answer in their place, I must stay in the Court in order to prevent the Bolsheviki from gaining control. . . . " (As quoted in C. Herman Pritchett, *The Roosevelt Court* [New York: The Macmillan Co., 1948], p. 18.) Justices Grier, Field, and McKenna, all three in various stages of senility after lengthy service, had to be coaxed off the bench by their colleagues, who were driven to resort to some ingenious devices. See also the California Commission on Judicial Performance's removal for "senility" of Supreme Court Justice Marshall F. McComb in 1977.

Removal. The removal of federal judges who wish to remain on the bench can be effected only by the process of impeachment and conviction. However, not only has it evidently been legal for some time for the Judicial Council of a U.S. Circuit to discipline one of its federal judges by stripping him or her of duties and authority while permitting the retention of both title and salary,[57] in 1980 Congress enacted legislation creating authority in the judicial councils of the (now thirteen) judicial circuits to *discipline*, but not to remove, for misconduct all federal judges except those of the Supreme Court.[58] In accordance with constitutional requirements, impeachment for "Treason, Bribery, or other high Crimes and Misdemeanors"[59] may be voted by a simple majority of the members of the House of Representatives, there being a quorum on the floor. Trial is then held in the Senate, which may convict by a vote of two-thirds of the members of the Senate present and voting, if a quorum is present.

Considerable controversy exists as to the exact meaning intended by the framers of Article II, Section 4, when they spoke of "other high Crimes and Misdemeanors." Some—Gerald Ford, for one—have contended that an impeachable offense is whatever a majority of the House views as such (although he came to insist that he referred only to the appointed members of the judicial branch, not to the elected President). Others, among them the followers of James Madison and Alexander Hamilton, insist, with those Founding Fathers, that the concept of "misdemeanor" is broad enough to encompass "any offense against society" and/or any offense "against the state" committed by a public official, be it criminal or not. Still others, President Nixon's defense team, for example, claimed that there can be no impeachment in the absence of a criminal act and that that act, moreover, would have to be an *indictable* offense, while, in the same breath, they insisted that no President can be indicted while in office. A close reading of the Constitution and the works of its framers, and a careful study of the publications of such leading constitutional experts as Harvard legal scholar Raoul Berger, The Committee on Federal Legislation of the Bar Association of the City of New York, and other legal bodies lead to the considered conclusion that neither a criminal act nor an indictment is a necessary requirement for

---

[57]This was done by the Tenth Circuit's Judicial Council in the case of U.S. District Court Judge Stephen S. Chandler of Oklahoma in 1966. He appealed unsuccessfully to the Supreme Court for review. (*Chandler v. Judicial Council of the Tenth Circuit*, 382 U.S. 1003 [1966].) A related matter concerns the power of an upper court (here a six-member tribunal of Court Judge Miles W. Lord of Minnesota) for "great bias" and "substantial disregard for the mandate of this court." (*The New York Times*, January 7, 1976, p. 1.)

[58]For a detailed description of the new statute's provisions, see 2 *Judicial Conduct Reporter* 3 (Fall 1980). For a comparison of the several circuits' rules and guidelines, see, ibid., No. 1 (Spring 1980). And for an updated explication as well as analysis, of the Judicial Councils Reform and Judicial Conduct and Disability Act of 1980, see "The Federal Judicial Discipline Act: Is Decentralized Self-Regulation Working?" by Stephen B. Burbank, who provides an inconclusive response. (67 *Judicature* 4 [October 1983]).

[59]Article II, Section 4.

a vote of impeachment by the House—which should not, however, drive us to embracing the Ford statement as a guide to a proper course of action. The Committee on the Judiciary of the House of Representatives, which voted three articles of impeachment against President Nixon in July 1974, clearly did not.

To date the House of Representatives has initiated a total of thirteen impeachment proceedings, of which ten were directed against federal judges (nine other judges resigned before formal charges were lodged against them[60]); one, in 1798, against U.S. Senator William Blount of Tennessee (charges against him were dismissed by the Senate by a 14:11 vote early in 1799 for want of jurisdiction, that body having already voted 25:1 to expel him six months earlier, on grounds of conspiracy to seize Spanish Florida and Louisiana with British and Indian help); one, in 1868, against President Andrew Johnson (who was acquitted by the margin of one courageous vote, 35:19, the House having charged him 126:47); and one, in 1876, against Secretary of War William Belknap (who was subsequently acquitted, 37:25, of taking kickbacks in office). President Nixon *resigned* on August 9, 1974, *before* the House of Representatives took a formal vote on the three counts of impeachment placed against him by its Committee on the Judiciary on July 27, 29, and 30 by votes, respectively, of 27:11 (for obstruction of justice), 28:10 (for unconstitutional abuse of power), and 21:17 (for failure to comply with a subpoena for tapes as evidence). However, following Nixon's public admission that he had withheld pertinent evidence, and his subsequent resignation, the Committee sent to the House a now *unanimous* report, charging that he had engaged in "deliberate, repeated, and continued deception of the American people" about the Watergate case. The House took no stand on its Committee's conclusions, but officially voted to "accept" its report, 412:3.[61]

Of the ten impeachment proceedings involving federal judges, nine went to trial, with five resulting in acquittals and four in actual removals; the tenth was not pursued by the House—U.S. District Court Judge Mark H. Delahay, who had been impeached by voice vote, resigned in 1873 before the articles of impeachment could be prepared. The five that ended in acquittal, briefly sketched in the following paragraphs, are headed, both chronologically and in importance, by the only impeachment trial to date that had involved a Justice of the Supreme Court, that of Associate Justice Samuel Chase.

[60]The last one was Seventh U.S. Court of Appeals Judge Otto Kerner, former Governor of Illinois, who resigned on July 24, 1974, having been only the second federal judge ever to be convicted of a felony (bribery). (The first was Second Court of Appeals Judge Martin Manton, also for bribery, in 1939). Kerner had served seven months of a three-year sentence when he was found to have lung cancer. Paroled, he underwent surgery; he died on May 9, 1976.

[61]The negative votes were cast by Representatives Earl Landgrebe (R.-Ind.), G. V. Montgomery (D.-Miss.), and Otto Passman (D.-La.). Landgrebe told a news conference that he would not vote for impeachment, even if Nixon were to defy the Court: "I believe in the man and I'm thankful for what he's done for America. I say praise Nixon and Praise America." (*The New York Times*, July 25, 1974, p. C23.)

1. *Samuel Chase* was a staunch and partisan convert to the Federalist cause, and one of President Washington's last appointments to the Supreme Court. Justice Chase was impeached by the House in March 1804 by a vote of 72:32. He had made himself obnoxious to the Jeffersonians and others by a long series of injudicious and often outrageous partisan attacks against them, both on and off the bench; by his "tyrannical trials [of opponents] under the Alien and Sedition Law [of 1798]"; by his obvious favoritism toward Federalists; and by his cavalier approach to the concept of impartial juries. His judicial posture was certainly not a happy one, but he had probably not committed any impeachable offense per se. Even so, the Senate tried him amidst great ceremony. Vice-President Aaron Burr presided, and Chief Justice Marshall was an important defense witness. Chase was justly acquitted in March 1805, the Senate failing to attain the required two-thirds majority for a conviction on any of the eight charges: with twenty-three votes needed for removal, the largest total attained against Chase on any count was nineteen. The result was a signal victory not only for the narrow interpretation of the impeachment process but also for the principle of an independent judiciary. Chase, somewhat contrite, remained on the highest bench until his death in 1811.[62]

2. *James H. Peck,* a judge of the U.S. District Court for the District of Missouri, impeached 123:49 in April 1830 for "misconduct in office by misuse of contempt power," was acquitted in January 1831 by a vote of 22:21.

3. *Charles Swayne,* a judge of the U.S. District Court for the Northern District of Florida, was impeached by voice vote in December 1904 on twelve charges of "padding expense accounts, using railroad property in receivership for his personal benefit; and misusing contempt of power," he was acquitted in February 1905 on all counts by varying votes.

4. *George W. English,* a judge of the U.S. District Court for the Eastern District of Illinois, was impeached by a vote of 306:2 in November 1926 for five counts of "partiality, tyranny, and oppression"; but proceedings in the Senate were dismissed, 70:9, when the accused resigned his office that December.

5. *Harold Louderback,* a judge of the U.S. District Court for the Northern District of California, impeached in February 1933 by a vote of 183:142 on five charges of "appointing incompetent receivers and allowing them excessive fees," was acquitted in May 1933 on all counts by diverse votes.

Of the four impeachment trials that resulted in conviction, the first was probably unconstitutional as well as unjust, the second was questionable, and the third and fourth were justified.

---

[62]For an authoritative commentary and interpretation, see Richard Tillich, "The Chase Impeachment," 4 *American Journal of Legal History* 49 (1960). See also Philip G. Henderson, "Marshall v. Jefferson: Politics and the Federal Judiciary in the Early Republic," 11 *Michigan Journal of Political Science* 2 (1983), pp. 54–55.

1. *John Pickering*, a judge of the U.S. District Court for the District of New Hampshire, who was known to be medically insane at the time, was impeached by the House in December 1803 on four counts of "irregular judicial proceedings, loose morals, and drunkenness" by a vote of 45:8. In March 1804 the Senate removed him from office by identical 19:7 votes on each of the articles. John Adams characterized the Pickering removal as "an infamous and certainly an illegal conviction." The unfortunate Pickering had been hopelessly insane and an alcoholic for three years, but he had committed no "High Crimes, and Misdemeanors."

2. *West H. Humphreys*, a judge of the U.S. District Court for the Middle, Eastern, and Western Districts of Tennessee, was impeached by voice vote in May 1862 on seven counts of "support of secession and holding Confederate office." In a one-day trial, on June 26, the Senate convicted Humphreys on all charges but one, removing him from office by a 38:0 vote and disqualifying him from holding any further office by a 36:0 vote.

3. *Robert W. Archbald*, an associate judge of the U.S. Commerce Court, which was abolished in 1915, was impeached in July 1912 by a 223:1 vote on thirteen serious charges of misconduct in office. The Senate removed him in January 1913 by voice vote after he had been convicted on five of the articles of impeachment. He was then disqualified from holding any further office by a 39:35 vote.

4. *Halsted L. Ritter* was the last jurist to date to be both impeached and convicted. A judge of the U.S. District Court for the Southern District of Florida, Ritter was impeached by the House, 181:146, in March 1936 on seven counts of "bringing his court into scandal and disrepute," including the receipt of corrupt payments, practicing law while on the bench, and falsifying income tax returns. That April the Senate acquitted him on six of the counts, but found him guilty on the seventh, 56:28. A motion to disqualify him from holding any further office lost 76:0, however.[63]

The undoubtedly fortunate failure of most impeachment attempts is not an indication of any lack of verbal efforts by legislators who, partly sincerely and partly for constituent consumption, are eager to "get" federal judges—in particular, the Justices of the Supreme Court—usually for decisions that the congresspersons have found repugnant for a variety of reasons. To cite but one modern example: In June 1953 a special subcommittee of five members was created by the House of Representatives to consider the impeachment of Supreme Court Justice William O. Douglas. The resolution for impeachment, which was brought to the House by Congressman W.M. Wheeler (D-

---

[63] When the U.S. Court of Claims refused to take jurisdiction in the Ritter case, Ritter appealed to the U.S. Supreme Court, which denied *certiorari*. (*Ritter v. United States*, 300 U.S. 368, [1937].)

Ga.), charged the jurist with "high crimes and misdemeanors in office," Douglas having granted a brief stay of the scheduled execution of convicted spies Julius and Ethel Rosenberg—a stay that had been set aside by the full Court almost at once. Nothing came of Mr. Wheeler's efforts.[64] (In fact, the attempt would be all but forgotten today were it not for a statement made by Gerald Ford on the floor of the House: "an impeachable offense is whatever a majority of the House of Representatives considers it to be at a given moment in history." Mr. Ford, then a Representative from Michigan, came to regret that assertion two decades later.) Such efforts are not confined to the poeple's representatives. In February 1957 a group of some two dozen men and women filed with the Clerk of the House Representatives a petition demanding that the House impeach the entire membership of the Supreme Court. It consisted of foot-long pages headed "Impeach Warren," a battle cry that was taken up with a vengeance by the John Birch Society, which widely advertised "The Warren Impeachment Packet" (obtainable for "One Dollar, Postpaid"). And the Georgia State Assembly, in a colorful brochure decorated with the state flag, distributed "A Resolution Requesting Impeachment of Six Members of the United States Supreme Court"—Justices Warren, Black, Reed, Frankfurter, Douglas, and Clark (Burton, Harlan, and Brennan escaping their wrath, somehow). The main charge: "Unconstitutional . . . pro-Communist racial integration policies."[65]

The majority of the states—in all but one of which judicial terms were fixed as of 1984—used to follow the federal pattern regarding removal of their appointed judges with lengthy tenure: impeachment and conviction being the normal process. Among the few states that had found it necessary to resort to it in the past were Tennessee, in the case of Criminal Court Judge Raulston Schoolfield, for "corrupt and injudicious conduct," in 1958, and Oklahoma, in that of its Supreme Court Justice Napoleon Bonaparte Johnson in 1965. But since the early 1970s most states have turned to other modes of removal, usually by resort to "commissions on judicial qualifications," "commissions on judicial performance," or "commissions on judicial disability and tenure." These commissions, composed frequently of both lawyers and non-lawyers,[66] serve as adjudicatory bodies, the ultimate removal power normally

[64] In July 1966 Rep. George W. Andrews (D.-Ala.) introduced another unsuccessful impeachment resolution against Douglas, this one on the ground of his "character," in view of the then sixty-seven-year-old Justice's fourth marriage. (His new wife was twenty-three.) Andrews was joined by Reps. Paul Findley (R.-Ill.) and Thomas G. Abernathy (D.-Miss.). And in 1970 Douglas's congressional enemies—led by Gerald Ford, who by then had become Republican Floor Leader—tried again to impeach him, and again failed.

[65] H. R. No. 174, "A Resolution," adopted on February 22, 1957, pp. 3-12.

[66] As of late 1983, there were forty-nine state plus several federal-level jurisdictions within the United States (e.g., the District of Columbia and Puerto Rico) that had boards, commissions, or courts charged in one fashion or another with the process of judicial discipline. In the spring of 1976 a total of 362 persons served on these bodies; of them 93 were non-lawyers,

being vested in the highest court of the state, generally its Supreme Court.[67] In a few states, for example, Alabama, Delaware, Illinois, and Kentucky, special courts or commissions are provided to serve both as the adjudicating *and* the removing body. Tennessee and West Virginia still cling to the impeachment process. New York has used three methods: prior to 1948 its legislature held judicial removal power; from 1948 through 1977 a special removal court, the now abolished *Court on the Judiciary,*[68] possessed that authority; and, as a result of a constitutional amendment, 1978 saw the beginning of the utilization of the 1975-established eleven-member *Commission on Judicial Conduct,* which hears all complaints against judges, conducts the trial, and imposes sanctions, subject to *de novo* review by the Court of Appeals, New

---

153 judges, and 116 lawyers who were not judges. (See Frank Greenberg, "The Task of Judging the Judges," 59 *Judicature* 10, [March 1976], pp. 458FF.) This District of Columbia established a seven-member "Commission of Judicial Disability and Tenure" under its 1975 reorganization statute. Its first challenge was an attempt to block the reappointment of District of Columbia Superior Court Judge Charles W. Halleck, who had come under attack because of his conduct in forty specific cases during his controversial first decade on that bench.

[67] Thus, in November 1970 the Louisiana Supreme Court, acting on the recommendation of the State Judicial Commission, removed from office, by a 6:1 vote, Judge Edward A. Haggerty, Jr., who had been arrested in a vice squad raid on a "stag party" in a local motel a year earlier. (*In re Judge Edward A. Haggerty, Jr.,* La. 241 So. 2d 469.) The dissenting judge could see no connection between Mr. Haggerty's personal and judicial conduct. In 1980 the Wisconsin Supreme Court suspended Circuit Judge Christ T. Seraphim for three years for "major violations of the Code of Judicial Ethics," including "gross personal misconduct with six women . . . that constituted unprivileged and nonconsensual physical conduct with offensive sexual overtones."

[68] That tribunal heard its first case in 1959, at which time it considered the removal of two Kings County jurists, Nathan R. Sobel and Samuel S. Liebowitz. It voted not to remove them, although it did "censure" them both for their public demeanor. In 1963, however, it did oust Supreme Court Justice Louis L. Friedman and Claim Court Judge Melvin H. Osterman in two separate actions: Friedman was removed on a vote of 4:2 for having engaged in "unethical judicial conduct" and having violated the "concept, spirit, and letter" of the canons of judicial ethics. He unsuccessfully appealed for U.S. Supreme Court review (*Friedman v. Court on the Judiciary,* 375 U.S. 10 [1963], certiorari denied). Osterman was removed on a 6:0 vote for his refusal to sign a waiver of immunity and answer questions before a New York grand jury investigating the 1963 New York State Liquor License Board scandals. His appeal to the U.S. Supreme Court also met with a terse "*certiorari* denied" response. (*Osterman v. Court on the Judiciary,* 376 U.S. 914 [1964].) Two other jurists, Michael M. D'Auria and Mitchell D. Schweitzer, resigned in 1971 and 1972, respectively, rather than face action by the Court on the Judiciary. In 1973, the latter removed Supreme Court Justice Joseph P. Pfingst, who had been under suspension for having been convicted of concealing a monetary conflict of interest. Pfingst, too, appealed his ousting to the U.S. Supreme Court, which once again sided with the Court of the Judiciary. (*Pfingst v. Court on the Judiciary,* 412 U.S. 941 [1973].) And in late 1975 the now-defunct New York tribunal "censured," but did not remove, Supreme Court Justice Wilfred A. Waltemade. Between 1978 and the spring of 1984 the Commission had removed seven full-time and 35 part-time judges (not counting four who were "saved" on appeal). In two instances the Court of Appeals ordered removal when the commission had failed to do so, most recently in April 1984 in the case of Buffalo City Court Judge Barbara M. Sims.

York's highest tribunal. In several western states, sitting judges may be recalled from office by popular vote—an intriguing and controversial manifestation of "direct democracy" of which the referendum and the initiative are illustrations along with the recall.

BRITAIN

The British have come a long way since the days of James I (1603–25) and Charles I (1625–49), when the English judges held their office *durante bene placito nostro* ("according to our good pleasure"). Most, but not all, English judges today, very much like their cousins in the United States, enjoy what to all intents and purposes is tenure for life. But since the Courts Act of 1971, "the Lord Chancellor may remove a circuit judge from office on the ground of incapacity or misbehavior."[69] Recorders—lower judges—are removable for "failure to comply with any requirements" of their appointment.[70] The custom of appointing judges for indefinite terms of office during their "good behavior" dates back to the Act of Settlement of 1701, which provided that judge's "commissions" be made *quam diu se bene gesserint* ("as long as they will have performed well"). One-significant recent change must be noted, however. As a result of the mandate of the Judicial Pensions Act of 1959 and the Courts Act of 1970 a seventy-two-year retirement limit for judges of the superior and circuit courts has been adopted for all appointments at that level, with a possible three-year extension. Recorders retire at seventy-two, but Higher Court judges may stay until seventy-five. Retirement pensions are paid on a graduated scale that rises from one-quarter of basic salary after five years of service to a maximum of half of the annual salary after fifteen years.

For practical purposes, the English judges, notably those of the superior courts, are irremovable, the Judicature Act of 1925 providing that all judges except the Lord Chancellor hold office "during good behaviour subject to a power of removal by His [now Her] Majesty on an address presented to His [now Her] Majesty by both Houses of Parliament.[71] However, the judges of the county courts are deemed to be removable at the insistence of the Lord Chancellor for "inability" and "misbehaviour" under various statutes, such as the County Courts Act of 1959. The justices of the peace are also removable for similar reasons of "misconduct" or "proved incapacity." In fact, the English judges are not protected in any way from a change by statute; Parliament retains its fundamental power to alter their tenure and emoluments of office. Suffice it to say that it is highly unlikely to do so in a detrimental sense! In any event, a dismissal of a judge for political reasons is impossible today for all practical purposes. Indeed, since the Act of Settlement of 1701, *only one* English judge has been removed on any grounds (although official com-

[69] Sec. 17 (4).
[70] Sec. 21 (6).
[71] Sec. 12 (1) of 15 & 16 G.O., ch. 49.

plaints have been lodged against seventeen). That single removal took place in 1830, when Sir Jonah Barrington, a superior judge—a judge in admiralty—was deprived of his office by petition of both houses of Parliament as a result of an inquiry into the Irish courts of justice carried out during that year.

The salaries of the judges (1983), £27,750 (for circuit judges), £28,950 (for the Lord Chancellor, which includes the £3,375 salary payable to the judge as Speaker of the House of Lords), and £52,500 (for the Lord Chief Justice of England), are set by an Act of Parliament,[72] but are, in effect, determined by the Lord Chancellor with the consent of the Prime Minister and the Chancellor of the Exchequer after a thorough discussion in Cabinet. The executive branch may not move to reduce these while the recipients hold office, and the legislature is similarly enjoined since judicial salaries do not even come up for parliamentary review. A further indication of effective judicial independence is the parliamentary custom that no questions at all may be asked about the conduct of courts in particular cases. Moreover, according to two court rulings now firmly regarded as *res judicata* in England,[73] a judge may not be held for civil or criminal proceeding because of anything he may have said or done in his judicial capacity, even if it is alleged to have been malicious or in bad faith. Given these cherished safeguards of judicial strength and independence, the English bench has reciprocated in full measure with a record of efficiency and impartiality not likely to be readily matched anywhere in the free world today. Sir Ivor Jennings was quite correct when he contended in 1954 that "no allegation" of partiality or corruption or political influence is ever made against judges of the United Kingdom—which does not mean that there is no criticism, especially on technical grounds.[74]

FRANCE

The career judges of the Fifth French Republic who, as we have seen, comprise a branch of the national civil service, also have life tenure. There is no doubt that they are at least as secure today as are their English and American counterparts. But it took a considerable while to attain that cherished goal. During the *ancien régime* judicial office went customarily to the favorites of the monarch, and especially to those who could afford to pay for it. *La révolution* replaced that interesting system of patronage *cum* purchase with popular election of judges, which was not much of an improvement, if any. Napoleon Bonaparte grandly eliminated that method and announced the principle of "irremovability," which, in practice, meant rather complete dependency on him. A period of minor changes and ameliorations was effected by the

[72]See Sec. 1 (2) of the Ministerial and Other Salaries Act of 1972 and N. B. Whittaker's *Almanac* for 1983.

[73]*Anderson v. Gorrie* 91 L.J.K.B. 897 (1922) and *Heddon v. Evans*, 35 T.L.R. 642 (1919). See also *Sirros v. Moore*, Q.B. 118 (1975).

[74]*The Queen's Government* (London: Penguin Books, 1954), p. 147.

institutions and individuals that succeeded the colorful Corsican until the days of the Third Republic, just a bit more than a century ago, when the status of the French judges improved—without, however, reaching a truly separate status.

Irremovability as an avowed policy for the career judiciary was resuscitated by a proclamation of the Provisional Government a few days after V-E Day in 1945. It was made a part of the basic document of the de Gaulle Republic by the specific verbiage of the Constitution of 1958, which asserts that these judges are "irremovable." Actually, that is technically incorrect, for they are removable, but solely for "misconduct in office," and then only on the recommendation of the High Council of the Judiciary, which acts as a disciplinary court for judges. When the council sits as such, the President of the *Cour de Cassation* is its presiding officer.

The judges of France are not quite as well paid as those across the Channel,[75] but there is no evidence that they are in any sense significantly more susceptible to corruption of injudiciousness than their English counterparts. Strengthened even more by the specific proviso of the de Gaulle Constitution making the President of the Repbulic the "guarantor of the independence of the judicial authority," and by the genuine protective power of the high Council of the Judiciary, they enjoy an extensive degree of both professional freedom and authority, notwithstanding sporadic criticism of their labors.

QUALIFICATIONS AND MOTIVATIONS: THE UNITED STATES

Although attitudes and practices regarding tenure of office do not differ significantly among the American, British, and French judiciaries, substantial, indeed, crucial, distinctions become immediately apparent in any consideration of the qualifications—background, experience, and training—of the judges in these countries. They represent distinctions that flow rather logically from different traditions and theories regarding the role of government in society, and they are attuned to what, for better or for worse, are deemed to be the needs and experiences of each land. With these thoughts in mind we turn to a consideration of the problem of judicial qualifications in the United States.

BASIC PREREQUISITES?

In contrast to the specialized requirements that obtain in Britain and France, there is but one standardized prerequisite for qualification as a U.S. *federal* judge today—the LL.B. or J.D. degree of the aspirant or, as was still true of

---

[75] The average annual salaries of the French judges in 1984 ranged from approximately $24,000 for the lowest echelon to $40,000 for the highest, *not* counting certain allowances that might add up to 20 percent. (Data provided by M. Raymond Exertier of the French Ministry of Justice, (November 21, 1984.)

seven states in 1983,[76] the completion of several years (usually three or four) of reading law or a combination of the latter plus a reduced attendance requirement in law school. The possession of these requirements is neither a constitutional nor a statutory requirement for appointment, yet custom would automatically exclude from consideration anyone who did not have them. Moreover, the legal profession, which, as already noted, has a very real voice in today's appointive process, would remonstrate so determinedly that the political powers of the government involved would assuredly acquiesce. (Still, at the *state* and local level not even a law degree is necessary in at least some instances.[77]) By 1985 only 55 of the 102 Justices on the Court had attended law school.

Theoretically, any graduate of an accredited bona fide school of law with his or her eye on a federal judgeship may thus look forward to an appointment to the coveted niche—provided that he or she is politically "available" *and* acceptable to the executive, legislative, and private forces that, in the order enumerated, constitute the powers-that-be underlying the paths of selection, nomination, and appointment in the judicial process. In the final analysis, of course, it is the President and his immediate advisers concerned—here usually the Attorney General and his Deputy—who take the crucial step of submitting the nominee to the Senate. Thus, all of America's chief executives except William Henry Harrison, Zachary Taylor, Andrew Johnson and Jimmy Carter have succeeded in seeing at least one nominee attain membership on the highest court of the land—our chief concern in these particular pages. Of the four exceptions, the first two were removed too quickly by death; Johnson was the victim of congressional machinations that successfully prevented him from filling several Supreme Court vacancies; and fate simply never presented Carter with an opportunity. Table 1 illustrates the number of Justices each President appointed and who *actually served*, including those not ultimately confirmed by the Senate. An example of the latter is John Rutledge, who was designated Chief Justice by President Washington in 1795 but the Senate, by a vote of 10:14, refused to confirm him. The senate had approved Rutledge as Associate Justice in 1789 but he had resigned that post less than two years later without ever sitting—although he had served on circuit duty—in order to accept the post of Chief Justice of the Supreme Court of South Carolina (and hence is listed as only one Washington appointment). Counting Justice Rutledge thus only once, and Justices E. D. White, Hughes, and Stone twice—since those three all actually served both as Associate Justice *and* as Chief Justice and were appointed by a *different* President in each instance—the 102 individual Justices who had served on the Court as of the beginning of the 1984–85 term provided thirty-five Presidents with 105 successful appointments.

---

[76]California, Maine, New York, Vermont, Virginia, Washington, and Wyoming. Alaska merely required "completion of certified clerkship."

[77]See ch. 4, *infra*, pp. 143–45 and fns. 6–8.

Table 1. Number of Presidential Appointments of U.S. Supreme Court Justices Who Actually Served on the Court (Arranged Chronologically)

President	Dates in Office	Number of Appointments
Washington	1789–1797	10
J. Adams	1797–1801	3
Jefferson	1801–1809	3
Madison	1809–1817	2
Monroe	1817–1825	1
J. Q. Adams	1825–1829	1
Jackson	1829–1837	6 (5)[a]
Van Buren	1837–1841	2 (3)[a]
W. H. Harrison	1841	0
Tyler	1841–1845	1
Polk	1845–1849	2
Taylor	1849–1850	0
Fillmore	1850–1853	1
Pierce	1853–1857	1
Buchanan	1857–1861	1
Lincoln	1861–1865	5
A. Johnson	1865–1869	0
Grant	1869–1877	4
Hayes	1877–1881	2
Garfield	1881	1
Arthur	1881–1885	2
Cleveland	1885–1889; 1893–1897	4[b]
B. Harrison	1889–1893	4
McKinley	1897–1901	1
T. Roosevelt	1901–1909	3
Taft	1909–1913	6
Wilson	1913–1921	3
Harding	1921–1923	4
Coolidge	1923–1929	1
Hoover	1929–1933	3
F. D. Roosevelt	1933–1945	9
Truman	1945–1953	4
Eisenhower	1953–1961	5
Kennedy	1961–1963	2
L. B. Johnson	1963–1969	2
Nixon	1969–1974	4
Ford	1974–1977	1
Carter	1977–1981	0
Reagan	1981–	1
		105

[a] Jackson had nominated Catron, but the latter was not confirmed until Van Buren had taken over.

[b] Two in each of his two terms, which were split by Harrison's single term.

JUDICIAL EXPERIENCE AND ITS ABSENCE

In view of the minimal basic need of the LL.B, or J.D., it is hardly astonishing that many a newly appointed U.S. jurist lacks practical judicial experience.[78] Among the appellate courts, this has been especially true of U.S. Supreme Court designees; those of the court level immediately below, the U.S. (Circuit) Court of Appeals, have often had some lower court experience on the U.S. District Court—the federal trial court. Among the 102 individual Justices who served on the Supreme Court between 1789 and the middle of 1984, only twenty-two had had ten or more years of previous judicial experience on any lower level, federal or state, at the time of their appointment, and forty-two had no judicial experience whatsoever. Yet, as Table 2 demonstrates, the list of the totally inexperienced contains many of the greatest and most illustrious names in America's judicial history. Among them are five of the fifteen Chief Justices—Taney, S. P. Chase, Waite, Fuller, and Warren—and Associate Justices Story, Miller, Bradley, Brandeis, Douglas, and Frankfurter, to name a few. (John Marshall had a mere three years in the very minor local Richmond, Virginia, City Hustings Court, from 1785–88.)

In a learned essay calling for selection of Supreme Court justices "wholly on the basis of functional fitness," Justice Frankfurter argued keenly that neither judicial experience nor political affiliation nor geographic considerations ought to play a significant role in the appointment of these highest jurists, whose job he viewed as necessarily requiring the qualities of *philosopher* ("but not too philosophical," commented his student Paul A. Freund), *historian, and prophet*.[79] Or, in the words of Justice Holmes, the judge should be a "combination of Justinian, Jesus Christ, and John Marshall."[80] Even though ill-equipped to do so (the task requires "poetic sensibilities" and the "gift of imagination"), the jurist must "pierce the curtain of the future ... give shape and visage to mysteries still in the womb of time,"[81] must "have antennae registering feeling and judgment beyond logical, let alone quantitative proof."[82] Thus, Felix Frankfurter asserted:

> One is entitled to say without qualification that the *correlation between prior judicial experience and fitness for the Supreme Court is zero*. The significance

[78] By way of contrast, in addition to other requirements, nominees to the intermediate appellate judiciary in Pakistan, for example, must have a minimum of ten years of judicial experience, and they need fifteen years for appointment to the Pakistan Supreme Court (including five years at the intermediate appellate level).

[79] To which, in a conversation with me in May 1964, Justice Brennan added "inordinate patience."

[80] As quoted by Judge Irving R. Kaufman, "Charting a Judicial Pedigree," *The New York Times*, January 24, 1981, p. 23.

[81] Charles Evans Hughes, who missed the presidency of the United States by a mere 3,000 California votes in 1916, described what he would have looked for as nominator of Supreme Court Justices, in the following order of priority: "strength of character, courage of convictions, sound learning, exact knowledge, painstaking study." (As quoted in *The New York Times*, February 22, 1970, p. 13.)

[82] Felix Frankfurter, *Of Law and Men* (New York: Harcourt, Brace and Co., 1956), p. 39.

Table 2. Prior Judicial Experience of U.S. Supreme Court Justices and Their
Subsequent Service

| Justice | Year Nominated[a] | Number of Years of Prior Judicial Experience | | | Years of Service on Supreme Court[b] |
		Federal	State	Total	
Jay[c]	1789	0	2	2	6
J. Rutledge[c,d]	1789 and 1795[c]	0	6	6	2
Cushing	1789	0	29	29	21
Wilson	1789	0	0	0	9
Blair	1789	0	11	11	7
Iredell	1790	0	½	½	9
T. Johnson	1791	0	1½	1½	2
Paterson	1793	0	0	0	13½
S. Chase	1796	0	8	8	15
Ellsworth[c]	1796	0	5	5	4
Washington	1798	0	0	0	31
Moore	1799	0	1	1	5
J. Marshall[c]	1801	0	3	3	34½
W. Johnson	1804	0	6	6	30
Livingston	1806	0	0	0	16
Todd	1807	0	6	6	19
Story	1811	0	0	0	34
Duval	1811	0	6	6	24
Thompson	1823	0	16	16	20
Trimble	1826	9	2	11	2
McLean	1829	0	6	6	32
Baldwin	1830	0	0	0	14
Wayne	1835	0	5	5	32
Taney[c]	1836	0	0	0	28
Barbour	1836	6	2	8	5
Catron	1837	0	10	10	28
McKinley	1837	0	0	0	15
Daniel	1841	4	0	0	19
Nelson	1845	0	22	22	27
Woodbury	1845	0	6	6	6
Grier	1846	0	13	13	23
Curtis	1851	0	0	0	6
Campbell	1853	0	0	0	8
Clifford	1858	0	0	0	23
Swayne	1862	0	0	0	19
Miller	1862	0	0	0	28
Davis	1862	0	14	14	15
Field	1863	0	6	6	34¾
S. P. Chase[c]	1864	0	0	0	8½
Strong	1870	0	11	11	10¾
Bradley	1870	0	0	0	22
Hunt	1872	0	8	8	10
Waite[c]	1874	0	0	0	14
Harlan I	1877	0	1	1	34

Table 2. Prior Judicial Experience of U.S. Supreme Court Justices and Their Subsequent Service

Justice	Year Nominated[a]	Number of Years of Prior Judicial Experience			Years of Service on Supreme Court[b]
		Federal	State	Total	
Woods	1880	12	0	12	6½
Matthews	1881	0	4	4	8
Gray	1881	0	18	18	21
Blatchford	1882	15	0	15	11
L. Q. C. Lamar	1888	0	0	0	5
Fuller[c]	1888	0	0	0	22
Brewer	1889	5	14	19	20
Brown	1890	16	0	16	16
Shiras	1892	0	0	0	11
H. E. Jackson	1893	7	0	7	2½
E. D. White[c]	1894 and 1910[c]	0	1½	1½	27
Peckham	1895	0	9	9	14
McKenna	1898	5	0	5	27
Holmes	1902	0	20	20	30
Day	1903	4	3	7	19
Moody	1906	0	0	0	4
Lurton	1909	16	10	26	4½
Hughes	1910 and 1930[c]	0	0	0	17
Van Devanter	1910	7	1	8	27
J. R. Lamar	1910	0	2	2	5
Pitney	1912	0	11	11	10
McReynolds	1914	0	0	0	27
Brandeis	1916	0	0	0	23
Clarke	1916	2	0	2	6
Taft[c]	1921	8	5	13	9
Sutherland	1922	0	0	0	16
Butler	1922	0	0	0	17
Sanford	1923	14	0	14	7
Stone[c,e]	1923 and 1941[c]	0	0	0	21
Roberts	1930	0	0	0	15
Cardozo	1932	0	18	18	6
Black	1937	0	1½	1½	34
Reed	1937	0	0	0	19
Frankfurter	1939	0	0	0	23
Douglas	1939	0	0	0	36½
Murphy	1940	0	7	7	9
Byrnes	1941	0	0	0	1
R. H. Jackson	1941	0	0	0	13
W. B. Rutledge	1943	4	0	4	6½
Burton	1945	0	0	0	13
Vinson[c]	1946	5	0	5	7
Clark	1949	0	0	0	18
Minton	1949	8	0	8	7
Warren[c]	1953	0	0	0	16

Table 2. Prior Judicial Experience of U.S. Supreme Court Justices and Their Subsequent Service

| Justice | Year Nominated[a] | Number of Years of Prior Judicial Experience | | | Years of Service on Supreme Court[b] |
		Federal	State	Total	
Harlan II	1955	1	0	1	16
Brennan	1956	0	7	7	
Whittaker	1957	3	0	3	5
Stewart	1958	4	0	4	22¾
B. R. White	1962	0	0	0	
Goldberg	1962	0	0	0	2¾
Fortas	1965	0	0	0	3½
T. Marshall	1967	3¾	0	3¾	
Burger[c]	1969	13	0	13	
Blackmun	1970	11	0	11	
Powell	1971	0	0	0	
Rehnquist	1971	0	0	0	
Stevens	1975	5	0	5	
O'Connor	1981	0	6½	6½	

[a] May be earlier than the date on which the successful nominee took the oath of office (e.g., Cushing, 1790, and Blair, 1790.
[b] Counted as of date of receipt of commission, following Senate confirmation.
[c] Indicates Chief Justice and date of is appointment and/or promotion.
[d] Rutledge's nomination as Chief Justice was rejected by the Senate, but he did serve in the post as a recess appointee for four months.
[e] Had no judicial experience when appointed as *Associate* Justice.

of the greatest among the Justices who had such experience, Holmes and Cardozo, derived not from that judicial experience but from the fact that they were Holmes and Cardozo. They were thinkers, and more particularly, legal philosophers.[83]

And on this point Justice Frankfurter was fond of quoting the distinguished Judge Learned Hand, who for so many years rendered outstanding service on the U.S. Court of Appeals for the Second Circuit (New York, Connecticut, and Vermont), but who never attained his richly merited promotion to the Supreme Court:

I venture to believe that it is as important to a judge called upon to pass on a question of constitutional law, to have a bowing acquaintance with Acton and Maitland, with Thucydides, Gibbon and Carlyle, with Homer, Dante, Shake-

[83] "The Supreme Court in the Mirror of Justices," 105 *University of Pennsylvania Law Review* 781 (1957). (Italics supplied.) "A copy of your lecture," wrote Sherman Minton, a recently retired colleague, to Frankfurter, "should be sent to each member of Congress. Your statement explodes entirely the myth of prior judicial experience. I am a living example that judicial experience [he had eight years on lower federal benches before coming to the Court] doesn't make one prescient." (Letter, dated April 18, 1957, Frankfurter Papers, Library of Congress.)

speare and Milton, with Machiavelli, Montaigne, and Rabelais, with Plato, Bacon, Hume, and Kant as with books which have been specifically written on the subject. For in such matters everything turns upon the spirit in which he approaches the questions before him. The words he must construe are empty vessels into which he can pour nearly everything he will. Men do not gather figs or thistles, nor supply institutions from judges whose outlook is limited by parish or class. They must be aware that there are before them more than verbal problems; more than final solutions cast in generalizations of universal applicability. They must be aware of the changing social tensions in every society which make it an organism; which demand new schemata of adaptation; which will disrupt it, if rigidly confined.[84]

Attitudes Toward Experience. Yet the experience factor for Supreme Court Justices,[85] although more or less dormant during some administrations, such as those of President Franklin D. Roosevelt, is sometimes revitalized by others, as it was by that of President Eisenhower. Roosevelt paid little, if any heed to it, whereas Eisenhower, after his initial appointment of Chief Justice Warren, insisted that his nominees have at least *some* judicial experience, no matter how slight. Of the nine men who sat on the Court as a result of President Roosevelt's appointments (or promotion to Chief Justice in the case of Stone), neither Chief Justice Stone nor Associate Justices Reed, Frankfurter, Douglas, Byrnes, and Jackson had any judicial experience whatsoever, while Justice Rutledge served on the Court of Appeals for the District of Columbia for four years and Justice Black saw one-and-a-half and Justice Murphy seven years, respectively, on state tribunals. President Truman followed his predecessor's habit of ignoring judicial background: of his four appointees, Associate Justices Burton and Clark had none at all; Chief Justice Vinson and Associate Justice Minton had five years and eight years, respectively, of prior service on the lower federal bench. President Eisenhower's four appointees subsequent to that of the Chief Justice—Associate Justices Harlan, Brennan, Whittaker, and Stewart—all had seen some prior service, although the total number of years for the four was but fifteen. Neither Associate Justices White and Goldberg, appointed by President Kennedy, nor Fortas, appointed by President Lyndon B. Johnson, had had any judicial experience, whereas Johnson's other appointee, Thurgood Marshall, had spent three and a half years on the federal bench below the Supreme Court. President Nixon's first two appointees, Chief Justice Burger and Associate Justice Blackmun, had served thirteen and eleven years, respectively, on lower federal benches, but Associate Justices Powell and Rehnquist had had no prior judicial experience at all when nominated. President Ford's sole appointee, Associate Justice John Paul Stevens, had seen five years of service on the U.S. Court of Appeals, and

---

[84] As quoted in *The New York Times Magazine*, November, 28, 1954, p. 14.

[85] One of the reviewers of my *Justices and Presidents*, op. cit., found that the twelve Justices rated "great" had a total of 40½ years of judicial experience prior to attaining the Supreme Court (with Holmes and Cardozo 28 of them!) while the fourteen rated as "failures" or "below average" had 64⅙ years!

President Reagan's appointee, Sandra Day O'Conner, had served six and a half years on the state of Arizona bench.

Congress, too, is hardly of one mind on the matter of the necessity or even the desirability of judicial experience as a prerequisite for appointment to the highest court in the land. Bills are continually introduced that would require future nominees to the Supreme Court to have upwards of five years of experience on lower court benches. In the 89th Congress, and again in the 91st, for example, thirteen bills of this type were sponsored by members on both sides of the aisle in both houses of Congress. But all of these measures have failed of enactment. Moreover, many legislators agree with what is clearly a majority of the closest observers of the Supreme Court, as well as with the thesis of Justice Frankfurter, that judicial experience, because of the special nature of that Court's work, is not essential. The Supreme Court is not a trial court in the sense that the federal district courts below are, nor is it called on to deal with a particular judicial constituency as are these courts of first instance and, to a considerably lesser extent, the federal courts of appeals that lie immediately above the district courts in the judicial hierarchy. Further, there is very little transition or connection between the experience in the lower federal constitutional courts and that of the highest—the procedural and jurisdictional frameworks are quite different. The type of private litigation at common law, so prevalent below, is practically extinct at the bar of today's Supreme Court; the highest Court is almost exclusively occupied with questions of public law, led by cases at constitutional law or with constitutional overtones, review of administrative actions, and other related questions. Experience on the courts below may well be theoretically desirable, although there are some observers who would not even grant that much, but it should not become a *requirement* for qualification for the Supreme Court. Again returning to Justice Frankfurter and Judge Learned Hand, the business of the Supreme Court today is "with the application of rather fundamental aspirations," what Judge Hand called *moods*, that are embodied in constitutional provisions such as the due process of law clauses of the Fifth and Fourteenth Amendments and the latter's equal protection of the laws mandate— clauses and concepts that were quite evidently deliberately designed "not to be precise and positive directions for rules of action." In the words of Justice Frankfurter:

> The judicial process in applying them involves a *judgment on the process of government*. The Court sits in judgment, that is, on the views of the direct representatives of the people in meeting the needs of society, on the views of Presidents and Governors, and by their construction of the will of legislatures *the Court breathes life, feeble or strong, into the inert pages of the Constitution and the statute books.*[86]

---

[86]Frankfurter, "The Supreme Court in the Mirror of Justices," op. cit., 793. (Italics supplied.) In an address at the University of Virginia a few years earlier, "F. F." had spelled out what he considered "essential" to service on the Court, as follows: "[Justices must] bring to their task, first and foremost, humility and an understanding of the range of the problems and of

Small wonder that this function calls for a combination of philosopher, historian, and prophet!

A Case Study. A brief survey of the judicial experience of the members of the 1978–79 Supreme Court may aid in demonstrating that even if that specific qualification is largely, or even wholly, absent in many instances, experience in other relevant areas of public service is often abundantly present. Of the members of the 1984–85 Court, which began its term on October 1, only five had past judicial experience, and in all but two or at most three of these cases it was rather negligible: as already noted, Chief Justice Burger had served thirteen years on the U.S. Court of Appeals for the District of Columbia, and Justice Blackmun eleven on the U.S. Court of Appeals for the Eighth Court. Justice Brennan had seen seven years of service on New Jersey state courts, Justice O'Connor six and a half on Arizona's. But Justices Stevens, Stewart, and Marshall had had a mere five, four, and three and a half years on the U.S. Court of Appeals for the Seventh, Sixth, and Second Circuit, respectively, and Justices White, Powell, and Rehnquist came to the Court without any prior judicial service.

Yet *all* of the members of the 1984–85 Court had a record of considerable experience in *public life*, frequently of an administrative nature, in addition to or in place of whatever judicial experience they might have had. Thus, in 1969, on his designation as Chief Justice at the age of sixty-one, Warren Earl Burger had practiced law for twenty-three years; had been mildly politically active in his native Minnesota; and for three years had been Assistant Attorney General, leading the civil division of the U.S. Department of Justice. William J. Brennan, Jr., had practiced law for fifteen years, was a decorated army officer during World War II, and had served the State of New Jersey when Governor Driscoll appointed him, at the youthful age of forty-three, to the state bench in 1949. Potter Steward had practiced law for more than a decade and had served on the City Council of Cincinnati for five years when the then thirty-nine-year-old first entered the federal judiciary in 1954. Byron R. White (known as "Whizzer" White)—that rare phenomenon of both Rhodes Scholar and professional athlete—had practiced law for fourteen years and was U.S. Deputy Attorney General when his wartime friend President Kennedy sent him to the highest bench in 1962. White was then forty-five, like Stewart one of the younger appointees in the Court's history (Douglas was a mere forty-one when F. D. R. sent him to the highest bench in 1941). President Johnson's second appointment, Thurgood Marshall—the first black to reach the highest Court—had practiced law for three decades,

---

their own inadequacy in dealing with them; disinterestedness, allegiance to nothing except the search, amid tangled words, amid limited insights, loyalty and allegiance to nothing except the effort to find their path through precedent, through policy, through history, through their own gifts of insight to the best judgment that poor fallible creatures can arrive at in that most difficult of all tasks, the adjudication between man and man, between man and state, through reason called law." (As quoted in *The Washington Post*, September 27, 1971, p. A20.)

much of it constitutional law at the bar of the Court he was destined to join, had been a nationally known leader in the civil rights movement; had served on the Second Circuit Court of Appeals from 1962 to 1965, and was the U.S. Solicitor General when the President thus honored him in 1967, at the age of fifty-nine. Harry A. Blackmun, President Nixon's second appointee, had practiced law in a Minneapolis firm for sixteen years and had served as general counsel to the Mayo Clinic in Rochester, Minnesota, for nine when he was named to the U.S. Court of Appeals for the Eighth Circuit by President Eisenhower in 1959, at the age of fifty-one. Lewis F. Powell, the third Nixon appointment (made late in 1971), sixty-four years old, had a long and distinguished career as a legal practitioner and civic leader in Virginia, including the chairmanship of the Richmond public school board in the late 1950s, and had been president of the American Bar Association. Nixon's fourth appointee, William H. Rehnquist, a youngish forty-seven when he was sent to the Court concurrently with Powell, had clerked for Justice Robert H. Jackson, had practiced law and been active in Arizona politics for a good many years, and was serving as U.S. Assistant Attorney General in charge of the Office of Legal Counsel at the time of his appointment to the Court. John Paul Stevens, fifty-five, the sole Ford appointee, had clerked for Justice Wiley Rutledge and practiced private law, specializing in antitrust matters, when he was appointed to the Circuit Court of Appeals for the Seventh Circuit in 1970, five years antecedent to coming to the Supreme Court. Sandra Day O'Connor, the first woman to reach the highest bench in the land, had seen service as a deputy county prosecutor in California, and as assistant attorney general of Arizona, had practiced private law, was active in Republican politics, served in the Arizona State Senate—where, as the first woman in the nation to hold such a post, she was elected as majority leader—and at fifty-one was in her seventh year on Arizona courts in 1981 when President Reagan's call came.

If, for the sake of argument, one were to grant the wisdom of judicial experience as a pertinent requirement for Supreme Court nominees, a background rich in nonjudicial experience, such as those just described, does not compensate in and of itself for the lack of actual experience on a lower bench. However, it does indicate that the men—until Sandra Day O'Connor there were no women on a federal court level *higher than* the Court of Appeals (the first at that was Judge Florence Allen of the Sixth Circuit[87])—who come to the

---

[87]It was not until 1979 that *every* state bench had at least one female judge. Of the 738 active *and* senior federal judgeships extant as of June 1979, twenty (six circuit and fourteen district) were held by women. (The first female federal judge was the Coolidge-appointed Genevieve R. Cline to the U.S. Customs Court in New York in 1928.) Judge Allen was appointed to the Sixth Circuit by President Roosevelt in 1934 from her position as the first woman on the Ohio State Supreme Court. She became Chief Judge of the Circuit in 1958—another "woman's first"—and retired from the bench at the age of seventy-five in 1959. She died in 1966.

Supreme Court of the United States, and for that matter to the lower federal courts, have had lengthy *legal* experience. Moreover *all* of the 10 who have actually *sat* on the highest bench, except Justice George Shiras (1892–1903), had engaged in at least *some* public service at various levels of government, often elective, or had participated in political activity. Nevertheless, unlike the jurists of France, for example, who are schooled and trained as jurists, a great many of the judges of the major courts in the United States have no *judicial* background—as distinguished from a *legal* one. England relies on still another system, to be discussed presently. Table 3 indicates the occupations of the Justices (using the full figure of 105 here) at the time of their appointment to the Supreme Court.

THE JUSTICES IN COMPOSITE

Whatever individual exceptions may be applicable, and keeping in mind the subjective attitude many an observer brings to bear on the qualifications and performance of the Justices of the Supreme Court of the United States, the caliber of that select group has been all but universally high. Indeed, no other unit of American government can readily match its general record of demonstrable competence and achievement. An overall analysis of the background and characteristics of the 102 Justices to date (1985–86 term) would produce the following composite:

Table 3. Occupations[a] of U.S. Supreme Court Designees at Time of Appointment[b]

Federal officeholder in executive branch	22
Judge of inferior federal court	22
Judge of state court	22
Private practice of law	18
U. S. senator	8
U.S. representative	4
State governor	3
Professor of law	3
Associate Justice of U.S. Supreme Court[c]	2
Justice of the Permanent Court of International Justice	1

[a]Many of the appointees had held a variety of federal or state offices, or even both, prior to their selection.
[b]In general, the appointments from state office are clustered at the beginning of the Court's existence; those from federal office are more recent.
[c]Justices E. D. White and Stone, who were *promoted* to the Chief Justiceship in 1910 and 1930, respectively.

Her earliest trail-blazing feat as a woman was her service on the Cleveland (Ohio) Court of Common Pleas from 1920 to 1922, from which she was elected to the seven-member Ohio Supreme Court. She had served for two six-year terms when F. D. R.'s call to the federal bench came. President Carter tripled the number of women on the federal bench. See the special issue of *Judicature*, "Women in the Judiciary," Vol. 65, No. 6 (December–January 1982).

Native-born (only six exceptions, most recent Justices Sutherland [England] and Frankfurter [Austria]), male (only one woman to date—mid-1985), Caucasian (the first black was appointed in 1967),[88] generally Protestant (six Catholic and five Jewish Justices), fifty to fifty-five years of age at the time of appointment, first-born (fifty-six, or 62 percent), of Anglo-Saxon ethnic stock (all except fifteen), of upper-middle to high social status, reared in a nonrural but not necessarily urban environment, civic-minded and politically active or at least politically aware, from an economically comfortable family, with a B.A. and LL.B or J.D. degress (one-third from "Ivy League" institutions),[89] having held some type of public office.[90]

MOTIVES THAT UNDERLIE APPOINTMENTS[91]

The only person who knows with certainty why a man is appointed to the Supreme Court is the President of the United States himself. However, historians and students of the judicial process can come close to the truth by interpreting the facts at their disposal: thus, a study of the records of the thirty-five Presidents who have fashioned members of the Supreme Court— an evaluation of their reasons for making the choices they did—points to several criteria that have been predominant in influencing presidential decisions. The following four have probably been the most important: (1) objective merit, (2) personal friendship, (3) balancing "representation or representativeness" on the Court, and (4) political and ideological compatibility.

When a President considers the objective merit of a candidate, he attempts to determine whether he or she possesses the ability and background requisite for a mastery of the vital and complicated issues that reach the Supreme Court. To achieve that end, he might look to the candidate's basic intellectual acumen, reputation for legal scholarship, competence in a particular area of the law, experience as a judge, lawyer, legislator, or executive, integrity and morals, judicial temperament, and work habits. Even age may be relevant. If the nominee is too young he or she may be lacking in judgment, wisdom, and experience; if too old, retirement, illness, or death may intervene.

---

[88] In October 1978 there were 525 black state and federal judges among the nation's 12,500—a number that accelerated dramatically with the enactment that month of the Omnibus Judgeship Bill of 1978, and with President Carter's previously described policies of pronounced affirmative action vis-à-vis appointments of females and minorities to federal judgeships.

[89] Of the 1984–85 Court, all except the Chief Justice and Justices Brennan, Marshall, and O'Connor were members of Phi Beta Kappa. Although the percentage began to decline in the late 1970s, "Ivy League" degrees still predominated on the high bench.

[90] For studies corroborating this "composite," see John R. Schmidhauser, "The Justices of the Supreme Court: A Collective Portrait," 3 *Midwest Journal of Political Science* 1 (1959); his *The Supreme Court: Its Politics, Personalities and Procedures* (New York: Holt, Rinehart and Winston, 1960), ch. 3, passim; and his *Judges and Justices: The Federal Appellate Judiciary* (Boston: Little, Brown and Co., 1979), chs. 3 and 4 passim. See also my *Justices and Presidents*, op cit., especially chs. 3 and 4.

[91] Much of the material in this section and in that on the role of the Senate is derived from chs. 1–4 of my *Justices and Presidents*, op. cit. fns. 28, 85, and 90.

Personal friendship is difficult to measure, but assuredly it has influenced a considerable number of nominations. In Taft's choice of Horace H. Lurton, in Wilson's of Louis D. Brandeis, in Truman's of Harold H. Burton, and in Kennedy's of Byron R. White, to cite some obvious illustrations, personal friendship figured prominently. Other examples are Truman's appointments of Chief Justice Fred M. Vinson and Associate Justices Tom C. Clark and Sherman Minton. It was probably the crucial consideration in the case of Minton, although the Indianan was a good Democrat and had seen eight years of service, however colorless, on the federal appelate bench. The most obvious and most discussed case in recent years was Lyndon Johnson's choice of Abe Fortas. Long Fortas's intimate personal friend, L. B. J. time and again urged him to accept a vacancy. Perhaps intuitively, Fortas was demonstrably reluctant. But he ultimately bowed to the President's entreaties and, with considerable lack of enthusiasm, accepted appointment to the seat vacated by Justice Goldberg when the latter resigned to become U.S. Ambassador to the United Nations in 1965.

Balancing "representation" on bases of religion, geography, race, and sex has also played a major role in presidential choice of Supreme Court nominees. Yet of the four key general factors that influence presidential selections, that of "representativeness" is patently the least defensible and the most emotion-charged. No matter how undesirable it may be in theoretical terms, however, it is not only here to stay in its long-established religion and geography components but, considering present-day group consciousness, it will very likely be markedly exacerbated by insistent demands for "representation" on the basis of both sex and race—demands avowedly championed by President Carter, for one.

The widespread notion that all sections of the land should be represented on the bench—to date the Justices have come from thirty-one of the fifty states—cannot be dismissed readily (see Table 4). It has considerable appeal as a matter of political equity. It was a primary consideration among almost all of the nineteenth-century Presidents; hence, Lincoln's successful search for "an outstanding trans-Mississippi lawyer" (Samuel F. Miller) and a Californian (Steven J. Field, a Democrat) and Cleveland's insistence on geographic appropriateness, best exemplified by his choice of a Chief Justice (Melvin Fuller). Among recent Presidents strongly influenced by the "geography factor" Richard Nixon stands out. Yet after the Haynsworth and Carswell rejections, he abandoned his much-publicized quest for a "Southern strict-constructionist" by choosing Judge Harry A. Blackmun, long time Minnesotan—an old and close friend of Chief Justice Burger, who was not only a Northerner but a resident of a state already "represented" twice on the Court.

On the other hand, a determined President will not permit geography to stand in the path of a desired appointment. Woodrow Wilson proved this with his insistence on the confirmation of Brandeis, notwithstanding the presence on the bench of Holmes, a fellow citizen of Massachusetts; so did Hoo-

Table 4. The 31 States from
which the 105 U.S. Supreme
Court Appointments Were
Made[a]

New York	15	Iowa	2
Ohio	9	Louisiana	2
Massachusetts	8	Michigan	2
Virginia	7	Minnesota	2
Pennsylvania	6	North Carolina	2
Tennessee	6	Arizona	2
Kentucky	5	Colorado	1
Illinois	4	Indiana	1
Maryland	4	Kansas	1
New Jersey	4	Maine	1
Alabama	3	Mississippi	1
California	3	Missouri	1
Connecticut	3	New Hampshire	1
Georgia	3	Texas	1
South Carolina	3	Utah	1
		Wyoming	1

[a]The state where the appointee then resided, not necessarily the state of his birth.

Table 5. Acknowledged Religion of the 102 Individual Justices of the U.S.
Supreme Court at Time of Appointment

Episcopalian	27	Jewish	5
Unspecified Protestant	25	Methodist	4
Presbyterian	17	Congregationalist	3
Roman Catholic	6	Disciples of Christ	2
Unitarian	6	Lutheran	1
Baptist	5	Quaker	1

ver when he finally appointed Cardozo in the face of the Court presence of fellow New Yorkers Stone and Hughes.

The religious factor is based on the notion that there should be a "Roman Catholic seat" and a "Jewish seat" on the Supreme Court. A development of dubious communal wisdom, the concept of religious-group representation has become one of the most emotion-charged characteristics of contemporary American political and judicial life (see Table 5)—one clearly here to stay.

Six men have occupied the "Catholic seat" to date: Chief Justice Roger B. Taney (Jackson, 1835), and Associate Justices Edward D. White (Cleveland, 1894—he was promoted to Chief Justice by Taft, 1910), Joseph McKenna (McKinley, 1898), Pierce Butler (Harding, 1922), Frank Murphy (Roosevelt, 1940), and William J. Brennan (Eisenhower, 1956). With the exception of the seven years between Justice Frank Murphy's death in 1949 (when President Truman deliberately ignored the unwritten rule of the "reserved" seat—"if he has the qualification, I do not care if he is a Protestant, Catholic or Jew" [*The New York Times*, July 29, 1949, p. 1]—and nominated Protestant Tom C. Clark to the vacancy created by Murphy's death) and Justice William J. Brennan, Jr.'s nomination in 1956, a Roman Catholic has been on the Supreme Court continuously since the White appointment.

The "Jewish seat" was established in 1916 with the appointment of Louis D. Brandeis. (Actually, President Fillmore had offered an appointment to Judah P. Benjamin of Louisiana in 1853, but the latter preferred to be in the U.S. Senate and declined. Brandeis was next, sixty-three years later.) That tradition, too, was broken when, in 1969, President Nixon successively nominated three Protestants (Haynsworth, Carswell, and Blackmun) to succeed Fortas. In 1971 Nixon had two opportunities to "atone" for this, but he again nominated two more Protestants, Lewis F. Powell, Jr. and William H. Rehnquist. Questioned on the continued "oversight" at one of his infrequent news conferences, Nixon gave the logical response: that merit, rather than religion, should and must govern—a laudable aim, provided it is in fact invoked. The five occupants of the "Jewish seat" to date have been Louis D. Brandeis (Wilson, 1916), Benjamin N. Cardozo (Hoover, 1932), Felix Frankfurter (Franklin D. Roosevelt, 1939), Arthur J. Goldberg (Kennedy, 1962), and Abe Fortas (Johnson, 1965).

In June 1967 Lyndon Johnson designated Thurgood Marshall, the first black ever to be nominated to the Supreme Court. The President, leaving no doubt that the nominee's race was probably the major factor in his decision, told the country, "I believe it is the right thing to do, the right time to do it, the right man and the right place."[92] It is fair to conjecture that there now exists a "black seat" on the bench that is more secure than the Catholic and the Jewish seats.[93] It is also highly likely that a "woman's seat" will be estab-

---

[92] *The New York Times*, June 14, 1967, p. 1. (By June, 1979 there were twenty-nine black federal jurists: one on the Supreme Court, six on the circuit courts, and twenty-one on district courts.)

[93] Felix Frankfurter, himself a Jew, had little patience with these "requirements": "*Tempore* Taft, his Secretary of War, one Stimson, told me that the President was desirous of putting a Jew on the federal bench in New York and has asked that I make a suggestion to that end. I told Stimson that racial and religious considerations seemed to me not only irrelevant in appointments to the bench but mischievously irrelevant. And that to appoint men for racial or religious reasons was playing with fire. Therefore, I would have no truck with it and I begged to be excused for what I regarded a highly indefensible and dangerous procedure." (Letter to Frank Buxton, Editor-in-Chief of the *Boston Herald*, Box 39, Manuscripts, National Archives.) See also Bruce A. Murphy, "A Supreme Court Justice as Politician: Felix Frankfurter and Federal Court Appointments," 21 *The American Journal of Legal History* 316–34 (1977), at 328.

lished. The presidential campaign of 1972 had featured public assurances by both candidates that a woman would be appointed: George McGovern promising that "the next vacancy" would go to a woman, and Richard Nixon, already on record with his abortive trial balloon Mildred Lillie nomination, speaking often of his desire to nominate "a qualified woman." Successful 1976 candidate Jimmy Carter repeatedly promised to send a woman to the Court at the first opportunity. He never had one, but Ronald Reagan did and appointed a woman as soon as the opportunity presented itself in mid-1981.

Political and ideological compatibility often go hand in hand in influencing presidential choices for the Supreme Court. Among the points a President is almost certain to consider are whether or not (1) his choice will render him more popular among influential interest groups, (2) the nominee has been a loyal member of the President's party, (3) the nominee favors presidential programs and policies (4) the nominee is acceptable, or at least not "personally obnoxious," to his home-state senators, (5) the nominee's judicial record, if any, meets the incumbent president's criteria of constitutional construction, (6) the President is indebted to the nominee for past political services, and (7) he feels "good" or "comfortable" about his choice.

It is an unwritten law of the judicial nominating process that the President will not normally select an individual from the ranks of the political opposition. To lessen charges of "court-packing," however, this rule is purposely relaxed now and then, but only within "political reason"—which seems to have meant roughly to the tune of 10 percent of all appointments to district and appellate tribunals and 15 percent to the Supreme Court. In at least thirteen instances of the latter, including two promotions to the post of Chief Justice, the appointee came from a political party other than that of the President. Thus, Whig President John Tyler appointed a Democrat, Samuel Nelson, and Republican Presidents Abraham Lincoln, Benjamin Harrison, William H. Taft, Warren G. Harding, Herbert Hoover, Dwight D. Eisenhower, and Richard M. Nixon appointed nine Democrats. Taft alone appointed three! The nine Justices and their nominators were Stephen J. Field (Lincoln), Howell E. Jackson (Benjamin Harrison), Horace H. Lurton, Edward D. White (to Chief Justice), and Joseph R. Lamar (Taft), Pierce Butler (Harding), Benjamin N. Cardozo (Hoover), William J. Brennan (Eisenhower), and Lewis F. Powell, Jr. (Nixon). And Democratic Presidents Woodrow Wilson, Franklin D. Roosevelt, and Harry S. Truman appointed three Republicans: Louis D. Brandeis (Wilson), Harlan F. Stone to Chief Justice (F. D. R.), and Harold D. Burton (Truman). Some would add, as a fourteenth case, F. D. R.'s selection of Felix Frankfurter, who labeled himself an Independent. What accounted for these thirteen or fourteen appointments from the ranks of "the other" party?

Crossing Party Lines. The naming of Nelson by President Tyler came after Tyler had been defeated by Democrat James K. Polk in the election of 1844. Eager to have history show at least one of his own nominees attain the

Supreme Court, the "lame duck" Tyler—after three of his four first Whig choices had to be withdrawn because of obviously decisive opposition, and the fourth one, John Spencer of New York, was rejected by the Senate 26:1— then designated Nelson, who had not been an active political figure.

In 1863 *Field*, who was to serve on the Court longer (34¾ years) than anyone to date but Douglas (36½ years), was chosen by Lincoln largely for three reasons. First, Field came from California, a part of the country not then represented on the Court—in fact, Congress created a tenth seat for that purpose—and even though he had been a Buchanan Democrat as late as 1861, Lincoln felt his nominee would help to "fuse" the Northern cause by preserving the loyalty of California and strengthening its polictical ties. Second, Field's many influential friends, including California's Governor Leland Stanford, put considerable pressure on the President. Third, Field's brother, David Dudley Field, a bitter and vocal opponent of slavery, had played a considerable role both in the organization of the Republican party and in Lincoln's nomination as its standard-bearer in 1860.

Harrison's choice of *Jackson* was motivated by reasons similar to those that governed the Tyler-Nelson case. Cleveland had already defeated Harrison when the vacancy on the Court occurred, the Democratic Senate was in no mood to confirm the Republican lame duck President's partisan choice, and happily, Harrison and Jackson, who had served in the Senate together, were close friends, as were their wives.

The Taft appointments of *Lurton* and *Lamar* and his promotion of *White*, all three Southern Democrats appointed by a good Republican, are attributable to a combination of personal friendship or esteem, ideological kinship, and politico-sectional expediency. Taft and Lurton had served together for eight years on the U.S. Circuit Court of Appeals for the Sixth Circuit, where they had become fast friends. Taft, who had been its Chief Judge, was very much impressed with the legal and judicial ability of the Tennessee Democrat who had succeeded him as Chief Judge when the future President went to the Philippine Islands. Conservative kinsmen, they were usually at one in their opinions from the bench and in their general philosophy of government. Taft called the nomination of his friend Lurton "the chief pleasure of my administration."[94] Although Joseph R. Lamar of Georgia was not as close to Taft personally as Lurton was, he readily met Taft's standards of conservatism and his general ideological bent. For example, the two men saw eye to eye on the tariff—a matter of the utmost importance to the President. And Taft perceived in the appointment of the Confederate Army veteran an additional opportunity for strengthening his position among Southern political leaders who, if they would not vote for him at election time, would at least

---

[94]Silas Bent, *Justice Oliver Wendell Holmes* (New York: Garden City Publishing Co., 1932), p. 248.

help him with his legislative program. He promoted White—then in his seventeenth year on the Court—in part because he considered him the ablest administrator among the Justices on the bench, in part because his fellow Justices apparently had petitioned the President to designate him rather than Hughes,[95] who had seemed to have the proverbial inside track ("White, Not Hughes, for Chief Justice," was the December 12, 1910 front-page headline in *The New York Times* when the announcement was made), in large part because in Taft's eyes he had voted "right" on the bench—among his votes there was one to uphold a military tariff in the Philippine Islands at the time Taft was governor there[96]—and, because of Taft's never-ceasing hopes of some day attaining that so ardently desired Center Chair, the sixty-five-year-old White was distinctly a more promising occupant than the forty-eight-year-old Hughes!

Wilson's hotly contested nomination of *Brandeis*, a registered Massachusetts Republican, was confirmed by the Senate by a vote margin of forty-seven to twenty-two after a delay of more than four months. Of the forty-seven affirmative votes, forty-four were cast from the forty-five Democratic senators present and voting; the three Republican votes in favor came from Senator Robert M. La Follette (Wisc.), George W. Norris (Neb.), and Miles Poindexter (Wash.). Twenty-one of the twenty-two negative votes came from the Republican senators present and voting.[97] The lone Democratic negative vote was cast by Senator Francis G. Newlands of Nevada. Twenty-seven senators, including the influential Borah, did not vote at all.[98] Brandeis, the famed "People's Lawyer," as Wilson was fond of calling him, was a personal friend of the President and a close ideological ally—a political and social liberal who shared Wilson's philosophy of life and government and who had worked hard for him in the 1912 campaign. It was primarily these two factors and his great regard for Brandeis's character and ability that prompted Wilson to ignore the sectional factor (Massachusetts was then already "represented" by Holmes); possible repercussions because of the nominee's religion (he was the first Jewish person to reach the Supreme Court); and the danger

[95] George Shiras III, *Justice George Shiras* (Pittsburgh: University of Pittsburgh Press, 1953), p. 130.

[96] Cf. William Howard Taft, *Our Chief Magistrate and His Power* (New York: Columbia University Press, 1916), pp. 99–102.

[97] Among these were illustrious and powerful men such as Henry A. du Pont, Henry Cabot Lodge, George Sutherland (a future colleague of the nominee!), Warren G. Harding, and Albert B. Fall. The remaining twenty-seven Senators did not vote; but twelve—all Republicans—were paired *against*, and twelve—ten Democrats and two Republicans (Moses E. Clapp of Minnesota and Asle J. Grenna of North Dakota)—*for*; three senators were absent and were not recorded at all.

[98] For a fascinating account of the Brandeis nomination and confirmation battle, see A. L. Todd's *Justice on Trial: The Case of Louis D. Brandeis* (New York: McGraw-Hill Book Co., 1964).

during the 1916 election year of designating a controversial personage such as Brandeis in the face of the violent opposition of the most influential segment of the bar and the business community, particularly in his New England home base. Ironically, despite his convictions regarding the "curse of bigness," Justice Brandeis never wrote an opinion in favor of the government in an antitrust case!

Harding's choice of *Butler*—vigorously promoted by the now Chief Justice Taft—had three motives. First, the President liked his record of almost four decades of service in the law and in public life; second, and probably most important, Harding found Butler's ideological ultraconservatism to be entirely sympathetic (he became one of the two leading avowed reactionaries on the bench); and third, the President deemed it politically advantageous to appoint a man who combined what would seem to be the desirable factor of being a "safe" Democrat—most Democrats refused to regard Butler as one of their number in roughly the same fashion as the Republicans did Brandeis—with that of being a member of an "unrepresented" minority religion (Roman Catholic) and a native Minnesotan, only the second nominee born west of the Mississippi to reach the bench. Initially rejected by the Senate, Butler was renominated by Harding on the following day and ultimately won confirmation easily, though he was veritably scorched by large segments of the public press.

The *Cardozo* appointment was almost literally forced on President Hoover by the country, despite the fact—conceivably detrimental or even fatal in the case of other nominees, depending on circumstances—that the nominee came from New York, already "represented" on the bench at that time by Chief Justice Hughes and Justice Stone, and that he was Jewish, a religion already "represented" by Justice Brandeis. Hoover raised these points during a command-visit by Republican Senator Borah of Idaho, chairman of the Committee on Foreign Relations, who had been very vocal in urging the Cardozo appointment, along with many others, including Justice Stone. (Stone, who was to play a major role in persuading the President to designate the man whom he had introduced to him initially, even offered to resign his own seat on the Court if that was what it would take to see his fellow New Yorker nominated.) Hoover handed Senator Borah a list of the names of several prominent individuals he was considering for the vacancy on the Court left by Justice Holmes's resignation. The last name on the list was that of the Chief Judge of the New York State Court of Appeals, Benjamin N. Cardozo. "Your list is all right," commented Senator Borah, "but you handed it to me upside down!"[99] When the President then strongly urged that his visitor consider the geographical situation involved, and mentioned "possible religious and sectarian repercussions," Senator Borah told him in no uncertain terms

[99]Claudius O. Johnson, *Borah of Idaho* (New York: Longman's Green and Co., 1936), p. 452.

that "Cardozo belonged as much to Idaho as to New York" and that geography should no more bar him than the presence of two Virginians on the high bench—John Blair and Bushrod Washington—should have prevented President John Adams from naming John Marshall Chief Justice.[100] Furthermore, Borah told Hoover, " . . . anyone who raises the question of race [sic] is unfit to advise you concerning so important a matter."[101] When the President bowed to what was all but unanimous professional as well as popular clamor for the Cardozo appointment, he became the recipient of much praise, typical of which was Senator Clarence Dill of Washington's remark that " . . . when President Hoover appointed Judge Cardozo . . . he performed the finest act of his career as President."[102]

President Franklin D. Roosevelt promoted *Stone*—who had been one of his professors at Columbia University Law School—largely as a manifestation of unity in the face of the incipient war crisis. When Chief Justice Hughes announced his intention to retire, speculation as to his successor revolved around Stone and the then Attorney General Robert H. Jackson. Roosevelt's heart was on the side of Jackson, who desperately craved the Chief Justice-ship, but he deemed it wiser and more politically astute and appropriate at this turbulent juncture of history to name Stone. In fact, he discussed the matter with Jackson, who agreed heavyheartedly and later, having become an Associate Justice of the Court, wrote that the need for judicial leadership and the "desirability for a symbol of stability as well as of progress" were evidently the reasons for Stone's elevation "in the interest of the [fostering of the] judiciary as an institution."[103] Moreover, the retiring Chief Justice himself had strongly urged Stone's elevation on the basis of his record, and had suggested that Roosevelt consult Justice Frankfurter in the matter. The latter told the President:

> . . . when war does come, the country should feel you are a national, the Nation's President, and not a partisan President . . . [to bolster this assessment] you [should] name a Republican, who has the profession's confidence, as Chief Justice.[104]

President Truman's nomination of *Burton*—the first of his four—is far too readily dismissed merely as a reward to "an old Senate crony."[105] The Republican senator from Ohio and mayor of Cleveland had served well and closely with the then Senator Truman on the latter's Special Committee to Investi-

---

[100] *The New York Times*, January 30, 1932.

[101] Johnson, loc. cit., p. 453.

[102] *The New York Times*, March 2, 1932, p. 13.

[103] Mason, *Harlan Fiske Stone*, op. cit., p. 573.

[104] Ibid., p. 567.

[105] For example, see Glendon A. Schubert, *Constitutional Politics* (New York: Holt, Rinehart and Winston, 1960), p. 38.

gate the National Defense Program (the "Truman Committee"). Unquestionably, Truman's personal affection for Burton was a factor in the appointment. But there were assuredly others: the advice given to the President that he designate a Republican to replace the retiring Justice Roberts, a Republican; Chief Justice Stone's advance approval of the nominee because of his valuable legislative experience; Truman's belief in Burton's judicial temperament; the absence of anyone from Ohio on the bench; the assumption that the nominee's Senate seat would be filled by a Democrat, as indeed it subsequently was, by the incumbent governor Lausche (though he was a rather unpredictable Democrat); plus the faithful support Burton had given to the Democratic party on foreign policy, and even on some domestic policy, throughout his tenure in the Senate.

President Eisenhower chose New Jersey Democrat *Brennan* for a variety of reasons. The President's initial choice had been that state's able Chief Justice, Arthur T. Vanderbilt, who had achieved an outstanding national reputation as head of the then recently reorganized New Jersey court system. Because of his advanced age and failing health (he died in 1957), Vanderbilt declined the appointment but he highly recommended the nomination of his colleague and protégé, Associate Justice Brennan of the State Supreme Court. This recommendation was strengthened by the support of Secretary of Labor James Mitchell, a New Jersey Republican; the two Republican senators from New Jersey, Clifford P. Case and Alexander H. Smith; and Democratic Governor Robert B. Meyner. Moreover, it was the very eve of the 1956 election, and the choice of a Roman Catholic from the metropolitan East would hardly hurt the President in the impending campaign. With only Republican Senator Joseph R. McCarthy of Wisconsin voting "no," the Brennan nomination was confirmed by the Senate in March 1957.

The most recent selection of a Supreme Court nominee from the opposition party is President Nixon's late 1971 choice of nominal Democrat Lewis F. Powell, Jr. Yet that distinguished Virginia ideological conservative seemed ideally fitted for the President's expressed qualifying criteria of "a philosophy for the Constitution similar to my own"—which he was fond of styling, not overly helpfully, as "strict construction." Powell did not meet the Nixon guidelines of "right age" (at sixty-four he was some ten years older than the preferred age) nor of "broad experience as an appeals judge" (he had no judicial experience whatsoever). But Powell came from a milieu sympathetic to the President both politically and personally: he was a recognized, visible leader of the Virginia Bar; he had seen important local and state civic service; he was a recent past president of the American Bar Associaton; and his writings in the "law-and-order" sector could not have been more pleasing to Mr. Nixon. Hence his professed formal party allegiance on the Democratic side was of small moment. Justice Powell's subsequent service on the Court proved the President's judgment of his third appointee's jurisprudential philosophy to be generally sound—but not without at least some "disappointments," such as the Justice's authorship of a unanimous opinion by the high bench (Justice Rehnquist not participating) clearly and unequivocally denying the existence of any "inherent" independent presidential power to wiretap in instances of suspected subversive *domestic* elements.[106]

There will always be some crossing of party lines, particularly at the lower court levels, in order to maintain at least the appearance of nonpartisanship in the judicial process and to placate the opposition, but the practice may be safely viewed as the exception rather than the rule (as Table 6 and the following statistics indicate). Many a President has been told by his political advisers to stay on his side of the fence, where surely there are just as many qualified and deserving lawyers as on the other side. "Think Republican," Republican National Chairman Rogers C. B. Morton frankly urged President Nixon when the latter was presented with his initial opportunity to fill two seats on the Supreme Court in the spring of 1969.[107] As Table 7 amply demonstrates, Morton's sentiments are not confined to *his* political party! After a consistent 1976 campaign promise of substituting "merit" for "politics" in nominating federal judges, President Carter had amassed a higher percentage by late 1980 than any other President except Woodrow Wilson. If the percentage of "other party" Supreme Court appointees has been higher than that of the lower federal courts, it is because the President recognizes that what matters more than anything else is the ideological compatibility of the candidate—what Teddy Roosevelt referred to as the nominee's "real" politics.

"PACKING THE COURT" AND THE NOMINEES' "REAL" POLITICS

Whatever the merits of the other criteria attending presidential motivations in appointments may be, what must be of overriding concern to any nominator is his perception of the candidate's "real" politics. The Chief Executive's crucial predictive judgment concerns itself with the nominee's likely future voting pattern on the bench, based on his past stance and commitment

Table 6. Avowed Political Affiliation of the 105 U.S. Supreme Court Justices at Time of Selection

Federalists	13	Republicans	41
Whig	1	Independent	1
Democrats	49		

[106] *United States v. United States District Court for the Eastern District of Michigan,* 407 U.S. 297 (1972).

[107] *The New York Times,* May 17, 1969, p. 1. "That's the name of the game," Morton continued, "[t]his is our opportunity and we ought to take it."

Table 7. Percentages of Federal Judicial Appointments Adhering to the Same
Political Party as the President, 1884–1985

President	Party	Percentage
Cleveland	Democratic	97.3
B. Harrison	Republican	87.9
McKinley	Republican	95.7
T. Roosevelt	Republican	95.8
Taft	Republican	82.2
Wilson	Democratic	98.6
Harding	Republican	97.7
Coolidge	Republican	94.1
Hoover	Republican	85.7
F. D. Roosevelt	Democratic	96.4
Truman	Democratic	93.1
Eisenhower	Republican	95.1
Kennedy	Democratic	90.9
L. B. Johnson	Democratic	95.2
Nixon	Republican	93.7
Ford	Republican	81.2
Carter	Democratic	94.8
Reagan	Republican	98.0 (as of mid-1985)

on matters of public policy, insofar as they are reliably discernible.[108] All Presidents have tried to thus "pack" the bench to a greater or lesser extent.

In the public eye Court-packing has been most closely associated with Franklin D. Roosevelt. Having had not a single opportunity to fill a Court vacancy in his first term (1933–37), and seeing his domestic programs consistently battered by the Court, the frustrated President attempted to get his

---

[108] An illuminating illustration is President Kennedy's selection of his long-time friend and ideological kinsman, Deputy Attorney General Byron J. White, to fill the first vacancy on the Court during his brief administration. As *Washington Star* reporter James E. Clayton reported the decision: "Thinking back on the process months later, the Attorney General [Robert F. Kennedy] tilted back his chair and said: 'You wanted someone who generally agreed with you on what role government should play in American life, what role the individual in society should have. You didn't think about how he would vote in a reapportionment case or a criminal case. You wanted someone who, in the long run, you could believe would be doing what you thought was best. You wanted someone who agreed generally with your views of the country.' Both he and the President believed that White and Arthur J. Goldberg met that test. They could not be as sure of the others on the list [Paul A. Freund of Harvard University and Judge William H. Hastie of the U.S. Court of Appeals for the Third Circuit]." As quoted in James E. Clayton's *The Making of Justice: The Supreme Court in Action* (New York: E. P. Dutton & Co., 1964), p. 52.

way all at once. His "Court-packing bill," however, died a deserved death in the Senate.

It is not surprising that Court-packing and the name of President Roosevelt have become synonymous. Yet even such popular heroes as Jefferson, Jackson, and Lincoln followed similar courses of action in the face of what they considered "judicial intransigence and defiance." Their approach was not as radical as Roosevelt's, but they very likely would have been sympathetic to his efforts. George Washington, though broadly regarded as far removed from "politics," had insisted that his fourteen nominees to the Court meet a veritable smorgasbord of qualifications.[109] In fact, every President who has made nominations to the Supreme Court has been guilty of Court-packing in some measure. It is entirely understandable that a President will choose men who will share his own philosophy of government and politics, at least to the extent of giving him a sympathetic hearing. Theodore Roosevelt, for example, in discussing the potential candidacy of Horace H. Lurton with Henry Cabot Lodge, put the issue well:

> The nominal politics of the man has nothing to do with his actions on the bench. His real politics are all important . . . He is right on the Negro question; he is right on the power of the federal government; he is right on the Insular business; he is right about corporations, and he is right about labor. On every question that would come before the bench, he has so far shown himself to be in much closer touch with the policies in which you and I believe than even [Associate Justice Edward D.] White because he has been right about corporations where White has been wrong.[110]

Lodge concurred in substance, but he replied that he could see no reason "why Republicans cannot be found who hold those opinions as well as Democrats."[111] Consequently, he strongly urged the candidacy of a Republican, whom T. R. then duly nominated—William H. Moody, Attorney General of Massachusetts.

Thus, concern with a nominee's real politics is a fundamental issue, and examples abound. It prompted Republican Taft to give half of his six appointments to Democrats who were kindred souls, Republican Nixon to appoint Democrat Powell, Democrat Roosevelt to promote Republican Stone, and Democrat Truman to appoint Republican Burton. Yet there is no guarantee that what a President perceives as real politics will not fade into a mirage. Hence Charles Warren, eminent chronicler of the Court, observed that

---

[109]Seven, to be exact. (See my *Justices and Presidents*, op. cit., p. 64.) Of Washington's fourteen nominees, thirteen were acted upon by the Senate, twelve were confirmed, but only ten served.

[110]Henry Cabot Lodge, *Selections from the Correspondence of Theodore Roosevelt and Henry Cabot Lodge, 1884–1918* (New York: Charles Scribner's Sons, 1925), Vol. 2, pp. 228, 230, 241.

[111]Ibid., p. 229.

nothing is more striking in the history of the Court than the manner in which the hopes of those who expected a judge to follow the political views of the President appointing him are disappointed.[112]

Few have felt the truth of that statement more keenly than Teddy Roosevelt did with Oliver Wendell Holmes, Jr., whose early "anti-administration" opinions in antitrust cases (notably in *Northern Securities v. United States*)[113] were entirely unexpected. A bare 5:4 majority in that case upheld the government's order, under the Sherman Anti-Trust Act, dissolving the Northern Securities Company, brainchild of E. H. Harriman and J. J. Hill, the wealthy and powerful owners of competing railroads who had organized the company in order to secure a terminal line into Chicago. Roosevelt had won that important litigaton, but he was furious about his recent appointee's "anti-anti-trust" vote in the case. He stormed: "I could carve out of a banana a Judge with more backbone that that!"[114] Holmes reportedly merely smiled when told the President's remark and noted his intention to "call the shots as I see them in terms of the legal and constitutional setting." Later, during T. R.'s second term of office (1905–9) Holmes expressed his sentiments to a labor leader at a White House dinner: "What you want is favor, not justice. But when I am on my job, I don't give a damn what you or Mr. Roosevelt want."[115]

James Madison, having refused to heed his political mentor, Thomas Jefferson, was similarly chagrined with his appointment of Justice Joseph Story. Jefferson had warned him that Story was an inveterate Tory who would become a rabid supporter of Chief Justice Marshall, and he was right: Story not only instantly joined Marshall's approach to constitutional adjudication and interpretation, but he even out-Marshalled Marshall in his nationalism. Perhaps even more chagrined was Woodrow Wilson when his appointee James C. McReynolds proved himself at once to be the antithesis of almost everything his nominator stood for and believed in.

More recently, Harry Truman observed that " ... packing the Supreme Court simply can't be done ... I've tried and it won't work ... Whenever you put a man on the Supreme Court he ceases to be your friend. I'm sure of that."[116] Future Presidents may be well advised to heed the admonition of Zechariah Chafee, Harvard's famed expert on the judicial process, who contended that to forecast the behavior of a future jurist it is wiser to consider the books in his library than the list of clients in his office.

There is indeed a considerable element of unpredictability in the judicial appointing process. To the often-heard "Does a person become any different when he puts on a gown?" Justice Frankfurter's sharp retort was always, "If

[112] *The Supreme Court in United States History*, rev. ed. (Boston: Little, Brown and Co., 1926), Vol. 2, p. 22.
[113] 193 U.S. 197 (1904).
[114] As quoted by James E. Clayton, op. cit., fn. 71, p. 47.
[115] As quoted by Arthur Krock, *The New York Times*, October 19, 1971, p. 431.
[116] Lecture at Columbia University, New York City, April 28, 1959.

he is any good, he does!" In the words of Alexander M. Bickel, "You shoot an arrow into a far-distant future when you appoint a Justice and not the man himself can tell you what he will think about some of the problems that he will face."[117] And late in 1969, reflecting on his sixteen years as Chief Justice of the United States, Earl Warren pointed out that he, for one, did not "see how a man could be on the Court and not change his views substantially over a period of years . . . for change you must if you are to do your duty on the Supreme Court."[118] It is a duty that, in many ways, represents the most hallowed in the governmental process of the United States.

ON THE ROLE OF THE U.S. SENATE

That the Senate takes its confirmation role seriously is documented by its refusal to confirm 27 of the 139 Supreme Court nominees forwarded to it in the less than two centuries of our history. True, even when counting the Senate's refusal to vote in the Fortas promotion, only four have been voted down during the present century, but, as the experiences of the Nixon Administration demonstrate, the possibility is ever present. Yet a return to the nineteenth-century record of one rejection for every three nominees would appear to be highly unlikely nowadays.

Just why were the twenty-seven rejected? Among the more prominent reasons have been (1) opposition to the nominating President, not necessarily to the nominee; (2) the nominee's involvement with a visible or contentious issue of public policy (i.e., "politics"); (3) opposition to the record of the incumbent Court, which the nominee was presumed, rightly or wrongly, to have supported; (4) senatorial courtesy (closely linked to the consultative nominating process); (5) a perceived "political unreliability" of the nominee. Usually several of these reasons figure in the rejection of a nominee, not one alone; the purpose of the previous list is merely to suggest some applicable prototypes.

Thus, a number of candidates were rejected because of Senate opposition to the nominating Chief Executive. For example, John Quincy Adams's nomination of John J. Crittenden in 1828 was "postponed" by the Senate in a strictly partisan vote of 17:23 two months after the nomination. The "loyalist" Democrats in the Senate thereby foiled Adams's last-minute Whig appointment and preserved the vacancy so that it could be filled instead by the President-elect, strong-party Democrat Andrew Jackson. In 1844 Whig President John Tyler sent six nominations to the upper house—which disapproved five and confirmed but one, the outstandingly qualified Chief Justice Samuel Nelson of New York's highest court. Of the former, John C. Spencer, an erstwhile Whig who had accepted high cabinet posts under

---

[117] As quoted in *Time Magazine*, May 23, 1969, p. 24.
[118] Comment to Anthony Lewis, "A Talk with Warren on Crime, the Court, the Country," *The New York Times Magazine*, October 19, 1969, pp. 128–29.

Tyler and whom the "loyalist" Whig followers of Henry Clay regarded as a traitor, was rejected by a formal roll call vote of 21:26; and action regarding Edward King, who was nominated twice, Ruben H. Walworth, and John M. Read was postponed by the Senate chiefly because of the mistaken expectation of the Clay Whigs that their leader would defeat James K. Polk in the presidential election of 1844. In 1852 action on George E. Badger, one of Whig President Millard F. Fillmore's nominees was postponed indefinitly—despite the fact that Badger was then a U.S. senator (Whig) from North Carolina—and no action at all was taken on his two others, Edward A. Bradford and William E. Micou. The purpose of the anti-Fillmore maneuvers was to preserve court vacancies for incoming Democratic President Franklin Pierce, yet Pierce succeeded in filling only one of them, he too falling victim to similar Senate tactics. Democrat James Buchanan's nomination of Jeremiah S. Black in December 1860, one month before his term ended, fell 25:26, chiefly because Republican senators wanted to hold the seat for Abraham Lincoln to fill. In 1866 Union President Andrew Johnson nominated his gifted Attorney General, Henry Stanberry, but the Senate's hostility to Lincoln's successor was such as to frustrate every attempt he made to fill a Supreme Court vacancy. Congress even went so far as to *abolish* the vacancy (thus "icing" Johnson's nominating impotence). A century later, in 1968, the Senate refused to approve Lyndon B. Johnson's attempt simultaneously to promote Abe Fortas to Chief Justice and to replace him with Judge Homer Thornberry of the U.S. Court of Appeals for the Fifth Circuit. Johnson failed largely because most members of the Senate "had had it" with the lame-duck President's nominations. Victory-scenting Republicans also wanted such plums as Supreme Court appointments for themselves; they had not had an opportunity to fill a vacancy on the bench since President Eisenhower's appointment of Justice Potter Stewart ten years earlier.

A good many illustrations are on record in which nominees failed to receive senatorial confirmation because of their involvement with public issues. Thus, in 1795 the Senate rejected John Rutledge as Chief Justice by a vote of 10:14 even though he had been serving as such for four months on a recess appointment, Congress not being in session. On John Jay's resignation from the Chief Justiceship Rutledge had asked Washington for the appointment, but he now found his fellow Federalists voting against him because of his vigorous opposition to the Jay Treaty of 1794. The Federalist senators refused to confirm a public figure who actively opposed the Treaty they had championed so ardently—even though he was able to meet Washington's staff criteria for service on the highest bench. Their cause was aided by an all-but-unanimous denunciation by the Northern Federalist press. In 1811, James Madison's nomination of Alexander Wolcott fell 9:24 because the Federalist senators, eagerly backed by the press, opposed Wolcott's vigorous enforcement of the embargo and nonintercourse acts when he was U.S. Collector of Customs in Connecticut. There was, however, also some genuine question as to Wolcott's legal qualifications.

The rejection of President Polk's nomination in 1845 of fellow Democrat George W. Woodward of Pennsylvania, although in part due to the opposition of Pennsylvania's Independent Senator Simon Cameron on the basis of "senatorial courtesy," was largely a result of what was termed Woodward's "gross nativist American sentiments." Chiefly because of these alleged sentiments, which were particularly offensive to Irish Americans, five Democratic senators joined Cameron and a phalanx of Whigs to defeat the nomination by a vote of 20:29. The President, however, saw the action as a power play calculated to weaken his Administration at its very outset. On December 15, 1869, Republican President Ulysses S. Grant nominated his eminently qualified and popular Attorney General Ebenezer R. Hoar. The debate over his nomination dragged on for seven weeks, until February 3, 1873, when Hoar was finally rejected by a vote of 24:33. Hoar had antagonized most of the Senators by his consistent refusal to back senatorial nominations for judgeships; by his publicly uncompromising insistence on "non-political" appointments throughout the government, and by his early championship of civil service reform. Moreover, he had made enemies of fellow Republicans by his outspoken opposition to the proposed impeachment of President Andrew Johnson. Few professional politicians appreciated Judge Hoar's high standards of excellence and assertive political independence, and the Court was deprived of an unusually promising candidate.

Another issue-oriented rejection was that of John J. Parker, Chief Judge of the U.S. Fourth Circuit Court of Appeals (Hoover, 1930). A prominent and distinguished Republican leader in North Carolina for many years, and an outstanding jurist, Judge Parker fell victim to the sustained opposition of the American Federation of Labor and the National Association for the Advancement of Colored People. Still, the Senate would not have had the votes to defeat the nomination—Parker lost by a two-vote margin, 39:41—had they not been aided by anti-Hoover Progressive Republicans, including such prominent and influential senators as Hiram Johnson of California, Robert M. La Follette, Jr., of Wisconsin, George W. Norris of Nebraska, and such powerful mavericks as William Borah of Idaho. The AFL's chief grudge against the nominee stemmed from the impression that he was "unfriendly" to labor and that it was he who had handed down an opinion affirming a lower court decision upholding "yellow dog" contracts.[119] However, a close reading of Judge Parker's opinion in the case indicates neither approval nor disapproval of "yellow dog" contracts; rather, it reflects the jurist's belief that he was bound by a U.S. Supreme Court precedent.[120] Yet the impression of anti-labor bias lingered, fostered by AFL President William Green and other influential labor spokesmen, who, on the other hand, did concede that Judge Parker's integrity, high standards, and professional qualifications were not in

---

[119] United Mine Workers v. Red Jacket Consolidated Coal and Coke Co., 18 F. 839 (1927).
[120] Hitchman Coal and Coke Co. v. Mitchell, 245 U.S. 229 (1917).

question. The NAACP contended that the nominee was opposed generally to black participation in politics and especially to black suffrage. Thus, Walter White of the NAACP leadership pointed out that Judge Parker, while stumping North Carolina as a gubernatorial candidate in 1920, had made an unfortunate remark: "The participation of the Negro in politics is a source of evil and danger to both races and is not desired by the wise men in either race or by the Republican Party of North Carolina."[121] Parker had uttered the statement in response to repeated taunts and charges by his Democratic opponents that he intended to enfranchise blacks and to alter the North Carolina Constitution to accommodate "them." Ironically, it was Judge Parker— he continued to sit on the Fourth Circuit bench after his rejection—who would write some of the earliest and most significant pro-black opinions on desegregation. Among them was *Rice v. Elmore* (1947), in which he sustained U.S. District Court Judge J. W. Waring's outlawing of South Carolina's machinations to bar blacks from primary elections.[122]

The next outright rejections were Judges Clement F. Haynsworth, Jr. and G. Harrold Carswell, both Nixon nominees, almost forty years later. Although their involvement with civil rights did play a considerable role in their rejection, especially in that of Carswell, the overriding and ultimately decisive margin of defeat lay elsewhere: in Haynsworth's case it was the question of judicial ethics; in Carswell's case it was lack of professional qualification. To his basic specifications Mr. Nixon had added a desire to choose a Southern jurist of conservative judicial bent. Of course, the Court already had at least one Southern strict constructionist, indeed, a constitutional literalist of the first magnitude, in the person of the distinguished Justice Hugo Lafayette Black of Alabama, but that was not exactly what the President had in mind. Haynsworth, a native of South Carolina and a Harvard Law School alumnus, a relatively able jurist meriting a "B-minus" grade in the minds of most Court watchers, fit all of the President's specifications—and, perhaps even more significantly, those of such influential Southern senators as Strom Thurmond (R.-S.C.), James O. Eastland (D.-Miss.), and John L. McClellan (D.-Ark.). He was also supported by the Attorney General, John N. Mitchell.

Most of the Senate seemed disposed to confirm Judge Haynsworth for the Fortas vacancy. But to the President's anger, frustration, and embarrassment, the hearings of the Senate Committee on the Judiciary provided clear evidence of the nominee's patent insensitivity to financial and conflict-of-interest improprieties. Apparently, as with Fortas, no actual legal infractions had taken place—but how could the senate confirm Haynsworth when it had played such an activist role in causing Fortas's resignation? It could not, and among those who vocally opposed the South Carolinian and voted against his

---

[121] *Hearings Before the Subcommittee of the Committee on the Judiciary, U.S. Senate, on the Confirmation of John J. Parker to Be an Associate Justice of the Supreme Court of the United States,* 71st Cong., 2d sess., 1930, p. 74.

[122] 165 F. 2d 387. (It sustained 72 F. Supp. 516, also decided in 1947.)

confirmation were such anti-Fortas, "strict constructionist" leaders as Senators Robert Griffin (R.-Mich.) and Jack Miller (R.-Iowa). Down went the Haynsworth nomination by a vote of 55:45 on November 21, 1969—largely for the reasons indicated, although he had also drawn considerable labor and minority-group fire for allegedly anti-civil libertarian and anti-civil rights stands. The livid President Nixon, however, chose to lay the blame for his nominee's defeat on "anti-Southern, anti-conservative, and anti-constructionist" prejudice, and he vowed to select another "worthy and distinguished protagonist" of Southern, conservative, and strict constructionist persuasion.[123]

To the dismay of those senators who had counseled confirmation of Judge Haynsworth lest a successor-nominee be even less worthy of the high post, the President, again on the recommendation of Attorney General Mitchell, quickly countered by nominating Judge G. Harrold Carswell of Florida, a little-known and little-distinguished ex-U.S. District Judge with only six months of experience on the U.S. Court of Appeals for the Fifth Circuit. "He is almost too good to be true," Mr. Mitchell was reported to have said.[124] The appointment was an act of vengeance—one intended to teach the Senate a lesson and to downgrade the Court. The Senate, intimidated by the President and the Attorney General, was disposed to confirm him. But suspicious reporters and researchers soon cast serious doubt on that "almost too good to be true" classification of the nominee. Immediately damaging was the discovery of a statement Carswell had made to a meeting of the American Legion on August 2, 1948, while he was running for a seat in the legislature of his native Georiga. "I yield to no man as a fellow candidate or as a fellow citizen in the firm, vigorous belief in the principles of White Supremacy, and I shall always be so governed."[125] To be sure, the nominee, pointing to his youth and inexperience (he was twenty-eight at the time), now disavowed that statement and any racism as well. But an examination of his record on the bench did more than cast further doubt on his objectivity in racial matters: While serving as U.S. Attorney in Florida, Carswell had been involved in the transfer of a public, municipally owned Tallahassee golf course—built with $35,000 of federal funds—to the status of a private club. It was a move obviously designed to circumvent a contemporary Supreme Court decision proscribing segregation in municipal recreation facilities.

Still, the administration appeared to have the votes for Senate confirmation, given the vivid memories of the Haynsworth battle, the intensive wooing of doubtful senators by the White House and the Justice Department, and the natural predisposition to give the President his choice, all things being equal. But things were far from equal, for as the Carswell opponents

[123] The New York Times, November 22, 1969, p. 20.
[124] Richard Harris, Decision (New York: E. P. Dutton & Co., 1971), p. 11.
[125] As quoted by Harris, op. cit., pp. 15–16; in The New York Times, January 23, 1970, p. 16; and by Senator Birch Bayh (D.-Ind.) in Congressional Record, Vol. 116, p. 6, p. 7498, 91st Cong., 2nd sess.

continued their attack it became apparent that, quite apart from the controversy surrounding his civil rights record, the candidate was patently inferior, simply on the basis of fundamental juridical and legal qualifications. If Judge Haynsworth had merited a "B-minus" grade, Judge Carswell scarcely merited a "D" on the scale of relevant ability. Senator Roman Hruska (R.-Neb.), the President's floor manager of the nomination, made a fumbling, pathetic attempt to convert the candidate's mediocrity into an asset: "Even if he is mediocre there are a lot of mediocre judges and people and lawyers. They are entitled to a little representation, aren't they, and a little chance? We can't have all Brandeises, Cardozos, and Frankfurters, and stuff like that there."[126] Hruska's remarkable assertion was seconded by Carswell-supporter Senator Russell Long (D.-La.), who intoned:

> Does it not seem . . . that we have had enough of those upside down, corkscrew thinkers? Would it not appear that it might be well to take a B student or a C student who was able to think straight, compared to one of those A students who are [sic] capable of the kind of thinking that winds up getting us a 100-percent increase in crime in this country?[127]

This line of agrument failed to convince the doubtful senators. Instead, they become increasingly aware of the lack of ability of the nominee, who among other debilitating features, held the dubious record of having been reversed by appellate courts more than any of the other federal jurists then sitting except eight! Yale Law School Dean Louis H. Pollak styled the Carswell nomination as one of "more slender credentials than any Supreme Court nominee put forth in this century."[128] Perhaps even more tellingly, the distinguished William Van Alstyne, professor of law at Duke University, opposed the nomination. Van Alstyne, an ardent and vocal backer of the Haynsworth nomination, now testified: "There is, in candor, nothing in the quality of the nominee's work to warrant any expectation whatever, that he could serve with distinction on the Supreme Court of the United States."[129] When the final vote on confirmation came on April 9, 1970—three months after the nomination—the President's choice went down by a vote of 51:45. Among the "no's" were such significant Republican votes as those of Margaret Chase Smith of Maine, Winston L. Prouty of Vermont, Marlow W. Cook of Kentucky, and Richard S. Schweiker of Pennsylvania.

It was indeed a bitter defeat for the President. Not only had he seen two nominees rejected within less than five months, but his carefully devised "Southern strategy" had suffered a serious blow. His reaction was swift and vitriolic. Conveniently ignoring the basic issues for his candidates' defeats, he blamed them instead on sectional prejudice, abject politics, and philosophical negations, and told the country:

---

[126] As quoted by Harris, op. cit., p. 110.
[127] *Congressional Record*, op. cit., p. 7487.
[128] Harris, loc. cit.
[129] As quoted by Harris, op. cit., p. 56.

... I have reluctantly concluded that—with the Senate as presently constituted—I cannot successfully nominate to the Supreme Court any federal
appellate judge from the South who believes as I do in the strict construction
of the Constitution. ... Judges Carswell and Haynsworth have endured with
admirable dignity vicious assaults on their intelligence, their honesty, and
their character. ... When all the hypocrisy is stripped away, the real issue was
their philosophy of strict construction of the Constitution—a philosophy that
I share. ...[130]

Quite the contrary, several distinguished federal jurists in the South were
eminently qualified to serve, jurists who indeed shared the President's philosophy of government and politics and whom the Seante assuredly would
have confirmed. It could not, in good conscience, given the Fortas precedent,
the public concern, and the nature and role of the Supreme Court, have confirmed Haynsworth or Carswell, especially not Carswell. The latter, ironically, was soon to be defeated by his constituents in the Florida senatorial
primary, during which he was photographed with a lettered sign around his
neck reading "Heah Come 'de Judge." It is an intriguing thought that had
Haynsworth been nominated after Carswell, he might well have been
confirmed.

President Nixon followed up his blast against the rejections with the pet-
ulant suggestion in a well-publicized letter to Senator Wiliam B. Saxbe (R.-
Ohio) that the Senate had denied him the right to see his choices appointed.
The right, he insisted, had been accorded all previous Presidents—a patently
false statement, in the face of twenty-seven rejections of nominees to the
Court on record. Moreover, the President's collateral suggestion to Saxbe and
the nation, that senatorial advice and consent to nominations (which is
expressly provided for in Article II, Section II, Clause 2 of the Constitution)
is merely a pro forma requirement, is utterly incorrect with regard to nominations to the judiciary in general and the Supreme Court in particular. Mr.
Nixon, fully familiar with the contrary judgment of practically all students of
constitutional law and history, as well as with Hamilton's equally contrary
assertions in The Federal Papers (Nos. 76 and 77), must have been aware of
how wrong he was. His anger and frustration were understandable, but his
historical misstatement was a distinct disservice to Country, Constitution,
and Court.

The Senate's 45:43 refusal to accept cloture in 1968 in order that the senators might vote on the promotion of Justice Fortas—no such vote was ever
taken—has been variously attributed to his "record" on the high bench on
such contentious issues as obscenity and criminal justice. In fact, although
those issues were dramatically vocalized by such powerful and committed
opponents to the nomination as Senators Strom Thurmond (R.-S.C.) and John
L. McClellan (D.-Ark.), they were not an important reason for the nomina-

---

[130]From the President's nationwide television address of April 9, 1970, as quoted in The New
York Times, April 10, 1970, p. 1, and in Time Magazine, April 20, 1970, p. 9.

tion's failure. It was fought with such ardor largely because of deep-seated opposition to the jurisprudential philosophy of the "Warren Court," whose approach to constitutional interpretation had resulted in the inevitable disaffection of numerous groups and individuals, both public and private. The Court's stance and record of "judicial activism" on such emotion-charged issues as desegregation, reapportionment and redistricting, criminal justice, separation of church and state, civil disobedience, and freedom of expression were bound to offend as well as to please.

Coming, as it did conveniently, at the close of the Johnson Administration, the Fortas nomination readily served as target and symbol of the pent-up frustrations against the Warren Court—but against the Court as a unit rather than against the individual Justices. One of the famous episodes surrounding the attacks against Fortas occurred early in the hearings on the nomination by the Senate Judiciary Committee, when Senator Thurmond shouted at Fortas: "Mallory! Mallory! I want that name to ring in your ears!" Thurmond's reference was to Andrew Mallory, a nineteen-year-old black from South Carolina who was arrested in 1954 on a charge of choking and raping a thirty-eight-year old Washington woman while she was doing her laundry. After a seven -hour interrogation by the police *prior* to his arraignment, Mallory had confessed. The trial was delayed for a year because doubts had been raised that he understood the proceedings against him, but ultimately Mallory was sentenced to the electric chair. He appealed to the Supreme Court on the grounds of coerced confession. In 1957, in what became the celebrated case of *Mallory v. United States*,[131] the Court unanimously reversed Mallory's conviction on the ground that the failure of the police to bring him before a magistrate "forthwith" constituted an "unnecessary delay," in violation of (congressionally sanctioned) federal rules of criminal law procedure, thereby giving "opportunity for the extraction of a confession." Released, Mallory resumed a life of drifting and crime that culminated in his 1960 arrest in Philadelphia and his subsequent apprehension for burglary, assault, and rape. He was convicted on the assault count, served eleven years in jail, and barely six months after his release in 1971 attacked and robbed a couple in a Philadelphia park. When discovered by two policemen, he aimed a gun at one and was killed by the other. It was the so-called Mallory Rule, as pronounced by the Supreme Court in 1957, that Senator Thurmond referred to in his outburst at Justice Fortas. Yet Fortas had never been connected with the case and had not even been appointed to the Court until 1965, eight years after the Mallory decision! (The Mallory Rule itself was modified by Congress in the Omnibus Crime Control Act of 1968.) Other charges were leveled at the nominee, some of them concerning decisions in obscenity cases rendered long before Fortas ever sat.

Senatorial courtesy, the fourth in our list of reasons for Senate refusal of Supreme Court nominations, has already been discussed. A fifth is broadly

[131] 354 U.S. 449.

styled "political unreliability," as perceived by the Senate. Perhaps the most obvious example of the application of this reason is another among the several unsuccessful Grant nominations—that of former Attorney General Caleb Cushing, who was the President's choice to assume the Chief Justiceship in 1874, following the death of Salmon P. Chase. Cushing's age—seventy-four— was noted prominently during debate, but the real reason for his rejection was the Senate's not-entirely-erroneous belief that Grant's close personal friend was a political chameleon. Indeed, Cushing had been in turn a Regular Whig, a Tyler Whig, a Democrat, a Johnson Constitutional Conservative, and, at last, a Republican. He had proved himself a first-rate practitioner and scholar; nevertheless, with opposition from almost all political factions growing daily, Grant withdrew Cushing from consideration.

A final reason for Senate refusal of a nominee is simply real or apparent lack of qualification to sit on the Supreme Court. Of course, the concepts of "quality" and "ability" are subject to diverse analysis; yet a number of ascertainable standards and guidelines clearly exist; A nominee's age, experience, and record in and out of public life are all available guidelines. Ulysses S. Grant, in choosing his Attorney General George H. Williams to fill the vacancy caused by the death of Chief Justice Chase, thus evoked an entirely justifiable storm of adverse reactions. Williams had seen service in the Senate and had been territorial governor of Oregon, but his record as Attorney General was undistinguished and his talents as a lawyer were clearly mediocre. (It was alleged that he had unnecessarily lost several important cases in private as well as public litigation.) Both the bar and the press were severely critical of his achievements and his promise. Stunned and hurt by this reaction, and despairing of a lengthy confirmation battle, Williams asked President Grant to withdraw his nomination in early January 1874.

It is fair to conclude that Presidents have avoided nominating patently unqualified individuals to the high tribunal, although a number of rather weak nominations have slopped past the Senate, such as James C. McReynolds (Wilson), Pierce Butler (Harding), Sherman Minton (Truman), and Charles E. Whittaker (Eisenhower).[132] The one nominee on whose lack of qualifications almost all fair-minded observers now agree is G. Harrold Carswell. With the calm hindsight of history President Nixon's choice still merits the characterization of a spite nomination. It is fortunate that the Senate simply would not accept Carswell.

Would any of the twenty-seven who failed in being confirmed have been approved if they had been members of the Senate at the time of their nomination? The evidence is persuasive that they would have: the Senate almost invariably treats as a cas d'honneur the presidential designation of a sitting member—and, normally, although not as predictably, of a past colleague in good standing. Among the many illustrations are Senators James F. Byrnes

---

[132]For a ranking of all Justices through Thurgood Marshall (1967), based on a poll conducted by sixty-five experts in 1970, see Appendix A in my *Justices and Presidents*, op. cit.

(D.-S.C.) and Harold H. Burton (R.-Ohio). Byrnes, highly respected and very much a member of the Senate's "inner club," was confirmed unanimously without even being scrutinized by the Committee on the Judiciary when President Roosevelt nominated him in 1941.[133] Burton's nomination, although that of a Republican by a Democratic President (Truman), was unanimously confirmed in 1945 on the same day it reached the Senate, which was then controlled by a Democratic majority.

That the special treatment accorded senatorial colleague-nominees is normally reserved for then sitting members is demonstrated by the case of ex-Senator Sherman Minton of Indiana. Minton, who had been defeated for re-election in 1940, largely because of his ardent espousal of the New Deal, was serving as a judge on the U.S. Court of Appeals for the Seventh Circuit when President Truman selected him for the Supreme Court in 1949. In part because of his support of the "Court-packing bill," the Senate judiciary committee voted 5:4 to ask him to testify before it. Minton refused, pointing to his position as a jurist and questioning the propriety of testifying lest conflicts arise concerning pending litigation. The committee relented and reported his nomination favorably, 9:2. But the Senate, led by prominent Republicans, took a formal vote on a motion to recommit Minton's nomination. It lost 45:21; thereafter he obtained quick confirmation, 48:16.

A notable exception to the unwritten rule of the all but automatic approval of sitting senatorial colleagues was Franklin D. Roosevelt's controversial nomination of Senator Hugo LaFayette Black (D.-Ala.) in August 1937. Black's nomination was referred to the judiciary committee for full hearings, an action not taken on a fellow-senator since 1888. The initial reasons for that move, over the strong objections by the chairman of the Committee, Senator Henry Ashurst (D.-Ariz.), were Black's strong support of the President's 1937 "Court-packing bill," his ardent New Deal partisanship, and his ruthless public investigations of the utility lobby. The attempt to increase the size of the Court was anathema to a majority of the Senate and the bar. And the controversy was compounded and exacerbated by rumors that Black had once been—and some alleged still was—a member of the Ku Klux Klan in his native Alabama. Even so, the Committee ultimately approved the nomination by a vote of 13:4 (two Democrats and two Republicans voting against him), and the Senate confirmed him 63:16, nine Republicans and six Democrats voting "nay." Meanwhile, reporter Ray Sprigle of the *Pittsburgh Post-Gazette* came up with evidence that Black had indeed belonged to the KKK. Black, however, faced the charges squarely, and in a candid, dramatic broadcast to the American people admitted a two-year KKK membership in the mid-1920s, but pointed to his established liberal record and vowed to be a fair and impartial jurist. During his tenure on the Court, which lasted more than a third of a century, he kept his word.

---

[133] After barely fifteen months, Byrnes resigned to become F. D. R.'s "Assistant President for Domestic Affairs."

The last test of the Senate's refusal to refer nominations of incumbent senators to the Judiciary Committee came with Burton in 1945; no senator has since been nominated. It was precisely the recognition of that rule which prompted leading supporters of President Nixon to urge him to nominate a senator after Judge Haynsworth's rejection in 1969. Evidently the President briefly toyed with the idea of nominating John Stennis (D.-Miss.) or Sam Ervin (D.-N.C.), both Southern Senators generally supportive of his "strict construction" views, but in his determination to "teach the Senate a lesson" he chose Carswell. Yet it will be recalled that one of "The Six" he had under consideration for the Black and Harlan vacancies in 1971 was Senator Robert C. Byrd (D.-W. Va.), a man arguably less qualified to serve on the Court than his colleagues Stennis and Ervin. Whether or not Nixon seriously contemplated the Byrd nomination, there is but scant doubt that his colleagues would have given their approval. Yet those same colleagues would have been far less likely to approve someone of equally marginal qualifications from outside the halls of the Senate.

In general, opposition to the confirmation of a Supreme Court Justice seems to reflect the existence of deep-seated concern in the nation. In the early years of the Court's history, relatively little interest was shown in the potentially "unfortunate effects" of Justices of uncertain, or certain, convictions. It became more frequent and noticeable as the influence of the Court became more apparent. At the present time, when there are so many issues in which large numbers of people are deeply concerned, almost every nominee is made to run the gauntlet; he may even feel slighted if his appointment is unopposed because this could be intepreted as a sign that he is not regarded as an individual who carries very much weight. The nomination and confirmation procedure has become one more battleground on which large issues are fought out before the public eye.

QUALIFICATIONS AND EXPERIENCE: THE SPECIAL CASES OF ENGLAND[134] AND FRANCE

In endeavoring to explain and analyze the staffing of the courts of England and France, and in comparing their respective judiciaries, it is necessary to remain cognizant of the two different types of law that govern the systems concerned—the common or Anglo-Saxon law in England and the civil or Roman law in France. There are fundamental differences between the laws of the two countries—and far greater ones become apparent, of course, in contrasting one or both with the prevalent norms and practices in the United States. But it is above all the very position of the judiciary that provides the key to these differences. Under the Roman law tradition of the Continent,

---

[134]The reader is reminded that "England," as understood for the purposes of this book, includes Wales (but *not* Scotland or Northern Ireland).

the judiciary is a part of the administrative-executive hierarchy (as will be explained in considerable detail in chapter 6) and it constitutes a *profession* distinctly separate from that of the practicing lawyer. Where the common law tradition holds, however, the legal profession is practically an autonomous body, the judges being drawn from its ranks—not withstanding the different mode and mood of selection that governs in England compared with that of the United States, where the common law tradition also holds.

Nevertheless, we have already observed that a common ideal, that of impartiality of the appointees, is held by all three lands for both selection and tenure of their judiciaries and that each is therefore willing, as it must be, to protect its independence and provide a large measure of immunity in order to achieve it. But the techniques of training and selecting judges and ensuring their impartiality differ widely.

ENGLAND

Unlike the United States, England divides its legal profession into two major groups—the *solicitors* and the *barristers*—and it is impossible to be both *concurrently*. The former deal mainly with the general public; they conduct about 95 percent of the ordinary legal business of the country, leaving the remaining highly important work of pleading and advocacy in the courts to the barristers, who see the layperson only when so instructed by a solicitor. The best analogy of the difference between the two groups is found in medicine: the difference between the general practitioner and the consultant and specialist. Barristers are consultants for the solicitors—the latter do all the ordinary work of the law and call in the barristers when they need or desire their services, either for advice or for conducting a case in court.

The Solicitors. The "office lawyers" of the legal structure, the solicitors are obviously its workhorses. It is they who deal directly with the clients, who do the routine legal office work, and who prepare the spadework for cases to be argued at the bar of the higher courts by the barristers. But they also enjoy the right of audience in the magistrates and county courts, and, at the discretion or "direction" of the Lord Chancellor, under section 12 of the Courts Act of 1971, at certain limited proceedings, in the Crown Court; in fact, they do a great deal of advocacy in these several courts. However, they are still not allowed to appear in the higher courts. They handle practically all of the drawing-up of legal documents, such as transfers of property. In short, the 42,984 practicing solicitors (1984) do the bulk of England's ordinary legal work. Having determined to become a solicitor on the conclusion of his or her educational career, and having undergone additional legal training,[135] the aspirant then takes a number of special professional examinations. Passing these, he or she becomes a "Solicitor of the Supreme Court" and commences a career. The solicitor will also probably join the Law Society, a voluntary

---

[135]See further description, *infra*, p. 92.

association of solicitors with certain statutory powers. Every *practicing* solicitor must become a member of this society. Incidentally, university training is not an absolute requirement—over half of the solicitors are not university products.

The Barristers. It is the 5,032 practicing barristers (1984) who constitute England's *best-known* legal talent. Their chief function is to render legal advice to clients (in the great majority of cases, on instructions given to them by solicitors), either generally or in preparation for trial, and, of course, to conduct cases, both civil and criminal. Thus, they argue all cases in the higher courts—cases that, by custom and tradition, are almost always given to them directly by the solicitors, who have processed them in a preliminary manner, rather than by the clients themselves. The barristers are professionally specialized and usually, although not inevitably, highly experienced members of the legal profession. Their specialization may lead them to practice in limited and specialized fields, such as Chancery, Common, or Criminal law, and Commercial law including Admiralty. It is from the ranks of the barristers that the Lord Chancellor normally selects the judges on behalf of the Crown. Indeed, with the exception of justices of the peace, the English and Welsh judges were always appointed from the ranks of practicing barristers until the passage of the Court Act of 1971, when solicitors became eligible for the posts of Recorder or Circuit Judge.[136]

The barristers are divided into two groups, or ranks: "junior barristers" and "Queen's Counsel." The latter are referred to colloquially as "silks" because they are entitled to wear a silk gown instead of the "stuff" gown worn by the junior barristers. The two gowns are different in style also: those worn by the Juniors are like academic gowns with flowing sleeves, those of the silks have simpler lines. One becomes a silk upon the recommendation of the Lord Chancellor, on reaching top status in the profession, seldom until the completion of ten years' successful practice, although it should be noted that some very distinguished lawyers never "take silk." Successful juniors usually apply for silk in their forties or fifties. In consultation with senior judges, the Lord Chancellor chooses between 40 and 50 names each year from the 180 or so who apply. The silks, who comprise 10 percent of the bar, constitute the elite among the barristers, and they generally receive higher fees than the junior barristers. Their main tasks include appearances in court, where they are usually accompanied by a junior. It is from the ranks of Queen's Counsel that judges are mainly chosen. Yet sometimes it is possible to become a judge without being a "Q.C."—for example, Lord Chief Justice Parker was made a judge as a junior. He had been junior counsel to the Treasury, the govern-

---

[136] A Recorder must now be a barrister or solicitor of at least ten years' standing; a Circuit Judge must be a barrister of at least ten years' standing or a Recorder who has held that judicial office for at least five years. A County Judge, however, must have been a barrister for at least seven years, a High Court Judge for at least ten, and a Lord Chief Justice of Appeal for at least fifteen.

ment advocate for Crown business in the High Court. Normally those who have taken silk for at least seven years, and, in the cases of the higher courts, for at least ten years, may expect to be considered for a judgeship in the event of a vacancy. But the number of superior court judges is low, and when one of the promotions does come it is viewed with a certain awe and respect by the legal profession and the public at large. Judges of the High Court are *invited* to become such by the Lord Chancellor—that is, they do not solicit the post—whereas those of the County Court are appointed from the ranks of those who have *applied* to the Lord Chancellor for consideration of appointment.[137]

All barristers are members of one of the four historic *Inns of Court* in London: Lincoln's Inn, Gray's Inn, Inner Temple, and Middle Temple.[138] In effect, they constitute both both a "law school" and a corporate professional organization. Separate colleges, each with its own hall, chapel—except that the Inner and Middle Temple share the Round Church—and library, they arose as a result of the lawyers' custom of living together during terms. Self-governing, historic organizations, officially dating back roughly to the time of Edward I, "Longshanks" (1272–1307), the Inns of Court have different histories, but they were generally modeled on the old trade guilds, to which they owe their origin. An Inn of Court was not so much a school of law as a school for Englishmen (as Sir John Fortescue so well described it in his epic *De Laudibus Legum Angliae*). The outlook developed in a university (Oxford and Cambridge) was purely scholastic; that in an Inn of Court was eminently national. In an Inn of Court the students lived together as one community. Fortescue describes the Inns of his time (fifteenth century) as not merely places for the students of the law, but as universities or schools of all com-

[137]In mid-1984, successful Q.C.s averaged around £60,000 a year. A handful of specialists—especially those in tax and company work—grossed over £200,000. Most established juniors ranged between £15,000 and £35,000, roughly at the same earning level as the average solicitor. But partners in the central London solicitors' firms (barristers may not engage in partnerships) average more than £40,000, and senior partners in top firms, very much like their counterparts in America, can earn in six figures annually, whereas those in small firms in poor areas of England and Wales may have to struggle to earn £12,000. (See "The Two Legal Professions," Part 2 of "English Justice," *The Economist*, August 6, 1983, pp. 46–47.)

[138]The Inner and Middle Temples derive their names from the Round Church, which was built by the Knights Templar in 1160, and stood, despite being widely damaged—as were the other two Inns—in the 1941 London blitz, between the Strand and the Thames. They were restored (and the church was rededicated) in the early 1960s. What is now known as the Inner Temple covers what used to be the consecrated portion of the grounds surrounding the Temple Church. The Middle Temple covers what used to be the unconsecrated part. Gray's Inn derives its name from Reginald de Grey, Justician of Chester, who lived there in the thirteenth century. (Sir Francis Bacon, one of Gray's Inn's most famous members, planned and planted its beautiful gardens, where he loved to walk and talk with such statesmen as Sir Walter Raleigh). Lincoln's Inn, whose records are continuous from 1942, owes its name to the Earl of Lincoln, who was a member of the King's Council, also in the thirteenth century.

mendable qualities. There, students as well as members of the bar would study, live, work, eat, and pray. But now they are no longer residences in the full sense of the term, although quite a few barristers still do live there, sometimes with their families.

Legal Education. In the past, under the tutelage of barristers, England's future lawyers were thus trained in the Inns rather than in a university law school, where Roman or civil law and canon law, as opposed to the common law, were taught. Today, these students may attend the lectures of the Council of Legal Education, a joint committee for education from the four Inns of Court. They are tested by examiners of the council, and on passing the examination and having kept their "dining terms," they apply to the "Benchers," the governing body of the Inn, for admission as barristers. This "dining term" rule is a relic of the days when students of the common law lived in the Inns of Court and had to frequent the hall of their Inn for dinner, for the exercises in "mooting," and for other forms of learning before becoming barristers. To this day they must dine in the hall on three nights in each dining term.

Once admitted to the bar, the young barrister remains under the general jurisdiction of his Inn of Court throughout his career—in fact, for life—and it is his Inn that constitutes both his professional protector and his disciplinarian. A full measure of *esprit de corps* flows naturally from life and membership in the Inn. Disciplinary problems are further under the supervision of the Genral Council of the Bar, a special body elected by the members of the Bar to act for it in a wide range of matters. Authority to expel a barrister for misconduct is given to the "Benchers" of the Inn of which he is a member. Disciplinary and other matters affecting the Bar generally also now come under the jurisdiction of the Senate of the Four Inns of Court, which has representative members of the four Inns and of the Bar Council.

The legal education provided by the Law Society for solicitors, who may have offices at the Inns but do not study there, differs from that given to the barristers. It is based on intensive courses, practical training, and a year's compulsory attendance at a recognized law school. The future barrister, on the other hand, must pass the bar examinations, which involve a background in general legal principles, although he may not have had specific training in these, he often does not attend the elaborate series of lectures provided by the Council of Legal Education, and he is not required to have practical training. However, recently a pledge has been exacted from candidates to spend six months as pupils in chambers.

The reason the future solicitor is given a thorough practical training in a solicitor's office by being apprenticed to the latter for three years if a university product and five years if not is because solicitors are entitled to practice from the moment they are admitted and can do legal work of practically any kind *at once* for the general public. But a barrister is never employed directly by a member of the public; he is employed, or instructed, by a solicitor and in practice is a highly trained lawyer before he gets work of any importance from a solicitor.

Even given the possibility of a judicial appointment, his or her attractive social status, and the "psychic income" he or she may receive from membership in the profession, the future of the barrister's branch of that profession is nevertheless undergoing some examination. One of the considerations is the relatively low income of many barristers, although big incomes are earned by those at the top of the profession. As of late 1984, the number of practicing barristers was 5,032, of whom 573 were women.[139] The former total represents a 70 percent increase since 1970, due in not inconsiderable measure to the rising legal aid work in Law Centres by barristers in both criminal and civil law—not necessarily their most desired type of practice.

Yet whatever the problems of the profession may be—and they have been exaggerated at times—the English judges are very likely the most highly esteemed, the most independent, and relatively speaking, the most generously paid in the West. There is little doubt that these three factors account in considerable degree for the generally higher quality of British justice, properly so often cited and envied by much of the rest of the world.

FRANCE

The Republic of France, together with several other states on the continent of Europe, goes considerably further than Britain in distinguishing between judges, public prosecutors, and officials of the powerful Ministry of Justice, on the one hand, and privately practicing lawyers on the other. Although there is a clear-cut distinction between the British solicitor and the barrister, both are nonetheless members of the legal profession and may commence their advanced legal training together. In France, however, the bench is a separate career; it is not viewed as a reward for legal excellence or renown as it is in both Britain and in the United States.

A future French student of the law must decide at the very outset of his or her schooling whether to become either a private lawyer or a judge or prosecutor or go to the Justice Ministry. If the former, he or she attends law school and chooses among six available specialties: *avocat*, roughly akin to the British barrister; *avoué*, the approximate equivalent of the British solicitor; *agrée*, who specializes in pleading before certain commercial tribunals, although these three specialties were, in effect, gradually being fused as of September 1972;[140] *notaire*, who is trained in drafting and registering of legal papers, related in name only to the American notary public who need not be a lawyer; *fiduciaire*, who specializes in tax matters; or *conseiller juridique*, who gives general legal advice. These six groups, including some 30,000 persons in 1984, comprise the French *legal*, not *judicial*, profession. The French

[139] Data supplied by courtesy of Alan H. Bray, M.A. (Oxon.), of Middle Temple Inn, London, Barrister-at-Law. Personal communication, April 28, 1984. See also the special issues of *The Economist*, "English Justice," July 30, August 6, 13, 20, and 27, and September 3, 1983.

[140] Pierre Drai, "Les 'Gens' de Justice," *Les Cahiers Francais*, 156–57, September–December 1972 (*La Documentation Francaise*, Paris 1972).

law student desirous of becoming a judge of the lower or appelate courts or a public prosecutor or member of the Ministry of Justice follows a totally separate path of training, for—as has been explained earlier—the judiciary of France is, in effect, a branch of the government, a part of the civil service.

Training for a Judgeship. Until the judicial reforms of 1958–59 took place, after finishing law school prospective members of the judiciary would initially gather some experience, a sort of apprenticeship, in a law office. From there they usually moved on to a minor office in a local court while awaiting appointment. In the meantime, when they deemed themselves sufficiently qualified, they would take an examination and, if successful, could then anticipate placement in the judicial system. It was common practice to be first assigned public prosecutor and then gradually effect promotion to a judgeship.

However, since 1959, as a result of a governmental decree designed to broaden and further professionalize their background, experience, and training, all potential applicants for judgeships as well as for legal posts in the executive branch, are required to attend the post-graduate (post–law school) level *École Nationale de la Magistrature* (National School for Jurists) for twenty-eight months: the first eleven of these are spent at the school's Bordeaux site in seminars, lectures, extrajudicial training (e.g., forensic medicine and criminology); in the next seventeen months the applicants gain practical experience in Paris and in the provinces. After a battle of examinations, and now having selected their careers, the candidates conclude their education with a special two-month preappointment training period. Those who wish to become matriculants of the *École Nationale* are selected on the basis of competitive examinations, in both legal subjects and the general liberal arts. Its students, who are paid by the government for attending the *École Nationale*, must have finished law school and be under twenty-seven years of age. Successful graduates are then assigned to one of the courts of first instance, the *tribunaux d'instance*, in accordance with their class standing—assuming they wish to become a judge. But they are also eligible for the *parquet*[141] (the office of the public prosecutor) or for service in the Ministry of Justice. The National School for Jurists was purposely designed to do for the judiciary what the National School of Administration *(École Nationale d'Administration)* has done so well for the upper echelons of the general civil service (and the members of the *Conseil d'Etat*,[142] some of whom at least think of themselves as judges): to create a competent, reputable, and esteemed group of public servants.

In the United States[143] and, to a more modified extent, in England, selection of a lawyer as a judge customarily represents the culmination of a long

---

[141] Explained in ch. 3, *infra*, especially pp. 101–3.

[142] Explained in ch 6 *infra*, pp. 279–82.

[143] Early in 1967 the American Bar Association endorsed, and Congress enacted into law that December, President Johnson's plan to establish a Federal Judicial Center in the Adminis-

and quite frequently distinguished career in the law—subject to certain obvious political contingencies in the United States. But in France the judge is chosen from the *judicial profession,* for which he or she is prepared by special schooling and examination[144]—a profession just as medicine, teaching, and the law are. Although it may not be particularly well paid, the judiciary enjoys considerable prestige and a high social rating. We shall now see it in action on the bench.

---

trative Office of the U.S. Courts (see ch. 4, *infra*) with the Chief Justice of the United States as chairman of its independent board. (Act of December 20, 1967, 81 Stat. 664.) Its purpose is "to further the development and adoption of improved judicial administration in the courts of the United States," as well as to train federal court employees, including federal judges, and to foster programs of continuing education for them. Other tasks of the Center, which is now quite properly regarded as the "research and development arm" of the federal judiciary, include keeping abreast of computer technology, conducting and stimulating research on methods to speed the handling of cases, and reducing case backlogs. In addition to the Chief Justice, the Center's membership consists of two circuit court judges and three district court judges, elected by the Judicial Conference of the United States and the Director of the Administrative Office of the U.S. Courts. The Center had a staff of ninety-four in early 1984.

[144] The education and training of the judges of the Federal Republic of Germany is again different from those discussed in the preceding pages. Whatever legal or judicial career may ultimately be pursued by a future member of the legal profession, the *same* preparation is followed, consisting of a two-stage process. The first is formal university study, lasting approximately five years (the minimum is three and a half in some thirty German universities with faculties of law). At the end of this formal educational stage, the student takes the "first state examination," and, if successful, is designated as *Referendar,* who is now ready to commence the second stage, a two-year period of practical training. During that period, the *Referendar* must work in five areas: in civil courts, in a criminal court or a prosecutors office, in an administrative office, in a private law office, and in one other approved legal or governmental activity. In each of these five areas the *Referendar* will spend from three to nine months. Regarded now as a temporary civil servant, the *Referendar* receives a government salary. At the end of the two-year practical period the difficult "second state examination" must be taken. Consisting of several days of written parts, it is followed by an oral examination, conducted by four individuals for different segments of the legal profession. If the *Referendar* passes, he or she now becomes an *Assessor*—eligible to enter any one of the five basic career branches of the law: judge *(Richter)*; prosecuting attorney *(Staatsanwalt);*—upper-level bureaucratic post; private practice attorney *(Rechtsanwalt);* private commercial enterprise or financial institution legal position. (*Additional* advanced university training would open the door for a sixth possibility, an academic career.) This disciplined, thorough composite of university education and practical training emphasizes a sameness of experience that has resulted in a highly professionalized career, one that other nations might well ponder. (Much of the above data are drawn from Daniel J. Meador, "German Appellate Judges: Career Patterns and American-English Comparisons," 67 *Judicature* 1 (June–July 1983).

3

Courts, Courtrooms, and Juries

TYPES OF COURTS: TRIAL AND APPELLATE

Each of the countries discussed in this book has a system of courts designed to serve its own needs and choice. Some have similar features, but no two are truly alike. Speaking broadly, however, each of these systems—and in fact practically every known judicial system in the world—has endeavored to separate the jurisdiction of *trial* (first instance) and *appellate* (review) courts. Some courts do fulfill both functions, but in that event, if justice is to have any meaning at all, they will at the very least separate dockets for each area. This applies, for example, to the English Crown Court and the French *Cour d'Assise*. In a rather limited sense, the Supreme Court of the United States is also constitutionally empowered to exercise jurisdiction in the trial as well as in the appellate area—termed *original* and *appellate* by Article III of the Constitution, in which these designations are found. However, that high tribunal's original jurisdiction docket is usually empty; seldom, if ever, has it exceeded more than a fraction of 1 percent of the volume of cases handled by the Court. The overwhelming number of cases and controversies that reach the highest tribunal in the American judicial hierarchy do so under its appellate jurisdiction. In fact, as will be explained in more detail in chapter 5, the Supreme Court may, except in the instance of litigation involving two or more of the fifty states, share its original jurisdiction with courts below— that is, its original jurisdiction is thus *concurrent* with them—which, in effect, means that seldom, if ever, will the Supreme Court decide such a case in its role of a trial court.

TRIAL COURTS

Trial courts perform the function their title clearly implies: they *try* cases in the first instance, as tribunals of original jurisdiction. Cases commence there because they are statutorily required to do so. More often than not they are also completed there upon the pronouncement of the verdict of guilt or acquittal, which may or may not, depending on organizational requirements and choice, have resulted from a trial by jury. Rather obvious illustrations of trial courts of varied jurisdiction are a U.S. District Court, a Court of Common Pleas in the Commonwealth of Pennsylvania, a French *Tribunal de Grande Instance*, and the Queen's Bench Division of the High Court of Justice of England and Wales.

Again depending somewhat on the law of the land and governmental subdivision concerned, both law and fact are taken into account at the bar of a trial court, and both parties to the litigation (plaintiff as well as defendant) are presumably accorded a full opportunity to present their respective sides of the case or controversy. In common law countries, such as most of the English-speaking lands, a single judge customarily, but by no means always, presides over a trial alone; in statutory law systems, such as those found in most continental European states, normally three or more judges sit *en banc*—sometimes joined by laypersons, such as the *rådmän* in Sweden. When a jury sits in a case, the judge *charges* (instructs) it at the conclusion of the presentation of pertinent evidence in the law and in the procedures attendant upon the case. The jury then returns a verdict on completion of its deliberations, which may last from a few hours to several days.

APPELLATE COURTS

The raison d'être of a court of appeals is to provide a forum for review of decisions rendered in trial court. Such appeals are presumably limited to questions of law at issue in the litigation below, but in some circumstances they may also deal with questions of fact, either collaterally or on their own merits. In any event, it is often extremely difficult to separate categorically matters of law and fact, and the final word on such a distinction, if it is crucial to the question of the grant of the petition for review, will necessarily lodge in the appellate tribunal itself. In large measure, this decision depends on the tribunal's statutory authority and the extent and nature of the discretionary review powers given to it. Some appellate courts *must* accept all cases properly presented to them for review, such as the U.S. (Circuit) Court of Appeals (assuming the presence of appropriate jurisdiction), which has no effective discretionary power to decline to accept appellate petitions. Others—for example, the U.S. Supreme Court—possess all but complete statutory *discretionary* authority as to whether or not to accept a case brought for review from below, although in theory there are *some* cases of mandatory review (as will be shown in chapter 5). Still other appellate tribunals, the British House of Lords for one (see chapter 6), have discretionary power to accept or reject cases, but are guided to a considerable degree by certification from the court below (here the Court of Appeal). Courts of appeals are usually multiple-member bodies; commonly, but not inevitably, at least, three judges sit *en banc* to hear the appeal without a jury.

A well-known appellate court, in addition to those already named, is England and Wales's important Court of Appeal (for civil and criminal cases). That court is empowered to *retry* a case, a departure from the normal role of appellate tribunals—but solely on the ground of fresh evidence having become available, and subject to the court's judgment that a retrial is indeed appropriate in the interests of justice.[1] It thus retries cases but rarely. Indeed, it is only in exceptional cases that fresh evidence is admitted in the Court of Appeal.[2] The *Cour de Cassation*, at the apex of the regular French judicial system, is another example of a court of appeals. In some appellate courts, such as the criminal division of the English Court of Appeals, appeals may be instituted only by the defendant. In the United States, although the federal government may usually appeal an adverse decision of a trial court on a point of *law*, unless it involves "double jeopardy," it is barred from appealing on a point of *fact*; this means that, in effect, the government cannot appeal an adverse verdict in a criminal proceeding on the basis of the factual evidence presented in court on pain of violating the double jeopardy safeguards of the Fifth Amendment to the U.S. Constitution (although, since a 1981 decision, it is permitted to appeal the length or brevity of certain sentences).[3] Until the Supreme Court so ruled in 1969, that Bill of Rights provision had not automatically applied to the states.[4]

COURTROOM PROCEDURE: GENERAL

There are essentially two methods by which society, through its judicial and legal organs, may approach a member of its body politic accused of an offense—either by presuming his innocence until it has effectively succeeded in proving him guilty under due process of law, or, in effect if not in theory, by presuming his guilt unless he successfully disproves that assumption under similar processes.

"INNOCENT-UNTIL-PROVED-GUILTY": THE ACCUSATORIAL PROCEDURE

It is a cornerstone of Anglo-Saxon justice that an accused is presumed innocent unless and until proved guilty beyond a reasonable doubt. Few, if any, concepts are more deeply rooted in our traditions. Admittedly, that principle has been violated from time to time, especially during periods of war and

---

[1] See Administration of Justice Act of 1964 (See. 5).
[2] See *Ladd v. Marshall* 1956 1 W.C.R.1489.
[3] Based on a provision contained in the Organized Crime Control Act of 1970, and here upheld 5:4 in an opinion written by Justice Blackmun. (*United States v. DiFrancesco*, 449 U.S. 117.)
[4] *Benton v. Maryland*, 395 U.S. 784. The 1960s had witnessed an increasing number of "applications," "absorptions," or "incorporations" of provisions of the Bill of Rights, by virtue of a series of landmark rulings of the Supreme Court. For a full discussion of this intriguing constitutional problem, see my *Freedom and the Court: Civil Rights and Liberties in the United States*, 4th ed. (New York: Oxford University Press, 1982), ch 3, "The Applicability of the Bill of Rights to the States."

other emergencies when an occasional departure from it has been justified on the grounds of constitutionally sanctionable expediency, however distasteful. Thus, writing painfully for a divided (6:3) bench that " . . . hardships are part of war, and war is an aggregation of hardships . . . " Justice Black, one of the foremost civil libertarians in the life of the Supreme Court of the United States, upheld the compulsory evacuation of 112,000 persons of Japanese ancestry from their homes on the West Coast—among them some 70,000 native-born American citizens, none of whom had been *specifically accused* of disloyalty.[5] On the whole, however, the record of the common law countries, such as Britain and the United States, has been good in this regard. The layperson may quite naturally be quick to adjudge a person guilty in his or her own mind, and he or she is sometimes joined by the press, particularly in America; but the Anglo-Saxon legal profession on both sides of the Atlantic Ocean, and throughout the English-speaking world, has done its best to adhere to the time-honored principle that an accused person is presumed to be innocent until proved otherwise beyond a reasonable doubt by due process of law. As Justice Brennan wrote for the Supreme Court in a decision highly unpopular with Congress and the public at large, in which the Court by a vote of 7:1 reversed the conviction of one Clinton Jencks, a suspected Communist perjurer who had not been permitted to attempt to impeach testimony given to the Federal Bureau of Investigation on the basis of which he had been convicted in the trial court: " . . . the interest of the United States in a criminal prosecution . . . is not that it shall win a case, but that justice shall be done."[6] And, in the words of Justice Frankfurter's majority opinion in a coerced confession case in 1961, " . . . ours is an accusatorial and not an inquisitorial system—a system in which the State must establish guilt by evidence independently and freely secured and may not by coercion prove its charge against an accused out of his own mouth."[7] Of course, this jurisprudential posture applies equally to any civil proceeding, whether or not the government is a party to it. In the gravamen of one of Justice Robert H. Jackson's opinions concerning one attorney's right to compel another to disclose certain papers involved in the litigation concerned, "A *common law* trial is and always should be an adversary proceeding."[8]

Thus, the presumption of the innocence of the accused is transformed into courtroom procedure in the Anglo-Saxon countries. Essential to it are the ancient, basic safeguards inherent in that philosophy of the law, safeguards which, to a greater or lesser degree, are fundamental to the notions of liberty and justice that pervade the political system of the liberal democratic West. Among these are the privilege against compulsory self-incrimination; the

[5] *Korematsu v. United States,* 323 U.S. 214 (1944).
[6] *Jencks v. United States,* 353 U.S. 657 (1957), at 668. With some paraphrasing, he in effect was quoting Justice Sutherland's opinion in *Berger v. United States,* 295 U.S. 78 (1935), at 88.
[7] *Rogers v. Richmond,* 365 U.S. 534, at 540-41.
[8] *Hickman v. Taylor,* 329 U.S. 495, at 516 (1946). (Italics supplied.).

right to cross-examine witnesses; the writ of *habeas corpus*—perhaps the most basic right of all—and many others in the same general category.

The Judge's Role. An important feature of the accusatorial type of procedure is that the judge does *not*—except as noted later, and in rare instances in order to call forth certain types of evidence, usually of a technical nature— insert himself into the substantive questioning during the trial, although the English trial judge is decidedly more interventionist than the American. Quite naturally, he or she does, indeed must, hand down rulings on various motions, points of order, and other problems that may arise during the course of the trial. The judge is, or certainly is expected to be, in complete charge of courtroom procedure, and as such possesses a considerable residue of what in legal parlance is termed *judicial discretion*. In this connection, that intriguing compound noun demands an application

> ... enlightened by intelligence and learning, controlled by sound principles of law, of firm courage combined with the calmness of a cool mind, free from partiality, not swayed by sympathy nor warped by prejudice nor moved by any kind of influence save alone the overwhelming passion to do that which is just. ... [9]

In that discretion, the judge will question a witness only to avert grave injustice, not to advance the case for either side. He or she is not in any sense an active elicitor of truth regarding the testimony presented unless becoming convinced, as did U.S. District Court Judge John J. Sirica in the initial "Watergate" trial, that there were gross prevarications. (His tactics were subsequently challenged in, but upheld by, the U.S. Court of Appeals.[10]) In essence, the judge is an independent arbiter between the state and the individual or between the litigating parties. This is a concept basic to the common law adversary proceeding mentioned by Justice Jackson, a system that "sets the parties fighting." According to Professor Max Radin, one of the giant interpreters of jurisprudential theory and practice, that system has been in vogue since its adoption in Rome in the fourth or fifth century B.C., when— for better or for worse, and quite conceivably the latter—the judge's task changed from determining the truth to the umpiring of a competition.[11] There is little doubt that many, probably most, of today's lawyers would have great difficulty of conceiving of a trial as anything else. It is thus often viewed, not at all inaccurately, as a grim game.

"GUILTY-UNTIL-PROVED-INNOCENT": THE INQUISITORIAL PROCEDURE

In France, to use the most obvious example, a different philosophy regarding the legal process obtains. For while in England and the United States the

---

[9] *Davis v. Boston Elevated Railway*, 235 Mass. 482, at 496–97. Quoted by Felix Frankfurter, *The Case of Sacco and Vanzetti* (Boston: Little, Brown, and Co., 1927), pp. 90–91.
[10] *Nixon v. Sirica*, 487 F. 2d 700 (1973). See the illuminating article by Robert M. Smith, "T-R-U-T-H or T-R-I-A-L," *The New York Times*, November 4, 1973, p. C37.
[11] Max Radin, "The Permanent Problems of the Law," 15 *Cornell Law Quarterly* 10–11 (1929).

basic question is whether or not the accused can be proved guilty, in France it is simply to determine "who did it." Not independent arbiters, the French judges are part of the machinery of the state, and courtroom procedure in criminal trials is characterized by the *inquisitorial* method, known as the *enquête*. Here the presumption may almost be regarded as implicitly one of guilt, although it is doubtful that any civilized land actually proceeds on such an assumption. Indeed, Radin refers to the notion of presumption of guilt as a "curiously persistent calumny," and views the presumption of innocence as "inherent in the French Declaration of the Rights of Man and the Citizen."[12] Still, so much painstakingly accumulated preliminary investigation by a professional judge—the *juge d'instruction* (examining magistrate)—has already preceded the courtroom trial that the French judge or judges presiding at the trial may well all but presume the defendant to be guilty of the offense charged. Nonetheless, the presiding judges—who are quite different actors in the judicial process from the *juges d'instruction*—actively, often vehemently and acidly, participate in the courtroom questioning of witnesses as well as of the accused—who, incidentally, cannot invoke the Anglo-Saxon privilege of refusing to take the stand on grounds of possible self-incrimination. Yet had the investigating judge been unable to find any evidence of apparent guilt, the accused would very likely never have been brought to trial regardless of the police's wishes. In a sense, this preliminary "investigation" (the *enquête*) is an advanced, combined form of grand jury investigation and indictment, still so prevalent in the American courts, but with the significant distinction that whereas the *enquête* in France is conducted by professional magistrates the American grand jury is composed entirely of laypersons.

The Juge d'Instruction *and the* Enquête. The office of the *juge d'instruction*—which is not a uniquely French institution—combines the powers of prosecutor and magistrate, but the *juge d'instruction* is not a member of the prosecution per se. His or her function is to determine the truth on behalf of the state, with the aid of the police. Yet the *juge* may commence an investigation only upon notification by a member of the *parquet*, that is, the public prosecutor (*procureur*),[13] who must have been advised of the crime by the police, which will have begun its own investigation. The powers of the *juge d'instruction* are awesome indeed: he or she may call witnesses and question them intensely, ask suspects to reenact the alleged crime, open mail and tap telephone wires, even keep people in jail indefinitely (although since 1974,

---

[12] *The Law and You* (New York: Mentor M34, 1948), p. 99. Prof. Radin took specific and strong exception to my characterization in an interview shortly before his death on June 22, 1950. Going beyond his written statement, he insisted that the presumption of innocence may be regarded as guaranteed by the Declaration in express terms (a view also propounded by Professor Margherita Rendel of the University of London Institute of Education, a specialist in the French judiciary, in a letter to me, August 8, 1984).

[13] The role of *parquet* is roughly similar to that of the U.S. Attorney General and his associates when they act as public prosecutors.

those accused of committing "minor transgressions" can be jailed for only six months without being brought before a *juge*)[14]; the revered Anglo-Saxon institution of the writ of *habeas corpus* is unknown in France. The *juge* may commission experts to investigate and report on special aspects. But perhaps the most potent weapon in the *juge d'instruction's* considerable arsenal is the famous *confrontation de témoins* (confrontation of witnesses), which is unlike anything in Anglo-American legal procedure. When two or more witnesses tell contradictory stories, they are called into the *juge d'instruction's* office for a confrontation. There, under watchful and experienced eyes and ears, and in the presence of a court official who writes down every uttered syllable, each witness is quoted repeatedly, with the other(s) invited to point out "errors" or "discrepancies" in his or her testimony. The questioning of witnesses may of course proceed after the *confrontation*—presumably it also took place before—with a witness's lawyer present in all instances. As a result of the *confrontation*, perjured testimony in criminal cases has been almost eradicated.

When all the evidence, including that obtained by the police on its own, has been procured in a case, and both the defense and prosecution lawyers—the latter headed by the *procureur*—have had access to the complete *dossier*, the *juge d'instruction*, who will usually consult the *procureur*, can now send the case to trial on his or her own authority. Because that is highly unlikely unless he or she is convinced of the presence of guilt, the resultant trial itself turns largely into a public verification of the accumulated record, *including* any previous criminal record. In the event of a statutorily designated *serious* crime, the entire record of the investigation must be reviewed before it is admitted to trial by a *chambre d'accusation*, a judicial body at the appellate court level. (There were 522 *juges d'instruction* in 1985.)

Although the broad powers accorded to the *juge d'instruction* are sometimes criticized even by French legal scholars as being akin to a "star chamber" proceeding, that charge is grossly exaggerated. The *juge d'instruction* operates in a system that simply refuses to concede to the contending parties control over the presentation of evidence—either its submission or its impeachment by cross-examination. During the trial such control becomes the duty of the presiding judge. In the absence of cross-examination, the data procured by the *enquête* are necessary to ensure the accuracy of testimony. However "tough" it may be, the *enquête* is characterized by a patient, painstaking discovery procedure, one that has presumably solved mysteries and eliminated discrepancies in testimony. All the evidence is recorded in the *dossier*, enabling the *juge d'instruction* and the *procureur* to build the case against the accused. But it does more: it permits the presiding judge to conduct the trial free from the many "games" inherent in the adversary process, especially as it is so frequently practiced in American courtrooms.

---

[14]Some disagreement exists on this point, with certain observers contending that the *juge* can in effect do so only for twenty days.

In its final impact, the French system of the enquête would appear to be at least as effective as the Anglo-American accusational method, in which all the evidence is brought out for the first time, in the manner of a contest, by testimony and cross-examination in open court before trial judge and jury. A grand jury indictment, after all, requires only a prima facie case. One may well contend that a criminal trial in a French court is truly a bona fide investigation, rather than the characteristic American battle between two opposing platoons of learned counsel—a "sporting theory" battle that, in the words of one legal authority, denotes "a bitter adversary duel" rather than a disinterested investigation—in which the duelers indulge in trickery and fight with "make believe" evidence that often bears scant relation to the facts at issue.[15]

VOX DEI OR VOX POPULI IN ACTION: THE JURIES

There is no doubt that the institution of the jury is at once one of the most fascinating and one of the most controversial aspects of the judicial process and that justice in the West owes a great debt to the jury system. Sundry types of juries exist; but in essence a jury is a group of ordinary citizens of predetermined number whom a duly constituted public official has called together for the purpose of answering a question. Used in Athens as long ago as five or six centuries before the birth of Christ, they appeared in Rome some ten centuries later and in France in the ninth century. The modern Western world traces their origin to the England of some eight hundred years ago, where, in the early stages, they were regarded simply as a body of men to aid the monarch in dispensing justice by attesting to certain facts—that is, the jurors did not determine guilt or innocence, but instead were witnesses. Whatever their age, juries have been praised and attacked ever since. Although many countries, not necessarily excluding dictatorships, still resort to juries—apart from English-speaking lands they exist today largely in Austria, Belgium, Denmark,[16] Greece, Norway, some Latin American countries, and some Swiss cantons—the institution has clearly declined. This is more true of the grand jury than it is of the trial (petit) jury, but use of both types has decreased, especially in England and Wales, where the grand jury was abolished by the Administration of Justice (Miscellaneous Provisions) Act of 1933, and where the use of the trial jury in civil cases was seriously curtailed by the same law. Today, the latter jury is used in fewer than 5 percent of all cases in the British Isles (to be exact, juries serve in fewer than 1 percent of civil cases, but they are used in all "grave" criminal ones—approximately 4 percent of the total—in which there is a plea of "not guilty"). In France, of course, the grand jury is not employed at all, because of the role of the juge

---

[15]See James Marshall, Law and Psychology in Conflict (Garden City, N.Y.: Doubleday & Co., 1969), p. 7. The Mitterand Government announced important changes as of 1988.

[16]Iceland, although still essentially adhering to the Danish judicial system, uses no juries at all.

d'instruction. Juries are still generally widely prevalent in the United States. In many of the fifty states, however, juries, notably grand juries, have fallen into at least partial disuse. Indeed, more and more trials everywhere are decided by judges sitting without a jury, sometimes as a result of statutory or constitutional provisions, sometimes by the agreed-upon choice of the parties to the suit. Today it seems almost unbelievable that the courts of Athens in the fifth century B.C. were composed of a jury only—there was no judge at all! Moreover, the more significant the nature of the case was, the more jurors there were. Thus, Socrates was tried by a panel of 501 in the fourth century B.C., and Alcibiades's trial on charges of treason in the fifth featured 1,501 jurors. These able Attics were drawn from all over the Athenian communities by a complicated but apparently popular lot system.[17]

The foundation of the English jury system is traceable to the French empire under the Carolingian kings. As part of their successful attempt to unite their empire, a procedure called the *inquisition*, or *inquest*, was devised. Carried out by representatives of the monarch, its purpose was to call together various bodies of neighbors to ask questions and explain the sovereign's "immemorial" rights. The Norman conquerors subsequently carried the concept of the inquest to England, where they used it first in the compilation of the 1086 *Domesday Book*.[18] This tome, which listed the ownership of all English land, was compiled from data obtained from royal administrators who gathered neighbors together in various parts of the country and used them as their source of information. This served to establish the right of the state to obtain data from its citizenry, and thus furthered the concept of the jury system (which many insist is thus essentially Anglo-Saxon in origin).

The first true juries were used to discover facts under the various writs of the *Possessory Assizes*; for example, litigant neighbors decided who was dispossessed—which, in most instances, they already knew—and who owned a certain piece of land under the writ of *Novel Disseisin* ("newly dispossessed"). Thus, trial by jury was closely linked with the protection of possessions; indeed, Norman dukes and English kings sometimes specifically granted, both to private persons and to churches, the privilege of having their rights ascertained by this method. However, these juries merely filled a particular need at a particular moment in English history; they were permitted to die out and are hence not the bona fide predecessor of the modern English jury. The latter institution, initially used for civil cases only, was founded under King Henry II in the sixth decade of the twelfth century. Today, it would look strange in its original form, for then it represented what in effect was a combination grand jury and trial jury that enabled the accusing body (the modern *grand* jury) also to pass judgment on the guilt of the accused (the

---

[17]See Charles P. Curtis, *It's Your Law* (Cambridge: Harvard University Press, 1954), p. 102.
[18]*Doom* is an Anglo-Saxon word, whereas *law* is derived from the Danish *lov*.

modern *trial* jury). Ultimately these two functions were separated, heralding the now axiomatic difference between them.[19]

THE GRAND JURY

The chief distinction between a grand jury and a petit (trial) jury is that the former does not decide a defendant's innocence or guilt. The grand jury merely determines whether or not, in its considered judgment, sufficient evidence exists or has been brought to its attention to justify a trial on criminal charges. (Grand juries do not ordinarily sit in civil charges.) A trial jury, on the other hand, determines whether to convict or acquit. Hence a grand jury does not return a verdict; it listens to a bill of evidence presented by the legal representative of the prosecuting authority, who must draw up the formal written accusation, and who almost invariably dominates its deliberations—given the absence of a judge or other "neutral" in the grand jury room. The grand jury then decides whether or not the evidence warrants an *indictment*, also known as a *true bill*, which it returns in approximately ninety-five out of one hundred instances. In effect, an indictment thus charges one or more persons with having committed a crime—be it a felony or misdemeanor. The party called before the grand jury does not actually have an opportunity to give his or her full story; if indicted that day will come in the courtroom in the event of a trial. Nor may counsel be brought into the jury room (except in a handful of states, including New York), though the respondent may return to an antechamber to consult with counsel. He or she is entitled to know the names of, yet not confront, let alone cross-examine, witnesses that have appeared before the grand jury, but little else—except, of course, the evidence presented at the preliminary hearing before the committing magistrate.[20] There is no *right* to appear before the grand jury; one is invited or ordered to come before it—and there is no right to advance notice of the nature and scope of the crime being investigated. When the grand jury does

---

[19]See Frederick G. Kempin, Jr., *Development of the Common Law* (Philadelphia: Lecture Note Fund, University of Pennsylvania, 1959), I-3-2 and I-3-7. For an excellent source on the origin and history of the jury, see F. W. Maitland, *The Constitutional History of England* (Cambridge: Cambridge University Press, 1979 [a reprint of the 1908 ed.]).

[20]In May 1977, the U.S. Supreme Court handed down two rulings by the decisive margins of 9:0 and 7:2, respectively, reaffirming, as it were, that grand juries are not trial juries and that those who appear before them have but limited procedural rights. Thus, in the first case (*United States v. Wong*, 431 U.S. 174), it held that a suspect under investigation, who is indicted for perjury on the basis of statements to a grand jury, may not have the grand jury testimony excluded from evidence at the trial stage simply because of the lack of an effective notice of the Fifth Amendment privilege of remaining silent to avoid self-incrimination. In the second case (*United States v. Washington*, 431 U.S. 181) the Court held that testimony given by a grand jury witness suspected of wrongdoing *could* be used against him in a later prosecution for a substantive criminal offense, even though he had not been warned in advance of his testimony that he was a potential defendant in danger of indictment. (The two dissenters in the latter case were Justices Brennan and Marshall.)

not find sufficient evidence, it issues what is known as an *ignoramus*, or a *no bill*, in which case the would-be-defendant is not brought to trial.

By most accounts, the institution of the grand jury antedates the Magna Carta of 1215, but its origin is a source of considerable disagreement. Some have claimed to find its traces among the Athenians, but Athenian history, though mentioning the trial jury repeatedly, is quite silent on any body of citizens whose duty it was merely to accuse. The first grand jury, then called a *presenting jury*, was created by the Assize of Clarendon in 1166 under King Henry II as an accusatory body–composed of twelve knights or twelve "good and lawful men" in each community. It provided

> . . . that inquiry be made in each county and in each hundred, by twelve lawful men of the hundred and four lawful men of every township—who are sworn to say truly whether in their hundred or township there is a man accused of being or notorious as a robber, or a murderer or a thief, or anybody who is a harborer of robbers, or murderers, or thieves, since the king began to reign. And this let the justice and sheriffs inquire, each before himself.

Interestingly enough, this provision was not included to protect the liberties of freemen, but rather to protect the King's interests. By 1352, in the reign of Edward III, the principle that a man's indictors were not to serve both as grand and trial jurors was firmly established. The modern concept of the grand jury dates from 1368, when Edward III impaneled twenty-four men to act as county inquisitorial boards. It was not until three centuries later, however, that a grand jury became truly independent: in two successive cases— *Colledge's Case* and *Earl of Shaftesbury's Case*[21]—it for the first time refused to return an indictment on the grounds of *ignoramus*, that it "knew nothing." According to at least one historian, the immediate reason for the *ignoramus* in one of the cases was that the sheriff and many of the grand jurors were friends of the Earl of Shaftesbury![22]

Information. In England and Wales, where the grand jury was abolished as a result of the aforementioned statute of 1933 after a century of decreasing use, and in many parts of the United States, the fast and easy method of *information* has been adopted in its place. This is a simple and efficacious device whereby the public prosecutor merely submits his charges in the form of an affidavit of evidence, supported by sworn statements, to a count of original jurisdiction. Usually a preliminary hearing has been held before a committing magistrate here, too, and after these brief procedures the accused is ready to stand trial. In France, the *enquête* by a professional judge performs the functions of the grand jury. Only in the United States is the common law heritage of that body still relatively popular.

The documented history of the process of information is not nearly as complete as that of the grand jury and the trial jury. However, Blackstone noted

---

[21] 8 How St. Tr. 550 (1681) and 8 How St. Tr. 759 (1681).
[22] George J. Edwards, Jr., *The Grand Jury* (Philadelphia: George T. Bisel Co., 1906), p. 29.

in his *Commentaries* that "there can be no doubt that this mode of prosecutions by information filed on record by the King's Attorney General, or by his coroner or master of the crown office in the court of the King's bench . . . is as ancient as the common law itself."[23] Although its usage lagged until the twentieth century, the process did figure prominently in the famous case of Peter Zenger, commonly recalled as a milestone in the battle against press censorship. In 1735 an attempt was made to indict that courageous editor of the *New-York Weekly Journal* for libel against the conduct of the royal government, as personified by Governor William Cosby. When the grand jury—symbolizing its independence in North America—ignored the bill of charges against him, Zenger was then held on the basis of an information filed by the attorney general of the province. After a celebrated trial in which he was ably defended by famed Philadelphia attorney Andrew Hamilton, Zenger was acquitted. It was the English settlers who had brought the grand jury with them from their native land, together with all of the other civil rights they had enjoyed there. America's revolutionaires thought of it later as a means to prevent political prosecutions.

Grand Jury Guarantees Today. The opening sentence of the Fifth Amendment to the Constitution of the United States in effect guarantees grand jury action on the *federal* level. Exempting members of the armed forces, it specifies that no person may be held for a "capital, or otherwise infamous crime," unless on a presentment or indictment of a grand jury. But the grand jury provision of the Fifth Amendment is not applicable to the *states,* the Supreme Court of the United States having held repeatedly and consistently that its absence in these constituent parts of the nation does not in itself violate those "fundamental principles of liberty and justice which lie at the base of all our civil and political institutions."[24] Indeed, fewer than one-half of the fifty states—twenty as of late 1984—still retain the grand jury system, and some of these use it solely to investigate crime and corruption among public officials in a limited number of cases, such as homicide and treason. The balance of the states have replaced it with the device of "information," which may also be employed by the federal government in noncapital cases[25] at the

---

[23] IV *Commentaries on the Laws of England* 309, (ch. 23, "Of the Several Modes of Prosecution.")

[24] *Palko v. Connecticut,* 302 U.S. 319 (1937). See also *Hurtado v. California,* 110 U.S. 516 (1884). The Supreme Court again refused to consider its "incorporation" in 1968. (*Gyuro v. Connecticut,* 393 U.S. 937.)

[25] The future availability of capital punishment on any level of government in the United States was placed into serious constitutional doubt by a 5:4 decision of the Supreme Court in 1972, which ruled that capital punishment, as then constituted, statutorily violated the prohibition against "cruel and unusual punishment" of the Eighth and Fourteenth Amendments. (*Furman v. Georgia,* 408 U.S. 238.) However, the Court altered course in a major 1976 ruling that upheld 7:2 the constitutionality of capital punishment, although in highly circumscribed, carefully delineated circumstances. (*Gregg v. Georgia,* 428 U.S. 153.) As a result, the first person to be executed in a decade went before a firing squad in Utah early in 1977 (by his

district court level, as it was in the 1972–74 Watergate scandals in the instance of one-time counsel to President Nixon, John W. Dean III, and, generally, in civil cases, a famous early example of which is the 1886 case of *Boyd v. United States.*[26]

Today's *federal* grand jury consists of a panel of twenty-three members, chosen at random from registered voters, followed by questioning by a judge and the U.S. Attorney. *State* grand juries range the proverbial gamut from five to seven (Virginia) to twenty-three (Maryland, Massachusetts, New Hampshire, and New Jersey). The selection process varies, but it is usually at random from the local register of voters. The appropriate judge selects the foreman and the deputy. Unlike the trial jury, the grand jury need not be unanimous even at the federal level, but an average minimum of twelve jurors—ranging from a low of four (Virginia) to sixteen (Minnesota) must agree on an indictment or an *ignoramus;* on the federal level, sixteen constitute a quorum and twelve are needed to indict. A grand jury is usually impaneled for a period of three to eighteen months at a time, unless it is discharged earlier by the judge to whom it reports,[27] and it is called together (and paid $30.00 a day plus 20¢ a mile at the federal level in 1984) during that time whenever need for its services arises, usually a few days each week. Because no one is being "tried," its proceedings are secret—all witnesses are heard *in camera*—and may not be released to the public. The latter *caveat*, which is protective of both the accused and the grand jurors, is an essential and traditional aspect of the grand jury system, which, unfortunately, has not been demonstrably foolproof.[28] With but a number of exceptions, such as New York since 1978, as already explained, not only are no defense attorneys allowed to be present, not even a judge is permitted *inside* the grand jury chamber. All witnesses thus testify alone. The grand jury normally deliberates with remarkable speed: the prosecutor appears before it; briefly outlines the government's case, and asks for an indictment, almost always succeeding in getting it.

Presentments. Grand juries may do considerably more than determine the sufficiency or lack of evidence submitted to them; they may also, and often do, conduct certain types of public investigations, enabling them to hand up a finding known as a *presentment.* Such an action represents a formal accusation against one or more individuals, made on the grand jury's own motion,

---

own request and under highly dramatized circumstances). By November 1985 a total of forty-nine had been executed, several by their own request.

[26] 116 U.S. 616.

[27] But the "Watergate" grand jury, impaneled by Judge Sirica, served for two and a half years—with Congress statutorily extending its term from the usual maximum of eighteen months. (It disbanded in a brief ceremony on December 5, 1976, a grand jury that will go down in history as having rendered important service to government and society.)

[28] See the troubling account by Ronald J. Ostrow, "Disclosures from Grand Juries Rampant," *The Virginian-Pilot*, October 24, 1980, p. A9.

calling attention to alleged illegal or improper activities—but *not* including an indictment.[29] The first presentment on record came in England in 1683; it charged certain Whigs, including the Earl of Macclesfield, with disloyal and seditious conduct. The accused brought an action for libel, but the court held for the grand jury, thus establishing the propriety of its report.[30]

Presentments have a habit of stirring up the public as well as the bar, quite frequently giving rise to general anguish. Thus, when a New York grand jury during the "quiz-show" scandals in 1959 on its own initiative handed up a presentment highly critical of the television and radio industry, General Sessions Court Judge Mitchell D. Schweitzer impounded and permanently sealed it. He declared that no grand jury had a right to return a report dealing with the activities or morals of a *private* individual or corporation. A bill designed to embody Judge Schweitzer's position in a law subsequently failed to pass the New York State legislature.[31] However, the matter was reopened tangentially two years thereafter, when the New York State Court of Appeals ruled 4:3 in the *Wood* case that a grand jury has the following choices: return an indictment, dismiss the charge, or remain silent.[32] Because this case involved *public* officials only, the ban seemed to have been extended to all elements of the citizenry. The action in the suit was brought by one James F. Wood, the foreman of a Schenectady county grand jury, to compel Judge Charles M. Hughes of the New York Supreme Court to make public a report the jury had filed on its own motion regarding the county highway department.

The narrowly decided *Wood* case, which overruled a prerogative in existence since 1688, put the role of the grand jury and its problems into closer focus. The majority decision, written by Judge Stanley H. Fuld—and applauded by most of the lawyers' associations of the State of New York—declared that the jury involved made an inquiry that, by its own admission, failed to find "willful and corrupt conduct" by a public official. The phrase

---

[29]Thus, in early 1975 a Manhattan grand jury, while returning an *ignoramus* on criminal charges in a 1973 hotel collapse, (1) called for a change in New York City's laws to require thorough annual inspections of all buildings constructed before 1901 and (2) urged other steps designed to avert disasters in old buildings, including speedier processing by city agencies of hazardous building violations and jail sentences rather than merely fines where building laws and regulations are violated. (*The New York Times*, January 24, 1975, p. M29.) In 1980 a special grand jury, looking into an unsolved murder of a policeman in a Harlem mosque in 1972, charged that the New York City Police Department's own investigation of the death "was curtailed in deference to fears of civil unrest in the black community." (*The New York Times*, January 24, 1980, p. B3.) None of the police or other public officials who were criticized in the report were named, however, because a state law forbids (see p. 110, *infra*) grand juries to criticize publicly an identified or identifiable person, except under specified "special circumstances."

[30]10 How St. Tr. 1330 (1684).

[31]A similar bill, but one which outlawed *all* presentments, had passed in 1946 but was vetoed by Governor Dewey. But note the 1964 statute (p. 110, *infra*).

[32]*Wood v. Hughes*, 212 N.Y.S. 2d 33 (1961).

quoted came from the statute under which the jury had been impaneled and charged, yet the jurors had simply decided to chart a course of action on their own, one that was both unauthorized and publicly deprecatory of reputations. The dissenters, on the other hand, urged that such action by the grand jury was simply a reaffirmation of a basic American principle under common law and of considerations of ethics in government—namely, that an authorized body of citizens may, indeed must, take appropriate action to counter the suppression or burial of evidence of "tyranny and corruption in public office." In April 1961 Judge Schweitzer augmented his earlier action by expressly warning four grand juries he impaneled that "under no circumstanes" were they to submit a presentment to his court. And the New Jersey State Supreme Court ruled that presentments must not be used to rebuke individuals in the absence of conclusive proof of wrongdoing. On the other hand, Philadelphia Common Pleas Court Judge Joseph E. Gold permitted a 1962 special grand jury charged to investigate municipal corruption in Philadelphia to hand up a stinging presentment in 1963, publicly naming individuals as well as organizations.[33] When, in 1964, the New York legislature finally agreed on a bill to deal with grand jury presentments, it turned out to be a compromise: under it a grand jury is empowered to criticize a public official or employee, but *only* if its main purpose is to recommend remedial administrative or legislative action. And U.S. District Judge John J. Sirica agonized for two weeks in early 1974 before he forwarded his sealed Watergate Grand Jury's presentment regarding President Nixon's involvement in the case to the U.S. House of Representative's Committee on the Judiciary for its consideration in weighing impeachment charges against the President. No wonder he agonized! It was later revealed that the Grand Jury in that presentment had cited Nixon, 19:0, as an "unindicted co-conspirator." It had refrained from indicting him only because Special Prosecutor Leon Jaworski had expressed the arguable opinion that a President was not indictable—an issue the Supreme Court pointedly refused to come to grips with in its momentous 8:0 "tapes" decision against the President late in July 1974 (*United States v. Nixon* and *Nixon* and *Nixon v. United States*[34]).

Whatever one's judgment of the merits of these developments may be, there is little doubt that although grand-juries have traditionally been vested with broad powers to investigate crimes, such powers are not, and cannot be, either unlimited or unbridled. Grand juries are not powers unto themselves,

---

[33] For details of the presentment, see *The Philadelphia Inquirer*, March 9, 1963, p. 1. The most celebrated "runaway" grand jury is the one that, in 1935, requested Governor Herbert Lehman of New York to supersede the District Attorney, who, the jury said, was trying to hamstring its investigation into organized vice and racketeering. The governor responded by naming Thomas E. Dewey as special prosecutor, and indictments and convictions followed.

[34] 417 U.S. 683. (In that same eventful year the Court ruled in *United States v. Calandra*, 414 U.S. 338 that the contentious judge-made "exclusionary rule does not apply to grand jury proceedings.")

but are essentially lay bodies whose actions are subject to judicial scrutiny and remedial relief. In that role grand juries have existed for such interesting and significant investigatory and stand-by purposes as juvenile delinquency, waterfront crime, narcotics traffic, subversive activities, quiz-show manipulation, official and private corruption, "kickbacks," tax evasion (e.g., the Agnew case in 1973), and the Watergate scandals of 1972–74.[35] Necessarily, grand juries became fairly well steeped in their particular area of jurisdiction. And they have often done a good job. The grand jury may well be cumbersome, amateurish, time-consuming, annoying, emotional, and a fifth wheel in the legal process, but on balance—as was well demonstrated by the persistent 1973–74 Watergate grand jury—it does appear to serve as a potentially powerful arm of direct democracy, if one is willing to accept the philosophy of the institution in the first place and if one has faith in the competence and intelligence of one's fellow citizens.[36]

THE TRIAL OR PETIT JURY

Normally, when the average person or the public press refers to a jury, he or she has the trial or petit jury in mind.[37] As has been indicated, the trial jury has suffered a decline in many parts of the world, but it is still a popular institution. In England and Wales it is employed mainly, but limitedly, in criminal cases, only very sparingly in civil cases; the same is true of France, possibly more so. In Switzerland only ten of the twenty-five cantons permit its use in criminal cases, none in civil cases. Its last important, and evidently secure, stronghold in the Western world is in the United States, where the concept of a trial by a jury of one's peers still thrives.

In England and Wales, where trial by jury, first for civil and later for criminal cases, effectively commenced during the reign of King Henry II (1154–

[35] In a post-Watergate book-length study of the grand jury, *The Grand Jury: The Use and Abuse of Political Power* (New York: Quadrangle/New York Times Book Co., 1975), Leroy D. Clark proposes a number of reforms, including more protection for witnesses, making the grand jury independent of the prosecutor's office, and limiting its ability to examine news reporters, scholars, and government officials. See all Congressman Joshuah Eilberg (D.-Pa), "A Proposal for Grand Jury Reform," in 60 *Judicature* 8 (March 1977), pp. 390–94. and the critical symposium, "The Grand Jury Under Examination: It Has Fallen on Hard Times," *The New York Times*, June 26, 1977, Sec. 4, p. E20. A highly negative view of grand juries is advanced by Judge Marvin E. Frankel and Gary P. Naftalis in their 1977 book, *The Grand Jury* (New York: Hill and Wang); a favorable one by Richard D. Younger, *The People's Panel: The Story of the Grand Jury* (Providence: Brown University Press, 1963).

[36] A basic question that immediately arises in the face of the type of drastic reforms in the grand jury system advanced by such opponents as, for example, Messrs. Clark and Eilberg, is whether, in effect, their projected schema would not transform the grand jury into another layer of trial jury and thus further hinder the concept of a speedy and fair trial. Congressman Eilberg's bill to review grand juries (H.R. 94) died in the 95th Congress. (Its author, accused of a series of criminal infractions involving "kickbacks," was defeated for re-election that fall.)

[37] In some areas, such as in parts of Pennsylvania, it is still known as the *traverse* jury, a term deriving from medieval days when Norman French was beginning to displace Latin as the official language of the Court of England.

89), the accused is still entitled—with some qualifications—to call for such a trial for all serious crimes and for a very limited number of substantial civil infractions, save in the highest and lowest courts, but the defendant may waive the privilege. Today fewer than 1 percent of all English civil cases are tried by juries—only those involving fraud and libel—and many of the erstwhile English-speaking colonies and possessions have either abolished the right to civil jury trial or have severely restricted it. However, at least in theory, a jury is always impaneled in criminal cases if the accused pleads not guilty to a serious offense. Still, as a result of the aforementioned 1933 statute, the English and Welsh courts have been given such wide discretion whether or not to call a jury even into a criminal case that it is hardly astonishing that jury impaneling has dramatically diminished. Indeed, 90 percent of criminal prosecutions are now decided by a judge or magistrate without a jury. However, if a trial jury is employed in a case, it is composed, as far as possible, of local people, and it consists of twelve persons (except ten to twelve in Coroner's Court). Their verdict of guilt or acquittal was, for seven hundred years, required to be unanimous, a requirement that was discarded when Parliament enacted the Criminal Justice Act of 1967 and 1971 permitting trial juries to convict by 10:2, 10:1, or 9:1.[38] The trial jury declined in England and Wales for a number of reasons, among which the more important are that (1) a judge sitting alone was believed to be able to perform at least as well as, and usually better than, the jury, (2) a speedy trial was desired, (3) juries tended to award very high damages in personal injury cases, and (4) the litigants rather than Her Majesty's government pay the jurors' fees.

The French Republic resorts to jury trials solely at the level of the assizes, the courts of original jurisdiction for serious crimes. Trial by jury has no deep roots in France. Indeed, although it once did exist as part of customary procedure in some parts of the country in the fifteenth century, it disappeared during the reign of Charles VII, and was not reimported from England until the Revolution. Today, it consists of nine local *citoyens* (who sit with one or more judges): there is no unanimity requirement, and frequently the verdict is rendered by a simple majority vote. The French have no great fondness for the jury system, and their adherence to the inquisitorial mode in the judicial process leaves little or no genuine purpose for a trial jury per se. In any event, they generally view the jury as an instrument designed to confuse the issues in a case.

But the United States, where a total of approximately 3 million jurors[39] serve in some 300,000 cases each year in the approximately 3,000 jury-employing federal and state courts, has remained broadly faithful to the concept of a trial by jury—although only one in ten of the cases on court calendars actually gets to a jury. Still, 85 percent of the world's criminal jury trials

---

[38]In Scotland, where juries may consist of fifteen persons in some cases, a simple majority of 8:7 suffices to convict. There juries may also render a verdict of "not proven."

[39]*Juror* is Latin for "to swear." A total of 667,264 *federal* jurors served in 1983–84.

take place here. This is necessarily true at the level of the *federal* courts because of the express requirements of the Sixth and Seventh Amendments to the Constitution. The Sixth ascertains a trial by jury in *all* federal criminal cases; the Seventh does the same for all civil cases in which the value of the controversy exceeds the sum of $20, which today means in practically every instance. Although all fifty states had also provided for at least *some* type of trial by jury, the specific mandating guarantees of the federal Bill of Rights to a trial by jury did not automatically apply to them until the Supreme Court, in 1968, ruled that this procedural right was "implicit in the concept of ordered liberty."[40] The highest tribunal had long insisted that a defendant in a state proceeding be given a *fair trial*, on pain of a violation of the Fourteenth Amendment's due process of law and equal protection of the laws clauses. Among the several state practices affecting juries that had *inter alia* been held thus to constitute an *unfair* trial, are *systematic* exclusion of blacks from juries[41] and the labeling of black jurors with brown, and white jurors with white, selection tickets.[42]

However, because each of the states may prescribe its own brand of jury system, a variety of practices exists, and many of these would be unconstitutional if practiced by the federal authorities. Thus, some states grant no jury trials in *civil* cases at all, others do in just a handful. The frequency of jury trials may thus vary widely—from only 3 per 100,000 accused in Connecticut to 144 per 100,000 in Georgia just a few years ago.[43] At the federal level, it is generally possible to *waive* a trial by jury, *provided* that common consent of the parties to the suit and of the judge assigned to the case is obtained,[44] but many states will not permit such a waiver, especially in certain criminal cases.[45] Other significant procedural differences between federal and

---

[40] *Duncan v. Louisiana*, 391 U.S. 145. But the Court ruled in 1970 that it does not reach crimes classified by states as "misdemeanors" if the penalty therefore does not exceed six months' incarceration. (*Baldwin v. Connecticut*, 399 U.S. 66.)

[41] *Norris v. Alabama*, 294 U.S. 587 (1935); *Hill v. Texas*, 316 U.S. 400 (1942); *Patton v. Mississippi*, 332 U.S. 463 (1947); *Whitus v. Georgia*, 385 U.S. 545 (1967).

[42] *Avery v. Georgia*, 345 U.S. 559 (1953). On the other hand, if non-whites in an assembled jury pool are excluded from jury duty on the basis of the use of intelligence tests administered equitably to all members in the pool, such exclusion is not *ipso facto* a prima facie denial of due process. (See *Donaldson v. California*, 404 U.S. 968, 1971, *certiorari* denied.) Nor is the systematic exclusion of young people such a denial. (*Ross v. United States*, 410 U.S. 990, 1973.)

[43] *Time Magazine*, August 12, 1966, p. 26.

[44] In 1965, in *Singer v. United States*, 380 U.S. 24, the Supreme Court ruled unanimously that a defendant in a federal trial does *not* have a constitutional right to insist on trial by a judge rather than by a jury if the government insists on a jury.

[45] According to the seminal study by Harry Kalven, Jr., and Hans Zeisel, *The American Jury* (Boston: Little, Brown and Co., 1966), regional custom apparently determines whether or not a defendant will waive jury trial, with the percentage of jury waivers varying from a high of 79 percent in Wisconsin to 3 percent in the District of Columbia and to 0 percent in Montana! Also significant is the category of crime: jury waiver occurs in 70 percent of drug vio-

state practices pertain to the size of juries and the requirement of unanimity. As a result of a series of significant Supreme Court decisions in the 1960s and 1970s, the following constitutional posture has emerged: Federal juries must still render unanimous verdicts in both civil[46] and criminal cases, but the English common law tradition of having twelve jurors is no longer constitutionally required in civil cases;[47] indeed, all but nine of the ninety-four federal trial courts either permitted[48] six-member juries in civil cases or even required them as of 1984—a mere 2.9 percent of such cases having been tried by juries.[49] State juries were long ago deemed not to be controlled by the federal unanimity jury rule,[50] and the states had adopted a host of diverse numerical requirements in both civil and criminal cases which repeatedly passed judicial muster. They were again exempted from the rule by two 1972 Court decisions that specifically sanctioned a 10:2 Oregon criminal jury verdict[51] and a 9:3 Louisiana one,[52] with Justice White's opinion for the 5:4 majority holding that, in noncapital cases such as these, nonunanimous rulings could equally well serve "the interests of the defendant in having the judgment of his peers interposed between himself and the officers of the state who prosecute and judge him. . . . "[53] (But the Court hedged as to the precise cutoff point at which even lower numerical nonunanimity would constitute a denial of due process of law.) Juries of fewer than twelve on the state level had been Court-approved for some time—even as small a panel as Florida's six-member criminal trial jury,[54] one of which convicted, and another subse-

---

lation cases (in which the judge is presumed to be less emotionally involved than lay jurors), whereas the jury is waived in only 13 percent of homicide cases (pp. 20–26).

[46] But note the 9:3 verdict permitted by U.S. District Judge Don J. Young in the "Kent State Victims" civil damage suit (*Krause and Scheuer, et al v. Rhodes and White, et al*, decided August 27, 1975). Apparently, that verdict was allowed because of a Rule 48 stipulation by both parties, given the nature of the case (*civil*) and the Court's approval of the use of six-member civil case juries in *Colgrove* (fn. 47, *infra*).

[47] *Colgrove v. Battin*, 413 U.S. 149 (1973).

[48] Reports of the Administrative Office of the U.S. Court for 1979ff.

[49] E.g., the U.S. District Court for the Southern District of New York, which mandated the six-member civil jury for all of its twenty-seven judges as of August 1, 1973. (See *The New York Times*, July 22, 1973, p. 16.)

[50] *Minneapolis & St. Louis Railroad Co. v. Bombolis*, 241 U.S. 211 (1916). In 1898 the Court had declared a constitutionally required standard of twelve-member federal juries in *Thompson v. Utah*, 170 U.S. 343, when Utah was still a federal territory. And just one year later it extended that requirement to federal civil trials as well. (*Capital Traction Co. v. Hof*, 174 U.S. 1.)

[51] *Apodaca v. Oregon*, 406 U.S. 404 (1972). In murder cases, however, all twelve members must vote for conviction.

[52] *Johnson v. Louisiana*, 406 U.S. 356 (1972).

[53] *Apodaca v. Oregon*, loc. cit., at 411.

[54] *Williams v. Florida*, 399 U.S. 78 (1970). Justice White here again expressed his conviction— one he altered in 1978, however—that size has no bearing on the essential feature of a jury. He viewed the latter as the "interposition between the accused and the accuser of the common sense judgment of a group of laymen, and in the community participation and shared

quently acquitted, Clarence Earl Gideon in his celebrated constitutional battle regarding the incorporation of the right to counsel in all criminal cases.[55] Today, approximately 80 percent of the states sanction jury verdicts by 75 percent of the jurors in civil cases, with 20 percent of the states extending this form of split verdict also to noncapital criminal cases. Three-fourths of the states now authorize various trials with juries of fewer than twelve members, often six,[56] but the Court specifically interdicted the use of juries of *fewer than six* in criminal cases in a unanimous, albeit badly split five-opinion, 1978 decision, striking down the use of *five-member* juries even if unanimous, in Georgia and in 1979 of a 5:1 split in a six-member Louisiana one.[57] The governing question concerning these state practices is not one of comparison or method but the essential one of whether or not the defendant received a fair trial under conditions of due process of law.

SELECTION AND IMPANELING OF JURIES

Since the enactment by Congress of the Jury Selection and Service Act of 1968—largely the work of Senator Joseph D. Tydings (D.-Md) and U.S. Court of Appeals Judge Irving R. Kaufman—federal grand and petit juries in the United States must be drawn by lot [58] from the "voter registration lists or the lists of actual voters" of the political subdivision's citizens by the jury clerk, who uses these names to form a jury panel or *venire*.[59] The statute, long

---

responsibility that results from that group's determination of guilt or innocence" (at 100). For a tentative conclusion that six-member juries convict fewer defendants than twelve-member juries, see 61 *Judicature* (September 1977), pp. 225–29; for one finding "no significant differences in conviction/acquittal rates or proportion of hung juries," see 62 *Judicature* (September 1978), pp. 153–54. But an extensive 1980 study of 110 juries, composed of nearly one thousand jurors, indicated that size does indeed affect a jury's behavior. See Robert T. Roper, "Jury Size and Verdict Consistency: 'A Line Has to Be Drawn Somewhere?'" 14 *Law and Society Review* (Summer 1980). Thus, he proves, for example, that twelve-member juries "hang" significantly more often than do smaller juries.

[55] *Gideon v. Wainwright*, 372 U.S. 335 (1963). In 1976 the Connecticut Supreme Court upheld the constitutionality of a law reducing the size of Connecticut juries from twelve to six for all criminal cases except murder. (*The New York Times*, August 11, 1976, p. C27.) New Jersey has mandated six-member civil case juries unless the judge requests twelve members.

[56] Why twelve was initially selected for a jury's composition remains a mystery. However, that number has been mathematically significant ever since the days of the Sumerians, 5000 B.C., and also has religious significance: twelve signs of the Zodiac; twelve tribes of Israel; twelve Christian apostles.

[57] *Ballew v. Georgia*, 435 U.S. 223 on *Burch v. Louisiana*, 441 U.S. 130, respectively.

[58] The statute speaks of "a master jury wheel (or a device similar in purpose and function)." In its broad statement of policy the statute proclaims: "It is the policy of the United States that all litigants in federal courts entitled to trial by jury shall have the right to grand and petit juries selected at random from a fair cross section of the community in the district or division wherein the court convenes." (28 U.S.C. 1861.)

[59] Two challenges to the confining of the lists to registered voters were turned aside by the Court by 1975. (*Thompson v. Sheppard*, 420 U.S. 984 and *Bowman v. Presiding Judge of*

requested by both public and private observers, became all but a foregone conclusion when a federal court of appeals ruled that a particular defendant's rights had been violated precisely because his or her jury had not been selected from "a cross section" of the community,[60] but under the so-called key man system.

That key man system, widely used until 1968 on the federal as well as the state level, still obtains in some of the latter jurisdictions, but it is dying out. Under it, the jury clerk asks "upstanding" citizens of the community to submit names of individuals whom *they* believe to be potentially qualified jurors, with the panel ultimately being selected by the clerk from these lists. A time-honored practice, it nonetheless lends itself to the possibility of considerable mischief as well as being unrepresentative, and the day may be close when the states too will either abandon it voluntarily or do so as a result of court "due process" requirements. The cross-section mandate requirement was buttressed with the enactment of the Jury Selection and Service Act of 1975. But note that neither by law nor by the terms of the Constitution does a jury need to be a microcosm of the larger community. *Systematic* exclusion is forbidden, but proportional representation is not required.

In England and Wales juries are selected by the sheriff from a list of householders compiled by local authorities; in France they are chosen from departmental lists of citizens of thirty years of age and over who possess all civic and political rights. In Switzerland juries sitting with the Criminal Chamber of the Federal Tribunal to try certain criminal cases are *elected* by the people for six-year terms on the basis of 1 juror for each 3,000 inhabitants. In Sweden they are elected by county councils for four-year periods. Happily, in more and more jurisdictions, notably in the United States, automation has entered, with electronic data-processing systems increasingly taking over the task of clerks who pick names from mahogany drums or glass jars to choose the jurors to be called for service, thus reducing to an average of twenty minutes a process that formerly took two days! Theoretically, any citizen of voting age is eligible for jury duty and may expect a call, unless he or she has served for more than a year in prison on a criminal charge and has not been pardoned for that offense.[61] This limiting proviso is statutorily applicable only to the

---

Superior Court, 421 U.S. 1011, both *certiorari* denied.) For a suggestion to combine voters and drivers as jury source lists, see Charles H. Logan and George F. Cole, "Reducing Bias in a Jury Source List by Combining Voters and Drivers," 67 *Judicature* (August 1983), pp. 87–94.

[60] *Scott v. Walker*, 358 F.2d 561 (1966). Because he viewed the prospective jury list in Erie County, N.Y. (Buffalo), to be less than a true cross section, State Supreme Court Justice Edward Brovenzano discharged the entire list of 110,000 for the county in July 1974! (*The New York Times*, July 4, 1974, p. 1.) The "cross-section" requirement was embraced by the Supreme Court in 1946 in *Thiel v. Southern Pacific Co.*, 329 U.S. 217. In 1983 Hamptom County, S.C., still resorted to a quaintly antique system in which a child under ten or a blind person sits in court and pulls the names of potential jurors from a metal box!

[61] The official qualifications for *federal* jurors, which are similar to those in the several states,

federal government, but most of the fifty states now have the same, or at least a similar, requirement. Although everyone else of voting age may thus expect to get a jury call at one time or another, not only is it relatively easy to avoid jury duty—which, incidentally, is one of the chief criticisms leveled against the jury system—but entire segments of the body politic are exempt either by permissible judicial rule, by law, or by custom. Among the occupational groups generally exempt in the vast majority of jurisdictions, especially in the United States, are professionals such as lawyers (a jury composed of arguing and advocating lawyers would indeed be an interesting, if hardly an edifying, experience!), licensed physicians and dentists (too busy to serve), members of the armed forces (often absent from the community), officers of all three branches of government (possible conflict of interest), police officers and fire fighters (indispensable professionally), clergy (a jury must deliberate, not pray), teachers (essential occupation). Other busy employed people can avoid jury service by submitting affidavits of indispensability from employers. Still others, such as nursing mothers and those with a large family of young children,[62] will normally have to do little more than write a letter to the court concerned to be excused by the judge.[63] But failure to do at least that much may conceivably result in a citation for contempt of court, which occurred in the case of one thirty-seven-year-old Waterloo, Iowa, mother who repeatedly flouted requests to serve on a criminal trial jury and finally found herself sentenced to be incarcerated for six months, in Rockwell City Women's Reformatory, for criminal contempt of court.[64] Moreover, the U.S. Supreme Court ruled 8:1 in 1975 that *women* as a class can no longer be excluded or be given *automatic* exemption based *solely* on sex if the consequence is that criminal jury *venires* are almost totally male.[65]

---

are (1) U.S. citizenship—aliens are ineligible, (2) attainment of at least eighteen years of age, (3) one year's residence in the district, (4) no prior conviction punishable for more than one year unless pardoned or amnestied, (5) ability to read, write, and understand English, and (6) no mental or physical disabilities that would hamper efficient jury service. In a 1976 holding the Court unanimously affirmed the exclusion of aliens from federal and/or state juries. (*Perkins v. Smith*, 426 U.S. 913.)

[62]In 1975 the Supreme Court upheld a Florida law that, *on their request*, exempts pregnant women and mothers of children under eighteen. (*Marshall v. Gavin*, 420 U.S. 907).

[63]Under new rules adopted following the enactment of the 1968 statute, the U.S. District Court for the Southern District of New York (Manhattan) now excuses the following *on written request:* lawyers; persons over 70; actively engaged ministers and members of religious orders; women with children under ten; practicing physicians, dentists, and registered nurses; persons who have served on juries thirty days in the preceding two years; sole proprietors of businesses who have no help; teachers, supervisors, or administrators of schools; and anyone living more than fifty miles from the Foley Square Court House.

[64]*The Philadelphia Inquirer*, May 18, 1952, p. 13. However, her conviction was reversed on procedural grounds on appeal by the Iowa Supreme Court. (*Watson v. Charlton*, 50 N.W. 2d 605.)

[65]The White-authored ruling—which overturned a fourteen-year-old decision that had allowed states to excuse women from jury duty automatically *unless* they went to the courthouse and

If none of the reasons cited is acceptable to the court as a bona fide excuse, an irresponsible citizen can, of course, still evade his civic duty by confessing to one of the many otherwise validly disqualifying factors in jury impaneling (which, the Supreme Court ruled 9:0 in 1984, must be open to the public and the press).[66] Among these are confession of prejudice for or against one of the litigants (although in England there is no right to *examine* a jury for prejudice and, since a 1973 rule established by the Lord Chief Justice, jurors are not to be excused on such "general grounds" as race, religion, political beliefs, or occupation),[67] acquaintance with either party to the suit, however slight, allegation of sympathy with or opposition to certain pertinent philosophies of life involved in the case, no matter how tangentially, and so forth. However, only those who are really willing and able to serve will normally do so in the long run. On the other hand, in 1968 the Supreme Court ruled 6:3 that persons expressing general conscientious scruples against the death penalty could no longer *automatically* get off, or be kept off, juries in capital cases; consequently, no death sentence could stand if it had been propounded by a jury *purged* of all persons who said they opposed the death penalty or had conscientious scruples against it—absent a juror's expression of views that would "prevent or substantially impair the performance of his duties as a juror in accordance with his instructions or oath."[68]

Challenges. Jurors may naturally be removed from a panel for any of the preceding reasons or a myriad of others by the procedure of appropriate *challenges* (first given credence by Roman tribunals during the Empire's heyday, when one was allowed to object to a jury trying any particular case), which are granted to both the defense and the prosecution as a matter of regular courtroom procedure in England and France as well as the United States,

---

volunteered for such duty (*Hoyt v. Florida*, 368 U.S. 57)—struck down, with Justice Rehnquist in lone dissent, Louisiana's jury law that was a carbon copy of Florida's in terms of its "volunteer only" rule for women. (*Taylor v. Louisiana*, 419 U.S. 522.) Actually, all other states, including Florida, had repealed such laws in the interim between the *Hoyt* and *Taylor* decisions. However, the Court declined to make *Taylor* retroactive. (*Daniel v. Louisiana*, 420 U.S. 31 [1975].) Early in 1979, with Justice ReHnquist again the sole dissenter, it went beyond the *Taylor* holding by ruling 8:1 that a state law allowing women to claim an automatic exemption from jury duty had deprived a murder defendant of his constitutional right to be tried by a jury composed of a cross section of the community. (*Duren v. Missouri*, 47 LW 4089.) But see fn. 62, *supra*.

[66]*Press Enterprise Co. v. Superior Court of California*, 52 LW 4113.

[67]See John Baldwin and Michael McConville, "Does the Composition of an English Jury Affect Its Verdict?," 64 *Judicature* 3 (September 1980), p. 137. The authors demonstrate convincingly that English juries are not representative of the whole community, but that their verdicts generally do *not* reflect their imbalance. (Ibid., pp. 133ff.)

[68]*Witherspoon v. Illinois*, 391, U.S. 510. While the *Witherspoon* holding was expanded in 1976 to cover even "just" exclusion (*Davis v. Georgia*, 429 U.S. 122) it was markedly narrowed in 1985 when the Court ruled 7:2 that a juror may be excluded if he (or she) expresses views that would "prevent or substantially impair the performance of his (or her) duties as a juror..." (*Wainwright v. Witt*, 53 LW 4108).

although the procedure is much more limited in the former two than in the last. Federal judges in the United States have clear authority to conduct all jury qualification questioning, as do the judges in twenty-two states, although judges may, and usually do, share that authority with the trial attorneys. In twenty-eight states, however, the latter control the process.

Most frequently employed in the United States, challenges are essentially of two types, *peremptory* and *for cause.* They come at the *voir dire* level of jury selection[69] and play a major role in the adversary process. A peremptory challenge entitles either party to the suit to request the removal of a would-be juror by *fiat*—no reason need be given; the mere request, whatever the motivation, will be honored. As the Supreme Court held in 1965, in a 6:3 decision written by Justice White that upheld the peremptory striking of all blacks available on the petit jury venire, " . . . the essential nature of the peremptory challenge is that it is one exercised without a reason stated, without inquiry, and without being subject to the court's control."[70] It is a critical, often crucial element in the lawyer's strategy—one consistently upheld at the *federal* level (again in 1983). But at the *state* level (e.g., New York, California, Illinois, Massachusetts, and New Mexico) appellate courts have begun to disallow prosecutors' use of peremptory challenges to exclude arbitrarily all members of a race or other identifiable class from a jury.[71] What *is* subject to court control, however, is the *number* of these challenges granted—although that is often determined by statute. It is customary to permit the defense more peremptory challenges than the prosecution, but this is not inevitably the case. In federal trial courts, one to three such challenges per juror are normally permitted each side, depending on the nature of the offense, twenty to each side in capital offenses. Yet in the 1974 Mitchell–Stans trial for perjury, conspiracy, and obstruction of justice, which resulted in the defendants' acquittal, U.S. District Court Judge Lee P. Gagliardi, citing "acute pre-trial publicity," assigned twenty peremptory challenges to the defense but only eight to the prosecution. In Pennsylvania, the usual rule for murder cases is

---

[69]See Arthur J. Stanley, Jr., and Robert G. Gegam, "Who Should Conduct *Voir Dire?*," 61 *Judicature* 2 (August 1977), pp. 70–78. (Examination of jurors is governed by Rules 47(a) and 24(b) of the Federal Rules of Civil and Criminal Procedure, respectively, which are subject to amendment by the Supreme Court.)

[70]*Swain v. Alabama,* 380 U.S. 202, at 220. The Court reconfirmed the constitutionality of the practice of "group" or "class" striking by way of challenges in the instances of two 1975 decisions upholding the exclusion of women from a man's trial jury. (*Lawson v. Edwards* and *Quick v. Harris,* 420 U.S. 907.) The cases were decided after *Taylor v. Louisiana, supra,* fn. 59. The 1983 case noted in the preceding text was *McCray v. Abrams,* 461 U.S. 961, in which the Court (7:2) pointedly refused to reexamine its 1965 *Swain* decision. The two dissenters were Justices Brennan and Marshall. Justices Blackmun, Powell, and Stevens wrote separate concurring opinions supporting the states' prerogatives of "serving the laboratories," and backing the Court's vote to deny review in the case. However, in late April 1985, the Court agreed to take another look at the issue (*Batson v. Kentucky,* 53 LW 3757).

[71]See Angel Castillo, "Courts Using State Constitutions to Bar Biased Selections of Juries," *The New York Times,* March 1981, p. B9.

twenty for the defense and twenty for the prosecution. In the sensational trial of Richard Speck, who was ultimately convicted of the murder of eight student nurses in Chicago in 1966, Illinois Judge Herbert C. Paschen, endeavoring to be scrupulously fair and guarding against reversals on appeal, permitted the unprecedented total of 320 peremptory challenges! Each side was permitted twenty for *each* of the eight murder charges—and a grand total of 2,500 jurors were questioned in a *voir dire* proceeding that ran for twenty-seven days.[72] In the notorious Pontiac Ten trial, involving the killing of three prison guards in the Pontiac, Michigan, state prison riot of 1978, each side was given 120 peremptory challenges. (The Ten were all jury acquitted.) On the other hand, in the famed Pentagon Papers (espionage, theft, and conspiracy) federal trial of Dr. Daniel Ellsberg and Anthony J. Russo in 1973, the defense was allowed a total of fourteen such challenges, the prosecution only six.

When a panelist is challenged for *cause*, however, the challenger must be in a position to advance a bona fide reason for his demand for the disqualification, and it will have to be one sufficiently related to the substantive or procedural aspects of the litigation involved in order to be acceptable in the eyes of the court. There are no limits to the *number* of challenges for cause, but, to point to one often-raised *quaere*, there is emphatically no constitutional or legal right to an all-black or all-white or all-male or all-female jury!

These challenges, whose procedures are regulated by the court concerned, frequently delay the impaneling of the trial jury for days, occasionally even for weeks. For instance, it took four months to select the twelve-member jury in the 1971 Connecticut murder trial of Bobby G. Seale—with a total of 1,550 jurors being called to the venire, 1,035 of whom were questioned.[73] And the arduous and delicate task of selecting a jury to sit in the trial of the eleven top-echelon members of the Communist Party-U.S.A. in Judge Harold Medina's U.S. District Court for the Southern District of New York in 1949 consumed a total of six weeks. Because of the nature of the charges of the case, which ultimately resulted in the conviction of all eleven (although with varying sentences),[74] both defense and prosecution were painstaking in their questioning of the prospective jurors, many of whom managed to extricate themselves from serving by simply acknowledging that they could not possibly have an open mind regarding the alleged guilt of the accused.

It is not astonishing, therefore, that jury selection has become not only an art but a game, albeit a grim one—one that often takes longer than the trial itself—in which defense and prosecution frequently go to extreme lengths to jockey for a jury panel favorable to their side. Thus, in 1972 defense attorneys employed psychologists and handwriting analysts to help select the Angela Davis jury which acquitted her. A team of social scientists went to Harris-

---

[72] See the accounts in *Time Magazine*, March 24 and April 7, 1967.
[73] *The New York Times*, March 12, 1971, p. 43.
[74] *United States v. Dennis*, 72 F. Supp. 417 (1949).

burg, Pennsylvania, three months prior to the 1973 trial of Father Philip Berrigan—accused of plotting to raid draft boards, blow up heating tunnels in Washington, D.C., and kidnap Dr. Henry A. Kissinger—to help the defense in its efforts to get a "sympathetic" jury impaneled from the final venire of forty-six prospective jurors. Their suggested "ideal" was "a female Democrat with no religious preference and a white collar or skilled blue collar job."[75] The jury that tried Dr. Carl Coppolino for murder in New Jersey in 1966 was selected from a panel of 275 that had been the object of the closest professional scrutiny and weeks-long attention of experienced Asbury Park lawyer Joe Mattice, who had been hired by the crack defense attorney, F. Lee Bailey, "to pick the jury" that would acquit. It did.[76] A "jury and trial consultant," Houston-based Cathy E. Bennett—one of now more than one hundred professionals rendering similar services across the country—orchestrated the selection of the jury that stunned prosecutors and the public by declaring millionaire former automaker John Z. DeLorean not guilty of drug conspiracy charges, despite the patently demonstrable evidence of five hours of videotape of DeLorean discussing a cocaine deal with undercover agents. Ms. Bennett coached defense attorneys in their ultimately successful quest of attaining a panel of jurors of well-educated, talented, sensitive professionals, who responded sympathetically to the defense's hard-hitting allegations of government entrapment.[77] On the other hand, the jury that found would-be Reagan assassin John Hinckley "not guilty by reason of insanity" consisted of a wholly opposite educational and social profile. The five men and seven women were hardly Hinckley's peers, they included a janitor, a cafeteria worker, a garage attendant, a secretary, and only one of the twelve was white.[78] The aforementioned New York jury that acquitted Messrs. Mitchell and Stans was constructed with the professional aid of one Marty Herbst, the president of a self-styled "communications think tank," following a profile that called for blue-collar workers, primarily Roman Catholics, who earned an average of $8,000 to $10,000 annually and read the *Daily News*. The profile had no place for Jews (none were impaneled), nor for people with college degrees (none were impaneled, although one alternate, who ultimately served, did have one), nor for those whom Herbst called "limousine liberals" (there were none). As Herbst told Martin Arnold of *The New York Times*, "We wanted people

---

[75] After some sixty hours of deliberations, the jury—nine women and three men—reported itself "hopelessly deadlocked" on all of the charges and found Father Berrigan and Sister Elizabeth McAllister guilty simply of "letter smuggling." (*The Philadelphia Bulletin*, May 6, 1973, pp. 10ff.) For an account of the operation of the team of social secintists at work here (and in two other famous cases), see *Time Magazine*, January 28, 1974, p. 60 and "Recipe for a Jury," *Psychology Today*, May 1977, p. 40.

[76] See the colorful report by Joe McGinnis in *The Philadelphia Inquirer*, December 19, 1966, p. 29.

[77] See Jay Mathews, "DeLorean Jury Selected with Expert Help," *The Washington Post*, August 17, 1984, p. A1.

[78] See "Insane on All Counts," *Time Magazine*, July 5, 1982, pp. 17–20.

who were home established, to the right, more concerned with inflation than Watergate"—jurors who would associate the dour John Mitchell with John Wayne.[79] It is no wonder that the prosecutor remarked bitterly after the acquittal that he had lost the case at the impaneling stage. He might have explained, too, that, although the defense had indeed employed its own impaneling tactics, the composition of the jury was also in no small measure determined by Judge Gagliardi, who eliminated an unusually large number of potential jurors at the voir dire "for possible prejudice" because they were "politically interested" and "better educated"! That kind of action taken by a trial judge, although a controversial practice, is neither uncommon nor illegal.[80] No wonder that, as Daniel Schorr commented on the jury selection system (he served on a federal jury in 1975): "Jury service has tended to become an activity for those whose regular activities are not valued by society."[81] Or, as U.S. District Court Judge Gerard L. Goettel put it during his frustrating presiding over the difficult impaneling of a jury in the Reverend Sun Myung Moon tax evasion case of 1982: "The choice is being narrowed to those who don't read much, don't talk much, and don't know much."[82]

In a completely different vein, it has proved so difficult at times to impanel a jury that clerks of courts literally have had to stoop to grabbing people off the streets in search of a trial panel, under the traditional common law right of going to the streets "to impress citizens into duty"—which is what happened on two occasions to strolling unemployeds near City Hall in Philadelphia in 1965 and 1966, and to a UN delegate taking a walk in Paterson, New Jersey, in 1958. A judge in Kentucky, in an unsuccessful attempt to impanel jurors for a case involving the murder of two deputy sheriffs in 1962, sent out state troopers; New Jersey sheriffs collared seventeen Morristown residents for service within forty minutes on an October day in 1967; and in 1981, in Prince Georges County, Maryland, a judge, impatient over a shortage of jurors, sent sheriff's deputies to scour the streets and shopping centers, causing twenty unhappy denizens to be dragged in for possible jury service.[83]

Blue Ribbon Juries. Among the charges voiced frequently against juries, both grand and petit, are that they merely give vent to the established community prejudices, that they are utterly unqualified to render judgment in other than simple, routine cases, and that, worse still, they are composed quite consistently of people who not only are uninformed in civic affairs, but

---

[79] May 5, 1974, p. 1.

[80] See the disturbing account in The New York Times, May 5, 1974, p. 1, in particular of the role played by an alternate juror, Andrew Choa, who had replaced a regular juror because of the latter's illness and became the most influential juror cum persuador in the case.

[81] The New York Times, April 25, 1974, p. C39.

[82] The Washington Post, December 29, 1983, p. A16.

[83] The New York Times, April 15, 1962; The New York Times, October 26, 1967; Readers Digest, April 1981, p. 126; and Time Magazine, September 28, 1981, p. 45. (The second example cited was for the trial of LeRoi Jones, the black poet and playwright, and two others on a weapons charge following the bloody 1967 riots in Newark, New Jersey.)

are actually not interested. In Illinois, at least for a while, the names of those persons who consistently failed to vote were placed at the top of prospective jury lists. This interesting practice was apparently based on the assumption that nonvoters make excellent jurors! In large part to meet the general criticism of unsatisfactory juries, some states in America have statutorily adopted either a special jury test, or, more commonly, the *blue ribbon jury*. This device, as used at various times and in sundry jurisdictions of a quarter of the states,[84] sees judges of certain courts giving potential veniremen a series of test questions involving legal terminology that the jurors would almost certainly encounter. If an otherwise eligible juror misses more than one or two of these chiefly multiple-choice and matching questions, disqualification is almost certain.

Blue ribbon juries (then called *struck juries*) made their first appearance in England in 1730. They were employed solely at the level of the King's Bench and only for "trials of great consequence" or when the subject matter of the case was beyond "discussion of the ordinary freeholder." Court officials would choose forty-eight men who were "competent, intelligent, and less prejudiced than the ordinary juror." Somewhat later, the privilege to impanel such a blue ribbon or "special" jury was extended to all courts, who could authorize it for either of the two preceding reasons or, generally, when an ordinary jury "could not be impaneled." However, they were finally statutorily abolished in England in 1971.

It is hardly astonishing that the institution of the blue ribbon jury would ultimately face a test at the bar of the highest court of the United States. It came in 1947 and 1948, in both instances not surprisingly involving the New York County special jury—which, in existence since the turn of the century, consisted of a "special jury" panel of some 3,000 eligibles out of a total pool of 60,000 veniremen,[85] and it was closely followed barely one year later by a similar test. By the narrowest of margins, 5:4 in each case, the Supreme Court of the United States upheld the statute and the practice against the dual challenge that it violated both the due process of law and the equal protection of the law clauses of the Fourteenth Amendment to the Constitution. The majority of the Court contended that the professionals and white collar workers, so dominant on the jury, could well come from widely varying salary groups and that neither clause cited requires that a jury must represent all components of society. As Justice Jackson wrote for the Court in the first case: "Society also has a right to a fair trail. The defendant's right is a neutral jury. He has no constitutional right to friends on a jury."[86] Furthermore, the major-

---

[84]E.g., Alabama, Delaware, Indiana, Michigan, New York, New Jersey, Tennessee, Vermont, Virginia, West Virginia.

[85]*Fay v. New York*, 332 U.S. 261 (1947) and *Moore v. New York*, 333 U.S. 565 (1948).

[86]*Fay v. New York*, loc. cit., at 288. Almost four decades later, the Supreme Court unanimously echoed Jackson's pertinent conclusion when it ruled 9:0, speaking through Justice Rehnquist, that a litigant "is entitled to a fair trial but not to a perfect one, for there are no perfect trials."

ity felt that a state might reasonably use blue ribbon juries as a means of rendering the administration of justice more efficient. But four Justices—Murphy, Black, Douglas, and Rutledge—dissented vigorously in an opinion written by Murphy, who had been President Franklin D. Roosevelt's Attorney General. He insisted that an accused person was entitled to be tried by a jury fairly drawn from a true cross section of the population, and that a blue ribbon jury simply could not be representative.

> One is constitutionally entitled to be judged by a fair sampling of all one's neighbors, . . . not merely those with superior intelligence or learning. . . . The vice lies in the very concept of "blue ribbon" panels—the systematic exclusion of all but the "best" or most learned or most intelligent of the general jurors. Such panels are completely at war with the democratic theory of our jury system, a theory formulated out of the experience of generations.[87]

The majority decision in that case has never been overruled and thus stands as *res judicata*. Yet its abolition on the *federal* level by the terms of the Jury Selection and Service Act of 1968 may well herald its demise in the states also—although, without a judicial decision to the contrary, its constitutionality prevails and its desirability in cases involving "highly technical" matters was specifically endorsed by Justice Powell as recently as 1981.[88] A blue ribbon jury may be both unfair and undemocratic, but these qualifications do not render it *ipso facto* unconstitutional. Furthermore, it may be well to reiterate that the notion that juries should be composed of men and women from all walks of life is a relatively recent one. At its English origins, the jury was composed of favorites of the Crown, men of position, or men who were indebted to the Crown. In the early history of the jury in the United States, it comprised a handful of propertied men. Several decades passed before being male and owning property, to name but the two more obvious qualifications, were no longer prerequisties to participation in jury duty.

THE TRIAL JURY AT WORK

A trial jury (which always contains one or more alternates to guard against a case of sudden indisposition of a juror) sits *en banc* throughout the course of the trial. It does so no matter how long the trial may take, and the jurors are compensated, generally inadequately, on a daily fee basis.[89] Each of its mem-

---

(*McDonough Power Co.* v. *Greenwood*, 52 LW 4126 [1984] at 4127. Rehnquist quoted from *Brown* v. *United States*, 411 U.S. 223 (1973) at 231–32, which, in turn, had quoted from *Bruton* v. *United States*, 391 U.S. 123 (1968) at 135 and *Lutwak* v. *United States*, 344 U.S. 604 (1953) at 619.

[87] *Moore* v. *New York*, loc. cit., at 570.

[88] Interview, *The Cavalier Daily*, (University of Virginia, Charlottesville, Va., October 21, 1981) p.1.

[89] In 1984 the juror's fee on the federal level was $30 daily and 20¢ a mile. In 1974, U.S. Senator Gaylord Nelson (D.-Wisc.) unsuccessfully proposed that federal jurors' pay be raised to the equivalent of their "on-the-job" income. (*The New York Times*, March 31, 1974, p. C17.)

bers is presumed to listen impartially and with an open mind to both sides of the case; is not to discuss the trial with anyone, no matter how near or dear; and, at least in theory, is not permitted to read, view or hear any media of communication that might conceivably have some bearing on the ongoing trial. In fact, most judges ban resort to *any media whatsoever* during the trial. The latter requirement may well be an illusory one: there is every reason to believe that, regardless of a juror's conscientiousness and dedication, few public-spirited individuals would in fact literally deny themselves the news of the day. However, if either side in the litigation succeeds in presenting incontrovertible proof of such an aberration, it may move for a mistrial or even a directed verdict of acquittal. Ordinarily (there are exceptions[90]) the jurors are not permitted to take notes, for they are expected to "register the evidence as it is given, on the tablets of (their) memory and not otherwise."[91] When the presiding judge has delivered his charge (see later) to the jury at the end of the trial, the jury retires for its deliberation until it reaches a verdict—which, according to the findings of a host of knowledgeable students of the jury system, they may well have decided *prior* to their deliberations![92]

If the deliberative proceedings stretch into the night, the jury is locked up ("sequestered") in a nearby hotel and subsequently continues its work on the following day or days. According to the results of research on jury deliberations conducted by one expert, 50 percent of the average jury's deliberation time is spent exchanging "personal experiences," 25 percent on "procedural matters," 15 percent on reviewing facts, and exactly 8 percent on discussing the judge's instruction.[93] If, after a reasonable period of time and repeatedly unsuccessful balloting, a trial jury is unable to arrive at a verdict of guilt or acquittal, the judge will declare it to be a *hung jury*, dismiss it, and remit the case to the docket for a trial *de novo* before an entirely different judge and jury. *But* the average judge will battle hard to avoid a deadlock. Thus, U.S.

One year later he introduced legislation to pay federal jurors as much as $100.00 per day "to offset hardship." On the latter issue, see "The Economic Hardship of Jury Duty," 58 *Judicature* 493–501 (1975). Senator Nelson, undaunted, tried again in 1977–78—once more *sans* success. In 1981 jury fees at the state level ranged from $45 a day in Kewannee County, Wisconsin, to $5 for civil cases in San Francisco. (*Time Magazine*, September 28, 1981, p. 45.)

[90]For example, Circuit Court Judge John C. Beatty, Jr., of Multnomah County, Oregon, has allowed the taking of notes since 1970, and he even provides stenographic pads and pencils. (See 64 *Judicature* 3 [September 1980], p. 3.)

[91]Indiana Supreme Court, as quoted by L. L. Bromberger, "Jurors Should Be Allowed to Take Notes," 32 *Journal of the American Judicature Society* 57–8 (1948). For a rather persuasive argument that jurors be permitted to take notes under carefully controlled guidelines, see Victor E. Flango, "Would Jurors Do a Better Job If They Could Take Notes?" 63 *Judicature* 9 (April 1980) pp. 436–43.

[92]Donald M. Gillmore, *Free Jury and Free Trial* (Washington, D.C.: Public Affairs Press, 1966), pp. 201–10.

[93]Ibid., quoting Rita M. James, "Status and Competence of Jurors," 64 *American Journal of Sociology* 563 (1959).

District Judge Edward Weinfeld of New York declined to accept the request of a long-deadlocked jury in 1962, sending it back to a midtown hotel with orders to return to his court at 9 A.M. It did, redeliberated, and later that day returned a verdict of "guilty."

"Hung" Juries. A famous example of a hung jury was that of the first Alger Hiss case,[94] in which the jury deadlocked 8:4 for conviction after countless ballots, and U.S. District Judge Samuel Kauffman declared it hung. Not long thereafter, Hiss was convicted of perjury in a new trial and with a new jury before U.S. Judge Henry W. Goddard.[95] A sensationalized illustration of not just one but two hung juries in succession was the highly publicized Finch–Tregoff murder–conspiracy case in California. The first trial ended in a hung jury in March 1960, after thirteen weeks of courtroom action, with the jury hopelessly deadlocked after thirty-seven hours of deliberation. At that time it stood 10:2 for convicting Dr. R. Bernard Finch, but 8:4 for his mistress Carole Tregoff's acquittal. The retrial was completed in November 1960, and again ended in a hung jury, this time having lasted seventeen weeks, with the jury taking fifty-nine ballots during seventy full hours of active deliberation. Edwin Fry, foremen and the only male on the jury, reported that the twelve jurors had unanimously found Dr. Finch guilty of the murder of his wife, but were divided 9:3 on the degree of murder to be charged, three jurors stubbornly insisting on a second-degree finding. On Miss Tregoff the jury had split 9:3 on the degree as well as the guilt—and that same count held against both regarding the conspiracy charge! Another seemingly interminable trial finally resulted, ending the fiasco in March 1961 with a clear-cut verdict against the two defendants: Dr. Finch was convicted of first-degree murder and conspiracy to commit murder, Miss Tregoff of second degree murder and conspiracy to commit murder. Both were given life sentences. She was out on parole in 1969, he in 1971, after having served eight and ten years, respectively. A contemporary example of three hung juries in succession following an initial, reversed conviction—with the governement then despairing of a fourth trial—was that of Black Panther co-founder Huey Newton, who had been charged with the killing of Oakland, California, policeman John Frey in a 1967 gun battle. Newton had been found guilty of manslaughter in his initial trial in 1968, but a new trial was ordered by the California Supreme Court because of judicial error in the charge to the first jury. In the first two subsequent trials the jury deadlocked, that is, was "hung" 6:6 and 11:1 for conviction; the third—which did not come until 1979—resulted in another hung jury, this time 10:2 for acquittal.

One determined juror can, of course, hang any jury that requires unanimity. This was demonstrated forcefully in 1979, when one elderly juror, proudly

---

[94] United States v. Hiss. Jury hung in August 1949.
[95] United States v. Hiss, 88 F. Supp. 559 (1950). See also United States v. Hiss, 107 F. Supp. 128 (1952).

stipulating that Congressman Daniel Flood (D.-Pa.) was indeed guilty of bribery, conspiracy, and perjury as charged, *hung* the 11:1 for conviction jury because he considered the seventy-five-year-old Flood "too old" to pay for his crimes.[96] (Reference is sometimes made to a *hanging jury*, which is a *grand jury* that has earned a reputation for almost certain indictments.)

INSTRUCTING THE JURY: THE JUDGE'S CHARGE

One of the highlights of a trial in the pertinent federal and state courts of the United States, and a crucial point in its evolvement, is the presiding judge's *charge* to the trial jury on completion of testimony, arguments, and motions by all concerned. It comes after the summations by the prosecution and the defense, the latter customarily speaking last. Much thought goes, or should go, into this charge, which is intended as an exposition of the law and is delivered orally in most, although not all, cases.[97] The judge must take great care to ascertain that its contents are clear, to the point, comprehensive, and illuminating and that they pose readily discernible alternatives to the jury panelists, who may well ask for further instructions on details. But as a rule the jury may not take copies of the charge to the jury deliberation room,[98] nor may they taperecord it. No wonder that jury comprehension remains generally low. It is a highly complicated business, but it need not be. Thus, in the words of an appellate tribunal:

> The trial judge should not as a rule limit himself to stating good set terms of law culled from the codes and the reports. Jurors need not legal definitions merely. They require proper instructions as to the method of applying such definitions after reaching their conclusions on the facts.[99]

---

[96] See the accounts in *The Philadelphia Inquirer*, August 9, 1971, p. 1, and *The Philadelphia Evening Bulletin*, December 16, 1971, p. G68. For an interesting examination of hung juries, replete with statistics, see Leo J. Flynn, "Does Justice Fail When the Jury Is Deadlocked?" 61 *Judicature* 3 (September 1977) pp. 129–34. For an account of the hung Flood jury see *Time Magazine*, February 19, 1979, p. 97.

[97] An interesting study of jury-charging attitudes by fifty randomly selected federal district court judges in 1970, conducted by Jerry K. Frye of Texas Christian University, pointed to among other things, the extreme importance judges assign to *oral* instructions, its "meaningfulness" to the jurors, an average length of one and one-half hours, a strong disinclination to permit any written material to accompany the jury to the deliberation room, and considerable confidence in the average juror's listening and comprehension ability. (See letter to author, plus chart, dated February 5, 1970.) Two-thirds of the states (e.g., Colorado, Illinois, Michigan) have tried to make "pattern," that is, standard, model, uniform instructions by judges mandatory. (See 62 *Judicature* 185 [October 1978].)

[98] There are exceptions, such as Iowa State courts, where juries are permitted to take written instructions to the deliberation room. Oregon statutorily permits the judge in his discretion to deliver his instructions orally and then send an exact copy to the jury.

[99] *People v. Odell*, 230 N.Y. 481 (1921) at 487–88. It has been repeatedly suggested that both the testimony and the instructions in litigation be *videotaped* so as to be readily available, and "recallable" by and to deliberating juries. See David U. Strawn and G. Thomas Munsterman, "Helping Juries Handle Complex Cases," 65 *Judicature* (March–April 1982), pp. 444–48.

As one recent careful research project again demonstrated convincingly, it is far from impossible to develop understandable jury instructions. Rewriting instructions can improve comprehensibility dramatically.[100]

Moreover, the judge must see to it that the charge is scrupulously fair to both sides in the dispute and it is naturally of overriding importance to the accused. It should be "the safeguard of fairness and impartiality and the guarantee of judicial indifference to individuals."[101] Many a charge has, ultimately, been instrumental in causing a mistrial; many another has been found by appellate courts to be defective on points of law. In brief, the judge's charge to the jurors, which is almost always necessarily complicated, sums up the case, pinpoints the chief issues involved, and concludes with the admonition that the jury must bring in a verdict of "guilty" or "not guilty"—addressing itself to each of the charges and/or counts at issue and, if a choice is permissible under law in homicide cases, determining the degree of punishment. Any verdict of "guilty" must have taken into account the absence of *reasonable doubt*, often a very difficult open-ended problem. There are no in-between stages of a verdict, although in some instances, in several of the fifty American states, juries are empowered to mitigate their judgment of guilt in homicide cases by a recommendation of mercy, which is normally binding on the judge. It was just such a binding recommendation by the third jury in the Finch–Tregoff murder case that saved Finch from the electric chair.

Under certain limited circumstances, a judge may express a value judgment on the evidence in charging the jury, but this is valid only in isolated instances, and, indeed, has been judicially interdicted in others (e.g., in Pennsylvania)[102]. Superior Judge Leroy Dawson in the second Finch–Tregoff case startled courtroom observers by telling the deadlocked jury that the evidence showed "a willful and deliberate taking of human life." When one of the defense attorneys repeatedly attempted to stop the judge from reading his comments, he found himself twice cited for contempt. Judge Dawson cited a 1934 amendment to the California Constitution as his authority and a San Diego case in 1958 as his precedent.[103] Since his own case resulted in a hung jury, Dawson's action was not challenged further. On the other hand, judges everywhere are free to comment on a jury's verdict once it has been announced, although many jurists believe this practice, too, to be at least unwise if not unethical; but it is not illegal unless expressly interdicted by constitutional, statutory, or judicial mandate.

Setting a Verdict Aside. In *civil* cases, but generally less commonly in *criminal* cases since only a few states permit it, a judge may *reverse* the jury's

[100] Amiram Elwork, James J. Alfini, and Bruce D. Sales, "Toward Understandable Jury Instructions," 65 *Judicature* (March–April 1982), pp. 432–43.

[101] *People v. Odell,* loc. cit., at 488.

[102] Philip R. Goldsmith, "Judges' Comments to Jurors Curbed," *The Philadelphia Inquirer,* April 22, 1972, p. 8.

[103] *The Philadelphia Evening Bulletin,* November 6, 1960, p. 1.

verdict. This frequently occurs in so-called *negligence* or *compensation award* cases, in which jury lawlessness, in the form of excessive verdict, is not uncommon. A much-publicized illustration of the latter is the overturning by U.S. District Court Judge Joseph Stevens of a $500,000 jury award in the alleged sex discrimination case involving onetime Metromedia anchorwoman Christine Craft. Stevens ruled that "plaintiff was not discriminated against because of her sex," that Metromedia's actions "with respect to her appearance were necessary and appropriate."[104] A federal case example of the negligence issue, one widely featured in the public press in 1959 because of an open clash between Justices Whittaker and Douglas, was *Inman v. Baltimore and Ohio Railroad*.[105] A District of Columbia jury had held the railroad negligent in stationing Inman where he could be knocked down by a drunken driver, and it awarded him $25,000. However, the judge who presided over the trial in the U.S. District Court set the verdict aside as being "irrational."[106] When the U.S. Court of Appeals upheld the district judge, Inman appealed to the U.S. Supreme Court, which, in a 5:4 opinion, affirmed the judgment below. What provoked the headlined outburst by Justice Douglas, and his insistence that the Supreme Court has a duty to enforce the guarantee of a jury trial and to prevent the lower courts from setting too strict a standard, was Justice Whittaker's concurring opinion. In it Whittaker had scoffed at the idea that the railroad had been negligent and suggested that the only way it could have prevented the accident was to have the employee encased in an army tank. This, in the full glare of an "Opinion Monday" (to be described in detail in chapter 5), Douglas denounced, in person and from the bench, as "smart-alecky." Barely one year later, however, with Justices Black and Douglas dissenting vehemently, the Supreme Court itself, for the first time in twenty-four years, reversed a jury's verdict awarding damages to an injured railroad worker.[107] Judge Charles E. Wyzanski, Jr., of the federal trial court below had upheld the jury's verdict but denounced it in no uncertain terms, asserting the case was devoid of "any evidence of negligence." He had refrained from setting it aside solely because he felt bound by what until then had been Supreme Court doctrine in these cases.[108] Of course, courts may also reverse and remand an award as being "too low," although this occurs far less frequently. Thus, the U.S. Court of Appeals for the Second Circuit held a $32,000 jury-awarded payment to a widow for the death of her husband killed in an automobile accident "as grossly inadequate," basing the decision on

---

[104] *Craft v. Metromedia, Inc.*, 572 F. Supp. 868 (1983).

[105] 361 U.S. 138.

[106] An example of a state court reversal of a verdict is the action by Philadelphia Court of Common Pleas, Judge Theodore L. Reimel in setting aside a $25,000 verdict by a jury for a local attorney's claim for fees due as being "excessive and perverse." (*The Philadelphia Evening Bulletin*, January 16, 1962, p. 13).

[107] *New York, New Haven, and Hartford v. Hennagan*, 364 U.S. 441 (1960).

[108] Ibid. As reported in 272 F. 2d 153 (1959) at 155–56.

what Judge Irving R. Kaufman noted as the unfair influence of the trial judge's charge to the jury.[109] A dramatic example of an overruling in a criminal case came in 1984 when Mobile County (Alabama) Judge Braxton Kittrell, Jr., overruled a jury that had unanimously sentenced a member of the Ku Klux Klan to life imprisonment without parole for the killing and hanging of a young black man. Judge Kittrell, rejecting the verdict as insufficient, instead sentenced the convicted Henry Francis Hay to death in the electric chair and set an execution date.[110]

Judges may also set aside a jury verdict if it is clearly based on an obviously mistaken notion of the law involved in a case. A recent instance is U.S. District Court Judge Oliver Gasch's setting aside of a $2 million libel judgment against *The Washington Post* for a story about Mobile Oil Corporation President William Tavoulares. Gasch ruled that the necessary evidence required in the case of a public figure under the legal precedent established in *New York Times v. Sullivan*[111] of proof of "knowing lies or statements made in reckless disregard of the truth" had neither been submitted nor established.[112] Yet all these practices in American courts are a far cry from Continental systems, in which the trial judge is permitted, if not expected, to comment on the weight of the evidence and the credibility of witnesses throughout the course of the trial and to allow the jury to know his or her opinion on the merits of the case.[113] On the other hand, the average judge in the United States, too, has the power in all cases to order a verdict of *directed acquittal* before a case goes to the jury—a motion made often by defense counsel almost as a routine matter, but rarely granted. If granted, however, it is not subject to reversal by any higher court on the *federal* level. Moreover, the judge may take a case out of the jury's hands if it becomes evident that only questions of law are involved and no facts are in dispute. And among the myriad of reasons why a judge may order a *retrial* is the finding of a clear case of basic confusion among the jurors—one that obviously affected the verdict in such a fashion that there is grave doubt in the mind of the presiding judge that the jury has fulfilled its part in seeing justice is done. Thus, in a New Jersey automobile accident case the jury had returned from its deliberations, and its foreman upon being asked by the judge, "Have you agreed upon a verdict, Mr. Foreman?" answered, "My name isn't Foreman. My name is Admerman." When the trial judge refused to recognize this interesting reply as a sufficient reason to declare a mistrial, defendant Naomi Haberli appealed

---

[109] *Caskey v. The Village of Wayland,* 362 F. 2d 1789 (1967).

[110] See the account in *The New York Times,* February 3, 1984, p. A16.

[111] 376 U.S. 254 (1964).

[112] *The Washington Post v. Tavoulares,* 527 F. Supp. 676 (D.C.-D.C., 1983).

[113] In sixteenth-century England, and until 1670, the so-called writ of atteint (the remote ancestor of today's "directed verdict") enabled a judge to refuse to accept any jury verdict he did not approve, no matter what the evidence. A new trial, with a larger jury, was then customarily held.

to the Appellate division of the New Jersey State Superior Court, which unanimously ordered a retrial, citing Mr. Admerman's response, as well as the grossly excessive award granted by his fellow jurors, as a prima facie example of the type of "basic confusion" necessitating a new trial.[114] Not a matter of confusion was the mistrial in a rape case declared by District of Columbia Superior Judge Fred B. Ugast in 1981. When a jury of eleven was unable to reach a verdict, the Judge, upon inquiry, received the following message from jury foreman Robert W. Smoot: "Your Honor, we cannot reach a decision in this case unless two jurors are replaced. . . . Drinking problem." Two jurors had been having a veritable ball during deliberations by drinking from cups of "Seven-Up," laced with a little good Bourbon ensconced in their purses![115] But it should be understood that no trial or appellate judge will readily tamper with a jury's verdict, no matter what his or her private opinion may be.

"*General*" *and* "*Special*" *Verdicts*. On the basis of the somewhat questionable assumption that the jury fully comprehends the judge's instructions concerning the applicable substantive legal rules, it is usually required to return a *general* or *overall* verdict in favor of one party or another. Theoretically, as already indicated, this jury verdict is based on the *facts* of the case, the judge himself having determined the rules of *law*—although it is not always possible to separate facts and law, and the U.S. Supreme Court has repeatedly dismissed challenges to statutory provisions that make juries the sole judges of the law as well as the facts in criminal trials.[116] In practice, however, the general verdict permits the jury to do what it pleases: it gives no details, simply reports its decision, and no one either really knows or may safely predict just what facts a jury found from the evidence. Judge Jerome Frank, a life-long and severe critic of the jury system as a fact-finding institution, viewed the judge's charge as little more than an elaborate ceremonial routine, and he argued that of all the possible ways that could be devised to arrive at the falsity or truth of testimony, " . . . *none could be conceived that would be more ineffective than trial by jury.*"[117] He and many other legal authorities have long contended that *special*, or *fact*, verdicts—employed in England for centuries, and reconfirmed with the Courts Act of 1971—in which the jury is asked to answer a *specific* question of fact, are a far preferable method of arriving at a verdict that is just to all concerned. In a special verdict procedure, which is now used in several of the fifty states and was authorized for federal *civil* suits in 1938 (but is very rarely used), the trial judge charges the jury to report its findings—presumably even if these are simply beliefs—about certain particular issues of fact raised during the course

[114] *The New York Times*, December 15, 1960, p. 27.
[115] As reported by *The Washington Post*, May 4, 1981, p. A18.
[116] See, for example, *Giles v. Maryland*, 372 U.S. 767 (1962).
[117] Jerome Frank, *Courts on Trial* (Princeton, NJ: Princeton University Press, 1949), p. 20 (Italics supplied.) This is one of the great books on the judicial process.

of the trial, facts that a jury should be able to weigh and determine with a modicum of accuracy and reliability. To those facts thus "found" the judge then applies the appropriate legal rule. It has been frequently and thoughtfully suggested that a jury's ability to find appropriate facts would be enormously enhanced were it permitted to submit written interrogatories to witnesses during the course of a trial (through the presiding judge).[118] In effect, some judges have begun to experiment with such procedures in complex cases.[119] Whatever the type of jury verdict advocated, the degree of perfection one may expect from the human institutions that constitute the judicial process is necessarily a limited one.

English and Welsh judges employ a charge rather similar to that found in the tribunals of the United States, but they provide somewhat more guidance to the jury during the trial. No charge is used in the courts of France. Instead, the French presiding judge, who actively directs the proceedings in the courtroom by interrogating the accused and witnesses, submits to the jury—in the infrequent instances of its presence in a case—a list of questions which the nine panelists are required to answer with a simple "yes" or "no." Standard examples of these queries would be, "Did the accused prove his alibi?"; "Was the accused present at the scene of the crime when it was committed?"; "Was the act of homicide one of self-defense?"; and, always, "If you find the defendant guilty, were there any extenuating circumstances?" Clearly, by his interrogation the judge tries to give to the jury the most lucid picture possible as a matter of guidance. The jury, its members voting individually and in secret, answers these questions specifically and thereby reaches its verdict—if necessary by a *majority* vote, in contrast to the *unanimity* requirements of the American federal judicial system. However, should the divisions among the jurors prove to be uncomfortably close, such as 7:5 or even 6:6, the presiding judge may assume the power of determining the verdict with the aid of the two associate judges (there are always three judges at the assized-trial level). But in that event the verdict is almost certain to be one of acquittal.

In West Germany today the entire courtroom examination in criminal trials is conducted by the judges, while the prosecuting attorney and counsel for the defense sit mute and take notes. Counsel is privileged to put a question only when the judges have completed an examination calculated to bring out fully and fairly all that a witness might tell. Jurors are taken from a local list of "outstanding" citizens and impaneled for a term of one year. Judge and jury sit on the bench together and participate jointly and equally in deliberation on a case—a procedure known as a *fused* jury.

JURIES: BLESSING OR EVIL?

It is not easy to be objective about juries—and few observers are. Certainly there is but little doubt that juries throughout the Western world have dec-

---

[118]See, e.g., Strawn and Munsterman, op. cit., p. 131, and Elwork, Alfini, and Sales, ibid.
[119]See Irving R. Kaufman, "The Verdict on Juries," *The New York Times Magazine*, April 1, 1984, pp. 42ff.

lined both in significance and esteem during the past century. Often, when they are not held in utter contempt by the professional critics, they are merely tolerated as a necessary, and at times admittedly convenient, evil. In large measure, the juries have brought this opprobrium on themselves—no matter how innocent and perhaps even understandable their response to the demands of the legal process may be. But it is not easy to defend the institution in the face of so many jury-created fiascos.

Thus, we again turn to the aforementioned Finch–Tregoff case, this time the first 1960 trial, to find the jury system at its worst. According to an interview (!) granted to United Press International by one of the female members of the panel of five men and seven women that had just been declared a hung jury,

> ... at one point a near fight broke out. At the height of one heated debate, a male juror threatened to throw another [a female] out of a window and turned over the jury table—he used to be a boxer—before she ran to the door. She was hysterical and pounded on the door for the bailiff.[120]

A different woman juror also readily and beamingly gave an interview to UPI, reporting that at least three "propositioning" notes had been passed to one of her female colleagues on the panel. An extra bailiff was then brought in to stand guard at another woman's hotel room door after those notes came to light.[121] A further illustration is the young mother from Bedford, Indiana, who confessed that as a member of a jury panel in the 1950s she had voted to convict the accused of rape—despite the fact that she believed him to be innocent. She did so against her own judgment, she readily admitted, because "I knew I had those children at home and we would never get out of there if we tried to argue it out with the others."[122] Similar "interviews" were granted by jurors in the Wallace Butts-Curtis Publishing Co. 1963 libel suit. In 1977, T. Cullen Davis, the "victor" in his six-month, $3 million plus costs jury trial for the murder of his twelve-year-old stepdaughter, joined several jurors (and the presiding judge, the bailiff, his mistress, and friends) for a raucous victory party in Amarillo, Texas.[123] And to conclude the unfortunately almost inexhaustible instances of the kind of antics that have served to bring widespread opprobrium on the institution: In March 1961, under the guise of registering a *coup* in what it called "public service," the Hearst Corporation-owned station WBAL-TV in Baltimore induced, evidently without any difficulty, nine of twelve jurors to appear before the studio camera and reenact their deliberations that resulted in the conviction of one Melvin Davis Rees, Jr., for murder and kidnapping. This intriguing performance, which featured in great detail the thoughts and reasoning that culminated in the verdict, came on the

---

[120] *The New York Times*, March 13, 1960, p. 42.
[121] Ibid. But judges may enjoin interviews (e.g., *U.S. v. Driscoll*, 276 F. Supp. 333, 1967).
[122] As quoted by John F. X. Irving, "The Jury May Be Out Permanently," *National Review* 177 (September 1958).
[123] *The [Charlottesville] Daily Progress*, November 18, 1977, p. A8.

evening *prior* to the scheduled sentencing of the convicted man! As a result, defense counsel succeeded in obtaining at least a temporary postponement of sentencing, and he raised a series of legal questions based on this jury TV debut, which the *Baltimore News Post*, also a Hearst-owned medium, termed "a reportorial breakthrough of the traditional silence of the jury room."[124] Considerations of law, ethics, morals, and taste were evidently deemed insignificant. And within hours of their acquittal of John Z. DeLorean of drug conspiracy charges in 1984, jurors were on TV—including the morning shows—providing detailed insight into their deliberations and offering sundry gratuitous advice to the government.

Evil? It is tempting to underscore the questioning of the efficacy of the institution of the jury—which Honoré Balzac once defined as "twelve men to decide who has the better lawyer," Herbert Spencer called "a group of twelve people of average ignorance," and Erwin Griswold styled "the apotheosis of the amateur"—by noting that there is considerable evidence that the average jury reaches its verdict in most instances by a kind of "happy" compromise. Not being able to agree on a financial award in a civil case, for example, each panelist will write down his or her own figure; then the jury will add the total, divide it by the number of jurors, and thus attain peace of mind![125] In homicide cases a host of revelations again and again points to jury compromises. Thus, unless they are expressly forbidden to do so by statute or by the judge's charge, jurors will frequently decide a case of murder by "compromising" between first-degree murder and acquittal by settling for a second-degree conviction, even if it is not justifiable by the facts in the case. For example, the 1967 Naples, Florida, jury that convicted Dr. Carl Coppolino of the poison-murder of his first wife, Carmela, brought in a verdict of murder in the *second* degree, when, obviously, the very use of purchased poison carries with it premeditation, which calls for a first-degree murder conviction. Evidently, the jury had "compromised." Sometimes the flip-of-the-coin or lot method is employed in order to get the nasty business over with. Or, as was demonstrated in a Hancock County, Kentucky, case, the jury became so confused as a result of its own deliberations that it formally "retracted" an already rendered verdict![126]

Even with the best of intentions, it may well be almost impossible for the wandering mind of the ordinary juror to overcome conclusively the histrionics that so often characterize presentation by counsel. Both prosecution and defense generally conduct what is to all intents and purposes a legal sporting combat, with each side following evidence by counterevidence, examination by cross-examination, witness by counter-witness, each one sworn to tell the truth, the whole truth, and nothing but the truth. Not infrequently, this

---

[124]See Jack Gould's article in *The New York Times*, March 25, 1961, p. 49.

[125]In some jurisdictions (e.g., Iowa) this "averaged" verdict, known as a "quotient" verdict, if ascertained to have occurred, does become grounds for a possible reversal.

[126]*The New York Times*, April 15, 1962, Sec. 4, p. E8.

alleged search for the truth results in statements in open court that are clearly out of order. But even if the judge so holds, as he often does, and asks the jury to disregard the statement at issue, it has been uttered, of course, and it is conjectural at best whether or not it can be wiped from the jurors' minds. To arrive at the truth behind what one long-time observer of juries styled "the curtain of flimflam and obfuscation"[127] the jury may well have to decide which side, in its judgment, seemed to tell fewer lies, and in that way reach a verdict. Hence, in the words of Judge Frank, based on his many years of active experience in the legal and judicial processes:

> ... the jury is the worst possible enemy of the "supremacy of the law." For "jury-made law" is, par excellence, capricious and arbitrary, yielding the maximum in the way of lack of uniformity, of unknowability.... To my mind a better instrument than the usual jury trial could scarcely be found for achieving uncertainty, capriciousness, lack of uniformity, disregard of the [rules], and unpredictability of decisions.[128]

Accordingly, he and others would prefer the trial judges to hear and decide cases alone, the assumption being that judges are trained in the law, which jurors are not, and that they function in a setting that is open to considerably more scrutiny than juries. Yet the "Chicago Jury Project"[129] pointed to a significant 83 percent agreement on verdicts between judges and juries!

Blessing? A natural and main source of endorsement of the jury system is the trial lawyer, who has a vested interest in influencing it—even if this is done by persuading the generally bewildered jurors that A is really B. Few, if any, defense lawyers in a criminal case would argue against it. But the venerable institution's defense does not need to rest its case on such pragmatic grounds. Many a legal scholar, far from decrying the factors of emotion, prejudice, and sympathy that are undeniably major determinants in jury verdicts, holds that these very factors advance the cause of justice because they represent the "socially adapted intuitive law" of the various communities to which we belong. Thus, Thomas Lambert of the American Trial Lawyers Association noted in 1968 that "the glory of the jury is its beautiful lawlessness.... [It represents] the yeasty independence of the average man over officialdom"[130]—a view of the jury generally seconded and even expanded recently by Jon M. Van Dyke in a full-length work on jury selection, replete with a host of statistical trial data.[131] Charles P. Curtis and Harold J. Berman

---

[127] David A Dressler, "Trial by Combat in American Courts," 222 *Harper's Magazine* 32 (April 1960).

[128] Frank, op. cit., pp. 123, 132. Mark Twain often voiced similar sentiments! For example: "The jury system puts a ban upon intelligence and honesty, and a premium upon ignorance, stupidity and perjury." (As re-quoted in *Time Magazine*, September 28, 1981, p. 47.)

[129] See p. 136 and fn. 135, *infra*.

[130] *Time Magazine*, July 26, 1968, p. 80.

[131] *Jury Selection Procedures: Our Uncertain Commitment to Representative Juries* (Cambridge, MA: Ballinger Publishing Co., 1977).

have contended repeatedly that the jury reflects "the intuitive part of us," which they view as a necessary counterbalance to the equally essential "intellectual part of us" in the judge.[132] This is particularly appropriate if one keeps in mind that, in the final analysis, the first and foremost function of a jury is to choose between conflicting testimony, testimony so frequently beclouded by histrionics and legalistics as to render an "intuitive" judgment all but inevitable—at least up to a point. Something can certainly be said for the time-honored principle of being judged by a group of one's peers. Jurors, as Holmes once put it, "introduce into their verdicts a certain amount—a very large amount. . . . of popular prejudice, and this keeps the administration of the law in accord with the wishes and feelings of the community."[133] Moreover, much of the adverse criticism would appear to depend on which side of the case one's interests lie and whether the jury sits in a civil or criminal case.

One of the most articulate and influential champions of the jury system was the distinguished John Henry Wigmore, who advanced four main arguments in favor of the principle: First, it prevents popular distrust of official justice because it gives the average member of the body politic a share in the political process—a kind of communal enactment of the democratic ideal. Second, it provides for some necessary flexibility in legal rules and regulations in that it enables an adjustment of the "general rule of law to the justice of a particular case," whereas the judge is rightly expected to be consistent and consequential in his rulings for all. Third, it educates the ordinary citizen in the administration of justice by cultivating the judicial habit in him and by creating in him a respect for law and order, thus making him conscious of his duty to society and his share in the governmental process. Fourth, it ameliorates the verdict because it is based on the amalgam of a host of temperaments and viewpoints.[134] In essence, this is a plea on behalf of the institution based on the recognition of the role of common sense in the judicial process. It is a plea echoed by law professors Harry Kalven, Jr., and Hans Zeisel of the University of Chicago after a monumental study of the jury system, involving the questioning of 550 judges who presided over 3,576 jury trials across the country. Their conclusion was that the freedom of a jury to inject its own sense of justice is one of the greatest strengths of the system. But it also acknowledged that "jury legislation," or the jury's conscious modification of the law to make it conform to community views of what it ought to be, was a factor in fully 50 percent of the disagreements between judge and jury of what *the law* in a given case *is*.[135]

---

[132] See Curtis, op. cit., pp. 101–4.

[133] Oliver Wendell Holmes, Jr., *Collected Legal Papers* (New York: Harcourt, Brace, and Howe, 1920), p. 237.

[134] As discussed and quoted by William Wirt Blume, "The Place of Trial in Criminal Cases," 43 *Michigan Law Review* (1944), pp. 64–65.

[135] The study, Ford Foundation–financed, and known as the "Chicago Jury Project," was published under the title *The American Jury* (Boston: Little, Brown and Co., 1966). See also

Unquestionably, the Wigmore roster of exhortation is subject to serious exception—especially since it is based, at least in part, on a rather optimistic view of human nature and a belief in the willingness as well as the ability of the average citizen to accept and adapt to these laudatory notions of participation in the responsibilities of society and state. Some of the illustrations presented in connection with the adverse criticism of the institution would appear to raise some crucial doubts regarding Professor Wigmore's analysis. Be that as it may, despite its shortcomings the jury system has been generally regarded by the public at large as a laudable instrument in the quest for justice. "It is so justly regarded," once applauded Joseph H. Choate, "as the best and perhaps the only known means of admitting the people to a share in maintaining their wholesome interest in the administration of justice. . . . "[136] The ultimate questions remain, however: Is it? And does it? It is difficult to still the haunting doubts.[137]

FROM OFFENSE TO TRIAL: A PROCEDURAL NOTE

The practices and customs that characterize the judicial process differ widely in the various jurisdictions discussed herein. This also applies to the procedures followed in the lengthy and often difficult path that leads from the commission of the offense to its ultimate adjudication in or out of the courtroom—for the vast majority of cases are in fact settled by mutual agreement before they reach the trial stage. Indeed, on the whole it is only the so-called trouble cases—or "hard" cases, as Holmes preferred to style them—that actually traverse the tedious process through the entire courtroom sequence. The purpose of this procedural note is to illustrate, in necessarily brief and generalized fashion, the various stages that confront participants in a full-length legal proceeding. The model employed, which will distinguish between civil and criminal cases, is a typical jurisdictional unit in the United States of America. And it should be noted that the very nature of an American court case requires the presence of the following four conditions: (1) an adversary process, (2) a justiciable issue, (3) ripeness for judicial determination, and (4) an actual disposition.[138]

Gary J. Jacobsohn, "Citizen Participation in Policy-Making: The Role of the Jury," 39 *The Journal of Politics* 1 (February 1977), pp. 73–96, particularly for the discussion on "jury nullification."

[136] As quoted by Justice Bernard Botein, *Trial Judge* (New York: Simon and Schuster, 1952), p. 195. Thomas Jefferson described the jury system as "the only anchor ever yet imagined by man by which government can be held to principles of its constitution." (As quoted in *Time Magazine*, September 28, 1981, p. 44.)

[137] See the Symposium, "The Jury in Complex Litigation," 65 *Judicature* 8–9 (March–April 1982), which analyzes key aspects of the problem in a series of several articles. (See especially those by Peter W. Sperlich, Mark A. Nordenberg, and William V. Luneberg.)

[138] See ch. 9 *infra*, in this connection. For a reference to the British system, see Doreen J. McBarnet, "Pre-Trial Procedure and the Construction of Conviction," *The Sociology of Law*, ed. by Pat Carlen (Sociological Review Monograph, no. 23, 1976).

PROCEDURE IN CIVIL CASES

A civil case is one in which individuals or groups bring adjudicatable actions in court against other individuals or groups by whom they contend to have been wronged. *Step 1 is the commencement of the action by the plaintiff,* the party bringing the suit, against the *respondent* or *defendent.* If it is a matter of an *appeal* rather than the bringing of an initial suit, the party who appeals is known as the *appellant,* the other side as the *respondent* or *appellee.* The plaintiff or appellant may also be termed *petitioner.* A word of caution: although it is easy to determine who the two sides to a respective suit are at the initial stage of a new suit, once that proceeding has reached the various appellate stages, it is considerably more difficult, and the only safe way to do so is to read the first few paragraphs of the case. In order to bring the suit, a plaintiff will have to do at least three things: (1) select the correct and proper tribunal, (2) have the defendant or his or her possessions brought before it, and (3) present the charges and ask for appropriate remedies.

In order to achieve the second requirement, the plaintiff must ask the proper authorities to serve a *summons,* which is issued after the petitioner has "sworn it out." Presumably it will be obeyed. Failure to respond to the summons will normally result either in a judgment against the respondent by default or in contempt proceedings. An even more compelling order to appear is a *subpoena,* a writ that, unlike the summons, must always be served on the respondent or witness in person; it directs his or her appearance on pain of being held in contempt of court (or of whatever other judicial or quasi-judicial authority may be empowered to issue the writ). A subpoena *duces tecum,* a related writ, requires the respondent to *bring something* along, a specific document, for example. If the respondent resides outside of the court's jurisdiction, but owns property therein, the latter may be *attached* in order to commence a suit, but only if the property attached is itself the subject matter of the suit. If it is not, the respondent cannot be brought into court by attachment of business property, even if he or she resides within the jurisdiction.

Closely related to the three tasks the plaintiff performs to commence the action is an attempt by the two parties to the suit to narrow the factual and legal issues involved by virtue of an exchange of one formal written statement, or a series of them, stating the claim at issue. Such statements are called *pleadings.* These follow logically as a result of the plaintiff's initiation of his or her *complaint. Step 2 is designed solely to formulate the issues in the case* and consists of the formal pleadings, now presumably involving the legal battery for both sides. This stage of the pleadings features the formal exchange of documents between the two sides, with the respondent required to file an *answer.* Often the lawyers are able to settle matters at this stage, but since we are concerned here with a sketch of the entire procedure, we assume that instead of there being acquiescence or agreement, the future defendant will file a *motion to dismiss* the complaint, sometimes also known as a *demurrer.*

If the plaintiff rejects these formal counterclaims, the stage will now have been set for the docketing of the case on the calendar of the court of proper jurisdiction. A *pretrial conference with the judge* may conceivably settle matters at this juncture and avoid an actual trial—it will very likely serve to further narrow some of the problems involved. The next formal stage is the trial itself.

The nature and character of *step 3*, the *trial*, depend largely on whether the issue between the litigants is one of law or one of fact. If the issue is solely one of *law*, the court receives the case by means of a legal *argument* presented by the attorneys for both sides. Because there are no facts to be determined, jury and witnesses are not called; the judge decides the dispute strictly on the basis of the law, as he or she sees it. But if the dispute is either "mixed" or strictly of *facts*, the case will be tried before judge and jury, depending somewhat on its nature and, as has been described earlier in the chapter, on whether or not a jury trial is waived by mutual consent when that is possible and desirable. The next four steps, *verdict, judgment, appellate review* (if any), and *enforcement*, if not self-explanatory, have already been delineated or will be discussed in subsequent chapters.

PROCEDURE IN CRIMINAL CASES

Because of the very nature of the offense, the procedure in a criminal case is *ipso facto* both more formal and more elaborate, and it involves the machinery of the state to a much greater degree. Above all, the state, as was demonstrated in chapter 1, *necessarily* is a party to the suit—at least in the sense that it is responsible for the prosecution of the offense. It is responsible because criminal proceedings pertain to actions by individuals or groups who are charged with having committed one or more antisocial acts that society, through its governmental processes, has defined as a "crime" in public law. *Step 1* in a criminal case, therefore, is very simply the *apprehension* of the prospective defendant within the territorial limitations of the governmental jurisdiction concerned—who, unless he or she voluntarily surrenders to the authorities, is literally caught and arrested, either in the act of commission, while fleeing, or as a result of an arrest warrant, which the arresting officer must obtain in advance from properly constituted authority. *Step 2*, closely related to the first, sees the arrested person—who, if indigent, is entitled to the appointment of counsel as of the arrest stage—brought before a magistrate (known until the 1960s as a "commissioner" on the federal level[139]) for the *preliminary* examination, in order to determine whether he or she shall be released or *held to answer*. If the latter, the accused will be held either in *custody* or released on *bail* to await the decision of the public prosecutor or the grand jury on the question of whether or not an *information* or an *indictment* shall be filed against him or her. The preliminary examination is a cru-

---

[139]See p. 167, *infra*, for a brief explanation of this office.

cial and highly significant stage in criminal procedure, if for no other reason than that well over half of those arrested are released here, which customarily closes the books on the matter.

Step 3 represents the formal *accusation* by grand jury indictment or by the process of "information," depending on the statutory requirements or practices in the several jurisdictions concerned. This is logically followed by the *arraignment* and pleading—although the accused may already have entered a plea at the preliminary hearing stage—which constitutes *step 4*. An arraignment consists simply of the official, formal reading of the terms of the indictment or information to the accused by the court of jurisdiction,[140] and it concludes with the question, "How do you plead?"—giving the accused the choice of "*guilty*" or "*not guilty.*"[141] Here the two parties often try to reach a settlement to avoid a formal trial; known as "plea bargaining"—a practice strongly discouraged in England—it is conducted between the prosecution and the defense, frequently with the assistance of the judge.[142] In sheer statistical terms it is employed about fifteen times more frequently than juries to "resolve" cases.

Step 5 is the *trial* itself. In a jury trial, the verdict is always the jury's to render—unless the judge directs the jury to find the defendant "not guilty." If there is no trial by jury, the judge's verdict takes its place, as happens in many, but not all, pleadings of guilty. A host of proceedings, with which we need not concern ourselves here, antedates the trial—including various motions for dismissal of the case, change of pleadings, placing of dispositions, request for changes of *venue*, plea bargaining, possible dismissal or change of charges. The trial is conducted by the judge, either with or without a jury as the case and jurisdiction may mandate, and the process terminates with the next four steps: *verdict, judgment and sentencing,*[143] *appellate review,* if any,

---

[140]In 1978 the Idaho Supreme Court gave effect to a new rule (43.2) governing arraignments that satisfy its requirements "either in person or by electronic audio-visual devices in the discretion of the magistrate." See Warren H. Gilmore, "Arraignment by Television: A New Way to Bring Defendants to the Courtroom," 63 *Judicature* 8 (March 1980), pp. 396ff.

[141]Under some circumstances the accused may plead *nolo contendere*, or "no contest"—specifically, "I do not wish to contend"—by which he throws himself on the mercy of the court. In effect an admission of guilt without so stating formally, the *nolo contendere* penalties are potentially the same as for the plea of guilty; but the judge more often than not displays leniency in such cases—some say if for no other reason than that the plea saves time, effort, and money. Vice-President Spiro T. Agnew's plea of *nolo contendere* in federal district court in October 1973 to a charge of income tax evasion is a famous case illustration. (Concurrently he announced his resignation from the high office, to which he was succeeded by Gerald Ford.)

[142]Plea bargaining—which has had official U.S. Supreme Court sanction (e.g., *Bordenkircher v. Hayes*, 98 S. Ct. 663 [1978])—played a prominent role in the Agnew case in 1973 and in many, in fact most, of the Watergate culprits' cases. Indeed, in 1978 the U.S. Department of Justice estimated that 90 percent of the country's *criminal* cases "are now resolved by the process of persuading the accused to plead guilty to a lesser crime." (*The New York Times,* January 19, 1978, p. A7.) As of 1984 all states except Alaska permitted plea bargaining.

[143]In 1977 the Supreme Court of Pennsylvania ruled that henceforth all *criminal* defendants

and *execution of the sentence imposed,* if any. Of course, no bare procedural sketch such as this can take into account the sundry aspects and ramifications of the manifold practices, procedures, and safeguards that surround this fascinating aspect of the judicial process; it should be regarded merely as the outline of its essential framework.

Despite the relatively drastic distinctions in judicial theory and practice between the common law lands and the statutory law lands of the free West, the justice meted out under both legal systems is similar in its ultimate degree of fairness if not in its efficiency. Each system is characterized by obvious advantages and disadvantages that govern its "costs" and each features methods that are peculiar to the needs or predispositions of the particular governmental jurisdiction concerned. As is so preeminently true of most practices in the realm of free government, they, too, are specifically adapted to the needs of the people directly involved. They are steeped in their own culture and tradition, and it is sheer folly for outsiders to endeavor to impose their own systems, even in theory. Sir Stafford Cripps once remarked wisely that methods and institutions of government are not simply commodities of international commerce, thus echoing the statement made by Alexis de Tocqueville in his *Democracy in America* in 1831:

> The more I see of this country [the United States] the more I admit myself penetrated with this truth: that there is nothing absolute in the theroretical value of institutions, and that their efficiency depends almost always on the original circumstances and the social conditions of the people to whom they are applied.

---

should receive a statement of *reasons* for any sentences imposed on them. (*Commonwealth v. Riggins,* Pa. 507.)

4

Courts at Home: I—The Lesser Tribunals

A DUAL SYSTEM OF COURTS

As a result of the federal system that prevails in the United States, the national government and fifty state governments all make and enforce law. In effect, this means that there exist, side by side, two major court systems—one could quite accurately even say fifty-one—which are wholly distinct bodies, in the sense that they are created under different basic authorities—the respective national and state constitutions. This is in marked contrast with federal India, for example, whose Constitution of 1950 provides for a single integrated judicial system, with the Supreme Court of India at the apex and subordinate (district) courts at the base. The jurisdiction of America's two systems may, and in some highly significant instances does, regularly "merge" at the bar of the final interpretative authority of the U.S. Supreme Court. However, such a "merger" can come about only if a *substantial* federal question has been validly raised in the proper state court below and, after all remedies at the state level are duly exhausted, successfully brought to the *discretionary* attention of the Supreme Court in all but a handful of cases. It is axiomatic that the path to the highest court in the land is long, expensive, arduous, and difficult—thus it is not traveled frequently. Other than in this appellate process, and possibly in the vexatious and procedurally intricate realm of injunctive relief, the national and state courts in the United States are separate entities. Nonetheless, it should be noted that through its constitutional power to establish "*inferior courts*,"[1] Congress possesses the power to draw a rigid line between the *jurisdiction* of these federal and state courts.

[1] U.S. Constitution, Art. III, Sec. 1, Para. 1. (Italics supplied.)

But it has not seen fit to do so except in certain civil rights areas, notably, some types of racial discrimination,[2] and in a number of fields of relatively narrow jurisdiction, such as matters involving admiralty, bankruptcy, copyright, and patent. "Judicial federalism"—the distribution of power between national and subnational judiciaries—remains a very significant, yet often overlooked, "parity" principle element of American federalism. There is no question that it raises "political, jurisdictional, and administrative stress"[3]— yet, as Chief Justice Burger contended warmly, federal and state courts must not grow too similar on pain of constituting "a possible threat to individual rights and to the quality of the state courts."[4]

THE STATE COURTS

It is in the courts of the fifty states that the great majority of the legal business of the American public begins and ends. The character, jurisdiction, quality, and complexity of these courts vary considerably from state to state in accordance with the myriad considerations of public policy, need, size, and constitutional practice that characterize the heterogeneous component parts of the nation. Every state constitution either establishes a judicial branch for its invariably tripartite government or, either in whole or in part—as is true for the national level under Article III of the Constitution of the United States— authorizes the legislature to provide for a judicial system. Although the terminology and structure among the state courts differ significantly, a discernible structural pattern does exist. The base consists of a system of justices of the peace and trial courts, with the pyramid gradually winding its way upward through a more or less elaborate appellate system, culminating in a supreme court (not invariably termed "Supreme Court," however).

THE JUSTICE OF THE PEACE

With rare exception, the lowest court at the state level—and there are those who would put the noun "court" into quotation marks in this particular connection—is the *Justice of the Peace*, originally a fourteenth-century Anglo-Saxon office. The officeholder is often, and sometimes irreverently, referred to as the "J. P." (standing for "Justice for the Plaintiff," in some eyes). The J. P. is also occasionally styled *squire* and *magistrate* increasingly in many cities (e.g., New York). By no means necessarily a lawyer, this official is usually elected for a two- to six-year term in counties, townships, and towns; but sometimes he or she is appointed for a term of similar length by the executive

---

[2]For example, see certain provisions of the Civil Rights Acts of 1957, 1960, 1964, and 1968 and the Voting Rights Act of 1965, as amended in 1970, 1975, and 1982.

[3]See the perceptive article by John W. Winkle, III, "Dimensions of Federalism," in 406 *The Annals* 67–76 (November 1974).

[4]As quoted in *The Washington Post*, June 11, 1980, p. A12. The Chief Justice was addressing the American Law Institute.

in the cities. The office has an honorable and, indeed, ancient tradition that came to the colonies from England. It was initially designed to aid in the administration of justice in minor matters at the local level. Today the Justice of the Peace, who is usually also a notary public, still performs a modicum of court work, but many of the duties are quasi-legislative, quasi-judicial, and quasi-administrative, including, characteristically, performance of civil marriages. Most of these tasks are undertaken on a fee basis—probably a regrettable practice in view of its close link to meting out justice. The J. P. does, however, retain at least the appearance of a court of first instance in minor civil and criminal matters. In the former, the jurisdiction normally extends only to cases involving less than $300; in the latter, it is limited almost exclusively to misdemeanors.

With notable exceptions, again usually confined to some urban areas—for example, New York City, where the magistrates have legal background, are appointed for ten-year terms of office, and receive about $45,000 annually, an unusually high figure for that office, which normally commands a far lower remuneration—the Justice of the Peace's lack of training and qualifications is exceeded only by a sure-fire penchant for convictions, which have averaged 96 percent in civil cases and 80 percent in criminal cases.[5] A study conducted in 1956 of the minor judiciary of North Carolina, found that not a single J. P. in that state then had a law degree, that 75 percent had never gone to college, and that 40 percent had never even attended high school![6] A similar study for Virginia a decade later showed that, of 411 past and present members of the Association of Justices of the Peace of Virginia, a mere four were lawyers, 71 percent has never gone to college, only five of the 29 percent who did were graduated, and 18 percent were not even high school graduates.[7] In Oregon only nine of seventy J. P.s had law degrees in 1966.[8] Even in such a cosmopolitan city as Philadelphia, only six of its twenty-eight elected magistrates held a law degree in 1968. All this represents an unfortunate state of affairs, for, given suitable attributes of integrity and proper qualification, the Justice of the Peace might well still provide able and inexpensive adjudication and settlement of minor legal problems in the judicial process. But Philadelphia's

---

[5]In 1962 in Pennsylvania, of 63,040 criminal cases handled by the then 4,305 J. P.s, 51,997, or about 83 percent, resulted in convictions; another 6,375, or 10 percent, were bound over for court trial; and 4,668, or about 7 percent, were dismissed (XI Horizons for Modern Governments 5, May 1963, p. 4). For examples of conviction rates from 95 to 99.2 percent in Michigan, Mississippi, and Tennessee counties, see Mitchell Dawson, "The Justice of the Peace Racket," in Robert Morlan and David L. Martin, Capitol Courthouse and City Hall, 6th ed. (Boston: Houghton Mifflin Co., 1981).

[6]Isham Newton, "The Minor Judiciary in North Carolina" (Unpublished Ph.D. thesis, University of Pennsylvania, 1956).

[7]"Justice of the Peace in Virginia: A Neglected Aspect of the Judiciary," 52 Virginia Law Review 151 (January 1966), describing a survey conducted by Weldon Cooper of the Institute of Government of the University of Virginia.

[8]The Christian Science Monitor, May 9, 1967, p. 5.

then Chief Magistrate, Joseph J. Hersch, insisted in a 1961 interview, seconded in 1968 by his successor, John Patrick Walsh, that the job of a magistrate is "more social than legal"; he decried the increasing clamor for a law
degree, stating:

> A law degree doesn't make a magistrate more qualified. Living with people is
> more essential than going to a law library to find our what it's all about. . . . If
> you take Purdon's law books away from them [the lawyers], they're out of
> business.[9]

Yet evidence of questionable judicial qualifications and aberrent on-bench
behavior that have continued to surface with some consistency are not likely
to stop the drive for an end to lay-judge staffing of the office. However, as
noted earlier, in 1976 the U.S. Supreme Court ruled in a Kentucky case that
a non-lawyer[10] jurist may preside even at a criminal trial involving possible
jail sentences, at least when the defendant has an opportunity, through an
appeal, to obtain a second trial before a judge who *is* a lawyer. In the case at
issue, the lay City Judge, C. B. Russell, had not only proved himself incompetent, but outrageously so![11] But, following the U.S. Supreme Court's holding, a number of state supreme courts (e.g., New Hampshire, Washington,
Idaho, and Florida) upheld the utilization of lay judges in sundry cases.[12] On
the other hand, North Carolina enacted a statute *requiring all* judges to have
a law degree.

THE MUNICIPAL COURT

Again because of varying needs, different nomenclature attends the *Municipal Court,* the next higher level of court ordinarily found in the several states.
Some of the most common designations are *Traffic Court, City Court, Night
Court, General District Court,* and *Police Court.* The Municipal Court,
whatever it may be called, is almost always a court of original jurisdiction,
and normally also the first court of record[13] in the judicial hierarchy of the
state. Its jurisdiction is customarily limited to about $500 to $1,000 in civil
cases and to misdemeanors when it does have criminal jurisdiction. The
municipal-level courts provide the parties before them with a fast and inex-

---

[9]Interview with author, December 18, 1961.

[10]*North v. Russell,* 427 U.S. 328. (See ch. 2, p. 23, fn. 1.)

[11]See the description of Allen Ashman and Pat Chapin, "Is the Bell Tolling for Non-Lawyer
Judges?," 59 *Judicature* 9 (April 1976).

[12]Thus, New Hampshire's Supreme Court, following *North,* upheld a similar arrangement for
its state, which allows a *de novo* trial in the Superior Court following a lay-judge court decision below.

[13]Although all courts are, presumably, required to keep records today, the expression "court of
record" is still used to distinguish between courts presided over by members of the minor
judiciary (magistrates of justices of the peace) and other courts of original jurisdiction presided
over by judges.

pensive procedure, and they are generally staffed by judges who possess legal training.[14]

THE COUNTY COURT

The next court in line is the workhorse of the average judiciary, the *County Court*. It is a court of general civil and criminal jurisdiction, as a rule covering three major types of cases and controversies: ordinary civil beyond the limit of the court of jurisdiction just below, criminal except for routine misdemeanors, plus probate and inheritance. As its name implies, the County Court's geographical jurisdiction is limited to the level of that subdivision of the state. If juries are used by a state judiciary at all—and they usually are, although there is still no *state* obligation, except in above-misdemeanor-level *criminal* cases,[15] always to provide juries under the wording and interpretation of the Bill of Rights in the *federal* Constitution—they will be found here. Although Philadelphia, for one, has a separate tribunal called the County Court (with jurisdiction over juveniles, domestic relations cases, certain crimes, and some civil matters), a whole coterie of allied or subsidiary courts is either present at this level or takes the place of the County Court. Among these may well be all or some of the following often self-explanatory, judicial county helpmates: *Common Pleas* (a court to hear and determine civil cases, usually where the amount in controversy is in excess of $5,000); *Oyer and Terminer* (a criminal court with jurisdiction over capital crimes and other felonies—e.g., murder, manslaughter, treason, robbery, rape, kidnapping); *Quarter Sessions* (a predominantly criminal court with jurisdiction over a few technical civil cases and over crimes not tried by Oyer and Terminer, which usually meets four times annually, and sometimes consists of the same personnel as Oyer and Terminer); *Orphans*; *Probate* (for wills, estates, and deeds); *Juvenile* (for youthful offenders); *Domestic Relations*; *Surrogate* (similar to Probate in some counties); *Chancery* (specializing in equity matters); and *Equity*.[16]

---

[14]Frequently found at the Municipal Court level is the *Court of Small Claims*. Its jurisdiction is usually limited to claims in civil disputes ranging from $150 (Texas) to $3,000 (Louisiana). Its speedy and inexpensive procedures are characterized by low court costs (averaging only $35 in 1984), no juries, often no appeals (except for a trial *de novo*), sometimes not even counsel—generally a simplified process that rarely takes more than six weeks to settle a complaint. A careful 1978 study by the National Center of Courts (see p. 175, *infra*) gave high marks to the Courts of Small Claims throughout the states.

[15]See *Duncan v. Lousisana*, 391 U.S. 145 (1968), ch. 3, p. 113 and fn. 40, *supra*. with respect to *criminal* cases.

[16]A highly promising "non-court" system of case-disposition in the judicial process is Philadelphia's (and Pittsburgh's) fascinating system of "compulsory arbitration" of *civil* cases—except equity cases and those involving title to real estate—involving claims of up to $20,000 (exclusive of interest and costs). Actually found administratively at the level of the County Court (Court of Common Pleas) in Philadelphia since its statutory adoption by the state in 1958, it consists of teams of three-member lawyer panels who hear and decide a vast number of cases that would otherwise linger on the court dockets. The lawyers are appointed by the Arbitra-

THE INTERMEDIATE COURT OF APPEALS

Beyond the County Court lies the intermediate court, or courts, of appeals, usually termed *Appellate Division, State Appellate Court, Superior Court,* or *Intermediate Court of Appeals.* The jurisdiction of this tribunal is almost wholly appellate—certain writs being the exception in some states. It receives and adjudges appeals from decisions of the County Court and the Municipal Court, and in rare cases, from others. More often than not its decisions are final, although it is, of course, possible to go up from here to the final level since it is an *intermediate* appellate court. Only about half of the states resort to such an intermediate stage, but all of the larger ones do. Some of these have an elaborate structure, indeed. New York has an intricate system of more than 150 appellate courts at this level, and the appellate structure of California enabled Caryl Whittier Chessman to file fourteen appeals in its system (which he augmented with twenty-eight appeals to the federal courts between 1948 and 1960 in an ultimately unsuccessful battle to escape San Quentin's gas chamber). Happily, in recent years several states have taken considerable strides toward the adoption of more integrated hierarchical judicial pyramids—in large measure owing to the fine example set by New Jersey under its Chief Justice, Arthur T. Vanderbilt, in the 1950s—Virginia's 1976 reorganization being a case in point.[17]

---

tion Commissioners from an alphabetical list of volunteers: no matter how long a hearing takes, the lawyers are each paid a nominal fee of $40.00 per case, the chairperson $70.00. The average cost per "trial" to date has been but $199.50! Not only their time and expertise but also their quarters and any necessary secretarial help are provided by these volunteer members of the bar. The atmosphere of the proceedings is judicial and judicious, but rules of evidence are given liberal construction. Any appeal taken from a panel's decision is heard by a County Court judge *de novo* with or without a jury. But such appeals have averaged only 10 percent per annum, and the successful processing of an average of 8,500 cases annually by these arbitration panels is proof positive of the system's success and common sense. (For details see the *Annual Reports* of the Commissioner of the Compulsory Arbitration Division of the County Court of Philadelphia, 1958ff.) Philadelphia, beset—as are almost all jurisdictions—by clogged dockets, is also moving lesser *criminal* offenses out of the regular court structure. Charges that carry penalties of two years or less imprisonment are handled by *special* judges who settle the cases without a jury. Any defendant dissatisfied with the result may have a formal court trial, but to date fewer than 4 percent have so requested. This has resulted in a marked decrease of untried cases. Cf. Atlanta, Baltimore, and Miami.

An intriguing development is the founding, in 1984, of "Judicate," known as "the National Private Court System." It is one of several concerns created in recent years to offer alternatives to the often costly and overcrowded legal systems. In essence "Judicate" and its prototypes are entirely private organizations that settle cases on the basis of state law, with an ironclad agreement by the parties to the suit—be it of a civil or criminal nature—that they will abide by the decision. These private "tribunals," or arbitration units, are usually headed by former judges, who preside in robes, hear lawyers for both sides, and question witnesses under oath. While state law and procedures are followed, there are no juries, and the public is excluded from the deliberations. Crucial is the advance agreement by all involved to abide by and accept the "judge's" decision. (See the articles by Martin Tolchin in *The New York Times,* May 12, 1985, p. 38, and August 4, 1985, p. E5.)

[17]See Larry C. Berkson, "The Emerging Ideal of Court Unification," 60 *Judicature* 8 March

THE FINAL COURT OF APPEALS

At the apex of each state sytem lies its *Final Court of Appeals,* which receives and adjudicates appeals on major questions emanating from the courts below, normally from the intermediate appellate level. It will not lightly accept cases that are merely concerned with questions of fact; its main purpose is to find the law. Usually this highest state court is known as the Supreme Court, but not always. In New York, for instance—where the "Supreme Court" is a trial court at the lower rung of the state judiciary and its lowest court of record— the high tribunal is called the *Court of Appeals;* in Maine and Massachusetts it is termed the *Supreme Judicial Court.* It has the last word in the state on all constitutional questions. Its decisions are final and authoritative as to state and, by virtue of the unitary structure involved, local law. Although there are some exceptions,[18] the U.S. Supreme Court insists that "all remedies below" must have been exhausted before it will consider a request for review from a party that "lost" in the final court of appeals of a state. Nevertheless, if a federal question of a substantial nature is allegedly involved, and if that question has been properly raised below, a chance, however slim, does exist that the highest court in the land will accept the case for review. In rare instances, the Supreme Court of the United States theoretically must accept a case appealed from the highest court—but, as will be described in the next chapter, this presumed duty is not without significant loopholes.

THE FEDERAL COURTS

When we look at the other prong of the "dual system of courts" at issue, we are confronted with the federal system, which is in many ways considerably less varied and confusing than the understandably heterogeneous state system(s). Certainly the federal courts are infinitely less numerous and, indeed, the hierarchical and jurisdictional arrangements of the three major constitutional courts—demonstrated later in Chart A—are readily comprehensible and clear-cut. Nevertheless, there is more to the structure and organization of the federal system of courts than is immediately apparent. Above all, there

---

1977), pp. 372–82, for a comprehensive, up-to-date analysis of the problem. In 1976 Virginia reorganized its judiciary with commendable economy of levels, to embrace from low to high: (1) General District Courts, one judge sitting, (2) Circuit Courts, the first court-of-record level, again just one judge sitting, and (3) the seven-member Virginia Supreme Court (chosen by the legislature). An intermediate Court of Appeals of ten members (selected in the same manner) was created in 1983 to become operative as of January 1985.

[18] *Fay v. Noia,* 372 U.S. 391 (1963), governing certain types of *habeas corpus* appeals. But cf. *Stone v. Powell.* 428 U.S. 465 (1976) and *Wainright v. Sykes,* 433 U.S. 72 (1977), rejecting at least part of the essence of the *Fay v. Noia* holding, and *Engle v. Isaac,* 456 U.S. 107 (1982), the latter insisting that objections to state trial proceedings be raised at the time of the trial. See also *Rose v. Lundy,* 455 U.S. 509 (1982), generally following the same trend of deference to the state criminal justice process in *habeas corpus* review attempts, and, similarly, *United States v. Frady,* 456 U.S. 152 (1982).

are two major *types* of federal courts from the point of view of their creation and functions: the *constitutional* courts and the *legislative* courts. Briefly, the former are created under Article III, the judiciary article of the Constitution, whereas the latter are created under Article I, its legislative article. Consequently, the safeguards of tenure, salary, and independence that accrue to judges of the constitutional courts by virtue of the explicit and inherent safeguards of Article III are not necessarily present for the judges of the legislative courts. However, because they are created by Congress, nothing prevents that body from clothing the judges of the legislative courts by statute with the same or similar prerogatives as are constitutionally guaranteed to those of the constitutional courts. In fact, even before Congress changed the status of three erstwhile legislative courts—the U.S. Court of Claims,[19] the U.S. Customs Court, and the U.S. Court of Customs and Patent Appeals[20]—to that of constitutional courts in 1953, 1956, and 1958, respectively, it had already granted them the same "good behavior" tenure provisions enjoyed by the judges of the constitutional courts. (As described later, the Court of Claims was reestablished as an Article I—i.e., legislative—court in 1982.) A more significant difference between the two types of courts is that the legislative courts are endowed with functions that are nonjudicial, that is, legislative and administrative, as well as judicial. Moreover, although they are tied into the constitutional appellate structure for certain purposes, they are primarily created to aid in the *administration* of specified congressional statutes. Nonetheless, their judgments are as much *res judicata* (authoritative settled law) as are those of the constitutional courts.

THE FEDERAL LEGISLATIVE COURTS

As its basic power for the establishment of *legislative* courts, Congress utilizes Article I, Section 8, Clause 9, which extends to it "the power to create tribunals inferior to the Supreme Court." The lawmakers then expressly or implicitly join the fundamental power through the "necessary and proper" clause, the famous "implied powers" clause (I-8-18) of the Constitution,[21] with that congressional authority in the particular field in which the court is to perform its main function—for example, the taxing power (I-8-1) for the U.S. Customs Court (now a constitutional court, known as the Court of International Trade) or the power to "make rules for the government and regulation

---

[19]The constitutionality of the change was challenged, but it was upheld by the Supreme Court in a 5:2 decision in 1962. (*Glidden Co. v. Zdanok*, 370 U.S. 530). It held the Court of Claims to be a court properly created under Article III of the federal Constitution, and that therefore its judges may sit on all federal district and appellate courts.

[20]The same verdict as that accorded to the constitutionality of the Court of Claims was applied in a challenge to the U.S. Court of Customs and Patent Appeals, and for the same reasons. (*Lurk v. United States*, 370 U.S. 530.)

[21]See *McCulloch v. Maryland*, 4 Wheaton 315 (1819). The first federal court originated in November 1775 as a Congressional Committee on Appeals and emerged in 1780 as the autonomous Court of Appeals in Cases of Capture.

of the land and naval forces" (I-8-14) for the U.S. Court of Military Appeals. Other legislative courts have existed in the past, of which the defunct (as of 1915) *U.S. Commerce Court,* created under congressional power over interstate and foreign commerce (I-8-3), is an example. But today, if we exempt the now officially transformed and reconstituted U.S. Court of Claims, U.S. Court of Customs, and U.S. Court of Customs and Patent Appeals, there are only three bona fide legislative courts: the U.S. Court of Military Appeals, the U.S. Tax Court, and the several Territorial Courts.

The U.S. Tax Court. Originally part and parcel of the executive branch under the Internal Revenue Service, the U.S. Tax Court was transformed into a legislative court by Congress under its taxing power (I-8-1) in 1969—heeding a long-standing recommendation of the Hoover Commission. It consists of nineteen judges—including its Chief Judge, elected by his or her colleagues for a two-year term in that post—who are appointed by the President with the advice and consent of the Senate for fifteen-year terms of office at $76,024 annually (1985), and who are still removable in the same manner as members of the independent regulatory commissions. Ten other special trial judges hear small tax cases, in which the tax due is less than $5,000. Notwithstanding its change to a legislative tribunal, the U.S. Tax Court is probably still viewable as, in effect, a quasi-administrative agency independent of the Internal Revenue Service rather than a court *qua* court. Its jurisdiction comprises the review of governmentally proposed deficiency assessments (or overpayments) of income, gift, self-employment, and prior excess profit taxes that have been challenged by the taxpayers concerned. The U.S. Commissioner of Internal Revenue is thus necessarily always the defendant party. The Tax Court, which may conduct trials anywhere in the United States—and did so in 100 cities in 1984, for example—is a busy agency, indeed, its workload having risen from 17,000 in 1979 to 42,000 as of early 1985. It is organized into subdivisions, each of which is headed by a judge. Each trial session is conducted by a single judge or by one of the five commissioners who are appointed by the Chief Judge.

The U.S. Court of Military Appeals. This "G.I.'s Supreme Court" was created in 1950 as part of the revised Uniform Code of Military Justice, as amended subsequently (most recently in 1983), which Code had been created earlier largely because of the severe criticism heaped on the military's concepts and practice of justice before, and especially during and after, World War II. That system of justice, steeped in the court-martial tradition, had been predominantly concerned with notions of military efficiency and chain of command, and had lodged all but dictatorial powers in the persons of the various commanding officers. Other than the unlikely "court of last resort" in the person of the President of the United States, all appeals from its judgments were to higher military commanders. The new code altered this arrangement drastically and dramatically by granting accused military personnel new rights before a court-martial and by creating the civilian U.S. Court of Military Appeals (USMCA), which Chief Justice Warren dubbed the "civilian supreme court of the military." *De minimis* this meant that service personnel now had a genuine appellate tribunal to apply and interpret military law (while retaining their right of eventual appeal to the Secretary of the Army, Navy, or Air Force and, of course, the President). In effect, the door was opened for civilian observance and at least a modicum of civilian control, and as the 1950s ripened into the 1960s it became clear that the service man had gained considerably more: the application of most of the Bill of Rights. Thus, in 1965 military personnel were assured that the Sixth Amendment's right to counsel entitled them not only to a lawyer in a military case, but to a *trained* lawyer. In April 1967 the "G.I.'s Supreme Court" ruled 2:1 that the limitations on police interrogation and confessions announced in 1966 by the Supreme Court of the United States in its historic *Miranda v. Arizona* decision[22] must also be applied in military law, because, in the words of the majority opinion written by Judge Homer Ferguson, it announced standards for the enforcement of the Fifth Amendment, which is binding on *all* federal courts—including the U.S.C.M.A.[23] And the Military Justice Act of 1968, authored by Senator Sam J. Ervin (D.-N.C.), contained sweeping safeguard provisions, including for the first time bail and insulation of military legal officers from local command pressure on court-martial decisions. The law permits defendants to demand trial by a military judge alone, instead of a jury of officers, in general courts-martial cases; and, if the defendant objects, forbids a single officer to act as prosecutor, defense counsel, judge, and jury in summary courts-martial.[24] Further liberalizations are contained in the Code's 1983 amendments.

The U.S. Court of Military Appeals is staffed by three judges who receive $80,392 (1985) annually; they must be appointed from civilian life, but may hold a reserve commission in "any armed force." They are nominated for staggered fifteen-year terms of office by the President, subject to confirmation by the Senate, and are eligible for reappointment. The President, who has the power to designate the Chief Judge, may, upon notice and hearing, remove a member of the court only for neglect of duty, malfeasance in office, or because of a mental or physical disability, but for no other cause. No more than two of the judges may be from the same political party. Those who had been appointed through 1984 had all had judicial and/or other public service, not necessarily excluding past military duty.[25] Indeed, the statute requires that all appointees be members of the bar of a federal court or of the highest state court. The USCMA, which determines its own rules of procedure, is authorized to review *at its discretion* decisions of courts-martial involving bad

---

[22] 384 U.S. 436.

[23] *United States v. Tempia*, 16 USCMA 629 (1976), at 635.

[24] P.L. 90-632.

[25] For example, as of the time of his appointment in 1956 by President Eisenhower, Judge Homer Ferguson had been an attorney-at-law, a judge, a U.S. senator, and ambassador to the Philippine Islands; he had seen no military service.

conduct discharges and prison sentences of more than one year, on being petitioned by the accused servicemen, provided that the petition had already
been passed on by a Court of Military Review appointed by the Judge Advocate General. The USCMA *must* review all courts-martial decisions, as
affirmed by a Court of Military Review, in which the death penalty was
decreed below, regardless of the rank of the accused, in all cases certified for
its review by the Judge Advocate General after initial review by a Court of
Military Review (consisting of commissioned officers or civilians, each of
whom must be a member of a bar of a federal court or of the highest state
court), or on "petition of the accused for good cause shown" in cases reviewed
by a Court of Military Review. However, the court's powers of review extend
solely to matters of law, not of fact—although that line, as we shall have occasion to note repeatedly, is sometimes a very fine one. The USCMA decides
about two hundred of the 3,000 cases that now reach it yearly.

An illustration of one type of decision the Court of Military Appeals may
render is the case of one Russo, a member of the Air Force, whom a duly
convened court-martial had found guilty of premeditated murder and sentenced to death. On reviewing the record of the case, the staff judge advocate
recommended approval of the sentence by the convening authority, but concurrently recommended that it be commuted to a dishonorable discharge
from the Air Force, coupled with life imprisonment. When a Court of Military Review received the case, it indicated its belief that the suggested com-
mutation was appropriate. However it held that it was "powerless to effect
the change in penalty . . . [because] Congress had not granted that power to
Boards of Review." Hence, it affirmed both the findings of guilt and the originally imposed sentence. Because this judgment involved a death penalty and
had been approved by a Court of Military Review below, review by the
Court of Military Appeals was mandatory. In a decision again written by
Judge Ferguson, the USCMA denied various other points of appeal advanced
by Russo but held that both a court-martial convening authority and a Court
of Military Review have the authority to lessen the severity of a death penalty. The USCMA then reversed the judgments below and returned the
record of the Russo trial to the Judge Advocate General of the Air Force for
action consistent with its decision.[26] More than half of all cases heard there
to date have won reversals in the Court of Military Appeals. One that did
not was that brought by First Lt. William L. Calley, who thus unsuccessfully
appealed from the twenty-year court-martial sentence meted out for his role
in the slaying of "at least twenty-two" Vietnamese civilians in the 1968 My
Lai massacre.[27] In 1974 that sentence was reduced by the Secretary of the
Army; his conviction was overturned by a federal district court but was rein-
stated 8:5 by the U.S. Court of Appeals for the Fifth Circuit.[28] He then

[26] *United States v. Russo*, 11 USCMA 252, 29 CMR 168 (1960).
[27] *United States v. Calley*, 22 MSCMA 534 (1973).
[28] *United States v. Calley*, 519 F.2d 184 (1975).

appealed to the U.S. Supreme Court which, without comment, refused to review his conviction.[29] He was freed in 1976.

Until the drastic amendments to the Military Justice Act, enacted by Congress in 1983 (see later), there was no direct appeal from the final judgments of the Court of Military Appeals. However, the U.S. Supreme Court, as well as the other federal constitutional courts, were able to exercise jurisdiction to review or "pick up" a case in an *habeas corpus* proceeding, such as claims of illegal detention, illegal procedure, or deprivation of fundamental constitutional rights. In 1953, the Supreme Court did indicate that it had that power in the much-discussed *Burns* case[30] that featured four separate opinions; but a majority of the Justices went on to point out that under the law federal constitutional court review would probably be limited to determinations of military court jurisdiction and considerations of "fair claims of justice." Justices Black and Douglas dissented vigorously, contending that *all* of the rights under the Fifth and Sixth Amendments of the U.S. Constitution should be held to apply to military as well as civilian trials. Regardless of the merits of the dissent, or of speculation on how the highest tribunal would "go" today, the Fifth Amendment issue has become moot in the face of the Court of Military Appeals' aforementioned 1967 confession and interrogation case,[31] in which Judge Ferguson wrote:

> The time is long since past when this court will lend an attentive ear to the argument that members of the armed forces are, by reason of their status, *ipso facto* deprived of all protections of the Bill of Rights.

The 1983 amendments governing Supreme Court review authorize the parties to petition that Court to review decisions of the USCMA through discretionary writs of *certiorari*. Given the concerns about the Supreme Court's overcrowded docket, however, the amendments were drafted in a manner that would limit the number of cases subject to direct review. Thus, cases in which the USCMA has declined to grant a petition for review are excluded, and the Supreme Court has *complete discretion* to refuse to grant petitions for writs of *certiorari*.

Without necessarily guaranteeing the application of *all* aspects of the Bill of rights in *all* circumstances to service personnel, the previously quoted Ferguson opinion, coupled with reforms readily undertaken by the armed forces themselves (led by the Air Force); the broad sweep of the Supreme Court's decisions in the 1960s matters affecting Amendments Four (applied and expanded again in 1982)[32] Five, Six, Seven, and Eight; the impact of the Ervin Military Justice Act of 1968 which, among others, provides protection against searches and seizures even broader than the Fifth Amendment; and the lib-

---

[29] *Calley v. Hoffman,* 425 U.S. 11 (1976).
[30] *Burns v. Wilson,* 346 U.S. 137, at 144, 147.
[31] *United States v. Tempia,* op. cit., at 635.
[32] *United States v. Kalscheuer,* 11 USCMA 373.

eralizing 1983 provisions for Supreme Court review, it seems safe to say that
the serviceman's constitutional protection now comes very close to that of
the American in mufti, that most, although not all (e.g., standing to sue superior officers),[33] lingering differences are being reduced or eradicated. Thus, a
form of random jury selection was sanctioned by the USCMA in 1974,[34] and
in 1980 President Carter approved changes in the Manual for Courts-Martial
that largely extend to the military the same evidentiary rules that are applicable in federal criminal trails.[35] Moreover, the Supreme Court had further
liberalized the rights of servicemen with a 1969 holding that gave the *civil*
courts authority over "off-base, non-service connected" offenses committed
in the United States in peacetime.[36] On the other hand, in 1975 the Court
applied brakes to the extent of ruling 6:3 that a federal District Court could
not halt a pending court-martial proceeding against an Army captain for possession and sale of marijuana simply on the grounds that his offense was not
"service connected" and therefore not under military jurisdiction. In effect,
the Court thus extended to military trials the rule that federal courts will not
interfere in state criminal trials *until* they have been concluded.[37] The Court
also held 5:3 in 1976 that *summary* courts-martial are not "criminal prosecutions" and that hence the Sixth Amendment's guarantee of representation
by counsel does not apply.[38] Yet in *bona fide* military criminal cases now not
only will the defendant have the services of a lawyer free of charge but he or
she will be able to *select* that lawyer, who must then be assigned "if reasonably available"—a provision going considerably beyond provisions governing
assignment of free counsel in civilian proceedings.

The Territorial Courts. Perhaps the several Territorial Courts are in a
slightly different category from the standard legislative courts, but they are
established by Congress under its power to "make all needful rules and regulations respecting the territory or other property belonging to the United
States. . . . " (IV-3-2). Created for, and located in, such diverse areas as Guam
(1900), Puerto Rico (1900), the Virgin Islands (1917), and the Northern Mariana Islands (1978),[39] these courts have jurisdiction that is, necessarily,
extremely varied.[40] Generally—but specifically excluding Puerto Rico, where

---

[33] *Chappell v. Wallace*, 462 U.S. 296 (1983).

[34] *United States v. Yager*, 7 MJ 171 (CMA 1979).

[35] See the informative article by Eugene R. Fidell, "Military Justice: Same Target, But Different
Steps and Tactics," *The New York Times*, May 30, 1980, p. 8E. See also the booklength
study by Harold F. Nufer, *American Service Members' Supreme Court: Impact of the U.S.
Court of Military Appeals on Military Justice* (Washington, D.C.: University Press of America, 1982).

[36] *O'Callahan v. Parker*, 395 U.S. 258.

[37] *Schlesinger v. Councilman*, 420 U.S. 738.

[38] *Middendorf v. Henry*, 425 U.S. 25.

[39] The Canal Zone had such a court from 1912 to 1982.

[40] For statistical purposes *only*, these courts and their judges have been counted throughout
this work as "U.S. District Courts."

they have federal jurisdiction only, Puerto Rico having a set of separate local courts—it includes matters analogous to those in the jurisdiction of state and local courts as well as the federal District Courts. The judges of the Territorial Courts are appointed in the usual manner by the President and confirmed by the Senate; but their term of office, which varies from four to eight years, represents an uncommonly brief period for members of the federal judiciary. Responding to pleas, Congress in 1966 provided for lifetime ("good behavior") tenure for Puerto Rico's federal judges. In creating the various Territorial Courts, Congress has generally followed the wise policy of tailoring them to specific local needs, while retaining the *fundamental*, as distinguished from the *formal*, safeguards of the Constitution of the United States.[41]

EX-LEGISLATIVE "SPECIAL" CONSTITUTIONAL COURTS

Until their conversion by Congress from their status as legislative to that of constitutional courts in the 1950s, the three most important and best known of these federal legislative courts were the Court of Claims (which was redesignated as such in 1982—see later), the Court of Customs (now the Court of International Trade), and the court of Customs and Patent Appeals (in 1982 consolidated with jurisdictional aspects of the old Court of Claims into the constitutional *U.S. Court of Appeals for the Thirteenth Circuit*). Although they are now constitutional courts, they nevertheless still occupy a special niche in the federal court system; they may be regarded as special constitutional courts with special court duties. Despite their new station, they thus still perform, or at least may be viewed as performing, certain quasi-legislative and quasi-administrative functions. However, there is no doubt that public laws by Congress specifically changed their former status, and it must be assumed theoretically that Congress will henceforth not bestow upon these three the kind of nonjudicial powers that have always been considered inappropriate for members of the constitutional courts.

The *U.S. Court of Claims*. Created in 1855, after four earlier bills seeking to establish it had failed, the Court of Claims consisted of seven judges[42] who, aided by fifteen "commissioners," were given the task of adjudicating citizens' suits for damages against the government of the United States. Most, but certainly not all, of these suits represented claims arising out of public contracts. Others involved just compensation for the taking of private property for public use. Some represented suits for injuries caused by negligent or wrongful behavior of a government employee. The court was, in fact, an institutionally arranged denial of the age-old theory that the sovereign cannot be

---

[41] See the series of *Insular Cases* (1901–05), especially *Hawaii v. Manchiki*, 190 U.S. 197 (1903) and *Rasmussen v. United States*, 197 U.S. 516 (1905), for an elaboration of the distinctions between the two terms. See also Justice Cardozo's memorable opinion for the Court in *Palko v. Connecticut*, 302 U.S. 319 (1937).

[42] The first woman to become a judge on the Court of Claims was Charlotte Murphy, in August 1973.

sued. Through the Court of Claims, sometimes referred to as "the keeper of the nation's conscience," the federal government did permit itself to be sued by affected persons—and thus became the only proper defendant—but only within rather narrow limits, such as the contractual disputes already mentioned. Because of the heavy volume of these complaints and the time consumed in their adjudication—it hears the largest number of claims in the world—the existence of the Court of Claims, with its jurisdiction extending to territories and possessions as well as the United States proper, represents a genuine blessing to the general courts, whose dockets might otherwise be clogged considerably more than they already are. Moreover, the Court of Claims as well as the other specialty-area courts proved to be a welcome time-and-trouble-saving device for Congress itself; for there is no question that a good many of the matters now handled and adjudicated by these courts would otherwise have come to the halls of the federal legislature in the form of requests for special or local bills or of amendments to general statutes.

Essentially, the nationwide jurisdiction of the Court of Claims was limited to *original* jurisdiction in all contractual, tax, injury, and other *non-tort*[43] claims against the government of the United States. All suits against that government for money damages are tried here if the amount exceeds $10,000 (except in tax refund claims in which District Courts have concurrent jurisdiction and in tort claims in which the District Courts have exclusive jurisdiction). However, the Federal Tort Claims Act of 1946, as amended in 1959, permits claims of $2,500 or less against the government to be settled by administrative officials in instances involving damages caused by a negligent act or omission by the government or one of its agents. The Court of Claims possessed a very limited power of *concurrent appellate review* with the U.S. Circuit Courts of Appeals in certain tort actions against the federal government decided in the U.S. District Courts. Decisions of the Court of Claims are subject to Supreme Court review in appropriate instances, and some of the latter's more famous cases did in fact "come up" from the Court of Claims, among them *Humphrey's Executor (Rathbun) v. United States*,[44] which arose out of a suit against the United States to recover a sum of money allegedly due the deceased Humphrey. In 1931 William Humphrey had been reappointed a member of the Federal Trade Commission for a second seven-year term; in 1933 President Franklin D. Roosevelt removed him. Contending that he had been illegally removed, Humphrey—and, upon his death, his executor, one Rathbun—sued to recover his salary. The Court of Claims, evidently somewhat uncertain of its grounds, certified some questions regarding the President's removal power to the Supreme Court (see Chart B, p. 188). That tribunal subsequently held unanimously that the Chief Executive had no authority to remove summarily members of independent regulatory

---

[43] A tort is any wrongful act, *other than a breach of contract*, for which an injured party may bring a civil action against the alleged wrongdoer.
[44] 295 U.S. 602 (1935).

commissions clothed with quasi-legislative, quasi-judicial, quasi-executive powers, thereby decisively restricting his power of removal. This decision stands today, reaffirmed and reinforced by a 1958 case that involved President Eisenhower's dismissal of War Claims Commissioner Wiener.[45]

Redesignated in 1982 as a *legislative* court, and restructured, now known as the *U.S. Claims Court*, the new/old tribunal has inherited all of its predecessor U.S. Court of Claims Court's *trial* jurisdiction, except for federal tort claims cases (which will continue to go to the U.S. District Courts and the regional U.S. Courts of Appeals. The new Claims Court has sixteen judges, appointed by the President with Senate advice and consent, who serve for fifteen-year terms and are paid $76,024 per annum (1985).

The U.S. Court of Customs and Patent Appeals. In 1910, utilizing the severally delegated powers to regulate commerce with foreign nations and among the states (I-8-3), to levy taxes (I-8-1), and "to promote the progress of science and useful arts" (I-8-8), Congress established the now defunct Court of Customs and Patent Appeals. Its five members, appointed in the customary manner, served "during good behavior." The functions of the court were primarily threefold: to review (1) decisions of the *Customs Court* regarding duties levied on goods imported into the United States and the classification of such goods, (2) those of the *Patent Office* regarding decisions on patents and trademarks, and (3) on a more legally restricted scale, those of the *Tariff Commission* relating to import practices.

For example, in one case on record the Tariff Commission (redesignated in 1974 as the *U.S. International Trade Commission*) on reviewing an appeal by an importer, held that the attempted importation and sale of certain synthetic sapphires and rubies described in an established U.S. patent represented not only "unfair methods of competition," but also "unfair acts in importation," both of which tended substantially to injure the industry of the patent's owner. The commission consequently recommended proceedings against the importer involved, and the latter appealed to the Court of Customs and Patent Appeals. The court held that the evidence at hand amply supported the findings below that the patent owner's industry was operated efficiently and economically within the United States, that the imported stones fell within the description of the patented articles, that the patent had been properly secured, that the importer's actions had a tendency substantially to injure the aforesaid owner within the meaning of the statute, and that where no holding of invalidity of patent was alleged, it would be regarded as valid.[46]

A rather different instance of the work of the court concerned an action in August 1955 by President Eisenhower, who, pursuant to a recommendation of the Tariff Commission, had set certain new import duty rates on bicycles

---

[45] *Wiener v. United States,* 357 U.S. 349.

[46] *Re Von Clemm,* 229 F.2d 441 (1955). For a more recent case involving the "comtervailing duty," see *Zenith Radio Corp. v. United States,* 562 F.2d 1209 (1978).

manufactured abroad. However, in so doing he had neither acted within the time limit prescribed by law nor really followed the Tariff Commission's advice—instead his announced rates represented a *compromise* with it. The importers filed a suit in the Customs Court that held against the U.S. government. The latter appealed on the legal issue involved to the Court of Customs and Patent Appeals. The court ruled that, by following the course of action described, the President had violated the basic statute, which provides that Tariff Commission recommendations must be either accepted or rejected outright.[47] All parties concerned acquiesced in that 1960 decision. The Court of Customs and Patent Appeals, unlike the Court of Claims, possessed only *appellate* jurisdiction, and was confined to matters of law. Appeals from its decisions could go to the Supreme Court.

The already alluded-to reorganizations of the judiciary in 1982 saw the abolition of the U.S. Court of Customs and Patent Appeals. Its functions, coupled with the trial jurisdiction (see earlier) of the old U.S. Court of Claims were consolidated into a new appellate tribunal, the twelve-member *U.S. Court of Appeals for the Federal Circuit*, the thirteenth such circuit in the federal appellate structure. This new tribunal hears appeals, including patent appeals from all federal district courts, in suits against the government for damages or refunds of federal taxes, appeals from the Court of International Trade, appeals from the Patents and Trademark Office, and a few other agency review cases. Review of its decisions are by writ of *certiorari* to the U.S. Supreme Court.

The U.S. Customs Court. Its nomenclature changed to *U.S. Court of International Trade* in 1980, but still commonly known as the Customs Court, the busy tribunal consists of nine members, who receive $76,084 annually (1985). No more than five may be from the same political party. Growing out of the U.S. Board of General Appraisers, and with roots extending back to pre-Revolutionary days, the modern version of the court was created by Congress in 1926 under its commerce and taxing powers. Sitting in three sections or divisions of three judges each, this special court, which meets in New York headquarters and all other ports of entry in both the continental United States and the territories and insular possessions, has jurisdiction to review the rulings and appraisals on imported goods by collectors of customs. As noted, appeals from its decisions now go to the Court of Appeals for the Federal Circuit although, in rare instances, it is possible to go directly to the Supreme Court.

An illustration of the work of the Court of International Trade—which handles roughly 3,500 cases yearly—is a case involving International Packers, Ltd., in 1959. The firm contended that it should be permitted to deduct from the appraised value of goods imported from Argentina a certain percentage of the purchase price it had to pay to the Argentine authorities on their

---

[47] *United States v. Schmidt Pritchard & Co.*, 47 CCPA 152, C.A.D. 750. For a leading recent work on the U.S. Court of Customs and Patent Appeals, see Lawrence Baum, "The Court of Customs and Patent Appeals," 11 *Law and Society Review* (1977), 823–50.

export. The U.S. government's customs officials rejected this claim. On bringing action for adjudication in the Court of International Trade (then still officially the Customs Court), the plaintiff convinced that body that the 15 percent levy exacted by the Argentine government was a "necessary expense
from the place of shipment to the place of delivery." Accordingly, the court
ruled that the percentage involved was properly allowable as a deduction in
computing the United States value of the merchandise under the Tariff Act.[48]

Review of tariff controversies by the Court of International Trade is not
limited to the statutory provisions of the various congressional enactments.
The right to sue before it applies to practically every legal controversy
between an importer-taxpayer and the federal government. The fact that the
Secretary of the Treasury or some other public official might have handed
down an administrative ruling does not preclude an appeal to this interesting
watchdog court.[49]

THE FEDERAL CONSTITUTIONAL COURTS

We now turn to the three chief *constitutional* courts, the U.S. District
Courts, the U.S. (Circuit) Courts of Appeals, and the U.S. Supreme Court—
but the most important of these, the Supreme Court, will be the sole subject
of the next chapter. All three were created under Article III of the U.S. Constitution. In its key Section 1, that article mentions only "one supreme court,"
but it goes on to point to "such inferior Courts as the Congress may from
time to time ordain and establish." The two lower of these three constitutional courts hence owe their origin to one of the very first acts passed by the
First U.S. Congress, the Judiciary Act of 1789, of which Senator Oliver
Ellsworth, who had been a delegate from Connecticut to the Constitutional
Convention and who would soon be the second Chief Justice of the United
States, was a leading author. The act established and fairly well spelled out
the national system of constitutional courts, which, as has been demonstrated,
received no hierarchical additions until the Court of Claims was designated
a constitutional court in 1953, followed by the Customs Court in 1956 and
the Court of Customs and Patent Appeals in 1958. Constitutional courts and
their judges are clothed with the significant and essential benefits of life (literally, "good behavior") tenure, irreducible salary, prestige, and independence. In the opinion of many an observer of the American scene, including
the author of this book, there are no positions of greater desirability and pres-

---

[48] *International Packers, Ltd. v. United States,* 171 F. Suppl 854.

[49] Another type of special Article III constitutional court, the *Foreign Intelligence Surveillance
Court,* was created in 1978 to regulate the use of electronic surveillance in foreign intelligence
cases. It reviews government requests for such surveillance of suspected spies, terrorists, and,
in exceptional cases, American citizens with information deemed essential to national security. In 1981 the seven U.S. District Court judges—who serve part time on the tribunal—
approved all of the 431 requests it received. (*U.S. News & World Report,* January 1, 1982,
p. 56.)

tige in the entire structure of American government than those occupied by the members of the three leading constitutional courts.

General Jurisdiction. Omitting the jurisdiction (discussed earlier) of the several past and/or present "special" federal courts, constitutional as well as legislative, the general jurisdiction of these three top federal constitutional courts is amazingly well spelled out by Article III, Section 2, of the Constitution. In what is surely one of the most succinctly worded segments of the basic document, the first sentence of the first paragraph of that section makes clear at once that the judicial power of the United States "shall extend to all Cases, in Law and Equity, arising under this Constitution, the Laws of the United States, and Treaties made, or which shall be made under their Authority. . . . " Thus, in addition to announcing the sweeping realm of overall jurisdiction, that wording comes to grips with one of the crucial aspects of the jurisdictional process, namely, that it is limited to "Cases" (and "Controversies," by subsequent phrases in the Section). This signifies the necessity of the presence of a bona fide case or controversy involving litigants of opposing points of view who bring to the federal courts a genuine conflict of interest. In the absence of these fundamental elements, the three constitutional courts have no jurisdiction—which pinpoints the important truth that they neither can nor will accept manufactured or trumped-up cases or controversies devoid of the essential elements described, nor can or will they render *advisory* opinions per se.[50] This collective ban is as applicable to official as it is to private personages, and even extends to the influential government official who might feel the urge of convenience to run to the chambers of the Supreme Court with a fervent plea for an opinion on the legality of an issue, be it pending or dormant. Thus, as early as 1792–93, the Supreme Court declined to advise the government because it deemed the advisory function to be one more properly belonging to the Cabinet—a precedent that has not been violated.[51]

After having disposed of that crucial aspect, the constitutional paragraph at issue goes on to outline the particular type of jurisdiction available to these courts. Generally speaking, these fall into two groups or classifications: (1) those that are based on the character or nature of the *subject matter of the case* and (2) those that are based on the character or nature of the *parties* to the suit. Under group 1 the courts may hear and dispose of cases and controversies in law and equity arising under the following:

(a) The Constitution, a federal law, or a treaty.

(b) Admiralty and maritime laws.

Under the necessarily larger and more complex group 2 the courts may hear and dispose of cases and controversies in law and equity in the following cases:

[50]For a detailed analysis of the "case and controversy" and other "maxims" of the judicial process, see ch.9, *infra.*

[51]See pp. 323–24, *infra.*

(a) The United States is a party to the suit.

(b) One of the fifty states is a party to the suit (*but*, in accordance with the provisions of the Eleventh Amendment, *not* if the suit was commenced or prosecuted *against* a state by either an individual—*any* individual—or a *foreign* country).

(c) They are between citizens of different states.

(d) They affect ambassadors and other duly appointed bona fide representatives of an accredited *foreign* country.

(e) They arise between citizens of the *same* state because of a dispute involving land grants claimed under titles of two or more states.

However, despite this very specific and extensive jurisdiction it does not necessarily follow that the federal courts will inevitably exercise it. There is no barrier in the language of the Constitution against congressional assignment of certain aspects of it (theoretically, probably even all of it!) to the fifty states, either on a concurrent or even exclusive basis—for example, the requirement that the value of a controversy in civil suits between citizens of different states must exceed $10,000 to qualify for original federal jurisdiction. Moreover, Congress may distribute the seven areas of federal jurisdiction among the various federal courts. It has done so and continues to do so in accordance with felt need, more often than not as a result of suggestions by the members of the judicial branch itself.

Overlapping Federal and State Jurisdiction. Whether or not Congress assigns concurrent or even exclusive jurisdiction in *federal* matters to *state* courts, it is axiomatic, of course, that in some areas the *state* courts have *exclusive* jurisdiction. It may be possible to raise a *federal issue* in a matter arising under state law or the state constitution, but the *original* jurisdiction of state courts over their own affairs is exclusive, as is that of the federal courts in their own sphere. However, there are some areas in which *both* court systems have jurisdiction[52]—as in the case of state bank embezzlement involving a federally insured bank—or in that of the theft of an automobile that subsequently crosses state lines—and where, consequently, the guilty party or parties are theoretically subject to prosecution and punishment by *both*. The U.S. Supreme Court has held repeatedly that such dual prosecution and even dual punishment violates neither the Bill-of-Rights ban of double jeopardy nor the "due process of law" clause under the Fourteenth Amendment.[53]

---

[52] The overall problem of jurisdiction remains a major bone of contention: for as long as a defendant can appeal an unfavorable verdict from state to federal courts, and as long as state courts can "distinguish" federal court orders, finality is often both illusory and elusive. See the perceptive book by Judge Carl McGowan of the U.S. Court of Appeals for the District of Columbia, *The Organization of Judicial Power in the United States* (Evanston: Northwestern University Press, 1969).

[53] See *Bartkus v. Illinois*, 359 U.S. 121 (1959) and *Abbate v. United States*, 359 U.S. 187 (1959). But note the replete-with-the-possibility-of change 6:3 *per curiam* ruling by the Court in *Rinaldi v. United States*, 434 U.S. 22 (1977).

As indicated earlier, Congress has purposely granted *exclusive* jurisdiction over certain federal matters to the states. More often than not it has done this to reduce the federal work load in otherwise routine areas, such as the vast realm of diversity of citizenship disputes (i.e., suits between citizens of different states.)[54] It was for these cases that it enacted the requirement of a minimum value of $10,000 as the admission ticket to the federal court of jurisdiction, here the U.S. District Court. Going beyond that proviso, however, Congress has seen fit to grant *concurrent* jurisdiction in diversity of citizenship cases to the states even when the value meets or exceeds $10,000—provided the parties to the suit are willing to go there. As a further aid to the over-docketed federal courts, especially the workhorse District Courts, Congress in the late 1950s enacted a long overdue statute dealing with the citizenship status of corporations for purposes of legal actions. As a result, corporations are now viewed as "citizens" not only of the states in which they have been incorporated—which had been the case heretofore—but also as "citizens" of those states in which they have their principal place of business, regardless of their status of incorporation in them.

On the other hand, Congress has seen fit to vest *exclusive* original jurisdiction in the federal courts in a number of areas: suits between two or more of the fifty states (Supreme Court only), cases involving *foreign* ambassadors and other accredited *foreign* representatives, all bankruptcy proceedings, and all prosecutions for violations of *federal* criminal laws. Chart A demonstrates the overall jurisdiction of the three major federal constitutional courts.

The U.S. District Courts. By all odds the workhorses of the federal judiciary, the ninety-four District Courts, with their 575 active judges[55]—perpetually an insufficient total—comprise the trial courts of the federal system. Established under the Judiciary Act of 1789, their jurisdiction extends to the initial trial of almost all civil and criminal cases arising in the vast realm of federal jurisdiction. It is here that the U.S. government commences, and usually ends, its prosecutions—for example, the government's victorious anti-trust suit against the electrical appliance concerns for illegal price-fixing, which began and terminated in the U.S. District Court for Eastern Pennsylvania in Philadelphia in February 1961, Judge J. Cullen Ganey rendering the famous decision that saw a number of astonished top executives go to jail.[56] It is here also that most suits arising under the federal statutes begin and end (viz., one Paul Abrikossoff's action to recover certain property that had been

---

[54]More than one-quarter of all civil federal cases now fall into that category of litigation! Indeed, they now represent the single highest category of civil cases filed in district courts. They comprise mostly insurance litigation, automobile accident cases, and other personal injury suits.

[55]Nearly half of these judgeships have tended to come from the ranks of one-time prosecutors.

[56]Case not reported in F. Supp. See Reporter's Transcript in Office of the Clerk, U.S. District Court, Eastern District of Pennsylvania. Also see Clerk Gilbert W. Ludwig's letter to author, dated June 8, 1961.

Chart A. The Jurisdiction of the Three Major Federal Constitutional Courts of the United States (1985)

Courts Created Under Article III of the Federal Constitution[a]

1 Supreme Court of the United States, nine judges, has:
Original jurisdiction in actions or controversies:
   1. Between the United States and a state.[b]
   2. Between two or more states.
   3. Involving *foreign* ambassadors, other *foreign* public ministers, and *foreign* consuls or their "domestics or domestic servants, not inconsistent with the law of nations."[b]
   4. *Commenced by a state against* citizens of another state or aliens, or *against* a foreign country.[b] (N.B.: If these actions are *commenced by the citizen or alien against a* state, or by a foreign country *against* a state, the suit must *begin in* state court, according to the provisions of Amendment XI.)
Appellate jurisdiction from:
   1. All lower federal *constitutional* courts; most, but not all, federal *legislative* courts, and the *territorial* courts.
   2. The highest state courts having jurisdiction, when a "substantial federal question" is involved.

13 U.S. (Circuit) Courts of Appeals, 168 judges,[c] have:
Appellate jurisdiction *only* from:
   1. U.S. District Courts.
   2. U.S. Territorial Courts, the U.S. Tax Court, the U.S. Claims Court, and some District of Columbia Courts.
   3. The U.S. Court of International Trade.
   4. The U.S. Independent Regulatory Commissions.
   5. Certain federal administrative agencies and departments (for review, but also for *enforcement* of certain of their actions and orders).

94 U.S. District Courts,[d] 576 judges,[e] have:
Original jurisdiction *only*[f] over:
   1. All crimes against the United States.
   2. All civil actions arising under the Constitution, laws, or treaties of the United States, wherein the matter in controversy exceeds $10,000 (unless the U.S. Supreme Court has jurisdiction as outlined previously).
   3. Cases involving citizens of different states or citizens and aliens, provided the value of the controversy is in excess of $10,000.[b]
   4. Admiralty, maritime, and prize cases.
   5. Review and *enforcement* of orders and actions of certain federal administrative agencies and departments.[b]
   6. All such other cases as Congress may validly prescribe by law.[g]

---

[a]For the purposes of this chart, the "special" constitutional courts (discussed on pp. 155–59) are omitted.

[b]*Jurisdiction not exclusive*—that is, while according to Article III of the Constitution cases are to originate here, legal arrangements may be made to have them handled by a different level court. For example, Congress has the power to give the federal District Courts *concurrent original jurisdiction* over cases affecting foreign ambassadors and *some* cases in which a state is a party to the suit. See *United States v. Ravara*, 2 Dallas 297 (1793); *Bors v. Preston*, 111 U.S. 252 (1884); and *Ames v. Kansas*, 111 U.S. 449 (1884). And in late 1964 the Supreme Court

disposed of by the Alien Property Custodian under the Trading with the Enemy Act).[57] And it is here that the trial (petit) juries sit in the federal system; they do so in roughly half of all cases commenced at that level. The District Courts have *original* jurisdiction only. However, when necessary, they do have the obligation to *enforce* as well as review actions and orders of certain federal administration agencies and departments; certain actions tried before U.S. magistrates, formerly known as commissioners (see later), may be reviewed by them; and certain other classes of cases may be *removed* to them from the state courts under certain specific statutory authorization. Hence, in the vast majority of instances, the decisions of the District Courts are, in effect, final. And there is a veritable flood of business: they now decide upwards of 600,000 cases annually. In 1983–84, a total of 642,605 proceedings were *commenced* in the District Courts.[58] No wonder delays are common here, as well as elsewhere in the understaffed, overly litigous American judicial system.[59] At the level of the *federal* courts the time interval between the point when a case was "at issue" and the trial itself ranged from 4.1 months to 39.1 months in 1959; from 3.9 to 48.7 months in 1965–66; and from 1.0 months to 52.0 months in 1982–83. In the *state* courts, it varied from 1.0 months to 52.9 months in 1959; from 4.3 to 69.5 months in 1965–66; and then from 0.6 months to 59.1 months in 1982–83.[60] A poignant and pertinent illus-

---

[57] *Abrikossoff v. Brownell*, 145 F. Supp. 18 (1956).

[58] To be precise: 261,485 civil, 36,845 criminal, and 344,275 bankruptcy cases—representing an overall increase of about 50 percent in ten years (*Annual Reports* of the U.S. District Courts). (The case backlog doubled between 1960 and 1975 and again since.)

[59] In 1976 alone a total of 5,320 civil rights suits were brought against employers—a 1500 percent increase since 1970! (*The New York Times*, May 22, 1977, Section 4, p. E7.) *Civil* suits filed between 1960 and 1980 tripled!

[60] See the symposium, "Lagging Justice," 328 *The Annals of the American Academy of Political and Social Science* (March 1960); the series by Howard James in *The Christian Science Monitor*, "Crisis in the Courts," April–July 1967, and James's book, *Crisis in the Courts*, rev. ed. (New York: David McKay Co., 1971); the statistics cited by Victor G. Rosenblum in *The 50 States and Their Local Governments*, ed. by James W. Fesler (New York: Alfred A. Knopf, 1967), pp. 434–35; and the *Annual Reports* of the Administrative Office of the U.S. Courts, 1972ff. See also the special issues of *Judicature* 65–66 (August 1981 and June–July

---

declined to review a Ninth Circuit Court decision that U.S. District Courts have jurisdiction over suits *by the United States against a state.* (*California v. United States*, 379 U.S. 817.)

[c] Plus (as of 1985) "senior" (retired appeals judges, voluntarily serving part or even full time. Not counted are the 232 bankruptcy judges who are distributed over the 94 districts.)

[d] Includes the district courts for Guam, the Virgin Islands, and the Northern Mariana Islands, all of which have local as well as federal jurisdiction.

[e] Plus about 110 "senior" (retired) district judges, voluntarily serving part or even full time.

[f] A case can be made for the contention that it also has a measure of *appellate* jurisdiction, involving certain actions tried before especially designated U.S. magistrates.

[g] As Congress did, for example, when in 1984 it restructured the bankrupt courts by assigning to the U.S. District Courts jurisdiction over Title 11 of the U.S. Code.

tration: a ten-year-old girl, Nancy Verona, was hit by a car while riding her bike. When her case at last came to trial, she was a young mother, aged nineteen, who brought her baby to the court with her![61]

The Speedy Trial Act of 1974, enacted by Congress to be effective as of July 1, 1975, set up a schedule to be implemented over a four-year period on the federal level (with sundry states expected, and likely, to adopt similar measures). It provided for time limits, ultimately reaching 100 days (July 1, 1979), within which *criminal* charges must either be brought to trail or dismissed. Indeed, as of November 1980, 96 percent of District Court criminal cases reached trial within those 100 days. Not astonishingly, this legislation found itself quickly in a number of procedural as well as interpretative difficulties. It came under heavy constitutional challenge, chiefly on separation of powers grounds, and was held unconstitutional by U.S. District Court Judge Joseph Young in *United States v. Howard*, 440 F. Supp. 1106 (1977). His decision was promptly appealed by the government. No final disposition having been rendered as of fall 1979, Congress postponed the law until July 1, 1980. The courts subsequently managed to skirt the constitutional issue, and the statute has proved to be generally successful.

Each of the fifty states of the Union, the District of Columbia, Puerto Rico, Guam, the Canal Zone, the Northern Mariana Islands, and the Virgin Islands contains at least one federal district with a District Court and a District Court judge, who receives $76,024 (1985) annually. There is no cutting across state lines, but in many instances the large number of cases to be adjudicated compels a subdivision of labor within a particular district. Almost all districts today (1985) have two or more judges, although there are still a few districts with only one. The Southern District of New York (New York County, i.e., Manhattan; Bronx County; and the adjacent suburban counties to the north),[62] with its high proportion of complex commercial litigation, had the 1984 maximum—twenty-seven. Almost half of all litigation occurs in the twelve District Courts that are located in the larger metropolitan areas. The Chief Justice of the United States (the Chief Justice of the Supreme Court) has the authority to transfer district judges temporarily from their home circuit to a more congested one, but only with their consent. These judges are then known as "visiting" or "designated" judges. It was as Visiting Judge for the Eastern District of Arkansas that U.S. District Judge Ronald N. Davies, whose home district was North Dakota, issued the now famous injunction[63] against Governor Orval E. Faubus and other state officials of Arkansas in September 1957, after they had actively interfered with an earlier court order

---

1982), "Court Delay: Diagnosing the Problem, Testing New Treatments," and "U.S. Courts Being Swamped ..." *The New York Times*, July 9, 1984, p. Al.

[61] Cited by Louis Banks, "The Crisis in the Courts," 64 *Fortune Magazine* 86 (December 1961) at 88.

[62] Columbia, Dutchess, Greene, Orange, Putnam, Rockland, Sullivan, Ulster, and Westchester.

[63] *United States v. Faubus*, 156 F. Supp. 220 (1957).

upholding the Little Rock School Board's desegregation plan.[64] Judge Davies had been temporarily transferred to help deal with a mounting backlog of cases. To cite one other procedural example: in order to remedy a staggering backlog of civil jury cases in the U.S. District Court for the Southern District of New York, Chief Justice Warren, acting on the urging of Chief Judge Sidney Sugarman of that court in 1968, to help clear the accumulation, assigned ten district judges from other parts of the country (one each from Oregon, California, Iowa, Kansas, Utah, Tennessee, New Mexico, and the Eastern District of New York, and two from Connecticut). The team did just that within two months. In 1978, however, the Justice Department's Office for Improvement in the Administration of Justice proposed new limits in such assignments, confining the latter to instances covering a regular judge's absence from his or her home circuit because of "illness, disability, or official business, or a vacancy exists . . . ," but not merely because of a heavy work load.

No matter how many judges may be permanently or temporarily assigned to a federal district, it is customary for a lone District Court judge, sitting with a jury—unless that institution has been validly waived—to preside over a trial in the roughly 400 localities where they now are held in the United States. However, in some instances of particular importance, Congress has statutorily provided for adjudication by *three-judge District Courts*. They customarily consist of two district judges and one circuit judge, the Judicial Code providing that at least one judge must be from the circuit—the next higher echelon in the judicial system. As a matter of practice, the Chief Judge of the Circuit Court involved, rarely, if ever, assigns more than that absolute minimum. Suits required to be heard by these three-judge District Courts— from which lies direct appeal to the Supreme Court of the United States as a matter of right in appropriate cases—are usually those seeking to restrain by an *injunction*, on grounds of unconstitutionality, the enforcement, operation, or execution of both federal and state statutes and orders of state administrative agencies dealing with apportionment or reapportionment of legislative districts and, similarly, in instances in which such a court is required by specific act of Congress, for example, the Civil Rights Act of 1964 and the Voting Rights Act of 1965, as amended, and the Federal Election Campaign Act of 1974.

Considerable sentiment exists for the discontinuation of the use of these three-judge tribunals—more than tripling in the number of cases handled by them during the past decade—for they have unquestionably added to the judicial workload, in general, and to Supreme Court review, in particular. Chief Justice Burger has been a leading and insistent spokesman for their abolition,[65] and, though not abolishing the three-judge tribunals, Congress, in

---

[64] *Aaron v. Cooper,* 143 F. Supp. 855 (1956).
[65] See the "Freund Report," published by the Federal Judicial Center, January 1973; *The New*

1976, restricted the type of cases in which they may henceforth be impaneled,[66] resulting in a drop of almost 50 percent in their caseload over a two-year period.

The busy judges of the District Courts are provided with a number of assistants to carry on their tasks, all of whom are appointed by the judges themselves (some were mentioned in chapter 3). Among them are the U.S. magistrates, law clerks, bailiffs, court reporters, stenographers, clerks, probation officers, and, as of 1971, professional administrators to relieve the chief judges of management duties at the appellate level as well as here at the trial level. These positions are more or less self-explanatory, except for that of the important, parajudicial *U.S. Magistrate*, who is not only in charge of some of the preliminary steps involved in the pre-trial process but has been granted considerably enhanced powers. Thus, he or she may issue arrest warrants, hear evidence to determine whether or not to hold an accused person for grand jury action and, if so, set the bail, and assume jurisdiction in certain minor federal offenses when the defendant waives the right to confront a federal judge and jury. Moreover, a magistrate is active in pre-trial and discovery proceedings, considers preliminary petitions, and appoints legal counsel for indigent defendants under the Criminal Justice Act of 1964.[67] As a result of the Federal Magistrates Act of 1979, full-time magistrates can now try *any* civil case, with the consent of all parties, as well as all misdemeanors, again such consent being granted, and the cases may be heard with or without a jury. As of 1979, too, appeals from a magistrate's judgements may, in a civil case, be taken directly to the U.S. Court of Appeals. In the instance of magistrate-conducted *criminal* misdemeanor trials, defendants must explicitly waive their right to a trial by a U.S. District Court judge, however. The 1979 statute details requirements for merit appointments: candidates are appointed by District Court judges for eight- and four-year terms of office, and they must have been members of the bar for at least five years prior to their selection. In 1982 there were about 500 authorized positions for magistrates plus a staff of 400. Salaries are geared to work load—up to about $50,000 annually—but gone are the days when magistrates (then called commissioners) were paid out of court fees.[68] In 1983–84 the magistrates handled 376,168

York Times, August 15, 1972, p. 1; and *U.S. News and World Report*, August 21, 1972, p. 41, for illustrative commentary. (See also Winkel, op. cit.)

[66] See p. 188, *infra* for specifics.

[67] In 1976 the Supreme Court specifically, and unanimously, upheld the power of U.S. magistrates to review preliminary law suits involving Social Security benefits and have them prepare proposed decisions and finding for U.S. District Court judges. (*Mathews v. Weber*, 423 U.S. 261.)

[68] For an excellent article on recent developments in this little-known office, see Steven Pruro, Roger L. Goldman, and Alice Padawer-Singer's authoritative article in 64 *Judicature* 10 (May 1981).

items of judicial business, including 106,138 pre-trial hearings in criminal cases.[69] Their 1979 statute-strengthened powers and duties[70] were specifically upheld by the U.S. Supreme Court, largely because a *judge* retains authority to accept, reject, or modify any rulings by a magistrate.[71]

The two most significant officers at the district level are the *U.S. Marshal* and the *U.S. Attorney*. Appointed for each of the districts by the President with the advice and consent of the Senate—with the senators of the President's political party the prime source of recommendation—the U.S. Attorney functions under the authority of the Attorney General (rather than that of the district judge). The "A.G." also appoints a number of Assistant U.S. Attorneys, often in conjunction with the patronage wishes of influential members of his political party. The U.S. Marshal,[72] appointed in the same manner as the U.S. Attorney, makes arrests, guards and transports prisoners, determines where a prisoner is to serve his sentence, disburses federal judicial funds, serves court orders, writs, and processes,[73] guards and transports all federal court documents, from jury notices to Supreme Court orders, ascertains the security of witnesses, generally maintains the decorum of the courtroom of the District Court of the United States, and, when called upon, aids in riot control. In 1984 there were ninety-four such marshals and 1600 deputy and chief deputy marshals.[74]

The U.S. (Circuit) Courts of Appeals. Initially established in 1891 as a group of nine, and standing immediately above the U.S. District Courts in the federal constitutional court hierarchy, are the thirteen U.S. (Circuit) Courts of Appeals, twelve of these on geographic lines. The thirteenth (described briefly earlier)[75] the 1982-created U.S. Court of Appeals for the Federal Circuit, does not have a specific regional/geographic base, but "counts" as a full-fledged circuit court of appeals. They are all essentially what their name implies: *appellate* courts only. They do, however, have a statutory obligation to *enforce*, when necessary, as well as review actions of a host of federal executive agencies that are clothed with quasi-judicial functions. Among these, to cite but a few, are certain rulings of the National Labor Relations Board, wage orders of the Administration of Wage and Hour

[69] *Annual Report,* Administrative Office of the United States Courts, 1984.

[70] P.L. 96-82, 93 Stat. 643.

[71] *United States v. Raddox,* 447 U.S. 667 (1980).

[72] The origin of the office traces back to medieval England, where the Old French word *mareshal* (groom) came to mean a sort of royal sheriff in charge of procuring witnesses for the monarch.

[73] This is a task that frequently takes considerable ingenuity. For example, to serve a desegregation injunction on the evasive and defiant Alabama Governor George Wallace in 1963, one deputy marshal stowed away in the men's room aboard the governor's plane!

[74] See *Annual Report* of the U.S. District Courts. Appointees must have attained a qualifying grade on the Treasury Enforcement Examination and have at least five years of investigative experience.

[75] See p. 155, *supra.*

Division of the Department of Labor, and orders under antitrust or unfair practice laws of the Interstate Commerce Commission, the Federal Communications Commission, the Civil Aeronautics Board, and the Board of Governors of the Federal Reserve System. But even if one were to classify aspects of the review and enforcement of the activities of these quasi-judicial units of the federal government as original jurisdiction—and they are that only by stretching the concept considerably—the vast majority of the work of the U.S. Courts of Appeals is clearly appellate. It is, in the words of an astute commentator, a "mini Supreme Court in the vast majority of cases,"[76] for, in effect, it is at once the first and last stop for appeals from below in all instances but those that go on up to the U.S. Supreme Court and those few that are permitted to bypass it from below en route to the Supreme Court. Other than the appeals from the highest state courts of record, which go directly to the Supreme Court without touching the other federal courts, the Circuit Courts of Appeals may be validly bypassed only if (1) direct appeal lies from a decision by a three-judge District Court, as explained before, (2) there is a direct appeal statutorily authorized to the Supreme Court from a limited number of ordinary District Court cases, such as a case in which a federal statute has been held unconstitutional by a District Court and the United States is a party to the suit, and (3) it is shown that a case is of "such imperative public importance as to justify the deviation from normal appellate process and require immediate settlement [in the Supreme Court]," as was true in such momentous controversies as those represented by the 1952 *Steel Seizure* and 1974 *Nixon Tapes* Cases.[77]

But in all other instances, both civil and criminal, the Circuit Court of Appeals is the natural appellate tribunal for the approximately 32,000 cases—an increase of 1600 percent between 1942 and 1982 (and 1200 percent between 1962 and 1982)—that now come up to it annually from the U.S. District Courts in the fifty states, the District of Columbia, and the territories, and from the many independent regulatory commissions, agencies, and cabinet departments that are endowed with quasi-judicial powers and functions. In effect, it *finally* decides approximately 85 percent of all federal cases. For example, the Court of Appeals for the District of Columbia, sometimes referred to as the Eleventh Circuit, held, on reviewing the denial of one Shachtman's passport application by the Department of State, that the latter had violated the due process of law clause of the Fifth Amendment in the circumstances at issue.[78] The Department of State subsequently complied

[76]J. Woodford Howard, Jr., *Courts of Appeals in the Federal Judicial System* (Princeton, N.J.: Princeton University Press, 1981), p. 58.

[77]*Youngstown Sheet and Tube Co. v. Sawyer*, 343 U.S. 579 and *United States v. Nixon*, 417 U.S. 683, respectively.

[78]*Shachtman v. Dulles*, 225 F. 2d 938 (1955).

with the court's mandate. Illustrations of cases arising from a decision of a District Court rather than that of an administrative agency or department are the (unsuccessful) appeal to the U.S. Court of Appeals for the Second Circuit by Alger Hiss for reversal of his conviction on perjury charges in connection with the theft of U.S. government documents and the (equally unsuccessful) appeal by President Nixon to the Court of Appeals for the District of Columbia from Judge John J. Sirica's order to turn nine of the Watergate tapes over to him for scrutiny.[79]

Although officially stripped of the term *circuit* in 1948, the courts on this important level in the federal judicial process—they were created under the landmark Judiciary Act of 1891—are still generally referred to as Circuit Courts. There are eleven such *numbered* circuits in the United States plus an unnumbered twelfth one, known as the *Court of Appeals for the District of Columbia*,[80] and the thirteenth, the *Court of Appeals for the Federal Circuit*, a 1982-created consolidation of parts of the jurisdiction of the old Court of Claims and the Court of Customs and Patent Appeals:

First Circuit:	Maine, Massachusetts, New Hampshire, Rhode Island, Puerto Rico
Second Circuit:[81]	Connecticut, New York, Vermont
Third Circuit:	Delaware, New Jersey, Pennsylvania, Virgin Islands
Fourth Circuit:	Maryland, North Carolina, South Carolina, Virginia, West Virginia
Fifth Circuit:	Louisiana, Mississippi, Texas
Sixth Circuit:	Kentucky, Michigan, Ohio, Tennessee
Seventh Circuit:	Illinois, Indiana, Wisconsin
Eighth Circuit:	Arkansas, Iowa, Minnesota, Missouri, Nebraska North Dakota, South Dakota
Ninth Circuit:	Arizona, California, Idaho, Montana, Nevada, Oregon, Washington, Hawaii, Alaska, Guam, Northern Mariana Islands
Tenth Circuit:	Colorado, Kansas, New Mexico, Utah, Oklahoma, Wyoming
Eleventh Circuit:	Alabama, Florida, Georgia

---

[79] *United States v. Hiss*, 185 F. 2d 822 (1950) and *Nixon v. Sirica*, 487 F. 2d 700 (1973), respectively.

[80] In 1933 the U.S. Supreme Court ruled that both the U.S. District Court for the District of Columbia *and* the U.S. Court of Appeals for the District of Columbia are at the same time "constitutional" and "legislative" courts. (*O'Donoghue v. United States*, 289 U.S. 516.) In 1930 it had held that "it is recognized that the courts of the District of Columbia are not created under the judiciary article of the Constitution but are legislative courts. . . . " (*Federal Radio Commission v. General Electric Company*, 281 U.S. 464, at 468.) But, of course, *O'Donoghue* governs today. However, the Court ruled unanimously in 1977 that these federal courts have no jurisdictional role in purely local criminal cases—that the judges of the home-ruled District of Columbia court structure have the competence to decide *all*, even constitutional problem, cases (*Swain v. Pressley,430 U.S. 372.*)

[81] Styled by the then President-elect of the American Bar Association, Lawrence E. Walsh, as

Each of these circuits is theoretically headed by one of the nine justices of the U.S. Supreme Court. By tradition they are said to be "riding circuit"—the junior Justices usually, but not necessarily, being assigned the "extra" circuits.[82] Indeed, this is what the Justices used to do, literally—and a frightful physical burden it was![83]—at the beginning of America's nationhood, but the practice fell into disuse approximately three-quarters of a century later with the enactment of the Judiciary Acts of 1869 and 1891. Today, lack of time prevents them from more than nominal participation, although they continue to be faithfully and formally "assigned" at the beginning of each term. And, of course, they do retain the power to act on certain pleas that arise from court actions, particularly dispositive orders, in "their" circuits. A typical illustration is Justice White's refusal to set aside an Oklahoma District Court decision that had nullified the state's May 1964 primary and had ordered a new primary for that September on a "one-man, one-vote" basis. White, as the Justice in administrative charge of the Tenth Circuit, of which Oklahoma is a part, simply wrote "stay denied," and "that," in Justice Holmes's language, "was that!" Supreme Court Justices are also empowered to preside over U.S. District Court proceedings but seldom do so (a rare exception being Justice Rehnquist's trial of *Heislup v. Town of Colonial Branch* on June 18–19, 1984).[84]

The thirteen Circuit Courts of Appeals comprise a total of 168 (1985) judges—salaried at $80,392 (1985) annually—who, except for the judges of the District of Columbia, must be residents of the assigned circuit during the time they serve and even thereafter, because, though they may have retired, they are still subject to assignments by the Chief Justice of the United States. Each of the Circuit Courts has a Chief Judge, who is customarily the judge with the longest service and who may serve for a total of seven years. (No one is eligible for the post if over the age of sixty-four at the time his or her seniority-based turn comes.) Upon reaching the voluntary retirement age of seventy, the incumbent Chief Judge retains powers as a full-fledged member of the court—assuming the judge neither chooses to retire nor has accumulated sufficient time to do so on full salary—but ceases to be its head. This arrangement also applies in the District Courts that have two or more judges but *not* in the Supreme Court.

"for practical purposes, the court of last resort for the most important commercial and financial problems of one of the great financial centers of the world." (*The New York Times*, April 27, 1975, sec. 4, p. 5.)

[82] In 1977–78 they were instead assigned to the two most senior members of the Court, Chief Justice Burger and ranking Associate Justice Brennan.

[83] Justice Iredell commented that he felt like a "travelling postboy" in the 1790s, as he rode over 4,000 miles to cover the Southern Circuit. (Quoted in John P. Frank's *The Marble Palace* [New York: Alfred A. Knopf, 1958], p. 10).

[84] 84-340R. Justice Rehnquist served at the invitation of U.S. District Court Judge D. Dortch Warriner of the Eastern District of Virginia, trying the case in Richmond.

Figure 2. The Thirteen Federal Judicial Circuits (*See* 28 U.S.C.A. § 41)

Each court consists of between four and twenty-six judges, depending on the amount of work in the circuit.[85] Usually three judges sit to decide cases; a quorum is two. In rare instances the entire membership of circuits sits *en banc*. Proceedings before the Courts of Appeals are conducted on the basis of the record established below—that is, before the U.S. District Courts or one of the administrative agencies. The most important cases are selected for rare oral argument—for example, the constitutionality of the Federal Election Campaign Act of 1974[86]—while the lesser ones, who are the majority, are decided on the basis of submitted documents (except in the Second Circuit, which has a history of hearing oral argument in *all* cases). At least in theory, *new* evidence may not be presented at the bar of this appellate tribunal, just as it may not be introduced in the appellate cases reaching the highest ranking court in America's judicial hierarchy, the Supreme Court of the United States. The Courts of Appeals' decisions are subject to review on appeal to the U.S. Supreme Court. More often than not the tendency is to affirm the intermediate appellate tribunal, but by no means inevitably. Thus, in the 1983–84 term, by May 1984 the Supreme Court had issued full opinions in fifteen of the Ninth Circuit's decisions, and in all fifteen had totally or substantially reversed that Court's judgments. It might be noted that sixteen of the then twenty-three active Ninth Circuit Court judges were appointed by President Carter.[87]

ADMINISTERING THE FEDERAL JUDICIARY

Before turning to a discussion of the Supreme Court, something should be said about the administration of the federal judicial system. While considerable thought may well have been given for many years to the establishment of a centralized administrative structure for these courts, it was actually not until shortly prior to the second quarter of this century that the judicial and legislative branches, particularly the former, recognized the urgency of the problem to the extent of doing something about it—other than to declaim and exhort on what had become an increasingly deplorable state of administrative anarchy. Fortunately, Congress yielded to mounting pressure by bar, bench, and interested laypersons, and the establishment of the Judicial Conference of the United States and the Administrative Office of the U.S. Courts in 1922 and 1939, respectively, effected considerable involvement.

The Judicial Conference of the United States. The 1922 statute requires "the Chief Justice . . . to submit to Congress an annual report of the proceedings of the Judicial Conference and its recommendation for legislation." This is done faithfully and to considerable advantage by the "Chief," who is head

---

[85] In 1985 the Ninth had twenty-eight, the Fifth had sixteen, and the Eleventh had twelve.
[86] *Buckley v. Valeo*, 519 F.2d 821 (1975).
[87] *The Washington Post*, May 23, 1984, p. A19.

of that body. In addition to him, it consists (1985) of the chief judge of each of the thirteen federal judicial circuits, thirteen district court judges, one from each of these circuits except the thirteenth (the U.S. Court of Appeals for the Federal Circuit)—chosen for a term of three years by the judges of the Circuit at its annual judicial Conference and two bankruptcy judges. The Judicial Conference meets at least twice a year at the Supreme Court in absolute secrecy for the legislatively established purpose of making a "comprehensive survey of the conditions of business in the courts of the United States and [of preparing] plans for assignment of judges to or from circuits or districts where necessary." It is also required to submit suggestions to the various courts "in the interest of uniformity and expedition of business." This vital body of prestigious and influential experts has made an excellent job of keeping abreast of the needs of an efficient judiciary and has done its utmost—in conjunction with the Administrative Office of the U.S. Courts, for which it establishes policy—to realize these needs. In that capacity, to cite an example of its administrative and personnel role, it sent out the following admonition to all federal judges: "No justice or judge of the United States shall serve in the capacity of officer or director or employee of any corporation organized for profit."[88] Repeatedly, it has called on all federal trial courts to adopt rules limiting what lawyers may say publicly about criminal cases.[89]

Although not all of the Judicial Conference's policy recommendations have either been adopted, or adopted speedily, by Congress—this applies especially to those involving the creation of new judgeships—the legislative branch has displayed considerable regard for the wisdom of the Judicial Conference and its committee. Thus, in 1958 Congress passed a Conference-recommended law authorizing the Judicial Conference to set up committees of judges, lawyers, and law professors to study the rules of procedure in the federal courts. On receiving such committees' recommendations, the Judicial Conference passes judgment on them and then sends them on to the Supreme Court for its action. Adopted changes become effective in ninety days unless they are specifically disapproved by Congress during that time. Congress also acquiesced in the Conference's request for federally appropriated funds for the defense of the indigents in federal courts, a move that resulted in the Criminal Justice Act of 1964,[90] and in the late 1970s it yielded to repeated calls for an increase in judicial salaries as well as in the number of sitting federal judges.

The Administrative Office of the U.S. Courts. This judicial housekeeping agency (and veritable gold mine of statistics) is the executive arm of the Judicial Conference. It is headed by the director and the deputy director, both of

---

[88] As quoted in its *Annual Report* for 1978.

[89] *The Philadelphia Evening Bulletin*, September 20, 1968, p. 12ff.

[90] See the article on the subject and related issues by Anthony Lewis, *The New York Times*, October 14, 1964.

whom are appointed by the Chief Justice of the Supreme Court.[91] The director possesses no administrative jurisdiction vis-à-vis the Supreme Court, but the director and the director's subordinates are crucially involved in the administrative business of the subordinate federal courts. (Indeed, an increasing number of the fifty states have begun to establish similar bodies—e.g., California, Iowa, New York, and Pennsylvania.) Among these tasks of the now more than 500-staffers agency are the compilation of the suggested budgets, determination of personnel needs, examination of the dockets, auditing of accounts, procurement and allocation of supplies, preparation of all vital statistics in connection with the business of the courts (its *Annual Report* has become essential for all those interested in the judicial process), and all such other duties as may be assigned to the director and his staff by either the Supreme Court or the Judicial Conference—both of which are headed by the Chief Justice of the United States. The Administrative Office of the U.S. Court has become an essential arm of the judicial system; it has been widely and justly acclaimed; it has, in effect, become indispensable to the orderly and successful operation of the courts. Judge John J. Parker, who characterized it at the time of its creation in 1939 as "probably the greatest piece of legislation affecting the judiciary since the Judiciary Act of 1789,"[92] was quite correct in his analysis. Nonetheless, constant efforts to bring about further improvement in the operation and function of the courts, high as well as low, are essential. The establishment in 1967 of the Federal Judicial Center as the research and training agency of the federal judicial system, with the Chief Justice of the United States as chairman of the board and the director of the Administrative Office of the U.S. Courts one of its members, is a highly commendable step in the right direction.[93] So is the creation of State/Federal Judicial Councils in almost all of the states (to alleviate friction between the two jurisdictions and to resolve overlapping between the two court systems) largely due to the efforts to Chief Justice Burger, the Chief Justice's call for a National Institute of Justice (to devise proposals to ameliorate various aspects of the judicial process), the establishment of the Institute for Court Management in Denver in 1970, and the 1972 creation of the National Center for State Courts in historic Williamsburg, Virginia (to assist those courts in research and development to meet cascading burdens of litigation and adjudication).[94] There remains much room, of course, for additional improvement,

---

[91] The statute refers to appointment "by the Supreme Court of the United States."

[92] As quoted by James Willard Hurst, *Thw Growth of American Law: The Law Makers* (Boston: Little, Brown and Co., 1950), pp. 114, 454.

[93] For a brief sketch of the Center's functions, see fn. 143, p. 95, ch. 2, *supra*. In 1973, the F.J.C. provided training for 1,600 federal judicial employees, including 129 judges. (See *The New York Times*, Jan. 7, 1974, p. C16.)

[94] See the interview with Chief Justice Warren E. Burger, "New Ways to Speed Up Justice," *U.S. News and World Report*, August 21, 1972, pp. 38–46; "Burger Renews Pleas for Agency," *The New York Times*, December 7, 1972, p. 31; and his comprehensive, forthright

especially in the realm of judicial education in which, however, aided by the establishment of some of these bodies—plus the American Academy of Judicial Education—major studies are being undertaken to maintain and improve professional competence through, as the American Bar Association put it, "continuing professorial education."[95]

annual "State of the Judiciary"messages to the profession and to the country, 1972ff. See also the imaginative new Judicial Fellows program.

[95] See 60 Judicature 7 (February 1977), pp. 334–42. As of 1975 at least three states—Minnesota, Iowa, and Wisconsin—made "refresher courses" for sitting judges compulsory. Early in 1978 Chief Justice Burger, in a series of much publicized lectures and speeches well received publicly, reportedly charged that up to "50 percent" of the lawyers who practiced in trial courts were inadequate.

5

Courts at Home: II—The Supreme Court

AT THE ZENITH: THE U.S. SUPREME COURT

The most dazzling jewel in the judicial crown of the United States is the revered and often controversial U.S. Supreme Court. It is the sole court mentioned specifically in Article III or in any other part of the Constitution, all other federal courts having been created by statute. The Supreme Court, the national symbol of justice, stands at the very pinnacle of the judiciary: there is no higher court, and all others bow before it—or, at least, are expected to do so. It is, in Alpheus Thomas Mason's words—so prophetic for the Watergate crisis of 1974—"the American counterpart of the British Crown, but unlike a queen on the throne, the Court has real power. It can bring Congress, President, state governors and legislators to heel."[1] At times having had as few as five, and at other times as many as ten, Justices in the first eighty years of its venerable history, the Court has stood at nine ever since the first term of President Grant in 1869. Before that date, and as dictated by various policy considerations, its membership, which is fixed by Congress, comprised five in 1789, six in 1790, seven in 1807, nine in 1837, ten in 1863, and eight in 1866.

The Supreme Court consists of the Chief Justice and eight Associate Justices, the former being currently rewarded with an annual salary of $104,728, the latter with $100,568 each,[2] subject to annual increments.[3] But the non-

---

[1]"Judicial Activism: Old and New," 55 *Virginia Law Review* 411 (1969).

[2]An illustration of petty congressional pique vis-à-vis the Supreme Court, motivated chiefly by its momentous and trail-blazing civil rights and civil liberties decisions of the 1950s and 1960s, was the refusal of Congress in 1964 and again in 1965 to give the Chief Justice and his associates on the Court the same $7,500 pay increase then granted all lower federal court judges. Instead, the members of the highest tribunal had to settle for a $4,500 raise.

[3]Under the Federal Salary Act of 1975, which provided for these incremental arrangements, the percentage is left to Presidential discretion—or, as President Carter ordered for 1978-79, they may be omitted entirely. The increments have ranged from 4.3 to 8.7 percent.

salary compensations, frequently called "psychic income" by college professors, are undoubtedly considerable. (The retirement prerogatives were discussed in chapter 2.)

ORIGINAL JURISDICTION

The U.S. Supreme Court has both *original* and *appellate* jurisdiction, but it exercises the former only in rare instances. Moreover, the Eleventh Amendment to the Constitution, ratified in 1798, has seriously abridged that phase of its work by removing from its, and the lower federal courts', jurisdiction all those cases in which one of its own citizens or one of another state or of a foreign country, or even a sovereign foreign country itself, wishes to sue one of the states of the United States. In effect, the Eleventh Amendment enacted the necessity of obtaining *a state's permission to sue it* in all litigation involving these categories.

The Eleventh Amendment was adopted as a direct result of a Supreme Court decision in 1793 in the case of *Chisholm v. Georgia*.[4] There the Court, in a broad decision, but in accordance with the terminology of Article III of the Constitution, held 4:1[5] that Chisholm, a citizen of one state (South Carolina), could sue another state (Georgia) in the federal courts—an outrageous and shocking pronouncement in the eyes of citizens with confirmed states-rights views. It was especially galling because the matter involved debts owed to a then-deceased British creditor, one Robert Farquhar, a merchant who had resided in Charleston, S.C., for whom Chisholm acted as an executor. (But it ought to be noted that the debts were for supplies sold in 1777 to Georgia in full accordance with the wishes and at the direction of Georgia's Executive Council.) The Supreme Court's judgment, which had been handed down without benefit of argument by Georgia, triggered instantaneous and profound opposition. For example, the lower house of the legislature of the State of Georgia passed a bill to punish by hanging "without benefit of clergy" any person endeavoring to aid in the enforcement of the decision! Merely two days had passed after the announcement in *Chisholm v. Georgia* when the future Eleventh Amendment was introduced into both houses of Congress.

Thereafter, the *original* jurisdiction docket of the Supreme Court became a very minor factor in its work. Not counting *memorandum orders* (to be explained later), at the outset of its 1984–85 term the Court had *rendered decisions* under the original jurisdiction clause of the Constitution—Article III, Section 2, Paragraph 2, as amended—in only 156 cases since its first term

---

[4] 2 Dallas 419. Actually, *Chisholm* involved the review of a case that had reached the Court from the Circuit Court below, entitled *Farquhar v. Georgia* (*Farquhar's Executor v. Georgia*). (Case File, Records of U.S. Circuit Court, District of Georgia, Case A, Box 1.)
[5] William Paterson had been commissioned an Associate Justice in 1793, but he did not participate in the case.

in 1789.[6] The cases that now still presumably commence there under it do so as a *matter of right* under its provisions. Theoretically, they comprise the following four categories of cases or controversies: (1) those between the United States and one of the fifty states,[7] (2) those between two or more states; (3) those involving *foreign* ambassadors, other *foreign* public ministers, and *foreign* consuls, or their "domestics or domestic servants not inconsistent with the law of nations"; and (4) those *commenced by a state* against citizens of another state or aliens or *against* a foreign country. (But note that if these actions are *commenced by the citizens*[8] or *alien or even the foreign country*[9] against a state, that litigation *must begin in state court*, in accordance with the provisions of the Eleventh Amendment.)

However, the Supreme Court does not exercise *exclusive* original jurisdiction even in the four categories cited, with the sole exception of category 2, that is, cases or controversies involving two or more of the several states. There it, and it alone, exercises original jurisdiction. But Congress, with the hearty approval of the Court, has extended *concurrent original* jurisdiction to the federal District Courts in litigation affecting category 3 and in *some*, but not all, cases in categories 1 and 4 in which a state is party to the suit at issue. Hence, most of the cases the Supreme Court has heard on its original jurisdiction docket have indeed involved two or more states. For example, the nine successive actions the state of Virginia filed against West Virginia in the lengthy and trying history of their debt controversy were all heard at the bar of the Supreme Court.[10] More recent controversies have involved Michigan and Ohio in a possession dispute over a 200-square-mile tract in the Maumee Bay area of mineral-rich Lake Erie,[11] California and Arizona in their persistent water rights squabbles,[12] a river boundary dispute between Louisiana and Texas,[13] Delaware's unsuccessful attempt to have the Court declare unconstitutional the electoral college vote count in presidential elections,[14]

[6]For a detailed analysis, including a list of 123 of these cases as of June 1959, see "The Original Jurisdiction of the United States Supreme Court," 11 *Stanford Law Review* (July 1959), pp. 665–719.

[7]E.g., *United States v. Maine*, 420 U.S. 515 (1975), involving the always live question of whether the states or the federal government have jurisdiction over oil deposits outside the three-mile limit. The federal government emerged victorious, 8:0, the White opinion being largely based on a *stare decisis* interpretation, bottomed on the 1953 Submerged Lands and Outer Continental Shelf Acts, as construed in, for example, *United States v. California* II, 381 U.S. 139 (1965).

[8]See *Hans v. Louisiana*, 134 U.S. 1 (1890).

[9]See *Monaco v. Mississippi*, 292 U.S. 313 (1934).

[10]E.g., *Virginia v. West Virginia*, 246 U.S. 565 (1918).

[11]*Michigan v. Ohio*, 386 U.S. 1029 (1967).

[12]*Arizona v. California*, 370 U.S. 906 (1961); ibid., 373 U.S. 546 (1963); ibid., rehearing denied, 375 U.S. 892 (1963). But see its "return" in 1983: 460 U.S. 605.

[13]*Texas v. Louisiana*, 410 U.S. 702 (1973).

[14]*Delaware et al., v. New York et al.*, 385 U.S. 895 (1966).

the evidently eternal Virginia–Maryland "war of the oyster beds,"[15] a Mississippi river bed area dispute between Mississippi and Arkansas,[16] and another river border dispute between Ohio and Kentucky.[17] All of these cases must, and do, commence in the Supreme Court. Yet if a determination of *facts* is required, the Court here often utilizes the device of referring these disputes to a special *master*—frequently an ex-jurist—for a hearing and report to it, as it did in the Virginia–Maryland oyster dispute, the Western water litigation cases, the 1966 suit by Ohio against Kentucky in a dispute over their boundary, and in the federal–state jurisdictional squabble over offshore oil deposits.[18]

APPELLATE JURISDICTION

The primary task of the Court is *appellate*. In that capacity it serves as the final arbiter in the construction of the Constitution of the United States and it thus provides a uniform interpretation of the law, although its very power to do so also enables it to change its mind from case to case. However, at least to a considerable degree, it attempts to adhere to precedent, the aforementioned doctrine known as *stare decisis*, that is, let the decision stand, giving to precedents the authority of established law. (We shall examine this philosophy of law and the extent of its success in chapter 8.)

Appellate cases come to the Supreme Court from the subordinate federal courts and the state courts of last resort (which are usually, but not always, the state supreme courts). Actually, there are five different sources of the appellate cases that reach the Court: (1) the state court of last resort having jurisdiction in a particular action, provided that a federal question has been raised validly, and further provided that all remedies have been duly exhausted below, (2) the thirteen U.S. Circuit Courts of Appeals, (3) the U.S. District Courts, and (4) one of the special constitutional legislative, and territorial courts, if permissible under the laws that establish it.

---

[15] E.g., *Virginia v. Maryland*, 355 U.S. 946 (1958).

[16] *Mississippi v. Arkansas*, 415 U.S. 302 (1974), involving the so-called Luna Bar.

[17] *Ohio v. Kentucky*, 444 U.S. 335 (1980); rehearing denied, 445 U.S. 939.

[18] The four masters involved in these decisions were, respectively, retired U.S. Supreme Court Associate Justice Stanley F. Reed, retired U.S. District Court Judge Simon H. Rifkind, retired U.S. Court of Appeals Judge Percy Foreman, and retired U.S. Court of Appeals Judge Albert B. Maris. Masters' reports are normally accepted by the Court, but not always—for example, in 1974 the Court rejected a master's proposal in connection with a long-standing dispute between New York and Vermont over water pollution in Lake Champlain. (*Vermont v. New York*, 415 U.S. 270). And, on occasion, a disappointed litigant may seek Court reconsideration of an accepted master's recommendation, as Maine and eleven other states did in 1975 opposing Master Maris's ruling against the states and in favor of the federal government as to jurisdiction over offshore Atlantic Coast oil deposits outside the three-mile limit. (*United States v. Maine*, 420 U.S. 515.) The Court, basing its decision both on Judge Maris's recommendation and *stare decisis*, stuck to its holding that it was indeed the federal government that owned the rights to the deposits in question.

Cases or controversies normally reach the Supreme Court for purposes of review under its appellate jurisdiction in one of three principal ways—with each member of the Court considering every application for review: (1) on a writ of appeal, as a matter of right (usually simply called *appeal*), (2) on a writ of *certiorari*, as a matter of Court discretion (usually simply called *certiorari* or *cert.*), and (3) by certification. The old writ of *error*, a common law process roughly akin to today's writ of appeal, was statutorily discontinued in the federal courts in 1928. It brought the entire record of a proceeding in a lower court before the Supreme Court for its consideration of "errors of law," allegedly committed below. We may also quickly dispose of *certification*. Rarely employed, it presents the Court with even fewer cases than those on its original jurisdiction docket. It covers "any question of law in any civil or criminal case in which instructions are desired" by the lower court, usually a Court of Appeals or the Court of Claims. Another way for cases to reach the Court is by "extraordinary writ," such as *habeas corpus* or *quo warranto*.

Appeal. In the instance of a writ of *appeal*, the aggrieved party—known as the *appellant*, the answering party being the *appellee* or *respondent*—has an absolute, *statutorily granted right* to carry a case to the U.S. Supreme Court, which in theory must review it. However, since 1928 the high tribunal has had the very considerable discretionary power to reject such an appeal on the ground that the federal question, otherwise validly raised, is "insubstantial." Moreover, the federal question must have been validly raised early in the state court—when the matter begins as a state issue—and even then the Supreme Court may not take the case if the state court's judgment can be sustained on an independent ground of state law. This highly significant multiple discretionary element in the area of the Court's so-called compulsory appellate jurisdicton caused it to dismiss over 90 percent of the appeals and petitions presented to it in the 1983–84 term. Of these, at least half were rejected "for want of a substantial federal question," or a "properly presented" one,[19] the balance on other jurisdictional grounds. An average of 50 to 60 percent of the writs of appeal are dismissed or the judgment below affirmed without printing the record or oral argument, and Justice Douglas contended in an important statistical article that, as a rule, the Court actually grants no more than 15 percent.[20]

Hence, the appeal is used but sparingly, to date in only about 9 percent of all cases or controversies *presented* to the Court, but Douglas claimed that this 9 percent constitutes 90 percent of all "meritorious" cases.[21] Yet whatever

---

[19] *Albanese v. United States*, 350 U.S. 845 (1955), *certiorari* denied (the Court's refusal to interfere with a Connecticut law that allows a person injured by a drunk to sue the person who sold the drink) and *Doe v. Delaware*, 450 U.S. 382, (1981) *per curiam*, respectively.

[20] William O. Douglas, "The Supreme Court and Its Case Load," 45 *Cornell Law Quarterly* 401 (Spring 1960) at 410.

[21] Ibid., at 409.

the practice, there are a total of five instances in which an aggrieved party may resort to it: (1) if a state court of last resort has declared a federal law or treaty, or parts thereof, unconstitutional;[22] or (2) if a state court *upholds a state law* or a provision of a state constitution *against a substantial challenge that it conflicts* with a provision of a federal law or treaty, or the U.S. Constitution;[23] (3) if any federal court declares a federal law or treaty, or parts thereof, unconstitutional, provided the United States is a party to the suit;[24] (4) if a federal Court of Appeal *strikes down a state law as being contrary to a federal law, treaty, or the Constitution;*[25] and (5) in certain statutorily specified cases from the federal District Courts and all other "courts of the United States" (e.g., if a case, required to be heard by any three-judge federal District Court, has resulted in an order granting or denying an injunction).[26] By far the largest number of cases on appeal come to the Supreme Court either from a state court of last resort—usually its highest court—or from one of the special three-judge courts at the federal District Court level (which must include at least one federal Circuit Court of Appeals judge). Many of the segregation-integration cases have reached the Supreme Court by the latter route.[27] In a potentially highly significant development Congress moved in 1979 to *remove* much of the Court's obligatory "appeal by right" jurisdiction and substitute thereafter *writ of certiorari*. But it was still in limbo before Congress in late 1985.

Certiorari. In all other cases involving a "federal question of substance" the disappointed litigant in a suit has *no right* to appeal to the Supreme Court the adverse decision he sustained; however, he does have the *privilege* of petitioning the highest bench in the land to grant him a writ of *certiorari*— a Latin term meaning "made more certain," or "better informed." Generally, each such petition,[28] a copy of which goes to every Justice with a record of the proceedings below, comprises the two sides' arguments both for and against its grant—the party bringing the action known as the *plaintiff* or *petitioner*, the other as the *respondent*. Ninety percent of the cases decided by

---

[22]E.g., *Reynolds v. Katzenbach*, 248 F. Supp. 593 (1965), consolidated with *South Carolina v. Katzenbach*, 383 U.S. 301 (1966).

[23]E.g., *Torcaseo v. Watkins*, 366 U.S. 488 (1961) and *Hill v. Stone*, 421 U.S. 289 (1975). In the latter case the Supreme Court threw out provisions of the Texas Constitution and a Texas statute on the same Fourteenth Amendment equal protection of the laws grounds.

[24]E.g., *Missouri v. Holland*, 252 U.S. 416 (1920).

[25]E.g., *Reynolds v. Sims*, 377 U.S. 533 (1964).

[26]E.g., *Wickard v. Filburn*, 317 U.S. 111 (1942), and *Ray v. Atlantic Richfield Co.*, 435 U.S. 151 (1978).

[27]E.g., *Brown v. Board of Education of Topeka*, 347 U.S. 483 (1954) and *Swann v. Charlotte-Mecklenburg Board of Education*, 402 U.S. 1 (1971).

[28]The petition must set forth the basis for the Court's jurisdiction, frame the questions presented for review, state the facts material to a consideration of those questions, and, in the words of Chief Justice Vinson, "explain why it is vital that the questions involved be decided finally by the Supreme Court." (From his talk to a group of University of Pennsylvania students, April 16, 1952.)

the Supreme Court reach it by that method, and most of these come to it from the Circuit Courts of Appeal. Neither in *certiorari* nor in *appeal* proceedings is a formal printed record necessary until such time as the writ of *certiorari* is granted or the appeal noted. However, forty copies of the petition must be filed within thirty to ninety days, depending on the type of case,[29] after final judgment and denial of rehearing in the lower courts, and they must be accompanied by a $100 fee.

The grant of *certiorari* signifies the willingness of the Supreme Court to review a case, based on a written petition initiated by the plaintiff together with a reply from the other side, which often urges a denial of *certiorari*. A grant of the petition—"petes for cert.," Justice Holmes used to call them—directs the lower court to send up the record in the case for review so that the decision "may be made more certain." Needless to say, the Court is quite chary of granting its writs of *certiorari* and, unless it detects an issue of substantial significance or controversy in the case or happens to be especially interested in it, chances are that the application for the writ will be rejected with a terse "*certiorari* denied"—as is evident from the published listing of a large number of petitions thus disposed of. The Court's own Rule 19 states that *certiorari* will be granted only "when there are special and important reasons therefor." Among these, according to the language of Rule 19 of the Court's Revised Rules of 1967, are the following: (1) when two federal Circuit Courts of Appeals or two three-judge federal District Courts have rendered conflicting decisions (e.g., in one case, two diametrically opposed judgments involving the constitutionality of the so-called Blue Laws were handed down by two three-judge federal District Courts, sitting in Boston and Philadelphia, striking down and upholding such Massachusetts and Pennsylvania laws, respectively, [30] and, in another case, equally opposing judgments, this time on the constitutionality of the Public Accommodations Title of the Civil Rights Act of 1964, were rendered by two three-judge courts in the *same* circuit—the Fifth—in Atlanta and Birmingham, respectively, upholding and striking down that title of the Act[31], (2) when a state court or a federal appellate court has passed on an important question of federal law on which the Supreme Court has never passed, [32] (3) when these lower courts have rendered a deci-

---

[29]The Court's *Rules* require a thirty-day deadline in *federal criminal* cases, ninety days in *federal civil*, cases, and ninety days also in *any state case*. (Letter from Clerk's Office, October 9, 1976.)

[30]*Crown Kosher Super Market v. Gallagher*, 176 F. Supp. 466 (1959), and *Two Guys from Harrison Allentown v. McGinley*, 179 F. Supp. 944 (1959).

[31]*Heart of Atlanta Motel v. United States*, 231 F. Supp. 393 (1964), and *McClung v. Katzenbach*, 233 F. Supp. 815 (1964). Another, more recent illustration was the issue of "selective" prosecution of individuals failing to register for the draft, with the Ninth Circuit approving and the Sixth Circuit disapproving: *United States v. Wayte*, 710 F.2d 1385 (CA 9) and *United States v. Schmucker*, 721 F. 2d 1046 (CA 6), respectively. (The U.S. Supreme Court ultimately ruled 7:2 in favor of the Ninth Circuit in 1985 in *Wayte v. United States*, 53 LW 4319.)

[32]*Furman v. Georgia*, 408 U.S. 238 (1972).

sion that conflicts with applicable precedent established by the Supreme Court, [33] or (4) when a federal court has so far departed from the accepted canons of judicial proceedings as to call for exercise of the Supreme Court's power of supervision.[34] In any case, as Justice Frankfurter viewed the Court's power to control its docket, ". . . [it] carries with it the responsibility of granting review only in cases that demand adjudication of the basis of importance to the operation of our federal system; importance of the outcome merely to the parties is not enough."[35] In an address to a group of Illinois lawyers he illustrated what the Chief Justice, who plays an important role in *certiorari* grants, might say:

> This is a very interesting and important question . . ., but we can't do any better than Judge Julian Mack [late judge of the U. S. Court of Appeal] did with it below. He really knows more about this field of law than the rest of us. I suggest we deny this petition for *certiorari*.[36]

This posture is symptomatic of what Justice Frankfurter used to term the need for "alert deference" to lower court opinions in general. It echoes Chief Justice Vinson's contention that the Supreme Court "is not, and never has been, primarily concerned with the corrections of errors in lower court decisions. . . . [Its] function is, therefore, to resolve conflict of opinions on federal questions of wide import under the Constitution, laws and treaties of the United States, and to exercise supervisory power over the lower courts."[37]

Still, a case of substance is not necessarily a "big" or "major" case. For example, the Supreme Court once reached down to the Police Court of Louisville, Kentucky, to set aside, as a violation of the due process of law clause of the Fourteenth Amendment to the Constitution, two $10 fines for loitering and disorderly conduct.[38] This case symbolizes the willingness of the highest court in the land to look at the smallest matters if it is necessary to do so to ensure justice. Here, in a criminal proceeding, one Sam Thompson, a man who had been convicted of disorderly public conduct for "shuffling" in a cafe, successfully took his claim of lack of evidence to the Supreme Court on *certiorari* because, under Kentucky law, the fines involved were too small to be reviewed by any state appellate court.[39] Speaking for the unanimous

---

[33] E.g., *Biddle v. Perovich,* 274 U.S. 480 (1927), and *United States v. O'Brien* plus *O'Brien v. United States,* 391 U.S. 367 (1969).

[34] E.g., *United States v. District Court (United States v. Haley),* 371 U.S. 18 (1962).

[35] Quoting from *Wilkerson v. McCarthy,* 336 N.J. 53 (1949).

[36] As quoted by Anthony Lewis, "How the Supreme Court Reaches Decisions," *The New York Times Magazine,* December 1, 1957, pp. 51–54.

[37] Address to the Annual Meeting of the American Bar Association, St. Louis, Mo., September 7, 1949. See also Justice Harlan's similar sentiments in *Cohen v. California,* 403 U.S. 15 (1971).

[38] *Thompson v. City of Louisville et al.* 362 U.S. 199 (1960).

[39] Actually, it was the family for whom he worked who urged Thompson to appeal his case, for they felt that the police had been harassing him; they hired Louis Lusky, a distinguished lawyer with an abiding interest in civil liberties, to take the case.

Court, Justice Black noted: "Our examination of the record presented in the petition for *certiorari* convinced us that *although the fines here are small, the due process questions presented are substantial and we* therefore granted *certiorari* to review the police court's judgment."[40] And, in the oral argument before the Court, the case was given *twice* the customary time allotted!

Since the Court has complete discretionary power over grants of *certiorari*—a power bestowed on it by the necessary and desirable "Judges Bill" of 1925,[41] which was largely the creation of Chief Justice Taft and Justice Van Devanter—it denies between 85 and 90 percent of all *certiorari* applications, and does not usually explain its reason for the denial.[42] Prior to the 1925 statute the Court's appellate jurisdiction was obligatory to the extent of some 80 percent of its business. Gone now are the days when the Court, its docket jammed with mandatory appeals, was expected to devote an all-too-large portion of its valuable time and energy merely to correcting errors of lower courts that primarily affected the rights of parties to a particular case or controversy. Today, it must concentrate on those cases whose resolution will have immediate importance far beyond the particular facts and parties involved. On the other hand, the Court has never forgotten the oft-quoted admonition of Chief Justice Marshall in *Cohens v. Virginia*, back in 1821:

> It is most true that this Court will not take jurisdiction if it should not: but it is equally true that it must take jurisdiction if it should. The judiciary cannot, as the legislature may, avoid a measure because it approaches the confines of the Constitution. We cannot pass it by because it is doubtful. With whatever doubts, with whatever difficulties, a case may be attended, we must decide it if it be brought before us. We have no more right to decline the exercise of jurisdiction which is given than to usurp that which is not given. The one or the other would be treason to the Constitution.[43]

Indeed, a glance at the subject matter represented on the Court's 1984–85 docket points to a veritable *smörgasbord*, ranging the alphabetical gamut

---

[40]Ibid., at 203. (Italics supplied.) See also the charming 1976 case of the "Nevada One Inch Pupfish" (*Cappaert v. United States*, 426 U.S. 128) and the 1978 case of the three-inch "Tennessee Snail Darter" (*Tennessee Valley Authority v. Hill*, 437 U.S. 153).

[41]43 Stat. 936.

[42]An examination of a forty-year period (1945–85) indicates that it does so in less than 1 percent of all such denials. However, on occasion one or more disappointed judges will write an *opinion*, or a note, on the Court's refusal to grant *certiorari* in a certain case—for example, Justice Douglas's lengthy one from the Court's refusal to hear a test of the constitutionality of New York's criminal syndicalism law in 1968. (*Epton v. New York*, 390 U.S. 29.) But the more common approach is simply to record a dissent from the Court's negative action on the request to grant the writ—as Chief Justice Burger and Justice Douglas did, for example, in *Buckley v. American Federation of T.V. and Radio Artists*, 419 U.S. 1093 (1974) See also the bitter dissenting opinion by Justice Rehnquist, joined by Chief Justice Burger and Justice White, from the Court's refusal to grant *certiorari* in the potentially highly significant affirmative action/reverse discrimination case of *Bushey v. New York State Civil Service Commission*, 53 LW 3477 (1985).

[43]6 Wheaton 264, at 404.

from abortion to zoning discrimination. However, there exists a distinct tendency on the Court's part to favor reviews sought by the federal government as a petitioning party. This is true both in terms of fully discussed cases and in the decisions of the Chief Justice (and the Clerk of Court) to "special list" cases for possible review in the first place.

To grant *certiorari*, at least four of the Justices must vote to do so. That decision is reached and formalized at the Court's weekly Conference, in which those petitions deemed worthy of consideration by any one Justice have been put on the Conference discussion list, each Justice, without direct consultation with any other, having reached his or her own conclusions as to whether the application should be considered at all. The Justice may have reached that decision either by reading a particular petition personally, by having shared that task with his or her law clerks, or by having asked them for a summary or "bench" memorandum. A novel Burger Court development has been the so-called *cert.* pool, an arrangement presently (1985) subscribed to by six[44] of the nine Justices, under which their respective law clerks work together in analyzing petitions for *certiorari*. A working rule devised by the Court itself, this Rule of Four also applies to noting probable jurisdiction on writs of appeal—an interesting development in view of the important distinction that theoretically governs the two writs. Of course, the Court can change its mind on a grant for review; there is nothing to prevent it, on thinking the matter over, from ultimately dismissing a writ as having been "improvidently granted."[45] According to a statute of 1863, however, six Justices constitute a quorum to hand down a decision.[46] This means that a plurality of four Justices can *decide* a case. In the event of a tie vote, the decision of the lower court stands as the final word in the controversy at issue.[47] But a single Justice may—unless, or until, overruled by action of his peers on the bench—grant a stay of execution or a writ of *habeas corpus*. A pertinent illustration of this significant prerogative is the grant of a request for a stay of execution, although denying a request for a writ of *habeas corpus*, by Justice Douglas, in the sensational case of the convicted atom spies, Ethel and Julius Rosenberg, in June 1953. While vacating the stay of execution just twenty-four hours after it had been granted, Chief Justice Vinson took note inferentially of the intemperate reaction in the public press, and especially in Con-

---

[44]Burger, White, Blackmun, Powell, Rehnquist, and O'Connor.

[45]E.g., *Cichos v. Indiana*, 385 U.S. 76 (1966), a state double jeopardy case which it had originally accepted for review; the "smut" case of *Carlos v. New York*, 396 U.S. 119 (1969); one aspect of *Nixon v. United States*, 418 U.S. 683 (1974); and *Florida v. Casal and Garcia*, 462 U.S. 637 (1983).

[46]Early in 1970, when Justice Harlan abruptly removed himself from an important case involving oil shale mining rights, the niceties of judicial ethics dictated the cancellation of a Supreme Court hearing in mid-argument—for Harlan's departure left but five Justices on the bench. (The *New York Times*, January 22, 1970, p. 22.)

[47]E.g., Maryland's highest court's 1971 finding that the Swedish film *I Am Curious (Yellow)* was obscene. (*Grove Press, Inc. v. Maryland State Board of Censors*, 401 U.S. 480.)

gress (where bills of impeachment were at once introduced in the House of Representatives), by writing that "Mr. Justice Douglas had power to issue the stay. No one has disputed this, and we think the proposition is indisputable."[48]

Considerable disagreement exists, not only among the many observers of the Court, but among the Justices themselves, as to the true meaning of a denial of an application for a writ of *certiorari*. Justice Jackson viewed "sincere worthiness" as a tacit agreement by a quorum of the Justices that the decision below is good enough to stand. "The fatal sentence," he wrote, "that in real life writes finis to many causes cannot in legal theory be a complete blank."[49] Justice Frankfurter, however, always insisted that no significance attaches to the denial of *certiorari*, that it "in no wise" implies Court approval of the decision below. All it means, he would point out, is that, for reasons seldom if ever disclosed, six or more Justices evidently do not think that a case ought to be adjudicated on its merits. On one occasion he spelled out his reasoning:

> . . . [it] seemed . . . to at least six members [of the Court] . . . that the issue was either not ripe enough or too moribund for adjudication; that the question had better wait for the perspective of time or that time would bury the question or, for one reason or another, it was desirable to wait and see; or that the constitutional issue was entangled with nonconstitutional issues that raised doubt whether the constitutional issue could be effectively isolated; or for various other reasons not related to the merits.[50]

No matter which of these two contrasting views may be "correct," the effect in the eyes of the disappointed petitioner is necessarily the same: at least for the present, he or she has lost.[51]

WORK LOAD

All cases to be disposed of are placed on one of the Court's three dockets: the *original*, the *appellate*, and the *miscellaneous*. In the 1983–84 term the Court had 5155 cases on these dockets and *disposed* of 4162 with finality. But of those many cases the Court disposed of, it decided only 285 *on the merits*,

---

[48] *Rosenberg v. United States*, 346 U.S. 273 (1953), at 285. Each Supreme Court Justice is responsible for considering appeals for stays in any matters that come up in his or her circuit. However, if someone seeking a stay is turned down by the Justice presiding over the circuit, the petitioner can further appeal to any or all of the other members of the Court for relief. When Douglas was savagely attacked for granting the Rosenbergs' stay, Senator William Langer (R.-N.D.) offered him solace: "Douglas, they have thrown several buckets of shit over you. But by God, none of it stuck. And I am proud." (*Go East, Young Man. The Early Years: The Autobiography of William O. Douglas* [New York: Random House, 1974], p. 469.)

[49] Concurring opinion in *Brown v. Allen*, 344 U.S. 443 (1953), at 543.

[50] Dissenting opinion in *Darr v. Burford*, 339 U.S. 200 (1950), at 227. See, similarly, Justice Brennan's statement in "State Court Decisions and the Supreme Court," 31 *Pennsylvania Bar Association Quarterly* (1960), pp. 399–400.

[51] See pp. 190–197, *infra*.

Chart B. U.S. Supreme Court Review

Cases Normally Reach the U.S. Supreme Court for Purposes of Review (as distinct from original jurisdiction) in One of Two Principal Ways:

    1. On APPEAL, i.e., as a matter of right.
    2. On a writ of *CERTIORARI*, as a matter of Court discretion.

(A third way, by CERTIFICATION, will be omitted for present purposes. It is rarely used, presenting the court with even fewer cases than those on its original docket. It covers "any question of law in any civil or criminal case as to which instructions are desired" by the lower court, usually a Court of Appeals.[a] The old writ of ERROR, a common law process strongly akin to (1) above, was statutorily discontinued in the federal courts in 1928. It brought the entire record of a case proceeding in a lower court before the Supreme Court for its consideration for alleged "errors of law" committed below.)

N.B.: Title 28 of the U.S. Code, formulated as a result of congressional legislation, governs the types of review available to an appellant. (See ch. 81, Secs. 1257 and 1254.)

I. *Cases reaching the U.S. Supreme Court on APPEAL* (i.e., the Court reviews because it *must*).

    A. *From the State Court of Last Resort* having statutory jurisdiction in any particular case (usually, but not always, the *highest state court*, which normally, but not always, is the state supreme court).
        1. When a state court has declared a federal law or a federal treaty, or provisions thereof, unconstitutional.
        2. When a state court has *upheld* a state law or a provision of the state constitution *against* the challenge that it *conflicts* with the federal Constitution, a federal law, a federal treaty, or any provision thereof.

    B. *From the U.S. (Circuit) Courts of Appeals:*
        1. When a state law or a provision of a state constitution has been *invalidated* because of a conflict with a federal law, a federal treaty, or a provision of the federal Constitution.
        2. When a federal law has been held *unconstitutional, provided* the United States, or one of its agencies, officers, or employees, is a party to the suit.

    C. *From the U.S. District Courts:*
        1. When a federal statute has been held *unconstitutional, provided* the United States, or one of its agencies, officers, or employees, is a party to the suit.
        2. When the United States is a party to a *civil* suit under the federal interstate-commerce, communication, or antitrust laws.
        3. When a *special three-judge District Court* (which must include at least one circuit judge) has granted or denied an interlocutory or permanent injunction in any proceeding required to be heard by such a court. These three-judge courts now sit only in suits brought to restrain, on grounds of unconstitutionality, *enforcement, operation, or execution of federal or state statutes* dealing with apportionment or reapportionment of legislative districts; in actions challenging the constitutionality of any statewide legislative body; and in instances in which such a court is *required* by specific acts of Con-

gress, such as the Civil Rights Act of 1964 and the Voting Rights Act of 1965, both as amended, and the Presidential Election Campaign Act of 1974.[b]

D. From "Any [other] Court of the United States" (comprising constitutional, legislative, and territorial courts)—specifically comprising courts not included under A, B, and C, above.

    1. When a federal statute has been held unconstitutional in any civil action, suit, or proceeding, provided the United States, or one of its agencies, officers, or employees is a party to it.[c]

II. Cases reaching the U.S. Supreme Court on a writ of CERTIORARI (i.e., because a minimum of four Supreme Court Justices has agreed to a review). Writs of certiorari are granted or denied at the discretion of the Court—subject always to the latent power of Congress to define and limit the appellate power of the Court.

A. From the State Court of the Last Resort having statutory jurisdiction in any particular case (usually, but not always, the highest state court, which normally, but not always, is the state supreme court).

    1. In all cases, other than those for which the remedy is APPEAL (see I.A. 1 and 2 above), in which a "substantial federal question" has been properly raised. (The Court itself determines just what constitutes such a question.)

B. From U.S. (Circuit) Courts of Appeals (and, in all pertinent cases, from other lower courts of the United States, such as certain legislative courts).

    1. When a decision involves the application or interpretation of a federal law, a federal treaty, the federal Constitution, or provisions thereof.

    2. Where the U.S. Court of Appeals has upheld a state law or a provision of a state constitution against the challenge that it conflicts with a federal law, a federal treaty, the federal Constitution, or provisions thereof.

---

[a]One of the very infrequent illustrations of its use is that by the Fifth U.S. Circuit Court of Appeals in 1963, which certified the question of whether or not its criminal contempt citation of Governor Ross R. Barnett and Lieutenant Governor Paul B. Johnson, Jr., of Mississippi necessitated a trial by jury. The intermediate appellate tribunal was evenly divided (4:4) when it turned to the Supreme Court in this ticklish case, which had arisen out of the admission of Negro James H. Meredith to the University of Mississippi at Oxford. (United States v. Barnett, 375 U.S. 805.) The highest tribunal ruled 5:4 against Barnett and Johnson (ibid., 376 U.S. 681) in 1964. But one year later the Circuit Court cleared the two because of "changed circumstances and conditions." (Ibid., 346 F. 2d 99.)

[b]Until Congress, heeding repeated entreaties by Chief Justice Burger and other students of the judicial process, limited these courts' jurisdiction in 1972 and, even more dramatically in 1976, their authority embraced a host of other areas, for example, orders of the Interstate Commerce Commission.

[c]But in a 5:4 District of Columbia decision in 1977, the Supreme Court ruled that it has no automatic duty to review any decision in a local court striking down a local law written by Congress; that there is, in other words, no automatic right of appeal to the Supreme Court when District of Columbia local courts strike down an Act of Congress that applies only in the District. (Key v. Doyle, 434 U.S. 59.)

with *full written opinions* handed down in just 163 cases (an average number), the remainder being disposed of either *per curiam* or by *memorandum orders* (e.g., "affirmed," "reversed," or "dismissed," (i.e., "vacated").[52] Yet it must be recognized that the Court does *act* on every case of which it disposes, whatever the nature of that disposition. The large number of cases docketed and disposed of, representing a major increase in the work load over previous years, has come chiefly in the so-called *miscellaneous* cases, which are largely handwritten or typewritten papers filed by indigent persons, often prison inmates, and, unlike the formal petitions for *certiorari* on the appellate docket, need not follow a particular form or even contain material normally considered essential in petitions. Indigents obtain authority to file from the federal *in forma pauperis* statute,[53] which gives to a citizen of the United States the right to enter proceedings in any federal court, provided he or she executes such an oath. Of course, this does not guarantee a Supreme Court review, although of the cases the Court heard in its 1983–84 term, more than half came to it *in forma pauperis!* Naturally, it did summarily vacate or reverse a fair number of other lower court decisions challenged by indigent persons, most of these cases being "frivolous" or without a substantial federal claim. The purpose of this interesting statute clearly was to protect indigent persons—a large proportion of whom, according to a bitter remark by Justice Jackson, represent "our convict population." And Justice Douglas, certainly a sympathetic friend of the underdog, once commented that the claims made in these pauper cases "are often fantastic, surpassing credulity ... [and] are for the most part frivolous."[54] Nevertheless, many vital criminal cases have reached the Court by this path—indeed, they have increased more than fortyfold since 1930, and today represent well over half of all case filings. Among them was the momentous *Gideon v. Wainwright*[55] in 1963, which resulted in the overruling of the *Betts v. Brady*[56] precedent that had stood for two decades. Clarence Earl Gideon had petitioned the Supreme Court for a writ of *habeas corpus*—the principal device available to those who attack state judgments—in a hand-penciled letter from his Florida prison cell.[57]

Of the total number of 5155 cases filed during the 1983–84 term, 993 were not disposed of, and thus went over to the 1984–85 docket. That residue is an average number of cases carried forward, the record—since the Clerk of the Supreme Court began to keep these statistics in 1930—coming with the

---

[52]Such "summary" decisions *cum* dispositions are not infrequently targets of strong intra-Court adverse criticism (e.g., see a sixteen-page memorandum by Justices Brennan and Marshall, described in detail in *The New York Times*, November 9, 1976, p. C24).

[53]28 USC 1915 (a). See also Supreme Court Rule 53.5.

[54]Address to the Cornell University School of Law, April 15, 1960.

[55]372 U.S. 335.

[56]316 U.S. 455 (1942).

[57]See the superb book on the *Gideon* case by Anthony Lewis, *Gideon's Trumpet* (New York: Random House, 1964), which, in addition to its basic story, is highly instructive in the judicial process.

1203 cases not disposed of by the 1973–74 term of the Court. Although there is some disagreement among the Justices themselves on the point, notably on the part of Douglas, who insisted time and again that the Court is "underworked—not overworked,"[58] most observers of the work of the Court believe firmly that it is overburdened with cases. In large measure, this is due to the flood of petitions that reach it; but to some degree it may also be because the Court has persisted in taking cases that are at best trivial, sometimes dealing simply with issues that did not present any truly imperative constitutional questions. This, of course, is a matter of judgment. Yet it would seem that at least in tax cases or in railroad and maritime injury-negligence cases, particularly the latter, which usually involve a question of fact as to who was at fault in the accident, the Court has at times unnecessarily overextended itself in granting petitions for review. That a good many of the Justices feel quite strongly about the matter is indicated by a veritable stream of comments by Justice Frankfurter, who, in case after case in this field, would pen a comment to the effect that "the case . . . is so trivial that the Court should dismiss its grant of review as improvident." And in one dispute, answering in the affirmative the question whether or not a jury should hear the case of a wrench falling on a seaman's "left great toe," Justice Harlan, speaking for a minority of four Justices, delivered a three-page dissent that began:

> At the opening of a term which finds the court's docket crowded with more important and difficult litigation than in many years, it is not without irony that we should be witnessing among the first matters to be heard a routine negligence . . . case involving only issues of facts. I continue to believe that such cases, distressing and important as they are for unsuccessful plaintiffs, do not belong in this Court.[59]

Justice Frankfurter went even further here, contending the Court should not even have agreed to consider such an issue in the first place; and he once again voiced his long-standing lament against consideration of minor negligence cases.

Among several suggestions advanced in the mid-1970s by the blue-ribbon Study Group on the Case Load of the Supreme Court, usually referred to as the Freund Committee (after Prof. Paul A. Freund of Harvard University Law School), was one to abandon the appellate jurisdiction of the Court and leave a writ of *certiorari* as the only means of obtaining review by the Supreme Court. In other words, direct appeals to the highest judicial body, whether from a one-judge court under the antitrust Expediting Act or from

---

[58] E.g., again in an interview on December 7, 1972 (*The Daily Progress*, Charlottesville, Va., p. 2). His colleague Brennan formally seconded Douglas in an interesting article in 59 *American Bar Association Journal* 835 (August 1973), "Justice Brennan Calls National Court of Appeals Proposal 'Fundamentally Unnecessary and Ill Advised.'" Douglas reiterated this view in 1975: "I found it a comfortable burden carried even in the months of my hospitalization." (*The New York Times*, June 27, 1975, p. C17.)

[59] *Michalic v. Cleveland Tankers, Inc.*, 364 U.S. 325 (1960) at 332–33.

a three-judge court convened to consider the constitutionality of a state or federal statute, would be abolished other than through *certiorari*. Congress began to talk about the proposal in 1979; but it had acted neither on it nor on the Freund Committee's widely discussed, Chief Justice Burger–backed proposal to create a new appellate court, known at the National Court of Appeals, as a "buffer" between the U.S. Court of Appeals and the U.S. Supreme Court.

An intriguing, and possibly highly significant, decision by the Court during its 1960–61 term gave Justice Frankfurter additional reasons for expounding on the theme of unwise, non-jurisdictional, unnecessary case work. Over his lone fifty-eight-page dissenting opinion, the eight-man majority held that policemen and other local officials who violated a citizen's constitutional rights under the Civil Rights Act of 1871 could be sued for damage in *federal* courts *even if these officials acted without state authority*. Frankfurter in his dissent not only charged the majority with violating federal–state relationships—relying heavily on the legislative history of the act as he saw it to prove his point—but he also decried what he viewed as rank court interference. Envisaging a veritable flood of petitions, he insisted that the broad construction adopted here by the Supreme Court made the federal Constitution

> a law to regulate the quotidian business of every traffic policeman, every registrar of elections, every city inspector or investigator, every clerk in every municipal license bureau in this country.[60]

Whatever the number of cases docketed, it ought to be fairly obvious that the lawyer who grandiosely and proudly informs both his client and the public press that "we'll fight this case all the way to the Supreme Court," really means that *if* the funds are present he will *attempt* to do so—unless a pauper's oath is involved the standard case will consume a solid outlay of upward of $10,000—and *if* the Court will grant review he will *endeavor* to convince it of the righteousness of his client's case. An average case takes from two to five years to reach the highest bench. The preparation and printing of the

---

[60] *Monroe v. Pape*, 365 U.S. 167 (1961). Frankfurter would have been repulsed in the face of 1978 and 1980 decisions by the Court which, going well beyond the 1961 holding, in effect stripped away the long immunity enjoyed by local (and, by implication, by federal) governments, ruling that such governments were subject to lawsuits for violations of civil rights and that having acted in "good faith" was not an acceptable defense. (*Monell v. New York Department of Social Services*, 436 U.S. 658 and *Owen v. City of Independence, Missouri*, 445 U.S. 622, respectively.) *Ergo*, a "person" in such litigation now extends to municipalities and other governmental entities; it is no longer limited to their officials. He would have been even more repulsed had he lived to note the Court's astonishing 6:3 decision in *Maine v. Thiboutot*, 448 U.S. 1 (1980), holding that not only can state and local officials be sued for damages for violations of civil rights, as established previously, but that the Civil Rights Act of 1871 *also* created a right to sue those officials for alleged denial of *any* federal benefit provided through them (e.g., food stamps, educational benefits, and other welfare programs enacted by the federal government). (See p. 277, *infra* for related explications of suits against governments and their officials.)

record and the writing of briefs alone normally consume five months. Seldom does the Court actually *hear oral arguments* on more than 125 to 150 of the cases it disposes of annually; the balance is dismissed on procedural or some other jurisdictional ground. Of those actually heard, formal *written opinions* by the Court are usually handed down in 75 to 85 percent of the cases, the others being decided *per curiam*—an anonymous opinion expressing the summary judgment of the Court as a whole and not the opinion of a single Justice with whom the others concur. In other words, a *per curiam* is an *unsigned*, normally very brief, opinion for the Court, applying *res judicata* (settled law), its authorship unknown to the outside world, although, in Professor Schubert's opinion, "it seems probable that most . . . are written by the Chief Justice or for him by one of his . . . law clerks."[61] For example, it was employed in the initial disposition of the controversial 1972 *Capital Punishment Cases*.[62] Usually *per curiam* opinions are written for a unanimous Court, but there are exceptions. For instance, in 1966 Justice Clark wrote a formal dissenting opinion to the Court's *per curiam* in *Riggan v. Virginia*[63] in which he was specifically joined by his colleagues Black, Harlan, and Stewart. There, the now readily identifiable majority of five (Warren, Douglas, Brennan, White, and Fortas) reversed *without briefs or arguments* a lower court decision upholding the validity of a search warrant issued by a Virginia tribunal. Considerable criticism about the increasing resort to *per curiam* decisions has ensued. However, it may very well be that this simply constitutes an attempt by the Court to resolve the conflict between rendering fully reasoned opinions and affording the finality of Supreme Court adjudication to as large a number of litigants as possible. Or it may simply represent a stopgap expedient, such as the Court's *per curiam* decision in a group of obscenity cases in 1967,[64] an area that has defied a firm, universally applicable rule of law— notwithstanding continuing attempts to determine one.[65]

Reconsideration. A petitioner whose request for review has been *denied* by the Court for one or more of the reasons discussed earlier is not, of course, barred from trying again. Accordingly, some sanguine souls are rather persistent in these efforts—although they rarely, if ever, succeed unless their new petition serves to convince four Justices of the merits of the renewed appeal. Thus, in a two-sentence statement included on the forty-second page of a forty-five page list of orders in nearly one thousand cases filed at the start of

---

[61] Glendon Schubert, *Judicial Policy-making: The Political Role of the Courts* (Glenview, IL.: Scott, Foresman and Co., 1965), p. 73. The statement concerning the role of the law clerks is subject to considerable doubt, however. (See, in this book, pp. 251–56 *infra*.)

[62] *Furman v. Georgia,* 408 U.S. 238.

[63] 384 U.S. 152.

[64] *Redrup v. New York, Austin v. Kentucky,* and *Gent v. Arkansas,* 386 U.S. 767 (decided together).

[65] See, for example, the Court's efforts in a series of 5:4 decisions handed down in 1973. (*Miller v. California* 413 U.S. 15 and *Paris Adult Theatre v. Slaton,* 413 U.S. 49).

the Court's 1976–77 term, it refused to reconsider[66] its July 2, 1976 decision[67] upholding the death penalty for murder, thus lifting the stay that had been blocking the states from implementing that decision. Among well-known illustrations of such unsuccessful attempts are the cases of Morton Sobell, convicted of complicity in the atomic espionage case of Ethel and Julius Rosenberg, and the doomed Caryl Chessman. Sobell filed eight formal petitions for review of his conviction between 1953 and 1958; all were denied by the Court without comment.[68] Chessman filed fully sixteen petitions for review with the Court between his conviction in 1948 for seventeen crimes (including kidnapping, attempted rape, sex perversion, robbery, and car theft) and his execution in 1960, prompting even Justice Douglas to comment: "The conclusion is inevitable that Chessman is playing a game with the courts, stalling for time. . . . This is not a case of a helpless man who was given no opportunity to participate in the settlement of the record."[69] Chessman's battle ended in failure only after he had filed a total of forty-two appeals[70] with various federal and state courts! The struggle covered twelve years, caused extensive debates on the merits of capital punishment, and made Chessman's name a household word throughout the world.[71] A rare occurrence in this realm of the judicial process is a Court-*solicited* or -encouraged reconsideration, such as that specifically requested by the 1961–62 bench when, in granting review to prison inmate Gideon,[72] it requested argument on the specific *quaere*[73] whether or not it should now reconsider its 1942 ruling in *Betts v. Brady*.[74] An embarrassing illustration is the Court's request to the parties in

---

[66] *Gregg v. Georgia*, 428 U.S. 1301 (1976).

[67] *Gregg v. Georgia*, 428 U.S. 153 (1976).

[68] He came close with his ninth attempt, in 1968, when he gained the vote of three of the necessary four Justices (Douglas, Harlan, and Brennan). He was released after his tenth appeal one year later.

[69] *Chessman v. Teets*, 354 U.S. 156 (1957), at 170.

[70] Emphasizing the need to limit repeated, seemingly endless, challenges and appeals in criminal convictions, the Court, speaking through Justice O'Connor, ruled in 1982 that there would simply have to be some limits to that game. (*United States v. Frady*, 456, U.S. 152; *Rose v. Lundy*, 455 U.S. 509; and *Engle v. Issac*, 456 U.S. 107.)

[71] Chessman's record years on death row were exceeded in 1966 by the thirteen years spent by both Edgar Labat and Clifton Alton Poret, two blacks who had been convicted of raping a young white woman in 1950. However, not only were they released from death row, but they were ordered freed from jail by the Fifth U.S. Circuit Court of Appeals because they had been convicted by juries from which blacks were *systematically* excluded. Their death row record was exceeded in turn by Edgar H. Smith, freed in 1971 after having served more than fourteen years for the murder of a fifteen-year-old girl. (A few years later he was back in jail for a new felony.)

[72] *Gideon v. Cochran*, 370 U.S. 908 (1962). (See fn. 57, *supra*.)

[73] "Should this Court's holding in *Betts v. Brady*, 316 U.S., be overruled?" In *Betts* the Court had held 6:3 that indigent state criminal defendants are automatically entitled to state-furnished counsel *only in capital criminal cases*—unless certain "special circumstances" attended the case (and, in the Court's judgment, they did not in *Betts*).

[74] 316 U.S. 455 (1942). When the *Gideon* decision came down in 1963, *Betts v. Brady* stood

an already-decided case "to address an additional question," namely, the possible modification of the Fourth Amendment's "exclusionary rule" to permit a "good faith" exception—only to conclude, "with apologies to all," that because "the issue we framed for the parties was not presented to the Illinois courts [we] . . . do not address it [here and now]."[75] It would, in fact, be tackled one year later.[76]

Rehearing. On the other hand, it is also possible for a *defeated* litigant to petition the Supreme Court for a *rehearing* within twenty-five days after the announcement of an unfavorable decision, in the dim hope that the Court, in the person of one or more of the Justices, may undergo a change of mind on rehearing the case. This is especially true when the original decision was a very close one and featured a sharply divided Court. But under the Court's rules, such a rehearing may not be granted unless a member of the *majority* in the original decision votes for one, and the Court in effect granted only six rehearings between 1950 and 1975, to cite an otherwise especially active quarter-century.

A notable illustration of one of the infrequent successes gained by a petitioner on rehearing—one of but three such victories in the twenty-five year period indicated—was the group of "military justice" cases, involving Mesdames Clarice Covert and Dorothy Smith-Krueger, both civilians, who killed their unfaithful Master Sergeant and Colonel spouses with ax and knife, respectively, while with them at overseas bases. The cases had been argued together at the bar of the Supreme Court initially in 1956, the constitutional issue being the validity of the section of the U.S. Uniform Military Code of Justice that authorized the military trial of civilians accompanying the armed forces abroad.[77] The Court had upheld the disputed section in a 5:3 decision, delivered by Justice Clark, whereas the three dissenters—Warren, Black, and Douglas—had protested they were being rushed at term's end, and Justice Frankfurter had refused to participate other than to file a "reservation" because of "lack of adequate time to consider" the issues involved and "their complexity." Clearly, this was the type of decision in which counsel for defendants might well see a distinct hope for a rehearing. A motion for one was duly filed; it was accepted by a 5:3 vote, the three original dissenters and Justice Frankfurter being joined in approving the petition for rehearing moved by Justice Harlan, a member of the original majority.[78] Matters certainly seemed to look up for the widows!

---

unanimously overruled—in a triumphant opinion for the Court by Justice Black, one of the three dissenters in *Betts* (*Gideon* v. *Wainwright*, 372 U.S. 335).

[75] *Illinois* v. *Gates*, 462 U.S. 213 (1983), at 217.

[76] *United States* v. *Leon* and *Massachusetts* v. *Sheppard*, 52 LW 5155 and 5177 (1984), respectively.

[77] *Kinsella* v. *Krueger*, 351 U.S. 470 and *Reid* v. *Covert*, 351 U.S. 487 (June 11, 1956).

[78] *Reid* v. *Covert* and *Kinsella* v. *Krueger*, 352 U.S. 901 (November 5, 1956). On petition for rehearing.

The case was duly reargued early in 1957, and during the waning days of that term the Court handed down its decision, reversing itself by declaring the section in question unconstitutional by a 6:2 vote.[79] Only Justices Clark and Burton remained of the former majority; Justices Minton and Reed having retired from the Court, Justice Harlan having changed his mind, and a new member, Justice Brennan, joining the majority. The ninth member, Justice Whittaker, just appointed to replace Justice Reed, did not participate in the decision. It should be reemphasized, however, that a grant of a petition for rehearing is the exception to the rule. The latter finds support in the prominent example of a petition for a rehearing of the so-called Hyde Amendment case, *Harris v. McRae*, brought in 1980 by 286 organizations and 70 law professors. The Court refused, thus staying with its original 5:4 ruling that had upheld a four-year-old ban on the use of Medicaid funds for abortions (with certain exceptions).[80] An indication of a possible chance for a rehearing, but certainly no assurance, is, of course, an officially announced change of mind from the bench, such as Justice Douglas's announcement, in the *New York Prayer Case*,[81] that he now believed the *New Jersey Bus Case* of 1947, in which he had provided the crucial fifth vote,[82] to have been wrongly decided! Yet the latter has never been overruled.

Reargument. A related, but distinct, practice is an order for *reargument*, in which the Court, for reasons best known to itself, orders a case back on the docket for reargument rather than hand down a decision. At the end of what became known as the "libertarian 1956–57 term," it did this in ten cases that had already been briefed and argued before it. The famed *Segregation Cases*[83] are a pertinent earlier example. Initially argued in December 1952, they were ordered reargued in December 1953 and were decided in May 1954. Another illustration is the aforementioned controversial water-dispute case between Arizona and California, which the Supreme Court ordered reargued in 1962—as an original jurisdiction case—despite the fact that the Court had spent a week hearing arguments in that complex litigation during the preceding January. A crucial reason for this order was Chief Justice Warren's voluntary disqualification—he had been governor of California—coupled with Justice Frankfurter's illness and Justice Whittaker's retirement, Whittaker's successor—Justice White—not having heard the initial arguments. A decision was ultimately handed down, in June of 1963, with the Chief Justice not participating, but with both Justice Goldberg, who had replaced the then-retired Justice Frankfurter, and Justice White taking part and siding with the 7:1 Black majority opinion.[84] A later petition for a rehearing by the "loser,"

---

[79] *Reid v. Covert* and *Kinsella v. Krueger*, 354 U.S. 1 (June 10, 1957). On rehearing.
[80] 448 U.S. 297.
[81] *Engel v. Vitale*, 370 U.S. 421 (1962), at 443.
[82] *Everson v. Board of Education of Ewing Township*, 330 U.S. 1.
[83] *Brown v. Board of Education of Topeka*, 347 U.S. 483 (1954), and *Bolling v. Sharpe*, 347 U.S. 497 (1954).
[84] *Arizona v. California*, 373 U.S. 546.

California, was denied.[85] And in the spring of 1985 Justice Powell requested reargument in five of the 57 cases he had missed because of a protracted illness, all five of which had ended in 4:4 ties.

THE U.S. SUPREME COURT AT WORK

The preceding concluding sections illustrate a marginal function of the Court. But how does this most impressive and most dignified of all governmental bodies in the United States *generally* conduct its work? Since 1873 it has customarily sat for thirty-six weeks annually, from the first or second Monday in October until the end of June.[86] Now and then, as in the 1972 *Pentagon Papers Case*[87] and in the dramatic Nixon tapes ruling of 1974,[88] the Court may briefly extend its term because of the felt necessity to render a decision prior to adjournment. And on rare occasions, such as in the case involving the Little Rock, Arkansas, school desegregation crisis in August–September 1957[89] and in that of the seven German saboteurs in 1942,[90] a Special Session may be convened, although there have been only four such sessions in this century. Yet it must be stated at once that the business of judging, at least at the level of the federal government, is a year-round occupation, regardless of the formal calendar.

All of the Court's sessions are now held in its own magnificent Greek-style, Corinthian-order, white marble structure, at 1 First Street, S.E., near Capitol Hill in Washington, D.C. The Court's present home,[91] (its construction

---

[85] 375 U.S. 892 (1963). But the issue has continued to percolate: cf. *Arizona v. California,* 460 U.S. 605 (1983). *United States v. Brewster,* 404 U.S. 1055 (1972), which dealt with the range and extent of senatorial immunity, represents a recent and pertinent illustration of a reargument order, as does a counsel case, *Kirby v. Illinois,* 406 U.S. 683 (1973), and two cases dealing with rights of aliens, *Weinberger v. Diaz,* 426 U.S. 77 and *Hampton v. Mow Sun Wong,* 426 U.S. 88, both 1976 actions.

[86] Its longest session to date (1977–78) ended on July 7, 1978.

[87] *The New York Times Co. v. United States* and *United States v. The Washington Post Co.,* 403 U.S. 713.

[88] *United States v. Nixon,* 417 U.S. 683, respectively.

[89] *Cooper v. Aaron,* 358 U.S. 1.

[90] *Ex parte Quirin,* 317 U.S. 1.

[91] The first term of the Supreme Court was the February term 1790—Jay and his colleagues failing initially of a quorum because of mired roads (other than the Chief Justice, only Justices James Wilson of Pennsylvania and William Cushing of Massachusetts were in attendance of the original six appointees). It began on February 2 of that year and was held in the Royal Exchange Building—designed as an open air market for butchers, with meeting facilities on the second floor—in New York City, which was then the seat of the federal government. That term lasted ten days, devoted to the admission of attorneys who wished to practice before it. The second term lasted two days! In July 1790, Congress moved the young nation's capital to Philadelphia, where in February 1791 the Court began to sit in the (now restored) State House, later known as Independence Hall, on Fifth and Chestnut streets. It met there for one term and then moved to nearby Old City Hall until August 1800—where it had to share space with the Mayor's Court. It switched to the County Court House for one term,

began in 1932 and was completed in 1935) is patterned after the Temple of Diana at Ephesus, the noble words "Equal Justice Under Law" carved above the two great 6½ ton bronze doors of the majestic entrance. The resplendent 82-by-91-foot courtroom itself, which is ringed on three sides by the Justices' chambers, has a 44-foot dome, supported by twenty-four Ionic columns of light Siena old convent marble from the Liguria region of Italy, and ivory vein marble walls from Alicante, Spain. The carvings on the walls depict both real and symbolic judicial figures (on one wall those of the pre-Christian era, on the other those of the Christian). Here convenes the Supreme Court of the United States, its nine Justices clad in black judicial vestments—which Judge Jerome Frank always wanted to banish.[92] (The building still houses its own seamstress to sew those judicial robes as well as a woodworking shop to repair the chairs.) They are seated behind the raised half-hexagon bench of marble and Honduran mahogany in high-backed black leather, swivel rocking chairs of various sizes,[93] which stand against a background of full purplish red draperies. At the appointed hour, the drapes part and from behind them appears the Chief Justice, followed by the eight Associate Justices, *seriatim* in order of seniority. They, as well as all those assembled in the courtroom, remain standing until the Marshal has completed his time-honored introduction: "Oyez, Oyez, Oyez! All persons having business before the Honorable, the Supreme Court of the United States, are admonished to draw near and give their attention, for the Court is now sitting. God save the United States and this Honorable Court" (a remark that has been the butt of a number of tasteless jokes).[94] The Justices' seats are arranged according to length of continuous

---

but in February 1801 joined the government in its move to Washington, D.C., to the office of the Clerk of the Senate (on the main floor of the East Wing of the then still unfinished Capitol Building). It remained there until its own beautiful chamber in that edifice, created by famed American architect Benjamin Henry Latrobe, was readied in 1810, although it had to meet in rented houses and private homes because of the destruction wrought in the War of 1812 when the British had used Supreme Court documents to set fire to the Capital. (Fully restored to its 1860 splendor in 1975, it is now open to the public, designated as the "Old Supreme Court Chamber.") In 1860, the court moved directly above to what is today known as the "Old Senate Chamber," where it functioned until 1935, more or less restricted to a total of four rooms, when the Cass Gilbert–designed present beautiful structure was ready for its occupancy across the plaza. Congress had appropriated $9,740,000 for the latter's construction; $93,532.02 was returned unexpended! The magnificent edifice stands as one of the greatest construction bargains in history. Unfortunately, neither Gilbert, its architect (who died in 1934) nor Chief Justice Taft, its "midwife" (who died in 1930) lived to see its completion.

[92]See his amusing "The Cult of the Robe" in his classic *Courts on Trial: Myth and Reality in American Justice* (Princeton, NJ: Princeton University Press, 1949), ch. 18.

[93]In late 1974 Chief Justice Burger let it be known that he was desirous of uniformity in the chairs; but at least some of his colleagues demurred.

[94]At the Court's first session of each new term in October, the Chief Justice will announce, as Warren E. Burger did on that occasion in 1984: "I have the honor to announce that the October 1984, term of the Supreme Court of the United States has convened." (October 1, 1984.)

service on the bench; the Chief Justice sits in the center, flanked by the Senior Associate Justice on his immediate right, the second-ranking on his immediate left, then alternating in that manner in declining order of seniority.

ORAL ARGUMENT

In this impressive setting, guarded by its special thirty-three-member police detail on round-the-clock security, and attended by four court attendants[95] (since 1963 mercifully no longer in knickers, long black stockings, and double-breasted jackets), the Court listens to oral arguments—in the cases it has agreed to hear—normally for the first three, but sometimes four, days in two weeks out of each month. (Until 1955 it used to sit for oral argument five days each week.) Its Justices spend the other two weeks behind closed doors considering cases and writing opinions. Accompanied by a $100 fee, forty copies of the printed briefs to be presented in the case at bar—one set going to each Justice—have to be filed with the Clerk of the Court well in advance (to be exact, within forty-five days after the case is placed on the docket by the party bringing suit) and the answering brief has to be filed thirty days after this.[96] The briefs, which are filed in accordance with prescribed format and nowadays are preferably no longer than twenty-five pages,[97] generally state the

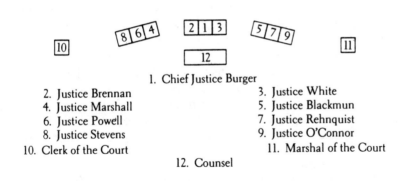

1. Chief Justice Burger

2. Justice Brennan   3. Justice White
4. Justice Marshall   5. Justice Blackmun
6. Justice Powell   7. Justice Rehnquist
8. Justice Stevens   9. Justice O'Connor
10. Clerk of the Court   11. Marshal of the Court

12. Counsel

Figure 3. The Supreme Court of the United States 1985–1986

[95] For the first time in its 182-year history the Court, in September 1972, appointed a *girl* as page—fourteen-year-old Deborah Gelin of Rockville, Md. At the beginning of the October term 1975, the Court discontinued the practice of utilizing teenage "pages," which originated in 1865, and replaced them with mature "court attendants," usually night students at area colleges and universities.

[96] All printed documents filed in the Court must be on 6½- by 9¼-inch paper, with type no smaller than 11-point, "adequately leaded," and the paper must be "opaque and unglazed."

[97] In 1974 the Court *rejected* a 107-page brief by L. S. Huffman, the prosecuting attorney of Allen County, Ohio, as not being brief enough under its rules. In rejecting it, the Justices cited a rule that all briefs be "concise and free from burdensome, irrelevant, immaterial and scandalous matter." Mr. Huffman, who had lost below in a case involving his attempts to close down a movie theater for allegedly showing an obscene film, had also attached an appendix comprising more than 4,500 small photos of sexual acitvity from the film! In 1976, visibly

facts, issues, questions to be presented, decisions of lower courts, and all relevant legal arguments, together with the statutes and citations of cases to which they apply—contemporarily also laced with social science data as part and parcel of a so-called Brandeis Brief, that is, one that stresses such data explicitly and usually extensively; it was first used by Louis D. Brandeis when he argued for Oregon in the 1908 maximum hour law case of *Muller v. Oregon*, 208 U.S. 412. (As already explained, those bona fide paupers whose cases are treated on the special miscellaneous docket may file handwritten or typewritten briefs.)

Oral argument, now heard on designated days from 10:00 A.M. to 12:00 P.M. and from 1:00 P.M. until 3:00 P.M.,[98] is at once the most significant, the most human, and the most fascinating aspect of the *public* portion of the Court's work. (All oral argument began to be taperecorded in 1955; all tapes are being preserved but become publicly available only three years after the ultimate decision date.) Of the 300 seats available, 112 are allotted to the Justices' families, members of the bar, and the media (nineteen positions complete with writing desks) with the remaining 188 being available to the general public strictly on a "first come, first served" basis.[99] Usually there are two public queues for those seats—one a three-minute-stay line, the other a "stay as long as you wish" one.)

There is at least a chance that skillful oral arguments, in supplementing the printed brief by oral emphasis,[100] may sway members on the spot, although this is far less likely in the great than in the small cases. Still, first impressions count—and Justice Douglas, for one, insisted that " . . . oral arguments win or lose the case."[101] Chief Justice Warren, on the other hand, regarded oral argument as "not highly persuasive."[102] And Justice Holmes seldom found it significant, often taking catnaps during it. The pressure on the arguing lawyers, who must speak from the floor level, naturally is enormous; they must indeed be quick of tongue and feet! They are frequently ques-

---

irritated, Chief Justice Burger veritably roasted Sylvester Petro, a Winston-Salem, N.C., lawyer who had filed a 216-page brief. (*The* [Charlottesville, Va.] *Daily Progress*, November 10, 1976, p. A3.)

[98] From 1873 until 1961 the Court met from 12:00 P.M. until 4:30 P.M., and from 1898 until 1970 it allowed but half an hour for lunch. Then Chief Justice Burger ordered the more humane break of one hour, now in force.

[99] By adding chairs in spare spaces, 500 people (including 14 additional media positions in the alcoves behind the regular 19) may be admitted on days of maximum public interest—such as oral argument in the 1974 *Nixon tapes case*—but that is rarely done. (*United States v. Nixon*, 417 U.S. 683.)

[100] See John M. Harlan, "What Role Does Oral Argument Play in the Conduct of an Appeal?" 41 *Cornell Law Quarterly* 6 (1955).

[101] *The Philadelphia Inquirer*, April 9, 1963, "Oral argument," as Frankfurter once put it, "has a force beyond what the written word conveys." (As quoted by Kenneth Turan, "Let Them Entertain You," *The Washington Post*, "Potomac." February 2, 1975, p. 11.

[102] "Seminar with Mr. Chief Justice Warren," University of Virginia Legal Forum, April 25, 1973, p. 9.

tioned sharply by the Justices, who often have a bench memorandum prepared before the argument, and their questions may conceivably forecast the ultimate decision of the Court, although in few, if any, instances is it possible, let alone safe, to give an accurate prognosis. Some Justices (e.g., Douglas and Powell) customarily ask very few questions; others (Frankfurter, the most impassioned advocate of oral argument, who would not read the briefs antecedent to it, and Stevens) have a habit of asking a great many. John P. Frank reported that in one particular case he witnessed—perhaps a somewhat extreme illustration—the Justices interrupted counsel 84 times during 120 minutes of oral argument, with 93 questions and interpolations, chargeable to Justice Frankfurter alone![103] Woe to the counsel who is ill-prepared or uncertain—and the Justices frown on reading from the prepared text. In fact, the Court's Rule 44 states that it looks "with disfavor" on such a practice. But the Justices may also well prove to be helpful to counsel. Thus, during one oral argument heard in the 1960–61 term, Justice Frankfurter sharply questioned an obviously flustered lawyer several times, only to see Justice Douglas intervene each time with a helpful answer! "I thought you were arguing this case," shot Frankfurter to grateful counsel, who responded, "I am, but I can use all the help I can get."[104] It should be clear that the Court, as Frankfurter once put it, does not see itself as "a dozing audience for the reading of soliloquies, but as a questioning body, utilizing oral argument as a means for exposing the difficulties of a case with a view to meeting them."[105]

Unlike the old days, especially during Chief Justice John Marshall's reign, when argument often seemed interminable, and when a Daniel Webster would sometimes address the Court with mounting eloquence for days, present-day lawyers are severely limited in the time granted to them for argument. Normally, the limit is one-half hour for each side; sometimes an hour is allotted. One of the rare suspensions of the time limit rule took place in the case of *United Steel Workers of America v. United States*,[106] involving

---

[103] *The Marble Palace* (New York: Alfred A. Knopf, 1958), pp. 104–5.

[104] As reported by Anthony Lewis in "The Justices' Supreme Job," *The New York Times Magazine*, June 11, 1961. (Italics supplied.)

[105] From "Memorial for Stanley M. Silverberg," *Of Law and Men*, ed. by Philip Elman (New York: Harcourt, Brace and Co., 1956), pp. 320–21. (Which does not mean that there has never been dozing on the high bench!) Almost all the Justices agree on the desirability and the significance of oral argument, but there are exceptions—for example, Justice Minton, who was always restive and bored during oral argument. Of course, the Court does not have to hear oral argument in order to render a formal decision in a case. Thus, in 1978, without hearing oral argument, and basing their judgment entirely on the legal papers submitted—a procedure they use infrequently—the Justices held 7:2 that reducing the benefits of welfare recipients who move from the United States to Puerto Rico is not a violation of their constitutional right to travel. (*Califano v. Torres*, 435 U.S. 1.) Also in the 1981 holding in *California v. Prysock*, 453 U.S. 355, in which it ruled 6:3, without hearing formal argument, that the *Miranda* warnings do not require "talismanic incantation" from the police.

[106] 361 U.S. 49 (1959). Six hours were provided in that case. Another was *Arizona v. California*,

the legality of the injunctive provisions of the Taft-Hartley Act. In the average term only about 250 hours of argument are allotted to the attorneys for their oral presentations.[107] They use a lectern to which two lights are attached; five minutes before time is up a white light flashes; when the second light, appropriately a red one, flashes, the lawyer must stop instantly, unless he is granted permission by the Chief Justice to continue. According to one of Chief Justice Hughes's law clerks, the "Chief" was so strict on the score of time that he once stopped a leader of the New York Bar in the middle of the word "if"; on another occasion, on being asked by the same attorney how much time remained, Hughes replied icily, "Fourteen seconds, Mr. Counsel."[108]

To argue cases at the bar of the Supreme Court a lawyer must be admitted to practice before it. This is now a relatively routine matter,[109] one that requires two sponsors, three years of good standing before the highest court of a state, and payment of a $100 fee. Gone are the days, in vogue until 1970, when the Chief Justice would formally welcome and chat with each lawyer newly admitted to practice before the Court.[110] The $100 "admission fee" is used by the Supreme Court to cover travel and printing expenses of Court-assigned lawyers who represent indigent parties that come before it. Admission may, however, be revoked—as occurred, for example, in the case of attorney Wilmer D. Rekeweg of Paulding, Ohio, in June 1967. Because of certain professional aberrations resulting in his disbarment from the practice of law in all courts of Ohio by order of the Supreme Court of Ohio, the Supreme Court of the United States, after a "show cause" procedure, suspended and then disbarred him in a special Order, which read: " ... it is ordered that the said Wilmer D. Rekeweg be, and he is hereby disbarred, and that his name be stricken from the roll of attorneys admitted to practice before the bar of this court."[111] A similar fate befell G. Gordon Liddy, one of the convicted Watergate burglars, who was disbarred in 1973,[112] and former White House Counsel, John W. Dean, III, in 1975.[113] In July 1976 the Court, 7:0, accepted ex-President Nixon's resignation from the Court's bar. (He was disbarred in New York.) Former Attorney General John N. Mitchell and former White House Assistant John D. Ehrlichman were disbarred by the Court

---

sixteen hours (!) in 1962; a third was *Brown v. Board of Education II* in 1955, for which fourteen hours were allotted. (370 U.S. 906 and 349 U.S. 294, respectively.)

[107] In the 1977–78 term, for example, 225 hours.

[108] Edwin McElwain, "The Business of the Supreme Court as Conducted by Chief Justice Hughes," 63 *harvard Law Review* 6 (1949).

[109] But see Chief Justice Burger's objections to one Daniel S. Zevin in 1984, forcing a formal vote on his admission, which Burger lost 6:3. (See *The New York Times*, May 1, 1984, p. A10.)

[110] In the 1975–76 term, for example, the Court admitted *sage und schreibe* 5,691 persons to practice before it! (*Washington Counsel*, September–October 1976, p. 49.)

[111] "Actions in United States Supreme Court," June 5, 1967 (as reported in *The New York Times*, June 6, 1967). (Order 1346 Misc.)

[112] *In the Matter of the Disbarment of George Gordon Liddy*, 414 U.S. 1037.

[113] *In the Matter of Disbarment of John W. Dean, III*, 421 U.S. 985.

in 1977.[114] And so was former Attorney General Richard G. Kleindienst, by a vote of 7:0, in 1982.[115]

The Solicitor General. The *Solicitor General* is the third-ranking official in the U.S. Department of Justice, following the Attorney General and the Deputy Attorney General. Because of its special relationship to the Supreme Court, the post of Solicitor General has always enjoyed a high reputation in legal circles, has been eagerly sought by members of the legal profession, and has not infrequently been filled by legal scholars (viz., President Kennedy's 1961 appointment of Professor Archibald Cox of Harvard University Law School, President Johnson's of Cox's Dean, Erwin N. Griswold,[116] in 1967, succeeding Thurgood Marshall, President Nixon's of Yale Law School Professor Robert M. Bork in 1973, and President Reagan's of Brigham Young Law School Dean Rex Lee in 1981).

The Solicitor General is in charge of all of the government's litigation in the Supreme Court, which constitutes in excess of 50 percent of the Court's total work load. He and his staff argue all of the government's cases before it. His office supervises all government briefs filed in the Court, and he must personally approve or disapprove any case before the government takes it to the Court. Moreover, the Solicitor General has supervisory authority over other government appeals. Only if he gives his approval may the government appeal from an adverse decision in a trial court—but, of course, it must be remembered that both the federal and state governments are checked by the Fifth (and Fourteenth) Amendment safeguards against double jeopardy. Sometimes, to the chagrin of certain members of both the executive and legislative branches, the Solicitor General's office exercises its commendable tradition of alertness toward any unfairness in government cases. When he detects such unfairness, the Solicitor General will usually file a "Confession of Error" in the Supreme Court, in which he asks that it set aside a victory won by the government in the lower court. Although this practice is of the very essence of justice—which, after all, should be the aim of all litigation—it may well be doubted that a large number of private counsel would be similarly willing to forgo a victory. All too frequently litigation is viewed as a courtroom battle between two opposing teams of high-powered trial lawyers bent on "victory" rather than on the triumph of justice.

BEHIND CLOSED DOORS

During the Court's term, each Friday and, at Chief Justice Burger's behest, since 1974 also at 3:00 P.M. on Wednesdays, is *Conference Day.*[117] On that

---

[114] *In the Matter of Disbarment of Richard G. Kleindienst,* 459 U.S. 811 (1982).

[115] *In re Mitchell* and *in re Ehrlichman,* 434 U.S. 917.

[116] Griswold was before the bench a total of 114 times—more than any other modern Solicitor General.

[117] Until changed by Chief Justice Warren, Saturday was Conference Day, and it used to go on until seven or eight at night! (As quoted by Jim Mann, *Los Angeles Times,* May 10, 1983, p. D1.)

day (there are about thirty each term of Court) the Justices, summoned by a buzzer five minutes before the hour, meet in a strictly closed session, usually from 9:30 or 10:00 A.M. until 5:30 or 6:00 P.M. (with a ten-minute mid-morning refreshment break and less than one hour for lunch) in the beautiful, oak-paneled conference chamber on the first (main) floor, under the chairmanship of the Chief Justice, whose offices are adjacent to it.[118] The role of the "Chief" is that of *primus inter pares*, although some have tended to be more *primus* than *pares*, and vice versa (as we shall presently see). Here the Justices discuss the cases they have heard, as well as all pending motions and applications for *certiorari*—although upwards of three-quarters of the latter are dismissed without even having merited conference discussion. Among petitions Justice Brennan thus considered frivolous in 1973 were the following propounded questions: "Are Negroes in fact Indians and therefore entitled to Indians' exemption from federal income taxes?" "Are the federal income tax laws unconstitutional insofar as they do not provide a deduction for the depletion of the human body?" "Is the Sixteenth Amendment unconstitutional as a violation of the Fourteenth Amendment?" and "Does a ban on drivers' turning right on a red light constitute an unreasonable burden on interstate commerce?"[119] Each Justice is expected to be ready to indicate his tentative stand, which he normally will have noted on his copy of the agenda, having been previously advised which cases would be up for discussion—generally those just heard by the Court on the three or four "argument days" during that week or those recently heard in the course of conferences meeting during the two recess weeks in which no oral arguments are presented. The conference "list" may run from 25 to 150 items; 75 is about normal. The importance of this traditional conference, or for that matter any conference of appellate judges at which law cases and controversies are reviewed, was stated ably by Justice Jesse W. Carter of the California Supreme Court:

> ... [The conference] is not a prayer meeting where everyone is expected to nod "amen"; it is more like a battleground where opposing philosophies meet in hand-to-hand combat.[120]

Or, as Justice Powell observed almost two decades later:

> [The conference] affords the principal opportunity for discussion, debate, and group deliberation. Justices may speak as frequently and as long as they wish ... and not infrequently a conference has altered my original tentative view.[121]

The Justices are seated around a large rectangular mahogany conference table, each of the nine highbacked chairs bearing a nameplate; about twenty-

---

[118]The conference room is a large ceremonial anteroom between the two offices occupied by the Chief Justice.

[119]59 *Journal of the American Bar Association* 846 (August 1973).

[120]As quoted in *The New York Times*, March 16, 1959, p. 31.

[121]As quoted by Richard L. Williams, *Smithsonian*, February 1977, p. 89.

five carts loaded with needed data stand nearby. In accordance with a tradition established by Chief Justice Fuller in 1888, all shake hands with one another on entering the room. The Chief Justice sits at the south end and the Senior Associate Justice at the north end. Three of the other Justices sit on one side, four on the other, but not necessarily in the usual order of seniority.[122] Looking down on this scene is the sole portrait in the room—that of Chief Justice John Marshall. The incumbent Chief Justice, whose personality and administrative talent loom large in these meetings, customarily gives his own view first in the case up for discussion, and he is followed by the other Justices in order of seniority. Each Justice—refreshed by coffee from a silver urn—must be prepared to recite and do so persuasively, if he or she feels strongly about an issue involved. Upon completion of this phase of their deliberations, the nine members of the Court take a tentative vote on the case, the Justice with the lowest seniority usually, but not always,[123] voting first this time, presumably so that he will not be influenced by the votes of his more experienced colleagues—a somewhat debatable rationale, which Justice Goldberg characterized as "ridiculous."[124] In any event it is not a rigid procedural rule. Each Justice has a hinged, lockable docket book, in which all votes are duly recorded.

The Role of the Chief Justice. Although he is theoretically merely *primus inter pares*—and he does have but one vote among nine—the "Chief" has a potential influence that may well outweigh that of any ordinary presiding officer. Justice Hughes suggested some reasons for this:

> Popular interest naturally centers in the Chief Justice as the titular head of the Court. He is its executive officer; he presides at its sessions and its conferences, and announces its orders. By virtue of the distinctive function of the Court he is the most important judicial officer in the world; he is the Chief Justice of the United States.[125]

---

[122]In a letter to me, dated September 28, 1970, Justice Brennan described the Court's seating arrangement at that time as follows: "The Chief Justice sits on one end and Justice Black on the other end of the table. On the Chief's right sit Justice Marshall, myself, and Justice Douglas in that order. On his left sit Justice Stewart, Justice White, Justice Blackmun, and Justice Harlan in that order," In an article in *The New York Times* (February 6, 1975, p. M31) Warren Weaver professed to have knowledge of a quite different contemporary seating arrangement, based strictly on "clockwise by seniority," with Douglas beginning the order on Burger's left. But in a letter to me, dated August 4, 1975, Barrett McGurn, the Court's information officer, declared Weaver to be wrong and, having checked with the Clerk of the Court, provided a diagram, which is very close to the data on the seating of the Justices supplied by Justice Brennan.

[123]In his account, loc. cit., Weaver reports that "this practice has been dropped" and that the voting, like the discussion, now proceeds on the basis of seniority—a claim supported by Justice Blackmun. My own account was reliably reconfirmed in early 1979, however, and again in 1982 by Chief Justice Burger.

[124]Statement to me, February 24, 1976, at University of Virginia Student Legal Forum.

[125]As quoted in *The New York Times*, June 24, 1969, p. 25.

Several of his functions lend themselves ideally to the exercise of that influence: one is the chairmanship of the Court's own conference, including his highly important role in the sifting of writs of *certiorari*, the other his assignment of opinions (to be more fully described later in this section). When the "Chief" opens discussion of a case by giving his own views first, he has an excellent opportunity to state the case as he sees it, to indicate the questions to be decided, and to give his opinions on the issue or issues involved. This "speak first" rule is a far from inconsiderable power, for there is a chance that his initial analysis of a problem will have at least some influence on that of others in the room. It is, of course, by no means inevitable that the person who selects the issues to be discussed will dominate or determine the ultimate results—to which the lasting and profound differences in reading the meaning of the Constitution among Justices on a host of issues bear witness. Still, there is a good chance that such will indeed be the case.

An interesting example, gleaned from the Harold H. Burton papers, among others, is Chief Justice Warren's role in speaking first in the Court's Conferences on the *1954 and 1955 Segregation Cases*.[126]

And other tasks, implied or actual, confront a Chief Justice and play a role in history's regard of him as an effective or ineffective leader. Among these is the ability to keep peace among the several Justices, who are often deeply divided along intellectual and personal lines. Justices Jackson and Black, for example, became increasingly hostile during the waning days of Chief Justice Stone's tenure (partly due to Jackson's long assignment in Nürnberg), resulting, or so it is believed, in President Truman's compromise "peacemaker appointment" of Fred Vinson as Stone's successor on the latter's death in 1946. Vinson, a person of far less judicial and intellectual stature than Stone, had a reputation as a conciliator and, apparently, succeeded at least in keeping the feud between the two Justices *en famille*. Justice McReynolds, a confirmed anti-Semite, refused even to speak to his newly appointed colleague, Justice Brandeis, from 1916 to 1919. Chief Justice White was unable to alter the situation, but the amiable and popular Chief Justice Taft apparently succeeded in mitigating it somewhat. Still, McReynolds caused Taft constant difficulties, too. For instance, he refused to sit for the Court's annual photograph in 1924 because he would have found himself seated to Brandeis in seniority—and no photo was taken! And two years earlier he had refused to accompany the Court to a Philadelphia ceremony, writing to Taft: "As you know, I am not always to be found when there is a Hebrew aboard. Therefore,

---

[126] *Brown v. Board of Education of Topeka*, 347 U.S. 483 (1954); ibid., 349 U.S. 294 (1955); and *Bolling v. Sharpe*, 347 U.S. 497 (1954). See the account by S. Sidney Ulmer in *Courts as . . . Small Groups* (New York: General Learning Press, 1971), pp. 23–26; the Warren obituary, *The New York Times*, July 11, 1974, p. A35; and Richard Kluger's *Simple Justice* (New York: Alfred A. Knopf, 1975).

my 'inability to attend' must not surprise you.'"[127] In 1939 he refused to attend Felix Frankfurter's robing ceremony; he would not sign the Court's routine retirement resolution when Brandeis left; and he habitually turned his back on Justice Cardozo. Other McReynolds quirks were almost constant carping at practically every opinion authored by Stone, whom he disliked for philosophical reasons, and his overt hostility toward Justice John H. Clarke. McReynolds, who, as Wilson's Attorney General, had played a role in Clarke's appointment to the bench, felt "betrayed" because Clarke failed to vote on the Court as McReynolds thought he should and would.[128] Although he was by no means able to stop entirely the public barbs exchanged on the bench on occasion between, for example, Justices Frankfurter and Whittaker on the one hand, and Justices Black and Douglas on the other, Chief Justice Warren apparently smoothed over many a ruffled feeling, despite his personal involvement in an outburst or two, as some of the illustrations to follow will indicate. Yet it is vital to be aware of a basic fact of life on the Court: *no Chief Justice can command the beliefs of his associates*, and the Court has never lacked for strong personalities and strong convictions, nor will it henceforth.

Another significant facet of the Chief's work is to keep an eye on the clock during the conference, with a view of getting its tasks accomplished. Although there has been disagreement on the extent of the Court's burden, there is little doubt that the pressure of case work is enormous. Unless a firm hand rules the conference, time will flee, especially as the Justices are, quite naturally, given to extensive speaking—Justice Oliver Wendell Holmes, Jr., interestingly enough, being a notable exception. No Chief Justice since Marshall controlled his flock so firmly as did Hughes, whom most students and observers of the Court, as well as those who served with him on the high tribunal, have generally regarded as the most effective—even if on occasion somewhat arbitrary—organizer, leader, and disciplinarian since Marshall's taut judicial regime.[129]

For example, Hughes would accord an average of three and one-half minutes of conference time, and no more, to a petition for *certiorari*—having himself gone through and thoroughly analyzed all of them *before* the conference and being fully prepared to make recommendations on each to his col-

---

[127] As quoted by Alpheus T. Mason in his *William Howard Taft: Chief Justice* (New York: Simon and Schuster, 1965), pp. 216–17.

[128] Any of the following types of applicants to a clerkship were disqualified with McReynolds: those who were "smokers," 'drinkers," Jews, married, or engaged!

[129] This does not mean that even Hughes was able to control the idiosyncracies of the cantankerous Justice McReynolds, who, upon being informed by a messenger from the Chief Justice that it was time to convene for a Court session, sent the messenger packing with the reply that he did "not work for" the Chief Justice. As reported by James F. Simon, *In His Own Image: The Supreme Court in Richard Nixon's America* (New York: David McKay Co., 1973), p. 55.

leagues. And he would often force the end of a discussion that he viewed as unprofitable or dilatory by intoning: "Brethren, the only way to settle this is vote. So let us do just that—now." Justice Stone, whose philosophy of his role as Chief was drastically different, declined to put any time on either *certiorari* discussions or a particular series of cases. Stone simply refused to engage in what he viewed as "high pressure tactics." Thus, whereas Hughes finished a conference docket in four hours, Stone would require four days for a similar docket. This did not make Stone a less qualified jurist, but it probably made him a far less effective Chief than Hughes—or Taft, another effective, resourceful, and popular Chief Justice, whose caliber, however, was certainly considerably below that of Stone as a *jurist*. (Taft was infinitely happier as Chief Justice than as President; he regarded the former office as possessing both more power and more prestige than the latter.) Some observers, although distinctly a minority, believe that the virtues of Hughes as Chief Justice were overstated and those of Stone underrated. One of these, John P. Frank, a law clerk for Justice Black, complained that Hughes's tactics of "business efficiency" meant that " ... discussion in conference was perforce a statement of conclusions more than an exchange of mutually stimulating ideas ..." and he charged the Chief Justice with "intellectual flexibility for the sake of the appearance of unanimity."[130] Be that as it may, Chief Justice Hughes was immensely popular as a leader of his bench, and he was the only member of the Court to whom Justice McReynolds would defer. We have Justice Frankfurter's word that " ... if he made others feel his moral superiority, they merely felt a fact ... all who served with him recognized [his] extraordinary qualities. ... To see him preside was like [seeing] Toscanini leading an orchestra."[131] Justice Black attested to his own "more than impersonal and detached admiration [for Hughes's] extraordinary intellectual gifts."[132] And Justice Roberts wrote that "Men whose views were as sharply opposed as those of Van Devanter and Brandeis, or those of Sutherland and Cardozo, were at one in their admiration and affectionate regard for their presiding officer."[133] There is little, if any, doubt that Charles Evans Hughes was the epitome of a great Chief Justice. And history may arguably place Earl Warren into a similar bracket—perhaps even higher, next to John Marshall. For to both Warren and Marshall the Court was more than "a mystically passive weigher of 'the law,' but also a participant, along with other agencies of the government, in the practical process of realizing the objectives set out in the Constitution's preamble."[134]

---

[130] John P. Frank, "Harlan Fiske Stone: An Estimate," 9 *Stanford Law Review* 692n (1957).

[131] *Of Law and Men,* op. cit., pp. 133, 148.

[132] Black to Hughes, June 3, 1941. Hughes Papers.

[133] New York County Lawyers' Association, December 12, 1948.

[134] Alpheus Thomas Mason, "Judicial Activism: Old and New," 55 *Virginia Law Review* 424 (1969). Fred Graham placed Warren just below Marshall and above Taney in an interesting evaluative article, "180 Years of Chief Justices: Some Nonentities, Some Giants," *The New York Times,* June 24, 1969, p. 25.

ASSIGNING AND WRITING OPINIONS

As Eugene V. Rostow wrote when he was dean of the Yale School of Law, "Judges must write down their reasons for a decision because they are partners with us, the citizenry, in an agreed procedure for reaching responsible decisions."[135] The practice of writing the Opinion of the Court[136] goes back to the days of Chief Justice John Marshall. Prior to his adoption of this time-saving procedure, the Justices usually delivered their opinions *seriatim*[137] in about one-quarter to one-third of the cases—a practice still prevalent with the Law Lords of the British House of Lords, and one that Jefferson, as President, wanted to institutionalize in the face of Marshall's powerful objections. Marshall realistically believed that the Court's power and prestige would be enhanced if it were to speak with a single voice.[138] Today, full opinions are written for the Court (some of these *per curiam*, as we have seen) in all cases heard by it on the merits, other than those decided by memorandum order. However, if there is a tie vote, no opinion is written, and the Court does not announce on which side of the tie the Justices stood. In the event of such a vote, the decision of the highest court below, from which the case came to the Supreme Court, is sustained; for example, the Court's 4:4 vote in the case of *Bailey v. Richardson*[139] affirmed the 2:1 upholding of the loyalty dismissal of Dorothy Bailey by the federal government in the Court of Appeals for the District of Columbia. In this instance the even division of the Court came about as a result of Justice Tom Clark's failure to participate in the case; because he had been the U.S. Attorney General at the time of Miss Bailey's travail and dismissal, he deemed it unethical to be involved in the disposition of her appeal. A more recent illustration is the Court's failure, because of Justice John Paul Steven's refusal to agree with either side, to resolve an important jury instruction controversy.[140]

Abstentions. The members of today's Supreme Court, unlike most members of Congress, are extremely cautious about even the faintest taint of con-

---

[135] *The Sovereign Prerogative: The Supreme Court and the Quest for Law* (New Haven: Yale University Press, 1962), p. 89.

[136] John P. Frank, a careful observer and student of the Court, once divided the writing styles of the Justices into four categories: "legal lumpy," "legal massive," "rock-bottom contemporary," and "legal lucid." *The Marble Palace*, op. cit., pp. 295 ff.

[137] A well-know illustration is the group of *seriatim* opinions by Associate Justices Chase, Paterson, and Iredell in the 1796 case of *Hylton v. United States*, 3 Dallas 171.

[138] The judges of Italy's Constitutional Court, the highest tribunal in the land (see ch. 7 *infra*, pp. 317ff.) are statutorily *forbidden* to file individual opinions and, in general, to make their votes known.

[139] 341 U.S. 918 (1951). Two other recent illustrations are the Court's 4:4 split (Justice Lewis F. Powell, a prominent Richmond educational leader, abstaining) in the 1973 Richmond school consolidation cases (*School Board of Richmond v. Bradley* and *Bradley v. State Board of Education of the Commonwealth of Virginia*, 411 U.S. 913, and a freedom of expression case affirming *per curiam* 4:4 a lower court's declaration of unconstitutionality (*Common Cause v. Schmitt*, 455 U.S. 129 [1982].)

[140] *Connecticut v. Johnson*, 460 U.S. 73 (1983).

flict of interest, be it of a social, economic, personal, or political nature.[141] Among the Justices, "When in doubt, do not sit" is a firmly established custom, called "recusing," partially reinforced by two federal statutes and a canon of the American Bar Association.[142] This was not always so, particularly not in the early days of the Court—witness Marshall's refusal to disqualify himself in *Marbury v. Madison*,[143] in which he was personally and directly involved.

Assignments Generally. The work load of preparing opinions of the Court is usually very well distributed. If the Court is unanimous, or if the Chief Justice is in the majority, he may, and often does, write the opinion of the Court himself. In the latter instance, provided he speaks for at least four other Justices, it would be known as the *majority opinion.*

But, of course, nothing prevents the Chief from asking another member of the Court to write the opinion either when it is unanimous or when he is on the side of the majority. The only exception to this practice is the long-standing tradition of permitting every newcomer to the Court to select the first opinion he will write. Long gone are the days of Chief Justice Marshall who, especially during his early years on the bench, would himself write practically every opinion—no doubt at least partly because his fellow Justices were rather lethargic (some would say browbeaten).[144] In fact, during his first four full years (1801–5) he personally authored all but two of the opinions of the Court![145] Chief Justice Warren, on the other hand, in assigning 80 percent of all the Court's opinions during his sixteen-year tenure, self-assigned but 10

---

[141] As a fledgling member of the Court in 1972, Justice Rehnquist, notwithstanding the highly critical reaction of large segments of the legal and academic communities, refused to disqualify himself in at least three 5:4 decisions that had been within his jurisdiction as an official in the Justice Department prior to his appointment to the Supreme Court—but he did *not* participate in *United States v. Nixon.*

[142] For their exact verbiage, see Title 29, Sec. 454, U.S.C.A., Title 28, Sec. 455, U.S.C.A., and the Fourth Canon of the American Bar Association's Canons of Judicial Ethics. The frequent abstentions of the then still recently appointed Justice Thurgood Marshall in his first term on the Court (1967–68)—largely because he had been Solicitor General of the United States as well as a prominent civil rights attorney—caused considerable consternation. By the end of the first five months of the term he had abstained in thirty-one of the forty-four formally decided cases!

[143] 1 Cranch 137 (1803).

[144] According to a wistful 1822 letter from Justice William Johnson to Thomas Jefferson, the former soon perceived the real reason his Chief, John Marshall, "delivered all the opinions. . . . Cushing was incompetent, Chase could not be got to think or write—Patterson [sic] was a slow man and willingly declined the trouble, and the other two judges [Marshall and Bushrod Washington] are commonly estimated as one judge. . . . ("Letter of December 10, 1822, quoted in Donald G. Morgan, *Justice William Johnson: The First Dissenter.* Columbia: University of South Carolina Press, 1954, pp. 181–82.()

[145] In all, he wrote 519 of his Court's 1,106 opinions, dissenting only nine times in his thirty-four and one-half years on the high bench; and he wrote 36 of the 62 decisions involving constitutional questions (See Robert J. Steamer, *The Supreme Court in Crisis: A History of Conflict* (Amherst: University of Massachusetts Press, 1971), p. 35.

percent, and Chief Justice Burger during his first fifteen terms (1969–84) self-assigned a similar percentage in assigning 84.8 percent of all cases.[146]

When the Chief Justice is on the minority side of a decision, however, the Senior Associate Justice on the side of the majority either writes the opinion of the Court himself or assigns it to one of the other members among the majority. All assignments are made by sending a formal note to the prospective author a few days following the conference. Professor Spaeth's significant study of Chief Justice Burger's assignment practices documents a remarkable record of distributive equality—better than any of his five immediate predecessors (Warren, Vinson, Stone, Hughes, and Taft).[147] The 1983–84 term serves as an illustration of an equitable distribution of the workload[148] of preparing the 163 written *opinions of the Court:* Justice Rehnquist wrote 19; Justice White and Justice Powell 18; Justice O'Connor 17; the Chief Justice and Justices Brennan, Blackmun, and Stevens 16 each; and Justice Marshall 15. (Twelve opinions were *per curiam.*) Of the sixty-eight written concurring *opinions* filed, Justice Stevens led his colleagues with 18; next was Justice Powell with eleven; Justices Brennan and O'Connor wrote ten each; Justices White and Blackmun wrote six; Justice Rehnquist penned three; and the Chief Justice and Justice Marshall brought up the rear with two each. Justice Stevens led the Court in its 127 written *dissenting opinions* by a wide margin with thirty-four; he was followed by Justice Brennan's twenty-nine; Justice Marshall wrote sixteen; Justice Rehnquist fourteen; Justices White, and Blackmun, and O'Connor authored nine each; Justice Powell wrote seven; and the Chief Justice penned none at all. (There were an additional 180 dissents *without* written opinions.)

Although until circa 1930 the Court tended to be unanimous in approximately 80 to 85 percent of its decisions, as a rule *unanimous opinions* have since then been rendered in a minority of full opinion cases, averaging 25 to 30 percent through the years, and only barely 20 percent in 1967–77—although 1982–83 and 1983–84 witnessed a welcome climb to 39 and 44 percent, respectively. A partial explanation for that fifty-odd year drop in the number of unanimous decisions is the plethora of complex and novel cases that the Court has had to deal with contemporarily. In the 1981–82 term thirty-three cases—nearly one-fifth of the all full opinions issued—were decided by a one-vote margin, twice as many as in the previous term of the

[146] Harold J. Spaeth, "Distributive Justice: Majority Opinion Assignments in the Burger Court," 67 *Judicature* 6 (December–January 1984), p. 301.

[147] Ibid., Table 1 and accompanying text.

[148] During his thirty-six-and-one-half-year tenure—which ended on November 15, 1975—Justice Douglas wrote more than 1,200 full majority, concurring, and dissenting opinions. In 1972–73 he authored a record 53 (!) of the latter. His 486 written dissents rank him as the most prolific dissenter to date (1985). Holmes, although known as the "great dissenter," wrote only 72, ranking him eleventh in that category. However, Holmes wrote more opinions on behalf of the *entire* Court (873) than anyone else. Douglas penned the most opinions *qua* opinions (1,232).

Court. That figure changed little in 1982–83 and 1983–84, with 19 and 21 percent, respectively. Memorandum orders, which, quite naturally, enjoy a far higher degree of unanimity, were up to 82.1 percent.[149] Most opinions are rendered as *majority* opinions, but an unfortunately increasing number do not command a majority and are thus delivered as *plurality* opinions. In the latter, the Court, although ruling on the issue(s) at hand, commands only a plurality of the Justices in favor of that particular ruling; that is, there may be a 4:3:2 decision—seven favoring the side of the "winner" but for dissimilar reasons. Until 1953 only forty-seven plurality decisions had been rendered in the Court's history; but the Warren Court handed down forty in the ensuing fifteen years, and the Burger Court presented the annals with eighty-eight between 1969 and 1981.[150] The ensuing three terms saw no improvement in the trend.

Dissenting Opinions. As these statistics demonstrate, dissenting and concurring opinions as well as simple dissents and concurrences are now quite common.[151] Yet only when the formal opinion method of registering disagreement with the decision and/or the opinion of the majority is employed does the practice become meaningful for the governmental process. A simple *dissent*, without explanation, such as "Mr. Justice Butler dissents" in *Palko v. Connecticut*,[152] represents as a vote on the other side; but it says little to the expert and layperson alike, save that a Justice, for reasons known only to himself, or herself, chose to dissent. It is entirely possible, of course, for honest, competent jurists to arrive at sharply divided opinions in a case; hence, *dissenting opinions*, both short and long, are quite common. In fact, the first *reported* decision of the Supreme Court was rendered by a divided Court, Justices William Cushing and Thomas Johnson dissenting from the Court majority's grant of an injunction to Georgia.[153] Thomas Jefferson believed early that dissents rendered the Court a more open, a more democratic institution—and that belief represented a major reason why he wanted the Court always to render *seriatim* opinions (a practice opposed, and discarded, by John Marshall when he became Chief Justice). As one of the best-known dissenters, Justice Holmes, said, "General propositions do not decide particular cases." One of the classic statements on the subject was made by the then ex-Associate Justice and future Chief Justice Charles Evans Hughes:

---

[149]Several good sources for these statistics exist; among others are the *Annual Report of the Director of Administrative office of the U.S. Courts* and the law reviews, especially the November issue of the *Harvard Law Review.*

[150]*The Washington Post,* June 25, 1981, p. A13.

[151]Apparently there exists a tradition—albeit not an unbroken one—that precludes *any* qualifying opinion in a decision involving a new Justice's first opinion for the Court. See Wallace Mendelson's "Neo-Behavioralism—A Rebuttal," 57 *American Political Science Review* 952 (December 1963), fn. 7.

[152]302 U.S. 319 (1937).

[153]*Georgia v. Braisford,* 2 Dallas 402 (1792).

A dissent in a court of last resort is an appeal to the brooding spirit of the law, to the intelligence of a future day, when a later decision may possibly correct the error into which the dissenting judge believes the court to have been betrayed.[154]

This from the pen of a jurist who rarely wrote dissenting opinions himself, who rarely dissented, and who exerted a greater dominance over the Court than any other Chief Justice save Marshall! Hughes often expressed the view that there is no reason to expect more unanimity on difficult problems of law than in the "higher reaches" of physics, theology, or philosophy. Justice Carter, the colorful state of California jurist mentioned earlier, was fond of observing: "I welcome dissents, for they test the soundness of my own opinions. . . . The dissenting opinion is . . . a forecast of things to come. The writers of dissents are usually men who look forward—not back, nor to the immediate present, but to the future."[155] Or, as Roscoe Pound once remarked, " . . . dissenting opinions may be the symptom of life in the law of time."[156] To Thomas Reed Powell they were " . . . most valuable equilibrators in the undulating course of the law."[157] And in his very last public statement on the last day of his sixteen-year tenure as Chief Justice of the United States, Earl Warren, responding to President Nixon, said:

We do not always agree [on the bench]. I hope the Court will never agree on all things. I am sure that its virility will have been sapped because it is composed of nine independent men who have no one to be responsible to except their own conscience.[158]

Many among the most memorable opinions of the Court initially on the dissenting side have eventually become majority opinions—especially some by famed spokesmen of erstwhile minority viewpoints, such as Justices William Johnson, Harlan, Sr., Holmes, Brandeis, Stone, and Black. One obvious example is the lone Harlan dissenting opinion in 1896, his eloquent remonstrance against the "separate but equal" doctrine in *Plessy v. Ferguson*,[159] which became the unanimous opinion of the Court in 1954 in Brown v. Board of Education of Topeka.[160] Another is the lone dissenting opinion of Stone in 1940 in the *Gobitis* case;[161] Stone argued forcefully, but unsuccessfully, against the compulsory flag salute required by the Minersville, Pennsylvania, school district even from those who found it to be religiously objectionable.

---

[154]C. Evans Hughes, *The Supreme Court of the United States* (New York: Columbia University Press, 1928), p. 68.

[155]As quoted in *The New York Times*, March 16, 1959, p. 31.

[156]"Preface," in *Justice Musmanno Dissents* (Indianapolis: Bobbs-Merrill, 1956).

[157]"The Logic and Rhetoric of Constitutional Law," 15 *Journal of Philosophy, Psychology, and Scientific Method* 654 (1918).

[158]As quoted in *The New York Times*, June 24, 1969, p. 1.

[159]163 U.S. 537. Harlan's memorable words: "Our Constitution is color-blind, and neither knows nor tolerates classes among citizens" (at 559).

[160]347 U.S. 483.

[161]*Minersville School District v. Gobitis*, 310 U.S. 586.

Scarcely three years later this became the opinion of the Court when a majority of six—over a memorable dissent by Justice Frankfurter—held a similar West Virginia Board of Education requirement to be an unconstitutional attachment of freedom of religion in the *Barnette* case.[162] Justice Cardozo, also a frequent dissenter, viewed the dissenting opinion as an entirely proper place for recording "the best inspiration of the time," for instruction in moral values still battling for general acceptance in the political process.[163] "It's grand to fight," once remarked Justice Black. "The Supreme Court does disagree. I hope it always will. It does have men who express their differences. I hope it always will have. Because I subscribe to the theory that there is no progress when differences are stifled."[164] It was Black who was given the honor of writing the opinion for the unanimous Court in the 1963 *Gideon* case, which extended to indigents the right to be furnished counsel in noncapital as well as capital criminal cases—a decision that overruled the *Betts* case of 1942 in which Black had vigorously dissented (joined by his brothers Douglas and Murphy).[165]

There is little doubt that a dissenting opinion is preeminently the result of a profoundly held conviction; consequently, it may well be regarded as strengthening rather than weakening the authority of a particular case. However, as Learned Hand contended, it may also weaken the Court's authority. Moreover, it may also serve to muddy the waters, to force extremist positions, and to confuse the public. For example, there are those students of the *Dred Scott* case—and not necessarily only the apologists for Chief Justice Taney—who contend that Taney's extremist position for the majority was a reaction to the extremist position taken by the politically ambitious Justice McLean in his dissenting opinion.[166] (It should be noted here that dissent is much less common in the fifty state courts, in which the average rate of dissent at the highest appellate level is but one case in ten.)[167] *De minimis*, as Harlan Fiske

---

[162] *West Virginia State Board of Education v. Barnette*, 319 U.S. 624 (1943).

[163] Benjamin M. Cardozo, *Selected Writings*, ed. by Margaret E. Hall (New York: Fallon Publishers, 1947), p. 274.

[164] Quoted in *The New York Times*, June 5, 1961, p. 10

[165] See fns. 57, 72, 73, 74, *supra*.

[166] In his essay on "politically minded" Justices, Alexander M. Bickel calls McLean the "most notoriously so." See his *Politics and the Warren Court* (New York: Harper & Row, 1965), p. 135. Indeed, McLean was a presidential candidate of sorts five times: in 1832 as an Anti-Mason, in 1836 as an Independent, in 1848 as both a Whig and a Free-Soiler; in 1852 he refused the Native American party's nomination; and in 1856 came his most serious candidacy, as a Republican. No doctrinaire he! See Francis P. Weisenburger, *The Life of John McLean: A Politician on the United States Supreme Court* (Columbus: Ohio State University Press, 1937).

[167] See the interesting article by Robert J. Sickles, "The illusion of Judicial Consensus," 59 *The American Political Science Review* 100 (March 1965). See also Steven A. Peterson and Kenneth N. Vines, "Acceptance of Dissent by American Legal Elites." (Paper prepared for delivery at the Southern Political Science Association's annual meetings in Atlanta, Georgia, November 4–6, 1976.)

Stone observed at the outset of his Chief Justiceship, dissent "is some assurance to counsel and to the public that decision has not been perfunctory, which is one of the most important objects of decision-writing."[168] Dissent is indeed essential to an effective judiciary in democratic society.[169]

Concurring Opinions. At times the reasoning of the Justice assigned to write the opinion of the Court may not be palatable to all of the members of the majority side. In that event, one or more *concurring opinions* may be written—an increasingly common practice during the past few decades. Broadly speaking, it usually signifies the concurrence of its author in the *decision*, but not in the *reasoning* of the Court. One illustration would be the two separate concurring opinions of Justices Black and Douglas in the 8:0 decision of the Supreme Court in *Rochin v. California*.[170] While agreeing with the Court that the State of California had engaged in grossly brutal, and hence obviously illegal, conduct in its apprehension and conviction of Rochin, a narcotics peddler, the two Justices strongly disagreed with the *ground* on which the Court based its reversal of Rochin's conviction: violation of the due process of law clause of the Fourteenth Amendment of the U.S. Constitution. In the firmly held judgment of Black and Douglas, California had actually violated individual liberty safeguards specifically enumerated in the Bill of Rights—in fact thus contending, as they had done ever since their appointment to the Court in 1937 and 1939, respectively, that the specific provisions are per se applicable to the states (by means of the Fourteenth Amendment) as well as to the federal government.[171]

Another example of the use of the concurring opinion is that by Justice Frankfurter—a frequent "concurrer"—in *Cooper v. Aaron (The Little Rock Case)*,[172] which was decided in the Special Session in the summer of 1958. There, not only in order to show its continuous unanimity in cases basically following *Brown v. Board of Education*,[173] but also to make clear that those Justices (Harlan, Brennan, and Whittaker) who had not participated in *Brown* were at one with the remaining six members of that historic opinion, the Supreme Court issued its opinion in the unique format of a joint authorship, with the names of each of its nine unanimous members specifically listed *seriatim* at the head of the "Opinion of the Court." However, Justice Frankfurter was obviously deeply grieved and disturbed by the clear flouting of the law and crass defiance of the federal judiciary by the officials of the State of

---

[168]"Dissenting Opinions Are Not Without Value," 26 *Journal of the American Judicature Society* 78 (1942).

[169]See Justice Frankfurter's opinion in *Ferguson v. Moore-McCormack Lines*, 352 U.S. 528 (1957) and, generally, Steven A. Peterson, "Dissent in American Courts," 43 *The Journal of Politics* 412 (May 1981).

[170]342 U.S. 165 (1952).

[171]See my *Freedom and the Court: Civil Rights and Liberties in the United States*, 4th ed. (New York: Oxford University Press, 1982), ch. 3.

[172]358 U.S. 1 (1958).

[173]347 U.S. 483 (1954).

Arkansas, led by Governor Orval E. Faubus—so much so that, notwithstanding the unusual joint authorship described, he was moved to write a separate concurring opinion, which was issued and published some weeks thereafter (an action that infuriated Chief Justice Warren, who had understood that there would be no separate opinion of any kind!). In it, Frankfurter gave what, in effect, was a profound and moving lecture to the country in general, and the South in particular, on the meaning of "the supreme Law of the Land" and the federal system. Written with scholarship and feeling, this independent statement nevertheless probably somewhat diminished the effect of the joint opinion of the Court. There are many legal scholars who are convinced that, whereas *dissenting* opinions are both eminently justifiable and necessary, *concurring* opinions are neither—that they are frequently nothing more than ego manifestations and/or "quibbling," which would more profitably be confined to footnotes in the body of the majority opinion. Chief Justice Warren, for one, strongly opposed resort to concurring opinions.[174] Yet there is no doubt that the concurring opinion is a significant tool in the judicial process.

Techniques of Assignment. The preceding discussion raises the interesting problem of the selection of the opinion writers by the Chief Justice, or by the Senior Associate Justice when the duty of designation devolves on him. Giving due attention to the need of distributing the work load relatively evenly (and, as explained earlier, permitting a Court newcomer to select his own first opinion to write), the average Chief Justice's assignments—approximately 80 to 85 percent of the cases—may well be said to follow a fairly common pattern. It is a pattern, based on the considerable influence that governs the actions of the Chief in making his selections, that will take account of all of the following considerations. First, the so-called great, big, or important constitutional cases—although these are necessarily somewhat subjective concepts[175]—should be authored by the Chief himself; for example, Chief Justice Warren speaking for the unanimous Court in *Brown v. Board of Education,*[176]—of which, as he was quoted after his retirement, he had written "every blessed word."[177]

> I assigned myself to write the decision, for it seemed to me that something so important ought to issue over the name of the Chief Justice of the United States. In drafting it, I sought to use low-key, unemotional language and to keep it short enough so that it could be published in full in every newspaper

[174]"Seminar with Mr. Chief Justice Warren," op. cit., p. 5.

[175]In his impressively researched, ably analytical study (see fn. 146, p. 211, *supra*), Harold J. Spaeth deals with the vexatious concept of "important" cases and their assignments during the first twelve Burger Court years (1969–80). Surprisingly, of the 170 cases styled as important that the Chief Justice assigned, Burger self-assigned only 43 (a total of 25.3 percent). Justice Brennan, on the other hand, when assignment devolved on him as Senior Associate Justice, self-assigned 12 of his 31, that is, 38.7 percent (op. cit., pp. 303–04).

[176]347 U.S. 483 (1954).

[177]As quoted by James F. Simon, *In His Own Image: The Supreme Court in Richard Nixon's America* (New York: David McKay Co., 1973), p. 55.

in the country. I kept the text secret (it was locked in my safe) until I read from the bench.[178]

In Chief Justice Hughes's majority opinion for the narrowly divided Court (5:4) in the immensely significant case of *West Coast Hotel Co. v. Parrish*,[179] upholding the state of Washington minimum wage law for women—sometimes, perhaps flippantly but probably not altogether unjustly, called "the-switch-in-time-that-saved-nine" case—the Court departed from its erstwhile stubborn adherence to the narrow construction of the concept of "freedom of contract" under the Fifth and Fourteenth Amendments to the Constitution by overruling the specific precedent of *Adkins v. Children's Hospital*[180] (in which it had struck down [5:3] a similar, though federal, law for the District of Columbia). That departure clearly indicated a change of position by the Chief Justice *and* Justice Roberts. The latter's switch was especially significant because before that he had normally represented the "swing vote" between the so-called pro- and anti-New Deal factions on the Court. His new stance heralded more or less clear sailing, at least on constitutional grounds, for the legislative programs enacted by the then still high-riding New Deal Roosevelt Administration.

In 1974 it was Chief Justice Burger who assigned himself the writing of the momentous opinion for his unanimous Court in *United States v. Nixon*[181] (consisting also of Justices Douglas, Brennan, Stewart, White, Marshall, Blackmun, and Powell). Obviously, he had and/or managed the necessary votes—which is not always the case, of course, as the 1978 decision in the long-anticipated *Bakke* ruling proved only too well to the chagrin of a good many students of the judicial process. In *Bakke*, instead of a unified and unifying holding written by the Chief, a badly split six-opinion, 154-page divider came down, authored by Justice Powell, who mustered a bare 5:4 margin in

---

[178] *The New York Times*, July 11, 1974, p. A35. He had elaborated in his University of Virginia "Seminar," op. cit. fn. 102, *supra*:

> I decided that the opinion in *Brown* would be short and that it would be written in simple, easy to understand English. I wanted the full text of the opinion to be short enough to be carried in every newspaper in the country in total and I wanted every citizen to be able to read and understand our decision since it would affect their lives. Frankfurter wrote his opinions for the legal experts. He thought that if they could understand them, they could explain them to others and that was all that was necessary. I didn't agree with that philosophy. I wrote my opinions for the common man to read. I don't deserve any credit for the *Brown* decision. Some say I united the Court in that decision. But I didn't. [Yet see p. 223, *infra*, for a rather different interpretation.] The real individuals who deserve credit for the *Brown* decision are the men from the South who were on the Court, that is Black from Alabama, Reed from Kentucky, and Clark from Texas. These men are responsible for the full Court or unanimous Court. These men couldn't go back home to their states for ten years after the decision in the case. A decision with three dissents from the Court's Southern members would not have been as persuasive as was the unanimous decision.

[179] 300 U.S. 379 (1937).

[180] 262 U.S. 525 (1923).

[181] 417 U.S. 683 Justice Rehnquist, a one-time Assistant Attorney General in the Nixon Administration, recused himself in the case.

the two prongs of this potentially significant "reverse discrimination/affirmative action" controversy.[182] Five years later, it was once again Chief Justice Burger who spoke for his 7:2 (or 6:3, depending on one's analysis of Justice Powell's concurring opinion) Court, when the high tribunal declared unconstitutional the then fifty-year-old practice of the one-house or two-house "legislative veto," imbedded in 212 statutes (62 of these active) over executive action. A decision of momentous significance, it was a "natural" for the Chief Justice's authorship.[183]

Second, no matter what the importance of a case, the selection of a Justice to write the opinion must take into account the possible importance of the decision as a precedent. Justices may well differ in their views on whether the decision should be lodged on a broad or a narrow construction of the issue and on the ground on which the decision is to be based. For instance, the movie *Lady Chatterley's Lover* had been banned by the New York State Board of Regents on grounds of a statutory provision that forbade showing of films that present "acts of sexual immorality, perversion or lewdness" as being "desirable, acceptable, or proper patterns of behavior," and the Court agreed unanimously that the movie did not fall under that ban. But a majority of only five Justices (Warren, Black, Douglas, Brennan, and Stewart) would join in Stewart's opinion for the Court holding that particular provision of the New York licensing statute to be an unconstitutional violation of the Fourteenth and First Amendments. There were five *concurring* opinions, of which the principal opinion by Harlan (joined by Frankfurter and Whittaker), while agreeing that the New York statute could not be validly applied in this case, argued that the Court should have reversed New York on *statutory construction* grounds without reaching the *constitutional issues*. Frankfurter also penned an individual concurrence, and Clark noted that he concurred "in the result." Black and Douglas, although members of the majority of five, joined one another in the two remaining concurring opinions, in which they contended that this statute, like all other prior censorship of movies, should be thrown out as being "unconstitutional on its face" as a prior restraint on freedom of speech and press.[184] Obviously, here the Chief Justice's assignment had to take into account which prospective authorship would be sufficiently acceptable, or least offensive, to five Justices—in this case, evidently Stewart's.

Third, although some observers would disagree, there is considerable evidence that the Chief is conscious of an element of public relations in designating his opinion writer. This is particularly true in cases that are undoubtedly going to be unpopular to a sizable segment of the population. In other words, he is not unmindful of the importance of making a decision acceptable

[182] *Regents of the University of California v. Bakke*, 429 U.S. 953.

[183] *Immigration and Naturalization Service v. Chadha*, 462 U.S. 919 (1983).

[184] *Kingsley International Pictures Corporation v. Regents*, 360 U.S. 684 (1959)—which featured a total of six opinions.

to the public, or, when necessary, of coating the bitter pill that must be swallowed. A fascinating illustration of this point was brought to light by Professor Alpheus T. Mason in his fine biography, *Harlan Fiske Stone: Pillar of the Law*.[185] In 1944 the Court conference on the Texas "White Primary" case, *Smith v. Allwright*,[186] had clearly evidenced that all of the Justices save Roberts were agreed that this constitutionally challenged Texas statute was unconstitutional as a violation of the Fifteenth Amendment. The South was bound to react with great vehemence. Chief Justice Stone assigned the opinion to Justice Frankfurter, an eloquent stylist and a profoundly serious and scholarly jurist, not given to pamphleteering. One day after the conference, having discussed his strong misgivings with some of his colleagues, Justice Jackson—a good friend of the principals involved—wrote a highly unusual, and, indeed, probably quite unprecedented, letter to the Chief Justice, candidly and fervently suggesting that the nature and the importance of the issue in the case were so far-reaching and made of such emotional matter that the Frankfurter selection was bound to "grate on Southern sensibilities." He explained:

> Mr. Justice Frankfurter unites in a rare degree factors which unhappily excite prejudice. In the first place, he is a Jew. In the second place, he is from New England, the seat of the abolition movement. In the third place, he has not been thought of as a person particularly sympathetic with the Democratic party in the past.[187]

Jackson went on to point out that he realized a consideration of every one of the listed factors was utterly distasteful and he mentioned them only with the greatest reluctance and "frank fear of being misunderstood." He had, of course, discussed the matter with Frankfurter and had advised him of his intention to write to the Chief Justice. Evidently persuaded by Jackson's argument, Stone, with Frankfurter's knowledge and agreement, substituted Justice Stanley Reed, who was (a) an old-line Kentuckian, (b) a Protestant, (c) native-born, in contrast to Justice Frankfurter, who was born in Vienna, and (d) a Democrat of long standing. This did not render the wounds of the South less severe, but at least they were administered, in a manner of speaking, by a one-time kinsman.

In the same general vein, the Chief Justice will normally make it a practice to assign so-called liberal opinions of the Court to "conservative" Justices and so-called conservative opinions to "liberal" Justices—again in the hope of making them more palatable. Thus, Chief Justice Stone assigned to one of the Court's leading liberals, Justice Black, the majority opinion in what has

---

[185]Alpheus T. Mason, *Harlan Fiske Stone: Pillar of the Law* (New York: The Viking Press, 1956), pp. 614–15.

[186]321 U.S. 649 (1944).

[187]Mason, loc. cit., p. 615. Justice Frankfurter was not exactly pleased about the publicity given this event—in fact, the revelation infuriated him.

been widely labeled as the "most racist" decision in this century's history of the tribunal, *Korematsu v. United States*.[188] There the Court upheld 6:3 the forcible exclusion of 112,000 persons of Japanese ancestry, including 77,000 native-born American citizens, and their removal from their West Coast homes to inland war relocation centers. Although not one of these evacuees had been specifically accused of disloyalty, the Black opinion upheld the exclusion order as a validly authorized emergency measure necessitated by the facts of life of wartime, as an "exercise of power of the government to take steps necessary to prevent espionage and sabotage in an area threatened by Japanese attack." When the Court, in a 7:1 opinion in 1957, severely limited the application of the Smith Act in the prosecution of Communist party leaders and members, Chief Justice Warren assigned the case to a member usually found on the conservative side, Justice Harlan.[189] When the Court, in the emotion-charged field of religion, in 1963 decided 8:1 that no state or locality may either require or sanction the recitation of the Lord's Prayer or the reading of verses from the Holy Bible in the public schools, the Chief Justice assigned that delicate case to Justice Clark, a Presbyterian who was active in the affairs of his church. (He was joined, in separate concurring opinions, by the Court's only Catholic, Justice Brennan, and its only Jew, Justice Goldberg.)[190] And in 1976 Chief Justice Burger assigned to his only black colleague, Justice Marshall, the writing of the opinion in a case charging employer discrimination against whites. Speaking for a unanimous Court, Marshall held that the provisions of the Civil Rights Act of 1964, barring such discrimination, are "not limited to discrimination against members of any particular race."[191] Such strategy or tactic is not always employed, but it is resorted to with sufficient regularity to make a distinct pattern, mild and unpredictable though it may be.

Fourth, when the conference has indicated a split decision, no matter how many Justices may be in the latent minority, the Chief Justice will endeavor to assign the opinion to a Justice whose views come closest to the would-be dissenters, without, however, being one of them. The theory here is that the Justice would, in this case—and probably in others—be a "center Justice," whose "middle" approach would be acceptable, more or less, to both majority and minority.[192] For example, in *United States v. Butler*[193] a majority of six declared the Agricultural Adjustment Act of 1933 unconstitutional, as an illegal use by Congress of its powers over taxation and commerce at the expense

[188]323 U.S. 214 (1944).

[189]*Yates v. United States*, 354 U.S. 298.

[190]*Abington School District v. Schempp* and *Murray v. Curlett*, 374 U.S. 203.

[191]*McDonald v. Santa Fé Transportation Co.*, 427 U.S. 273.

[192]For an able and extensive discussion of this and related points, see the interesting paper by David J. Danelski, "The Influence of the Chief Justice in the Decisional Process of the Supreme Court," presented at the 1960 American Political Science Association Meeting, New York City, September 9, 1960.

[193]297 U.S. 1 (1936).

of the principle of "dual federalism." This was one of thirteen New Deal laws or provisions thereof that the Court would invalidate on constitutional grounds in little more than one year's time during 1935–36. Reasoning that an opinion by one of the four "ultra-conservative" justices—Butler, McReynolds, Van Devanter, and Sutherland—would only serve to increase the fury of both the executive and legislative branches, Chief Justice Hughes assigned Justice Roberts to speak for the Court. The latter wrote an opinion that adopted the broad Hamilton–Story interpretation of the "general welfare" clause of the Constitution (I-8-1) but struck down the particular tax at issue as substantially an illegal regulation of local affairs. There is evidence that the Chief Justice went along with the majority only because Roberts wrote the opinion—and there was enough in that opinion to permit the minority of three, and their allies on both ends of Pennsylvania Avenue, to nourish hopes for a better day! It came scarcely a year later.

The critical role of the Chief Justice in assigning opinions is thus axiomatic. Much depends on his skill, diplomacy, tact, and sheer powers of persuasion. On retiring, Chief Justice Warren was frankly proud of the record of "his" Court on that score: "During all the years I was there I never had any of the Justices urge me to give them opinions to write, nor did I ever have anyone object to any opinion that I assigned to him or anyone else."[194] "My biggest consideration," he elaborated shortly prior to his death, "was always who could best express the wishes of the majority; who could write it best; and who could best unite the rest." He rejected any notions of "expertise" on the part of individual Justices, but he did

> sometimes assign an opinion to a Justice because he had an interest in a particular area and evinced a desire to write the opinion.... I often did that with Justice Black who, I knew, wanted to write the majority opinions in cases which adopted ideas he had expressed in dissent years earlier. He had been on the Court many years, and it was something I could do for him.[195]

The Chief Justice's assignment to Black of the Court's unanimous opinion in *Gideon v. Wainwright* is prominent confirmation of that point.[196] No other Chief, in the opinion of Justice Frankfurter, a longtime member of the bench who served under four Chief Justices and knew three others, "equalled Chief Justice Hughes in the skill and wisdom and disinterestedness with which he made his assignments." He closed his observations with this wise admonition:

> The grounds for the assignment may not always be obvious to the outsider. Indeed, they are not always so to the members of the Court; the reasons normally remain within the breast of the chief justice. But these involve, if the

---

[194]Comment to Anthony Lewis, "A Talk with Warren on Crime, the Court, the Country," *The New York Times Magazine*, October 19, 1969, p. 130.

[195]"Seminar with Chief Justice Warren," op. cit., pp. 1–2.

[196]372 U.S. 335 (1963). *Gideon* overruled *Betts v. Brady*, 316 U.S. 455 (1952), in which Justice Black had written the dissenting opinion. (See p. 194, *supra.*)

duty is wisely discharged, perhaps the most delicate judgment demanded of the chief justice.[197]

Yet no matter how hard he may try, or how skillful he may be, a Chief Justice cannot compel unanimity. As we have already seen, separate opinions are the rule rather than the exception. It is thus not at all uncommon to find five, six, seven, eight, and occasionally even nine opinions in a single case. The *Dred Scott Case*, the *License Cases*, the 1971 *Pentagon Papers Case*, and the 1972 *Capital Punishment Cases* each featured nine such opinions![198] The *Steel Seizure Case*[199] had seven; the *Connecticut Birth Control Case*,[200] *Baker v. Carr*,[201] the 1973 *Abortion Cases*,[202] the *Nixon Recordings and Materials Case* of 1977,[203] and the 1978 *Bakke "Reverse Discrimination" Case*[204] each six; and *Dennis*,[205] the *Bible Reading Cases*,[206] *Ginzburg v. United States*,[207] and the 1982 *Free Public Education for Children of Illegal Aliens Case*[208] each had five opinions. The practice of writing separate opinions may be valuable and intriguing, yet it hardly lends itself to certainty in the judicial process. However, certainty is not inevitably an end in itself; indeed, certainty and unanimity in the law are generally possessed only under a dictatorial system of government—to which, in fact, they are indispensable.

Drafting and Circulating Opinions: The Key Stage. Following the assignment of opinions—which does not take place at the Conference itself, but formally, in writing, a few days to two weeks thereafter—the laborious task of drafting commences. The power of persuasion by the author, presumably actively supported by the Chief Justice, whenever feasible, looms large in this phase of the judicial decision-making process. An opinion, as Justice Holmes once commented, not only must be informative and persuasive, it must show that the " ... judge can dance the sword dance; that is he can justify an

---

[197] *Of Law and Men*, op. cit., pp. 137, 142. Frankfurter regarded Marshall, Taney, and Hughes as the greatest Chief Justices.

[198] *Dred Scott Case*, 19 Howard 393 (1857): Taney (Opinion of the Court); Wayne, Nelson, Grier, Daniel, Campbell, and Catron (Concurring Opinions), and McLean and Curtis (Dissenting Opinions). *License Cases*, 7 Howard 283 (1849). *Pentagon Papers Case: The New York Times v. United States* and *United Stated v. The Washington Post*, 403 U.S. 713. *Capital Punishment Cases*, *Furman v. Georgia*, 408 U.S. 238.

[199] *Youngstown Sheet and Tube Co. v. Sawyer*, 343 U.S. 579 (1952).

[200] *Griswold v. Connecticut*, 381 U.S. 479 (1965).

[201] 369 U.S. 186 (1962).

[202] *Roe v. Wade*, 410 U.S. 113, and *Doe v. Bolton*, 410 U.S. 179. In his memoir of his father, *My Father: A Remembrance* (New York: Random House, 1975), Hugo Black, Jr., touches on those decisions' controversial impact: "When Justice Harry Blackmun wrote the 'abortion' opinion, poor Daddy in his grave contemplating infinity, was crucified about the decision—he actually received over 1,000 letters of protest" (p. 148).

[203] *Nixon v. Administrator of General Services*, 433 U.S. 425.

[204] *Regents of the University of California v. Bakke*, 438 U.S. 265.

[205] *Dennis v. United States*, 341 U.S. 494 (1951).

[206] *Abington School District v. Schempp* and *Murray v. Curlett*, 374 U.S. 203 (1963).

[207] 383 U.S. 463 (1966).

[208] *Plyler v. Doe*, 457 U.S. 202 (1982).

obvious result without stepping on either blade of opposing fallacies."[209] Again, we know but little of what takes place during these backstage activities, but from those few sources that are available—papers, biographies, former law clerks, various memoirs, and, lately, the research of persistent political scientists—we do acquire an outline of this terminal phase of the preparation of a Supreme Court opinion, collective as an end product but with the distinct imprint of the minds and labor of nine individuals. As opinions are drafted, and on whatever side of the tentative decision they may be, printed "proof" copies are circulated by their authors among the members of the Court. These copies—indeed all of the Court's publications—are composed by a special unit of printers who labor in secrecy (to the extent of locking themselves in during working hours) and utilize the basement of the Court building for their work rather than the Government Printing Office. A private Supreme Court library, with a staff of fourteen and all conceivable facilities, is at the disposal of the Justices and their law clerks at all times.

Depending on comments by his or her colleagues, an author of an opinion may draw additional drafts in an attempt to gain adherence or a concurrence rather than a dissent; or he or she may use any one of the other devices that may soften disagreement where disagreement exists, or make more forceful an opinion where unanimity seems attainable. Justice Brennan reported that once he circulated ten printed drafts before one was accepted as the Opinion of the Court,[210] and Justice Powell acknowledged having rewritten one opinion at least ten times also.[211] This labor of persuasion is undertaken irrespective of how the several Justices may have voted in conference, the theory being that there is always hope for their views to win out in future years. The process of opinion writing is frequently a difficult and laborious task, sometimes running into months, occasionally even years—although the normal length of the labor ranges from thirty-five to fifty-eight days. The opinion for *Brown v. Board of Education* was in various stages of writing from 1952 to 1954, probably largely owing to Chief Justice Warren's herculean efforts to obtain not only a unanimous Court, but also a single opinion, undoubtedly a delicate and difficult matter on the subject at issue—the declaration of unconstitutionality of compulsory racial segregation in the public schools.[212]

---

[209] Alpheus T. Mason, reviewing *The Holmes-Einstein Letters* (New York: St. Martin's Press, 1965), in *The New York Times Book Review*, November 22, 1964, p. 60. See, for example, some of the important work concerning the innards of the Conference by lawyer-political scientists David J. Danelski of Cornell University, S. Sidney Ulmer of the University of Kentucky, and Walter F. Murphy of Princeton University. See also the excellent article by J. Woodford Howard, Jr., "On the Fluidity of Judicial Choice," 52 *American Political Science Review* 43 (March 1968) which, relying heavily on Murphy papers, provides fascinating and important insights.

[210] "Inside View of the High Court," *The New York Times Magazine*, October 6, 1963.

[211] J. Harvie Wilkinson, III, *Serving Justice: A Supreme Court Clerk's View* (New York: Charterhouse, 1974), p. 93.

[212] As he reported some years later:

Although still very much a case of conjecture, apparently the last holdout on the Court was Justice Reed.[213] It is certain that this decision was the collective product of inordinately painstaking labor.

We do know of many specific cases of persuasion—"bargaining" would not at all be an inappropriate term here—thanks to the papers left by the Justices. In one instance, Justice Butler, who had voted in conference to reverse the decision of the lower court, evidently succumbed to the persuasive powers of his colleague Stone. Sending a copy of his "surrender" to Chief Justice Taft, who ever tried to turn a dissenting opinion into silent acquiescence, he wrote to case-author Stone as follows:

> I voted to reverse. While this sustains your conclusion to affirm, I still think reversal would be better. But I shall in silence acquiesce. Dissents seldom aid in the right development or statement of the law. They often do harm. For myself I say: "lead us not into temptation."[214]

It is quite clear that all of the Justices, at one time or another, are thus willingly constrained by group and institutional concerns. About another and later Stone opinion, Chief Justice Hughes wrote to him: "I choke a little at swallowing your analysis, still I do not think it would serve any useful purpose to expose my views."[215] Although, as Chief Justice, Stone exercised far less persuasive pressure than Hughes, he did work for unanimity whenever possible. At times, this would involve—as it does quite frequently—a switch from a decisional ground initially agreed on to another. For example, in one of the cases brought during Stone's tenure, *Edwards v. California*,[216] he successfully persuaded Justice Byrnes to change his conference vote. Now delivering the opinion of the Court, Byrne's switch resulted in adopting a *ground* for the decision on which five members of the Court could agree—the inter-

---

Ordinarily, the Justices at our Friday conferences stated their positions, offered debate and then voted. But in Brown we were all conscious of the case, so I held off a vote from conference to conference while we discussed it. If you'll remember, Brown was argued in the fall of 1953, and I did not call for a vote until the middle of the following February, when I was certain we would be unanimous. We took one vote, and that was it.

(*The New York Times*, July 11, 1974, p. A35.) For a view that strongly *disapproves* of this obviously so deliberately planned and achieved unanimity, see Charles S. Hyneman, *The Supreme Court on Trial* (New York: Atherton Press, 1963), pp. 211–14.

[213] According to Yale Law Professor Fred Rodell, three Justices (evidently Reed and Jackson plus either Burton, Clark, or Minton) came close to dissenting, and the bare minimum of four had voted to grant *certiorari* in the case. See his "It Is the Earl Warren Court," *The New York Times Magazine*, March 13, 1966, p. 93. In a letter to Reed, Frankfurter noted there probably would have been four dissenters (Reed one of them) had the case been decided just one term earlier. (Letter displayed in Retrospective Memorial Exhibit in honor of Justice Felix Frankfurter's Ninety-fifth Birthday, October 21, 1977.)

[214] As quoted by David J. Danelski in "The Influence of the Chief Justice in the Decisional Process of the Supreme Court," pp. 19–20. See fn. 192, *supra*.

[215] Danelski loc cit., at p. 21. The case was *Stanford v. Commissioner*, 308 U.S. 39 (1939).

[216] 314 U.S. 160 (1941).

state commerce, rather than the "privileges and immunities" clause of the Constitution. Four Justices concurred in the decision, thus rendering it unanimous, but indicated their preference for the latter ground. An extreme example of the drive for agreement was provided in a difficult double jeopardy case in 1959, when Justice Brennan wrote the opinion of the Court *and a separate opinion* in which he expressed views he had evidently been unable to persuade his colleagues to accept, stating that " . . . it cannot be suggested that in cases where the author is the mere instrument of the Court he must forego expression of his own convictions."[217] It is essential to recognize that Justices may shift positions between the Conference and their final vote—a "testament," as Professor Howard put it, "to the limitations of conference and the effectiveness of the argumentation system."[218]

Much of what has been said of the backstage give-and-take is documented by an excellent study by Professor Alexander M. Bickel of Yale University Law School (one of Justice Frankfurter's law clerks) entitled *The Unpublished Opinions of Mr. Justice Brandeis.*[219] Based on the private papers of Louis Dembitz Brandeis as they relate to his career as Justice of the Supreme Court of the United States from 1916 to 1939, the book is rich in illustrations of the persuasive processes that accompany the drafting of opinions for ultimate delivery. One or two examples will suffice: a photograph of a note from Holmes to Brandeis indicates that Holmes had revised his opinion in *Bullock v. Florida*[220] by adopting the result Brandeis had urged on him. Having been persuaded by Brandeis's point of view, Holmes did so willingly enough; but his note showed much concern lest his changed opinion cause dissatisfaction among the former majority and perhaps result in a reassignment of the case to someone else. That did not happen, however.[221]

In another instance, it was Brandeis's turn to give in. He had felt quite strongly about the construction of a statute at issue in a 1924 railroad case opinion, which had been assigned to Justice McReynolds.[222] In discussing the case some years later with then Professor of Law Felix Frankfurter, Brandeis said that he had told the Chief Justice (Taft) that "he couldn't stand for"

---

[217] *Abbate v. United States,* 359 U.S. 187 (1959), at 196, fn. 1. Other similar illustrations cited by Brennan are the actions of Justice Jackson in *Wheeling Steel Corporation v. Glander,* 337 U.S. 562 (1949) at 576; those of Justice Cardozo in *Helvering v. Davis,* 301 U.S. 619 (1937) at 639–41; and Justice Blackmun's in *Logan v. Zimmerman Brush Co.,* 455 U.S. 438–42 (1982). There, Blackmun, writing the majority opinion, turned around and also penned a separate plurality "addendum" to his own opinion. The lawyers in the case noted that they were still trying to figure out just what it meant. See also Justice Stevens's intriguingly diverse actions in *South Carolina v. Regan,* 52 LW 4232 (1984), at 4241, in which he registered a dissent along with a partial concurrence.

[218] Howard, loc cit., p. 47. (Justice Brennan told me that post-Conference "line-up" switches are far more common than is generally believed.)

[219] (Cambridge: Harvard University Press, 1957.) Subtitled, *The Supreme Court at Work.*

[220] 254 U.S. 513 (1921).

[221] Bickel, loc cit., insert between pp. 118–19, last photographic plate.

[222] *Railroad Commission of California v. Southern Pacific Railway Co.,* 264 U.S. 331.

McReynolds's opinion, that it contained too much that would "bother us in the future." Justice Van Devanter, continued Brandeis,

> worked with McReynolds and made changes, and the Chief asked me whether that will remove my sting. The corrections weren't adequate, and finally the Chief took over the opinion and put out what is now the Court's opinion and I suppressed my dissent, because, after all, it's merely a question of statutory construction and the worst things were removed by the Chief.[223]

On the other hand, the persuasion *cum* bargaining may well be blunt and direct, as evidenced by a memorandum sent by the usually gentle Justice Stone to the not-so-gentle Justice Frankfurter: "If you wish to write [the opinion] placing the case on the ground which I think tenable and desirable, I shall cheerfully join you. If not, I will add a few observations for myself."[224]

Toward the End Product. By far the most important fact revealed by this glimpse into the Supreme Court's inner sanctum is that many, if not all, of the Court's opinions, though ostensibly the work of one person are really the product of many minds, in the sense that the Justice who writes the opinion often has to add to, delete, or modify the original draft in order to be able to retain the support of his colleagues, many of whom are far from agreeing with him or with each other. If this involves changes of mind, even reversals, so be it—such behavior is very human. In fact, one close student of the Court's 1940 decade was tempted to avow that hardly any decision during that period "was free from significant alteration of vote and language before announcement to the public."[225] Moreover, studies based on the Justices' papers make abundantly clear that Justices of *all* ideological persuasions ponder, bargain, and argue in the course of reaching their decisions—even at the risk of compromising their ideologies.[226] Those who see facile niches and categories for the Justices may need to do a bit more applied research. It is essential to recognize that each member of the Court participates in every stage of the consideration of a case. Once we grasp this, we can readily understand why a considerable number of the Court's decisions are vague or contain several apparently contradictory statements. Because the views reflected in a given opinion are rarely identical, it may well turn out to be either ambiguous or maintain several varying postures, in order that each Justice who supports it will be able to reconcile it with his or her own particular position. A pertinent example is the laborious forging of Chief Justice Stone's majority opinion in *In Re Yamashita*,[227] in which the Court upheld the conviction by a U.S. mil-

---

[223] As quoted and described by Bickel, loc cit., pp. 209–10.

[224] Quoted by Mason in *Harlan Fiske Stone*, op. cit., p. 501. (Stone's letter was dated January 20, 1941.)

[225] Howard, op. cit., p. 44.

[226] See, for example, ibid., pp. 55–56.

[227] 327 U.S. 1 (1946).

itary commission of the Japanese general who was accused of violating the laws of war in failing to prevent his troops from committing atrocities against American and Philippine citizens. The decision is quite unclear on the question of whether the due process clause of the Fifth Amendment is binding on such a military commission. On the whole, the opinion tends to give the impression that the answer to this question is in the negative, but some slight support can be found for the contrary view. According to Professor Mason, Stone's biographer, the latter's original draft contained the assertion that Yamashita's trial would have to adhere to the requirement of this clause. However, to meet at least in part the objections of Justices Black and Reed, who apparently were of the opinion that these commissions were not bound by the provisions of the due process clause, Stone deleted the assertion and made some confusing additions that Black and Reed could more or less reconcile with their own views on this matter.[228] The end product, though it did not entirely satisfy either its readers or the bench as a whole, at least had the virtue—if that it be—of receiving the support of the majority of the Court.

Secrecy of Deliberations. Even though these various data undoubtedly are intriguing and are important to an understanding of the Court's *modus operandus* the absolute secrecy that attends the backstage work and deliberations of the Supreme Court—the "Purple Curtain," as Professor Fowler Harper once called it—is essential. Until 1910 it was customary for two page boys to be present, but since that time (the Justices suspected a leak by one or more of the pages in a decision) no one but the nine Justices has been present in the conference; no record of the discussions is kept. When clerks bring messages, the Justice who is junior in seniority, no matter what his or her chronological age, goes to the door to get them. There simply are no leaks. This is not to say, however, that no leaks have ever occurred. The most serious of these on record came in connection with the *Dred Scott* case.[229] In that case not only did the pro-slavery Justice John Catron evidently tell President-elect James Buchanan the "line-up" of the Justices in the pending decision one month prior to its announcement, but segments of the Northern press published the dissenting opinion of Justice Curtis. The incoming President, troubled and weak, used the Catron information in his inaugural address on March 4, 1857, and told the country that the Court would soon settle the much disputed territorial question. Two days later Chief Justice Taney delivered the 7:2 opinion of the Court, which, as history proved all too soon, did anything but settle the problem. Indeed, it acted as a catalyst in bringing on the Civil War.

[228] Mason, op. cit., pp. 667–69.

[229] *Dred Scott v. Sandford*, 19 Howard 393 (1857). See Stanley I. Kutler, *The Dred Scott Decision: Law or Politics* (Boston: Houghton Mifflin Co., 1967); Vincent C. Hopkins, S. J., *Dred Scott Case* (New York: Atheneum, 1967); and D. E. Fehrenbacher, *The Dred Scott Case* (New York: Oxford University Press, 1978) for book-length analyses.

However, that instance was a rare and crass exception.[230] Complete secrecy does, and must, exist. The Court can neither open its backstage deliberations to the public nor hold news conferences. To do either would fatally affect its position as well as its effectiveness. For a description of what goes on behind the doors, we depend almost entirely on the kind of papers and biographies of the Justices discussed earlier, duly analyzed by scholars, and, on occasion, on revelations, usually appearing after the death of the Justice involved, by their former law clerks. Yet even these revelations are more often than not confined to matters of procedure. This is emphatically as it should be. We know enough of the operation and functions of the highest court in the land to enable us to appreciate, study, and, we hope, understand them in the context of the Court's significant role in the process of free government. To repeat, the secrecy of the Court's proceedings behind that "Purple Curtain" is a necessary by-product of its work. In a widely read article endeavoring to explain Justice Roberts's famous so-called switch-in-time to the side of the "liberals" on the Court in 1937, Justice Frankfurter viewed the Court's reticence in these terms:

> Disclosure of Court happenings not made public by the Court itself, in its opinions and orders, presents a ticklish problem. The *secrecy that envelops the Court's work is not due to love of secrecy or want of responsible regard for the claims of a democratic society to know how it is governed.* That the Supreme Court should not be amenable to the forces of publicity to which the Executive and the Congress are subjected is essential to the effective functioning of the Court. But the passage of time may enervate the reasons for this restriction, particularly if disclosure rests not on tittle-tattle or self-serving declarations. . . . [231]

OPINION DAY(S)

The final stage in the Supreme Court's decision-making process occurs on *Opinion Day.* On that important occasion, now commonly tied into the pub-

---

[230] Justice Jackson's biographer, Eugene C. Gerhart, buttressed by other Court observers and biographers, professes to be satisfied of proof of about six to eight decisional leaks, commencing with *Luther v. Borden* 7 Howard 1 (1849) and ending with *United States v. South-East Underwriters Assn.*, 22 U.S. 533 (1944). See *America's Advocate: Robert H. Jackson* (Indianapolis: The Bobbs-Merrill Co., 1958), pp. 258–69. He points to Drew Pearson and his friendship with Justices Black and Douglas as the culprits. Two years prior to Gerhart's assertions, Alpheus Thomas Mason had already related in his *Harlan Fiske Stone: Pillar of the Law* that Pearson obtained advance leaks from the Conference room through Douglas in at least two cases, citing *United States v. Hope Natural Gas Co.*, 320 U.S. 59 (1944) as well as the *South-Eastern Underwriters* case. (Mason, op. cit., p. 625.) See also the allegations surrounding the Court's denial of *certiorari* in 1977 in the "Watergate Three" conviction case and the two alleged "print shop" leaks in 1979.

[231] "Mr. Justice Roberts" 104 *University of Pennsylvania Law Review* 313 (1955). (Italics supplied.) For further insights "behind the scenes," see Walter F. Murphy, *Elements of Judicial Strategy* (Chicago: University of Chicago Press, 1964), especially ch. 3, "Marshalling the Court."

lic oral argument hearing days of each month during the term,[232] the Court announces, or "hands down," the decisions it has reached. Other than those disposed of *per curiam* or decided by memorandum order,[233] the now made-public cases—all of which are filed with the Clerk of the Court—cover the full reasoning of the Court and set forth all viewpoints expressed by the Justices. Commencing with the junior Justices, and proceeding in ascending order of seniority, the various opinions may be either read verbatim or para-phrased or summarized—the customary and Chief Justice-preferred method—by their authors as the spirit and the occasion may dictate; some-times simply the decision is given by the author or by the Chief Justice. Justice Whittaker used to read from his text, whereas Justice Frankfurter never looked at his, but would expound from memory. Thus, techniques vary widely.[234] The reading of the opinions may run from a few minutes to more than an hour[235]—although the Chief Justice would almost certainly try to dis-courage the latter. And although the process has indeed been increasingly speeded up of late, normally resulting merely in a summary by the author of the majority opinion, a visitor to the Supreme Court on an Opinion Day ought to be prepared for the possibility, albeit no longer the probability, of two hours' duration—as was true of the *Bakke* case opinions in late June of 1980 and was similarly true of Justice Stewart's stinging dissenting opinion in

---

[232] Until April 11, 1965, when Chief Justice Warren announced that he and the Court saw no reason why decisions should be announced only on Mondays, that day of the week was in fact "reserved" for that purpose. And in the 1970–71 term of "his" Court, Chief Justice Burger commenced a pointed—although but marginally, successful—effort to avoid Mon-days, chiefly to vitiate the high overtime payments to printers in the Court's printshop incurred by first-day-of-the-week pressures. By the 1980s, except for the third Monday in each series of announcements of opinions, Tuesdays and Wednesdays had become standard Opinion Days.

[233] A device increasingly, and controversially, resorted to, for example, the Court's 1976 sum-mary 6:3 affirmation of a 2:1 three-judge District Court action that had rejected a challenge to a Virginia law prohibiting even private, adult consensual sodomy. (*Doe v. Common-wealth Attorney for City of Richmond*, 425 U.S. 901.) See the interesting article by John P. McKenzie, "4-Word High Court Rulings Questioned," *The Washington Post*, April 18, 1976, p. 2, highly critical of "the judgment is affirmed" syndrome. For another simple sum-mary affirmance without oral argument of a very significant voting rights issue, see *Missis-sippi Republican Executive Committee v. Brooks*, 53 LW 3361 (1984).

[234] See Donald D. Gregory and Stephen L. Wasby, "How to Get an Idea from Here to There: The Court and Communication Overload," 3 *Public Affairs Bulletin* 5 (November–Decem-ber 1970), passim.

[235] One of Justice Holmes's many virtues was brevity, which one of his most ardent on-the-bench admirers, Justice Robert H. Jackson, attributed to Holmes's lifelong practice of writing his opinions in longhand while *standing* at a desk of draftsman's height. When fatigue set in, Holmes would write finis to the opinion. See Eugene C. Gerhart, *Robert H. Jackson: Lawyer's Judge* (Albany: Q Corporation, 1961), pp. 109–10. The average length of Holmes's opinions was 3.54 pages—by far the briefest among the Justices who served with him; the longest, 12.24 pages per opinion, were written by Justice Horace Gray.

the 1980 *Fullilove* case, an opinion he read aloud in full.[236] This interesting practice of announcing opinions orally is not generally followed in the lower courts, in which a case is "announced" simply by filing its disposition with the clerk. Prior to the Chief Justiceship of Charles Evans Hughes, the Court's announcements were even lengthier, for the Justices generally persisted in reading opinions word for word, not infrequently in an unrelieved monotone. Hughes, however, sensing a golden opportunity—in the words of Edwin McElwain, who was one of his law clerks—to make "a public demonstration of the dignity and responsibility of the Court to the bar and to the thousands of visitors who came to the new Supreme Court Building during his regime,"[237] not only encouraged paraphrasing and summarizing of opinions, but also impressed on his colleagues of the bench the need to deliver them forcefully and convincingly. The Chief Justice himself was such an impressive figure—with his magnificent head, white beard, and sonorous voice—that visitors to an Opinion Day, hearing him deliver one of his opinions with dramatic impact, often likened him to a latter-day Moses, a concept not entirely displeasing to Hughes, not so much for himself, but for Court and Law.

Even after the Justices have assembled for the announcement of their opinions, should any one of their number have some last-minute qualms regarding one about to be handed down, all he has to do is to ask the Chief Justice to "let it go over"—such is the concern with each Justice's sensibilities. It cannot be emphasized too strongly that *each and every Justice* passes on all aspects of a case, at *each* of its stages; the Court most emphatically does not function by committee, panel, or section. The now published opinions presumably confine themselves to the issue involved in the various cases, but the voicing of profoundly held beliefs, and at times even a swipe at a colleague, is quite common. Thus, cleavages among the Justices of an intellectual, policy, and, at times, even personal nature become apparent in the written opinions—no matter how skilled an arbiter the Chief Justice may be. Fortunately, less frequent are *ad hoc* outbursts from the bench on Opinion Day; these are not found in the written record, but they do occur. Perhaps the most famous one is Justice McReynolds's explosion in 1935, while reading his dissent in the *Gold Clause Cases*,[238] when he veritably screamed from the bench: "This is Nero at his worst. The Constitution is gone!"

Judicial Tempers. To give some brief, contemporary illustrations of this aspect of Opinion Day: In November 1960, Justice Douglas, having just heard Justice Whittaker read the 6:3 opinion for the Court in a tax case,[239] com-

---

[236]*Regents of the University of California v. Bakke*, 438 U.S. 265 and *Fullilove v. Klutznick*, 448 U.S. 448, respectively. The 1901 *Insular Cases* took six hours to deliver.

[237]"The Business of the Supreme Court as Conducted by Chief Justice Hughes," 63 *Harvard Law Review* 20 (1949).

[238]*Norman v. Baltimore & Ohio Railroad Co.* 294 U.S. 240.

[239]*Meyers et al. v. United States*, 364 U.S. 410 (1960).

mented acidly from the bench that the issue decided this day was "narrow and technical"; that he would not have filed a dissent had not the "majority's error been so egregious"; and he closed with the observation: "But six make the law, and sometimes very bad law." Earlier that year, Justice Frankfurter had characterized as a "judicial somersault" an opinion for the Court by Justice Stewart in a criminal law case.[240] On Opinion Monday, March 30, 1959, Justice Frankfurter, while reading the majority opinion upholding the successive federal and state trials of one Bartkus for the same criminal act, against the charge of double jeopardy, made a passing reference to "the so-called Bill of Rights." When Justice Black's turn came to read his dissent in the case, he declared passionately: "This case concerns the Bill of Rights, not the 'so-called Bill of Rights'!"[241] Eight years later, the normally gentle Black, dissenting from a new interpretation of the constitutionality of eavesdropping in the *Katz* case, accused his brothers of being "language-stretching judges" whose aim was to "rewrite" the Constitution, who lacked "scholarship, common sense and candor," who had engaged in "clever word juggling."[242] On an Opinion Monday in April 1971, the usually affable Justice Brennan began his dissent from the Court's 5:4 decision ruling that some foreign-born U.S. Citizens could lose their citizenship merely on certain residential grounds by bitterly observing: "Since the Court this term has already downgraded citizens receiving public welfare, and citizens having the misfortune to be illegitimate, I suppose today's decision downgrading citizens born outside the United States should have been expected."[243]

During the waning days of the 1960–61 term, the public and the Court were treated to two serious *ad hoc* outbursts from the bench on two Opinion Days, involving Chief Justice Warren and, again, Justice Frankfurter. In the first instance, a sharp dissent by the latter provoked an oral rebuttal by the former, which was even more unusual because the Chief Justice, on the side of the 5:4 majority, had written no opinion in the case. But in stating his dissent, Justice Frankfurter took nearly fifteen minutes to sharpen the written language and heighten his criticism of the majority opinion in the criminal case at issue. Evidently hurt and annoyed by Frankfurter's tone of voice and the contents of his summation, the Chief Justice told the courtroom that "since so much has been said here that was not in any written opinion," he wanted to add a word as to why he joined the majority.[244]

An even more serious manifestation of judicial temper-flaring occurred several Opinion Days later, again featuring the same two Justices. The Court, once again by a 5:4 vote, as is so frequently the case in criminal cases involv-

---

[240] *Elkins and Clark v. United States*, 364 U.S. 206 (1960).

[241] As reported by Anthony Lewis, "Justice Black at 75: Still the Dissenter," *The New York Times Magazine*, February 26, 1961, p. 74.

[242] Comment from the bench in *Katz v. United States*, 389 U.S. 347, on December 18, 1967.

[243] *Rogers v. Bellei*, 401 U.S. 815.

[244] As reported in *The New York Times*, March 21, 1961, p. 18.

ing Bill-of-Rights interpretations, had reversed the murder conviction of one Willie Lee Stewart. In a ringing dissent, Justice Frankfurter, going far beyond anything he had written, accused the majority of "plucking out" of the lengthy trial record an isolated episode, and suggested that judges find in the record "what the mind is looking for." He went on to categorize the majority opinion as an "indefensible example of finicky appellate review of criminal cases" and warned against "turning a criminal appeal into a quest for error." When he had finished, Chief Justice Warren leaned forward, his face deeply flushed, and with evident emotion stated that the dissent just heard was not a proper statement of an opinion, but rather a

> lecture . . . a closing argument by a prosecutor to a jury. It is properly made, perhaps, in the conference room [of the Court], but not in the court room. . . . The purpose of reporting an opinion [here] is to inform the public and is not for the purpose of degrading this Court.

Warren then turned to Frankfurter, who was seated to his immediate left, and whispered an invitation to respond. Frankfurter said: "The Chief Justice urges me to comment on what he said, but of course I won't. I have another case."[245] Yet at the end of the session the two adversaries were engaged in friendly and cordial conversation! Even Supreme Court Justices are human. . . .[246]

---

[245] As reported in *The Philadelphia Evening Bulletin*, April 25, 1961, p. 3, and in *The New York Times*, April 25, 1961, p. 27. (The case is *Stewart v. United States*, 366 U.S. 1.)

[246] Since the preceding exchanges took place, there have been other memorable judicial outbursts—among them an unusually sharp attack by Justice Douglas on his brother Black in *Arizona v. California*, 373 U.S. 546 (1963); an acid exchange between Black and Justice Harlan in the congressional redistricting case of *Wesberry V. Sanders*, 376 U.S. 1 (1964); Harlan's scathing attack on the entire Court in the key reapportionment cases of 1964, headed by *Reynolds v. Sims*, 377 U.S. 533; Justice White's sarcastic references to his colleague Goldberg's reasoning in the now famous case of *Escobedo v. Illinois*, 378 U.S. 478 (1964); Justice Black's blistering attack on what he regarded as the "loosest construction of the Constitution in this court's history" by its two leading alleged and avowed "strict constructionists," Chief Justice Burger and Justice Blackmun, in the "gratis divorce proceedings case" of *Boddie v. Connecticut*, 401 U.S. 371 (1971); Justice Stewart's angry charge in a 1974 repossession case (*Mitchell v. W. T. Grant Co.*, 416 U.S. 600) that "recent changes in the Court's composition—instead of principles of law—caused a break with precedent less than two years old!"; and Justice Blackmun's biting comment that Justice Stewart's 5:4 majority opinion for the Court in the late 1976 complicated tax case of *United States v. Foster Lumber Co.*, 429 U.S. 32, was "a wooden and unimaginative reading of the tax law," and his characterization of another Stewart Opinion in a 1981 custody case as "virtually incredible." (*Lassiter v. Department of Social Services*, 452 U.S. 18.) In a much-quoted outburst Justice Rehnquist accused his colleagues of continuing "to evade some responsibility for this mockery of our criminal justice system [the Court's reluctance to uphold death sentences]," charging the "Court and the lower Federal courts" of having "converted the constitutional limits upon imposition of the death penalty by the States and the Federal Government into arcane niceties which parallel the equity court practices described in Charles Dickens's 'Bleak House.'" (*The New York Times*, April 28, 1981, p. D23.) Rehnquist returned to the fray in the 1983 reversal of a drug suspect's "airport profile" conviction, commenting sarcastically

Ratio Decidendi and Obiter Dictum. It is important to distinguish—although this is sometimes far more easily said than done—between the *ratio decidendi* of an opinion and the frequently present *obiter dictum* or *obiter dicta. Ratio decidendi* refers to the essence, the vitals, the necessary legal or constitutional core of the decision; *obiter dictum* is a more or less extraneous point, presumably unnecessary to the decision, made by the author of an opinion. In other words, the former constitutes the legal rule to be followed and adhered to; the latter is an expression of a belief, viewpoint, or sentiment, which, at least in theory, has no binding effect. It is not surprising, however, that, on occasion, an *obiter dictum* lives long after the *ratio decidendi* has been forgotten! Moreover, as U.S. District Court Judge P. M. Hall of California once put the matter, "I am not unmindful of the fact that in the last analysis the Judges of the Supreme Court are the final arbiters as to what is or is not *dicta* in a previous opinion."[247] Justice Brennan once observed that *obiter dicta* reflected "the gas on the stomach felt by the Justice at the time he was writing the decision."[248] But it is the *ratio decidendi* that makes the decided case one of record and renders the matter at issue *res judicata*, that is, a matter on which a competent court of law has passed judgment.

One of the most famous expounders of the *obiter dictum* was Chief Justice John Marshall, who delighted in employing that technique as a medium for the constitutional education of the public. His celebrated opinions in *Marbury v. Madison*,[249] *McCulloch v. Maryland*,[250] and *Gibbons v. Ogden*,[251] for example, are full of *dicta* that history has so merged with the *ratio decidendi* in these cases that the two concepts are almost indistinguishable. Nor has that

---

that the Court's plurality opinion "betrays a mindset more useful to those who officiate at shuffleboard games, primarily concerned with which particular square the disk has landed on, than to those who are seeking to administer a system of justice whose twin purposes are the conviction of the guilty and the vindication of the innocent." (*Royer v. Florida*, 460 U.S. 491, at 520.) Earlier, Justice Brennan had accused Rehnquist and his allies of "judicial activism," "sheer demagoguery," and "unvarnished hostility to constitutional claims." (*The Washington Post*, April 22, 1982, p. A11.) Justice O'Connor—much sniped at by some of her brethren—returned fire on one occasion by finding Justice Brennan's views on at least one instance to "carry more rhetorical force than substance" and referring to a Blackmun opinion as simply an "absurdity." (*The Washington Times*, November 18, 1982, p. A10.) And, beginning in 1982, Justice Stevens commenced a continuing barrage of public criticism of his colleagues for what he considered a "pro-prosecution" tilt, a charge in which he was joined by Justices Marshall and Blackmun. (E.g., *The* [Charlottesville, Va.] *Daily Progress*, August 7, 1982, p. A3; *The Washington Post*, April 24, 1984, p. A4; *The New York Times*, Aug. 5, 1984, p. 1; and *The Washington Post*, Sept. 24, 1984, p. A1 and Oct. 26, 1985, p. A8.)

[247] *Odikubo v. Bonesteel*, 60 F. Supp. 916 (1945) at 930, fn. 28. As Lord Loyd of Hamstead once observed in his *Introduction to Jurisprudence*, 3d ed., discussing the use of *dicta*: "A battery of howitzers off the target is more impressive than a pop gun on it." (New York: Praeger Publishers, 1972, p. 711.)

[248] Remark made to me, December 18, 1969, in the Justice's chambers.

[249] 1 Cranch 137 (1803).

[250] 4 Wheaton 316 (1819).

[251] 9 Wheaton 1 (1824).

approach become extinct in our own day, to which illustrations on two levels of the judiciary bear witness: In the case of *Shachtman v. Dulles*,[252] three judges of the U.S. Circuit Court of Appeals for the District of Columbia held unanimously that the grounds for the Secretary of State's denial of a passport to the petitioner constituted an arbitrary, and hence unconstitutional, denial of due process of law under the Fifth Amendment. That was the *ratio decidendi* of the case, but the author of the opinion of the tribunal, Circuit Judge Fahy, in an interesting *obiter dictum*, based the privilege of a passport on the "natural right" to travel, "to go from place to place as the means of transportation permit." At the level of the Supreme Court, *Watkins v. United States*[253] dealt with the refusal of a former labor organizer, John T. Watkins, to answer certain questions put to him by a subcommittee of the House Committee on Un-American Activities, which was investigating "Communist activities in the Chicago area." In a 6:1 decision, speaking through Chief Justice Warren, the Court set aside Watkins's conviction for contempt of Congress in the District Court below because neither Congress nor the Committee had ever satisfactorily apprised him whether or not the questions he had refused to answer were "pertinent to the subject under inquiry." This failure on the part of the legislature was thus held to render the conviction void on the ground of vagueness under the due process of law clause of the Fifth Amendment. Here we have the *ratio decidendi* of the *Watkins* case. But, resorting to the device of the *obiter dictum*, Chief Justice Warren also discussed matters, however related, which had not really been specifically raised by the petitioner Watkins in his allegations. In the face of charges of "overstatement" and "lily-gilding," Warren's long and fervent *dictum* clearly represented a lecture to Congress—and, he hoped, to the public at large—on the rights of individuals and Congress's abuse of its power to investigate. In it was this admonition: "We have no doubt that there is no congressional power to expose for the sake of exposure."[254] Another important example is the Court's footnote *dictum* in *United States v. Barnett*,[255] which indicated that anyone convicted of criminal contempt by a judge could not be given a sentence more severe than might be imposed for a "petty offense."

After the announcement and reading of an opinion the case is presumably finished, insofar as the members of the Court are concerned, and no further public comment thereon will normally emanate from the Justices. On rare occasion, however, the public reception of a decision may move a Justice to comment further. This occurred, for example, as a result of the New York Prayer Case,[256] when Justice Clark seized upon the occasion of a public speech to take note of the decision's critical reception by "explaining" his

[252] 225 F. 2d 938 (1955).

[253] 354 U.S. 178 (1957).

[254] Ibid., at 200.

[255] 376 U.S. 681 (1964), at 695 fn. 12.

[256] *Engel v. Vitale*, 370 U.S. 421 (1962).

vote as a member of the majority. Referring to the Court's 8:1 judgment that New York's state-composed twenty-two-word nondenominational prayer for use in the state's public schools constituted a violation of the principle of separation of church and state as imbedded in the First and Fourteenth Amendments, he stated simply: "No to me means no. That is all the court decided, not that there should be no recognition of a supreme being."

COMPLIANCE

When officially announced as decided, the case becomes binding on all lower federal courts and on all state courts when and where applicable. It is now *the* controlling opinion, *res judicata*—the law of the land—as enunciated and/or interpreted by its highest tribunal. It is then duly recorded and published—printed by a computer for the first time in October 1981—by the federal government in an invaluable series of volumes known as the *United States Reports*, which, duly compiled and edited by the Supreme Court's Reporter of Decisions, constitute the sole *official* record of the actions of the Court. Several unofficial publications are also available.[257] (The *Reports* and their forerunners are on file back to 1790.) However, although compliance with the Court's decisions may be expected to be a foregone conclusion insofar as the lower *federal* courts are concerned (Chapter 8 will discuss some of the problems of compliance, and of enforcement by *nonjudicial* governmental bodies generally), it is not always necessarily simple and automatic.

By Federal Courts. For example, in September 1960, Judge Ashton Williams of the U.S. District Court for South Carolina disqualified himself from a desegregation suit on the ground that *he* considered the Supreme Court's decision and subsequent order in *Brown v. Board of Education*[258] to be unconstitutional. He announced that another judge would have to hear the case, brought by four Charleston blacks, which involved compulsory segregation of the Charleston municipal golf course. Contending that the Supreme Court's decision barring separate facilities for whites and blacks in such public recreational facilities was based "on no constitutional grounds," he nonetheless stepped aside rather than disobey, and declared: "Since as a Federal judge I have to follow that decision I will disqualify myself because I have taken an oath to sustain the Constitution."[259]

Another U.S. District Court jurist, the then eighty-seven-year-old Judge William H. Atwell of Texas, went considerably further in 1956; he simply *refused* to carry out the desegregation ruling of the Court, and resorted to every conceivable judicial roadblock to prevent it. Although his ruling had been reversed by the Fifth U.S. Circuit Court of Appeals,[260] after his initial

---

[257]For example, the *Supreme Court Reporter*, the *Lawyers' Edition of the Opinions of the United States Supreme Court*, and *United States Law Week*.

[258]347 U.S. 483 (1954) and 349 U.S. 294 (1955).

[259]As reported in *The New York Times*, September 8, 1960, p. 27.

[260]*Brown v. Rippy*, 233 F. 2d 796 (1956).

rejection of the plaintiffs' petition,[261] he again refused to set a date of desegregation of the Dallas school district because such a step would cause "civil wrongs." In order to make quite clear where he stood on the issue, Atwell announced:

> I believe that it will be seen that the [Supreme] Court based its decision on no law but rather on what the Court regarded as more authoritative, more psychological knowledge.... It will be recalled that in 1952, Mr. Justice Frankfurter said it [the Supreme Court] was not competent to take judicial notice of "claims of social scientists."[262]

The Court of Appeals, naturally, again reversed the second Atwell decision in short order.[263] But far from acquiescing, Judge Atwell now embarked on a course of action in the opposite extreme by ordering all Dallas schools integrated in the middle of the academic year.[264] This decision was also reversed by the higher court.[265] Three or four years later, Atwell retired permanently—he had been recalled for temporary duty—and another federal District Court judge ultimately ordered a "mild" form of desegregation. This was broadened and amended by the Fifth Circuit Court of Appeals in accordance with the Supreme Court's 1954 and 1955 mandates,[266] with desegregation scheduled to begin on a one-grade-a-year basis in September of 1961[267]— which indeed it did, without incident. It should be pointed out, however, that the nature of the implementation order, as handed down by the Court in the second Brown case,[268] was tailor-made for dilatory tactics by federal District Court judges. It vested in them inherent authority to use their discretion in ordering desegregation by suggesting that they take notice of the peculiarities of the local situation. In effect, they were guided solely by the Court's mandate that the judges require a "prompt and reasonable start toward full compliance" and that they take such action as may be necessary to bring about the end of racial segregation in the public schools "with all deliberate speed."[269] This open-ended order has naturally also resulted in contentious,

---

[261] Bell v. Rippy, 133 F. Supp. 811 (1955).

[262] Bell v. Rippy, 146 F. Supp. 485 (1956) at 486.

[263] Borders v. Rippy, 247 F. 2d 268 (1957).

[264] 2 Race Relations Law Reporter 985 (1957).

[265] Rippy v. Borders, 250 F. 2d 690 (1957).

[266] Brown v. Board of Education, 347 U.S. 483 (1954), and ibid., 349 U.S. 294 (1955).

[267] Boston v. Rippy, 275 F. 2d 850 (1960).

[268] Loc. cit., 349 U.S. 294 (1955).

[269] Ibid., at 296. The term "all deliberate speed" was suggested by Justice Frankfurter, who lifted it from Justice Holmes's opinion in Virginia v. West Virginia, 222 U.S. 17 (1911) at 30—a case dealing with a monetary controversy between the two states. After more than fourteen years of "deliberate speed" compliance, the Court unanimously abandoned that doctrine in October 1969, ordering desegregation "at once" by and for all school systems so as henceforth to "operate now and hereafter only unitary schools." (Alexander v. Holmes County Board of Education of Mississippi, 396 U.S. 19. Rehearing denied, 396 U.S. 976 [1969].)

far-reaching, "judicial activist" desegregation orders, increasingly utilized by a plethora of U.S. District Court Judges as of the mid-1960s, and even accelerating in the 1970s. Examples are Judge W. A. Garrity, Jr.'s orders in connection with the Boston school desegregation controversy of 1974–75, including a federal takeover of the school system and some of the extensive compliance orders by, for instance, U.S. District Court Judge Frank M. Johnson of the Middle District of Alabama, *inter alia* requiring such specific mandates as college degrees for the athletic coaches and dieticians of state institutions and *x* number of feet of urinal space for each male inmate of a state prison or mental institution.[270]

But lest the impression arise that all defiance and deviation from the law as stated by the Court are confined to the segregation–integration controversy, we have another, and quite different example, this one involving an eminent jurist, Chief Judge John J. Parker of the Fourth U.S. Circuit Court of Appeals. In 1940 the Supreme Court had held 8:1 in the first of the *Flag Salute cases*[271] that Pennsylvania could validly require children of Jehovah's Witnesses attending public schools to salute the flag, despite claims of violation of their constitutionally guaranteed freedom of religion. Only Justice Stone had dissented. But no Supreme Court reversal still having taken place two years later, Judge Parker held an *identical* West Virginia statute unconstitutional.[272] He went to some length to point out that this really was not defiance, because three members of the 1940 majority had publicly confessed error on the occasion of a different case involving another constitutional claim by Jehovah's Witnesses,[273] and two others[274] had retired from the bench in the two-year interim, thus leaving the supporters of the compulsory flag salute in a minority of three.[275] His analysis and implied prediction proved to be correct, because the Court did specifically overrule itself, 6:3, when that very same West Virginia case[276] reached it—but, of course, Judge Parker

---

[270] *Morgan v. Hennigan,* 379 F. Supp. 410 (Mass., 1974), schools; Alabama: *Wyatt v. Stickney,* 344 F. Supp. 373 (1972), Bryce Hospital; *Pugh v. Locke,* 406 F. Supp. 318 (1976), prisons, E.g., *Pugh* required "in working order one toilet per 15 inmates, one urinal or one foot of urinal trough per 15 inmates, one shower per 20 inmates, and one lavatory per 10 inmates," at 334. "Each inmate who requires a special diet for reasons of health or religion shall be provided a diet to meet his or her individual need," at 334. "Visitors shall not be subjected to any unreasonable searches," at 334. "Qualified staff sufficient to maintain institutional order and to administer programs shall be employed," at 335.

[271] *Minersville School District v. Gobitis,* 310 U.S. 586 (1940).

[272] *Barnette v. West Virginia,* 47 F. Supp. 251 (1942) at 253.

[273] *Jones v. Opelika,* 316 U.S. 584 (1942) at 623–24. The three were Justices Black, Douglas, and Murphy.

[274] Chief Justice Hughes and Justice Byrnes.

[275] Justices Roberts, Reed, and Frankfurter. The six constituting the new majority were the new Chief Justice (Stone), the three "confessors-of-error" (Black, Douglas, and Murphy), and the two newcomers to the bench, Justices Jackson and Rutledge.

[276] *West Virginia State Board of Education v. Barnette,* 319 U.S. 624 (1943).

could neither safely predict that event, nor did it lessen the fact of his deviation.[277]

A grotesque illustration of defiance on the lower federal court level, is the astonishing case of the then eighty-six-year-old U.S. District Court Judge T. Whitfield Davidson of Dallas. In 1962, fully four years after he had been ordered to do so by the Supreme Court of the United States, Judge Davidson refused resolutely to impose a $506.11 penalty on a Texas farmer who had wilfully and illegally exceeded his planting allotment of wheat under federal regulations by forty-three acres. The venerable judge simply insisted on his own conclusions that the statute involved was unconstitutional—despite several Supreme Court holdings to the precise contrary[278]—and he further ruled that the highest court had no jurisdiction in the case at bar! When the federal authorities ultimately appealed Judge Davidson's obstructions to the Supreme Court, the latter made clear, in a curt and unsigned opinion, that it did indeed have jurisdiction and that it wanted its orders carried out forthwith "without delay."[279] They were! Had they not been, the Court could have issued a writ of *mandamus* to him—as it did in 1969 to U.S. District Judge John F. Dooling, Jr., of Brooklyn, who not only had ignored a trial jury's guilty verdict and dismissed the grand jury's indictment against four members of the "Mafia," but had ignored a writ by the U.S. Court of Appeals for the Second Circuit.[280]

And, as a last example of a lower federal jurist's fling of the gauntlet of outright refusal to abide by a Supreme Court ruling, we have the contemporary action by U.S. District Court Judge W. Brevard Hand of the Southern District of Alabama, who in 1983 declared unconstitutional the highest tribunal's 1962 ban on state-mandated prayers in public schools.[281] Hand's sixty-six-page ruling[282] was bottomed on the proposition that the Supreme Court had misread history by incorporating the First Amendment and misinterpreted the separation of church and state clause when it handed down its historic decision. Hand's order was stayed by Justice Powell, pending action on appeal by the U.S. Court of Appeals for the Eleventh Circuit. The latter subsequently reversed Judge Hand unanimously.[283]

However, these illustrations of deviations by lower court *federal* judges are exceptions to the general rule of compliance with the orders emanating from

---

[277]For an enlightening article on compliance generally, see Walter Murphy, "Lower Court Checks on Supreme Court Power," 53 *American Political Science Review* (December 1959), pp. 1017–31.

[278]The leading, and unanimous, decision was *Wickard v. Filburn* 317 U.S. 111 (1942), which upheld the constitutionality of the Agricultural Adjustment Act of 1938.

[279]*United States v. District Court (United States v. Haley)*, 371 U.S. 18.

[280]*Perzico v. United States*, 395 U.S. 911 (1969).

[281]*Engel v. Vitale*, 370 U.S. 421.

[282]*Jaffree v. Board of School Commissioners of Mobile County*, 554 F. Supp. 1104 (USDC S. Ala.).

[283]Ibid., 705 F. 2d 1526 (CA 11) (1983).

the highest tribunal. There may be disagreement with such an order, but one must, and may, expect that it be followed. The following comments by U.S. District Court Judge Charles E. Wyzanski, Jr., of Boston are in the best tradition of compliance, no matter how extensive the substantive disagreement. At issue was one of those time-consuming negligence cases, involving a trial jury's grant of $30,000 in damages to an injured New Haven Railroad worker, one Mrs. Henagan. The New Haven, on receiving the jury's verdict in Judge Wyzanski's court, asked him to set it aside. He replied that he would if he could, but that he was not free to do so because the Supreme Court had consistently held in favor of railroad employees in similar cases and that the Court's precedent commanded his obedience. But he went on to indicate his feelings in no uncertain terms:

> I cannot read the record as a whole in a way to find any evidence of negligence [by the New Haven]. But I know that my method of reading the record is different from that of a majority of the Supreme Court of the United States as exhibited in past cases, and I hope *I am a lawful judge,* and I recognize the limits of my authority whether appellate judges do or not.[284]

Ironically, as matters developed, the Supreme Court, for the first time in a quarter of a century of rulings in Federal Employers' Liability Act cases, a short time thereafter reversed a jury verdict by a 6:2 majority because it found insufficient negligence on the part of the railroad—and the case was Mrs. Henagan's![285]

It should also be noted that the Court, by special order, may bypass proceedings in the lower federal courts, although this is not commonly done, as Congressman Adam Clayton Powell (D.-N.Y.) found out in 1967 when he unsuccessfully sought a Supreme Court order to bypass the U.S. Court of Appeals, where his appeal from an adverse decision from a U.S. District Court on his exclusion from the U.S. House of Representatives then lodged. However, an example of a successful plea is a 1964 antitrust action under the Clayton Act commenced by the federal government against the El Paso Natural Gas Co. There, Justice Douglas directed that El Paso divest itself of a firm it had acquired "without delay"—and without "further proceedings in the lower courts,"—an order from which only Justice Harlan dissented.[286]

By State Courts. When it comes to compliance with Supreme Court decisions by *state* courts, an entirely different element enters. In effect, the Supreme Court has no power to make a *final determination* of any case in

---

[284] *New York, New Haven, & Hartford v. Henagan,* as reported in 272 F. 2d 153 (1959), at 155–56. (Italics supplied.) For a similar stance see the statement of U.S. Court of Appeals for the Fifth Circuit in *Griffin v. Breckenridge,* 410 F. 2d 817 (1969), a case it wanted to overrule but did not, because "[s]ince we may not adopt what the Supreme Court has expressly rejected, we obediently abide the mandate in [*Collins v. Hardyman,* 341 U.S. 651, 1951, at 826–27]."

[285] *New York, New Haven, & Hartford, v. Henagan,* 364 U.S. 441 (1960).

[286] *United States v. El Paso Natural Gas Co.,* 376 U.S. 251.

which it reviews *state* court judgments. All it can do in these instances is to *decide the federal issue* and *remand* it to the state court below for final judgment "not inconsistent with this opinion."[287] Because the state courts possess the power to raise new issues—issues based on "independent and adequate state grounds"[288]—after they receive the case back from above, they are provided with an opportunity to evade the substantive effects of the reversal by the Supreme Court in a number of ways.[289] And once a new issue is raised, the ultimate disposition of the case may, of course, go either way. A notorious illustration is the case of Virgil Hawkins, a then forty-two-year-old Florida black, who was denied admission to the University of Florida Law School in 1949. After lengthy legal stratagems, delays, and assorted maneuvers on all levels of the judiciary over a period of nine years, Hawkins was finally ordered admitted by the U.S. Supreme Court after the Florida Supreme Court continued to stall—yet he was in fact never allowed to go to the university, and he gave up.[290] He finally earned his law degree at the New England School of Law in 1965, when he was fifty-eight years of age, and he was at last admitted to the Florida Bar—without having to take the bar examination—in 1976, at age 70! That this whole matter of spotty and often unpredictable state court compliance is not an illusory conclusion is well demonstrated by, for instance, certain statistics gathered and published by the *Harvard Law Review* some years ago.[291] For example, from 1941 to 1951, the Supreme Court remanded 175 cases to the various state courts for further proceedings "not inconsistent with this judgment." In 46 of these (almost 27 percent of the total), further litigation ensued, with 22 of the parties who *won* in the Supreme Court now *losing* in the state courts as a result of the final judgment below. In the decade immediately preceding, the Court had reviewed 187 state court cases and remanded them. In 34 of these (somewhat above 18 percent), new issues were

---

[287] E.g., see the grisly history of the case of *Williams v. Georgia*, 349 U.S. 375 (1955) and 350 U.S. 950 (1956).

[288] See *Murdock v. City of Memphis*, 87 U.S. 590 (1874). However, to be independent that state ground must not depend for its support on, or be intertwined with, the federal question.

[289] E.g., the New York State Court of Appeals' "reviving" of that state's eavesdropping law in 1967 (*People v. Kaiser*, 286 N.Y. 52 & 801), notwithstanding the U.S. Supreme Court's mandate of unconstitutionality pronounced six months earlier in *Berger v. New York*, 388 U.S. 41.

[290] Among the seven Hawkins cases were: *Florida ex rel Hawkins v. Board of Control*, 347 U.S. 971 (1954); ibid., 350 U.S. 413 (1956); and ibid., 355 U.S. 839 (1957). See the account of the Hawkins dilemma in Walter F. Murphy and C. Herman Pritchett, *Courts, Judges, and Politics* (New York: Random House, 1961), pp. 606–18. For another, see Daryl Paulson and Paul Hawkes, "Desegregating the University of Florida Law School: Virgil Hawkins v. The Florida Board of Control," 12 *Florida State University Law Review* 1 (Spring 1984).

[291] See the two *Notes*, "Final Disposition of State Court Decisions Reversed and Remanded by the Supreme Court, October Term 1931 to October Term 1940," 55 *Harvard Law Review* 1357 (1942), and "Evasion of Supreme Court Mandates in Cases Remanded to State Courts since 1941," 67 *Harvard Law Review* 1251 (1954).

raised below, and in a mere 9 of these the ultimate state court decision favored the party who had "won" in the Supreme Court of the United States. Especially certain state supreme courts, who are very much the creatures of the political system in which they operate, may invoke "judicial federalism" by relying on state constitutions as independent sources of constitutional authority.[292]

Whatever the difference in the degree of compliance with the decisions of the highest court in the land,[293] it is fair to conclude that their nationwide impact is often uneven. The many diverse local conditions that characterize the federal system are all but tailor-made for considerable latitude in compliance. This fact of constitutional life clearly accounts for the spotty, often utter lack of compliance in the 1954 and 1955 decisions concerning desegregation, yet, conversely, also for the amazingly speedy acceptance and compliance, however varied, with the reapportionment-redistricting decision of the 1960s, following the historic Supreme Court ruling in *Baker v. Carr.*[294] On the other hand, some public school districts, egged on by local and state authorities, openly defied, and others circumvented by "interpretations" that seemed to ignore, the language of the Supreme Court's ruling in the *Prayer and Bible Reading Cases* of 1962 and 1963.[295] Indeed, nearly 13 percent of the nation's public schools—and 50 percent of those in the South—were continuing their defiance as the 1960s turned into the 1970s[296]—although, happily, the nationwide figure had dropped to 10 percent by early 1975.[297] But there are more than a few examples of continuing efforts of defiance, such as Alabama's during 1981–83.[298] And until the Court issued its contentious but specific and plainly understood rules in its historic criminal justice decision in *Miranda v. Arizona,*[299] different state courts—even so sophisticated a court as the

---

[292]See the illuminating article by Mary Cornelia Porter and G. Alan Tarr, "The New Judicial Federalism and the Ohio Supreme Court: Anatomy of a Failure," 45 *Ohio State Law Journal* 1 (1984).

[293]For a study that found no significant degree of difference in the compliance rate of federal and state courts, see Edward N. Beiser, "A Comparative Analysis of State and Federal Judicial Behavior: The Reapportionment Cases," 62 *American Political Science Review* 788 (September 1968).

[294]369 U.S. 186 (1962). Barely six years later all but a handful of states had either complied voluntarily or done so as a result of U.S. District Court orders. What had once been an average deviation of close to 11 percent in population representation had sunk to less than 1 percent—an amazing manifestation of compliance!

[295]See, for example, "The Supreme Court and the Bible Belt: Tennessee Reaction to the 'Schempp' Decision," by Robert H. Birkby, 10 *Midwest Journal of Political Science* 3 (August 1966). Also see Henry J. Abraham and Robert R. Benedetti, "The State Attorney General: A Friend of the Court?" 117 *University of Pennsylvania Law Review* 6 (April 1969).

[296]*The New York Times,* March 26, 1969, p. 1.

[297]*The New York Times,* February 5, 1975, p. 24.

[298]See p. 238, *supra.*

[299]384 U.S. 436 (1966).

Supreme Court of New Jersey—interpreted the decision in *Miranda's* antecedent, *Escobedo v. Illinois*,[300] in a host of diverse, frequently clearly defiant, ways. If properly supported by responsible public and private sources of power and influence, the Court will of course ultimately generally have its way, more or less—unless it is reversed by legislative action or constitutional amendment, or if it overrules or modifies its own decisions (of which much more will be said in chapters 7 and 8). But it must be accorded appropriate executive support—as indeed it was in Little Rock, Arkansas, Oxford, Mississippi, and Tuscaloosa, Alabama—for, as will be emphasized and reemphasized in these pages, the Court's only effective power is the power to persuade: purse and sword, as Hamilton noted so presciently in *Federalist No. 78*, are in other hands.

OUTSIDE INFLUENCES ON COURT PERSONNEL

Much has been written and pronounced on various outside sources that allegedly prey on and lobby the Court and endeavor to influence its decision-making process. A good deal of this commentary has been exaggerated; much has been spurious; some has been made with nothing less than evil intent and ill will; and some has been sheer nonsense. Of course, the Justices are subject to "influence." Any governmental body with the power to make significant discretionary choices, which the Court assuredly possesses, may be expected to be a target of interest groups and interest seekers. But it is an entirely different type of "influence" from that normally associated with lobbying. Let it be stated at once and unequivocally, the sort of lobbying and the buttonholing and back-slapping approaches used to influence (1) legislators and (2) executives and administrators, not only would not work with the members of the federal judiciary in general, and the Justices of the Supreme Court in particular, but would meet with withering disdain. As the British would say, "this simply is not done!" Moreover, the so welcome and necessary independence of the federal judiciary, and the almost Olympian position of awe, if not necessarily always majoritarian regard and esteem, the Justices rightfully enjoy in the popular mind would militate against any of the Myriad approaches, ingenuous or ingenious, to which the average official or unofficial lobbyist resorts in Washington and the various other seats of federal and state power in the United States of America. If, however, we mean by "influence" a well-reasoned and ably written brief, be it by one of the litigants or a brief *amicus curiae* (see later); a persuasive oral argument on behalf of an issue at bar; a timely, thoughtful, and convincing book, monograph, speech, or, notably, law review article on the general or specific issue; a strategically timed use of a bona fide test case—*that* type of influence, as well as the intriguing

[300]378 U.S. 478 (1964).

concept of the "climate of public opinion" (to be discussed in chapter 7), falls into a different category. In the final analysis, here the Justices remain the complete masters of their own house.

In elaborating somewhat on the several sources of outside influence that may bear on the Court, we may omit the more obvious and self-explanatory, such as the well-written brief, the persuasive oral argument, and most literature. Some others do deserve separate treatment, including the alleged "gray eminences" behind the Justices, the law clerks.

LEGAL PERIODICALS

Articles that appear in law reviews and other legal periodicals undoubtedly have exerted a formative influence on the law for some time. This is only natural, because the best legal thinking finds expression in these periodicals (only the top law students "work on" law reviews while in law school). The jurists are part of the legal process and are quite naturally generally familiar with the thinking that presents itself in the pages of the reviews; indeed, they must be familiar with it if they wish to keep their fingers on the pulse of the profession and, as Justice Holmes put it so cogently, "the felt necessities of the times." In a pioneering article based on work leading to his doctorate, Chester A. Newland presented the results of a close study of the use made by the Supreme Court of legal periodicals during the period between 1924 and 1956.[301] In most cases the law review and other articles cited by the Justices constituted minor references in the opinions concerned, although a few seemed to be close to the *ratio decidendi*. An avowed and indeed acknowledged illustration of the latter is Justice Brandeis's significant opinion in the landmark case of *Erie v. Tompkins* of 1938,[302] which overruled the century-old precedent on the judicial application of common law laid down in *Swift v. Tyson*.[303] Brandeis, who is generally regarded at the principal originator of the use of law review articles, made a point of crediting "the research of a competent scholar"—Charles Warren's article, "New Light on the History of the Federal Judiciary Act of 1789," 37 *Harvard Law Review* 49 (1923).[304] In any event, there were numerous references in each term after 1937, with an average of twenty-five opinions (or about one-fifth of the number handed down by the Court in a typical term) citing a total of between forty and seventy periodicals. Not surprisingly, the Justices varied in the frequency of use

---

[301] "Legal Periodicals and the United States Supreme Court," 3 *Midwest Journal of Political Science* 58–74 (February 1959).

[302] 304 U.S. 64.

[303] 16 Peters 1 (1842). As a result of *Erie*, the Judicial Code now provides that "the laws of the several states . . . shall be regarded as rules of decision in trials at common law in the courts of the United States." Equity, admiralty, and criminal cases are excluded from the clause's operation, however.

[304] 304 U.S. 64, at 72–73.

they made of these references, depending, more or less, on their scholarly bent and interest. Of the Justices appointed after 1937 and before 1957 who cited legal periodicals in at least twenty opinions during that period, Justice Rutledge, with a per-term average of 7.4 opinions, headed the list; next came Justice Frankfurter with 5.5; third was Justice Jackson with 4.1; low man was Justice Burton with 2.0. For whatever significance it may have, the statistics also indicate that the four most frequently cited journals during the thirty-two-year period covered by Professor Newland's study, and the number of times they were referred to, were *The Harvard Law Review* (399); *Yale Law Journal* (194), *The Columbia Law Review* (176), and *The Michigan Law Review* (165).

There is little doubt that reliance on the legal periodicals by both bar and courts has increased further. Thus, a study published a generation after Newland's demonstrated, *inter alia*,[305] that the U.S. Supreme Court used thirty-six law review references in *Miranda v. Arizona*, (1966), forty-five in *Furman v. Georgia*, (1972), and fifteen in *Stone v. Powell* (1976).[306] Although difficult to determine objectively, this particular genre of the written word exerts a formative influence, and it does, of course, represent an outside influence. Yet it may well be asked how much "outside" this particular type of influence is. Moreover, commentators as well as students of the legal process hardly agree on its extent. To cite one of the more extreme points of view on the matter, in a speech in the House of Representatives, Congressman Wright Patman (D.-Tex.) viewed any reliance on legal periodicals as all but evil and sinister, and contended that it was subversive of traditional judicial processes:

> In adopting and relying upon such pseudo-legalistic papers disseminated by the lobbyist-authors thereof the result is that the theories advanced by these pretended authorities were presented and received by the Court in an ex parte fashion.[307]

Replying to Patman in his article, Professor Newland charged the veteran congressman with "some measure of naïveté," and pointed out that if law reviews and other legal journals were not to limit their interests solely to the past, they were bound to be vehicles for the expression of views on current policy issues.[308] He concluded his observations by putting the problem into its proper focus:

> Critics may properly object that some views expressed in legal periodicals and adopted by the courts are contrary to policies which they deem desirable. But no greater unanimity of opinion usually exists among law faculties and reviews

---

[305] Steven R. Schlesinger, *The Facts, Evidence, and Law* (Lanham, MD: University Press of America, 1983), pp. 37–42.

[306] *Congressional Record, 85th Cong. 1st sess.*, Vol. 103, Part 12, p. 16160.

[307] Newland, op. cit., pp. 73–74.

[308] Ibid., p. 74.

than exists on the Supreme Court. Legal periodicals appear to be "political" in somewhat the same way that the Courts are.[309]

SOCIAL SCIENCE DATA

Related to the judicial use of legal periodicals, but in a rather different category, is the resort by members of the Court to *social science data*, either on the basis of independent research and utilization by the Justices themselves or, more frequently, because of their presentation in briefs by the litigants. The literature on the phenomenon is still sparse but has begun to increase markedly, and a 1978 "Report on the Uses of Social Science in Judicial Decision Making" by Professor Victor G. Rosenblum of Northwestern University and colleagues throws considerable, if perhaps inconclusive, light on the matter. What follows relies heavily on that interesting study.[310]

"Social science data" (or "materials") are usually bracketed under the disciplines of political science, economics, sociology, psychology, history, anthropology, and a few others. Accepting that classificiation, the Rosenblum research examined the use of such data as a tool of decisional aid by members of the Supreme Court during the 1954, 1959, 1964, 1969, and 1974 terms— 1954, of course, including the *Brown v. Board* desegregation decision, which made frank use of social science data, and 1969 representing the end of the Warren and the beginning of the Burger eras. During that twenty-year period, the sitting Justices numbered twenty-one—ranging in order of seniority from Black through Rehnquist—and wrote about 800 majority and concurring opinions and 470 dissenting opinions in a total of 601 cases. In roughly one-third of their opinions the Justices resorted to identifiable social science materials, although these were not necessarily crucial to the *ratio decidendi* in a case. The cases featuring the usage were almost evenly divided between civil and criminal suits and similarly divided between those coming to the Court on appeal or a writ of *certiorari*. In descending order of frequency, the social science disciplines represented (with their appearance frequency noted in parentheses) were political science (43 percent), economics (20.1 percent), sociology (18.8 percent), psychology (9.4 percent), history (4.0 percent), anthropology (1.3 percent), and others (3.4 percent). By far the heaviest concentration of utilization by the Justices occurred in four fields of litigations: legislative apportionment, criminal procedure, racial discrimination, and election and voting laws. Almost 60 percent of the total were brought on "equal protection of the laws" grounds, with those coming up under "due process of law" a clear but distant second (13 percent).

Among some of the both interesting and significant findings of the Rosenblum study were the following: A larger percentage of use and reliance on social science materials occurred on the *winning* side of the cases involved. Unexpectedly, perhaps, there was *no* correlation between the use of social

[309]384 U.S. 436; 408 U.S. 238; and 428 U.S. 465, respectively.
[310]Unpublished manuscript, April 1978. (Used by permission of the author.)

science data and so-called liberal and conservative Justices. The four most frequent *absolute* users were, in descending order, Harlan, Douglas, White, and Stewart; the most frequent *relative* ones were, in the same order, White, Goldberg, Marshall, and Frankfurter. Three of the twenty-one Justices *never* employed social science data, namely, Burton, Minton, and Whittaker—but they were among the least productive opinion authors and, arguably, the least widely read. Some Justices utilized the materials *solely* in majority opinions, never in dissent: Frankfurter, Warren, Goldberg, Burger, and Powell; others resorted to them chiefly in dissenting opinions: Black, Douglas, and Stewart. Certain members of the Court proved themselves to be demonstrably comfortable with the use of social science findings, for example, Warren, Marshall, and White, whereas others, for example, Black and Clark, in particular, were extremely wary of them. Whatever conclusions one may draw from it, the phenomenon is one to be reckoned with in the judicial process and bids fair to find continued, and very likely increased, utilization.[311]

TEST CASES

Because the American federal judicial system is based on the concept of litigation by virtue of an actual case or controversy brought before the courts by parties directly concerned, who must have standing to sue either as individuals or as personally and directly involved members of a class (see chapter 9), the solution of an issue in the judicial process depends on the decision handed down by the tribunal having jurisdiction. Consequently, neither the U.S. Supreme Court nor any of the lower constitutional courts can decide an issue unless it is before that court. Hence the employment of "test cases" becomes *a fortiori* crucial, and both the timing and the presentation of the case are of the utmost importance. As long as the plaintiff or petitioner is a bona fide litigant it does not matter whether or not he or she pays for the almost always considerable expenses involved; nor does it matter to the outcome whether he or she personally is vitally interested in the decision. Provided that any individual is directly involved and is willing to go to court, it is of no legal significance that, in effect, he or she may thus well act as a front or a foil. Some states do have laws against "barratry"—a form of induced litigation— but it is extremely difficult to prove that barratry has been practiced unless a litigant so acknowledges. This is particularly unlikely in those "class action" cases (see chapter 9) epitomized by the segregation–integration controversy.

The first really important case in that realm came before the Supreme Court through the auspices of a Missouri black, Lloyd Gaines, to whom that

[311]See the critical analysis of the phenomenon by David M. O'Brien, "The Seduction of the Judiciary: Social Science and the Courts," 64 *Judicature* (June–July 1980), and its defense by Peter W. Sperlich, "Social Science Evidence and the Courts," ibid. 63 (December–January 1980).

state had statutorily denied admission to its public law school,[312] but who mysteriously disappeared just a few days prior to his significant 7:2 victory in the Court. (Gaines was never heard from again.) Ever since that time, test cases have been brought with increasing frequency by blacks who have been discriminated against—with the active encouragement, backing, and financing of the interest groups such as the National Association for the Advancement of Colored People (NAACP). It is neither surprising nor subject to doubt that that organization, dedicated to the aim inherent in its title, has acted, and will assuredly continue to act, very much like a strategy board of a field command, with due regard to the manifold tactical and strategic problems that beset such a command. In that sense, it resorts to the device of the test case to get its day in court, as do a host of other organizations for their own purposes. The American Civil Liberties Union is a similarly apposite example of the practice.

Another illustration of the practice is the concerted drive by the Jehovah's Witnesses to obtain a maximum of religious freedom, as the Witnesses conceive of it, through the device of testing in the courts what they consider to be restrictions and attacks on their members. During the second quarter of this century, individual members of that sect, actively supported by the parent body, brought more than fifty bona fide test cases to the Supreme Court. Of these they won all but five! Nor is this practice confined to so-called minority groups. Almost every segment of the body politic has resorted to the device of the test case to gain—or lose—a point. The question arises, just how much pressure or influence-peddling on the Court *is* involved here? Those who suspect a burglar under every judicial bed quite naturally view test cases as an all but subversive scheme. Yet test case or regular case, a case is a case, provided it meets the jurisdicitional requirements of the Court. And the line between a "plotted" or "instigated" case and a "real" or "natural" one is so thin that it almost defies detection except in the most obvious instances. Moreover, the Court is the master of its own calendar and will not accept frivolous litigation, much less hand down a decision on it. Finally, if an issue of constitutional magnitude is duly and properly brought before the Court—all legal remedies below having been exhausted, and all the requirements of the judicial process having been met—and the Court has agreed to review it, does it *really matter* whether the issue was instigated or just happened in the natural course of events?

THE BRIEF AMICUS CURIAE

Closely related, indeed often essential, to the technique of test cases encouraged and supported by interest groups is the resort to the brief *amicus curiae*. It is a partisan brief filed by an outside individual or group—almost always a

---

[312]*Missouri ex rel Gaines v. Canada*, 305 U.S. 337 (1938).

formal organization in the latter category—who is not a litigant in the suit but is vitally interested in a decision favorable to the side it espouses. Long gone is the original concept of the *amicus curiae*—namely, that it "acts for no one, but simply seeks to give information to the Court."[313] The device of the brief *amicus curiae*, that is, "friend of the court," which may well be a misnomer in some situations, "friend of the *cause*" being far more accurate,[314] enables the interested party filing these briefs to enter the case, however tangentially, either by way of a written statement, or by participating in oral argument, or both. But there are obstacles as well as limitations to the filing of an *amicus curiae*. If all parties consent to the filing of such a brief, the Supreme Court's rules require its own acquiescence thereto. However, mutual consent by the litigants is by no means always readily forthcoming. In that event, a party may petition the Court itself for permission to file an *amicus curiae*, a request that may or may not be granted, depending entirely on the judgment of the Justices.[315] Moreover, in cases in which the U.S. government is a party to a suit, which is true of approximately one-half or even more of the total number of all cases before the Supreme Court, consent for leave to file briefs *amici curiae* must, at least in theory, be given by the Solicitor General before the Court will admit them. In general, that high government official has been quite willing to do so, but on some occasions the Court has granted organizational requests for briefs *amici curiae* over his refusal to consent. The same general approach is true of cases involving *state* government—as was demonstrated by the Supreme Court's acceptance of briefs *amici curiae* in the 1965 case testing Connecticut's birth control statute over that state's objections.[316]

Who files these briefs? Theoretically any interested party may do so; in practice, however, most briefs *amici curiae* come from active civic organizations and other pressure groups and, not surprisingly, from the federal government itself through the Solicitor General. According to an authoritative study of applicants for leave to file during relatively recent times,[317] most requests have been filed by the following organizations: the ACLU (a tireless and effective battler for civil rights and liberties);[318] the NAACP (persistent and broadly successful spokesperson for blacks); the American Jewish Congress and the American Jewish Committee (in roughly the same category as the ACLU, but with emphasis on cases concerning matters involving its own

---

[313] *Campbell v. Swasey*, 12 Ind. 70 (1859) at 72.

[314] See the persuasive article, "'Friend of the Court' More Properly Means 'Friend of the Cause,'" by Fred Barbash, *The Washington Post*, December 27, 1980, p. A4.

[315] Thus, in *Lemon v. Kurtzman*, 397 U.S. 1042 (1969), probable jurisdiction noted, the Court granted one motion to file an *amicus curiae* and denied another.

[316] *Griswold v. Connecticut*, 381 U.S. 479. See the illuminating article in *Time Magazine*, February 26, 1965, pp. 50–51.

[317] Clement E. Vose, "Litigation as a Form of Pressure Group Activity," 319 *Annals of the American Academy of Political and Social Science* (September 1958), pp. 20–31.

[318] Between 10 and 20 percent of the cases the Court agreed to review in the last generation.

particular interests); and the chief interest group for the vast labor movement the AFL-CIO. Also very active have been the American Bar Association, sundry consumer groups (often led by Ralph Nader and Common Cause), various veterans' pressure groups, led by the American Legion, and, quite often of late in matters involving reapportionment–redistricting, sexual discrimination, and segregation–integration (but not only those), the U.S. government.[319] Such requests have often, but by no means always, been granted.

To cite a specific example of the successful use of an *amicus curiae* by the last, the government filed such a brief in a 1960 case, *Boynton v. Virginia*,[320] through the auspices of Solicitor General J. Lee Rankin. Here a bus terminal restaurant in Richmond, Virginia, segregated passengers according to color, regardless of their destination. The plaintiff rested his brief on the equal protection of the laws clause of the Fourteenth Amendment, under which so many cases in the area of racial segregation had been won by black petitioners. However, the Solicitor General's brief *amicus curiae* used an entirely different approach, contending that since the restaurant involved was an "integral part" of a bus line's interstate passenger service, the Interstate Commerce Act of 1887—a federal statute—forbade such segregation. More or less ignoring the litigants' arguments and briefs, the Supreme Court fastened on the contents of Mr. Rankin's *amicus curiae* and decided 7:2 in the plaintiff's favor. Justice Whittaker, however, in a dissenting opinion in which he was joined by Justice Clark, chided the Court majority for deciding the case on the commerce clause which had been raised *solely* by the government as *amicus curiae*.

Unless the evidence is as clear-cut as it was in the preceding instance, it is very difficult to determine how far, if at all, the Court's decision and opinion make use of briefs *amici curiae*. What some commentators in this field report as the gospel's truth is not infrequently laced with conjecture and sheer guesswork, and some of it with prejudiced motivation. On the other hand, it would be fair to state that the flood of briefs *amici curiae* filed by the NAACP in the area of its own special interest had at least some persuasive influence in the outcome of the many cases handed down by the Court in the fifteen years

---

[319]In one fairly typical stretch of six terms of Court (1962–68), the U.S. government participated as *amicus curiae* in 121 cases (about 15 percent of the total number of cases heard by the Court). Roughly half of these 121 dealt with race and apportionment matters. See Samuel Krislov, *The Role of the Attorney General as* Amicus Curia (Washington, D.C.: American Enterprise Institute for Public Policy Research, July 1968), pp. 71–103. In the 1970s, discrimination other than on the basis of race replaced apportionment as the government's second major concern. A more recent study by Karen O'Connor demonstrates the continuing, and indeed mounting, *amicus curiae* role of the federal government in Supreme Court litigation. Thus, in the decade from 1970 through 1979 covered by her research, the Office of the Solicitor General of the United States participated as *amicus curiae* in 285 cases, comprising a total of 17 percent of all cases. (But the government also took part as the direct party in an *additional* 713 cases, comprising an additional 42 percent of all cases. See 66 *Judicature* 6 [December–January 1983], pp. 257–64.)

[320]364 U.S. 454.

between the end of World War II and 1960, for example—in which cases the cause espoused by the NAACP gained fifty victories! A specific illustration of one of these is the momentous decision by the Court in *Shelley v. Kraemer*, the most important of the *Restrictive Covenant cases*.[321] That case held the record for the number of main briefs and briefs *amici curiae* filed and accepted until 1963: nineteen by the NAACP and others favorably disposed to its point of view, five by opposing groups, chiefly real-estate interests, and one by Solicitor General Philip B. Perlman on behalf of the U.S. Department of Justice, siding with the black plaintiff.[322] Speaking for the unanimous six-man Court—Justices Reed, Jackson, and Rutledge having disqualified themselves from participation—Chief Justice Vinson ruled that although racially restrictive *private* covenants did not in themselves violate the Fourteenth Amendment of the Constitution, *court enforcement* of such contracts would constitute state action and thereby violate the equal protection of the laws clause of that Amendment—a signal victory for the cause of the NAACP.

Other illustrations of the use of briefs *amici curiae* on *both* sides are *Gideon v. Wainwright*, the influential 1963 decision that extended the right of indigents to be assigned counsel for *noncapital* as well as capital criminal cases; *DeFunis v. Odegaard* which, in 1974, raised the delicate question of "reverse discrimination" in university admissions; and *Regents of the University of California v. Bakke*, which re-raised that issue insistently in 1977–78 after the Court had "mooted" it in *DeFunis*.[323] In *Gideon*, twenty-four such briefs were filed on behalf of Clarence Earl Gideon, two on behalf of Florida Prison Warden Wainwright, thus toppling the erstwhile record submittals. In *DeFunis*, eight briefs were filed for law student Marco DeFunis and nineteen for University of Washington President Charles Odegaard, another record. It was surpassed, however, in *Bakke* with the filing of 120 briefs, 83 on the side of the University of California, 32 for Alan Bakke, and 5 that were "neutral." But that record, too, was shattered in 1984, in *Sony Corporation of America v. Universal City Studios*, when 140 briefs *amici curiae* entered the fascinating fray involving the right of American citizens regularly to copy television programs at home on videotape recorders, such as those manufactured by Betamax.[324]

Surely, briefs *amici curiae* may, and sometimes do, influence members of the Court. To acknowledge that entirely plausible, and in many cases quite conceivably salutary, phenomenon is one thing; to lower it to the level of a sinister or subversive cops-and-robbers plot is quite another. In this realm of

---

[321]334 U.S. 1 (1948) plus *Hurd v. Hodge*, 334 U.S. 24 (1948) and *Barrows v. Jackson*, 346 U.S. 249 (1953).

[322]Clement E. Vose, *Caucasians Only: The Supreme Court, the NAACP, and the Restrictive Covenent Cases* (Berkeley and Los Angeles: University of California Press, 1959), Ch. VIII.

[323]372 U.S. 335; 416 U.S. 312; and 429 U.S. 109 respectively. (One of the briefs *amici curiae* for Alan Bakke was filed by Marco DeFunis.)

[324]52 LW 4090.

alleged outside influence, as well as in those discussed earlier, the fact remains that, when all is said and done, the Justices have the final word on whether or how far, if at all, they permit themselves to be influenced within the accepted framework of the judicial process.

THE LAW CLERKS

In a somewhat different category among the "pressures" on the Court are its law clerks. Depending on the point of view advanced, these able and intelligent young aides to the Justices, all recent law-school graduates in their mid-twenties, are in the category either of a private secretary aide-de-camp to their Justices or of a gray eminence, a sort of judicial Rasputin—indeed, the veritable power behind the throne! Thus, in an angry 1958 speech on the Senate floor, U.S. Senator John Stennis (D.-Miss.), a vigorous critic of the Court's attitude on segregation and subversion cases took pains to call for an investigation of the activities of the clerks, the establishment of statutory minimum qualifications for them, and their confirmation by the Senate just like the Justices themselves—all this because of what the Senator termed "their ever-increasing importance and influence." The law clerks, he said, might be occupying roles in government far more important than those occupied by undersecretaries and assistant secretaries of the executive branch, and that

> [to] the extent that they participate in shaping the work of the court, they are deciding vital questions of national effect. Within the Judicial branch, these are equivalent to policy-level decisions in the executive branch.[325]

Yet we have the word of ex-law clerk after ex-law clerk that their influence on the Justices to whom they were assigned was nil insofar as the actual judicial decision-making process was concerned. John P. Frank, once clerk to Justice Black, wrote that, in his years at the court, "my Justice made approximately one thousand decisions, and I had precisely no influence on any of them."[326] Frank related that a Douglas clerk, having substantially taken it upon himself to reorganize a draft opinion by his Justice, was told by the latter: "I can see you've done a lot of work, but you are off base here. If and when you get appointed to the Supreme Court, you can write opinions as you choose."[327] "Sometimes," commented another Black clerk, "a clerk can get a word or comma accepted, but the substance and decision are never anything but Black's alone."[328] Dean Acheson, one of several of Justice Brandeis's law clerks who later rose to national prominence, reported that his Justice would

[325] As reported in *The New York Times*, May 7, 1958, p. 27.
[326] *The Marble Palace*, op. cit., p. 119. See his "The Supreme Court: The Muckrakers Return," *Journal of the American Bar Association* (February 1980), pp. 160ff.
[327] "... The Muckrakers Return," loc. cit., p. 164.
[328] Daniel J. Meador, "Justice Black and His Law Clerks," 15 *Alabama Law Review* 57 (1962) at 59–60.

sometimes let him work on a draft opinion, largely for the sake of criticism, but:

> When I finished my work on a draft which had been assigned to me or got as far as I could, I gave it to him. [As is evident from the Brandeis files] he tore it to pieces, sometimes using a little, sometimes none [of it].[329]

Justice Byron R. White, who clerked for Chief Justice Vinson (1946–53), recalled later: "I don't think anything I ever did or said influenced my Justice. I felt I was doing him a service by making sure that relevant considerations were placed before him. . . . "[330] "Judging is not delegated!" snapped Justice Brennan once in response to a reporter's taunt.[331] And of all the law clerks who have written or otherwise reported on their experiences behind the "Purple Curtain," only one, William H. Rehnquist[332]—who was appointed to the Supreme Court by President Nixon late in 1971 from his former position of U.S. Assistant Attorney General—suggested the possibility of some "*unconscious* slanting of material by clerks."[333] But even he, who had served as Justice Jackson's clerk in the 1952–53 term, readily admitted that the notion of the law clerk "exerting an important influence on the cases actually decided by the Court, may be discarded at once . . . I certainly learned of none."[334] During his often heated confirmation hearings, a memorandum came to light in which Rehnquist had argued to Jackson that the "separate but equal" doctrine in education should not be overturned because it "was right and should be reaffirmed."[335] Yet Jackson subsequently joined the unanimous Court in declaring that doctrine unconstitutional in 1954.[336]

These law clerks, almost without exception, have gone on to notable careers.[337] Just who are they, and how are they selected? As indicated, they are recent law-school graduates of the highest caliber, and all were men until the first two women, Lucille Loman and Margaret Corcoran, were appointed by Justices Douglas and Black, respectively, in 1944 and 1966. Each is chosen

---

[329] As quoted by Bickel, *The Unpublished Opinions . . . , op. cit.,* p. 92.

[330] As quoted by Williams, op. cit., fn. 113, pp. 90–91.

[331] *Time Magazine,* June 5, 1964, p. 67.

[332] Rehnquist was the second of three contemporary Supreme Court Justices to have served as law clerks themselves, the other two being White and John Paul Stevens (the latter for Wiley Rutledge in 1947–48).

[333] "Who Writes Decisions of the Supreme Court?" *U.S. News and World Report,* December 13, 1957, p. 275.

[334] Ibid.

[335] *The New York Times,* December 7, 1971, p. C20.

[336] *Brown v. Board of Education of Topeka,* 347 U.S. 483 (1954) and *Bolling v. Sharpe,* 347 U.S. 497 (1954). See also Kluger's account, op. cit. (fn. 126 surpa).

[337] E.g., Dean Acheson (U.S. Secretary of State), Francis Biddle (U.S. Attorney General), Irving Olds (President of U.S. Steel Corp.), David Riesman (famed professor of sociology), Elliot Richardson (Attorney General, Secretary of Defense, Undersecretary of State, Secretary of Health, Education and Welfare, and Secretary of Commerce), and the aforementioned Associate Justices White, Rehnquist, and Stevens (see fn. 33 *supra*).

by an individual Justice to work for him or her for a year, sometimes for two.[338] The practice[339] was initiated in the Supreme Court in 1882 by Justice Horace Gray, who had begun using the clerks during his tenure on the Massachusetts bench. Gray, whose opinions were consistently longer than those of his colleagues, hired recent top Harvard Law School graduates for one year, and he paid his clerks out of his own pocket until 1886, when Congress appropriated $1,600 annually for a "stenographic clerk" for each Justice.[340] That figure had risen to $30,549 by 1984-85. Today (1985) each Associate Justice usually selects four (except Justice Stevens who uses only two and Justice Rehnquist who uses three), and the Chief Justice selects five (actually four and one special assistant). Since 1972 the Chief also has been entitled to an "Administrative Assistant to the Chief Justice," a post created by Congress to help in planning, leadership, and administrative responsibilities for the federal judiciary.

Some Justices do their own selecting of clerks, either by personal interview or by considering written data, almost always the former; others rely chiefly on experts' recommendations (viz., Justice Frankfurter, whose clerks were chosen for him by Professors Sachs and Freund at the Harvard Law School), as indeed "F. F." used to select all of Justice Brandeis's clerks, and as Justice Brennan has members of that faculty do now. From there, Professor of Law Felix Frankfurter sent a number of his own outstanding students, sometimes referred to as "Felix's Happy Hot Dogs," to the Court as clerks[341] (and to government service with the New Deal). In short, the clerks are really the purely personal patronage of the Justices, who are free to base their selections on whatever criteria they desire. John P. Frank avowed that his Justice, Hugo Black tried "to get Southern boys—and tennis players where possible."[342] Justice Stewart preferred Yale Law School graduates, Justice Murphy those from Michigan, Justice Butler Minnesotans, Justice Minton Indianans, Chief Justice Vinson those who had their degrees from Northwestern University, Chief Justice Warren Californians, Justice Clark graduates of lesser-known law schools, and Justice Powell Virginians. Justice Harlan ordinarily chose one applicant from Harvard and one from a New York City law school, and

---

[338]But Justice Joseph McKenna (1898-1925) kept his first clerk for twelve years and had only two other clerks during his remaining twelve years on the Court. And there was one law clerk who served with four Justices, beginning with Justice J. Rufus Peckham (1896-1909) in 1905 and ending with Justice George Sutherland (1922-38) in 1924, for a record total of nineteen years! (See Wilkinson, op. cit., pp. 48-49.)

[339]At the state level the practice has generally been customary only since circa 1950, and it has become extensive only since 1970. (See John B. Oakley and Robert S. Thompson, *Law Clerks and the Judicial Process.* Berkeley: University of California Press, 1981.)

[340]Until 1973, when each of the Justices was at last assigned two secretaries, they had to content themselves with just one, plus the use of the stenographic pool.

[341]In 1948 "F. F." appointed the first black Supreme Court clerk, William T. Coleman (who would later serve as Secretary of Transportation under President Ford).

[342]*The Marble Palace,* op. cit., pp. 115-16.

Justice Douglas usually turned to a West Coast law school for his choice. Alone among his colleagues to do so, Justice Stevens selected a *state* supreme court clerk as one of his two clerks for 1984–85. In the 1965–66 term of the Court, to cite one Court's pattern, nineteen law clerks were chosen by the nine members of the court, Chief Justice Warren selecting three, Justice Douglas one, and all the others two; there was also one assigned jointly to retired Justices Reed and Burton, who were still "on call" for lower federal court spot tasks, as assigned by the Chief Justice. The young lawyers came from ten different law schools: six from Harvard University, three each from Yale University and the University of Pennsylvania, two each from the University of Virginia and Stanford University, and one each from Columbia University, the University of Texas, and the University of North Carolina. The 1984–85 "lineup" (excluding Chief Justice Burger's four), reflecting the increased number of clerks allotted as well as greater diversity, provided the following data, in descending order of frequency: Harvard, five; Chicago and Columbia, four; Yale, three; Stanford, two; and one each from George Washington, U.C.L.A., Maine, Virginia, Illinois, Howard, Pennsylvania, Georgetown, New York University, Michigan, Tulane, and Boston University.

Exactly what work a Justice assigns or delegates to his clerk depends on the former's inclination—or, as Justice Jackson once stated, "on the Justice's temperament and experience." Apparently, most but by no means all of the Justices use their clerks to wade through the manifold petitions for *certiorari* that are filed annually (Justices Frankfurter and Brennan[343] are on record as being notable exceptions to the practice). Typically, a law clerk may read such a petition and the opposing party's response and then type or pen a brief memorandum to his or her Justice stating the issues involved and setting forth arguments for and against a grant of the desired writ. Suffice it to note that the Justice concerned will, of course, make up his or her own mind; yet the *certiorari* work by the clerks may well become crucial in the Court's endeavor to handle the ever-mounting case load.[344] In the manifestation of unusual public self-criticism *cum* confessional, Justice Stevens observed that he had "found it necessary to delegate a great deal of responsibility in the review of petitions [of *certiorari*]" to his law clerks. "They examine them all and select a small minority that they believe I should read myself. As a result, I do not even look at the papers in over 80 percent of the cases that are filed."[345] No wonder, then, that the *Brethren* would attribute such an exaggerated degree of importance to the law clerks![346]

---

[343] See 59 *American Bar Association Journal* 836 (August 1973) for Justice Brennan's assertions on the issue.

[344] For an interesting analysis, which contends that the Court could not function without the clerks' *certiorari* role, see Arthur S. Miller, "High Court Secrets," *The New York Times*, November 17, 1971, p. M45.

[345] Address to the American Judicature Society, San Francisco, August 8, 1982.

[346] Bob Woodward and Scott Armstrong, *The Brethren: Inside the Supreme Court* (New York: Simon and Schuster, 1979), passim.

Some of the Justices may go somewhat further in employing their clerks, asking for a so-called bench memorandum on a particular case now and then. Such a memorandum may note whether the case is properly before the Court, state what federal issues are presented and how these were decided by the courts below, summarize the positions of the parties pro and con on the grant of the writ, propound certain approaches and points of precedent, and thereby suggest questions to be asked of counsel by the Justices during oral argument. The most intensive task performed by the law clerks is probably that of the necessary drudgery of research once an opinion has been assigned to a particular Justice. Then commences the time-consuming chore of investigating, of sorting and checking precedents, citations, historical data, congressional records—the host of materials so vital to the decision-making process. Beyond that, the chief role of the law clerk is to serve as a foil, friend, critic, and sounding board. In the final analysis, however, as one former clerk wrote:

> In the course of my year, we never changed the Justice's mind on the result of any case. Our influence was close to nil. There was the fullest discussion, but he made the decisions. . . . The judge will listen if you say that some statement in his draft opinion is too broad or that a case is cited incorrectly. But if you tell him that such-and-such a constitutional amendment doesn't mean what he believes, you might as well stay in bed.[347]

The clerks are important tools for the Justices in the judicial process,[348] perhaps indispensable ones, yet they are hardly classifiable as veritable powers behind the throne. The picture painted in *The Brethren*—a highly controversial book, based to a very considerable extent on the assertions of 170 anonymous law clerks—is misleading.[349] In the words of Justice Powell's first clerk: "The idea that law clerks represent some independent force of resistance within the Court or that they somehow thwart or undermine a Justice's personal will, is a piece of mythology that ought to be rejected."[350] Essentially, they are law *clerks*—able, intelligent, and undoubtedly often, if not always, of considerable procedural aid to their Justices. But they are not members of the Court in any sense of the term. And, as has been contended repeatedly in connection with the entire matter of influence on it, the Supreme Court of the United States is, in fine, master of its own house—which does not,

---

[347] As quoted anonymously in *The New York Times*, October 14, 1957, p. 29.

[348] See Michael Slaughter, "Judicial Clerkships in Perspective," 59 *Judicature* 5 (December 1975), pp. 248–52.

[349] *The Brethren*, op. cit.

[350] Wilkinson, op. cit., p. 61. Justice Frankfurter's then law clerk, Philip Elman, tried unsuccessfully to dissuade the Justice from penning his famous dissenting opinion in *West Virginia State Board of Education v. Barnette*, 319 U.S. 624 (1943) at 646. (See pp. 237–38, *supra*.) Frankfurter told his clerk with some acerbity: "This is my opinion, not yours." (As reported by Israel Shenker, *The New York Times*, October 23, 1977, p. 34.)

however, mean that it is not aware of the existence of other houses both in and out of the governmental compound.

As we conclude this extensive consideration of the Supreme Court of the United States at work, it is both easy and natural to assent to a perceptive statement made by *The New York Times* Supreme Court reporter Anthony Lewis as he left his seven-year coverage of the Court for a new assignment in London in 1965: "The wonderful thing about the Supreme Court is that it does its work. It decides, as it has to decide. There has never been a Rules Committee to save the Justices on tough problems.... [T]he Supreme Court ... is the last stronghold of personal responsibility for decision."[351]

---

[351] *The New York Times Magazine*, January 17, 1965, pp. 56–58.

6

Courts Abroad

Wherever appropriate, reference has been made to the practices and theories of jurists and judicial systems of sundry lands, since the comparative element is one of the essential characteristics of this work. Newly emergent states of the world adapt their needs to the legal and social patterns of older ones. The United States has both profited from and contributed to other systems. Basically English in origin and design, features of its judicial system and process nevertheless both resemble, and differ drastically from, its progenitor as well as that of others. The legal systems of England and Wales, France, and the Soviet Union are most useful in an analysis in this connection. In the following pages a relatively brief view of the courts of these three countries will be presented.

THE COURTS OF ENGLAND AND WALES

It is incorrect to think of the courts of Great Britain or of the United Kingdom as a unified judicial system. For actually *three different systems* exist in the United Kingdom of Great Britain and Northern Ireland: one for England and Wales, one for Scotland, and one for Northern Ireland. Only at the ultimate appellate level of the House of Lords is it possible to speak with accuracy of a unified system for the United Kingdom; because that body in its judicial role represents the final court of appeals—in those very few cases that manage to reach it—from the judgments of the highest courts of Scotland and Northern Ireland as well as from those of England and Wales. The following description is of the judicial system of England and Wales—for convenience hereafter referred to as England—unless specified otherwise.[1]

In the United States the *same* tribunals ordinarily have *both* civil and criminal jurisdiction, with some minor exceptions for certain low-level state courts, such as the Court of Small Claims in Pennsylvania. But in the England of today justice is meted out in two separated judicial hierarchies, one for civil cases and one for criminal cases, although the sitting judges are often the same individuals. (There are fewer than 500 full-time judges in England, but they are augmented by more than 25,000 lay magistrates or justices of the peace.) The separation between civil and criminal court jurisdiction is based on the Supreme Court of Judicature (Consolidation) Act of 1925, as amended, the progeny of a series of Judicature Acts which commenced in 1873. That statute brought order into what had been a truly bewildering array of distinct tribunals—for example, some seven or eight leading courts had original jurisdiction in civil cases! However, unlike France, neither England nor the United States has a bona fide system of administrative courts, although some of the English administrative courts such as Railway Rate Tribunals existed long before World War II, and others have begun to make their appearance since the war; also, some of the special and/or legislative tribunals in the United States are at least quasi-administrative.[2]

THE CRIMINAL COURTS' HIERARCHY

It is perhaps somewhat unorthodox to discuss the criminal courts' hierarchy before that of the civil courts, but the English structure lends itself peculiarly well to such a procedure—in part because of a considerable amount of interchange of judges between the two hierarchies, despite the rigid structural segregation inherent in the system. Jurisdiction over criminal offenses has been exercised as a separate entity for some 700 years.

The Justice of the Peace or Magistrate and the Stipendiary Magistrate. At the base of the criminal courts hierarchy in England is the unpaid, volunteer lay magistrate, the *Justice of the Peace or Magistrate*, who must live within fifteen miles of the judicial area of jurisdiction. It is an office established by law in 1326 or 1327 during the reign of Edward II. The approximately 25,600 J.P.s or Magistrates are at work today (1985) in some 500 magistrate courts. In most of the larger cities, but also in a few smaller ones. In the larger cities there is instead the *Stipendiary Magistrate*—London alone, where he or she is called Metropolitan Magistrate, has roughly thirty-five of these officials—

---

[1] These courts are presided over by judges who often, but certainly no longer always, wear wigs—either shoulder-length ("full-bottomed") or short—and robes of office, with the color of their robes depending on the law they administer. Common law judges as well as those who administer to the criminal law wear scarlet robes; the others wear black. The atmosphere in an English courtroom remains much more formal than in an American one, but English judges have become rather tolerant of the manner in which people dress in court.

[2] See chapter 4, *supra*, for details.

who, unlike the Justice of the Peace or Magistrate, must be a full-time professional lawyer, usually a barrister, and is salaried at £25,750 (1983), again
unlike the unpaid lay J.P.s or Magistrates. With the exception of the Duchy
of Lancaster, where they are designated by its own Chancellor, the Magistrates at this lowest level of the criminal hierarchy are appointed on behalf
of the Crown by the Lord Chancellor after careful screening and recommendation by local advisory committees in each county.[3] This politically designated officer, who was discussed earlier,[4] is not only the highest judicial officer
in the British system, he is also a member of the Cabinet, its foremost legal
adviser, and a member as well as *ex officio* presiding officer of the House of
Lords.

Sitting *en banc* in twos or threes (more often the latter) without a jury—
the Stipendiary Magistrate sits alone—the Justice of the Peace or Magistrate,
in his or her role (10,000, or 40 percent were women in 1983)[5] as a tribunal
of first instance, is exclusively a court of summary jurisdiction for criminal
offenses. Indeed, more than nine out of ten criminal cases begin and end
there. But he or she may also double as a committing judicial officer by holding an accused for action by a higher court in the event of "indictable"
offenses. These would normally require grand jury action at the federal level
in the United States; but in England, since the statutory abolition of the grand
jury in 1933, the process of "information" has replaced it. Except for minor
matters, trials at this lowest level of original jurisdiction are conducted by one,
two, or three justices of the peace, but by only one Stipendiary Magistrate—
a vital distinction between the two similar types of officials. The latter's chief
function is to try relatively minor criminal offenses, although they have an
important jurisdiction in certain domestic relations—matrimonial, bastardy,
and rate cases, and some administrative functions, such as licensing—and, as
indicated, to determine whether or not evidence is sufficient to commit the
alleged offender for trial before a jury in a higher court. Barristers and solicitors have equal rights of access in these tribunals.

Many of the offenses handled by the J.P. or Magistrate or the Stipendiary
Magistrate concern traffic violations with limited fines.[6] Generally speaking,
his or her jurisdiction is now (1985) restricted to cases involving a maximum
fine of £1,000 or a six-months jail sentence, or both, although there are exceptions, such as customs cases. In many instances the accused is permitted the
option of a trial before the Justice of the Peace or Magistrate or the Stipendiary Magistrate or before a higher judge (and jury, when appropriate). Expe-

---

[3]For an excellent discussion of the magistrate level of the English judiciary, see E. C. Friesen
and I. R. Scott, *English Criminal Justice* (Birmingham: Institute of Judicial Administration,
University of Birmingham, 1977).

[4]See chapter 2, *supra*.

[5]*The Economist* (August 13, 1983, p. 51) claims 98 percent to be a more accurate figure.

[6]A late 1970s study found three-quarters of nontraffic sentences in the Magistrate-level courts
to be in the form of fines.

rience has demonstrated that the accused will often choose the lower-level tribunal because of considerations of expeditiousness, but he or she may have the right to a trial and wish to exercise it.

Still apropos the first level of the judiciary, when two or more Justices of the Peace or Magistrates or one Stipendiary Magistrate are sitting, a *Court of Petty Sessions* is said to exist. As will be explained subsequently, appeals from this level are possible either to the Crown Court or to a three-judge Divisional Court of the Queen's Bench Division of the High Court of Justice, depending on the nature of the appeal and provided that the defendant did not plead guilty—although in London he or she is free to appeal even in the latter event if the sentence is more than one month in prison or a fine of more than £3. Appeals in matrimonial cases go to the Divisional Court of the Family Division of the High Court of Justice.

The Crown Court. Immediately above the J.P. level is the *Crown Court*, established by the Courts Act of 1971; it replaced the fourteenth-century *Court of Quarter Sessions* and the twelfth-century *Assize Courts*. Clothed with appellate as well as original jurisdiction, it is the first court in which an accused, given the proper circumstances, is entitled to a trial by jury. The Crown Court is statutorily enabled to sit anywhere in England and Wales and is staffed by High Court judges, the newly created Circuit judges, and Recorders. They sit with Justices of the Peace or Magistrates in case of appeals and committals of sentence, but no more than nine members of the Court may sit *en banc* in any given case. In some boroughs the Court consists merely of the paid *Recorder*, usually selected from barristers of at least five years' experience. A Recorder sits only occasionally as such, however, and continues in practice as a barrister. Ordinarily, the Court's session is presided over by a professional Circuit judge or, on limited occasions, by a High Court of Justice (a civil court) in London. It was Lord Parker, the Lord Chief Justice, who, in his capacity as a judge of its Queen's Bench Division, presided over the important Blake spy trial that took place in the spring of 1961 in England's capital. (The Lord Chief Justice, who is England's highest judicial officer, is the head of the Queen's Bench Division.)

Because of the nature of the offenses tried before them—all trials on indictment, including all major felonies such as homicide, robbery, larceny, and rape—the assizes still always sit with a jury. Much traditional pageantry and fanfare attend their sessions, the proper judicial manner being very much in evidence. The Crown Court for Metropolitan London is the Central Criminal Court, widely known as the "Old Bailey" because of the name of the building where it meets for its twelve sessions annually, one each month.[7]

Appeals from judgments of the Crown Court are possible to the next higher level court, the Court of Appeal, on both points of law and fact. On

---

[7]"Bailley" was the tenth-century English word for "enclosure," and the Old Bailey stands on the site of an enclosure, originally part of Newgate Prison, where public executions took place until 1868.

the former, any convicted defendant may appeal; and he or she may do so on a point of fact with leave of the Crown Court judge or that of the Court of Appeal itself. The latter permission is mandatory for an appeal against the sentence.

The Court of Appeal. Appeals from the two lower levels in the hierarchy, to which only the defendant is entitled—the Prosecution may not appeal from a verdict of acquittal, although the Attorney General may refer a point of law—were formerly taken directly to the *Court of Criminal Appeal,* created in 1907. Recently, however, the separate Court of *Criminal Appeal* was abolished, and its functions taken over by a *Criminal Division* of the *Court of Appeal*—an arrangement of chiefly administrative importance. Appeals come to the Criminal Division in the same way they used to go to the Court of Criminal Appeal, assuming the necessary jurisdiction is present and leave to file has been obtained. It is the most important tribunal of appellate jurisdiction in the criminal hierarchy of England. Sitting without a jury, it hears appeals based on the transcripts of the evidence taken at the trial. The Court of Appeal is composed of the legally qualified and salaried judges of the Queen's Bench Division of the High Court of Justice and often there may be one or two members of the Lords Justices who form the Court of Appeal. Usually there are three members—the customary quorum—but in civil cases sometimes only two.

Because of the stipulated assumption that any appeal constitutes a "retrial," the Court of Appeal has the power to revise (i.e., alter or vary) the original sentence in three situations: (1) if it is not legally justified, (2) if it was based on improper evidence, and (3) if the length or severity of the sentence points to an error in "some matter of principle" by the trial court. The Court of Appeal may even substitute conviction on another offense for the initial one if it appears that the defendant should have been convicted for it rather than for the one for which he or she was convicted below. But it has no power to order a trial *de novo* unless there has been a mistrial in the lower court.

The House of Lords. In rare instances, the accused—never the Prosecution—has one last and very much restricted path of appeal, from the Court of Appeal to the *House of Lords* (an institution to be more fully described in connection with the civil hierarchy). Yet such an appeal is possible only when a point of law of "general public importance" is involved, and leave to file for appeal to that august body must be given by the Court of Appeal or the Divisional Court of the Queen's Bench Division of the High Court of Justice, or by the House of Lords itself if the appeal is refused by the aforementioned tribunals. Moreover, since the House of Lords often confines its rulings on the specific, sometimes narrow, point of law involved, broad legal pronouncements are uncommon.[8]

---

[8]See Richard M. Jackson, *The Machinery of Justice in England,* 7th ed. (Cambridge: Cambridge University Press, 1977). This is an excellent book, and one of the very few relatively

Until a statutory change was effected in 1960,[9] permission to appeal to the House of Lords was even more circumscribed than the present procedure. Leave to appeal could be granted only by the Attorney General, the senior law officer of the Crown, and then only if the point of law involved was deemed of "*exceptional* public importance." Thus, in the famous Guenther Padola loss-of-memory murder case of 1959, the Attorney General, Sir Reginald Manningham-Buller, refused to grant such permission. All other channels of appeal had previously been exhausted, and the Old Bailey jury had decided in the trial court that the alleged amnesia was faked. The accused consequently paid the ultimate penalty.

THE CIVIL COURTS' HIERARCHY

Although some of the terminology will be similar and some of the judicial personnel are in fact, the same, the existing hierarchical distinctions between the criminal and civil courts are highly pertinent to a proper understanding of the judicial process in England. Again, we commence at the lowest level of the courts.

The County Court. The court of first instance in civil matters is the County Court—so called by virtue of the adoption of the ancient name of the local courts of the county in early Anglo-Norman times, despite the fact that the jurisdiction of these tribunals today does not necessarily coincide with county boundaries. Indeed, it has nothing to do with them. The districts they serve are arranged so that a County Court is within ready reach everywhere; they are subject to geographic alteration by the Lord Chancellor. The more than 500 county courts are grouped into over fifty circuits, with at least one judge for each such circuit, who holds court in each district at least once a month but daily in busy circuits. The judges, called "circuit judges" since the Courts Act of 1971, are appointed by the Crown on the advice of the Lord Chancellor—again with the exception of those in the Duchy of Lancaster, as in the case of the Justices of the Peace. To qualify, they must be barristers in good standing with at least seven years of experience. They retire at seventy-two or, exceptionally, at seventy-five.

The County Court judges, who earn £29,750 (1983), are prone to live in their districts. They hold court daily in London and once or twice a month in appropriate towns, referred to as their circuit, depending on the work load docketed. Each County Court is assigned a *Registrar*, a senior practicing barrister or solicitor appointed by and subject to removal by the Lord Chancellor, who is not only in charge of the court's office staff but who may also act as a lesser judge. By leave of his or her county court judge, and in the absence of objections by any of the parties, the Registrar deals mainly with matters not involving more than £75 but may exercise wider jurisdiction with the consent of the litigants.

---

up-to-date ones available on the British judiciary. It presents a superb explanation and analysis of its subject matter.

[9]See fn. 13, p. 265, *infra*, for explanation.

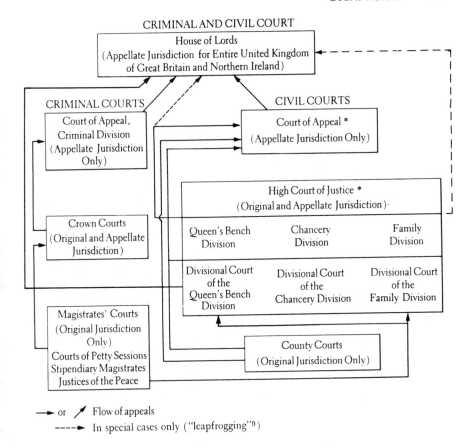

CRIMINAL AND CIVIL COURT

*or ✓ Flow of appeals
----► In special cases only ("leapfrogging"[9])

* The Court of Appeal and the High Court of Justice form the *Supreme Court of Judicature* (known simply as "The Supreme Court") which, in effect, however, is neither "supreme" nor a "court". (See p. 265, *infra*.)

Figure 4. The criminal and civil courts of England and Wales (1985)

The jurisdiction of the County Court, although strictly limited statutorily, is extensive, and the number of cases commenced at this level is vast. In 1982, for instance, a total of 2,301,364 proceedings were entered in the county courts.[10] Broadly speaking, the large majority of cases fall into the area of actions based on contract and tort claims up to a maximum of £1,000, with a handful of exceptions (e.g., libel and slander). Yet many of these cases do not exceed £150 in value. Other areas of County Court jurisdiction include equity matters up to £5,000, real-estate actions for the recovery of land in which the net annual value of the land's rating is not above the County Court limit, and a limited range of admiralty and bankruptcy matters. And a highly significant field of its jurisdiction arises under so-called social or collectivist

[10]Bray, op. cit., ch. 2, p. 97, fn. 137.

statutes, a by-product of today's welfare state. Since 1934, an appeal from the County Court must be taken directly to the Court of Appeal, thus bypassing the next higher court level.

The High Court of Justice. Immediately above the County Court in the hierarchy of the civil courts stands the *High Court of Justice*—an ancient institution deriving from the Norman *curia regis*, which was the monarch's personal instrument for dispensing justice. It has chiefly original but also some divisionally restricted appellate jurisdiction. This famous tribunal, established in 1837, is now (1985) staffed by eighty (seventy-seven plus three senior pending judges) distinguished *puisne* judges,[11] salaried at £45,500 (1983), who have had a minimum of ten years of experience as barristers—many have had twenty or twenty-five years. The three divisions of the "High Court," as it is commonly called, thus comprise the forty-nine–member *Queen's Bench Division*, including its presiding officer, the Lord Chief Justice of England who ranks immediately after the Lord Chancellor in the judicial hierarchy; the thirteen-member *Chancery Division*, plus its non-sitting presiding officer, the Lord Chancellor; and the President and sixteen judges of the *Family Division* (formerly known as the *Probate, Divorce, and Admiralty Division*).

Of the three, the Queen's Division is by far the largest and busiest, partly because its judges must participate also in the work of the criminal courts as a matter of exercising original jurisdiction—as was explained earlier—and partly because, with three or five of its judges sitting as the *Divisional Court* of the Queen's Bench Division, it hears certain appeals in criminal cases from the courts of summary jurisdiction, that is, the Justice of the Peace or Magistrate and Stipendiary Magistrate Court and the Crown Court. Coupled with its jurisdiction over the general field of the common law, its work range thus extends to (1) ordinary civil actions (normally those claims with more than £5,000 at stake), (2) its appellate and supervisory jurisdiction *en banc* in its mantle of Divisional Court of the Queen's Bench Division, (3) appellate functions exercised by a single judge, and (4) its limited original criminal jurisdiction.

As the presiding officer of the Queen's Bench Division, the Lord Chief Justice enjoys a considerable degree of authority and prestige. In his capacity he is the directing figure of the criminal courts of England—although, unlike the Lord Chancellor, he has no direct say in government. The L.C.J.'s stature depends on a good deal on his individual personality; yet what he says on any

---

[11] The first woman to be appointed to the High Court of Justice was County Court Judge Elizabeth Lane, Q.C., who reached her country's No. 3 tribunal in August 1965. A minor crisis arose over what to call the first woman judge. Would it be "Mr. Justice" or "Your Lordship"? Not at all, decreed the Lord Chancellor, Lord Gardiner: Instead, upon her confirmation by Queen Elizabeth it was announced that "henceforth and hereafter" Dame Elizabeth Lane would be addressed as "The Honorable Mrs. Justice Lane," and inside the court room she would be addressed as "My Lady" or "Your Ladyship." (*The Christian Science Monitor,* September 19, 1965, p. 11.)

given occasion may influence not only the other judges but also the lawyers, the magistrates, and even the police. The Lord Chief Justice is regarded with much awe, confidence, and respect.

The Chancery Division has exclusive jurisdiction in some cases and concurrent jurisdiction with the Queen's Bench Division in others. In the extensive former category are equity matters of bankruptcy, companies, tax, finance, execution of trusts, wardships, patent cases, foreclosures of mortgages, and so on. Appeals from county courts in bankruptcy matters lie to a *Divisional Court of the Chancery Division.*

The Family Division has jurisdiction in the areas implied by its name: giving valid title to the estate of deceased persons; matrimonial decrees as to divorce (the new growth area for English lawyers), nullity, restitution of conjugal rights, judicial separation, presumption of death, and dissolution of marriage; and declaration of legitimacy. Its *Divisional Court* hears appeals from the Magistrates' Courts level in matrimonial cases. The Family Division also used to have jurisdiction over various matters affecting ships under maritime law, but since the administration of Justice Act of 1970 there is an Admiralty Court as part of the Queen's Bench Division to take Admiralty business.[12]

In addition to its specialized jurisdiction, just explained, the High Court of Justice has overall jurisdiction in all cases that are eligible for hearings in the County Court as well as those that lie outside that tribunal's jurisdiction. But, if it is asked to take cases under its original jurisdiction when these can be handled by the County Court, for example, routine controversies with a value of less than £1,000, even the successful plaintiff may have to pay court costs. Together with the Court of Appeal, the High Court of Justice forms the *Supreme Court of Judicature,* which usually sits in London. It is a body that is actually neither supreme nor a court, but serves as a type of cover-all for the Common Law and Chancery branches of the civil courts system.

The Court of Appeal. Appeals from any of the Divisions of the High Court of Justice go to the *Court of Appeal,*[13] which consists of the Master of the Rolls (England's third highest judicial officer), who is the presiding judge in the Court of Appeal, plus seventeen Lord Justices of Appeal, the regular sitting members—usually in groups of three—who must have had fifteen years of experience as barristers or been High Court judges. The Court of Appeal's

---

[12]In popular lingo, the Family Division used to be referred to as "Wrecks" Division, because it was said to deal with "wills, wives, and wrecks." Lord Goddard, who was Lord Chief Justice for twelve years, amended this jest by quipping that the Division deals with "wrecks of wills ... marriages ... and ships." (Lord Goddard, "Organization and Jurisdiction of the Courts of England," 44 *Journal of the American Judicature Society* 62 [August 1960]. See his entire article for a fine description, pp. 60–65.)

[13]The Administration of Justice Act of 1969 provides for appeals in some cases directly from the High Court to the House of Lords, thus "leapfrogging" the Court of Appeal. Thus, under its Part II, appeals from the High Court in certain civil proceedings may be brought directly to the House of Lords ("leapfrog" over the Court of Appeal) on the certificate of the High Court and leave of the House of Lords.

appellate jurisdiction extends to points of law arising out of civil cases from the County Court or the High Court of Justice. There may now also be appeals on fact from High Court decisions, but they rarely succeed.

Appeals on points of law coming from the County Court reach the Court of Appeal as a matter of right if the amount of the claim involved exceeds £ 20, or when the remedy is an injunction. In other appeals the judge below must give permission. In the cases coming from the High Court, appeal is automatic on points of law but not on points of fact. If the Court of Appeal grants an appeal, retrial of the case will normally take place below; however, it may also reconsider the evidence itself, but without taking new testimony from witnesses.

The House of Lords. From the Court of Appeal, if the matter of law involved is deemed to be of sufficient importance, there remains the final path of appeal to the *House of Lords* (an expensive one—£1,000 for printing costs alone is an average expenditure, the cost of reaching the Lords commonly running to £20,000) provided that the appeal has been certified by the Court of Appeal[14] or granted by the House of Lords itself, a historic right dating back to the practices of the Norman institution of the *magnum concilium,* the Great Council. The Lords do not, of course, sit in a mass body for that purpose—there were 1,170 members in 1983 (although the average daily attendance was but 290).[15] Instead, the legal section of the House of Lords comprises a small, highly skilled, distinguished group of judicial experts, the nine *Law Lords,* known as the *Lords of Appeal in Ordinary,* plus the Lord Chancellor, the presiding officer of the House of Lords. These ten officials, who thus constitute the final court of appeal, are augmented by any other peer who has held, or now holds, high judicial office under the Crown.

This small group of appellate[16] experts, who sit in *bancs* of five, was created originally by the Appellate Jurisdiction Act of 1876 to supplement the judicial strength of the House of Lords. It remains the sole kingdomwide judicial body, and as such always has some members from Scotland (usually two) and, on occasion, one from Northern Ireland. These few dignitaries, who have

---

[14] A famous illustration of a refusal by the Court of Appeal so to certify an appeal was the case of Dr. Robert A. Soblen in 1962. The sixty-one-year-old psychiatrist had fled the United States while under a life sentence for wartime espionage for the Soviet Union, and asked Britain to grant him asylum. The British Home Office refused, and Soblen commenced a lengthy, ultimately unsuccessful, series of legal maneuvers to escape deportation. He later committed suicide rather than be sent back to the States.

[15] *The International Yearbook and Statesmen's Who's Who* (East Grinstead, West Sussex, England: Thomas Skinner Directories, Ltd., 1983).

[16] The House of Lords has *original* jurisdiction in civil cases of claims to peerages and decisions as to disputed elections. (In criminal matters it has both original and appellate jurisdiction, but it is very rarely exercised.) All in all, the Law Lords handle about sixty cases annually. See Louis Blom-Cooper and Gavin Drewry, *Final Appeal: A Study of the House of Lords in its Judicial Capacity* (New York: Oxford University Press, 1972), and Alan Paterson, *The Law Lords* (Toronto: University of Toronto Press, 1982).

backgrounds of at least fifteen years as barristers in England or Northern Ireland or as practicing advocates in Scotland, or of two years in high judicial office, are all professional, paid judges with life peerages, and ordinarily take no part whatever in the political business of the Lords; they constitute the Supreme Court of the United Kingdom of Great Britain and Northern Ireland. But unlike the Supreme Court of the United States, and the other U.S. federal and state courts, neither the House of Lords nor any other English or Welsh court, no matter how high, possesses the power of judicial review—that ultimate power of *striking down* legislative and executive actions as being unconstitutional—which will be fully described in the following chapter.

The Judicial Committee of the Privy Council. One other major appellate tribunal, sitting somewhat astride the regular court system just described, exists in the British Isles. It is the important *Judicial Committee of the Privy Council*, which constitutes the final court of appeal for cases from the ecclesiastical courts of the Church of England, colonies, protectorates, trust territories, the Isle of Man, and the Channel Islands. It is also available as the ultimate appellate body for all those members of the Commonwealth that might wish to avail themselves of its services. But in recent years, with the exception of isolated cases from Ceylon, New Zealand, Australia, Ghana, Jamaica, Singapore, Hong Kong, and Malaya, Commonwealth members have normally preferred to adjudicate their problems in their own judicial structure. This is conclusively the case with India, for example. The Judicial Committee of the Privy Council constituted the final court of appeal from Canada on constitutional matters until 1949, when the right to appeal to it was abolished there by statute.

Only privy councilors are eligible for membership on the Judicial Committee. In practice, most of the work has been done by the Law Lords of the House of Lords, but other high judicial officers from the United Kingdom, as well as from the Commonwealth and other jurisdictions that the Judicial Committee serves, have participated in its functions.

THE COURTS OF FRANCE

If imitation may be regarded as indication of approval, the popularity and acceptance of the French judicial system among the older as well as the newer states of the world represent such approval in the highest degree. The French administration of justice, far more than the Anglo-American, has become a model abroad. To a large extent this is attributable to its base—those legendary civil, criminal, penal, commercial, and procedural codes, drafted under the often personal direction of Napoleon Bonaparte at the end of the eighteenth century, and especially at the beginning of the nineteenth, culminating in the famous, and still very much alive, *Code Napoleon*. With full justice the French codes have been called "well-balanced pieces of jurisprudential art, utterly systematic and conveniently accessible."[17] Here French logic was truly at its best.

Yet the judicial structure that applies the codes—which, of course, have been periodically amended—is far from a simple and readily comprehensible one. A maze of tribunals stud the countryside—just as in Napoleon's time, despite a number of revisions in the hierarchy of one of the two major court systems under the de Gaulle Republic in 1959, 1963, 1965, and 1967, and under Charles de Gaulle's successors, Georges Pompidou, in 1972, Valéry Giscard d'Estaing, in 1974 and 1979, and François Mitterand, in 1981–82. The French authorities have gone so far as to take due public cognizance of the problem in an official governmental release, which noted that "judicial organization in France is exceptionally complex," but they went on to point out that "it is the product of successive contributions from centuries of our history, and in it, tradition continues to play a very important role."[18] This acknowledgment may not be of much comfort to the student of the system, but it does serve as an explanation. The government bulletin might have added that one of the reasons for the complexity and profusion of the French courts is the generally admirable notion that justice should be provided quickly, efficiently, inexpensively, and conveniently.

TWO MAJOR DIVISIONS

The courts of France are characterized by two quite separate and distinct hierarchies: first, the ordinary or regular courts; second, the administrative courts. (A substructure of commercial and certain other special courts need not concern us at this juncture; they may be viewed as falling generally under the ordinary courts, although appeal from some of them lies to the Conseil d'État.) In case of doubt as to proper jurisdiction, the eight-member Tribunal des Conflits (Tribunal of Conflicts), created especially for that umpire-role and headed by the Minister of Justice, who votes only in case of a tie, determines unappealably to which of the two major court systems a case goes.

Again, the chief reason for this division of responsibility between the two judicial hierarchies is an historic one. Fearful that the ordinary courts might interfere with the administrative or executive branch of the government, the legislative bodies of France, dating all the way back to the days of the Revolution, wrote into laws and constitutions specific provisions that expressly forbade judicial bodies to intervene. For example, the Law of December 22, 1789, provided: " . . . Judicial power should not trouble local administrative agencies in the exercise of their functions." And that of August16–24, 1790, spelled the matter out more clearly:

---

[17]Robert G. Neumann, European and Comparative Government, 4th ed. (New York: McGraw-Hill Book Co., 1968), p. 330. On the other hand, a good many women have considered them still hostile toward egalitarianism.

[18]As quoted in European Political Systems, 3d ed., ed. Taylor Cole (New York: Alfred A. Knopf, 1959), p. 234.

The judicial functions are and will remain forever separate from the administrative functions. The judges will not be allowed, under penalty of forfeiture, to disturb in any manner whatsoever, the activities of the administrative corps, nor to summon before them the administrators, concerning their functions.[19]

This was all very well in theory, but it soon became clear that someone or something would be needed to check certain administrative excesses of power beyond the mediating and advisory services rendered by the *Conseil d'État* on matters in dispute between the citizen and the government. Hence the eventual adoption of the system of administrative courts—comprising the *Conseil* plus developing subordinate administrative tribunals—designed to check administrative abuses and at the same time retain the cherished principle of separation of powers insofar as the judicial and executive–administrative functions are concerned. The separated hierarchies have flourished, and they survive essentially unchanged in design and principle, although not in certain organizational structure and nomenclature.

THE ORDINARY OR REGULAR COURTS' HIERARCHY

On March 1, 1959, the de Gaulle government effected the first group of several contemporary judicial reforms, chiefly designed to give the courts a corps of more specialized judges and to distribute these more equitably geographically in a rearranged system of ordinary courts, geared more closely to modern demands and realistic population distribution. The effect of these changes, as augmented in 1963, 1965, and 1967, most recently and extensively in 1972, and again in 1981, is reflected in the following description.

The Court of Instance (TRIBUNAL D'INSTANCE). The first de Gaulle Reorganization Bill abolished the time-honored but outdated lowest of the ordinary courts, the local *Juge de Paix*—again our friend, the Justice of the Peace—and replaced that popular institution with a new local court of first instance in all minor civil cases, the *Tribunal d'Instance*. Theretofore *juges de paix*, armed with law diplomas, unlike most of their English and American counterparts, had brought justice, more or less, to the 3,040 cantons of France by way of a completely informal, inexpensive, and often inconsequential procedure in the usual type of petty, chiefly civil, infractions, which obliged them to "ride circuit." Since 1959, however, the new *tribunaux d'instance*, numbering 455, have existed in the capitals of the various *arrondissements*—the administrative geographical levels above the canton. Each of these courts may have several judges, who are required to live in the area of jurisdiction of the tribunal, but decisions are rendered by a single judge. The *tribunaux d'instance* and their judges have been given considerably more effective adjudicatory power than that possessed by the old *juges de paix*. Indeed, they are

[19]Stephan Riesengeld, "The French System of Administrative Justice: A Model for American Law," 18 *Boston University Law Review* 48 (1938). See also Margherita Rendel's excellent work, *The Administrative Function of the French Conseil d'État* (London: Weidenfeld and Nicolson, 1970).

fully intended to become the most important basic unit in the revised judicial system.

The Court of Major Instance (TRIBUNAL DE GRANDE INSTANCE). The old civil Court of First Instance (Tribunal de Première Instance), one of which was located in every arrondissement, gave way to the newly created Tribunal de Grande Instance. The erstwhile criminal section of this level, the Correctional Court (Tribunal Correctionnel), has been retained but was moved to the criminal side of the judicial structure (see Figure 5). In place of the original 359 courts, the new 172 tribunaux de grande instance have unlimited civil jurisdiction throughout the département—the highest administrative subdivision in France—not merely in a single arrondissement. According to the number of inhabitants and the "degree of economic activity,"[20] the larger départements are entitled to two or more of the tribunals. Each case is tried by several judges sitting en banc, usually three, but always an uneven number, with the decision reached by majority vote. Appeals from the tribunaux de grande instance lie to the Courts of Appeals.

The reforms established Police Courts (Tribunaux de Police) as the basic tribunal for minor offenses (e.g., parking violations) on the criminal side of the organizational ledger. Numbering 455 like the tribunaux d'instance, its judge (or judges) may well be the same individual as that at the basic civil level. The Police Court's jurisdiction is limited to offenses not exceeding penalties of sixty days in prison and/or small fines.

At the next higher level of the criminal hierarchy of the ordinary courts are the aforementioned Correctional or Criminal Courts (Tribunaux Correctionnels). Like their counterparts on the civil side, the tribunaux de grande instance, there are 172 units, composed of three or more judges. Their jurisdiction extends to more serious offenses, covering penalties of up to five years' imprisonment and fines upward of F.F. 200.

The Assize Court (COUR D'ASSISE). The original tribunal for most criminal cases above the tribunaux correctionnels and for most appeals is the Assize Court (Cour d'Assise). Its original jurisdiction thus extends to all major criminal cases, such as homicide, its penalty power ranging from fines to life imprisonment. It does not sit with a jury when acting as an appellate tribunal; rather, a lot-chosen jury of nine "de simples citoyens" (plain citizens), plus three judges sit in cases of original jurisdiction. (A verdict of guilty requires a majority of eight votes.) There are ninety-five assizes, one in each département, each being usually staffed with three judges from the twenty-seven units of the courts of appeal above. However, depending on the work load and the availability of personnel, two of the three judges may be drafted from a local lower tribunal, but the presiding judge is invariably a member of the Cour d'Appel.

The Court of Appeal (COUR D'APPEL). The 1959 and subsequent reforms did not make any substantial changes in the structure of the Court of Appeal

---

[20] Ambassade de France, French Affairs Bulletin No. 84 (May, 1959), p. 32.

(Cour d'Appel), the appellate tribunal for civil cases from below, and none at all in the number of the twenty-seven judicial districts *(Chambres)*—each of which includes several *départements*—in which one of these tribunals operates. However, the jurisdiction of the *Cour d'Appel* was naturally extended not only to take appeals on all matters of fact from both the civil and criminal courts below but also to include the special courts alluded to earlier, and other newly created ones, particularly in the field of social and economic legislation. Thus, in addition to criminal appeals from the *assises*, and civil ones from the *tribunaux de grande instance*, appeals to a *Cour d'Appel* may come from such as any one of the following (in addition to the considerable number of appeals that come up from the *tribunaux de grande instance* in the regular hierarchy below): The *Labor Conciliation Board (Conseil de Prud'hommes)*, composed of an equal number of employers and employees who, chosen by their own groups for six years (one-half retiring every three years), hear disputes arising out of industrial contracts and arbitrate these; the *Commercial Court (Tribunal de Commerce)*, consisting of business persons elected by their local peers for two-year terms to act in certain statutorily designated commercial cases; the *Juvenile Court (Tribunal pour Enfants)*, one judge sitting for three years, chosen from a *tribunal de grande instance*; the *Farm Lease Court*, found at the seat of each *tribunal d'instance*; the *Social Security Court*, which consists of one judge from the *tribunal d'instance* plus two representatives of "interested parties," and the similarly composed *Rent Tribunal (Tribunal de Baux Rureaux)*. All of these special courts have several court units throughout the country. Each of the twenty-seven courts of appeal, with from three to five judges sitting—seven in the Parisian tribunal—hears a case before it entirely *de novo*; their decisions on points of fact are final. On points of *law* further appeal lies to the *Cour de Cassation*.

In 1963, Parliament created a complicated and controversial special tribunal to combat "subversive activity," the *Permanent Court of State Security (Cour de Sûreté de l'État)*, largely as a direct result of terrorist activity by both civil and military elements involved in the government's attempts to settle the difficult problem of Algeria. The tribunal, which consisted of civilian judges and senior military officers and sat without a jury, the sole appeal from its decisions being to the *Cour de Cassation*, was abolished in June 1981 as one of the Mitterand Administration's first acts.

The Supreme Court of Appeal (Cour de Cassation). At the pinnacle of the regular courts of France stands its Supreme Court of Appeal *(Cour de Cassation)*. Although it was largely unaffected by the Judicial Reorganization Acts of 1959, 1963, and 1965, the 1967 reforms did reach it. Appropriately sitting in Paris—as ever, the heart and pulse of *la patrie*—it consists of eighty-three judges, or, more precisely, seventy-seven counselors *(conseillers)*, the Chief Justice *(Premier Président)*, and five presidents of sections. Its jurisdiction, which is interpretatively final in both civil and criminal cases on points of *law*, extends throughout the French Republic. The high tribunal enjoys great prestige and respect.

The *Cour de Cassation* is divided into five sections (*chambres*) of fifteen judges, each headed by a *président*, a favorite French title, with the entire tribunal presided over by the First President, or Chief Justice. Seven judges constitute a quorum to hear a case. Two sections deal with civil matters (personal and family status and property); one of these, known as the Screening Section, receives and evaluates all petitions and requests for review, conducts a preliminary inquiry into their merits, dockets those it deems worthy of review by the court, and rejects all others. The other three *chambres* handle commercial, social, and criminal matters, respectively. Like the House of Lords, but unlike the Supreme Court of the United States, the *Cour de Cassation* has no original jurisdiction; all cases that come to it through the hierarchy of the ordinary courts do so by way of appeal from the assizes (a majority of the cases) and the courts of appeal below.

Casser, the French for "to break," or "to smash," indicates the actual role of this respected and dignified tribunal. That role is distinctly limited, for the *Cour de Cassation* rules only on the legal appropriateness of the decision rendered—that is, it merely passes judgment on *the point of law involved in the decision*, emphatically not on the substance of the case. It neither "decides" nor "retries" a case. It simply possesses the power to quash (*casser*) the legal point of a case, and *then to remand it below for retrial* by a court of the same category and rank as the one from which it came, but not to the same court. In the event of a second appeal in a case that it had sent back down initially, the Court will give an authoritative interpretation which must be followed by the lower tribunal. In sum, the *Cour de Cassation's* legal holdings are binding on all lower courts.

In no sense does the *Cour de Cassation*, "an offspring of the revolutionary legislators' profound distrust of the judges,"[21] have the power of judicial review—although in 1974 President Giscard d'Estaing's government promised to consider its adoption in a future reform of the judiciary. Indeed, as the Court itself ruled, in a case involving the newspaper *Le National*, a law that had been "deliberately promulgated according to constitutional forms" is beyond attacks on grounds of unconstitutionality under the French system of separation of powers.[22] The absence of *bona fide* judicial review[23] is a deficiency of power the French courts have shared with their friends across the Channel. However, a system of what might be called quasi-judicial review, lodged in an extra-judicial body lying outside the judicial hierarchy, the *Constitutional Council* (*Conseil Constitutionnel*)—to be described in the following chapter—was adopted by the Constitution of the Fifth Republic as a suc-

[21] Mauro Cappelletti, *Judicial Review in the Contemporary World* (Indianapolis: The Bobbs-Merrill Co., 1971), p. 13.

[22] See 7 *Political Studies* 51–53 and 60–61 (February 1959).

[23] Except insofar as the *Conseil d'État* (see pp. 279ff., *infra*) reviews decrees under Arts. 38 and 39 of the Constitution. For recent developments see William Safran, *The French Polity* (New York: David McKay Co., 1978).

cessor to its rather anemic relative of the Fourth Republic, the *Constitutional Committee (Comité Constitutionnel)*. But as will be readily perceived, the French system of quasi-judicial review is a far cry from the *bona fide* power and authority vested in the U.S. judiciary—although it may have been undergoing a modicum of strengthening since 1974.

ADMINISTRATIVE TRIBUNALS GENERALLY

We now turn to what is unquestionably the more interesting, because more novel, second judicial hierarchy in France, the popular and entirely separate *administrative courts*, which are more or less foreign to the Anglo-Saxon world. Despite some significant post-World War II modifications, especially in England and Wales, beginning with the Rules of the Supreme Court of 1977 that radically amended its Order 53 and were incorporated into the Supreme Court Act of 1981 (see later), the United Kingdom and the United States still hold, by and large, to the ancient Anglo-Saxon principle that "the King can do no wrong"—which, in effect, signifies that the sovereign, the state, cannot be sued without its expressed consent. This concept of governmental immunity, dating from the reign of Henry II (1154–89), has its legal roots in the prerogatives of the King of England, who was the "Fountainhead

Figure 5. The regular (ordinary) courts of the fifth French Republic (1985)

of Justice and Equity" under the law of the feudal state. During the sixteenth century, the personal immunity of the monarch was enlarged to include that of the state—hence the King (State) can do no wrong. Accordingly, in the Anglo-Saxon world of our day the acts of government officials are viewed as the acts of ordinary citizens and are judged by exactly the same rules of law and before the same courts. After all, it is one of the underlying principles of the philosophy of democratic government that any citizen is presumably capable of participating in it (a notion dear to the heart of President Andrew Jackson, and well popularized by him, who used it to justify, and some erroneously contend, to invent, the "spoils system"). Thus, as one of Britain's great students of government, A. V. Dicey, often put it, every government official, from the Prime Minister on down to the lowliest clerk, is "under the same responsibility for every act done without legal justification as any other citizen."[24]

Until fairly recently (see earlier) this has meant that a British or American citizen who believes himself or herself to have been aggrieved or injured by a government official in either of the two lands and wants to take action would *have to sue that official*—who, in turn, would have to justify his actions at the bar of the regular courts. Thus, if citizen John Smith believes that he has been wronged or maltreated by Sheriff James Doe in the latter's capacity as an officer of the law, he may bring suit. But such a suit must be brought against Sheriff James Doe, in a regular court of jurisdiction, *not* against Doe's state of Virginia, whose laws he was presumably enforcing (or not against the United States, if the arresting officer had been a federal official), and the suit will normally read *Smith v. Doe*. Moreover, to collect damages, which would presumably come out of Doe's pocket, citizen Smith must demonstrate successfully that Sheriff Doe has exceeded his discretionary authority under the law—an extremely difficult task in most instances. However, as alluded to earlier, the adoption in England and Wales of new rules, capped by the Supreme Court Act of 1981, render feasible the application of what the British term "judicial review" in order to seek redress through prerogative writs, such as *mandamus, certiorari,* or prohibition. *Not* judicial review in the same sense as it is understood in the United States, the English and Welsh practice facilitates application for redress for alleged grievances against government *directly to a court of law*.[25]

Whatever the underlying philosophical justifications for personal liability of governmental officials, its practical implications are often unsatisfactory, to say the least, and may well be fraught with danger both to the individuals involved and the system they serve and under which they live. Among these implications and the lessons of experience are the possibility that an official

[24]For example, see his *Introduction to the Study of the Law of the Constitution,* 10th ed. (New York: The Macmillan Co., 1961).

[25]See especially H. W. R. Wade, *Administrative Law,* 5th ed. (Oxford: Oxford University Press, 1982), particularly pp. 572–76.

may perform his or her duties timidly or haphazardly or not perform them in accordance with his or her most considered judgment but according to expediency; the difficulty, already alluded to, of collecting from an individual government servant; and the question why, in performing a governmental duty, a civil servant should be personally responsible in the first place. Moreover, there are the inevitable delays in getting a case docketed in the courts; the slowly grinding judicial process, especially in as large and litigation-happy a country as the United States; and the inconvenience and expense of bringing a case to court. All these represent factors that may well, and often do, outweigh any monetary recompense that might eventually accrue to the plaintiff.

In recognition of these very real problems, England and the United States have gradually begun to provide tribunals in which the state may be sued directly. No abandonment of the old philosophy of a single, unified judiciary has taken place, nor is it likely to take place in the near future. However, both countries have shown considerable interest in the institution of the Scandinavian *ombudsman*,[26] a sort of "people's watchdog" over administrative abuses, who commands a good deal of influence and esteem, though little direct power, and who disposes of some thousand cases annually with dispatch and expertise. Indeed, with the enactment of the Parliamentary Commissioner Act of 1967, Britain adopted a limited, rather restricted, and watered down version of it.

Moreover, both Britain and the United States have taken some tangible steps in the direction of rendering matters a bit more palatable to government employees and citizens alike. Thus, Britain adopted the Crown Proceedings Act of 1947, which, under certain circumstances, makes the government responsible for the actions of its servants. Purposely provided with many loopholes and exceptions, the act nevertheless now enables ordinary citizens to sue the government in the same manner and before the same tribunals "as if the Crown were a fellow-citizen." Hence, the injured or aggrieved party sues the state as a matter of right.[27] Furthermore, the act makes government departments responsible for common law as well as statutory duties. However, it should be noted that the act confines itself, more or less, to the *non-law-enforcing* agencies of government, thus leaving unchanged the path of claims that might arise under the law-enforcing units, such as police, military

---

[26]See the compendium on the *ombudsman*, edited by D. C. Rowat, *The Ombudsman: Citizen's Defender*, 2d ed. (London: Allen & Unwin, 1968), containing chapters on Britain and the United States; the chapter on the United States is my "The Need for Ombudsmen in the United States." See also my "Denmark's *Folketingets Ombudsmand:* A People's Watchdog," 20 *Public Administration Review* 152 (Summer 1960), and the compendium, edited by Roy V. Peel, "The Ombudsman or Citizen's Defender: A Modern Institution," 377 *The Annals* (May 1968), pp. iii–240.

[27]Thus, if a citizen is run over by a Post Office van, he can sue the Post Office instead of proceeding against the Attorney General by Petition of Right.

services, foreign affairs. Nevertheless, this unquestionably valuable statute does represent a wholesome and welcome change.[28]

What this statute did for Britain, the Tort Claims Act of 1946 had done, broadly speaking, for the United States one year earlier, insofar as the federal government is concerned. Under it, a citizen who feels he has been injured or aggrieved by an employee of the federal government, or the government itself, may bring suit in any civil action other than a breach of contract, which is not a tort, against the United States for negligence or wrongful acts, no maximum monetary ceiling existing on the claim. The statute, as amended in 1966, also renders possible making claims of less than $25,000—and above that with the approval of the Attorney General—directly to the head of any federal agency alleged to be responsible for a loss caused by "negligent or wrongful act of omission of an employee," but the agency is *not required* to sanction such claims. Appeals under the provisions of the Tort Claims Act may be taken to the new U.S. Court of Appeals for the Federal Circuit and, under certain conditions, to the regular constitutional court hierarchy.

The Court of Claims, established in 1855 and redesigned and reconstituted as the U.S. Claims Court in 1982 (as was demonstrated in some detail in chapter 4), is itself a vehicle for citizens to sue the federal government for damages and as such represents a modification of the "sovereign-can-do-no-wrong" principle. But its limited jurisdiction is confined to contractual, tax, and other non-tort claims against the government of the United States. The Tort Claims Act contains, as its British counterpart, many deliberate exceptions and ambiguities. For example, it excludes

> any claim based upon an act or omission of an employee of the Government exercising due care, in the exercise of a statute or regulation, whether or not such statute or regulation be valid, or based upon the exercise or performance or the failure to exercise or perform a discretionary function or duty on the part of a federal agency or an employee of the Government, whether or not the discretion involved be abused. . . . [29]

but it is hoped that it personifies a salutary trend in adjudication.[30] In effect, the act, together with the U.S. Claims Court and the U.S. Tax Court (see pp.

---

[28] For a brief evaluation of the Act, see Harry Street, *Government Liability: A Comparative Study* (Cambridge: Cambridge University Press, 1953).

[29] It should not be forgotten, of course, that in both countries exist numerous *quasi-judicial* agencies and/or tribunals that, among other duties, *adjudicate administratively* claims on the government. These are, for example, the "independent" regulatory commissions and agencies in the United States, and the ministerially appointed "special administrative tribunals" in the United Kingdom—established to deal with cases arising out of the application of social policy, for example, the Licensing Authority for Public Service Vehicles. An important development in connection with these British tribunals was the creation of the Council on Tribunals, established under the Tribunals and Inquiries Act of 1958, following the Franks Committee Report; it is charged with general supervision over all British administrative tribunals. For a perceptive explanation and analysis, see H. W. R. Wade, "The Council on Tribunals," *Public Law* 351 (1960).

[30] For an article that is still informative on the status of the doctrine of tort liability in the

150ff., *supra*), represents one of three forms of "consent in advance" under which a citizen may now bring suit against the *federal* government.[31]

Mention should be made of the remarkable series of Burger Court cases stripping government officials of their immunity from damage suits for violating rights established under the federal Constitution or federal law. In *Butz v. Economou*, 438 U.S. 478 (1978), the Court permitted suits against federal officials who were or should have been aware that they were violating constitutional rights except when it is demonstrated that absolute immunity is essential for conducting the public business. In *Monell v. New York City Dept. of Social Services*, 436 U.S. 658 (1978), local governments were made subject to damage suits for civil rights violations. In *Owen v. City of Independence, Missouri*, 445 U.S. 622 (1980), the Court made it clear that a municipality may not assert the good faith of its officials as a defense. If a constitutional violation occurs, a city may be held accountable for damages for the actual loss in court. An even more liberal decision was *Maine v. Thiboutot*, 448 U.S. 1 (1980), in which the Court ruled that private citizens, under the Civil Rights Act of 1871, are entitled to sue their own states whenever state policy allegedly violates any federal law. By reducing the barrier to suing government officials, the Court has made it easier for private citizens to assert equal protection and due process claims. That there are limits to the Court's largesse, however, was demonstrated by two 1981 rulings (both 6:3). In the first, the Court held that local governments are immune from "*punitive* damages" that go beyond *compensating* the victim for injuries caused by violations of constitutional rights (*Newport v. Fact Concerts*, 453 U.S. 247). In the second, the Court determined that individuals could not sue for damages against alleged unconstitutional behavior by state and local officials if the laws involved in the claim *themselves* provide adequate remedies for the alleged violations—here the federal water pollution laws (*Middlesex County v. National Sea Clammers*, 453 U.S. 1). In 1984 the Court, dividing 5:4, ruled that state and local (and, by implication, federal) judges may be subjected to limited civil suits for damages to pay the legal fees of criminal suspects whose rights they had allegedly violated *(Pulliam v. Allen and Nicholson*, 52 LW 4525).

THE FRENCH ADMINISTRATIVE COURTS

The hierarchy of courts that administers the *droit administratif* in France is very much part and parcel of the governmental system, however separated it is from the ordinary courts. To the French—and to many careful observers

---

several states of the United States, see Robert A. Leflar and Benjamin E. Kantrowitz, 29 *New York University Law Journal* 1363 (1954), especially the "Five Major Groupings," pp. 1407–8.

[31] For an approach designed to simplify as well as facilitate suits against government, see Peter H. Schuck, *Suing Government: Citizen Remedies for Official Wrongs* (New Haven: Yale University Press, 1983).

in the Anglo-Saxon world as well—theirs is the only logical system of supervising the administrative branch of the government, not only because of its rapid, convenient, and efficient adjudicatory process, but also because of the expertise inherent in the judicial personnel that staff its administrative courts. This is even more remarkable because the French administrative courts are actually more closely linked to the executive than to the judicial branch. Evolving gradually since revolutionary days, the predominantly "judge-made" *droit administratif* has a long and honorable history, beginning with the creation of the first *Council of State (Conseil d'État)* under Napoleon Bonaparte in the year VIII (1799).

The structure of the French administrative court system is infinitely less complicated than the regular court system. It consists of but two levels: first, the *Regional Councils* or *Administrative Tribunals (Tribunaux Administratifs)*, since they are arranged no longer in *départements*, as of yore, but in twenty-three national regions plus Paris; second, the famous multipurpose and powerful *Council of State (Conseil d'État)* at the apex. (There is also a number of special collateral administrative tribunals, sometimes known as "inferior councils"—such as the *Council of Public Instruction [Conseil d'Instruction Publique]* and the *Draft Review Board [Conseil Militaire de Revision]*, which may be omitted for present purposes.)

The Regional Councils (TRIBUNAUX ADMINISTRATIFS). It is to the *Tribunal Administratif* of the appropriate region that a French citizen with a complaint against the administrative branch of *La République* or local authorities turns initially. In almost all instances involving the *droit administratif*, the *Tribunal Administratif* acts as the administrative court of first instance. It has power either to annul an illegal decision or action or to cause payment of damages. It is staffed by able, experienced civil servants of whom three-quarters have been recruited either directly from the *École Nationale d'Administration* (see later), or from the administrative branch itself—provided they have law degrees—or they are merit appointees who have passed competitive examinations; a few have come from political or semipolitical posts.[32] The caliber of the four to six members of each *tribunal administratif*—one *président*, of course, and three to five *conseillers*—is almost always outstanding even at this first instance level.

The administrative court system of France is both simple and inexpensive: all a plaintiff at the bar of his *Tribunal Administratif* has to do is to execute and file the official complaint form, which costs practically nothing. Normally, the tribunal will conduct the investigation of the complaint by way of written statements to both sides of the complaint. Sometimes an oral hearing is held, at which the litigants may either present arguments personally or through legal counsel. When the tribunal is ready to render a decision it will do so

[32]Margherita Rendel, "The Political Impact of the French *Conseil d'État*." Paper presented at the meeting of the International Political Science Association, Montreal, Canada, Aug. 21, 1973, p. 3.

publicly; usually that settles the matter. Far more often than not, the complaining *citoyen* wins his or her suit, and can then look forward to normally speedy compensation from the public treasury for any damages. So prevalent have these citizen victories been that considerable criticism has ensued among both legal scholars and practitioners who believe that the administrative court system has caused the French government to be "too tough on itself," that there exists what might be viewed as a distinct bias *against* it.

The Council of State (LE CONSEIL D'ÉTAT). With its appellate jurisdiction from the *tribunaux administratifs*—approximately 20 to 25 percent of the lower tribunals' decisions are appealed[33]—as well as original jurisdiction in certain stipulated "important" and/or "delicate" cases, the *Conseil d'État*, housed in the Palais-Royal, justly enjoys enormous prestige. Actually, it is far more than a merely administrative tribunal; only one of its seven sections— a most renowned one, the *Litigation Section (Section du Contentieux)*— deals with the *droit administratif*. The other six are concerned with drafting of legislation for the cabinet, giving advisory opinions on legislative and executive matters, supervising rules of public administration, and performing sundry other significant functions in the governmental process. In the words of one of the foremost students of the *Conseil d'État*, it is its policy "to ensure a reasonable and proper administrative method, and to try to achieve consistency and completeness, so that administrative agencies are not driven to stretching or twisting the law in order to carry out their policies."[34] Plainly, it will insist on what it regards as proper procedures.

Roughly one-half of the Council's membership of 271, headed titularly by the Minister of Justice but effectively by its vice-president, works in the administrative court section, and its personnel, supported by twenty-two high-ranking *fonctionnaires*, is uniquely trained and qualified. The members of that Litigation Section are recruited in two ways, as are those of the other branches of the council: the "second class auditors" *(auditeurs de 2e classe)*— those who enter the council at the bottom of the ladder—are drawn from graduates of the three-year course at the justly celebrated École Nationale *d'Administration*, which provides expert personnel destined for the highest levels of the corps of civil servants in France. Admission to the École is by stiff competitive examination, most of the applicants having had some training in the law or in political science. The school graduates only about 150 students annually—a figure that represents at most 5 percent of the initial applicants—and those who do obtain their diplomas are indeed highly trained and qualified. The personnel of the higher echelons of the council come from either the upper levels of the ministries, the ranks of the prefects, or the legal profession, or are promoted from lower echelons. France is justly proud of her

---

[33] *Les Cahiers Français*, Nos. 156–157, September–December 1972, "La Justice," Notice 1 (Paris: La Documentation Française, 1972).
[34] Margherita Rendel, *The Administrative Function of the French Conseil d'État*, op. cit., p. 248.

distinguished corps of *conseillers* in the Council of State; it is truly an elite civil service body and richly merits its great prestige and acclaim.

Nine subsections, numbered chronologically, constitute the section of the council which handles the *droit administratif.* Each of these subsections consists of a *président* and a number of *conseillers.* Although all the subsections operate independently in readying cases for decision, they may hear cases either singly or in pairs. Important cases are considered by the full "judicial section," consisting of the President of the section, the two Deputy Presidents, the *conseillers* (who are also members of the Administrative Section), and the *rapporteurs.* The highest organ of the *Conseil d'État* is its Litigation Assembly, for which are reserved cases of "extreme importance." It is composed of the Vice-President of the *Conseil,* the Presidents of the sections, the Deputy Presidents of the Litigation Section, the Presidents of the subsections that originally dealt with the case, and the *rapporteur.* Decisions by all of these organs are of equal weight, and they are final and binding.

Review Procedure. As already illustrated briefly, the procedure for obtaining review in the French administrative court hierarchy is as simple as it is inexpensive. In large measure, it is inexpensive because the French state assumes responsibility for investigating both the facts and the law involved in a plaintiff's petition. Moreover, because under the French inquisitorial procedure the judiciary plays an active role throughout the administration of justice, the role of the petitioner is reduced to a summary statement as to the alleged facts and the relief prayed. He or she may request either of two types of review actions: (1) proceedings for the annulment of an *ultra vires*—beyond powers—administrative act *(recours pour excès de pouvoir)* or (2) proceedings to order some type of affirmative administrative action, such as payment of monetary damages *(recours de pleine juridiction).* Most petitions for review fall into the first category. Having received the petition, the administrative tribunal takes over; petitioner need not even retain legal counsel in the first type of case unless he or she chooses to do so. In any event, the petitioner need not worry: his or her interests will be amply guarded by the mills of the *droit administratif.* Moreover, the Council of State, *on its own cognizance,* has added a third ground for review going beyond the concept inherent in *ultra vires* (i.e., an official action beyond the scope of legal authority) namely, the famous French administrative law concept of *détournement de pouvoir,* best translated as rank *abuse* of power. In its eyes, *abuse* of power is a concept different from that of an illegal *application* of power, which is governed by the first review category under *ultra vires.* Its deliberations are secret.

Once the Council of State has granted the availability of review, it must define the extent or scope of its reviewing power on the merits. This is especially true in the first category cases, under which the legality of an administrative action may be challenged on three grounds, all of which fall under the *ultra vires* concept: (1) lack of jurisdiction, (2) failure to observe procedures defined by law, (3) error of law. To these three the special category of abuse of power is then added.

Even President de Gaulle had to bow to a Council ruling in 1962 under the *excès de pouvoir* category: He had set up a special military tribunal to try terrorists who aided European extremists in Algeria. But when the lawyer for one of the leaders of the terrorist secret army charged de Gaulle with "an illegal administrative act" in setting up the tribunal, and took the matter to the Council of State, the latter agreed and ruled it illegal indeed! (One year later Parliament created the now abolished Court of State Security described earlier.) On the other hand, later that year the Council found itself impotent in the face of its defiance by de Gaulle in connection with his call for a national referendum on direct election of the *Président* (see p. 313, *infra*). It did, however, win a qualified victory over him in May 1968 when, following its declaration of unconstitutionality of de Gaulle's proposed national referendum on his leadership during a series of sustained student uprisings, the *Président*—sensing a hostile political climate—yielded. (Yet he won an unprecedented victory in the national *elections* he then called instead of the abortive referendum.) The *Conseil d'État's* role of constitutional watchdog, manifested in these illustrations, prompted one expert, Professor Mauro Cappelletti, to assert that it has come near to assuming the power to invalidate statutes per se—since it seems now ready to review "all *executive* acts, decrees, and ordinances, even those legislative in nature ... in adversary, party-initiated proceedings for conformity with applicable statutes, the provisions of the Constitution, and the general principles of law."[35] But it still lacks actual power to declare a law unconstitutional.

Evaluation. It is hardly surprising that the Council of State is literally swamped with petitions for action and review! The same applies to the lower rung of the administrative court system. The French people look up to it as a reliable and virile guardian of individual rights against administrative encroachment. Moreover, they have great faith in the ability of these high-class civil servants to dispose of the thousands upon thousands of cases that reach them every year—as well they might. Small wonder that Anglo-Saxon states have given considerable thought to the adoption of a similar system. The Task Force of the Second Hoover Commission in the United States, for one, urgently suggested some form of administrative court system for our federal government.

Not only does the French system provide for fuller review of administrative action than the average Anglo-Saxon one, but the cost of litigation is smaller, accessibility to the courts is greater, review is more easily available, scope of review is larger, state liability for damages is less circumscribed, and settlement is far more prompt and efficient. The French state, whatever the

---

[35] *Judicial Review in the Contemporary World*, op cit., p. 18. Margherita Rendel (see fns. 19, 32, 34 and 36 of this chapter) concurs readily.

wisdom of its philosophy of government here may be, simply considers itself totally liable for service-connected faults of public officers and state agencies. That liability has even been extended to cover most cases in which the damage is caused by personal fault of public officials, for the administrative courts have held that such faults are often inseparably connected with the administrative service of which the official is an agent. In such cases, the state indemnifies the damages to the injured citizen, and the officer at fault becomes personally liable to the state.

Yet the French state accepts liability not only for fault under the *droit administratif* but, as outlined earlier, also for risk. In other words, if proper administrative action results in an unequal burden on, or a social injustice to, a citizen, the state bears the cost of equalizing the burden—without the need to introduce a private bill in the legislature. In effect, the *droit administratif* is developing in the direction of absolute liability to ensure equitable sharing among all citizens of the burden of government action. This may well be far from an unmixed blessing, but the French administrative court system, with the *Conseil d'État* standing at its apex, has operated so successfully and has proved to be such a bulwark against arbitrary actions by the centralized state, that it richly merits the careful attention that has increasingly been extended to it by students and practitioners of government alike. And the political implications of its jurisdictional growth in constitutional matters—perhaps "its most important development in the last quarter of [the] century"[36]—will undoubtedly enhance that attention.

SOME NOTES ON THE JUDICIARY OF THE SOVIET UNION

Because of the oligarchical nature of the effective instrumentalities of government in the Union of Soviet Socialist Republics, law and judiciary—the entire judicial process—are in a category of their own. Despite the series of mild reforms that were adopted in the mid and late 1930s and the far more significant ones of the post-Stalin era, especially those of 1957–59, 1961–63 and 1977, law in the Russia of today is still employed principally as a tool of the state; it is utilized for purposes of conformity; it is an organ of state power *par excellence*. The rights of the citizens under such a system are often illusory. Moreover, certain rights specifically enumerated under the Constitution of the USSR, are qualified by such tellingly realistic phrases as " . . . unless otherwise provided by law . . . ," such as Article III of the Constitution of 1936, as amended, dealing with the right to public trial, and Article 39 of that of 1977 regarding "basic rights, liberties, and duties of USSR citizens," which warns that the "exercise of rights and liberties by citizens must not injure the

---

[36]Margherita Rendel, "The Political Impact of the French *Conseil d'État*," op. cit. p. 12.

interests of society and the state or the rights of other citizens."[37] However, the post-1953 Soviet law reforms, especially the "Fundamental Principles of Criminal Procedural Legislation," adopted in 1958, have rendered this and a host of other substantive and procedural concepts more meaningful, if in a limited manner.[38]

Although theoretically all law is inherently coercive and conformist, the fundamentally arbitrary characteristic of Soviet law is a logical by-product of the traditional concept of Marxism, which views law as an instrument of domination, as a coercive tool of the state in its transition from socialism to communism, in which the *duties* of a citizen prevail over his or her *rights*. This characteristically coercive interpretation has been embraced quite naturally by the Soviet jurists, who follow Lenin's dictum that law is "nothing if there is no apparatus adapted to coerce people into observing its provisions."[39] Hence the absence of meaningful guarantees to freedom under Soviet rule. It should be noted, however, that the legal system and machinery of justice in the Soviet Union, which in its outward structure and functioning was derived largely from the French system and generally follows that as well as the German Continental model, grinds in an entirely different manner when it deals with an ordinary transgression than with one involving the state as a politico-economic institution per se. In the former case, adjudication will be effected by the tribunals involved in roughly the same manner known throughout the world; but in the latter, law becomes the political organ of state power, the instrument of the class that constitutes the regime of the land, a mere adjunct of state power in pursuit of conformity within Soviet society. Its collective interests, as interpreted by its jurists, are simply paramount to any individual interest.

THE ABSENCE OF AN INDEPENDENT JUDICIARY

There is not—indeed there cannot be—a truly independent judiciary under Soviet Rule. Although the 1977 Constitution provides, as did its predecessor, that "Judges are independent and subject only to the law,"[40] any meaningful power to check and balance the other branches of the government—assuming there are purposeful distinctions at all—is necessarily illusory. On the con-

---

[37] *Constitution (Fundamental Law) of the Union of Soviet Socialist Republics* (Moscow: Foreign Languages Publishing House, 1962), p. 91; and *Constitution (Basic Law) of the Union of Soviet Socialist Republics*, 1977, respectively.

[38] For an informative analysis see Harold J. Berman, "Legality vs. Terror: The Post-Stalin Law Reforms," in *Politics in Europe: Five Cases in European Government*, ed. Gwendolyn M. Carter and Alan F. Westin (New York: Harcourt, Brace and World, 1965), pp. 179–205. See also the excellent recent study by Robert Sharlet, *The New Soviet Constitution of 1977* (Brunswick, OH: King's Court Press, 1978).

[39] Quoted by George C. Guins, *Soviet Law and Soviet Society* (The Hague: Martinus Nijhoff, 1954), p. 45. See also Donald D. Barry and Carol Barner-Barry, *Contemporary Soviet Politics: An Introduction* (Englewood Cliffs, N.J.: Prentice-Hall, 1978).

[40] Constitution of June 4, 1977, Art. 155 and December 5, 1936, Art. 112.

trary, both the legislature and the judiciary are instruments (Stalin called them "transmission belts") of the party. There have been criticisms in the Soviet press of direct party interference in certain cases, but this happens rarely. The judges are, after all, politically reliable—almost all are party members—and thus need neither instructions nor "cues."

The judiciary does not, of course, possess the power of effective judicial review. If that power exists anywhere at all in the USSR (really an academic question) it resides in the Presidium of the Supreme Soviet, which is specifically charged under the Constitution with the interpretation of the laws.[41]

Moreover, throughout the judicial hierarchy, both the professional and the lay judges, known as *assessors*, are *elected* for short terms of office, not exceeding five years, by legislative bodies *(soviets)* or residents of the districts in which they serve, and they are all subject to recall at any time. Either faithful party members or politically acceptable "non-party Bolsheviks," these judges—aged twenty-five and over—reflect the political power of the state, and the eyes of the dominant elements of Soviet society are constantly fixed on them.

THE COURT HIERARCHY

One of the most salient features of the judicial hierarchy of the USSR is its high degree of centralization, despite the federal structure of the government and despite the myriad courts in the various and manifold geographic subdivisions below. The sole "federal" court is the Supreme Court of the USSR, which enjoys corrective power over the lower courts. But more important is the overriding supervisory power of the "boss" of the entire judicial system, the Procurator-General, the "supreme overseer of Soviet legality" (who will be described more fully later).

The Comrades' Court. At the lowest level of the Soviet judiciary is the *Comrades' Court*, a unique institution that actually falls outside the regular hierarchy. More appropriately, these units, which may be found at local levels everywhere in the land, have been called "social" or "honour courts."[42] Staffed by local citizens for the adjudication of disputes between individuals, Comrades' Courts are organized as *ad hoc* bodies in villages, farm cooperatives, apartment houses, factories, or any other place of work or dwelling where they might be needed to deal with the sundry petty offenses that invariably take place among people everywhere, whatever their political philosophy may be. The "judges" of the Comrades' Court in a particular unit or locality are normally elected for each case that arises by the membership of the residential or occupational unit concerned, or they may comprise all those

[41]Constitution of 1977, Art. 121 (5). The "Supreme Soviet" is the highest legislative body in the USSR, which meets infrequently. Its "Presidium" is its small "executive committee" that functions continuously; it issues decrees, which have the force of law, but it has no administrative responsibilities; its tasks are essentially executive and ceremonial.
[42]Robert G. Neumann, op. cit., pp. 627–28.

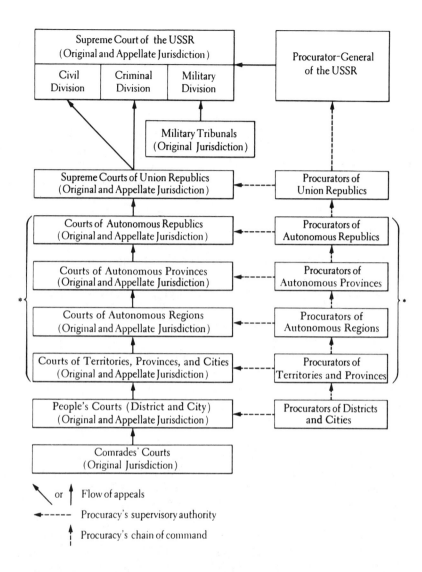

Supreme Court of the USSR
(Original and Appellate Jurisdiction)

| Civil Division | Criminal Division | Military Division |

Procurator-General of the USSR

Military Tribunals
(Original Jurisdiction)

Supreme Courts of Union Republics
(Original and Appellate Jurisdiction)

Procurators of Union Republics

Courts of Autonomous Republics
(Original and Appellate Jurisdiction)

Procurators of Autonomous Republics

Courts of Autonomous Provinces
(Original and Appellate Jurisdiction)

Procurators of Autonomous Provinces

Courts of Autonomous Regions
(Original and Appellate Jurisdiction)

Procurators of Autonomous Regions

Courts of Territories, Provinces, and Cities
(Original and Appellate Jurisdiction)

Procurators of Territories and Provinces

People's Courts (District and City)
(Original and Appellate Jurisdiction)

Procurators of Districts and Cities

Comrades' Courts
(Original Jurisdiction)

↖ or ↑ Flow of appeals

◀----- Procuracy's supervisory authority

↑ Procuracy's chain of command

* These provincial or territorial subdivisions and levels are not necessarily present everywhere in the USSR, nor do they necessarily carry identical nomenclature in the various jurisdictions marked–facts that pertain to the procuracy as well as the courts. (This chart was compiled from the text of the 1977 Constitution.) See "The New USSR Constitution," in 29 *The Current Digest of the Soviet Press* 41 (November 9, 1977), pp. 1-13.

Figure 6. The judiciary and procuracy of the USSR (1985)

present at a meeting of that unit. Their jurisdiction was materially extended with the 1963 court reforms, so they can now deal with petty hooliganism, petty thefts in the case of first-time offenders, and petty speculation, plus a host of other minor infractions. They may also levy reprimands and small fines, order an offender to apologize, administer "public censure," propose that an offender be evicted from his dwelling, propose that he be transferred to a job paying less, or require the payment of damages to the victim of up to 50 rubles ($70.00 in 1984). Probably the most important cases tried by these courts—which since 1963 may also operate in factories and other places of work to make, non-obligatory recommendations to management for "corrective action"—are those involving breaches of "labor discipline" and "standards of behavior in communal apartments." In the words of a leading authority on Soviet courts, the basic aim is "reform" of the "anti-social offender" and "the entire procedure is conceived as a lesson in communist morality."[43]

But because these Comrades' Courts are really not recognized as courts per se, their decisions are subject to annulment by the level immediately above, the People's Court. This is true for all judgments *except* a new classification, devised in 1959, and confirmed and expanded in 1963, concerning decisions of special Comrades' Courts in connection with "speculators, hooligans, unemployed elements, etc." and generally "unsocialist behavior." Those found guilty of one of these offenses at a meeting of "friends and neighbors" constituted as the Comrades' Court of jurisdiction, may be punished by banishment from their place of residence.[44] The People's Court may not review that type of decision, although the local *soviets* (legislatures) do have that power.

The People's Court. If we omit the level of the quasi-tribunal just discussed, the base of the Soviet judiciary is actually occupied by the *People's Court.* Organized on a district and city basis throughout the Soviet Union, the People's Courts are strictly courts of original jurisdiction in both criminal and civil cases, except for their tangential supervisory power over the Comrades' Courts. As the workhorse courts of the entire system, the People's Courts handle the bulk of the minor criminal and civil cases in the USSR. The Council of Ministers of the pertinent Union or Autonomous Republic concerned determines the number of these courts to be established in each district *(raion)* or city. They are locally staffed by one judge, as chairman, and two assessors; the former is elected by the inhabitants of the district or city for five years and the latter for two. The judge is not statutorily required to be a professional, although he or she usually is;[45] the assessors, being "lay judges," have no formal judicial or legal background.

[43] Harold J. Berman, *Justice in the U.S.S.R.*, rev. ed., enl. (New York: Vintage Books, 1966), pp. 289–91.
[44] Neumann, loc. cit., p. 628.
[45] Ninety-three percent were lawyers in 1975—representing a change from earlier years when

Assessors, who come from all walks of life and who usually serve only for a brief period, perhaps up to two weeks annually, are emphatically not to be regarded as jurors in the typical Western sense. No juries as the West knows them exist in the Soviet Union—although there have been periodic suggestions, ignored by the authorities, that they be introduced. When the assessors hear and decide a case, they act as judges: they have a full voice and vote on the various aspects of the facts and law of a case as well as in the decision itself. Although the views of the professional judge on the People's Court almost always prevails (it is "very rare" for the two assessors to outvote the judge, conceded Voroshilev District Chief Judge Konstantin Bakhamov in a late 1983 interview),[46] the assessors do play a role, however minor, and are part and parcel of the judicial process there.[47]

The Courts of the Autonomous Region, Autonomous Province, and Autonomous Republic. Now matters become somewhat more complicated. At the next level, or really at the next three levels, lie the intermediate courts, arranged according to territorial divisions that bridge the hierarchical gap between the level of the People's Court and that of the *Supreme Court of the Union Republic.* Not *all* multiple rungs of these intermediate courts will inevitably be present in *all* union republics, certainly not in the smaller ones, although sometimes there will even be a fourth (simply styled "territories, provinces, and cities" in the Constitution[48]), but they are sufficiently standardized to represent a definite pattern. Their jurisdiction is both original and appellate. In the exercise of the appellate function, they review decisions coming to them from the sundry People's Courts of their respective territories, and when an appeal has been decided by a minimum of three regular judges sitting *en banc* it is final.

The courts of the regions, autonomous regions, and autonomous republics have original jurisdiction in the more serious criminal and civil cases. Among the former, according to the revised criminal code, are "anti-state activities, crimes against administrative order when they involve particular danger to the state, the pillaging of socialist property, and other important economic

---

many Soviet Union judges had either little or no formal training. See Barry and Barry, op. cit., fn. 33, p. 141.

[46]Granted to a group of thirty American lawyers and judges on tour in the Soviet Union. See Timothy Harper, "A Rare Look into Soviet Courts," 69 *American Bar Association Journal* (October 1983), p. 1495.

[47]In the United States, Vermont's Constitution provides for an intriguing system of laypersons or "side judges" who exercise substantial authority in the country courts of that state. In 1985 there were twenty-eight such citizen judges, two in each of the fourteen counties; they are elected by the county to serve with a judge. Although forty-four other states used a total of 14,000 similar "side judges" in 1979, none possessed the kind of authority exercised by those in Vermont. (*Time Magazine*, September 26, 1983, p. 62.) It should also be noted that the institution of "assessors" is present, whatever its particular nomenclature, in several countries of Continental Europe and in European-based legal systems elsewhere.

[48]The Constitution of 1977, op. cit. See fns. 37, 40, and 41, and the note in Figure 6, *supra.*

crimes." The realm of civil jurisdiction embraces cases involving the state and social institutions, public enterprises, and organizations. The work of these courts is usually performed by panels of five professional judges and assessors, holding the titles of chairman, deputy chairman, members, and people's assessors, all of whom are elected for five-year terms by the *soviets* of the areas or regions concerned.

The Supreme Court of the Union Republic. In each Union Republic—the largest constituent part of the federal structure of the Soviet Union—lies a *Supreme Court of the Union Republic*, constituting the highest judicial body of that division. Its members, headed by five professional judges, but also comprising the ubiquitous assessors, are elected for five-year terms by the Supreme Soviet of the Union Republic. These high courts have both original and appellate jurisdiction. In the latter sphere of their work, they are empowered to set aside the decisions of any inferior court in the Republic; and appellate decisions rendered by them become binding. Related to that jurisdiction is their power to supervise all inferior courts by receiving and acting on "protests" against verdicts rendered below, coming to them from the Procurator-General or the Chairman of the Supreme Court of the USSR or by the corresponding officials of the lower echelons—one of the more intriguing practices in the Soviet Union, which, in effect, institutionalizes double jeopardy at the discretion of the state! The Supreme Court of the Union Republic has original jurisdiction in the more serious criminal and civil cases, including those involving infractions committed in office by the higher officials of government in the Republic. Its decisions are final.

The Supreme Court of the USSR. At the pinnacle of the judicial hierarchy in the Soviet Union stands the *Supreme Court of the USSR*, classified by Article 104 of the Constitution of 1936 as its "highest judicial organ." Elected by the Supreme Soviet of the USSR for five-year terms of office, its membership consists of a chairman, two vice chairmen, nine professional judges, and twenty people's assessors. Moreover, attached to it as members *ex officio* are the fifteen chairman of the supreme courts of the union republics, but these do not necessarily sit on a steady basis. The regular members of the Supreme Court are divided into three specialized *collegia* (panels), one each for civil, criminal, and military matters, but the entire Court is charged to meet at least once every three months in plenary session (the *plenum*). The chairman may preside over any case before the Court and he has the power to relieve or discharge any inferior court in the Soviet Union of a case to "protest" it in plenary session—sessions that are invariably attended by the Procurator-General.

Despite the implications of the Supreme Court's division of labor and jurisdiction, it is basically a court of review and appeals, a supervisory court. As such it also has the authority to recommend, even to draft for the Supreme Soviet, legislation dealing with the judicial system. Yet, as already explained, the Supreme Court emphatically lacks the power of judicial review; nor does it possess the authority to interpret laws, a function theoretically reserved, as is the former, to the Presidium of the Supreme Soviet of the USSR—to whom it may give advice in cases of interpretation. Nevertheless, the civil and criminal *collegia* do serve as tribunals of original jurisdiction in cases of exceptional nationwide significance. When it exercises original jurisdiction, a *collegium* consists of one professional judge as chairman and two assessors; in its appellate or review jurisdiction all its members are regular judges. The remaining *collegium*, the military, has jurisdiction in a small number of particularly significant cases of treason, espionage, and other high crimes against the state. It may also review appeals from, and protests against, the judgments of lower military tribunals. Except in the sense that there is always the possibility of an appeal to the Presidium of the Supreme Soviet, decisions of the Supreme Court of the USSR are final and binding. But far more significant on the scales of power and authority in the judicial system of the Soviet Union than any court is the Procurator-General and the extensive hierarchy of procurators throughout the land.

THE PROCURATOR-GENERAL

The best indication of the subordination, centralization, and lack of independence of the judicial hierarchy in the Soviet Union is the existence of the *Procurator-General*, sometimes known as Public Prosecutor or Public Procurator. No official associated with the legal or judicial process of comparable authority exists anywhere else today—certainly not in the free world. An institution conceived by Tsar Peter the Great in 1722 and revived by Lenin after a five-year lapse in 1922, the Procurator-General combines a position atop the entire judiciary with that of watchdog of the application and interpretation of both civil and criminal law on all levels of government, either directly or indirectly. Chosen by the Supreme Soviet of the USSR for a term of five years, the Procurator-General, in turn, either directly appoints or exercises considerable input in the appointment by the Secretariat of the various procurators for five-year terms on the lower levels throughout the USSR. The Procurator-General's posture is truly a centralized and centralizing one, and although he or she is technically responsible for all actions to the Supreme Soviet, in effect the P.-G. is responsible solely to the Communist party's top echelon, the Politbureau and the Secretariat. The subordinate procurators, too, are independent of all local organs of government: as guardians of local conformity they are responsible solely to their chief, the Procurator-General in Moscow—and, of course, to top party authorities (sometimes even to subordinate ones).

Powers and Functions. Always held by a high-ranking, trusted member of the Communist party, the position of Procurator-General is eagerly sought and is one of pronounced influence. Andrei Vyshinsky, who occupied the office during the famous purge trial years in the late 1930s, whence he steadily advanced, ultimately to become Foreign Minister and the Soviet Union's Representative to the United Nations, described the Procurator-General as the "watchman of socialist legality, the leader of the policy of the Communist party and of Soviet authority, the champion of socialism."[49] Even if this appraisal is somewhat embellished, it comes close to the verities of a system of law in which the Procurator-General personifies an omnipotent force. In Nikita Khrushchev's words, he "must stand guard over the laws of the Soviet Union."[50]

The Procurator-General possesses significant prerogatives beyond the basic authority outlined in Artlces 164–68 of the Constitution of 1977—namely, to ensure the strict observance of the law by all ministries and institutions as well as by all officials and citizens of the Soviet Union at large and, under a 1955 statute, to exercise the function of "general superviser" over the "legality of acts of all state organs." These other prerogatives include the following: to conduct a *juge d'instruction* type of pre-trial preliminary investigation (as may also the KGB—the secret police—and the regular police), to act in the nature of a Scandinavian *ombudsman* (see pp. 275ff., *supra*), which the Soviet Union claims to have invented, to exercise the right to appear in any civil case on behalf of either party at any point during a trial, to re-open a completed or closed trial by means of the now familiar "protest," although the period of time during which this can be done seems to have been shortened from five years to two by the reforms of 1957, and to review the judgment of any court, regardless of whether the case was adjudicated in a lower court or the plenum of the Supreme Court of the USSR. Moreover, the Procurator-General sits with the latter and thus has a strategic perch from which to operate. In brief, the Procuracy *(prokuratura)* combines the basic authority of bringing people to justice before the judiciary with that of supervising the execution of the laws by all institutions of government, public officials, and private citizens. This represents a unique and awe-inspiring compendium of power but one that is not inconsistent with the dissent-stifling, dissent-punishing system under which the Procurator-General functions.

---

[49] *The Law of the Soviet State* (New York: The Macmillan Co., 1948), p. 537.
[50] Quoted in Glenn G. Morgan, *Soviet Administrative Legality: The Role of the Attorney General's Office* (Stanford: Stanford University Press, 1962), citing *Izvestia* of January 25, 1958. Professor Morgan's fine book is devoted exclusively to the Soviet procuracy.

7

Judicial Review: I—The Supreme Power

DEFINING JUDICIAL REVIEW

Certainly the most controversial and at the same time the most fascinating role of the courts of the United States in general, and of the Supreme Court in particular, is the exercise of the power of *judicial review*. It is commonly viewed with almost equal amounts of reverence and suspicion. Edward S. Corwin regarded it as "American democracy's way of hedging its bet."[1] Although about sixty-five countries—chiefly in Western Europe, Latin America, Africa, and the Far East—had adopted some form of judicial review by late 1985, in its full majesty and range it is a power that the *ordinary* courts (i.e, those that are part of the formal judicial hierarchy) of only a handful of lands possess effectively. Chief among these are Austrialia, Brazil, Burma, Canada, India, Pakistan, and Japan, of whom all except Japan have federal systems of government, with Australia and Canada being closest to the American model.[2] Experience has demonstrated that countries which have exhib-

---

[1] Review of Benjamin F. Wright's article, "Growth of American Constitutional Law," 56 *Harvard Law Review* 487 (1942).

[2] For an informative summary discussion, see K. C. Wheare, *Federal Government*, 4th ed. (New York: Oxford University Press, 1964, reprinted in 1980), ch. 4, "The Constitution, the Courts, and the Law." Judicial review in Switzerland is confined to cantonal legislation, but serious consideration has been given to its introduction at the *federal* level. India's Supreme Court had been flexing its muscles increasingly in the 1950s and 1960s. For example, it struck down 10:1 Prime Minister Indira Gandhi's Bank Nationalization Act, ruling that the July 1969 takeover of the fourteen biggest banks was "hostile discrimination" because other Indian banks and foreign banks were excluded. (*The New York Times*, February 11, 1970, p. 1). By 1975 it had held more than one hundred federal and state laws unconstitutional. But late in

ited stable or moderately stable traditions of judicial review are generally characterized by (1) regime stability, (2) a competitive political party system, (3) significant horizontal power distribution, (4) a strong tradition of judicial independence, and (5) a high degree of political freedom.[3]

Briefly stated, judicial review in the United States comprises the power of any court to *hold unconstitutional and hence unenforceable any law, any official action based on a law, or any other action by a public official that it deems*— upon careful, normally painstaking, reflection and in line with the canons of the taught tradition of the law as well as judicial self-restraint—*to be in conflict with the basic law, in the United States its Constitution*. In other words, by invoking the power of judicial review—which, of course, may "approve" as well as "veto"—a court applies the *superior* of two laws, which at the level of the federal judiciary of the United States signifies the Constitution instead of the legislative statute or some action by a public official allegedly or actually based on it.

In the United States, the chief subject in this treatment of judicial review, this highly significant instrument of power—"the principled process of enunciating and applying certain enduring values of our society"[4]—is possessed theoretically by every court of record, no matter how high or low on the judicial ladder. Although admittedly it happens rarely, it is not at all impossible for a judge in a low-level court of one of the fifty states to declare a federal law unconstitutional; such a decision would quite naturally at once be appealed to higher judicial echelons for review. Conscious of the nature and purpose of federalism and, especially, the need to permit legislative bodies to act in accordance with their judgment, no matter how unwise that may be at

---

that year came Mrs. Gandhi's "emergency" usurpation of all effective governmental power, and the Indian judiciary, especially its Supreme Court, lay low. However, on Mrs. Gandhi's defeat in early 1977, the Court reasserted itself markedly. See Robert L. Hardgrave, Jr., *India: Government and Politics in a Developing Nation*, 3d ed. (New York: Harcourt Brace Jovanovich, 1980). Yet it did not take very long on her return to power in 1980 to note an indubitable return to the *status quo ante*. (See, among others, Ved Metha, *A Family Affair: India Under Three Prime Ministers* (New York: Oxford University Press, 1982) and Aroun Thourie, *Mrs. Gandhi's Second Reign* (New Delhi: Vikas Publishing House Pvt. Ltd., 1983). Buttressed by the enactment in 1982 of the Canadian Charter of Rights and Freedom, Canada's Supreme Court evinced rapid cognizance of its implied powers to flex its interpretative muscle, frequently citing America's initial embrace of judicial review under the leadership of John Marshall. (See, for example, Michael T. Kaufman, "Canada's Judiciary Starts Using New Powers," *The New York Times*, May 6, 1984, p. 14.) See also Christopher S. Wren, "Canada Supreme Court Rules Solely English Laws Invalid," ibid., June 14, 1985, p. A3. Sweden adopted judicial review in 1974, but had not employed it as of mid-1985.

[3]See the perceptive paper by Donald P. Kommers, "Cross-National Comparisons of Constitutional Courts: Toward a Theory of Judicial Review," presented at the Annual Meeting of the American Political Science Association, Los Angeles, Calif., September 11, 1970.

[4]Alexander M. Bickel, *The Least Dangerous Branch* (Indianapolis: The Bobbs-Merrill Co., 1962), p. 58.

times, courts are understandably loath to invoke the judicial veto. Yet their power to do so, and particularly that of the Supreme Court of the United States, serves as an omnipresent and potentially omnipotent check on the legislative and executive branches of government. Thus, although that highest tribunal has to date (summer 1985) declared but 134 or 135 provisions of *federal* laws unconstitutional in whole or in part, out of a total of almost 91,000 public and private laws enacted, some 970 *state* laws and provisions of *state* constitutions[5] have run wholly or partly afoul of that judicial checkmate since 1789—about 850 of these coming after 1870. An example of the latter action is the Court's unanimous ruling in *Torcaso v. Watkins:*[6] there it struck down a provision of the Maryland Constitution on the ground that to compel officeholders to declare belief in God constituted a "religious test for public office" that invaded the individual's right to religious freedom. In many ways, the Court's power over state actions is of more significance to the federal system than the much more publicized and more well-known power over federal actions. It ought to be added that approximately 100 *federal* executive branch ordinances have also been invalidated since the turn of the century.

Tables 8 and 9 illustrate in some detail the power of judicial review over *legislative enactments* as exercised by the Supreme Court at the *federal level only.* But it is interesting to note that more statutes of the State of Louisiana have been declared unconstitutional than those of any other state, Louisiana being the only one of the fifty to employ *civil law* as its judicial system. Regarding the sparse number of federal statutes held unconstitutional by the post-"anti New Deal" Supreme Court in recent times, the sixty-two provisions of congressional enactments that as of this writing (summer 1985) have fallen since 1937—actually since 1943—all but seven did so because they infringed on certain personal rights and liberties safeguarded under the Constitution. Those sixty-two instances were as follows:

1. *Tot v. United States* (1943).[7] A statutory presumption that a known criminal in possession of firearms or ammunition must have carried them in violation of the Federal Firearms Act of 1938, Section 2(f), was invalidated 8:0 as a violation of the due process of law clause of the Fifth Amendment.

2. *United States v. Lovett* (1946).[8] Section 304 of the Urgent Defense Appropriation Act of 1943, which barred the salaries of certain specifically named federal employees, was struck down 8:0 as violative of the constitutional prohibition against a Bill of Attainder.

---

[5]In an unpublished monograph, "Judicial Review of State Laws and the National Policy-Making Role of the Supreme Court in Protecting Fundamental Rights," David G. Barnum suggests the appropriate figure to be 848 between 1809 and 1974. (Undated manuscript, p. 11.) That would appear to be on the low side, however.

[6]367 U.S. 488 (1961).

[7]319 U.S. 463.

[8]328 U.S. 303.

Table 8. U.S. Supreme Court Declarations of Unconstitutionality of Federal
Statutes (in Whole or in Part), I (arranged chronologically in accordance with
tenure of Chief Justices)[a]

Time Span	Chief Justice	Number of Declarations of Unconstitutionality	Commentary
1798–1801	Jay	0	
	J. Rutledge	0	Weak, placid Court
	Ellsworth	0	
1801–1835	Marshall	1	1803: *Marbury v. Madison*
1836–1864	Taney	1	1857: *Dred Scott v. Sandford*
1864–1873	Chase	10	1870: *Legal Tender cases*
1874–1888	Waite	9	1833: *Civil Rights cases*[b]
1888–1910	Fuller	14 (15)	1895: *Income Tax cases*
1910–1921	White	12	1918: *Child Labor case*
1921–1930	Taft	12	1923: *Minimum Wage case*
1930–1936	Hughes	14	Of these, 13 came in 1934–36!
1936–1941	Hughes	0	The New Deal Court emerges following the "switch-in-time that saved nine" in 1937
1941–1946	Stone	2	New Libertarian emphasis
1946–1953	Vinson	1	Abstemious Court
1953–1969	Warren	25	High watermark of Libertarianism
1969–present[a]	Burger	33	Chiefly First, Fifth, and Fourteenth Amendment concerns
		134 (135)	

[a] As of fall 1985.
[b] Consolidated five different cases in *one* opinion (here counted as one).

3. *United States v. Cardiff* (1952).[9] Section 704 of the Food, Drug, and
Cosmetic Act, which deals with factory inspection, fell 8:1 as unconstitution-
ally vague under the due process clause of the Fifth Amendment.

4. *Bolling v. Sharpe* (1954).[10] The federal companion case to the *Public
School Segregation Cases*, involving an 1862 federal statute that, insofar as
pertinent here, provided for separate schools for white and black children,
was unanimously held unconstitutional as a violation of the due process of
law clause of the Fifth Amendment.

[9] 344 U.S. 174.
[10] 347 U.S. 497. (The states cases' citation is *Brown v. Board of Education of Topeka, Kansas,
et al.*, 347 U.S. 483.)

Table 9. U.S. Supreme Court Declarations of Unconstitutionality of Federal Statutes (in Whole or in Part), II[a]

Under Chief Justice	Recorded Declaration Number	Citation of Case and Year Decided	Vote
Marshall	1	Marbury v. Madison, 1 Cranch 137 (1803)	4:0
Taney	2	Dred Scott v. Sandford, 19 Howard 393 (1857)	7:2
Chase	3	Gordon v. United States, 2 Wallace 561 (1865)	8:2
Chase	4	Ex parte Garland, 4 Wallace 33 (1867)	5:4
Chase	5	Reichart v. Felps, 6 Wallace 160 (1868)	8:0
Chase	6	The Alicia, 7 Wallace 571 (1869)	8:0
Chase	7/8/9[b]	Hepburn v. Griswold, 8 Wallace 603 (1870)	4:3
Chase	10	United States v. DeWitt, 9 Wallace 41 (1870)	9:0
Chase	11	The Justices v. Murray, 9 Wallace 274 (1870)	9:0
Chase	12	United States v. Klein, 13 Wallace 128 (1872)	7:2
Waite	13	United States v. Reese, 92 U.S. 214 (1876)	7:2
Waite	14	United States v. Fox, 95 U.S. 670 (1878)	9:0
Waite	15/16[c]	Trade Mark cases, 100 U.S. 82 (1879)	9:0
Waite	17	United States v. Harris, 106 U.S. 629 (1883)	8:1
Waite	18	Civil Rights cases,[d] 109 U.S. 3 (1883)	8:1
Waite	19	Boyd v. United States, 116 U.S. 616 (1886)	7:2
Waite	20	Baldwin v. Franks, 120 U.S. 678 (1887)	7:1
None[e]	21	Callan v. Wilson, 127 U.S. 540 (1888)	8:0
Fuller	22	Monongahela Nav. Co. v. U.S., 148 U.S. 312 (1893)	8:0
Fuller	23	Pollock v. Farmers' L. & T. Co., 157 U.S. 429 (1895)	6:2
Fuller	23A[f]	Pollock v. Farmers' L. & T. Co., 158 U.S. 601 (1895)	5:4
Fuller	24	Wong Wing v. United States, 163 U.S. 228 (1896)	8:0

Table 9 (Continued)

Under Chief Justice	Recorded Declaration Number	Citation of Case and Year Decided	Vote
Fuller	25	Kirby v. United States, 174 U.S. 47 (1899)	6:2
Fuller	26	Jones v. Meehan, 175 U.S. 1 (1899)	9:0
Fuller	27	Fairbank v. United States, 181 U.S. 283 (1901)	5:4
Fuller	28	James v. Bowman, 190 U.S. 127 (1903)	6:2
Fuller	29	Matter of Heff, 197 U.S. 488 (1905)	8:1
Fuller	30	Rassmussen v. United States, 197 U.S. 516 (1905)	9:0
Fuller	31	Hodges v. United States, 203 U.S. 1 (1906)	7:2
Fuller	32	Employers' Liability cases, 207 U.S. 463 (1908)	5:4
Fuller	33	Adair v. United States, 208 U.S. 161 (1908)	6:2
Fuller	34	Keller v. United States, 213 U.S. 138 (1909)	6:3
Fuller	35	United States v. Evans, 213 U.S. 297 (1909)	9:0
White	36	Muskrat v. United States, 219 U.S. 346 (1911)	9:0
White	37	Coyle v. Oklahoma, 221 U.S. 559 (1911)	7:2
White	38	Choate v. Trapp, 224 U.S. 665 (1912)	9:0
White	39	United States v. Hvoslef, 237 U.S. 1 (1915)	8:0
White	40	Thames & Mersey Mar. Ins. Co. v. United States, 237 U.S. 19 (1915)	8:0
White	41	Hammer v. Dagenhart, 247 U.S. 251 (1918)	5:4
White	42	Knickerbocker Ice Co. v. Stewart, 253 U.S. 149 (1920)	5:4
White	43	Eisner v. Macomber, 252 U.S. 189 (1920)	5:4
White	44	Evans v. Gore, 253 U.S. 245 (1920)	7:2
White	45	United States v. Cohen Grocery Co., 255 U.S. 81 (1921)	6:2
White	46	Weeds, Inc. v. United States, 255 U.S. 109 (1921)	6:2
White	47	Newberry v. United States, 256 U.S. 232 (1921)	5:4

Table 9 (Continued)

Under Chief Justice	Recorded Declaration Number	Citation of Case and Year Decided	Vote
Taft	48	United States v. Moreland, 258 U.S. 433 (1922)	5:3
Taft	49	Child Labor Tax case, 259 U.S. 20 (1922)	8:1
Taft	50	Hill v. Wallace, 259 U.S. 44 (1922)	9:0
Taft	51	Keller v. Potomac Electric Co., 261 U.S. 525 (1923)	9:0
Taft	52	Adkins v. Children's Hospital, 261 U.S. 525 (1923)	5:3
Taft	53	Washington v. Dawson, 264 U.S. 219 (1924)	7:2
Taft	54	Miles v. Graham, 268 U.S. 501 (1925)	8:1
Taft	55	Trusler v. Crooks, 269 U.S. 475 (1926)	9:0
Taft	56	Myers v. United States, 272 U.S. 52 (1926)	6:3
Taft	57	Nichols v. Coolidge, 274 U.S. 531 (1927)	9:0
Taft	58	Untermyer v. Anderson, 276 U.S. 440 (1928)	6:3
Taft	59	National Life Insurance Co. v. United States, 277 U.S. 508 (1928)	6:3
Hughes	60	Heiner v. Donnan, 285 U.S. 312 (1932)	6:2
Hughes	61	Booth v. United States, 291 U.S. 339 (1934)	9:0
Hughes	62	Lynch v. United States, 292 U.S. 571 (1934)	9:0
Hughes	63	Panama Refining Co. v. Ryan et al., 293 U.S. 388 (1935)	8:1
Hughes	64	Perry v. United States, 294 U.S. 330 (1935)	5:4
Hughes	65	Railroad Retirement Bd. v. Alton R. R., 295 U.S. 330 (1935)	5:4
Hughes	66	Schechter Poultry Corp. v. United States, 295 U.S. 495 (1935)	9:0
Hughes	67	Louisville Joint Stock Land Bank v. Radford, 295 U.S. 555 (1935)	9:0
Hughes	68	United States v. Constantine, 296 U.S. 287 (1935)	6:3
Hughes	69	Hopkins Federal Savings and Loan Association v. Cleary, 296 U.S. 315 (1935)	9:0
Hughes	70	United States v. Butler, 297 U.S. 1 (1936)	6:3

Table 9 (Continued)

Under Chief Justice	Recorded Declaration Number	Citation of Case and Year Decided	Vote
Hughes	71	*Rickert Rice Mills v. Fontenot,* 297 U.S. 110 (1936)	9:0
	72	*Carter v. Carter Coal Co.,* 298 U.S. 238 (1936)	5:4
Hughes	73	*Ashton v. Cameron County Water Improvement District,* 298 U.S. 513 (1936)	5:4
Stone	74	*Tot v. United States,* 319 U.S. 436 (1943)	8:0
None[g]	75	*United States v. Lovett,* 328 U.S. 303 (1946)	8:0
Vinson	76	*United States v. Cardiff,* 344 U.S. 174 (1952)	8:0
Warren	77	*Bolling v. Sharpe,* 347 U.S. 497 (1954)	9:0
Warren	78	*United States ex rel Toth v. Quarles,* 350 U.S. 11 (1955)	6:3
Warren	79	*Reid v. Covert* and *Kinsella v. Krueger,*[h] 354 U.S. 1 (1957)	6:2
Warren	80	*Trop v. Dulles,* 356 U.S. 86 (1958)	5:4
Warren	81	*Kinsella v. United States ex rel Singleton,*[h] 361 U.S. 234 (1960)	7:2
Warren	82	*Grisham v. Hagan,* 361 U.S. 278[h] (1960) plus *McElroy v. United States,* 361 U.S. 281 (1960)[i]	6:2
Warren	83	*Kennedy v. Mendoza-Martinez* plus *Rusk v.*	5:4
Warren	84	*Cort*[j] 372 U.S. 144 (1963)	
Warren	85	*Schneider v. Rusk,* 377 U.S. 163 (1964)	5:3
Warren	86	*Aptheker v. Secretary of State,* 378 U.S. 500 (1964)	6:3
Warren	87	*Lamont v. Postmaster-General* plus *Fixa v. Heilberg,*[j] 381 U.S. 301 (1965)	8:0
Warren	88	*United States v. Brown* 381 U.S. 437 (1965)	5:4
Warren	89	*United States v. Romano,* 382 U.S. 136 (1965)	9:0
Warren	90	*Afroyim v. Rusk,*[k] 387 U.S. 253 (1967)	5:4
Warren	91	*United States v. Robel,* 389 U.S. 258 (1967)	6:2
Warren	92	*Marchetti v. United States,* 390 U.S. 39 (1968)	7:1

Table 9 (*Continued*)

Under Chief Justice	Recorded Declaration Number	Citation of Case and Year Decided	Vote
Warren	93	Grosso v. United States, 390 U.S. 62 (1968)	7:1
Warren	94	Haynes v. United States, 390 U.S. 85 (1968)	7:1
Warren	95	United States v. Jackson, 390 U.S. 569 (1968)	6:2
Warren	96	Washington v. Legrant (Shapiro v. Thompson) 394 U.S. 618 (1969)	6:3
Warren	97–101[l]	Leary v. United States, 395 U.S. 6 (1969)	9:0
Burger	102	Turner v. Untied States, 396 U.S. 398 (1970)	6:2
Burger	103	Schacht v. United States, 398 U.S. 58 (1970)	5:4
Burger	104	Oregon v. Mitchell, 400 U.S. 112 (1970)	5:4
Burger	105/106[m]	Blount v. Rizzi and United States v. The Book Bin, 400 U.S. 410 (1971)	9:0
Burger	107	Tilton v. Richardson, 403 U.S. 672 (1971)	9:0
Burger	108	Chief of Capitol Police v. Jeanette Rankin Brigade, 409 U.S. 972 (1972)	9:0
Burger	109[l]	Richardson v. Davis and Richardson v. Griffin, 409 U.S. 1069 (1972)	6:3
Burger	110	United States Department of Agriculture v. Murry, 413 U.S. 508 (1973)	5:4
Burger	111	United States Department of Agriculture v. Moreno, 413 U.S. 528 (1973)	7:2
Burger	112/113[n]	Frontiero v. Richardson, 411 U.S. 677 (1973)	8:1
Burger	114	Jiminez v. Weinberger, 417 U.S. 628 (1974)	8:1
Burger	115	Weinberger v. Wiesenfeld, 420 U.S. 636 (1975)	8:0
Burger	116/117[o]	Buckley v. Valeo, 421 U.S. 1 (1976)	8:0/6:2
Burger	118/119[p]	National League of Cities v. Usery, 426 U.S. 833 (1976)	5:4
Burger	120	Califano v. Goldfarb, 430 U.S. 199 (1977)	5:4
Burger	121	Califano v. Silbowitz, 430 U.S. 924 (1977)	9:0
Burger	122	Railroad Retirement Board v. Kalina, 431 U.S. 909 (1977)	9:0

Table 9 (Continued)

Under Chief Justice	Recorded Declaration Number	Citation of Case and Year Decided	Vote
Burger	123	Marshall v. Barlow's, Inc. 436 U.S. 307 (1978)	5:3
Burger	124	Califano v. Westcott, 443 U.S. 76 (1979)	9:0
Burger	125/126[q]	United States v. Will, 449 U.S. 200 (1981)	8:0
Burger	127	Common Cause v. Schmitt, 455 U.S. 129 (1982)	4:4[r]
Burger	128	Railway Labor Executive Association v. Gibbons, 455 U.S. 457 (1982)	9:0
Burger	129	Northern Pipeline Construction Co. v. Marathon Pipeline Co., 458 U.S. 50 (1982)	6:3
Burger	130	United States v. Grace, 46 U.S. 171 (1983)	8:1
Burger	131[s]	Immigration and Naturalization Service v. Chadha, 462 U.S. 919 (1983)	7:2
Burger	132	Bolger v. Youngs Drugs, 463 U.S. 60 (1983)	8:0
Burger	133	FCC v. League of Women Voters of California, 52 LW 5008 (1984)	5:4
Burger	134	Regan v. Time, Inc., 52 LW 5084 (1984)	8:1
Burger	135	F.E.C. v. National Conservative Pol. Action Comm. 53 LW 4293 (1985)	7:2

[a] As of summer 1985

[b] Same case but parts of three statutes.

[c] Same case but two different statutes.

[d] Consolidated five cases, in one opinion.

[e] Chief Justice Waite died before the case was heard and was not replaced by Chief Justice Fuller until after it had been decided.

[f] Rehearing of the earlier case.

[g] Chief Justice Stone had died before the case was heard and Chief Justice Vinson did not take his place on the bench until after it had been decided. (Counted under Stone.)

[h] See pp. 301-2, infra, for elaboration.

[i] Two separate cases but the same statute and the same citation.

[j] The two cases were reported under the same citation, but there were two declarations of unconstitutionality involving segments of two separate statutes. (See pp. 301-2, infra.)

[k] Although the holding refers specifically only to one aspect of the statute, its breadth may be interpreted as reaching several more.

[l] One citation but involving four provisions of one statute and one of another.

[m] Two separate cases invalidating two different statutes, but same citation.

[n] One citation but involving two different statutes.

[o] Two different provisions of the same statute, but differing votes: 8:0 on constitutionality, 6:2 on expenditure limits.

Table 9 (*Continued*)

Under Chief Justice	Recorded Declaration Number	Citation of Case and Year Decided	Vote

ᵖTwo different amendments to the same statute.

�q Same case and same issue, but two different statutes.

ʳAffirmed by an equally divided Court (4:4), Justice O'Connor not sitting, *per curiam*, but with full opinion affirming the declaration of unconstitutionality by two lower federal courts of record.

ˢCase could be read (6:3) as declaring unconstitutional 212 statutes with similar provisions, 62 of these still active. But here *Chadha* is viewed as just a *single* declaration of unconstitutionality.

5. *United States ex rel Toth v. Quarles* (1955).[11] The Court held unconstitutional 6:3, Article 3A of the Uniform Code of Military Justice when applied to a *former* member of the U.S. Air Force as violative of the guarantees of the civilian judicial process inherent in Article III of the Constitution.

6-8. *Reid v. Covert* and *Kinsella v. Krueger* (1957), later coupled with *Kinsella v. United States ex rel Singleton* and *Grisham v. Hagan* and *McElroy v. United States* (1960).[12] These cases concerned a series of related decisions in which the Court, over a three-year period, dealt with several aspects of Article 2(11) of the Uniform Code of Military Justice, and, by votes ranging from a high of 7:2 to a low of 5:4, found some of these unconstitutional as applied to various civilians accompanying the armed forces. The pertinent sections of the Code in these multiple cases fell as violative of the individuals' rights under Article III and Amendments V and VI of the Constitution, including the right to a trial by jury, indictment by grand jury, and public trial in a civilian court before an impartial jury of one's peers.

9. *Trop v. Dulles* (1958).[13] Here the narrowly divided Court struck down Section 401(G) of the Nationality Act of 1940, holding that Congress had exceeded its military and expatriation powers in making desertion in time of war punishable by expatriation. The Court ruled 5:4 that to expatriate for such a reason constituted "cruel and unusual punishment," forbidden by Amendment VIII.

10 and 11. *Kennedy v. Mendoza-Martinez* and *Rusk v. Cort* (1963).[14] Although these two cases were decided together (and under the same citation), the Court's 5:4 decision in effect held two sections of different congressional statutes unconstitutional as violative of procedural safeguards found in Amendments V and VI. Thus affected were Section 349(a)(10) of the Immigration and Nationality Act of 1952 and Section 401(j) of the Nationality Act

[11] 350 U.S. 11.
[12] 354 U.S. 1; 361 U.S. 234; 361 U.S. 278 and 361 U.S. 281, respectively.
[13] 356 U.S. 86.
[14] 372 U.S. 144.

of 1940, which had provided for automatic expatriation of U.S. citizens who, in order to evade military service, either fled the country or refused to return upon draft-board notification.

12. *Schneider v. Rusk* (1964).[15] In another citizenship decision the Supreme Court here invalidated 5:3 Section 352(a)(1) of the 1940 Nationality Act, chiefly on due process of law grounds under the Fifth Amendment. Section 352 had deprived *naturalized* American citizens of their citizenship if they returned to the territory of their birth and then resided there for more than three years.

13. *Aptheker v. Secretary of State* (1964).[16] Here a 6:3 majority of the Court declared unconstitutional on its face Section 6 of Title I of the Subversive Activities Control Act of 1950, which proscribed the application for or the use of a U.S. passport by any member of an organization required to register under the Act's provisions. The Court held that Section 6 " . . . too broadly and indiscriminately restricts the right of travel and thereby abridges the liberty guaranteed by the Fifth Amendment."

14. *Lamont v. Postmaster-General* and *Fixa v. Heilberg* (1965).[17] In its first decision voiding an Act of Congress on the ground that it violated the freedom of speech guarantee of the First Amendment, the Court unanimously declared unconstitutional a section of the Postal Services and Federal Employees Salary Act of 1962, which provided that all mail matter originating abroad, except first class mail, that the Secretary of the Treasury held to be "communist political propaganda" was to be detained and that the addressee was to be notified that it could be delivered only if the addressee sent a card stating that desire.

15. *United States v. Brown* (1965).[18] The Court, in one of its rare applications of the Bill of Attainder prohibition, held 5:4 that Section 504 of the Labor–Management Reporting and Disclosures (Landrum–Griffin) Act of 1959, making it a crime for a member of the Communist party to serve as an officer or employee of a labor union, was in fact such an unconstitutional piece of legislation.

16. *United States v. Romano* (1965).[19] Unanimously, the Court reversed a conviction under a section of the Internal Revenue Code providing that the presence of a defendant at the site of an illegal still was sufficient to authorize a conviction for possession and control of that still, unless the defendant satisfactorily explained his or her presence to the jury. It held such a statutory presumption of guilt to be an unconstitutional violation of substantive due process of law under the Fifth Amendment.

[15]377 U.S. 163.
[16]378 U.S. 500.
[17]381 U.S. 301.
[18]381 U.S. 437.
[19]382 U.S. 136.

17. *Afroyim v. Rusk* (1967).[20] Here, in an enormously significant decision, the Court ruled 5:4 that Congress, under Section 1 of Amendment Fourteen, lacks the constitutional authority to pass any laws that strip American citizens of their nationality *without their express consent.* Specifically, it declared unconstitutional that section of the already tattered Nationality Act of 1940 which deprived U.S. citizens of their nationality if they voted in a foreign election—and thereby overruled a 1958 decision that had held 5:4 to the contrary.[21]

18. *United States v. Robel* (1967).[22] On that term's last Opinion Day, the Court struck down 6:2 as an unconstitutional infringement of the freedom of association guarantees of the First Amendment a section of the much-battered Subversive Activities Control Act of 1950 that made it a crime for Communist party members to work in defense plants.

19-21. *Marchetti v. United States* and *Grosso v. United States* and *Haynes v. United States* (1968).[23] Here, in three separate 7:1 decisions delivered simultaneously, the Court declared unconstitutional as a violation of the Fifth Amendment's privilege against compulsory self-incrimination two separate sections of the Gambling Tax Act of 1951 in the first two cases named and one of the Firearms Act's of 1934 in the third.

22. *United States v. Jackson* (1968).[24] A section of the "Lindberg Anti-Kidnapping Law" (12-1A of the Title 18 of the Criminal Code), dealing with pleas and sentencing, fell as violative of the self-incrimination and jury guarantees of Amendments V and VI, respectively.

23. *Washington v. Legrant* (1969).[25] The Court declared unconstitutional, as a violation of the Fifth Amendment's due process of law, a District of Columbia statutory provision that denied welfare assistance to those residents of the District who had not resided there for at least one year prior to their application for assistance.

24-28. *Leary v. United States* (1969).[26] Unanimously, the Court here struck down five provisions of two federal laws dealing with marijuana controls as violative of the Fifth Amendment's strictures against compulsory self-incrimination. One law required payment of a tax for transportation of marijuana; the other established that anyone with marijuana in his or her possession upon entrance into the United States could be presumed to have imported it knowingly.

---

[20] 387 U.S. 253.
[21] *Perez v. Brownell*, 356 U.S. 44.
[22] 389 U.S. 258.
[23] 390 U.S. 39; 390 U.S. 62; and 390 U.S. 85, respectively. (Two separate laws were involved, the two cases first cited coming under the first.)
[24] 390 U.S. 569.
[25] 394 U.S. 618 (This is usually cited under *Shapiro v. Thompson*, the state welfare case with which it was consolidated.)
[26] 395 U.S. 6.

29. *Turner v. United States* (1970).[27] Similarly to the *Leary* decisions, the Court subsequently held unconstitutional 6:2 a provision of the Narcotics Import and Export Act that created a presumption that possessors of cocaine knew of its illegal importation into the United States.

30. *Schacht v. United States* (1970).[28] Down unanimously, on grounds of crass violation of First Amendment freedom of expression, went a quaint federal law that made it a crime for an actor to wear U.S. military apparel in a theatrical production if the portrayal reflected "discredit" on the armed forces—it was perfectly acceptable to wear it if it was a "favorable" portrayal!

31. *Oregon v. Mitchell* (1970).[29] While the Court *upheld* 5:4 a newly enacted federal law that provided for the lowering of the voting age to eighteen in *national* elections, it ruled unconstitutional (Justice Black, the author of both opinions, switching to the other side) a collateral provision of the law that would also have lowered the voting age similarly for *state and local* elections as violative of Article I, Sec. 2 of the U.S. Constitution governing state electoral authority.

32 and 33. *Blount v. Rizzi* and *United States v. The Book Bin* (1971).[30] Two so-called "mail block" laws were unanimously held to constitute unconstitutional invasions of First Amendment guarantees of freedom of expression, because they authorized the Post Office Department to cut off postal service to mail order houses that deal in pornography, without providing prompt judicial review of the issues of "pornography."

34. *Tilton v. Richardson* (1971).[31] A provision of the Federal Higher Educational Assistance Act of 1963 here fell unanimously afoul of First Amendment strictures against the violation of the principle of separation of church and state, by permitting church-affiliated schools to use buildings erected with federal construction funds for religious purposes after a twenty-year hiatus.

35. *Chief of Capitol Police v. Jeannette Rankin Brigade* (1972),[32] saw another unanimous declaration of unconstitutionality of a federal statute, one enacted in 1882, on First and Fifth Amendment invasion grounds. The law, adjudged an impermissibly vague restriction of free speech and assembly, had banned "all unauthorized demonstrations" on the grounds of the U.S. Capitol.

36. *Richardson v. Davis* and *Richardson v. Griffin* (1972).[33] Here the Court struck down 6:3, as an unconstitutional infringement of due process of law

---

[27] 396 U.S. 398.
[28] 398 U.S. 258.
[29] 400 U.S. 112.
[30] 400 U.S. 410.
[31] 403 U.S. 672.
[32] 409 U.S. 972.
[33] 409 U.S. 1069.

guarantees under the Fifth Amendment, Section 203(a) of the Social Security Act of 1935, as amended, which provided that "illegitimate children get benefit payments only to the extent payments to widows and other children of wage earners do not exhaust 'maximum family' benefits."

37 and 38. *United States Department of Agriculture v. Murry* and *United States Department of Agriculture v. Moreno* (1973).[34] By votes of 5:4 and 7:2, respectively, the Court here backed challenges to the constitutionality of Sections 5(b) and 3(e) of the Food Stamp Act of 1964, as amended, as violations of due process of law under the Fifth Amendment. In the former instance, the program denied eligibility to certain household residents on "over-age" grounds, in the latter to "unrelated" persons; the Court's majorities regarded both provisions as at war with the legislation's stated purpose.

39 and 40. *Frontiero v. Richardson* (1973).[35] With only Justice Rehnquist in dissent, the Court struck down as violative of the due process of law clause of the Fifth Amendment sections of 37 and 10 U.S.C. that provided for greater statutory dependency benefits to servicemen than to servicewomen.

41. *Jiminez v. Weinberger* (1974).[36] Again with only Justice Rehnquist dissenting, the Court declared unconstitutional, again on due process grounds, a provision of the Social Security Act of 1935, as amended—42 U.S.C. 416(h)(3)(B)—which denied benefits to illegitimate children of a disabled mother just because they were born after the disability began.

42. *Weinberger v. Wiesenfeld* (1975).[37] Unanimously (8:0) the Court, also on due process grounds, struck down another provision of the Social Security Act, Section 402(g), which authorized survivors' benefits for the widows of deceased workers with children but denied them to widowers in the same position.

43 and 44. *Buckley v. Valeo* (1976).[38] By vote of 6:2 and 8:0 the Court threw out two separate provisions of the Federal Election Campaign Act of 1974, the former on First Amendment (freedom of expression) grounds, the latter as a violation of the separation of powers because of the manner in which the FEC commissioners were to be appointed.

45 and 46. *National League of Cities v. Usery* (1976).[39] By identical 5:4 votes the Court declared unconstitutional as an impermissible extension of the congressional power over interstate commerce two amendments to the Fair Labor Standards Act, added in 1966 and 1974, that mandated the application of the act's minimum wage provisions to state and municipal employees. The majority held the amendments to be coercive.

[34]413 U.S. 508 and 413 U.S. 528, respectively. (This involved two separate decisions governing two distinct sections of the statute.)
[35]411 U.S. 677. (The provisions of the two separate statutes were disposed of in the same case.)
[36]417 U.S. 628.
[37]420 U.S. 636.
[38]421 U.S. 1.
[39]426 U.S. 833.

47. *Califano v. Goldfarb* (1977).[40] Another 5:4 decision declared unconstitutional as a violation of due process of law of the Fifth Amendment an OASDI requirement that rendered it more difficult for widowers than for widows to collect Social Security survivor's benefits. (42 U.S.C., Section 402[f][1][D].)

48. *Califano v. Silbowitz* (1977).[41] In a summary *per curiam* decision the Court, without recorded dissent, struck down, again on due process grounds, yet another OASDI provision, 42 U.S.C., Section 402(c)(1)(C), that required men but not women seeking Social Security benefits through their spouse's earned benefits *to prove* that they received at least one-half of their support from said spouse.

49. *Railroad Retirement Board v. Kalina* (1977).[42] In still another deprivation of due process holding, the Court declared unconstitutional 45 U.S.C., Section 231(a)(c)(3)(ii), which permitted the wife of a retired railroad employee to qualify for her spouse's annuity without a showing of actual dependency, while requiring the husband of a retired female railroad employee to demonstrate actual dependency in order to qualify for such benefits. (The vote was 9:0.)

50. *Marshall v. Barlow's, Inc.* (1978).[43] A fractured 5:3 Court here held unconstitutional the statutory authorization for warrantless inspections pursuant to Section 8(a) of the Occupational Health and Safety Act (OSHA) of 1970, deeming it violative of the Fourth Amendment.

51. *Califano v. Westcott* (1979).[44] One more Social Security case saw a provision of 42 U.S.C. Section 407 fall 9:0 (5:4) on violation of due process *cum* equal protection grounds. It had provided for welfare payments to families with an unemployed father but *not* in cases in which a mother became unemployed. The Court was unanimous on the provision's unconstitutionality, but it split 5:4 on statutory construction grounds.

52 and 53. *United States v. Will* (1981).[45] Two statutes (enacted in 1977 and 1982, respectively) that rescinded judicial pay increases *after* they had already gone into effect were declared unconstitutional 8:0 as a violation of Article III, Section 1. (Public Laws 94–440, 90 Stat. 1439 and 96–86, 93 Stat. 565).

54. *Common Cause v. Schmitt* (1982).[46] U.S. Court of Appeals decision that Presidential Election Campaign Fund Act's prohibition against expenditure over $1,000 by unauthorized political committees to further a presidential candidate's election violates the First Amendment (and that federal

[40] 430 U.S. 199.
[41] 430 U.S. 934.
[42] 431 U.S. 909.
[43] 436 U.S. 307.
[44] 443 U.S. 76.
[45] 449 U.S. 200.
[46] 455 U.S. 129.

district courts lack jurisdiction to hear private citizens' suits to enforce the act) were affirmed by an equally divided 4:4 Court.

55. *Railway Labor Executives' Association v. Gibbons* (1982).[47] Unanimously, the Court held unconstitutional Section 701 of the Staggers Rail Act of 1980, which had reenacted an earlier lower-federal-court-voided segment (Sects. 106 and 110) of the Rock Island Railway Transition and Employee Assistance Act (RITA) that had been deemed an uncompensated taking of private property for a public purpose in violation of the Just Compensation Clause of the Fifth Amendment. The Supreme Court ruled 9:0 that the Staggers Act's provisions as reenacted are repugnant to Article I, Section 8, Clause 4 of the Constitution, which empowers Congress to enact "uniform Laws on the subject of Bankruptcies throughout the United States."

56. *Northern Pipeline Construction Co. v. Marathon Pipeline Co.* (1982).[48] Struck down 6:3 Section 241(a) of the Bankruptcy Act of 1978 for giving excessive power to bankruptcy judges who lacked the constitutional protections of Article III judges (such as "good behavior" tenure and guarantees against salary reductions while in office).

57. *United States v. Grace* (1983).[49] A section of federal law, barring the distribution of leaflets or picketing on the public sidewalk surrounding the Supreme Court of the United States in Washington, D. C., was declared unconstitutional 8:1 as a *prima facie* violation of the First Amendment's freedom of speech, press, and assembly guarantees.

58. *Immigration and Naturalization Service v. Chadha* (1983).[50] The "one house" legislative veto provisions, contained in Section 224(c)(2) of the federal immigration and naturalization statute, were declared unconstitutional 7:2 as "severable" encroachment on executive power and as *ultra vires* congressional authority under Article I, Section 7. (In effect, the Court's sweeping holding declared unconstitutional 6:3 one- and/or two-house legislative vetos in fully 212 statutes enacted by Congress since 1932, with sixty-two of these still active in 1983.)[51]

59. *Bolger v. Youngs Drugs* (1983).[52] Section 3001(e)(2) of Title 39 U.S.C., which prohibited the mailing of unsolicited advertisements for contraceptive devices, was declared unconstitutional 8:0 as a violation of First Amendment guarantees of freedom of expression.

60. *FCC v. League of Women Voters of California* (1984).[53] In a 5:4 decision, the Court declared unconstitutional the provision of 47 U.S.C. 399, which had barred editorials on public radio and TV stations that receive

---

[47] 455 U.S. 457.
[48] 458 U.S. 50.
[49] 461 U.S. 171.
[50] 462 U.S. 919.
[51] *Chadha* is here counted as just a *single* declaration of unconstitutionality, however.
[52] 463 U.S. 60.
[53] 52 LW 5008.

funding from the Corporation for Public Broadcasting, as an impermissible violation of the First Amendment's freedom of expression.

61. *Regan v. Time, Inc.* (1984).[54] A complex and multiopinioned 8:1 ruling struck down as a First Amendment violation 18 U.S.C. Section 504's mandated *exception* to 18 U.S.C. 474's ban on use of photographic reproductions of U.S. currency "for philatelic, numismatic, educational, historical, or newsworthy purposes," as discriminating on basis of *content* of the photograph and message it conveys "and thus cannot survive First Amendment challenge as reasonable time, place, and manner regulation."

62. *F.E.C. v. National Conservative Political Action Committee* (1985).[55] By a 7:2 vote the Court struck down as an unconstitutional infringement on First Amendment rights of free speech and association 9012 (f) of 26 U.S.C. 9011, which limited the amount of money political action committees (PACs) could spend on behalf of presidential nominees.

State legislation, too, has thus been held unconstitutional largely because of infringement of civil rights and liberties, although there have been some exceptions, and a number of instances involved cases of state interference with national interests, especially in the realm of interstate commerce.[56]

After the famous decision in *Marbury v. Madison* in 1803 in which Chief Justice Marshall enunciated the doctrine of judicial review—although it was not really the first instance of its application (see this chapter, pp. 323–24) no other federal legislation and only thirty-six state statutes were declared unconstitutional by his Court during the remaining thirty-two years of his long tenure of thirty-four years.[57] Nevertheless, the Marshall Court wielded immense power and, guided by the dominant figure of the great Chief Justice, probably did more than either of the other two branches of the national government to make the young United States a strong, vigorous, powerful nation, and its Constitution a living, effective, elastic basic law. Not until Chief Justice Taney's painful decision in *Dred Scott v. Sandford* (19 Howard 393) in 1857 was another federal statute struck down by the Court; and the greatest crisis evoked by that power of the Supreme Court did not arrive until, dominated by the doctrinaire conservatives among the so-called Nine Old Men, the Court in 1934–36 declared unconstitutional no fewer than thirteen New Deal laws.

JUDICIAL REVIEW ABROAD

As already indicated, the practice of judicial review in its ultimate and awesome U.S. application of striking down, of utterly negating, legislative and/or

---

[54] 52 LW 5084.

[55] *F.E.C. v. National Conservative Political Action Committee*, 53 LW 4293 (1985).

[56] *Morey v. Doud*, 354 U.S. 451 (1957) for the former category and *Great Atlantic and Pacific Tea Co. v. Cottrell*, 424 U.S. 366 (1976) for the latter.

[57] The Circuit Court of Appeals for the District of Columbia did strike down by a vote of 2:1 a congressional statute in *U.S. v. Benjamin More* only six months after *Marbury v. Madison.*

executive action, is not likely to be found in nonfederal states. Hence the other two major subject lands of this study either do not (as in the case of Britain, except in the sense of the aforedescribed "application for judicial review" under the Supreme Court Act of 1981) or did not, until the adoption of the Constitution of 1958 (in the case of France), clothe their courts with the *bona fide* power of judicial review as it is known in America, Australia, and Canada, for example. And in the instance of the French Fifth Republic, it is "judicial review" only to a limited degree, if indeed it is classifiable as "judicial review" at all. But as noted earlier, the Giscard d'Estaing government, which came into office in May 1974, pledged moves toward *bona fide* judicial review. Although it had not achieved that when it gave way to the Mitterand adminsitration in 1981, it did see enacted into law a provision expanding the role of the Constitutional Council (see later).

BRITAIN

In Britain, Parliament is supreme in the sense that any law that has been enacted by it and has received the routine approval of the Crown becomes the law of the land and is *ipso facto* beyond overturning by the British courts. By virtue of the ancient English writ of *quo warranto*[58] the courts do, of course, possess the authority to interpret legislation (which also continually crops up in ordinary litigation), and particularly administrative action based on it, for all government officials are potentially accountable to the courts for their actions. The construction, the interpretation, and the meaning of the words of an act of Parliament are a matter of law for the courts. *But the courts may not strike down the law itself.* In the immortal words of Walter Bagehot, the famous British economist and journalist, "there is nothing the British Parliament cannot do except transform a man into a woman and a woman into a man." Although he expressed this fact of governmental life more than a century ago, it is still fundamentally true today (albeit not in medical contemplation!).

The people of Britain, although no longer as homogeneous as of yore, are deeply steeped in the common experience of centuries, tradition, custom, and a firm if hardly uncritical faith in Westminster and Whitehall, and they continue to be generally resolved to entrust their treasured freedoms to the good judgment of their representatives assembled in Parliament. These representatives are duly checked—"controlled" is a more appropriate term—by the powerful executive arm, the political parties, the continuing dedication to the "cricket" factor, and public opinion itself. The British courts are broadly revered and esteemed as necessary concomitants of the democratic process, but emphatically not to the degree of being ultimate guardians of the Constitution as are the American courts. On the other hand, as recent muscle-

---

[58]It requires a person to show by what authority he or she exercises a "public office, franchise, or liberty."

flexing by the Law Lords has indicated,[59] the British judiciary will endeavor to guard the Constitution in its own way by taking on Cabinet ministers. Even if that should turn out to be merely symbolic in the long run, it nonetheless points to the presence of a guardianship that could be regarded as both tentative and revisionist.

FRANCE

The French, too, insisting that a law is the expression of the sovereign will, had not endowed their courts with authority to declare laws unconstitutional, even in a limited manner, until the proclamation of the Constitution of the Fifth Republic in 1958. However, prior to it they did devise a rather interesting safeguard in order to ascertain that suggested legislation of dubious constitutionality did not become law per se short of an amendment to the Constitution. That safeguard was established by the framers of the Constitution of the Fourth Republic in the form of a special thirteen-member committee known as the *Constitutional Committee (Comité Constitutionnel)*.

Chaired by the President of the Republic, the Constitutional Committee consisted, in addition to the President of the National Assembly and the President of the Council of the Republic, of three members selected by the latter and seven by the former branch of the legislature. In each instance these ten were chosen from personnel outside the membership of the respective chambers, usually professors of law in general concord with the several political parties represented in Parliament. Whenever it was requested to do so—and only then!—by the President of the Council of the Republic and an absolute majority of its members, the committee was empowered to examine a law prior to its final promulgation to determine whether or not it was of such a nature as to require its recasting as a *constitutional amendment* rather than simply pass as a *law*. If the committee concurred that a law did in fact imply an amendment to the Constitution, it was sent back to the National Assembly for appropriate action. Not surprisingly, the Constitutional Committee was hardly a very busy institution; it was called on in merely a few cases, and only one or two of these gave it an opportunity to perform a significant role. Whatever its performance, the institution was a far cry from bona fide judicial review.

The Constitutional Council. However, France moved a bit closer to the latter, without actually attaining it, with the adoption of a provision in the de Gaulle Constitution of 1958 calling for a *Constitutional Council (Counseil Constitutionnel)*. Not a court at all, it actually lies outside the judicial system of the government; neither individual citizens nor groups (except as noted on p. 312, *infra*) nor courts of law can appeal to it. The council is composed of all the ex-Presidents of France—regardless of which Republic they may have

[59]For two examples, see *Laker Airways v. Department of Trade* (1977) Q.B. 643 and *Padfield v. Minister of Agriculture, Fisheries, and Food* (1968) A.C. 977.

headed—plus nine other distinguished personages, of whom the President of the Republic, the President of the Senate, and the President of the National Assembly each select three. M. *le président* of the council is chosen from among its membership by the incumbent President of the Republic. The members may hold no public office of any kind, other than already held civil service appointments, for it was the intention of the authors of the institution that its membership be wholly independent, exercising no outside remunerative public activity whatsoever.

The nine appointive members of the Constitutional Council—usually lawyers who have been active in politics (five of the original nine had been active Gaullists)—serve for one nonrenewable, staggered nine-year term of office, whereas all ex-Presidents of France serve for life. In theory, the latter may not resign, but one, the venerable Vincent Auriol, first President of the Fourth Republic, announced on July 2, 1960, that, in protest of three allegedly unconstitutional actions taken by President de Gaulle, he would no longer participate in the Council's work. The disputed actions were, first, a measure to increase vastly state aid to denominational schools, second, de Gaulle's refusal, in March 1960, to convene Parliament in special session despite a request by a majority of the deputies, duly backed by a constitutional provision, and, third, the short-cut procedure employed to revise the Constitution on the structure of the French Community. The then seventy-five-year-old popular Socialist, who had done much to bring de Gaulle to power in the dark days of May 1958, concluded his letter of resignation to Council President Léon Noel as follows:

> This lack of deference for the national sovereignty and our fundamental charter orients the constitutional regime of 1958 toward a system of personal and arbitrary power in opposition to the essential rules and principles of democracy. . . . [T]hus, not wanting to remain powerless and mute before attacks on the national sovereignty, I regret to inform you that I will no longer sit with the Constitutional Council.[60]

The Council has the preventive power to declare unconstitutional all *organic laws* (e.g., appointment and removal of high officials; finance bills) and *standing orders* (rules of procedure) of the houses of Parliament; both these categories *must* be submitted to the council prior to their promulgation. It is also empowered to strike down those *ordinary laws*, *treaties*, and *protocols* that *may* be voluntarily referred to it before final enactment or ratification by the President of the Republic, the Premier, or the Presidents of the two houses of Parliament. Thus, Senate President Alain Poher—who had unsuccessfully opposed President Georges Pompidou in the 1969 elections—referred an antifreedom of association bill to it in 1971. It was a measure that had been bitterly criticized by liberals and leftists and passed over the Senate's objections. In a milestone decision, the Council declared it unconstitu-

---

[60] As reported by Robert C. Doty in *The New York Times* (International Edition), July 2, 1960.

tional, marking the first time that the body, dominated by the ruling Gaullist party, had effectively opposed the government on a fundamental point of law.[61]

Normally, the Council is expected to hand down a decision within one month, but if the government categorizes a referred measure as "urgent," it must rule on the matter within eight days. Among the other main functions of the Council are supervision of the "regularity" of the elections of the President of the Republic, the members of Parliament—the Constitutional Council, not Parliament, establishes the credentials of the deputies[62] and senators—and of all popular referenda; it may decide disputes between the government (the Ministry) and Parliament regarding the "delimitation of executive and legislative competence";[63] and it must be consulted by the President of the Republic when he is contemplating the assumption of emergency powers under Article 16 of the Constitution, as de Gaulle did in April 1961, with regard to both the existence of the emergency and the measures he proposes to take under it.

The Council (which meets in camera) could not itself initiate action in constitutional cases until 1974; but it may now do so and it is autonomous regarding the other delimited areas of its power just outlined. A quorum for a valid decision is seven members, yet an absolute majority is required to certify Presidential disability—another of its responsibilities. A single opinion is delivered in behalf of the entire body (there are no concurring or dissenting opinions), but all decisions of the Council must be written. Its decisions, which are based on written documents and briefs, there being no oral argument at all, are final and binding and are not appealable to "any jurisdiction whatsoever." Yet the Council has no power to enforce its decisions, other than the power to persuade.

Given its limited range of power and authority,[64] it would be highly misleading to characterize the functions of the Constitutional Council as full judicial review per se. For there are three debilitating weaknesses: First, the inability of private individuals to challenge the constitutionality of a law, because only the high public officers named previously and, since 1974, sixty

---

[61] Decision of July 16, 1971. (See the articles in the International Edition of the Herald Tribune, July 19, 1971, and The New York Times, July 18, 1971, p. 13.)

[62] Thus, after the November 1962 elections to the National Assembly, the Council invalidated the results in four assembly districts.

[63] By the end of 1969, the Council had decided sixty-six such disputes. See Roy Pierce, French Politics and Political Institutions, 2d ed. (New York: Harper & Row, 1973), pp. 94–95. In only seven of the disputes did the Council side with Parliament.

[64] Between 1958 and 1975, the Council rendered 484 decisions, including 35 certifications of results of elections and referenda. During that same period it examined the constitutionality of organic laws just twenty times, that of ordinary laws eleven times, and that of treaties just once. (Louis Favoreu and Loic Philip, "La jurisprudence du Conseil constitutionnel," 91 Revue du droit et de la science politique, January–February 1975, pp. 165–200.) See the latter journal's subsequent annual volumes for current statistics.

deputies or senators—acting in a group petition—possess that right as an adjunct of their official station. Second, a challenge to the constitutionality of a law even by those authorized to do so is possible solely as to the *substance* of the law and not as to its procedural application (one of the most frequent causes of court review in the United States, for example). Third, the extremely short period of time permitted to the Council for its deliberation on a validly challenged measure makes all but a mockery of the concept of an appeal—especially since its power is exercisable only *prior* to promulgation. On the other hand, its record to date (1985) indicates a definite inclination to assert itself in the constitutional evaluation of the writing of parliamentary rules. It remains to be seen whether this inclination is a harbinger of more assertion in other areas of its presumed competence, but this is unlikely. In the still apposite opinion of one of the most astute commentators on the French scene, *le conseil constitutionnel* is best thought of as an adjunct to the President of the Republic in his endeavors to ensure respect for the 1958 Constitution.[65] This appraisal was assuredly vindicated when President de Gaulle in October 1962 called for a national referendum on direct election of the President—despite the Council's objections, and those by the *conseil d'état*, to such a referendum call on the obvious ground that the Constitution of 1958 did not provide for such direct action and that, indeed, the President's call represented a patent violation of the letter and the spirit of the basic document. But when, predictably, de Gaulle refused to be stopped, held the referendum, won it (albeit by a narrow margin), and then saw his action and the attendant results challenged at the bar of the Council, the latter promptly declared itself "incompetent" to rule on the "subject matter approved" by and in the referendum. The French Constitutional Council is no Supreme Court of the United States, despite the efforts implicit in the Giscard d'Estaing reforms of 1974 that, in theory, indeed may represent "un gramme de démocratie."[66] Indeed, in 1977 the Giscard government did push through further legislation to expand the watchdog role of the Council, which has used it a number of times, including on a budget. But there is still a long way to go, even under a Socialist administration, such as Mitterand's. Yet there is no doubt that the past decade has witnessed what one of its leading interpreters regards as a "profound transformation" leading to a "heretofore unimaginable stature of genuine prestige."[67]

SOME OTHER SPECIAL CONSTITUTIONAL TRIBUNALS

Several countries—perhaps recognizing traditional distinctions between natural and positive law—have created judicial bodies that approach or even

[65] William Pickles, *The French Constitution, October 4, 1958* (London: Stevens & Co., Ltd., 1960), p. 33.

[66] See Maurice Duverger, "Un gramme de démocratie," *Le Monde*, October 11, 1974.

[67] Louis Favoreu, "Le droit constitutionnel jurisprudentiel en 1981–1982," *Revue du Droit Public et de la Science Politique en France et a L'Étranger*, February 1983, pp. 337–39.

feature some of the manifestations of the power of judicial review, yet they are usually found *outside* or astride the ordinary court structure. Among the more visible of these bodies are the constitutional courts of West Germany, Italy, and Austria, all of which practice at least some measure of judicial review. There are others, but a brief treatment of these three will suffice to illustrate the point. The three states, each in a post–World War II development, empowered their special constitutional courts to guard against infringement of their constitutions by simple legislation and other governmental action, such as any action that would violate the constitutional guarantee, present in almost identical form in all three lands, that "all persons shall be equal before the law." There has been fairly general acceptance of their purpose and functions.[68]

By far the most active and most successful among the three is West Germany's *Federal Constitutional Court (Bundesverfassungsgericht)*, created in 1951—responding to U.S. advocacy of an independent judiciary and the power of judicial review—under the Basic Law of 1949, as amended in 1970, and seated in Karlsruhe. (The framers of the Weimar Republic had rejected judicial review because of what they regarded as the "stultifying actions" of the U.S. Supreme Court!)[69] It consists of sixteen judges of at least forty years of age; all have considerable past judicial, legal, professional, or other high public experience and are elegible for judicial office as well as for election to the *Bundestag* (though they cannot be members of it). They are elected half by the lower house *(Bundestag)* by a special committee of twelve electors set up by it on the basis of proportional representation in the *Bundestag*—hence dominated by the major parties—with eight of the twelve votes necessary for selection, and half by the upper house *(Bundesrat)* of Parliament by a two-thirds majority. The *Bundesrat* is representative of the partisan and regional interests of the *Länder* (states). The selections by the two houses are made from a list provided by the Ministry of Justice. It comprises *all* federal judges eligible for elevation to the *Bundesverfassungsgericht* as well as any other legally trained candidates who are nominated by the federal government, by the *Länder*, and by the political parties. Only six of those selected—three from each of its two eight-member chambers[70]—*must* come from the ranks of professionally trained, sitting federal judges; the others may, but need not, be drawn from such judgeships. As of 1970 all judges serve for nonrenewable twelve-year terms of office; they must retire at age sixty-eight.

In response to disputes or cases brought by agencies, institutions, and individuals empowered to invoke its jurisdiction, the Federal Constitutional

[68]See the informative article by Taylor Cole, "The Constitutional Courts: A Comparison," in 53 *American Political Science Review* (December 1959), pp. 963–84. See also Mauro Cappelletti, *Judicial Review in the Contemporary World* (Indianapolis: The Bobbs-Merrill Co., 1971), ch. 3, "The Modern Systems of Judicial Review: The Organs of Control," pp. 45–68.

[69]The High State Court *(Staatsgerichtshof)* did, however, have express authority to settle constitutional conflicts between levels and branches of government.

[70]Each house of Parliament elects one-half of each of the two chambers (senates).

Court possesses the extensive power to decide all disputes involving the meaning and interpretation of the Basic Law *(Grundgesetz)*; it decides the constitutional validity of any federal or state *(Land)* statute, whether or not a case involving it has already come before one of the regular courts; and it adjudicates disputes between organs of government at the national level. Out of these powers arise the Court's two most significant functions: jurisdiction over disputes between the Federal Republic and the *Länder* regarding the latter's administration of the former's statutes,[71] and guardianship over the fundamental rights and privileges of citizens as determined by the Basic Law both on substantive and procedural grounds—like judicial review in the United States and unlike its restricted, if conceivably ultimately widening, practice in France.

As indicated, the *Bundesverfassungsgericht*[72] is composed of two chambers or senates of eight judges each. Initially, one handled all cases dealing with civil and constitutional rights and the other handled all other cases. But to even out the caseload *both* senates now decide individual rights or constitutional complaints. The first senate thus has jurisdiction over complaints involving the interpretation of Articles 1-17 (speech, religion, equal protection, right to trade, etc.), whereas the second senate decides complaints involving procedural due process rights (Articles 101, 103, and 104).[73] Votes in the former are not recorded, but the latter publishes the division in cases and identifies authors. The *Bundesverfassungsgericht* has been a busy and assertive court—now exceeding 3,500 cases annually (approaching the work load of the U.S. Supreme Court)—and to the surprise of many a skeptic it has acted with considerable courage and vigor. For example, it braved the wrath and power of Chancellor Konrad Adenauer when, in a momentous decision early in 1961, it declared unconstitutional, as a violation of principles of federalism guaranteed in Article 30 of the Basic Law, his executive action setting up a federally controlled second television network that was to be financed largely through commercials[74]—a plan that had been expressly rejected by Parliament earlier! The decision was particularly remarkable because it resulted from a suit filed some months earlier by four *Länder* dominated by the Chancellor's opposition, the Social Democrats.

---

[71] See the excellent study on the Court's federalism jurisprudence by Philip M. Blair, *Federalism and Judicial Review in West Germany* (Oxford: Clarendon Press, 1981).

[72] There are several modes of access to the *Bundesverfassungsgericht*, the three most important ones being (1) *Richterklage*—request by an inferior court to have the BVG render a judgment on a constitutional question in a pending case; (2) *Parteienklage*—appeal by a constitutional organ (federal or state); (3) *Bürgerklage* or *Verfassungsbeschwerde*—in cases concerning questions of violation of basic rights of individuals involving any statute, judicial decision, or administrative act or in the case of local governments, "the right of self-government." (No cases had been filed under category 1 as of late 1984.)

[73] This division of jurisdiction was announced in 14/BVerfGE (1971).

[74] 12 BVerfGE 60 (1961).

Two other significant decisions served to declare unconstitutional both the Communist party in 1956 and the socialist *Reich* party (a neo-Nazi organization) in 1952 as being militantly resistant to the constitutional and democratic order of the state.[75] And as another illustration of the Court's virility and assertiveness, it did not hesitate to strike down an executive decree based on what the Court viewed as unconstitutional delegation of legislative power by the *Bundestag* to the Executive.[76] The reasoning employed here was quite similar to that used by the U.S. Supreme Court in 1935, in the "Hot Oil" cases,[77] when it declared unconstitutional, as an illegal delegation of legislative power to the Chief Executive, an important section of the National Industrial Recovery Act, which was soon to fall in its entirety. A further example of the Court's versatile jurisdictional determination came in 1966 when it declared unconstitutional the federal statutes under which the three major political parties had been subsidized from public funds to the tune of DM 38 million (about $14 million) annually. The Court held that such funds could be authorized only for legitimate election campaign expenses, not for general propaganda, and would have to be made available to splinter parties as well. "In a free society," said the tribunal, "the process of forming public opinion should be free of the state, and should move from the people themselves to the state institutions rather than from the state down to the people."[78] And the BVG made worldwide headlines early in 1975 when it struck down 6:2, as unconstitutional, a federal law permitting abortions on request during the first three months of pregnancy, holding the 1974 statute to violate the Constitution's guarantee that "everyone shall have the right to life." In the words of the unidentified majority opinion's author, "[T]he bitter experience of the Nazi period in Germany provides historical grounds for determining that protection of human life should receive absolute priority."[79] It is fair to say that the *Bundesverfassungsgericht* has assumed an importance hardly predictable, and that it has thus become a significant and prestigious element in the constitutional *modus operandi* of the new German federalism. Between 1951 and 1980 it declared 107 statutes unconstitutional, partly or entirely. In the judgment of one seasoned observer, "the Court clearly has become the most important source of judicial influence in German politics and the most active and powerful tribunal in Western Europe."[80] On the other hand, there are those who would conclude, with Professor Fritz Nova, that the BVG "has checked its exercise of power with a strong sense of self-

[75] BVerf GE 85 (1956) and 2 BVerf GE 1 (1952).
[76] 1 BVerf GE 14 (1951).
[77] *Panama Refining Co. v. Ryan*, 293 U.S. 388 (1935).
[78] 20 BVerf GE 56–59, 119, 134 (1966).
[79] 39 BVerf GE 1–95 (1975). See the incisive analysis by Donald P. Kommers, "Abortion and Constitution: United States and West Germany," 25 *The American Journal of Comparative Law* 2 (Spring 1977).
[80] Lewis J. Edinger, *Politics in Germany: Attitudes and Processes*, 2d ed. (Boston: Little, Brown and Co., 1976), p. 323.

restraint" and that the latter phenomenon, coupled with limited creativity, has "characterized its performance."[81] As another expert on the BVG concludes, while the tribunal's impact has indeed been "substantial," it would be wise at this time to avoid "an inflated conception of the Court's significance in the German system."[82]

Yet another modern special Constitutional tribunal is Italy's *Constitutional Court (Corte Costituzionale)*, established under the Italian Constitution of 1948—although it did not begin to function until January 1, 1956. This fifteen-member body is staffed with distinguished, mature personages who have had at least twenty years of experience as practicing lawyers, or who are experienced judges or professors of law. (Once more we note the high esteem in which the professor is still held in Europe.) The members of the Court are appointed for staggered nine-year terms, five selected by the President of the Republic of Italy with the Premier's countersignature (a mere *pro forma* requirement, for the selection is exclusively the President's jealously guarded prerogative); five by a three-fifths vote of Parliament in joint session, and five by the "ordinary and administrative judiciary"—that is three by the *Corte di Cassazione* (Court of Cassation), one by the *Consiglio di Stato* (Council of State), and one by the *Corte dei Conti* (Court of Accounts). The Court is the final interpreter of the Constitution; it has the power to declare both national and regional laws unconstitutional—as it did in the case of a 1934 law that denied Sunday rest to shepherds and, a decade later, in that of a government ban on foreign cable TV[83]—and it serves as arbiter in disputes between organs of government at the national level. In that role it also acts as legitimator—for example, it validated the controversial Divorce Act of 1971, a law enacted only after a long and bitter Parliamentary struggle, that for the first time in Italy's history enables married people to dissolve their wedlock.[84] Access of individuals to it is considerably less readily available than in West Germany and that fact, plus a general tendency to tread much more gingerly, at first rendered the *Corte Costituzionale* less of a peacemaker in matters of

---

[81]"Political Innovation of the West German Federal Constitutional Court: The State of Discussion on Judicial Review," 70 *The American Political Science Review* 1 (March 1976), p. 124.

[82]Donald P. Kommers, *Judicial Politics in West Germany: A Study of the Federal Constitutional Court* (Beverly Hills: Sage Publications, 1976), p. 301. See also C. C. Schweitzer, Taylor Cole, Donald P. Kommers et al (eds.), *Politics and Government in the Federal Republic of Germany* (London: Berg Publishers, Ltd., 1983; New York: St. Martins, 1984).

[83]Decisions of July 22, 1962 and 1974, respectively. A few months prior to the former decision, the *Corte Costituzionale* upheld the constitutionality of articles 559 and 560 of Italy's penal code which had provided for sterner punishment for adulterous wives than for unfaithful husbands. That judgment, however, was overruled on contemporary egalitarian grounds in 1968, the Court holding that the different responsibilites and punishments established thereunder for men and women were violative of Act III of the Italian Constitution's "equal protection clause." (Giurprudenza Corte Costituzionale No. 126 [1968], overruling Guir. Cost. No. 64 [1961], resp.)

[84]Giur. Cost. No. 169 (1971).

constitutional checks than its counterpart north of the Alps. The *Corte's* average annual caseload has been less than two hundred to date. Nevertheless, it has sporadically asserted itself, and particularly so when dealing with the now familiar illegal delegation of legislative power to the executive branch, and in the realms of family relations, women's rights, and criminal procedure. This has prompted two knowledgeable commentators to conclude, perhaps somewhat expansively, that the Court has not only "insisted upon its prerogatives and successfully defended its position," but that it has "become a bulwark for freedom in Italian society."[85] On the other hand, although the Court's decisions are generally obeyed, other decisions have been deliberately ignored by officials—one such instance in 1957 causing the resignation of Enrico De Nicola, the Court's first Presdient, when a cabinet minister resolutely refused to adhere to a decision of the Court.[86] Thus, antagonism between the judicial and other branches has indeed flared sporadically. But the Court has been generally cautious and deferential. By and large, it is fair to conclude, with Professor Giovanni Bognetti, that the Court to date had chosen to exercise what has been aptly called "only a discreet presence in Italian political life"—that, all things being equal, the Italian Constitutional Court prefers "exhortations to orders."[87]

Austria, too, has its Constitutional Court, the *Verfassungsgerichtshof*. This fourteen-member tribunal (there are always six substitute members available) was reinstituted in 1945, based on the Austrian Constitution of 1920, as amended in 1925 and 1929. Its members are appointed by the President of the Republic of Austria from nominees of the federal government, partly on the recommendations of the lower house (National Council) and the upper house (Federal Council) of Parliament for life tenure—unlike the German and Italian justices—up to the compulsory retirement age of seventy. The tribunal has the power to review the constitutionality of legislation and to decide jurisdictional disputes between the courts and administrative authorities. Until 1975 individuals had less ready access to the *Verfassungsgerichtshof* than their German neighbors had to their constitutional court but more than Italians to theirs. As a result of a constitutional amendment adopted in that year, however, individuals are entitled to file complaints (*Beschwerde*) not merely because they believe their constitutionally guaranteed rights to have been violated by an act of the *administration*—as they had been able to do since at least 1920—but now also if they believe one of their rights to have been violated by a *law* (an act of the legislature). Thus,

---

[85] Guglielmo Negri and Joseph La Palombara, "Principles of Italian Constitutional Law and the Structure of Central Government," in Guglielmo Negri, *Three Essays on Comparative Politics* (Milano: D. A. Ciuffre, 1964), pp. 33–37 and p. 8, respectively.

[86] See Norman Kogan, *The Government of Italy* (New York: Thomas Y. Crowell Co., 1965), p. 120.

[87] "The Political Role of the Italian Constitutional Court," 49 *Notre Dame Lawyer* 5 (June 1974), pp. 982–98.

there has been a *rapprochement* to the German conception of judicial review. The Austrian *Verfassungsgerichtshof*, too, now asserts itself; it has not been loath to examine challenged legislation, even legislation that, like the subject of an increasing number of cases handled by the Italian *Corte Costituzionale*, extends to the socioeconomic and egalitarian realm: for example, it held unconstitutional a section of the Income Tax Law that differentiated between the sexes for tax purposes (decision of March 29, 1958). In the view of at least one astute Austrian lawyer-political scientist observer, the *Verfassungsgerichtshof*—which customarily disposes of about 500 cases annually—is now a type of "upper house" of the Austrian political system.[88]

Yet of all the issues that have confronted these three constitutional courts of Europe, by far the greatest number has concerned the interpretation and application of respective constitutional provisions in the vexatious areas of delegation of legislative authority, federalism, and equality before the law. With varying emphasis, they are very much in the constitutional weather eye of the U.S. judiciary as well—contemporarily especially the latter.

A HISTORICAL NOTE

The notion that courts, or some other body, should exercise judicial review as the guaradian of the theoretical primacy of a basic law or constitution[89] stems primarily from the early European rejection of the idea of the inviolability of an enacted law. One of the first statements clamoring for a type of judicial review in that connection was made in England—oddly enough in view of its subsequent rejection of the concept. It arose out of the famous *Dr. Bonham's Case* in 1610. The King, pursuant to an Act of Parliament, had granted to members of the London College of Physicians the exclusive right to issue licenses to practice medicine in that city. Dr. Bonham was charged with practicing medicine illegally, for he was not a member of that College, the latter having refused to license him. The College then fined him, confiscating half of the fine for itself! When the case came before Sir Edward Coke, the Lord Chief Justice, he declared the charter void as a violation of the common law. Holding the latter to be supreme, Sir Edward simply stated that the courts could declare acts of Parliament null and void; therefore, he held in the now famous dictum: "[W]hen an act of Parliament is against common right and reason, or repugnant, or impossible to be performed, the common

---

[88]Manfried Welan, "*Der Verfassungsgerichtshof—eine Nebenregierung?*" in Heinz Fischer, *Das Politische System Österreichs* (Wien: Europaverlag, 1977), p. 313.

[89]An intriguing development on that front, albeit a still somewhat unreliable one, in terms of its genuine role and meaning, is the establishment in 1964 of Yugoslavia's eleven-member Constitutional Court, elected by the Federal Assembly for a once renewable eight-year term of office. See Winston M. Fisk and Alvin Z. Rubinstein, "Yugoslavia's Constitutional Court," 15 *East Europe* 7 (July 1966). It has evinced some muscle-flexing by taking on a number of local fiefdoms, but it does not seem to be destined for a genuine counterfoil to medium- and upper-level governmental authority.

law will controul it and adjudge such act to be void."[90] Parliament then simply reenacted the statute! If Sir Edward's view of judicial review was ever seriously adopted at all anywhere in England, it found itself promptly superseded when the Glorious Revolution of 1688 clearly established the supremacy of Parliament. In fact, already in 1653 Lord Coke's peers had held in *Captain Streater's Case*[91] that " . . . we must submit to the legislative power else things would run around."[92]

Nevertheless, the concept of judicial review—a product of our common Western history and the "logical result of centuries of European thought and colonial experience"[93]—subsequently found its way across the Atlantic Ocean to the British Colonies, there to be nurtured by several colonial courts. In eight or nine separate early judgments these courts refused to enforce legislative enactments that they deemed to be against "the laws of nature" (shades of Locke and future events) or "the laws of natural equity"—in a sense against the latent, unwritten Constitution.[94]

JUDICIAL REVIEW AT HOME

Yet if the principle of judicial review was imbedded in the minds of the American Founding Fathers, they assuredly failed to spell it out literally— although the records of the Constitutional Convention in Philadelphia in 1787 prove conclusively that the idea of judicial review was widely recognized and accepted; that the matter was very much on the minds of the delegates, who after all distrusted unrestrained popular government; and that it was widely debated. In any event, the massed evidence is quite persuasive that a vast majority of the delegates, Anti-Federalists as well as Federalists, favored it, although for quite different reasons. Between twenty-five and thirty-two of the forty delegates—including three-fourths of the Convention's leaders—are generally considered to have called for it. Distinguished constitutional atuhorities, such as Professors Beard, Corwin, Berger, and Mason, fully agree on that interpretation of the wishes of the delegates[95] who, with

---

[90] 8 Co. 188a.

[91] 5 How St. Trs. 365.

[92] However, there are those who argue—a bit tortuously—that, in effect, by their common law power of *interpreting* legislation, the courts of England *do* practice judicial review. See, for example, A. Wilson, in "the Doctrine and Practice of Judicial Review of Legislation," 4 *Me Judice* 20 (January 1962).

[93] Mauro Cappelletti, *Judicial Review in the Contemporary World*, op. cit., p. 25.

[94] See fn. 99 and accompanying text, p. 322, *infra*.

[95] See Charles Beard, "The Supreme Court—Usurper or Grantee?" 27 *Political Science Quarterly* 1 (1912); Max Farrand, *The Framing of the Constitution of the United States* (New Haven, CT: Yale University Press, 1913); Edward C. Corwin, *The Doctrine of Judicial Review; Its Legal and Historical Basis and Other Essays* (Princeton, NJ: Princeton University Press, 1914); John Schmidhauser, *The Supreme Court as Final Arbiter in Federal-State Relations, 1789–1957*, (Chapel Hill: University of North Carolina Press, 1958), especially chs. 1

less than a handful of dissenters, in effect concurred in the pronouncement by Gouverneur Morris of Pennsylvania that the courts should decline to give the weight of law to "a direct violation of the Constitution." Morris admitted that such control over the legislature might have "its inconveniences," but that it was nonetheless necessary because even the "most virtuous citizens will often as members of a legislative body concur in measures which afterwards in their private capacity they will be ashamed of."[96]

So prominent a framer as Alexander Hamilton declared in his famous *Federalist Paper* No. 78 that judicial review was definitely meant to be incorporated into the prerogatives of the judiciary; that "the courts were designed to be an intermediate body between the people and the legislature, in order among other things, to keep the latter within the limits assigned to their authority. The interpretation of the laws is the proper and peculiar province of the courts." *Federalist* No. 78 should be read in conjunction with Nos. 79, 80, 81, and 83 to derive fuller benefit of Hamilton's view of judicial power, of which a crucial ingredient was his conviction, as he put it in No. 80, that "no man ought certainly to be a judge in his own cause, or in any cause in respect to which he has the least interest or bias." The "Father of the Constitution" himself, James Madison, wrote:

> Judiciary is truly the only defensive armor of the Federal Government, or rather for the Constitution and laws of the United States. Strip it of that armor and the door is wide open for nullification, anarchy and convulsion.[97]

And in his famed Philadelphia lectures of 1790–91, James Wilson, probably the most influential Founding Father after James Madison, and by then an Associate Justice of the U.S. Supreme Court, observed that the Constitution was supreme law, that it was for the judges to declare and apply it, that what was subordinate must give way, and that because one branch of the government infringed the Constitution was no reason that another should abet such infringement.[98] Despite this solid evidence it is still a matter of some academic dispute whether or not the framers intended the power of judicial

---

and 11. See also Beard's classic, *The Supreme Court and the Constitution*, rev. ed., with an introduction by Alan F. Westin (Englewood Cliffs, NJ: Prentice-Hall, 1962). Benjamin F. Wright, however, puts the number of "pro"-delegates at the much lower level of seven to seventeen. One reason for the difference in numbers may well be that the larger figure may include those delegates who embraced the idea of a "Council of Revision," which would have consisted of the President and "a convenient number of the National Judiciary" empowered to examine every act of Congress and by its dissent to constitute a veto. The Founding Fathers rejected the Council, however. They also rejected the "Congressional Negative," which would have empowered Congress to disallow *state* laws deemed to contravene the Constitution.

[96] As quoted by Alpheus T. Mason and Richard H. Leach, *In Quest of Freedom* (Englewood Cliffs, NJ: Prentice-Hall, 1959), p. 124.

[97] As quoted by Charles Warren in *The Supreme Court in United States History* (Boston: Little, Brown and Co., 1937), vol. I, p. 740.

[98] Ibid., vol. 1, p. 460.

review to be given to the courts. But there are sundry additional grounds for the conclusion that such doubts as still remain ought to be laid to rest—that the debate over the legitimacy of judicial review has been settled by history.

FURTHER HISTORICAL ROOTS

The Constitution itself, while admittedly not providing for the power of judicial review in so many words, assuredly alludes to it by implication. The supremacy clause of Article VI (Section 2) relating to the duty of state judges, may very well be viewed as implying judicial review by federal tribunals over *state actions*. Moreover, that same provision of the Constitution requires acts of Congress to be made "in pursuance thereof," which would seem to call for someone to act as arbiter. It may be well to quote the entire supremacy clause:

> This Constitution, and the laws of the United States which shall be made in pursuance thereof, and all treaties made or which shall be made under the authority of the United States, shall be the supreme law of the land; and the judges in every state shall be bound thereby, anything in the Constitution or laws of any state to the contrary notwithstanding.

Another clearly relevant provision of the basic document is to be found in Article III, Section 2, which states the following:

> The judicial power shall extend to all cases, in law and equity, arising under this Constitution, the laws of the United States and treaties made or which shall be made, under the authority. . . .

If nothing else, this section strongly articulates the authority of the judiciary over cases in a vast area of constitutional interpretation and thus implies its finite power as to the legality of those cases.

Moreover, as has already been briefly indicated, it is noteworthy that in the colonial period the British Privy Council had *established* judicial review over acts passed by the colonial legislatures—and indeed exercised it 469 times in the seventeenth and eighteenth centuries.[99] At least eight states' ratifying conventions expressly discussed and accepted the power to pronounce legislative acts null and void.[100] Furthermore, between 1789 and 1803 the courts in ten of the states had *exercised* that power by declaring state laws to be in conflict with state constitutions, and prior to 1789 eight instances[101] of state court judicial review deciding against their state legislature took place. And Section 25 of the Judiciary Act 1789, the law under which the First Con-

[99]Robert K. Carr, *The Supreme Court and Judicial Review* (New York: Farrar & Rinehart, 1942), p. 43.
[100]Virginia, Rhode Island, New York, Connecticut, Massachusetts, New Jersey, North Carolina, and South Carolina. For examples of its application in several cases, see Charles Grove Haines, *The American Doctrine of Judicial Supremacy*, 2d ed., rev. and enl. (Berkeley: University of California Press, 1959).
[101]E. G., *Holmes v. Walton* (New Jersey, 1780) and *Trevett v. Wheeden* (Rhode Island, 1786).

gress created the national judiciary, *conferred* on the federal government specific authority to *reverse* provisions of state laws and state constitutions that conflicted with the "Constitution, treaty, statute, or commission of the United States."[102] Still, because neither the Constitution for any level of government nor the Judiciary Act of 1789 for the national level *specifically* provided for judicial review, it remained for the Supreme Court of the United States to do so. This it did in 1803, in *Marbury v. Madison*[103]—though, as Thomas Reed Powell noted in his *Vagaries and Varieties in Constitutional Interpretation*, no one "had any premonition that the point of judicial review would be relevant to the disposition of the controversy."[104]

SPELLING IT OUT: MARBURY V. MADISON

With the possible exception of *McCulloch v. Maryland*[105]—of which James Bradley Thayer and Felix Frankfurter thought "that the conception of the nation which Marshall derived from the Constitution and set forth [in it] is his greatest single judicial performance"[106]—and, perhaps, *Gibbons v. Ogden*[107] (but for different reasons), no more important case at constitutional law exists than the hallowed and revered *Marbury v. Madison*, which has been called "the rib of the Constitution."[108] All three were written by that great national constitutionalist, Chief Justice John Marshall, who had himself been a delegate to the Ratifying Convention of Virginia and a one-term congressman from that state. The background of the *Marbury* decision is so colorful, and the decision itself so important, that no treatment of the judicial process would be complete without at least a brief analysis of the case—one that is still frequently cited by courts not only in the United States but also in other countries, for example, Italy, Japan, and India!

Prompt enactment of the Judiciary Act of 1789 enabled the national judiciary to begin to function at once in the fledging United States, but questions of the existence of the power of judicial review and any possible challenge of it did not arise immediately. However, the issue was simmering. For example, in *Hayburn's case* Associate Justices Blair and Wilson, riding circuit in Pennsylvania in 1792, had refused to carry out a congressional statute that they deemed contrary to the Constitution, contending that they could not perform certain duties imposed on them by the law because they were not "judicial

---

[102] Act of September 24, 1789, c.20, 25, I Statutes at Large 73, 87.

[103] 1 Cranch 137.

[104] (New York: Columbia University Press, 1956), p. 11.

[105] 4 Wheaton 315 (1819).

[106] "John Marshall and the Judicial Function," in *Government Under Law* (Cambridge: Harvard University Press, 1956), p. 8. For an incisive study and analysis of Thayer's influential "reasonable doubt" test, see Sanford B. Gabin, *Judicial Review and the Reasonable Doubt Test* (Port Washington, NY: Kennikat Press Corp., 1980).

[107] 9 Wheaton 1 (1824).

[108] Glendon A. Schubert, *Constitutional Politics* (New York: Holt, Rinehart and Winston, 1960), p. 178.

in nature."[109] Together with District Judge Peters they were to pass on disputed pension claims of invalid war veterans, with *their* determination subject to review by the Secretary of War and Congress! If nothing else, this judicial refusal to carry out a legislative act called attention to the constitutional problem. Three years later, in *Van Horne's Lessee v. Dorrance*[110] Justice William Paterson—who had been a delegate to the Constitutional Convention from New Jersey—held for the Court: "Whatever may be the case in other countries, yet in this *there can be no doubt that every act of the Legislature repugnant to the Constitution, is absolutely void.*"[111] A similar judgment was expressed by Justice Samuel Chase on another occasion soon thereafter.[112]

Moreover, the Supreme Court had struck down at least two relatively minor *state* enactments,[113] although, in fact, the second of these decisions was of considerable importance because it held state laws subject to treaties by ruling that the Anglo-American Peace Treaty overrode a Virginia law on the delicate and potentially explosive issue of debts owed to British subjects by Americans.[114] Furthermore, depending on the historical source, the Supreme Court even held an insignificant *federal* pension claim law unconstitutional in the case of *United States v. Yale Todd*, which was decided in 1794 but not officially reported until it became a footnote almost sixty years later in *United States v. Ferreira*.[115] Nevertheless, this was evidently the first instance of the declaration of unconstitutionality of a federal statute. Finally, two years after *Yale Todd*, the Court—with three of its six justices not participating—expressly *upheld* a congressional statute imposing a duty on carriages as not being a "direct tax" and therefore not unconstitutional.[116] (Exactly ninety-nine years later the Supreme Court in effect overruled this decision in the *Second Income Tax Case*,[117] thus precipitating the Sixteenth Amendment.) Yet regardless of these aforegone instances of incipient concern with judicial review, it was not until 1803 and *Marbury v. Madison* that matters actually came to a climax.

The Factual Setting. The second President of the United States, John Adams, had been defeated in his bid for re-election in 1800 by his political arch-rival, Thomas Jefferson. Laboring desperately to salvage something for his prostate Federalist party, Adams was determined to pack the federal judiciary with as many judgeships as humanly and statutorily possible. With the aid of a more than obliging lame-duck Federalist Congress, which passed both

---

[109] 2 Dallas 409 (1792). See also the unreported *Chandler v. Secretary of War* (dec. 2/14/1794).
[110] 2 Dallas 304 (1795).
[111] Ibid., at 308. (Italics supplied.)
[112] *Cooper v. Telfair*, 2 Dallas 14 (1800) at 19.
[113] *Clerke v. Harwood*, 3 Dallas 342 (1797) and *Ware v. Hylton*, 3 Dallas 199 (1796).
[114] *Ware v. Hylton*, loc. cit.
[115] 13 Howard 40 (1851)
[116] *Hylton v. United States*, 3 Dallas 171 (1796).
[117] *Pollock v. Farmers Loan & Trust Co.*, 158 U.S. 601 (1895).

the Circuit Court Act[118] and the District of Columbia Organic Law Act early in 1801, Adams, before leaving office on March 3, 1801, was able to nominate, have approved by the Senate, and commission the following into office: sixteen new circuit judges (under the Circuit Court Act), forty-two new Justices of the Peace (under the District of Columbia Act), and one Chief Justice of the U.S. Supreme Court—his own Secretary of State, the forty-five-year-old staunch Federalist John Marshall (who in 1798 had refused Washington's offer of an Associate Justiceship). These nominees have often been called "Adams' Midnight Judges" because the President devoted his waning hours in office to signing their commissions of appointment.

It fell to the outgoing premier of the cabinet—Marshall, whose appointment Adams came to regard as the single most important act of his administration (just as President Hoover would ultimately regard his of Cardozo more than 125 years later)—to affix to them the Great Seal of the United States and then to deliver the new judgeship commissions to the various appointees. But Marshall, at once fatigued and exhilarated on Inauguration Eve, failed to deliver seventeen of the forty-two Justices of the Peace commissions, although, aided by his brother James, he worked until late into the evening and indeed had taken care of all the important new circuit judgeships plus most of the other appointments. However, he would begin his first full day as Chief Justice in the morning, a post to which he had been appointed almost two months earlier upon the resignation of the elderly and feeble Oliver Ellsworth in favor of a diplomatic position,[119] and upon John Jay's summary refusal to accept Adam's proffered second appointment as Chief Justice—duly confirmed by the Senate—because, as Jay felt, the Court, at the head of a judicial "system so defective," lacked "energy, weight, and dignity."[120] As head of the Court, Marshall would have the somewhat less than delightful duty of administering the oath of the Presidency to his avowed political enemy (and distant cousin) Thomas Jefferson, who would later frequently refer to Marshall as "that gloomy malignity." He left the undelivered commissions to the incoming Secretary of State, James Madison.[121] The stage

---

[118]The Act, which was repealed in March 1802 at Jefferson's insistence, also provided that the next vacancy on the Supreme Court should *not* be filled, thus reducing the Court's membership from six to five and thereby rendering impossible any automatic vacancy-filling appointment by the incoming Jefferson, a "Democratic-Republican" rather than a Federalist. Barely one year later the new President succeeded in having Congress reestablish the membership at six.

[119]See Albert J. Beveridge, *The Life of John Marshall* (Boston: Houghton Mifflin Co., 1919).

[120]See Frank Monaghan's biography, *John Jay: Defender of Liberty* (New York: The Bobbs-Merrill Co., 1935). See p. 357 *infra*, for additional data on the matter.

[121]For a penetrating analysis of the more technical aspects of *Marbury v. Madison*, see Justice Harold H. Burton's article, "The Cornerstone of Constitutional Law: The Extraordinary Case of *Marbury v. Madison*," 36 *American Bar Association Journal* 805 (October 1950). See also the more historical piece by John A. Garraty, "The Case of the Missing Commissions," in his *Quarrels that Have Shaped the Constitution* (New York: Harper & Row, 1964),

was thus set for a towering battle of three veritable titans of the early days of Constitution and Nation.

Preliminaries. Angry because of the sustained packing of the judiciary with Federalist appointees, Jefferson on taking office was delighted to find the seventeen undelivered Justice of the Peace commissions on the desk of the Secretary of State (Madison arrived somewhat later). The new President, subsequently seconded enthusiastically by his new Secretary of State, determined not to deliver them, declaring that the " . . . nominations crowded in by Mr. Adams after he knew he was not appointing for himself I treat as mere nullities."[122] And, according to one account, the commissions at issue were "disposed of with the other waste paper and rubbish of the office."[123] Neither subsequent pleas nor threats by such disappointed office-seekers as William Marbury were to sway them. Marbury, a forty-one-year-old Washingtonian, and three other staunch Federalists—Denis Ramsay, William Harper, and Robert Townshend Hooe—subsequently sought aid of counsel and hired Charles Lee, Attorney General under George Washington and John Adams.

Lee turned to the law and to the courts. He found what he believed to be the applicable law in a provision of the Judiciary Act of 1789: Section 13 of that important statute extended to the Supreme Court of the United States the power to issue a *writ of mandamus* (Latin for "we command"), an old Anglo-Saxon writ used as early as the twelgth-century reign of Henry II, commanding a public official to perform his official, ministerial, nondiscretionary duty. Invoking that provision, Lee petitioned the Court for appropriate action, and, at the next term of the Court in 1803 (Congress's angry Jeffersonian majority having canceled the Court's 1802 term), *Marbury v. Madison* reached the original docket of the highest court of the land. It could readily have dismissed the petition for want of jurisdiction under the 1789 statute in this type of case, but, as will become apparent, this would hardly have suited the purposes of the Chief Justice. For presiding over the Supreme Court now, of course, was Jefferson's mortal political enemy and Adam's loyal supporter, John Marshall, who had transmitted an order to Madison, who promptly ignored it, to show cause why the requested writ of mandamus should not be issued against him. Surely Marshall's decision would be in favor of Marbury, especially in view of the seemingly clear language of Section 13!

Marshall, C. J., for the Court. But both the Federalists and the Jeffersonian Republicans had underestimated the boldness and judiciousness, the craftsmanship and shrewd political acumen, the farsightedness and statesmanship, and above all, the powerful dedication to the Constitution—*as he saw it and wanted to see it*—of the fourth Chief Justice of the U.S. Supreme Court. And it was John Marshall who spoke for the unanimous Court in a twenty-seven-

---

and a recent analysis by George L. Haskins, "Law Versus Politics in the Early Years of the Marshall Court," 130 *University of Pennsylvania Law Review* (November 1981), pp. 1–27.
[122]Warren, op. cit., vol. I, p. 201.
[123]Charles S. Hyneman, *The Supreme Court on Trial* (New York: Atherton Press, 1963), p. 75.

page opinion, despite the fact that he had a direct personal interest in the case at bar, which today would almost certainly result in self-disqualification (recusing) from the case. Whatever one may think of his failure to abstain, it is not difficult to agree with Professor Corwin that "his compact presentation of the case marches to its conclusion with all the precision of a demonstration of Euclid."[124] The Chief Justice was confronted with a dilemma: if he were to grant the writ in the face of almost certain disobedience by Madison, the Court would be powerless, and if he were to refuse to grant it, Jefferson would triumph.

Marshall's heart, of course, was on the side of Marbury's cause—which happened to be that of his fellow Federalists—and he did not hesitate to chide Jefferson and Madison from the bench, to castigate them for their "rascality." Moreover, he distinctly concurred with the plaintiff's contention that (1) he had a legal right to the commission and (2) the laws of the land afforded him a remedy. These 9,000 words of *obiter dicta* consumed twenty of the twenty-seven pages! But as to the remedy, Marshall—an experienced political savant, here confronted with an utterly political situation—announced unmistakably that a writ of mandamus, issued by the Supreme Court under Section 13 of the Judiciary Act, was definitely *not* such a remedy, for it was *unconstitutional!*

It was unconstitutional, explained Marshall for himself and his unanimous Associate Justices, Paterson, Chase, and Washington (Cushing and Moore not sitting in the case), because by *incorporating it into the Judiciary Act of 1789, Congress had added to the original jurisdiction of the Supreme Court by law*—an action which Article III, the judicial article of the Constitution, does not sanction. And, continued Marshall in an unprecedented, pithy, 1,500-word display of judicial self-abnegation combined with judicial assumption of power (for there is no doubt that judicial review,"the ultimate conservative response to the 'evils of democracy,'"[125] was a goal of the democracy-distrusting Federalists) in Section 13 Congress had given the Court a power it could not legally receive. (That section of the act had actually figured in earlier Supreme Court decisions, yet no one had chosen to raise the present constitutional issue.) "*An act repugnant to the Constitution is void,*" explained Marshall, thus echoing Hamilton's *Federalist* No. 78, and, in so stating the matter, he enunciated clearly the doctrine of judicial review.[126] He elaborated:

[124] A lecture at Princeton University, September 25, 1950.

[125] Wallace Mendelson, *Capitalism, Democracy, and the Supreme Court* (New York: Appleton-Century-Crofts, 1960), p. 20.

[126] For a different view, though wholly "pro" judicial review, see Charles L. Black, Jr., *The People and the Court: Judicial Review in a Democracy* (New York: The Macimillan Co., 1960), pp. 25ff. Black contends that judicial review had already been firmly established by then, and he calls a "myth" the usual belief that it was Marshall who gave it authoritative expression.

It is empahtically the province and duty of the judicial department to say what the law is. Those who apply the rule to particular cases, must of necessity expound and interpret that rule. . . . A law repugnant to the Constitution is void; . . . courts as well as other departments are bound by that instrument.[127]

Significance and Summary. In brief, John Marshall—thus ingeniously having managed to have his cake and eat it too, in what Senator Albert J. Beveridge of Indiana, his most famous biographer, perhaps somewhat extravagantly described as "a coup as bold in design and as daring as that by which the Constitution had been framed"[128]—clearly, cogently, and quite emphatically enunciated and interpreted three principles of the utmost significance to the young nation: (1) that the courts have the power of judicial review, (2) that the Constitution of the United States is the supreme law of the land, (3) that the *original* jurisdiction of the Supreme Court cannot be changed by simple law of Congress, since that particular jurisdiction is specifically limited by the language of the Constitution—although, plainly, the *appellate* jurisdiction may indeed be changed by simple legislation because the letter of the Constitution so permits.

This, of course, has been done since, with the most pertinent example being the intriguing post-Civil War case of *ex parte McCardle*.[129] Here the Supreme Court had under consideration an appeal, already argued before it in an 1868 *habeas corpus* proceeding, which was specifically authorized under a statute of 1867—having unanimously rejected the government's motion to dismiss it for want of jurisdiction—in which the constitutionality of one of the Reconstruction Acts was at issue. Fearful that the Court might declare the act involved unconstitutional, and thus conceivably strike a mortal blow against the entire Reconstruction program, Congress, over President Andrew Johnson's courageous but fruitless veto that March quickly amended the 1867 statute defining the appellate jurisdiction of the Supreme Court in these cases. Congress did this, in a rider to a customs and revenue appeals bill, by withdrawing from that jurisdiction direct appeals to the Supreme Court from the circuit courts in certain classes of *habeas corpus* proceedings, including the present one.[130] Incidentally, the majority of the Court who, led by Chief Justice Salmon P. Chase, had simply postponed action pending the legislative and executive moves, was far from displeased about the congressional victory,

---

[127] *Marbury v. Madison,* 1 Cranch 137 (1803).

[128] Op. cit., vol. 1, p. 223, and vol. III, p. 142.

[129] 7 Wallace 506 (1869). Colonel William H. McCardle, editor of the *Vicksburg [Miss.] Times* in the Fourth Reconstruction District, whose paper had been vociferously critical of Reconstruction policies and forces under the command of General Edward O. C. Ord, had been charged with numerous offenses, court-martialed, and sentenced to be shot.

[130] In a letter to his son, Battle, shortly before he died (he was released by the military in due course and never tried in civil court for his alleged crimes and lived to a ripe old age). McCardle wrote that the Supreme Court had actually agreed to decide the case in his favor before Congress acted, the vote being 5:3 to hold his arrest unconstitutional. (He did not say how he became privy to that data.)

although Associate Justices Field and Grier issued a bitter public dissent against what they viewed as an evasion of constitutional responsibility and deliberate procrastination. But the Court was unanimous in upholding the action of Congress—and the Reconstruction Acts were never tested by it.

Whether or not one accepts Leonard Baker's enthusiastic encomium, namely, that Marshall's opinion in *Marbury v. Maryland* "was one of civilization's finest hours, one of mankind's greatest achievements,"[131] the importance of Marshall's decision in *Marbury v. Madison* to American constitutional development can hardly be overestimated.[132] There is no question that judicial review is crucial to the governmental process in the United States under its federal character, its separation of powers principle—the whole nature of its constitutionalism. Yet it cannot be gainsaid that Marshall strained the judicial process in making *Marbury v. Madison* his vehicle for the announcement of the doctrine of the judicial veto. We have already noted that he should probably have disqualified himself from sitting in the case because of his direct and personal involvement with both its fundamental issue and its *dramatis personae*—after all, the case in effect arose out of his own negligence or apathy—and that, in any event, he did not really have to accept the case for review. He could readily have dismissed it for lack of original jurisdiction in this case. Moreover, based on available precedent, he could easily have interpreted Section 13 and its empowering provision—indeed, he probably should have—in such a manner as to raise no substantial questions regarding *substantive* statutory additions to the Court's original jurisdiction. For a good case could be made for the contention, based on the intent of its framers in the First Congress (which included future Chief Justice Oliver Ellsworth), that Section 13 signified nothing more than that the Court had the *procedural* power to grant writs of mandamus in all instances when such a remedy would be appropriate in the disposition of cases duly and properly brought before it, either on its original or its appellate docket. Specifically, the section stated that the Supreme Court could issue the writ to "persons holding office under the authority of the United States"—and the justices *had* issued that writ in earlier cases without questioning Section 13 for a moment.[133] By no means was Section 13 thus necessarily intended to enlarge the original jurisdiction of the Court, but Marshall now claimed that the Court could not issue a writ of mandamus *except* in cases that came to it on appeal from a lower court.

Yet none of the preceding suggested alternate courses of action would have suited Marshall's purposes—one of which also was to avoid the potential

---

[131] *John Marshall: A Life in Law* (New York: The Macmillan Co., 1974), p. 409.

[132] Marbury and his fellow litigants disappeared into the obscurity from which they had come at the conclusion of the case, although Marbury did become president of a Georgetown bank in 1814. He died in the same year as Marshall, 1835.

[133] See, for example, Beveridge's *Marshall, op. cit.*, vol. III, p. 130, fns. 1 and 2 and 1 Cranch, generally.

embarrassment that would have resulted from the almost certain defiance by President Jefferson. Having said and recognized that, however, we should acknowledge the genius of that powerful figure in American history and of the great service he performed in expounding the doctrine of judicial review when he did—a doctrine for which he fought hard in the Virginia Ratification Convention. Far from being a usurpation, it has powerful claims to authenticity, based on more than a century of history, a strong line of precedents, and convincing contemporary literature. That debate on the justification and wisdom of the doctrine ensued almost at once, and that it has never really ceased, merely serves to add stature to its progenitor.[134] In the words of Charles P. Curtis, John Marshall "snatched from the majority and offered to our courts, the function of rendering our political decencies and aspirations into immanent law. What we owe to Marshall is the opportunity he gave us of combining a reign of conscience with a republic."[135]

[134]For a thoughtfully advocative contention that John Marshall, far from being a "usurper" or a "judicial activist," merely "followed [the] basic design [of the Founding Fathers] to create a system in which the parts could no longer emasculate the whole," see Wallace Mendelson, "Was Chief Justice Marshall an Activist?" in S. C. Halpern and C. M. Lamb (eds.), *Supreme Court Activism and Restraint* (Lexington, Mass.: Lexington Books, 1982), pp. 57–76.

[135]"Review and Majority Rule," in *Supreme Court and Supreme Law*, ed., by Edmond Cahn (New York: Simon and Schuster, 1971), p. 198, Professor Cahn's own essay in his collection, "An American Constitution," is a fascinating analysis of both the wisdom *and* the justification of judicial review.

8

Judicial Review:
II—Controversy and
Limitations

JUDICIAL REVIEW IN A DEMOCRATIC STATE: SAINT OR SINNER?

That no other federal law, or section thereof, was declared unconstitutional by the Supreme Court between *Marbury v. Madison*[1] in 1803 and the *Dred Scott* case,[2] a full fifty-four years later, did not lessen the debate on the doctrine of judicial review. That it has remained fresh, indeed, and has lost none of its controversial characteristics, is testified to vividly and contemporarily by—to employ an obvious illustration—the widespread public, often emotion-charged, debate surrounding the unanimous decision for the Court by Chief Justice Warren in the 1954 *Segregation cases*[3] —in a sense the grandchildren of the Taney Court's decision in *Dred Scott*. The charge against the Warren Court: in holding compulsory segregation on account of race in the public schools to be a violation of the "equal protection of the laws" clause of the Fourteenth Amendment to the U.S. Constitution in the state cases, and the due "process of law" clause of the Fifth in the federal case, the Court had not *judged*, not *interpreted*, not *reviewed*, but *legislated*. Two decades later, to use an even more contemporary illustration, the same indictment would be levied against the Burger Court's historic and contentious *Abortion cases*[4] by what came to be known as the "pro-life" forces (with the "pro-choice" forces on the other side). The indictment of judicial legislation is

[1] 1 Cranch 137.
[2] *Dred Scott v. Sandford*, 19 Howard 393 (1857).
[3] *Brown v. Board of Education*, 347 U.S. 483 (1954) and *Bolling v. Sharpe*, 347 U.S. 497 (1954). *Brown* was a Kansas case; *Bolling* came from the District of Columbia.
[4] *Roe v. Wade* and *Doe v. Bolton*, 410 U.S. 113 and 410 U.S. 179 (1973), respectively.

directly related, of course, to the power and doctrine of judicial review, once characterized as "the people's institutionalized means of self-control."[5]

INVOKING AUTHORITY

Unfortunately, all too few professional observers of the judicial process and quite naturally even fewer laypersons, however informed they may be, are resolutely consistent in their attitude toward either judicial review or the institution that exercises the power. To abide by Paul A. Freund's exhortation that "criticism ... be informed by perspective and informed by philosophy"[6] is difficult. More often than not "it all depends whose ox is being gored," to employ Al Smith's pungent phrase. Yet it is entirely feasible to determine both articulate and reasonable "con" and "pro" positions regarding the doctrine without embracing the postures of the more passionate partisans of the controversy. Although a great deal of literature on the subject is available, we may well permit two of America's most honored and most literate governmental personages to speak for the two sides. It is fair to say that, had they not lived and functioned considerably more than a century apart, they would have respected and admired one another and would have made a worthy set of opponents in any public debate on the issue: Thomas Jefferson *con*, and Benjamin Cardozo *pro* judicial review! With due allowance for certain deviations, their points of view, even their verbiage, are today very much representative of the two divergent attitudes on the question.

Con. Although, as a strong believer in the necessity of an independent judiciary, he was in fact among the first to suggest judicial review as a means of harmonizing the federal system, and although evidence contained in at

---

[5]Charles L. Black, Jr., *The People and the Court: Judicial Review in a Democracy* (New York: The Macmillan Co., 1960), p. 20. For some other vital contemporary works on judicial review, with varying points of view, cf. Alexander M. Bickel, *The Least Dangerous Branch* (Indianapolis: The Bobs-Merrill Co., 1962) and his *The Supreme Court and the Idea of Progress* (New York: Harper & Row, 1970); Herbert Wechsler, *Principles, Politics and Fundamental Law* (Cambridge: Harvard University Press, 1961); Charles S. Hyneman, *The Supreme Court on Trial* (New York: Atherton Press, 1963); Howard E. Dean, *Judicial Review and Democracy* (New York: Random House, 1966); Arthur A. North, S. J., *The Supreme Court: Judicial Process and Judicial Politics* (New York: Appleton-Century-Crofts, 1966); Louis Lusky. *By What Right? A Commentary on the Supreme Court's Power to Revise the Constitution* (Charlottesville, Va: The Michie Co., 1975); Raoul Berger, *Government by Judiciary: The Transformation of the Fourteenth Amendment* (Cambridge: Harvard University Press, 1977); Jesse H. Choper, *Judicial Review and the National Political Process* (Chicago: University of Chicago Press, 1980); John Hart Ely, *Democracy and Distrust: A Theory of Judicial Review* (Cambridge: Harvard University Press, 1980); Sanford B. Gabin, *Judicial Review and the Reasonable Doubt Test* (New York: Kennikat Press, 1981); Arthur S. Miller, *Toward Increased Judicial Activism: The Political Role of the Supreme Court* (Westport, CT: Greenwood Press, 1982); and Michael J. Perry, *The Constitution, the Courts, and Human Rights: An Inquiry into the Legitimacy of Policy-Making by the Judiciary* (New Haven, CT: Yale University Press, 1982).

[6]*The Supreme Court of the United States* (Cleveland and New York: The World Publishing Co., 1961), p. 77.

least two letters written from Paris to James Madison is persuasive that Thomas Jefferson had favored some type or degree of direct judicial control at the time of the framing of the Constitution in Philadelphia and even almost two years later,[7] the great Virginian certainly never accepted the notion of judicial review as it was subsequently expounded by his political opponent, John Marshall. Some observers[8] trace the genesis of his hostility to the enforcement of the hated Alien and Sedition Acts of 1798—prior to this he was demonstrably not opposed to judicial review, at least not in theory. In any event, Jefferson's opposition to overriding judicial power was based on two major concepts: first, that the doctrine of judicial review—and certainly as applied by Marshall, for he saw no one else do it—violates that of the constitutionally mandated theory of the separation of powers, and second, that it represents a patent denial of the veritable popular will, the majority will, as expressed by the sovereign people through their duly elected representatives "in Congress assembled" (and in any other properly constituted legislative body). That the second assertion did not, however, blind him to the potential excesses of these representatives, is indicated clearly in one of his letters to Madison, to whom he voiced the fear that " . . . the tyranny of the legislatures is the most formidable dread at present and will be for many years."[9]

Nonetheless, Jefferson vehemently rejected the contention that the Founding Fathers had intended to give to one of the three branches the sole right to prescribe rules for the government of the others "and to that one, too, which is unelected by and independent of the nation." He insisted that each of the three branches, being independent, "has an equal right to decide for itself the meaning of the Constitution in the cases submitted to its action; where it is to act ultimately without appeal; [and that] the court is neither more learned nor more objective than the political branches of the government.[10] He did grant its salutory role in protecting constitutional rights.[11] Yet in fine, to Jefferson, the doctrine of judicial review, with its inherent possibilities of leading to judicial supremacy, was both elitist and antidemocratic—although, of course, on close examination one sees that all agencies of government have their "undemocratic" aspects. Moreover, it is entirely possible to categorize the sage of Monticello's stance on judicial review not so much

---

[7]December 20, 1787, and March 15, 1789.

[8]E.g., Wallace Mendelson "Jefferson on Judicial Review: Consistency through Change," 29 University of Chicago Law Review (Winter 1962), pp. 327–37.

[9]Letter of March 15, 1789.

[10]From his letter to Judge Spencer Roane of the Virginia Supreme Court, September 6, 1819. See also his letter to Abigail Adams, September 11, 1804, when he wrote: "You seem to think it devolves on the judges to decide on the validity of the Secition Law. But nothing in the Constitution gives them a right to decide for the executive, more than the executive to decide for them." As quoted by Saul K. Padover, A Jefferson Profile (New York: The John Day Co., 1956), p. 154.

[11]Letter to William Jarvis, September 28, 1820.

as opposition *qua* opposition, but opposition based on its presence as a tool in the hands of John Marshall.

Jefferson's position on the nonexclusiveness of the power to interpret the Constitution has been echoed frequently since, but by none better than Justice John B. Gibson of the Supreme Court of Pennsylvania, a contemporary of Jefferson and essentially an advocate of legislative supremacy, who was probably the most able adversary of judicial review in his day. From that bench in 1825, in his now famous dissenting opinion in *Eakin v. Raub*,[12] in which his colleagues upheld the power of Pennsylvania's state courts to declare state statutes unconstitutional, Gibson, insisting that "[t]he oath to support the Constitution is not peculiar to the judges, but is taken indiscriminately by every officer of the government...," lucidly and forcefully challenged Marshall's argument in *Marbury v. Madison* along the lines of the Jeffersonian response. One of his key points was the classic concept of popular democracy—that it is a "postulate in the theory of our government ... that the people are wise, virtuous, and competent to manage their own affairs."[13] Yet Gibson had apparently modified his viewpoint twenty years later. When an attorney, pleading his case before the Pennsylvania Supreme Court, cited the Gibson dissent in *Eakin v. Raub*, that Justice replied from the bench that he had changed his opinion for two reasons: one, that the Pennsylvania Constitutional Convention of 1838, by remaining silent on judicial review, had "sanctioned the pretensions of the court to deal freely with the act of the legislature," and two, "from experience of the necessity of the case."[14] This does not necessarily connote a change of mind, but it assuredly does indicate at least that Justice Gibson, true to his philosophy of the representative legislative function, had accepted the latter's "surrender" to the doctrine. It ought to be noted here that Gibson never intended his opposition to judicial review to extend to the *federal* judiciary's power to declare *state* laws unconstitutional. For *that* power he perceived as clearly stipulated by the obligations of Article VI of the U.S. Constitution, the supremacy clause. Nonetheless, when Gibson, supported by John C. Calhoun, was under consideration for the U.S. Supreme Court vacancy caused by Justice Bushrod Washington's death in 1829, his well-known *Eakin* rationale truncated his candidacy.

Pro. Although he greatly admired Jefferson as a human being, a democratic leader, and a political philosopher, Benjamin N. Cardozo, who served for eighteen years on the New York State Court of Appeals as well as an Associate Justice of the U.S. Supreme Court for the regrettably brief period from 1932 to 1938, disagreed strongly with Jefferson's approach to, and rejection of, judicial review. Cardozo anchored his belief in that doctrine on the firm conviction that although it must be employed cautiously and sparingly, as he

---

[12] 12 S. & R. (Pa. S. Ct.) 330.

[13] Ibid., at 355.

[14] See *Norris v. Clymer*, 2 Pa. St. 277 (1845) at 281, as reported by Robert F. Cushman, *Cases in Constitutional Law*, 6th ed. (Englewood Cliffs, NJ: Prentice-Hall, 1984), p. 12.

himself did, it serves nonetheless as a necessary and proper check on possible excesses by both the federal and state legislatures. But it would be utterly wrong to label him a "judicial activist." More than a decade prior to his universally hailed appointment to the Supreme Court, where he mounted the seat vacated by Justice Oliver Wendell Holmes, Jr., Cardozo had advanced his key contention that it is the *restraining influence of its presence* rather than the frequency of its application that renders judicial review so vital to the governmental process in the United States of America. His characteristically beautiful style and language must be quoted directly:

> By conscious or subconscious influence, the presence of this restraining power aloof in the background, but none the less always in reserve, *tends to stabilize and rationalize the legislative judgment*, to infuse it with the glow of principle, to hold the standard aloft and visible for those who must run the race and keep the faith. . . . The restraining power of the judiciary does not manifest its chief worth in the few cases in which the legislature has gone beyond the lines that mark the limits of discretion. Rather shall we find *its chief worth in making vocal and audible the ideals that might otherwise be silenced, in giving them continuity of life and expression, in guiding and directing choice within the limits where choice ranges.* This function should preserve to the courts the power that now belongs to them; if only the power is exercised with insight into social values, and with suppleness of adaption to changing social needs.[15]

The great jurist whom Cardozo had succeeded was familiar with this passage, fully concurred in its sentiment and credo, and had practiced it throughout his three decades on the highest bench of the land. However, although Holmes was willing to grant that the United States would not "come to an end if we lost our power to declare an Act of Congress void," he firmly insisted that " . . . the Union would be imperiled if we could not make that declaration as to the laws of the several states."[16] U.S. Circuit Court Judge Learned Hand, the distinguished contemporary of Holmes and Cardozo, frequently echoed this Holmesian creed. But Hand went considerably further than Holmes when, writing several years after his retirement from the bench, he endeavored to devise a test that would provide another modification of the doctrine. Although agreeing that the Supreme Court must have the power and authority to review *grants* of power to and by Congress, he believed that it should not possess these sanctions regarding "a review of how the power has been *exercised*."[17] It is difficult to see how such an amendment of the doctrine of judicial review would not wound it seriously, if not fatally.

---

[15]Benjamin N. Cardozo, *The Nature of the Judicial Process* (New Haven, CT: Yale University Press, 1921), pp. 93–94. (Italics supplied.)

[16]Oliver Wendell Holmes, Jr., "Law and the Court," in *Collected Legal Papers* (New York: Harcourt, Brace, 1920), p. 295.

[17]Learned Hand, *The Bill of Rights* (Cambridge: Harvard University Press, 1958), pps. 66, 93–94. (Italics supplied.)

The Jefferson and Cardozo viewpoints—and their attempted modifications—have manifold ardent and articulate adherents.[18] Yet there is no longer any doubt that judicial review is a permanent fixture in the American structure and operation of government, notwithstanding the repeated frontal and guerilla attacks from both public and private sources.[19] It is, after all, an essential adjunct of our constitutional firmament, a normal fact of American governmental life—ringingly reconfirmed in such seminal decisions as *United States v. Nixon* in 1974 and *Immigration and Naturalization Service v. Chadha* in 1983.[20]

DRAWING THE LINE—OR ATTEMPTING TO DO SO

Directly and intimately entwined in the controversy over the doctrine of judicial review is the thus perpetually voiced charge that the Supreme Court of the United States—and in varying lesser degrees the lower componets of the judiciary—is guilty of *judicial legislating;* in other words, that many of its decisions are tantamount to legislating rather than juding. More than often not, this indictment of the judiciary admits, and indeed grants, that the Court must have the power to *interpret* legislation and, if "absolutely necessary," hold unconstitutional a law that is *clearly* contrary to the Constitution— although no yardstick is provided on the connotation of the modifier "clearly." But this school of thought insists that a line msut be drawn between the exercise of judicial *judgment* and the imposition of judicial *will.* Judicial will is accordingly equated with legislating, presumably reserved to Congress and the legislatures of the fifty states. Like all fine lines, the one between

---

[18]For a conveniently "tabularized" list of arguments in favor and against judicial review, see Alan F. Westin's "Introduction" to the paperback edition of Charles A. Beard's classic, *The Supreme Court and the Constitution* (Englewood Cliffs, NJ: Prentice-Hall, 1962), pp. 6–7.

[19]For summary analysis of attempted legislative checks on the power, see Sheldon D. Elliott, "Court-Curbing Proposals in Congress," 33 *Notre Dame Lawyer* (August 1958), pp. 597–605. Five excellent books dealing with the problem are Walter F. Murphy, *Congress and the Court* (Chicago: University of Chicago Press, 1962); C. Herman Pritchett, *Congress versus the Supreme Court* (Minneapolis: University of Minnesota Press, 1961); Raoul Berger, *Congress v. The Supreme Court* (Cambridge: Harvard University Press, 1969); Adam C. Breckenridge, *Congress Against the Court* (Lincoln: University of Nebraska Press, 1971); and John R. Schmidhauser and Larry L. Berg, *The Supreme Court and Congress: Conflict and Interaction, 1945–1968* (New York: The Free Press, 1972). See also the important study in the late 1960s, undertaken by Stuart S. Nagel, which demonstrates that between 1802 and 1959 there were seven periods of high-frequency and an equal number of low-frequency Court-curbing legislation. He found a total of 165 bills introduced in Congress durint those 157 years that were designed to curb the power of the Court: 49 were aimed at changing or eliminating the power of judicial review, 49 at changing its personnel, 45 at limiting its jurisdiction, and 22 represented miscellaneous "curbing" proposals. See "Court Curbing Periods in American History," in his *The Legal Process from a Behavioral Perspective* (Homewood, IL: Dorsey Press, 1969), pp. 285–93. In the first five months of 1981 alone, 23 Court-curbing proposals were introduced in the House and 4 in the Senate!

[20]417 U.S. 683 and 462 U.S. 919, respectively.

"interpreting" or "judging" and "legislating" is highly tenuous. How is it to be drawn? by whom? where? under what circumstances? Clearly there is no simple or single response to these questions, so crucial to line-drawing in general, and the line at issue in particular—ever conscious of Justice Robert H. Jackson's memorable exhortation *cum caveat*, one year prior to his death in 1954, that "We are not final because we are infallible; but we are infallible only because we are final."[21]

JUDICIAL LEGISLATING

The polar extremes in the endless controversy over the absence or presence of the concept of judicial legislating become readily apparent in the following two quotes, taken from active and honorable participants on both sides of the aisle—institutionally as well as philosophically. Early in 1930, rising on the floor of the U.S. Senate, of which he was one of the finest and most purposeful members for many years, George W. Norris of Nebraska, the "gentle-knight of progressive ideals," shouted:

> We have a legislative body, called the Hosue of Representatives, of over 400 men. We have another legislative body, called the Senate, of less than 100 men. We have, in reality, another legislative body, called the Supreme Court, of nine men; and they are more powerful than all the others put together.[22]

The diametrically opposite point of view is represented in a passage from an address to the New York State Bar Association in 1893 by Justice David Brewer of the U.S. Supreme Court:

> They [courts and judges] make no law, they establish no policy, they never enter into the domain of popular action. They do not govern. Their functions in relation to the state are limited to seeing that popular action does not trespass upon right and justice as it exists in written constitutions and natural law.[23]

Both expressions are equally extreme in their thesis, of course; they represent gross oversimplifications, notwithstanding the sincerity and conviction of the two speakers involved. Indeed, most of the Justices of the highest tribunal do not claim to have a pat answer to the vexatious question presented by the controversy over *the line*. But they have often come to grips with the crux of the matter in recognizing the human element that is so inevitably involved in the judicial process. In the realistic words of Justice John H. Clarke:

> I have never known any judges, no difference how austere of manner, who discharged their judicial duties in an atmosphere of pure, unadulterated rea-

---

[21] *Brown v. Allen*, 344 U.S. 443 (1953), at 540, concurring opinion.
[22] *Congressional Record*, 71 Cong. 2d Sess., Vol. 72, Part 4, p. 3566 (February 13, 1930).
[23] Address to the New York State Bar Association, *Proceedings* (1893).

son. Alas! we are all "the common growth of Mother Earth,"—even those of us who wear the long robe.[24]

The blunt-spoken Justice McReynolds insisted that a judge should not be "an amorphous dummy, unspotted by human emotions"—and he was more than a little spotted! "Judges are men, not disembodied spirits," once remarked Justice Frankfurter; " . . . as men they respond to human situations. They do not reside in a vacuum." "Our judges are not monks or scientists," wrote Chief Justice Warren, "but participants in the living stream of our national life, steering the law between the dangers of rigidity on the one hand and formlessness on the other."[25] He thus echoed the realistic appraisal made by Thomas Reed Powell four decades earlier, who had commented:

> Judges have preferences for social policies as you and I. They form their judgments after the varying fashions in which you and I form ours. They have hands, organs, dimensions, senses, affections, passions. They are warmed by the same winter and summer and by the same ideas as a layman is.[26]

In any event, the Justices are agreed that they endeavor to judge the cases and controversies that reach the Court in accordance with the perceived commands of the Constitution and the laws of the land. There is no doubt that the nine Justices—in fact the judges on all levels of the judicial process—necessarily "legislate" in interpreting constitutional phraseology. The question is how much and how far they are justified in such judicial legislating. The often quoted jurist, however apocryphal the story may be, who responded to the question of whether judges make law replied, "Of course we do; made some myself last Monday," is undoubtedly close to the truth. One of the wisest among those who graced the bench of the Supreme Court, the revered Justice Holmes—who has been so well described as the official judicial philospher for the modern age[27]—also recognized "without hesitation" that judges *do and must legislate*"; but he added that they " . . . can do so only interstitially; they are confined from molar to molecular motions."[28] In a valedictory interview, Chief Justice Warren readily acknowledged that the Court, in effect, does make law:

> It doesn't make it consciously, it doesn't do it by intending to usurp the role of Congress but because of the very nature of our job. When two litigants come into court, one says the act of Congress means this, the other says the act of Congress means the opposite of that, and we say the act of Congress

---

[24]Hoyt L. Warner, *The Life of Mr. Justice Clarke* (Cleveland: Western Reserve University Press, 1959), p. 69.

[25]"The Law and the Future," 52 *Fortune* 106 (November 1955).

[26]"The Logic and Rhetoric of Constitutional Law," 15 *Journal of Philosophy, Psychology, and Scientific Method* 656 (1918).

[27]Fred V. Cahill, Jr., *Judicial Legislation* (New York: The Ronald Press, 1952), p. 32.

[28]*Southern Pacific Co. v. Jensen*, 244 U.S. 205 (1916), at 221. (Italics supplied.)

means something—either one of the two or something in between. We are making law, aren't we?[29]

Chief Justice Marshall, however, who was fully aware of the problem at issue, nevertheless insisted that "judicial power, as contradistinguished from the power of the law, has no existence. Courts are the mere instruments of the law, and can will nothing."[30] Yet this statesman, who is generally recognized as the most influential, competent, and successful of all the Chief Justices to date and is ranked among the two or three most powerful and influential jurists ever to sit on the Supreme Court, was hardly loath to interpret broadly the Constitution and legislation passed under its authority—and in accordance with what Justice Holmes later referred to as "the felt necessities of the time." After all, had not that same Marshall written, in the great *McCulloch v. Maryland* decision, that our laws were made under a Constitution that was "intended to endure for ages to come, and consequently,to be adapted to the various *crises* of human affairs"?[31] Probably no Justice has done more of this "adapting," and more incisively, than did Chief Justice Marshall, who often reminded his fellow citizens that "we must never forget that it is a *Constitution* we are expounding!"[32] Did he *interpret* or did he *legislate?* Undoubtedly both.

More on the Line and on the Goring of Oxen. Marshall's long-term successor, Chief Justice Roger B. Taney, stared into the heart of the problem when, in rendering the majority opinion in the *Dred Scott* case, he held that the Constitution

> speaks not only in the same words, but with the same meaning and intent with which it spoke when it came from the hands of its framers, and was voted on and adopted by the people of the United States. Any other rule of construction would abrogate the judicial character of this court, and make it the mere reflex of the popular opinion or passion of the day.[33]

But the *Dred Scott* decision has been denounced more often as sheer "legislation" than any other decision of the Court, with the possible exception of the 1954 *Segregation cases.*[34] When he was informed of the decision in *Dred Scott,* Senator Hale of New Hampshire introduced a resolution to *abolish* the Supreme Court. Yet again depending on the point of view, those people who hailed the 1857 *Dred Scott* judgment as "statesmanlike interpretation" would

---

[29]Sacramento, California, June 26, 1969, as quoted in *The New York Times,* June 27, 1969, p. 17.

[30]*Osborn v. United States Bank,* 9 Wheaton 739 (1824) at 865.

[31]Wheaton 315 (1819) at 413. (Italics in original.)

[32]Justice Frankfurter considered this Marshall statement to be "the single most important utterance in the literature of constitutional law—most important because most comprehensive and comprehending." ("John Marshall and the Judicial Function," 69 *Harvard Law Review* 217 [1955] at 219.)

[33]*Dred Scott v. Sandford,* 19 Howard 393 (1857).

[34]*Brown v. Board of Education,* 347 U.S. 483 (1954) and *Bolling v. Sharpe,* 347 U.S. 497 (1954).

have violently denounced the 1954 *Segregation cases* as "blatant legislation," whereas the champions of the latter decisions would have roundly denounced the former! Indeed, some of the torrent of abuse poured on the Court by the latter day *Segregation cases* critics is almost identical in verbiage to that employed by the enemies of their Southern ancestors, the Radical Republicans of the North, in attacking *Dred Scott!* Could it be that the popular judgment does, in fact, depend on whose ox is being gored?

Justice Owen J. Roberts, always searching for, it not inevitably contributing to, a modicum of consistency on the bench, attempted to draw the line once and for all in 1936—"the slot machine theory," commented Roscoe Pound acidly—when he spoke for a majority of six in the significant case of *United States v. Butler*, in which the Court struck down the New Deal's Agricultural Adjustment Act of 1933:

> When an act of Congress is appropriately challenged in the Courts as not conforming to the constitutional mandate the judicial branch of the Government has only one duty—*to lay the article of the Constutition which is invoked beside the statute which is challenged and to decide whether the latter squares with the former.*[35]

"Bravo," applauded the *opponents* of the New Deal, "great judicial statesmanship, proper and precise interpretation of the Constitution!" "An unwarranted, outrageous assumption of legislative authority," countered the *proponents* of the New Deal, "arrogant disregard of constitutional limitations of judicial power." And President Roosevelt, scarcely one year after *Butler*, moved unsuccessfully to pack the Court by statutory provision, setting off one of the most interesting, most heated, and most sustained controversies in the entire history of Court and nation.[36]

It was in the *Butler* case that the issue was perhaps most nearly joined by Justice Harlan Fiske Stone, not too many years later to be the Chief Justice, when he dissented from the opinion of the majority and admonished the members on that side of the decision that

> [w]hile unconstitutional exercise of power by the executive and legislative branches is subject to judicial restraint, *the only check on our own exercise of power is our own sense of self-restraint.* . . . Courts are not the only agency of government that must be assumed to have capacity to govern. . . . For the removal of unwise laws from the statute books appeal lies not to the courts but to the ballot and to the processes of democratic government.[37]

---

[35] 297 U.S. 1 (1936) at 62. (Italics supplied.)

[36] For two engagingly written accounts, see Joseph Alsop and Turner Catledge, *The 168 Days* (New York: Doubleday, Doran, 1938) and Leonard Baker, *Back to Back: The Duel Between F.D.R. and the Supreme Court* (New York: The Macmillan Co., 1967).

[37] *United States v. Butler*, 297 U.S. 1 (1936) at 78, 88. (Italics supplied.) In an intriguing, if hardly noncontroversial, analysis, Professor Bradley C. Canon identifies six specific elements or dimensions that give general structure to the concept of "judicial activism": (1) *Majoritari-*

This would seem to be as close to the facts of judicial life as is attainable. In a sense, and although he would very likely have disapproved of the comparison, the Stone comment was almost an echo of a famous statement made twenty years earlier by Charles Evans Hughes while he was the Republican presidential nominee. He had just become an ex-Associate Justice of the U.S. Supreme Court, was an ex-Governor of New York, a future member of the Permanent Court of Arbitration and Judge of the Permanent Court of International Justice, a future Secretary of State in the Administrations of Presidents Harding and Coolidge, and ultimately would ascend the Court for a second tenure, this time as Chief Justice. While stumping during the campaign, a campaign which almost won him the presidency, he publicly repeated a pronouncement he had made in 1907 while he was still governor: "*We are under Constitution, but the Constitution is what the judges say it is. . . .*"[38] That assertion represents both too drastic and too simplified an analysis of the complex position of the judiciary and the Court, and it is subject to considerable substantive modification. Surely, in the final analysis, the Constitution is or becomes what the people of the nation want it to be or to become—a fact of political life that is very much on the mind of judges—and it must be considered, as Holmes said, "in the light of our whole experience and not merely in that of what was said a hundred years ago." In the words of his long-time friend and colleague, Brandeis:

> Our Constitution is not a straight jacket. It is a living organism. As such it is capable of growth—of expansion and adaptation to new conditions. Growth implies changes, political, economic, and social. Growth which is significant manifests itself rather in intellectual and moral conceptions than in material things.[39]

Moreover, for the sake of argument, the Constitution may well be what the judges say it is, but this by no means makes certain appropriate compliance, as has been repeatedly demonstrated. With these essential qualifications in mind, however, the Hughes campaign statement, coupled with the

---

anism—the degree to which policies adopted through democratic processes are judicially negated. (2) *Interpretive stability*—the degree to which earlier court decisions, doctrines, or intrpretations are altered. (3) *Interpretive fidelity*—the degree to which constitutional provisions are interpreted contrary to the clear intentions of other drafters or the clear implications of the language used. (4) *Substance/democratic process distinction*—the degree to which judicial decisions make substantive policy rather than affect the preservation of democratic political processes. (5) *Specificity of policy*—the degree to which a judicial decision establishes policy itself as opposed to leaving discretion to other agencies or individuals. (6) *Availability of an alternate policymaker*—the degree to which a judicial decision supersedes serious consideration of the same problem by other governmental agencies. "Defining the Dimensions of Judicial Activism," 66 *Judicature* 6 (December–January 1983), pp. 237–47.

[38] Charles Evans Hughes, *Addresses*, 2d ed. (New York: Putnam, 1916), p. 185 (Italics supplied.)

[39] An unpublished passage in *United States v. Moreland*, 258 U.S. 433 (1922), as quoted by Alexander Bickel in his *The Supreme Court and the Idea of Progress* (New York: Harper & Row, 1970), p. 20.

Stone dissent in the *Butler* case, could serve largely as the definitive view of the Court's attitude. It has frequently been echoed by other articulate members of the highest bench, such as that philosophical devotee of British legislative supremacy and majority rule, Justice Frankfurter, who, in dissenting in the controversial expatriation case of *Trop v. Dulles*, lectured that

> All power is, in Madison's phrase, "of an encroaching nature." . . . Judicial power is not immune against this human weakness. It must also be on guard against encroaching beyond its proper bounds, and not the less so since *the only restraint upon it is self-restraint.* . . .[40]

Vast differences about this aspect of the vexatious line exist now, and have always existed, among the Justices themselves, but most, in fact probably all, would candidly subscribe to the essence of the suggested Stone–Hughes formula, however at variance their interpretation and application of it may be. One thing is above all clear—in the realistic words of Justice Cardozo, not only one of the most proficient and most beloved Justices ever to sit on the Supreme Court but also one of its finest and most haunting stylists: *"The great tides and currents which engulf the rest of men, do not turn aside in their course, and pass the judges idly by."*[41]

Justice George Sutherland, one of the six-man majority in the *Butler* case, justified judicial activism—which he and his jurisprudential soulmates, Justices Van Devanter, McReynolds, and Butler applied chiefly in the economic *laisser faire* camp—as natural judicial involvement. As one Sutherland student analyzed his posture, the oath of office taken by each Justice required him to decide cases in terms of his own best judgment. As he put it: "Self-restraint, therefore, had no place among judicial duties. To surrender one's deliberate judgment, indeed, except as it might be modified by the persuasion of those holding different views, would constitute a violation of his oath of office."[42] To quote Sutherland directly from his dissenting opinion in the 1937 "switch-in-time-that-saved-nine" *West Coast Hotel* case:

> Self-restraint belongs in the domain of will and not of judgment. The check upon the judge is that imposed by his oath of office, by the Constitution, and by his own conscientious and informed convictions. . . .[43]

It is delicious irony that his jurisprudential and philosophical opposite, Justice William O. Douglas, could just as easily have written these words and applied them to *his* posture in the realm of civil rights and liberties! In any event, as Justice Frankfurter put the matter cogently, the Court cannot, in the long run, escape judging; it must adjudicate; it must decide. Not one to judge

---

[40]356 U.S. 86 (1958) at 113. (Italics supplied.)

[41]Benjamin N. Cardozo, *The Nature of the Judicial Process*, op. cit. p. 168 (Italics supplied.)

[42]Carl Brent Swisher, *The Growth of Constitutional Power in the United States*, 2d ed. (Chicago: University of Chicago Press, 1963), p. 221.

[43]*West Coast Hotel Co. v. Parrish*, 300 U.S. 379, at 402.

lightly or hastily—Professor Wallace Mendelson has aptly called him a "humilitarian" among jurists with respect to the judicial process[44]—Frankfurter, while deeply dedicated to the concept of judicial self-restraint, nevertheless clearly faced the problem in his concurring opinion in the well-known *Sweezy* case:

> To be sure, this [opinion] is a conclusion based on a judicial judgment in balancing two contending principles—the right of a citizen to political privacy, as protected by the Fourteenth Amendment, and the right of the State to self-protection. And striking the balance implies the exercise of judgment. This is the inescapable judicial task in giving substantive content, legally enforced, to the Due Process Clause, and it is a task ultimately committed to this Court. It must not be an exercise of whim or will. *It must be an overriding judgment founded on something much deeper and more justifiable than personal preference. As far as it lies within human limitations, it must be impersonal judgment. It must rest on fundamental presuppositions rooted in history to which widespread acceptance may fairly be attributed.* Such a judgment must be arrived at in a spirit of humility when it counters the judgment of the State's highest court. *But, in the end, judgment cannot be escaped—the judgment of this Court.*[45]

That this awesome and even agonizing duty of finding and drawing the line between judicial will and judicial judgment in rendering a necessary decision conscientiously is not confined to the highest level of the federal judiciary may be illustrated by a decision of the Supreme Court of Michigan. In a consortium case replete with human factors, a closely divided (4:3) Court not only reversed a lower court decision but negated precedent of long standing. Speaking for the majority, Justice Talbot Smith recognized that the decision represented a drastic departure from the past and would surely be viewed as judicial legislating. Yet having braved the expected storm, he admitted that the decision to permit the wife of a man seriously injured in an automobile accident to sue for loss of consortium (i.e., marital comfort, affection, and companship) marked a stride away from the "outworn legal views" derived from old English and Roman law that a wife is merely a "vassal, chattel, and household drudge." He concluded:

> Were we to rule upon precedent alone, we would have no trouble with this case. We would simply tell this woman to be gone, and take her shattered husband with her.... Legally today, the wife stands on a par with her husband.... *The obstacles to the wife's [court] action were judge-invented and they are herewith judge-destroyed.*[46]

---

[44]"Mr. Justice Frankfurter—Law and Choice," 10 *Vanderbilt Law Review* 333 (February 1957).

[45]*Sweezy v. New Hampshire, by Wyman, Attorney-General,* 354 U.S. 234 (1957) at 266–67. (Italics supplied.)

[46]*Montgomery v. Stephan,* 359 Mich. 33 (1960). Eight years later the New York Court of Appeals handed down an almost identical decision, and also by a 4:3 vote! (*Millington v. Southern Elevator Co.,* 293 N.Y.S. 2d 305.)

The anticipated critical storm of charges of crass judicial legislating broke over the heads of author and Court at once. Yet, perhaps Justice Smith had simply been unusually frank in writing his opinion as he did—rather than disguising it in judicial semantics. Perhaps he had not been unaware of the famous expression of judicial philosophy by Chancellor Kent of New York a century and a half earlier:

> I saw where justice lay, and the moral issue decided the court [Kent] half the time; and I then sat down to search the authorities. . . . I might once in a while be embarrassed by a technical rule, but I almost always found principles suited to my views of the case. . . .[47]

In summary, depending, of course, on the facts and posture of each individual case, both verbiage and line are very much matters of degree. But, as Justice Frankfurter took pains to admonish, to say that courts make law just as legislatures do is ". . . to deny essential features in the history of our democracy. It denies that legislation and adjudication have had different lines of growth, serve vitally different purposes, function under different conditions, and bear different responsibilities."[48]

JUDGES LIMITED: THE TAUGHT TRADITION OF THE LAW

Moreover, it must be clearly understood that judges are not free agents in rendering their decisions, regardless of the impression given by some. Again in Frankfurter's words: "We do not sit like a kadi under a tree dispensing justice according to considerations of individual expediency."[49] A deplorable tendency exists in the mind of the public to oversimplify the process of judicial decision making, the area of government obviously least understood by the average citizen. Although it may perhaps overstate the case somewhat, there is much merit in the contention of the just-cited Justice Talbot Smith, that "we are rigidly bound within walls that are unseen" (by the layperson).[50] These walls are built of the heritage of the law, the spirit of the Anglo-Saxon law, the impact of the cases as they come down through the years—in brief, *the taught tradition of the law*. No one has expressed the heart of the matter better than Justice Cardozo:

> A jurist is not to innovate at pleasure. He is not a knight-errant, roaming at will in pursuit of his own ideal of beauty or of goodness. He is to draw his inspiration from consecrated principles. He is not to yield to spasmodic sentiment, to vague and unregulated benevolence. He is to exercise a discretion

[47]William Kent, ed., *The Memoirs and Letters of James Kent* (Boston: Little, Brown and Co., 1898), pp. 158–59.
[48]"Reflections on Reading Statutes," 2 *The Record* 213 (June 1947).
[49]*Terminiello v. Chicago*, 337 U.S. 1 (1949) at 11.
[50]Statement to author, August 15, 1958 (Madison, Wisconsin).

informed by tradition, methodized by analogy, disciplined by system, and subordinated to the primordial necessity of order in the social life.[51]

Among the vital aspects of his taught tradition of judicial self-restraint[52] are an abiding sense of judicial integrity, a close and necessary regard for the rules of procedure, considerations of equal treatment before the law, the deference shown to legislative enactments, judicial recognition of the realities of the cultural, ideological, and institutional setting the judges share with their fellow citizens, not excluding the political realities, and *stare decisis*, the adherence to precedent.

STARE DECISIS

The desirability and, indeed, the need for certainty in planning our affairs, in both their internal (professional) and external aspects, render reliance on precedent an attractive and useful doctrine. "Imitation of the past," observed Justice Holmes, "until we have a clear reason for change, no more needs justification than appetite. It is a form of the inevitable to be accepted until we have a clear vision of what different things we want."[53] Yet, be it noted at once that *stare decisis* is a principle of policy and not a mechanical formula of adherence to the latest decision, "however recent and questionable, when such adherence involves collision with a prior doctrine more embracing in its scope, intrinsically sounder, and verified by experience."[54] "*Stare decisis*," in the words of Justice Brandeis,

is usually the wise policy, because in most matters it is more important that the applicable rule of law be settled than it be settled right.... This is commonly true even where the error is a matter of serious concern, *provided correction can be had by legislation.* But in cases involving the Federal Constitution, where correction through legislative action is practically impossible, this Court has often overruled its earlier decisions. The Court bows to the lessons of experience and the force of better reasoning, recognizes that the process of trial and error, so fruitful in the physical sciences, is appropriate also in the judicial function.[55]

---

[51] Benjamin N. Cardozo, *The Nature of the Judicial Process*, op. cit., p. 141.

[52] Professor Philip B. Kurland makes six basic assumptions for the doctrine of judicial self-restraint:

> One is history and the obligation that constitutionalism imposes to adhere to the essential meaning put in the document by its framers. A second is the intrinsically undemocratic nature of the Supreme Court. A third is a corollary to the second, an abiding respect for the judgments of those branches of the government that are elected representatives of their constituents. A fourth is the recognition that judicial error at this level is more difficult of correction than other forms of judicial action. A fifth is respect for the judgments of earlier courts. But [sixth], the essential feature of judicial restraint that has gained most attention and aroused the greatest doubts probably because few men are themselves big enough to abide by its command—is the notion of rejection of personal preference. [*Mr. Justice Frankfurter and the Supreme Court* (Chicago: University of Chicago Press, 1971), p. 5.]

[53] "Holdsworth's English Law," in *Collected Legal Papers* (Boston: A. Harcourt, 1920), p. 290.

[54] Justice Frankfurter, for the Court, in *Helvering v. Hallock*, 309 U.S. 106 (1940) at 110.

[55] *Burnet v. Coronado Oil & Gas Co.*, 285 U.S. 293 (1932) at 406. (Italics supplied.)

Thus, quoting the first sentence of the preceding statement some fourteen years later, Justice Douglas went on to observe that "... throughout the history of the Court *stare decisis* has had only a limited application in the field of constitutional law. And it is a wise policy which largely restricts it to those areas of the law *where correction can be had by legislation.* Otherwise the Court loses the flexibility necessary if it is to serve the need of succeeding generations."[56]

The doctrine of *stare decisis* requires a careful weighing in each doubtful case "of the advantages of adherence to precedent and the necessity for judicially planned social and economic progress."[57] The law, as Dean Pound has stated, must be stable and yet it cannot stand still. Or, as Viscount Kilmuir, then the Lord High Chancellor of Britain, told a distinguished audience of legal scholars in 1960: "Critics are apt to allege that we treat existing law with such reverence that every antique is replaced unaltered. I believe in an occasional spring cleaning."[58] Just such a "spring cleaning" occurred in an intriguing 9:0 decision by the Court in 1975, when it ruled that liability in a maritime collision must be *apportioned* among the ships involved according to their *proportionate* ("relative") degree of responsibility, thus abolishing the then 120-year-old rule that damages be divided "equally."[59]

Reliance on precedent presents difficult problems to the judge, especially since the question to be resolved comes, normally speaking, to a *choice* of precedents. "Sometimes," commented Justice Jackson wistfully in his last book, "one is tempted to quote his former self, not only to pay his respects to the author, but to demonstrate the consistency of his views, if not their correctness."[60] Precedents abound and not all precedents are of equal rank; a good many judges generally seem to accord considerably more sanctity to very old and hallowed "precedents," such as most of Chief Justice John Marshall's decisions, than to those of relatively recent vintage. Progress, in any event, does not stand still, and a precedent may have to be overruled or reversed in time. "Our assurance that our children will live, as we have, under a constitutional democracy," commented the then U.S. Solicitor General Stanley F. Reed, "rests upon the power of the form of government to adjust itself.... The position of the Supreme Court on *stare decisis* makes that adjustment possible."[61] In at least 150 decisions made between 1810 and 1984, the Supreme Court of the United States *overruled* its own previous deter-

[56]*New York v. United States,* 322 U.S. 572 (1946) at 590–91 (Italics supplied.)

[57]Robert A. Sprecher, "The Development of the Doctrine of Stare Decisis and the Extent to Which It Should Be Applied," 31 *American Bar Association Journal* 501–9 (1945).

[58]Speech on the occasion of the dedication ceremony of the University of Chicago Law Center, April 30, 1960.

[59]*United States v. Reliable Transfer Co.,* 421 U.S. 397, overruling *Schooner Catherine v. Dickinson,* 17 Howard 170 (1854).

[60]Robert H. Jackson, *The Supreme Court in the American System of Government* (Cambridge: Harvard University Press, 1955), p. 11.

[61]"Stare Decisis," 35 *Pennsylvania Bar Association Journal Quarterly* 150 (1938).

minations.[62] Many additional cases are *distinguished* from precedent, which is somehow viewed as a less disrespectful device. "From age to age," commented Justice Douglas in an able treatment of the issue,

> the problem of constitutional adjudication is the same. It is to keep the power of government unrestrained by the social or economic theories that one set of judges may entertain. *It is to keep one age unfettered by the fears or limited vision of another.*[63]

Or, as Justice Potter Stewart admitted after twelve years on the Court, in an important 1970 labor case, quoting Justice Frankfurter: "Wisdom too often never comes, and so one ought not to reject it merely because it comes late."[64] Precedents, as Justice Talbot Smith said, being "judges-invented," may thus be "judge-destroyed." The judge must speak and through him society speaks. His function, as one leading student of constitutional law put it so lucidly, is "necessarily something more than to be a grammarian . . . [but] it is decidely less than to be a zealot."[65] Lord Coke's practice to the contrary, few, if any, judges today would create a maxim out of whole cloth and then recite, "as the old maxim saith. . . ." (Yet it was the same Lord Coke who lauded *stare decisis* as "the known certaintie of the law which is the saftie of all."[66]) "The rule of *stare decisis*," in New York Court of Appeals' Chief Judge Stanley H. Fuld's words, "was intended not to effect a petrifying rigidity, but to assure the justice that flows from certainty and stability. If, instead, adherence to precedent offers not justice but unfairness, not certainty but doubt and confusion, it loses its right to survive and no principle constrains us to follow it."[67]

To sum up, the judge is assuredly not a free agent. Indeed, the second Justice John Marshall Harlan underscored that fact of judicial life poignantly, when he wrote a concurring memo in a coerced confession case:

> [D]espite my strong inclination to join in the dissent of my Brother White, I can find no acceptable avenue of escape from *Miranda v. Arizona* [384 U.S. 436, 1966] in judging this case. . . . Therefore, and purely out of respect for *stare decisis*, I reluctantly feel compelled to acquiesce in today's decision of the Court, at the same time observing that the constitutional condemnation of this perfectly sensible, proper, and indeed commendable police work, highlights the unsoundness of *Miranda*.[68]

---

[62]For a list of ninety of these instances and a discussion of the entire "overruling" problem, see A. P. Blaustein and A. H. Field, "Overruling Opinions in the Supreme Court," 57 *Michigan Law Review* 2 (1957).

[63]William O. Douglas, *Stare Decisis* (New York: The Association of the Bar of the City of New York, 1949), p. 31.

[64]*Boys Market v. Retail Clerks' Union*, 398 U.S. 235 (1970) at 255.

[65]Paul A. Freund, *The Christian Science Monitor*, March 27, 1956, p. 16.

[66]Robert von Moschzisker, "Stare Decisis," 37 *Harvard Law Review* 409 (1924) at 429.

[67]*Time Magazine*, May 10, 1971, p. 43.

[68]*Orozco v. Texas*, 394 U.S. 324 (1969) at 327–28.

But Stewart joined White's dissent, responding to Harlan's action with the statement: "It seems to me that those who dissented [in Miranda] remain free not only to express our continuing disagreement with that decision, but also to oppose any broadening of its impact."[69]

No matter what it may be termed or how it may be styled, of necessity the judge "makes" the law—to some degree, at least. The delicate question will ever be how to aid its development without violating the confines of the constitutional structure. Let Justice Cardozo state the case:

> ... [but] no doubt the limits for the judges are narrower. He legislates only between gaps. He fills the open spaces of the law. How far he may go without traveling beyond the walls of the interstices cannot be staked out for him upon a chart. He must learn it for himself as he gains the sense of fitness and proportion that comes with years of the practice of an art.... None the less, within the confines of those open spaces and those of precedent and traditions, choice moves with a freedom which stamps its actions as creative. The law which is the resulting product is not found, but made. The process, being legislative, demands the legislator's wisdom.[70]

Surely, to echo a comment once made by Max Lerner, "... judicial decisions are not babies brought by constitutional storks." They are the carefully considered, more or less practical, judgments by the human beings who, sensitive to their calling, wield judicial authority—as judges, not as legislators.[71]

OTHER LIMITATIONS ON JUDICIAL POWER AND EFFECTIVENESS

Yet there remain several other qualifying considerations—checks may be a better term—on judicial authority, even at the highest level of the federal courts. First, the Supreme Court's rulings may be effectively reversed by other participants in the processes of government; second, they are almost inevitably responsive to overall policy formulations, sooner or later; third, for enforcement they must look to the executive branch of the government; and fourth, as demonstrated in chapter 5, compliance with them is not necessarily automatic.

---

[69] Ibid., at 331. Justice Tom C. Clark retrospectively contended that he had developed what a biographer called a "no subsequent dissent" rule. Not entirely convincing on the record, the rule professed a policy of dissenting from a precedent *only* during the term in which it was established. Thereafter, it would be the law of the land, and Clark would consider himself bound by it—unless he could later marshal a majority of his colleagues in establishing a new precedent in the older one's place. See Dennis D. Dorin, "Tom C. Clark: The Justice as Administrator," 61 *Judicature* 6 (December–January 1978).

[70] *The Nature of the Judicial Process,* op. cit., pp. 113–15.

[71] See the perceptive historical analysis by Robert J. Harris, "Judicial Review: Vagaries and Varieties," 38 *The Journal of Politics* 173 (August 1976).

REVERSING THE COURT

In a variety of ways, although not without some toil and trouble, the Supreme Court of the United States may be reversed by direct or indirect action of other institutions in the political process. Although its decisions unquestionably constitute the supreme law of the land—as they must if government under law is to have any meaning in American society—and are thus final and binding, even that high body may have the last say "only for a time." This truth is readily documented by briefly examining the fate of the aforementioned 134 or 135 cases in which the Court, as of the autumn of 1985 and unanimously in almost one-third of these instances—had struck down as unconstitutional provisions of federal laws.

On several, although not numerous, occasions Congress passed legislation that has had the effect of reversing the Court either totally or in substantial measure—as it did in passing the Federal Employers' Liability Act of April 22, 1908, designed to replace that of 1906 which the Court had declared unconstitutional 5:4 as an illegal invasion of instrastate commerce in the *First Employers' Liability cases*[72] earlier in 1908. Since Congress seemed to have corrected the alleged constitutional deficiency of the earlier statute, the Court found no difficulty in unanimously upholding it when the test came in the *Second Employers' Liability cases*[73] in 1912. Two better-known recent illustrations are Congress's 1978 overturning by statutory amendment of Title VII of the Civil Rights Act of 1964 of a 1976 Court ruling that had upheld private employers in their refusal to provide "disability benefits" for pregnant workers[74], and its speedy 1982 legislative overturning of a 1981 Court holding that had upheld a federal statute declaring retirement pension pay to regular and reserve army commissioned officers "off limits" in divorce settlements.[75] In other instances the circumstances or situation of the controversy had either changed or become moot, thus rendering insignificant or totally unimportant the erstwhile decision handed down by the Court—as, for example, the withdrawal of improperly delegated legislative power by action of the legislature or the revocation or amendment of a challendged administrative or executive order, both actions coming prior to the full effect of the Court's decisions.[76] In some instances it simply *distinguished* cases from often very similar earlier

---

[72] 207 U.S. 463.

[73] 223 U.S. 1. Another instance was the Court's declaration of unconstitutionality of a federal municipal bankruptcy act in 1936 (*Ashton v. Cameron County Water Improvement District*, 298 U.S. 513), which Congress "corrected" with the enactment of a slightly revised law that was upheld by the Court two years later (*United States v. Bekins*, 304 U.S. 27).

[74] *General Electric Co. v. Gilbert*, 429 U.S. 125. For two tables concentrating on congressional reversal action, see Robert A. Dahl's updated 1957 article (as explained in fn. 91 *infra*) in Thomas P. Jahnige and Sheldon Goldman, eds., "The Supreme Court's Role in National Policy Making," in *The Federal Judicial System: Readings in Process and Behavior* (New York: Holt, Rinehart and Winston, 1968), pp. 358–63.

[75] *McCarty v. McCarty*, 453 U.S. 210.

[76] E.g., *Lewis Publishing Co. v. Wyman*, 228 U.S. 610 (1913).

decisions—as it did when it upheld the second New Deal Agricultural Act of 1938 in *Mulford v. Smith*[77] in 1939 even though it had struck down the first A.A.A. in *U.S. v. Butler*[78] three years earlier. True, the statutes were not exactly alike, and the personnel of the Court had changed, but the essential features, impact, and purpose of the statutes were unchanged. In other cases, the Court itself questioned, reversed, modified, or even negated its earlier judgments—by no means solely because of changes in its personnel—as it did so prominently in the four *Covert-Krueger cases* between 1955 and 1960.[79] And in six to nine (depending on one's point of view)instances, Amendments to the Constitution were passed in order to reverse the Court: the *Eleventh* (1798), reversing the 1793 decision in *Chisholm v. Georgia*,[80] by amending the original jurisdiction of the Supreme Court to hear certain suits against the several states; the *Thirteenth, Fourteenth,* and *Fifteenth* (the Civil War Amendments, adopted in 1865, 1868, and 1870, respectively), reversing various Supreme Court decisions, including the *Dred Scott case*,[81] dealing with suffrage, slavery, and civil rights; the *Sixteenth* (1913), the Income Tax Amendment, giving Congress power to tax incomes from whatever source derived, thereby effectively reversing the 1895 decisions in *Pollock v. Farmers' Loan and Trust Co.*,[82] which had held various income tax *statutes*, designed to accomplish the same end, unconstitutional as a violation of Article 1, Section 9, Clause 4; and the *Twenty-Sixth*, overturning the Court's 1970 ruling in *Oregon v. Mitchell*[83] by granting the franchise to eighteen-year-olds in *state* elections (the Court having upheld the statute insofar as it dealt with *federal* elections). Some would include the *Seventeenth* (direct election of U.S. Senators), the *Nineteenth* (women's suffrage, 1920), and the *Twenty-Fourth* (abolition of the poll tax in federal elections). The adoption of a constitutional amendment is the most authoritative and most certain method of reversing the Court, but it is also usually the most difficult politically to attain and almost always the most time-consuming.[84]

Going beyond the 134 provisions struck down by it, the Court *overruled* 138 of its decisions between 1937 and 1985, beginning with the immediate post-"switch-in-time-that-saved-nine" era. Prior to this, the Court had over-

---

[77] 307 U.S. 38.

[78] 297 U.S. 1.

[79] 'Kinsella v. Krueger, 357 U.S. 470 and Reid v. Covert 351 U.S. 487 (June 11, 1956); 352 U.S. 901 (November 5, 1956); 354 U.S. 1 (June 10, 1957); and Kinsella v. Singleton 361 U.S. 234 and Grisham v. Hagan, 361 U.S. 278 (January 18, 1960).

[80] 2 Dallas 419.

[81] Dred Scott v. Sandford, 19 Howard 393 (1857).

[82] 158 U.S. 601 and 157 U.S. 429.

[83] 400 U.S. 112.

[84] By spring 1985 some 10,000 amendments had been proposed in Congress, but only 33 were passed by both houses and sent to the states for ratification procedures. See Gary L. McDowell, "On Meddling with the Constitution," 5 *Journal of Contemporary Studies* 4 (Fall 1982), pp. 8–9.

ruled itself at least 44 times. (These two figures cover not only overrulings of provisions previously held unconstitutional, but also those made on other than constitutional grounds.)[85] Unless it seems to be absolutely necessary, however, the Court is disinclined to resort to the strong concept of *overruling*. Thus, in only 10 instances among the aforementioned 134 did the Court in subsequent decisions *specifically* and *literally* acknowledge an overruling— as it did, for example, in upholding the entire federal Fair Labor Standards Act of 1938 in the case of *United States v. Darby*[86] in 1941. There, among others, addressing itself to the child labor provisions of that statute, it *specifically* overruled its 1918 decision in *Hammer v. Dagenhart*,[87] in which it had declared the federal Keating-Owen Child Labor Law of 1916 unconstitutional. An interesting example of the Court's overruling one of its own precedents of long standing came in 1976 when by an 8:0 vote, it unanimously overturned an 1871 (!) decision[88]—*Low v. Austin*, 13 Wall. 29—declaring it "wrongly decided" and thereby opened the way for state and local governments to place taxes on imported goods still in their original package but stored in warehouses, a type of taxation heretofore forbidden by the holding in the *Low v. Austin* case. Overruling differs from reversing in definition: technically speaking, a case may be *reversed* only on rehearing; thus, the original decision and the reversing decision are applicable to the *identical case*. An example of that procedure is the Court's decision in *Jones v. Opelika*, 316 U.S. 584, on June 8, 1942, upholding 5:4 an Opelika, Alabama, statute which required payment of the usual license tax or fee even by those groups (here the Jehovah Witnesses) that claimed exemption on grounds of freedom of religion—a decision that the Court vacated 5:4 on rehearing less than eleven months later, in *Jones v. Opelika*, 319 U.S. 103, on May 3, 1943, and then *reversed* on the same day in *Murdock v. Pennsylvania*, 319 U.S. 105.

The various statistics just cited do not take into account the many instances in which the Court overrules precedents *sub silentio*—that is, when it overrules an earlier decision without saying so but the effect is clearly the same as an expressed overruling—as it did on several occasions in the last quarter of the past century and the first quarter of this century in the realm of commerce and taxation. Nor do these figures account for those instances in which Congress, disagreeing with the Supreme Court's reading of a statute, simply rewrites or repeals it. For example, between 1944 and 1984 alone, Congress took sixty-three actions in economic matters that collectively overturned eighty-nine Supreme Court rulings.

Thus, although most of the Supreme Court's decision on questions of constitutionality last, quite a few are ultimately modified or neutralized by the

---

[85] For all overrulings between 1790 and 1972, see *The Constitution of the United States of America* (Washington, DC: U.S. Government Printing Office, 1973).
[86] 312 U.S. 100.
[87] 247 U.S. 251.
[88] *Michelin Tire Co. v. Wages*, 423 U.S. 276.

Court itself or by valid action of other branches of the government, led by Congress. America's system of judicial review, as Professor Freund has noted cogently, indeed produces frustrations, but it has a saving grace of resiliency.

POLICY FORMULATIONS AND CONSIDERATIONS

In any case, the policy views of the Court, the members of which, after all, are "children of their times,"[89] never remain for long out of line with the policy views of the lawmaking majority—with the probable, but not inevitable, exception of decisions involving the Bill of Rights, particularly those made between 1940–49 and 1954–57 when the Court on a good number of occasions stood as a veritable bastion against the popular majority viewpoint. On major public policy issues, both the Chief Executive and Congress may be expected to succeed, speaking generally and *in the long run*— "... and the run must not be too long either!," as Professor Edward S. Corwin once observed—[90] although in the short run they may well have to bow. If the Court is to thrive, as Professor Wallace Mendelson has said so well, it "must respect the social forces that determine elections and other major political settlements. No court can long withstand the morals of its era."[91] It is the "child of its time." The Court, however, cannot be a mere register of public opinion; it must be the latter's sporadic molder and leader. Yet, in the final analysis, as Francis Biddle well noted, its Justices "must not get away too far from life and should continually touch earth for renewed vitality."[92] An intriguing suggestion to formalize the issue was dramatically, albeit unsuccessfully, propounded by President Theodore Roosevelt in a speech in Columbus, Ohio, in 1912 when he called for a popular right of petition to bring before the voters "at some subsequent election" whether or not the judicial "interpretation of the Constitution" in a particular case, about which the public feels strongly, "is to be sustained ... or reversed," that is recalled![93]

Judicial alignment with the other two major branches on overriding policy matters may not always follow axiomatically, but it comes very close to real-

---

[89]Robert G. McCloskey, *The American Supreme Court* (Chicago: University of Chicago Press, 1961), p. 182.

[90]*Court Over Constitution* (Princeton NJ: Princeton University Press, 1938), p. 127.

[91]*Justices Black and Frankfurter: Conflict in the Court*, 2d ed. (Chicago: University of Chicago Press, 1966), pp. 75–76. On this point see also the intriguing, although somewhat interpretatively misleading, article by Robert A. Dahl, "Decision-Making in a Democracy: The Supreme Court as a National Policy-Maker," 6 *Journal of Public Law* 279 (1957), updated a decade later (see fn. 74), *supra*). For a telling response to Dahl, pointing out convincingly that the Court's policy-making influence is considerably more extensive than Dahl's rather narrowly based thesis would have us believe, see Jonathan D. Casper, "The Supreme Court and National Policy Making," 70 *The American Political Science Review* 1 (March 1976), pp. 50–63.

[92]*Justice Holmes, Natural Law, and the Supreme Court* (New York: The Macmillan Co., 1961), p. 73.

[93]See Stephen Stagner, "The Recall of Judicial Decisions and the Due Process Debate," 24 *The American Journal of Legal History* 3 (July 1980), pp. 257–58.

ity. Some observers of the scene have even contended that far from representing a dependable means of preventing "legislative tyranny," judicial review of national policy seems to have but marginal value.[94] Whatever the actual merits of this contentious judgment may be, the Court is well aware of the limitations on its powers. Justice Frankfurter, the "conscience of the Court" during most of his length tenure, thus addressed himself to the question of reversing the Supreme Court in his now well-known separate concurring opinion in the unanimously decided Little Rock School case, *Cooper v. Aaron*,[95] in which he quoted at length from his concurring opinion in the *United Mine Workers* case of 1947:

> Even this court has the last say only for a time. Being composed of fallible men, it may err. But revision of its errors must be by orderly process of law. The court may be asked to reconsider its decisions, and this has been done successfully again and again throughout our history. Or, what this court has deemed its duty to decide may be changed by legislation; as it often has been, and, on occasion, by constitutional amendment.[96]

He might have added that one of the major catalysts in revision and reconsideration is the inevitably changing personnel composition of the Court—yet any recognition of that crucial element in judicial decision-making must carefully guard against a pat and oversimplified catch-all analysis of its significance. In any event, reversal of judicial action is possible, and it has frequently been effectuated. Decisions running counter to the broad consensus simply dod not last *in the long run*. The toast offered in 1801 at a dinner honoring the Justices, "To the Judiciary of the United States—independent of party, independent of power, independent of popularity!"[97] merits skeptical analysis. Still, time and again the Court has come through nobly when the constitutional chips have been down, as it did in July 1974, when it was confronted with the expansive claims of Executive privilege advanced by President Nixon during the Watergate controversy. Its unanimous 8:0 ruling[98] against these claims constituted a—probably *the*—major catalyst in his subsequent resignation from office on August 9 of that fateful year.

---

[94]E.g., S. Sidney Ulmer, "Judicial Review as Political Behavior: A Temporary Check on Congress," 4 *Administrative Science Quarterly* 426 (March 1960).

[95]358 U.S. 1 (1958).

[96]*United States v. United Mine Workers*, 330 U.S. 258. An embattled U.S. District Court Judge, James B. McMillan, sitting in key desegregation cases in the Western District or North Carolina, put it similarly:

> In the long run . . . a majority of the people will have their way. . . . If the Constitution is amended or the higher courts rule so as to allow continued segregation in the local public schools, this court will have to be governed by such amendment or decisions. In the meanwhile the duty of this and other courts is to seek to follow the Constitution in the light of the existing rulings of the Supreme Court, and under the belief that the constitutional rights of people should not be swept away by temporary local or national public opinion or political manipulation. [Swann v. Charlotte-Mecklenburg Board of Education, 318 F. Supp. 786.].

[97]As quoted in *Connecticut Courant*, February 9 and 16, 1801.

[98]*United States v. Nixon*, 417 U.S. 683.

COMPLIANCE AND ENFORCEMENT

But there is more to be said. Aspects of chapter 5 demonstrated at some length that the judgments of the Supreme Court of the United States are not necessarily accepted as automatically binding by those who ought to be bound. A decision may be simply ignored, as was proved by, for example, the continuation of the practice of "released time"[99] in numerous public secondary schools in situations and settings identical to that struck down as an unconstitutional violation of the principle of separation of state and church in *McCollum v. Board of Education.*[100] In 1966, four years after the decisions in the *Prayer and Bible Reading cases,*[101] some 60 percent of the states reported continued violations of the Court's mandates.[102] Or a decision may be circumvented, and even opposed by force, to which the history of the 1954 and 1955 *Segregation cases* and their progeny bear ample witness. And there is the already described host of calculated, interminable delays in compliance.[103]

Moreover, with the very few exceptions of its original jurisdiction docket cases, the Court formulates *general* policy. It is the lower federal and state courts, as the case may be, that *apply* it, presumably "not inconsistent with this opinion," as the Supreme Court's mandate normally reads. In so applying the opinion, the lower courts may, and often do, materially modify the Supreme Court's determination. These modifications, moreover, are not at all astonishing in view of the not infrequent habit of Supreme Court Justices to mix dogma with dicta. On the other hand, some of the so-called modifications or interpretations clearly have been little short of outright defiance—especially by state courts.[104] Indeed, as an astute observer of judicial power noted confidently, "a material gap exists between what the Court orders to be done and what the people will do."[105]

There is also the obvious fact that, lacking any source of physical power of its own, the Supreme Court depends on the political branches of the government for the enforcement of its mandates, in particular on the Chief Executive, who has the vital obligation to ascertain obedience to all Court orders.

[99] For an explanation and an analysis of "released time" see my *Freedom and the Court: Civil Rights and Liberties in the United States,* 4th ed. (New York: Oxford University Press, 1982), ch. 6.

[100] 333 U.S. 203 (1948).

[101] *Engel v. Vitale,* 370 U. S. 421 (1962) and *Abington School District v. Schempp* and *Murray v. Curlett,* 374 U.S. 203 (1963).

[102] See Ellis Katz, "Patterns of Compliance with the *Schempp* Decision," 14 *Journal of Public Law* 2 (1966); and Henry J. Abraham and Robert R. Benedetti, "The State Attorney-General: A Friend of the Court?" 117 *University of Pennsylvania Law Review* 795 (April 1969).

[103] See ch. 5, pp. 235–45, *supra.*

[104] On this general point see the informative article by Walter Murphy. "Lower Court Checks upon Supreme Court Power," 53 *American Political Scienc Review* (December 1959), pp. 1017–31.

[105] Choper, *Judicial Review and the National Political Process,* op. cit., p. 150, fn. 5.

If the Court fails to obtain that cooperation in those instances in which it is vital for compliance, it necessarily stands helplessly on the sidelines. The most famous case in point is the comment, perhaps apocryphal, by President Andrew Jackson who, according to Chief Justice Marshall's biographer, exploded, "John Marshal has made his decision:—*now let him enforce it!*"[106] The outburst reputedly occurred as a result of Marshall's decision in *Worcester v. Georgia,*[107] in which his Court upheld the rights of the Cherokee Indians in a dispute with Georgia, and in which he strongly implied in his opinion that it was the President's duty to honor and back the Cherokee Nation's rights under federal law. Aprocryphal or not, the Jackson comment illustrates the Court's dependence and its quandary when the necessary executive support is not forthcoming. Its effectiveness in the absence of the executive sword is as limited as its operations in general would be without the necessary appropriations from the legislative purse, and the legislative assent to its jurisdictional and procedural needs. In essence, as Justice Jackson starkly stated this fact of judicial life, " . . . [the Court] can perform but one function—that of deciding litigations—and can proceed in no manner except by the judicial process.[108] Thus, he echoed an oft-quoted remark by Justice Samuel Miller that "in the division of the powers of government between the three great departments, executive, legislative, and judicial, the judicial is the weakest for purposes of self-protection and for the enforcement of the power which it exercises."[109] But not only do we often expect too much from the Court, we let it, or wish it would, settle *policy* matters that ought to be settled by one of the other two branches, notably the legislative, but which for a variety of reasons, chiefly political, are not.[110] Glaring illustrations of such policy matters are reapportionment/redistricting, segregation/desegregation—"let the Court decide!" urged Senators Paul Douglas (D.-Ill.) and Kenneth Keating (R.-N.Y.) during the acrimonious debates on controversial provisions of the Civil Rights Act of 1964[111]—and aspects of criminal justice. And there is a host of others in which the proverbial buck has been passed eagerly to the judicial branch!

---

[106] Albert J. Beveridge, *The Life of John Marshall,* vol. 4 (Boston: Houghton Mifflin Co., 1919), p. 551. (Italics supplied.)

[107] 6 Peters 515 (1832). Worcester, a citizen of Vermont, was a missionary preaching the gospel, who had entered the territory of the Cherokee Nation under President Jackson's authorization, but without the permission that the state of Georgia required by statute. The Court declared the statute unconstitutional; yet, ironically, Jackson now sided with Georgia! It may well be that he did so because he did not wish to drive Georgia into the South Carolina-led tariff nullification camp.

[108] *The Supreme Court in the American System of Government* (Cambridge: Harvard University Press, 1955), p. 12.

[109] *In re Neagle,* 135 U.S. 1 (1890), at 63.

[110] On that point see the address by Justice Harlan at dedication ceremonies of the American Bar Center at Chicago, Illinois, August 13, 1963.

[111] 110 *Congressional Record* 13434 (1964).

MACHTKAMPF: THE SUPREME COURT
IN THE POLITICAL POWER STRUGGLE

Whatever the implications of the preceding paragaphs, the Supreme Court has indeed been a participant in what may be viewed as a continuous struggle by the three "separated branches" of the federal government to attain a position of dominance, if not ultimate control, in the American political system. Because it lacks the potent weapons of the other two branches, especially weapons that would aid its self-protection and its enforcement of the powers it exercises, the Court has neccessarily been less prominent in this *Machtkampf* (struggle for power); but its own important tool of judicial review has provided it with a genuine measure of authority. And, as just pointed out, it has often been propelled into action precisely because the other organs of government have failed to fulfill their own responsibilities.

Victory in the *Machtkampf* of the three branches has been in the form of supremacy, which has alternated from branch to branch; although sometimes the struggle has been featured by a quasi-alliance of two branches against the third over a period of time. A pertinent example is the frustrated and frustrating protracted effort of the closely allied New Deal legislature and New Deal executive commencing in 1933, which, on many major issues, had to wait for victory over the Supreme Court until four years later, when the "switch-in-time-that-saved-nine" took place.

In general, however, the *tone* of dominance has been set by the person and personality of the elected Chief Executive, who, after all, is the sole individual in the American federal governmental process to have a nationwide constituency, and who, within limits, is in the position of interpreting his power narrowly or broadly. In other words, whenever the President has been of the category commonly called "active" or "strong" (e.g., Washington, Jackson, Polk, Lincoln, Wilson, the two Roosevelts, and Lyndon Johnson) the executive branch, *in the long run*, has been able to acquire supremacy. Where he has been "passive" or "weak," perhaps did not manifest sufficient concern for, understanding of, or even interest in the political process, or simply lacked sufficient support in Congress or by the people (e.g., John Quincy Adams, Pierce, Buchanan, Andrew Johnson, Grant, McKinley, Harding, Coolidge, Hoover, Eisenhower, Ford, and Carter), supremacy was acquired by Congress or, on occasion, by the Supreme Court. In several instances no clear-cut supremacy can be pinpointed. This is true, for example, of the presidencies of Madison and Monroe, Hayes, Cleveland, Taft, Truman, the end of Eisenhower's second term after the dismissal of Sherman Adams and the death of John Foster Dulles (ther is no doubt about the presence of congressional supremacy during Eisenhower's first term in office), Kennedy, and Reagan. It should also be noted that during some presidencies, or at least parts thereof, the executive has tended to dominate in foreign affairs and Congress in internal matters (e.g., Truman, Eisenhower, and Kennedy). The abortive presidency of Richard M. Nixon falls into a special category: Expansive assertions and practices of presidential power enabled him to engage in sundry policy innovations in foreign affairs at the expense of domestic tranquiltiy and achievements. His perceptions of Executive power and privilege escalated until the "Watergate syndrome" engulfed him and his administration, ultimately resulting in his resignation from office on August 9, 1974—the first President to resign in the history of the Republic. The precipitous "full, free, and absolute" pardon, granted but one month later by the Nixon-selected successor, Gerald Ford, for all offenses "committed or that may have been committed" by the resignee in the course of his entire presidency, exacerbated prevalent national frustrations and anger and raised fundamental questions for the principle of equal justice under law as well as for the future of the separation of powers and checks and balances.

At the risk of some oversimplification and generalization—which inevitably attend categorization and classification—Table 10 is designed to indicate periods of American history in which existed fairly discernible tendencies toward supremacy by one branch or two allied branches against a third. Some periods are necessarily listed in more than one category: for example, the first four years of the New Deal era, when presidential supremacy was unquestioned—or, rather, when Congress surrendered to President Roosevelt, but during which time the Supreme Court proved to be a major roadblock to the New Deal program.

There is no doubt that the Supreme Court of the United States has sporadically challenged the authority of both President and Congress. But in spite of the four or five indicated periods of tendencies toward judicial supremacy, the Court has never really actively bid for the role of dominant governmental agency of the land, although a good case could be made for there having been such a bid during the era of Chief Justice Marshall. During that period, as well as during the heyday of the Hughes anti-New Deal Court, we may speak of periodic "government by judiciary" or "judicial supremacy," yet even then there was never any genuine likelihood that the Court would in the final analysis effectively dominate the executive and/or the legislative branches. When all is said and done, the Supreme Court of the United States does not possess the political power, the arsenal of potent weapons of government, the tools of the publicity media, or the strategic position in the government or in the body politic generally enjoyed by the other two branches.

A Historical Note. If we take a closer look at the Supreme Court's role in the Machtkampf on the American political scene we see that the high tribunal began on a very inauspicious note. Its dozen or so pre-Marshall years, during which three Chief Justices came and went—the second of whom, John Rutledge, was not confirmed by the Senate—were characterized by a lack of popular esteem and understanding, little work, and dissatisfied personnel. The first Chief Justice, John Jay, so thoroughly disliked his job and so loathed circuit-riding that he not only spent one year during his tenure in England on a diplomatic mission, but twice ran for governor of New York, succeeding on the second try. whereupon he happily resigned the Chief Justiceship!

Table 10. Periods of Discernible Tendencies Toward Supremacy of Branches of the Government

Years	President(s)	Chief Justice(s)	Commentary
A. *Tendencies Toward Legislative Supremacy*			
1809–29	Madison Monroe J. Q. Adams	Marshall	Supremacy facilitated and advanced by powerful Court
1837–45	Van Buren W. H. Harrison Tyler	Taney	Aided by strong Court and passive Presidents
1849–61	Taylor Fillmore Pierce Buchanan	Taney	Nadir of presidency *Dred Soctt* case
1865–85	Johnson Grant Hayes Garfield Arthur	S. P. Chase Waite	Partially effective opposition by Johnson and Hayes
1919–21	Wilson	White	Defeat of League President ill
1921–33	Harding Coolidge Hoover	Taft Hughes	Co-operative Court Weak, passive Presidents
1953–59	Eisenhower	Warren	Strong Court Passive President
1974–77	Ford	Burger	"Healing" President
1977–81	Carter	Burger	Tentative, cautious President
B. *Tendencies Toward Executive Supremacy*			
1789–97	Washington	Jay Rutledge Ellsworth	Cooperative Congress and Court Weak, docile Court
1801–09	Jefferson	Marshall	Some doubt about Executive Supremacy, but generally present. Strong Court
1829–37	Jackson	Marshall Taney	President in high form Last years of Marshall Court
1845–49	Polk	Taney	Underrated President
1861–65	Lincoln	Taney S. P. Chase	High-water mark of Presidency Civil War
1901–08	T. Roosevelt	Fuller	Popular President Assertive Court

Years	President(s)	Chief Justice(s)	Commentary
1913–19	Wilson	White	President lost control to Republican congressional majority in 1919, however
1933–45	F. D. Roosevelt	Hughes	Revolution on Court, 1937 "Packing"
		Stone	Powerful President
1945–47	Truman	Vinson	Truman "honeymoon"
1963–68	L. B. Johnson	Warren	Powerful President
1969–74	Nixon	Burger	Vast claims to presidential power—truncated by Watergate

C. *Tendencies Toward Judicial Supremacy*

Years	President(s)	Chief Justice(s)	Commentary
1801–29	Jefferson Madison Monroe J. Q. Adams	Marshall	The great Chief Justice at power's peak
1857	Pierce Buchanan	Taney	The *Dred Scott* fiasco
1889–1901	B. Harrison Cleveland McKinley	Fuller	Judiciary's embrace of *laissez-faire*
1935–36	F. D. Roosevelt	Hughes	Thirteen New Deal Laws declared unconstitutional
1954–57	Eisenhower	Warren	Civil libertarian activism

D. *Supremacy Tendencies Not Readily Discernible*

Years	President(s)	Chief Justice(s)	Commentary
1797–1801	John Adams	Ellsworth	President and Congress shared power
1885–89	Cleveland	Waite Fuller	Probably President, but . . .
1910–13	Taft	White	Uncertainty (Taft wants to be on Court.)
1947–53	Truman	Vinson	Divided foreign and domestic tendencies but strong, assertive President
1959–60	Eisenhower	Warren	Sudden assertion of power by President. Strong, activist Court Democratic congressional majority
1961–63	Kennedy	Warren	Divided foreign and domestic tendencies. Strong, activist Court

Table 10 (Continued)

Years	President(s)	Chief Justice(s)	Commentary
1968–69	Johnson	Warren	Vietnam War becomes Johnson's political Waterloo
1981–	Reagan	Burger	Strong, persuasive president, but powerful congressional opposition, centered in House

When President Adams offered to reappoint him as Chief Justice in 1800, he refused categorically. Nonetheless, Adams appointed him on December 19, 1800; the Senate confirmed him: Adams and Marshall signed his commission; but Jay declined on January 2, 1801, citing his health (which was good). And, as already pointed out, the third Chief Justice, Oliver Ellsworth, eagerly left his office for a diplomatic post in France, where he then resigned, allegedly because of ill health. The Court did, however, soon make clear that it intended to act as an arbiter in disputes between the states and the federal government; and it became quickly apparent that its judicial sympathies lay with the latter.

The Marshall era, of course, brought about a drastic metamorphosis in the Supreme Court's prestige. The Chief Justice completely dominated the Court[112]—with dissents confined almost solely to Justice William Johnson who is justly regarded as "the father" of both dissenting and concurring opinions. It is quite clear that Marshall, more than any other man in the history of the judiciary, determined the character of America's federal constitutional system. From its lowly, if not discredited, level John Marshall raised the U.S. Supreme Court to a position of equality with the executive and the legislature—perhaps even one of dominance during the heyday of his Chief Justticeship. He called his constitutional interpretations as he saw them, always adhering to his previously discussed, oft-expressed doctrine that " ... it is a *constitution* we are expounding ... intended to endure for ages to come and, consequently, to be adapted to the various crises of human affairs."[113] Yet, as we know, he hastened to insist that "[j]udicial power, as contradistinguished from the power of law, has no existence. Courts are the mere instruments of the law, and can will nothing."[114] Thus, "willing nothing," Marshall handed down, among many others, four of the most momentous decisions in the history of, and the future for, Court, Constitution, and country, without which it is at best doubtful that the nation would have grown and prospered as it has: (1) *Marbury v. Madison*[115] (judicial review, supremacy of the U.S. Con-

[112]See ch. 5, *supra*, esp. fn. 144.
[113]*Osborn v. United States Bank*, 9 Wheaton 739 (1824) at 865.
[114]*McCulloch v. Maryland*, 4 Wheaton 315 (1819).
[115]1 Cranch 137 (1803).

stitution), (2) *McCulloch v. Maryland*[116] (implied powers of Congress, reaffirmation of the supremacy of the U.S. Constitution, federal immunity from involuntary state taxation, federal government held to have its powers directly from the people rather than from the states), (3) *Gibbons v. Ogden*[117] (plenary federal authority over interstate and foreign commerce), and (4) *Dartmouth College v. Woodward*[118] (inviolability of contracts). Truly, the Court led and, leading, gave the federal government the means to develop and work.

Whereas the Marshall Court had by its decisions placed the emphasis on the national commercial-creditor-propertied classes, its successor, the also powerful Taney Court, pursued a different emphasis. The sanctitiy of property remained a primary consideration of the tribunal, but it devolved on a different segment of society and, incidentally, of the country. A Southerner from Maryland, the Jackson-appointed Roger B. Taney, a Democrat and a Catholic—the first of his religious persuasion to be on the bench—by his decisions favored states' rights and *agrarian* property, that is, land and slaves. From a totally different milieu than the powerful constitutional nationalist who preceded him, Taney, and with him a majority of his Court, demonstrated a faithful attachment to the economic interests of the South and the rapidly developing frontier of the West. But disaster loomed on the horizon: after pursuing the aforementioned policies determinedly, and with little, if any, interference from the other two branches for twenty years, Taney, then in his eightieth year, lonely and frustrated, met his and the Court's judicial Waterloo in 1857 with his opinion in *Dred Scott v. Sandford*[119]—the thrust of which was leaked in advance by Justice John Catron to President Buchanan,[120] the sole known major breach of secrecy on record, although a handful of alleged others have been reported.[121]

This decision—"more than a crime ... a blunder"[122]—by his Southern-dominated Court, with but two Justices dissenting, John McLean[123] and Benjamin Curtis (Curtis's opinion having been circulated in advance in the Northern press), featured nine separate opinions, including Taney's. It stipulated among other things that no Negro could be a citizen, that the Negro was "a person of an inferior order," that he was a slave and thus his master's permanent property no matter whether the latter took him to slave or free

---

[116]Op. cit., fn. 114.

[117]9 Wheaton 1 (1824).

[118]4 Wheaton 518 (1819).

[119]19 Howard 393.

[120]Justice Robert O. Grier had also *scienter* to the leak; indeed, it was he who encouraged Catron to spill the proverbial beans.

[121]See Ch. 5, *supra*, fn. 230, for illustrations.

[122]Bickel, *The Least Dangerous Branch*, op cit., p. 45. (The phrase is Talleyrand's.)

[123]For a discussion of McLean's political motivations and aspirations see fn. 166, ch. 5, *supra*. See also Bickel's commentary in his *Politics and the Warren Court* (New York: Harper & Row, 1965), p. 135.

parts of the country, that the Missouri Compromise was unconstitutional, and that no individual of African descent was "a portion of this American people." *Dred Scott* permanently beclouded Taney's reputation—notwithstanding his towering contributions to constitutional development—dragged the Supreme Court of the United States into its lowest depths, and hastened the dawn of the Civil War and with it the Emancipation Proclamation and the Civil War Amendments (XIII, XIV, and XV). In the words of a Washington newspaperman, "If epithets and denunciations could sink a judicial body, the Supreme Court of the United States would never be heard of again"[124]

With *Dred Scott*, which has been widely viewed as the most disastrous opinion ever issued by the high bench,[125] the Court invited a violent congressional reaction. While that took a while to enter concrete form, the influence of the Court declined at once. The country as a whole was hardly willing to consider, let alone accept, Justice James M. Wayne's anxious explanation *cum* plea in his concurring opionion that

> ... there had become such a difference of opinion that the peace and harmony of the country required the settlement of the slavery issues by judicial decision. ... In our action we have only discharged our duty as a distinct and efficient department of the Government, as the framers of the Constitution meant the judiciary to be. ...[126]

Far from alleviating the incipient sectional strife, the Court had aggravated it. During and after the Civil War, with Taney reduced to bitterness and unhappiness, Congress demonstrated its utter contempt of the Supreme Court by *thrice* changing its size in six years: up from nine to ten in 1863, down from ten to seven in 1866, up again from seven to nine in 1869. Quite obviously, all this was done for policy purposes. And, as seen earlier in these pages, when in 1868–69 the post-Taney Court indicated a possible declaration of unconstitutionality of some of the military Reconstruction Acts, an angry Congress, acting under its powers derived from the Constitution to limit the Court's appellate jurisdiction, simply deprived it of the power to decide the case.[127] This was the beginning of the Chief Justiceship of the politically ambitious Salmon P. Chase (1864–74)[128] and of Morrison R. Waite (1874–88), both Northern Republicans, during whose tenure the Court, predictably, was chiefly concerned, in addition to safeguarding property, with maintaining the status quo: state authority over individuals and federal authority over interstate commerce—the two great post-Civil War problems.

[124]As quoted by Hyneman, op. cit., p. 31.

[125]E.g., McCloskey, op. cit., p. 94.

[126]*Dred Scott v. Sandford*, loc. cit., at 454–55.

[127]*Ex parte McCardle*, 7 Wallace 506 (1869).

[128]Prior to his assumption of the Chief Justiceship, Chase had been a candidate at the Republican presidential conventions of 1856 and 1860. In 1868, while on the highest bench, he unsuccessfully sought the presidential nomination on *both* tickets!

The former included the Waite Court's nullification of the attempted use of the due process of law clause of the Fourteenth Amendment by the federal government as a national arm to protect civil rights in the states in the historic *Civil Rights Cases*[129]—something the Chase Court had already done in connection with the Amendment's "privileges or immunities" clause when citizens of Louisiana attempted to invoke it.[130] Indeed, the Chase Court, in a burst of judicial activism, did declare nine acts of Congress unconstitutional; but, as explained earlier, in the final analysis it bowed before the power of the Radical Republicans in Congress, and it was effectively "packed" by President Grant in 1871, thus nullifying within fifteen months its briefly successful attempt to battle for what it had regarded as stable currency in the *Legal Tender cases*.[131] One important contribution of the Waite Court to be noted, notwithstanding its generally proprietarian bent, was the highly significant development of the "affectation with the public interest" doctrine, announced by the Chief Justice himself in his opinion for a majority of seven in the leading *Granger* case of *Munn v. Illinois*.[132] There, while still clinging to the notion of due process laid down in *The Slaughterhouse cases*,[133] Waite held that, under certain circumstances, the state police power could be employed to regulate private property in the public interest.

With the long Chief Justiceship of the Cleveland-appointed Melville W. Fuller of Illnois, however, the Court all but bid for policy leadership. It did this, above all, by striking out on a path designed to reassure the sanctitiy of property, as the majority of the Court saw it. This majority was now composed of a group of highly conservative, property-conscious Justices, who, when given the opportunity, began to strike down as unconstitutional a fair number of federal and state laws in the conomic and social sphere. *Laissez faire* seemed secure, indeed! Until roughly this time, state laws, for example, had been held unconstitutional largely because they were viewed as conflicting either with the interstate commerce or the obligation-of-contract clauses of the Constitution. Of 128 state laws invalidated by the federal courts *before* 1888, 50 involved the former clause, 50 the latter, and only one the taking of property "without due process of law." The Fuller Court, on the other hand, ultimately struck down a large number of state laws on that last ground, holding that the several legislative "experimentations" at issue deprived "persons" of liberty and property without *substantive* due process of law. Substantive due process had truly come of age! The Supreme Court had become the arbiter "between the voters on the one hand and the property owners on

---

[129] 109 U.S. 3(1883).

[130] *The Slaughterhouse Cases*, 16 Wallace 36 (1873).

[131] 12 Wallace 457 (1871) and *Hepburn v. Griswold*, 8 Wallace 603 (1870).

[132] 94 U.S. 113 (1877).

[133] 16 Wallace 36 (1873). See my *Freedom and the Court: Civil Rights and Liberties in the United States*, 4th ed. (New York: Oxford University Press, 1982), pp. 41–49.

the other."[134] And the concept of "persons" now also included *corporations*, thanks to a unanimous Court ruling in the *Santa Clara* case,[135] a decision invalidating assessments on portions of railroad property. It was featured by a casual *announcement*, without benefit of argument, by Chief Justice Waite, who did not even write the opinion: "The Court does not wish to hear argument on the question whether the provision in the Fourteenth Amendment ot the Constitution, which forbids a State to deny to any person within its jurisdiction the equal protection of the laws, applies to these Corporations. We are all of the opinion that it does."[136] This was a rather cavalier manner of disposing of a highly significant constitutional issue—one that was neither before the Court nor had been argued in the case at bar!

The states, however, and, considerably later, the federal government insistently wished to pioneer in the realm of economic and social legislation, as they deemed that to be the desire of the majority of the voters. Yet in most areas (viz., maximum hours, minimum wages, working conditions, regulation of woman and child labor, compulsory arbitration, employer liability, and many others), the legislatures ran into the judicial vetoes not only of the Fuller Court, but also those of his successors, the White and Taft Courts and, until 1937, the Hughes Court—despite the established Waite "affectation with the public interest" doctrine. Throughout this period the Supreme Court demonstrated again and again a remarkable regard for the protection of *property* under its interpretations of the "liberty and property" phrases of the "due process of law" clauses of the Fifth and Fourteenth Amendments to the U.S. Constitution. But, oddly enough, the Court found these clauses no barrier against legislative invasions of the *cultural and political* realms, often referred to as "civil rights" or "civil liberties."

From the turn of the century on, when the great Oliver Wendell Holmes, Jr., was appointed by President Theodore Roosevelt to what was to be his thirty-year tenure on the Court, dissenting voices to the majority's policies were increasingly heard. As of 1916 Holmes was joined in dissents, although frequently for different reasons, by his colleague Louis D. Brandeis; and with the advent of Justices Harlan F. Stone in 1925 and Benjamin N. Cardozo in 1932, the dissenting voices in this area had settled to just one short of a majority. The previously described switch by Chief Justice Hughes, and, to a lesser extent, by Justice Owen D. Roberts, ultimately brought on what the eminent American constitutionalist Edward S. Corwin aptly called "a Constitutional Revolution." Having lost the battle of packing the Court in February 1937, President F. D. Roosevelt won the war when fate, in the form of deaths and resignations, weeded out the remaining four ultra-conservative Justices on the bench between 1937 and 1941—Associate Justices Willis Van Devanter,

[134]Arthur J. Hadley, "The Constitutional Position of Property in America," 64 *The Independent* 837 (1904).
[135]*Santa Clara County v. Southern Pacific Railroad Co.*, 118 U.S. 394 (1886).
[136]Ibid., at 396.

George Sutherland, James C. McReynolds, and Pierce Butler—ultimately allowing him to fill nine vacancies on the court[137] (second only to Washington's ten).[138]

By no means did all of these Roosevelt appointees see the law at all times as he had hoped they would; but certainly the New Deal now had clear sailing, and there was no doubt that the new Justices rejected outright the "thou-shalt-not-pass" doctrines of their predecessors relative to legislative experimentation in the economic-proprietarian sphere. As Justice Black was to comment later: "Whether the legislature takes for its textbook Adam Smith, Herbert Spencer, Lord Keynes, or some other is no concern of ours."[139] Judicial self-restraint on legislative policymaking in these areas of public life became the avowed policy of the Court—just as the "Old Court" had practiced a similar restraint on legislative policies in the cultural and political realms (e.g., the "separate but equal" concept and abridgement on speech, press, and assembly). Yet, interestingly enough, the "New Court" immediately commenced to complete the cycle of policy reversal by throwing up judicial vetoes in the face of a good many legislative encroachments, as the Court saw them, on civil rights and liberties. Thus, the nature and character of the Court's labors began to change dramatically. Of the 160 decisions in which it had written opinions in the 1935–36 term, a mere two had dealt with civil rights and liberties. That ratio began to climb steadily so that a decade later twenty times as many opinions fell into that category, and fifteen years later fully fifty-four cases dealt with that vital area of public life—a fact of judicial life that has not only continued to the present, but has accelerated, with well over half of the Court's written opinions now regularly concerning the libertarian sector (87 of 160 and 84 of 150, respectively, in the Court's 1976 and 1981 terms, for example).

When Justices Murphy and Wiley Rutledge joined Chief Justice Stone and Justices Black and Douglas in the early 1940s, these "libertarian activists" were generally in firm control—certainly until the death of the Chief Justice in April 1946. They briefly relinquished that control during the last four years of the Vinson Court upon the deaths of Justices Murphy and Rutledge in 1949 and their replacement by Justices Clark and Minton, when the Court tended, broadly speaking, to side with government rather than the individual in the general field of national security, that so difficult and emotion-charged Cold War problem. But they more or less regained it during the first four years of the Warren Court, from 1953 to 1957, Chief Justice Warren having replaced Chief Justice Vinson on Vinson's death. However, with the Court led by the consistently "nonactivist" Justice Frankfurter, the 1957–58 term saw a return to readily discernible judicial self-restraint even in *that* area of

---

[137]Black, Reed, Frankfurter, Douglas, Murphy, Stone (promotion to Chief Justice), Byrnes, Jackson, and Rutledge.
[138]See text, p. 76 and fn. 109, ch. 2, "Staffing the Courts,", *supra.*
[139]*Ferguson v. Skrupa,* 372 U.S. 726 (1963), at 732.

public and constitutional policy—some would contend largely as a result of the veritable barrage of congressional and public criticism against the Court following its spate of "pro-civil liberty" decisions in 1956–57. Yet with the retirement of Justices Whittaker and Frankfurter in 1962 and their replacement by Justices Byron White and Arthur Goldberg, the latter in turn yielding to Abe Fortas in 1965, plus the Thurgood Marshall replacement of Justice Clark, the libertarian image of the Warren Court was restored. It continued and indeed mounted until the Chief Justice's resignation in 1969. His replacement by Warren Earl Burger has been characterized by a somewhat moderating tenor and by some retrenchment in the criminal justice sector, but there are no indications of a general return to pre-Warren Court doctrine. The overriding concern for civil rights and liberties will almost surely continue to characterize a majority of cases reaching the highest tribunal for adjudication.

Finally, when the great issues of executive power that had arisen in the Watergate affair reached the Burger Court in July 1974, it took on President Nixon, in *United States, Petitioner, v. Richard M. Nixon, President of the United States.*[140] In an 8:0 decision, the unanimous Court, including three of the Nixon appointees (the fourth, Justice Rehnquist, having disqualified himself), ruled, in effect, that no man was above the law, that the President was duty-bound to comply with a valid judicial order to turn over evidence desired in a criminal trial, and that there was no "absolute, unqualified presidential privilege of immunity from judicial process under all circumstances." Here, fifteen days prior to Nixon's resignation, Chief Justice Burger, resorting to John Marshall's immortal words, told the President, the nation, and the world: "We therefore reaffirm that it is 'emphatically the province and the duty' of this Court 'to say what the law is.'"

If we reflect on these several considerations in this analysis of the *Machtkampf*, the work of the Supreme Court and the force and implications of its decisions come into closer focus. At times the Court has clearly led the a country (e.g., the Marshall era); at other times it has more or less held the line (e.g., the Chase–Waite era—with important qualifications); at times it has deliberately stimulated social and economic progress (e.g., the post-1937 Court); at others it has deliberately delayed it (e.g., the Fuller Court). At times it has looked to a majority sentiment, as it were, by following the election returns (e.g., the *Insular* decisions at the turn of the last century)[141] at others it has defied majority sentiment (e.g., some fo the 1956–47 term civil liberties decisions).[142] At times its decisions have been seemingly motivated by sectional or class considerations (e.g., *Dred Scott,*[143] proclaiming corpora-

---

[140]417 U.S. 683.

[141]*Downes v. Bidwell,* 182 U.S. 244 (1901) and *De Lima v. Bidwell,* 182 U.S. 1 (1901).

[142]E.g, *Watkins v. United States,* 354 U.S. 178; *Jencks v. United States,* 353 U.S. 657; *Yates v. United States,* 354 U.S. 298.

[143]*Dred Scott v. Sandford,* loc. cit.

tions as "persons,"[144] and the 1954 *Segregation cases*[145]); at others they have been truly national in spirit and effect (e.g., the four major Marshall decisions, cited earlier).[146] In a very real sense, the Court through the years has thus been the conscience of the country. In a measure, it has represented the Rousseauist *volonté générale* of the land, in a qualitative rather than a quantitative sense. It has done this through its decisions, speaking through its Justices, who—almost always of a rather high caliber—have interpreted the Constitution as they saw it, in line with the taught tradition of the law.

Of course, the Supreme Court of the United States is engaged in the political process, but, in Justice Frankfurter's admonitory prose, it is "the Nation's ultimate judicial tribunal, not a super-legal aid bureau."[147] His jurisprudential heir, Justice John Marshall Harlan, seconded and extended this point by observing that the "Constitution is not a panacea for every blot upon the public welfare, nor should this Court, ordained as a judicial body, be thought of as a general haven for reform movements."[148] Of course, the Justices—who, in the words of E. V. Rostow, are "inevitably teachers in a vital national seminar"[149]—consult their own policy preferences. But they do so in an institutional setting that forces responsibility on them. They must meet and maintain high standards of integrity, intelligence, logic, reflectiveness, and consistency. They must ever demonstrate a sense of history complete with the realities and vagaries of public affairs, a task that Judge J. C. Hutcheson, Jr., of Texas once called "the hunch of intuition about the inner life of American democracy."[150] They have the exciting, yet delicate task of heeding the "felt necessities of the time"—to employ once again Justice Holmes's inspired phrase[151] while holding aloft the banner of constitutional fundamentals. It was Daniel Webster, not a present-day observer or participant of the governmental process, who put his finger on what should be obvious. Speaking in the House of Representatives in support of a judiciary bill, he intoned that "the maintenance of the judicial power is essential and indispensable to the very being of this government. The Constitution without it would be no constitution; the government no government."[152]

---

[144]Santa Clara County v. Southern Pacific Railroad Co., loc. cit.

[145]*Brown v. Board of Education*, 347 U.S. 483 and *Bolling v. Sharpe*, 347 U.S. 497.

[146]See p. 360 supra.

[147]*Uveges v. Pennsylvania*, 335 U.S. 437 (1948) at 450.

[148]*Reynolds v. Sims*, 377 U.S. 533 (1964), dissenting opinion, at 624.

[149]"The Democratic Character of Judicial Review," 66 *Harvard Law Review* 195 (1952).

[150]As quoted by Rostow in his *The Sovereign Prerogative: The Supreme Court and the Quest for Law* (New Haven, CT: Yale University Press, 1962), p. 110.

[151]Oliver Wendell Holmes, Jr., *The Common Law* (Boston: Little, Brown and Co., 1881), p. 1.

[152]As quoted by Chief Justice Earl Warren, "Webster and the Court," *Dartmouth College Alumni Magazine*, May 19, 1969, p. 34.

9

Coda:
A Realistic
Bulwark

If the foregoing analysis of the role of the Supreme Court of the United States in the political process has proved anything at all, it ought to be that there is a recognition of the overriding need for judicial self-restraint. Its acceptance plays an omnipresent and omnipotent part in the attitude of the nine members of the highest court in the United States. No matter how the judicial record of these nine individuals may appear on a chart or graph; no matter how predictable or unpredictable their position on certain issues may be—a factor that on balance is probably far more of a blessing than a curse—they are fully aware of their role in, and responsibility to, the democratic body politic they serve with such dedication. They serve as a collective institution of government; but it is an institution that is characterized by individual absorption in the tasks at hand, an absorption that calls for direct personal evaluation and decision making. As has been demonstrated throughout these pages, *each member of the Supreme Court* normally participates in every stage of the consideration of a case—from the review stage through the evaluation of briefs, through oral argument, through discussion and vote in Conference, to the writing of or participation in the ultimate opinion of the Court. At every stage of the life of a case the Justices are fully aware of their responsibilites as members of the governmental process, and thus practice much procedural as well as substantive judicial self-restraint—both in the type of cases they will hear and in the kind of decisions they will render. This emphasis on what Alexander Bickel wisely termed "passive virtues"[1] is a sim-

---

[1] *The Least Dangerous Branch: The Supreme Court at the Bar of Politics* (Indianpolis: The Bobbs-Merrill Co., 1962), title of ch. 4.

ple, and yet immensely complicated, fact of judicial life—whatever the opinion of expert as well as lay outsiders on judicial legislating may be. But there is little doubt that the Justices believe with Johann Wolfgang von Goethe that "self-limitation is the first mark of the master."[2]

Throughout the almost two centuries of its existence, the Court has developed a host of unwritten laws, practices, precedents, and attitudes which we may well view as a code of behavior for the highest judicial body in the United States—a series of significant *maxims of judicial self-restraint*. In analyzing the most commonly accepted of these, the reader should be aware that any such enumeration will necessarily involve some generalization and that maxims, like rules, are sometimes broken quite deliberately.

THE SIXTEEN GREAT MAXIMS OF JUDICIAL SELF-RESTRAINT[3]

There is nothing sacred about either the number of these maxims or the order in which they will appear. They are presented roughly in the order in which they would normally confront the Justices as an issue reaches the Supreme Court in the form of a case of controversy—presumably when it has become "ripe" for adjudication.

ONE: Before the Court will even glance at a particular issue or dispute officially, a definite "case" or "controversy" at law or in equity between bona fide adversaries under the Constitution must exist, involving the protection or enforcement of valuable legal rights, or the punishment, prevention, or redress of wrongs directly concerning the party or parties bringing the justiciable suit. Justice Jackson viewed this maxim as "perhaps the most significant and least comprehended limitation upon the judicial power."[4] The judicial system of the United States is constructed on specific cases with specific facts. Thus, when a group of federal employees endeavored to join one George P. Poole in a suit testing the validity of that portion of the Hatch Act of 1939 which forbids members of the executive civil service to take an active part in "political management or in political campaigns," the Supreme Court disqualified them as appellants because they, unlike Poole, had not violated the provision in question.[5] Refusing to take jurisdiction, the Court thereby reiterated its oft-expressed stand against "every form of pronouncement on abstract, contingent, or hypothetical issues."[6] Except for Poole's claims, no

---

[2]From the sonnet "*Was Wir Bringen*," 1802. ("*In der Beschränkung zeigt sich erst der Meister..*")

[3]An astute critic has observed that "self-interpretation" would be a more cogent appellation. (Letter from Wilmer Douglas Bentley, October 16, 1975.

[4]Robert H. Jackson, *The Supreme Court in the American System of Government* (Cambridge: Harvard University Press, 1955), p. 11.

[5]*United Public Workers of America v. Mitchell*, 330 U.S. 75 (1947). The *Poole* case issue is also apposite to the "standing" maxim, item "Two," *infra*.

[6]Jackson, loc., cit., p. 12.

case or controversy directly involving the interest of the appellants was involved here in the face of the Supreme Court's first maxim, regardless of what lower tribunals might have held. Probably the most famous illustration of the "case or controversy" problems is the Court's 1911 decision in *Muskrat v. United States.*[7] At issue was an act of Congress that had authorized Muskrat and others to bring suit in the U.S. Court of Claims, wtih an appeal to the Supreme Court to *determine the validity of certain acts of Congress* that altered the terms of some prior allotments of Cherokee Indian lands. Speaking for a unanimous Court, Justice Day rejected the appeal as not meeting the "case or controversy," requirement. "If such actions as are here attempted, to determine the validity of legislation are sustained," lectured Day, "the result will be that this court, instead of keeping within the limits of judicial power and deciding cases or controversies arising between opposing parties, as the Constitution intended it should, will be required to give opinions in the nature of advice concerning legislative action, *a function never conferred upon it by the Constitution. . . .*"[8]

TWO: Closely related to the need for the presence of a case or controversy is the logical demand that the *party or parties bringing suit must have "standing."* The gist of the question of standing, as the Court elucidated it in *Baker v. Carr*, "is whether the party seeking relief has alleged such a personal stake in the outcome of the controversy as to assure that concrete adverseness which sharpens the presentation of issues upon which the court so largely depends for illumination of difficult constitutional questions."[9] There are two major aspects to the difficult and intricate concept of standing.[10] The *first*, to raise a constitutional issue with proper standing, is that it must be shown that the one who seeks to challenge the statute or action is personally and substantially injured by it, or is in substantial danger of such injury. A relaxation of that rule, at least in the sensitive free speech area, was introduced with the Court's landmark 1965 ruling in *Dombrowski v. Pfister*, where it held 5:2 that federal district judges should have the power to

---

[7]219 U.S. 346.

[8]Ibid., at 362. (Italics supplied.) President Nixon's counsel unsuccessfully argued the absence of a "case" or "controversy" in *United States v. Nixon*, 417 U.S. 683 (1974).

[9]369 U.S. 186 (1962), at 204.

[10]"Standing," quoted and noted Chief Justice Warren on one often reported occasion, "has been called 'one of the most amorphous [concepts] in the entire domain of public law.' Some of the complexities peculiar to standing problems result because standing 'serves on occasion, as a shorthand expression for all the various elements of justiciability.' In addition, there are at work in the standing doctrine the many subtle pressures which tend to cause policy considerations to blend into constitutional limitatons." (*Flast v. Cohen*, 392 U.S. 83 [1968] at 92.) For other pithy references to the incredible difficulties surrounding the issue and concept of "standing," see the excellent article, and its important footnotes, especially 1 and 3, by Karen Orren, "Standing to Sue: Interest Group Conflict in the Federal Courts," 70 *The American Political Science Review* (September 1976), pp. 723–41; and the similarly perceptive one by Tinsley E. Yarbrough, "Litigant Access Doctrine and the Burger Court," 31 *Vanderbilt Law Review* (January 1978), pp. 33–70.

enjoin the enforcement of unconstitutional laws (i.e., laws presumed unconstitutional "on their face"), if these laws, as per Justice Brennan's majority opinion, pose a "chilling effect" on freedom of expression by mere "fact of prosecution, unaffected by the prospects of its success or failure....[Thus, courts may] avoid making vindication of freedom of expression await the outcome of protracted litigation."[11] But the relaxation was short-lived. District judges, prodded by aggressive attorneys for litigants, followed the Supreme Court's *Dombrowski* ruling with such gusto that state laws on obscenity, abortion, subversion, homosexuality, vagrancy, and so on, began to fall like tenpins; in 1971 the Burger Court called a halt, in a significant decision which instructed the lower federal courts to estop state prosecutions *only* when state officials were "cynically harassing" defendants, causing "irreparable injury."[12] In other words, six years after *Dombrowski* the Court substituted a test of "irreparable injury" for "chilling effect."

The *second* aspect of standing is that a petitioner, endeavoring to speak for a group or "class" of similarly affected and/or interested parties, must not only have a personal and substantial interest infringed by the statute or action but must also "bring himself, by proper averment and showing, within the class as to whom the act thus attacked is unconstitutional."[13] Thus, the

[11] 380 U.S. 479, at 487.

[12] *Younger v. Harris*, 401 U.S. 37 (1971). The Court applied its *Younger* ruling to six cases before it on the same day as the parent case (February 23, 1971). The opinions in *Younger* and the six were written by Justice Black, with but Douglas in dissent.

[13] *Southern Railroad Co. v. King.* 217 U.S. 524 (1910) at 534. The reference to "class" in the quotation points to the vexatious legal phenomenon called a "class action" that is, a suit filed by the person allegedly wronged on behalf of himself or herself and perhaps hundreds or thousands of unnamed others *who can be classifed with him or her as similarly wronged.* Thus, class actions, when successful, provide a way for the claims of many individuals to be settled at one time, eliminating repetitious litigation and establishing an economical route to obtaining redress, since the legal fees can be taken from the total damages awarded. Celebrated illustrations of successful class action suits are the school desegregation cases of 1954 and the "one-person, one-vote" cases of 1964. In the decade that followed more and more class action suits were brought (they doubled between 1970 and 1975) and finally the Burger Court began to draw a line. The first such limiting decision was rendered late in 1973, in a 6:3 vote against the plaintiff in a pollution case. Although certain kinds of class actions, such as those involving antitrust and civil rights suits, will still not be affected by the Court's herein pronounced limitation since they have no statutory minimum requirement (e.g., *U.S. Steel Corporation v. Dickerson*, 421 U.S. 948 [1975], involving charges of discrimination brought by three black employees on behalf of *all* blacks working in the company's plant), the new policy brought the following changes: When, for example, parties from different states are henceforth involved (i.e., in diversity of citizenship cases which *do* call for a $10,000 minimum—see ch. 4 *supra*), every plaintiff must now meet the $10,000 damage allegation requirement *separately!* No longer will a "collective" total of $10,000 thus bring proper class action standing (*Zahn v. International Paper Co.*, 414 U.S. 291 [1974]. A further narrowing of class action availability came with a unanimous ruling handed down in May 1974, that hereafter a person bringing such a suit must notify *all* members of the class potentially benefitting *and* bear the costs of such notice, even it that should be prohibitively high (*Eisen v. Carlisle and Jacqueline*, 416 U.S. 1979), which the court in 1978 unanimously expanded to

Supreme Court ruled 6:3 in late 1970 that the Commonwealth of Massachusetts lacked *standing* to litigate the question of the constitutionality of the
Vietnam War by attempting to challenge it in behalf of its individual citizens.[14] A lower appellate court did accept the war-legality question as a justiciable controversy a year later, and then upheld its legality, but the Supreme
Court, predictably, denied *certiorari*.[15] Among the federal judiciary's pruden-
tial limitations, thus, is found the rule that "normally" it will not grant standing when the harm alleged "is a 'generalized grievance' shared in substantial
measure by all or a large class of citizens,"[16] the strong implication being that
legislative redress ought to be sought instead. Nor, as the Court lectured in
a 5:4 opinion written by Justice Rehnquist in 1982, will it condone the use
of the federal courts by citizen groups who seem to endeavor to employ them
as if they were "constituted as ombudsmen of the general welfare" or as "college debating societies" or as podiums for those who "would roam the country
in search of governmental wrong doing."[17]

One of the most famous illustrations of a *lack of standing* on record is the
case of Dr. Wilder Tileston, a Connecticut physician who wanted to chal-

---

extend to the *compiling* of the names and address of the affected class in *Oppenheimer Fund
v. Sander*, (437 U.S. 340). Consequently, the Court thus quickly declined to review a ruling
below that had held a group of *Carte Blanche* credit card holders could *not* bring a class
action suit on behalf of all 800,000 such owners in order to challenge financing provisions
imposed by the issuing company (*Katz v. Carte Blanche Corporation*,419 U.S. 885 [1974]).
And a lower federal court accordingly ruled that one S. L. Cartt's suit, challenging Standard
Oil of California's claims for its F-310 gasoline, could not proceed until she notified *each* of
the 700,000 Standard credit card holders in the state. (That would have cost her $42,000, and
as she was unable to raise that amount, her class action suit failed.) While the early 1980s
saw a number of split decisions that seemed to strengthen procedural opportunities to file
class action suits (e.g. *Deposit Guarantee National Bank v. Roper*, 445 U.S. 326 (1980); *U.S.
Parole Commission v. Geraghty*, 445 U.S. 388 [1980]; *Merrill Lynch v. Curran*, 456 U.S. 353
[1982]; and *Board of Education v. Pico*, 457 U.S. 853 [1982]) that same time period also witnessed the contrary (e.g., *Middlesex Country Sewer Authority v. Sea Clammers*, 453 U.S. 1
[1981] and *Los Angeles v. Lyons*, 46 U.S. 95 [1983]. The last word has hardly been spoken
here; but one should not expect a return to the easy-access days of the 1950s–1970s.
[14]*Massachusetts v. Laird*, 400 886, Justices Douglas, Harlan, and Stewart dissenting.
[15]*Orlando v. Laird*, 404 U.S. 869 (1971), Justices Douglas and Brennan dissenting. (The Circuit
Court's citation was 443 F. 2d 1039.) Another attempt in 1972 also failed. (*DaCosta v. Laird*,
405 U.S. 979, *certiorari denied*, with Justice Douglas dissenting from the denial.)
[16]Thus, see the heavily criticized decision in *Warth v. Seldin*, 422 U.S. 490 (1975) at 498–99,
quoting *Baker v. Carr*, op. cit., fn. 9, *supra*, holding 5:4, through Justice Powell's majority
opinion, that city taxpayers of Rochester, New York, residents of a zoned suburb, a builders'
association looking for work in the suburb, and a citizen housing group lacked standing to
sue to challenge the suburban zoning restriction at issue just as much as central city low- and
moderate-income dwellers did. See also the Court's 5:3 opinion in *Allen v. Wright*, authored
by Justice O'Connor, holding that a lower federal court had improperly permitted a group of
black parents to challenge the manner in which the IRS grants tax exemption to private
schools. (52 LW 5110 [1984].).
[17]*Valley Forge Christian College v. Americans United for the Separation of Church and State*,
454 U.S. 464, at 473, 487.

lenge the constitutionality of that state's statutory probibition[18]—enforced but three times between the time of its birth in 1879 and its death at the bar of the U.S. Supreme Court in 1965[19]—of the "use of drugs or instruments to prevent conception, and the giving of assistance or counsel in their use." Having lost his appeal in the Connecticut Supreme Court of Errors below, he endeavored to get federal Supreme Court review. Because of their importance to the concept of standing, the pertinent sections of that court's *per curiam* decision should be quoted:

> Appellant [Dr. Tileston] alleged that the statute, if applicable to him, would prevent his giving professional advice concerning the use of contraceptives to three patients whose condition of health was such that their lives would be endangered by child-bearing, and that appellees [Abraham S. Ullman and other law enforcement officers of the state], intend to prosecute any offense against the statute and "claim or may claim" that the proposed professional advice would constitute such an offense. The complaint set out in detail the danger to the lives of appellant's patients in the event that they should bear children, but *contained no allegation asserting any claim under the Fourteenth Amendment of infringement of appellant's liberty or his property rights.* The relief prayed was a declaratory judgment [to be explained in the next maxim] as to whether the statutes are applicable to appellant and if so whether they constitute a valid exercise of constitutional power "within the meaning and intent of Amendment XIV of the Constitution of the United States prohibiting a state from depriving any person of *life* without due process of law." . . .
>
> We are of the opinion that the proceedings in the state courts *present no constitutional question which appellant has standing to assert. The sole constitutional attack upon the statutes under the Fourteenth Amendment is confined to their deprivation of life—obviously not appellant's but his patients'.* There is no allegation or proof that appellant's life is in danger. *His patients are not parties to this proceeding* and there is no basis on which we can say that he has standing to secure an adjudication of his patient's constitutional right to life, *which they do not assert in their own behalf.* . . . *No question is raised in the record with respect to the deprivation of appellant's liberty or property in contravention of the Fourteenth Amendment.* . . . Since the appeal must be dismissed on the grounds that appellant has no standing to litigate the constitutional question which the record presents, it is unnecessary to consider whether the record shows the existence of a genunie case or controversy essential to the exercise of jurisdiction of this Court. . . . Dismissed.[20]

In short, Dr. Tileston had no standing to sue: his patients might well have had such, but they did not bring suit; he might have had such, but he brought suit on nonjusticiable grounds. The Court was not about to get into the del-

---

[18]*Tileston v. Ullman*, 318 U.S. 44 (1943).
[19]*Griswold v. Connecticut*, 381 U.S. 479.
[20]*Tileston v. Ullman*, loc. cit., at 46. (Italics supplied.)

icate matter of birth control if it could avoid doing so (it would ultimately get involved—and amidst withering criticism—two decades later[21]).

Not to be outdone, opponents of the Connecticut statute tried again in 1961, and this time with patients *and* a physician as plaintiffs. The Supreme Court was hard pressed to reject the appeal for adjudication of the issue and thus continue to refuse to get enmeshed in the sticky problem. But it managed: Led, not surprisingly, by Justice Frankfurter, and narrowly dividing 5:4, the majority held the controversy *not* to be "fit for adjudication", that no one had in fact been injured, such as being jailed or fined, and that consequently, " . . . this Court cannot be umpire to debates concerning harmless, empty shadows."[22] Frankfurter pointed out that the law in question had rarely been the subject of a prosecution, that perhaps it had died of disuse and would therefore not ever be enforced. Yet the statute's opponents were not mollified: more determined than ever to test its constitutionality, they continued to try to obtain standing to challenge it. They opened a birth-control clinic in New Haven, frankly advertising its existence—and, to their utter delight, the state decided to prosecute them! Best of all, Mrs. Estelle T. Griswold, the executive director of the Planned Parenthood League of Connecticut, and Dr. C. Lee Buxton, a licensed physician, who served as medical director for the league's New Haven Center, found themselves convicted and fined $100 each. Now they had standing at last! Losing in the courts below, they appealed to the Supreme Court on the ground that the Connecticut statute, as applied to them, violated the Fourteenth Amendment. In 1965 the Court granted their appeal, pointing out that persons prosecuted under a relevant statute must surely have standing to challenge it. And by a vote of 7:2 in an expansive, heavily criticized opinion by Justice Douglas—plus three concurring and two dissenting opinions—it declared the law to be an unconstitutional infringement not only of Amendment XIV, but also of Amendments I, III, IV, V, and IX by way of "penumbras formed by emanations" therefrom.[23] Whatever the merits of the Connecticut case may be, standing is assuredly essential to an orderly and efficacious judicial process.[24]

---

[21] *Roe v. Wade and Doe v. Bolton,* 410 U.S. 113 and 410 U.S. 179 (1973), respectively.

[22] *Poe v. Ullman and Buxton v. Ullman,* 367 U.S. 497 (1961).

[23] *Griswold v. Connecticut,* 381 U.S. 479 (1965) at 484.

[24] Another fascinating and contentious aspect of this problem is the precedent established by the Supreme Court ruling in *Frothingham v. Mellon,* 262 U.S. 447 (1923), which determined that an "ordinary taxpayer" is generally precluded from contesting the constitutionality of *federal* expenditures, such as expenditures to sectarian schools and other institutions, on the ground that he or she does not possess "sufficient interest" to bring suit. In *Frothingham* (often identified as *Massachusetts v. Mellon,* the two were argued, considered, and disposed of together). Justice Sutherland held for the unanimous Court that a taxpayer's interest in the moneys of the Treasury (here regarding the Federal Maternity Act) "is shared with millions of others; is comparatively minute and indeterminable; the effect upon future taxation . . . is so remote . . . that no basis is afforded for an appeal to the preventive power of the Court." As a consequence, a *federal* taxpayer (but not necessarily a *state* taxpayer in his capacity as

THREE: The Court does not render advisory opinions, that is, judicial rulings on the constitutionality of governmental action in the absence of a case or controversy requiring such a ruling for its disposition—nor do the lower federal constitutional courts. In effect, this was settled as early as 1793, when President Washington addressed the members of the Supreme Court, asking them to define for him the authority given him by the Constitution to decide certain questions involved in the U.S. policy of neutrality with respect to a war such as the one then in progress in Europe. Chief Justice Jay responded for the Court that it would not and could not tender legal advice— that its role was confined to the decision of cases that arose in the course of bona fide litigation. *Legislative* courts, however, may give advisory opinions, and so may many of the courts of the fifty states, such as Colorado, Massachusetts, and South Dakota.

All courts, on the other hand, are empowered to render *declaratory judgments*—a device that enables courts generally to enter a final judgment between litigants *in an actual controversy*, defining their respective rights

---

a state citizen, for many states do allow such "taxpayer suits"), whose rights guaranteed by, for example, the First Amendment, are actually deemed violated, may be without a judicial remedy. This dilemma became particularly acute with the passage of the Federal Elementary and Secondary Aid ot Education Act of 1965, given its attendant overtones of the separation of church and state controversy. Consequently, legislation to provide for judicial review of the constitutionality of grants and loans under seven specific federal statutes, including the aid-to-education measure just mentioned, plus any other statute administered by the Department of Health, Education, and Welfare—was introduced. Although it had early rough going—it passed the Senate on four occasions, only to die in the House in each instance— two bills formally authorizing the Court to review the constitutionality of legislation dealing with such aid as that prescribed in the 1965 statute, became law in 1965 and 1967. And in a dramatic development the Court in October 1967 decided to hear arguments of seven taxpayers (*Flast v. Gardner*, 389 U.S. 895) who contended that they had a right as federal citizens to challenge the constitutionality of federal aid to parochial schools, notwithstanding the *Frothingham* precedent. In June 1968 the Court agreed, 8:1, in *Flast v. Cohen*, 392 U.S. 83, provided that the taxpayer can establish a two-part "nexus": (1) that he or she establish a "logical link between that [taxpayer] status and the type of legislative enactment attacked [which legislation must be based on the congressional exercise of its taxing and spending power under I-8:1]; and (2)) that he or she can show that the challenged enactment exceeds specific constitutional limitations imposed upon the exercise of the congressional taxing and spending power . . ." (at 102–3). Abuse of legislative power *must* be demonstrated. Thus, in two celebrated late 1974 cases, the Court ruled *against* two taxpayer suits based on *Flast*, denying standing in both instances. The first (*United States v. Richardson*, 418 U.S. 166) sought to have declared unconstitutional congressional legislation authorizing the nondisclosure of Central Intelligence Agency receipts and expenditures under the CIA Act of 1949, the suit alleging that the arrangement violated the requirement for regular accounting of public fund expenditures under 1-9-7 of the Constitution. The second (*Schlesinger v. Reservists Committee to Stop the War*, 418 U.S. 208) challenged the reserve status of members of Congress, alleging violation of the "incompatability" clause of the Constitution (I-6-2). In both instances the prevailing Court majorities, 5:4 and 6:3, respectively, saw either a failure of a sufficient *Flast* "nexus" especially its part 1, or regarded the taxpayer claims as being of the nonjusticiable "general citizen" or "voter grievance" type or both. It is a fair question to ask whether the Court distinguished or in effect contracted *Flast*.

under a statute, contract, will, or other document, *without* attaching to the otherwise binding judgment any consequential or coercive relief. The crucial distinction between a declaratory judgment and an advisory opinion is the presence of an actual controversy in the case of a declaratory judgment, whereas an advisory opinion would deal with an abstract, hypothetical question insofar as the judicial process is concerned. Today, three-quarters of the states[25] and the federal government under the Federal Declaratory Judgment Act of 1934, permit declaratory judgments. In the words of the federal statute, such a judgment—which is reviewable above—answers the following question in an actual controversy: " . . . whether or not further relief is or could be prayed." As Justice Rehnquist put it on one occasion: "A declaratory judgment is simply a statement of rights, not a binding order."[26] It was for just such a declaratory judgment that Dr. Tileston had pleaded initially, and unsuccessfully, because he then lacked standing.

The Supreme Court itself has admitted the obvious: that the line between advisory opinions and declaratory judgments is a thin one, and that "it would be difficult, if it would be possible, to fashion a precise test for determining in every case whether there is such a controversy [as is demanded by a declaratory judgment]."[27] But it insisted in the *Ashwander* case[28] that the Federal Declaratory Judgment Act "does not attempt to change the essential requisites for the exercise of judicial power"; and, on another occasion, it stated that it cannot be invoked to "obtain an advisory decree upon a hypothetical state of facts."[29]

FOUR: Not only must the complainant in federal court expressly declare that he or she is invoking the Constitution of the United States—"the ultimate touchstone of constitutionality," in Justice Frankfurter's phrase—but a specific live rather than dead constitutional issue citing the particular provision on which he or she relies in that document must be raised by him or her; the Court will not entertain generalities. Indeed, it has held specifically that an attack on a statute as "violative of the Constitution of the United States" is insufficient on its face.[30] Nor will a simple contention that a statute

---

[25] A famed declaratory judgment was the 7:0 fifty-nine pages ruling by the New Jersey Supreme Court, authorizing the father of Karen Ann Quinlan, Joseph T. Quinlan, to have her life terminated medically by arranging for the disconnection of the life-sustaining machinery that had kept the comatose Karen Ann alive for over a year as of 1976. The state of New Jersey appealed its highest court's verdict to the U.S. Supreme Court, but the latter denied review. (*Garger v. New Jersey*, 429 U.S. 922, [1976].) (*In the Matter of Karen Ann Quinlan*, decided March 31, 1976.) This action was taken shortly following the judicial decision, but the stricken girl "lived" comatose for almost ten more years; death came in June 1985.

[26] *Steffel v. Thompson*, 415 U.S. 452 (1974) at 482

[27] *Maryland Casualty Co. v. Pacific Coal and Oil Co.*, 312 U.S. 270 (1941) at 273.

[28] *Ashwander v. Tennessee Valley Authority*, 297 U.S. 288 (1936) at 325.

[29] *Electric Bond & Share Co. v. Securities & Exchange Commission*, 303 U.S. 419 (1938) at 443.

[30] *Herndon v. Georgia*, 295 U.S. 441 (1935).

is "in violation of the Fifth or Seventh Amendments to the Constitution" do.[31] Specific, careful, closely reasoned documentation is essential. Moreover, the issue must be raised *seasonably; that is timely* assertion of the constitutional issue must be made before a tribunal having proper jurisdiction, and it must be reasserted at every opportunity in the course of the litigation. The Court is not concerned with dead or moot and thus inappropriate problems— as, for example, one caused by the death of the defendant in an appeal in a criminal action.[32]

FIVE: The Court looks askance on any attempt to have the judicial decision-cake and eat it too. Thus, *it will not pass on the constitutionality of a statute or of an official action at the instance of one who has availed himself or herself of its benefits, but then decides to challenge its legality anyway.* An illustration is the case of a St. Louis, Missouri, casting company, in the role of owner of property within a special sewer district who connected his premises with a freshly constructed sewer and availed himself of its benefits. But then he challenged the validity of the statute that permitted a tax levy against him as a recipient of the services as being an unconstitutional infringement of his property rights under the Fourteenth Amendment.[33] The Supreme Court held unanimously that by accepting and availing himself of the benefits of the construction and zoning involved, the owner was "estopped from maintaining a suit" on the grounds and under the circumstances here involved.

SIX: All remedies in the pertinent lower federal and/or state courts must have been exhausted, and prescribed lower court procedure duly followed before making application to the U.S. Supreme Court for review. As Judge Augustus N. Hand of the U.S. Court of Appeals for the Second Circuit Court once observed, the rule of exhaustion is the only rule which is consistent with orderly government." Thus, the highest court of the land will not review a judgment of a state court unless on the face of the record it affirmatively appears that a *federal question constituting an appropriate ground* for such review was presented in, and expressly or necessarily decided by, such a state court. For example, in 1963 the Court ruled 6:3 that a New York state judgment had not been taken to the highest New York court empowered to consider it, as statutorily required for Supreme Court review. Hence it dismissed a writ it had granted earlier to hear the case as having been "improvidentially

---

[31] *Chapin v. Frye*, 179 U.S. 127 (1900).

[32] *List v. Pennsylvania*, 131 U.S. 396 (1888). See also *DeFunis v. Odegaard*, 416 U.S. 312 (1974) for a controversially "mooted" case (that had nothing to do with death). See also the Court's mooting in *National Organization of Women v. Idaho*, 459 U.S. 809 (1982) and in *Carmen v. Idaho*, 459 U.S. 809 (1982) of two interesting questions involving the proposed Equal Rights Amendment: (1) whether or not states could change a "yes" vote to a "no" vote and (2) whether or not Congress had acted constitutionally when it extended the ERA ratification date by simple majority vote rather than by a two-thirds vote. The Court held both questions moot because even the majority-vote extension of three years had expired on June 30, 1982.

[33] *St. Louis v. Prendergast Co.*, 260 U.S. 459 (1923).

granted."[34] A decade later, the Court sternly and unanimously rejected a challenge by a group of legal rights organizations to a new system of New York State court registration and supervision being applied to charitable corporations practicing law in that state by the Appellate Division of the New York State Supreme Court. The U.S. Supreme Court held that the groups had to apply to the Appellate Division for an exception to the registration requirements and be refused *before* they could bring a constitutional challenge to the supervision system.[35] No matter how vital, inviting, timely, or attractive the issue involved may be, the Supreme Court will not accept a case unless the remedies below have been exhausted; nor does it matter that a lower tribunal might not be "friendly" to the substance of a suit—as has occurred frequently in connection with state court adjudication of such contentious problems as desegregation, criminal justice, and Bible-reading in the public schools.[36] Orderly procedure is of the very essence of the judicial process; judicial and administrative chaos is the alternative.

SEVEN: *Assuming it has been properly raised, the federal question at issue must be substantial rather than trivial; it must be the pivotal point of the case; and it must be part of the plaintiff's case rather than a part of his adversary's defense.* Whatever the subjective overtones of the term "substantial" may be, it is normally not an overwhelming job to distinguish between a "substantial" and a "trivial" federal question. For example, the controversies surrounding the extent of the federal government's authority in connection with the Tennessee Valley Authority projects, raised in sundry respects in the famous case of *Ashwander v. T.V.A.,*[37] and the attempts by the State of California to close its borders to a destitute non-citizen traveling in interstate commerce as well as those by Connecticut and others to deny welfare benefits to persons recently migrated from other states,[38] are pertinent instances of substantial federal questions. On the other hand, the endeavors of some Greek-letter fraternities on various campuses in New York and Colorado to have the Supreme Court review requirements by the Trustees of the State University of New York, those of the University of Colorado setting deadlines on removing restrictive racial and/or religious clauses from fraternity "constitutions" on pain of revocation of campus privileges, and a student's legal challenge to an "F" he received in a Chemistry course were summarily—and quite predictably—turned aside as not involving such a substantial question.[39]

---

[34] *Gotthilf v. Sills,* 375 U.S. 79. See also *United States v. Raines,* 362 U.S. 17 (1960) at 21.

[35] *Young Lords Party v. Supreme Court of New York,* 414 U.S. 1088 (1973).

[36] E.g., *Michel v. Louisiana,* 350 U.S. 91 (1955) and *Wallace v. Jaffree,* 52 LW 3719 (1984). See also *Fay v. Noia,* 372 U.S. 319 (1963) for both sides of the exhaustion controversy.

[37] *Ashwander v. Tennessee Valley Authority,* 297 U.S. 288 (1936).

[38] *Edwards v. California,* 314 U.S. 160 (1941) and *Shapiro v. Thompson,* 394 U.S. 618 (1969), respectively.

[39] *Webb v. State University of New York,* 348 U.S. 867 (1954); *The New York Times,* June

EIGHT: Although it would be an oversimplification, if not entirely incorrect, to state that the Supreme Court reviews only questions of law, it is nonetheless generally true that *questions of fact—as distinct from questions of law—are not normally accepted as proper bases for review.* This is especially true of the area of judicial review of administrative construction of statutes, when a *purely* factual question has no chance of a hearing, for Congress has statutorily provided for the finality of administrative finding of fact.

However, it is axiomatic that the problem of which questions are of "law," which are of "fact," and which are "mixtures" is a difficult one. Any attempt to draw a rigid line poses a genuine problem because of the very nature of the two concepts—as was demonstrated again in a station house "show-up" identification case in late 1972, in which the Court, dividing 5:3, held that the dispute between the litigants was not so much over "the elemental facts" as over the "constitutional significance to be attached to them."[40] In the words of an expert on the subject, ". . . matters of law grow downward into roots of fact, and matters of fact reach upward, without a break, into matters of law."[41] In any event, the Court will not permit administrative procedures, which most frequently are at issue in this particular dichotomy, to fall below what it is prone to regard as a "constitutional minimum," a concept that is clearly a matter of law subject to judicial review.

NINE: While, as already indicated, Britain's highest tribunal, the House of Lords, considered itself *bound* by its own prior decisions until it publicly and expressly modified that doctrine in 1966,[42] *the Supreme Court of the United States has never held itself absolutely bound by its precedents.* It has often adhered to many of these, of course, and will presumably continue to do so, but it has not permitted itself to become enslaved by past decisions. Nor could it do so—the law does not stand still; Justice Holmes's aforementioned "felt necessities of the time" are ever-compelling facts of governmental life. We must not expect from the Court, in Chief Justice Hughe's trenchant warning, "the icy stratosphere of certainty." And in Justice Cardozo's immortal truth: "Somewhere between worship of the past and exaltation of the present, the path of safety will be found."[43] But a decision of the Supreme

---

18, 1965, p. 1 and *ibid.*, September 3, 1966, p. 10; and *Mercurio v. Board of Regents of the University of Nebraska*, 463 U.S. 1214 (1983), respectively.

[40] *Neil v. Biggers*, 409 U.S. 188. The majority comprised the Chief Justice and Associate Justices Powell (the author of the opinion), White, Blackmun, and Rehnquist; in dissent were Douglas, Brennan, and Stewart. (Marshall did not participate.)

[41] John Dickinson, *Administrative Justice and the Supremacy of Law* (Cambridge: Harvard University Press, 1927), p. 55.

[42] See the Lord Chancellor's (Lord Gardiner's) announcement, in *House of Lords Official Reports*, vol. 276, no. 43, col. 677, July 26, 1966. *Parliamentary Debate (Hansard Weekly)* and 1 W.L.R. 1234 (1966). For an interesting, pertinent, recent House of Lords decision, see *Broome v. Cassell & Co.* [1972] 2 W.L.R. 645, in particular Lord Diplock, at 721.

[43] Benjamin N. Cardozo, *The Nature of the Judicial Process* (New Haven, Ct: Yale University Press, 1921), p. 160.

Court is utterly binding *in federal matters* on all courts below, state as well as federal, regardless of sporadic foot-dragging and aberrations.[44]

TEN: The Court has been inclined to defer to certain legislative or executive actions by classifying an issue otherwise quite properly before it as a political question—hence refusing to come to grips with it. Depending on one's point of view—after all, is not every constitutional question or decision "political" to some extent?—this intriguing practice or formula is either a mere *device* for transferring the responsibility for a question or decision to another branch of the government, or it is in fact *required* by the constitutionally explicit or implicit realities and necessities of the presence of the separation of powers principle. What really *is* a "political question"? Giving short shrift to this inquiry, Justice Holmes, coming to the core of an issue briskly and pithily as always, once characterized it as " . . . little more than a play on words."[45] He would have no part of the concept as a judicial mechanism, though nevertheless fully recognizing, of course, the realities of the political facts of life. Jefferson, on the contrary, regarded all questions involving the constitutionality of acts of Congress that might come before the Court as "political questions."

Professor Edward S. Corwin essayed the following, perhaps not entirely helpful, definition of the vexatious verbiage in his last monumental annotation of the Constitution:

> . . . a political question relates to the possession of political power, of sovereignty, of government, the determination of which is vested in Congress and the President, and whose decisions are binding on the courts.[46]

In a different vein, Professor J. W. Peltason, one of the students of the revered Princeton scholar, preferred to view political questions as "those which judges choose not to decide, and a question becomes political by the judges' refusal to decide it."[47] Professor Charles C. Post regarded the term as an "open sesame word" that "instantly relieved [the Court] of all control over the problem."[48] And Judge Learned Hand labeled it—insofar as its scope is undefined—as a "stench in the nostrils of strict constructionists."[49] A good many of the Supreme Court's decisions, though not necessarily invalidating Corwin's analysis, would seem to support Peltason's more realistic evaluation. However, judges can, and do, change their minds, depending on the posture and setting of an issue; what may be rejected or avoided as a political question

---

[44]See pp. 235–45 and 354–56, *supra*.

[45]*Nixon v. Herndon*, 273 U.S. 536 (1927) at 540.

[46]Edward S. Corwin, *The Consitution of the United States*, revised and annotated (Washington, DC: U.S. Government Printing Office, 1953), p. 547.

[47]Jack W. Peltason, *Federal Courts in the Political Process* (Garden City, NY: Doubleday, 1955), p. 10.

[48]*The Supreme Court and Political Questions* (Baltimore: The Johns Hopkins University Press, 1936), p. 11.

[49]*The Bill of Rights* (Cambridge: Harvard University Press, 1958), p. 15, n. 3.

today may quite conceivably be accepted for review on its merit at a later date, of which the legislative reapportionment–redistricting decisions are pertinent illustrations.

For years—to be precise, until its precedent-shattering decision in what must be regarded as one of the two or at most three most significant Supreme Court decisions of the twentieth century, namely *Baker v. Carr* in 1962[50]—the Court simply would not get involved in the question of the constitutionality or even the justiciability of the way in which legislatures and constitutions either did or did not apportion or district state and/or congressional districts, no matter how obvious, how outrageous, and even how illegal the apportionment or districting or lack of it might have been! The Court, in the words of the main advocate of this determined and consistent stand, Justice Frankfurter (to whom Fred Rodell liked to refer as "the Court's Emily Post"), was not going to get itself involved in such a "patently political question," in such a "political thicket," which in his view was, after all, an area of the "exclusive authority" of legislatures.[51]

Thus, the constitutionality of the well-known county unit system of Georgia—a prime example of anti-urban, pro-rural legislative gerrymandering—had been before the Court on several occasions. Under that system, each of the various counties received a minimum of two and a maximum of six electoral votes for the eight most populous counties, including Fulton County (Atlanta), with each county's electoral vote going to the candidate receiving the highest popular vote therein. The net effect had been that the one million inhabitants of Fulton County—of whom a considerable proportion of registered votes were black—received but one-third more votes than the handful of residents in numerous small rural counties. In other words a vote in the small counties of Georgia had from 11 to 120 times as much weight as one in Fulton! Yet attempts to have the Supreme Court come to grips with the matter had come to naught as recently as 1950, 1951, 1958, and 1959. The Court stood by its pronouncement in the first of these cases, *South v. Peters*,[52] that "a state's geographical distribution of electoral strength among its political subdivision" is a political question. Thereby the Court continued to cling to the general philosophy and tactics it had enunciated in *Colegrovev. Green* in 1946,[53] a case concerning congressional districts in Illinois. Here appellants had contended that the Illinois law apportioning them was unconstitutional because the various districts were characterized by rank inequalities. For example, one in Chicago had 914,053 inhabitants, whereas one in southern Illinois comprised a mere 112,116. But in its decision the Supreme Court, with only seven Justices participating, and these split three ways, neverthe-

---

[50]369 U.S. 186.
[51]See his opinion for the Court in *Colegrove v. Green*, 328 U.S. 549 (1946) and his dissenting opinion in *Baker v. Carr*, 369 U.S. 186 (1962), both discussed later.
[52]339 U.S. 276 (1950).
[53]328 U.S. 549.

less held, through Justice Frankfurter and Associate Justices Reed and Burton, that it could not intervene in such a political question, which it regarded as being up to the legislature to determine and alleviate. If the Court did intervene, wrote Frankfurter, it would be entering into a "political thicket," and that, anyway, it is "hostile to a democratic system to involve the judiciary in the politics of the people."[54] Justice Black, speaking also for Justices Douglas and Murphy, dissented vigorously, contending that the state of Illinois's failure to redistrict was tantamount to "willful legislative discrimination" and constituted a denial of the equal protection of the laws presumably guaranteed by the Fourteenth Amendment ot the Constitution of the United States.

But the days of the "political question" doctrine in *this* sector of public law were clearly numbered when the Court, after twice having noted probable jurisdiction in its 1960–61 term, agreed to hear argument in a 1961 Tennessee case involving that state's outright refusal to reapportion the General Assembly among its ninety-five counties, seats that had been arbitrarily and capriciously apportioned by a 1901 statute—and never touched since, despite an almost fivefold growth of eligible voters and major shifts of population from rural to urban areas generally. The case was *Baker v. Carr*. Knowing its significance, the Supreme Court ordered three and a half hours of oral argument,[55] with U.S. Solicitor General Archibald Cox arguing as *amicus curiae* on the side of the plaintiff on behalf of the U.S. government. The mere willingness to accept *Baker v. Carr* for review served notice of the possibility, if not the probability, of a dramatic "political question" shift. And it was dramatic, indeed! There were six opinions, covering a total of 165 pages, with Justice Frankfurter's agitated and angry dissenting opinion for Justice Harlan and himself consuming 65 pages alone! Still what Justice Brennan actually decided in his opinion for the Court can be described quickly: (1) that the federal courts *do* have jurisdiction in apportionment–districting cases, (2) that the Baker complaint did present a *justiciable controversy*, and (3) that Baker and his co-appellants had *standing* to bring the suit. Notwithstanding Frankfurter's deeply felt warnings, in what was to prove his last opinion prior to his retirement for reasons of health later that year (1962), that the judiciary was damaging itself by getting into such "political matters," that it was immersing itself dangerously and wrongly in a "mathematical quagmire," the Court majority of six (Justice Whittaker had not participated in the case), without addressing itself to the specific merits of Baker's contentions, (a)

---

[54] Ibid., at 554. The decisive fourth vote in the case was provided by Justice Rutledge who, in effect, agreed with the three dissenters that the issue *per se* was justiciable, but nonetheless chose to concur in the Frankfurther opinion for the Court in view of "the shortness of time remaining" before the next election and the difficulties of an election at large in a state with so many congressional districts. Justice Jackson did not sit; he was at the Nuremberg war crimes trials. Chief Justice Stone had just died, and his successor, Fred M. Vinson, had not yet been sworn in.

[55] *Baker v. Carr*, 368 U.S. 804 (1961).

regarded them as eminently justiciable in the courts (i.e., capable of adjudi-cation) and (b) remanded the case to the lower federal court from which it came for purposes of such adjudication. (Ultimately, Tennessee was ordered to redistrict. It complied, albeit haltingly.) In short, rejecting the Frankfurter admonition that " . . . in a democratic society like ours, relief [for political mischief] must come through an aroused popular conscience that sears the conscience of the people's representatives,"[56] the highest court in the land in effect reformulated the "political question" concept and doctrine. No longer would it apply to the matter at issue. In Brennan's words, the political ques-tion doctrine relates properly to "the relationship between the judiciary and the coordinate branches of the Federal Government, and not the federal judi-ciary's relationship to the states . . ."[57] Over Frankfurter's specific disagree-ment on the point, Brennan thus confined "political questions," by way of the *Baker v. Carr* decision, to "a function of the separation of powers."[58]

As a logical result of the decision, the Supreme Court subsequently struck down as unconstitutional the infamous, although by then somewhat revised, Georgia County Unit System for state legislative apportionment in *Gray v. Sanders* in 1963,[59] plus state legislative malapportionment of congressional districts in 1964 in *Wesberry v. Sanders.*[60] Later in 1964, in the most far-reaching and most contentious of all of the myriad of post-*Baker v. Carr*–related decisions, the Court required that *both* houses of state legislatures be apportioned on the basis of *population*—a decision handed down in a six-case "package" known by its lead case, *Reynolds v. Sims.*[61] In 1968 the principle was extended to local government,[62] and in 1969 the Court made clear, 6:3, that states would have to justify *any* numerical deviation between districts on pain of findings of unconstitutionality.[63] Decisions in 1970 held the "one-person one-vote" rule to apply to all elective bodies exercising "general gov-ernmental authority"[64]—even school boards (although not all of them)[65]—but *not* to those that, like the New York City Board of Estimate, do not possess that kind of power,[66] nor, accordingly, to elected *judges.*[67] Ultimately, devia-

[56]Ibid., 369 U.S. 186 (1962) at 270.
[57]Ibid., at 210.
[58]Ibid., at 217.
[59]372 U.S. 368. (Its famed "one-person, one-vote" statement is at 381.)
[60]376 U.S. 1.
[61]377 U.S. 533.
[62]*Avery v. Midland County,* 390 U.S. 474.
[63]*Wells v. Rockefeller,* 394 U.S. 542.
[64]E.g., *Hadley v. Junior College District of Metropolitan Kansas Cityy,* 397 U.S. 50.
[65]*Rosenthal v. Board of Education of Central High School,* 420 U.S. 985 (1975), where a central school board of eight appointees was selected: two each from four districts of elected town school board memberships. On the other hand, the Court applied the "one-person, one-vote" principle anew by refusing to review its embrace below in the 1975 case of *Regional High School District # 5 v. Baker,* 423 U.S. 995.
[66]*Bergerman v. Lindsay,* 398 U.S. 955.
[67]*Wells v. Edwards,* 409 U.S. 1095 (1973).

tions were sanctioned for certain political boundaries at the state level,[68] but not even as much as 0.7(!) percent for congressional districts,[69] and there are distinct limits on how much even a state may deviate.[70]

It should be clear, however, that the important contraction brought about by *Baker v. Carr* has by no means removed the concept of "political question" doctrine as such. A case like the well-known 1849 *Luther v. Borden*[71] would today assuredly continue to be treated, in line with the new Brennan formula announced in *Baker v. Carr*, as a political question. *Luther v. Borden* arose out of the Rhode Island Dorr Rebellion, early in America's history. Very briefly, the facts of the case were such that the Supreme Court found itself confronted with the crucial decision as to *which one* of two governments battling for legal supremacy in Rhode Island in 1842 was *the* legal one. The Court concluded that this was clearly a "political question": For the President of the United States, John Tyler, in reserving the right to exercise the power, conferred on the Chief Executive by Congress in 1795, to send federal troops to aid states in suppressing insurrection, had, by mobilizing the militia (though short of calling it out) in response to the Charter government's plea, indicated that he regarded the original (the "Charter") government as the lawful one of the two, and that this judgment was binding on the judiciary.

If one accepts the concept of the political question at all, the *Luther* example is obviously a much more clear-cut one than those involving legislative apportionment. Yet what a political question *is* remains difficult to determine. Generalization of the doctrine is still virtually impossible. Moreover, as Justice Brennan pointed out in *Baker v. Carr*, " ... the mere fact that [a] suit seeks protection of a political right does not mean it presents a political question. Such an objection is little more than a play upon words."[72] As his colleague Clark put the matter in his concurring opinion, " ... national respect for the courts is more enhanced through the forthright enforcement of [basic national rights such as fair legislative apportionment] than by rendering them nugatory through the interposition of subterfuges."[73] And, as Professor Louis Henkin asked suggestively: "Would not the part of the courts in our system, the institution of judicial review, and their public and intellectual acceptance, fare better if we broke open that package, assign its components elsewhere, and threw the package away?"[74] However attractive in the-

---

[68] *City of Virginia Beach v. Howell*, 410 U.S. 315 (1973); *Gaffney v. Cummings*, 412 U.S. 735 (1973); and *White v. Regester*, 412 U.S. 755 (1973).

[69] *Karcher v. Daggett*, 462 U.S. 725 (1983).

[70] See, e.g., the Court's unanimous "no" in 1975 to a North Dakota attempt to institute multi-member senatorial districts and to deviate up to 20 percent. (*Chapman v. Meier*, 420 U.S. 1.)

[71] 7 Howard 1.

[72] Opinion for the Court, 369 U.S. 186, at 209.

[73] Ibid., at 261–62. See also the Court's forthright disposition of potentially delicate political issues in *Powell v. McCormack*, 395 U.S. 486 (1969).

[74] "Is There a 'Political Question' Doctrine?" 85 *Yale Law Journal* 597 (1976), p. 625.

ory, the "political question" maxim is a treadmill; perhaps to a fatal degree its supporting logic is circular.

ELEVEN: In the event of a validly challenged statute, the presumption of its constitutionality is always in its favor. As early as 1827, Justice Bushrod Washington wrote:

> It is but a decent respect to the wisdom, integrity, and patriotism of the legislative body, by which any law is passed, to presume in favor of its validity, until its violation of the Constitution is proved beyond a reasonable doubt.[75]

Hence, as the history of the Court shows, if a legislative enactment can be construed to be in reasonable harmony with the Constitution, a majority of the Court will almost always do so. Obviously, the views of the Justices have differed somewhat, often drastically, on the meaning of the word "reasonable." Thus, though there is today practically no judicial interference with legislation dealing with economic and social matters, the Court remains seriously divided on what constitutes "reasonable" legislative restrictions in certain areas of civil rights and liberties, such as the national security sector in the face of the specific guarantees under the First Amendment. For example, generally speaking, a hard core of five members of the 1966–67 Warren bench—the Chief Justice himself and Justices Black, Douglas, Brennan, and Fortas—would brook little, if any, legislative encroachments in this sector, whereas a hard core of three—Justices Clark, Harlan, and White—would exercise more or less judicial self-restraint, with Justice Stewart more unpredictable here, given his pronounced concern both for freedom of expression and judicial abstemiousness.

In any event, the Court will not normally formulate a rule of constitutional law broader than is required by the precise facts to which it is to be applied. "The cardinal principle of statutory construction," wrote Chief Justice Hughes in a famous case,

> is to save and not to destroy. We have repeatedly held that as between two possible interpretations of a statute, by one of which it would be unconstitutional and the other valid, our plain duty is to adopt that which will save the act. Even to avoid a serious doubt the rule is the same.[76]

On the other hand, Justice Stone, normally a firm adherent to the philosophy of presumption of constitutionality, implied an important exception to the general rule in his footnote in the otherwise rather unimportant *Carolene Products* case.[77] which footnote became one of the most famous of all time! It was there that he stated that perhaps there might be occasion for departing from the normal presumption of constitutionality for legislation in cases where *the legislative action in question involved a restriction or curtailment*

---

[75] *Ogden v. Saunders*, 12 Wheaton 213 (1827).
[76] *N.L.R.B. v. Jones & Laughlin Steel Corporation*, 301 U.S. 1 (1937).
[77] *United States v. Carolene Products Co.*, 304 U.S. 144 (1938) at 152–53, fn. 4.

of the ordinary political processes which could generally be expected to be employed to bring about the negation of undesirable legislation, or where it appeared to be within "a specific prohibition of the Constitution, such as those of the first ten amendments, which are deemed equally specific when held to be embraced within the Fourteenth.[78] And as of the late 1960s, the Burger Court adopted a posture of judicial "suspicion" under which it began to regard legislative activity in certain categories as "suspect," notably in those of race, national origin, alienage, and sex. In those areas, legislatures (and executives) would henceforth have to prove the existence of a "compelling state interest" rather than, as heretofore, a mere "rational relationship" in order to see their actions survive "close" judicial scrutiny.

TWELVE: In the exercise of what some commentators have been fond of styling "judicial parsimony," *if a case or controversy can be decided on any other than constitutional grounds—such as by statutory construction, which constitutes the greatest single area of the Court's work, or if it can rest on an independent state ground—the Court will be eager to do so.* For normally it will not decide questions of a constitutional nature unless absolutely necessary to the decision of the case, and even then it will draw such a decision as narrowly as possible, being ever loath to formulate a rule of constitutional law broader than is clearly required by the precise facts to which it is to be applied. Nor will it anticipate a question of constitutional law in advance of the necessity of deciding it. As Justice White put it in an "obscenity" case, the proper approach is "not to invalidate . . . but to construe . . . narrowly."[79] Justice Frankfurter succinctly underscored the point of anticipation in an edifying exchange with Thurman Arnold, who was acting as counsel for Dr. J. P. Peters, petitioner in the loyalty-security case of *Peters v. Hobby.*[80] Mr. Arnold pleaded with the Court that he would not like to win the case on the narrow procedural, statutory ground to which a majority of the members of the bench was evidently inclining. Responded Justice Frankfurter: "The question is not whether you want to win the case on that ground or not. This Court reaches constitutional issues last, not first." He might well have quoted Justice Brandeis's famous assertion that the " . . . most important thing we do is not doing." And "not doing" is what Justice Rehnquist did in 1977 by putting off a potentially significant decision on parental commitment of unwilling children to Pennsylvania mental institutions, ruling: "The fact that it would be convenient for the parties and the public to have promptly decided whether this legislation assailed is valid cannot justify a departure from these settled rules of status and class."[81]

---

[78] Ibid., (italics supplied). On the issue of what has been regarded as a judicial "double standard," see my *Freedom and the Court: Civil Rights and Liberties in the United States,* 4th ed. (New York: Oxford University Press, 1982), ch. 2.

[79] *United States v. Thirty-Seven (37) Photographs,* 402 U.S. 363 (1971) at 375, plurality opinion.

[80] 349 U.S. 311 (1955). The exchange is reported in 23 *U.S. Law Week* 265–66 (1955).

[81] *Kremens v. Bartley,* 431 U.S. 119 (1977), quoting Justice Brandeis's opinion in *Ashwander v. Tennessee Valley Authority,* 297 U.S. 288 (1936).

The loyalty-security field affords a host of pertinent illustrations of the Court's preference for a resort to its potent weapon of statuory construction rather than to constitutional grounds. This delicate and emotion-laden area of public policy is tailor-made for such an approach, which preserves the statute while sometimes smoothing certain ragged edges. Thus, the Court effects a gain, however moderate it may be, for individual civil rights, while retaining the generally popular and politically desirable law. To cite some instances: it is precisely what the Court did in narrowing executive authority to dismiss government employees under the Summary Suspension Act of 1950 by ruling that the act did not authorize dismissal of employees holding "non-sensitive" positions,[82] in limiting the power of the Secretary of State to withhold a passport from a citizen "for any substantive reason he may choose," holding that the Immigration and Nationality Act of 1952 did not authorize such sweeping discretionary powers,[83] and in holding that, while the Magnuson Seaman's Act of 1950 had given the executive branch the authority to act to prevent sabotage, it had emphatically not provided it with the authority to inquire into seamen's beliefs and associations before granting them seamen's licenses.[84] In each of these instances, congressional reaction was to the effect that "we did so intend to authorize what you say we did not," but in the absence of the passage of any clarifying or amplifying amendments the two statutes stood as judicially construed. After all, statutory construction is an act of judgment and, as Justice Holmes once observed succinctly, applies to cases "in which there is a fair contest between two readings." On the other hand, there are also instances when there is really no contest—as the Court held unanimously in no uncertain terms when, in 1975, it rejected the President's "impounding" of $9 billion in water pollution funds because the legislation establishing the program had clearly not given him that authority.[85]

THIRTEEN: The Court will not ordinarily impute illegal motives to the lawmakers. "So long as Congress acts in pursuance of its constitutional power," explained Justice Harlan in a much-debated decision upholding certain aspects of the investigative authority of the House Committee on Un-American Activiites,[86] "the judiciary lacks authority to intervene on the basis of the motives which spurred the exercise of that power." This sentiment was echoed by Justice Black in one of his last opinions, in which he wrote that no precedent existed for holding a law violative of "equal protection solely because of the motivations of the men who voted for it."[87] And as early as 1810 Chief Justice Marshall had written that it "may well be doubted how

---

[82] Cole v. Young, 351 U.S. 536 (1956).

[83] Kent and Briehl v. Dulles, 357 U.S. 116 (1958).

[84] Schneider v. Smith, 390 U.S. 17 (1968). For an excellent more recent illustration, see T.W.A. v. Hardison, 432 U.S. 63 (1977).

[85] Train v. City of New York, 420 U.S. 35.

[86] Barenblatt v. United States, 360 U.S. 109 (1959). (Italics supplied.)

[87] Palmer v. Thompson, 403 U.S. 217 (1971), majority opinion at 224.

far the validity of a law depends upon the motives of its framers."[88] Indeed, the Court is not supposed to consider *motives* at all; but, as Max Radin once wrote, that concept is indeed a "transparent and absurd fiction"[89]—to which the decision in the *Child Labor Tax case*[90] of 1922, for example, bears eloquent witness.

However, to compound the problem, the Supreme Court is expected to, and very frequently does, take legislative *intent* or *purpose* into account; yet, it is no easy task to separate motives and intent, and Justice Frankfurter, for one, consistently refused to do so. The Court, however, has to essay judgments: thus, it answered in the negative, although by a margin of but one vote (5:4), the question of whether or not anything in the current patent laws demonstrated a congressional intent to deny patents to *inventions that happen to be alive*, thereby in effect telling the scientific community that it may patent new forms of life.[91] Justice Holmes wrote, "I only wnat to know what the words mean." Still: "A ... word is not a crystal, transparent and unchanged, it is the skin of a living thought and may vary greatly in color and content according to the circumstances and time in which it is used."[92] And he found *policy* in words.[93] Or, as Justice Cardozo wrote so appropriately, "a great principle of constitutional law is not susceptible of comprehensive statement in an adjective."[94] The *Steel Seizure case*[95] of 1952, in which seven separate opinions were written, provided a basis for an opinion for the Court only because a sufficient number of Justices was able to agree on the single point that Congress, in enacting the Taft–Hartley Act, had deliberately *intended* not to provide for presidential authority to seize struck plants. Here the intent of Congress proved to be the basis for the Court's judgment that the Chief Executive had usurped legislative power, with the Justices, as is their custom, equating intent with legislative history.

This approach is sometimes styled "psychoanalyzing Congress" by some of the less reverent observers of the governmental scene, who have considerable—and perhaps well-grounded—doubt of the infallibility of the Holmesian contention, frequently quoted by Justice Frankfurter, that " ... a page of history is worth a volume of logic."[96] yet whatever their merits otherwise, for this purpose at least the *Congressional Record* and the reports of the var-

---

[88] *Fletcher v. Peck*, 6 Cranch 87, at 130.
[89] "Statutory Interpretation," 43 *Harvard Law Review* 863d (April 1930).
[90] *Baily v. Drexel Furniture Co.*, 259 U.S. 20.
[91] *Diamond v. Chakrabarty*, 447 U.S. 303 (1980).
[92] *Town v. Eisner*, 245 U.S. 418 (1917) at 424.
[93] See Felix Frankfurter, "Some Reflections on the Readings of Statutes," Sixth Annual Benjamin N. Cardozo Lecture before the Association of the Bar of the City of New York, March 8, 1947. (Reprinted in 47 *Columbia Law Review* (1947), 527–46.)
[94] *Carter v. Carter Coal Co.*, 298 U.S. 238 (1936) at 327.
[95] *Youngstown Sheet and Tube Co. v. Sawyer*, 343 U.S. 579.
[96] *New York Trust Co. v. Eisner*, 256 U.S. 345 (1921) at 349.

ious committees of Congress are a constant and evidently fertile source of reference for the members of the Supreme Court. Thus, in unanimously upholding the Voting Rights Act of 1965, the Court repeatedly referred to congressional intent to eradicate the "substantial voting discrimination" in specific sections of the country because it "knew" about these and wanted to remove them. Again and again Chief Justice Warren used the term "Congress knew," thus underscoring its intent or purpose.[97] Conversely, we have the example of utter disregard by a five-member Court majority, led by Justice Brennan, in its contentious 1979 Weber racial quotas-in-employment case, wherein it disregarded not only the express language of Title VII of the Civil Rights Act of 1964, but also its demonstrable congressional intent![98]

FOURTEEN: If the court does find that it must hold a law unconstitutional, it will usually try hard to confine the holding to that particular section of the statute which was successfully challenged on constitutional grounds — provided such a course of action is at all feasible. It would not be feasible, of course, if the section at issue constituted the veritable heart of the legislation, in which case the Court would follow a well-established rule of statutory construction: if the various parts of a statute are inextricably connected to such degrees as to warrant the assumption that the legislature intended the law to function as a whole, then if some portions of the statute are unconstitutional the law must be treated as unconstitutional in its entirety.[99] "Sectionalized" unconstitutionality is known as separability—sometimes as severability[100]—for which Congress now customarily, and quite specifically, provides in its statutes, although it neither always does so nor is it required by the courts to do so.[101] A typical separability clause, taken from the War Powers Resolution of 1973, reads:

> If any provision of this joint resolution or the application therof to any person or circumstance is held invalid, the remainder of the joint resolution and the application of such provision to any other person or circumstance shall not be affected thereby.

This not only serves to have those sections not affected by the Court's particular decision, but it may also act to preserve the law's entire structure for a test involving different litigants.

---

[97] South Carolina v. Katzenbach 383 U.S. 301 (1966), opinion for the Court.

[98] United Steel Workers v. Weber, 443 U.S. 193.

[99] For example, see Pollock v. Farmers' Loan and Trust Co., 158 U.S. 601 (1895).

[100] A recent (1983) example is the severability of No. 244 (c)(2) of the Immigration and Naturalization Code, declaring the congressional veto (here by one house) unconstitutional (7:2), but also applying it (6:3) to all of the other similar 211 laws that contained one- or two-house vetoes. (Immigration and Naturalization Service v. Chadha, 462 U.S. 919.)

[101] See Chief Justice Burger's opinion in Tilton v. Richarson, 403 U.S. 672 (1971), in which a portion of a federal statute was declared unconstitutional despite the acknowledged "absence of an express separability provision."

The series of decisions declaring portions of the Uniform Code of Military Justice Act of 1950 unconstitutional[102] are cases in point; certain powers delegated to the armed services under it are no longer valid, but the balance of the act stands and is enforced. On the other hand, although initially it was merely the "hot oil" provisions of the National Industry Recovery Act of 1933—standing apart from those provisions of the act dealing with codes of fair competition—that fell as an unconstitutional delegation of legislative power in January 1935,[103] four months later the codes, too, and with them the entire structure of the act, fell on similar grounds.[104]

FIFTEEN: A legislative enactment—or an executive action—may be unwise, junust, unfair, undemocratic, injudicious, " . . . if you like . . . even tyrannical,"[105] or simply stupid, but still be constitutional in the eyes of the Court. Much deference is thus paid to the legislature, and justly so under the American system of separation of powers and division of powers. In the clipped language of a Holmes opinion: "We fully understand . . . the very powerful argument that can be made against the wisdom of this legislation, but on that point we have no concern."[106] Justice Holmes once stated this constitutional and judicial philosophy in typically colorful fashion to the then sixty-one-year-old Justice Stone:

> Young man, about 75 years ago I learned that I was not God. And so, when the people . . . want to do something I can't find anything in the Constitution expressly forbidding them to do, I say, whether I like it or not, "Goddamit, let 'em do it.[107]"

Or, as he said to John W. Davis on another occasion: "Of course I know, and every other sensible man knows, that the Sherman law [the Sherman Anti-Trust Act of 1890] is damned nonsense, but if my country wants to go to hell, I am here to help it."[108] The man who was appointed to the Holmes seat on the Court after Justice Cardozo's death in 1938, Justice Felix Frankfurter, continued to champion that philosophy of judicial self-restraint eloquently, repeatedly, and consistently. It was one he had articulated often, even prior to ascending the Court. For example, in a 1925 article, when he wrote: "Even the most rampant worshiper of judicial supremacy admits that wisdom and justice are not the tests of constitutionality."[109] On the Court, true to that

---

[102] United States ex rel Toth v. Quarles, 350 U.S. 11 (1955); Reid v. Covert 354 U.S. 1 (1957); Kinsella v. Singleton, 361 U.S. 234 (1960), among others.

[103] Panama Refining Co. v. Ryan, 293 U.S. 388.

[104] Schechter v. United States, 295 U.S. 495.

[105] Justice Holmes, dissenting in Lochner v. United States, 198 U.S. 45 (1905).

[106] Noble State Bank v. Haskell, 219 U.S. 575 (1910), opinion for the Court, at 580.

[107] As quoted by Charles P. Curtis in his Lions Under the Throne (Boston: Houghton Mifflin Co., 1947), p. 281.

[108] As told by Francis Biddle, Justice Holmes, Natural Law and the Supreme Court (New York: The Macmillan Co., 1961), p. 9.

[109] "Can the Supreme Court Guarantee Toleration?" 43 New Republic 85 (1925) at 87.

philosophy, he thus dissented vigorously from the majority's declaration of unconstitutionality of a section of the Immigration and Nationality Act of 1940 in *Trop v. Dulles*:

> It is not easy to stand aloof and allow want of wisdom to prevail, to disregard one's own strongly held view of what is wise in the conduct of affairs. But it is not the business of this Court to pronounce policy. It must observe a fastidious regard for limitations on its own power, and this precludes the Court's giving effect to its own notions of what is wise or politic. That self-restraint is of the essence in the observance of the judicial oath, for the Constitution has not authorized the judges to sit in judgment on the wisdom of what Congress and the Executive Branch do.[110]

But once again much, if not all, depends on how the Justices see the line between self-restraint, which they indubitably all recognize as an essential element in the judicial process, and *ultra vires* legislative and executive actions. If, in drawing this line, some Justices, on some issues, are prone to address themselves more to the judicial heart than the judicial mind, who is to say where and how the Founding Fathers of the Constitution of the United States would today distinguish between that document's heart and mind? They too were men, just as judges are men, "not disembodied spirits," in Justice Frankfurter's words; they are men who "respond to human situations . . . [who] do not reside in a vacuum." And his mentor, Holmes, believed that judges "should not be too rigidly bound to the tenets of judicial self-restraint in cases involving civil liberties."[111] Of course, even pedigreed champions of the latter may well disagree on the point in certain specific cases—as is intriguingly demonstrated by Justices Black and Douglas in the *Connecticut Birth Control case* of 1965.[112] There, speaking for the seven-man majority that held the state's anti-birth-control law unconstitutional on a host of grounds, Douglas insisted that " . . . we do not sit [in rendering this decision] as a super-legislature to determine the wisdom, need, and propriety of laws that touch economic problems, businsess affairs, or social conditions. This law, however, operates directly on an intimate relation of husand and wife, and their physician's role in one aspect of that relation."[113] Black, however, dissenting together with his colleague Stewart, regarded the Court's action as one "based on subjective considerations of 'natural justice' [a formula that] is no less dangerous when used to enforce this Court's views about personal rights than those about economic rights."[114] Judges are men (and women). . . .

---

[110]356 U.S. 86 (1958) at 120.

[111]As quoted by Chief Justice Stone to Professor Clinton Rossiter, April 12, 1941, related by Alpheus T. Mason in *Harlan Fiske Stone: Pillar of the Law* (New York: The Viking Press, 1956), p. 516

[112]*Griswold v. Connecticut*, 381 U.S. 479.

[113]Ibid., at 482.

[114]Ibid., at 522.

SIXTEEN: The Supreme Court has reiterated time and again that it *is not designed to serve as a check against inept, unwise, emotional unrepresentative legislators.* Chief Justice Waite put it well when he wrote in 1876 that for *"protection against abuses by legislatures the people must resort to the polls, not the courts."*[115] Some eighty years later, Justice Douglas reiterated this point of view forcefully: "Congress acting within its constitutional powers, has the final say on policy issues. If it acts unwisely the electorate can make a change."[116] This fundamental truth lies at the very core of the democratic process—a process that enables the people and their representatives at once to rise to soaring heights of wisdom and magnanimity and to descend to the depths of folly and pettiness. Yet that process, under law, proscribes *unconstitutional* action.

THE BULWARK

The Supreme Court of the Untied States of America—which Woodrow Wilson viewed as "the balance wheel of our whole constitutional system ... a vehicle of the Nation's life ..."—[117] may be perpetually steeped in controversy; it may not always have exercised all of its power, or exercised it wisely when it did; it may on occasion have gone well beyond its presumed functions; it may have deliberately avoided issues that might have proved to be potentially troublesome; it may not always have been able to make its decisions "stick"; and there may well be considerable room for improvement. No institution of government can be devised by human beings that will be satisfactory to all people at all times. The Court is much better at saying what the government may *not* do, or what it may do, than in prescribing what public policy the government ought to chart and how to go about doing it. Indeed, the Court should resolutely shun prescriptive policymaking.[118] It has quite enough to do in statutory and constitutional applicaton and interpretation. To reiterate the second Justice Harlan's often-quoted admonition: "The Constitution is not a panacea for every blot upon the public welfare; nor should this Court, ordained as a judicial body, be thought of as a general haven for reform ovements."[119] Paraphrasing Professor Freund, the question is not whether the Court can do everything, but whether it can do something. Of course, it can escape neither controversy nor criticism—nor should it. In

---

[115] *Munn v. Illinois,* 94 U.S. 113, at 134. (Italics supplied.)

[116] *Railway Employees' Department v. Hansen,* 351 U.S. 225 (1956).

[117] *Constitutional Government in the United States* (New York: Columbia University Press, 1907), p. 142.

[118] On this point see Alexander M. Bickel's *The Supreme Court and the Idea of Progress* (New York: Harper & Row, 1970); Raoul Berger, *Government by Judiciary: The Transformation of the Fourteenth Amendment* (Cambridge: Harvard University Press, 1977); and Sanford B. Gabin, *Judicial Review and the Rational Doubt Test* (Port Washington, NY: Kennikat Press Corp., 1980).

[119] *Reynolds v. Sims,* 377 U.S. 533 (1964), dissenting opinion, at 624.

Justice Holmes's oft-quoted words: "We are very quiet there, but it is the quiet of a storm center, as we all know." As an institution at once legal, prolitical, governmental, and human, the Court possesses both the assets and the liabilities that attend these descriptive characteristics.

Yet, when all is said and done, the Court, at the head of the U.S. judiciary, is not only the most fascinating, the most unfluential, and the most powerful judicial body in the world, it is also "the living voice of the Constitution,"[120] as Lord Bryce, who knew America well indeed, once phrased it. As such it is both arbiter and educator and, in essence, represents the sole solution short of anarchy under the American system of government as we know it. It acts, in the words of one commentator, "as the instrument of national moral values that have not been able to find other governmental expression"[121]—assuming, of course,that it functions within its authorized sphere of constitutional adjudication. In that role it operates "as the collective conscience of a sovereign people."[122] And, as Alexander Meiklejohn once observed, no other institution "is more deeply decisive in its effect upon our understanding of ourselves and our government."[123] It defines values and proclaims principles. It is a corrective force in our life.

Beyond that, moreover, the Supreme Court of the United States is the chief protector of the Constitution, of its great system of balances—as *United States v. Nixon* and *Immigration and Naturalization Service v. Chadha*, for example, proved again so tellingly in 1974 and 1983, respectively[124]—and of the peoples' liberties. It is the greatest institutional sfafeguard we possess. It may have retreated, even yielded to pressures now and then, but without its vigilance our liberties would scarcely have survived. Few have sounded this call more eloquently than did Justice Black in his memorable opinion for the Court in *Chambers v. Florida*:

> Under our constitutional system, courts stand against any winds that blow as havens of refuge for those who might otherwise suffer because they are helpless, weak, outnumbered, or because they are non-conforming victims of prejudice and public excitement. No higher duty, no more solemn responsibility, rests upon this Court, than that of translating into living law and maintaining this constitutional shield deliberately planned and inscribed for the benefit of every human being subject to our Constitution—of whatever race, creed, or persuasion.[125]

Within the limits of procedure and deference to the presumption of constitutionality of legislation, the Court—our "sober second thought," as Chief

---

[120] *The American Commonwealth* (New York: The Macmillan Co., 1905), vol. 1, p. 272.

[121] Anthony Lewis, *The New York Times Magazine*, June 17, 1962, p. 28.

[122] Judge J. Skelly Wright, "The Role of the Courts: Conscience of a Sovereign People," 29 *The Reproter* 5 (September 29, 1963).

[123] *Free Speech and Its Relation to Self-Government* (New York: Harper & Brothers, 1948), p. 32.

[124] 417 U.S. 683 and 462 U.S. 919, respectively.

[125] 309 U.S. 227 (1940), at 241.

Justice Stone called it[126]—is the natural forum in our society for the individual and for the small group. The Court's essential function, as Chief Justice Warren told the Centennial Convocation of the New York School of Law, "is to act as the final arbiter of minority rights."[127] It thereby serves as a primary rather than an auxiliary check. In Justice Douglas's words: "The people should know that when filibusters occupy the forums, when oppressions are great, when the clash of authority between the individual and the State is severe, they can still get justice in the courts"[128]—assuming the existence of constitutional warrant therefor. It represents a power that so astute an observer of the American scene as Alexis de Toqueville (Montesquieu's student) viewed as "one of the most powerful barriers that have been devised against tyranny of political assemblies."[129]

Thus, the Court must be prepared to say "no" to the government—which Madison, the father of the Bill of Rights, hoped fervently it would always do. There are many citizens—indeed, most citizens, once they have given the problem the careful thought it merits—who will feel far more secure in the knowledge of *that* guardianship, one generally characterized by common sense, than if it were primarily exercised by the far more easily pressured, more impulsive, and more emotion-charged legislative or executive branches. Far too easily do these two yield to the politically expedient and the popular, for they are close, indeed, to what Judge Learned Hand called "the pressure of public hysteria, public panic, and public greed." Hence—and again in Earl Warren's words—"the Court must always stand ready to advance the rights of . . . minority interests if the executive and the legislative branches falter."[130] His Court did just that, moving dramatically from deference to the prerogatives of the other two branches and of the states to aggressive protection of the constitutional rights of the individual—as the Court perceived these, and it did so amidst withering criticism from a host of diverse quarters, both lay and professional.

The Court, which often has had to act as a "moral goad" to public panic and public greed, is neither engaged nor interested in a popularity contest—its function is *not* one of counting constituents. Should the time ever arrive when that is the Court's function, the supreme judicial tribunal wil have lost its meaning. "[W]e have no constituency," mused Warren on the last day of his sixteen-year tenure as Chief Justice of the United States, just prior to swearing in his succesor, Warren Earl Burger. "We serve no minority. We serve only the public interest as we see it, guided only by the Constitution and our own conscience."[131]

[126]"The Common Law in the United States," 50 *Harvard Law Review* 25 (1936).
[127]New York City, October 3, 1968.
[128]*Bell v. Maryland*, 378 U.S. 226 (1964), concurring opinion, at 242–43.
[129]*Democracy in America* (New York: Alfred A. Knopf, 1948), vol. 1, p. 103.
[130]As quoted in *The Philadelphia Inquirer*, October 4, 1968, p. 2.
[131]As quoted in *The New York Times*, June 24, 1969, p. 24.

Even if a transfer of that guardianship to other institutions of government were theoretically desirable, which few thoughtful citizens believe, it would be politically impossible. "Do we desire constitutional questions," asked Charles Evans Hughes when off the bench, in his fine book on the Court, " ... to be determined by political assemblies and partisan division?"[132] The response must be a ringing "no!" In the 1955 Godkins Lectures, which he was preparing to deliver at Harvard University when death intervened, Justice Jackson expressed this conviction eloquently and ably:

> The people have seemed to feel[133] that the Supreme Court, whatever its defects, is still the most detached, dispassionate, and trustworthy custodian that our system affords for the translation of abstract into concrete constitutional commands.[134]

And we may well agree with Thomas Reed Powell that the logic of American constitutional law is the common sense of the Supreme Court.

As a commentary on the point, that distinguished observer of Court and Constitution reported an incident that took place after the turn of the century in a debate on the floor of the U.S. Senate between Senators John C. Spooner of Wisconsin and "Pitchfork Ben" Tillman of South Carolina. At one juncture of the proceedings, Tillman exclaimed: "I am tired of hearing what the Supreme Court says. What I want to get at is the common sense of the matter." Rejoined Spooner: "I too am seeking the common sense of the matter. But, as for me, I prefer the common sense of the Supreme Court of the United States to that of the Senator from South Carolina."[135]

In the long run common sense has always served the Supreme Court of the United States well in its ceaseless striving, as a voice of reason, to maintain the blend of change and continuity which is the *sine qua non* for desirable stability in the governmental process of a democracy. In that role it will, because it must, live in history.

---

[132] *The Supreme Court of the United States* (New York: Columbia University Press, 1928), p. 236.

[133] On this point see the interesting findings and reflections by Gregory Casey, "The Supreme Court and Myth: An Empirical Investigation," 8 *Law & Society* 385 (Spring 1974).

[134] Jackson, op. cit., fn. 4, p. 23. (The lectures were delivered by his son.)

[135] "The Logic and Rhetoric of Constitutional Law," 15 *Journal of Philosophy, Psychology, and Scientific Method* 656 (1918).

Appendices

APPENDIX A. MEMBERS OF THE SUPREME COURT OF THE UNITED STATES*

Name	Place of Birth	Year of Birth	State App't From	Appointed by President	(A) Judicial Oath Taken	Date Service Terminated	(B) Service Terminated By	Years of Service	Year of Death
Chief Justices:									
Jay, John	N.Y.	1745	N.Y.	Washington	Oct. 19, 1789(a)	June 29, 1795	resigned	5	1829
Rutledge, John	S.C.	1739	S.C.	Washington	Aug. 12, 1795(C)	Dec. 15, 1795	rejected†	¾	1800
Ellsworth, Oliver	Conn.	1745	Conn.	Washington	Mar. 8, 1796	Dec. 15, 1800	resigned	4	1807
Marshall, John	Va.	1755	Va.	Adams, J.	Feb. 4, 1801	July 6, 1835	Death	34	1835
Taney, Roger Brooke	Md.	1777	Md.	Jackson	Mar. 28, 1836	Oct. 12, 1864	Death	28	1864
Chase, Salmon Portland	N.H.	1808	Ohio	Lincoln	Dec. 15, 1864	May 7, 1873	Death	8½	1873
Waite, Morrison Remick	Conn.	1816	Ohio	Grant	Mar. 4, 1874	Mar. 23, 1888	Death	14	1888
Fuller, Melville Weston	Maine	1833	Illinois	Cleveland	Oct. 8, 1888	July 4, 1910	Death	21	1910
White, Edward Douglass	La.	1845	La.	Taft	Dec. 19, 1910(C)	May 19, 1921	Death	10	1921
Taft, William Howard	Ohio	1857	Conn.	Harding	July 11, 1921	Feb. 3, 1930	retired	8	1930
Hughes, Charles Evans	N.Y.	1862	N.Y.	Hoover	Feb. 24, 1930(C)	June 30, 1941	RETIRED	11	1948
Stone, Harlan Fiske	N.H.	1872	N.Y.	Roosevelt, F.	July 3, 1941(C)	Apr. 22, 1946	Death	5	1946
Vinson, Frederick Moore	Ky.	1890	Ky.	Truman	June 24, 1946	Sept. 8, 1953	Death	7	1953
Warren, Earl	Calif.	1891	Calif.	Eisenhower	Oct. 5, 1953	June 23, 1969	RETIRED	15	1974
Burger, Warren Earl	Minn.	1907	Va.	Nixon	June 23, 1969				
Associate Justices:									
Wilson, James	Scotland	1742	Penn.	Washington	Oct. 5, 1789(b)	Aug. 21, 1798	Death	8	1798
Blair, John	Va.	1732	Va.	Washington	Feb. 2, 1790(c)	Jan. 27, 1796	resigned	6	1800
Cushing, William	Mass.	1732	Mass.	Washington	Feb. 2, 1790(b)	Sept. 13, 1810	Death	20	1810
Rutledge, John	S.C.	1739	S.C.	Washington	Feb. 15, 1790(c)	Mar. 5, 1791	resigned	1	1800
Iredell, James	England	1751	N.C.	Washington	May 13, 1790(b)	Oct. 20, 1799	Death	9	1799
Johnson, Thomas	Md.	1732	Md.	Washington	Aug. 6, 1792(c)	Feb. 1, 1793	resigned	¾	1819
Paterson, William	Ireland	1745	N.J.	Washington	Mar. 11, 1793(a)	Sept. 9, 1806	Death	13½	1806
Chase, Samuel	Md.	1741	Md.	Washington	Feb. 4, 1796	June 19, 1811	Death	15	1811
Washington, Bushrod	Va.	1762	Va.	Adams, J.	Feb. 4, 1799(c)	Nov. 26, 1829	Death	31	1829

Name		Birthplace	Birth year	Appointed by	Oath/Commission	End of service	Reason	Years	Year of death
Livingston, Henry Brockholst	N.Y.	1757	Jefferson	Jan. 20, 1807	Mar. 18, 1823	Death	16	1823
Todd, Thomas	Va.	1765	Jefferson	May 4, 1807(a)	Feb. 7, 1826	Death	18	1826
Duvall, Gabriel	Md.	1752	Madison	Nov. 23, 1811(a)	Jan. 14, 1835	resigned	23	1844
Story, Joseph	Mass.	1779	Madison	Feb. 3, 1812(c)	Sept. 10, 1845	Death	33	1845
Thompson, Smith	N.Y.	1768	Monroe	Sept. 1, 1823(b)	Dec. 18, 1843	Death	20	1843
Trimble, Robert	Ky.	1777	Adams, J.Q.	June 16, 1826(a)	Aug. 25, 1828	Death	2	1828
McLean, John	Ohio	1785	Jackson	Jan. 11, 1830	Apr. 4, 1861	Death	31	1861
Baldwin, Henry	Conn.	1780	Jackson	Jan. 18, 1830	Apr. 21, 1844	Death	14	1844
Wayne, James Moore	Ga.	1790	Jackson	Jan. 14, 1835	July 5, 1867	Death	32	1867
Barbour, Philip Pendleton	Va.	1783	Jackson	May 12, 1836	Feb. 25, 1841	Death	4	1841
Catron, John	Tenn.	1786	Van Buren	May 1, 1837	May 30, 1865	Death	28	1865
McKinley, John	Va.	1790	Van Buren	Jan. 9, 1838(c)	July 19, 1852	Death	14	1852
Daniel, Peter Vivian	Va.	1784	Van Buren	Jan. 10, 1842(c)	May 31, 1860	Death	18	1860
Nelson, Samuel	N.Y.	1792	Tyler	Feb. 27, 1845	Nov. 28, 1872	retired	27	1873
Woodbury, Levi	N.H.	1789	Polk	Sept. 23, 1845(b)	Sept. 4, 1851	Death	5	1851
Grier, Robert Cooper	Pa.	1794	Polk	Aug. 10, 1846	Jan. 31, 1870	retired	23	1870
Curtis, Benjamin Robbins	Mass.	1809	Fillmore	Oct. 10, 1851(b)	Sept. 30, 1857	resigned	5	1874
Campbell, John Archibald	Ga.	1811	Pierce	Apr. 11, 1853(c)	Apr. 30, 1861	resigned	8	1889
Clifford, Nathan	Maine	1803	Buchanan	Jan. 21, 1858	July 25, 1881	Death	23	1881
Swayne, Noah Haynes	Va.	1804	Lincoln	Jan. 21, 1862	Jan. 24, 1881	retired	18	1884
Miller, Samuel Freeman	Ky.	1816	Lincoln	July 21, 1862	Oct. 13, 1890	Death	28	1890
Davis, David	Md.	1815	Lincoln	Dec. 10, 1862	Mar. 4, 1877	resigned	14	1886
Field, Stephen Johnson	Conn.	1816	Lincoln	May 20, 1863	Dec. 1, 1897	retired	34¾	1899
Strong, William	Conn.	1808	Grant	Mar. 14, 1870	Dec. 14, 1880	retired	10¾	1895
Bradley, Joseph P.	N.J.	1813	Grant	Mar. 23, 1870	Jan. 22, 1892	Death	21	1892
Hunt, Ward	N.Y.	1810	Grant	Jan. 9, 1873	Jan. 27, 1882	disabled	9	1886
Harlan, John Marshall	Ky.	1833	Hayes	Dec. 10, 1877	Oct. 14, 1911	Death	34	1911
Woods, William Burnham	Ohio	1824	Hayes	Jan. 5, 1881	May 14, 1887	Death	6¼	1887
Matthews, Stanley	Ohio	1824	Garfield	May 17, 1881	Mar. 22, 1889	Death	7	1889
Gray, Horace	Mass.	1828	Arthur	Jan. 9, 1882	Sept. 15, 1902	Death	20	1902
Blatchford, Samuel	N.Y.	1820	Arthur	Apr. 3, 1882	July 7, 1893	Death	11	1893
Lamar, Lucius Quintus C.	Ga.	1825	Cleveland	Jan. 18, 1888	Jan. 23, 1893	Death	5	1893
Brewer, David Josiah	Asia Minor	1837	Harrison	Jan. 6, 1890	Mar. 28, 1910	Death	20	1910
Brown, Henry Billings	Mass.	1836	Harrison	Jan. 5, 1891	May 28, 1906	retired	15	1913
Shiras, George, Jr.	Pa.	1832	Harrison	Oct. 10, 1892	Feb. 23, 1903	retired	10	1924

APPENDIX A (Continued)

Name	Place of Birth	Year of Birth	State App't From	Appointed by President	(A) Judicial Oath Taken	Date Service Terminated	(B) Service Terminated By	Years of Service	Year of Death
Jackson, Howell Edmunds	Tenn.	1832	Tenn.	Harrison	Mar. 4, 1893	Aug. 8, 1895	Death	2½	1895
White, Edward Douglass	La.	1845	La.	Cleveland	Mar. 12, 1894	Dec. 18, 1910	promoted	16	1921
Peckham, Rufus Wheeler	N.Y.	1838	N.Y.	Cleveland	Jan. 6, 1896	Oct. 24, 1909	Death	13	1909
McKenna, Joseph	Penn.	1843	Calif.	McKinley	Jan. 26, 1898	Jan. 5, 1925	retired	26	1926
Holmes, Oliver Wendell	Mass.	1841	Mass.	Roosevelt, T.	Dec. 8, 1902	Jan. 12, 1932	retired	29	1935
Day, William Rufus	Ohio	1849	Ohio	Roosevelt, T.	Mar. 2, 1903	Nov. 13, 1922	retired	19	1923
Moody, William Henry	Mass.	1853	Mass.	Roosevelt, T.	Dec. 17, 1906	Nov. 20, 1910	disabled	4	1917
Lurton, Horace Harmon	Ky.	1844	Tenn.	Taft	Jan. 3, 1910	July 12, 1914	Death	4½	1914
Hughes, Charles Evans	N.Y.	1862	N.Y.	Taft	Oct. 10, 1910	June 10, 1916	resigned	5	1948
Van Devanter, Willis	Ind.	1859	Wyo.	Taft	Jan. 3, 1911	June 2, 1937	RETIRED	26	1941
Lamar, Jospeh Rucker	Ga.	1857	Ga.	Taft	Jan. 3, 1911	Jan. 2, 1916	Death	5	1916
Pitney, Mahlon	N.J.	1858	N.J.	Taft	Mar. 18, 1912	Dec. 31, 1922	disabled	10	1924
McReynolds, James Clark	Ky.	1862	Tenn.	Wilson	Oct. 12, 1914	Jan. 31, 1941	RETIRED	26	1946
Brandeis, Louis Dembitz	Ky.	1856	Mass.	Wilson	June 5, 1916	Feb. 13, 1939	RETIRED	22	1941
Clarke, John Hessin	Ohio	1857	Ohio	Wilson	Oct. 9, 1916	Sept. 18, 1922	resigned	5	1945
Sutherland, George	England	1862	Utah	Harding	Oct. 2, 1922	Jan. 17, 1938	RETIRED	15	1942
Butler, Pierce	Minn.	1866	Minn.	Harding	Jan. 2, 1923	Nov. 16, 1939	Death	16	1939
Sanford, Edward Terry	Tenn.	1865	Tenn.	Harding	Feb. 19, 1923	Mar. 8, 1930	Death	7	1930
Stone, Harlan Fiske	N.H.	1872	N.Y.	Coolidge	Mar. 2, 1925	July 2, 1941	promoted	16	1946
Roberts, Owen Josephus	Pa.	1875	Pa.	Hoover	June 2, 1930	July 31, 1945	RESIGNED	15	1955
Cardozo, Benjamin Nathan	N.Y.	1870	N.Y.	Hoover	Mar. 14, 1932	July 9, 1938	Death	6	1938
Black, Hugo Lafayette	Ala.	1886	Ala.	Roosevelt, F.	Aug. 19, 1937	Sept. 17, 1971	RETIRED	34	1971
Reed, Stanley Forman	Ky.	1884	Ky.	Roosevelt, F.	Jan. 31, 1938	Feb. 25, 1957	RETIRED	19	1980
Frankfurter, Felix	Austria	1882	Mass.	Roosevelt, F.	Jan. 30, 1939	Aug. 28, 1962	RETIRED	23	1965
Douglas, William Orville	Minn.	1898	Conn.	Roosevelt, F.	Apr. 17, 1939	Nov. 12, 1975	RETIRED	36½	1980
Murphy, Frank	Mich.	1890	Mich.	Roosevelt, F.	Feb. 5, 1940	July 19, 1949	Death	9	1949
Byrnes, James Francis	S.C.	1879	S.C.	Roosevelt, F.	July 8, 1941	Oct. 3, 1942	resigned	1	1972
Jackson, Robert Houghwout	Pa.	1892	N.Y.	Roosevelt, F.	July 11, 1941	Oct. 9, 1954	Death	13	1954
Rutledge, Wiley Blount	Ky.	1894	Iowa	Roosevelt, F.	Feb. 15, 1943	Sept. 10, 1949	Death	6½	1949

Name	State			President					
Clark, Thomas Campbell	Texas	1899	Texas	Truman	Aug. 24, 1949	June 12, 1967	RETIRED	18	1977
Minton, Sherman	Ind.	1890	Ind.	Truman	Oct. 12, 1949	Oct. 15, 1956	RETIRED	7	1965
Harlan, John Marshall	Ill.	1899	N.Y.	Eisenhower	Mar. 28, 1955	Sept. 23, 1971	RETIRED	16	1971
Brennan, William Joseph, Jr.	N.J.	1906	N.J.	Eisenhower	Oct. 16, 1956				
Whittaker, Charles Evans	Kansas	1901	Mo.	Eisenhower	Mar. 25, 1957	Mar. 31, 1962	DISABLED§	5	1973
Stewart, Potter	Mich.	1915	Ohio	Eisenhower	Oct. 14, 1958	July 3, 1981	RETIRED	22¾	
White, Byron Raymond	Colo.	1917	Colo.	Kennedy	Apr. 16, 1962				
Goldberg, Arthur Joseph	Ill.	1908	Ill.	Kennedy	Oct. 1, 1962	July 25, 1965	Resigned	2¾	
Fortas, Abe	Tenn.	1910	Tenn.	Johnson, L.	Oct. 4, 1965	May 14, 1969	Resigned	3½	1982
Marshall, Thurgood	Md.	1908	N.Y.	Johnson, L.	Oct. 2, 1967				
Blackmun, Harry A.	Ill.	1908	Minn.	Nixon	June 9, 1970				
Powell, Lewis Franklin, Jr.	Va.	1907	Va.	Nixon	Jan. 7, 1972				
Rehnquist, William Hubbs	Wisc.	1924	Ariz.	Nixon	Jan. 7, 1972				
Stevens, John Paul	Ill.	1920	Ill.	Ford	Dec. 19, 1972				
O'Connor, Sandra D.	Texas	1930	Ariz.	Reagan	Sept. 15, 1981				

NOTES: The acceptance of the appointment and commission by the appointee, as evidenced by the taking of the prescribed oaths, is here implied; otherwise the individual is not carried on this list of the Members of the Court. Examples: Robert Hanson Harrison is not carried, as a letter from President Washington of February 9, 1790, states Harrison declined to serve. Neither is Edwin M. Stanton, who died before he could take the necessary steps toward becoming a member of the Court. Chief Justice Rutledge is included because he took his oaths, presided over the August term of 1795, and his name appears on two opinions of the Court for that term.

(A) The date a member of the Court took his judicial oath (the Judiciary Act provided "That the Justice of the Supreme Court, and the district judges, before they proceed to execute the duties of their respective offices, shall take the following oath . . . .") is here used as the date of the beginning of his service, for, until that oath is taken, he or she is not vested with the prerogatives of the office. However, Senate confirmation may well have come earlier, for example, Bushrod Washington's (on December 20, 1798). Dates without lowercase-letter references are taken from the Minutes of the Court or from the original oath which is in the Clerk's file. The lowercase letter (a) denotes the date is from the Minutes of some other court, (b) from some other unquestionable authority, (c) from authority that is questionable, and better authority would be appreciated.

(B) Explanation of terms used in identifying nature of termination of services:

1. A member of the Court of seventy or more years of age and of ten or more years of service who, pursuant to the Act of April 10, 1869, or subsequent acts, retired or resigned and continued to receive the salary which he was receiving when he retired or resigned, is here carried as "retired."

2. A member retiring since the Act of March 1, 1937 (50 Stat. 24) is granted the same privileges with regard to retiring, instead of resigning, that are granted to judges other than Justices of the Supreme Court. He may be assigned to perform such judicial duties as he is willing to undertake, and during the remainder of his lifetime continues to receive the salary of the office. Such member is here carried as "RETIRED."

3. A member of less than seventy years of age or having less than ten years of service, who resigned and who thereafter did not continue to draw pay based on his age or service, or who resigned before the Act of April 10, 1869, became effective, as Justice Duvall did, is here carried as "resigned."

4. A member of seventy or more years of age and ten or more years of service, resigning since the Act of March 1, 1937, who continues to receive the salary he was receiving when he resigned is here carried as "RESIGNED."

5. Justices Hunt, Moody, and Pitney, who retired under Special Acts, are here carried as "disabled."

6. A member retiring for disability under the general provisions of 28 U.S. Code 372 is here carried as "DISABLED."

(C) For Chief Justice's service as Associate Justice, see under the latter rubric.

*Adapted from a table revised by Frank M. Hepler, Marshal of the Supreme Court of the United States, 1972; revised 1985.

†Served under a recess appointment from August 12, 1795, to December 15, 1795.

§Resigned September 30, 1965.

	Judiciary Act of 1789 provided for a Chief Justice and 5 Associate Justices					
Year	John Jay 1789-1795	John Rutledge 1789-1791	William Cushing 1789-1810	James Iredell 1790-1799	James Wilson 1789-1798	John Blair 1789-1796
1789 1790	John Jay 1789-1795	John Rutledge 1789-1791	William Cushing 1789-1810	James Iredell 1790-1799	James Wilson 1789-1798	John Blair 1789-1796
	John Rutledge 1795 Oliver Ellsworth 1796-1799	Thomas Johnson 1791-1793 William Paterson 1793-1806			Bushrod Washington 1798-1829	Samuel Chase 1796-1811
1800	John Marshall 1801-1835			Alfred Moore 1799-1804 William Johnson 1804-1834		
		Henry B. Livingston 1806-1823				
1810			Joseph Story 1811-1845			Gabriel Duval 1811-1836
1820		Smith Thompson 1823-1843				
1830					Henry Baldwin 1830-1844	
	Roger B. Taney 1836-1864			James M. Wayne 1835-1867		Philip P. Barbour 1836-1841
1840						Peter V. Daniel 1841-1860
		Samuel Nelson 1845-1872	Levi Woodbury 1846-1851		Robert C. Grier 1846-1870	
1850			Benjamin R. Curtis 1851-1857 Nathan Clifford 1858-1881			
1860	Salmon P. Chase 1864-1873			*Act of July 23, 1866, provided for reduction of the Court to 7 members as vacancies should occur.*		Samuel F. Miller 1862-1890
1870	Morrison R. Waite 1874-1888	Ward Hunt 1872-1882			William Strong 1870-1880	
1880		Samuel Blatchford 1882-1893	Horace Gray 1881-1902		William B. Woods 1880-1887	
	Melville W. Fuller 1888-1910				Lucius Q. C. Lamar 1888-1893	Henry B. Brown 1890-1906
1890		Edward D. White J 1894 CJ 1910-1921			Howell E. Jackson 1893-1895 Rufus W. Peckham 1895-1909	
1900			Oliver Wendell Holmes 1902-1932			William H. Moody 1906-1910
1910	Edward D. White J 1894 CJ 1910-1921	Willis Van Devanter 1910-1937			Horace H. Lurton 1909-1914	Joseph R. Lamar 1910-1916
					James C. McReynolds 1914-1941	Louis D. Brandeis 1916-1939
1920	William H. Taft 1921-1930					
1930	Charles E. Hughes 1930-1941		Benjamin N. Cardozo 1932-1938			
		Hugo L. Black 1937-1971	Felix Frankfurter 1939-1962			William O. Douglas 1939-1975
1940	Harlan F. Stone J 1925 CJ 1941-1946				James F. Byrnes 1941-1942 Wiley Rutledge 1943-1949 Sherman Minton 1949-1956	
1950	Fred M. Vinson 1946-1953					
	Earl Warren 1953-1969				William J. Brennan 1956	
1960			Arthur J. Goldberg 1962-1965 Abe Fortas 1965-1969			
	Warren E. Burger 1969					
1970		Lewis F. Powell, Jr. 1972	Harry A. Blackmun 1970			
1980						John Paul Stevens 1975

*Adapted from a table revised by Frank M. Hepler, Marshal of the Supreme Court of the United States, 1972; revised 198

						1789
						1790

Act of February 24, 1807, provided for increase of the Court to 7 members.

Thomas Todd
1807-1826

Act of March 3, 1837, provided for increase of the Court to 9 members.

Act of March 3, 1863, provided for increase of the Court to 10 members.

Act of April 10, 1869, provided for increase of the Court to 9 members.

Act of July 23, 1866, provided for reduction of the Court to 7 members as vacancies should occur. (Actually the Court fell to 8.)

Act of July 23, 1866, provided for reduction of the Court to 7 members as vacancies should occur.

1800

Robert Trimble
1826-1828

John McLean
1829-1861

John Catron
1837-1865

John McKinley
1837-1852

1810

1820

1830

John A. Campbell
1853-1861

1840

1850

Noah H. Swayne
1862-1881

David Davis
1862-1877

Stephen J. Field
1863-1897

Joseph P. Bradley
1870-1892

1860

John M. Harlan
1877-1911

1870

Stanley Matthews
1881-1889

David J. Brewer
1889-1910

1880

George Shiras, Jr.
1892-1903

Joseph McKenna
1898-1925

William R. Day
1903-1922

1890

1900

Charles E. Hughes
1910-1916

Mahlon Pitney
1912-1922

John H. Clarke
1916-1922

1910

George Sutherland
1922-1938

Edward T. Sanford
1923-1930

Harlan F. Stone
J 1925
CJ 1941-1946

Pierce Butler
1922-1939

1920

Owen J. Roberts
1930-1945

1930

Stanley F. Reed
1938-1957

Frank Murphy
1940-1949

Robert H. Jackson
1941-1954

Harold H. Burton
1945-1958

Tom C. Clark
1949-1967

1940

1950

Charles E. Whittaker
1957-1962

Potter Stewart
1958-1981

John M. Harlan
1955-1971

Byron R. White
1962

Thurgood Marshall
1967

1960

Wm. H. Rehnquist
1972

1970

Sandra D. O'Connor
1981

1980

Selected
Bibliographies

I. AMERICAN CONSTITUTIONAL LAW: CLASSIFIED LISTING OF SELECTED TOPICAL WORKS

ADMINISTRATIVE LAW AND JUSTICE

(Administrative law and Agencies in the United States; Independent Regulatory commissions.)

Association of American Law Schools. *Selected Essays on Constitutional Law.* Foundation Press, 1938.

Carter, L. H. *Administrative Law and Policy: Cases and Comments.* Little, Brown, 1983.

Cushman, R. E. *The Independent Regulatory Commissions.* Oxford University, 1941.

Cortner, R. C. *The Bureaucracy in Court: Commentaries and Case Studies in Administrative Law.* Kennikat Press, 1982.

Davis, K. C. *Administrative Law.* 3d ed. West, 1972.

———. *Administrative Law and Government.* 2d ed. West, 1975.

———. *Discretionary Justice: A Preliminary Inquiry.* Louisiana State University, 1969.

Dickinson, J. *Administrative Justice and the Supremacy of Law.* Russell, 1959.

Dimock, M. E. *Law and Dynamic Administration.* Praeger, 1980.

Dodd, L. C., and R. L. Schott. *Congress and the Administrative State.* Wiley, 1979.

Fesler, J. W. *Area and Administration.* University of Alabama, 1949.

Frank, J. F. *If Men Were Angels.* Harper, 1942.

Freedman, J. C. *Crisis and Legitimacy: The Administrative Process and American Government.* Cambridge University, 1979.

Friendly, H. J. *The Federal Administration Agencies: The Need for Definition of Standards.* Harvard University, 1962.

Gellhorn, W. *Administrative Law and Process in a Nutshell.* 2d ed. West, 1972.

———. *Administrative Law: Cases and Comments.* 6th ed. Foundation Press, 1974.

———. *Federal Administrative Proceedings.* Johns Hopkins University, 1941.

Goodnow, F. *Comparative Administrative Law.* Dabor, 1978.

Gould, D. J. *Law and the Administrative Process.* University Press of America, 1979.

Heffron, F., and N. McFeeley. *The Administrative Regulatory Process.* Longman, 1983.

Hood, C. C. *The Limits of Administration.* Wiley, 1976.

Jacobini, H. B., A. P. Melone, and C. Kalvelage. *Research Essentials of Administrative Law.* Palisades, 1983.

Jaffe, L. L. *Judicial Control of Administrative Action.* Little, Brown, 1965.

———, and N. Nathanson. *Administrative Law: Cases and Materials.* Little, Brown, 1961.

Jowell, J. L. *Law and Bureaucracy: Administrative Discretion and the Limits of Legal Action.* Kennikat Press, 1975.

Kagan, R. A. *Regulating Justice.* Sage Publications, 1978.

Langallatag, A. *The Department of Justice of the United States.* Johns Hopkins University, 1927.

Linde, H. A., and G. Bunn. *Legislative and Administrative Processes.* Foundation Press, 1976.

Lorch, R. S. *Democratic Justice and Administrative Law.* Wayne State University, 1969.

McFarland, C. *Judicial Control of the F.T.C. and the I.C.C.* Harvard University, 1933.

Mashaw, J. L. *Bureaucratic Justice: Managing Social Security Disability Claims.* Yale University, 1982.

Mayers, L. *The American Legal System.* Rev. ed. Harper & Row, 1964.

Nachmias, D., and D. H. Rosenbloom. *Bureaucratic Government USA.* St. Martin's Press, 1980.

Nichols, P. *Power of Eminent Domain.* Boston Book, 1909.

Nonet, P. *Administrative Justice: Advocacy and Change in a Government Agency.* Sage Publications, 1969.

Paulson, M. C., ed. *Legal Institutions Today and Tomorrow.* Columbia University, 1959.

Pound, R. *Administrative Law: Its Growth, Procedure, Significance.* University of Pittsburgh, 1942.

Redford, E. S. *The Regulatory Process.* University of Texas, 1969.

Rich, M. C., and W. E. Brucar. *The Central Panel System for Administrative Law Judges.* University Press of America, 1984.

Schwartz, B. *An Introduction to American Administrative Law.* 2nd ed. Oceana, 1962.

———. *The Professor and the Commissions.* Knopf, 1959.

———., and H. W. R. Wade. *Legal Control of Government: Administrative Law in Britain and the United States.* Oxford University, 1972.

Shapiro, M. *The Supreme Court and Administrative Agencies.* Free Press, 1968.

Sharkinsky, I. *Public Administration: Policy-Making in Government Agencies*. 4th ed. Rand McNally, 1978.

Sturm, F. F. *Customs Law and Administration*. 2d ed. American Importers Association, 1979.

Tucker, E. W. *Cases and Problems on Administrative Law, Regulation of Enterprise and Individual Liberties*. West, 1975.

Wade, H. W. R. *Administrative Law*. 5th ed. Oxford University, 1983.

Welborn, D. M. *Governance of Federal Regulatory Agencies*. University of Tennessee, 1977.

Wilson, J. Q. *The Politics of Regulation*. Basic Books, 1980.

Weaith, R. E., and R. G. Hutcheson. *Administrative Tribunals*. Allen & Unwin, 1973.

APPORTIONMENT, GERRYMANDERING, AND REDISTRICTING

Bain, C. W. *Annexation in Virginia: The Use of the Judicial Process for Readjusting City-County Boundaries*. University of Virginia, 1966.

Baker, G. E. *The Reapportionment Revolution: Representation, Political Power, and the Supreme Court*. Random House, 1966.

———. *Rural Versus Urban Political Power*. Random House, 1955.

———. *State Constitutions: Reapportionment*. National Municipal League, 1962.

———. ed. *Representation and Redistricting Issues of the 1980s*. Lexington Books, 1981.

Ball, H. *The Warren Court's Conception of Democracy*. Fairleigh Dickinson University, 1971.

Birch, A. H. *Representation*. Praeger, 1971.

Boyd, W. J. D. *Changing Patterns of Apportionment*. National Municipal League, 1965.

Bushnell, E. B., ed. *Impact of Reapportionment on the Thirteen Western States*. University of Utah, 1970.

Claude, R. *The Supreme Court and the Electoral Process*. Johns Hopkins University, 1970.

Commission on Intergovernmental Relations. *Apportionment of State Legislatures*. Government Printing Office, 1962.

Congressional Quarterly. *Representation and Apportionment*. Congressional Quarterly Press, 1966.

Cortner, R. E. *The Apportionment Cases*. University of Tennessee, 1970.

David, P. T., and E. Eisenberg. *Devaluation of the Urban and Suburban Vote*. Bureau of Public Administration, University of Virginia, 1961–1962.

de Grazia, A. *Apportionment and Representative Government*. Praeger, 1963.

Dixon, R. G., Jr. *Democratic Representation*. Oxford University, 1968.

Elliott, W. E. Y. *The Rise of Guardian Democracy: The Supreme Court's Role in Voting Rights Disputes, 1945–1969*. Harvard University, 1974.

Goldwin, R. A., ed. *Representation and Misrepresentation*. Rand McNally, 1968.

Graham, G. S. *One Man, One Vote: Baker v. Carr and the American Levelers*. Little, Brown, 1972.

Griffith, E. C. *The Rise and Development of the Gerrymander*. Arno Press, 1964.

Grofman, B., et al. *Representation and Redistricting Issues*. Lexington Books, 1982.

Hacker, A. *Congressional Districting: The Issue of Equal Representation*. Rev. ed. Brookings Institution, 1964.

Hamilton, H., ed. *Legislative Apportionment: Key to Power*. Harper & Row, 1964.

Hardy, L., A. Helsop, and S. Anderson, eds. *Reapportionment Politics*. Sage Publications, 1981.

Havard, W. C., and L. C. Beth. *The Politics of Mis-Representation*. Atherton, 1962.

Jewell, M. E., ed. *The Politics of Reapportionment*. Atherton, 1962.

Larson, J. E. *Reapportionment and the Courts: A Survey of Recent Cases*. University of Alabama, 1962.

Lee, C. B. T. *One Man, One Vote: WMCA and the Struggle for Equal Representation*. Scribner, 1967.

McKay, R. B. *Reapportionment: The Law and Politics of Equal Representation*. Twentieth Century Fund, 1965.

———. *Reapportionment and the Federal Analogy.* National Municipal League, 1962.

National Municipal Review. *Court Decisions on Legislative Reapportionment.* National Municipal Review, 1962.

O'Rourke, T. B. *The Impact of Reapportionment.* Transaction Books, 1980.

———. *Reapportionment: Law, Politics, Computers.* American Enterprise Institute, 1972.

Polsby, N. W., ed. *Reapportionment in the 1970s.* University of California, 1971.

Schubert, G. A., ed. *Reapportionment.* Scribner, 1965.

Taper, B. *Gomillion v. Lightfoot: Apartheid in Alabama.* McGraw-Hill, 1962.

———. *Gomillion v. Lightfoot: The Tuskegee Gerrymander Case.* McGraw-Hill, 1962.

Wieck, W. M. *The Guarantee Clause of the U.S. Constitution.* Cornell University, 1972.

Zeller, B., ed. *American State Legislatures.* Committee on American Legislatures, American Political Science Association, 1954.

ASPECTS OF AMERICAN CONSTITUTIONAL DEMOCRACY

GENERAL WORKS

(Works dealing with many areas of our system, but not specifically with any one feature — many are cross-referenced in other categories.)

Association of American Law Schools. *Selected Essays on Constitutional Law.* Foundation Press, 1938.

Aumann, F. A. *The Instrumentalities of Justice: Their Forms, Functions, and Limitations.* Ohio State University, 1956.

Beard, C. A. *The Republic.* Viking Press, 1943.

Berman, H. J. *Talks on American Law.* Random House, 1961.

Black, C. L., Jr. *Perspectives in Constitutional Law.* Prentice-Hall, 1963.

Burdick, C. K. *The Law of the American Constitution: Its Origins and Development.* Putnam, 1922.

Burlingame, R. *The American Conscience.* Knopf, 1957.

Cardozo, B. N. *Law and Literature and Other Essays.* Harcourt, Brace, 1931.

Cohen, L. K., ed. *The Legal Conscience: Selected Papers of Felix S. Cohen.* Yale University, 1960.

Collyer, R., comp. *In Defense of the Constitution: Excerpts from Addresses and Opinions of the Chief Justices of the United States.* Yale University, 1960.

Commager, H. S. *The American Mind.* Yale University, 1950.

Cooley, T. M. *The General Principles of Constitutional Law in the United States of America.* Dabor, 1978.

Corwin, E. S. *The General Principles of Constitutional Law in the United States of America.* Dabor, 1978.

Corwin, E. S. *A Constitution of Powers in a Secular State.* University of Virginia, 1951.

———. *Our Expendable Constitution.* University of Illinois, 1955.

Curtis, O. P. *It's Your Law.* Harvard University, 1954.

Dahl, R. A. *A Preface to Democratic Theory.* University of Chicago, 1956.

Daniels, J. *Frontier on the Potomac.* Macmillan, 1946.

Denning, A. *The Road to Justice.* Stevens, 1955.

Dewey, D. O. *Union and Liberty: A Documentary History of American Constitutionalism.* McGraw-Hill, 1969.

Dietze, G., ed. *Essays on the American Constitution.* Prentice-Hall, 1964.

Dilliard, I., ed. *The Spirit of Liberty: Papers and Addresses of Learned Hand.* Knopf, 1959.

Douglas, W. O. *Being an American.* Way, 1948.

———. *We the Judges.* Doubleday, 1956.

Edel, W. *A Constitutional Convention: Threat of Challenge.* Praeger, 1981.

Edwards, N. *The Courts and the Public Schools.* University of Chicago, 1962.

Fainsod, M., and L. Gordon. *Government and the American Economy.* Norton, 1948.

Fesler, J. W. *Area and Administration.* University of Alabama, 1949.

Fisher, L. *The Constitution Between Friends: Congress, President, and the Law.* St. Martin's Press, 1978.

Frankfurter, F. *Law and Politics.* Harcourt, Brace, 1939.

———. *Of Law and Men: Papers and Addresses,* ed. Phillip Elman. Harcourt, Brace, 1956.

———. *The Public and Its Government.* Oxford University, 1930.

Freedman, V. *Society on Trial: Current Court Decisions and Social Change.* Thomas, 1965.

Garrison, L. K., et al. *The Legal Process.* Rev. ed. Chandler, 1961.

Garvey, G. *Constitutional Bricolage.* Princeton University, 1971.

The Gaspar Bacon Lectures on the Constitution of the United States, 1940–1950. Boston University, 1953.

Gordon, R. M. *Nine Men Against America.* Devin-Adair, 1958.

Hagrath, E. P., ed. *The Constitutional System.* Scott, Foresman, 1966.

Hall, K. L., H. M. Hyman, and L. V. Sigal, eds. *The Constitutional Convention as an Amending Device.* American Political Science Association, 1981.

Hare, J. I. C. *American Constitutional Law.* Brown, 1889.

Holcombe, A. N. *The Constitutional Law.* Rev. ed. Scott, Foresman, 1968.

Kaplan, B., and L. Hall, eds. *Judicial Administration and the Common Man.* Lippincott, 1953.

Kauper, P. G. *Frontiers of Constitutional Liberty.* University of Michigan, 1956.

Laski, H. J. *The American Democracy.* Viking Press, 1948.

Lasswell, H. D. *Power and Personality.* Norton, 1948.

Lieberman, J. K. *Milestones.* West, 1976.

McCloskey, R. G. *Essays in Constitutional Law.* Knopf, 1957.

McKay, R. B., ed. *The American Constitutional Law Reader.* Oceana, 1958.

McLaughlin, A. S. *The Courts, the Constitution, and Parties.* University of Chicago, 1912.

Marshall, G. *Constitutional Theory.* Oxford University, 1971.

Mason, A. T., and W. M. Beaney. *The Supreme Court in a Free Society.* Rev. ed. Prentice-Hall, 1968.

Matthews, J. M. *The American Constitutional System.* McGraw-Hill, 1940.

Mayers, L. *The American Legal System.* Rev. ed. Harper & Row, 1964.

Miller, A. S. *Democratic Dictatorship: The Emergent Constitution of Control.* Greenwood Press, 1981.

Morlan, R. L. *Capitol, Courthouse, and City Hall.* 3d ed. Houghton Mifflin, 1966.

Paulson, M. C., ed. *Legal Institutions Today and Tomorrow.* Columbia University, 1959.

Pearson, S. A., ed. *The Constitutional Policy: Essays on the Founding Principles of American Politics.* University Press of America, 1983.

Pekalis, A. H. *Law and Social Action.* Cornell University, 1950.

Pomeroy, J. N. *An Introduction to the Constitutional Law of the U.S.* Hurd and Houghton, 1886.

Pritchett, C. H. *The American Constitutional System.* 4th ed. McGraw-Hill, 1976.

———. *Constitutional Law of the Federal System.* Prentice-Hall, 1984.

Read, C., ed. *The Constitution Reconsidered.* Rev. ed. and preface by R. B. Morris. Columbia University, 1968.

Rickard, J. A., and J. H. McCrocklin. *Our National Constitution.* Stackpole Books, 1956.

Rottschaefer, H. *The Constitution and Socio-Economic Change.* University of Michigan Law School, 1949.

Schechter, A. H. *Contemporary Constitutional Issues.* McGraw-Hill, 1972.

Schrag, P. G. *Behind the Scenes: The Politics of a Constitutional Convention.* Georgetown University, 1985.

Schwartz, B. *A Commentary on the Constitution of the U.S. Part 1: The Powers of Government.* Macmillan, 1963.

———. *American Constitutional Law.* Harvard University, 1955.

———. *From Confederation to Nation: The American Constitution, 1835–1877.* Johns Hopkins University, 1973.

———. *The Powers of Government*. Macmillan, 1965.

Shapiro, M. M., ed. *The Supreme Court*. Scott, Foresman, 1967.

———. *The Supreme Court and Constitutional Law*. Scott, Foresman, 1965.

Smith, H. R. *Democracy and the Public Interest*. University of Georgia, 1960.

Sutherland, A. E., ed. *Constitutionalism in America*. Blaisdell, 1964.

———. *Government Under Law*. Harvard University, 1956.

———. *The Law and One Man Among Many*. University of Wisconsin, 1956.

Taft, W. H. *Popular Government*. Yale University, 1913.

Tiffany, J. *A Treatise on Government and Constitutional Law*. W. C. Little, 1867.

Truman, D. B. *The Governmental Process*. Knopf, 1951.

Vanderbilt, A. T. *The Doctrine of Separation of Powers and Its Present Day Significance*. University of Nebraska, 1963.

Watson, D. K. *The Constitution of the United States: Its History, Application, and Construction*. Callaghan, 1910.

Weaver, S. P. *Constitutional Law and Its Administration*. Callaghan, 1946.

Wechsler, H. *Principles, Politics, and Fundamental Law: Selected Essays*. Harvard University, 1961.

Welch, J. *The Constitution*. Houghton, Mifflin, 1956.

Westin, A. F. *The Uses of Power: Seven Cases in American Politics*. Harcourt, Brace & World, 1962.

Wilson, W. *Constitutional Government in the United States*. Columbia University, 1908.

Wright, B. F. *Growth of American Constitutional Law*. Reynal and Hitchcock, 1942; rpt. University of Chicago (Phoenix Books), 1967.

CASEBOOKS—AMERICAN CONSTITUTIONAL LAW AND CONSTITUTIONAL HISTORY

Aldisert, R. J. *The Judicial Process: Readings, Materials and Cases*. West, 1976.

Aqueduct Books, eds. *Decisions of the U.S. Supreme Court, 1963–1964 Term–* . Aqueduct Books, 1965– .

Areen, J., et al. *Law, Science and Medicine*. Foundation Press, 1984.

Ball, H. *Constitutional Power: Cases on the Separation of Power and Federalism*, West, 1980.

Barrett, E. L., Jr. *Constitutional Law: Cases and Materials*. 7th ed. Foundation Press, 1985.

———, and W. Cohen. *Constitutional Law: The Structure of Government*. Foundation Press, 1985.

Bartholomew, P. C. *American Constitutional Law*. 2d ed. Littlefield, Adams, 1978.

———. *Ruling American Constitutional Law*. Littlefield, Adams, 1974.

———. *Summaries of Leading Cases on the Constitution*. 11th rev. ed. by J. F. Menez. Littlefield, Adams, 1981.

Berman, H. J., and W. R. Greiner. *The Nature and Functions of Law*. 3d ed. Foundation Press, 1972.

Berns, W. F. *Constitutional Cases in American Government*. Cornell University, 1963.

Birkby, R. H. *The Constitution and Public Policy*. Congressional Quarterly Press, 1983.

Bodenheimer, E., J. B. Oakley, and J. C. Love. *An Introduction to the Anglo-American Legal System*. West, 1980.

Bonsignore, J., et al. *Before the Law: An Introduction to the Legal Process;* 3d ed. Houghton Mifflin, 1983.

Brest, P. *Processes of Constitutional Decisionmaking: Cases and Materials*. Little, Brown, 1975.

Cahill, P. V., and R. J. Steamer. *The Constitution: Cases and Comments*. Ronald Press, 1959.

Chase, H. W., and C. R. Ducat. *Constitutional Interpretation*. 2d ed. West, 1979.

Conant, M. *The Constitution and Capitalism*. West, 1974.

Cushman, R. E., and R. F. Cushman. *Cases in Constitutional Law*. 6th ed. Appleton-Century-Crofts, 1984.

———. *Leading Constitutional Decisions*. 15th ed. Appleton-Century-Crofts, 1977.

Dodd, W. F. *Cases and Materials on Constitutional Law*. West, 1954.

Dowling, N. T. *Cases on Constitutional Law*. 6th ed. Foundation Press, 1959.

———, and R. A. Edwards. *American Constitutional Law*. Foundation Press, 1954.

———, and G. Gunther. *Constitutional Law*. 7th ed. Foundation Press, 1968.

Ducat, C. R. *Modes of Constitutional Interpretation*. West, 1978.

Evans, L. B. *Cases on American Constitutional Law*. 6th ed. Callaghan, 1952.

Fairman, C. *American Constitutional Decisions*. Holt, 1950.

Feeley, M. M., and S. Krislov. *Constitutional Law*. Little, Brown, 1985.

Fein, B. E. *Significant Decisions of the Supreme Court, 1974–75 Term*. American Enterprise Institute, 1976.

Fenwick, C. G. *Evans Cases on Constitutional Law*. 7th ed. Callaghan, 1957.

Fischer, T. C., and R. F. Zehnle. *Introduction to Law and Legal Reasoning*. West, 1977.

Ford, S. D. *The American Legal System—Its Dynamics and Limits*. 2d ed. West, 1974.

Forkosch, M. D. *Constitutional Law*. 2d ed. Foundation Press, 1969.

Frank, J. P. *Cases and Materials on Constitutional Law*. Rev. ed. McGraw-Hill, 1952.

Freund, P. A., et al. *Constitutional Law*. Little, Brown, 1961.

Friedelbaum, S. H. *Contemporary Constitutional Law*. Houghton Mifflin, 1972.

Garrity, J. A., ed. *Quarrels That Have Shaped the Constitution*. Harper & Row, 1964.

Goldman, S. *Constitutional Law and Supreme Court Decision-Making: Cases and Essays*. Harper & Row, 1982.

Grad, F. P. *Environmental Law: Sources and Problems*. Bender, 1972.

Greenberg, J. *Cases and Materials on Judicial Process and Social Change*. West, 1976.

Grillot, H. J. *Introduction to Law and the Legal System*. 3d ed. Houghton Mifflin, 1983.

Grossman, J. B., and R. S. Wells, eds. *Constitutional Law and Judicial Policy Making*. 2d ed. Wiley, 1980.

Gunther, G. *Cases and Materials on Constitutional Law*. 11th ed. Foundation Press, 1985.

Hall, J. P. *Cases on Constitutional Law*. West, 1913.

Hare, J. I. C. *American Constitutional Law*. Brown, 1889.

Heller, F. H. *Introduction to American Constitutional Law*. Harper, 1952.

Jackson, P. E. *Dissent in the Supreme Court: A Chronology*. University of Oklahoma, 1969.

Jacobstein, J. M., and R. M. Mersky, eds. *Fundamentals of Legal Research 1977*. Foundation Press, 1977.

Jones, R. W. *The Law of Journalism*. Washington Law Book, 1940.

Kauper, P. G. *Constitutional Law—Cases and Materials*. Little, Brown, 1961.

Ketcham, O. W., and M. G. Paulsen. *Cases and Materials Relating to Juvenile Courts*. Foundation Press, 1967.

Kutler, S. I. *The Supreme Court and the Constitution: Readings in American Constitutional History*. 3d ed. Norton, 1984.

Linde, H. A., and G. Bunn. *Legislative and Administrative Processes*. Foundation Press, 1976.

Lockard, D., and W. F. Murphy. *Basic Cases in Constitutional Law*. Macmillan, 1980.

Lockhart, W. B., Y. Kamisar, and J. H. Choper, eds. *American Constitutional Law*. 4th ed. West, 1975.

———. *Cases and Materials on the American Constitution*. 4th ed. West, 1975.

———. *Dodd's Cases on Constitutional Law*. West, 1962.

McKay, R. B., ed. *The American Constitutional Law Reader*. Oceana, 1958.

Maddex, J. L. *Cases and Comments on Constitutional Law*. West, 1974.

Mason, A. T., and W. B. Beaney. *American Constitutional Law: Introductory Essays and Selected Cases*. 6th ed. Prentice-Hall, 1978.

Mendelson, W. *The American Constitution and the Judicial Process*. Dorsey Press, 1980.

———. *The Constitution and the Supreme Court*. 2d ed. Dodd, Mead, 1965.

Mishkin, P. J., and C. Morris. *On Laws and Courts: An Introduction to Judicial Development of Case and Statute Study*. Foundation Press, 1965.

Monahan, J., and L. Walker. *Cases and Materials on Social Science in Law*. Foundation Press, 1985.

Mott, K. F. *The Supreme Court and the Living Constitution*. University Press of America, 1981.

Nowak, J. E., R. D. Rotunda, and J. N. Young. *Handbook on Constitutional Law*. West, 1978.

Pollack, L. H., ed. *The Constitution and the Supreme Court*. New American Library (Meridian Books), 1965.

Presser, S. B., and J. S. Zainaldin. *Law and American History: Cases and Materials*. West, 1980.

Pritchett, C. H. *American Constitutional Issues*. McGraw-Hill, 1962.

——. *The Federal System in Constitutional Law*. Prentice-Hall, 1978.

——, and A. F. Westin, eds. *The Third Branch of Government*. Harcourt, Brace, & World, 1963.

Rosenblum, V. G., and A. D. Castberg. *Cases on Constitutional Law: Political Roles of the Supreme Court*. Dorsey Press, 1973.

Rossum, R. A., and G. A. Tarr. *American Constitutional Law: Cases and Interpretation*. St. Martin's Press, 1983.

Ruddy, F. S., ed. *American International Law Cases, 1969–1978*. Oceana, 1980.

Saye, A. B. *American Constitutional Law: Cases and Texts*. 2d ed. West, 1979.

——. *Cases and Materials on Constitutional Law*. 2d ed. Callaghan, 1974.

Schantz, W. T., *The American Legal Environment: The Individual, His Business, and His Government*. West, 1976.

Schechter, A. H. *Contemporary Constitutional Issues*. McGraw-Hill, 1972.

Schlesinger, S. R. *The United States Supreme Court*. University Press of America, 1983.

Schmidhauser, J. R. *Constitutional Law in American Politics*. Brooks/Cole, 1984.

——. *Constitutional Law in the Political Process*. Rand McNally, 1963.

Schwartz, B. *American Constitutional Law*. 2d ed. Macmillan, 1979.

Scott, J. B. *Judicial Settlement of Controversies Between States of the American Union*. Oxford University (Clarendon Press), 1918.

Shapiro, M., and D. Hobbs. *American Constitutional Law: Cases and Analyses*. Winthrop, 1978.

——. *The Politics of Constitutional Law*. Winthrop, 1974.

Shapiron, M. and R. J. Tresolini. *American Constitutional Law*. 6th ed. Macmillan, 1983.

Shuman, S. I., and N. D. West. *American Law: An Introductory Survey of Some Principles, Cases, and Text*. Wayne State University, 1971.

Sigler, J. A. *Courts and Public Policy: Cases and Essays*. Dorsey Press, 1969.

Slane, A. *Major Supreme Court Decisions in American Government*. University Press of America, 1982.

Spaeth, H. J. *Classic and Current Decisions of the United States Supreme Court*. Freeman, 1977.

——. *The Warren Court: Cases and Commentary*. Chandler, 1966.

Stephens, O. H., and G. J. Rathjen. *The Supreme Court and the Allocation of Constitutional Power: Introductory Essays and Selected Cases*. Freeman, 1980.

Story, J. N., and L. M. Ward. *Perspectives of American Law: Cases on Law and Society*. West, 1974.

Swisher, C. B. *Historic Decisions of the Supreme Court*. Toronto, 1958.

Thayer, J. B. *Cases on Constitutional Law*. Macmillan, 1959.

Tresolini, R. J. *American Constitutional Law*. 3d ed. Macmillan, 1970.

——. *Constitutional Decisions in American Government*. Lippincott, 1965.

——. *Justice and the Supreme Court*. Lippincott, 1963.

Tribe, L. H. *American Constitutional Law: A Treatise*. Foundation Press, 1978.

Tucker, E. W. *Text, Cases, and Problems on the Adjudication of Social Issues*. 2d ed. West, 1977.

———. *Text, Cases and Problems on Legal Regulations of the Environment*. West, 1972.

Wheeler, R. R., and H. R. Whitcomb. *Judicial Administration: Text and Readings*. Prentice-Hall, 1977.

White, G. E. *Tort Law in America*. Oxford University, 1979.

Williams, J. S. *Constitutional Analysis in a Nutshell*. West, 1979.

Woll, P. *Constitutional Law: Cases and Comments*. Prentice-Hall, 1981.

COMPARATIVE ASPECTS

(Chiefly domestic aspects; for comparative aspects overseas, see Bibliography III. See also Judicial Process and Judicial Review.

Abraham, H. J. *The Judicial Process: An Introductory Analysis of the Courts of the United States, England, and France*. 5th ed. Oxford University, 1986.

Andrews, W. G., ed. *Constitutions and Constitutionalism*. 2d ed. Van Nostrand, 1963.

Becker, T. L. *Comparative Judicial Politics*. Rand McNally, 1970.

Borchard, E. M. *Declaratory Judgments*. 2d ed., Bands-Baldwin, 1941.

Bowie, R. R., and C. J. Friedrich, eds. *Studies in Federalism*. Little, Brown, 1954.

Burgess, J. W. *Political Science and Comparative Constitutional Law*. Ginn, 1980.

Cappelletti, M. *Judicial Review in the Contemporary World*, Bobbs-Merrill, 1971.

Dawson, J. P. *A History of Lay Judges*. Doubleday, 1956.

Douglas, W. O. *We the Judges*. Doubleday, 1956.

Friedrich, C. J. *Constitutional Government and Democracy*. 5th ed. Blaisdell, 1968.

Glick, H. R. *Supreme Courts in State Politics*. Basic Books, 1971.

Gray, C. M. *Copyhold, Equity, and the Common Law*. Harvard University, 1963.

Harding, A. L., ed. *The Administration of Justice in Retrospect*. Southern Methodist University, 1957.

Haynes, E. *The Selection and Tenure of Judges*. National Press Conference of Judicial Councils, 1944.

Karlen, D. *Appellate Courts in the United States and England*. New York University, 1956.

Kempin, F. G., Jr. *Legal History: Law and Social Change*. Prentice-Hall, 1963.

Kolasa, B. J., and B. Kolasa. *Legal Systems*. Prentice-Hall, 1978.

Macmahon, A. W. *Federalism Mature and Emergent*. Doubleday, 1953.

McWhinney, W. *Judicial Review in the English-Speaking World*. 4th ed. University of Toronto, 1969.

Murphy, W. F., and J. Tanenhaus. *Comparative Constitutional Law: Cases and Commentaries*. St. Martin's Press, 1977.

———. *The Study of Public Law*. Random House, 1971.

Newan, R. A. *Equity and Law: A Comparative Study*. Oceana, 1961.

Pollock, Sir F. *Essays in the Law*. Macmillan, 1922.

Read, C., ed. *The Constitution Reconsidered*. Columbia University, 1938.

Rice, W. G. *A Tale of Two Courts: Judicial Settlement of Controversies Between the States of the Swiss and American Federations*. University of Wisconsin, 1967.

Robson, W. A. *Justice and Administrative Law: A Study of the British Constitution*. Stevens, 1951.

Schubert, G., and D. J. Danelski, eds. *Comparative Judicial Behavior*. Oxford University, 1969.

Schwartz, B. *The Code Napoleon and the Common Law World*. New York University, 1956.

Shapiro, M. *Courts: A Comparative and Legal Analysis*. University of Chicago, 1981.

Spiro, H. *Government by Constitution*. Random House, 1959.

Stannard, H. *The Two Constitutions: A Comparative Study of British and American Constitutional Systems*. Van Nostrand, 1959.

Sutherland, A. E., ed. *Government Under Law*. Harvard University, 1956.

Wagner, W. J. *Federal States and Their Judiciary: Comparative Study in Constitutional Law and Organization of Courts in Federal States.* Mouton, 1959.

Wheare, K. C. *Federal Government.* 14th ed. Oxford University, 1964.

———. *Modern Constitutions.* Oxford University, 1951.

THE CONGRESS

(The legislative organ—a branch of the separation of powers of our national government. See also The Presidency)

AFL-CIO. *Why Richard M. Nixon Must Be Impeached—Now.* AFL-CIO, 1974.

American Civil Liberties Union. *Why President Richard Nixon Should Be Impeached.* ACLU, 1974.

Americans for Democratic Action. *The Case for Impeachment.* ADA, 1974.

Arnold, R. D. *Congress and the Bureaucracy: A Theory of Influence.* Yale University, 1979.

Barber, S. A. *The Constitution and the Delegation of Congressional Power.* University of Chicago, 1975.

Benedict, M. L. *The Impeachment and Trial of Andrew Johnson.* Norton, 1973.

Ben-Veniste, R., and G. Frampton, Jr. *Stonewall: The Real Story of the Watergate Prosecution.* Simon and Schuster, 1977.

Berger, R. *Congress versus the Supreme Court.* Harvard University, 1969.

———. *Executive Privilege: A Constitutional Myth.* Harvard University, 1974.

———. *Impeachment: The Constitutional Problem.* Harvard University, 1973.

Black, C. L., Jr. *Impeachment: A Handbook.* Yale University, 1974.

Bolton, J. R. *The Legislative Veto.* American Enterprise Institute, 1977.

Boyan, A. S., Jr. *Constitutional Aspects of Watergate: Documents and Materials.* Oceana, 1976.

Brant, I. *Impeachment: Trials and Errors.* Knopf, 1972.

Breckinridge, A. C. *Congress Against the Court.* University of Nebraska, 1971.

Brenner, P. *The Limits and Responsibilities of Congress.* St. Martin's Press, 1983.

Clausen, A. R. *How Congressmen Decide: A Policy Focus.* St. Martin's Press, 1973.

Congressional Quarterly. *Impeachment.* Congressional Quarterly Press, 1974.

———. *Impeachment and the U.S. Congress.* Congressional Quarterly Press, 1975.

———. *Powers of Congress.* Congressional Quarterly Press, 1976.

———. *Watergate: Chronology of a Crisis.* Congressional Quarterly Press, 1975.

Dash, S. *Chief Counsel: Inside the Ervin Committee—The Untold Story of Watergate.* Random House, 1976.

Davidson, R. H., and W. J. Oleszek. *Congress Against Itself.* Indiana University, 1977.

Dean, J. W., III. *Blind Ambition: The White House Years.* Simon and Schuster, 1976.

Deantonio, E., and D. Talbot. *Point of Order! A Documentary of the Army-McCarthy Hearings.* Norton, 1964.

Dewitt, D. M. *The Impeachment and Trial of Andrew Johnson.* Russell & Russell, 1902.

Dionisopoulos, P. A. *Rebellion, Racism, and Representation: The Adam Clayton Powell Case and Its Antecedents.* Northern Illinois University, 1970.

Dobrovir, W. A., et al. *The Offenses of Richard M. Nixon: A Lawyer's Guide for the People of the U.S.A.* Zill, 1974.

Dodd, L. C., and B. I. Oppenheimer, eds. *Congress Reconsidered.* 2d ed. Congressional Quarterly Press, 1981.

Doyle, J. *Not Above the Law: The Battles of Watergate Prosecutors Cox and Jaworski.* Morrow, 1977.

Ehrlich, W. *Presidential Impeachment: An American Dilemma.* Forum, 1974.

Ettrude, D. J., ed. *The Power of Congress to Nullify Supreme Court Decisions.* H. W. Wilson, 1924.

Fenno, R. F., Jr. *The Power of the Purse.* Little, Brown, 1966.

Fisher, L. *The Constitution Between Friends: Congress, the President, and the Law.* St. Martin's Press, 1978.

———. *The President and Congress: Power and Policy.* Free Press, 1972.

———. *Constitutional Conflicts Between Congress and the President.* Congressional Quarterly Press, 1985.

Goehlert, R. *Congress and Law-Making.* ABC-Clio, 1979.

Goldfarb, R. L. *The Contempt Power.* Columbia University, 1963.

Griffith, E. S., and F. R. Valeo. *Congress: Its Contemporary Role.* 5th ed. New York University, 1976.

Harris, J. P. *The Advice and Consent of the Senate: A Study of the Confirmation of Appointments by the United States Senate.* University of California, Berkeley, 1953.

Hinckley, B. *Stability and Change in Congress.* 2d ed. Harper & Row, 1978.

Hoffer, P. C., and N. E. H. Hull. *Impeachment in America, 1635–1805.* Yale University, 1985.

Hurst, J. W. *The Growth of American Law: The Lawmakers.* Little, Brown, 1950.

Jacobson, G. C. *Money in Congressional Elections.* Yale University, 1980.

Jaworski, L. *The Right and the Power.* Crowell, 1976.

Jewell, M. E., and S. C. Patterson. *The Legislative Process.* 3d ed. McGraw-Hill, 1977.

Kernochan, J. F. *The Legislative Process.* Foundation Press, 1981.

Labovitz, J. R. *Presidential Impeachment.* Yale University, 1978.

Lawson, J. F. *The General Welfare Clause.* Privately printed. 1934.

Lowi, T. J., ed. *Legislative Politics USA.* 2d ed. Little, Brown, 1950.

Lurie, L. *The Impeachment of Richard Nixon.* Berkeley Publishing, 1973.

Mansfield, H. C., Sr. *Congress Against the President.* Academy of Political Science, 1975.

Mason, A. T., and W. B. Beaney. *The Supreme Court in a Free Society.* Prentice-Hall, 1959.

Morgan, D. L. *Congress and the Constitution: A Study of Responsibility.* Harvard University, 1967.

Murphy, W. F. *Congress and the Court.* University of Chicago, 1962.

Nichols, E. R. *Congress or the Supreme Court: Which Shall Rule America?* Noble, 1935.

Orfield, G. *Congressional Power: Congress and Social Change.* Harcourt Brace Jovanovich, 1976.

Paulson, M. D., ed. *Legal Institutions Today and Tomorrow.* Columbia University, 1959.

Polsby, N. W. *Congress and the Presidency.* 3d ed. Prentice-Hall, 1976.

Price, D. *Who Makes the Law?* Schenckman, 1972.

Pritchett, C. H. *Congress Versus the Supreme Court.* University of Minnesota, 1961.

Rapoport, D. *The House: From Adam Clayton Powell to Peter Rodino.* Follett, 1975.

Schick, A. *Congress and Money.* Urban Institute Press, 1980.

Schmidhauser, J. R., and L. L. Berg. *The Supreme Court and Congress: Conflict and Interaction, 1945–1968.* Free Press, 1972.

Smith, G. *High Crimes and Misdemeanors: The Impeachment and Trial of Andrew Johnson.* Morrow, 1977.

Schnapper, M. B., ed. *Presidential Impeachment: A Documentary Overview.* Public Affairs Press, 1974.

Simpson, A. *A Treatise on Federal Impeachments.* Philadelphia Bar Association, 1916.

U.S. House of Representatives. Committee on the Judiciary. *Impeachment Inquiry, 1974.* Superintendent of Documents, 1975.

Vinyard, D. *Congress.* Scribner, 1969.

Weeks, K. M. *Adam Clayton Powell and the Supreme Court.* Kennikat Press, 1971.

Wilson, W. *Congressional Government.* Houghton Mifflin, 1885.

FEDERALISM

IN GENERAL

Allen, R. S. *Our Sovereign States*. Vanguard Press, 1949.

Ames, H. V., ed. *State Documents on Federal Relations, 1789–1861*. University of Pennsylvania, 1900.

Anderson, W. *The Nation and the States: Rivals or Partners?* University of Minnesota, 1955.

Association of American Law Schools. *Selected Essays on Constitutional Law*. Foundation Press, 1938.

Benson, G. C. S. *The New Centralization*. Rinehart, 1941.

Bloch, C. *States Rights: The Law of the Land*. Harrison, 1958.

Bordon, M., ed. *The Anti-Federalist Papers*. Michigan State University, 1965.

Bowie, R. R., and D. J. Friedrich, eds. *Studies in Federalism*. Little, Brown, 1954.

Brannon, H. *A Treatise on the Rights and Privileges Guaranteed by the Fourteenth Amendment to the Constitution of the United States*. Anderson, 1901.

Bridwell, R., and R. U. Whitten. *The Constitution and the Common Law: The Decline of the Doctrines of Separation of Power and Federalism*. Lexington Books, 1977.

Clark, J. P. *The Rise of a New Federalism*. Columbia University, 1938.

Cooley, R. M. *Constitutional Limitations*. 17th ed. Little, Brown, 1954.

Corwin, E. S. *The Doctrine of Judicial Review*. Princeton University, 1914.

———. *National Supremacy: Treaty Power Versus State Power*. Holt, 1913.

Davis, S. R. *The Federal Principle: A Journey Through Time in Quest of Meaning*. University of California, 1978.

Dealey, G. Q. *Growth of American State Constitutions*. Da Capo Press, 1972.

Dietze, G. *The Federalist: A Classic on Federalism and Free Government*. Johns Hopkins University, 1960.

Dodd, W. F. *The Revision and Amendment of State Constitutions*. Johns Hopkins University, 1910.

Douglas, W. O. *We the Judges*. Doubleday, 1956.

Elazar, D. *American Federalism: A View from the States*. 3d ed. Harper & Row, 1984.

Engdahl, D. E. *Constitutional Power: Federal and State*. West, 1974.

Fogelson, R. M., and L. E. Susskind. *American Federalism*. Arno Press, 1977.

Guthrie, W. D. *Lectures on the 14th Article of Amendment to the Constitution of the United States*. Little, Brown, 1898.

Hamilton, A., J. Jay, and J. Madison. *The Federalist Papers*. McLean, 1788.

Harris, R. J. *The Judicial Power of the United States*. Kennikat Press, 1940.

Hart, H. M., Jr., and H. Wechsler. *The Federal Court and the Federal System*. Foundation Press, 1953.

Hawkins, R. B., Jr., ed. *American Federalism: A New Partnership for the Republic*. Institute for Contemporary Studies, 1982.

Heins, A. J. *Constitutional Restrictions Against State Debt*. University of Wisconsin, 1963.

Hicks, U. K. *Federalism: Failure and Success—A Comparative Study*. Oxford University, 1979.

Hopkins, V. C. *Dred Scott's Cases*. Fordham University, 1951.

House, P. W., and W. A. Steger. *Modern Federalism: An Analytic Approach*. Lexington Books, 1982.

Howitt, A. M. *Managing Federalism*. Congressional Quarterly Press, 1983.

Hutchins, R. M. *Two Faces of Federalism*. Center for the Study of Democratic Institutions, 1962.

Hyman, H. M. *A More Perfect Union: The Impact of the Civil War and Reconstruction on the Constitution*. Knopf, 1973.

Kettl, D. F. *The Regulation of American Federalism*. Louisiana State University, 1983.

Kilpatrick, J. J. *The Sovereign States*. Regnery, 1957.

King, P. *Federalism and Federation.* Johns Hopkins University, 1982.

Lien, A. J. *Concurring Opinion.* Washington University, St. Louis, 1957.

Livingston, W. S. *Federalism and Constitutional Change.* Oxford University, 1956.

Macmahon, A. W., ed. *Federalism Mature and Emergent.* Doubleday, 1955.

Main, J. R. *The Antifederalist Critics of the Constitution, 1781–1788.* Quadrangle, 1964.

Mason, A. T. *Free Government in the Making.* 3d ed. Oxford University, 1965.

———. *The States' Rights Debate: Antifederalism and the Constitution.* 2d ed. Oxford University, 1972.

Merriam, C. E. *The Written Constitution and the Unwritten Attitude.* R. R. Smith, 1931.

Miller, A. S. *The Supreme Court and American Capitalism.* Free Press, 1968.

Morley, F. *Freedom and Federalism.* Regnery, 1959.

Orfield, L. B. *The Amending of the Federal Constitution.* Callaghan, 1942.

Peltason, J. W. *Fifty-Eight Lonely Men: Southern Federal Judges and School Desegregation.* Harcourt, Brace & World, 1961.

Pound, R., C. H. McIlwain, and R. F. Nichols. *Federalism as a Democratic Process.* Rutgers University, 1942.

Powell, T. R. *Vagaries and Varieties in Constitutional Interpretations.* Columbia University, 1956.

Ramaswamy, M. *The Creative Role of the Supreme Court of the United States.* Stanford University, 1956.

Reagan, M. D. *The New Federalism.* 2d ed. Oxford University, 1981.

Roberts, O. J. *The Court and the Constitution.* Harvard University, 1951.

Rockefeller, N. A. *The Future of Federalism.* Harvard University, 1962.

Schmidhauser, J. R. *The Supreme Court as Final Arbiter of Federal-State Relations.* University of North Carolina, 1958.

Sprague, J. D. *Voting Patterns of the United States Supreme Court: Cases in Federalism, 1889–1959.* Bobbs-Merrill, 1968.

Ten-Broek, J. *Anti-Slavery Origins of the Fourteenth Amendment.* University of California, 1951.

Upshur, A. P. *A Brief Enquiry into the Fine Nature and Character of Our Federal Government.* Ruffin, 1840.

Warren, C. *The Supreme Court and Sovereign States.* Princeton University, 1924.

Wheare, K. *Federal Government.* 4th ed. Oxford University, 1964.

White, L. D. *The States and the Nation.* Louisiana State University, 1956.

Wieck, W. M. *The Guarantee Clause of the United States Constitution.* Cornell University, 1972.

Wilcox, T. *States' Rights v. the Supreme Court.* Little, Brown, 1960.

Wright, D. *Understanding Intergovernmental Relations.* PWS (Duxbury Press), 1978.

THE COMMERCE CLAUSE

Baxter, M. G. *Daniel Webster and the Supreme Court.* University of Massachusetts, 1967.

Benson, P. R., Jr. *The Supreme Court and the Commerce Clause, 1937–1970.* Dunellen, 1971.

Cooke, F. H. *The Commerce Clause of the Federal Constitution.* Baker, Voolins, 1908.

Corwin, E. S. *The Commerce Power Versus States Rights.* Princeton University, 1936.

Frankfurter, F. *The Commerce Clause Under Marshall, Taney and Waite.* Univesrity of North Carolina, 1937.

Gavit, B. C. *The Commerce Clause of the United States Constitution.* Principia, 1956.

Hartman, J. P. *State Taxation of Interstate Commerce.* Dennis, 1953.

Kallenbach, J. E. *Federal Cooperation with the States Under the Commerce Clause.* University of Michigan, 1942.

Kurland, P. B., ed. *The Supreme Court and Patents and Monopolies.* University of Chicago, 1975.

Mahany, M. M. *Commerce Clause Tax Problems.* Wilkinson, 1940.

Melder, F. E. *State and Local Barriers to Interstate Commerce in the United States.* University of Maine, 1937.

Meyer, B. H. *A History of the Northern Securities Case.* University of Wisconsin, 1906; rpt. Da Capo Press, 1972.

Ramaswamy, M. *The Commerce Clause in the Constitution of the United States.* Longmans, Green, 1948.

Ribble, F. D. G. *State and National Power over Commerce.* Columbia University, 1937.

Rottschaefer, H. *The Constitution and Socio-Economic Change.* University of Michigan, 1948.

Rutledge, W. B. *A Declaration of Legal Faith.* University of Kansas, 1947.

Wood, S. B. *Constitutional Politics in the Progressive Era.* University of Chicago, 1967.

THE CONTRACT CLAUSE

Ackerman, B. A. *Private Property and the Constitution.* Yale University, 1977.

Atiyah, P. S. *The Rise and Fall of Freedom of Contract.* Oxford University, 1981.

Gilmore, G. *The Death of Contract.* Ohio State University, 1974.

Magrath, P. B. *Yazoo: Law and Politics in the New Republic, the Case of Fletcher v. Peck.* Brown University, 1967.

Shirley, J. M. *The Dartmouth College Cases and the Supreme Court of the United States.* University of Chicago, 1895; rpt. Da Capo Press, 1971.

Wright, B. F. *The Contract Clause of the Constitution.* Harvard University, 1938.

FULL FAITH AND CREDIT

Jackson, R. H. *Full Faith and Credit: The Lawyer's Clause in the Constitution.* Columbia University, 1945.

THE GUARANTEE CLAUSE

Gettleman, M. E. *The Dorr Rebellion.* Random House, 1973.

Wieck, W. M. *The Guarantee Clause of the United States Constitution.* Cornell University, 1972.

POLICE POWER

Roettinger, R. *The Supreme Court and the State Police Power: A Study in Federalism.* Public Affairs Press, 1957.

RELATIONSHIP AMONG THE STATES

Ames, H. V., ed. *State Documents on Federal Relations.* University of Pennsylvania, 1900–1906.

Leach, R. H., and R. S. Sugg, Jr., *The Administration of Interstate Compacts.* Louisiana State University, 1959.

Ridgeway, M. E. *Interstate Compacts: A Question of Federalism.* Southern Illinois University, 1971.

Scott, J. B. *Judicial Settlement of Controversies Between States of the American Union.* Oxford University (Clarendon Press), 1918.

Thursby, V. B. *Interstate Cooperation: A Study of the Interstate Compact.* Public Affairs Press, 1953.

Warren, C. "The Supreme Court and Disputes Between States." *Bulletin of the College of Virginia* 34, no. 5 (June 1940).

Zimmerman, F. L., and M. Wendell. *The Interstate Compact Since 1925.* Council of State Governments, 1951.

STATE COURTS AND FEDERAL RELATIONSHIPS

Berkson, L. C., S. W. Hays, and S. J. Carbon, eds. *Managing the State Courts: Text and Readings.* West, 1977.

Council of State Governments. *Courts of Last Resort of the States*. Council of State Governments, 1955.
———. *State Court Systems*. Council of State Governments. 1970.
Elliott, S. D. *Improving Our Courts*. Oceana, 1959.
Foster, L., and C. Boast. *Subject Compilation of State Laws: Research Guide and Annotated Bibliography*. Greenwood Press, 1981.
Friendly, H. J. *Federal Jurisdiction: A General View*. Columbia University, 1973.
Gazell, J. A. *The Future of State Court Management*. National University Publications, 1978.
———. *State Trial Courts as Bureaucracies*. Kennikat Press, 1975.
Glick, H. R. *Supreme Courts in State Politics*. Basic Books, 1971.
———, and K. N. Vines. *State Court Systems*. Prentice-Hall, 1972.
Jacobs, C. E. *The Eleventh Amendment and Sovereign Immunity*. Greenwood Press, 1972.
Klein, F. J. *Federal and State Court Systems—A Guide*. Ballinger, 1978.
Mitchel, W. *Relations Between Federal and State Courts*. Columbia University, 1950.
Morris, T. R. *The Virginia Supreme Court: An Institutional and Political Analysis*. University of Virginia, 1979.
Porter, M. C., and G. A. Tarr, eds. *State Supreme Courts: Policymakers in the Federal System*. Greenwood Press, 1982.
Stott, E. K., Jr., T. J. Fetter, and L. L. Crites. *Rural Courts: The Effects of Space and Distance on the Administration of Justice*. National Center for the State Courts, 1977.
Tarr, G. A. *Judicial Impact and State Supreme Courts*. Heath, 1977.
Vanderbilt, A. T. *Minimum Standards of Judicial Administration*. New York University, 1949.
Wendell, M. *Relations Between the Federal and State Courts*. Rev. ed. Columbia University, 1953.

THE TAXING POWER AND OTHER MONETARY PROBLEMS

Bernard, M. M. *Constitutions, Taxation, and Land Policy*. Lexington Books, 1980.
Dunne, G. T. *Monetary Decisions of the Supreme Court*. Rutgers University, 1960.
Friedman, L. M. *Contract Law in America: A Social and Economic Case Study*. University of Wisconsin, 1965.
Hansen, A., and H. Perloff. *State and Local Finance in the National Economy*. Norton, 1944.
Heins, A. J. *Constitutional Restrictions Against State Debt*. University of Wisconsin, 1963.
Maxwell, J. A. *Financial Impact of Federalism in the United States*. Harvard University, 1946.

HISTORY

IN GENERAL

(Sweeping surveys as well as specific eras and institutions)

Alfange, D. *The Supreme Court and the National Will*. Doubleday, 1937.
Alloway, C. C. *United States Constitutional Law, 1850–1875*. Oceana, 1958.
Angell, E. *Supreme Court Primer*. Reynal and Hitchcock, 1937.
Bates, E. S. *The Story of the Supreme Court*. Bobbs-Merrill, 1936; rpt. Cornerstone Library, 1963.
Bauer, E. K. *Commentaries on the Constitution, 1790–1860*. Columbia University, 1952.
Beck, J. M. *The Constitution of the United States*. Doran, 1922.
Beitzinger, A. J. *A History of American Political Thought*. Dodd, Mead, 1972.
Beth, L. P. *The Development of the American Constitution, 1877–1917*. Harper & Row, 1971.
Billikopf, D. M. *Judicial Power: 1789–1864*. Vantage, 1973.
Boudin, L. B. *Government by Judiciary*. Godwin, 1932.
Bourguignan, H. J. *The First Federal Court: The Federal Appellate Prize Court of the American Revolution, 1775–1787*. American Philosophical Society, 1977.

Brown, E. S. *Ratification of the 21st Amendment to the Constitution of the United States.* Da Capo Press, 1970.

Burdick, C. K. *The Law of the American Constitution: Its Origins and Development.* Putnam, 1922.

Burgess, J. W. *The Civil War and the Constitution, 1859–1865.* Dunellen, 1901.

Carson, H. L. *The History of the Supreme Court of the United States.* Keller, 1891.

Commager, H. S., ed. *Documents of American History.* 6th ed. Appleton-Century-Crofts, 1948.

Cooley, T. M. *Constitutional History of the U.S.* Putnam, 1889.

Cover, R. M. *Justice Accused: Antislavery and the Judicial Process.* Yale University, 1975.

Crosskey, W. W. *Politics and the Constitution in the History of the United States.* University of Chicago, 1953.

———, and W. Jeffrey, Jr. *Politics and the Constitution in the History of the United States.* Vol. 3 of *The Political Background of the Federal Convention.* University of Chicago, 1981.

Cummings, H. W., and C. McGarland. *Federal Justice.* Macmillan, 1937.

Curtis, G. T. *Constitutional History of the United States.* Da Capo Press, 1984.

Dargo, G. *Roots of the Republic: A New Perspective on Early American Constitutionalism.* Praeger, 1974.

Donald, P. *The Politics of Reconstruction.* Louisiana State University, 1966.

Edmunds, P. D. *Law and Civilization.* Public Affairs Press, 1959.

Ernst, M. L. *The Ultimate Power.* Doubleday, 1937.

Fairman, C. *The Bacon Lectures on the Constitution of the United States, 1940–1950.* Boston University, 1953.

———. Part 1 of *Reconstruction and Reunion, 1864–1888.* Vol. 6 of *The Oliver Wendell Holmes Devise History of the Supreme Court of the United States.* Gen. ed. P. A. Freund. Macmillan, 1973.

Feerick, J. D. *The Twenty-Fifth Amendment: Its Complete History and Earliest Application.* Fordham University, 1976.

Fenn, P. T. *The Development of the Constitution.* Appleton-Century-Crofts, 1948.

Flack, H. B. *The Adoption of the Fourteenth Amendment.* Johns Hopkins University, 1908.

Fox, J. C. *The History of Contempt of Court.* Oxford University, 1927.

Frankfurter, F. *The Commerce Clause Under Marshall, Taney, and Waite.* University of North Carolina, 1937.

Freund, P. A., gen. ed. *The Oliver Wendell Holmes Devise History of the Supreme Court of the United States.* 11 vols. Macmillan, 1973– .

Fribourg, M. G. *The Supreme Court in American History.* Macrae Smith, 1965.

Friedman, L. M. *A History of American Law.* Simon and Schuster, 1973.

———, and H. N. Schreiber, eds. *American Law and Constitutional Order: Historical Perspectives.* Harvard University, 1978.

Friedrich, C. J., and R. G. McCloskey. *From the Declaration of Independence to the Constitution.* Bobbs-Merrill, 1964.

Fuess, C. M. *Daniel Webster.* Little, Brown, 1930.

Goebel, J., Jr. *Antecedents and Beginnings to 1801.* Vol. 1 of *The Oliver Wendell Holmes Devise History of the Supreme Court of the United States.* Gen. ed. P. A. Freund. Macmillan, 1971.

Graham, G. G., and S. G. Graham, eds. *Founding Principles of American Government.* Chatham House, 1984.

Guthrie, W. D., Jr. *Lectures on the Fourteenth Amendment to the Constitution of the United States.* Little, Brown, 1898.

Haines, C. G. *The Role of the Supreme Court in American Government and Politics, 1789–1835.* University of California, 1944; rpt. Da Capo Press, 1971.

———, and F. H. Sherwood. *The Role of the Supreme Court in American Government and Politics, 1835–1864.* University of California, 1957; rpt. Da Capo Press, 1973.

Hall, K. L., ed. *A Comprehensive Bibliography of Constitutional and Legal History, 1896–1979.* Kraus, 1982.

Hamilton, W. H., and D. Adair. *The Power to Govern: The Constitution Then and Now.* Norton, 1937.

Hartz, L. *Economic Policy and Democratic Thought.* Harvard University, 1948.

Hawke, D. F. *Honorable Treason: The Declaration of Independence and the Men Who Signed It.* Viking Press, 1976.

Hendrick, B. J. *Bulwark of the Republic.* Little, Brown, 1939.

Hockett, C. H. *The Constitutional History of the U.S., 1826–1876.* Macmillan, 1939.

Hyman, H. M. *A More Perfect Union: The Impact of the Civil War and Reconstruction on the Constitution.* Knopf, 1973.

Jackson, R. H. *The Struggle for Judicial Supremacy.* Knopf, 1941.

Jacobs, C. E. *Law Writers and the Courts.* University of California, 1954.

James, J. B. *The Framing of the Fourteenth Amendment.* University of Illinois, 1956.

Jameson, J. F., ed. *Essays in the Constitutional History of the U.S. in the Formative Period, 1775–1789.* Da Capo Press, 1970.

Jensen, M. D. *The Articles of Confederation.* University of Wisconsin, 1940.

Kelly, A. H., W. Harbison, and A. H. Belz. *The American Constitution: Its Origin and Development.* 6th ed. Norton, 1983.

Kempin, F. G., Jr. *Historical Introduction to Anglo-American Law in a Nutshell.* 2d ed. West, 1973.

———. *Legal History: Law and Social Change.* Prentice-Hall, 1963.

Kendrick, B. J. *Journal of the Joint Committee of Fifteen on Reconstruction.* Scribner's, 1914.

Kutler, S. I. *Judicial Power and Reconstruction Politics.* University of Chicago, 1968.

———, ed. *The Supreme Court and the Constitution: Readings in American Constitutional History.* 3d ed. Morton, 1984.

Lacy, C. *The Meaning of the American Revolution.* New American Library, 1960.

Lasson, N. B. *The History of the Development of the Fourteenth Amendment.* Johns Hopkins University, 1937.

Leedham, C. *Our Changing Constitution.* Dodd, Mead, 1964.

Levy, L. *Judgments: Essays in American Constitutional History.* University of Chicago, 1972.

Lieberman, J. *Milestones.* Oxford University, 1976.

McCloskey, R. G. *The American Supreme Court.* University of Chicago, 1960.

McCune, W. *The Nine Young Men.* Harper, 1947.

McIllwain, C. H. *Constitutionalism, Ancient and Modern.* Rev. ed. Cornell University, 1947.

McLaughlin, A. C. *The Constitutional History of the United States.* Appleton-Century, 1935.

———. *The Courts, the Constitution and Parties.* University of Chicago, 1912.

Mason, A. T. *The Supreme Court from Taft to Warren.* Rev. and enl. Louisiana State University, 1968.

Maverick, M. *In Blood and Ink.* Modern Age, 1939.

Mendelson, W. *Capitalism, Democracy, and the Supreme Court.* Appleton-Century-Crofts, 1960.

Miller, P., ed. *The Legal Mind in America: From Independence to the Civil War.* Doubleday, 1962.

Millett, S. M. *A Selected Bibliography of American Constitutional History.* Clio, 1975.

Morgan, E. S. *The Birth of the Republic.* University of Chicago, 1956.

Munro, W. B. *The Makers of the Unwritten Constitution.* Macmillan, 1930.

Murray, W. H. *The Supreme Court, the President, and Seven Senators.* Meador, 1959.

Myers, G. *History of the Supreme Court of the United States.* Kerr, 1912.

Padover, S. K. *The Living United States Constitution.* Rev. ed. Meador, 1968.

Paludan, P. S. *A Covenant with Death: The Constitution, Law, and Equality in the Civil War.* University of Illinois, 1975.

Paul, A. M. *Conservative Crisis and the Rule of Law: Attitudes of Bar and Bench, 1887–1895.* Cornell University, 1960.

Pollack, L. H., ed. *The Constitution and the Supreme Court: A Documentary History*. World, 1966.

Pomeroy, J. N. *An Introduction to the Constitutional Law of the United States*. Houghton Mifflin, 1886.

Pritchett, C. H. *The American Constitution*. 3d ed. McGraw-Hill, 1977.

Rachlis, F. *They Came to Kill*. Random House, 1961.

Randall, J. G. *The Civil War and Reconstruction*. Heath, 1937.

———. *Constitutional Problems Under Lincoln*. Rev. ed. Peter Smith, 1963.

Read, C., ed. *The Constitution Reconsidered*. Columbia University, 1938.

Ribble, F. D. G. *State and National Power over Commerce*. Columbia University, 1937.

Rodell, F. *Nine Men: A Political History of the Supreme Court from 1790–1955*. Random House, 1955.

Rodick, B. C. *American Constitutional Custom: A Forgotten Factor in the Founding*. Philosophical Library, 1953.

Rogers, H. S., ed. *Constitutional History of the United States as Seen in the Development of American Law*. Bender, 1890.

Rosen, P. L. *The Supreme Court and Social Science*. University of Illinois, 1972.

Schovler, J. *Constitutional Studies*. Dodd, Mead, 1897.

Schubert, G. *The Constitutional Polity*. Boston University, 1970.

Schwartz, B. *The Reins of Power: A Constitutional History of the United States*. Hill & Wang, 1963.

Semonche, J. E. *Charting the Future: The Supreme Court Responds to a Changing Society, 1890–1920*. Greenwood Press, 1978.

Silver, D. M. *Lincoln's Supreme Court*. University of Illinois, 1956.

Smith, J. M., and P. L. Murphy. *Liberty and Justice*. Knopf, 1958.

Steamer, R. J. *The Supreme Court in Crisis: A History of Conflict*. University of Massachusetts, 1971.

Story, J. *A Familiar Exposition on the Constitution of the United States: Containing a Brief Commentary*. Petersburgh, 1940.

Swindler, W. F. *Court and Constitution in the 20th Century: The Old Legality, 1889–1932*. Bobbs-Merrill, 1969.

———. *The New Legality, 1932–1968*. Bobbs-Merrill, 1970.

Swisher, C. B. *American Constitutional Development*. 2d ed. Houghton Mifflin, 1954.

———. *The Taney Period, 1836–64*. Vol. 5 of *The Oliver Wendell Holmes Devise History of the Supreme Court of the United States*. Gen. ed. P. A. Freund. Macmillan, 1974.

Thorpe, F. N. *The Constitutional History of the United States, 1765–1895*. Da Capo Press, 1971.

Tocqueville, A. de. *Democracy in America*. H. G. Langley, 1841.

Towle, N. *A History and Analysis of the Constitution of the United States*. Little, Brown, 1860.

Twiss, B. R. *Lawyers and the Constitution: How Laissez Faire Came to the Supreme Court*. Princeton, 1942.

Wallace, H. A. *Whose Constitution?* Reynal and Hitchock, 1936.

Warren, C. *The Supreme Court in United States History*. Rev. ed. Little, Brown, 1926.

Wills, G. *Inventing America: Jefferson's Declaration of Independence*. Doubleday, 1978.

Wright, B. F. *The Contract Clause of the Constitution*. Harvard University, 1938.

TWO AREAS OF MAJOR HISTORICAL INTEREST—SPECIFIC WORKS

1. Origin, Formation, and Ratification of the Constitution

Adams, W. P. *The First American Constitution*. University of North Carolina, 1981.

Baldwin, H. *A General View of the Origin and Nature of the Constitution and Government of the United States*. Clark, 1837.

Bancroft, G. *History of the Formation of the Constitution of the United States of America.* Appleton, 1882.

Beard, C. A. *An Economic Interpretation of the Constitution of the United States.* Macmillan, 1913.

Becker, C. L. *The Declaration of Independence: A Study in the History of Political Ideas.* Knopf, 1942.

Bowen, C. D. *Miracle at Philadelphia: The Story of the Constitutional Convention, May to September 1787.* Little, Brown, 1966.

Brant, I. *The Bill of Rights.* Bobbs-Merrill, 1965.

———. *James Madison: Father of the Constitution, 1787–1800.* Bobbs-Merrill, 1950.

Brown, R. E. *Charles Beard and the Constitution: A Critical Analysis of an Economic Interpretation of the Constitution.* Princeton University, 1956.

Buchanan, J. M., and G. Tullock. *The Calculus of Consent: Logical Foundations of Constitutional Democracy.* University of Michigan, 1956.

Butzner, J., comp. *Constitutional Chaff: Rejected Suggestions of the Constitutional Convention of 1787 with Explanation on Argument.* Columbia University, 1941.

Corwin, E. S. *American Constitutional History.* Ed. A. T. Mason and G. Harvey. Harper & Row, 1963.

Dietze, G. *The Federalist: A Classic on Federalism and Free Government.* Johns Hopkins University, 1960.

Dilliard, I., ed. *Building the Constitution.* Post-Dispatch Educational Program, 1937.

Elliot, J., ed. *The Debates in the Several State Conventions on the Adoption of the Federal Constitution.* 2d ed. Lippincott, 1854.

Farrand, M. *The Framing of the Constitution of the United States.* Yale University, 1926.

———. *The Records of the Federal Convention of 1787.* Yale University, 1926.

Fiske, J. *The Critical Period of American History, 1783–1789.* Houghton Mifflin, 1888.

Goebel, J., Jr. *Antecedents and Beginnings to 1801.* Vol. 1 of *The Oliver Wendell Holmes Devise History of the Supreme Court of the United States.* Gen. ed. P. A. Freund. Macmillan, 1971.

Graham, H. J. *Everyman's Constitution.* Norton, 1968.

Hamilton, Jay, and Madison. *The Federalist Papers.* McLean, 1788; rpt. Random House, 1972.

Horwitz, R. H., ed. *The Moral Foundations of the American Republic.* 2d ed. University of Virginia, 1982.

Hunt, C., and J. B. Scott, eds. *The Debates in the Federal Convention of 1787.* Oxford University, 1920.

Hyneman, C. S., and G. W. Davy. *A Second Federalist: Congress Creates a Government.* Appleton-Century-Crofts, 1966.

Jaffa, H. V. *American Conservatism and the American Founding.* Carolina Academic Press, 1983.

Jameson, J. F. *Essays in the Constitutional History of the United States in the Formative Period, 1775–1789.* Houghton Mifflin, 1889.

Jenson, M. O. *The Making of the American Constitution.* Krieger (Anvil Series) 1964.

Konefsky, S. S. *John Marshall and Alexander Hamilton: Architects of the American Constitution.* Macmillan, 1965.

Kruschke, E. R. *An Introduction to the Constitution of the United States.* American Book, 1968.

Latham, E., ed. *The Declaration of Independence and the Constitution.* Heath, 1956.

Levy, L. W., ed. *Essays on the Making of the Constitution.* Oxford University, 1972.

Long, B. *Genesis of the Constitution of the United States of America.* Macmillan, 1926.

Lyon, W. *The Constitution and the Men Who Made It.* Houghton Mifflin, 1936.

McCloskey, P. N., Jr. *The United States Constitution.* Addison-Wesley, 1964.

McDonald, F. *A Constitutional History of the United States.* Watts, 1982.

———. *We the People: The Economic Origins of the Constitution.* University of Chicago, 1958.

McLaughlin, A. C. *The Confederation and the Constitution, 1783-1789.* Harper, 1905.

Madison, J. *Journal of the Federal Convention.* Langtree and O'Sullivan, 1840.

Mason, A. T. *The States Rights Debate: Antifederalism and the Constitution.* 2d ed. Prentice-Hall, 1972.

Miller, J. C. *Origins of the American Revolution.* Little, Brown, 1943.

Montross, L. *Reluctant Rebels: The Story of the Continental Congress.* Harper, 1950.

Morrison, S. F. *Sources and Documents Illustrating the American Revolution, 1764-1788, and the Formation of the Federal Constitution.* 2d ed. Oxford University, 1929.

Murphy, P. L. *The Constitution in Crisis Times, 1918-1969.* Harper & Row, 1972.

Pearson, S. A., Jr., ed. *The Constitutional Polity.* University Press of America, 1984.

Prescott, A. T., comp. *Drafting the Federal Constitution.* Louisiana State University, 1941.

Rossiter, C. *Seedtime of the Republic.* Harcourt, Brace, 1953.

———. *1787: The Grand Convention.* Macmillan, 1966.

Rossum, R. A., and G. L. McDowell, eds. *The American Founding: Politics, Statesmanship and the Constitution.* Kennikat Press, 1981.

Schachner, N. *The Founding Fathers.* Putnam Press, 1954.

Schuyler, R. N. *The Constitution of the United States: An Historical Survey of Its Formation.* Macmillan, 1923.

Scott, J. B. *The Declaration of Independence, the Articles of Confederation, the Constitution of the United States.* Oxford University, 1917.

Shapiro, M., ed. *The Constitution of the United States and Related Documents.* Appleton-Century-Crofts, 1966.

Smith, E. C., ed. *The Constitution of the United States.* Harper & Row, 1975.

Solberg, W. N. *The Federal Convention and the Formation of the Union of American States.* Liberal Arts, 1958.

Stevens, C. E. *Sources of the Constitution of the United States.* Macmillan, 1894.

Story, J. *Commentaries on the Constitution of the United States.* Little, 1833.

Tugwell, R. G. *The Compromising of the Constitution: Early Departures.* University of Notre Dame, 1976.

Van Doren, C. C. *The Great Rehearsal: The Story of the Making and Ratifying of the Constitution of the United States.* Viking Press, 1948.

Warren, C. *The Making of the Constitution.* Little, Brown, 1937.

Wright, B. F. *Consensus and Continuity, 1776-1787.* Boston University, 1958.

2. The Franklin D. Roosevelt Era

Alsop, J., and T. Catledge. *The 168 Days.* Doubleday, 1938.

Baker, L. *Back to Back: The Duel Between FDR and the Supreme Court.* Macmillan, 1967.

Barnes, W. R., and A. W. Littlefield. *The Supreme Court Issue and the Constitution.* Barnes & Noble Books, 1937.

Brant, I. *Storm over the Constitution.* Bobbs-Merrill, 1936.

Burns, J. M. *The Lion and the Fox.* Harcourt, Brace, 1956.

Cope, A. H., and F. Krinsky. *Franklin D. Roosevelt and the Supreme Court.* Heath, 1952.

Cortner, R. *The Wagner Act Cases.* University of Tennessee, 1964.

Corwin, E. S. *Constitutional Revolution, Ltd.* Claremont, 1941.

Eriksson, E. M. *The Supreme Court and the New Deal.* University of California at Los Angeles, 1940.

Goldberg, L., and E. Levenson. *Lawless Judges.* Rand School Press, 1935.

Jackson, R. H. *The Struggle for Judicial Supremacy.* Knopf, 1941.

Johnson, J. E. *Reorganization of the Supreme Court.* H. W. Wilson, 1937.

Lippmann, W. *The Supreme Court: Independent or Controlled?* Harper, 1937.

Mason, A. T. *The Supreme Court: Vehicle of Revealed Truth or Power Group, 1930/-1937.* Boston University, 1953.

Pearson, D., and R. S. Allen. *The Nine Old Men.* Doubleday, 1936; rpt. Da Capo Press, 1973.

———. *The Nine Old Men at the Crossroads.* Doubleday, 1937; rpt. Da Capo Press, 1973.

Pritchett, C. H. *The Roosevelt Court: A Study in Judicial Politics and Values, 1937-1947.* Macmillan, 1947.

Pusey, T. R. *The Supreme Court Crisis.* Macmillan, 1937.

Sommer, F. H. *Reforming the Supreme Court.* New York University, 1951.

U.S. Senate, 75th Congress, 1st Session. Committee on the Judiciary. *Reorganization of the Federal Judiciary.* Government Printing Office, 1937.

INTERPRETATIONS OF THE CONSTITUTION

(Analysis and interpretations of the written Constitution, clause by clause. Also, aspects of the "unwritten" Constitution practices which modify the written document.)

Ackerman, B. A. *Private Property and the Constitution.* Yale University, 1976.

American Academy of Political and Social Sciences. *The Bicentennial Conference on the United States Constitution.* University of Pennsylvania, 1980.

American Bar Association. *Amendment of the Constitution by the Convention Method Under Article V.* ABA, 1974.

American Enterprise Institute. *A Constitutional Convention: How Well Would It Work?* AEI, 1979.

Antieua, C. J. *Commentaries on the Constitution of the United States.* University of Buffalo, 1960.

Baldwin, L. D. *Reframing the Constitution: An Imperative for Modern America.* ABC-Clio, 1972.

Barber, S. A. *The Constitution and the Delegation of Congressional Power.* University of Chicago, 1975.

———. *On What the Constitution Means.* Johns Hopkins University, 1983.

Bayard, J. *A Brief Exposition of the Constitution of the United States.* Hogan & Thompson, 1833.

Berger, R. *Government by Judiciary: The Transformation of the Fourteenth Amendment.* Harvard University, 1977.

Bobbitt, P. *Constitutional Fate: Theory of the Constitution.* Oxford University, 1982.

Boutwell, G. *The Constitution of the United States at the End of the First Century.* Heath, 1895.

Brannon, H. *A Treatise on the Rights and Privileges Guaranteed by the Fourteenth Amendment to the Constitution of the United States.* Anderson, 1961.

Burdick, C. *The Law of the American Constitution.* Putnam, 1922.

Cooke, E. F. *A Detailed Analysis of the Constitution.* 4th ed. Littlefield, Adams, 1975.

Cooley, T. M. *A Treatise on the Constitutional Limitations.* Da Capo Press, 1972.

Corwin, E. S. *The Constitution and What It Means Today.* 14th ed. Ed. H. W. Chase and C. R. Ducat. Princeton University, 1973.

———, ed. *Constitution of the United States: Analysis and Interpretation.* Government Printing Office, 1964.

Crews, K. D. *Edward S. Corwin and the American Constitution: A Bibilographical Analysis.* Greenwood Press, 1985.

Cullop, F. G. *The Constitution of the United States: An Introduction.* New American Library (Signet), 1964.

Ducat, C. R. *Modes of Constitutional Interpretation.* West, 1978.

Dumbauld, E. *The Constitution of the United States.* University of Oklahoma, 1964.

Eckhardt, B., and C. L. Black, Jr. *The Tides of Power: Conversations on the American Constitution.* Yale University, 1977.

Edelman, M. *Democratic Theories and the Constitution.* State University of New York, 1984.

Eidelberg, P. *The Philosophy of the American Constitution: A Re-Interpretation of the Intentions of the Founding Fathers.* Free Press, 1968.

Feerick, J. D. *The Twenty-Fifth Amendment: Its Complete History and Earliest Applications.* Fordham University, 1976.

Foster, R. *Commentaries on the Constitution of the United States.* Boston Book, 1896.

Graham, H. J. *Everyman's Constitution.* Norton, 1968.

Grimes, A. P. *Democracy and the Amendment to the Constitution.* Lexington Books, 1978.

Gunther, G., ed. *John Marshall's Defense of McCulloch v. Maryland.* Stanford University, 1969.

Guthrie, W. D. *Lectures on the 14th Amendment to the Constitution of the United States.* Little, Brown, 1898.

Hamilton, Jay, and Madison. *The Federalist Papers.* McLean, 1788; rpt. Random House, 1972.

Harmon, M. J., ed. *Essays on the Constitution of the United States.* Kennikat, 1978.

Heathcock, C. L. *The United States Constitution in Perspective.* Allyn & Bacon, 1963.

Henkin, L. *Foreign Affairs and the Constitution.* Foundation Press, 1972.

Holder, A. R. *The Meaning of the Constitution.* Barron's, 1974.

Horwill, H. W. *The Usages of the American Constitution.* Oxford University, 1925.

Howard, A. E. D. *Commentaries on the Constitution of Virginia.* University of Virginia, 1974.

Jacobs, C. E. *The Eleventh Amendment and Sovereign Immunity.* Greenwood, 1972.

Jayson, L. S., and J. H. Killian. *The Constitution of the United States of America: Analysis and Interpretation.* Government Printing Office, 1973.

Jones, P. F., ed. *The Constitution of the United States, 1787-1962.* University of Pittsburgh, 1963.

Kauper, P., ed. *The Article V Convention Process: A Symposium.* University of Michigan, 1968.

Keller, M. *Affairs of State.* Harvard University, 1977.

Kruschke, E. R. *An Introduction to the Constitution of the United States.* American Book, 1968.

Leedham, C. *Our Changing Constitution.* Dodd, Mead, 1964.

Levy, L. W. *Judgments: Essays on American Constitutional History.* Quadrangle, 1972.

Lieberman, J. K. *Understanding the Constitution.* Walker, 1967.

Liston, R. A. *The Tides of Justice: The Supreme Court and the Constitution in Our Time.* Dell (Delacorte Press), 1966.

McBain, H. L. *The Living Constitution.* Macmillan, 1927.

McDowell, G. L. *Taking the Constitution Seriously: Essays on the Constitution and the Constitutional Law.* Kendall/Hunt, 1981.

McIlwain, C. M. *The American Revolution: A Constitutional Interpretation.* Da Capo Press, 1971.

Matthews, J. M. *Legislative and Judicial History of the Fifteenth Amendment.* Johns Hopkins, 1909; rpt. Da Capo Press, 1971.

Merrian, C. C. *The Written Constitution and the Unwritten Attitude.* R. R. Smith, 1931.

Meyer, H. N. *The Amendment that Refused to Die.* Beacon Press, 1978.

Michigan Law Review. *The Article V Convention Process: A Symposium.* Da Capo, 1970.

Miller, A. S. *Social Change and Fundamental Law: America's Enduring Constitution.* Greenwood, 1979.

Mitchell, B., and L. P. Mitchell. *A Biography of the Constitution of the United States.* Oxford University, 1964.

Mott, K. F. *The Supreme Court and the Living Constitution.* University Press of America, 1981.

Murphy, P. L. *The Constitution in Crisis Times.* Harper & Row, 1972.

Orfield, L. B. *The Amending of the Federal Constitution.* Callaghan, 1942.

Padover, S. K., ed. *The Living United States Constitution.* New American Library (Mentor Books), 1953.

Peltason, J. W. *Corwin and Peltason's Understanding the Constitution.* 10th ed. Holt, Rinehart and Winston, 1985.

Pomeroy, J. *An Introduction to the Constitutional Law of the United States.* Hurd and Houghton, 1870.

Price, D. K. *America's Unwritten Constitution: Science, Religion, and Political Responsibility.* Louisiana State University, 1983.

Pritchett, C. H. *The American Constitutional System.* 5th ed. McGraw-Hill, 1981.

Rawle, W. *A View of the Constitution of the United States.* Nicklin, 1829.

Rottschaefer, H. *The Constitution and Socio-Economic Change.* University of Michigan, 1948.

———. *Handbook of American Constitutional Law.* West, 1939.

Schouler, J. *Constitutional Studies.* Dodd, Mead, 1897; rpt. Da Capo Press, 1971.

Schwartz, B. *A Commentary on the Constitution of the United States. Part 1: The Powers of Government.* Macmillan, 1963.

Shapiro, M., ed. *The Constitution of the United States and Related Documents.* AHM, 1973.

Sheppard, F. *The Constitutional Textbook.* Childs, 1855.

Shogan, R. *A Question of Judgment.* Bobbs-Merrill, 1972.

Small, N. J., ed. *Constitution of the United States of America.* Rev. and annotated Government Printing Office, 1964. ·

Smith, O. G. *The Convention and the Constitution: The Political Ideas of the Founding Fathers.* St. Martin's Press, 1964.

Story, J. *Commentaries on the Constitution of the United States.* Little, 1833.

———. *A Familiar Exposition on the Constitution of the United States: Containing a Brief Commentary.* Petersburg, 1840.

Taylor, J. *Construction Construed and Constitutions Vindicated.* Shepherd & Pollard, 1820.

Ten-Broek, J. *Anti-Slavery Origins of the Fourteenth Amendment.* University of California, 1951.

Tiedeman, C. G. *The Unwritten Constitution of the United States.* Dabor, 1978.

Tiffany, J. *A Treatise on Government and Constitutional Law.* W. C. Little, 1867.

Towle, N. *A History and Analysis of the Constitution of the United States.* Little, Brown, 1860.

Tucker, J. *The Constitution of the United States.* Callaghan, 1899.

Tugwell, R. G. *The Compromise of the Constitution: Early Departures.* University of Notre Dame, 1976.

———. *The Emerging Constitution.* Harper & Row, 1974.

———. *Model for a New Constitution.* Freel, 1970.

Vose, C. *Constitutional Change.* Heath, 1972.

Walker, T. *American Politics and the Constitution.* PWS (Duxbury Press), 1978.

Wasson, R. *The Constitution of the United States: Its History and Meaning.* Bobbs-Merrill, 1927.

Watson, D. *The Constitution of the United States.* Callaghan, 1910.

Whiting, W. *War Powers Under the Constitution of the United States.* L. J. Shepard, 1874.

Willoughby, W. W. *The Constitutional Law of the United States.* Baker, Voorhis, 1929.

Wood, G. S. *The Confederation and the Constitution: The Critical Issues.* University Press of America, 1979.

JUDGES AND JUSTICES
(The men and women and their behavior in their decision-making function.)
(See also especially Bibliography II and Staffing the Courts infra.)

Abraham, H. J. *Justices and Presidents: A Political History of Appointments to the Supreme Court.* 2d ed. Oxford University, 1985.

American Enterprise Institute. *Judicial Discipline and Tenure Proposals.* AEI, 1979.

Asch, S. H. *The Supreme Court and Its Great Justices.* Arco, 1971.

Ashman, C. *The Finest Judges Money Can Buy.* Nash, 1973.

Baxter, M. G. *Daniel Webster and the Supreme Court*. University of Massachusetts, 1967.

Becker, T. *Political Behavioralism and Modern Jurisprudence*. Rand McNally, 1965.

Berger, R. *Impeachment: The Constitutional Problems*. Harvard University, 1973.

Bickel, A. M. *Politics and the Warren Court*. Harper & Row, 1966.

Blaustein, A. P., and R. M. Mersky. *The First One Hundred Justices: Statistical Studies on the Supreme Court of the United States*. Shoe String Press, 1978.

Borkin, J. *The Corrupt Judge*. Potter, 1962.

Botein, B. *Trial Judge*. Simon and Schuster, 1952; rpt. Cornerstone Library, 1963.

Braithwaite, W. T. *Who Judges the Judges? A Study of Procedure for Removal and Retirement*. American Bar Foundation, 1971.

Brant, I. *Impeachment: Trials and Errors*. Knopf, 1972.

Bruce, A. A. *The American Judge*. Macmillan, 1924.

Burris, W. *The Senate Rejects a Judge: A Study of the John J. Parker Case*. University of North Carolina, 1962.

Cardozo, B. N. *The Nature of the Judicial Process*. Yale University, 1921.

Chase, H. W. *Federal Judges: The Appointing Process*. University of Minnesota, 1973.

——, et al., eds. *Biographical Dictionary of the Federal Judiciary*. Yale University, 1977.

Coffin, C. M. *The Ways of a Judge: Reflections from the Federal Appellate Bench*. Houghton Mifflin, 1980.

Danielski, D. J. "The Chief Justices of the Supreme Court." Ph.D. diss., University of Illinois, 1961.

Davenport, W. H., ed. *Voices in Court*. Macmillan, 1958.

Dawson, J. P. A. *A History of Lay Judges*. Little, Brown, 1960.

——. *The Oracles of the Law*. University of Michigan, 1968.

Douglas, W. O. *We, the Judges*. Doubleday, 1956.

Dubois, P. L. *From Ballot to Bench: Judicial Elections and the Quest for Accountability*. University of Texas, 1980.

Edwards, G. *George Edwards, Pioneer at Law: A Legacy in the Pursuit of Justice*. Norton, 1975.

Escovitz, S. S., F. Kurland, and N. Gold. *Judicial Selection and Tenure*. 2d ed. American Judiciary Society, 1975.

Ewing, C. A. M. *The Judges of the Supreme Court, 1789–1937*. University of Minnesota, 1938.

Frank, J. *A Man's Reach: The Philosophy of Judge Jerome Frank*. Greenwood, 1977.

Freund, P. A. *On Law and Justice*. Harvard University, 1968.

Friedman, L., and F. L. Israel, eds. *The Justices of the United States Supreme Court, 1789–1969: Their Lives and Major Opinions*. Chelsea & Bowker, 1969.

Friendly, H. J. *Benchmarks*. University of Chicago, 1967.

Glennon, R. J. *The Iconoclast as Reformer: Jerome Frank's Impact on American Law*. Cornell University, 1985.

Goldberg, L., and L. Levenson. *Lawless Judges*. Rand School Press, 1935.

Goulden, J. C. *The Benchwarmers: The Private World of the Powerful Federal Judges*. Weybright and Talley, 1974.

Griffith, K. *Judge Learned Hand and the Role of the Federal Judiciary*. University of Oklahoma, 1973.

Hall, K. L. *The Politics of Justice: Lower Federal Judge Selection and the Second Party System, 1829–61*. University of Nebraska, 1980.

Harris, R. *Decision*. Dutton, 1971.

Hurst, J. S. *The Growth of American Law: The Lawmakers*. Little, Brown, 1950.

Jackson, D. D. *Judges: An Inside View of the Agonies and Excesses of an American Elite*. Atheneum, 1974.

Jaffe, L. L. *English and American Judges as Lawmakers*. Oxford University, 1970.

Kennedy, R. F., Jr. *Judge Frank M. Johnson, Jr*. Putnam, 1978.

Kirchheimer, O. *Political Justice: The Use of Legal Procedure for Political Ends*. Princeton University, 1961.

Kitchin, W. *Federal District Judges: An Analysis of Judicial Perceptions.* College Press, 1978.

Klein, F. W., and J. S. Lee, eds. *Selected Writings of Arthur T. Vanderbilt.* Oceana, 1966.

Knox, J. C. *A Judge Comes of Age.* Scribner, 1940.

Kristein, B. F., ed. *A Man's Reach: The Philosophy of Judge Jerome Frank.* Macmillan, 1965.

Leflar, R. A., ed. *The Compleat Judge (Appellate Genus): Appellate Judicial Opinions.* West, 1974.

Levy, L. W. *The Law of the Commonwealth and Chief Justice Shaw.* Harvard University, 1957.

Lide, L. D. *The Trial Judge in South Carolina.* University of South Carolina, 1953.

Lummus, H. T. *The Trial Judge.* Foundation Press, 1937.

MacKenzie, J. P. *The Appearance of Justice.* Scribner, 1974.

Maddi, D. L. *Judicial Performance Polls.* American Bar Foundation, 1977.

Miller, A. S. *A "Capacity for Outrage": The Judicial Odyssey of J. Skelly Wright.* Greenwood Press, 1984.

Mitchell, B., and L. P. Mitchell. *A Biography of the Constitution of the United States.* Oxford University, 1975.

Nagel, S. *Comparing Elected and Appointed Judges.* Sage Publications, 1973.

———. *"Judicial Characteristics and Judicial Decision-Making."* Ph.D. diss., Northwestern University, 1961.

Peltason, J. W. *Fifty-Eight Lonely Men: Southern Federal Judges and School Desegregation.* Rev. ed. Harcourt, Brace, & World, 1971.

Philip, C. O., P. A. Nejelski, and A. Press. *Where Do Judges Come From?* Institute of Judicial Administration, 1977.

Porter, E. S. *Conscience of the Court.* Prentice-Hall, 1962.

Pritchett, C. H. *The Roosevelt Court: A Study in Judicial Politics and Values, 1937–1947.* Macmillan, 1947.

Pyne, T. S. *Judicial Retirement Plans.* American Judicial Society, 1980.

Reincke, M., and J. Wilhelm, eds. *The American Bench: Judges of the Nation.* Reginald Bishop Forster, 1978.

Roe, G. E. *Our Judicial Oligarchy.* Huebsch, 1912.

Rosenblum, V. G. *Law as a Political Instrument.* Doubleday, 1955.

Ryan, J. P., et al. *American Trial Judges: Their Work Styles and Performance.* Free Press, 1980.

Schick, M. *Learned Hand's Court.* Johns Hopkins University, 1970.

Schmidhauser, J. *Judges and Justices: The Federal Appellate Judiciary.* Little, Brown, 1978.

Schubert, G. A. *Constitutional Politics.* Holt, Rinehart and Winston, 1960.

———. *Judicial Behavior: A Reader in Theory and Research.* Rand McNally, 1964.

———, ed. *Judicial Decision-Making.* Free Press, 1959.

———. *The Judicial Mind: The Attitudes and Ideologies of the Supreme Court, 1943–1963.* Northwestern University, 1965.

———. *The Judicial Mind Revisited: Psychometric Analysis of Supreme Court Ideology.* Oxford University, 1974.

———. *Quantitative Analysis of Judicial Behavior.* Free Press, 1959.

Shanks, H. *The Art and Craft of Judging.* Macmillan, 1968.

Sheldon, C. H. *The Supreme Court: Politicians in Robes.* Glencoe, 1970.

Shientag, B. L. *Moulders of Legal Thought.* Viking Press, 1943.

Shogan, R. *A Question of Judgment: The Fortas Case and the Struggle for the Supreme Court.* Bobbs-Merrill, 1972.

Simon, J. F. *In His Own Image: The Supreme Court in Richard Nixon's America.* McKay, 1973.

———. *The Judge.* McKay, 1976.

Stansbury, A. J. *Report of the Trial of James H. Peck.* Hilliard, Gray, 1833.

Steamer, R J. *The Supreme Court: Constitutional Revision and the New "Strict Constructionism."* Burgess, 1973.

Stein, D. *Judging the Judges: The Cause, Control and Cure of Judicial Jaundice.* Exposition Press, 1975.

Stoltz, P. *Judging Judges: The Investigation of Rose Bird and the California Supreme Court.* Free Press, 1981.

Todd, A. L. *Justice on Trial: The Case of Louis D. Brandeis.* McGraw-Hill, 1964.

Tomkins, D. C. *The Supreme Court of the United States: A Bibliography.* University of California, 1959.

Tresolini, R. J. *Justices and the Supreme Court.* Lippincott, 1963.

Ulc, O. *The Judge in a Communist State.* Ohio State University, 1972.

Ulman, J. N. *A Judge Takes the Stand.* Knopf, 1933.

Umbreit, K. B. *Our Eleven Chief Justices.* Harper, 1938.

Vanderbilt, A. T. *Judges and Jurors: Their Functions, Qualifications, and Selection.* Boston University, 1956.

Westin, A. F. *The Supreme Court: Views from Inside.* Norton, 1961.

White, G. E. *The American Judicial Tradition: Profiles of Leading American Judges.* Oxford University, 1976.

Winters, G. R., ed. *Handbook for Judges.* Rev. ed. American Judiciary Society, 1975.

Wolfman, B., et al. *Dissent Without Opinion: The Behavior of Justice William O. Douglas in Federal Tax Cases.* University of Pennsylvania, 1975.

Wyzanski, C. E., Jr. *Whereas—A Judge's Premise: Essays in Judgment, Ethics, and the Law.* Atlantic, Little, Brown, 1965.

Yarbrough, T. E. *Judge Frank Johnson and Human Rights in Alabama.* University of Alabama, 1981.

THE JUDICIAL PROCESS

GENERAL AND SPECIFIC WORKS
(The federal judicial process and court system, especially the Supreme Court and its jurisprudence)
(See also Judicial Review)

Abraham, H. J. *Courts and Judges: An Introduction to the Judicial Process.* Oxford University, 1959.

———. *The Judicial Process: An Introductory Analysis of the Courts of the United States, England, and France.* 5th ed. Oxford University, 1986.

———. *The Judiciary: The Supreme Court in the Governmental Process.* 6th ed. Allyn & Bacon, 1983.

Acheson, P. C. *The Supreme Court: America's Judicial Heritage.* Dodd, Mead, 1961.

Aldisert, R. J. *The Judicial Process: Readings, Materials, and Cases.* West, 1976.

Alfange, D. *The Supreme Court and the National Will.* Kennikat Press, 1937.

American Enterprise Institute. *An Imperial Judiciary: Fact or Myth?* American Enterprise Institute, 1979.

Aranson, P. H., ed. *Supreme Court Economic Review.* Macmillan, 1982– .

Arneson, B. A. *Elements of Constitutional Law.* Harper, 1928.

Auerbach, C. A., et al. *The Legal Process.* Rev. ed. Chandler, 1961.

Auerbach, J. S. *Justice Without Law? Resolving Disputes Without Lawyers.* Oxford University, 1983.

Aumann, F. R. *The Changing American Legal System: Some Selected Phases.* Ohio State University, 1940.

Baade, H. W., ed. *Jurimetrics.* Duke University, 1963.

Baer, J. A. *The Chains of Protection: The Judicial Response to Women's Labor Legislation.* Greenwood Press, 1973.

Balbus, I. D. *The Dialectics of Legal Repression: Black Rebels Before the American Criminal Courts.* Russell Sage Foundation, 1973.

Baldwin, S. E. *The American Judiciary.* West Virginia University, 1925.

Ball, H. *Courts and Politics: The Federal Judicial System.* Prentice-Hall, 1980.

———. *Judicial Craftsmanship or Fiat? Direct Overturn by the United States Supreme Court.* Greenwood Press, 1978.

Bannan, J. F. and R. S. Bannan. *Law, Morality and Vietnam: The Peace Militants and the Courts.* Indiana University, 1974.

Bartee, A. F. *Cases Lost, Causes Won: The Supreme Court and the Judicial Process.* St. Martin's Press, 1984.

Baum, L. C. *The Supreme Court.* Congressional Quarterly Press, 1984.

Beck, C., ed. *Law and Justice: Essays in Honor of Robert T. Rankin.* Luke, 1969.

Becker, T. L., and M. M. Feeley. *The Impact of Supreme Court Decisions.* 2d ed. Oxford University, 1973.

———, and V. Murray. *Government Lawlessness in America.* Oxford University, 1971.

Bent, J. A. *The Independent Judiciary.* Morgantown, 1925.

Berger, R. *Government by Judiciary.* Harvard University, 1977.

Berkson, L. C. *The Supreme Court and Its Publics.* Lexington Books, 1978.

Bickel, A. M. *The Least Dangerous Branch: The Supreme Court as the Bar of Politics.* Bobbs-Merrill, 1963.

———. *Politics and the Warren Court.* Da Capo Press, 1973.

———. *The Supreme Court and the Idea of Progress.* Rev. ed. Yale University, 1978.

———, et al. *Watergate, Politics, and the Legal Process.* American Enterprise Institute, 1974.

———. *The Morality of Consent.* Yale University, 1976.

Birkby, R. H. *The Court and Public Policy.* Congressional Quarterly Press, 1983.

Black, C. L. *Decision According to Law.* Norton, 1981.

———. *Structure and Relationship in Constitutional Law.* Louisiana State University, 1969.

Blandford, L. A., and P. R. Evans, eds. *Supreme Court of the United States, 1789–1980: An Index to Opinions Arranged by Justice.* Supreme Court Historical Society, 1983.

Blasi, V., ed. *The Burger Court: The Counterrevolution That Wasn't.* Yale University, 1983.

Bolner, J., and R. Shanley. *Busing: The Political and Judicial Process.* Praeger, 1974.

Bonsignore, J., et al. *Before the Law: An Introduction to the Legal Process.* 2d ed. Houghton Mifflin, 1979.

Bosmajian, H., ed. *Dissent: Symbolic Behavior and Rhetorical Strategies.* Allyn & Bacon, 1972.

Boudin, L. B. *Government by Judiciary.* Godwin, 1932.

Boyum, K. O., and L. Mather, eds. *Empirical Theories About Courts.* Longman, 1983.

Brigham, J. *Constitutional Language: An Interpretation of Judicial Decision.* Greenwood Press, 1978.

Callison, I. P. *Courts of Injustice.* Twayne, 1956.

Canon, B. C., and C. A. Johnson. *Judicial Politics: Implementation and Impact.* Congressional Quarterly Press, 1984.

Cardozo, B. N. *The Nature of the Judicial Process.* Yale University, 1921.

Carp, R. A., and C. K. Rowland. *Policymaking and Politics in the Federal District Courts.* University of Tennessee, 1983.

Carp, R. A., and R. Stidham. *Federal Courts.* Congressional Quarterly Press, 1985.

Carter, J. D. *The Warren Court and the Constitution: A Critical View of Judicial Activism.* Pelican, 1973.

Carter, L. H. *Contemporary Constitutional Lawmaking: The Supreme Court and the Art of Politics.* Pergamon Press, 1985.

Casper, G., and R. A. Posner. *A Study of the Supreme Court's Caseload.* American Bar Federation, 1974.

———. *The Workload of the Supreme Court.* American Bar Federation, 1976.

Channels, N. L., *Social Science Methods in the Legal Process.* Rowman & Allanheld, 1985.

Cicourel, A. *The Social Control of Juvenile Justice.* Wiley, 1968.

Clayton, J. E. *The Making of Justice: The Supreme Court in Action*. Dutton, 1964.

Congressional Quarterly. *The Supreme Court: Justice With Law*. 2d ed. Congressional Quarterly Press, 1977.

———. *Guide to the U.S. Supreme Court*. Congressional Quarterly Press, 1979.

Cook, B. B. *The Judicial Process in California*. Dickinson, 1961.

Cooke, W. W., ed. *Fundamental Legal Concepts as Applied in Judicial Reasoning*. Yale University, 1964.

Cooley, R. M. *Constitutional Limitations*. Putnam, 1868.

Cooley, T. M. *Principles of Constitutional Law*. 2d ed. Little, Brown, 1891.

Corsi, J. R. *Judicial Politics: An Introduction*. Prentice-Hall, 1984.

Cover, R. M. *Justice Accused: Antislavery and the Judicial Process*. Yale University, 1975.

Cox, A. *The Role of the Supreme Court in American Government*. Oxford University, 1976.

———. *The Warren Court: Constitutional Decision as an Instrument of Reform*. Harvard University, 1968.

Coy, H. *The First Book of the Supreme Court*. Watts, 1958.

Curtis, C. P. *Lions Under the Throne*. Houghton Mifflin, 1947.

Davis, A. L. *The United States Supreme Court and the Uses of Social Science Data*. MSS, Information Corp., 1973.

Dolbeare, K. M. *Trial Courts in Urban Politics*. Wiley, 1967.

———, and P. E. Hammond. *The School Prayer Decisions: From Court Policy to Local Practice*. University of Chicago, 1971.

Douglas, W. O. *We, the Judges*. Doubleday, 1956.

Eckhardt, B., and C. L. Black, Jr. *The Tides of Power*. Yale University, 1976.

Eisenstein, J. *Politics and the Legal Process*. Harper & Row, 1973.

Empey, L. T., ed. *Juvenile Justice: The Progressive Legacy and Current Reforms*. University of Virginia, 1978.

Epstein, A. L. *Juridical Techniques and the Judicial Process*. Rhodes-Livingstone, 1954.

Ernst, M. L. *The Great Reversals: Tales of the Supreme Court*. Weybright and Talley, 1973.

Ervin, S. J., Jr., and R. Clark. *Role of the Supreme Court: Policy-Maker or Adjudicator*. American Enterprise Institute, 1972.

Farnsworth, E. A. *An Introduction to the Legal System of the United States*. Oceana, 1963.

Felscher, H., and M. Rosen. *The Press in the Jury Box*. Macmillan, 1966.

Fish, P. G. *The Politics of Federal Judicial Administration*. Princeton University, 1973.

Fiss, O. M. *The Civil Rights Injunction*. Indiana University, 1978.

Fleming, M. *The Price of Perfect Justice*. Basic Books, 1974.

Ford, S. D. *The American Legal System: Its Dynamics and Limits*. 2d ed. West, 1974.

Forte, D. F. *The Supreme Court in American Politics: Judicial Activism v. Judicial Restraint*. Heath, 1972.

Frank, J. *Courts on Trial: Myth and Reality in American Justice*. Princeton University, 1959.

———. *If Men Were Angels*. Harvard University, 1942.

———. *Law and the Modern Mind*. Brentano's, 1930.

Frank, J. P. *The Marble Palace: The Supreme Court in American Life*. Knopf, 1958.

Freund, P. A. *On Understanding the Supreme Court*. Little, Brown, 1949.

———. *The Supreme Court of the United States: Its Business, Purposes, and Performances*. New American Library (Meridian Books), 1961.

Funston, R. *A Vital National Seminar: The Supreme Court in American Political Life*. Mayfield, 1978.

———. *Constitutional Counterrevolution: The Warren Court and the Burger Court*. Schenckman, 1977.

Gambitta, R. L., M. L. May, and J. C. Foster, eds. *Governing Through Courts*. Sage Publications, 1981.

Gardiner, J. A. *Public Law and Public Policy*. Praeger, 1976.

Ginger, A. F., ed. *The Law, the Supreme Court and the People's Rights*. AFG Legal Publics, 1975.

Glick, H. R. *Courts, Politics, and Justice.* McGraw-Hill, 1983.

———. *Supreme Courts in State Politics.* Basic Books, 1971.

Goldberg, A. J. *Equal Justice: The Warren Era of the Supreme Court.* Northwestern University, 1971.

Goldman, S., and T. P. Jahnige. *The Federal Courts as a Political System.* 3d ed. Harper & Row, 1985.

———, and A. Sarat. *American Court Systems: Readings in Judicial Process and Behavior.* Freeman, 1978.

Goldstein, A. *The Passive Judiciary.* Louisiana State University, 1981.

Goulden, J. C. *The Benchwarmers: The Private World of the Powerful Federal Judges.* Weybright and Talley, 1974.

Graglia, L. A. *Disaster by Decree: The Supreme Court Decisions on Race and the Schools.* Cornell University, 1976.

Gray, D. L. *The Supreme Court and the News Media.* Northwestern University, 1968.

Greenberg, J. *Cases and Materials on Judicial Process and Social Change.* West, 1977.

Grossman, J. B., and J. Tanenhaus, eds. *Frontiers of Judicial Research.* Wiley, 1969.

Grossman, J. B., J. Tanenhaus, and R. S. Wells, eds. *Constitutional Law and Judicial Policy-Making.* Wiley, 1972.

Grunbaum, W. *Judicial Policymaking: The Supreme Court and Environmental Quality.* General Learning Press, 1976.

Halpern, S. C., and C. S. Lamb, eds. *Supreme Court Activism and Restraint.* Lexington Books, 1982.

Harris, M. K., and D. P. Spiller, Jr. *After Decision: Implementation of Judicial Decrees in Correctional Settings.* American Bar Association, 1976.

Harris, R. J. *The Judicial Power of the United States.* Louisiana State University, 1940.

Hart, H. M., and H. Wechsler. *The Federal Courts and the Federal System.* Foundation Press, 1953.

Harvard Law Review. *Social Science Approaches to the Judicial Process.* Da Capo Press, 1971.

Haskins, G. L. and H. A. Johnson. *Foundations of Power: John Marshall, 1801–1815.* Macmillan, 1981.

Heumann, M. *Plea Bargaining.* University of Chicago, 1978.

Hirschfield, R. *The Constitution and the Court.* Random House, 1960.

Hoffman, P. *Courthouse.* Hawthorn Books, 1979.

Horn, R. A. *Groups and the Constitution.* Stanford University, 1956.

Horwitz, D. L. *The Courts and Social Policy.* Brookings Institution, 1977.

———. *The Jurocracy: Government Lawyers, Agency Programs, and Judicial Decisions.* Heath, 1977.

Hughes, C. E. *The Supreme Court of the United States.* Columbia University, 1928.

Hughes, G. *The Conscience of the Courts: Law and Morals in American Life.* Doubleday, 1975.

Hyneman, C. S. *The Supreme Court on Trial.* Atherton, 1963.

Jackson, P. E., ed. *The Wisdom of the Supreme Court.* University of Oklahoma, 1962.

Jackson, R. H. *The Supreme Court in the American System of Government.* Harvard University, 1955.

Jacob, H. *Debtors in Court: The Consumption of Governmental Services.* Rand McNally, 1969.

———. *Justice in America: Courts, Lawyers, and the Judicial Process.* 4th ed. Little, Brown, 1984.

———. *Law, Politics and the Federal Courts.* Little, Brown, 1968.

Jacobson, G. J. *Pragmatism, Statesmanship, and the Supreme Court.* Cornell University, 1977.

Jahnige, T. P., and S. Goldman, eds. *The Federal Judicial System: Readings in Process and Behavior.* Holt, Rinehart and Winston, 1968.

Jenkins, A. H. *Social Order and the Limits of the Law.* Princeton University, 1980.

Johnson, C. A., and B. A. Canon. *Judicial Politics: Implementation and Impact*. Congressional Quarterly Press, 1984.

Johnson, G. W. *The Supreme Court*. Morrow, 1962.

Johnson, R. M. *The Dynamics of Compliance: Supreme Court Decision-Making from a New Perspective*. Northwestern University, 1968.

Journal of Public Law (Symposium). *Policy-Making in a Democracy: The Role of the United States Supreme Court*. 1977.

Judson, R. N. *The Judiciary and the People*. Yale University, 1913.

Kadish, M. R., and S. H. Kadish. *Discretion to Disobey: A Study of Lawful Departures from Legal Rules*. Stanford University, 1973.

Karlen, D. *Appellate Courts in the United States and England*. New York University, 1963.

Kirschheimer, O. *Political Justice: The Use of Legal Procedure for Political Ends*. Princeton University, 1961.

Klein, M. M., and L. Herschhower, eds. *Courts and Law in Early New York: Selected Essays*. Kennikat Press, 1976.

Klein, M. S. G. *Law, Courts, and Policy*. Prentice-Hall, 1984.

Klonoski, J. R., and R. I. Mendelsohn. *The Politics of Local Justice*. Little, Brown, 1970.

Kohlmeier, L. M., Jr. *"God Save This Honorable Court!"* Scribner, 1973.

Krislov, S. *The Supreme Court in the Political Process*. Macmillan, 1965.

——, et al. *Compliance and the Law: A Multidisciplinary Approach*. Sage Publications, 1971.

Kurland, P. B. *Politics, the Constitution, and the Warren Court*. University of Chicago, 1973.

——, ed. *The Supreme Court and the Judicial Function*. University of Chicago, 1975.

——, and G. Casper, eds. *Landmark Briefs and Arguments of the Supreme Court of the U.S.* University Publications of America, annually, 1977– .

——. *The Supreme Court Review*. University of Chicago, 1960– .

Kutler, S. I., ed. *The Dred Scott Decision: Law or Politics*. Houghton Mifflin, 1967.

Levi, E. H. *An Introduction to Legal Reasoning*. University of Chicago, 1948.

Levin, A. L., and R. R. Wheeler, *The American Judiciary*. Sage Publications, 1982.

Levy, L. W., ed. *The Supreme Court Under Earl Warren*. New Viewpoints, 1972.

Lewis, M., J. L. Hague, and W. Bundy. *An Introduction to the Courts and Judicial Process*. Prentice-Hall, 1978.

Lieberman, J. K. *The Litigious Society*. Basic Books, 1981.

Llewllyn, K. N. *The Bramble Bush*. Oceana, 1960.

Loewen, J. W. *Social Science in the Courtroom: Statistical Techniques and Research Methods for Winning Class-action Suits*. Heath, 1982.

Loh, W. D., ed. *Social Research in the Judicial Process*. Russell Sage Foundation, 1984.

Lyttle, C. M. *The Warren Court and Its Critics*. University of Arizona, 1968.

McCloskey, R. G. *The American Supreme Court*. University of Chicago, 1960.

——. *The Modern Supreme Court*. Harvard University, 1972.

McDonald, W. F., and J. A. Cramer, eds. *Plea Bargaining*. Heath, 1980.

McDowell, G. L. *Equity and the Constitution: The Supreme Court, Equitable Relief, and Public Policy*. University of Chicago, 1982.

McLauchlan, W. P. *American Legal Processes*. Wiley, 1977.

McRuer, J. C. *The Evolution of the Judicial Process*. Clark, Irvin, 1959.

Magrath, C. P., ed. *Constitutionalism and Politics: Conflict and Concerns*. Scott, Foresman, 1968.

Manwaring, D. R., D. R. Reich, and S. L. Wasby. *The Supreme Court as Policy Maker: Three Studies on the Impact of Judicial Decisions*. Public Affairs Research Bureau, 1968.

Markowitz, J. D. *Plea Bargaining: An Annotated Bibliography*. American Judicial Society, 1978.

Marvell, T. B. *Appellate Courts and Lawyers: Information Gathering in the Adversary System*. Praeger, 1979.

Mason, A. T. *The Supreme Court: Instrument of Power or of Revealed Truth?* Boston University, 1953.

————. *The Supreme Court: Palladium of Freedom.* University of Michigan, 1962.

Mather, L. M. *Plea Bargaining or Trial?* Lexington Books, 1980.

Mayers, L. *The Machinery of Justice: An Introduction to Legal Structure and Process.* Prentice-Hall, 1963.

Melone, A. P., and C. Kalvelage. *Primer on Constitutional Law.* Palisades, 1982.

Mendelson, W. *The Supreme Court: Law Versus Discretion.* Bobbs-Merrill, 1967.

Menez, J. F. *Decision Making in the Supreme Court of the United States: A Political and Behavioral View.* University Press of America, 1984.

Miller, A. S. *The Supreme Court: Myth and Reality.* Greenwood Press, 1978.

Milner, N. A. *The Court and Local Law Enforcement: The Political Impact of Miranda.* Sage Publications, 1971.

Monahan, J., and L. Walker. *Social Science in Law.* Foundation Press, 1985.

Moore, R. F. *Stare Decisis.* Simons-Boardman, 1958.

Moreland, C. C. *Equal Justice Under the Law.* Oceana, 1957.

Morris, G. H. *The Insanity Defense: A Blueprint for Legislative Reform.* Lexington Books, 1975.

Murphy, W. F. *Elements of Judicial Strategy.* University of Chicago, 1973.

————, and J. Tanenhaus. *The Study of Public Law.* Random House, 1971.

————, and D. Kastner. *Public Evaluations of Constitutional Courts.* Sage Publications, 1974.

————, and C. H. Pritchett, eds. *Courts, Judges, and Politics.* 3d ed. Random House, 1979.

Nader, L. *No Access to Law: Alternatives to the American Judicial System.* Academic Press, 1980.

Nagel, S. S. *Improving the Legal Process.* Heath, 1975.

————. *Legal Policy Analysis: Finding an Optimum Level Mix.* Lexington Books, 1976.

————. *The Legal Process from a Behavior Perspective.* Dorsey Press, 1969.

————. *The Legal Process: Modeling the System.* Sage Publications, 1977.

Neely, R. *How Courts Govern America.* Yale University, 1981.

Neier, A. *Only Judgment: The Limits of Litigation in Social Change.* Wesleyan University, 1982.

Neubauer, D. W. *America's Courts and the Continental Judicial System.* PWS (Duxbury Press), 1979.

Newman, R. P., and D. R. Newman. *Evidence.* Houghton Mifflin, 1971.

Newmyer, R. K. *The Supreme Court Under Marshall and Taney.* Harlan Davidson, 1984.

North, A. A. *The Supreme Court: Judicial Process and Judicial Politics.* Appleton-Century-Crofts, 1966.

Norton, T. J. *Losing Liberty Judicially.* Macmillan, 1928.

————. *Undermining the Constitution.* Devin-Adair, 1950.

Oakley, J. B., and R. S. Thompson. *Law Clerks and the Judicial Process: Perceptions of the Quality and Functions of Law Clerks in American Courts.* University of California, 1980.

Peltason, J. W. *Federal Courts in the Political Process.* Doubleday, 1955.

Posner, R. A., *The Federal Courts.* Harvard University, 1985.

Post, C. G., Jr. *The Supreme Court and Political Questions.* Johns Hopkins University, 1936; rpt. Da Capo Press, 1969.

Provine, D. M. *Case Selection in the United States Supreme Court.* University of Chicago, 1980.

Pugh, D. J., et al. *Judicial Rulemaking: A Compendium.* University Publications of America, 1985.

Pusey, M. J. *The Supreme Court Crisis.* Da Capo Press, 1972.

Radcliffe, J. E. *The Case-or-Controversy Provision.* Pennsylvania State University, 1978.

Ramaswamy, J. *The Creative Role of the Supreme Court of the U.S.* Stanford University, 1956.

Ransom, W. L. *Majority Rule and the Constitution.* Carey and Lea, 1921.

Rembar, C. *The Evolution of Our Legal System.* Simon and Schuster, 1980.

Rich, M. C., and W. E. Brucan, *The Central Panel System for Administrative Law Judges.* University Publications of America, 1985.

Richardson, R. J., and K. N. Vines. *The Politics of the Federal Courts.* Little, Brown, 1970.

Roberts, O. J. *The Court and the Constitution.* Harvard University, 1951.

Roche, J. I., and L. W. Levy, eds. *The Judiciary: Documents in American Government.* Harcourt, Brace & World, 1964.

Rodgers, H. R. *Community Conflict, Public Opinion, and the Law.* Merrill, 1969.

Rohde, D. W., and J. H. Spaeth. *Supreme Court Decision Making.* Freeman, 1976.

Rosen, P. L. *The Supreme Court and Social Science.* University of Illinois, 1972.

Rosenblum, V. *Law as a Political Instrument.* Random House, 1955.

Ross, H. L. *Settled Out of Court.* Aldine, 1969.

Rubin, H. T. *Juvenile Justice: Policy, Practices, and Law.* Goodyear, 1970.

Saks, M. J., and C. H. Baron, eds. *The Use/Nonuse/Misuse of Applied Social Research in the Courts.* Abt, 1980.

Salomon, L. E., ed. *The Supreme Court.* H. W. Wilson, 1961.

Sarri, R., and Y. Hasenfeld, eds. *Brought to Justice? Juveniles, the Courts and the Law.* University of Michigan, 1977.

Sax, J. L. *Defending the Environment.* Knopf, 1971.

Sayer, R. H., B. B. Boyer, and R. E. Gooding, Jr. *The Warren Court: A Critical Analysis.* Chelsea House, 1968.

Schlesinger, S. R. *The United States Supreme Court: Fact, Evidence, and Law.* University Press of America, 1983.

Schmandt, H. J. *Courts in the American Political System.* Dickinson, 1968.

Schmidhauser, H. R. *The Supreme Court: Its Politics, Personalities, and Procedures.* Holt, Rinehart and Winston, 1960.

Schubert, G. A. *Constitutional Politics.* Holt, Rinehart and Winston, 1960.

———. *The Constitutional Polity.* Boston University, 1970.

———. *Judicial Policy Making.* 2d ed. Scott, Foresman, 1974.

———. "Judicial Process and Behavior, 1963–1971." In *Political Science Annual 3,* ed. J. A. Robinson. Bobbs-Merrill, 1972.

———. *Quantitative Analysis of Judicial Behavior.* Free Press, 1959.

Schuck, P. H. *Suing Government: Citizen Remedies for Official Wrongs.* Yale University, 1983.

Schwartz, B. *The Supreme Court: Constitutional Revolution in Retrospect.* Ronald Press, 1954.

Scigliano, R. G. *The Courts: A Reader in the Judicial Process.* Little, Brown, 1962.

Semonche, J. E. *Charting the Future: The Supreme Court Responds to a Changing Society, 1890–1920.* Greenwood Press, 1978.

Shapiro, M. *Courts: A Comparative and Political Analysis.* University of Chicago, 1981.

———. *Law and Politics in the Supreme Court: New Approaches to Political Jurisprudence.* Stanford University, 1964.

———. *The Supreme Court and Public Policy.* Scott, Foresman, 1969.

———, and D. Hobbs. *The Politics of Constitutional Law.* Winthrop, 1976.

Sheldon, C. H. *The Judicial Process: Models and Approaches.* Dodd, Mead, 1974.

Sigler, J. A. *An Introduction to the Legal System.* Dorsey Press, 1968.

Spaeth, H. J. *An Introduction to Supreme Court Decision Making.* Chandler, 1965.

———. *Supreme Court Policy Making.* Freeman, 1979.

Starr, I. *The Federal Judiciary.* Oxford University, 1957.

Steamer, R. J. *The Supreme Court: Constitutional Revision and the New "Strict Constructionism."* Burgess, 1973.

Strelb, V. L. *Juvenile Justice in America.* Kennikat Press, 1978.

Strick, A. *Injustice for All.* Viking Penguin, 1979.

Strum, P. *The Supreme Court and "Political Questions": A Study in Judicial Evasion!* University of Alabama, 1974.

Swigert, V. L., ed. *Law and the Legal Process.* Sage Publications, 1982.

Swisher, C. B. *The Growth of Constitutional Power in the United States.* 2d ed. University of Chicago, 1963.

———. *The Supreme Court in Modern Role.* Rev. ed. New York University, 1965.

———. *The Taney Period, 1836-64.* Macmillan, 1974.

Tarr, G. A. *Judicial Impact and State Supreme Courts.* Lexington Books, 1977.

Tate, A., Jr., and D. W. Goliwas. *Treatises for Judges: A Selected Bibliography.* 3d ed. Louisiana State University, 1977.

Theberge, L., ed. *The Judiciary in Democratic Society.* Heath, 1979.

Thomas, W. H. *The Burger Court and Civil Liberties.* Rev. ed. King's Court, 1980.

Traynor, R. J. *Quo Vadis, Prospective Overruling: A Question of Judicial Responsibility.* University of Birmingham, 1976.

Truman, D. B. *The Governmental Process.* 2d ed. Knopf, 1971.

Tully, A. *Supreme Court.* Simon and Schuster, 1963.

Ulmer, S. S. *Courts as Small and Not So Small Groups.* General Learning Press, 1971.

———. *Courts, Law, and the Judicial Process.* Free Press, 1981.

———. *Political Decision Making.* Van Nostrand, 1971.

University Publications of America, eds. *The Complete Oral Arguments of the Supreme Court of the United States.* University Publications of America, 1981-.

Vanderzell, J. H., ed. *The Supreme Court and American Government.* Crowell, 1968.

Vines, K. N., and H. Jacob. *Studies in Judicial Politics.* Tulane University, 1962.

von Moschzisker, R. *Star Decisis, Res Indicata, and Other Selected Essays.* Dixon, 1929.

Walker, M. W. *The Evolution of the United States Supreme Court.* General Learning Press, 1974.

Warren, E. *A Republic . . . If You Can Keep It.* Quadrangle, 1972.

Wasby, S. L. *Continuity and Change: From the Warren Court to the Burger Court.* Goodyear, 1976.

———. *The Impact of the United States Supreme Court.* Dorsey Press, 1970.

———. *The Supreme Court in the Federal Judicial System.* Holt, Rinehart and Winston, 1984.

Wasserstrom, R. A. *The Judicial Decision: Toward a Theory of Legal Justification.* Stanford University, 1969.

Wessel, M. R. *Science and Conscience.* Columbia University, 1980.

Westin, A. F. *The Supreme Court: Views from Inside.* Norton, 1961.

Whitehead, J. W. *The Stealing of America.* Crossway, 1983.

Wilkinson, J. H., III. *Serving Justice.* Charterhouse, 1974.

Willoughby, W. F. *Principles of Judicial Administration.* Brookings Institution, 1929.

Winter, G. R., and E. J. Schoenbaum. *American Courts and Justice.* American Judicial Society, 1976.

Witkin, B. E. *Manual on Appellate Court Opinions.* West, 1977.

Wolfman, B., J. L. F. Silver, and M. A. Silver. *Dissent Without Opinion: The Behavior of Justice William O. Douglas in Federal Tax Cases.* University of Pennsylvania, 1975.

Wunder, J. R. *Inferior Courts, Superior Justice.* Greenwood Press, 1979.

Zelermyer, W. *The Legal System in Operation: A Case Study from the Procedural Beginning to the Judicial Conclusion.* West, 1977.

JUDICIAL REVIEW
(See also The Judicial Process)

Abraham, H. J. Chapters 6-9 in *The Judicial Process: An Introductory Analysis of the Courts of the United States, England, and France.* 5th ed. Oxford University, 1986.

Agresto, J. *The Supreme Court and Constitutional Democracy.* Cornell University, 1984.

Alfange, D. *The Supreme Court and the National Will.* Doubleday, Doran, 1937.

Association of American Law Schools, *Selected Essays on Constitutional Law*. Foundation Press, 1938.

Ball, H. *Judicial Craftsmanship or Fiat? Direct Overturn by the United States Supreme Court*. Greenwood Press, 1978.

Beard, C. A. *The Supreme Court and the Constitution*, Rev ed. with new introduction by A. F. Westin. Prentice-Hall, 1962.

Beck, J. M. *The Changed Conception of the Constitution*. University of Rochester, 1952.

Becker, T. L. *The Supreme Court Decision: Readings on Causes and Effects*. Oxford University, 1969.

Berger, R. *Government by Judiciary*. Harvard University, 1977.

Black, C. L., Jr. *Old and New Ways in Judicial Review*. Bowdoin College, 1957.

———. *The People and the Court: Judicial Review in a Democracy*. Macmillan, 1960.

Bobbitt, P. *Constitutional Fate: Theory of the Constitution*. Oxford University, 1982.

———. *The Doctrine of Judicial Review*. Princeton University, 1914.

———. *The Establishment of Judicial Review*. Princeton University, 1930.

———. *Our Constitutional Revolution and How to Round It Out*. Philadelphia Brandeis Lawyer Society, 1951.

Boudin, L. B. *Government by Judiciary*. Godwin, 1932.

Cahn, E., ed. *Supreme Court and Supreme Law*. Indiana University, 1954; rpt. Simon and Schuster, 1971.

Carr, R. K. *Democracy and the Supreme Court*. University of Oklahoma, 1936.

———. *The Supreme Court and Judicial Review*. Farrar and Rinehart, 1942.

Cassinelli, C. W. *The Politics of Freedom*. Putnam, 1868.

Choper, J. H. *Judicial Review and the National Political Process*. University of Chicago, 1980.

Corwin, E. S. *Court over Constitution: A Study of Judicial Review as an Instrument of Popular Government*. Princeton University, 1938.

Coxe, B. *An Essay on Judicial Power and Unconstitutional Legislation*. Kay, 1893; rpt. Da Capo Press, 1970.

Crosskey, W. W. *Politics and the Constitution in the History of the United States*. University of Chicago, 1953.

Cushman, R. E. *The Role of the Supreme Court in a Democratic Nation*. Public Affairs Committee, 1938.

———. *The Supreme Court and the Constitution*. Public Affairs Committee, 1940.

———. *What's Happening to Our Constitution*. Public Affairs Committee, 1940.

Davis, H. A. *The Judicial Veto*. Houghton Mifflin, 1914; rpt. Da Capo Press, 1971.

Dean, H. *Judicial Review and Democracy*. Random House, 1966.

Dougherty, J. H. *The Power of the Federal Judiciary over Legislation*. Putnam, 1912.

Elliott, W. E. Y. *The Rise of a Guardian Democracy*. Harvard University, 1974.

Ely, J. H. *Democracy and Distrust: A Theory of Judicial Review*. Harvard University, 1979.

Fennell, W. G. *The "Reconstructed Court."* New York University, 1942.

Field, O. P. *The Effect on an Unconstitutional Statute*. University of Minnesota, 1935; rpt. Da Capo Press, 1971.

Forte, D. F., ed. *The Supreme Court in American Politics: Judicial Activism v. Judicial Restraint*. Heath, 1972.

Freedman, M., W. H. Beaney, and E. V. Rostow. *Perspectives on the Court*. Northwestern University, 1967.

Gabin, S. B. *Judicial Review and the Reasonable Doubt Test*. Kennikat Press, 1979.

Garvey, G. *Constitutional Bricolage*. Princeton University, 1971.

Gilbert, W. C., comp. *Provisions of Federal Law Held Unconstitutional by the Supreme Court of the United States*. Government Printing Office, 1936.

Goldberg, L. P., and E. Levenson. *Lawless Judges*. Da Capo Press, 1970.

Haines, C. G. *The American Doctrine of Judicial Supremacy*. 2d ed., rev. and enl. University of California, 1959; rpt. Da Capo Press, 1977.

———. *A Government of Laws or a Government of Men.* University of California at Los Angeles, 1929.

Haller, W. *Supreme Court und Politik in den U.S.A.: Fragen der Justiziabilität in der hochstrichterlichen Rechtsprechung.* Verlag Stämpfli, Bern, Switzerland, 1981.

Hand, L. *The Bill of Rights.* Harvard University, 1958; rpt. Atheneum, 1964.

Henry, J. M. *Nine Above the Law: Our Supreme Court.* Lewis, 1936.

Higgins, T. J. *Judicial Review Unmasked.* Christopher Publications, 1981.

Hyneman, C. S. *The Supreme Court on Trial.* Atherton, 1963.

Johnson, J. E., ed. *Limitation of the Power of the Supreme Court to Declare Acts of Congress Unconstitutional.* H. W. Wilson, 1935.

Johnston, R. E. *The Effect of Judicial Review in Federal-State Relations in Australia, Canada, and the United States.* Cambridge University, 1970.

Levy, B. H. *Our Constitution: Toll or Testament.* Knopf, 1941.

Lewinson, J. L. *Limiting Judicial Review.* Parker, Stane and Braid, 1937.

Loewenstein, K. *Political Power and the Governmental Process.* University of Chicago, 1956.

Long, H. A. *Usurpers, Foes of Free Men.* Post, 1957.

Lusky, L. *By What Right? A Commentary on the Supreme Court's Right to Revise the Constitution.* Michie, 1975.

McCloskey, R. G. *American Conservatism in the Age of Enterprise.* Harvard Universtiy, 1957.

———. *The American Supreme Court.* University of Chicago, 1960.

McKay, R. B., ed. *The American Constitutional Law Reader.* Oceana, 1958.

McLaughlin, A. C. *The Courts, Constitution and Parties.* University of Chicago, 1912.

McWhinney, E. *Judicial Review in the English-Speaking World.* 4th ed. University of Toronto, 1969.

Mason, A. T. *The Supreme Court: Palladium of Freedom.* University of Michigan, 1962.

Meigs, W. M. *The Relation of the Judiciary to the Constitution.* Neale, 1919; rpt. Da Capo Press, 1971.

Miller, A. S. *Toward Judicial Activism: The Political Role of the Supreme Court.* Greenwood Press, 1982.

Moore, B. F. *The Supreme Court and Unconstitutional Legislation.* Columbia University, 1913.

Nichols, E. R. *Congress or the Supreme Court: Which Shall Rule America?* Noble, 1935.

"The Role of the Supreme Court in the American Constitutional System." *Notre Dame Lawyer.* Notre Dame Law School Symposium, 1959.

Perry, M. J. *The Constitution, the Courts, and Human Rights: An Inquiry into the Legitimacy of Constitutional Policymaking by the Judiciary.* Yale University, 1982.

Powell, T. R. *Vagaries and Varieties in Constitutional Interpretations.* Columbia University, 1956.

Roe, G. E. *Our Judicial Oligarchy* Huebsch, 1912.

Rosenblum, V. G. *Law as a Political Instrument.* Random House, 1955.

Rostow, E. V. *The Sovereign Prerogative: The Supreme Court and the Quest for Law.* Yale University, 1962.

Senior, M. R. *The Supreme Court: Its Power of Judicial Review with Respect to Congressional Legislation.* George Washington University, 1937.

Smith, F. A. *Judicial Review of Legislation in New York, 1906–1938.* Columbia University, 1952.

Statsky, W. P. *A Text on Legal Reasoning: Legislative Analysis: How to Use Statutes and Regulations.* West, 1975.

Syracuse Law Review. "Controversy over the Supreme Court: A Symposium." Spring, 1959.

Tompkins, D. C. *The Supreme Court of the United States: A Bibliography.* University of California, 1959.

Tribe, L. H., *Constitutional Choices.* Harvard University, 1985.

Von Moschzisker, R. *Judicial Review of Legislation.* National Association for Constitutional Government, 1923; rpt. Da Capo Press, 1971.

Warren, C. *Congress, the Constitution, and the Supreme Court*. Little, Brown, 1935.

Wechsler, H. *Principles, Politics and Fundamental Law*. Harvard University, 1961.

Wright, B. F. *The Growth of American Constitutional Law*. Reynal and Hitchcock, 1942.

JURIES

Administrative Office of United States Courts. *Juror Utilization in the United States Courts*. Government Printing Office, 1971.

Abraham, H. J. *The Judicial Process: An Introductory Analysis of the Courts of the United States, England, and France*. 5th ed. Oxford University, 1986.

Alfini, J. J. *Pattern Jury Instructions*. American Judicial Society, 1972.

Austin, A. D. *Complex Litigation Confronts the Jury System: A Case Study*. University Press of America, 1985.

Barber, D., and G. Gordon, eds. *Members of the Jury*. Wildwood House, 1976.

Bentham, J. *The Elements of the Art of Packing as Applied to Special Juries*. Effingham-Wilson, 1821.

Ben-Veniste, R., and G. Frampton, Jr. *Stonewall: The Real Story of the Watergate Prosecution*. Simon and Schuster, 1977.

Bloomstein, M. J. *Verdict: The Jury System*. Dodd, Mead, 1968.

Busch, F. X. *Law and Tactics in Jury Trials*. Bobbs-Merrill, 1963.

Chester, G. *The Ninth Juror*. Random House, 1971.

Clark, L. D. *The Grand Jury: The Use and Abuse of Political Power*. Quadrangle, 1975.

Clementson, G. B. *Special Verdicts and Special Findings by Juries*. West, 1905.

Crook, J. *Law and Life of Rome*. Cornell University, 1967.

Ellwork, A., B. Sales, and J. J. Alfini. *Making Jury Instructions Understandable*. Michie/Bobbs-Merrill, 1982.

Forsyth, W. *History of Trial by Jury*. New ed. Cockcroft, 1875.

Francis, P. *How to Serve on a Jury*. Oceana, 1953.

Frank J. *Courts on Trial: Myth and Reality in American Justice*. Princeton University, 1949.

Frankel. M. E., and G. P. Naftalis. *The Grand Jury: An Institution on Trial*. Hill & Wang, 1977.

Ginger, A. F., ed. *Jury Selection in Criminal Trials: New Techniques and Concepts*. AFG Legal Publications, 1975.

Gleisser, M. *Juries and Justice*. Barnes, 1968.

Green, L. *Judge and Jury*. Vernon, 1930.

Harris, R. *Freedom Spirit*. Little, Brown, 1976.

Hastie, R., S. D. Penrod, and N. Pennington. *Inside the Jury*. Harvard University, 1983.

Joiner, C. W. *Civil Justice and the Jury*. Prentice-Hall, 1962.

Kadish, M. R., and S. H. Kadish. *Discretion to Disobey: A Study of Lawful Departures from Legal Rules*. Stanford University, 1973.

Kairys, D., ed. *The Jury System: New Methods for Reducing Prejudice*. National Jury Project, New York, 1975.

Kalven, H., Jr., and H. Zeisel. *The American Jury*. University of Chicago, 1966.

Keeney, B. C. *Judgment by Peers*. Harvard University, 1949.

Lermack, P. *Materials on Juries and Jury Research: An Annotated Bibliography*. American Judicial Society, 1977.

Levlin, Sir P. *Trial by Jury*. Stevens, 1956.

Lubbers, J. *Annotated Bibliography on the Grand Jury*. American Judicial Society, 1973.

McBride, R. L. *The Art of Instructing the Jury*. W. H. Anderson, 1969.

McCart, S. *Trial by Jury: A Complete Guide to the Jury System*. Chelton, 1965.

Martin, G. *Lawyers Speak the Truth About Counsel-Conducted Voir Dire*. American Judicial Society, 1970.

Mathes, W. C., and E. J. Devitt. *Federal Jury Practice and Instructions, Civil and Criminal.* West, 1965.

Miller, G. R., and N. E. Fontes. *Videotape of Trial: A View from the Jury Box.* Sage Publications, 1979.

Nieland, R. G. *Patterning Jury Instructions: A Critical Look at a Modern Movement to Improve the Jury System.* American Judicial Society, 1979.

Osborn, A. S. *The Mind of the Juror.* Boyd, 1937.

Polier, J. W. *A View from the Bench.* National Council on Crime and Delinquency, 1964.

Saks, M. J. *Jury Verdicts.* Lexington Books, 1977.

Sales, B., ed. *The Jury, Judicial, and Trial Processes.* Plenum, 1979.

Scigliano, R. G. *The Michigan One-Man Grand Jury.* Michigan State University, 1957.

Shields, D. C., and J. F. Cragan. *Justice and the Jury.* Campus, 1971.

Simon, R. J. *The Jury and the Plea of Insanity.* Little, Brown, 1968.

———. *The Jury: Its Role in American Society.* Lexington Books, 1979.

———, ed. *The Jury System in America: A Critical Overview.* Sage Publications, 1975.

Stoever, W. *A Comparison of Six- and Twelve-Member Civil Juries in New Jersey Superior and County Courts.* Institute of Judicial Administration, 1972.

Timothy, M. *Jury Woman.* Emty Press, 1974.

Vanderbilt, A. T. *Judges and Jurors: Their Functions, Qualifications, and Selection.* Boston University, 1956.

Van Dyke, J. *Jury Selection Procedures: Our Uncertain Commitment to Representative Panels.* Ballinger, 1977.

Villasenor, V. *Jury: The People vs. Juan Corona.* Little, Brown, 1976.

Wehnke, R. A. *The Art of Selecting a Jury.* Parker, 1980.

Wellman, F. L. *Gentlemen of the Jury.* Macmillan, 1936.

Winters, G. R. *The Jury: Selected Readings.* American Judicial Society, 1971.

Younger, R. D. *The People's Panel: The Grand Jury in the United States, 1634–1941.* Brown University, 1963.

Zerman, M. B. *Call the Final Witness: The People vs. Darrell R. Mathes as Seen by the Eleventh Juror.* Harper & Row, 1976.

JURISDICTION AND ORGANIZATION OF COURTS

Abraham, H. J. *The Judicial Process: An Introductory Analysis of the Courts of the United States, England, and France,* 5th ed. Oxford, 1986. Chapters 3–5.

American Judicature Society. *Court Studies.* University Publications of America, 1985.

Annual Reports of the Director of the Administrative Office of the U.S. Courts. Government Printing Office.

Bator, P. M., et al. *Hart and Wechsler's The Federal Courts and the Federal System.* 2d ed. Foundation Press, 1973.

Berkson, L., and S. Carbon. *Court Unification: History, Politics, and Implementation.* American Judicial Society, 1978.

Bourguignon, H. J. *The First Federal Court: The Federal Appellate Prize Court of the American Revolution, 1775–1787.* American Philosophical Society, 1977.

Brantingham, P. L., and T. G. Blomberg. *Courts and Diversion.* Sage Publications, 1979.

Brennan, W. J. *Modernizing the Courts.* Institute of Judicial Administration, 1957.

Bunn, C. W. *A Brief Survey of the Jurisdiction and Practice of the Courts of the United States.* 5th ed. West, 1949.

Bureau of Municipal Research. *The Magistrate Courts of Philadelphia.* Rev. ed. Pennsylvania Economy League, 1958.

Callender, C. M. *American Courts: Their Organization and Procedure.* McGraw-Hill, 1927.

Carlton, C. *The Court of Orphans.* Humanities Press, 1974.

Carp, R. A., and C. K. Rowland. *Policymaking and Politics in the Federal District Court.* University of Tennessee, 1983.

Comer, J. P. *The Forging of the Federal Indigent Code.* Principia, 1966.

Countryman, E. *The Supreme Court of the United States.* Bender, 1913.

Dobie, A. N. *Handbook of Federal Jurisdiction and Procedure.* West, 1928.

Early, S. T., Jr. *Constitutional Courts of the United States.* Littlefield, Adams, 1977.

Eisenstein, J. and H. Jacob. *Felony Justice: An Organizational Analysis of Criminal Courts.* Little, Brown, 1977.

Feeley, M. M. *The Process Is the Punishment: Handling Cases in a Lower Criminal Court.* Sage Publications, 1979.

Ferguson, J. H., and D. L. Cowells. *Minor Courts in Pennsylvania: A Study of the Justices of the Peace and Aldermen.* Pennsylvania State University, 1962.

Fins, H. O. *Federal Jurisdiction and Procedure.* Bobbs-Merrill, 1960.

Fox, S. J. *Law of Juvenile Courts in a Nutshell.* West, 1971.

Flanders, S. *Case Management and Court Management in the United States District Courts.* Federal Judicial Center, 1977.

Frank, J. F. *Courts on Trial.* Princeton University, 1959.

Frankfurter, F., and N. Greene. *The Law Injunction.* Macmillan, 1930.

Friendly, H. J. *Federal Jurisdiction: A General View.* Columbia University, 1973.

Gazell, J. A. *The Future of State Court Management.* National University Publications, 1978.

———. *State Trial Courts as Bureaucracies: A Study in Judicial Management.* Dunellen, 1975.

Glick, H. *State Trial Courts in State Politics: An Investigation of the Judicial Role.* Basic Books, 1971.

———, and K. N. Vines. *State Court System.* Prentice-Hall, 1973.

Goldfarb, R. L. *The Contempt Power.* Columbia University, 1963.

Goldman, S., and T. Jahnige. *The Federal Courts as a Political System.* Harper & Row, 1971.

Gressman, E., and R. L. Stern. *Supreme Court Practice.* 4th ed. Bureau of National Affairs, 1969.

Harding, A. L., ed. *The Administration of Justice in Retrospect.* Southern Methodist University, 1957.

Harris, R. J. *The Judicial Power of the United States.* Louisiana State University, 1940.

Hart, H. M., Jr. and H. Wechsler. *The Judicial Code and Rules of Procedure in the Federal Courts.* Foundation Press, 1954.

Hays, S. W. *Court Management: The Administrators and Their Judicial Environment.* Lexington Books, 1978.

Howard, J. W., Jr. *Courts of Appeal in the Federal Judicial System.* Princeton University, 1981.

Institute of Public Administration. *The Minor Courts in Pennsylvania.* Pennsylvania State University, 1962.

Johnson, T. A. *An Introduction to the Juvenile Justice System.* West, 1975.

Kalven, D. *Appellate Courts in the United States and England.* New York University, 1956.

Klein, M. W., ed. *The Juvenile Justice System.* Sage Publishers, 1976.

Knab, K. M. *Courts of Limited Jurisdiction: A National Survey.* Government Printing Office, 1977.

Laurent, F. *The Business of a Trial Court.* University of Wisconsin, 1959.

Lepawsky, A. *The Judicial System of Metropolitan Chicago.* University of Chicago, 1932.

McGowan, C. *The Organization of Judicial Power in the United States.* Northwestern University, 1969.

Marvell, T. B. *Appellate Courts and Lawyers: Information Gathering in the Adversary System.* Greenwood Press, 1978.

Meador, D. J., ed. *The Office of Chief Justice.* Miller Center of Public Affairs, University of Virginia, 1984.

Moley, R. *Our Criminal Courts.* Minton, Balch, 1930.

Morris, T. R. *The Virginia Supreme Court: An Institutional and Political Analysis.* University of Virginia, 1975.

Osthus, M. O. *Intermediate Appellate Courts.* 2d ed. American Judicial Society, 1976.
———. *State Intermediate Appellate Courts.* American Judicial Society, 1980.
Paulsen, M., ed. *The Problem of Juvenile Courts and the Rights of Children.* The American Law Institute, 1975.
Post, C. G., Jr. *The Supreme Court and Political Questions.* Johns Hopkins University, 1936.
Pound, R. *Organization of Courts.* Little, Brown, 1940.
Presser, S. B. *Studies in the History of United States Courts of the Third Circuit.* Government Printing Office, 1982.
Richardson, R. W., and K. N. Vines. *Politics of the Federal Courts.* Little, Brown, 1970.
Robertson, R. *Jurisdiction of the Supreme Court of the United States.* Bender, 1951.
Rose, J. C. *Jurisdiction and Procedure of Federal Courts.* Bender, 1938.
Rosenberg, M. *The Pretrial Conference and Effective Justice.* Columbia University, 1964.
Rovner-Pieczenic, R. *The Criminal Court: How It Works.* Lexington Books, 1976.
Rubin, T. *The Courts: Fulcrum of the Justice System.* Goodyear, 1976.
Sayre, W. S., ed. *State Court Systems.* Prentice-Hall, 1973.
Schick, M. *Learned Hand's Court.* Johns Hopkins University, 1970.
Schuck, P. H. *The Judiciary Committees: A Study of the House and Senate Committees.* Grossman, 1975.
Stone, C. D. *Should Trees Have Standing? Toward Legal Rights for Natural Objects.* Avon Books, 1976.
Sunderland, E. R. *Judicial Administration.* Callaghan, 1939.
Tachau, M. K. B. *Federal Courts in the Early Republic: 1789–1816.* Princeton University, 1976.
Teitlebaum, L. E., and A. R. Gough, eds. *Beyond Control: Status Offenders in the Juvenile Courts.* Sage Publications, 1978.
Senate. Committee on the Judiciary. *Composition and Jurisdiction of the United States Supreme Court.* Superintendent of Documents, 1954.
———. *Reorganization of the Federal Judiciary.* Superintendent of Documents, 1937.
Warren, G. *Traffic Courts.* Little, Brown, 1942.
Wheeler, R. R., and H. R. Whitcomb, eds. *Judicial Administration: Text and Readings.* Prentice-Hall, 1976.
Winters, G. R., ed. *Selected Readings on Courthouses and Courtrooms.* American Judicial Society, 1976.
Wolfson, R. F., and P. Kurland. *Jurisdiction of the Supreme Court of the United States.* Rev. ed. Bender, 1951.
Wood, M. L., and R. Kast. *Court Studies: An Annotated Bibliography.* American Judicial Society, 1976.
Wright, B. F. *Federal Courts.* West, 1963.
———. *Handbook of the Law of Federal Courts.* 2d ed. West, 1970.

THE LAW
(Principles of law. What the law is. Development of the law.)
(See also Philosophical and Theoretical Aspects of Law.)

Ackerman, B. *Reconstructing American Law.* Harvard University, 1984.
Allen, C. K. *Law in the Making.* 7th ed. Oxford University, 1964.
Arens, R., and H. D. Lasswell. *In Defense of Public Order: The Emerging Field of Sanction Law.* Columbia University, 1961.
Arneson, B. A. *Elements of Constitutional Law.* Harper, 1928.
Aumann, F. R. *The Changing American Legal System.* Ohio State University, 1940.
Ballow, H. *A Treatise of Equity.* Abraham Small, 1820.
Banks, M. A. *Using a Law Library.* 2d ed. Carswell, 1974.

Barkun, M. *Law Without Sanctions: Order in Primitive Societies and the World Community.* Yale University, 1968.

Berman, H. J., ed. *Talk on America's Law.* Random House, 1961.

———, and W. R. Greiners. *The Nature and Function of Law.* Foundation Press, 1966.

Berman, H. J. *Law and Revolution.* Harvard University, 1985.

Billias, G. *Law and Authority in Colonial America.* Barre, 1965.

Bishin, W. R., and C. D. Stone. *Law, Language, and Ethics: An Introduction to Law and Legal Method.* Foundation Press, 1972.

Black, C. L., Jr. *The Occasions of Justice: Essays Mostly in Law.* Macmillan, 1964.

———. *Structure and Relationships in Constitutional Law.* Louisiana State University, 1969.

Black, D. *The Behavior of Law.* Academic Press, 1976.

Bloustein, E. J., ed. *Nuclear Energy, Public Policy and the Law.* Oceana, 1964.

Blumberg, A. S., ed. *Law and Order.* Aldine, 1970.

Borchard, E. M. *Declaratory Judgments.* 2d ed. Banks-Baldwin, 1941.

Bridwell, R., and U. Whitten. *The Constitution and the Common Law.* Lexington Books, 1978.

Bromberg, W. *The Use of Psychiatry in the Law.* Greenwood Press (Quorum Books), 1979.

Brownell, E. A. *Legal Aid in the United States* (with Supplement). Lawyers' Cooperative, 1961.

Buckland, W. W., and A. D. McNair. *Roman Law and the Common Law.* Rev. ed. Cambridge University, 1952.

Calabresi, G. *A Common Law for the Age of Statutes.* Harvard University, 1982.

Carter, J. *Law: Its Origin, Growth, and Function.* Putnam, 1907.

Carter, L. H. *Reason in Law.* 2d ed. Little, Brown, 1984.

Cataldo, B. F., et al. *Introduction to Law and the Legal Process.* Wiley, 1965.

Cohen, M. L. *How to Find the Law.* 7th ed. West, 1976.

———. *Legal Research in a Nutshell.* 3d ed. West, 1978.

Cooley, T. M. *Constitutional Limitations.* Putnam, 1868.

Cooper, F. E. *Living the Law.* Bobbs-Merrill, 1958.

Corry, J. A. *The Power of the Law.* CBC Learning Systems, 1971.

Cosgrove, R. A. *The Rule of Law: Albert Dicey, Victorian Jurist.* University of North Carolina, 1980.

Curran, B. *The Legal Needs of the Public.* American Bar Foundation, 1978.

Cushing, J. D., ed. *The Colony Laws of North America.* Glazier, 1979.

Daube, D. *Roman Law: Linguistic, Social, and Philosophical Aspects.* Aldine, 1969.

Davenport, W. H., ed. *Voices In Court.* Macmillan, 1958.

Davis, F. J., et al. *Society and the Law: New Meaning for an Old Profession.* Free Press, 1962.

D'Entrèves, A. P. *Natural Law.* 2d ed. Hutchinson, 1970.

Desmond, C. S. *Through the Courtroom Window.* West, 1959.

Donnelly, R. C., J. Goldstein, R. D. Schwartz. *Criminal Law.* Free Press, 1962.

Edmunds, P. D. *Law and Civilization.* Public Affairs Press, 1959.

Edwards, M. *The Courts and the Public Schools.* University of Chicago, 1962.

Ehrlich, J. W., ed. *Blackstone.* Capricorn, 1959.

Eisenstein, J. *Politics and the Legal Process.* Harper & Row, 1973.

Field, O. P. *The Effect of an Unconstitutional Statute.* University of Minnesota, 1935.

Fischer, T. C., and R. F. Zehnle. *Introduction to Law and Legal Reasoning.* West, 1977.

Flaherty, D. *Essays in the History of Early American Law.* University of North Carolina, 1969.

Ford, S. *The American Legal System: Its Dynamics and Limits.* 2d ed. West, 1976.

Fordham, J. B. *Local Government Law.* Foundation Press, 1949.

Freemann, M. D. A. *The Legal Structure.* Longman, 1974.

Freund, E. *The Police Power, Public Policy, and Constitutional Rights.* Callaghan, 1904.

Friedman, L. M. *A History of American Law.* Simon and Schuster, 1973.

———. *An Introduction to American Law.* Morton, 1984.

———. *Law and Society.* Prentice-Hall, 1977.

————, and H. N. Scheiber, eds. *American Law and the Constitutional Order.* Harvard University, 1978.

Fuller, L. L. *The Anatomy of Law.* Random House (Modern Library), 1969.

————. *The Law in Quest of Itself.* Beacon Press, 1940.

————. *Legal Fictions.* Stanford University, 1967.

————. *The Morality of Law.* Yale University, 1964.

Gavong, C. K., and R. W. Pearce. *Law and Society.* Irwin, 1965.

Gilmore, G. *The Ages of American Law.* Yale University, 1977.

Grad, F. P., A. L. Goldberg, and B. A. Shapiro. *Alcoholism and the Law.* Oceana, 1971.

Gray, C. M. *Copyhold, Equity, and the Common Law.* Harvard University, 1963.

Gray, J. C. *The Nature and Sources of the Law.* 2d ed. Beacon Press, 1963.

Greiner, W. R. *The Nature and Function of Law.* Foundation Press, 1975.

Green, L. *Judge and Jury.* Vernon Law Book, 1930.

Green, L. C. *Law and Society: Essays in the Sociology of Law.* Oceana, 1975.

Griswold, E. N. *Law and Lawyers in the United States: The Common Law Under Stress.* Harvard University, 1964.

Harding, A. L., ed. *Origins of the Natural Law Tradition.* Kennikat Press, 1954.

Hare, J. I. C. *American Constitutional Law.* Brown University, 1889.

Hart, H. L. A. *The Concept of Law.* Oxford University, 1961.

Hartland, E. C. *Primitive Law.* Kennikat Press, 1964.

Hartzler, H. R. *Justice, Legal Systems, and Social Structure.* Kennikat Press, 1976.

Havinghurst, C. C., ed. *Air Pollution Control.* Oceana, 1969.

————. *Medical Progress and the Law.* Oceana, 1969.

Hayek, F. A. *Law, Legislation, and Liberty.* University of Chicago, 1978.

Hazard, G. C., Jr. *Law in a Changing Society.* Prentice-Hall, 1968.

Henderson, G. C. *The Position of Foreign Corporations in American Constitutional Law.* Harvard University, 1960.

Henson, R. D., ed. *Landmarks of Law: Highlights of Legal Opinion from 1890 to the Present.* Harper & Row, 1960; Beacon Press, 1963.

Hoebel, E. A. *The Law of Primitive Man.* Harvard University, 1964.

Hogue, A. R. *Origins of the Common Law.* University of Indiana, 1966.

Hohfeld, W. N. *Fundamental Legal Conceptions.* Yale University, 1964.

Holdsworth, Sir W. *A History of English Law.* Goodhart and Hanbury, 1956.

Holmes, O. W. *The Common Law.* Little, Brown, 1881; New edition ed. by M. DeWolfe Howe, Harvard University, 1963.

Home, H., Lord Kames. *Principles of Equity.* Bell and Bradfute, 1825.

Honnold, J. *The Life of the Law: Readings on the Growth of Legal Institutions.* Free Press, 1964.

Horwitz, M. J. *The Transformation of American Law, 1780–1860.* Harvard University, 1977.

Houghteling, J. L., Jr. *The Dynamics of Law.* Harcourt Brace Jovanovich, 1968.

Hurst, J. W. *Law and Social Order in the United States.* Cornell University, 1977.

————. *The Law of Treason in the United States: Collected Essays.* Greenwood Press, 1971.

Jackson, P. E. *Justice and the Law.* Michie, 1964.

Jahr, A. D. *The Law of Eminent Domain: Valuation and Procedure.* Boardman, 1953.

Jolowicz, H. F. *Roman Foundations of Modern Law.* Oxford University, 1957.

Jones, H. W. *The Efficacy of Law.* Northwestern University, 1969.

Jowell, J. L. *Law and Bureaucracy.* Dunellen, 1975.

Kairys, D., ed. *The Politics of Law: A Progressive Critique.* Pantheon Books, 1982.

Keeton, R. E. *Legal Cause in the Law of Torts.* Ohio State University, 1963.

Kent, J. *Commentaries on American Law.* 5th ed. Little, Brown, 1830.

Kirchheimer, O. *Political Justice: The Use of Legal Procedure for Political Ends.* Princeton University, 1961.

Kornstein, D. *The Music of the Laws.* Everest House, 1982.

Lee, L. T. *Consular Law and Practice.* Praeger, 1961.

Lefcourt, R., ed. *Law Against the People: Essays to De-mystify Law, Order, and the Courts.* Knopf, 1971.

Lieberman, J. K. *Milestones! 200 Years of American Law.* West, 1977.

Llewellyn, K. N. *The Common Law Tradition: Deciding Appeals.* Little, Brown, 1960.

Lloyd of Hamstead, Lord. *Jurisprudence.* Praeger, 1972.

Lobenthal, J. *Power and Put-On: The Law in America.* Outerbridge & Dienstfrey, 1970.

London, E. *The World of Law.* 2 vols. Simon and Schuster, 1960.

Lunt, D. C. *The Road to Law.* Norton, 1962.

McCormick, O. T. *Handbook of the Law of Evidence.* West, 1954.

McKean, D. *The Integrated Bar.* Houghton Mifflin, 1963.

Macmillan, H. P. *Law and Other Things.* Cambridge University, 1937.

Maine, Sir H. *Ancient Law.* J. Mirray, 1930; rpt. Beacon Press, 1963.

Maitland, F. W. *Equity.* Cambridge University, 1936.

———. *The Forms of Action at Common Law.* Cambridge University, 1962.

Manning, B. *Federal Conflict of Interest Law.* Harvard University, 1964.

Marshall, J. *Law and Psychology in Conflict.* Bobbs-Merrill, 1968; rpt. Doubleday (Anchor Books,) 1969.

Mellinkoff, D. *The Language of the Law.* Little, Brown, 1963.

Morris, R. B. *Studies in the History of American Law.* Lippincott, 1959.

Muir, W. K., Jr. *Law and Attitude Change.* University of Chicago, 1973.

Nader, L. *Law in Culture and Society.* Aldine, 1969.

New York Times, The, eds. *American Law: The Formative Years.* Arno Press, 1971.

Nelson, W. E. *Americanization of the Common Law: The Impact of Legal Change on Massachusetts Society, 1760–1830.* Harvard University, 1975.

Newan, R. A. *Equity and Law: A Comparative Study.* Oceana, 1961.

Niblett, B., ed. *Computer Science and Law.* Cambridge University, 1980.

Nice, R. W., ed. *Treasury of Law.* Philosophical Library, 1964.

Oceana Publications, Inc., eds. *Annual Survey of American Law.* Oceana, 1960–.

———. *The Legal Almanac Series.* 1955– .

Oran, D. *Law Dictionary for Non-Lawyers.* West, 1975.

Palmer, E. E., ed. *Current Law and Social Problems.* University of Toronto, 1963.

Perkins, R. M. *Cases on Criminal Law and Procedure.* Foundation Press, 1959.

Phelps, C. E. *Elements of Judicial Equity.* King, 1890.

Plucknett, F. T. A. *A Concise History of the Common Law.* 3d ed. Butterworth, 1940.

Pollock, Sir F. *Essays in the Law.* Macmillan, 1922.

———. *The Expansion of the Common Law.* Macmillan, 1904.

———. *A First Book in Jurisprudence.* 4th ed. Macmillan, 1918.

———. *Jurisprudence and Legal Essays.* St. Martin's Press, 1962.

———, and F. W. Maitland. *The History of English Law Before the Time of Edward I.* Cambridge University, 1895; rpt. 1968.

Posner, R. A. *Economic Analysis of Law.* Prentice-Hall, 1963.

Pound, R. *The Formative Era of American Law.* Little, Brown, 1938.

Radin, M. *The Law and Mr. Smith.* Bobbs-Merrill, 1938.

———. *The Law and You.* New American Library (Mentor Books), 1948.

Rawls, J. *A Theory of Justice.* Harvard, 1971.

Raz, J. *The Concepts of a Legal System.* Oxford University, 1970.

———. *Practical Reasons and Norms.* Hutchinson Ross, 1975.

Re, E. D., ed. *Selected Essays on Equity.* Oceana, 1955.

Robinson, J., ed. *An American Legal Almanac: The Law in All States, Summary and Update.* Oceana, 1978.

Rodell, F. *Woe Unto You Lawyers.* Rev. ed. Pageant, 1956.

Rodes, R. E., Jr. *The Legal Enterprise.* Dunellen, 1976.

Rodgers, H. S. *Constitutional History of the United States as Seen in the Development of American Law.* Bender, 1890.

Ross, M. J. *Handbook of Everyday Law.* Rev. and enl. Harper & Row, 1967.

Rostov, E. V. *The Ideal in Law.* University of Chicago, 1978.

Rottschaefer, H. *Handbook of American Constitutional Law.* West, 1939.

Sales, B. D., ed. *Law and Human Behavior.* Plenum, 1982.

Schnapper, M. B. *Constraint by Copyright.* Public Affairs Press, 1962.

Schoenfeld, C. G. *Psychoanalysis and the Law.* Thomas, 1973.

Schur, E. M. *Law and Society: A Sociological View.* Random House, 1969.

Schwartz B., ed. *American Law, The Third Century: The Law Bicentennial Volume.* New York University School of Law, 1976.

———. *The Law in America: A History.* McGraw-Hill, 1974.

Schwartz, M. L., ed. *Law and the American Future.* Prentice-Hall, 1976.

Schwartz, R., and J. Skolnick. *Society and the Legal Order.* Basic Books, 1970.

Seagle, W. *Law, the Science of Inefficiency.* Macmillan, 1952.

———. *The Quest for Law.* Knopf, 1941.

Shapo, M. S. *The Duty of Act: Tort Law, Power, and Public Policy.* University of Texas, 1978.

Shartel, B. *Our Legal System and How It Operates.* University of Michigan Law School, 1950.

Sigler, J. A., and B. R. Beede. *The Legal Sources of Public Policy.* Lexington Books, 1977.

Simon, T. R. *The Tradition of Natural Law.* Fordham University, 1965.

Simpson, S. P., and J. Stone. *Law and Society.* West, 1948–49.

Sloan, I. J. *Environment and the Law.* Oceana, 1971.

———. *Youth and the Law.* Oceana, 1970.

Soper, P. *A Theory of Law.* Harvard University, 1984.

Steigleman, W. A. *The Newspaperman and the Law.* Brown, 1950.

Story, J. *Commentaries on Equity Jurisprudence.* Little and Brown, 1836.

———. *Commentaries on Equity Pleadings.* Little and Brown, 1840.

Surrency, E., B. Field, and J. Crea. *A Practical Guide to Legal Research.* 2d ed. Oceana, 1959.

Sutherland, A. E. *An Introduction to Law.* Harvard University, 1957.

———. *Statutes and Statutory Construction.* 3d ed. Horack, 1943.

Taylor, J. *Elements of the Civil Law.* 4th ed. S. Sweet, 1828.

Thayer, J. B. *Legal Essays.* Boston Book, 1908.

Twining, W., ed. *H. L. A. Hart Jurists: Profiles in Legal Theory.* Stanford University, 1981.

University of Michigan Law School 1955 Conference. *Aims and Methods of Legal Research.* University of Michigan, 1958.

Van Caenegem, R. C. *The Birth of the English Common Law.* Cambridge University, 1973.

Vanderbilt, A. T. *Studying Law.* 2d ed. New York University, 1955.

Vining, J. *Legal Identity: The Coming of Age of Public Law.* Yale University, 1978.

Waddams, S. M. *Introduction to the Study of Law.* Carswell, 1979.

Walker, T. *Introduction to American Law.* Micklin and Johnson, 1837.

Wasserstein, B., and H. J. Green. *With Justice for Some.* Beacon Press, 1970.

Weaver, S. P. *Constitutional Law and Its Administration.* Callaghan, 1946.

Weinberg, L. S., and J. W. Weinberg. *Law and Society: An Interdisciplinary Introduction.* University Press of America, 1980.

Weisbrod, B. A. *Public Interest Law: An Economic and Institutional Analysis.* University of California, 1978.

Weissman, J. *Law in a Business Society.* Prentice-Hall, 1963.

White, G. E. *Patterns of American Legal Thought.* Michie, Bobbs-Merrill, 1978.

———. *Tort Law in America: An Intellectual History.* Oxford University, 1980.

White, J. B. *The Legal Imagination.* Little, Brown, 1973.

Wigmore, J. H. *Wigmore on Evidence.* 3d ed. Little, Brown, 1940.

Willoughby, W. W. *The Constitutional Law of the United States.* Baker, 1929.

Wolff, H. *Roman Law: A Historical Introduction.* University of Oklahoma, 1951.

Wolff, R. *The Rule of Law.* Simon and Schuster, 1971.

Wormser, R. A. *The Story of Law.* Simon and Schuster, 1962.

Wortley, B. A. *Jurisprudence.* Oceana, 1966.

Wright, C. A. *Handbook of the Law of Federal Courts.* West, 1970.
Yale Law School. *Two Centuries' Growth of American Law, 1701-1901.* Scribner, 1901.

THE LEGAL PROFESSION
(Lawyers, attorneys, court officers: The men and women, their work, their education.)
(See also Procedure in the Courts; Judges and Justices and Staffing the Courts.)

American Bar Association. *Code of Professional Responsibility and Code of Judicial Conduct.* American Bar Association, 1974.
Arnold, T. *Fair Fights and Foul: A Dissenting Lawyer's Life.* Harcourt, Brace & World, 1965.
Auchincloss, L. *The Partners.* Houghton Mifflin, 1973.
Auerbach, J. S. *Justice Without Law? Resolving Disputes Without Lawyers.* Oxford University, 1983.
———. *Unequal Justice: Lawyers and Social Change in Modern America.* Oxford University, 1976.
Bell, G. *Taking Care of the Law.* Morrow, 1982.
Belli, M. *Melvin Belli: My Life on Trial.* Morrow, 1977.
———. *Ready for the Plaintiff.* Holt, 1956.
Bent, A. E. *The Politics of Law Enforcement.* Lexington Books, 1974.
Ben-Veniste, R., and G. Frampton, Jr. *Stonewall: The Real Story of the Watergate Prosecution.* Simon and Schuster, 1977.
Bishop, J. W., Jr. *Obiter Dicta: Opinions, Judicial and Otherwise, on Lawyers and the Law.* Atheneum, 1971.
Black, J., ed. *Radical Lawyers: Their Role in the Movement and in the Courts.* Avon Books, 1971.
Blaustein, A. D., and C. O. Porter. *The American Lawyer.* University of Chicago, 1954.
Bloom, M. T. *The Trouble with Lawyers.* Simon and Schuster, 1969.
Bloomfield, M. H. *American Lawyers in a Changing Society, 1776-1876.* Harvard University, 1976.
Bonner, R. J. *Lawyers and Litigants in Ancient Athens: the Genesis of the Legal Profession.* University of Chicago, 1927.
Botein, B. *The Prosecutor.* Simon and Schuster, 1956.
Bowen, C. D. *The Lion and the Throne: The Life and Times of Sir Edward Coke, 1552-1634.* Little, Brown, 1957.
Brakel, S. J. *Public Funds, Private Lawyers, and Poor People.* American Bar Foundation, 1974.
Brown, C. G. *You May Take the Witness.* University of Texas, 1955.
Brown, E. L. *Lawyers, Law Schools and the Public Service.* Russell Sage Foundation, 1948.
Butler, C. H. *A Century at the Bar of the Supreme Court.* Putnam, 1942.
Carlin, J. E. *Lawyer's Ethics: A Survey of the New York City Bar.* Russell Sage Foundation, 1966.
———. *Lawyers on their Own: A Study of Individual Practitioners in Chicago.* Rutgers University, 1962.
Carter, L. H. *The Limits of Order.* Heath, 1974.
Casper, J. D. *American Criminal Justice: The Defendant's Perspective.* Prentice-Hall, 1972.
———. *Lawyers Before the Warren Court: Civil Liberties and Civil Rights, 1957-1966.* University of Illinois, 1972.
Chambers, M. M. *College and the Courts.* Columbia University, 1952.
Choust, A. H. *The Rise of the Legal Profession in America.* University of Oklahoma, 1965.
Christensen, B. F. *Lawyers for People of Moderate Means.* American Bar Foundation, 1970.
Conner, R. F., and C. R. Huff. *Attorneys as Activists.* Sage Publications, 1979.
Countryman, V., and T. Finnan, eds. *The Lawyer in Modern Society.* Little, Brown, 1965.
Couric, E., ed. *Women Lawyers: Perspectives on Success.* Harcourt Brace Jovanovich, 1984.

Curran, B. A., and F. O. Spaulding. *The Legal Needs of the Public.* American Bar Foundation, 1974.

Curtis, C. P. *It's Your Law.* Harvard University, 1954.

Davenport, W. H., ed. *Voices in Court.* Macmillan, 1958.

Donovan, J. W. *Modern Jury Trials.* Jennings, 1929.

Drinker, H. S. *Legal Ethics.* Columbia University, 1953.

Eisenstein, J. *Counsel for the United States: U.S. Attorneys in the Political and Legal System.* Johns Hopkins University, 1978.

Elliff, J. T. *Crime, Dissent and the Attorney General: The Justice Department in the 1960's.* Sage Publications, 1971.

Eulau, A. and J. D. Sprague. *Lawyers in Politics: A Study in Professional Convergence.* Bobbs-Merrill, 1964.

Fordham, E. W. *Notable Cross-Examinations.* Macmillan, 1957.

Frank, J. P. *Lincoln as a Lawyer.* University of Illinois, 1961.

Frank, M. M. *The Diary of a D.A.* Holt, Rinehart and Winston, 1960.

Freedman, M. H. *Lawyers' Ethics in an Adversary System.* Bobbs-Merrill, 1975.

Garland, A. H. *Experience in the United States Supreme Court.* J. Byrne, 1898.

Gerson, A., ed. *Lawyers' Ethics.* Transaction Books, 1978.

Ginger, A. F., ed. *The Relevant Lawyers.* AFG Legal Publications, 1975.

Goodhart, A. L. *Five Jewish Lawyers of the Common Law.* Oxford University, 1959.

Goulden, J. C. *The Million Dollar Lawyers.* Putnam, 1978.

———. *The Superlawyers: The Small and Powerful World of the Great Washington Law Firms.* Weybright and Talley, 1972.

Green, M. J. *The Other Government: The Unseen Power of Washington Lawyers.* Grossman, 1975.

Greenbaum, E. S. *A Lawyer's Job: In Court, in the Army, in the Office.* Harcourt, Brace & World, 1968.

Grosman, B. A. *The Prosecutor: An Inquiry Into the Exercise of Discretion.* University of Toronto, 1976.

Grossman, J. *Lawyers and Judges.* Wiley, 1965.

Gruzenberg, O. O. *Yesterday: Memoirs of a Russian-Jewish Lawyer.* Lexington Books, 1982.

Handler, J. F. *The Lawyer and His Community: The Practicing Bar in a Middle-Sized City.* University of Wisconsin, 1968.

———, E. J. Hollingsworth, and H. S. Erlanger. *Lawyers and the Pursuit of Legal Rights.* Academic Press, 1978.

Harbaugh, W. H. *Lawyer's Lawyer: The Life of John W. Davis.* Oxford University, 1978.

Harris, R. *Justice: The Crisis of Law, Order, and Freedom in America.* Dutton, 1970.

Heinz, J. P., and E. O. Laumann. *Chicago Lawyer: The Social Structure of the Bar.* Basic Books, 1984.

Hine, R. L. *Confessions of an Un-Common Attorney.* Macmillan, 1945.

Hoffman, P. *What the Hell is Justice? The Life and Trials of a Criminal Lawyer.* Playboy Press, 1975.

Horowitz, D. L. *The Jurocracy: Government Lawyers, Agency Programs, and Judicial Decisions.* Lexington Books, 1977.

Horton, J. T. *James Kent: A Study in Conservatism.* Appleton-Century, 1939.

Hurst, J. W. *The Growth of American Law: The Lawmakers.* Little, Brown, 1950.

Huston, L. A., et al. *Roles of the Attorney General of the United States.* Legislative Reference Service, 1968.

Irons, P. H. *The New Deal Lawyers.* Princeton University, 1982.

Johnson, E., Jr. *Justice and Reform: The Formative Years of the O.E.O. Legal Services Program.* Russell Sage Foundation, 1974.

Karlen, D. *The Citizen in Court: Litigant, Witness, Juror, Judge.* Holt, Rinehart & Winston, 1964.

Knox, J. D. *A Judge Comes of Age.* Scribner, 1940.

Kutner, L. *The Lawyer*. Dodd, Mead, 1966.

Lawson, W. D., ed. *Great American Lawyers*. Winston, 1907.

Lieberman, J. K. *Crisis at the Bar: Lawyers' Unethical Ethics and What to Do About It*. Norton, 1978.

Llewellyn, K. N. *The Bramble Bush: On Our Law and Its Study*. Oceana, 1957.

Luban, D., ed. *The Good Lawyer: Lawyers' Role and Lawyers' Ethics*. Rowman & Allanheld, 1984.

McKean, C. *The Integrated Bar*. Houghton Mifflin, 1963.

Marks, F. R. *The Lawyer, the Public and Professional Responsibility*. American Bar Foundation, 1972.

———, and D. Cathcart. *Discipline Within the Legal Profession: Is it Self-Regulation?* American Bar Foundation, 1974.

Matthews, D. *Who Needs the B*st*rds?* Arbor House, 1975.

Mayer, M. *The Lawyers*. Harper & Row, 1966.

Medcalf, L. *Law and Identity: Lawyers, Native Americans, and Legal Practice*. Sage Publications, 1978.

Melone, A. P. *Lawyers, Public Policy, and Interest Group Politics*. University Press of America, 1977.

Miller, F. W. *Prosecution*. Little, Brown, 1969.

Morgan, R. R. *Disabling America: The "Rights Industry" in Our Time*. Basic Books, 1985.

Morris, C. *How Lawyers Think*. Ohio University (Swallow Press), 1962.

———. *The Justification of the Law*. University of Pennsylvania, 1971.

Musmanno, M. M. *Verdict*. Doubleday, 1958.

Navasky, V. S. *Kennedy Justice*. Atheneum, 1971.

Nissman, D. M., and E. Hagen. *The Prosecution Function*. Lexington Books, 1981.

Nizer, L. *My Life in Court*. Doubleday, 1961.

Nolan, D. R. *Readings in the History of the American Legal Profession*. Michie, Bobbs-Merrill, 1980.

Oakley, J. B., and R. S. Thompson. *Law Clerks and the Judicial Process: Perceptions of the Qualities and Functions of Law Clerks in American Courts*. University of California, 1981.

Park, W. R., ed. *Manual for Legal Assistants*. West, 1979.

Parness, J. A. *The Expanding Role of the Parajudge in the United States*. American Judicial Society, 1973.

Partridge, B. *Country Lawyer*. Charles Evans Hughes Press, 1939.

Paulson, M. C., ed. *Legal Institutions Today and Tomorrow*. Columbia University, 1959.

Pike, J. A. *Beyond the Law: The Religious and Ethical Meaning of the Lawyer's Vocation*. Doubleday, 1963.

Pound, R. *The Lawyer from Antiquity to Modern Times*. West, 1953.

Prest, Wilfred, ed. *Lawyers in Early Modern Europe and America*. Homes & Meier, 1981.

Rodell, F. *Woe unto You, Lawyers!* Reynal and Hitchcock, 1939.

Rosenblatt, S. M. *Malpractice and Other Malfeasances*. Stuart, 1977.

———. *Trial Lawyer* Stuart, 1984.

Rosenthal, D. E. *Lawyer and Client: Who's in Charge?* Transaction Books, 1977.

Rossman, G. *Advocacy and the King's English*. Bobbs-Merrill, 1960.

Rutherford, M. L. S. "The Influence of the American Bar Association on Public Opinion and Legislation." Ph.D. diss., University of Pennsylvania, 1937.

St. John, A. R. *Final Verdict*. Doubleday, 1962.

Sayer, J. E. *Clarence Darrow: Public Advocate*. Kennikat Press, 1978.

Scheingold, S. A. *The Politics of Rights: Lawyers, Public Policy, and Political Change*. Yale University, 1974.

Schientag, B. L. *Moulders of Legal Thought*. Viking Press, 1943.

Schmidhauser, J. R. *The Supreme Court: Its Politics, Personalities, and Procedures*. Holt, 1960.

Seymour, W. N. *United States Attorney: An Inside View of "Justice" in America Under the Nixon Administration*. New York University, 1975.

Shayne, N. T. *The Paralegal Profession: A Career Guide*. Oceana, 1977.

Sheresky, N. *On Trial: Masters of the Courtroom*. Viking Press, 1977.

Simon, J. F. *The Judge*. McKay, 1976.

Smigel, E. O. *The Wall Street Lawyer*. Indiana University, 1969.

Smith, T. *Lawyer: Opportunities for Careers in the Legal Profession*. Macmillan, 1961.

Stewart, J. B. *The Partners*. Simon and Schuster, 1983.

Stolz, P. *Judging Judges: The Investigation of Rose Bird and the California Supreme Court*. Free Press, 1982.

———. *The Legal Needs of the Public: A Survey Analysis*. American Bar Foundation, 1968.

Stryker, E. P. *The Art of Advocacy*. Simon and Schuster, 1954; rpt. Cornerstone Library, 1963.

Sunderland, E. R. *Judicial Administration*. Callaghan, 1939.

Taylor, G. C. *Fifty Years in the Law*. Philosophical Library, 1963.

Tierney, K. *Darrow: A Biography*. Crowell, 1979.

Twiss, B. *Lawyers and the Constitution*. Princeton University, 1942.

Vanderbilt, A. T. *Men and Measures in the Law*. Knopf, 1949.

———. *Studying Law*. 2d ed. New York University, 1955.

Ware, G., ed. *From the Black Bar*. Capricorn, 1976.

Warkov, S., and J. Zelan. *Lawyers in the Making*. Aldine, 1965.

Warren, C. *A History of the American Bar*. Little, Brown, 1911.

Wasserstein, B., and M. J. Green, eds. *With Justice for Some*. Beacon Press, 1970.

Wellman, F. L. *The Art of Cross-Examination*. 4th ed. Macmillan, 1936.

———. *Day in Court*. Macmillan, 1910.

Weinberg, A., and I. Weinberg, eds. *Clarence Darrow's Verdicts out of Court*. Quadrangle, 1963.

Weyrauch, W. O. *The Personality of Lawyers*. Yale University, 1964.

Whitney, M. O. *Life on the Circuit with Lincoln*. Estes-Lauriat, 1892.

Wice, P. B. *Criminal Lawyers: An Endangered Species*. Sage Publications, 1978.

Williston, S. *Life and Law*. Little, Brown, 1940.

Winters, G. R. *Bar Association Organization and Other Activities*. American Judicature Society, 1954.

Wood, A. L. *Criminal Lawyer*. Yale University, 1967.

THE MILITARY:

(LAW, COURTS, CONTROL)

(See also *Bibliography IV*, Section V, "Military Justice and Selective Service in Peace and War.")

Ambrose, S. E., and J. A. Barber, Jr., eds. *The Military and American Society*. Free Press, 1972.

Aycock, W. B., and B. W. Wurfel. *Military Law Under the Uniform Code of Military Justice*. University of North Carolina, 1955.

Bachman, J. G., J. D. Blair, and D. R. Segal. *The All-Volunteer Force*. University of Washington, 1977.

Binkin, M., and S. J. Bach. *Women and the Military*. Brookings Institution, 1977.

Bishop. J. W., Jr. *Justice Under Fire: A Study of Military Law*. Charterhouse, 1974.

Corwin, E. S. *Total War and the Constitution*. Knopf, 1947.

Davis, J. W., Jr., and K. M. Dolbeare. *Little Groups of Neighbors: the Selective Service System*. Markham, 1968.

Edwards, M. O., and C. L. Decker. *The Serviceman and the Law*. Stackpole Books, 1951.

Everett, R. O. *Military Justice in the Armed Forces of the United States.* Military Service, 1956.

Feld, B. A. *A Manual of Courts: Martial Practice and Appeal.* Oceana, 1957.

Generous, W. T., Jr. *Swords and Scales: The Development of the Uniform Code of Military Justice.* Kennikat Press, 1973.

Goodpaster, A. J., et al. *Civil-Military Relations.* American Enterprise Institute, 1977.

Huntington, S. P. *The Soldier and the State.* Random House (Vintage Books), 1963.

Karsten, P. *Law, Soldiers, and Combat.* Greenwood Press, 1978.

Levantrossier, W. F. *Congress and the Citizen-Soldier: Legislative Policy Making for the Federal Armed Forces Reserve.* Ohio State University, 1968.

McNair, L. and A. D. Watts. *The Legal Effects of War.* 4th ed. Cambridge University, 1966.

Mayers, L. *The American Legal System* Rev. ed. Harper & Row, 1964.

Miller, J. C., III, ed. *Why the Draft? The Case for a Volunteer Army.* Penguin Books, 1968.

Millis, W. *The Constitution and the Common Defense.* Fund for the Republic, 1959.

Nofer, H. F. *American Servicemembers' Supreme Court.* University Press of America, 1982.

Pusey, M. J. *The Way We Go To War.* Houghton Mifflin, 1969.

Smith, L. *American Democracy and Military Power: A Study of Civil Control of the Military Power in the United States.* University of Chicago, 1951.

Sofaer, A. D. *War, Foreign Affairs and the Constitutional Power.* Ballinger, 1977.

Spanier, J. W. *The Truman-MacArthur Controversy and the Korean War.* Harvard University, 1959.

West, L. C. *They Call It Justice: Command Influence and the Court Martial System.* Viking Press, 1976.

Wiener, F. B. *The Uniform Code of Military Justice.* Combat Forces Press, 1950.

Yarmolinsky, A., ed. *The Military Establishment: Its Impact upon American Society.* Harper & Row, 1971.

PHILOSOPHICAL AND THEORETICAL ASPECTS OF LAW (JURISPRUDENCE)
(See also The Law.)

Anderson, W. R., ed. *Studies in Legal Philosophy.* Vanderbilt University Law School, 1961.

Arnold, T. W. *The Symbols of Government.* Yale University, 1935.

Association of the Bar of the City of New York. *Conflict of Interest and Federal Service.* Harvard University, 1960.

Aubert, V., ed. *Sociology of Law.* Penguin Books, 1969.

Bannan, J. F., and R. S. Bannan. *Law, Morality and Vietnam: The Peace Militants and the Courts.* Indiana University, 1974.

Benditt, T. M. *Law as Rule and Principle: Problems of Legal Philosophy.* Stanford University, 1978.

Berman, H. J. *Talks on American Law.* Random House, 1961.

——, and W. R. Greiner. *The Nature and Function of Law.* 3d ed. Foundation Press, 1972.

Beutel, F. K. *Some Potentialities of Experimental Jurisprudence as a New Branch of Social Science.* University of Nebraska, 1957.

Blackstone, W. *Commentaries on the Laws of England.* Oxford University, 1765–69; rpt. University of Chicago, 1979.

——. *Of Public Wrongs.* Beacon Press, 1963.

Bodenheimer, E. *Jurisprudence.* McGraw-Hill, 1947.

——. *Jurisprudence: The Philosophy and Method of the Law.* Harvard University, 1976.

Boorstin, D. J. *The Mysterious Science of the Law.* Beacon Press, 1963.

Brandt, R. B., ed. *The Concept of Social Science.* Prentice-Hall, 1962.

Bronaugh, R., ed. *Philosophical Law: Authority, Equality, Adjudication, Privacy.* Greenwood Press, 1978.

Brown, B. F., ed. *The Natural Law Reader.* Oceana, 1960.

Burgess, J. W. *Political Science and Comparative Constitutional Law*. Ginn, 1890.

———. *Recent Changes in American Constitutional Theory*. Columbia University, 1923.

Burin, F. S., and K. L. Shell, eds. *Politics, Law and Social Change: Selected Essays of Otto Kirchheimer*. Columbia University, 1969.

Cahill, F. V. *Judicial Legislation: A Study in American Legal Theory*. Ronald Press, 1952.

Cahn, E. *The Moral Decision: Right and Wrong in the Light of American Law*. 2d ed. Indiana University, 1959.

———, ed. *The Predicament of Democratic Man*. Macmillan, 1961.

———. *The Sense of Injustice*. New York University, 1951.

Cahn, L., ed. *Confronting Justice: The Edward Cahn Reader*. Little, Brown, 1966.

Cain, M., and A. Hunt. *Marx and Engels on Law*. Academic Press, 1980.

Calabresi, G. *Ideals, Beliefs, Attitudes, and the Law*. Syracuse University, 1985.

Calhoun, J. C. *A Disquisition on Government*. Appleton, 1854; rpt. Political Science Classics, 1947.

Cardozo, B. N. *The Growth of the Law*. Yale University, 1924.

———. *Law and Literature and Other Essays and Addresses*. Harcourt, Brace, 1931.

———. *The Nature of the Judicial Process*. Yale University, 1921.

———. *The Paradoxes of Legal Science*. Columbia University, 1928.

Carlin, J. E., J. Howard, and S. Messenger. *Civil Justice and the Poor*. Sage Publications, 1968.

Carpenter, W. S. *Foundations of Modern Jurisprudence*. Appleton-Century-Crofts, 1958.

Carter, L. H. *Reason in Law*. Little, Brown, 1979.

Chambliss, W. J., and R. B. Seidman. *Law, Order and Power*. Addison-Wesley, 1971.

———. *Sociology of the Law: A Research Bibliography*. Glendessary Press, 1970.

Christie, G. C. *Jurisprudence*. West, 1973.

Cohen, L. K., ed. *The Legal Conscience: Selected Papers of Felix S. Cohen*. Yale University, 1960.

Cohen, M., ed. *Donald Dworkin and Contemporary Jurisprudence*. Rowman & Allanheld, 1984.

Cohen, M. R. *Law and Social Order*. Harcourt, Brace, 1933.

———. *My Philosophy of Law*. West, 1941.

———. *Reason and Law*. Collier, 1961.

———. *Reason and Nature*. Harcourt, Brace, 1931.

Corwin, E. S. *Constitutional Revolution, Ltd*. Claremont, 1941.

———. *The Higher Law Background of American Constitutional Law*. Cornell University, 1929.

———. *The Twilight of the Supreme Court: A History of our Constitutional Theory*. Yale University, 1934.

Cowan, T., ed. *The American Jurisprudence Reader*. Oceana, 1955.

Currie, B. *Selected Essays on the Conflict of Laws*. Drake, 1963.

Curtis, C. P. *Law as Large as Life*. Simon and Schuster, 1959.

Dalzell, G. W. *Benefit of Clergy in America and Related Matters*. Blair, 1955.

D'Amato, A. *Jurisprudence: A Descriptive and Normative Analysis of Law*. Martinus Nijhoff, 1984.

Davis, K. C. *Discretionary Justice: A Preliminary Inquiry*. University of Illinois, 1972.

Davitt, T. B. *The Basic Values in Law*. American Philosophical Society, 1968.

D'Entrèves, A. P. *Natural Law*. 2d ed. Hutchinson, 1970.

Dias, R. M. W., and G. B. J. Hughes. *Jurisprudence*. Butterworth, 1957.

Dilliard, I., ed. *The Spirit of Liberty: Papers and Addresses of Learned Hand*. Knopf, 1959.

Durkheim, E. *The Division of Labor in Society*. Free Press, 1933.

Duster, T. *The Legislation of Morality*. Free Press, 1970.

Dworkin, R. M., ed. *The Philosophy of Law*. Oxford University, 1977.

Ehrenzweig, A. A. *Psychoanalytic Jurisprudence*. Oceana, 1971.

Ehrlich, E. *Fundamental Principles of the Sociology of Law*. Harvard University, 1936.

Einaudi, M. *The Physiocratic Doctrine of Judicial Control*. Harvard University, 1938.

Evan, W. M., ed. *Law and Sociology*. Free Press, 1962.

Feinberg, J. *Philosophy of Law*. Dickinson, 1975.

Fleming, M. *The Price of Perfect Justice*. Basic Books, 1974.

Frank, J. F. *Law and the Modern Mind*. 2d ed. Brentano's, 1949; rpt. Doubleday (Anchor Books), 1963.

Friedman, L., and S. Macaulay, eds. *Law and the Behavioral Sciences*. Bobbs-Merrill, 1969.

———, and B. Neuborne. *Unquestioning Obedience to the President*. Norton, 1972.

Friedman, L. M. *The Legal System: A Social Science Perspective*. Russell Sage Foundation, 1975.

Friedman, W. *Law in a Changing Society*. 2d ed. Penguin Books, 1972.

———. *Legal Theory*. 5th ed. Columbia University, 1967.

Friedrich, D. J., and J. W. Chapman, eds. *Justice*. Atherton, 1963.

———. *The Philosophy of Law in Historical Perspective*. 2d ed. University of Chicago, 1962.

———. *Transcendent Justice: The Religious Dimensions of Constitutionalism*. Duke University, 1963.

Fuchs, J. *Natural Law: A Theological Investigation*. Sheed and Ward, 1965.

Fuller, L. *Morality of Law*. Rev. ed. Yale University, 1969.

Gerhart, E. *American Liberty and National Law*. Beacon Press, 1953.

Gierke, O. von. *Natural Law and the Theory of Society*. Trans. E. Barker. Cambridge University, 1934; Beacon Press, 1963.

Ginsberg, M. *On Justice in Society*. Penguin Books, 1965.

Golding, M. P., ed. *The Nature of Law: Readings in Legal Philosophy*. Random House, 1966.

———. *Philosophy of Law*. Prentice-Hall, 1975.

Hacker, P. M. S., and J. Rax, eds. *Law, Morality, and Society: Essays in Honour of H. L. A. Hart*. Oxford University, 1977.

Haines, C. G. *The Revival of Natural Law Concepts*. Harvard University, 1930.

Hall, J. *Foundations of Jurisprudence*. Bobbs-Merrill, 1973.

———. *Readings in Jurisprudence*. Bobbs-Merrill, 1938.

Harding, A. L., ed. *The Administration of Justice in Retrospect*. Southern Methodist University, 1957.

Hare, J. I. C. *American Constitutional Law*. Brown, 1889.

Harris, R. W. *Justice: The Crisis of Law, Order, and Freedom in America*. Dutton, 1970.

Hart, H. L. A., ed. *Austin's The Problems of Jurisprudence Determined*. Oxford University, 1981.

———. *The Concept of Law*. Oxford University, 1961.

———. *Essays in Jurisprudence and Philosophy*. Oxford University, 1983.

Hartzler, H. R. *Justice, Legal Systems and Social Structure*. Kennikat Press, 1976.

Hayek, F. A. *Law, Legislation, and Liberty*. University of Chicago, 1973.

Henson, R. D., ed. *Landmarks of Law: Highlights of Legal Opinion from 1890 to the Present*. Harper, 1960.

Holcombe, A. N. *Our More Perfect Union: From 18th Century Principles to 20th Century Practice*. Harvard University, 1950.

Holmes, O. W. *The Common Law*. Little, Brown, 1881; rpt. Harvard University, 1963.

Hook S., ed. *Law and Philosophy: A Symposium*. New York University, 1964.

Hughes, G. *The Conscience of the Courts: Law and Morals in American Life*. Doubleday (Anchor Books), 1975.

Hunt, A. *The Sociological Movement in Law*. Temple University, 1978.

Hurst, J. W. *Law and Social Process in United States History*. University of Michigan, 1960.

Jackson, P. E., comp. *Justice and the Law*. Michie, 1964.

Jenkins, I. *Theory of Law and Legal Action*. Princeton University, 1980.

Kant, I. *The Metaphysical Principles of Justice*. Trans. John Ladd. Bobbs-Merrill, 1965.

Kamenka, E., R. Brown, and A. Ehr-soon Tay, eds. *Law and Society: The Crisis in Legal Ideals*. St. Martin's Press, 1978.

Kaplan, M. A. *Justice, Human Nature, and Political Obligation*. Free Press, 1977.

Kelsen, H. *General Theory of Law and State, Harvard University, 1945.*
———. *The Pure Theory of Law.* University of California, 1980.
———. *What Justice?* University of California, 1980.
Konvitz, M. R., ed. *Law and Social Action.* Cornell University, 1950.
Le Boutillier, C. *American Democracy and Natural Law.* Columbia University, 1950.
Lefcourt, R., ed. *Law Against the People: Essays to Demystify Law, Order and the Courts.* Random House, 1971.
Levi, E. H. *An Introduction to Legal Reasoning.* University of Chicago, 1949.
Levitt, M., and B. Rubenstein. *Orthopsychiatry and the Law.* Wayne State University, 1971.
Llewellyn, K. N. *The Bramble Bush.* Oceana, 1968.
———. *Jurisprudence: Realism in Theory and Practice.* University of Chicago, 1962.
Lloyd, D. ed. *Introduction to Jurisprudence.* Praeger, 1960.
Louthan, W. C. *Politics of Justice.* Kennikat Press, 1978.
McCloskey, R. C. *American Conservatism in the Age of Enterprise.* Harvard University, 1957.
McKinnon, H. R. *The Higher Law.* Gillick, 1946.
McIlwain, O. H. *The American Revolution: A Constitutional Interpretation.* Macmillan, 1928.
———. *Constitutionalism, Ancient and Modern.* Rev. ed. Cornell University, 1947.
———. *Constitutionalism and the Changing World.* Macmillan, 1939.
Maritain, J. *Man and the State.* Univerity of Chicago, 1951.
———. *The Rights of Man and Natural Law.* Centenary Press, 1958.
Marshall, J. *Intention in Law and Society.* Funk & Wagnalls, 1968.
Mason, A. T., and R. R. Leach. *In Quest of Freedom: American Political Thought and Practice.* Prentice-Hall, 1959.
Moore, R. G. *Stare Decisis.* Simmons-Boardman, 1958.
Morris, C., ed. *The Great Legal Philosophers: Selected Readings in Jurisprudence.* Rev. ed. University of Pennsylvania, 1971.
———. *The Justification of the Law.* University of Pennsylvania, 1971.
Mullin, O. *In Quest of Justice.* University of Minnesota, 1931.
Murphy, J. G., and J. L. Coleman. *The Philosophy of Law: An Introduction to Jurisprudence.* Rowman & Allenheld, 1984.
Nader, L., ed. *Law in Culture and Society.* University of California, 1971.
Nagel, S. S. *Law and Social Change.* Sage Publications, 1970.
Nejelski, P. *Social Research In Conflict with Law and Ethics.* Ballinger, 1977.
Newman, R. E., ed. *Essays in Jurisprudence in Honor of Roscoe Pound.* Greenwood Press, 1973.
Nice, R. W. ed. *Treasury of Law.* Philosophical Library, 1965.
Noonan, J. T., Jr. *Persons and Masks of the Law.* Farrar, Straus & Giroux, 1976.
Northrup, F. C. S. *The Complexity of Legal and Ethical Experience.* Little, Brown, 1959.
Olafson, F. A., ed. *Justice and Social Policy.* Prentice-Hall, 1965.
———. *Society, Law, and Morality.* Prentice-Hall, 1961.
Paton, G. W., and D. P. Durham, eds. *A Textbook of Jurisprudence.* 4th ed. Oxford University, 1972.
Patterson, C. P. *Constitutional Principles of Thomas Jefferson.* University of Texas, 1953.
Patterson, E. S. *Jurisprudence.* Foundation Press, 1953.
Paul, A. M. *The Conservative Crisis and the Rule of Law.* 2d ed. Harper & Row, 1969.
Paul, J. *The Legal Realism of Jerome N. Frank: A Study of Fact-Skepticism and the Judicial Process.* Martinus Nijhoff, 1959.
Petrazycke, L. J. *Law and Morality.* Harvard University, 1955.
Pollack, E. H. *Jurisprudence: Principles and Applications.* Ohio State University, 1977.
Pollack, Sir F. *Essays in the Law.* Macmillan, 1922.
———. *Jurisprudence and Legal Essays.* St. Martin's Press, 1961.
Posner, R. A. *An Economic Analysis of Law.* Little, Brown, 1977.
Pound, R. *Contemporary Juristic Theory.* Claremont, 1940.
———. *Interpretations of Legal History.* Harvard University, 1946.

————. *An Introduction to the Philosophy of Law.* Rev. ed. Yale University, 1959.

————. *The Future of the Common Law.* Harvard University, 1937.

————. *Justice According to Law.* Yale University, 1951.

————. *Law and Morals.* University of North Carolina, 1924.

————. *Law Finding Through Experience and Reason.* University of Georgia, 1960.

————. *New Paths of the Law.* University of Nebraska, 1950.

————. *Social Control Through Law.* Yale University, 1942.

————. *The Spirit of the Common Law.* Marshall, Ones, 1931; rpt. Beacon Press, 1963.

————. *The Task of Law.* Franklin and Marshall College, 1944.

Radin, M. *The Law as Logic and Experience.* Yale University, 1940.

Rawls, J. *A Theory of Justice.* Harvard University, 1957.

Reagan, R. *Private Conscience and Public Law: The American Experience.* Fordham University, 1972.

Reuschlein, H. G. *Jurisprudence—Its Prophets: A Survey of Taught Jurisprudence.* Greenwood Press, 1951.

Robson, W. S. *Civilization and the Growth of Law.* Macmillan, 1935.

Rodes, R. E., Jr. *The Legal Enterprise.* Kennikat Press, 1976.

Rommen, H. A. *The Natural Law.* Herder, 1947.

Ross, A. *On Law and Justice.* Stevens, 1959.

————. *Towards a Realistic Jurisprudence.* Munksgaard, 1946.

Rossiter, C. L. *Seedtime of the Republic.* Harcourt, Brace, 1953.

Rostow, E. V. *The Ideal in Law.* University of Chicago, 1978.

————. *The Sovereign Prerogative: The Supreme Court and the Quest for Law.* Yale University, 1962.

Rumble, W. E., Jr. *American Legal Realism: Skepticism, Reform, and the Judicial Process.* Cornell University, 1968.

Saks, M. J., and R. Hastie. *Social Psychology in Court.* Van Nostrand, 1978.

Salmond, J. W. *Jurisprudence.* 3d ed. Stevens & Haynes, 1910.

Sawer, G. *Law in Society.* Oxford University, 1965.

Schubert, G. *Human Jurisprudence: Public Law as Political Science.* University of Hawaii, 1975.

Selznick, P. *Law, Society, and Industrial Justice.* 2d ed. Transaction Books, 1978.

Shientag, B. L. *Moulders of Legal Thought.* Kennikat Press, 1943.

Sholar, J. N. *Legalism.* Harvard University, 1964.

Shuman, S. I. *Legal Positivism: Its Scope and Limitations.* Wayne State University, 1963.

Simon, R. J. *The Sociology of Law.* Chandler, 1968.

Simon, Y. R. *The Tradition of Natural Law.* Fordham University, 1965.

Simpson, S. P., and J. Stone. *Law and Society.* West, 1948–49.

Smith, A. *Lectures on Jurisprudence.* Ed. R. L. Meek, D. D. Raphael, and P. G. Stein. Oxford University, 1977.

Smith, J. A. *The Spirit of American Government.* Macmillan, 1907.

Stone, J. *Human Law and Human Justice.* Stanford University, 1966.

————. *Law and the Social Sciences in the Second Half Century.* University of Minnesota, 1966.

————. *Legal Systems and Lawyers' Reasonings.* Stanford University. 1964.

————. *The Province and Function of Law.* Harvard University, 1950.

————. *Social Dimensions of Law and Justice.* Stanford University, 1966.

Strauss, L. *Natural Right and History.* University of Chicago, 1953.

Strieb, V. I. *Juvenile Justice in America.* Kennikat Press, 1978.

Summers, R., ed. *Essays in Legal Philosophy.* University of California, 1968.

————. *More Essays in Legal Philosophy.* University of California, 1971.

Sutherland, A. E., ed. *Government Under Law.* Harvard University, 1956.

————. *The Law and One Man Among Many.* University of Wisconsin, 1956.

Tapp, J. L., and F. J. Levine. *Law, Justice and the Individual in Society: Psychological and Legal Issues.* Holt, Rinehart and Winston, 1977.

Taylor, T. *Perspectives on Justice.* Northwestern University, 1975.

Thoreau, H. D. *Walden and Civil Disobedience.* Washington Square Press, 1967.

Tiedman, C. G. *The Unwritten Constitution of the United States.* Putnam, 1890.

Timasheff, N. S. *An Introduction to the Sociology of Law.* Harvard University, 1939.

Tocqueville, A. de. *Democracy in America.* H. G. Langley, 1841.

Toulmin, S. *The Place of Reason in Ethics.* Cambridge University, 1953.

Tuck, R. *Natural Rights Theories: Their Origin and Development.* Cambridge University, 1980.

Tullock G. *The Logic of the Law.* Basic Books, 1971.

Unger, R. M. *Law in Modern Society: Toward a Criticism of Social Theory.* Free Press, 1977.

University of Notre Dame. *Natural Law Institute Proceedings.* University of Notre Dame, 1947–51.

Vinogradoff, P. *Common Sense in Law.* 3d ed. Oxford University, 1949.

———. *Outlines of Historical Jurisprudence.* Oxford Unviersity, 1920.

Von Moschzisher, R. *Stare Decisis, Res Judicata, and Other Essays.* Cyrus Dixon, 1929.

Wasserstrom, R. A. *The Judicial Decision: Toward a Theory of Legal Justification.* Stanford University, 1961.

Weber, M. *Max Weber on Law in Economy and Society.* Harvard University, 1954.

Wharton, F. *Commentaries on Law.* Kay, 1884.

Whitehead. A. N. *Symbolism.* Macmillan, 1927.

Wigdor, D. *Roscoe Pound: Philosopher of Law.* Greenwood Press, 1974.

Wormuth, F. D. *Essays in Law and Politics.* Kennikat Press, 1978.

———. *The Origins of Modern Constitutionalism.* Harper, 1949.

Wright, B. F. *American Interpretations of Natural Law.* Harvard University, 1931.

Wu, J. C. H. *Foundation of Justice.* Sheed and Ward, 1959.

Zelermyer, W. *The Process of Legal Reasoning.* Prentice-Hall, 1963.

THE PRESIDENCY

(The executive organ of the United States government: A branch in the separation of powers of our national government.)
(See also The Congress)

Abraham, H. J. *Justices and Presidents: A Political History of Appointments to the Supreme Court.* 2d ed. Oxford University, 1985.

Alley, R. S. *So Help Me God: Religion and the Presidency.* Knox Press, 1972.

American Civil Liberties Union. *Why President Nixon Should be Impeached.* American Civil Liberties Union, 1974.

AFL-CIO. *Why Richard M. Nixon Must Be Impeached.* AFL-CIO, 1974.

Americans for Democratic Action. *The Case for Impeachment.* ADA, 1974.

Bach, S., and G. T. Sulzner. *Perspectives on the Presidency: A Collection.* Heath, 1964.

Bailey, H. A., Jr., ed. *Classics of the American Presidency.* Moore, 1980.

Ball, H. *No Pledge of Privacy: The Watergate Tapes Litigation, 1973–1974.* Kennikat Press, 1977.

Barber, J. D. *The Presidential Character.* Prentice-Hall, 1973.

Barger, H. M. *The Impossible Presidency: Illusions and Realities of Executive Power.* Scott, Foresman, 1984.

Benedict, M. L. *The Impeachment and Trial of Andrew Johnson.* Norton, 1973.

Ben-Veniste, R., and G. Frampton, Jr. *Stonewall: The Real Story of the Watergate Prosecution.* Simon and Schuster, 1977.

Berger, R. *Executive Privilege: A Consititutional Myth.* Harvard University, 1974.

———. *Impeachment: The Constitutional Problem.* Harvard University, 1973.

Bernstein, C., and B. Woodward. *All the President's Men.* Simon and Schuster, 1974.

Bessette, J. M., and J. Tulis, eds. *The Presidency in the Constitutional Order.* Louisiana State University, 1981.

Binkley, W. E. *The Powers of the President.* Russell & Russell, 1937.

———. *President and Congress.* 3d rev ed. Knopf. 1962.

Black, C. L., Jr. *Impeachment: A Handbook.* Yale University, 1974.

Brant, I. *Impeachment: Trials and Errors.* Knopf, 1972.

Breckenridge, A. C. *The Executive Privilege: Presidential Control over Information.* University of Nebraska, 1974.

———. *The Power to Lead: The Crisis of the American Presidency.* Simon and Schuster, 1984.

Burns, J. M. *Presidential Government: The Crucibile of Leadership.* Houghton Mifflin, 1973.

———. *The Power to Lead: The Crisis of the American Presidency.* Simon and Schuster, 1984.

Ceaser, J. W. Presidential Election Theory and Development. Princeton University, 1979.

Commager, H. S. *The Defeat of America: Presidential Power and the National Character.* Simon and Schuster, 1975.

Congressional Quarterly. *Impeachment.* Congressional Quarterly Press, 1974.

———. *Impeachment and the United States Congress.* Congressional Quarterly Press, 1975.

Corwin, E. S. *The President: Office and Powers.* 5th ed. New York University, 1984.

———. *Total War and the Constitution.* Knopf, 1947.

Cotter, C. P., and J. M. Smith. *Powers of the President During National Crisis.* Public Affairs Press, 1959.

Cronin, T. E., ed. *The Presidential Advisor System.* Harper & Row, 1969.

———. *The State of the Presidency.* 2d ed. Little, Brown, 1981.

———, and R. G. Tugwell. *The Presidency Reappraised.* 2d ed. Praeger, 1977.

D'Amato, A. A., and R. M. O'Neil. *The Judiciary and Vietnam.* St. Martin's Press, 1972.

Davis, V., ed. *The Post-Imperial Presidency.* Transaction Books, 1980.

Dewitt, D. M. *The Impeachment and Trial of Andrew Johnson.* Russell & Russell, 1902.

DiClerico, R. E. *The American President.* Prentice-Hall, 1979.

Dobrovir, W. A. *The Offenses of Richard M. Nixon: A Lawyer's Guide for the People of the United States of America.* Ziff, 1974.

Dolce, P. C., and G. H. Skau, eds. *Power and the Presidency.* Scribner, 1976.

Doyle, J. *Not Above the Law: The Battles of Watergate Prosecutors Cox and Jaworski.* Morrow, 1977.

Eagleton, T. A. *War and Presidential Power.* Liveright, 1974.

Egger, R. *The President of the United States.* 2d ed. McGraw-Hill, 1972.

———, and J. P. Harris. *The President and Congress.* McGraw-Hill, 1963.

Ehrlich, W. *Presidential Impeachment: An American Dilemma.* Forum Press, 1974.

Feerick, J. D. *From Failing Hands: The Story of Presidential Succession.* Fordham University, 1965.

Finer, H. *The Presidency: Crisis and Regeneration.* University of Chicago, 1973.

Finley, J., and J. Sanderson. *The American Executive and Executive Methods.* Century, 1908.

Fisher, L. *Constitutional Conflicts Between Congress and the President.* Congressional Quarterly Press, 1985.

———. *The Constitution Between Friends: Congress, the President, and the Law.* St. Martin's Press, 1978.

———. *The Politics of Shared Power: Congress and the Executive.* Congressional Quarterly Press, 1981.

———. *President and Congress: Power and Policy.* Free Press, 1972.

Friedman, L., ed. *United States v. Nixon: The President Before the Supreme Court.* Bowker, 1974.

Genovese, M. A. *The Supreme Court, the Constitution, and Presidential Power.* University Press of America, 1980.

Gilbert, A. M. *Executive Agreements and Treaties, 1946–1973.* Thomas-Newell, 1973.

Glick, H. R. *Courts, Politics, and Justice.* McGraw-Hill, 1982.

Goldsmith, W. M. *The Growth of Presidential Power: A Documented History.* Bowker, 1975.

Greenstein, F. I. *The Hidden-Hand Presidency: Eisenhower as Leader.* Basic Books, 1982.

Grundstein, N. D. *Presidential Delegation of Authority in Wartime.* University of Pittsburgh, 1961.

Griffith, E. S. *The American Presidency: The Dilemma of Shared Power and Divided Government.* New York University, 1976.

Haight, D., and L. Johnson, eds. *The Presidency.* St Martin's Press, 1967.

———. *The Presidency: Roles and Powers.* Rand McNally, 1965.

Halperin, M., and D. N. Hoffman. *Governmental Secrecy and the Founding Fathers.* New Republic Books, 1977.

Hardin, C. M. *Presidential Power and Accountability.* University of Chicago, 1974.

Hargrove, E. C. *The Power of the Modern Presidency.* Random House, 1974.

Hart, J. *The Ordinance Making Powers of the President of the United States.* Johns Hopkins University, 1925.

———. *The Presidential Branch.* Pergamon Press, 1985.

Hecht, M. B. *Beyond the Presidency: The Residues of Power.* Macmillan, 1976.

Heller, F. H., ed. *The Truman White House: The Administration of the Presidency, 1945–1953.* University of Kansas, 1980.

Henkin, L. *Foreign Affairs and the Constitution.* Foundation Press, 1973.

Hess, S. *Organizing the Presidency.* Brookings Institution, 1976.

Hirschfield, R. S., ed. *The Power of the Presidency.* 3d ed. Aldine, 1982.

Hoffman, D. N. *Governmental Secrecy and the Founding Fathers.* Greenwood Press, 1981.

Hoxie, R. G. *Command Decision and the Presidency.* Reader's Digest Press, 1977.

Hoy, J. C., and M. H. Bernstein, eds. *The Effective President.* Palisades, 1976.

Hughes, E. J. *The Living Presidency.* Coward, McCann & Geoghegan, 1973.

Humbert. W. H. *The Pardoning Power of the President.* American Council on Public Affairs, 1941.

Hurst, J. W. *The Growth of American Law: The Lawmakers.* Little Brown, 1974.

James, D. B. *The Contemporary Presidency.* 2d ed. Bobbs-Merrill, 1974.

Jaworski, L. *The Right and the Power.* Crowell, 1976.

Jensen, C. *The Pardoning Power in the American States.* University of Chicago, 1922.

Kallenbach, J. E. *The American Chief Executive.* Harper & Row, 1966.

Koenig, L. W. *The Chief Executive.* 4th ed. Harcourt Brace Jovanovich, 1984.

———. *The President and the Crisis: Powers of the Office from the Invasion of Poland to Pearl Harbor.* King Crown, 1944.

Kurland, P. B. *Watergate and the Constitution.* University of Chicago, 1978.

Labovitz, J. R. *Presidential Impeachment.* Yale University, 1978.

Latham, E. *Kennedy and Presidential Power.* Heath, 1972.

Learned, H. B. *The President's Cabinet.* Yale University, 1912.

Loss, R., ed. *Presidential Power and the Constitution: Essays by Edward S. Corwin.* Cornell University, 1976.

Lurie, L. *The Impeachment of Richard Nixon.* Berkley Publishing Co., 1973.

McConnell, G. *The Modern Presidency.* 2d ed. St. Martin's Press, 1976.

———. *The President Seizes the Steel Mills.* University of Alabama, 1960.

———. *Steel and the Presidency, 1962.* Norton, 1963.

McKay, R. B., ed. *The American Constitutional Law Reader.* Oceana, 1958.

Mankiewicz, F. *U.S. v. Richard M. Nixon: The Final Crisis.* Quadrangle, 1975.

Marcus, M. *Truman and the Steel Seizure Case: The Limits of Presidential Power.* Columbia University, 1977.

Mason, A. T., and W. B. Beaney. *The Supreme Court in a Free Society.* Prentice-Hall, 1959.

May, E. R. *The Ultimate Decision: The President as Commander in Chief.* Braziller, 1960.

Merry, H. J. *Constitutional Function of Presidential-Administrative Separation.* University Press of America, 1978.

Miller, A. S. *Presidential Power in a Nutshell.* West, 1977.

Mondale, W. F. *The Accountability of Power: Toward a Responsible Presidency.* McKay, 1975.

Morgan, R. P. *The President and Civil Rights.* St Martin's Press, 1970.

Mosler, P., ed. *Judicial Protection Against the Executive.* Oceana, 1972.

Mullen, W. F. *Presidential Power and Politics.* St Martin's Press, 1970.

Murphy, J. F. *The Pinnacle: The Contemporary American Presidency.* Lippincott, 1974.

Nathan, R. P. *The Administrative Presidency.* Wiley, 1983.

———. *The Plot that Failed: Nixon and the Administrative Presidency.* Wiley, 1975.

Nelson, M. *The Presidency and the Political System.* Congressional Quarterly Press, 1984.

New York Times. *The Assassination of a President.* Viking Press, 1964.

Neustadt, R. E. *Presidential Power: The Politics of Leadership from FDR to Carter.* Wiley, 1980.

Nixon, R. M. *RN: The Memoirs of Richard Nixon.* Grosset & Dunlap, 1978.

Orman, J. M. *Presidential Secrecy and Deception.* Greenwood Press, 1980.

Page, B. I., and M. Petracca. *The American Presidency.* McGraw-Hill, 1982.

Pious, R. M. *The American Presidency.* Basic Books, 1979.

Polsby, N. W. *Congress and the Presidency.* 3d ed. Prentice-Hall, 1976.

Pusey, M. N. *The Way We Go to War.* Houghton Mifflin, 1969.

Randall, J. C. *Constitutional Problems Under Lincoln.* Rev. ed. University of Delaware, 1956; rpt. University of Illinois, 1964.

Rankin, R. S., and W. R. Lallmayr. *Freedom and Emergency Powers in the Cold War.* Appleton-Century-Crofts, 1964.

Reedy, G. E. *The Presidency in Flux.* Columbia University, 1972.

———. *The Twilight of the Presidency.* Mentor Books, 1971.

Reveley, W. J., III. *War Powers of the President and Congress.* University of Virginia, 1981.

Rich, B. N. *The President and Civil Disorder.* Brookings Institution, 1941.

Roscoe Pound-American Trial Lawyers Foundation. *The Power of the Presidency.* RPTLF, 1977.

Rosenman, S., and D. Rosenman. *Presidential Style: Some Giants and A Pygmy in the White House.* Harper & Row, 1976.

Rossiter, C. L. *The American Presidency.* Rev. ed. New American Library (Mentor Books), 1960.

———. *Constitutional Dictatorship: Crisis Government in the Modern Democracies.* Princeton University, 1948.

———. *The Supreme Court and the Commander-in-Chief.* Rev. ed. Cornell University, 1976.

Schaffter, D., and D. Matheus. *The Powers of the President as Commander-in-Chief of the Army and Navy of the United States.* Da Capo Press, 1971.

Schandler, H. Y. *The Unmaking of a President: Lyndon Johnson and Vietnam.* Princeton University, 1977.

Schlesinger, A. M., Jr. *The Imperial Presidency.* Houghton Mifflin, 1973.

Schnapper, M. B., ed. *Conscience of the Nation: The People Versus Richard M. Nixon.* Public Affairs Press, 1974.

Schubert, G. A. *The Presidency in the Courts.* University of Minnesota, 1957.

Scigliano, R. *The Supreme Court and the Presidency.* Free Press, 1970.

Sego, M. A. *The Issues of Watergate.* Regal Books, 1974.

Seymour-Ure, C. *The American President: Power and Communication.* St. Martin's Press, 1982.

Shull, S. A. *Presidential Policy Making: An Analysis.* King's Court. 1979.

Sickles, R. J. *The Presidency: An Introduction.* Prentice-Hall, 1980.

Simpson, A. *A Treatise on Federal Impeachments.* Philadelphia Bar Association, 1916.

Sirica, J. J. *To Set the Record Straight.* Norton, 1979.

Small, N. J. *Some Presidential Interpretations of the Presidency.* Johns Hopkins University, 1932; rpt. Da Capo Press, 1970.

Smith, G. *High Crimes and Misdemeanors: The Impeachment and Trial of Andrew Johnson.* Morrow, 1977.

Smith, N. J., and C. P. Cotter. *Powers of the President During Crisis.* Public Affairs Press, 1960.

Sorensen, T. C. *Watchmen in the Night: Presidential Accountability and Watergate.* MIT, 1975.

Spangler, E. *Presidential Tenure and Constitutional Limitation.* University Press of America, 1977.

Spragens, W. C. *The Presidency and the Mass Media in the Age of Television.* University Press of America, 1978.

Taft, W. H. *Our Chief Magistrate and His Powers.* Columbia University, 1916.

Thach, C. C., Jr. *The Creation of the Presidency, 1775–1789: A Study in Constitutional History.* Johns Hopkins University, 1923, 1969.

Thomas, A. V. W., and A. J. Thomas, Jr. *War-Making Powers of the President: Constitutional and International Law Aspects.* Southern Methodist University, 1982.

Thomas, N., and H. W. Baade. *The Institutionalized Presidency.* Oceana, 1972.

Thompson, K. W. *The President and the Public Philosophy.* Lousisana State University, 1983.

Tourtellot, A. B. *The Presidents and the Presidency.* Russell & Russell, 1964.

Tugwell, R. G., and T. E. Cronin. *The Presidency Reappraised.* Praeger, 1974.

U.S. House of Representatives. Committee on the Judiciary. *Impeachment: Selected Materials.* Superintendent of Documents, 1975.

———. *Impeachment Inquiry. Superintendent of Documents, 1975.*

Vinyard, D. *The Presidency.* Scribner, 1971.

Wayne, S. J. *The Legislative Presidency.* Harper & Row, 1978.

Westin, A. F. *Anatomy of a Constitutional Law Case.* Macmillan, 1958.

White, T. H. *Breach of Faith: The Fall of Richard Nixon.* Atheneum, 1975.

Wildavsky, A. *Perspectives on the Presidency.* Little, Brown, 1975.

Winter, R. K., Jr. *Watergate and the Law: Political Campaigns and Presidential Power.* American Enterprise Institute, 1974.

Wolk, A. *The Presidency and Black Civil Rights: Eisenhower to Nixon.* Fairleigh Dickinson University, 1971.

Woodward, B., and C. Bernstein. *All the President's Men.* Simon and Schuster, 1975.

———. *The Final Days.* Simon and Schuster, 1976.

PROCEDURE IN THE COURTS
(See also *The Legal Profession*)

Adams, E. *Courts and Computers.* American Judicature Society, 1972.

Alfini, J. J., and G. R. Winters, comps. and eds. *Selected Readings on Courtroom Design.* American Judicature Society, 1973.

American Bar Association. *The Improvement of the Administration of Justice: A Handbook.* 4th ed. ABA, 1961.

Annual Reports of the Director of the Administrative Office of the United States Courts. Government Printing Office.

Bailey, F. L., and J. Greenya. *For the Defense.* Atheneum, 1975.

Balbus, I. D. *The Dialectics of Legal Repression: Black Rebels Before the American Criminal Courts.* 2d ed. Transaction Books, 1977.

Barron, W. W., and A. Holtzoff, *Federal Practice and Procedure.* Thompson, 1950–58.

Bennett, W. L., and M. S. Feldman. *Reconstructing Reality in the Courtroom.* Rutgers University, 1981.

Berkson, L. C., S. W. Hays, and S. C. Carbon, eds. *Managing the State Courts: Text and Readings.* West, 1977.

Borchard, E. M. *Convicting the Innocent.* Yale University, 1932.

Buckle, S. R. T., and L. G. Buckle. *Bargaining for Justice: Case Disposition and Reform in the Criminal Courts.* Praeger, 1977.

Bureau of Municipal Research. *The Magistrate Courts of Philadelphia.* Rev. ed. Pennsylvania Economy League, 1958.

Bush, F. X. *Law and Tactics in Jury Trials.* Bobbs-Merrill, 1963.

Callendar, C. N. *American Courts: Their Organization and Procedure.* McGraw-Hill, 1927.

Clark, R. *Contempt.* Ohio University (Swallow Press), 1970.

Cohen, M. L. *Legal Research in a Nutshell.* 2d ed. West, 1971.

Dangel, E. M. *Contempt.* National Lawyers Manual, 1939.

Davenport, W. H., ed. *Voices in Court.* Macmillan, 1958.

Doble, A. M. *Handbook of Federal Jurisdiction and Procedure.* West, 1928.

Dolbeare, K. M. *Trial Courts in Urban Politics: State Court Policy Impact and Functions in a Local Political System.* Wiley, 1967.

Douglas, W. O. *Stare Decisis.* Association of Bar of City of New York, 1949.

Drechsel, R. E. *Newsmaking in the Trial Courts.* Longman, 1983.

Early, S. T., Jr. *Constitutional Courts of the United States.* Littlefield, Adams, 1976.

Eisenstein, J., and H. Jacob. *Felony Justice: An Organizational Analysis of Criminal Courts.* Little, Brown, 1976.

Epstein, L. *Conservatives in Court.* University of Tennessee, 1985.

Feeley, M. M. *The Process is the Punishment: Handling Cases in a Lower Criminal Court.* Bank, 1979.

Finns, N. O. *Federal Jurisdiction and Procedure.* Bobbs-Merrill, 1960.

Fiss, O. M. *The Civil Rights Injunction.* Indiana University, 1978.

Fleming, M. *The Price of Perfect Justice.* Basic Books, 1974.

Foster, G. W., Jr. *The Status of Class Action Litigation.* American Bar Foundation, 1974.

Fox, J. C. *The History of Contempt of Court.* Oxford University, 1927.

Fox, S. J. *Juvenile Courts in a Nutshell.* West, 1971.

Frank, J. F. *Courts on Trial.* Princeton University, 1959.

———, and B. Frank. *Not Guilty.* Doubleday, 1957.

Gavit, B. C. *Procedure in State Courts.* Practicing Law Institute, 1946.

Glaser, W. A. *Pretrial Discovery and the Adversary System.* Sage Publications, 1969.

Goldfarb, R. L. *The Contempt Power.* Rev. ed. Doubleday, 1971.

Goldman, J. *Ineffective Justice: Evaluating the Pre-Appeal Conference.* Sage Publications, 1980.

Goldstein, A. S. *The Insanity Defense.* Yale University, 1967.

———. *The Passive Judiciary: Prosecutorial Discretion and the Guilty Plea.* Louisiana State University, 1982.

Grau, C. *Judicial Rolemaking: Administration, Access and Accountability.* American Judicature Society, 1978.

Gressman, B., and R. L. Stern. *Supreme Court Practice.* 4th ed. Washington Bureau of National Affairs, 1969.

Grey, D. L. *The Supreme Court and the News Media.* Northwestern University, 1968.

Hall, L., and Y. Kamisar. *Modern Criminal Procedure.* West, 1965.

Harding, A. L., ed. *The Administration of Justice in Retrospect.* Southern Methodist University, 1957.

Hart, H. M., Jr., and H. Wechsler. *The Judicial Code and Rules of Procedure in the Federal Courts.* Foundation Press, 1954.

Heumann, M. *Plea Bargaining: The Experiences of Prosecutors, Judges, and Defense Attorneys.* University of Chicago, 1978.

Jacob, H. *Debtors in Court.* Rand McNally, 1969.

James, P. *Criminal Procedure.* Little, Brown, 1965.

Karlen, D. *The Citizen in Court: Litigant, Witness, Juror, Judge*. Holt, Rinehart and Winston, 1964.

———. *Judicial Administration: The American Experience*. Oceana, 1970.

———. *Primer on Procedure*. Campus, 1950.

Klein, J. F. *Let's Make a Deal*. Heath, 1976.

Korbaken, C. A., J. J. Alfini, and C. W. Grau. *Judicial Rulemaking in the State Courts: A Compendium*. American Judicature Society, 1978.

Kunstler, W. M. *First Degree*. Oceana, 1970.

Laurent, F. W. *The Business of a Trial Court*. University of Wisconsin, 1959.

Leavitt, M. R. *Calen 9: A Calendaring and Assignment System for Court of Appeals*. Federal Judiciary Center, 1978.

Leflar, R. A. *Internal Operating Procedures of Appellate Courts*. American Bar Foundation, 1977.

Llewellyn, K. N. *The Common Law Tradition: Deciding Appeals*. Little, Brown, 1960.

Loftus, E. F. *Eyewitness Testimony*. Harvard University, 1980.

McCarty, D. G. *Psychology for the Lawyer*. Prentice-Hall, 1929.

MacDougal, C. D. *Covering the Courts*. Prentice-Hall, 1946.

McLaughlan, W. P. *American Legal Processes*. Wiley, 1977.

———. *Federal Court Caseloads*. Praeger, 1983.

Marvell, T. B. *Appellate Courts and Lawyers: Information Gathering in the Adversary System*. Greenwood Press, 1978.

Matthews, P. *How to Try a Criminal Case*. Dennis, 1960.

Meador, D. J. *English Practices and American Reforms*. University of Virginia, 1973.

Moldovsky, J., and R. DeWolf. *The Best Defense*. Macmillan, 1975.

Moore, R. F. *Stare Decisis*. Simmons-Boardman, 1958.

Munsterberg, H. *On the Witness Stand*. Simmons-Boardman, 1925.

Newman, R. P., and D. R. Newman. *Evidence*. Houghton Mifflin, 1970.

Osthus, M. O. *Intermediate Appellate Courts*. American Judicature Society, 1973.

———, and R. A. Shapiro. *Congestion and Delay in the State Appellate Courts*. American Judicature Society, 1974.

Oswald, J. F. *Contempt of Court*. Butterworth, 1911.

Peck, D. A. *Decision at Law*. Dodd, Mead, 1961; rpt. Simon and Schuster (Cornerstone Library), 1963.

Perkins, R. M. *Cases on Criminal Law and Procedure*. Foundation Press, 1959.

Porter, E. S. *Conscience of the Court*. Prentice-Hall, 1962.

Pound, R. *Appellate Procedure in Civil Cases*. Little, Brown, 1941.

Robertson, J. A. *Rough Justice: Perspectives on Lower Criminal Courts*. Little, Brown, 1975.

Rose, J. C. *Jurisdiction and Procedures of Federal Courts*. Bender, 1938.

Rosenberg, M. *The Pretrial Conference and Effective Justice*. Columbia University, 1965.

Rosett, A., and D. R. Cressey. *Justice by Consent: Plea Bargaining*. Lippincott, 1976.

Rovner-Pieczenik, R. *Pretrial Intervention Strategies*. Lexington Books, 1976.

Saari, D. J. *American Court Management: Theories and Practices*. Greenwood Press (Quorum Books), 1982.

St. John, A. R. *Final Verdict*. Doubleday, 1962.

Spurrier, R. L., Jr. *Inexpensive Justice: Self-Representation in the Small Claims Court*. Kennikat Press, 1980.

Strick, A. *With Injustice for All*. Putnam, 1977.

Stryker, L. P. *The Art of Advocacy*. Charles Evans Hughes Press, 1979.

———. *Courts and Doctors*. Macmillan, 1932.

Taylor, G. C. *Fifty Years in the Law*. Philosophical Library, 1963.

Thomas, C. H. *Problems of Contempt of Court*. Horn-Shafer, 1943.

Thompson, D. C. *Court Organization and Administration: A Bibliography*. Institute of Governmental Studies, 1973.

Tierney, K. *How To Be a Witness*. Oceana, 1971.

Uhlman, T. M. *Racial Justice: Black Judges and Defendants in an Urban Trial Court*. Lexington Books, 1979.

Vanderbilt, A. T. *Cases and Other Materials on Modern Procedure and Judicial Administration*. Washington Square Press, 1952.

———. *Men and Measures in the Law*. Knopf, 1949.

Von Moschzisker, R. *Stare Decisis, Res Judicata, and Other Essarys*. Cyrus Dixon, 1929.

Weaver, S. *Decision to Prosecute*. MIT, 1979.

Wheeler, R. R. and H. R. Whitcomb, eds. *Judicial Administration: Text and Readings*. Prentice-Hall, 1977.

Wood, M. L. and R. Kast, eds. *Court Studies: An Annotated Bibliography*. American Judicature Society, 1976.

Wright, B. F. *Federal Courts*. West, 1963.

Zeisel, H., H. Kalven, Jr. and B. Buchholz. *Delay in the Court*. Little, Brown, 1959.

Zelermyer, W. *The Legal System in Operation*. West, 1977.

REFORMS

(Discussion of change in the Constitution and the courts.)

Alsop, J. and T. Cartledge. *The 168 Days*. Doubleday, 1938.

American Bar Association. *The Improvement of the Administration of Justice*. ABA, 1971.

Association of the Bar of the City of New York. *Conflict of Interest and Federal Service*. Harvard University, 1960.

Baker, L. *Back to Back: The Struggle Between FDR and the Supreme Court*. Macmillan, 1967.

Bureau of Municipal Research. *The Magistrate Courts of Philadelphia*. Rev. ed. Pennsylvania Economy League, 1958.

Carr, W. S. *A Selected Chronology and Bibliography of Court Organization and Reform*. American Judicature Society, 1970.

Cohn, R. G. *To Judge With Justice: History and Politics of Illinois Judicial Reform*. University of Illinois, 1973.

Downie, L., Jr. *Justice Denied: The Case for Reform of the Courts*. Praeger, 1971.

Dubois, P. L., ed. *The Analysis of Judicial Reform*. Lexington Books, 1982.

———. *The Policy of Judicial Reform*. Lexington Books, 1982.

Elliot, W. Y. *The Need for Constitutional Reform* Whittlesey House, 1935.

Empey, L. T., ed. *Juvenile Justice: The Progressive Legacy and Current Reforms*. University of Virginia, 1980.

Federal Judicial Center. *Report of the Study Group on the Case Load of the Supreme Court*. Administrative Office of the U.S. Courts, 1972.

Feeley, M. M. *Court Reform on Trial: Why Simple Solutions Fail*. Basic Books, 1983.

Fleming, M. *The Price of Perfect Justice*. Basic Books, 1973.

Friendly, H. F. *Federal Jurisdiction: A General View*. Columbia University, 1973.

Freisen, E. C., Jr;, E. C., and N. M. Gallas. *Managing the Courts*. Bobbs-Merrill, 1971.

Goodnow, F. J. *Social Reform and the Constitution*. Macmillan, 1911.

Hays, S. W. *Court Reform*. Lexington Books, 1978.

Hazlitt, H. *A New Constitution Now*. McGraw-Hill, 1942.

Hehmeyer, A. *Time for a Change: A Proposal for a Second Constitutional Convention*. Rinehart, 1943.

James, H. *Crisis in the Courts*. Rev. ed. McKay, 1977.

Johnson, E., Jr. *Justice and Reform: The Formative Years of the American Legal Service Program*. Transaction Books, 1977.

McGuigan, P. B., and R. R. Rader. *A Blueprint for Judicial Reform*. Free Congress Foundation, 1981.

Meador, D. J. *Criminal Appeals: English Practice and American Reforms*. University of Virginia, 1973.

Miller, G. R., and N. E. Fontes. *Videotape on Trial: A View from the Jury Box.* Sage Publications, 1980.

Nagel, S. S. *Improving the Legal Process: Effect of Alternatives.* Lexington Books, 1975.

Neely, R. *Why Courts Don't Work.* McGraw-Hill, 1983.

Pound, R. *The Causes of Popular Dissatisfaction with the Administration of Justice.* American Judicature Society, 1906.

Seron, C. *Judicial Reorganization: The Politics of Reform in the Federal Bankruptcy Court.* Lexington Books, 1978.

Seymour, W. N. *Why Justice Fails.* Morrow, 1973.

Strick, A. *With Injustice for All.* Putnam, 1977.

Vanderbilt, A. T. *The Challenge of Law Reform.* Princeton University, 1955.

Weinstein, J. B. *Reform of Court Rule-Making Procedures.* Ohio State University, 1977.

Wheeler, J. P., ed. *Salient Issues of Constitutional Revision.* National Municipal League, 1960.

Winter, G. R., and E. J. Schoenbaum, eds. *American Courts and Justice.* American Judicature Society, 1976.

STAFFING THE COURTS
(Selection, tenure, discipline, removal, and compensation.)

Abraham, H. J. *The Judicial Process: An Introductory Analysis of the Courts of the United States, England, and France.* 5th ed. Oxford University, 1986.

———. *Justices and Presidents: A Political History of Appointments to the Supreme Court.* 2d ed. Oxford University, 1985.

American Bar Association. *Judicial Discipline and Disability Retirement.* American Bar Association, 1978.

American Judicature Society. *Judicial Disability and Removal Commissions: Courts and Procedures.* AJS, 1972.

Ashman, A., and J. J. Alfini. *The Key to Judicial Merit Selection: The Nominating Process.* American Judicature Society, 1974.

Barnett, R. *Law Clerks in the United States Courts and State Appellate Courts.* American Judicature Society, 1973.

Bashful, E. *The Florida Supreme Court: A Study in Judicial Selection.* Florida State University, 1958.

Bell, G., et al. *Whom Do Judges Represent?* American Enterprise Institute, 1981.

Berkson, L. C., and S. B. Carron. *The United States Circuit Judge Nominating Commission: Its Members, Procedures, and Candidates.* American Judicature Society, 1980.

Blaustein, A. P., and R. M. Mersky. *The First One Hundred Justices: Statistical Studies on the Supreme Court of the United States.* Shoe String Press, 1978.

Braithwaite, W. T. *Who Judges the Judges? A Study of Procedures for Removal and Retirement.* American Bar Foundation, 1971.

Carbon, S. B., and L. C. Berkson. *Judicial Retention Elections in the United States.* American Judicature Society, 1980.

Carpenter, W. S. *Judicial Tenure in the United States.* Yale University, 1918.

Chase, H. W. *Federal Judges: The Appointing Process.* University of Minnesota, 1972.

Connelly, V. J. *Compensation Commission.* American Judicature Society, 1973.

Council of State Governments. *Judicial Administration: Education and Training Programs.* Council of State Governments, 1975.

Danelski, D. J. *A Supreme Court Justice Is Appointed.* Random House, 1964.

Davis, C. *Judicial Selection in West Virginia.* Bureau for Government Research, 1959.

Davis, J. W. *Selecting Judges.* Andrews, 1933.

Downie, L. J., Jr. *Justice Denied.* Penguin Books, 1974.

Dubois, P. L. *From Ballot to Bench: Judicial Elections and the Quest for Accountability.* University of Texas, 1980.

Excovitz, S. S., with F. Kurland and N. Gold. *Judicial Selection and Tenure*. American Judicature Society, 1975.

Goulden, J. C. *The Benchwarmers*. Ballantine Books, 1974.

Grossman, J. B. *Lawyers and Judges*. Wiley, 1965.

Hall, K. L. *The Judges of the United States*. Government Printing Office, 1978.

———. *The Politics of Justice: Lower Federal Judicial Selection and the Second Party System*. University of Nebraska, 1979.

Harris, J. P. *The Advice and Consent of the Senate: A Study of the Confirmation of Appointments by the United States Senate*. University of California, 1953.

Hawley, W. D. *Nonpartisan Elections and the Case for Party Politics*. Wiley, 1973.

Haynes, E. *The Selection and Tenure of Judges*. National Conference of Judicial Councils, 1944.

Henderson, B., and T. C. Sinclair. *Judicial Selection in Texas*. University of Houston, 1964.

Hyde, L. M. *Merit Selection: The Missouri Experience*. American Judicature Society, 1973.

Karfunkel, T., and T. W. Ryley. *The Jewish Seat: Anti-Semitism and the Appointment of Jews to the Supreme Court*. Exposition Press, 1978.

Lowe, R. S., ed. *Resource Materials for (First) National Conference on Judicial Selection and Tenure*. American Judicature Society, 1974.

McGuigan, P. B., and R. R. Rader, eds. *A Blueprint for Judicial Reform*. Free Congress Research and Education Foundation, 1981.

McHargue, D. J. "Factors Influencing the Selection and Appointment of Members of the United States Supreme Court, 1784–1932." Ph.D. diss. University of California at Los Angeles, 1949.

Nagel, S. S. *Comparing Elected and Appointed Judicial Systems*. Sage Publications, 1973.

Parkhill, B. *Judicial Selection in Illinois*. American Judicature Society, 1974.

Rae, D. *The Political Consequences of Electoral Laws*. Yale University, 1967.

Schlesinger, J. *Ambition and Politics: Political Careers in the United States*. Rand McNally, 1966.

Schmidhauser, J. R. *Judges and Justices: The Federal Appellate Judiciary*. Little, Brown, 1979.

———. *The Supreme Court: Its Politics, Personalities and Procedures*. Holt, 1960.

Scigliano, R. G. *The Courts: A Reader in the Judicial Process*. Little, Brown, 1962.

Seymour, W. N., Jr. *Why Justice Fails*. Morrow, 1974.

Shogan, R. *A Question of Judgment: The Fortas Case and the Struggle for the Supreme Court*. Bobbs-Merrill, 1972.

Simon, J. F. *In His Own Image: The Supreme Court in Richard Nixon's America*. McKay, 1973.

Stein, D. *Judging the Judges: The Cause, Control and Cure of Judicial Jaundice*. Exposition Press, 1974.

Tesitor, I. A., and D. B. Sinks. *Judicial Conduct Organizations*. 2d ed. American Judicature Society, 1980.

Todd, A. L. *Justice on Trial: The Case of Louis D. Brandeis*. McGraw-Hill, 1964.

Vanderbilt, A. T. *Judges and Jurors: Their Functions, Qualifications, and Selection*. Boston University, 1956.

Watson, R. A., and R. G. Downing. *The Politics of Bench and Bar: Judicial Selection Under the Missouri Non-Partisan Court Plan*. Wiley, 1969.

Wheeler, R. R., and L. A. Levin. *Judicial Discipline and Removal in the United States*. Federal Judiciary Center, 1979.

Winters, G. R. *Fact and Fiction About Judicial Selection and Tenure*. American Judicature Society, 1973.

———, ed. *Judicial Discipline and Removal*. American Judicature Society, 1973.

———. *The Merit Plan for Judicial Selection and Tenure: Its Historical Development*. American Judicature Society, 1968.

———. *One-Man Judicial Selection*. American Judicature Society, 1973.

———, ed. *Selected Readings on Judicial Discipline and Removal*. American Judicature Society, 1973.

———, ed. *Selected Readings on Judicial Selection and Tenure*. Rev. ed. American Judicature Society, 1973.

———, and R. S. Lowe, eds. *Readings for the National Conference of Judicial Disability and Removal Commissions*. American Judicature Society, 1973.

II. BIOGRAPHIES, AUTOBIOGRAPHIES, AND RELATED WORKS OF AND BY JUSTICES OF THE SUPREME COURT OF THE UNITED STATES

(Listed by Justices in Alphabetical Order, Following a "General or Multi-Applicable Works" Section)

GENERAL OR MULTI-APPLICABLE WORKS

Abraham, H. J. *Freedom and the Court: Civil Rights and Liberties in the United States.* 4th ed. Oxford University, 1982.

———. *The Judicial Process: An Introductory Analysis of the Courts of the United States, England, and France.* 5th ed. Oxford University, 1986.

———. *Justices and Presidents.* 2d ed. Oxford University, 1985.

Asch, S. H. *The Supreme Court and Its Great Justices.* Arco, 1971.

Barbar, J. *The Honorable Eighty-Eight.* Vanguard Press, 1957.

Barnes, C. *Men of the Supreme Court: Profiles of the Justices, 1945–1976.* Facts on File, 1979.

Bates, E. S. *The Story of the Supreme Court.* Bobbs-Merrill, 1936.

Blandford, L. A., and P. R. Evans, eds. *Supreme Court of the United States, 1789–1980: An Index to Opinions Arranged by Justice.* Supreme Court Historical Society, 1983.

Blaustein, A. P., and R. M. Mersky. *The First One Hundred Justices: Statistical Studies on the Supreme Court of the United States.* Shoe String Press (Archon Books), 1978.

Brown, J. M. *Through These Men.* Harper, 1956.

Cahn, E., ed. *The Great Rigths.* Macmillan, 1963.

Campbell, T. W. *Four-Score Forgotten Men.* Pioneer, 1950.

Cannon, M., and D. M. O'Brien, eds. *Views from the Bench.* Chatham, 1985.

Carson, H. L. *The Supreme Court of the United States: Its History.* Huber, 1891.

Congressional Quarterly. *Guide to the U.S. Supreme Court.* 1979–.

Crosskey, W. W. *Politics and the Constitution in the History of the United States.* University of Chicago, 1953.

Danelski, D. J. "The Chief Justices of the Supreme Court" Ph.D. diss., University of Illinois, 1961.

Dunham, A., and P. B. Kurland, eds. *Mr. Justice.* Rev. and enl. University of Chicago, 1964.

Ewing, C. A. M. *The Judges of the Supreme Court, 1780–1937.* University of Minnesota, 1938.

Fairman, C. *Reconstruction and Reunion, 1864–88.* Macmillan, 1971.

Flanders, H. *The Lives and Times of the Chief Justices of the Supreme Court of the United States.* Lippincott, 1858.

Frank, J. P. "The Appointment of Supreme Court Justices: Prestige Principles and Politics." *Wisconsin Law Review* 1941: (Mar.): 172; (May): 343; (July): 461.

———. *Marble Palace: The Supreme Court in American Life.* Knopf, 1958.

Freund, P. A. *On Law and Justice.* Harvard University, 1968.

————, ed. *The Oliver Wendell Holmes Devise: History of the Supreme Court of the United States* (various volumes). Macmillan, 1971– .

Friedman, L., and F. L. Israel, eds. *The Justices of the United States Supreme Court, 1789–1978*. 5 vols. Chelsea House, 1980.

Goebel, J. *Antecedents and Beginnings to 1801*. Macmillan, 1971.

Grossman, J. B. *Lawyers and Judges: The ABA and the Process of Judicial Selection*. Wiley, 1965.

Harris, J. P. *The Advice and Consent of the Senate*. University of California, 1953.

Harris, R. *Decision*. Dutton, 1971.

Haynes, E. *Selection and Tenure of Judges*. National Conference of Judicial Councils, 1944.

Howell, R. F. "Conservative Influence on Constitutional Development, 1923–1937: The Judicial Theories of Justices Van Devanter, McReynolds, Sutherland, and Butler." Ph.D. diss., Johns Hopkins University, 1952.

Lewis, W. E. *Seven Great American Lawyers*. Lippincott, 1909.

Lieberman, J. K. *Milestones! 200 Years of American Law*. West, 1976.

London, E., ed. *The World of Law: The Law in Literature and the Law as Literature*. Simon and Schuster, 1960.

Mason, E., ed. *Chief Justices of the United States*. (Columbus) Dispatch Co., 1977.

McCloskey, R. G. *The American Supreme Court*. University of Chicago, 1960.

McCune, W. *The Nine Young Men*. Harper, 1947.

McHargue, D. S. "Factors Influencing the Selection and Appointment of Members of the United States Supreme Court, 1789–1932." Ph.D. diss., University of California at Los Angeles, 1949.

Merryman, J. H. *The Civil Law Tradition*. Stanford University, 1970.

Murphy, B. A. *The Brandeis/Frankfurter Connection: The Secret Political Activities of Two Supreme Court Justices*. Oxford University, 1982.

Noonan, J. T. B., *Persons and Masks of the Law: Cardozo, Holmes, Jefferson, and Wythe as Makers of the Law*. Farrar, Straus & Giroux, 1976.

Pritchett, C. H. *The Roosevelt Court: A Study in Judicial Politics and Values, 1937–1947*. MacMillan 1948.

Rodell, F. *Nine Men: A Political History of the Supreme Court of the United States from 1790–1855*. Knopf, 1955.

Schmidhauser, J. R. *Judges and Justices: The Federal Appellate Judiciary*. Little, Brown, 1979.

————. *The Supreme Court: Its Politics, Personalities, and Procedures*. Holt, Rinehart and Winston, 1960.

Schubert, G. A. *The Judicial Mind: The Attitudes and Ideologies of the Supreme Court, 1943–1963*. Northwestern University, 1965.

Seagle, W. *Men of Law: From Hammurabi to Holmes*. Macmillan, 1947.

Simon, J. F. *In His Own Image: The Supreme Court in Richard Nixon's America*. McKay, 1973.

Steamer, R. J. *The Supreme Court in Crisis: A History of Conflict*. University of Massachusetts, 1971.

"Studies in Judicial Biography: A Symposium." *Vanderbilt Law Review* 10, no. 2 (1957).

Thompson, D. C. *The Supreme Court of the United States: A Bibliography*. University of California, 1959.

Tresolini, R. J. *Justice and the Supreme Court*. Lippincott, 1962.

Umbreit, K. B. *Our Eleven Chief Justices: A History of the Supreme Court in Terms of Their Personalities*. Harper, 1938.

Van Santvoord, G. *Sketches of the Lives and Judicial Services of the Chief Justices of the Supreme Court of the United States*. Scribner 1854.

Warren, C. *The Supreme Court in United States History*. Little, Brown, 1922, 1926, 1935.

Westin, A. F., ed. *The Supreme Court: Views from Inside*. Norton, 1961.

White, G. E. *The American Judicial Tradition. Profiles of Leading American Judges*. Oxford University, 1976.

Woodward, B., and S. Armstrong. *The Brethren: Inside the Supreme Court.* Simon and Schuster, 1979.

WORKS ABOUT OR BY INDIVIDUAL JUSTICES

HENRY BALDWIN (1780–1844)

Baldwin, H. *A General View of the Origin and Nature of the United States.* Lippincott, 1837.

PHILIP P. BARBOUR (1783–1841)

Baldwin, H. *A General View of the Origin and Nature of the Constitution and Government of the United States.* J. C. Clark, 1837.

Cynn, P. P. "Philip Pendleton Barbour." 4 John P. Branch Historical Papers of Randolph-Macon College 67 (1913).

Scott, W. W. *History of Orange County.* Waddey, 1907.

HUGO LAFAYETTE BLACK (1886–1971)

Ball, H. *The Vision and the Dream of Justice Hugo L. Black: An Examination of a Judicial Philosophy.* University of Alabama, 1975.

Black, H. L. *A Constitutional Faith.* Knopf, 1968.

Black, H. L., Jr. *My Father: A Remembrance.* Random House, 1975.

Davis, H. B. *Uncle Hugo: An Intimate Portrait of Mr. Justice Black.* Privately published, 1965.

Dennis, E. E., et al., eds. *Justice Hugo Black and the First Amendment.* Iowa State University, 1978.

Dilliard, I. *One Man's Freedom: Mr. Justice Black and the Bill of Rights.* Knopf, 1963.

Dunne, G. T. *Hugo Black and the Judicial Revolution.* Simon and Schuster, 1977.

Frank, J. P. *Mr. Justice Black: The Man and His Opinions.* Knopf, 1949.

Hamilton, V. V. de V. *Hugo Black: The Alabama Years.* Louisiana State University, 1972.

———, ed. *Hugo Black and the Bill of Rights.* University of Alabama, 1978.

Magee, J. J. *Mr. Justice Black: Absolutist on the Court.* University of Virginia, 1980.

Mason, G. L. *Hugo Black and the United States Senate.* University of Kansas, 1964.

Meador, D. J. *Mr. Justice Black and His Books.* University of Virginia, 1974.

Mendelson, W., ed. *Justices Black and Frankfurter: Conflict in the Court.* 2d ed. University of Chicago, 1966.

"Mr. Justice Black: A Symposium." 65 *Yale Law Journal* (Feb. 1956).

Silverstein, M. *Constitutional Faiths: Felix Frankfurter, Hugo Black, and the Process of Decision-Making.* Cornell University, 1984.

Strickland, S. P., ed. *Hugo Black and the Supreme Court: A Symposium.* Bobbs-Merrill, 1967.

U.S. Congress. Joint Committee on Printing. *Hugo Lafayette Black, 1886–1971: Memorial Addresses and Tributes.* Government Printing Office, 1972.

Williams, C. *Hugo L. Black: A Study in the Judicial Process.* Johns Hopkins, 1950.

HARRY A. BLACKMUN (1908–   )

Pollett, M. "Harry A. Blackmun." In *The Justices of the United States Superior Court, 1789–1978,* ed. L. Friedman and F. L. Israel, vol. 5, p. 2. Chelsea House, 1980.

JOHN BLAIR, JR. (1732–1800)

Drinard, J. E. "John Blair, Jr." 39 *Proceedings of Virginia State Bar Association* 436 (1927).

SAMUEL BLATCHFORD (1820–1893)

Paul, A. M. "Samuel Blatchford." In *The Justices of the United States Supreme Court, 1789–1978,* ed. L. Friedman and F. L. Israel, vol. 2, p. 2. Chelsea House, 1980.

JOSEPH P. BRADLEY (1813-1892)

Bradley, C., ed. *Miscellaneous Writings of Joseph P. Bradley.* Harham, 1901.
Bradley, J. P. *Family Notes Respecting the Bradley Family of Fairchild.* Privately published, 1894.
Fairman, C. "Mr. Justice Bradley." In *Mr. Justice,* by A. Dunham and P. B. Knowland. University of Chicago, 1964.

LOUIS DEMBITZ BRANDEIS (1856-1941)

Baker, L. *Brandeis and Frankfurter: A Dual Biography.* Harper & Row, 1984.
Bickel, A. M. *The Unpublished Opinions of Mr. Justice Brandeis: The Supreme Court at Work.* Harvard University, 1957; rpt. Phoenix Books (University of Chicago), 1967.
DeHaas, J. *Louis D. Brandeis.* Block, 1929.
Dilliard, I., ed. *Mr. Justice Brandeis: Great American.* Modern View Press, 1941.
Fraenkel, O. K., ed. *The Curse of Bigness: Miscellaneous Papers of Louis D. Brandeis.* Viking, 1934.
Frankfurter, F. *Mr. Justice Brandeis.* Yale University, 1932; rpt. Da Capo Press, 1972.
Freund, P. A. *The Writings of Louis D. Brandeis.* Bobbs-Merrill, 1966.
Gal, A. *Brandeis of Boston.* Harvard University, 1980.
Goldman, S., ed. *The Words of Mr. Justice Brandeis.* Schuman, 1953.
Konefsky, S. J. *The Legacy of Holmes and Brandeis: A Study in the Influence of Ideas.* Macmillan, 1956; rpt. Da Capo Press, 1974.
Lief, A., ed. *Brandeis: The Personal History of an American Ideal.* Stackpole Books, 1936.
———. *The Social and Economic Views of Mr. Justice Brandeis.* Viewpoint, 1930.
Mason, A. T. *Brandeis—A Free Man's Life.* Viking Press, 1946.
———. *Brandeis and the Modern State.* National Home Library, 1936.
———. *Brandeis: Lawyer and Judge in the Modern State.* Princeton University, 1933.
———. *The Brandeis Way.* Princeton University, 1938.
Noble, I. *Firebrand for Justice: A Biography of Louis Dembitz Brandeis.* Westminster Press, 1969.
Paper, L. J. *Brandeis: An Intimate Biography of America's Truly Great Supreme Court Justice.* Prentice-Hall, 1983.
Peare, C. O. *The Louis D. Brandeis Story.* Crowell, 1970.
Pollack, E. H., ed. *The Brandeis Reader.* Oceana, 1956.
Strum, P. *Louis D. Brandeis: Justice for the People.* Harvard University, 1984.
Todd, A. L. *Justice on Trial: The Case of Louis D. Brandeis.* McGraw-Hill, 1964.
Urofsky, M. I. *Louis D. Brandeis and the Progressive Tradition.* Little, Brown, 1981.
———. *A Mind of One Piece: Brandeis and American Reform.* Scribner 1971.
——— and D. W. Levy, eds. *Letters of Louis D. Brandeis.* Vol. 1, 1870-1897: *Urban Reformer;* Vol. 2, 1897-1912: *People's Attorney;* Vol. 3, 1912-1916; Vol. 4, 1916-1921; Vol. 5, 1921-1941. State University of New York, 1972-1978.
Yale Law Library. *Louis Dembitz Brandeis, 1856-1941: A Bibliography.* Yale University, 1958.

WILLIAM J. BRENNAN, JR. (1906-   )

Friedman, S. J. *William J. Brennan, Jr.: An Affair with Freedom.* Atheneum, 1967.

DAVID J. BREWER (1837-1910)

Lardner, L. A. "The Constitutional Doctrines of Justice David Josiah Brewer." Ph.D. diss., Princeton University, 1938.

HENRY BILLINGS BROWN (1936-1913)

Kent, C. A. *Memoir of Henry Billings Brown.* Dunfield, 1915.
Paul, A. M. *Conservative Crisis and the Rule of Law.* Cornell University, 1960.

WARREN E. BURGER (1907-   )

Norman, A. E. "Warren E. Burger." In *The Justices of the United States Supreme Court, 1789-1978.* ed. L. Friedman and F. L. Israel, vol. 5, p. 2. Chelsea House, 1980.

HAROLD H. BURTON (1888-1965)

Berry, M. F. *Stability, Security, and Continuity: Mr. Justice Burton and Decisionmaking in the Supreme Court, 1945-1948.* Greenwood Press, 1978.

Hudson, E. G., ed. *The Occasional Papers of Mr. Justice Burton.* Bowdoin College, 1969.

Marquardt, R. G. "The Judicial Justice: Mr. Justice Burton and The Supreme Court." Ph.D. diss., University of Wisconsin, 1973.

Provine, D. M. *Case Selection in the United States Supreme Court.* University of Chicago, 1980.

PIERCE BUTLER (1866-1939)

Brown, F. J. *The Social and Economic Philosophy of Pierce Butler.* Catholic University, 1945.

Danelski, D. J. *A Supreme Court Justice is Appointed.* Random House, 1964.

JAMES F. BYRNES (1879-1972)

Byrnes, J. F. *All in One Lifetime.* Harper, 1958.

Petit, W. "Justice Byrnes and the Supreme Court." 6 *South Carolina Law Quarterly* 423 (1954).

JOHN A. CAMPBELL (1811-1889)

Conner, H. G. *John Archibald Campbell, Associate Judge of the United States Supreme Court, 1853-1861.* Houghton Mifflin, 1920.

Holt, J., Jr. "The Resignation of Mr. Justice Campbell." 12 *Alabama Law Review* 105 (1959).

BENJAMIN N. CARDOZO (1870-1938)

Bender, N., ed. *The Benjamin N. Cardozo Memorial Lectures.* Bender, 1971.

Cardozo, B. N. *The Growth of the Law.* Yale University, 1924.

———. *Law and Literature and Other Essays.* Harcourt, Brace, 1931.

———. *The Nature of the Judicial Process.* Yale University, 1921.

———. *Paradoxes of the Legal Science.* Columbia University, 1928.

Hall, M. E., ed. *Selected Writings of B. N. Cardozo.* Fallon, 1947.

Hellman, G. S. *Benjamin N. Cardozo—American Judge.* Whittlesey House, 1940.

Levy, B. H. *Cardozo and Legal Thinking.* Oxford University, 1938.

———. *Cardozo and the Frontiers of Legal Thinking: With Selected Opinions.* 2d ed. Case-Western Reserve University, 1970.

Pollard, J. P. *Mr. Justice Cardozo: A Liberal Mind in Action.* Yorktown Press, 1935.

Sainer, A. L. *Law Is Justice: Notable Opinions of Mr. Justice Cardozo.* Ad Press, 1938.

JOHN CATRON (1786-1865)

Gass, E. C. "The Constitutional Opinions of Justice John Catron." 8 *East Tennessee Historical Society's Publications* 54 (1936).

SALMON PORTLAND CHASE (1808-1873)

Chase, S. P. *Diaries and Correspondence.* Da Capo Press, 1971.

Hart, A. B. *Salmon Portland Chase.* Houghton Mifflin, 1899.

Johnson, B. T. *Reports on Cases Decided by Chief Justice Chase in the Circuit Court of the United States for the Fourth Circuit.* Da Capo Press, 1972.

Schuckers, J. W. *The Life and Public Services of Salmon Portland Chase.* Appleton, 1874.

SAMUEL CHASE (1741-1811)

U.S. Senate. *Trial of Samuel Chase, an Associate Justice of the Supreme Court Impeached by the House of Representatives for High Crimes and Misdemeanors Before the Senate of the United States.* 1805, 8th Cong., 2d sess.
Elsmere, J. *Justice Samuel Chase.* Janevar, 1980.

TOM C. CLARK (1899-1977)

Dorin, D. D. "Justice Tom Clark and the Right of Defendants in State Courts." Ph.D. diss., University of Virginia, 1974.
Dutton, C. B. "Mr. Justice Tom Clark." 26 *Indiana Law Journal* 169 (1951).
Kirkendall, R. J. *The Truman Period as a Research Field.* Columbia University, 1967.

JOHN H. CLARKE (1857-1945)

Levitan, D. M. "The Jurisprudence of Mr. Justice Clarke." 7 *Miami Law Quarterly* 44 (1952).
Warner, H. L. *The Life of Mr. Justice Clarke: A Testimony to the Power of Liberal Dissent in America.* Western Reserve University, 1959.

NATHAN CLIFFORD (1803-1881)

Clifford, P. G. *Nathan Clifford, Democrat.* Putnam 1922.
Magrath, C. P. *Morrison R. Waite: The Triumph of Character.* Macmillan, 1963.

BENJAMIN ROBBINS CURTIS (1809-1874)

Curtis, B. R., Jr. *A Memoir of Benjamin Robbins Curtis, L.L.D.* Little, Brown, 1897.
Leach, R. H. "Benjamin R. Curtis: Case Study of a Supreme Court Justice." Ph.D. diss., Princeton University, 1951.

WILLIAM CUSHING (1732-1810)

Cushing, J. D. "A Revolutionary Conservative: The Public Life of William Cushing, 1732-1810." Ph.D. diss., Clark University, 1960.

PETER V. DANIEL (1784-1860)

Frank J. P. *Justice Daniel Dissenting: A Biography of Peter V. Daniel, 1784-1860.* Harvard University, 1964.
Hendricks, B. M. *Bulwark of the Republic: A Biography of the Constitution.* Little, Brown, 1957.

DAVID DAVIS (1815-1886)

Fairman, C. *Mr. Justice Miller and the Supreme Court, 1862-1890.* Harvard University, 1939.
King, W. L. *Lincoln's Manager; David Davis.* Harvard University, 1960.
Kutler, S. I. *Judicial Power and Reconstruction Politics.* University of Chicago, 1968.

WILLIAM RUFUS DAY (1849-1923)

McLean, J. E. *William Rufus Day, Supreme Court Justice from Ohio.* Johns Hopkins University, 1947.

WILLIAM O. DOUGLAS (1898-1980)

Ashmore, H. S., ed. *The William O. Douglas Inquiry into the State of Individual Freedom.* Westview Press, 1979.
Bosmajian, H. *Justice Douglas and Freedom of Speech.* Scarecrow Press, 1980.
Countryman, V., ed. *Douglas of the Supreme Court: A Selection of His Opinions.* Doubleday, 1959.

——. *The Douglas Opinions*. Random House, 1977.

——. *The Judicial Record of Justice William O. Douglas*. Harvard University, 1974.

——. *The Right of the People*. Arena Lettres, 1972.

Douglas, W. O. *The Anatomy of Liberty: The Rights of Man Without Force*. Trident, 1963.

——. *The Bible and the Schools*. Little, Brown, 1966.

——. *The Court Years (1939–1975). The Autobiography of William O. Douglas*. Random House (Vintage Books), 1980.

——. *Democracy and Finance*. Yale University, 1940.

——. *Go East, Young Man*. Random House, 1974.

——. *International Dissent*. Random House (Vintage Books), 1974.

——. *A Living Bill of Rights*. Doubleday, 1961.

——. *Of Men and Mountains*. Harper & Row, 1950.

——. *The Supreme Court and the Bicentennial*. Associated University Press, 1978.

——. *We the Judges*. Doubleday, 1956.

——, ed. *Courts, Law and Judicial Process*. Free Press, 1981.

Duram, J. C. *Justice William O. Douglas*. G. K. Hall, 1981.

"Justices Frankfurter and Douglas." 26 *University of Chicago Law Review*. (Autumn 1958.)

Keller, R. H., Jr., ed. *In Honor of Justice Douglas: A Symposium on Individual Freedom and the Government*. Greenwood Press, 1981.

Simon, J. F. *Independent Journey: The Life of William O. Douglas*. Harper & Row, 1980.

Wolfman, B. J., L. F. Silver, and M. A. Silver. *Dissent Without Opinion: The Behavior of Justice William O. Douglas in Federal Tax Cases*. University of Pennsylvania, 1975.

GABRIEL DUVAL (1752–1844)

Dilliard, I. "Gabriel Duval." In *The Justices of the United States Supreme Court, 1789–1844*. Ed. L. Friedman and F. L. Israel, vol. 1, p. 2. Chelsea House, 1980.

OLIVER ELLSWORTH (1745–1807)

Brown, W. G. *The Life of Oliver Ellsworth*. Macmillan, 1905; rpt. Da Capo Press, 1970.

STEPHEN J. FIELD (1816–1899)

Field, S. J. *Personal Reminiscences of Early Days in California*. Privately published, 1893; rpt. Da Capo Press, 1968.

Swisher, C. B. *Stephen J. Field: Craftsman of the Law*. Brookings Institution, 1930; rpt. Phoenix Books (University of Chicago), 1969.

Turner, W. R., *Documents in Relation to the Charges Preferred by Stephen J. Field and Others*. Privately published, 1853.

ABE FORTAS (1910–1982)

Fortas, A. *Concerning Dissent and Civil Disobedience*. New American Library, 1968.

Heckart, R. J. "Justice Fortas and the First Amendment." Ph.D. diss., State University of New York at Albany, 1973.

Shogan, R. *A Question of Judgment: The Fortas Case and the Struggle for the Supreme Court*. Bobbs-Merrill, 1972.

FELIX FRANKFURTER (1882–1965)

Aronson, M. J. "The Juristic Thought of Mr. Justice Frankfurter." 5 *Journal of Social Philosophy* (1940).

Baker, L. *Brandeis and Frankfurter: A Dual Biography*. Harper & Row, 1983.

——. *Felix Frankfurter*. Coward, McCann, 1969.

Frankfurter, F., ed. *The Business of the Supreme Court*. Macmillan, 1927.

——. *The Case of Sacco and Vanzetti: A Critical Analysis for Lawyers and Layman*. Little, Brown, 1927, 1961, 1962.

——. *The Commerce Clause Under Marshall, Taney and Waite.* University of North Carolina, 1937.

——. *Extrajudicial Essays on the Court and Constitution.* Ed. P. B. Kurland. Harvard University, 1970.

——. *Of Law and Men.* Harcourt, Brace, 1956.

——. *Mr. Justice Brandeis.* Yale University, 1932; rpt. Da Capo Press, 1972.

——, ed. *Mr. Justice Holmes.* Coward, McCann, 1931.

——. *Mr. Justice Holmes and the Constitution.* Harvard University, 1938.

——. *Mr. Justice Holmes and the Supreme Court.* 2d ed. Atheneum, 1965.

——. *The Public and Its Government.* Beacon Press, 1964.

Freedman, M. *Roosevelt and Frankfurter: Their Correspondence, 1928–1945.* Little, Brown, 1968.

Hirsch, H. N. *The Enigma of Felix Frankfurter.* Basic Books, 1981.

Jacobs, C. E. *Justice Frankfurter and Civil Liberties.* University of California, 1961; rpt. Da Capo Press, 1974.

Justices Frankfurter and Douglas," *University of Chicago Law Review.* (Autumn 1958).

Konefsky, S. J., ed. *The Constitutional World of Mr. Justice Frankfurter.* Macmillan, 1949.

Kurland, P. B., ed. *Felix Frankfurter on the Supreme Court.* Harvard University, 1970.

——. *Mr. Justice Frankfurter and the Constitution.* University of Chicago, 1971.

——. *Of Law and Life and Other Things That Matter: Papers and Addresses of Felix Frankfurter, 1956–1963.* Harvard University, 1965.

Lash, J. P. *From the Diaries of Felix Frankfurter.* Norton, 1975.

MacLeish, A., and E. F. Prichard, Jr., eds. *Law and Politics: Occasional Papers of Mr. Justice Frankfurter.* Harcourt, Brace, 1939.

Mendelson, W., ed. *Felix Frankfurter: A Tribute.* Reynal and Hitchcock, 1964.

——, ed. *Felix Frankfurter: The Judge.* Reynal and Hitchcock, 1964.

——. *Justices Black and Frankfurter: Conflict in the Courts.* 2nd ed. University of Chicago, 1966.

"Mr. Justice Felix Frankfurter: A Symposium." 66 *Yale Law Journal* (December 1957).

Parrish, M. E. *Felix Frankfurter and His Times: The Reform Years.* Free Press, 1982.

Phillips, H. B., ed. *Felix Frankfurter: Scholar on the Bench.* Johns Hopkins University, 1960.

Silverstein, M. *Constitutional Faiths: Felix Frankfurter, Hugo Black, and the Process of Judicial Policy-Making.* Cornell University, 1984.

"Justices Frankfurter and Douglas." *University of Chicago Law Review.* (Autumn 1958).

MELVILLE WESTON FULLER (1833–1910)

King, W. L. *Melville Weston Fuller: Chief Justice of the United States, 1888–1910.* Macmillan, 1950; rpt. Phoenix Books (University of Chicago), 1967.

Wapz, W. E. "Chief Justice Fuller, The Individualist on the Bench." 10 *Maine Law Review* 77 (1917).

ARTHUR J. GOLDBERG (1908–)

Goldberg, A. J. *Equal Justice: The Supreme Court in the Warren Era.* Northwestern University, 1971.

——. *The Supreme Court of the United States.* Northwestern University, 1971.

Moynihan, D. P., ed. *The Defenses of Freedom: The Public Papers of Arthur J. Goldberg.* Harper & Row, 1966.

HORACE GRAY (1828–1902)

Mitchell, S. R. "Mr. Justice Horace Gray." Ph.D. diss., University of Wisconsin, 1961.

ROBERT C. GRIER (1794–1870)

Jones, F. R. "Robert Cooper Grier." 16 *Green Bag* 221 (1904).

JOHN MARSHALL HARLAN I (1833-1911)

Clark, F. B. *The Constitutional Doctrine of Justice Harlan.* Johns Hopkins University, 1915; rpt. Da Capo Press, 1969.

"John Marshall Harlan, 1833-1911: A Symposium." 46 *Kentucky Law Journal.* (Spring 1958.)

Latham, F. B. *The Great Dissenter—John Marshall Harlan.* Cowles, 1970.

Porter, M. C. A. "John Marshall Harlan and the Laissez-Faire Courts." Ph.D. diss., University of Chicago, 1970.

JOHN MARSHALL HARLAN II (1899-1971)

Levin, M. "Justice Harlan: The Full Measure of the Man." 58 *American Bar Association Journal* 579 (1972).

"Mr. Justice John Marshall Harlan: A Symposium."*Harvard Law Review* (Dec. 1971).

Shapiro, D., ed. *The Evolution of a Judicial Philosophy: Selected Opinions and Papers of Justice John M. Harlan.* Harvard University, 1969.

OLIVER WENDELL HOLMES, JR. (1841-1935)

Bander, E. J., comp. *Justice Holmes Cathedra.* Michie, 1966.

Bent, S. *Justice Oliver Wendell Holmes.* Vanguard Press, 1932.

Biddle, F. *Justice Holmes, Natural Law, and the Supreme Court.* Macmillan, 1961.

———. *Mr. Justice Holmes.* Scribner, 1942.

Bowen, C. D. *A Yankee from Olympus: Justice Holmes and His Family.* Little, Brown, 1944.

Burton, D. H., ed. *The Holmes-Sheehan Correspondence.* Kennikat Press, 1976.

———, ed. *Oliver Wendell Holmes, Jr., What Manner of Liberal?* Krieger, 1979.

———, ed. *Progressive Masks: Letters of Oliver Wendell Holmes, Jr., and Franklin Ford.* University of Delaware, 1981.

Frankfurter, F., ed. *Mr. Justice Holmes.* Coward, McCann, 1931.

———. *Mr. Justice Holmes and the Supreme Court.* 2nd ed. Atheneum, 1965.

Holmes, O. W., Jr. *Collected Legal Papers.* Harcourt, 1920.

———. *The Common Law.* Little, Brown, 1881; new ed., Harvard 1962, ed. Mark DeWolfe Howe.

———. *Speeches.* Little, Brown, 1891, 1896, 1913.

Howe, Mark DeWolfe ed. *The Holmes-Laski Letters, 1916-1935.* Harvard University, 1953; Atheneum, 1963.

———, ed. *The Holmes-Pollock Letters, 1874-1932.* Rev. ed. Harvard University, 1941; rpts. Atheneum, 1963.

———, ed. *Justice Holmes to Dr. Wu: An Intimate Correspondence, 1921-1932.* Central Books, 1935.

———. *Justice Oliver Wendell Holmes: The Proving Years, 1870-1882.* Harvard University, 1963.

———. *Justice Oliver Wendell Holmes: The Shaping Years, 1841-1870.* Harvard University, 1957.

———, ed. *The Occasional Speeches of Justice Oliver Wendell Holmes.* Harvard University, 1963.

———, ed. *Touched with Fire: Civil War Letters and Diary of Oliver Wendell Holmes, Jr., 1861-1864.* Da Capo Press, 1969.

Hurst, W. J. *Justice Holmes and Legal History.* Macmillan, 1964.

Konefsky, S. J. *The Legacy of Holmes and Brandeis: A Study in the Influence of Ideas.* Macmillan, 1956; rpt. Da Capo Press, 1974.

Lerner, M., ed. *The Mind and Faith of Justice Holmes.* Little, Brown, 1943.

Lief, A., ed. *The Dissenting Opinions of Mr. Justice Holmes.* Vanguard Press, 1943.

———. *Representative Opinions of Mr. Justice Holmes.* Greenwood Press, 1976.

Marke, J., ed. *The Holmes Reader.* 2nd ed. Oceana, 1964.

Morse, J. T., Jr., ed. *Life and Letters of Oliver Wendell Holmes.* Houghton Mifflin, 1896.

Peabody, J. B., ed. *Holmes-Einstein Letters.* Macmillan, 1964.

Pohlman, H. L. *Justice Oliver Wendell Holmes and Utilitarian Jurisprudence.* Harvard University, 1984.
Shriver, H. C., ed. *Justice Oliver Wendell Holmes: His Book Notice and Uncollected Letters and Papers.* Da Capo Press, 1973.
Wu, J., ed. *Justice Holmes to Dr. Wu: An Intimate Correspondence.* Central Books, 1947.

CHARLES EVANS HUGHES (1862–1948)

Danelsik, D. J., and J. S. Tulchin, eds. *The Autobiographical Notes of Charles Evans Hughes.* Harvard University, 1973.
Hendel, S. *Charles Evans Hughes and the Supreme Court.* Columbia University, 1951.
Hughes, C. E. *Addresses.* 2nd ed. Harper, 1916.
———. *The Supreme Court of the United States.* Columbia University, 1928.
Hughes, H. L. "They Don't Make Them Like That Anymore." *New York Review of Books,* May 30, 1974.
Kornberg, H. R. "Charles Evans Hughes in the Supreme Court: A Study in Judicial Philosophy and Voting Behavior." Ph.D. diss., Brown University, 1972.
Perkins, D. *Charles Evans Hughes and American Democratic Statesmanship.* Little, Brown, 1956.
Pusey, M. J. *Charles Evans Hughes.* Macmillan, 1951.
Ransom, W. L. *Charles Evans Hughes: The Statesman As Shown in the Opinions of the Jurist.* Dutton, 1916.
Warren, E. *Hughes and the Court.* Colgate University, 1962.
Wesser, R. F. *Charles Evans Hughes: Politics and Reform in New York, 1905–1910.* Cornell University, 1967.

WARD HUNT (1810–1886)

Obituaries: *New York Times* and *New York Daily Tribune.* March 25, 1886.
Wyman, T. B. *Genealogy of the Name and Family of Hunt.* Wilson, 1862.

JAMES IREDELL (1751–1799)

Connor, H. G. "James Iredell: Lawyer, Statesman, Judge, 1751–1799." 60 *University of Pennsylvania Law Review* 225 (1911–1912).
McRee, G. F., ed. *The Life and Correspondence of James Iredell.* Peter Smith, 1949.

HOWELL E. JACKSON (1832–1895)

Doak, H. M. "Howell Edmunds Jackson." 1897 *Proceedings of the Bar Association of Tennessee* 76.
Schiffman, H. E. "Howell E. Jackson." In *The Justices of the United States Supreme Court, 1789–1978.* Ed. L. Friedman and F. L. Israel, vol. 2, p. 2. Chelsea House, 1980.

ROBERT H. JACKSON (1892–1954)

Desmond, C. S., et al. *Mr. Justice Jackson: Four Lectures in His Honor.* Columbia University, 1969.
Gerhart, E. C. *America's Advocate: Robert H. Jackson.* Bobbs-Merrill, 1958.
———. *Robert H. Jackson: Lawyer's Judge.* "Q" Corp., 1961.
Jackson, R. H. *Full Faith and Credit: The Lawyer's Clause in the Constitution.* Columbia University, 1945.
———. *The Struggle for Judicial Supremacy: A Study of a Crisis in American Judicial Power.* Knopf, 1941.
———. *The Supreme Court in the American System of Government.* Harvard University, 1955.
"Mr. Justice Jackson: A Symposium." 8 *Stanford Law Review.* (Dec. 1955.)
Schubert, G., ed. *Dispassionate Justice: A Synthesis of the Judicial Opinions of Robert H. Jackson.* Bobbs-Merrill, 1969.

Seymour, W. N., et al., eds. *Mr. Justice Jackson: Four Lectures in His Honor.* Columbia University, 1969.

Steamer, R. J. "The Constitutional Doctrine of Mr. Justice Robert H. Jackson." Ph.D. diss., Cornell University, 1954.

JOHN JAY (1745–1829)

Jay, W. *The Life of John Jay.* Harper, 1833.

Johnston, H. P., ed. *The Correspondence and Public Papers of John Jay, 1763–1826.* 2 vols. Putnam, 1890, 1893.

Monaghan, F. *John Jay: Defender of Liberty.* Bobbs-Merrill, 1935.

Morris, R. B., ed. *John Jay, the Making of a Revolutionary: Unpublished Papers, 1745–1780.* Harper & Row, 1975.

———. *John Jay, the Nation and the Court.* Boston University, 1967.

THOMAS JOHNSON (1732–1819)

Delaplaine, E. S. *The Life of Thomas Johnson.* Hitchcock, 1927.

WILLIAM JOHNSON (1771–1834)

Morgan, D. G. *Justice William Johnson, the First Dissenter: The Career and Constitutional Philosophy of a Jeffersonian Judge.* University of South Carolina, 1954.

Schroeder, O., Jr. "Life and Judicial Work of Justice William Johnson, Jr." 95 *University of Pennsylvania Law Review* 164 (1946–1947).

JOSEPH RUCKER LAMAR (1857–1916)

Lamar, C. P. *The Life of Joseph Rucker Lamar, 1857–1916.* Putnam, 1926.

LUCIUS Q. C. LAMAR (1825–1893)

Cate, W. A. *Lucius Q. C. Lamar.* University of North Carolina, 1935.

Mayes, E. *Lucius Q. C. Lamar.* Barbee, 1895.

Murphy, J. B. *L. Q. C. Lamar.* Louisiana State University, 1973.

HENRY BROCKHOLST LIVINGSTON (1757–1823)

Livingston, E. B. *The Livingstons of Livingston Manor.* Knickerbocker, 1910.

HORACE H. LURTON (1844–1914)

Obituaries: 59 *Ohio Law Bulletin* 389, 1914; 12 *Ohio Law Register* 223, 1914; *New York Times,* July 13, 1914.

JOSEPH McKENNA (1843–1926)

McDevitt, M. B. *Joseph McKenna: Associate Justice of the United States.* Catholic University, 1946; Da Capo Press, 1974.

JOHN McKINLEY (1780–1852)

Hicks, J. "Associate Justice John McKinley: A Sketch." 18 *Alabama Law Review* 227 (1965).

JOHN MCLEAN (1785–1861)

Weisenburger, F. P. *The Life of John McLean: A Politician on the United States Supreme Court.* Ohio State University, 1937; Da Capo Press, 1974.

JAMES CLARK McREYNOLDS (1862–1946)

Blaisdell, D. P. "Mr. Justice James Clark McReynolds." Ph.D. diss., University of Wisconsin, 1948.

Early, S. T., Jr. "James Clark McReynolds and the Judicial Process." Ph.D. diss., University of Virginia, 1954.

Gilberts, S. P. *James Clark McReynolds.* Privately published, 1946.

McCraw, J. B. "Justice James Clark McReynolds and the Supreme Court, 1914-1941." Ph.D. diss., University of Texas, Austin, 1949.

JOHN MARSHALL (1755-1835)

Adams, J. S., ed. *An Autobiographical Sketch by John Marshall.* University of Michigan, 1837.
Baker, L. *John Marshall: A Life in Law.* Macmillan, 1974.
Beveridge, A. J. *The Life of John Marshall.* Houghton Mifflin, 1916.
Corwin, E. S. *John Marshall and the Constitution: A Chronicle of the Supreme Court.* Yale University, 1921.
Cotton, J. P., Jr., ed. *The Constitutional Decisions of John Marshall.* Putnam's 1905; Da Capo Press, 1969.
Cullen, C. T., and H. A. Johnson. *The Papers of John Marshall.* University of North Carolina, 1977.
Dillon, J. M., ed. *John Marshall: Complete Constitutional Decisions.* Callaghan, 1903.
Faulkner, R. K. *The Jurisprudence of John Marshall.* Princeton University, 1968.
Gunther, G., ed. *John Marshall's Defense of McCulloch v. Maryland.* Stanford University, 1969.
Haskins, G. L., and H. A. Johnson. *Foundations of Power: John Marshall, 1801-1815.* Macmillan, 1981.
Johnson, H. A., ed. *The Papers of John Marshall,* vol. 1, *Correspondence and Papers, No. 10, 1775-June 23, 1788.* University of North Carolina, 1974.
Jones, W. N., ed. *Chief Justice John Marshall: A Reappraisal.* Cornell University, 1956; Da Capo Press, 1971.
Konefsky, S. J. *John Marshall and Alexander Hamilton: Architects of the American Constitution.* Macmillan, 1964.
Loth, D. G. *Chief Justice: John Marshall and the Growth of the Republic.* Norton, 1949.
Mason, F. N. *My Dearest Polly: Letters of Chief Justice Marshall to His Wife, 1779-1831.* Garret & Massie, 1961.
Oliver, A. *The Portraits of John Marshall.* University of Virginia, 1976.
Palmer, B. W. *Marshall and Taney: Statesmen of the Law.* University of Minnesota, 1939.
Rhodes, I. S. *The Papers of John Marshall: A Descriptive Calendar.* University of Oklahoma, 1969.
————. *The Papers of John Marshall: A Descriptive Calendar.* University of Oklahoma, 1970.
Roche, J. P., ed. *John Marshall: Major Opinions and Other Writings.* Bobbs-Merrill, 1966.
Services, J. A. *A Bibliography of John Marshall.* U.S. Commission for Celebration of 200th Anniversary of Birth of John Marshall, 1956.
Severn, B. *John Marshall: The Man Who Made the Court Supreme.* McKay, 1969.
Stinchombe, W. C., and C. Cullen, eds. *The Papers of John Marshall.* Vols 1-3. University of North Carolina, 1975.
Stites, F. *John Marshall: Defender of the Constitution.* Little, Brown, 1981.
Surrency, E., ed. *The Marshall Reader.* Oceana, 1955.
Sutherland, A. E. *Government Under Law.* Harvard University, 1956.
Swindler, W. F. *The Constitution and Chief Justice Marshall.* Dodd, Mead, 1979.
Thayer, J. B. *John Marshall.* Houghton Mifflin, 1901; Phoenix Books (University of Chicago), 1967; rpt. Da Capo Press, 1974.

THURGOOD MARSHALL (1908-   )

Bland, R. W. *Private Pressure on Public Law: The Legal Career of Justice Thurgood Marshall.* Kennikat Press, 1973.
Fenderson, L. H. *Thurgood Marshall.* McGraw-Hill, 1969.

STANLEY MATTHEWS (1824-1889)

Greoe, C. J. "Stanley Matthews." In *Seven Great American Lawyers.* Ed. W. D. Lewis. Lippincott, 1909.

SAMUEL FREEMAN MILLER (1816–1890)

Fairman, C. *Mr. Justice Miller and the Supreme Court, 1862–1890.* Harvard University, 1939.
Gregory, C. N. *Samuel Freeman Miller.* State Historical Society of Iowa, 1907.
Miller, S. F. *Lectures on the Constitution.* Banks, 1891.

SHERMAN MINTON (1890–1965)

Wallace, H. L. "Mr. Justice Minton—Hoover Justice on the Supreme Court." 34 *Indiana Law Journal* 145 (1959).

WILLIAM HENRY MOODY (1853–1917)

Weiner, F. B. *The Life and Judicial Career of William Henry Moody.* Harvard University, 1937.

ALFRED MOORE (1755–1810)

Friedman, L. "Alfred Moore." In *The Justices of the United States Supreme Court, 1789–1978,* ed. L. Friedman and F. L. Israel, vol. 1, p. 2. Chelsea House, 1980.

FRANK MURPHY (1890–1949)

Fine, S. *Frank Murphy: The Detroit Years.* University of Michigan, 1975.
———. *Frank Murphy: The New Deal Years.* University of Chicago, 1979.
Howard, J. W., Jr. "Frank Murphy: A Liberal's Creed." Ph.D. diss., Princeton University, 1959.
———. *Mr. Justice Murphy: A Political Biography.* Princeton University, 1968.
Lunt, R. D. *The High Ministry of Government: The Political Career of Frank Murphy.* Wayne State University, 1965.
"Mr. Justice Frank Murphy: A Symposium." *Michigan Law Review.* (April 1950.)
Norris, H. *Mr. Justice Murphy and the Bill of Rights.* Oceana, 1965.

SAMUEL NELSON (1792–1873)

Countryman, E. "Samuel Nelson." 19 *Green Bag* 329, 1927.

SANDRA DAY O'CONNOR (1930–)

"Justice—At Last." *Time,* July 20, 1981.
Moore, R. H. Jr. "Justice O'Connor and the States." Paper presented at the annual meeting of the American Political Science Association, Birmingham, Alabama, November 3, 1983.

WILLIAM PATERSON (1745–1806)

Wood, G. S. *William Paterson of New Jersey, 1745–1806.* Fair Lawn Press, 1933.

RUFUS W. PECKHAM (1838–1909)

Duker, W. F. "Mr. Justice Rufus W. Peckham: The Police Power and the Individual in a Changing World." 47 *Brigham Young Law Review* (1980).
Hall, A. O. "Mr. Justice Peckham." 8 *Green Bag* (1896).

MAHLON PITNEY (1858–1924)

Breed, A. R., "Mahlon Pitney." Senior thesis, Princeton University, 1932.

LEWIS F. POWELL, JR. (1907–)

"Hon. Lewis F. Powell, Jr.: A Symposium." *Richmond Law Review.* (1977).
Wilkinson, J. H., III, *Serving Justice: A Supreme Court Clerk's View.* Charterhouse, 1974.

STANLEY F. REED (1884–1980)

Fitzgerald, M. J. "Justice Reed: A Study of a Center Judge." Ph.D. diss., University of Chicago, 1950.

O'Brien, F. W. *Justice Reed and the First Amendment: The Religion Clauses.* Georgetown University, 1958.

WILLIAM H. REHNQUIST (1924–   )

Rehnquist, W. H. "The Notion of a Living Constitution." 54 *Texas Law Review* 693 (1976).
———. "Political Battles for Judicial Independence." 50 *Washington Law Review* 835 (1975).

OWEN J. ROBERTS (1875–1955)

Leonard, C. A. *A Search for a Judicial Philosophy: Mr. Justice Roberts and the Constitutional Revolution of 1937.* Kennikat Press, 1971.
Roberts, O. J. *The Court and the Constitution.* Harvard University, 1951.

JOHN RUTLEDGE (1739–1800)

Barnwell, R. W. "Rutledge, 'The Dictator.'" 7 *Journal of Southern History* 215 (1941).
Barry, R. *Mr. Rutledge of South Carolina.* Duell, Sloan and Pearce, 1942.

WILEY B. RUTLEDGE (1894–1949)

Harper, F. W. *Justice Rutledge and the Bright Constellation.* Bobbs-Merrill, 1965.
Rutledge, W. B. *A Declaration of Legal Faith.* University of Kansas, 1947; rpt. Da Capo Press, 1971.
"Wiley B. Rutledge: A Symposium." 35 *Iowa Law Review.* (Summer, 1950).

EDWARD T. SANFORD (1865–1930)

Cook, S. A. "Rath to the High Bench: The Pre-Supreme Court Career of Justice Edward Terry Sanford." Ph.D. diss., University of Tennessee, 1977.
Sanford, E. T. *Blount College and the University of Tennessee.* University of Tennessee, 1894.

GEORGE SHIRAS, JR. (1832–1924)

Shiras III, G., ed. *Justice George Shiras, Jr., of Pittsburgh.* University of Pittsburgh, 1953.

JOHN PAUL STEVENS (1920–   )

Orland, L. "John Paul Stevens." In *The Justices of the United States Supreme Court, 1789–1978,* ed. L. Friedman and F. L. Israel, vol. 5, p. 2. Chelsea House, 1980.

POTTER STEWART (1915–   )

Barnett, H. M., and K. Levine. "Mr. Justice Stewart." 40 *New York University Law Review* 526 (1965).
Frank, J. B. *The Warren Court.* Macmillan, 1964.

HARLAN FISKE STONE (1872–1946)

Konefsky, S. J. *Chief Justice Stone and the Supreme Court.* Macmillan, 1946.
Mason, A. T. *Harlan Fiske Stone: Pillar of the Law.* Viking Press, 1956.
Stone, H. F. *Law and Its Administration.* Columbia University, 1915.
———. *Public Control of Business.* Howell, Soskin, 1940.

JOSEPH STORY (1779–1845)

Commager, H. S. "Joseph Story." In *Gaspar G. Bacon Lectures on the Constitution of the United States.* Ed. A. N. Holcombe et al., Boston University, 1953.
———. *The Writings of Justice Joseph Story.* Bobbs-Merrill, 1966.
Dunne, G. F. *Justice Joseph Story and the Rise of the Supreme Court.* Simon and Schuster, 1970.
McClellan, J. *Joseph Story and the American Constitution.* University of Oklahoma, 1971.

Newmyer, R. K., *Supreme Court Justice Joseph Story: Statesman of the Old Republic*. American Society for Legal History, 1985.

Schwartz, M. D., and J. C. Hogan. *Joseph Story: A Collection of Writings by an Eminent American Jurist*. Oceana, 1959.

Story, Joseph. *Commentaries on the Constitution of the United States*. Little and Brown, 1833.

Story, W. W., ed. *Life and Letters of Joseph Story*. Little, Brown, 1851.

———. *The Miscellaneous Writings of Joseph Story*. Little, Brown, 1852.

Warren, C. *The Story-Marshall Correspondence*. New York University, 1942.

WILLIAM STRONG (1808–1895).

Kutler, S. I. "William Strong." In *The Justices of the United States Supreme Court, 1789–1978*, ed. L. Friedman and F. L. Israel, vol. 2, p. 1. Chelsea House, 1980.

GEORGE SUTHERLAND (1862–1942)

Paschal, J. F. *Mr. Justice Sutherland: A Man Against the State*. Princeton University, 1951.

Sutherland, G. *Constitutional Power and World Affairs*. Columbia University, 1919.

NOAH H. SWAYNE (1804–1884)

Silver, D. M. *Lincoln's Supreme Court*. University of Illinois, 1956.

Swayne, N. W., comp. *The Descendants of Francis Swayne and Others*. Lippincott, 1921.

WILLIAM HOWARD TAFT (1857–1930)

Anderson, J. I. *William Howard Taft: An Intimate History*. Norton, 1981.

Mason, A. T. *William Howard Taft: Chief Justice*. Simon and Schuster, 1965.

McHale, F. *President and Chief Justice: The Life and Public Services of William Howard Taft*. Dorrance, 1931.

Pringle, H. F. *The Life and Times of William Howard Taft*. Farrar & Rinehart, 1939.

Taft, W. H. *The Anti-trust Act and the Supreme Court*. Harper 1914.

———. *Liberty Under Law: An Interpretation of the Principles of our Constitutional Government*. Yale University, 1922.

———. *Our Chief Magistrate and His Powers*. Columbia University, 1916.

———. *United States Supreme Court the Prototype of a World Court*. American Society for Judicial Settlement of International Disputes, 1915.

ROGER BROOKE TANEY (1777–1864)

Lewis, W. *Without Fear or Favor: A Biography of Chief Justice Roger Brooke Taney*. Houghton Mifflin, 1965.

Palmer, B. W. *Marshall and Taney: Statesmen of the Law*. University of Minnesota, 1939.

Smith, C. W., Jr. *Roger B. Taney: Jacksonian Jurist*. University of North Carolina, 1936; Da Capo Press, 1973.

Steiner, B. C. *Life of Roger Brooke Taney, Chief Justice of the United States Supreme Court*. Williams & Wilkins, 1922.

Swisher, C. B. *Roger B. Taney*. Macmillan, 1935.

———. *The Taney Period, 1836–64*. Macmillan, 1974.

Taylor, S. *Memoir of Roger Brooke Taney: Chief Justice of the Supreme Court of the United States*. J. Murphy, 1872; Da Capo Press, 1973.

SMITH THOMPSON, (1768–1843)

Roper, D. M. "Mr. Justice Thompson and the Constitution." Ph.D. diss., Indiana University, 1963.

THOMAS TODD (1765–1826)

O'Rear, E. C. "Justice Thomas Todd." 38 *Register of the Kentucky State Historical Society* 113 (1940).

ROBERT TRIMBLE (1776–1828)

Goff, J. T. "Mr. Justice Trimble of the United States Supreme Court." 58 *Register of the Kentucky Historical Society* 6 (1960).

WILLIS VAN DEVANTER (1859–1941)

Gould, L. L. "Willis Van Devanter in Wyoming Politics, 1884–1897." Ph.D. diss., Yale University, 1966.

Howard, J. O. B. "Constitutional Doctrines of Mr. Justice Van Devanter." Ph.D. diss., State University of Iowa, 1937.

FRED M. VINSON (1890–1953)

Bolner, J. "Chief Justice Vinson: A Study of His Politics and His Constitutional Law." Ph.D. diss., University of Virginia, 1962.

Frank, J. P. "Fred Vinson and the Chief Justiceship," 21 *University of Chicago Law Review* 212 (1954).

Pritchett, C. H. *Civil Liberties and the Vinson Court*. University of Chicago, 1954.

MORRISON R. WAITE (1816–1888)

Magrath, C. P. *Morrison R. Waite: The Triumph of Character*. Macmillan, 1963.

Trimble, B. R. *Chief Justice Waite: Defender of the Public Interest*. Princeton University, 1938.

EARL WARREN (1891–1974)

Bozell, L. B. *The Warren Revolution*. Arlington House, 1966.

Christman, H. M., ed. *The Public Papers of Chief Justice Earl Warren*. Simon and Schuster, 1959.

Frank, J. P., with Y. Karsh. *The Warren Court*. Macmillan, 1964.

Katcher, L. *Earl Warren: A Political Biography*. McGraw-Hill, 1967.

Pollack, J. H. *Earl Warren: The Judge Who Changed America*. Prentice-Hall, 1979.

Schwartz, B. *Super Chief Earl Warren and His Supreme Court: A Judicial Biography*. Columbia University, 1983.

Stone, I. *Earl Warren*. Prentice-Hall, 1948.

Warren, E. "All Men Are Created Equal." Association of the Bar of the City of New York, 1970.

———. *Hughes and the Court*. Colgate University, 1962.

———. *The Memoirs of Chief Justice Warren*. Doubleday, 1977.

———. *A Republic . . . if You Can Keep It*. Quadrangle, 1972.

Weaver, J. D. *Warren: The Man, the Court, the Era*. Little, Brown, 1967.

White, G. E. *Earl Warren: A Public Life*. Oxford University 1982.

BUSHROD WASHINGTON (1762–1829)

Binney, R. *Bushrod Washington*. Sherman, 1858.

Washington, C. B. "Justice Bushrod Washington." 9 *Green Bag* 329 (1897).

JAMES MOORE WAYNE (1790–1867)

Lawrence, A. A. *James Moore Wayne: Southern Unionist*. University of North Carolina, 1943.

BYRON R. WHITE (1917–)

Israel, F. L. "Byron R. White." In *The Justices of the United States Supreme Court, 1789–1978*, ed. L. Friedman and F. L. Israel, vol. 4, p. 2. Chelsea House, 1980.

EDWARD DOUGLAS WHITE (1845–1921)

Highsaw, R. B. *Edward Douglas White: Defender of the Conservative Faith*. Louisiana State University, 1981.

Hill, A. B. "The Constitutional Doctrine of Chief Justice White." Ph.D. diss., University of California, 1922.

Klinkhamer, Sister M. C. "Edward Douglas White, Chief Justice of the United States." Ph.D. diss., Catholic University, 1948.

CHARLES E. WHITTAKER (1901-1973)

Friedman, L. "Charles Whittaker." In *The Justices of the United States Supreme Court, 1789-1978*, ed. L. Friedman and F. L. Israel, vol. 4, p. 2. Chelsea House, 1980.

JAMES WILSON (1742-1798)

McCloskey, R. G., ed. *The Works of James Wilson*. Harvard University, 1967.

Smith, C. H., *James Wilson, Founding Father*. University of North Carolina, 1956.

Wilson, J. *Commentaries on the Constitution of the United States*. Extracted from debates. T. Lloyd, 1792.

———. *The Works of the Hon. James Wilson*. Bronson & Chaunch, 1804.

LEVI WOODBURY (1789-1851)

Woodbury, C. L., ed. *Writings of Levi Woodbury*. Little, Brown, 1852.

WILLIAM B. WOODS (1824-1887)

Proceedings of the Bench and Bar of the Supreme Court of the United States in Memoriam William B. Woods. 123 U.S. 761 (1887).

Proceedings of the Bench and Bar . . . William B. Woods. 15 *Washington Law Reporter* 357 (1887).

III. COMPARATIVE CONSTITUTIONAL AND ADMINISTRATIVE LAW

Aaron, B., ed. *Labor Courts and Grievance Settlement in Western Europe.* University of California, 1971.

Abbott, S., ed. *The Prevention of Racial Discrimination in Britain.* Oxford University, 1971.

Abel, A. S. *Laskin's Canadian Constitutional Law.* 4th rev. ed. Carswell, 1975.

Abel, R. L., ed. *The Politics of Informal Justice.* Academic Press, 1982.

Abel-Smith, E., and R. Stevens. *Lawyers and the Courts: A Sociological Study of the English Legal System, 1750-1965.* Heinemann, 1967.

———. *In Search of Justice: Society and the Legal System.* Heinemann, 1968.

———, B. M. Zander, and R. Brooke. *Legal Problems and the Citizen.* Heinemann, 1973.

Abrahams, G. *Police Questioning and the Judges' Rules.* Longman (Oyez) 1964.

Adams, M. *Censorship: The Irish Experience.* University of Alabama, 1968.

Agrawala, S. G. *Aircraft Highjacking and International Law.* Oceana, 1973.

Albinski, H. S. *Canadian and Australian Politics in Comparative Perspective.* University of Michigan, 1971.

Alcott, A. N., ed. *Judicial and Legal Systems in Africa.* Butterworth, 1962.

Alderfer, H. F. *Public Administration in New Nations.* Praeger, 1968.

Alexander, L. N. *The Law of the Sea.* University of Rhode Island, 1970.

Alexandrowicz, C. H. *Constitutional Developments in India.* Oxford University, 1957.

Allen, Sir C. K. *Administrative Jurisdiction.* Stevens, 1956.

———. *Law in the Making.* 7th ed. Oxford University, 1967.

———. *Law and Orders: An Inquiry into the Nature and Scope of Delegated Legislative and Executive Powers in England.* 3rd Ed. Stevens, 1953.

———. *The Queen's Peace.* Stevens, 1956.

Almond, G., and J. L. Coleman, eds. *The Politics of the Developing Areas.* Princeton University, 1960.

———, and S. Verba. *The Civic Culture: Political Attitudes and Democracy in Five Nations.* Little, Brown, 1956.

Alston, P., ed. *The International Dimensions of Human Rights.* Greenwood Press, 1982.

Amery, L. S. *Thoughts on the Constitution.* 2d ed. Oxford University, 1953.

Ames, W. L. *Police and Community in Japan.* University of California, 1981.

Amos, Sir. M. S. *British Criminal Justice.* Rev. ed. Longmans, Green, 1957.

———, and F. P. Walton, *Introduction to French Law.* Oxford University, 1935.

Anderson, J. N. D., ed. *Changing Law in Developing Countries.* Praeger, 1963.

———, *Islamic Law in the Modern World.* New York University, 1959.

Andrassy, J. *International Law and the Resources of the Sea.* Columbia University, 1970.

Andrews, J. A. *Criminal Justice.* University of Wales, 1968.

———, ed. *Human Rights in Criminal Procedures: A Comparative Study.* Martinus Nijhoff, 1982.

Anson, Sir. W. R. *Law and Custom of the Constitution.* Oxford University, 1922-35.

Anthony, K. *Feminism in Germany and Scandinavia.* Constable, 1966.

Appleman, J. A. *Military Tribunals and International Crimes.* Bobbs-Merrill, 1954.

Archbold, W. A. J. *Outlines of Indian Constitutional History—British Period.* Barnes & Noble Books, 1973.

Archer, P. *The Queen's Courts.* 2d ed. Pelican, 1963.

———. *Human Rights.* Fabian Society, 1969.

Arendt, H. *Eichman in Jerusalem*. Rev. ed. Viking Press, 1966.

Arthurs, H. W. *"Without the Law": Administrative Justice and Legal Pluralism in Nineteenth Century England*. University of Toronto, 1985.

Atiyah, P. S. *The Rise and Fall of Freedom of Contract*. Oxford University, 1981.

Atkins, S., and B., Hoggett, *Women and the Law*. Basil Blackwell, 1984.

Aubert, V., ed. *Sociology of Law*. Penguin Books, 1974.

Austin, J. *The Province of Jurisprudence Determined*. Weidenfeld & Nicholson, 1954.

Bagehot, W. *The English Constitution*. 2d ed. World's Classics, 1928.

Bailey, D. H. *Public Liberties in the New States*. Rand-McNally, 1964.

Bain, K. B. *Banned!* MacGibbon & Kee, 1967.

Baird, J. W., ed. *From Nuremberg to My Lai*. Heath, 1978.

Baker, H. C. *Legal Systems of Israel*. Israel University Press, 1968.

Baker, J. K. *An Introduction to English Legal History*. 2d ed. Butterworth, 1979.

Baker, R. D. *Judicial Review in Mexico: A Study of the Amparo Suit*. University of Texas, 1971.

Baldwin, J., and M. McConville. *Negotiated Justice: Pressure on Defendants to Plead Guilty*. Martin Robertson, 1977.

———. *Jury Trials*. Oxford University, 1979.

———, and K. Bottomley, eds. *Criminal Justice: Selected Readings*. Martin Robertson, 1978.

Banerjee, D. N. *Our Fundamental Rights: Their Nature and Extent (As Judicially Determined)*. World Press, 1960.

Bankowski, Z., and G. Mungham. *Images of Law*. Routledge & Kegan Paul, 1976.

Bannerjee, A. C., *The English Law in India*. Humanities Press, 1983.

Banton, M. *The Policeman in the Community*. Basic Books, 1964.

———. *Race Relations*. Basic Books, 1968.

———. *Racial Minorities*. Fontana Collins, 1972.

Barclay, W., K. Kumar, and R. P. Simms, eds. *Racial Conflict, Discrimination, and Power*. AMS Press, 1976.

Barker, Sir. E. *Church, State and Education*. University of Michigan, 1957.

Barkun, M. *Law Without Sanctions: Order in Primitive Societies and the World Community*. Yale University, 1968.

Barlow, R. B. *Citizenship and Conscience: A Study in the Theory and Practice of Religious Toleration in England During the Eighteenth Century*. University of Pennsylvania, 1963.

Barron, M. *Minorities in a Changing World*. Knopf, 1967.

Barry, B. *The Liberal Theory of Justice*. Oxford University, 1973.

Barry, D. D., and C. Barner-Barry. *Contemporary Soviet Politics: An Introduction*. Prentice-Hall, 1978.

Bartholomew, P. C. *The Irish Judiciary*. University of Notre Dame, 1971.

Bar-Yaacov, N. *Dual Nationality*. Praeger, 1961.

Bassiouni, M. C., ed. *The Islamic Criminal Justice System*. Oceana, 1982.

Basu, D. D. *Commentary on the Constitution of India*. 5th ed. Sarkar, 1965.

Bataille, A. *Inside the French Courts*. Hutchinson, 1941.

Bathhurst, M. E., et al. *Legal Problems of an Enlarged European Community*. Stevens, 1972.

Baumann, F. E., ed. *Human Rights and American Foreign Policy*. Kenyon College, 1982.

Baxi, U. *The Indian Supreme Court and Politics*. Eastern Book, 1980.

Bayley, D. H. *The Police and Political Development in India*. Princeton University, 1969.

———. *Forces of Order: Police Behavior in Japan and the United States*. University of California, 1978.

———. *Public Liberties in the New States*. Rand-McNally, 1964.

———, and H. Mendelsohn. *Minorities and the Police*. Free Press, 1969.

Bean, P. *Punishment: A Philosophical and Criminological Inquiry*. Martin Robertson, 1981.

Bebr, G. *Judicial Control of the European Communities*. Praeger, 1962.

Becker, T. L. *Comparative Judicial Politics: The Political Functionings of Courts.* Rand-McNally, 1970.

———, ed. *Political Trials.* Bobbs-Merrill, 1970.

Bedford, S. *The Faces of Justice: A Traveller's Report.* Simon and Schuster, 1961.

Bedi, A. S. *Freedom of Expression and Security: A Comparative Study of the Function of the Supreme Courts of the United States of America and India.* Asia Publishing, 1966.

Beer, L. W. *The Constitution of Japan: Major Judicial Decisions 1961–1970.* New Publications, 1976.

Bell, W., and W. E. Freeman, eds. *Ethnicity and Nation-Building: Comparative, International, and Historical Perspective.* Sage Publications, 1974.

Bellamy, J. *Crime and Public Order in England in the Later Middle Ages.* University of Toronto, 1973.

———. *The Tudor Law of Treason: An Introduction.* University of Toronto, 1979.

Bendix, R. *Nation-Building and Citizenship.* Wiley, 1964.

Benewick, R. *Political Violence and Public Order.* Allen Lane, 1969.

Bentham, J. *Rationale of Judicial Evidence.* Hunt and Clarke, 1827.

Benton, W. E., and G. Grimm, eds. *Nuremberg: German Views of the War Trials.* Southern Methodist University, 1955.

Berkeley, G. E. *The Democratic Policeman.* Beacon Press, 1969.

Berman, H. J. *Justice in Russia: An Interpretation of Soviet Law.* Rev. enl. ed. Random House (Vintage Books), 1963.

———. *Law and Revolution: The Formulation of the Western Legal Tradition.* Harvard University, 1983.

———. and J. W. Spindler. *Soviet Criminal Law and Procedure: The RSFSR Codes.* 2d ed. Harvard University, 1972.

———. and J. B. Quigley, Jr. *Basic Laws on the Structure of the Soviet State.* Harvard University 1968.

Bernier, I. *International Legal Aspects of Federalism.* Shoe String Press, 1973.

Berry, B. *Race and Ethnic Relations.* 3rd ed. Houghton Mifflin, 1965.

Beth, L. P. *The Development of Judicial Review in Ireland, 1937–1966.* Institute of Public Administration, Dublin, 1967.

Birch, A. H. *Federalism, Finance and Social Legislation in Canada, Australia, and the United States.* Oxford University, 1955.

Bishop, W. *International Law: Cases and Materials.* 2d, ed. Dennis, 1962.

Black, C. *Twentieth Century Europe.* 4th ed. Knopf, 1972.

Black, E. R. *Divided Loyalties: Canadian Concepts of Federalism.* McGill-Queen's University, 1975.

Blackstone, Sir W. *Commentaries on the Laws of England.* Oxford University, 1765–1769; rpt. Harper, 1854; Beacon Press, 1962; University of Chicago, 1979.

Blair, P. M. *Federalism and Judicial Review in West Germany.* Oxford University, 1981.

Blalock, H. *Toward a Theory of Minority-Group Relations.* Wiley, 1967.

Blanshard, P. *Freedom and Catholic Power in Spain and Portugal.* Beacon Press, 1962.

Blaustein, A. P., and G. H. Flanz. *Constitutions of the Countries of the World.* Oceana, 1971.

———, J. Sigler, and B. R. Beede, comps. *Independence Documents of the World.* Oceana, 1978.

Blom-Cooper, L., and G. Drewry. *The Final Appeal: A Study of the House of Lords in its Judicial Capacity.* Oxford University, 1972.

Blondel, J. *Comparative Legislatures.* Prentice-Hall, 1973.

———. *Comparative Political Systems.* Praeger, 1972.

Bloomfield, L. P. *International Military Forces.* Little, Brown, 1964.

Bodde, E., and C. Morris. *Law in Imperial China Exemplified by 190 Ch'ing Dynasty Cases.* Harvard University, 1968.

Bohannan, P. *Justice and Judgment Among the Tiv.* Oxford University 1957.

Bonner, R. J. *Lawyers and Litigants in Ancient Athens.* Barnes & Noble Books, 1969.

Borkin, J., *The Crime and Punishment of F. J. Farber*. Free Press, 1978.

Borrie, G. J., ed. *Judges on Trial: A Study of the Appointment and Accountability of the English Judiciary*. North Holland, 1976.

Bosch, W. J. *Judgment on Nuremberg*. University of North Carolina, 1970.

Bottoms, A. E., and J. D. McClean, *Defendants in the Criminal Process* Routledge & Kegan Paul, 1976.

Boulding, E. *Women in the Twentieth Century World*. Sage Publications, 1976.

Boutmy, E. G. *Studies in Constitutional Law: France, England, United States*. 2d ed. Macmillan, 1891.

Bowett, D. W. *The Law of International Institutions*. Praeger University, 1963.

Bowie, R. R. *International Crisis and the Role of Law*. Oxford University, 1974.

Bozeman, A. B. *The Future of Law in a Multicultural World*. Princeton University, 1971.

Bradley, A. W., ed. *Wade and Phillips, Constitutional and Administrative Law*. 9th ed. Longmans,Green, 1978.

Brady, J. P. *Justice and Politics in People's China: Legal Order or Continuing Revolution?* Sage Publications, 1983.

Braithwaite, J. *Inequality, Crime and Public Policy*. Routledge & Kegan Paul, 1979.

Brierly, J. L. *The Law of Nations*. 6th ed. Oxford University, 1963.

Brinkhorst, L. G., and J. G. Schermers. *Judicial Remedies in the European Community*. Rothman, 1969.

Brohi, A. K. *Fundamental Law of Pakistan*. Din Mahammadi Press, 1958.

Brookes, E. H., and J. B. Macaulay. *Civil Liberty in South Africa*. Oxford University, 1958.

Brotz, H. *The Politics of South African Democracy and Racial Diversity*. Oxford University, 1977.

Brown, E. G. *British Statutes in American Law, 1776–1836*. University of Michigan, 1965.

Browne, G. P., *The Judicial Committee and the British North America Act*. University of Toronto, 1967.

Browne, G. P., ed. *Documents on the Conf"eration of North America*. McClelland and Stewart, 1969.

Brownlie, I. *Principles of Public International Law*. Oxford University, 1968.

———. *Basic Documents on Human Rights*. Oxford University, 1971.

Brumberg, A. *In Quest of Justice*. Praeger, 1970.

Bryan, J. W. *The Development of the English Law of Conspiracy*. Johns Hopkins University, 1909.

Bryson, W. H. *The Equity Side of the Exchequer*. Cambridge University, 1975.

Buergenthal, T., ed. *Human Rights, International Law and the Helsinki Accord*. Allanheld, Osmum, 1979.

Bunche, R. *A World View of Race*. Kennikat Press, 1968.

Bunn, R., and W. G. Andrews, eds. *Basic Documents in Human Rights*. Oxford University, 1971.

———, eds. *Political and Civil Liberties in Europe*. Van Nostrand, 1967.

Bunyan, T. *The Political Police in Britain*. St. Martin's Press, 1976.

Burgess, J. W. *Political Science and Comparative Constitutional Law*. Dabor, 1978.

Burman, S. B., and B. E. Harrell-Bund, eds. *The Imposition of Law*. Academic Press, 1984.

Cahn, E. *The Sense of Injustice*. New York University, 1949.

Caiden, G. E. *International Handbook of the Ombudsman*. Greenwood Press, 1983.

Cam, H. M. *Law-Finders and Law-Makers in Medieval England*. Barnes & Noble Books, 1963.

Cameron, J. R. *Frederick William Maitland and the History of English Law*. University of Oklahoma, 1961.

Cameron, P. D. *Property Rights and Sovereign Rights: The Case of North Sea Oil*. Academic Press, 1983.

Campbell, C. M., and R. Wilson. *Lawyers and Their Public*. Martin Robertson, 1974.

Campbell, E. Q. *Racial Tensions and National Identity*. Vanderbilt University 1972.

Cantor, N. F. *William Stubbs on the English Constitution*. Cromwell, 1967.

Cappelletti, M. *Judicial Review in the Contemporary World*. Bobbs-Merrill, 1971.

Carey, J., ed. *Race, Peace, Law and Southern Africa*. Oceana, 1967.

————, ed. *United Nations Protection of Civil and Political Rights*. Syracuse University, 1971.

Carlen, P. *Magistrates' Justice*. Martin Robertson, 1976.

Carlton, C. *Bigotry and Blood: Documents on the Western Troubles*. Nelson-Hall, 1977.

Carlston, K. S. *Law and Organization in World Society*. University of Illinois, 1962.

Carlyle, A. J. *Political Liberty: A History of the Conception in the Middle Ages and Modern Times*. Cass, 1963.

Carr, Sir T. *Concerning English Administrative Law*. Columbia University, 1941.

Castaneda, J. *Legal Effects of United Nations Resolutions*. Columbia University, 1941.

Castlberg, F. *The European Convention on Human Rights*. Oceana, 1974.

————. *Freedom of Speech in the West*. Oceana, 1960.

————. *Problems of Legal Philosophy*. Allen and Unwin, 1958.

Cavenaugh, W. E. *Juvenile Courts, the Child and the Law*. Penguin, 1967.

Cecil, H. *The English Judge*. Stevens, 1970.

Central Office of Information. *The English Legal System*. Her Majesty's Stationery Office, 1964.

Chalidze, V. *To Defend These Rights: Human Rights and the Soviet Union*. Random House, 1974.

Chanders, J. *To Deprave and Corrupt*. Souvenir, 1962.

Chandler, D. *Capital Punishment in Canada*. McClelland and Stewart, 1976.

Chaney, E. M. *Supermadre: Women in Politics in Latin America*. University of Texas, 1979.

Chapman, B. *The Profession of Government*. Allen & Unwin, 1959.

Charles, R. *La Justice en France*. Presses Universitaires de France, 1958.

Charvet, J. *A Critique of Freedom and Equality*. Cambridge University, 1981.

Cheffins, R. I. *The Constitutional Process in Canada*. McGraw-Hill, 1969.

Chen, P. M. *Law and Justice: The Legal System in China 2400 BC–1960 AD*. Kennikat Press, 1974.

Chloros, A. G. *Yugoslav Civil Law: History, Family, Property*. Oxford University, 1970.

Christoph, J. B. *Capital Punishment and British Politics*. University of Chicago, 1962.

Claglett, H. *Administration of Justice in Latin America*. Oceana, 1952.

Claude, R. P., ed. *Comparative Human Rights*. Johns Hopkins University, 1976.

Clignet, R. *Liberty and Equality in the Educational Process*. Wiley, 1974.

Clinard, M. B. and D. J. Abbott. *Crime in Developing Countries: A Comparative Perspective*. Wiley 1973.

Clyde, W. M. *The Struggle of the Freedom of the Press from Caxton to Cromwell*. Oxford University, 1964.

Cockburn, J. S., ed. *Crime in England 1550–1800*. Princeton University 1977.

Cohen, M., ed. *Law and Politics in Space*. McGill University 1964.

Combin, J. *The Church and the National Security State*. Orbis Books, 1980.

Conot, R. E. *Justice at Nuremberg*. Harper & Row, 1983.

Conrad, J. P. *Crime and Its Correction: An International Survey of Attitudes and Practices*. University of California, 1965.

Conquest, R. ed. *Justice and the Legal System in the U.S.S.R.* Praeger, 1968.

————, ed. *The Soviet Police System*. Praeger, 1968.

Consumer Council. *Justice Out of Reach: A Case for Small Claims Courts*. Her Majesty's Stationery Office, 1970.

Coombs, O. ed. *Is Massa Day Dead: Black Moods in the Caribbean*. Doubleday (Anchor Books, 1974).

Cooray, J. A. L. *Constitutional Government and Human Rights in a Developing Society*. Colombo, Sri Lanka, 1969.

Coote, A. *Women's Rights*. Penguin Books, 1974.

Corbett, P. E. *The Growth of World Law*. Princeton University, 1971.

——. *Law in Diplomacy*. Princeton University, 1959.

Cornish, W. R. *The Jury*. Allen Lane, 1968.

Cosgrove, R. A. *The Rule of Law: Albert Vern Dicey, Victorian Jurist*. University of North Carolina, 1980.

Cowen, Z. *Federal Jurisdiction in Australia*. Oxford University, 1959.

——. *Individual Liberty and the Law*. Oceana, 1977.

Cracknell, D. G. Constitutional Law and the English Legal System. (Butterworth, 1968).

Cragg, G. *Freedom and Authority: A Study of English Thought in the Early Seventeenth Century*. Westminster Press, 1975.

Craig, A., *Suppressed Books*. World, 1963.

Craig, A. *The Banned Books of England and Other Countries*. Allen & Unwin, 1967.

Cramer, J. *The World Police*. Cassell 1964.

Cray, E. *The Big Blue Line: Police Power versus Human Rights*. Coward-McCann, 1967.

Crick, B., and W. A. Robson, eds. *Protest and Discontent*. Penguin Books, 1970.

Critchley, T. A. *A History of Police in England and Wales*. Constable, 1967.

——. *The Conquest of Violence: Order and Liberty in Britain*. Schocken Books, 1970.

Cropper, I. *Criminal Evidence*. Butterworth, 1965.

Cross, R. *An Introduction to Criminal Law*. 5th ed. Butterworth, 1964.

——. *Precedent in English Law*. 2d ed. Oxford University, 1968.

——. *The Golden Thread of the English Criminal Law: The Burden of Proof*. Cambridge University, 1976.

Curtis, M., ed. *Religion and Politics in the Middle East*. Westview, 1981.

D'Amato, A. A. *The Concept of Custom in International Law*. Cornell University, 1971.

Daniel, W. W. *Racial Discrimination in England*. Penguin Books, 1968.

Daube, D. *Roman Law: Linguistic, Social, and Philosophical Aspects*. Aldine, 1969.

David, H. E. *Government and Politics in Latin America*. Ronald Press, 1958.

David, R., and H. P. de Vries. *The French Legal System: An Introduction to Civil Law Systems*. Oceana, 1958.

——. and J. E. C. Brierly. *Major Legal Systems in the World Today: An Introduction to the Comparative Study of Law*. 2d ed. Carswell, 1978.

David, R. *French Law: Its Structure, Sources and Methodology*. Louisiana State University, 1972.

Davidson, E. *The Trial of the Germans: Nuremberg 1945–1946*. Macmillan, 1967.

Davis, K. C. *Discretionary Justice in Europe and America*. University of Illinois, 1976.

Davis, M., and Krauter, J. F. *The Other Canadians: Profiles of Six Minorities*. Methuen, 1971.

Davis, S. R. *The Federal Principle*. University of California, 1978.

Dawidowicz, L. S. *The War Against the Jews. 1933–1945*. Holt, Rinehart and Winston, 1975.

Dawson, F. P. *A History of Lay Judges*. Harvard 1960.

Dawson, J. P. *Gifts and Promises: Continental and American Laws Compared*. Yale University 1980.

Delany, V. T. H. *The Administration of Justice in Ireland*. Institute of Public Administration, Dublin, 1962.

Del de Lolme, J. L. *The Constitution of England*. Parker, 1838.

Denning, Sir A. *The Changing Law*. Stevens, 1953.

Deshpande, V. L. *Judicial Review of Legislation*. Eastern Book, 1975.

Deutsch, E. P. *An International Rule of Law*. University of Virginia, 1977.

Devlin, Sir P. *The Criminal Prosecution in England*. Yale University, 1958.

——. *The Enforcement of Morals*. Oxford University, 1965.

——. *The Judge*. Oxford University, 1979.

——. *Trial by Jury*. Stevens, 1956.

Diamond, A. S. *The Evolution of Law and Order*. Watts, 1951.

Dicey, A. V. *Introduction to the Study of the Law on the Constitution*. 10th ed. Macmillan, 1959.

———. *Law and Public Opinion in England During the Nineteenth Century*. Torch Publications, 1958.

Dietze, G. *Two Concepts of the Rule of Law*. Bobbs-Merrill, 1973.

Dinstein, Y. *Consular Immunity from Judicial Process*. Hebrew University, 1966.

Dillon, J. F. *The Laws and Jurisprudence of England and America*. Little, Brown, 1894.

Donner, A. *The Role of the Lawyer in the European Community*. Northwestern University, 1968.

Dorsey, G. L., ed. *Toward Equality and Freedom: An International Comparative Approach*. Oceana, 1975.

Dorsey, G. L. *Equality and Freedom: International and Comparative Jurisprudence*. Oceana, 1977.

Dowrick, F. E. *Justice According to the English Common Lawyers*. Butterworth, 1961.

Drewery, G. *Law, Justice and Politics*. Longman, 1975.

Driver, G. R., and J. C. Miles. *The Babylonian Laws*. Oxford University (Clarendon Press), 1952.

Du Cann, R. *The Art of the Advocate*. Penguin Books, 1964.

Duchacek, I. A. *Rights and Liberties in the World Today: Constitutional Promise and Reality*. ABC-Clio, 1973.

Duffet, J., ed. *Against the Crime of Silence: Proceedings of the International War Crimes Tribunal*. Bertrand Russell Peace Foundation, 1968.

Dugard, J. *Human Rights and the South African Legal Order*. Princeton University, 1978.

Duguit, L. *Law in the Modern State*. Huebsch, 1919.

Dumbauld, E. *The Life and Legal Writings of Ango Grotius*. University of Oklahoma, 1970.

Dworkin, R. *Taking Rights Seriously*. Harvard University, 1977.

———. *A Matter of Principles*. Harvard University, 1985.

Eaves, J., Jr., *Emergency Powers and the Parliamentary Watchdog*. Hansard Society, 1957.

Eddey, K. J. *The English Legal System*. 2d ed. Carswell, 1977.

Eder, P. J. *A Comparative Survey of Anglo-American and Latin-American Law*. New York University, 1950.

Edwards, S., *Female Sexuality and the Law*. Basil Blackwell, 1981.

Eide, A. *Human Rights in the World Society*. Coleman, 1980.

Ehrmann, H. W., *Comparative Legal Cultures*. Prentice-Hall, 1976.

Eldersveld, S. J., V. Jagannadham, and A. P. Barnabas. *The Citizen and the Administrator in a Developing Democracy*. Scott, Foresman, 1968.

Elias, T. O. *The Nature of African Customary Law*. Manchester University, 1956.

Elliott, J. L. *Minority Canadians*. Prentice-Hall, 1971.

Else-Mitchell, R., ed. *Essays on the Australian Constitution*. 2d ed. Law Book Co., Sydney, 1961.

Emden, C. S. *The People and the Constitution*. 2d ed. Oxford University, 1956.

Engel, S., with R. A. Metall, eds. *Law, State, and International Legal Order: Essays in Honor of Hans Kelsen*. University of Tennessee, 1964.

Englard, I. *Religious Law in the Israel Legal System*. Hebrew University, 1975.

Enloe, C. *Ethnic Conflict and Political Development*. Little, Brown, 1973.

———. *Police, Military and Ethnicity: Foundations of State Power*. Transaction Books, 1979.

Ensor, R. C. K. *Courts and Judges in France, Germany, and England*. Oxford University, 1933.

Erades, L., and W. L. Gould. *The Relations Between International Law and Municipal Law in the Netherlands and in the United States*. Oceana, 1960.

Esmein, A. *A History of Continental Criminal Procedure*. Parkhill, 1914.

Evan, W. M., ed. *Law and Sociology: Exploratory Essays*. Free Press, 1962.

Evans, A. E., and J. P. Murphy. *Legal Aspects of International Terrorism*. Lexington Books, 1978.

Evans, R. J. *The Feminists*. Harper & Row, 1979.

Facts on File, eds. *Political Prisoners: A World Report*. Facts on File, 1978.

Falk, R. A. *Human Rights and State Sovereignty*. Holmes & Meier, 1981.

————. *Legal Order in a Violent World*. Princeton University, 1968.

————. *The Role of Domestic Courts in the International Legal Order*. Syracuse University, 1964.

————. *The Status of Law in International Society*. Princeton University, 1970.

————, and C. E. Black, eds. *The Future of the International Legal Order*. Princeton University, 1970.

————, G. Kolks, and R. J. Lifton, eds. *Crimes of War*. Viking Press, 1971.

————, and S. H. Mendlovitz, eds. *The Strategy of World Order*. World Law Fund, 1966.

Falk, R. A., et al. *Essays on International Jurisdiction*. Ohio State University, 1961.

Fascell, D., ed. *International News: Freedom Under Attack*. Sage Publications, 1980.

Fawcett, J. C. S. *The Application of the European Convention on Human Rights*. Oxford University, 1969.

Fazal, M. A. *Judicial Control of Administrative Action in India and Pakistan*. Oxford University, 1969.

Feifer, G. *Justice in Moscow*. Simon and Schuster, 1964.

Fein, H. *Accounting for Genocide: National Response, and Jewish Victimization During the Holocaust*. Free Press, 1979.

Feldbrugge, F. J. M., ed. *Encyclopedia of Soviet Law*. Sythoff, 1973.

Fellman, D. *The Defendant's Rights Under English Law*. University of Wisconsin, 1966.

Ferencz, B. B. *An International Criminal Court: A Step Toward World Peace—Documentary History and Analysis*. Oceana, 1979.

Fernando, E. M. *The Bill of Rights*. Oceana, 1971.

————. *The Constitution of the Philippines*. Oceana, 1975.

Finer, S. E., ed. *Five Constitutions: Contrasts and Comparisons*. Penguin Books, 1979.

Fitzgibbon, R. H., ed. *The Constitution of the Americas*. University of Chicago, 1951.

Flaherty, D. H., ed. *Essays in the History of Canadian Law*. University of Toronto, 1981.

Flecher, J. K. *The British Courts: Traditions and Ceremonial*. Cassell, 1953.

Flender, H. *Rescue in Denmark*. Macfadden-Bartell, 1964.

Fliess, P. J. *Freedom of the Press in the German Republic. 1918-1933*. Louisiana State University, 1955.

Foot, P. *The Rise of Enoch Powell*. Penguin Books, 1967.

————. *Immigration and Race in British Politics*. Penguin Books, 1967.

Foreign Languages Publishing House. *Fundamentals of Soviet Criminal Legislation, The Judicial System, and Criminal Court Procedure*. FLPH, 1960.

Forsythe, D. P. *Human Rights and World Politics*. University of Nebraska, 1983.

Fosdick, R. B. *European Police Systems*. Century, 1915.

Fouilee, A., et al. *Modern French Legal Philosophy*. Macmillan, 1921.

Franck, T. M. *Comparative Constitutional Processes: Cases and Materials*. Praeger, 1968.

————. *Comparative Constitutional Process: Fundamental Rights in the Common Law Countries*. Sweet & Maxwell, 1968.

————, and E. Weisband. *Word Politics and Verbal Strategy Among the Super Powers*. Oxford University, 1971.

Freedeman, C. E. *The Conseil d'État in Modern France* Columbia University, 1961.

Friedland, M. L. *Detention Before Trial*. University of Toronto, 1974.

————, *Double Jeopardy*. Oxford University, 1969.

————, ed. *Courts and Trials: A Multi-Disciplinary Approach*. University of Toronto, 1975.

Friedman, J. R., and M. I. Sherman, eds. *Human Rights An International and Comparative Law Biography*. Greenwood Press, 1985.

Friedman, S. S. *Amcha: An Oral Testament of the Holocaust*. University Press of America, 1979.

Friedman, W. *The Changing Structure of International Law*. Columbia University, 1964.

————. *Law and Social Change in Contemporary Britain*. Stevens, 1951.

————. *Law in a Changing Society*. 2d ed. Penguin Books, 1965.

————. *Legal Theory*. 5th ed. Columbia University, 1967.

———. ed. *Transnational Law in a Changing Society*. Columbia University, 1972.

Friedrich, C. *The Impact of American Constitutionalism Abroad*. Boston University, 1967.

Friesen, E. C., and I. R. Scott, *English Criminal Justice: An Introduction for American Readers*. University of Birmingham, 1977.

Fry, G. K. *The Administrative Revolution in Whitehall*. Croom Helm, 1981.

Galbraith, V. H. *Domesday Book: Its Place in Administrative History*. Oxford University, 1975.

Gastil, R. D. *The Freedom in the World: Political Rights and Civil Liberties, 1982*. Greenwood Press, 1983.

Galeotti, S. *The Judicial Control of Public Authorities in England and in Italy*. Stevens, 1954.

Gall, G. L. *Canadian Legal System*. Carswell, 1977.

Garsia, M. *Criminal Law and Procedure in a Nutshell*. Sweet & Maxwell, 1964.

Geldart, W. M. *Elements of English Law*. 7th ed. Oxford University, 1966.

Gellner, J., and J. Smerek. *The Czechs and Slovaks in Canada*. University of Toronto, 1965.

Ghosh, S. K. *Freedom from Fear*. Satchidanda Prakashani, India, 1978.

———. *In Search of Justice*. Satchidanda Prakashani, India, 1976.

Gide, A. *Recollections of the Assize Court*. Hutchinson, 1941.

Giele, J. Z., and A. C. Smock, eds. *Women: Roles and Status in Eight Countries*. Wiley, 1977.

Gierke, O. F. *Associations and the Law*. Ed. and trans., George Herman. University of Toronto, 1977.

Gilbert, G. M. *Nuremberg Diary*. New American Library, 1960.

Giles, F. T. *The Criminal Law*. 3rd ed. Penguin Books, 1963.

———. *The Juvenile Courts: Their Work and Problems*. Allen & Unwin, 1946.

———. *The Magistrates' Courts*. Rev. ed. Stevens, 1964.

Ginsberg, M., ed. *Law and Opinion in England in the Twentieth Century*. University of California, 1959.

Giuttari, T. R. *The American Law of Sovereign Immunity: An Analysis of Legal Interpretation*. Praeger, 1970.

Glaser, K., and S. J. Possony. *Victims of Politics: The State of Human Rights*. Columbia University, 1979.

Glassey, L. K. J. *Politics and the Appointment of the Justices of the Peach, 1675–1720*. Oxford University, 1980.

Glazer, N., and K. Young, eds. *Ethnic Pluralism and Public Policy: Achieving Equality in the United States and Britain* (Lexington Books, 1983).

Gledhill, A. *The Republic of India: The Development of Its Law and Constitution*. 2d ed. Stevens, 1964; rpt. Greenwood Press, 1977.

Gluckman, M., ed. *Ideas and Procedures in African Customary Law*. Oxford University, 1969.

———. *The Ideas in Barotse Jurisprudence*. Yale University, 1965.

———. *The Judicial Process Among the Barotse of Northern Rhodesia*. 2d ed. University of Manchester, 1967.

———. *Politics, Law and Ritual in Tribal Society*. Aldine, 1965.

Goerner, E. A., ed. *Democracy in Crisis: New Challenges to Constitutional Democracy in the Atlantic Area*. University of Notre Dame, 1971.

Golay, O. F. *The Founding of the Federal Republic of Germany*. University of Chicago, 1958.

Golyakov, I. T. *The Role of the Soviet Court*. Public Affairs Press, 1948.

Goren, D. *Secrecy and the Right to Know*. Turtledove, 1979.

Goodhart, A. H. *English Law and the Moral Law*. Stevens, 1953.

———. *Precedent in English and Continental Law*. Stevens, 1934.

Goodnow, R. *Comparative Administrative Law*. Dabor, 1978.

Gottlieb, A., ed. *Human Rights, Federalism and Minorities*. Canadian Institute of International Affairs, 1970.

Gough, J. W. *Foundamental Law in English Constitutional History*. Oxford University, 1955.

Graham, J. W. *Conscription and Conscience: A History. 1916–1919*. Knopf, 1969.

Graham, M. H. *Tightening the Reins of Justice: A Comparative Analysis of the Criminal Jury Trial in England and the United States.* Greenwood Press, 1983.

Graulich, P. *Guide to Foreign Legal Materials.* Oceana, 1968.

Graveson, R. H. *The Conflict of Law.* Sweet & Maxwell, 1965.

Green, A. W. *Political Integration by Jurisprudence.* Martinus Nijhoff, 1969.

Green, E. *Judicial Attitudes Toward Sentencing.* Macmillan, 1961.

Green, L. C. *Law and Society.* Oceana, 1975.

Greenberg, S. B. *Race and State in Capitalist Development: Comparative Perspectives.* Yale University, 1979.

Greenwood, C. *Firearms Control: England and Wales.* Routledge and Kegan Paul, 1972.

Griffith, J. A. G. *The Politics of the Judiciary.* Fontana, 1977.

————, and J. Street. *Principles of Administrative Law.* 2d ed. Pitman, 1958.

Groves, H. E. *Comparative Constitutional Law.* Oceana, 1963.

Grzybowski, K. *Soviet Legal Institutions.* University of Michigan, 1962.

————. *The Socialist Commonwealth of Nations, Organizations and Institutions.* Yale University, 1964.

Gsovsky, V., and K. Grzybowski, eds. *Government, Law and the Courts in the Soviet Union and Eastern Europe.* Praeger, 1960.

Guins, G. C. *Soviet Law and Soviet Society.* Martinus Nijhoff, 1954.

Gulliver, P. H. *Disputes and Negotiations: A Cross-Cultural Perspective.* Academic Press, 1980.

Gurr, T. R., et al. *The Politics of Crime and Conflict: A Comparative Study of Four Cities.* Sage Publications, 1977.

————. *Rogues, Rebels, and Reformers: A Political History of Urban Crime and Conflict.* Sage Publications, 1976.

Gutteridge, H. C. *Comparative Law.* Cambridge University, 1946.

Guy, J. A. *The Cardinal's Court: The Impact of Thomas Molsey in Star Chamber.* (Bowman & Little, 1977).

Haas, E. B., *Human Righs and International Action.* Stanford University, 1970.

Hacker, P. M. S., and J. Raz, eds. *Law, Morality and Society: Essays in Honor of H.L.A. Hart.* Oxford University, 1977.

Hagerstrom, A. *Inquiries into the Nature of Law and Morals.* Oxford University, 1931.

Haksar, U. *Minority Protection and International Bill of Human Rights.* Allied, 1974.

Hale, Sir M., ed. *The History of the Common Law of England.* University of Chicago, 1971.

Haley, A. G. *Space Law and Government.* Appleton-Century-Crofts, 1963.

Hall, J. *Comparative Law and Social Theory.* Louisiana State University, 1963.

Halpern, M. *Applying a New Theory of Human Relations to the Comparative Study of Racism.* University of Denver, 1970.

Hampshire, S., ed. *Public and Private Morality.* Cambridge University, 1978.

Hamson, C. J. *Executive Discretion and Judicial Control: An Aspect of the French Conseil d'État.* Stevens, 1954.

Hanbury, H. G., and D. C. M. Yardley. *English Courts of Law.* 5th ed. Oxford University, 1979.

Hannum, H., ed *Guide to International Human Rights Practice.* University of Pennsylvania, 1984.

Harding, A. *A Social History of English Law.* Penguin Books, 1966; rpt. Peter Smith, 1973.

————. *The Law Courts of Medieval England.* Barnes & Noble Books, 1973.

————, ed. *Law-making and Lawmakers in British History.* Royal Historical Society, 1980.

Hargrove, J. L., ed. *Law, Institutions and the Global Environment.* Oceana, 1972.

Harries-Jenkins, G., and J. Van Doorn, eds. *The Military and the Problem of Legitimacy.* Sage Publications, 1976.

Harris, W. R. *Tyranny on Trial: The Evidence at Nuremberg.* Southern Methodist University, 1954.

Harrison, B. F. *The Work of a Magistrate.* Shaw, 1964.

Harrison, W. *The Government of Britain*. 6th ed. Hutchinson, 1960.

Hart, H. L. A. *Punishment and Responsibility: Essays in the Philosophy of Law*. Oxford University, 1968.

Hart, J. M. *The British Police*. Allen & Unwin, 1951.

Hassan, F. *The Concept of State and Law in Islam*. University Press of America, 1981.

Hauriou, M. *Droit Constitutionnel et Institutions Politiques*. Monchrestien, 1966.

Hausner, G. *Justice in Jerusalem*. Harper & Row, 1966.

Havighurst, C. C., ed. *International Control of Propaganda*. Oceana, 1967.

Hawgood, J. A. *Modern Constitutions Since 1787*. Macmillan, 1939.

Hay, P. *Federalism and Supranational Organizations: Patterns for New Legal Structures*. University of Illinois, 1966.

Hazard, J. N. *Communist's and Their Law*. University of Chicago, 1969.

———. *Law and Social Change in Soviet Society*. University of Toronto, 1953.

———. *Settling Disputes in Soviet Society: The Formative Years in Legal Institutions*. Rev. ed. Columbia University, 1960.

———, I Shapiro, and P. B. Maggs. *The Soviet Legal System: Post-Stalin Documentation and Historical Commentary*. 2d ed. Oceana, 1969.

Heineman, B. W., Jr. *The Politics of the Powerless: A Study of the Campaign Against Discrimination*. Oxford University, 1972.

Henderson, D. F. *The Constitution of Japan: Its First Twenty Years, 1947–67*. University of Washington, 1969.

Henderson, E. G. *Foundations of English Administrative Law: Certiorari and Mandamus in the Seventeenth Century*. Harvard University, 1963.

Henkin, L. *International Bill of Rights: The Covenant on Civil and Political Rights*. Columbia University, 1982.

Hepple, B. *Race, Jobs, and the Law in Britain*. Penguin Books, 1968.

Heuston, R. F. V. *Essays in Constitutional Law*. 2d ed. Stevens, 1964.

Hevener, N. K., ed. *The Dynamics of Human Rights in United States Foreign Policy*. Transaction Books, 1981.

Hewitt, P., *The Abuse of Power: Civil Liberties in Modern Britain*. Basil Blackwell, 1981.

Heyde, W. *The Administration of Justice in the Federal Republic of Germany*. German Information Office, 1971.

Heydecker, J. J., and J. Leeb. *The Nuremberg Trials*. Greenwood Press, 1975.

Hilberg, P. *The Destruction of the European Jews*. Harper & Row, 1983.

Hill, L.B. *The Model Ombudsman: Institutionalizing New Zealand's Democratic Experiment*. Princeton University, 1977.

Hiro, D. *Black British, White British*. Rampart, 1974.

Hoffman, S., et al. *In Search of France*. Harvard University, 1960.

Hogarth, J. *Sentencing as a Human Process*. University of Toronto, 1974.

Hogg, P. *Constitutional Law of Canada*. Carswell, 1977.

Holcombe, A. N. *Human Rights in the Modern World*. New York University, 1948.

Holdaway, S., ed. *The British Police*. Sage Publications, 1980.

Holdsworth, Sir. W. *A History of English Law*. 7th ed. Goodhart & Hanbury, 1956.

———. *Some Makers of English Law*. Rev. ed. Cambridge University, 1966.

Holloway, K. *Modern Trends in Treaty Law: Constitutional Law, Reservations and the Three Modes of Legislation*. Oceana, 1967.

Holmes, C. *Anti-Semitism in British Society. 1876–1939*. Holmes & Meier, 1979.

Holmes, J., and C. Sharman. *The Australian Federal System*. Allen & Unwin, 1978.

Holt, J. C. *Magna Carta*. Cambridge University, 1965.

Hosking, G. A. *The Russian Constitutional Experiment: Government and Duma, 1907–1914*. Cambridge University, 1973.

Howell, P. A. *The Judicial Committee of the Privy Council 1833–1876*. Cambridge University, 1980.

Hughes, C. *The Federal Constitution of Switzerland: Translation and Commentary.* Oxford University, 1954.

Hutchinson, T. W., ed. *Africa and Law: Developing Legal Systems in African Commonwealth Nations.* University of Wisconsin, 1968.

Hyde, H. M., Lord Justice. *The Life and Times of Lord Birkett of Ulverston.* Random House, 1965.

Iglitzin, L. G., and R. Ross, eds. *Women in the World: A Comparative Study.* (ABC-Clio, 1976.

Ingraham, B. L. *Political Crime in Europe: A Comparative Study of France, Germany and England* (University of California, 1980).

Inns of Court, The. *Rule of Law: A Study by the Inns of Court* Conservative Political Caucus, 1956.

Institute of Pacific Studies. *Pacific Courts and Justice.* Commonwealth Magistrates Association, 1977.

Ioffe, O. S. *Soviet Civil Law.* International Arts and Sciences Press, 1961.

————, and M. D. Shargorodskii. *Problems of Legal Theory.* International Arts and Sciences Press, 1961.

Jackson, R. H. *The Nuremberg Case.* Knopf, 1947.

Jackson, R. M. *Enforcing the Law.* Pelican Publishing Co., 1972.

————. *The Machinery of Justice in England.* 7th ed. Cambridge University, 1977.

Jacob, Sir. I. H. *The Reform of Civil Procedural Law and Other Essays in Civil Procedure.* Sweet & Maxwell, 1982.

Jacobini, H. B. *International Law: A Text.* Rev. ed. Dorsey Press, 1968.

Jaffe, L. L. *English and American Judges as Lawmakers.* Oxford University, 1970.

James, P. S. *Introduction to English Law.* 4th ed. Butterworth, 1959.

James, Viscount Stair. *The Institution of the Law of Scotland.* Yale University, 1981.

Jenks, C. W. *The Common Law of Mankind.* Praeger, 1959.

————. *Law in the World Community.* McKay, 1967.

————. *The Proper Law of International Organization.* Oceana, 1962.

————. *Space Law.* Praeger, 1965.

Jenks, E. *The Book of English Law.* 6th ed. Ohio State University, 1967.

Jennings, Sir. W. I. *The British Constitution.* 3rd ed. Cambridge University, 1950.

————. *Constitutional Law and the Commonwealth.* 3rd ed. Oxford University, 1957.

————. *The Law and the Constitution.* 4th ed. University of London, 1958.

Jessup, P. C. *The Price of International Justice.* Columbia University, 1971.

Johnson, C. *Conspiracy at Matsukawa.* University of California, 1972.

Johnson, E. L. *An Introduction to the Soviet Legal System.* Methuen, 1969.

Johnston, R. E. *The Effect of Judicial Review on Federal-State Relations in Australia, Canada, and the United States.* Louisiana State University, 1969.

Johnstone, Q., and D. Hopson, Jr. *Lawyers and Their Work.* Bobbs-Merrill, 1967.

Jolowicz, H. F., and B. Nicholas. *Historical Introduction to the Study of Roman Law.* 3rd ed. Cambridge University, 1972.

Jones, A. H. M. *Studies in Roman Government and Law.* Praeger, 1960.

Jones, D. *Crime, Protest, Community, and Police in Nineteenth-Century Britain.* Routledge & Kegan Paul, 1982.

Jones, G. *The Sovereignty of the Law.* University of Toronto, 1973.

Joyce, J. A. *Capital Punishment: A World View.* Nelson, 1961.

————. *Human Rights: International Documents.* Oceana, 1978.

Joyner, N. D. *Highjacking as an International Crime.* Oceana, 1974.

Kahin, G. McT. *Major Governments of Asia.* Cornell University, 1958.

Kamenka, E., and A. Ehr-Soon Tay, eds. *Human Rights.* St. Martin's Press, 1978.

Kaminskaya, D. *Final Justice.* Simon and Schuster, 1983.

Kaplan, M. A. *The Jewish Feminist Movement in Germany.* Greenwood Press, 1979.

Karlen, D. *Appellate Courts in the United States and England.* New York University, 1963.

———, in collaboration with G. Sawyer and E. M. Wise. *Anglo-American Criminal Justice.* Oxford University, 1967.

Karst, K. L., and K. S. Rosenn. *Law and Development in Latin America.* University of California, 1975.

Katz, M. *The Relevance of International Adjudication.* Harvard University, 1968.

Katznelson, I. *Black Men, White Cities.* Oxford University, 1974.

Keeton, G. W. *The Norman Conquest and the Common Law.* Barnes & Noble Books, 1966.

Keeton, G. W. *The Passing of Parliament.* 2d ed. Benn, 1954.

———, et al. *The United Kingdom, the Development of its Law and Constitution: England, Wales, Northern Ireland, the Isle of Man, Scotland, the Channel Islands.* Stevens, 1955.

Keir, Sr. D. L. *The Constitutional History of Modern Britain Since 1485.* 6th ed. Black, 1960.

———, and F. H. Lawson, eds. *Cases in Constitutional Law.* 5th ed. Oxford University, 1967.

Kellas, J. G. *The Scottish Political System.* 2d ed. Cambridge University, 1975.

Kelly, J. M. *Fundamental Rights in the Irish Law and Constitution.* 2d ed. Allen Figgis, 1967.

———. *Studies in the Civil Judicature of the Roman Republic.* Oxford University, 1976.

Kelly, W., and N. Kelly. *Policing in Canada.* Maclean-Hunter, 1975.

Kelsen, H. *The Communist Theory of Law.* Praeger, 1960.

———. *General Theory of Law and State.* Russell & Russell, 1961.

———. *Principles of International Law.* 2d ed. Holt, Rinehart and Winston, 1966.

Kempin, F. G., Jr. *Legal History: Law and Social Change.* Prentice-Hall, 1963.

Kessler, M.-C. *Le Conseil d'État.* Armand Colin, 1968.

Khadduri, M., *The Islamic Conception of Justice.* Johns Hopkins, 1984.

Kidd, R. *British Liberty in Danger.* Lawrence & Wishart, 1942.

Kili, S. *Turkish Constitutional Developments and Assembly Debates on the Constitutions of 1924 and 1961.* Robert College Press, 1972.

King, J. B. *Law Versus Order: Legal Process and Free Speech in Contemporary France.* Shoe String Press (Archon Books), 1975.

King, R. R. *Minorities Under Communism: Nationality as a Source of Tension Among Balkan Communist States.* Harvard University, 1973.

Kinnane, C. H. *Anglo-American Law.* 2d ed. Bobbs-Merrill, 1952.

Kiralfy, A. K. *The English Legal System.* 6th ed. Sweet & Maxwell, 1977.

Kiralfy, A. K. *Introduction to Jurisprudence.* 4th ed. Carswell, 1979.

Kiraly, B. K. *Tolerance and Movements of Religious Dissent in Eastern Europe.* Columbia University, 1976.

Kirchheimer, O. *Political Justice.* Princeton University, 1961.

Kohn, W. S. G. *Women in National Legislatures: A Comparative Study of Six Countries.* Yale University, 1980.

Kommers, D. P. *Judicial Politics in West Germany: A Study of the Federal Constitutional Court.* Sage Publications, 1976.

———, and G. D. Loescher. *Human Rights and American Foreign Policy.* University of Notre Dame, 1978.

Konstantinovsky, B. A. *Soviet Law in Action: The Recollected Cases of a Soviet Lawyer.* Harvard University, 1953.

Koopmans, T., ed. *Constitutional Protection of Equality.* Martinus Nijhoff, 1975.

Kramer, D. C. *Comparative Civil Rights and Liberties.* University Press of America, 1982.

Krauter, J. F. *Civil Liberties and the Canadian Minorities.* University of Michigan, 1969.

Krieger, L. *The German Idea of Freedom.* Beacon Press, 1957.

Kucherov, S. *The Congress of Soviet Administration of Justice: Soviet History and Operation.* Brill, 1970.

———. *Courts, Lawyers, and Trials Under the Last Three Tsars.* Praeger, 1953.

Kunkel, W. *An Introduction to Roman Legal and Constitutional History.* Oxford University, 1966.

Kuper, H., and L., eds. *African Law: Adaptation and Development.* University of California, 1965.

Kutner, L. *The Human Right to Individual Freedom: A Symposium on World Habeus Corpus.* University of Miami, 1970.

——. *World Habeas Corpus.* Oceana, 1962.

Lachlan, C. M. *Criminal Justice in Eighteenth-Century Mexico: A Study of the Tribunal of the Acordada.* University of California, 1974.

La Fave, W. R. *Law in the Soviet Society.* University of Illinois, 1966.

La Forest, G. V. *Disallowance and Reservation of Provincial Legislation.* Canadian Ministry of Justice, 1955.

——. *Extradiction to and from Canada.* Hauser, 1962.

Lambert, J. *Crime, Police and Race Relations.* Oxford University, 1970.

La Nauze, J. A. *The Making of the Australian Constitution.* University of Melbourne, 1972.

Landau, A. F. *Selected Judgments of the Supreme Court of Israel.* Transaction Books, 1971.

Lane, P. H. *The Australian Federal System with United States Analogues.* Law Book Co., Sydney, 1972.

Lapenna, I. *State and Law: Soviet and Yugoslav Theory.* Yale University, 1964.

Laqueur, W., and B. Rubin, eds. *The Human Rights Reader.* Temple University, 1979.

Larkin, M. *Church and State: After the Dreyfuss Affair: The Separation Issue in France.* Barnes & Noble Books, 1974.

Laskin B., ed. *Canadian Constitutional Law: Cases, Text and Notes.* 3rd ed. Carswell, 1969.

——. *The British Tradition in Canadian Law.* Stevens, 1967.

Lasky, H. J. *Studies in Law and Politics.* Allen & Unwin, 1932.

Laufer, H. *Verfassungsgerichtsbarkeit and Politischer Prozess.* Mohr, 1968.

Von Laun, R. *Stare Decisis.* Meissner's Verlag, 1984.

Lauterpacht, E., and J. G. Collier. *Individual Rights and the State in Foreign Affairs.* Praeger, 1977.

Lauterpacht, Sir. H. *The Development of International Law in the International Court.* Praeger, 1958.

——. *The Function of Law in the International Community.* Oxford University, 1933.

Lawson, F. H. *A Common Lawyer Looks at the Civil Law.* Oxford University, 1955.

——, et al. *Amos and Walton's Introduction to French Law.* 2d ed. Oxford University, 1963.

——, ed. *The Roman Law Reader.* Oceana, 1969.

Lawson, F. H. *The Rational Strength of English Law.* Stevens, 1951.

Leavitt, R. R., ed. *Women Cross-Culturally: Change and Challenge.* Mouton-Alaine, 1976.

Lederman, W. R., ed. *The Courts and the Canadian Constitution.* McClelland & Stewart, 1964.

Leech, N. E., C. T. Oliver, and J. M. Sweeney. *The International Legal System: Cases and Materials.* Foundation Press, 1973.

Lester, A., and G. Bindman. *Race and Law in Great Britain.* Penguin Books, 1972.

Letourneur, M., J. Bauchet, and J. Meric. *Le Conseil d'État et les Tribunaux Administratifs.* Armand Colin, 1970.

Levi, W. *Law and Politics in the International Society.* Sage Publications, 1976.

Levin, J., ed. *The Struggle for Racial Equality.* Longmans, Green, 1967.

Levine, D. H. *Religion and Politics in Latin America.* Princeton University, 1981.

Levy, H. P. *The Press Council: History, Procedure, and Cases.* St. Martin's Press, 1968.

Lewin, J. *Studies in African Law.* University of Pennsylvania, 1971.

Lewis, J. R. *Law in Action.* Allman, 1965.

Lewy, C., et al *Essays on French Law.* Washington Law Society, 1958.

Liang, H. H. *The Berlin Police Force in the Weimar Republic.* University of California, 1970.

Libbrecht, E. *Enterprises à Caractère Juridiquement International.* Martinus Nijhoff, 1974.

Lillich, R. B. *International Claims: Postwar British Practice.* University of Virginia, 1972.

Lillich, R. B., and B. H. Weston, eds. *International Claims: Contemporary European Practices.* University of Virginia, 1981.

Lissak, M. *Military Roles in Modernization: Civil-Military Relations in Thailand and Burma.* Sage Publications, 1976.

Lissitzyn, O. J. *The International Court of Justice.* Columbia University, 1951.

Llewellyn, K. *The Bramble Bush.* Knopf, 1930.

Lloyd, D. ed. *Introduction to Jurisprudence.* Rev. ed. Praeger, 1966.

Luard, E. *Conflict and Peace in the Modern International System.* Little, Brown, 1968.

———, ed. *The International Protection of Human Rights.* Praeger, 1967.

Lucas, J. R. *On Justice.* Oxford University, 1980.

Luchaire, F. *Le Counseil Constitutionnel.* Economica, 1980.

Lyon, J. N., and R. G. Atkey, eds. *Canadian Constitutional Law in a Modern Perspective.* University of Toronto, 1970.

Maarseveen, H. van, and G. van Dertang. *Written Constitutions: A Computerized Comparative Study.* Oceana, 1978.

McConville, S. *The History of English Prison Administration.* Routledge & Kegan Paul, 1981.

MacCormick, N *Legal Reasoning and Legal Theory.* Oxford University, 1978.

MacDonald, R. St. J., ed. *Changing Legal Objectives.* University of Toronto, 1963.

MacGuigan, M. R. *Jurisprudence: Readings and Cases.* 2nd ed. University of Toronto, 1963.

MacMillan, W. M. *The Road to Self-Rule: A Study in Colonial Evolution.* Taber, 1969.

MacNeill, J. G. *The Constitutional and Parliamentary History of Ireland Till the Union.* Kennikat Press, 1970.

Maggs, P. B. *The Soviet Legal System.* Oceana, 1966.

Maitland, F. W. *The Constitutional History of England.* Cambridge University, 1961.

———. *Selected Historical Essays.* Beacon Press, 1963.

Maki, J. M. *Court and Constitution in Japan: Selected Supreme Court Decisions, 1948–60.* University of Washington, 1964.

———, trans. and ed. *Japan's Commission on the Constitution: The Final Report.* University of Washington, 1980.

Malinowski, B. *Crime and Custom in Savage Society.* Harcourt Brace, 1926.

Mallory, J. R. *The Structure of Canadian Government.* St. Martin's Press, 1971.

Manchester, W. *A Modern Legal History of England and Wales, 1750–1950.* Butterworth, 1980.

Mann, A. *Judgment at Nuremberg.* New American Library, 1960.

Marke, J. J. *Vignettes of Legal History.* 2nd ser. Rothman, 1977.

Marsh, S. B. *Outlines of English Law.* Sweet & Maxwell, 1967.

Marshall, G. *Constitutional Theory.* Oxford University, 1971.

———. *Police and Government: The Status and Accountability of the British Constable.* Methuen, 1965, 1967.

Marshall, G., and G. C. Moodle. *Some Problems of the Constitution* Hutchinson, 1959.

Martin, R. *Personal Freedom and the Law in Tanzania.* Oxford University, 1974.

Maser, W. *Nuremberg: A Nation on Trial.* Scribner, 1979.

Mason, P. *Race Relations.* Oxford University, 1970.

McCable, S. and R. Purves. *Bypassing the Jury.* Basil Blackwell. 1972.

———. *The Jury at Work.* Basil Blackwell, 1972.

———. *The Shadow Jury at Work.* Basil Blackwell, 1974.

McDougal, M. S., and F. Feliciano. *Law and Minimum World Public Order.* (Yale, 1962).

———, H. D. Lasswell, and L.-C. Chen. *Human Rights and World Public Order.* Rev. ed. University of Chicago, 1980.

McGrath, W. T., (2d), *Crime and its Treatment in Canada.* 2nd. Macmillan, 1976.

McIlwain, C. H. *The High Court of Parliament.* Yale University, 1910.

McIntosh, M. *The Organization of Crime.* Macmillan, 1975.

McKechnie, W. S. *The New Democracy and the Constitution.* Kennikat Press, 1972.

McLennan, B., ed. *Political Opposition and Dissent.* Dunnellen, 1973.

McRuer, J. C. *The Evolution of the Judicial Process.* Clarke, Irwin, 1957.

McWhinney, E., ed. *Canadian Jurisprudence: The Civil Law and the Common Law in Canada.* Carswell, 1958.

———. *Comparative Federalism: States' Rights and National Power.* University of Toronto, 1963.

———. *Constitutionalism in Germany and the Federal Constitutional Court.* Martinus Nijhoff, 1962.

———. *Constitution-making.* University of Toronto, 1981.

———. *Judicial Review in the English-Speaking World.* 4th ed. University of Toronto, 1969.

———, and M. A. Bradley, *New Frontiers in Space Law.* Oceana, 1969.

Meador, D. J. *Criminal Appeals: English Practices and American Reforms.* University of Virginia, 1972.

Mecham, J. L. *Church and State in Latin America: A History of Politico-Ecclesiastical Relations.* Rev. ed. University of North Carolina, 1966.

Megarry, Q. C. *Lawyer and Litigant in England.* Stevens, 1962.

Merrilat, H. C. L. *Land and Constitution in India.* Columbia University, 1970.

Merryman, J. H. *The Civil Law Tradition: An Introduction to the Legal Systems of Western Europe and Latin America.* Stanford University, 1971.

Mezey, M. L. *Comparative Legislatures.* Duke University, 1979.

Miles, R., and A. Phizacklea, eds. *Racism and Political Action in Britain.* Routledge and Kegan Paul, 1979.

Millard, E. L. *Freedom in a Federal World.* 9th ed. Oceana, 1966.

Miller, D. *Social Justice.* Oxford University, 1976.

Miller, D. W. *Church, State and Nation in Ireland: 1898–1921.* University of Pittsburgh, 1974.

Miller, W. R. *Cops and Bobbies: Police Authority in New York and London.* University of Chicago, 1977.

Milner, A. *African Legal Systems.* Praeger, 1968.

Milner, J. B., ed. *Community Planning: A Casebook on Law and Administration.* University of Toronto, 1963.

Milsom, S. F. C. *The Legal Framework of English Federalism.* Cambridge University, 1970.

Milton, F. *The English Magistracy.* Oxford University, 1967.

Minear, R. H. *Victors' Justice: The Tokyo War Crimes Trial.* Princeton University, 1971.

Montrose, J. *Precedents in English Law and Other Essays.* Irish University Press, 1968.

Moore, J. N., ed. *Law and Civil War in the Modern World.* Johns Hopkins, 1974.

Morgan, G. G. *Soviet Administration Legality: The Role of the Authority General's Office.* Stanford University, 1962.

Morris, N., and C. Howard. *Studies in Criminal Law.* Oxford University, 1964.

Morrison, F. L. *Courts and the Political Process in England.* Sage Publications, 1973.

Moskowitz, M. *Human Rights and World Order.* Oceana, 1958.

———. *International Concern with Human Rights.* Oceana, 1975.

———. *The Politics and Dynamics of Human Rights.* 2d ed. Oceana, 1968.

Mosler, P., ed. *Judicial Prosecution Against the Executive.* Heymanns/Oceana, 1972.

Mower, A. G., Jr. *The United States, The United Nations, and Human Rights.* Greenwood Press, 1979.

Mueller, C. O. W., ed. *The French Criminal Procedure Code.* Rothman, 1964.

———. *The German Criminal Procedure Code.* Rothman, 1965.

Muhammad. V. A. S. *The Legal Framework of World Trade.* Praeger, 1958.

Murphy, W. F., and J. Tanenhaus. *Comparative Constitutional Law: Cases and Commentaries.* St. Martin's Press, 1977.

Napley, D. *A Guide to Law and Practice Under the Criminal Justice Act of 1967.* Sweet & Maxwell, 1967.

Nelson, J. L., and V. M. Green, eds. *International Human Rights: Contemporary Issues.* Coleman, 1980.

Newman, K. J. *Essays on the Constitution of Pakistan.* Dacca, 1956.

Newman, R. A. *Equity and Law: A Comparative Study.* Oceana, 1960.

Nicholas, B. *An Introduction to Roman Law.* Oxford University, 1962.

Nielson, N. C., Jr. *The Crisis of Human Rights.* Thomas Nelson, 1978.

Nordlinger, E. *Soldiers in Politics: Military Coups and Governments.* Prentice-Hall, 1977.

Norton, P. *The Constitution in Flux.* Martin Robertson, 1982.

Nwabueze, B. O. *Judicialism in Commonwealth Africa.* St. Martin's Press, 1977.

Nyerere, J. K. *Freedom and Development: Uhurn NaMaedeleo.* Oxford University, 1974.

Nyquist, O. *Juvenile Justice: A Comparative Study.* St. Martin's Press, 1960.

Ogilvie, Sir C. *The King's Government and the Common Law, 1471–1641.* Oxford University, 1958.

Okin, S. M. *Women in Western Political Thought.* Princeton University, 1979.

Olivecrona, K. *Law as Fact.* 2d ed. Stevens, 1971.

Oppler, A. C. *Legal Reform in Occupied Japan.* Princeton University, 1975.

Ostrower, A. *Language Law and Diplomacy.* University of Pennsylvania, 1965.

O'Sullivan, R. *The Inheritance of the Common Law.* Stevens, 1950.

Page, L. *Justice of the Peace.* Faber & Faber, 1967.

Palkhivala, N. A. *Our Constitution Defaced and Defiled.* Macmillan of India, 1978.

Papadatos, P. *The Eichmann Trial.* Praeger, 1965.

Parizea, U. A., and D. Szabo. *The Canadian Criminal Justice System.* Lexington Books, 1977.

Peteri, Z. and V. Lamm, eds. *Legal Development and Comparative Law.* Akademiai Kiado, 1982.

Parker, G. *An Introduction to Criminal Law.* Carswell, 1977.

Parker, J. *Some Aspects of French Law.* Scribner, 1929.

Parry, C. *Nationality and Citizenship Laws of the Commonwealth.* Steven's, 1960.

Paterson, A. *The Law Lords.* University of Toronto, 1982.

Paton, G. W., and D. P. Derham, eds. *A Textbook of Jurisprudence.* Oxford University, 1972.

Patterson, S. *Immigration and Race Relations in Britain, 1960–1967.* Oxford University, 1969.

Peaslee, A. J. *Constitutions of Nations.* 2d ed. Nijhoff, 1956.

Pennock, R. J., and J. W. Chapman, eds. *The Limits of Law.* Lieber-Atherton, 1974.

Phadnis, U. *Religion and Politics in Sri Lanka.* South Asia Books, 1976.

Phillips, A. *Report on Native Tribunals.* Nairobi Government Printer, 1945.

Phillips, O. H. *The Constitutional Law of Great Britain and the Commonwealth.* 2d ed. Sweet & Maxwell, 1957.

Plische, E. *Contemporary Government of Germany.* Houghton Mifflin, 1961.

Plucknett, T. F. T. *Early English Legal Literature.* Cambridge University, 1958.

———. *A Concise History of the Common Law.* 4th ed. Butterworth, 1948.

Podgorecki, A. *Law and Society.* Routledge and Kegan Paul, 1974.

Podgorecki, A., et al *Knowledge and Opinion About Law.* Martin Robertson, 1974.

Pollard, R. S. W., ed. *Administrative Tribunals at Work: A Symposium.* Stevens, 1950.

Pollis, A., and P. Schwab, eds. *Human Rights and Ideological Perspectives.* Praeger, 1980.

Pollock, Sir. F., and F. W. Maitland. *History of English Law.* Cambridge University, 1898.

Pomerance, M., *The Advisory Function of the International Court of Justice in the League and U.N. Eras.* Johns Hopkins, 1973.

Pompe, C. A. *Aggressive War: An International Crime.* Martinus Nijhoff, 1953.

Pospisil, L. *Anthropology of Law: A Comparative Theory.* Harper & Row, 1971.

Potter, H. *An Historical Introduction to English Law and Its Institutions.* 3d ed. Sweet & Maxwell, 1948.

Pound, R. *The Lawyer from Antiquity to Modern Times.* International Publishers, 1953.

Pratt, O. C. *Tort Liability of the State.* University of Illinois, 1947.

Pratt, W. F. *Privacy in Britain.* Bucknell University, 1979.

Prest, W., ed. *Lawyer in Early Modern Europe and America.* Holmes & Meier, 1981.

Pritchard, J. L. *A History of Capital Punishment.* Kennikat Press, 1972.

Proehl, P. O., ed. *Legal Problems of International Trade.* University of Illinois, 1959.

Pylee, M. V. *Constitutional Government in India.* 2d ed. Asia Publishing, 1965.

Rackman, E. *Israel's Emerging Constitution, 1948–1951.* Columbia University, 1951.

Radcliffe, G. R. Y., and G. Cross. *The English Legal System.* 6th ed. Ed. G. J. Hand and D. J. Bentley. Butterworth, 1977.

Radzinowicz, Sir. L. and J. King. *The Growth of Crime: The International Experience.* Basic Books, 1977.

———, and M. E. Wolfgang. *Crime and Justice.* Basic Books, 1971.

Ramachandran, V. G. *Fundamental Rights and Constitutional Remedies.* 2d ed. Eastern Book, 1970.

Ramundo, B. A. *The Soviet Legal System: A Primer.* American Bar Association, 1971.

Rao, S. P. *The Public Order of Ocean Resources: A Critique of the Contemporary Law of the Sea.* MIT, 1975.

Ratner, R. S., ed. *Equal Employment Policy for Women.* Temple University, 1979.

Rawls, J. *A Theory of Justice.* Harvard University, 1971.

Ray, S. *Judicial Review and Fundamental Rights.* Eastern Law House, 1974.

Raymond, E. *The Soviet State.* 2d ed. New York University, 1978.

Raz, J. *The Authority of Law: Essays on Law and Moralities.* Oxford University, 1979.

Reiner, R. *The Blue-Coated Worker: A Sociological Study of Police Unionism.* Cambridge University, 1978.

Reith, C. *A Short History of the British Police.* Oxford University, 1948.

Rendel, M. *The Administrative Functions of the French Conseil d'État.* Weidenfeld & Nicholson, 1970.

———, ed. *Women, Power and Political Systems.* St. Martin's Press, 1981.

Report of the Committee on Administrative Tribunals and Enquiries. Her Majesty's Stationery Office, 1957.

Reuschemeyer, D. *Lawyers and Their Society: A Comparative Study.* Harvard University, 1974.

Rice, W. G. *Law Among States in Federacy: A Survey of Decision of the Swiss Federal Tribinal in Intercantonal Controversies.* Thomas Nelson, 1959.

———, *A Tale of Two Courts: Judicial Settlement of Controversies Between the State of the Swiss and American Federations.* University of Wisconsin, 1967.

Richardson, H. G., and G. O. Sayles. *Law and Legislation from Aethelberht to Magna Carta.* University of Edinburgh, 1966.

Richardson, W. C. *A History of the World Court.* Claitor, 1978.

Richmond, A. H. *Readings in Races and Ethnic Relations.* Pergamon Press, 1972.

Roberts, G. D. *Law and Life.* W. H. Allen, 1964.

Robertson, A. H. *European Institutions.* Praeger, 1959.

———. *Human Rights in Europe.* Manchester University, 1963.

———, ed. *Human Rights in National and International Law* (Oceana, 1968).

———. *Privacy and Human Rights.* Praeger, 1959.

Robinson, J. *And the Crooked Shall Be Made Straight: The Eichmann Trial, the Jewish Catastrophe, and Hannah Arendt's Narrative.* Macmillan, 1965.

Robson, W. A. *Justice and Administrative Law: A Study of the English Constitution.* 3d ed. Stevens, 1951.

Rodger, H., and E. Weber. *The European Right: A Historical Profile.* University of California, 1966.

Romashkin, P. S., ed. *Fundamentals of Soviet Law.* Foreign Languages Publishing, 1961.

Ronning, C. N. *Law and Politics in Outer-American Diplomacy.* Wiley, 1963.

Rose, E. J. B. *Colour and Citizenship: A Report on British Race Relations.* Oxford University, 1969.

Rose, R., ed. *Electoral Behavior: A Comparative Handbook.* Free Press, 1975.

Rosenne, S. *The Law and Practice of the International Court.* Martinus Nijhoff, 1965.

———. *The World Court: What it is and How it Works.* 3d rev.ed. Oceana, 1974.

———, comp. and ed. *Documents on the International Court of Justice.* Oceana, 1975.

Ross, A. *On Law and Justice.* University of California, 1959.

Rothchild, D. *Racial Bargaining in Independent Kenya: A Study of Minorities and Decolonization.* Oxford University, 1973.

Royal Commission on the Police. *Final Report.* Her Majesty's Stationery Office, 1962.

Rudd, G. R. *The English Legal System.* Butterworth, 1962.

Ruddy, F. S., ed. *American International Law Cases, 1969–1978.* Oceana, 1980.

Rule, J. B. *Private Lives and Public Surveillances.* Allen Lane, 1973.

Runes, D. D. *The Disinherited and the Law.* Philosophical Library, 1964.

———. *The World Court.* Oceana, 1962.

Russel, P. H., ed. *Leading Constitutional Decisions.* Rev. ed. McClelland & Stewart, 1973.

———. *The Supreme Court of Canada as a Bilingual and Bicultural Institution.* Queen's Printer, 1969.

Ryan, K. W. *An Introduction to the Civil Law.* Law Book Co. of Australia, 1962.

Sachs, A. *Justice in South Africa.* University of California, 1973.

Said, A. *Human Rights and World Order.* Transaction Books, 1979.

St. John-Stevas, N. *Life, Death, and the Law: Law and Christian Morals in England and the United States.* Indiana University, 1961.

Salacuse, J. *An Introduction to Law in French-Speaking Africa.* Michie, 1971.

Samaha, J. B. *Law and Order in Historical Perspective: The Case of Elizabethan Essex.* Academic Press, 1974.

Sandifer, D. V. *Evidence Before International Tribunals.* Rev. ed. University of Virginia, 1977.

Sandifer, D. V., and L. R. Scheman. *The Foundations of Freedom.* Praeger, 1966.

Sartori, G. *Democratic Theory.* Praeger, 1965.

Sathe, S. P. *Contemporary India: Socio-Economic and Political Processes.* Continental Prakanshan, 1982.

Sauer, J., ed. *Zum Verhaltris von Staat und Kirche.* Bademia Verlag, 1976.

Sawer, G. *Australian Federalism in the Courts.* Cambridge University, 1969.

———, and E. M. Wise. *Anglo-American Criminal Justice.* Oxford University, 1967.

———, ed. *Cases on the Constitution of Australia.* 3d ed. Law Book Co. of Australia, 1964.

Schact, J. *An Introduction to Islamic Law.* Oxford University, 1964.

Schaefer, R. T. *The Extent and Content of Racial Prejudice in Great Britain.* R & E Research, 1976.

Schiff, G. S. *Tradition and Politics: The Religious Parties of Israel.* Wayne State University, 1977.

Schlesinger, R. B. *Comparative Law: Cases, Text, Materials.* 2d ed. Foundation Press, 1960.

———. *Formation of Contracts: A Study of the Common Core of Legal Systems.* Oceana, 1968.

———. *Soviet Legal Theory.* Routledge & Kegan Paul, 1964.

———. *Soviet Legal Theory: Its Social Background and Development.* Humanities Press, 1951.

Schmeiser, D. A. *Civil Liberties in Canada.* Oxford Univeristy, 1964.

Schmidt, F. F., and S. Strömholm. *Legal Values in Modern Sweden.* Bedminister, 1964.

Schoultz, L. *Human Rights and United States Policy Toward Latin America.* Princeton University, 1981.

Schubert, G., and D. J. Danelski. *Comparative Judicial Behavior: Cross-Cultural Studies in Political Decision-Making in the East and West.* Oxford University, 1969.

Schur, E. M. *Narcotics Addiction in Britain and America.* University of Indiana, 1962.

Schuyler, R. L. *British Constitutional History Since 1832.* Van Nostrand, 1962.

Schwartz, B., ed. *The Code Napoleon and the Common-Law World.* New York University, 1956.

———. *French Administrative Law and the Common-Law World.* New York University, 1954.

———. *Law and the Executive in Britain.* New York University, 1949.

———, ed. *The Root of Freedom: A Constitutional History of England.* Hill & Wang, 1967.

————, and H. W. R. Wade. *Legal Control of Government: Administrative Control in Great Britain and the United States*. Oxford University, 1972.

Schwarzenberger, G., and C. Holland, eds. *Law, Justice and Equity: Essays in Tribute to G. W. Keefon*. Oceana, 1967.

Schwelb, E. *Human Rights and International Community*. Quadrangle, 1964.

Schwoerer, L. G. *The Declaration of Rights, 1689*. Johns Hopkins University, 1981.

Scofield, C. L. *A Study of the Court of Star Chamber*. University of Chicago, 1960.

Scott, F. R. *Civil Liberties and Canadian Federalism*. University of Toronto, 1959.

Seervai, H. M. *Constitutional Law of India*. 2d ed. Tripathi, 1976.

Segal, R. *The Race War: The World-Wide Clash of White and Non-White*. Viking Press, 1967.

Shapiro, M. *Courts: A Comparative and Political Analysis*. University of Chicago, 1981.

Sharlet, R. *The New Soviet Constitution of 1977*. King's Court, 1978.

Sharma, J. D. *Modern Constitutions at Work*. Asia Publishing, 1962.

Sharswood, G. *Blackstone's Commentaries on the Laws of England*. Lippincott, 1891.

Shawcross, Sir. H. W. *The Functions and Responsibilities of an Advocate*. Association of the Bar of the City of New York, 1958.

Shepherd, G. W., Jr. and V. P. Nanda, eds. *Human Rights and Third World Development*. Greenwood Press, 1985.

Sherwood, R. *The Court of Oliver Cromwell*. Rowman & Littlefield, 1978.

Shetreet, S. *Judges on Trial: A Study of the Appointment and Accountability of the English Judiciary*. Elsevier, 1976.

Shientag, B. L. *Moulder of Legal Thought*. Kennikat Press, 1943.

Shoolbred, C. F. *The Administration of Criminal Justice in England and Wales*. Pergamon Press, 1966.

Shourie, A. *Mrs. Ghandi's Second Reign*. Viking Publishing, 1983.

Siebert, F. S. *Freedom of the Press in England: 1476–1776*. University of Illinois, 1952; rpt. 1965.

Sieghart, M. A. *Government by Decree*. Stevens, 1950.

Silvert, K. H., ed. *Churches and States: The Religious Institution and Modernization*. American University Field Staff, 1967.

Simon, G. *Church, State and Opposition in the U.S.S.R.* University of California, 1974.

Simpson, A. W. B. *A History of the Common Law of Contract*. Oxford University, 1975.

Simpson, J. L., and H. Fox. *International Arbitration: Law and Practice*. Praeger, 1959.

Sing, N. *Human Rights and International Cooperation*. Chand, 1969.

Singer, P. *Democracy and Disobedience*. Oxford University, 1974.

Singh, D. K., ed. *U. N. Shukla's Commentaries on the Constitution of India*. 6th ed. Lucknow, 1975.

Siyar, S. *The Islamic Law of Nations*. Johns Hopkins University, 1966.

Smith, A. *The Commerce Power in Canada and the United States*. University of Toronto, 1968.

————, ed. *Newspapers and Democracy*. MIT, 1979.

Smith, B. F. *Reaching Judgment at Nuremberg*. Basic Books, 1977.

————. *The Road to Nuremberg*. Basic Books, 1981.

Smith, D. E. *Religion and Political Modernization*. Yale University, 1974.

————, ed. *South Asian Politics and Religion*. Princeton University, 1968.

Smith, G. A. *A Constitutional and Legal History of England*. Scribner, 1955.

Smith, J. C. *Legal Obligation*. University of Toronto, 1976.

Smith, M. *The Developments of European Law*. Columbia University, 1928.

Smith, S. A. de, *Constitutional and Administrative Law*. 2d ed. Penguin Books, 1975.

————. *Judicial Review of Administrative Action*. Stevens, 1960.

Sohn, L. B., and Buergenthal, T. *International Protection of Human Rights*. Bobbs-Merrill, 1973.

Solaun, M., and S. Kronus. *Discrimination Without Violence: Miscegenation and Racial Conflict in Latin America*. Wiley, 1973.

Solomon, P. H., Jr. *Soviet Criminologists and Criminal Policy*. Columbia University, 1978.

Sommerich, O. C., and B. Busch. *Foreign Law—A Guide to Its Pleading and Proof*. Oceana, 1959.

Sorenson, M., ed. *Manual of Public International Law*. St. Martin's Press, 1968.

Sowle, C. R., ed. *Police Power and Individual Freedom*. Aldine, 1965.

Spinrad, W. *Civil Liberties*. Quadrangle, 1970.

Stacey, F. *British Government, 1966–1975: The Years of Reform*. Oxford University, 1975.

———. *A New Bill of Rights for Britain*. David and Charles, 1973.

———. *Ombudsmen Compared*. Oxford University, 1978.

Stanger, R. J., ed. *Essays on Espionage and International Law*. Ohio State University, 1962.

Stannard, H. *The Two Constitutions: A Comparative Study of British and American Constitutional Systems*. Van Nostrand, 1949.

Starke, J. G. *Introduction to International Law*. 5th ed. Butterworth, 1963.

Stead, P. J. *The Police of Paris*. Staples, 1957.

Stein, P. *Regulae Juris: From Juristic Rules to Legal Maxims*. University of Edinburgh, 1966.

Steiner, H. J., and D. F. Vagts. *Transnational Legal Problems*. Foundation Press, 1975.

Stephen, J. F. *A History of the Criminal Law of England*. Macmillan, 1883.

———. *Liberty, Equality, Fraternity*. Elgard, 1873.

Stephenson, C., and F. G. Marcham, eds. *Sources of English Constitutional History*. Harper, 1937.

Stevenson, R. B. *Law and Politics: The House of Lords as a Judicial Body, 1800–1976*. University of North Carolina, 1978.

———. *Questions and Answers on Constitutional Law and Legal History*. 7th ed. Sweet & Maxwell, 1959.

Stewart, J. B. *The Canadian House of Commons: Procedure and Reform*. McGill-Queen University, 1977.

Stewart, V. L. *The Changing Faces of Juvenile Justice*. New York University, 1977.

Stewart, Z., ed. *The Ancient World: Justice, Heroism and Responsibility*. Prentice-Hall, 1966.

Stone, J. *The International Court and World Crisis*. Carnegie Endowment for World Peace, 1962.

———. *Legal System and Lawyer's Reasonings*. Stevens, 1964.

———. *Social Dimensions of Law and Justice*. Stanford University, 1966.

Strauss, L. *Natural Right and History*. University of Chicago, 1955.

Strayer, B. L. *Judicial Review of Legislation in Canada*. University of Toronto, 1968.

Street, H. *Freedom: The Individual and the Law*. 2d ed. MacGibbon & Kee, 1967.

———. *Governmental Liability: A Comparative Study*. Cambridge University, 1953.

———, G. Howe, and G. Bindman. *Anti-discrimination Legislation: the Street Report*. Political & Economic Planning, 1967.

Strong, C. F. *A History of Modern Political Constitutions: An Introduction to the Comparative Study of the History and Existing Form*. Capricorn, 1964.

Stumpf, S. E. *Morality and the Law*. Vanderbilt University, 1966.

Sutherland, D. W. *The Assize of Novel Dissension*. Oxford University, 1973.

Syatauw, J. J. G. *Decisions of the International Court of Justice*. Oceana, 1963.

Szabo, I. *Socialist Concept of Human Rights*. Adadémiai Kiadó, Budapest, 1966.

Szirmai, A., ed. *Law in Eastern Europe*. Hillary, 1959.

Szladits, C. *Bibliography of Foreign and Comparative Law Books and Articles in English*. Oceana, 1955, 1961, 1969, 1975.

———. *A Guide to Foreign Legal Materials—French, German, Swiss*. Oceana, 1959.

Tarnapolsky, W. S. *The Canadian Bill of Rights*. Rev. ed. McClelland & Stewart, 1975.

Taswell-Langmead, T. P. *English Constitutional History*. 11th ed. Rev. by T.F.T. Plucknett. Houghton Mifflin, 1961.

Taylor, I., P. Walton, and J. Young. *The New Criminology*. Routledge & Kegan Paul, 1973.

————, eds. *Critical Criminology*. Routledge & Kegan Paul, 1975.

Taylor, T. *Nuremberg and Vietnam: An American Tragedy*. Quadrangle, 1970.

Teitler, G. *The Genesis of the Professional Officers' Corps*. Sage Publications, 1977.

Theberge, L. *The Judiciary in a Democratic Society*. Lexington Books, 1978.

Thibaur, J., and L. Walker. *Procedural Justice: A Psychological Analysis*. Halsted, 1975.

Thio, S. M. *Locus Standi and Judicial Review*. Singapore University, 1971.

Thomas, J. A. C. *Textbook of Roman Law*. North-Holland, 1976.

Triska, J. F. *Constitutions of the Communist Party States*. Stanford University, 1968.

————, and R. M. Slusser. *The Theory, Law, and Policy of Soviet Treaties*. Stanford University, 1962.

Trudeau, P. E. *A Canadian Charter of Human Rights*. Queen's Press, 1968.

————. *Federalism and the French Canadians*. Macmillan, 1968.

Tsamerican, J. P., and S. L. Ronin. *Equality of Rights Between Races and Nationalities in the U.S.S.R.* UNESCO, 1962.

Tuck, R. *Natural Right Theories: Their Origin and Development*. Cambridge University, 1980.

Tumin, M., ed. *Comparative Perspectives on Race Relations*. Little, Brown, 1969.

Turner, R. V. *The King and His Courts*. Cornell University, 1968.

Tusa, A., and J. Tusa. *The Nuremberg Trial*. Atheneum, 1984.

Tuttle, E. O. *The Struggle Against Capital Punishment in Great Britain*. Stevens, 1961.

Twining, W. *The Place of Customary Law in the National Legal Systems of East Africa*. University of Chicago, 1963.

Ulc, O. *The Judge in a Communist States*. Ohio State University, 1972.

Ullmann, W. *Law and Politics in the Middle Ages*. Cornell University, 1975.

Unger, R. M. *Law in Modern Society: Toward A Criticism of Social Theory*. Free Press, 1976.

United Nations. *International Court of Justice*. UN Publications, 1971.

Vallat, Sir F., ed. *An Introduction to the Study of Human Rights*. Europa, 1972.

Van Caenegem, R. C. *The Birth of the English Common Law*. Cambridge University, 1973.

Van Den Berghe, B. *Race and Racism: A Comparative Perspective*. Wiley, 1967.

Van Dyke, V. *Human Rights, the United States, and the World Community*. Oxford University, 1970.

Vedel, G. *Droit Administratif*. Presses Universitaires de France, 1968.

Veenhoven, W. A., et al, eds. *Case Studies on Human Rights and Fundamental Freedoms: A World Survey*. Martinus Nijhoff, 1976.

Verba, S. *Law and the Indo-China War*. Princeton University, 1972.

————, N. H. Nie, and J. C. Kim. *Participation and Political Equality: Seven-Nation Comparison*. Cambridge University, 1978.

Verhelst, T. *Safeguarding African Customary Law*. Oxford University, 1969.

Vile, M. J. C. *Constitutionalism and the Separation of Powers*. Oxford University, 1967.

Vinogradoff, Sir P. *Common Sense in Law*. 3d ed. Oxford University, 1959.

Von der Mehden, F. R. *Comparative Political Violence*. Prentice-Hall, 1973.

Von Glahn, G. *Law Among Nations*. 2d ed. Macmillan, 1970.

Von Jhering, R. *The Struggle for Law*. 2d ed. Callaghan, 1915.

Von Knieriem, A. *The Nuremberg Trials*. Regnery, 1959.

Von Mehren, A. T. *The Civil Law System: Cases and Materials for the Comparative Study of Law*. Little, Brown, 1957.

————, ed. *Law in Japan: The Legal Order in a Changing Society*. Harvard University, 1963.

Vyshinsky, A. Y. *Law of the Soviet State*. Macmillan, 1948.

Waddams, S. M. *Introduction to the Study of Law*. Carswell, 1979.

Wade, E. C. S. *Administrative Law*. 4th ed. Oxford University, 1977.

————. *Dicey's Introduction to the Study of the Law of the Constitution*. 10th ed. Macmillan, 1959.

————, and G. C. Phillips, eds. *Constitutional Law*. 7th ed. Longmans, Green, 1965.

Waden, H. W. R. *Administrative Law*. 5th ed. Oxford University, 1982.

――――. *Towards Administrative Justice*. University of Michigan, 1963.

Wagner, W. J. *Federal States and their Judiciary: Comparative Study*. Mouton, 1959.

Walker, D. M. *The Scottish Legal System*. Green, 1959.

Walker, M. G. *Criminal Law*. Sweet & Maxwell, 1964.

Walker, N. *Crime and Insanity in England: The Historical Perspective*. University of Edinburgh, 1968.

――――. *Crime and Punishment in Britain*. University of Edinburgh, 1965.

――――. *Crimes, Courts, and Figures: An Introduction to Criminal Statistics*. Penguin Books, 1971.

Walker, R. J. *The English Legal System*. 4th ed. Butterworth, 1976.

Waller, I. *Men Released from Prison*. University of Toronto, 1974.

Wallington, P., (ed.) *Civil Liberties 1984*. Basil Blackwell, 1984.

Walvin, J. *The Black Presence: A Documentary History of the Negro in England*. Schocken Books, 1972.

Watkins, R. D. *The State as a Party Litigant*. Johns Hopkins University, 1927.

Watson, A. *The Making of the Civil Law*. Harvard University, 1981.

Watson, J. S. and W. C. Costin. *The Law and Working of the Constitution: Documents, 1660-1914*. Adam and Charles Black, 1952.

Weeks, K. M. *Ombudsmen Around the World: A Comparative Chart*. 2d ed. University of California, 1978.

Wegenast, K., et al. *Trennung von Kirche und Staat*. Herbert Reich, 1975.

Wegner, J. R. *A Bibliography of Israel Law in English and Other European Languages*. Hebrew University, 1972.

Weil, G. L. *The European Convention on Human Rights*. Sijthoff, 1963.

Weiler, P. *In the Last Resort: A Critical Study of the Supreme Court of Canada*. Carswell, 1974.

Welch, C. E. Jr., *Civilian Control of the Military: Theory and Cases from Developing Countries*. Basic Books, 1977.

――――, ed. *Soldier and State in Africa: A Comparative Analysis of Military Intervention and Political Change*. Northwestern University, 1970.

Wetter, J. G. *The International Arbitral Process Public and Private*. Oceana, 1979.

Weyrauch, W. O. *The Personality of Lawyers: A Comparative Study of Subjective Factors in Law, Based on Interviews with German Lawyers*. Yale University, 1964.

Wheare, K. C. *The Constitutional Structure of the Commonwealth*. Oxford University, 1961.

――――. *Modern Constitutions*. 2d ed. Oxford University, 1966.

Whitaker, B. *The Police*. Eyre & Spottiswoode, 1964.

Whitaker, H. G. *Politics and Power: A Text in International Law*. Harper & Row, 1964.

White, G. M. *The Use of Experts by International Tribunals*. Syracuse University, 1965.

White, I. L., et al. *Law and Politics in Outer Space: A Bibliography*. University of Arizona, 1971.

White, S. E. *Sir Edward Coke and "The Grievances of the Commonwealth" 1621-1628*. University of North Carolina, 1979.

Whitehead, T. *Mental Illness and the Law*. 2d ed. Basil Blackwell, 1984.

Whittemore, E. P. *The Press in Japan Today: A Case Study*. University of South Carolina, 1968.

Whyte, J. D., W. R. Lederman, eds. *Canadian Constitutional Law*. Butterworth, 1975.

Wiener, F. B. *Civilians Under Military Justice: The British Practice Since 1689, especially in North America*. University of Chicago, 1967.

Wigmore, J. H. *A Panorama of the World's Legal Systems*. West, 1928.

Wiles, P. N. P., (ed.) *The Sociology of Crime and Delinquency in Britain*. Martin Robertson, 1976.

Wilkins, J. L. *Legal Aid in the Criminal Courts*. University of Toronto, 1975.

Williams, B., ed. *Obscenity and Film Censorship*. Cambridge University, 1982.

Williams, G. L. *Learning the Law*. 10th ed. Carswell, 1978.

————. *The Proof of Guilt.* 3d ed. Stevens, 1963.

————. *A Treatise on the Anglo-American System of Evidence.* Little, Brown, 1961.

Williams, W. J. *Moriarty's Police Law.* 18th ed. Butterworth, 1965.

Williams, W. L. *Intergovernmental Military Forces and World Public Order.* Oceana, 1971.

Wilson, G. *Cases and Materials on Constitutional and Administrative Law.* Cambridge University, 1976.

Wilson, H. *The Governance of Britain.* Harper & Row, 1977.

Wilson H. H., and H. Glickmann. *The Problem of Internal Security in Great Britain, 1948-1953.* Random House, 1954.

Wilson, R. R., ed. *International and Comparative Law of the Commonwealth.* Duke University, 1969.

Winks, R. *The Blacks in Canada: A History.* Yale and McGill Universities, 1971.

Wiseman, H. V. *The Cabinet in the Commonwealth.* Stevens, 1958.

Woetzel, R. *The Nuremberg Trials in International Law.* Rev. ed. Praeger, 1962.

Wolf-Phillips, L. *Constitutions and Modern States: Selected Texts and Commentary.* Praeger, 1968.

Wolfenden, Sir John, et al. *The Wolfenden Report.* Stein & Day, 1963.

Woodhouse, A. S. P. *Puritanism and Liberty.* 2d ed. University of Chicago, 1951.

Woodsworth, J. S. *Strangers Within Our Gates or Coming Canadians.* University of Toronto, 1972.

Woong, S. S. *Comparative Analysis of Korean and American Judicial Systems.* American Judicature Society, 1974.

Wormouth, F. D. *Essays in Law and Politics.* Kennikat Press, 1978.

Wortley, B. A. *Jurisprudence.* Oceana, 1967.

Wortman, R. A. *The Development of a Roman Legal Consciousness.* University of Chicago, 1976.

Wright, G., and A. Mejia, Jr. *An Age of Controversy.* Dodd, Mead, 1963.

Wynes, W. A. *Legislative, Executive, and Judicial Powers in Australia.* 4th ed. Law Book Co. of Australia, 1970.

Young, W. L., *Minorities and the Military: A Cross National Study in World Perspective.* Greenwood Press, 1982.

Zaitsev, Y., and O. Poltorak. *The Soviet Bar.* Foreign Languages Publishing, 1959.

Zander, M. *Lawyers and the Public Interest.* Weidenfeld and Nicholson, 1968.

Zile, Z. L., ed. *Ideas and Forces in Soviet Legal History.* College Printing and Publishing, Madison, 1970.

Zile, Z. L., R. Sharlet, and J. C. Love. *The Soviet Legal System and Arms Inspection.* Praeger, 1972.

Zines, L. *The High Court and the Constitution.* Butterworth, 1980.

Zurcher, A. J. *Constitutions and Constitutional Trends Since World War I,* 2d ed. New York University, 1955.

Zwiebach, B. *Civility and Disobedience.* Cambridge University, 1975.

IV. AMERICAN CONSTITUTIONAL LAW: CLASSIFIED LISTING OF SELECTED WORKS ON CIVIL RIGHTS AND LIBERTIES

I. GENERAL AND BACKGROUND

A. HISTORICAL

Avins, A., ed. *The Reconstruction Amendment Debates: The Legislative History and Contemporary Debates in Congress on the 13th, 14th, and 15th Amendments.* Virginia Commission of Constitutional Government, 1967.

Baer, J. A. *Equality Under the Constitution: Reclaiming the Fourteenth Amendment.* Cornell University, 1984.

Barrington, B. C. *Magna Carta.* 2d ed. Campbell, 1900.

Becker, Carl L. *The Declaration of Independence.* Harcourt Brace, 1922.

Berman, W. C. *The Politics of Civil Rights in the Truman Administration.* Ohio State University, 1970.

Brant I. *The Bill of Rights: Its Origins and Meaning.* Bobbs-Merrill, 1965.

Brauer, C. M. John F. Kennedy and the Second Reconstruction. Columbia University, 1977.

Brown, Stuart Gerry. *The First Republicans: Political Philosophy and Public Policy in the Party of Jefferson and Madison.* Syracuse University, 1954.

Carter, H. *The Angry Scar: The Story of Reconstruction.* Doubleday, 1959.

Casper, J. D. *Lawyers Before the Warren Court: Civil Liberties and Civil Rights, 1957–1966.* University of Illinois, 1972.

Castberg, Frede. *Freedom of Speech in the West.* Oceana, 1960.

Chafee, Z. *How Human Rights Got Into the Constitution.* Boston University, 1952.

Chicago, University of. *The People Shall Judge.* 2 vols. University of Chicago, 1949.

Collins, R. K. L. *Constitutional Government in America.* Carolina Academic Press, 1980.

Commager, H. S., and L. W. Levy. *The Bill of Rights.* Bobbs-Merrill, 1966.

Cortner, R. A. *The Supreme Court and the Second Bill of Rights.* University of Wisconsin, 1981.

Cover, R. *Justice Accused: Antislavery and the Judicial Process.* Yale University, 1974.

Cranston, M. *Freedom: A New Analysis.* Longmans, Green, 1953.

Daube, D. *Civil Disobedience in Antiquity.* Aldine, 1973.

Dietze, G. *Magna Carta and Property.* University of Virginia, 1965.

Dollard, J. *Mr. Lincoln and the Negroes: The Long Road to Equaltiy.* Atheneum, 1963.

Duchacek, I. D. *Rights and Liberties in the World Today: Constitutional Promise and Reality.* ABC-Clio Press, 1973.

Duker, W. F. *A Constitutional History of Habeas Corpus.* Greenwood Press, 1980.

Dumbauld, E. *The Bill of Rights and What It Means Today.* University of Oklahoma, 1957.

———. *The Declaration of Independence and What It Means Today.* University of Oklahoma, 1965.

Eaton, Clement. *Freedom of Thought in the Old South.* Duke University, 1940.

Ekirch, A. A. *The Decline of American Liberalism.* Longmans, Green, 1955.

Facts of File, comps. *Civiel Rights, 1960–1968.* Facts on File, 1967; rpt. 1973.

Fairman, C., and S. Morrison. *The Fourteenth Amendment and the Bill of Rights: The Incorporation Theory.* Stanford University, 1949.

Fetner, G. L. *Ordered Liberty: Legal Reform in the Twentieth Century.* Knopf, 1983.

Flack, H. B. *The Adoption of the Fourteenth Amendment.* John Hopkins University, 1908.

Friedman, L. M, and H.N. Schieber, eds. *American Law and the Constitutional Order.* Harvard University, 1981.

Grant, J. ed. *Black Protest: History, Documents and Analysis, 1619 to the Present.* Fawcett, 1968.

Harlan, L. B. *Separate and Unequal.* University of North Carolina, 1958.

Harris, R. J. *The Quest for Equality: The Constitution, Congress, and the Supreme Court.* Louisiana State University, 1960.

Harvey, J. C. *Civil Rights During the Kennedy Administration.* University of Mississippi, 1971.

Holt, J. C. *Magna Carta.* Columbia University, 1966.

———. *The Making of Magna Carta.* University of Virginia, 1965.

Horwitz, M. J. *The Transformation of American Law.* Harvard University, 1979.

Howard, A. E. D. *The Road from Runnymede: Magna Carta and Constitutionalism in America.* University of Virginia, 1968.

Hurst, J. W. *Law and the Conditions of Freedom in the Nineteenth Century United States.* University of Wisconsin, 1956.

Hyman, H. H. *To Try Men's Souls: Loyalty Tests in American History*. University of California, 1959.

Hyman, Harold M. *Era of the Oath: Northern Loyalty Tests During the Civil War and Reconstruction*. University of Pennsylvania, 1954.

James, J. B. *The Framing of the Fourteenth Amendment*. University of Illinois, 1956.

———. *The Ratification of the Fourteenth Amendment*. Mercer University, 1984.

Jensen, M. *The Articles of Confederation*. University of Wisconsin, 1960.

Johnson, D. *The Challenge of American Freedoms*. University of Kentucky, 1963.

Kelley, A. H. *Where Constitutional Liberty Came From*. Catt Memorial Fund, 1954.

Kemper, D.J. *Decade of Fear: Senator Hennings and Civil Liberties*. University of Missouri, 1965.

Knight, H. *With Liberty and Justice for All: The Meaning of the Bill of Rights Today*. Oceana, 1967.

Konvitz, M. R. *A Century of Civil Rights*. Columbia University, 1961.

Lasson, N. B. *The History of the Development of the Fourteenth Amendment*. Johns Hopkins University, 1937.

Levy, L. W. *Jefferson and Civil Liberties: The Darker Side*. Quadrangle, 1973.

———. *Legacy of Suppression: Freedom of Speech and Press in Early American History*. Harvard University, 1960.

Lewis, A., and *The New York Times*. *Portrait of a Decade*. Random House, 1965.

Lewis, F. P. *The Dilemma in the Congressional Power to Enforce the Fourteenth Amendment*. University Press of American, 1980.

Lien, A. J. *Concurring Opinion: The Privilege or Immunity Clause of the Fourteenth Amendment*. Washington University, 1957.

Linden, G. M. *Politics or Principles: Congressional Voting on the Civil War Amendments and Pro-Negro Measures, 1838–1969*. University of Washington, 1976.

MacIver, R. M., ed. *Great Expressions of Human Rights*. Harper, 1950.

Markmann, C. L. *The Noblest Cry: A History of the American Civil Liberties Union*. St. Martin's Press, 1965.

McPherson, J. M. *The Struggle for Equality: Abolitionists and the Negro in the Civil War and Reconstruction*. Princeton University, 1965.

Meador, D. J. *Habeas Corpus and Magna Carta: Dualism of Power and Liberty*. University of Virginia, 1966.

Mennix, D. P., and M. Cowley. *Black Cargoes: A History of the Atlantic Slave Trade, 1581–1865*. Viking Press, 1962.

Metz H. W., and C. A. H. Thomson. *Authoritarianism and the Individual*. Brookings Institution, 1950.

Meyer, H. N. *The Amendment That Refused to Die*. Beacon Press, 1978.

Miller, J. C. *The Federalist Era*. Harper & Row, 1960.

Muller, H. J. *Freedom in the Ancient World*. Harper, 1961.

———. *Freedom in the Western World*. Harper & Row, 1964.

Murphy, P. *World War I and the Origin of Civil Liberties in the United States*. Norton, 1979.

Myers, H. A. *Are Men Equal?* Cornell University, 1955.

Nelson, B. H. *The Fourteenth Amendment and the Negro Since 1920*. Russell & Russell, 1967.

Nye, R. B. *Fettered Freedom: Civil Liberties and the Slavery Controversy, 1930–1960*. Michigan State College, 1949.

Pallister, A. *Magna Carta: The Heritage of Liberty*. Oxford University Press, 1971.

Pole, J. R. *The Pursuit of Equality in American History*. University of California, 1978.

Pound, R. *The Development of Constitutional Guarantees of Liberty*. Yale University, 1957.

Preston, W., Jr. *Aliens and Dissensus: Federal Supression of Radicals, 1903–1933*. Harvard University, 1963.

Quarles, B. *Lincoln and the Negro*. Oxford University, 1961.

Randall, James G. *The Civil War and Reconstruction*. Heath, 1937.

———. *Constitutional Problems under Lincoln*. University of Illinois, 1951.

Raphael, D. D., ed. *Political Theory and the Rights of Man*. Indiana University, 1967.
Reitman, A. *The Pulse of Freedom: American Liberties, 1920-1970*. Norton, 1975.
Roche, J. P. *The Quest for the Dream: The Development of Civil Rights and Human Relations in Modern America*. Macmillan, 1963.
Rossiter, C. *Seedtime of the Republic: The Origin of American Tradition of Political Liberty*. Harcourt, Brace, 1953.
Rutland, R. A. *The Birth of the Bill of Rights, 1776-1791*. Collier, 1962.
Scheiber, H. N. *The Wilson Administration and Civil Liberties*. Cornell University, 1960.
Schwartz, B., ed. *The Bill of Rights: A Documentary History*. McGraw-Hill, 1971.
———. *The Great Rights of Mankind: A History of the American Bill of Rights*. Oxford University, 1977.
———. *The Roots of Freedom*. Hill & Wang, 1967.
———. *Roots of the Bill of Rights*. Chelsea House, 1973.
Sharpe, R. J. *The Law of Habeas Corpus*. Oxford University, 1976.
Shotwell, James T. *The Long Way to Freedom*. Bobbs-Merrill, 1960.
Silver, David M. *Lincoln's Supreme Court*. University of Illinois, 1956.
Smith, J. M. *Freedom's Fetters: The Alien and Sedition Laws and American Civil Liberties*. Cornell University, 1956.
Smith, M. H. *The Writs of Assistance Case*. University of California, 1978.
Sowell, T. *Ethnic America: A History*. Basic Books, 1981.
Stenton, D. M. *After Rynnymede: Magna Carta in the Middle Ages*. University of Virginia, 1965.
Stevens, W. O. *Footsteps to Freedom*. Dodd, Mead, 1954.
Swindler, W. F. *Magna Carta: Legend and Legacy*. Bobbs-Merrill, 1965.
Ten Broek, J., E. N. Barnhart, and F.W. Matson. *The Anti-Slavery Origins of the Fourteenth Amendment*. University of California, 1951.
———. *Equal Under Law*. Collier, 1965.
Thorne, S. E., et al. *The Great Charter*. New American Library (Mentor Books), 1969.
Weyl, N. *Treason: The Story of Disloyalty and Betrayal in American History*. Public Affairs Press, 1950.
Whipple, L. *The Story of Civil Liberty in the United States*. Vanguard Press, 1927.
White, W. *How Far the Promised Land?* Viking Press, 1955.
Wieck, W. M. *The Sources of Antislavery Constitutionalism in America, 1760-1848*. Cornell University, 1977.
Woodward, C. V. *The Strange Career of Jim Crow*. 3d ed. Oxford University, 1974.
Wright, Esmond. *Fabric of Freedom, 1763-1800*. Hill & Wang, 1961.
Wynes, C. E. *Race Relations in Virginia, 1870-1902*. University of Virginia, 1961.
Zabel, O. H. *God and Caesar in Nebraska: A Study of the Legal Relationship of Church and State, 1854-1954*. University of Nebraska, 1955.

B. DOCUMENTS AND REPORTS

Adams, A. J. and J.M. Burke. *Civil Rights: A Current Guide to the People, Organizations and Events*. Bowker, 1970.
American Civil Liberties Union. *Annual Report(s)*. ACL Union
Angle, Paul. *By These Words*. Rand McNally, 1954.
Bardolph, R. *The Civil Rights Record: Black Americans and the Law, 1849-1970*. Crowell, 1971.
Becker, Carl L. *The Declaration of Independence*. Princeton University, 1945.
Berman, D. M. *A Bill Becomes a Law: The Civil Rights Act of 1960*. Macmillan, 1962.
Boyd, Julian P. *The Declaration of Independence*. Princeton University, 1945.
Brookes, A. D., ed. *Civil Rights and Liberties in the U.S.* Civil Liberties Education Foundation, 1962.
Brown, Stuart Gerry, ed. *We Hold These Truths*. Harper, 1948.

Bullock, C. S., III and C. M. Lamb, eds. *Implementation of Civil Rights Policy*. Brooks/Cole, 1984.

Burke, J. M., ed. *Civil Rights: A Current Guide to People, Organizations and Events*. 2d ed. Bowker, 1974.

Chafee, Z. *Documents of Fundamental Human Rights: The Anglo-American Tradition*. Harvard University 1952; rpt. Atheneum, 1963.

———. *Three Human Rights in the Constitution of 1787*. University of Kansas, rev. ed., 1968.

Civil Rights Act of 1964: Test, Analysis, Legislative History. Bureau of National Affairs. 1964.

Cohen, W., M. Schwartz, and D. A. Sobul. *The Bill of Rights: A Sourcebook*. Benziger Bruce & Glencoe, 1968.

Commager, H. S., ed. *Documents in American History*. 4th ed. Appleton-Century-Crofts, 1949.

———. *Living Ideas in America*. Harper, 1951.

Congressional Quarterly. *The Rights Revolution*. Congressional Quarterly Press, 1979.

Davis, J. P., ed. *The American Negro Reference Book*. Prentice-Hall, 1966.

Dixon, R. G. and E. Plischke, eds. *American Government: Basic Documents and Materials*. Van Nostrand, 1950.

Dorsen, N. *Frontiers of Civil Liberties*. Pantheon Books, 1968.

Garling, M. *The Human Rights Handbook*. Facts on File, 1979.

Ginsberg, R. B. *Constitutional Aspects of Sex-Based Discrimination*. West, 1974.

Goldwin, R. A., and W. A. Schambra. *How Does the Constitution Secure Rights?* American Enterprise Institute, 1984.

Grant, J., ed. *Black Protest: History, Documents, and Analysis, 1619 to the Present*. Fawcett, 1968.

Hamilton, A., J. Madison, and J. Jay. *The Federalist*. Benjamin F. Wright, ed. Harvard University, 1961.

Hanson, H. A. et al. *Fighting for Freedom*. Winston, 1947.

Harris, R. *Freedom Spent: Tales of Tyranny in America*. Little, Brown, 1973.

Hurst, J. W. *The Law of Treason in the United States: Collected Essays*. Greenwood Press, 1971.

Kennett, L. and J. L. Anderson. *The Gun in America: The Origin of a Dilemma*. Greenwood Press, 1975.

King, D. B., and C. W. Quick, eds. *Legal Aspects of the Civil Rights Movement*. Wayne State University, 1965.

Monaghan, Frank. *Heritage of Freedom*. Princeton University, 1947.

Morgan, R. E. *Disabling America: The "Right's Industry" in Our Time*. Basic Books, 1985.

Murray, P. *Human Rights U.S.A., 1948-1966*. Board of Missions, Methodist Church, 1967.

———. *State Laws on Race and Color*. Christian Service, 1950.

Perry, R.L., ed. *Sources of Our Liberties: Documentary Origins of Individual Liberties in the U.S. Constitution and the Bill of Rights*. American Bar Foundation, 1959.

———. *Sources of Our Liberties: English and American Documents from Magna Charta to the Bill of Rights*. McGraw-Hill, 1964.

Pious, R. M., ed. *Identity and Authority: Civil Rights and Liberties in the 1970's*. Random House, 1973.

President's National Advisory Commission on Civil Disorders. *Report*. Bantam Books, 1968.

Rainwater, L., ed. *Social Problems and Public Policy: Inequality and Justice — A Survey of Inequalities of Class, Status, Sex, and Power*. Aldine, 1975.

Rankin, R. S. *State Constitutions: The Bill of Rights*. National Memorial League, 1960.

Reitman, A., ed. *The Price of Liberty*. Norton, 1968.

———. *The Pulse of Freedom: American Liberties, 1920-1970's*. Norton, 1975.

Rodgers, H. R., Jr., and C. S. Bullock III. *Law and Social Change: Civil Rights, Laws and Their Consequences*. McGraw-Hill, 1972.

Sandoz, E. *Conceived in Liberty: American Individual Rights Today*. PWS (Duxbury Press), 1978.

Sherrill, R. *The Saturday Night Special*. Penguin Books, 1975.

Sholnick, J. H., ed. *The Politics of Protest: A Task Force Submitted to the NCCPV*. Simon and Schuster, 1969.

Smith, James M. and Paul L. Murphy. *Liberty and Justice: An Historical Record of American Constitutional Development*. Knopf, 1958.

Sobul, D. *The Bill of Rights: A Handbook*. Benziger Bruce & Glencoe, 1968.

Witherspoon, J.P. *Administrative Implementation of Civil Rights*. University of Texas, 1968.

Yarbrough, J. E., ed. *The Reagan Administration and Human Rights*. Praeger, 1985.

C. CASEBOOKS (GENERAL AND SPECIFIC)

Abernathy, C. P. *Cases and Materials on Civil Rights*. West, 1980.

Abernathy, M. G. *Civil Liberties Under the Constitution*. 4th ed. University of South Carolina, 1985.

Amaker, N. C. *Civil Liberty and Civil Rights*. 4th ed. Oceana, 1966.

Barker, L. J., and T. W. Barker, Jr. *Civil Liberties and the Constitution: Cases and Commentaries*. Prentice-Hall, 1982.

———. *Freedoms, Courts, Politics: Studies in Civil Liberties*. Prentice-Hall, 1972.

Berney, A. L. *The Legal Problems of the Poor: Cases and Materials*. Sage Publications, 1974.

Birkby, R. H. *The Court and Public Policy*. Congressional Quarterly Press, 1983.

Bonnicksen, A. L. *Civil Rights and Liberties*. Mayfield, 1982.

Brigham, J. *Civil Liberties and American Democracy*. Congressional Quarterly Press, 1983.

Catterell, H. H., ed. *Judicial Cases Concerning American Slavery and the Negro*. Carnegie Institute, 1926–37.

Cohen, F. *Cases and Materials on the Law of the Deprivation of Liberty: A Study in Social Control*. West, 1980.

Cohen, W., and J. Kaplan. *Constitutional Law, Civil Liberty, and Individual Rights*, 2d ed. Foundation Press, 1982.

Cortner, R. C., *The Supreme Court and Civil Liberties Policy*. Mayfield, 1976.

———, and C. M. Lytle, Jr. *Modern Constitutional Law: Commentary and Case Studies*. Free Press, 1971.

Cushman, Robert F. *Cases in Civil Liberties*. 3d ed. Prentice-Hall, 1979.

Davidson, K. M., R. B. Ginsburg, and H.H. Kay. *Sex-Based Discrimination: Text Cases and Materials*. West, 1974.

Dionisopoulos, P. A., and C. R. Ducat. *The Right to Privacy: Essays and Cases*. West, 1976.

Dorsen, N., ed. *Discrimination and Civil Rights: Cases, Texts, and Materials*. Little, Brown, 1969.

———, P. Bender, and B. Neuborne. *Political and Civil Rights in the United States*. Little, Brown, 1976.

Duchacek, I. D. *Rights and Liberties*. ABC-Clio, 1975.

Emerson, T. I., et al. *Political and Civil Rights in the United States*. 4th ed. Little, Brown, 1976.

Fairman, Charles. *American Constitutional Decisions*. Holt, 1950.

Frankel, L. H. *Law, Power, and Personal Freedom*. West, 1975.

Franklin, M. *The First Amendment and the Fourth Estate: Communications Law for Undergraduates*. Foundation Press, 1977.

Freeman, W. *Society on Trial: Current Constitutional Decisions and Social Change*. Thomas, 1965.

Gordon, W. I. *Nine Men Plus: Supreme Court Opinions on Free Speech and Free Press*. Brown, 1971.

Greenberg, J. *Cases and Materials on Judicial Process and Social Change*. West, 1976.

Gunther, G., and N. T. Dowling. *Cases and Materials on Individual Rights in Constitutional Law*. Foundation Press, 1970.

Gunther, G. *Individual Rights in Constitutional Law*. 4th ed. Foundation Press, 1986.

Gweck, S. *Cases on Criminal Law and Its Enforcement*. West, 1951.

Haiman, F. S. *Freedom of Speech: Issues and Cases*. Random House, 1965.

Hays, A. C. *Let Freedom Ring*. Boni & Liveright, 1937.

Inbau, F. E., and C. Sowle. *Cases and Comments on Criminal Justice*. Foundation Press, 1960.

Israel, J. H., and W. R. LaFave. *Criminal Procedure in a Nutshell: Constitutional Limitations*. West, 1971.

Kamisar, Y., W. R. LaFave, and J. H. Israel. *Cases, Comments, and Questions on Basic Criminal Procedure*. 4th ed. West, 1974.

Kaplan, J., and J. Skolnick. *Criminal Justice: Introductory Cases and Materials*. 3d ed. Foundation Press, 1982.

Kemerer, F. R., and K. L. Deutsch. *Constitutional Rights and Student Life: Value Conflict in Law and Education*. West, 1980.

Kerper, H. B. *Introduction to the Criminal Justice System*. West, 1972.

————, and J. Kerper. *Legal Rights of the Convicted*. West, 1974.

Konvitz, M.R. *Bill of Rights Reader: Leading Constitutional Cases*. 4th ed. Cornell University, 1968.

————. *Expanding Liberties: The Emergence of New Civil Liberties and Civil Rights in Postwar America*. Viking Press, 1967.

Lapides, F. R, and D. F. Borrows. *Racism: A Casebook*. Crowell, 1971.

Lockhart, W. B., Y. Kamisar, and J. H. Choper. *Cases and Materials on Constitutional Rights and Liberties*. 5th ed. West, 1980.

Low, P., J. Jefferies, and R. Bonnie. *Criminal Law Cases and Materials*. Foundation Press, 1982.

Loewy, A. H. *Criminal Law in a Nutshell*. West, 1975.

Maddex, J. L. *Cases and Comments on Constitutional Law*. West, 1974.

Mason, A. P., and W. M. Beaney. *American Constitutional Law: Introductory Essays and Selected Cases*. 6th ed. Prentice-Hall, 1977.

Mendelson, W. *The American Constitution and Civil Liberties*. Dorsey Press, 1981.

Micheall, J., and H. Wechsler, eds. *Criminal Law and Its Administration: Cases, Statutes, and Commentaries*. Foundation Press, 1940.

Miller, F. W., et al. *The Police Function*. West, 1971.

Morgan, R. E., *The Law and Politics of Civil Rights and Liberties*. Knopf, 1985.

Newman, E. S. *Civil Liberty and Civil Rights*. 5th ed. Oceana, 1970.

Oddo, G. L. *Freedom and Equality: Civil Liberties and the Supreme Court*. Goodyear, 1979.

Parker, D., R. M. O'Neil, and N. Econopouly. *Civil Liberties: Case Studies and the Law*. Houghton Mifflin, 1965.

Paulsen, M. G., and S. H. Kadish. *Criminal Law and Its Processes*. Little, Brown, 1962.

Pollack, H., and A. B. Smith. *Civil Liberties and Civil Rights in the United States*. West, 1978.

Poulos, J.W. *The Anatomy of Criminal Justice*. Foundation Press, 1976.

Pritchett, C. Herman. *American Constitutional Issues*. McGraw-Hill, 1962.

Reimel, T. *Handbook on Criminal Law in Pennsylvania*. Bisel, 1958.

Scarboro, J.E., and J.B. White. *Constitutional Criminal Procedure: Cases, Questions and Notes*. Foundation Press, 1977.

Sheldon, C. *The Supreme Court: Politicians in Robes*. Free Press, 1970.

Sovern, M. I. *Cases and Materials on Racial Discrimination in Employment*. West, 1969.

Spinard, W. *Civil Liberties*. Quadrangle, 1970.

Story, J. N., and L. M. Ward. *Perspectives of American Law: Cases on Law and Society*. West, 1974.

Sweet, E. C. *Civil Liberties in America: A Casebook*. Van Nostrand, 1966.

Tresolini, R. J. *These Liberties: Case Studies in Civil Rights*. Lippincott, 1968.

Tribe, L. H. *The Constitutional Protection of Individual Rights*. Foundation Press, 1978.

Tucker, E. W. *Cases and Problems on the Adjudication of Social Issues*. 2d ed. West, 1977.

————. *Text, Cases, and Problems on Administrative Law, Regulation of Enterprise, and Individual Liberties*. West, 1974.

Vieira, N. *Civil Rights in a Nutshell*. West. 1978.

Weinreb, L.L. *Leading Constitutional Cases on Criminal Justice.* 4th ed. Foundation Press, 1985.

D. GENERAL OUTLINES

(See also II. B., Theories and Aspects of Freedom, Rights, and Liberties; specific rights.)

Abernethy, G. L. *The Idea of Equality: An Anthology.* John Knox, 1959.

Asch, S. *Civil Rights and Responsibilities under the Constitution.* Arco, 1968.

Antieau, C. J. *Rights of Our Fathers.* Coiner, 1968.

Barker, L. J., and T. W. Barker, Jr. *Freedom, Courts, Politics: Studies in Civil Liberties.* Prentice-Hall, 1965.

Barth, A. *The Rights of Free Men: An Essential Guide to Civil Liberties.* Knopf, 1984.

Bishop, H. M., and S. Hendel. *Basic Issues of American Democracy.* Appleton-Century-Crofts, 1961.

Bontecou, E., ed. *Freedom in the Balance: Opinions of Judge Henry W. Edgeton Relating to Civil Liberties.* Cornell University, 1953.

Brannon, H. A. *Treatise on the Rights and Privileges Guaranteed by the Fourteenth Amendment to the Constitution of the United States.* Anderson, 1901.

Brennan, W. J., Jr. *The Bill of Rights and the States.* Center for the Study of Democratic Institutions, 1961.

Brigham, J. *Civil Liberties and American Democracy.* Congressional Quarterly, 1984.

Brookes, E. H., and J. B. Maculay. *Civil Liberty in South Africa.* Oxford University, 1959.

Brooks, A. D. *Civil Rights and Liberties in the United States: An Annotated Bibiliography.* Civil Liberties Educational Foundation, 1962.

Bullock, C. S., III, and C.M. Lamb, eds. *Implementation of Civil Rights Policy.* Brooks/Cole, 1983.

Cahn, E. *Can the Supreme Court Defend Civil Liberties?* Sidney Hillman Foundation, 1956.
———. *The Great Rights.* Macmillan, 1963.

Cahn, Mrs. E., comp. *Confronting Injustice: The Edmond Cahn Reader.* Little, Brown, 1966.

Columbia University Teachers College, Citizenship Education Project. *When Men Are Free: Premises of American Liberty.* Houghton Mifflin, 1955.

Commager, H. S., et al. *Civil Liberties Under Attack.* University of Virginia, 1943.

Congressional Quarterly. *Revolution in Civil Rights.* 3d ed. Congressional Quarterly Press, 1968.
———. *The Supreme Court and Individual Rights.* Congressional Quarterly Press, 1980.

Creamer, J. S. *A Citizen's Guide to Legal Rights.* Holt, Rinehart and Winston, 1971.

Cushman, R. E., *Civil Liberties in the United States: A Guide to Current Problems and Experience.* Cornell University, 1956.

Davis, E. *But We Were Born Free.* Bobbs-Merrill, 1954.

Donovan, J. C. *The Politics of Poverty.* Bobbs-Merrill (Pegasus), 1967.

Douglas, W. O. *The Anatomy of Liberty.* Trident, 1963.
———. *A Living Bill of Rights.* Doubleday, 1961.
———. *The Rights of the People.* Doubleday, 1958.

Dorsen, N. *Frontiers of Civil Liberties.* Pantheon Books, 1968.

Dorsey, G. L. *American Freedoms: An Essay on the Bill of Rights. Hein,* 1974.

Edman, I. *Fountainhead of Freedom.* Reynal and Hitchcock, 1941.

Edwards, R. A. *The Fourteenth Amendment and Civil Liberty.* Catt Memorial Fund, 1955.

Fernando, E. M. *The Bill of Rights.* Oceana, 1971.

Fleishman, H. *Let's Be Human.* Oceana, 1960.

Frankel, O. K. *Our Civil Liberties.* Viking Press, 1964.
———. *The Rights We Have: A Handbook of Civil Liberties.* Cornell University, 1971.

Friedman, L. *The Civil Rights Reader: Basic Documents of the Civil Rights Movement.* Walker, 1967.

Gellhorn, W. *American Rights: The Constitution in Action.* Macmillan, 1960.

Ginger, A. F. *The Law, the Supreme Court and the People's Rights.* Barron's, 1974.

Hanely, T. O. B. *Their Rights and Liberties.* Newman Press, 1959.

Humphrey, H. H. *Beyond Civil Rights: A New Day for Equality.* Random House, 1968.

Hurwitz, L. *The State as Defendant: Governmental Accountability and the Redress of Individual Grievances.* Greenwood Press, 1981.

Hutchins, Robert M. *Freedom, Education and the Fund: Essays and Addresses, 1946-1956.* New American Library (Meridian Books), 1956.

Jacobs, C. E. *Justice Frankfurter and Civil Liberties.* University of California, 1961.

Kauper, P. G. *Civil Liberties and the Constitution.* University of Michigan, 1962.

———. *Frontiers of Constitutional Liberty.* University of Michigan, 1956.

Kemper, D. J. *Decade of Fear: Senator Hennings and Civil Liberties.* University of Missouri, 1956.

Kommers, D. P., and G. D. Loescher, eds. *Human Rights and American Foreign Policy.* University of Notre Dame, 1979.

Konvitz, M. R. *First Amendment Freedom: Selected Cases on Freedom of Religion, Speech, Press, Assembly.* Cornell University, 1963.

———, and C. Rossiter, eds. *Aspects of Liberty: Essays Presented to Robert E. Cushman.* Cornell University, 1958.

Kunstler, W. M. *. . . And Justice for All.* Oceana, 1962.

Kurland, P. B., ed. *Selections from the Supreme Court Review.* University of Chicago, 1975.

Lamont, C. *The Rights to Travel.* Basic Pamphlets, 1957.

Lee, F. G., ed. *Neither Conservative Nor Liberal: The Burger Court on Civil Rights and Liberties.* Krieger, 1983.

Lewis, A. *Portrait of a Decade.* Random House, 1964.

MacLeish, A. *A Continuing Journey.* Houghton Mifflin, 1967.

Nagel, S., ed. *The Rights of the Accused: In Law and Action.* Sage Publications, 1972.

Newman, E. S., ed. *Civil Liberty and Civil Rights.* 5th ed. Oceana, 1970.

———. *The Freedom Reader.* 2d ed. Oceana, 1963.

———. *The Hate Reader.* Oceana, 1964.

———. *The Law of Civil Rights and Civil Liberties.* Oceana, 1958.

Penrose, W. O. *Freedom Is Ourselves.* University of Delaware, 1952.

Pious, R. M., ed. *Civil Rights and Liberties in the 1970's.* Random House, 1973.

Pritchett, C. H. *Constitutional Civil Liberties.* Prentice-Hall, 1984.

Reppy, A. *Civil Rights in the United States.* Central Books, 1951.

Roche, John P. *Courts and Rights: The American Judiciary in Action.* 2d ed. Random House, 1966.

Rodgers, H. R., Jr., and C. S. Billock *Law and Social Change: Civil Rights, Law, and Their Consequences.* McGraw-Hill, 1972.

Rogge, J. O. *The First and the Fifth: With Some Excursions Into Others.* Thomas Nelson, 1960.

Schechter, A. H. *Contemporary Constitutional Issues.* McGraw-Hill, 1972.

Schwartzman, R., and J. Stein. *Law of Personal Liberties.* Oceana, 1955.

Senser, R. *Primer on Interracial Justice.* Helicon, 1962.

Shapiro, M. *The Court and Civil Rights.* Scott, Foresman, 1966.

Smith, T. V. *The Bill of Rights and Our Individual Liberties.* Catt Memorial Fund, 1954.

Starr, I. *Human Rights in the United States.* Rev. ed. Oxford University, 1964.

Starzinger, V. *Civil Rights.* St. Martin's Press, 1965.

Superintendent of Documents. *The Annual Report of the United States Commission on Civil Rights.* 1959- .

Thomas, N. C. *Politics, Administration, and Civil Rights.* Random House, 1966.

Wattenberg, W. W., ed. *All Men Are Created Equal.* Wayne State University, 1966.

Way, H. F. *Liberty in the Balance: Current Issues in Civil Liberties.* 5th ed. McGraw-Hill, 1981.

Wilcox, C., ed. *Civil Liberties Under Attack.* University of Pennsylvania, 1952.

Wirt, F. M., and W. D. Hawley. *New Dimensions of Freedom in America*. Chandler, 1969.
Yeager, F. B., and J. R. Start. *Your Inalienable Rights*. Public Affairs Press, 1960.

II. PHILOSOPHY OF CIVIL RIGHTS AND LIBERTIES

A. GENERAL

1. *Due Process (See also* IV, Criminal Justice, Law, and Procedure: VIII, Expression: Speech, Press, and Petition; IX, Assembly and Association; XIV, Internal Security.)

Annas, G. J. *The Rights of Hospital Patients*. Avon Books, 1974.
Bogan, E. C., et al. *The Rights of Gay People*. Avon Books, 1974.
Bonnicksen, A. L. *Civil Rights and Liberties*. Mayfield, 1982.
Collins, F. L. *The F.B.I. in Peace and War*. Ace Books, 1943.
Constans, H. P., Jr. *Fit for Freedom*. University Press of America, 1980.
Cunningham, M., et al. *Free man Versus His Government*. Southern Methodist University, 1958.
Ennis, B., and L. Siegel. *The Rights of Prisoners*. Avon Books, 1974.
Francis, P. *Protection Through the Law*. Oceana, 1965.
Gora, J. M. *The Rights of Reporters*. Avon Books, 1974.
Graham, F. P. *The Due Process Revolution*. Hayden, 1970.
Houseman, G. L. *The Right of Mobility*. Kennikat Press, 1979.
Law. S. *The Rights of the Poor*. Avon Books, 1974.
Levine, A., with E. Cary and D. Divoky. *The Rights of Students*. Avon Books, 1975.
Mashaw, J. L. *Due Process in the Administrative State*. Yale University, 1984.
Mott, R. L. *Due Process of Law*. Bobbs-Merrill, 1926; rpt. Da Capo 1973.
Nagel, S. S., ed. *The Rights of the Accused: In Law and Action*. Sage Publications, 1972.
Nash, R. H. *Freedom, Justice and the State*. University Press of America, 1980.
Newman, E. S. *Police, and Law and Personal Freedom*. Oceana, 1965.
Pennock, J. R., and J. W. Chapman, eds. *Due Process*. New York University, 1977.
Rivkin, R. *The Rights of Servicemen*. Avon Books, 1974.
Robertson, J. A. *The Rights of the Critically Ill*. Bantam Books, 1983.
Rosengart, O. *The Rights of Suspects*. Avon Books, 1974.
Ross, S. D. *The Rights of Women*. Avon Books, 1975.
Rubin, D., *The Rights of Teachers*. Avon Books, 1974.
Rudovsky, D. *The Rights of Prisoners*. Avon Books, 1974.
Sussman, A. N. *The Rights of Young People*. American Civil Liberties Union, 1977.
Walton, A. N. *Ethics of Withdrawal of Life-Support Systems*. Greenwood Press, 1983.
Wasby, S. L., ed. *Civil Liberties Police and Policy Making*. Southern Illinois University, 1977.
Williams, B. *Due Process*. Morrow, 1960.
Williams, E. B. *One Man's Freedom*. Atheneum, 1962.
Wood, V. *Due Process of Law, 1932–1949*. Louisiana State University, 1951.

2. *Equal Protection (See also* II.F, The Economic Sphere; IV, Criminal Justice, Law, and Procedure; VI, Segregation/Desegregation, Integration; VII, Voting and Suffrage; XIII, Immigration, Citizenship, and Alienage.)

Association of the Bar of the City of New York. *Equal Justice for the Accused*. Dodd, Mead, 1959.
Baer, J. A., *Equality Under the Constitution: Reclaiming the Fourteenth Amendment*. Cornell University, 1983.
Berger, M. *Equality by Statute: The Revolution in Civil Rights*. Rev. ed. Doubleday, 1967.
Berger, R. *Government by Judiciary: The Transformation of the Fourteenth Amendment*. Harvard University, 1978.
Dorn, E. *Rules and Racial Equality*. Yale University, 1979.
Dye, T. R. *The Politics of Equality*. Bobbs-Merrill, 1971.

Equal Rights Amendment Project. *The Equal Rights Amendment: A Bibliographic Study.* Greenwood Press, 1976.

Foster, J. C., and M. C. Segers. *Elusive Equality: Liberalism, Affirmative Action, and Social Change in America.* Associated Faculty Press, 1983.

Foundation of Federal Bar Association. *Equal Justice Under the Law.* Grosset & Dunlop, 1965.

Gross, B. R., ed. *Reverse Discrimination.* Prometheus Books, 1977.

Harris, R. J., *The Quest for Equality: The Constitution, Congress, and the Supreme Court.* Louisiana State University, 1960.

Levine, D. M., and M. J. Bane, eds. *The "Inequality" Controversy: Schooling and Distributive Justice.* Basic Books, 1974.

Lineberry, R. L. *Equality and Urban Policy.* Sage Publications, 1977.

Mayhew, L. H. *Law and Equal Opportunity.* Harvard University, 1968.

McMurrin, S. M., ed. *The Conditions for Educational Equality.* Committee for Economic Development, 1971.

McPherson, J. M. *The Struggle for Equality.* Princeton University, 1964.

Meyer, H. N. *XIV: The Amendment That Refused to Die.* 2d ed. Beacon Press, 1978.

Okun, A. M., *Equality and Efficiency: The Big Tradeoff.* Brookings Institution, 1975.

Pole, J. R. *The Pursuit of Equality in American History.* University of California, 1978.

Rae, D. *Equalities.* Harvard University, 1983.

Rainwater, L., ed. *Inequality and Justice.* Aldine, 1974.

Redenius, C. M. *The American Ideal of Equality: From Jefferson's Declaration to the Burger Court.* Kennikat Press, 1981.

Wallace, P. A., ed. *Equal Employment Opportunity and the AT&T Case.* MIT, 1976.

Warsoff, L. A. *Equality and the Law.* Greenwood Press, 1938.

Wilensky, H. L. *The Welfare State and Equality.* University of California, 1975.

Wilhoit, F. M. *Quest for Equality in Freedom.* Transaction Books, 1979.

Wise, A.E. *Rich Schools, Poor Schools: The Promise of Equal Educational Opportunity.* University of Chcago, 1968.

B. THEORIES AND ASPECTS OF FREEDOM, RIGHTS, AND LIBERTIES

Abraham, H. J. *Freedom and the Court: Civil Rights and Liberties in the United States.* 4th ed. Oxford University, 1982.

Adler, Mortimer. *The Idea of Freedom.* Vols. 1–2. Doubleday, 1958, 1961.

American Civil Liberties Union. *Freedom Through Dissent.* Oceana, 1963.

Angle, P. M., ed. *Created Equal: The Complete Lincoln-Douglas Debates of 1858.* University of Chicago, 1958.

Anshen, Ruth Nanda. *Freedom: Its Meaning.* Marcourt, Brace, 1940.

Bachrach, P. *Problems in Freedom.* Stackpole Books, 1953.

Barth, A. *Law Enforcement Versus the Law.* Collier, 1963.

———. *The Rights of Free Men.* Knopf, 1984.

Bay, C. *The Structure of Freedom.* Stanford University, 1958.

Bayer, R. *Homosexuality and American Psychiatry: The Politics of Diagnosis.* Basic Books, 1981.

Bayley, D. H. *Public Liberties in the New States.* Rand McNally, 1964.

Benokraitis, N. V., and J. F. Feagin. *Affirmative Action and Equal Opportunity: Action, Inaction, Reaction.* Westview, 1978.

Berdau, H. A., ed. *Civil Disobedience: Theory and Practice.* Bobbs-Merrill (Pegasus), 1969.

Berlin, I. *Four Essays on Liberty.* Oxford University, 1969.

Blalock, H. M., Jr. *Toward a Theory of Minority-Group Relations.* Capricorn, 1975.

Block, W. E., and Walker, M. A. *Discrimination, Affirmative Action, and Equal Protection.* Fraser Institute, 1983.

Buchanan, J. M. *The Limits of Liberty: Between Anarchy and Leviathan.* University of Chicago, 1975.

Chafee, Z. *The Blessings of Liberty*. Lippincott, 1956.

Chagla, M. C. *The Individual and the State*. Asia Publishing House, 1961.

Childress, J. F., *Civil Disobedience and Political Obligation*. Yale University, 1972.

Coffin, W. S., Jr., and C. E. Whitaker. *Law, Order, and Civil Disobedience*. American Enterprise Institute, 1967.

Cohen, M., T. Nagel, and T. Scanlon. *Equality and Preferential Treatment*. Princeton University, 1977.

Cohen, M. P. *The Faith of a Liberal*. Holt, 1946.

Collins, C. W. *The Fourteenth Amendment and the States*. Little, Brown, 1912.

Commager, H. S. *Freedom and Order: A Commentary on the American Political Science*. Braziller, 1966.

Corwin, E. S. *Liberty Against Government: The Rise, Flowering and Decline of a Famous Juridical Concept*. Louisiana State University, 1948.

Cowling, M. *Mill and Liberalism*. Cambridge University, 1963.

Cranston, M. *Freedom: A New Analysis*. Longmans, Green, 1953.

———. *What Are Human Rights?* Taplinger, 1973.

Dahl, R. A. *A Preface to Democratic Theory*. University of Chicago, 1956.

Dietze, G. *Two Concepts of the Rule of Law*. Liberty Fund, 1973.

Dorsen, N. *Our Endangered Rights*. Pantheon Books, 1984.

———, ed. *The Rights of Americans: What They Are, What They Should Be*. Random House (Vintage Books), 1971.

Douglas, W. O. *An Almanac of Liberty*. Doubleday, 1954.

———. *The Anatomy of Liberty*. Trident, 1963.

Dowden, W. S., and T. N. March, eds. *The Heritage of Freedom: Essays on the Rights of Free Men*. Harper & Row, 1962.

Dreyfuss, J., and C. Lawrence III. *The Bakke Case: The Politics of Inequality*. Harcourt Brace Jovanovich, 1979.

Dworkin, R. *Taking Rights Seriously*. Harvard University, 1977.

Eastland, T., and W. J. Bennett. *Counting by Race: Equality from the Founding Fathers to Bakke and Weber*. Basic Books, 1979.

Ekirch, A. A., Jr. *The Decline in American Liberalism*. Longmans, Green, 1955; rtp. Atherton, 1966.

———, ed. *Voices in Dissent: An Anthology of Individualist Thought in the United States*. Citadel Press, 1964.

English, R., ed. *The Essentials of Freedom*, Kenyon College, 1960.

Filler, L., ed. *Wendell Phillips on Civil Rights and Freedom*. Hill & Wang, 1965.

Fishkin, J. S. *Justice, Equal Opportunity, and the Family*. Yale University, 1983.

Flathman, R. *The Practice of Rights*. Cambridge University, 1977.

Fortas, A. *Concerning Dissent and Civil Disobedience*. New American Library, 1968.

Fosdick, D. *What Is Liberty?* Harper, 1939.

Franklin, J. H. *Racial Equality in America*. University of Chicago, 1976.

Friedman, D. *The Machinery of Freedom*. Harper & Row, 1973.

Friedrich, C. J. *Authority*. Harvard University, 1958.

Fullinwider, R. K. *The Reverse Discrimination Controversy: A Moral and Legal Analysis*. Rowman & Littlefield, 1980.

Gans, H. J. *More Equality*. Random House (Vintage Books) 1972.

Gerhart, E. C. *American Liberty and Natural Law*. Beacon Press, 1953.

Gillers, S. *Getting Justice: The Rights of People*. New American Library (Mentor Books, 1974).

Glazer, N. *Ethnic Dilemmas, 1964–1982*. Harvard University, 1983.

Goldman, A. H. *Justice and Reverse Discrimination*. Princeton University, 1979.

Graglia, L. A. *Disaster by Decree*. Cornell University, 1976.

Graham, H. J. *Everyman's Constitution: Historical Essays on the Fourteenth Amendment*,

"The Conspiracy Theory" and American Constitutionalism. National Historical Society of Wisconsin, 1968.

Green, J. F. *The United Nations and Human Rights.* Brookings Institution, 1956.

Green, P. *The Pursuit of Inequality.* Pantheon Books, 1982.

Greenawalt, K. *Discrimination and Reverse Discrimination.* Knopf, 1983.

Gross, B. R. *Discrimination in Reverse: Is Turnabout Fair Play?* New York University, 1978.

Hahn, H., and W. Holland. *American Government: Minority Rights Versus Majority Rule.* Wiley, 1975.

Halpern, S. C., ed. *The Future of Our Liberties: Perspectives on the Bill of Rights.* Greenwood Press, 1982.

Hand, L. *The Spirit of Liberty: Papers and Addresses of Learned Hand.* 3d ed. Knopf, 1960.

Handlin, O., and M. Handlin. *The Dimensions of Liberties.* Harvard University, 1961.

Harris, R. J. *The Crisis of Law, Order and Freedom in America.* Dutton, 1970.

Hartz, L. *The Liberal Tradition in America.* Harcourt, Brace, 1955.

Horn, R. A. *Groups and the Constitution.* Stanford University, 1956.

Jaffa, H. V. *The Conditions of Freedom.* Johns Hopkins University, 1975.

Johnson, G. W. *This American People.* Harper, 1951.

Kallen, H. M. *Liberty, Laughter, and Tears.* University of Chicago, 1975.

———. *A Study of Liberty.* Antioch College, 1959.

Kennedy, R. E. *The Pursuit of Justice.* Harper & Row, 1965.

Laski, R. *Liberty in the Modern State.* Viking Press, 1930.

Lester, R. A. *Reasoning About Discrimination.* Princeton University, 1979.

Levy, L. W. *Jefferson and Civil Liberties: THe Darker Side.* Harvard University, 1963.

Lewis, F. P. *The Dilemma in the Congressional Power to Enforce the Fourteenth Amendment.* University Press of America, 1982.

Lisber, F. *Civil Liberty and Self-Government.* 3d ed. Lippincott, 1875.

Livingston, J. C. *Fair Game? Inequality and Affirmative Action.* Freeman, 1979.

Lyons, D., ed. *Rights.* Wadsworth, 1979.

Machan, T. R. *Human Rights and Human Liberties.* Nelson-Hall, 1975.

McClosky, H., and A. Brill. *Dimensions of Tolerance.* Sage Publications, 1983.

MacIver, R. M. *Conflict of Loyalties.* Harper, 1952.

MacLeish, A. *Freedom in the Right to Choose.* Beacon Press, 1951.

Madden, E. *Civil Disobedience and Moral Law.* University of Washington, 1968.

Maritain, Jacques. *Man and the State.* University of Chicago, 1951.

Markman, C. L. *The Noblest Cry.* St. Martin's Press, 1965.

Mayer, M., ed. *The Tradition of Freedom.* Oceana, 1960.

Meiklejohn, A. *Political Freedom: The Constitutional Powers of People.* Oxford University, 1965.

Medina, H. R. *The Anatomy of Freedom.* Holt, 1959.

Mill, John Stuart. *On Liberty.* Appleton-Century-Crofts, 1851.

———. *Prefaces to Liberty: Selected Writings of John Stuart Mill.* Ed. B. Wishy. Beacon Press, 1959.

Miller, H. H. *The Case for Liberty.* University of North Carolina, 1965.

Milton, J. *Areopagitica.* Ed. C. E. Vaughan. Dent, 1925.

Mims, Edwin, Jr. *The Majority of the People.* Modern Age Books, 1941.

Morgan, Charles. *Liberties of the Mind.* Macmillan, 1952.

———. *A Time to Speak.* Harper & Row, 1964.

Morgan, Richard E. *Disabling America: The "Rights Industry" in Our Time.* Basic Books, 1985.

Muller, H. J. *The Individual in a Revolutionary World.* Ryerson, 1964.

———. *Issues of Freedom: Paradoxes and Promises.* Harper, 1960.

Newman, E. S. *Civil Liberty in a Revolutionary World.* Ryerson, 1964.

Nock, A. J. *Our Enemy the State.* Capton, 1946.

O'Neil, R. M. *The Price of Dependency: Civil Liberties in the Welfare State.* Dalton, 1970.

Oppenheim, F. E. *Dimensions of Freedom*. St. Martin's Press, 1961.

Orton, W. A. *The Liberal Tradition: Social and Spiritual Conditions of Freedom*. Oxford University, 1945.

Patterson, B. B. *The Forgotten Ninth Amendment*. Bobbs-Merrill, 1955.

Pennock, J. R. *Liberal Democracy*. Rinehart, 1950.

———, and J. W. Chapman. *Political and Legal Obligation*. Atherton, 1970.

Perry, M. J. *The Constitution, the Courts, and Human Rights*. Yale University, 1982.

Pfeffer, L. *The Liberties of an American: The Supreme Court Speaks*. 2d ed. Beacon Press, 1963.

Rogge, O. J. *The First and the Fifth*. T. Nelson, 1959.

Rossum, R. A. *Reverse Discrimination: The Constitutional Debate*. Dekker, 1980.

Russell, B. *Authority and the Individual*. Simon and Schuster, 1949.

Schaffer, D. L., ed. *The New Egalitarianism: Questions and Answers*. Kennikat Press, 1978.

Singer, P. *Democracy and Disobedience*. Oxford University, 1973.

Smity, Bernard. *The Democratic Spirit*. Knopf. 1941.

Spenser, H. *Man Versus the State*. Appleton, 1884.

Spinrad, W. *Civil Liberties*. New Viewpionts, 1970.

Spitz, D. *Essays on the Liberal Idea of Freedom*. University of Arizona, 1964.

Spurrier, R. L., Jr., *To Preserve These Rights: Remedies for the Victims of Constitutional Deprivations*. Kennikat Press, 1977.

Stern, F. M. *Life and Liberty: A Return to First Principles*. Crowell, 1975.

Stone, V. J., ed. *Civil Liberties and Civil Rights*. University of Illinois, 1977.

Stouffer, S. A. *Communism, Conformity and Civil Liberties: A Cross Section of the Nation Speaks Its Mind*. Doubleday, 1955.

Tawney, R. J. *Equality*. Barnes & Noble Books, 1965.

Thomas, N. *Great Dissenters*. Norton, 1954.

Thompson, K. W. *The Moral Imperatives of Human Rights*. University Press of America, 1980.

Thibault, J., and L. Walker. *Procedural Justice: A Psychological Analysis*. Halsted, 1976.

Thoreau, H. D. *On the Duty of Civil Disobedience*. Yale University, 1849.

Trueblood, D. E. *Declaration of Freedom*. Harper, 1955.

Truman, Harry S. *Freedom and Equality*. University of Missouri, 1960.

Tussman, J. *Obligation and the Body Politic*. Oxford University, 1960.

United Nations. *Yearbook on Human Rights*. Annual (1946–   ).

Van Dyke, V. *Human Rights, Ethnicity, and Discrimination*. Greenwood Press, 1985.

Verba, S., and G. Orren. *Equality in America*. Harvard University, 1985.

Walker, P. G. *Restatement of Liberty*. Hutchinson, 1951.

Wasby, S. L., ed. *Civil Liberties: Policy and Policy Making*. Lexington Books, 1976.

Whipple, L. *Our Ancient Liberties*. H.W. Wilson, 1927.

Wild, J. *Human Freedom and Social Order*. Duke University, 1961.

Williams, R. J. *Free and Unequal*. Liberty Press, 1979.

Woetzel, R. K. *The Philosophy of Freedom*. Oceana, 1966.

Woodhouse, A. S. P. *Puritanism and Liberty*. 2d ed. University of Chicago, 1951.

C. THE ROLE OF THE SUPREME COURT

(See also II.D, "Line Drawing.")

Abraham, H.J. *Freedom and the Court: Civil Rights and Liberties in the United States*. 4th ed. Oxford University, 1982.

———. *The Judiciary: The Supreme Court in the Governmental Process*. 6th ed. Allyn and Bacon, 1983.

Acheson, P. C. *The Supreme Court: American's Judicial Heritage*. Dodd, Mead, 1961.

Asch, S. H. *Civil Rights and Repsonsibilities Under the Constitution*. Arco, 1969.

Becker, C. L., et al. *Safeguarding Civil Liberty Today.* Cornell University, 1965.

Bickel, A. M. *Politics and the Warren Court.* Harper & Row, 1965.

Bonnickesen, A. L. *Civil Rights and Liberties: Privileges of Interpretation.* Mayfield, 1981.

Cahn, E. *Can the Supreme Court Defend Civil Liberties?* Sidney Hillman Foundation, 1956.

Carr, R. K. *Federal Protection of Civil Rights: Quest for a Sword.* Cornell University, 1945.

Casper, J. D. *Lawyers Before the Warren Court: Civil Liberties and Civil Rights.* University of Illinois, 1956.

Cover, R. *Justice Accused: Antislavery and the Judicial Process.* Yale University. 1974.

Cox, A. M., M. DeWolfe Howe, and J.R. Wiggins. *Civil Rights, the Constitution, and the Courts.* Harvard University, 1967.

Cushman, R. E., ed. *Safeguarding Civil Liberty Today.* Cornell University, 1945.

Dworkin, R. M., ed. *The Philosophy of Law.* Oxford University, 1977.

Fraenkel, O. K. *The Supreme Court and Civil Liberties.* 2d ed. Oceana, 1962; Supplement, 1966.

Freedman, M., W. M. Beaney, and E.V. Boston. *Perspectives on the Court.* Northwestern University, 1967.

Goldberg, A. J. *The Warren Era of the Supreme Court.* Northwestern University, 1971.

Gordon, Rosalie. *Nine Men Against America: The Supreme Court and Its Attack on American Liberties.* Devin-Adair, 1958.

Johnson, D. *The Challenge to American Freedom.* University of Kentucky, 1963.

Konvitz, M. R. *Expanding Liberties: The Emergence of New Civil Liberties and Rights in Postwar America.* Viking Press, 1967.

Laponce, J. A. *The Protection of Minorities.* University of California at Los Angeles, 1960.

Lee, F. F. *Negro and White in Connecticut Town.* Bookman. 1961.

Mason, A. T., and W. M. Beaney. *The Supreme Court in Free Society.* Prentice-Hall, 1959.

Mitau, G. T. *Decade of Decisions, 1954–1964.* Scribner, 1968.

McCloskey, R. G. *The American Supreme Court.* University of Chicago, 1960.

Morris, A. A. *The Constitution and American Education.* West, 1974.

Murphy, P. L. *The Constitution in Crisis Times, 1918–1969.* Harper & Row, 1972.

Pritchett, C. H. *Congress Versus the Supreme Court, 1957–1960.* University of Minnesota, 1961.

————. *The Political Offender and the Warren Court.* Boston University, 1958.

Roche, J. P. *Courts and Rights.* Random House, 1961.

Rotunda, R. R., ed. *Six Justices on Civil Rights.* Oceana, 1982.

Rubin, E. R. *Abortion, Politics, and the Courts: Roe v. Wade and Its Aftermath.* Greenwood Press, 1982.

Shapiro, H. H. *Federal Enforcement of the Criminal Civil Rights Statutes.* Rutgers University, 1960.

Spicer, G. W. *The Supreme Court and Fundamental Freedom.* 2d ed. Appleton-Century, 1967.

Tussman, J. *The Supreme Court on Racial Discrimination.* Oxford University, 1963.

Ziegler, B. M. *Desegregation and the Supreme Court.* Heath, 1958.

D. "LINE DRAWING"

(See also II.C, The Role of the Supreme Court.)

Abraham, H. J. *Freedom and the Court: Civil Rights and Liberties in the United States.* 4th ed. Oxford University, 1982.

Buchanan, J. M. *Between Anarchy and Leviathan: The Limits of Liberty.* University of Chicago, 1975.

Buckley, W. F., Jr. *God and Man at Yale.* Regnery, 1951.

Bullock, C. S., III, and C. M. Lamb, eds. *Implementation of Civil Rights Policy.* Brooks/Cole, 1984.

Casper, J. D. *The Politics of Civil Liberties.* Harper & Row. 1972.

Commager, H. S., ed. *Freedom and Order: A Commentary on the American Political Scene.* Braziller, 1966.

———. *Majority Rule and Minority Rights.* University of Virginia, 1943.

Cook. T. I. *Democratic Rights Versus Communist Activity.* Doubleday, 1954.

Dorsen, N., ed. *The Rights of Americans.* Pantheon Books, 1970.

Fiss, C. M. *The Civil Rights Injunction.* Indiana University, 1979.

Frankel, L. H. *Law, Power and Personal Freedom.* West, 1975.

Ginger, A. F. *The Law, the Supreme Court, and the People's Rights.* 2d ed. Barrows, 1977.

Graebner, N. A., ed. *Freedom in America: A 200-Year Perspective.* Pennsylvania State University, 1977.

Hand, L. *The Bill of Rights.* Harvard University, 1958.

Harris, R. *Freedom Spent.* Little, Brown, 1977.

Hayek, F. A. *Law, Legislation, and Liberty.* University of Chicago, 1974.

Hofstadter, R., and M. Wallace. *American Violence: A Documentary History.* Knopf, 1970.

Hook, S. *Heresy, Yes; Conspiracy, No!* John Day, 1953.

———. *The Paradoxes of Freedom.* University of California, 1962.

Kariel, H. *The Decline of American Pluralism.* Stanford University, 1961.

Katsch, M. E. *Taking Sides: Clashing Views on Controversial Legal Issues.* Dushkin, 1983.

Kerner Commission. *Report of the National Advisory Commission on Civil Disorders.* Bantam Books, 1968.

King, D. B., and C. W. Quick, eds. *Legal Aspects of the Civil Rights Movement.* Wayne State University, 1964.

Kluge, E.-H. W. *The Ethics of Deliberate Death.* Kennikat Press, 1980.

Masotti, L. H. and D. R. Bowen. *Riots and Rebellion.* Sage Publication, 1968.

Mendelson, Wallace. *Justice Black and Frankfurter: Conflict in the Court.* 2d ed. University of Chicago, 1967.

Morris, A. A. *The Constitution and American Education.* West, 1974.

Nielsen, K. *Equality and Liberty: A Defense of Radical Egalitarianism.* Rowman & Allanheld, 1985.

Northwestern University School of Law. *Perspectives on Justice.* Northwestern University, 1975.

Okun, A. M. *Equality and Efficiency: The Big Tradeoff.* Brookings Institution, 1975.

O'Neil, R. M. *The Courts, Government, and Higher Education.* Committee for Economic Development, 1971.

Rembar, C. *Perspective.* Arbor House, 1975.

Robb, H. E., and R. Sobel. *From Left to Right: Readings on the Sociopolitical Spectrum.* Benziger Bruce & Glencoe, 1968.

Sheldon, C. H. *The Supreme Court: Politicians in Robes.* Glencoe Press, 1970.

Sigler, J. A. *American Rights Policies.* Dorsey Press, 1975.

Skolnick, J. H., ed. *The Politics of Protest.* Simon and Schuster, 1969.

Sloan, I. J. *Youth and the Law: Rights, Privileges and Obligations.* Oceana, 1970.

Sowle, C. R., ed. *Police, Power and Individual Freedom: The Quest for Balance.* Aldine, 1962.

Stone, V. J. *Civil Liberties and Civil Rights.* Penguin Books, 1964.

Street, H. *Freedom, the Individual and the Law.* Penguin Books, 1964.

Sutherland, J. N., and M. G. Werthiaman. *Comparative Concepts in Law and Order.* Scott, Foresman, 1971.

Tussman, J. *Government and the Mind.* Oxford University, 1977.

Veysey, L., ed. *Law and Resistance: American Attitudes Toward.* Harper & Row, 1970.

Walker Commission. *Rights in Conflict: The Walker Report on Violence in Chicago.* Bantam Books, 1969.

Williams, R. J. *Free and Unequal.* Liberty Press, 1980.

Witherspoon, J. P. *Administrative Implementation of Civil Rights.* University of Texas, 1969.

E. STATES' RIGHTS

(See also III. E., The South and Its Viewpoint.)

Bloch, C. J. States' Rights: The Law of the Land. Harrison, 1958.

Brady, T. P. Black Monday. Mississippi Association of Citizens' Councils, 1955.

Collins, C. W. The Fourteenth Amendment and the States. Little, Brown, 1912.

Cortner, R. C. The Supreme Court and the Second Bill of Rights. University of Wisconsin, 1981.

Eastland, J. C. The Supreme Court's Modern Scientific Authorities in the Segregation Cases. Mississippi Association of Citizens' Councils, 1957.

Kilpatrick, J. J. The Sovereign States: Notes of a Citizen of Virginia. Regnery, 1957.

Marshall, B. Federalism and Civil Rights. Columbia University, 1964.

Putnam, C. Race and Reason. Public Affairs Press, 1961.

Virginia State Committee for Courts of Justice. The Doctrine of Interposition: Its History and Application. 1957.

Williams, J. B. Interposition: The Barrier Against Tyranny. University of Texas, 1956.

F. THE ECONOMIC SPHERE

Ackerman, S. Private Property and the Constitution. Yale University, 1977.

Baldwin, R. N. Civil Liberties and Industrial Conflict. Harvard University, 1938.

Becker, C. L. Freedom and Responsibility in the American Way of Life. Knopf, 1945.

Bendich, A. M. Privacy, Poverty, and the Constitution. University of California, 1966.

Berle, A. A., Jr. Economic Power and the Free Society. Fund for the Republic, 1957.

Brakel, S. J. Judicare: Public Funds, Private Lawyers, and Poor People. American Bar Foundation, 1974.

Cousins, F. R. Public Civil Rights Agencies and Fair Employment. Praeger, 1969.

Darnley, F., Jr. Creating Equality: The Failure of the Public Sector. Lexington Books, 1985.

Gellhorn, W. Individual Freedom and Governmental Restraints. Louisiana State University, 1956.

Gilmore, G. The Death of Contract. Ohio State University, 1974.

Gregory, C. O. Labor and Law. Norton, 1958.

Hale, R. L. Freedom Through Law. Columbia University, 1952.

Hayek, F. A. The Constitution of Liberty. University of Chicago, 1960.

Johnson, E., Jr. Justice and Reform: The Formative Years of the OEO Legal Services Program. Russell Sage Foundation, 1974.

Lehne, R. The Quest for Justice: The Politics of School Finance Reform. Longman, 1977.

Levitan, S. A., and R. Taggart. Still a Dream. Harvard University, 1975.

Liberman, E. Unions Before the Bar. Harper, 1950.

Lien, A. J. Concurring Opinion: The Privileges or Immunities Clause of the Fourteenth Amendment. Washington University, St. Louis, 1957.

Lineberry, R. L. Equality and Urban Policy: The Distribution of Municipal Public Services. Sage Publications, 1971.

Lockard, D. Toward Equal Opportunity: A Study of State and Local Anti-Discrimination Laws. Macmillan, 1960.

Mason, A. T. Security Through Freedom: American Political Thought and Practice. Cornell University, 1955.

Mason, L. The Language of Dissent. World, 1959.

Millis, H. A., and E. C. Brown. From the Wagner Act to Taft-Hartley. University of Chicago, 1950.

Morison, S. E. Freedom in Contemporary Society. Little, Brown, 1956.

Moskowitz, D. H. Exlusionary Zoning Litigation. Ballinger, 1977.

Nelson, R. H. Zoning and Property Rights. MIT, 1978.

Pincus, J. School Finance in Transition: The Courts and Educational Reform. Ballinger, 1974.

Polsky, S., ed. The Medico-Legal Reader. Oceana, 1956.

Reich, M. *Racial Inequality: A Political-Economy Analysis.* Princeton University, 1980.
Rostow, E. V. *Planning for Freedom.* Yale Univeristy, 1963.
Rottschaefer, H. *The Supreme Court and Socio-Economic Change.* University of Michigan, 1948.
Schnapper, M. B. *Constraint by Copyright.* Public Affairs Press, 1962.
Siegan, B. H. *Economic Liberties and the Constitution.* University of Chicago, 1980.
Tawney, R. H. *Equality.* 5th ed. Putnam, 1961.
Thomas, N. C. *Politics, Administration and Civil Rights.* University of Michigan, 1966.
Westin, A. F., and S. Salisbury. *Individual Rights in the Corporation.* Pantheon Books, 1979.
Wolkinson, B. W. *Blacks, Unions, and the EEOC.* Lexington Books, 1973.

III. PHILOSOPHY OF PREJUDICE, MINORITY GROUPS, SEX, AGE, AND RACE RELATIONS

A. GENERAL

Allport, G. W. *The Nature of Prejudice.* Doubleday, 1960.
————. *Personality and Social Encounter: Selected Essays.* Beacon Press, 1960.
Barrera, M. *Race and Class in the Southwest.* University of Notre Dame, 1979.
Barron, M. L., ed. *Minorities in a Changing World.* Knopf, 1967.
Baruch, D. W. *Glass House of Prejudice.* Morrow, 1946.
Barzun, J. *Race: A Study in Modern Superstition.* Harcourt, Bract, 1937.
Bayes, J. H. *Minority Politics and Ideologies in the United States.* Chandler & Sharp, 1982.
Bellush, J., and S. David. *Race and Politics in New York City: Six Studies in Policy Making.* Praeger, 1971.
Benedict, R. *Race: Science and Politics.* Viking Press, 1947.
Berger, M. *Equality by Statute: Legal Controls over Group Discrimination.* Columbia University, 1954.
Berson, L. E. *The Negro and the Jews.* Random House, 1971.
Bibby, C. *Race, Prejudice, and Education.* Praeger, 1961.
Blackstone, W. T., and R. D. Heslep, ed. *Social Justice and Preferential Treatment.* Praeger, 1978.
Bowser, B. P., and R. G. Hunt, eds. *Impacts of Racism on White Americans.* Sage Publications, 1980.
Brauer, C. M. *John F. Kennedy and the Second Reconstruction.* Columbia University, 1977.
Brink, W., and L. Harris. *Black and White: A Study of U.S. Racial Attitudes Today.* Simon and Schuster, 1967.
Bunch, R. J. *The Political Status of the Negro in the Age of FDR.* Ed. D. W. Grantham. University of Chicago, 1973.
Burkey, R. M. *Racial Discrimination and Public Policy in the United States.* Heath, 1971.
Burlingame, R. *The Sixth Column.* Lippincott, 1962.
Caditz, J. *White Liberals in Transition.* Halsted Press, 1976.
Carlson, L. H., and G. H. Colburn. *In Their Place: White American Defines Her Minorities, 1850-1950.* Wiley, 1972.
Catlin, J. B., J. Seeley, and M. Talburtt. *Affirmative Action: Its Legal Mandate and Organizational Implication.* University of Michigan, 1974.
Clarke, K. B. *Prejudice and Your Child.* Beacon Press, 1955.
Cohen, M., T. Nagel, and T. Scanlon, eds. *Equality and Preferential Treatment.* Princeton University, 1976.
Colburn, D. R., and G. E. Pozzetta, eds. *America and New Ethnicity.* Kennikat Press, 1978.
Cole, S., and M. W. Cole. *Minorities and the American Promise.* Harper, 1954.
Cortes, C. E., et al., eds. *Three Perspectives on Ethnicity in America: Blacks, Chicanos, and Native Americans.* Capricorn, 1976.

Cox, O. C. *Caste, Class and Race: A Study in Social Dynamics*. Doubleday, 1948.

Curran, C. E. *Issues in Sexual and Medical Ethics*. University of Notre Dame, 1978.

Davis, A., B. B. Gardner, and M. R. Gardner. *Deep South: A Social Anthropological Study of Caste and Class*. University of Chicago, 1954.

Dexter, H. H. *What's Right with Race Relations*. Harper, 1959.

Dimond, P. R. *Discrimination in the Provision of Public Services*. Lexington Books, 1978.

Dinnerstein, L., and F. C. Jaher, eds. *The Aliens: A History of Ethnic Minorities in America*. Appleton-Century-Crofts, 1970.

Dollard, J. *Cast and Class in a Southern Town*. 3d ed. Doubleday, 1957.

Dorn. E. *Rules and Racial Equality*. Yale University, 1979.

Dworkin, A. G., and R. J. Dworkin, eds. *The Minority Report*. Holt, Rinehart and Winston, 1976.

Dworkin, R. J. *Taking Rights Seriously*. Harvard University, 1977.

Dykeman, W., and J. Stokely. *Neither Black nor White*. Rinehart, 1957.

———. *Seeds of Southern Change: The Life of Will Alexander*. University of Chicago, 1962.

Fineberg, S. A. *Punishment Without Crime: What You Can Do About Prejudice*. Doubleday, 1949.

Gittler, J. P. *Understanding Minority Groups*. Wiley, 1956.

Glazer, N. *Affirmative Discrimination*. Basic Books, 1976.

———, and D. P. Moynihan, *Beyond the Melting Pot*. MIT, 1965.

———. *Ethnicity: Theory and Experience*. Harvard University. 1975.

Glock, C. Y., and E. Siegelman, eds. *Prejudice U.S.A.* Praeger, 1969.

Goldman, A. H. *Justice and Reverse Discriminiation*. Princeton University, 1979.

Goodman, M. E. *Race Awareness in Young Children*. Addison-Wesley, 1952.

Gordon, M. D. *Assimilation in American Life: The Role of Race, Religion, and National Origin*. Oxford University, 1964.

Greeley, A. M. *Why Can't They Be Like Us? America's White Ethnic Groups*. Dutton, 1971.

Greenberg, J. *Race Relations and American Law*. Columbia University, 1959.

Griessman, G. E. *Minorities: A Text with Readings in Intergroup Relations*. Holt, Rinehart and Winston, 1975.

Grimes, A. P. *Equality in America: Religion, Race and the Urban Majority*. Oxford University, 1964.

Gross, B. R., ed. *Reverse Discrimination*. Prometheus Books, 1977.

Handlin, O. *Race and Nationality in American Life*. Little, Brown, 1957.

———. *The Uprooted*. Little, Brown. 1951.

Hansen, M. L. *The Immigrant in American History*. Harvard University, 1940.

Herzog, S. J., ed. *Minority Group Politics: A Reader*. Holt, Rinehart and Winston, 1971.

Hirsch, S. G. *The Fears Men Live By*. Harper, 1955.

Holden, M., Jr. *The White Man's Burden*. Chandler, 1973.

Jahoda, M. *Race Relations and Mental Health*. Columbia University, 1960.

Katz, S., ed. *Negro and Jew: An Encounter in America*. Macmillan, 1967.

Kramer, J. *The American Minority Community*. Crowell, 1970.

Laponee, J. A. *The Protection of Minorities*. University of California at Los Angeles, 1960.

Lee, F. F. *Negro and White in Connecticut Town*. Bookman, 1961.

Lester, R. *Anti-bias Regulations at Universities*. McGraw-Hill, 1974.

Levine, C. H. *Racial Conflict and the American Mayor: Power, Polarization and Performance*. Lexington Books, 1974.

Lubell, S. *White and Black: Test of a Nation*. Harper & Row, 1964.

Makielski, S. J., Jr. *Beleaguered Minorities: Cultural Politics in America*. Freeman, 1973.

Marcus, L. *The Treatment of Minorities in Secondary School Textbooks*. Anti-Defamation League, 1961.

Marden, C. F., and G. Meyer. *Minorities in American Society*. American Book, 1968.

Mason, P. *Common Sense About Race*. Macmillan, 1961.

Masuoka, J., and P. Valien. *Race Relations: Problem and Theory.* University of North Carolina, 1961.

Meister, R. J. *Race and Ethnicity in Modern America.* Heath, 1974.

Myers, G. A. *History of Bigotry in the United States.* Random House, 1943.

Neuman, E. S., ed. *The Hate Reader.* Oceana, 1964.

Novak, M. *The Rise of the Unmeltable Ethnic.* Macmillan, 1972.

Palley, M. L., and M. B. Preston. *Race, Sex and Policy Problems.* Lexington Books, 1979.

Pettigrew, T. F., et al. *Prejudice.* Harvard University, 1980.

Polenberg, R. *One Nation Divisible: Class, Race, and Ethnicity in the United States Since 1938.* Viking Press, 1980.

Raab, E. *American Race Relations Today.* Doubleday, (Anchor Books), 1962.

————, and S. Lipset. *Prejudice and Society,* Anti-Defamation League, 1967.

Rawls, J. *A Theory of Justice.* Harvard University, 1971.

Rose, A. M. *Race Prejudice and Discrimination: Readings in Inter-Group Relations in the United States.* Knopf, 1951.

Rose, P. I. *They and We: Racial and Ethnic Relations in the U.S.* Random House, 1966.

Roy, R. L. *Apostles of Discord.* Beacon Press, 1953.

Saenger, G. *The Social Psychology of Prejudice.* Harper, 1953.

Schaeffer, D. L. *Justice or Tyranny: A Critique of John Rawls' Theory of Justice.* Kennikat Press, 1978.

Simpson, G. E., and J. M. Yinger. *Racial and Cultural Minorities: An Analysis of Prejudice and Discrimination.* Harper, 1965.

Snyder, L. L. *The Idea of Racialism: Its Meaning and History.* Van Nostrand, 1962.

Sowell, T. *Ethnic America: A History.* Basic Books, 1981.

Steinberg, S. *The Ethnic Mix: Race, Ethnicity, and Class in America.* Atheneum, 1981.

Steinfield, M. *Cracks in the Melting Pot: Readings in Racism and Discrimination in American History.* Glencoe Press, 1970.

Stember, C. H., *Sexual Racism: The Emotional Barriers to an Integrated Society.* Elsevier, 1976.

Thompson, E. T., and E. C. Hughes. *Race: Individual and Collective Behavior.* Free Press, 1958.

————. *Race Relations and the Race Problem.* Duke University, 1939.

Trager, H. G., and M. R. Yarrow. *They Learn What They Live: Prejudice in Young Children.* Harper, 1952.

Tumin, M. M., ed. *Race and Intelligence.* Anti-Defamation League, 1963.

UNESCO. *Race and Science: The Race Question in Modern Science.* Columbia University, 1961.

U.S. Commission on Civil Rights. *Justice.* Government Printing Office, 1961.

Vanden Zanden, J. W. *American Minority Relations: The Sociology of Peace and Ethnic Groups.* 2d ed. Ronald Press, 1966.

Vanderbilt University School of Law. *The Race Relations Law Reporter,* 1956–

Watts, W., and L. A. Free. *Aspirations and Social Concerns, Crime, Blacks, Inequality, and Women.* Potomac, 1977.

Weisbrod, R. G., and A. Stein. *Bittersweet Encounter: The Afro-American and the American Jew.* Negro Universities Press, 1970.

Westin, A. F., ed. *Freedom Now: The Civil Rights Struggle in America.* Basic Books, 1964.

Willie, C. V., ed. *Black, Brown, White Relations: Race Relations in the 1970s.* Transaction Books, 1977.

Wood, F. G. *Black Scare: The Racist Response to Emancipation and Reconstruction* University of California, 1970.

Yin, R. K. *Race, Creed, Color, or National Origin.* Peacock, 1973.

Young, W. M., Jr., *To Be Equal.* McGraw-Hill, 1964.

Zubaida, S., ed. *Race and Racialism.* Barns & Noble Books, 1970.

B. THE BLACKS

(See also VI, Segregation/Desegregation/Integration)

Aptheker, H. Soul of the Republic: The Negro Today. Marzani & Munsell, 1964.

Banton, M. Race Relations. Basic Books, 1967.

Barbour, F. B., ed. The Black Power Revolt. Porter, Sargent, 1968.

—————. The Balck Seventies. Horizon Press, 1971.

Bardolph, R., ed. The Civil Rights Record: Black Americans and the Law, 1849-1970. Crowell, 1970.

—————. The Negro Vanguard. Rinehart, 1961.

Barker, L. J. The Black in the American Political System. Winthrop, 1974.

—————, and J.J. McCorry, Jr. Black Americans and the Political System. 2d ed. Winthrop, 1980.

Bittker, B. I. The Case for Black Freedom. Random House, 1972.

—————. The Case for Black Reparations. Random House, 1973,.

Bontemps, A. 100 Years of Negro Freedom. Dodd, Mead, 1961.

Booker, S. Black Man's America. Prentice-Hall, 1964.

Brink W., and L. Harris. The Negro Revolution in America. Simon and Schuster, 1964.

Brown, I. C. The Story of the American Negro. Friendship Press, 1957.

Bullock, C. S., III, and H. R. Rodgers, Jr. Racial Equality in America: In Search of an Unfulfilled Goal. Goodyear, 1975.

Burkey, R. M. Racial Discrimination and Public Policy in the United States. Heath, 1971.

Burns, W. H. The Voices of Negro Protest in America. Oxford University, 1963.

Cartwright, J. H. The Triumph of Jim Crow: Tennessee Race Relations in the 1980s. University of Tennessee, 1976.

Conrad, E. Jim Crow America. Duell, Sloan and Pearce, 1947.

Crain, R. L., and C. S. Weisman. Discrimination, Personality, and Achievement: A Survey of Northern Blacks. Seminar, 1972.

Davie, Maurice R. Negroes in American History. McGraw-Hill, 1949.

Davis, J. character Assassination. Philosophical Library, 1951.

Draper, R. The Rediscovery of Black Nationalism. Viking Press, 1970.

DuBois, W. E. B., The Philadelphia Negro. Blom, 1967.

Eastland, T., and W. J. Bennett. Counting by Race: From the Founding Fathers to Bakke. Basic Books, 1979.

Ellison, M. The Black Experience: American Blacks Since 1865. Barnes & Noble Books, 1974.

Ehrlich, W. They Have No Rights: Dred Scott's Struggle for Freedom. Westport, 1979.

Essien-Udom, E. U. Black Nationalism: A Search for Identity in America. University of Chicago, 1962.

Farmer, J. Freedom—When? Random House, 1966.

Fehrenbacher, D.E. The Dred Scott Case: Its Significance in American Law and Politics. Oxford University, 1978.

Fischel, L. H., Jr., and B. Quarles. The Negro American: A Documentary History. Morrow, 1968.

Franklin, J. H. From Slavery to Freedom: A History of American Negroes. 4th ed. Knopf, 1974.

—————. Racial Equality in America. University of Chicago, 1976.

—————, and I. Harr, eds. The Negro in the Tewentieth Century: A Reader. Random House, (Vintage Books), 1967.

Frazier, E. F. Black Bourgeoisie. Free Press, 1957.

—————. The Negro in the United States. Rev. ed. Macmillan, 1957.

Froman, R. Racism. Dell (Delacorte Press), 1972.

Gaither, G. H. Blacks and the Populist Revolt. University of Alabama, 1976.

Gary, L. E., ed. Black Men. Sage Publications, 1981.

Georges-Abeyie, G. The Criminal Justice System and Blacks. Boardman, 1984.

Ginzberg, E., and A. S. Eichner. *The Troublesome Presence: American Democracy and the Negro*. Free Press, 1964.

Glenn, N. D., and C. M. Bonjean, eds. *Blacks in the United States: An Anthology*. Chandler, 1969.

Goldwin, R. A. *100 Years of Emancipation*. Rand McNally, 1964.

Graham, H. D. *Violence: The Crisis of American Confidence*. Johns Hopkins University, 1971.

Greenberg, E. S., N. Milner, and D. M. Olson. *Black Politics: The Inevitability of Conflict*. Holt, Rinehart and Winston, 1970.

Greger, R., and E. McDonald. *A Look Down the Lonesome Road*. Doubleday, 1964.

Grier, W. H., and T. M. Cobbs. *Black Rage*. Basic Books, 1968.

Griffin, J. H. *Black Like Me*. Houghton Mifflin, 1960.

Hall, R. L. *Black Separatism in the United States*. University Press of New England, 1978.

Hamilton, C. V. *The Politics of Civil Rights*. Random House, 1968.

Hansberry, L. *The Movement: Documentary of a Sruggle for Equality*. Simon and Schuster, 1965.

Harvey, J. C. *Black Civil Rights During the Johnson Administration*. Jackson State University, 1973.

———. *Civil Rights During the Kennedy Administration*. Jackson State University. 1971.

Hentoff, N. *The New Equality*. Viking Press, 1964.

Herskovits, M. J. *The American Negro*. Indiana University, 1968.

Higginbotham, A. L., Jr. *In the Matter of Color: Race and the American Legal Process—The Colonial Period*. Oxford University, 1978.

Hoover, D., ed. *Understanding Negro History*. New Viewpoints, 1968.

Isaacs, H. R. *The New World of Negro Americans*. Day, 1963.

Jacob, P. *Prelude to Riot: A View of Urban America from the Bottom*. Random House, 1968.

Javits, J. K. *Discrimination—U.S.A.* Harcourt, Brace, 1960.

Kalven, H., Jr. *The Negro and the First Amendment*. Ohio State University, 1965.

Kardiner, A., and L. Ovesey. *The Mark of Oppression*. New American Library (Meridian Books), 1962.

Katz, W. L., ed. *Eyewitness: The Negro in American History*. Pitman, 1968.

Kephart, W. M. *Racial Factors and the Urban Law Environment*. University of Pennsylvania, 1958.

Killiam, L., and C. Grigg. *Racial Crisis in America: Leadership in Conflict*. Prentice-Hall, 1964.

King, L. L. *Confessons of a White Racist*. Viking Press, 1971.

Kirby, J. B. *Black Americans in the Roosevelt Era: Liberalism and Race*. University of Tennessee, 1980.

Ladd, E. *Negro Political Leadership in the South*. Cornell University, 1966.

Ladner, J. A. *Tomorrow's Tomorrow: The Black Woman*. Doubleday, 1971.

Lane, A. J. *The Brownsville Affair: National Crisis and Black Reaction*. Kennikat Press, 1972.

Levitan, S. A., W. V. Johnson, and R. Taggart. *Still a Dream: The Changing Status of Balcks Since 1960*. Harvard University, 1975.

Levy, L. W., and D. L. Jones, eds. *Jim Crow in Boston: The Origins of the Separate But Equal Doctrine*. Da Capo Press, 1974.

Lincoln, E. R. *The Black Muslims in America*. Beacon Press, 1961.

Lipsky, M., and D. J. Olson. *Commission Politics: The Processing of Racial Crisis in America*. Transaction books, 1977.

Litt. E. *Ethnic Politics in America*. Scott, Foresman, 1970.

Litwack, L. F. *North of Slavery: The Negro in the Free States, 1790–1860*. University of Chicago, 1961.

Logan, R. W. *The Negro in the United States*. Van Nostrand, 1957.

Lomax, L. E. *The Negro Revolt*. Harper & Row, 1962.

Mangum, C. S. *The Legal Status of the Negro*. University of North Carolina, 1940.

Mannix, D. P., and M. Cowley. *Black Cargoes: A History of the Atlantic Slave Trade, 1581–1865.*

Marx, G. T. *Protest and Prejudice: A Study of Belief in the Black Community.* Rev. ed. Harper & Row, 1970.

McAdoo, H. P., ed. *Black Families.* Sage Publications, 1981.

Matthews, D. R., and J. W. Prothro. *Negroes and the New Southern Politics.* Harcourt, Brace & World, 1966.

McKissick, F. *Three Fifths of a Man.* Macmillan, 1969.

Meister, R. J. *Race and Ethnicity in Modern America.* Heath, 1974.

Mitchell, G. E., and W. H. Peace III. *The Angry Black South: Southern Negroes Tell Their Own Story.* Citadel Press, 1962.

Miller, K. S., and R. M. Drager. *Comparative Studies of Blacks and Whites in the United States.* Seminar, 1973.

Moreland, L. B. *White Racism and the Law.* Merrill, 1971.

Morris, M. D. *The Politics of Black America: An Annotated Bibliography.* Public Affairs Press, 1971.

Myrdal, G. *An American Dilemma: The Negro Problem and Modern Democracy.* Harper & Row 1962; rpt. Pantheon Books, 1975.

Newby, I. A. *Challenge to the Court.* Louisiana State University, 1967.

Nolan, V. A. *Communism Versus the Negro.* Regnery, 1951.

Nordhalt, J. W. *The People That Walk in Darkness: A History of the Negro People in America.* Ballantine Books, 1960.

Novak, D. A. *The Wheel of Servitude: Black Forced Labor After Servitude.* University of Kentucky, 1978.

Panetta, L. E., and P. Gall. *Bring Us Together: The Nixon Team and the Civil Rights Retreat.* Lippincott, 1971.

Parsons, T., and K. B. Clark, eds. *The Negro American.* Beacon Press, 1967.

Pease, J. H., and W. H. Pease. *Bound with Them in Chains: A Biographical History of the Antislavery Movement.* Greenwood Press, 1972.

Pinckney, A. *Black Americans.* Prentice-Hall, 1969.

President's National Advisory Commission on Civil Disorders. *Report.* Bantam Books, 1968.

Putnam, C. *Race and Reality.* Public Affairs Press, 1961.

Redding, J. S. *On Being Negro in America.* Bobbs-Merrill, 1951.

———. *They Came in Chains: Americans from Africa.* Rev. ed. Lippincott, 1973.

Ringer, B. B. *"We the People" and Others.* Tavistock, 1983.

Rose, A. *The Negro in America.* Beacon Press, 1956.

Rowan, C. *Go South to Sorrow.* Random House, 1957.

———. *South of Freedom.* Knopf, 1952.

Santa Cruz, H. *Racial Discrimination.* United Nations, 1971.

Shade, W. G., and R. C. Herrenkohl. *Seven on Black: Reflections on the Negro Experience in America.* Lippincott, 1969.

Sickels, R. J. *Race, Marriage, and the Law.* University of New Mexico, 1972.

Silberman, C. E. *Crisis in Black and White.* Random House, 1965.

Sloan, I. J. *The American Negro: A Chronology and Fact Book.* Oceana, 1965.

Sowell, T. *Civil Rights: Rhetoric or Reality.* Morrow, 1984.

Storing, H. J., ed. *What Country Have I? Political Writings by Black Americans.* St. Martin's Press, 1970.

Tushnet, M. V. *The American Law of Slavery.* Princeton University, 1981.

Uhlman, T. M. *Racial Justice: Black Judges and Defendants in an Urban Trial Court.* Lexington Books, 1979.

Warren, R. P. *Who Speaks for the Negro?* Random House, 1965.

Weisbord, R. G. *Genocide Birth Control and the Black American.* Greenwood Press, 1975.

Weyl, N. *The Negro in American Civilization.* Public Affairs Press, 1960.

Welsch, E. K. *The negro in the United States: A Research Guide.* Indiana University, 1965.

Wilson, E. G. *The Loyal Blacks.* Capricorn, 1976.

Wilson, W. J. *The Declining Significance of Race: Blacks and Changing American Institutions.* University of Chicago, 1978.

Yinger, J. M. *A Minority Group in American Society.* McGraw-Hill, 1965.

Young, W. M., Jr. *Beyond Racism.* McGraw-Hill, 1969.

C. OTHER MINORITY GROUPS: AMERICAN INDIANS, JEWS, JAPANESE et al.

Barsh, R. L., and J. Y. Henderson. *The Road: Indian Tribes and Political Liberty.* University of California, 1979.

Bauer, Y. *The Holocaust in Historical Perspective.* University of Washington, 1978.

Belth, N. C., ed. *Barriers: Patterns of Discrimination Against Jews.* Friendly House, 1958.

Bendetsen, K. R. *Final Report: Japanese Evacuation from the West Coast.* Superintendent of Documents, 1943.

Bloom, L., and R. Riemer. *Removal and Return.* University of California, 1949.

Bosworth, A. R. *America's Concentration Camps.* Norton, 1967.

Broun, H. C., and G. Britt. *Christians Only.* Da Capo Press, 1974.

Brown, D. *Bury My Heart at Wounded Knee.* Holt, Rinehart and Winston, 1971.

Burnette, R. *The Tortured Americans.* Prentice-Hall, 1971.

Cabrera, Y. A. *Emerging Faces: The Mexican-Americans.* Brown, 1971.

Collier, J. *The Indians of America.* U.S. Bureau of Indian Affairs, 1947.

Conrat, M., and R. Conrat. *Executive Order 9066.* University of California, 1972.

Daniels, R. *Concentration Camps, U.S.A.: Japanese-Americans and World War II.* Holt, Rinehart and Winston, 1971.

———. *The Decision to Relocate the Japanese-Americans.* Lippincott, 1975.

———. *The Politics of Prejudice: The Anti-Japanese Movement in California and the Struggle for Exclusion.* University of California, 1978.

Daniels, W. M. *American Indians.* H.W. Wilson, 1957.

Davis, E. *But We Were Born Free.* Bobbs-Merrill, 1954.

Deloria, V., Jr. *Custer Died for Your Sins: An Indian Manifesto.* Macmillan, 1969.

Dobkowski, M. N. *The Tarnished Dream: The Basis of American Anti-Semitism.* Greenwood Press, 1979.

Embrey, S. K., ed. *The Lost Years, 1942–1946.* University of California, 1972.

Epstein, B. R., and A. Forster. *"Some of My Best Friends . . ."* Farrar, Straus, 1962.

Fellows, D. K. *A Mosaic of America's Ethinic Minorities.* Wiley, 1972.

Forster, A., and B. R. Epstein. *Cross-Currents.* Doubleday, 1957.

———. *The New Anti-Semitism.* McGraw-Hill, 1974.

———. *The Trouble-Makers.* Doubleday, 1952.

Gallo, P. J. *Ethnic Alienation: The Italian-Americans.* Fairleigh Dickinson University, 1974.

Gessner, R. *Massacre: A Survey of Today's American Indians.* Da Capo Press, 1974.

Girdner, A., and A. Loftis, *The Great Betrayal.* Macmillan, 1969.

Glock, C. Y., G. J. Selznick, and J.L. Spaeth. *The Apathetic Majority: A Study Based on Public Responses to the Eichmann Trial.* Anti-Defamation League, 1966.

———. *Christian Beliefs and Anti-Semitism.* Anti-Defamation League, 1966.

Grebler, L., et al. *The Mexican-American People: The Nation's Second Largest Minority.* Free Press, 1971.

Grobman, A., and D. Landes, eds. *Genocide: Critical Issues of the Holocaust.* Simon Wiesenthal Center, 1982.

Grodzins. M. *Americans Betrayed: Politics and the Japanese Evacuation.* University of Chicago, 1949.

Handlin, O. *The Dimensions of Liberties.* Harvard University, 1961.

Herzog, S. J., ed. *Minority Group Politics.* Holt, Rinehart and Winston, 1971.

Higham, J. *Strangers in the Land: Patterns of American Nativism, 1869–1929.* Rutgers University, 1955.

Hosokawa, B. *Nisei: The Quiet Americans.* Morrow, 1969.

Howard, J. R., ed. *Awakening Minorities: American Indians, Mexican-Americans, Puerto Ricans*. Transcation Books, 1972.

Irons, P. *Justice at War: The Story of the Japanese American Internment Cases*. Oxford University, 1983.

Javits, J. K. *Discrimination—U.S.A*. Harcourt, Brace, 1960.

Josephy, A. M. *Red Power: The American Indian's Fight for Freedom*. McGraw-Hill, 1972.

Katz, J. *From Prejudice to Destruction: Anti-Semitism, 1700–1933*. Harvard University, 1981.

Kitagawa, D. *Issei and Nisei: The Internment Years*. Seabury Press, 1967.

Kitano, H. H. L. *Japanese Americans*. Prentice-Hall, 1969.

Konvitz, M. R. *The Alien and the Asiatic in American Law*. Cornell University, 1950.

Kramer, J. R., and S. Leventman. *Children of the Gilded Ghetto*. Yale University, 1961.

Krickus, R. *Pursuing the American Dream: White Ethnics and the New Populism*. Doubleday, 1976.

Leathers, N. L. *The Japanese in America*. Lerner Law Books, 1967.

Leighton, A. H. *The Governing Men*. Princeton University, 1945; rpt. 1964.

Lewis, H. D., ed. *The Chicanos*. Indiana University, 1975.

Mack, R. W., and T. S. Duster. *Patterns of Minority Relations*. Anti-Defamation League, 1965.

McWilliams, Carey. *Brothers Under the Skin*. Little, Brown, 1964.

———. *A Mask for Privilege*. Little, Brown, 1948.

———. *North from Mexico*. Lippincott, 1949.

———. *Prejudice: Japanese-Americans, Symbols of Racial Intolerance*. Little, Brown, 1944.

Mears, E. G. *Resident Orientals of the American Pacific Coast*. University of Chicago, 1928.

Modell, J. *The Economics and Politics of Racial Accommodation: The Japanese of Los Angeles, 1900–1942*. University of Illinois, 1977.

Nagler, M. *Perspectives on the North American Indians*. McClelland and Stewart, 1972.

Parkes, J. *Anti-Semitism*. Quadrangle, 1969.

Philliber, W. W., and C. B. McCoy, eds. *The Invisible Minority: Urban Appalachians*. University of Kentucky, 1979.

Piccigallo, P. R. *The Japanese on Trial: Allied War Crime Operations in the East, 1945–1951*. University of Texas, 1979.

Prohias, R. J., and L. Casal. *The Cuban Minority in the United States*. Arno Press, 1974.

Quinley, H. E., and C. Y. Glock. *Anti-Semitism in America*. Free Press, 1979.

Reel, A. F. *The Case of General Yamashita*. University of Chicago, 1949.

Reischauer, E. O. *The Japanese*. Harvard University, 1977.

Rosenstock, M. *Louis Marshall: Defender of Jewish Rights*. Wayne State University, 1966.

Rusaldo, R., R. A. Calvert, and G. L. Seligmann. *Chicano: The Beginnings of Bronze Power*. Morrow, 1974.

Samora, J., ed. *La Raza: Forgotten Americans*. University of Notra Dame, 1966.

Seldes, G. *"We Hold These Truths. . . ."* League of American Writers, 1939.

Selznick, G. J., and S. Steinberg. *The Tenacity of Prejudice: Anti-Semitism in Contemporary America*. Anti-Defamation League, 1969.

Servin, M. P. *An Awakened Minority: The Mexican-Americans*. Glencoe Press, 1974.

Sindler, A. P. *Change in the Contemporary South*. Duke University, 1964.

Smith, B. *Americans from Japan*. Lippincott, 1948.

Steiner, S. *La Raza: The Mexican-Americans*. Harper & Row, 1970.

Ten Broek, J., E. N. Barnhart, and F. W. Matson. *Prejudice, War and the Constitution: Causes and Consequences of the Japanese-Americans in World War II*. Rev. ed. University of California, 1968.

Thomas, D. S. *The Salvage*. University of California, 1952.

———, and R. S. Nishimito. *The Spoilage*. University of California, 1946.

Tumin, M. M. *An Inventory and Appraisal of Research on American Anti-Semitism*. Anti-Defamation League, 1961.

Van Every, D. *Disinherited: The Lost Birthright of the American Indian*. Morrow, 1966.

Weglyn, M. *Years of Infamy: The Untold Story of America's Concentration Camps.* Morrow, 1976.

Weintraub, R. G. *How Secure These Rights?* Doubleday, 1949.

Wyman, D. S. *The Abandonment of the Jews: America and the Holocaust, 1941–1945.* Pantheon Books, 1984.

Yinger, J. M. *Anti-Semitism: A Case Study in Prejudice and Discrimination.* Anti-Defamation League, 1964.

D. SEX (GENDER)

(See also IV. F, . . . Privacy; XII, Morals, Obscenity, and Censorship.)

Alder, F. *Sisters in Crime: The Rise of the New Female Criminal.* McGraw-Hill, 1975.

Amunden, K. *The Silenced Majority: Women and American Democracy.* Prentice-Hall, 1971.

Baer, J. A. *The Chains of Protection: The Judicial Response to Women's Labor Legislation.* Greenwood Press, 1978.

Bardwick, J. M. *The Great Revolution.* Holt, Rinehart and Winston, 1979.

Bardon, E. *The Sexual Arena and Women's Liberation.* Nelson-Hall, 1978.

Binkin, M., and S. J. Bach. *Women and the Military.* Brookings Institution, 1977.

Bird, C. *Born Females : The High Cost of Keeping Women Down.* McKay, 1968.

Boles, J. K. *The Politics of the Equal Rights Amendment: Conflict and the Decision Process.* Longman, 1979.

Boneparth, E., ed. *Women, Power and Policy.* Pergamon Press, 1982.

Callahan, D. *Abortion: Law, Choice and Morality.* Macmillian, 1970.

Chafe, W. H. *Women and Equality: Changing Patterns in American Culture.* Oxford University, 1977.

Chafetz, J. S., and A. G. Dworkin. *Female Revolt: The Causes of Mass Feminist Movements.* Rowman & Allanheld, 1985.

Chesler, P. *Women and Madness.* Doubleday, 1972.

Chapman, J. R., and M. Gates, eds. *The Victimization of Women.* Sage Publications, 1978.

Cohen, M., T. Nagel and T. Scanlon, eds. *The Rights and Wrongs of Abortion.* Princeton University, 1974.

Congressional Quarterly. *The Women's Movement.* Congressional Quarterly Press, 1977.

DeCrow, K. *Sexist Justice.* Random House (Vintage Books), 1975.

D'Emilio, J. *Sexual Politics, Sexual Communities: The Making of a Homosexual Minority in the United States, 1940–1970.* University of Chicago, 1983.

Diamond, I. *Sex Roles in the State House.* Yale University, 1977.

Datesman, S. K., ed. *Women, Crime, and Justice.* Oxford University, 1980.

Davidson, K. M., R. B. Ginsberg, and H. H. Kay. *Sex-Based Discrimination: Test, Cases, and Materials.* West, 1974.

Deckard, B. S. *The Women's Movement.* 2d ed. Harper & Row, 1978.

Delin, B. *The Sex Offender.* Beacon Press, 1978.

Denmark, F. *Who Discriminates Against Women.* Sage, Publications, 1974.

Ditzion, S. *Marriage, Morals, and Sex in America.* Bookman, 1953.

Edwards, S. *Female Sexuality and the Law.* Martin Robertson, 1981.

English, J., ed. *Sex Equality.* Prentice-Hall, 1977.

Epstein, C. F. *Women in Law.* Basic Books, 1981.

Epstein, L. K., ed. *Women in the Professions.* Heath, 1975.

Evans, R. *The Feminists.* Barnes & Noble Books, 1978.

Fishel, A. and J. Pottker. *National Politics and Sex Discrimination in Education.* Lexington Books, 1978.

Flexner, E. *Century of Struggle: The Women's Rights Movement in the United States.* Harvard University, (Belknap Press), 1959.

Foner, P. S., ed. *Frederick Douglass on Women's Rights.* Greenwood Press, 1976.

Freeman, J., ed. *The Politics of Women's Liberation.* McKay, 1975.

———. *Women: A Feminist Perspective.* Mayfield, 1975.

Friedan, B. *The Feminine Mystique.* Norton, 1963.

Frohock, F. M. *Abortion: A Case Study in Law and Morals.* Greenwood Press, 1983.

Fulenwider, C. K. *Feminism in American Politics.* Praeger, 1980.

Gager, N., ed. *Women's Rights Almanac.* Harper & Row, 1976.

Gelb, J., and M. L. Palley. *Women and Public Policies.* Princeton University, 1982.

Ginsberg, R. B. *Constitutional Aspects of Sex-Based Discrimination.* West, 1974.

Githens, M., and J. L. Prestage. *A Portrait of Marginality: The Political Behavior of the American Woman.* McKay, 1977.

Goldstein, L. F. *The Constitutional Rights of Women: Cases in Law and Social Change.* Longman, 1979.

Granfield, D. *The Abortion Decision.* Doubleday, 1969.

Greenberg, H., ed. and comp. *The Equal Rights Amendment: A Bibliographic Study.* Greenwood Press, 1976.

Gruberg, M. *Women in American Politics.* Academic Press, 1968.

Harley, S., and R. Terborg-Penn. *The Afro-American Woman.* Kennikat Press, 1978.

Harris, B. J. *Beyond Her Sphere: Women and the Professions in American History.* Greenwood Press, 1978.

Hayden, T. *Punishing Pregnancy.* American Civil Liberties Union, 1973.

Jaffe, F. S., B. L. Lindheim, and P. R. Lee. *Abortion Politics: Private Politics and Public Policy.* McGraw-Hill, 1981.

Jaquette, J., ed. *Women in Politics.* Wiley, 1974.

Kanowitz, L. *Equal Rights: The Male Stake.* University of New Mexico, 1981.

———. *Sex Roles in Law and Society.* University of New Mexico, 1972.

———. *Women and Law.* University of New Mexico, 1969.

Kirkpatrick, J. J. *Political Woman.* Basic Books, 1974.

Klein, E. *Gender Politics.* Harvard University, 1984.

Kraditor, A. S. *Up from the Pedestal.* Quadrangle, 1963.

Krason, S. M. *Abortion: Politics, Morality, and the Constitution.* University Press of America, 1984.

Kyle, P. A. eds. *Integrating the Neglected Majority.* King's Court, 1977.

Lader, L. *Abortion II: Making the Revolution.* Beacon Press, 1973.

McElroy, W., ed. *Freedom, Feminism, and the State.* Cato, 1982.

MacKinnon, C. A. *Sexual Harrassment of Working Women: A Case of Sex Discrimination.* Yale University, 1978.

Mead, M., and F. B. Kaplan. *American Women.* Scribner, 1965.

Millet, K. *Sexual Politics.* Doubleday, 1970.

Mohr, J. C. *Abortion in America.* Oxford University, 1978.

Montagu, A. *Sex, Man and Society.* Putnam, 1969.

Morgan, R., ed. *Sisterhood is Powerful.* Random House (Vintage Books), 1970.

Murphy, I. L. *Public Policies on the Status of Women.* Lexington, Books, 1973.

O'Connor, K. *Women's Organizations' Use of the Courts.* Lexington Books, 1980.

Peck, E. *A Funny Thing Happened on the Way to Equality.* Prentice-Hall, 1975.

Price, B. R., and N. J. Sokoloff. *The Criminal Justice System and Women.* Boardman, 1982.

Rabkin, P. A. *Fathers to Daughters: The Legal Foundations of Female Emancipation.* Greenwood Press, 1980.

Rodgers-Rose, L. A. F. *The Black Woman.* Sage Publications, 1980.

Ross, S. D., and A. Borcher. *The Rights of Women.* Bantam Books, 1983.

Rossi, A., ed. *Academic Women on the Move.* Sage Publications, 1973.

Rubin, E. R. *Abortion, Politics and the Courts: Roe v. Wade and its Aftermath.* Greenwood Press. 1982.

Ryan, M. P. *Womanhood in America: From Colonial Times to the Present.* New Viewpoints, 1975.

Saltman, J., and S. Zimering. *Abortion Today.* Thomas, 1973.

Sarvis, B., and H. Rodman. *The Abortion Controversy.* Columbia University, 1973.

Schwendinger, J. R., and Herman Schwendinger. *Rape and Inequality.* Sage Publications, 1983.

Simon, R. J. *Women and Crime.* Lexington Books, 1975.

Steiner, G. Y. *The Abortion Dispute and the American System.* Brookings Institution, 1983.

———. *Constitutional Inequality: The Political Fortunes of the Equal Rights Amendment.* Brookings Institution, 1985.

Stimpson, C. R., ed. *Discrimination Against Women.* Bowker, 1973.

———. *Women and the "Equal Rights" Amendment.* Bowker, 1972.

Tanner, L. B., ed. *Voices from Women's Liberation.* New American Library, 1972.

Taylor, G. R. *Sex in History.* Vanguard Press, 1954.

Tooley, M. *Abortion and Infanticide.* Oxford University, 1984.

Tong, R. *Women, Sex, and the Law.* Rowman & Allanheld, 1984.

Underwood, L. A. *Women in Federal Employment Programs.* Urban Institute, 1979.

Walbert, D. F., and J. D. Butler. *The Abortion Controversy.* Case Western Reserve University, 1973.

Wardle, L. D., and M. A. Q. Wood. *A Lawyer Looks at Abortion.* Brigham Young University, 1982.

Ware, C. *Woman Power: The Movement for Women's Liberation.* Tower, 1970.

Wright, H. *Sex and Society.* University of Washington, 1969.

E. THE SOUTH AND ITS VIEWPOINT

(See also II.E, States' Rights.)

Bartley, N. *The Rise of Massive Resistance: Race and Politics in the South During the 1950s.* Louisiana State University, 1969.

Black, E. *Southern Governors and Civil Rights: Racial Segregation as a Campaign Issue in the Second Reconstruction.* Harvard University, 1976.

Carter, H. *Southern Legacy.* Louisiana State University, 1950.

———. *The South Strikes Back.* Doubleday, 1959.

Cash, W. J. *The Mind of the South.* Knopf, 1956.

Chafe, W. H. *Civility and Civil Rights: Greensboro, North Carolina, and the Black Struggle for Equality.* Oxford University, 1980.

Chaze, E. *Tiger in the Honeysuckle.* Scribner 1965.

Clark, T. D. *The Emerging South.* Oxford University, 1961.

Collins, C. W. *Whither Solid South.* Pelican Books, 1947.

Cousins, R. E., et al. *South Carolinians Speak: A Moderate Approach to Race Relations.* University of North Carolina, 1957.

Dabbs, J. H. *The Southern Heritage.* Knopf, 1958.

Diamond, I. *Sex Roles in the State House.* Yale University, 1977.

Eaton, C. *The Mind of the Old South.* Louisiana State University, 1964.

Ely, J. W., Jr. *The Crisis of Conservative Virginia: The Byrd Organization and the Politics of Massive Resistance.* University of Tennessee, 1976.

Gates, R. L. *The Making of Massive Resistance.* University of North Carolina, 1965.

Graham. H. D. *Crisis in Print: Desegregation and the Press in Tennessee.* Vanderbilt University, 1967.

Grantham, D. W., Jr. *Hoke Smith and the Politics of the New South.* Louisiana State University, 1967.

Hays, B. A. *A Southern Moderate Speaks.* University of North Carolina, 1959.

Highsaw, R. B., ed. *The Deep South in Transformation.* University of Alabama, 1964.

Leiserson, A., ed. *The American South in the 1960's.* Praeger, 1965.

McGill. R, *The South and the Southerner.* Little, Brown, 1963.

McKean, K. F. *Cross Currents in the South.* Ohio University (Swallow Press), 1963.

Morris, W. *The South Today: 100 Years After Appomattox.* Harper & Row 1965.

Newby, I. A. *Challenge to the Court: Social Scientists and the Defense of Segregation, 1954–1966*. Louisiana State University, 1969.

———. *Jim Crow's Defenses: Anti-Negro Thought in America, 1900–1930*. Louisiana State University, 1965.

Nicholls, W. A. *Southern Tradition and Regional Progress*. University of North Carolina, 1960.

Norris, H., ed. *We Dissent*. St. Martin's Press, 1962.

Roland, C. P. *The Improbable Era: The South Since World War II*. University of Kentucky, 1975.

Rubin, L. D., and J. J. Kilpatrick. *The Lasting South*. Regnery, 1957.

Savage, H., Jr. *The Seeds of Time: The Background of Southern Thinking*. Holt, 1959.

Silver, J. W. *Mississippi: The Closed Society*. Enl. ed. Harcourt, Brace & World, 1966.

Simkins, F. R. *Pitchfork Ben Tillman*. Louisiana State University, 1967.

Sindler, A. P., ed. *Change in the Contemporary South*. Duke University, 1964.

Sosna, M. *Southern Liberals and the Race Issue: In Search of the Silent South*. Columbia University, 1977.

Sprigle, R. *In the Land of Jim Crow*. Simon and Schuster, 1949.

Thorp, W. *A Southern Reader*. Knopf, 1955.

Tisdale, J. W. *A Southerner's Reflection About the 1954 Supreme Court Decision Concerning Racial Segregation in the Public Schools*. Jarrett's Press, 1956.

Warren, R. P. *Who Speaks for the Negro?* Random House, 1965.

Watters, P. *The South and the Nation*. Pantheon Books, 1970.

Wirt, F. M. *Politics of Southern Equality: Law and Social Change in a Mississippi County*. Aldine, 1970.

Wood, F. G. *Black Scare: The Racist Response to Emancipation and Reconstruction*. University of California, 1968.

Zinn, H. *The Southern Mystique*. 2d ed. Simon and Schuster, 1972.

F. AGE

MacDonald, R. M. *Mandatory Retirement and the Law*. American Enterprise Institute, 1978.

Malinchak, A. A. *Crime and Gerontology*. Prentice-Hall, 1980.

Myerhoff, B., and A. Simic. *Life's Career: Aging*. Sage Publication, 1978.

IV. CRIMINAL JUSTICE, LAW, AND PROCEDURE

A. DUE PROCESS AND CRIMINAL JUSTICE GENERALLY
(*See also* Specific aspects below.)

Alexander, F. *The Criminal, the Judge, and the Public*. Free Press, 1961.

Allen, F. A. *The Borderland of Criminal Justice: Essays in Law and Criminology*. University of Chicago, 1969.

Alpert, G. P. *Legal Rights of Prisoners*. Heath, 1978.

Atkin, B. M. *The Invisible Justice System: Discretion and the Law*. Anderson, 1980.

Bakel, C. *The Right to Bear Arms*. McGraw-Hill, 1966.

Baker, R., and F. A. Meyer, Jr. *The Criminal Justice Game*. PWS (Duxbury Press), 1980.

Barth, A. *The Price of Liberty*. Viking Press, 1962.

Beck, C. *Law and Justice: Essays in Honor of Robert S. Rankin*. Duke University, 1970.

Belli, M. *The Law Revolution*. Sherbourne, 1969.

Bent, A. E. The Politics of Law Enforcement. Lexington Books, 1974.

Berk, R. A., et al. *The Measure of Justice: An Empirical Study of Criminal Law Change*. Academic Press, 1976.

Blumberg, A. S., ed. *The Scales of Justice*. 2d ed. Dutton, 1973.

Casper, J. D. *American Criminal Justice: The Defendant's Perspective*. Prentice-Hall, 1972.

———. *Criminal Courts: The Defendant's Perspective*. Government Printing Office, 1978.

Chambliss, W. J. *Crime and the Legal Process*. McGraw-Hill, 1969.
———. *Criminal Law in Action*. Hamilton, 1975.
Chute, C. L., and M. Bell. *Crime, Courts and Probation*. Macmillan, 1956.
Cohn, A., and R. Udolf. *The Criminal Justice System and its Psychology*. Anderson, 1982.
Cole, G. F. *The American System of Criminal Justice*. 3d ed. Brooks/Cole, 1983.
———. *Criminal Justice: Law and Politics*. 4th ed. Brooks/Cole, 1984.
———. *Politics and the Administration of Justice*. Sage Publications, 1973.
Columbia Law Review. *Criminal Law and its Administration*. Da Capo Press, 1971.
Cray, E. *The Big Blue Line*. Coward-McCann, 1967.
Cronin, T. E., T. Z. Cronin, and M. Molakovich. *U.S. v. Crime in the Streets*. Indiana University, 1981.
Cummings, H., and C. McFarland. *Federal Justice*. Da Capo Press, 1970.
Curtis, L. A. *Criminal Violence*. Lexington Books, 1974.
Davis, B. *Criminological Bibliographies*. Greenwood Press, 1978.
Decker. S. H. *Juvenile Justice Policy*. Sage Publications 1984.
Denfeld, D. *Streetwise Criminology*. General Learning Press, 1974.
Dershowitz, A. M. *The Best Defense*. Random House, 1982.
Dienstein, W. *Are You Guilty?* Thomas, 1954.
Donen, N. *The Rights of Americans*. Random House, 1970.
Eldridge, W. B. *Narcotics and the Law*. New York University, 1962.
Elison, K. W., and R. Buckhout. *Psychology and Criminal Justice*. Harper & Row 1981.
Fellman, D. *The Defendant's Rights*. Rinehart, 1958.
———. *The Defendant's Rights Today*. University of Wisconsin, 1976.
Felsher, H. and M. Rosen. *The Press in the Jury Box*. Macmillan, 1966.
Fingarette, H. *The Meaning of Criminal Insanity*. University of California, 1972.
Fleming, M. *The Price of Perfect Justice*. Basic Books, 1974.
Francis, P. *Protection Through the Law*. Oceana, 1965.
Frankel, S. *Beyond a Reasonable Doubt*. Stein & Day, 1971.
Galloway, J., ed. *Criminal Justice and the Burger Court*. Facts on File, 1977.
———, ed. *Supreme Court and the Rights of the Accused*. Facts on File, 1972.
Garbus, M. *Ready for the Defense*. Avon Books, 1974.
George, B. J., Jr. *Constitutional Limitations on Evidence in Criminal Cases*. University of Michigan, 1966.
Gerber, R. J., ed. *Contemporary Issues in Criminal Justice: Some Problems and Suggested Reforms*. Kennikat Press, 1975.
Gillers, S. *Getting Justice: The Rights of the People*. Basic Books, 1971.
Goldfarb, R. L. *The Contempt Power*. Columbia University, 1963.
———. *Jails: The Ultimate Ghetto of the Criminal Justice System*. Doubleday (Anchor Books), 1975.
Goldstein, J., A. M. Dershowitz, and R. D. Schwartz. *Criminal Law: Theory and Process*. Free Press, 1974.
Goldstein, J. H. *Aggressions and Crimes of Violence*. Oxford University, 1975.
Grant, J. A. *Our Common Law Constitution*. Boston University, 1960.
Gray, V., and B. Williams. *The Organizational Politics of Criminal Justice: Policy in Context*. Lexington Books, 1980.
Greenberg, M. H., and J. D. Olander. *Criminal Justice Through Science Fiction*. New Viewpoints, 1977.
Hagan, J., ed. *Deterrence Reconsidered: Methodological Innovations*. Sage Publication, 1982.
Harding, A. L., ed. *Fundamental Law in Criminal Prosecutions*. Southern Methodist University, 1959.
Harris, W. R. *Tyranny on Trial: The Evidence at Nuremberg*. Southern Methodist University, 1954.
Hawes, J., ed. *Law and Order in American History*. Kennikat Press, 1979.
Holten, N. G., and M. E. Jones. *The System of Criminal Justice*. 2d ed. Little, Brown, 1982.

Humphreys, H. M. *Contemporary Criminal Justice in America*. Public Insights, 1980.

Hunt, M. *The Mugging*. Atheneum, 1972.

Jacob, H. *Crime and Justice in Urban America*. Prentice-Hall, 1980.

————, ed. *The Potential for Reform of Criminal Justice*. Sage Publications, 1974.

————. *Urban Justice: Law and Order in American Cities*. Prentice-Hall. 1973.

Kamisar, Y., F. E. Inbau, and T. Arnold. *Criminal Justice in Our Time*. University of Virginia, 1965.

Kalmanoff, A. S. *Criminal Justice: Enforcement and Administration*. Little, Brown, 1976.

Kaplan, J. *Criminal Justice: Introductory Cases and Materials*. Foundation Press, 1973.

Karlen, D. *Anglo-American Criminal Justice*. Oxford University, 1968.

Katz, L. R. *The Justice Imperative: An Introduction to Criminal Justice*. Anderson, 1980.

Katzman, G. S. *Understanding the Criminal Process*. Pergamon Press, 1985.

Kennett, L. B., and L. Anderson. *The Gun in America: The Origins of a National Dilemma*. Greenwood Press, 1975.

Kirchheimer, O. *Political Justice: The Use of Legal Procedure for Political Ends*. Princeton University, 1961.

Klein, I. J. *Constitutional Law for Criminal Justice Professionals*. PWS (Duxbury Press), 1980.

Kukla, R. J. *Gun Control*. Stackpole Books, 1973.

Law Enforcement Assistance Administration. Institute of Law Enforcement and Criminal Justice. *Reducing Court Delay*. Government Printing Office, 1973.

LeGrande, J. L. *The Basic Processes of Criminal Justice*. Glencoe 1973.

Levin, A. L. *Evidence and the Behavioral Sciences*. University of Pennsylvania, Institute of Legal Research, 1966.

Levin, M. A. *Urban Politics and the Criminal Courts*. University of Chicago, 1977.

Levy, L. W. *Against the Law: The Nixon Court and Criminal Justice*. Harper & Row, 1974.

Lieberman, J. K. *How the Government Breaks the Law*. Penguin Books, 1973.

Loewy, A. H. *Criminal Law in a Nutshell*. West, 1974.

McDonald, W. F., ed. *Criminal Justice and the Victim*. Sage Publications, 1976.

McGuigan, P. B., R. R. Rader, and C. A. Keiper. *Criminal Justice Reform*. Regnery, 1983.

McIntyre, D. M. *Criminal Justice in the United States*. Rev. ed. American Bar Foundation, 1974.

Marks, T. C., and J. T. Reilly. *Constitutional Criminal Procedure*. PWS (Duxbury press), 1979.

Mathias, W., R. C. Rescoria, and E. Stephans. *Foundations of Criminal Justice*. Prentice-Hall, 1980.

Morash, M., ed. *Implementing Criminal Justice Policies*. Sage Publications, 1982.

Moreland, C. C. *Equal Justice Under Law*. Oceana, 1965.

Morris, H. *Freedom and Responsibility*. Stanford University, 1981.

Mott, R. L. *Due Process of Law*. Bobbs-Merrill, 1926.

Nagel, S. S. *Improving the Legal Process: Effect of Alternatives*. Lexington Books, 1975.

————, ed. *Modeling the Criminal Justice System*. Sage Publications, 1977.

————, ed. *The Political Science of Criminal Justice*. Thomas, 1983.

————. *Rights of the Accused*. Sage Publications, 1972.

Nardulli, P. F. *The Courtroom Elite: An Organizational Perspective on Criminal Justice*. Ballinger, 1979.

Navasky, J. S. *Kennedy Justice*. Atheneum, 1971.

Neubauer, D. W. *Criminal Justice in Middle America*. General Learning Press, 1974.

Newman, D. J. *Conviction: The Determination of Guilt or Innocence Without Trial*. Little, Brown, 1967.

Newman, E. S. *Police, the Law and Personal Freedom*. Oceana, 1964.

Oaks, D. H., and W. Lehman. *A Criminal Justice System and the Indigent*. 2d ed. University of Chicago, 1968.

Olander, J. D., and M. H. Greenberg, eds. *Criminal Justice Through Fiction*. New Viewpoints, 1978.

Orloski, R. J. *Criminal Law: An Indictment.* Nelson-Hall, 1977.

Orton, W. A. *The Liberal Tradition: Social and Spiritual Conditions of Freedom.* Oxford University, 1945.

Palmer, J. W. *Constitutional Rights of Prisoners.* 2d ed. Anderson, 1977.

Paulsen, M. G. *Equal Justice for the Poor Man.* Public Affairs Pamphlets, 1965.

Pelfrey, W. V. *The Evolution of Criminology.* Anderson, 1980.

Peterson, V. W. *Barbarians in Our Midst.* Little, Brown, 1952.

Pittman, D., and W. Gordon, *Revolving Door: A Study of the Chronic Police Case Inebriate.* Free Press, 1967.

Platt, T., and P. Takagi, eds. *Crime and Social Justice.* Barnes & Noble Books, 1981.

Ploscowe, M. *The Truth About Divorce.* Hawthorn Books, 1955.

Pound, R. *Criminal Justice in America.* Holt, 1945; rpt. Da Capo Press, 1975.

Putkammer, E. W. *Administration of Criminal Law.* University of Chicago, 1953.

Quinney, R. *Class, State, and Crime: On the Theory and Practice of Criminal Justice.* Longmans, Green, 1977.

———. *Criminal Justice in America: A Critical Understanding.* Little, Brown, 1974.

Richette, L. A. *The Throwaway Children.* Lippincott, 1969.

Rossum, R. A. *The Politics of the Criminal Justice System.* Dekker, 1978.

Rudofsky, D. *The Rights of Prisoners.* Avon Books, 1973.

Schaefer, W. V. *The Suspect and Society: Criminal Procedure and Converging Constitutional Doctrines.* Northwestern University, 1967.

Scheingold, S. A. *The Politics of Law and Order: Street Crime and Public Policy.* Longman, 1984.

Seagle, W. *Acquitted of Murder.* Regnery, 1958.

Shelden, R. G. *Criminal Justice in America: A Sociological Approach.* Little, Brown, 1982.

Sherrill, R. *The Saturday Night Special.* Charterhouse, 1973.

Sigler, J. *Understanding Criminal Law.* Little, Brown, 1981.

Silverstein, L. *Defense of the Poor.* American Bar Association, 1965.

Swigert, V. L., and R. A. Farrell. *Murder, Inequality, and the Law.* Lexington Books, 1976.

Taylor, H. *Due Process of Law and Equal Protection.* Callaghan, 1917.

Taylor, T. *Two Studies in Constitutional Interpretation.* Ohio State University, 1968.

Trebach, A. S. *The Rationing of Justice: Constitutional Rights and the Criminal Process.* Rutgers University, 1964.

Uviller, H. R. *The Processes of Criminal Justice Adjudication.* West, 1975.

Walker, S. *Popular Justice: A History of American Criminal Justice.* Oxford University, 1980.

Way, H. F. *Criminal Justice and the American Constitution.* PWS (Duxbury Press), 1980.

Weinreb, L. L. *Denial of Justice: Criminal Process in the United States.* Free Press, 1977.

Whitebread, C. H. *Criminal Procedure.* Foundation Press, 1980.

Wright, J. and P. Lewis. *Modern Criminal Justice.* McGraw-Hill, 1978.

Zinn, H., ed. *Justice: Eyewitness Accounts.* Beacon Press, 1977.

———. *The Responsibilities of Civil Disobedience: Nine Fallacies on Law and Order.* Random House, 1968.

B. FAIR TRIAL

Balbus, I. D. *The Dialectics of Legal Repression: Black Rebels Before the American Criminal Courts.* Sage Publications, 1973.

Blackburn, S., ed. *White Justice: Black Experience Today in America's Courtrooms.* Harper & Row, 1971.

Busch, F. X. *Law and Tactics in Jury Trial.* Bobbs-Merrill, 1961.

Carter, D. T. *Scottsboro: A Tragedy of the American South.* Louisiana State University, 1969.

Forer, L. G. *"No One Will Listen": How Our Legal System Brutalizes the Youthful Poor.* Day, 1970.

Friendly, A., and R. L. Goldfarb. *Crime and Publicity: The Impact of News on the Administration of Justice.* 20th Century Fund, 1967.

Heller, F. H. *The Sixth Amendment ot the Constitution of the United States: A Study in Constitutional Development.* University of Kansas, 1951.

Klaus, S., ed. *The Milligan Case.* Da Capo Press, 1971.

Loftus, E. F. *Eyewitness Testimony.* Harvard University, 1979.

Misner, R. L. *Speedy Trial: Federal and State Practices.* Michie, 1983.

Morris, G. H. *The Insanity Defense: A Blueprint for Legislative Reform.* Heath, 1976.

Newman, D. J. *Conviction: TheDetermination of Guilt or Innocence Without Trial.* Little, Brown, 1966.

Orfield, L. B. *Criminal Procedure from Arrest to Appeal.* New York University, 1947.

Strouse, V. *Up Against the Law: The Legal Right of People Under Twenty-One.* New American Library (Signet), 1970.

Sullivan, H. W. *Trial by Newspaper.* Patriot Press, 1961.

Wigmore, Sir J. H. *A Treatise on the Anglo-American System of Evidence in Trials at Common Law.* 3d ed. Little, Brown, 1940.

Williams, E. B. *One Man's Freedom.* Atheneum, 1962.

C. SELF-INCRIMINATION

Berger, M. *Taking the Fifth: The Supreme Court and the Privilege Against Self-Incrimination.* Lexington Books, 1980.

Griswold, E. N. *The Fifth Amendment Today.* Harvard University, 1955.

Hook, S. *Common Sense and the Fifth Amendment.* Criterion, 1959.

Inbau, F. E. *Self-Incrimination.* C. C. Thomas, 1950.

Levy, L. W. *Origins of the Fifth Amendment.* Oxford University, 1968.

Maguire, John N. *Evidence of Guilt: Restrictions upon Its Discovery or Compulsory Disclosure.* Littel, Brown, 1959.

Mayers, L. *Shall We Amend the Fifth Amendment?* Harper, 1959.

Meltzer, M. *The Right to Remain Silent.* Harcourt Brace Jovanovich, 1972.

Schwartzman, R., and J. Stein. *The Law of Personal Liberties.* Oceana, 1955.

Stephens, O. H., Jr. *The Supreme Court and Confessions of Guilt.* University of Tennessee, 1973.

D. CONFESSIONS

Baker, L. *Miranda: Crime, Law and Politics.* Atheneum, 1983.

Beisel, A. R. *Control over Illegal Enforcement of the Criminal Law: Role of the Supreme Court.* Boston University, 1955.

George, J. B., ed. *A New Look at Confessions: Escobedo—the Second Round.* University of Michigan, 1966.

Graham, F. P. *The Self-Inflicted Wound.* Macmillan, 1970.

Inbau, F. E., and J. E. Inbau. *Criminal Interrogation and Confessions.* 2d ed. Williams & Wilkins, 1967.

————. *Lie Detection and Criminal Interrogation.* Williams & Wilkins, 1953.

Kamisar, Y. *Police Interrogation and Confessions: Essays in Law and Policy.* University of Michigan, 1980.

Milner, N. A. *The Court and Local Law Enforcement: The Political Impact of Miranda.* Sage Publications, 1971.

Reid, J. E., and F. E. Inbau. *Truth and Deception: The Polygraph ("Lie Detector") Technique.* Williams & Wilkins, 1966.

Reik, T. *The Compulsion to Confess.* Farrar, Straus, Cudahy, 1959.

Rogge, O. J. *Why Men Confess.* Nelson, 1959; rpt. Da Capo Press, 1975.

Sampson, W. *The Catholic Question in America: Auricular Confession.* Da Capo Press, 1974.

Sobel, N. R. *The New Confession Standards: "Miranda v. Arizona."* Gould, 1966.

Stephens, O. H., Jr. *The Supreme Court and Confessions of Guilt.* University of Tennessee, 1973.

Tompkins, D. C., comp. *The Confession Issue, From Nabb to Miranda: A Bibliography.* University of California, 1968.
United States Commission on Civil Rights. *Justice.* Government Printing Office, 1961.

E. SEARCHES AND SEIZURES

Amsterdam, A. G. *Perspectives on the Fourth Amendment.* Minnesota Law Review Foundation, 1974.
Ashley, P. O. *Say it Safely.* University of Washington, 1956.
Beisel, A. R. *Control over Illegal Enforcement of the Criminal Law: Role of the Supreme Court.* Boston University, 1955.
Breckenridge, A. C. *The Rights to Privacy.* University of Nebraska, 1971.
Cantey, R. C. *The Law of Search and Seizure.* University of Georgia, 1957.
Cogan, J. J. *Law of Search and Seizure.* Oceana, 1950.
Donovan, J. B. *Strangers on a Bridge: The Case of Colonel Abel.* Atheneum, 1964.
Fisher, E. C. *Searches and Seizures.* Northwestern University, 1970.
Garrison, O. V. *Spy Government.* Stuart, 1967.
Griswold, E. N. *Search and Seizure: A Dilemma of the Supreme Court.* University of Nebraska, 1975.
Hirschel, J. D. *Fourth Amendment Rights.* Heath, 1979.
LaFave, W. R. *Search and Seizure: A Treatise on the Fourth Amendment.* West, 1980.
Landynski, J. W. *Search and Seizure and the Supreme Court.* Johns Hopkins University, 1966.
Lasson, N. B. *The History and Development of the Fourth Amendment to the United States Constitution.* Johns Hopkins University, 1937; rpt. Da Capo Press, 1970.
Maguire, John M. *Evidence of Guilt: Restrictions upon Its Discovery or Compulsory Disclosure.* Little, Brown, 1959.
Packard, V. *The Naked Society.* McKay, 1960.
Ringel, W. E. *Arrests, Searches, Confessions.* Gould, 1966.
———. *Lawyers' Guide to Legal and Illegal Searches.* Gould, 1965.
Schlesinger, S. R. *Exclusionary Injustice: The Problem of Illegally Obtained Evidence.* Dekker, 1977.
Schwartz, B. *A Commentary on the Constitution of the United States: Rights of the Person—Sanctity, Privacy, and Expression.* Macmillan, 1968.
Taylor, T. *Two Studies in Constitutional Interpretation: Search, Seizure, Surveillance . . .* Ohio State University, 1969.
Tiffany, L. P., D. M. McIntyre, Jr., and D. L. Rotenberg. *Detection of Crime: Stopping and Questioning, Search and Seizure, Encouragement and Entrapment.* Little, Brown, 1967.
Varon, J. A. *Searches, Seizures and Immunities.* Bobbs-Merrill, 1961.

F. WIRETAPPING, EAVESDROPPING, AND PRIVACY

(*See also* XII, Morals, Obscenity, and Censorship.)

American Enterprise Institute. *Privacy Protection Proposals.* AEI, 1979.
Ball, H. *No Pledge of Privacy: The Watergate Tapes Litigation, 1973–1974.* Kennikat, 1977.
Barth, A. *The Price of Liberty.* Viking Press, 1961.
Beisel, A. R. *Control over Illegal Enforcement of the Criminal Law: Role of the Supreme Court.* Boston University, 1955.
Bloustein, E. J. *Individual and Group Privacy.* Transaction Books, 1975.
Breckenridge, A. C. *The Right of Privacy.* University of Nebraska, 1970.
Brenton, M. *The Privacy Invaders.* Coward-McCann, 1964.
Carroll, J. M. *The Third Listener.* Dutton, 1969.
Cowan, P., et al., eds. *State Secrets: Police Surveillance in America.* Holt, Rinehart and Winston, 1974.
Dash, S., R. Schwartz, and R. E. Knowlton. *The Eavesdroppers.* Rutgers University, 1959.
Dienes, C. T. *Law, Politics, and Birth Control.* University of Illinois, 1972.

Dionisopoulos, P. A., and C. R. Ducat. *The Right to Privacy: Essays and Cases*. West, 1976.

Dorsen, N., and S. Gillers, eds. *None of Your Business: Government Secrecy in America*. Viking Press, 1974; rpt. 1975.

Engberg, E. *The Spy in the Corporate Structure and the Right to Privacy*. World, 1967.

Ernst, M. L., and A. U. Schwartz. *Privacy: The Right to Be Let Alone*. Macmillan, 1962.

Fogarty, M. S. *Issues of Privacy and Security in the Urban Informational System*. Northwest Regional Educational Laboratory, 1969.

Goldberg, E. M. *Privacy Problems in Municipal Informational Systems*. Claremont, 1972.

Gross, H. *Privacy: Its Legal Protection*. Oceana, 1965.

Hayden, T. *The Privacy Act*. American Civil Liberties Union Foundation, 1976.

Hirschel, J. D. *Fourth Amendment Rights*. Heath, 1979.

Hofstadter, S. H., and G. Horowitz. *The Right to Privacy*. Central Books, 1964.

Lapidus, E. J. *Eavesdropping on Trial*. Hayden, 1974.

Long, E. V. *The Intruders: The Invasion of Privacy by Government and Industry*. Praeger, 1967.

Michigan Law Review. *The Right of Privacy: A symposium on the Implications of Griswold v. Connecticut*. Da Capo Press, 1971.

Miller, A. R. *The Assault on Privacy; Computers, Data Banks, and Dossiers*. University of Michigan, 1971.

Murphy, W. F. *Wiretapping on Trial*. Random House, 1965.

O'Brien, D. M. *Privacy, Law, and Public Policy*. Praeger, 1979.

Pennock, J. R., and J. W. Chapman, eds. *Privacy*. Atherton, 1971.

Richards, D. A. J. *Sex, Drugs, and the Law*. Rowman & Allanheld, 1982.

Rosenberg, J. M. *The Death of Privacy*. Random House, 1969.

Rule, J. B. *Private Lives and Public Surveillance: Social Control in the Computer Age*. Schocken Books, 1974.

———, et al. *The Politics of Privacy*. New American Library (Mentor Books), 1980.

Slough, M. C. *Privacy, Freedom and Responsibility*. C. C. Thomas, 1969.

U. S. Superintendent of Documents, comp. *Legal Protections of Privacy*. Government Printing Office, 1975.

Westin, A. F., ed. *Information Technology in a Democracy*. Harvard University, 1971.

———. *Privacy and Freedom*. Atheneum, 1967.

———, and M. A. Bakers. *Databanks in a Free Society*. Quadrangle, 1973.

Whiteside, T. *Computer Capers: Tales of Electronic Thievery, Embezzlement, and Fraud*. Crowell, 1978.

Zelermeyer, W. *Invasion of Privacy*. Syracuse University, 1959.

C. COUNSEL

Baker. L. *Miranda: Crime, Law and Politics*. Atheneum, 1983.

Beaney, W. M. *The Right to Counsel in American Courts*. University of Michigan, 1955.

Carter, D. T. *Scottsboro: A Tragedy of the American South*. Louisiana State University, 1969.

Cheatham, E. E. *A Lawyer When Needed*. Columbia University, 1963.

Graham, F. P. *The Self-Inflicted Wound*. Macmillan, 1970.

Heller, F. H. *The Sixth Amendment to the Constitution of the United States: A Study in Constitutional Development*. University of Kansas, 1951.

Hermann, R., E. Single, and J. Boston, *Counsel for the Poor: Criminal Defense in Urban America*. Heath, 1978.

Lewis, A. *Gideon's Trumpet*. Random House, 1964.

Medalie, R. J. *From Escobedo to Miranda: The Anatomy of a Supreme Court Decision*. Lerner Law Books, 1966.

Milner, N. A. *The Court and Local Law Enforcement: The Political Impact of Miranda*. Sage Publications, 1971.

Norris, C., and S. D. Washington. *The Last of the Scottsboro Boys*. Putnam, 1979.

Silverstein, L. *Defense of the Poor in Criminal Cases in American State Courts.* American Bar Foundation, 1965.

Ulmer, S. S. *Military Justice and the Right to Counsel.* University of Kentucky, 1970.

H. DOUBLE JEOPARDY

Friedland, M. L. *Double Jeopardy.* Oxford University, 1969.

Miller, L. G. *Double Jeopardy and the Federal System.* University of Chicago, 1968.

Sigler, J. A. *Double Jeopardy: The Development of a Legal and Social Policy.* Cornell University, 1969.

I. JURIES

(*See also* Bibliography I, "Juries.")

Bloomstein, M. J. *Verdict: The Jury System.* Dodd, Mead, 1963.

Busch, F. X. *Law and Tactics in Jury Trials.* Bobbs-Merrill, 1963.

Heller, F. H. *The Sixth Amendment to the Constitution of the United States: A Study in Constitutional Development.* University of Kansas, 1951.

Kalven, H., Jr., and H. Zeisel. *The American Jury.* Little, Brown, 1966; rpt. University of Chicago (Phoenix Books), 1971.

Keeney, B. C. *Judgment by Peers.* Harvard University, 1949.

Orfield, L. B. *Criminal Procedure from Arrest to Appeal.* New York University, 1947.

Saks, M. J. *Jury Verdicts: The Role of Group Size and Social Decision Rule.* Heath, 1977.

Simon, R. J. *The Jury and the Defense of Insanity.* Little, Brown, 1968.

Spooner, L. *An Essay on the Trial by Jury.* Jewett, 1852.

Zeisel, H., H. Kalven, Jr., and B. Buchholz. *Delay in the Courts.* Little, Brown, 1959.

J. BAIL

Beeley, A. L. *The Bail System in Chicago.* University of Chicago 1927; rpt. 1966.

Clarke, S. *The Bail System in Charlotte, 1971–1973.* National Technical Information Society, 1975.

De Hass, E. *Antiquities of Bail: Origin and Historical Development in Criminal Cases to the Year 1275.* Columbia University, 1940.

Flemming, R. B. *Punishment Before Trial: An Organizational Perspective of Felony Bail Processes.* Longman, 1982.

Foote, C. *Studies in Bail.* International Press, 1967.

Freed, D. J., and P. M. Wald. *Bail in the United States.* U. S. Department of Justice and Vera Foundation, 1964.

Goldfarb, R. *Ransom: A Critique of the American Bail System.* Harper & Row, 1965.

Thomas, W. H., Jr. *Bail Reform in America.* University of California, 1976.

———. *Pretrial Release Programs.* National Institute of Law Enforcement, 1977.

Thompkins, D. C., ed. *Bail in the United States: A Bibliography.* University of California 1964.

Wald, P. *Bail in the United States.* Government Printing Office, 1964.

Wice, P. B. *Freedom for Sale: A National Study of Pretrial Release.* Lexington Books, 1974.

K. CRUEL AND UNUSUAL PUNISHMENT

Anslinger, H. J., and W. Oursler. *The Murderers.* Cudahy, 1961.

Barnes, H. E. *The Story of Punishment.* Stratford, 1930.

Becarria, C. *On Crime and Punishment.* Indiana University, 1963.

Berkson, L. C. *The Concept of Cruel and Unusual Punishment.* Lexington Books, 1975.

Carrington, F. G. *Neither Cruel nor Unusual.* Arlington House, 1978.

Chambliss, W. J. *The Deterrent Influence of Punishment.* Indiana University, 1972.

Eldridge, J. H. *Narcotics and the Law.* New York University, 1962.

Hawkins, G. *Punishment and Deterrence.* Indiana University, 1972.

Honderich, T. *Punishment: The Supposed Justifications.* Pelican Books, 1972.

Meltsner, M. *Cruel and Unusual: The Supreme Court and Capital Punishment.* William Morrow, 1954.

Newfield, J. *Cruel and Unusual Justice.* Holt, Rinehart and Winston, 1974.

Prettyman, B. E. Jr. *Death and the Supreme Court.* Harcourt, Brace, 1961.

L. POLICE AGENCIES AND ENFORCEMENT

Ahern, J. F. *Police in Trouble.* Hawthorn Books, 1972.

Alex, N. *Black in Blue.* Appleton-Century-Crofts, 1969.

Asch, S. H. *Police Authority and the Rights of the Individual.* Arco, 1967.

Banton, M. *The Police in the Community.* Basic Books, 1964.

Bayley, D. H., and H. Mendelsohn. *Minorities and the Police: Confrontation in America.* Free Press, 1969.

Becker, T. L., ed. *Government Lawlessness in America.* Oxford University, 1971.

Bennett, R. R., ed. *Police at Work: Policy Issues and Analyses.* Sage Publications, 1983.

Bent, A. E. *The Politics of Law Enforcement.* Lexington Books, 1974.

Berkeley, G. E. *The Democratic Policemen.* Beacon Press, 1969.

Blumberg, A. S., ed. *Law and Order: The Scales of Justice.* Aldine, 1970.

Bopp. W. J., *"O. W.": O. W. Wilson and the Search for a Police Profession.* Kennikat Press, 1977.

Bordua, D. J. *The Police: Six Sociological Essays.* Wiley, 1967.

Brown, J., and G. Howse, eds. *Police in the Community.* Lexington Books, 1975.

Carr-Hill, R. A., and N. G. Stern. *The Police and Criminal Statistics.* Academic Press, 1979.

Chapman, J. I. *The Impact of Police on Crime and Crime on Police.* Institute of Government and Public Affairs, 1977.

Chevigny, P. *Police Power: Police Abuses in New York City.* Pantheon Books, 1969.

Chicota, R. A., and M. C. Moran, eds. *Riot in the Cities: An Analytical Symposium on the Causes and Effects.* Fairleigh Dickinson University, 1970.

Clark, R. S. *Police and the Community.* New Viewpoints, 1979.

Cole, G. F. *Politics and the Administration of Justice.* Sage Publications, 1973.

Collins, F. L. *The F.B.I. in Peace and War.* Rev. and enl. by L. Demles. Berkley (Ace Books), 1962.

Cooper, J. L. *The Police and the Ghetto.* Kennikat Press, 1979.

Cray, E. *The Big Blue Line.* Coward-McCann, 1967.

Davis, K. C. *Police Discretion.* West, 1975.

Deutsch, A. *The Trouble with Cops.* Crown, 1955.

Edwards, G. *The Police on the Urban Frontier.* Institute of Human Relations, 1968.

Eldiff, T. J., ed. *Crime, Dissent, and the Attorney General: The Justice Department in the 1960s.* Sage Publications, 1971.

Elliston, F. A., and M. Feldberg, eds. *Moral Issues in Police Work.* Rowman & Allanheld, 1985.

Ferdico, J.N. *Criminal Procedure for the Law Enforcement Officer.* West. 1975.

Fink, J. and L. G. Sealy. *The Community and the Police: Conflict or Cooperation.* Wiley, 1974.

Freed, L. *Police Work.* Simon and Schuster, 1981.

Gardiner, J. A. *Traffic and the Police: Variations in Law Enforcement Policy.* Harvard University, 1969.

Goldstein, H. *Policing a Free Society.* Ballinger, 1977.

Grosman, B. A. *Police Command: Decisions and Discretion.* Macmillan, 1975.

Hahn, H., ed. *Police in Urban Society.* Sage Publications, 1971.

Halpern, S. C. *Police Association and Department Leaders: The Politics of Cooperation.* Lexington Books, 1975.

Harris, R. *Justice: The Crisis of Law, Order and Freedom in America.* Dutton, 1970.

Hopkins, E. *Our Lawless Police.* Viking Press, 1931.

Inbau, F. E., and J. R. Thompson, eds. "The Supreme Court and the Police." *The Journal of Criminal Law, Criminology, and Social Sciences.* September and December in 1966.

Kelling, G., et al. *The Kansas City Preventive Patrol Experiment.* Police Foundation, 1974.

Lavine, E. H. *The Third Degree.* Da Capo Press, 1974.

Leonard, V. A., ed. *Academy Lectures on Lie Detection.* C. C. Thomas, 1950.

Lipsky, M., ed. *Law and Order: Police Encounters.* 2d ed. Dutton, 1973.

Lowenthal, M. *The Federal Bureau of Investigation.* Sloane, 1950.

Manning, P. K. *Police Work: The Social Organization of Policing.* MIT, 1976.

Miller, W. R. *Cops and Bobbies: Police Authority in New York and London.* University of Chicago. 1977.

Millspaugh, A. C. *Crime Control by the National Government.* Brookings Institution, 1937.

Milner, N. *The Court and Local Law Enforcement.* Sage Publications, 1971.

Monkkonen, E. *Police in Urban America, 1860–1920.* Cambridge University, 1981.

Muir, W. K., Jr. *Police: Street Corner Politicians.* University of Chicago, 1977.

Murphy, P. V. *Commissioner: A View from the Top of American Law Enforcement:* Simon and Schuster, 1977.

Navasky, V. S. *Kennedy Justice.* Atheneum, 1971.

Niederhoffer, A. *Behind the Shield: The Police in Urban Society.* Doubleday, 1967.

Perry, D. C. *Police in the Metropolis.* Merrill, 1975.

Potholm, C. P., and R. E. Morgan. *Focus on Police: The Police in American Society.* Halsted Press, 1976.

Radano, G. *Walking the Beat: A New York Policeman Tells What It's Like on His Side of the Law.* World, 1968.

Radelet, L. A. *The Police and the Community: Studies.* Glencoe, 1973.

Reiss, A. J., Jr. *The Police and the Public.* Yale University, 1971.

Reston, J., Jr. *The Innocence of Joan Little: A Southern Mystery.* Times Books, 1977.

Rubinstein, J. *City Police.* Farrar, Straus & Giroux, 1973.

Ruchelman, L. *Police Politics: A Comparative Study of Three Cities.* Ballinger, 1974.

———, ed. *Who Rules the Police?* New York University, 1972.

Saunders, C. B., Jr. *Upgrading the American Police.* Brookings Institution, 1970.

Skolnick, J. H., and T. C. Gray. *Police In America.* Little, Brown, 1975.

Smith, B. *Police Systems in the United States.* Rev. ed. Harper, 1945.

Sowle, C. R., ed. *Police Power and Individual Freedom: The Quest for Balance.* Aldine, 1972.

Steadman, R. F., ed. *The Police and the Community.* Johns Hopkins University, 1972.

Steer, D. *Police Caution: A Study in the Exercise of Police Discretion.* Blackwell, 1971.

Sulnick, R. H. *Civil Litigation and the Police.* C. C. Thomas, 1976.

Summers, M. R., ed. *Law and Order in a Democratic Society.* Merrill, 1970.

Turner, W. *The Police Establishment.* Putnam, 1968.

Turner, W. W. *Invisible Witness: The Use and Abuse of the New Technology of Crime Investigation.* Bobbs-Merrill, 1968.

Uhnak, D. *Law and Order.* Simon and Schuster, 1972.

Ungar, S. J. *F.B.I.* Atlantic Monthly Press–Little, Brown, 1975.

United States Commission on Civil Rights. *Justice.* Government Printing Office, 1961.

Viano, E. C., and J. H. Reiman, eds. *The Police in Society.* Lexington Books, 1975.

Wasby, S. L. *Small Town Police and the Supreme Court.* Lexington Books, 1976.

Weiner, N. L. *The Role of the Police in Urban Society.* Bobbs-Merrill, 1976.

Westley, W. *Violence and the Police.* MIT, 1970.

Whitehead, D. *The F.B.I. Story: A Report to the People.* Random House, 1956.

Whittemore, L. H. *Cop! A Closeup of Violence and Tragedy.* Holt, Rinehart and Winston, 1969.

Wilson, J. Q. *Emerging Patterns of American Police Administration.* Sweet & Maxwell, 1971.

———. *Police Administration.* 4th ed. McGraw-Hill, 1977.

———. *Varieties of Police Behavior: The Management of law and Order in Eight Communities.* Harvard University, 1968.

Wilson, J. V., and P. Q. Fuqua. *The Police and the Media*. Little, Brown, 1975.

Wintersmith, R. *Police and the Black Community*. Lexington Books, 1974.

Wise, D. *The American Police State*. Random House, 1976.

Wolfle, J. L., and J. F. Heaphy, eds. *Readings on Productivity in Policing*. Heath, 1975.

Zarr, M. *The Bill of Rights and the Police*. Oceana, 1970.

M. ARRESTS AND PRELIMINARIES

Boudin, K., et al. *The Bust Book: What To Do Till the Lawyer Comes*. Grove Press, 1970.

Creamer, J. S. *The Law of Arrest, Search, and Seizure*. Saunders, 1968.

Dalbey, D. *Police Interrogation and the Miranda Rule*. Federal Bureau of Investigation National Academy, 1967.

Galton, F. *Finger Prints*. Macmillan, 1892.

Greenwood, P. W., et al. *Prosecution of Adult Felony Defendants*. Heath, 1976.

Lafave, W. R. *Arrest: The Decision to Take a Suspect into Custody*. Little, Brown, 1965.

Levin, A. L., and E. A. Wooley. *Dispatch and Delay*. University of Pennsylvania, 1961.

Machen, E. W., Jr. *The Law of Arrest*. University of North Carolina, 1950.

Miller, F. W. *Prosecution: The Decision to Charge a Suspect with a Crime*. Little, Brown, 1969.

Moenssens, A. *Fingerprints and the Law*. Chilton, 1969.

Murphy, J. *Arrest by Police Computer*. Lexington Books, 1975.

Newman, D., *Conviction: The Determination of Guilt or Innocence Without Trial*. Little, Brown, 1966.

Nimmer, R. *Two Million Unnecessary Arrests*. American Bar Association, 1971.

Orfield, L. B. *Criminal Procedure from Arrest to Appeal*. New York University, 1947.

Rosenberg, M. *The Pretrial Conference and Effective Justice*. Columbia University, 1964.

Smith H. M. *Arrest, Search and Seizure*. C. C. Thomas, 1959.

Tobias, M. W. *Pre-Trial Criminal Procedure*. C. C. Thomas, 1972.

Vera Institute of Justice. *Felony Arrests: Their Prosecution and Disposition in New York City's Courts*. Vera Institute of Justice, 1977

N. CAPITAL PUNISHMENT

Alix, E. K. *Ransom Kidnaping in America, 1874–1974: The Creation of a Capital Crime*. Southern Illinois University, 1981.

Bedau, H. A. *The Case Against the Death Penalty*. American Civil Liberties Union Foundation. 1973.

———. *The Courts, the Constitution, and Capital Punishment*. Lexington Books 1977.

———, ed. *The Death Penalty in America*. 3d ed. Oxford University, 1982.

———. *The Right to Life and Other Essays on the Death Penalty*. Bobbs-Merrill (Pegasus), 1969.

———, and C. M. Pierce, eds. *Capital Punishment in the United States*. AMS Press, 1982.

Berns, W. *For Capital Punishment: Crime and the Morality of the Death Penalty*. Basic Books, 1979.

Berger, R. *Death Penalties: The Supreme Court's Obstacle Course*. Harvard University, 1982.

Black, C. L., Jr. *Capital Punishment: The Inevitability of Caprise and Mistake*. Norton, 1975.

Bok, C. *Star Wormwood*. Knopf, 1959.

Bovee, M. H. *Christ and the Gallows, or Reasons for Abolishing Capital Punishment*. Lakeside, 1869.

Bowers, W. J. *Executions in America*. Lexington Books, 1974.

Bresler, F. *Reprieve: A Study of a System*. G. G. Harrap, 1966.

Burleigh, C. C. *Thoughts on the Death Penalty*. N. p. 1845.

Bye, R. T. *Capital Punishment in the United States*. Committee on Philanthropic Labor, 1919.

Calvert, E. R. *Capital Punishment in the Twentieth Century*. Kennikat, 1927.

Cheever, G. B. *Punishment by Death*. Harrap, 1842.

Chessman, C. *Cell 2455 Death Row*. Prentice-Hall, 1954.

Chevigny, P. G. *Police Power: Police Abuses in New York City*. Pantheon Books, 1968.

Christoph, J. B. *Capital Punishment and British Politics*. University of Chicago, 1962.

Cohen, B. L. *Law Without Order: Capital Punishment and the Liberals*. Regnery, 1970.

DiSalle, M. V. *The Power of Life or Death*. Random House, 1965.

Dos Passos, J. *Facing the Chair*. Da Capo Press, 1970.

Duffy, H. S., with A. Hirshberg. *88 Men and 2 Women*. Doubleday, 1962.

Enders, M. E. *The Morality of Capital Punishment*. Twenty-Third Publications, 1984.

Gardiner, G. A. *Capital Punishment as a Deterrent, and the Alternative*. Gollancz, 1956.

Gettinger, S. H. *Sentenced to Die: The People, the Crimes, and the Controversy*. Macmillan, 1979.

Gower, E. A. *A Life for a Life*. Chatto & Windus, 1956.

Hart, H. L. A. *Punishment and Responsibility*. Oxford University, 1968.

Joyce, J. A. *Capital Punishment: A World View*. Nelson, 1961.

Karpman, B. *The Sexual Offender and His Offenses: Etiology, Pathology, Psychodynamics and Treatment*. Julian, 1954.

Koestler, A. *Reflections on Hanging*. Macmillan, 1957.

Laurence, J. *A History of Capital Punishment*. Citadel Press, 1960.

Lawes, L. E. *Man's Judgment of Death*. Putnam, 1924.

McCafferty, J. A., ed. *Capital Punishment*. Aldine-Atherton, 1972.

McClellan, S. G. *Capital Punishment*. H. W. Wilson, 1961.

Mailer, N. *The Executioner's Song: A True-Life Novel*. Little, Brown, 1979.

Meltsner, M. *Cruel and Unusual Punishment: The Supreme Court and Capital Punishment*. Random House, 1973.

Morgan, P. M. *Deterrence: A Conceptual Analysis*. Sage Publications, 1977.

Prettyman, E. B., Jr. *Death and the Supreme Court*. Harcourt, Brace & World, 1961.

Pritchard, J. L. *A History of Capital Punishment*. Kennikat Press, 1972.

Roscoe Pound-American Trial Lawyers Foundation. *The Penalty of Death*. Roscoe Pound-American Trial Lawyers Foundation, 1980.

St. John Stevas, N. *Life, Death, and the Law*. Secker & Warburg, 1956.

Schuessler, K. F. *The Deterrent Influence of the Death Penalty*. Indiana University, 1972.

Schwed, R. E. *Abolition and Capital Punishment: The United States Judicial, Political, and Moral Barometer*. AMS Press, 1983.

Scott, G. R. *The History of Capital Punishment*. Kennikat Press, 1980.

Sellin, T. *Capital Punishment*. Harper & Row, 1967.

―――. *The Penalty of Death*. Sage Publication, 1980.

Spence, G. *Of Murder and Madness: A True Story of Insanity and the Law*. Doubleday, 1983.

Van den Haag, E., and J. P. Conrad. *The Death Penalty: A Debate*. Plenum, 1983.

Vialet, J. *Capital Punishment: Pro and Con Arguments*. Library of Congress, 1966.

Wolfe, B. H. *Pileup on Death Row*. Doubleday, 1973.

O. SENTENCING

Carr, W. S., and V. J. Connelly. *Sentencing Patterns and Problems: An Annotated Bibliography*. American Judicature Society. 1973.

Cederblom, J. B., and W. L. Blizek, eds. *Justice and Punishment*. Ballinger, 1977.

Council of State Governments. *Definite Sentencing: Four States*. University of Kentucky, 1976.

Davis, K. C. *Discretionary Justice*. Louisiana State University, 1969.

Dawson, R. O. *Sentencing: The Decision as to Type, Length and Conditions of Sentence*. Little, Brown, 1969.

Eldridge, W. *The Second Circuit Sentencing Study*. Federal Judiciary Center, 1974.

Frankel, M. *Criminal Sentences: Law Without Order*. Hill & Wang, 1974.

Gaylin, W. *Partial Justice: A Study of Bias in Sentencing*. Knopf, 1975.

Goldfarb, R., and L. R. Singer. *After Conviction*. Simon and Schuster, 1973.

Green, E. *Judicial Attitudes in Sentencing*. Macmillan, 1961.

Grupp, S. E. *Theories of Punishment.* Indiana University, 1971.

Heumann, M. *Plea Bargaining: The Experiences of Prosecutors, Judges, and Defense Attorneys.* University of Chicago, 1978.

Hogarth, J. *Sentencing as a Human Process.* University of Toronto, 1971.

Hood, R. *Sentencing in Magistrates' Courts.* Stevens, 1962.

Levin, M. A. *Urban Politics and the Criminal Courts.* University of Chicago, 1977.

Rosett, A., and D. R. Cressey. *Justice by Consent: Plea Bargaining in the American Courthouse.* Lippincott, 1976.

Sharples, K. S. *The Legal Framework of Judicial Sentencing Policy.* University of Amsterdam, 1972.

Sommer, R. *The End of Imprisonment.* Oxford University, 1977.

Tompkins, D. L. *Sentencing the Offender: A Bibliography.* University of California, 1971.

Twentieth Century Fund Task Force on Criminal Sentencing. *Fair and Certain Punishment.* McGraw-Hill, 1976.

Van Den Haag, E. *Punishing Criminals: Concerning a Very Old and Painful Question.* Basic Books 1977.

Walker, N. *Sentencing in a Rational Society.* Allen Lane, 1969.

Whinery, L. H., et al. *Predictive Sentencing.* Lexington Books, 1976.

P. PRINCIPLES OF CRIME AND CRIMINOLOGY

Alexander, F., and H. Staub. *The Criminal, the Judge, and the Public: A Psychological Analysis.* Macmillan, 1963.

Allen, F. A. *The Borderland of Criminal Justice.* University of Chicago, 1964.

———. *The Crimes of Politics: Political Dimensions of Criminal Justice.* Harvard University, 1974.

Allen, R. C., ed. *Readings in Law and Psychiatry.* Johns Hopkins University, 1968.

Alpert, G. P., ed. *Legal Rights of Prisoners.* Sage Publications, 1980.

American Enterprise Institute. *Reform of Federal Criminal Laws,* American Enterprise Institute, 1978.

Adenates, J. *Punishment and Deterrence.* University of Michigan, 1974.

Arens, R. *Insanity Defense.* Philosophical Library, 1974.

Bakal, C. *The Right to Bear Arms.* McGraw-Hill, 1966.

Barak, G. *In Defense of Whom? A Critique of Criminal Justice Reform.* Anderson, 1980.

Barnes, H. E., and N. K. Teeters. *New Horizons in Criminology.* Prentice-Hall, 1944.

Berk, R. A., H. Brackman, and S. L. Lesser. *The Measure of Justice.* Academic Press, 1976.

Blumberg, A. S. *Criminal Justice: Issues and Ironies.* 2d ed., New Viewpoints, 1979.

Blumstein, A., J. Cohen, and D. Nagin, eds. *Deterrence and Incapacitation.* American Academy of Sciences, 1972.

Browning, F., and J. Gerassi. *The American Way of Crime.* Putnam, 1980.

Caplan, L. *The Insanity Defense and the Trial of John W. Hinckley, Jr.* Godine, 1984.

Carter, L. H. *The Limits of Order.* Little, Brown, 1974.

Caughey, J. W. *Their Majesties the Mob.* University of Chicago, 1960.

Cederblom, J. B., and R. L. Blazek. *Justice and Punishment.* Ballinger, 1977.

Chaiken, J., et al. *Criminal Justice Models: An Overview.* Rand McNally, 1975.

Chang, D. H. *Crime and Delinquency.* Transaction Books, 1977.

Chappell, D., and J. Monahan, eds. *Violence and Criminal Justice.* Lexington Books, 1975.

Clark, R. *Crime and America: Observations on Its Nature, Causes, Prevention, and Control.* Simon and Schuster, 1970.

Cohn, A. N., ed. *Criminal Justice Planning and Development.* Sage Publications, 1977.

Cole, G. F. *The American System of Criminal Justice.* 2d ed. PWS (Duxbury Press), 1977.

———. *Criminal Justice: Law and Politics.* 3d ed. PWS (Duxbury Press), 1980.

Committee for Economic Development. *Reducing Crime and Assuring Justice.* CED, 1972.

Conklin, J. E. *The Impact of Crime.* Macmillan, 1975.

Congressional Quarterly. *Crime and Justice.* Congressional Quarterly Press, 1978.

Cook, F. J. *The F.B.I. Nobody Knows.* Macmillan, 1964.

Cooper, G. M., ed. *Insanity Defenses.* Rev. ed. National College for Criminal Defense, 1981.

Cressey, D. R., ed. *Crime and Criminal Justice.* Quadrangle, 1971.

————. *Theft of the Nation.* Harper & Row, 1969.

Crick, B. *Crime, Rape and Gin: Reflections on Contemporary Attitudes to Violence, Pornography and Addiction.* Prometheus Books, 1974.

Cronin, T. E., T. Z. Cronin, And M. E. Molakovich, *U.S. v. Crime in the Streets.* Indiana University, 1981.

Davis, B. L., comp. *Criminal Bibliographies.* Greenwood Press, 1978.

Daudistel, H. C., et al. *Criminal Justice: Situations and Decisions.* Holt, Rinehart and Winston, 1979.

Doig, J. W. *Criminal Corrections: Ideals and Realities.* Lexington Books, 1983.

Douglas, J. D. *Crime and Justice in American Society.* Bobbs-Merrill, 1971.

Duffee, D. *Correctional Policy and Prison Organization.* Sage Publications, 1975.

Edelhertz, H., and G. Geis. *Public Compensation to Victims of Crime.* Praeger, 1974.

Eldridge, W. B. *Narcotics and the Law.* Rev. ed. Aldine, 1967.

Elliff, J. T. *Crime, Dissent, and the Attorney General.* Sage Publications, 1971.

Ennis, B. J. *Prisoners of Psychiatry: Mental Patients, Psychiatry, and the Law.* Avon Books, 1974.

Evans, M. S., and M. Moore. *The Law Breakers: America's Number One Domestic Problem.* Arlington House, 1968.

Fogel, D. *"We Are the Living Proof."* Anderson, 1975.

Forer, L. G. *Criminals and Victims: A Trial Judge Reflects on Crime and Punishment.* Norton, 1984.

Fox, J. A., ed. *Models in Quantitative Criminology.* Academic Press, 1981.

Galliher, J. F., and J. L. McCartney. *Criminology: Bower, Crime, and Criminal Law.* Dorsey Press, 1977.

Gardiner, J. A., and M. Mulkey, eds. *Crime and Criminal Justice.* Lexington Books, 1975.

Geis, G., and R. F. Meier, *White Collar Crime.* Rev. ed. Free Press, 1977.

Gerber, R. J., ed. *Contemporary Issues in Criminal Justice: Some Problems and Suggested Reforms.* Kennikat Press, 1975.

Gibbs, J. P. *Crime, Punishment, and Deterrence.* Elsevier, 1975.

Glasser, D. *Crime in our Changing Society.* Holt, Rinehart and Winston, 1978.

————. *The Effectiveness of a Prison and Parole System.* Bobbs-Merrill, 1969.

Glueck, S., ed. *Law and Psychiatry: Cold War or Entente.* Johns Hopkins University, 1962.

Goldstein, A. S. *The Insanity Defense.* Viking Press. 1967.

Grad, F. P. *Alcoholism and the Law.* Oceana, 1971.

Greenberg, D. F., ed. *Corrections and Punishment.* Sage Publications, 1977.

Gross, H. *A Theory of Criminal Justice.* Oxford University, 1979.

Gurr, T., et al. *The Politics of Crime and Conflict: A Comparative Study of Four Cities.* Sage Publications, 1977.

Halleck, S. L. *Psychiatry and the Dilemmas of Crime.* University of California, 1974.

Hart, H. L. A. *Punishment and Responsibility.* Oxford University, 1968.

Hartjen, C. A. *Crime and Criminalization.* 2d ed. Holt, Rinehart and Winston, 1978.

Hartung, F. E. *Crime, Law and Society.* Wayne State University, 1971.

Haskell, M. R., and L. Yablonski. *Criminology: Crime and Criminality.* 2d ed. Rand Mcnally, 1977.

Hawes, J. M., ed. *Law and Order in American History.* Kennikat Press, 1979.

Hermann, D. H. J. *The Insanity Defense: Philosophical, Historical, and Legal Perspectives.* C. C. Thomas, 1983.

Inciardi, J. A. *Reflections on Crime.* Holt, Rinehart and Winston, 1978.

Jefferey, C. R. *Crime Prevention Through Environmental Design.* 2d ed. Sage Publications, 1977.

Johnson, E. H. *Crime, Correction, and Society: Introduction to Criminology.* 4th ed. Dorsey Press, 1978.

Johnson, K. A. *Public Order, Criminal Behavior and Criminal Laws.* R. & R. Research Association, 1977.

Jones, D. A. *Crime Without Punishment.* Lexington Books, 1974.

Kefauver, E. *Crime in America.* Doubleday, 1951.

Keilitz, I., and J. P. Fulton. *The Insanity Defense and Its Alternatives.* National Center for State Courts, 1984.

Kennett, L., and L. V. Anderson. *The Gun in America: The Origins of a National Dilemma.* Greenwood Press, 1975.

Kittrie, N. N. *The Right to Be Different: Deviance and Enforced Therapy.* Johns Hopkins University, 1971.

Levin, M. A. *Urban Politics and the Criminal Courts.* University of Chicago, 1977.

Mannheim, H. *Criminal Justice and Social Reconstruction.* Paul, French, Tuebner, 1946.

Marshall, J. *Law and Psychology in Conflict.* Bobbs-Merrill, 1966.

McDonald, D. *The Price of Punishment: Public Spending for Corrections in New York.* Westview, 1980.

McLennan, B. N., ed. *Crime in Urban Society.* Dunellan, 1970.

McNeely, R. L., and C. E. Pope, eds. *Race, Crime, and Criminal Justice.* Sage Publications, 1981.

Menninger, K. *The Crime of Punishment.* Viking Press, 1968.

Meyer, F. A., Jr., and R. Baker, eds. *Determinants of Law Enforcement Policies.* Lexington Books, 1979.

Miller, F. W. *Prosecution: The Decision to Charge a Suspect with a Crime.* Little, Brown, 1969.

Mitchell, R. S. *The Homosexual and the Law.* Arco, 1969.

Moran, R. D. *Knowing Right from Wrong: The Insanity Defense of Daniel McNaughton.* Free Press, 1981.

Morris, N. *The Future of Imprisonment.* University of Chicago, 1974.

———. *Madness and the Criminal Law.* University of Chicago, 1983.

Nagel, S. S., ed. *Modeling the Criminal Justice System,* Sage Publications, 1977.

———, E. Fairchild, and A. Champagne, eds. *The Political Science of Criminal Justice.* Thomas, 1983.

National Commission on the Insanity Defense. *Myths and Realities.* National Mental Health Association, 1983.

Newman, C. L., and B. R. Price. *Jails and Drug Treatment.* Sage Publications, 1977.

Ohlin, L., ed. *Prisoners in America.* Prentice-Hall, 1973.

Orland, L. *Prisons: Houses of Darkness.* Free Press, 1975.

Overstreet, H., and B. Overstreet. *The F.B.I. in Our Open Society.* Norton, 1969.

Packer, H. L. *The Limits of the Criminal Sanction.* Stanford University, 1968.

Pelfrey, W. V. *The Evolution of Criminology.* Anderson, 1982.

Pepinsky, H. E. *Crime and Conflict: A Study of Law and Society.* Academic Press, 1976.

Pincoffs, E. *The Rationale of Legal Punishment.* Humanities Press, 1966.

Polier, J. W. *The Rule of Law and the Role of Psychiatry. Johns Hopkins University,* 1968.

Popper, R. *Post-Conviction Remedies in a Nutshell.* West, 1978.

Quinney, R. *Class, State, and Crime: On the Theory and Practice of Criminal Justice.* Longman, 1977.

———, ed. *Crime and Justice in Society.* Little, Brown, 1969.

Radzinowicz, Sir L., and M. E. Wolfgang, eds. *Crime and Justice.* 3 vols. Wiley, 1971.

Reid, S. T. *Crime and Criminology.* 2d ed. Holt, Rinehart and Winston, 1979.

Reiff, R. *The Invisible Victim: The Criminal Justice System's Forgotten Responsibility.* Basic Books, 1980.

Robinson, D. N. *Psychology and Law: Can Justice Survive the Social Sciences?* Oxford University, 1980.

Robitscher, J. B. *Pursuit of Agreement: Psychiatry and the Law.* Lippincott, 1966.
Rosett, A. C., and D. C. Cressey. *Justice by Consent: Plea Bargains in the American Court House.* Lippincott, 1976.
Rubin, S. *Crime and Juvenile Delinquency.* 3d ed. Oceana, 1970.
———. *Illusion, Fiction and Myths.* Oceana, 1965.
———. *Law of Criminal Correction.* 2d ed. West, 1973.
———. *Psychiatry and Criminal Law.* Oceana, 1965.
Schafer, S. *The Political Criminal: The Problem of Morality and Crime.* Free Press, 1974.
Scheingold, S. A., *The Politics of Law and Order.* Longman, 1984.
Schever, J. H. *To Walk the Streets Safely.* Doubleday, 1969.
Schur, E. M. *Crimes Without Victims.* Prentice-Hall, 1965.
Silberman, C. *Criminal Violence, Criminal Justice.* Random House, 1978.
Silver, I., ed. *A National Strategy to Reduce Crime.* Avon Books, 1975.
Skolnick, J. H. *Justice Without Trial: Law Enforcement in Democratic Society.* Wiley, 1966.
———. *The Politics of Protest.* Simon and Schuster, 1969.
Smith, A. B., and J. Pollack. *Some Sins Are Not Crimes: A Plea for Reform of the Criminal Law.* New Viewpoints, 1975.
———, and L. Berlin. *Treating the Criminal Offender: Issues and Problems.* Oceana, 1974.
Stanley, D. T. *Prisoners Among Us: The Problem of Parole.* Brookings Institution, 1976.
Stinchcombe, A. L., et al. *Crime and Punishment: Changing Attitudes in America.* Jossey-Bass, 1980.
Strickland, K. G., and H. Bartelson. *Legal Rights for Women Prisoners.* Lexington Books, 1976.
Sutherland, E. M., and D. C. Cressey. *Principles of Criminology.* Lippincott, 1960.
Sutherland, E. W. *White Collar Crime.* Holt, Rinehart and Winston, 1961.
Szasz, T. S. *Law, Liberty and Psychiatry.* Macmillan, 1964.
———. *Psychiatric Justice.* Macmillan, 1965.
Talarico, S. M., ed. *Research in Criminal Justice.* Anderson, 1980.
Tappan, R. W. *Crime, Justice and Correction.* McGraw-Hill, 1960.
Thibaut, J., and L. Walker. *Procedural Justice: A Psychological Analysis.* Halsted Press, 1975.
Toplin, R. B. *Unchallenged Violence: An American Ordeal.* Greenwood Press, 1975.
Turk, A. T. *Criminality and Legal Order.* Rand McNally, 1972.
University of Chicago Law Review staff. *Criminal Justice in Extremis: Administration of Justice During the April, 1968 Chicago Disorders.* American Bar Foundation, 1970.
Van Den Haag, E. *Punishing Criminals: Concerning a Very Old and Painful Question.* Basic Books, 1977.
Von Hirsch, A. *Doing Justice: The Choice of Punishment.* Hill & Wang, 1976.
Walker, S. *Popular Justice: A History of American Criminal Justice.* Oxford University, 1980.
Whitlock, F. A. *Criminal Responsibility and Mental Illness.* Butterworth, 1963.
Wilson, J. Q., ed. *Crime and Public Policy.* I.C.S. Press, 1983.
———. *Thinking About Crime.* Rev. ed. Random House, 1985.
Winslade, W. J. and J. W. Ross. *The Insanity Plea: Uses and Abuses.* Scribner, 1983.
Wolfgang, M. E., R. M. Figlio, and T. Thornberry. *Evaluating Criminals.* Elsevier, 1978.
Woodson, R. L. *A Summons to Life: Mediating Structures and Prevention of Youth Crime.* American Enterprise Institute, 1980.
Zimring, F. E. *Perspectives on Deterrence.* National Institute of Mental Health, 1971.
———, and G. J. Hawkins. *Deterrence: The Legal Threat in Crime Control.* University of Chicago, 1973.

V. MILITARY JUSTICE AND SELECTIVE SERVICE IN PEACE AND WAR

A. GENERAL

(*See also* X, Religion; Bibliography I, "The Military.")

American Friends, Serivce Committee. *The Draft?* Hill & Wang, 1968.
Anthony, J. G. *Hawaii Under Army Rule.* Stanford University, 1955.

Baskir, L. M., and W. A. Strauss. *Reconciliation After Vietnam*. University of Notre Dame, 1977.

Bishop, J. W., Jr. *Justice Under Fire: A Study of Military Law*. Charterhouse, 1974.

Cochran, C. L., ed. *Civil-Military Relations: Changing Concepts in the Seventies*. Free Press, 1974.

Coffin, T. *The Passion of the Hawks*. Macmillan, 1964.

Corwin, E. S. *Total War and the Constitution*. Knopf, 1947.

Ellsberg, D. *Papers on the War*. Simon and Schuster, 1972.

Fairman, C. *The Law of Martial Rule*. Callaghan, 1943.

Finn, J., ed. *A Conflict of Loyalties: The Case for Selective Conscientious Objection*. Bobbs-Merrill (Pegasus), 1968.

Friedman, L., and B. Neuborne. *Unquestioning Obedience to the President: The ACLU Case Against the Legality of the War in Vietnam*. Norton, 1972.

Generous, W. T., Jr. *Swords and Scales: The Development of the Uniform Code of Military Justice*. Kennikat Press, 1973.

Goldman, N. L., and D. R. Segal, eds. *The Social Psychology of Military Service*. Sage Publications, 1976.

Herring, P. *The Impact of War*. Farrar & Rinehart, 1941.

Huntington, S. P. *The Soldier and the State: The Theory and Politics of Civil-Military Relations*. Havard University (Belknap Press), 1957.

Jacobs, C. E., and J. R. Gallagher. *The Selective Service Act*. Dodd, Mead, 1967.

Karsten P. *Soldiers and Society*. Greenwood Press, 1977.

Lovell, J. P., and P. S. Kronenberg. *New Civil-Military Relations: The Agonies of Adjustment of Post-Vietnam Realities*. Dutton, 1973.

Lynn, C. J. *How to Stay Out of the Army: A Guide to Your Rights Under the Draft Laws*. Grove Press, 1968.

Marmion, H. A. *Selective Service: Conflict and Compromise*. Wiley, 1968.

McNair, L., and A. D. Watts. *The Legal Effects of War*. Cambridge University, 1966.

Miller, J. C., III, et. al., eds. *Why the Draft? The Case for a Volunteer Army*. Penguin Books, 1968.

Millis W., et al. *Arms and the State: Civil-Military Elements in National Policy*. 20th Century Fund, 1958.

———. *Individual Freedom and the Common Defense*. Fund for the Republic, 1957.

Minear, R. H. *Victors' Justice: The Tokyo War Crimes Trial*. Princeton University, 1971.

Oppenheimer, M., ed. *The American Military*. 2d ed. Dutton, 1974.

Paxon, F. C. *America at War, 1917-1918*. Houghton Mifflin, 1939.

Peterson, H. C., and G. C. Fita. *Opponents of War, 1917-1918*. University of Wisconsin, 1957.

Rankin, R. S. *When Civil Law Fails: Martial Law and its Legal Basis in the United States*. Duke University, 1939.

Reel, A. F. *TheCase of General Yamashita*. University of Chicago, 1949.

Rossiter, C. *The Supreme Court and the Commander-in-Chief*. Cornell University, 1951.

Scheiber, H. N. *The Wilson Administration and Civil Liberties*. Cornell University. 1960.

Sherrill, K. L. *Military Justice Is to Justice as Military Music Is to Music*. Harper, 1970.

Smith, L. *American Democracy and Military Power*. University of Chicago, 1951.

Stein, H., ed. *American Civil-Military Establishment*. University of Alabama, 1963.

Summers, Robert E. *Wartime Censorship of Press andRadio*. H. W. Wilson, 1942.

Swormley, J. M. Jr. *The Military Establishment*. Beacon Press, 1964.

Tatum, A., and J. S. Tuchinsky, *Guide to the Draft*. Beacon Press, 1969.

Tax, S., ed. *The Draft: A Handbook of Facts and Alternatives*. University of Chicago, 1968.

Taylor. T. *Nuremberg and Vietnam: An American Tragedy*. Quadrangle, 1970.

Ulmer, S. S. *Military Justice and the Right to Counsel*. University of Kentucky, 1970.

Velvel, L. R. *Undeclared War and Civil Disobedience*. Dunellen, 1970.

Walzer, M. *Just and Unjust Wars*. Basic Books, 1977.

————. *Obligations: Essays on Disobedience, War and Citizenship.* Harvard University, 1970.

Welch, C. E., Jr., and A. K. Smith. *Military Role and Rule: Perspectives on Civil-Military Relations.* PWS (Duxbury Press), 1974.

Zahn, G. C. *War, Conscience and Dissent.* Hawthorn Books, 1967.

B. CIVILIANS

Anderson, M., ed. *The Military Draft: Selected Readings on Conscription.* Hoover Institution, 1982.

————, ed. *Registration and the Draft.* Hoover Institution, 1982.

Barnes, P. *Pawns: The Plight of the Citizen Soldier.* Knopf, 1972.

Berry, M. F. *Military Necessity and Civil Rights Policy: Black Citizenship and the Constitution, 1861–1868.* Kennikat Press, 1977.

Bloom, L., and R. Riemer. *Removal and Return.* University of California, 1949.

Cable, J. L. *Loss of Citizenship: Denaturalization—the Alien in Wartime.* National Law Book, 1943.

Childress, J. F. *Moral Responsibility in Nonviolence, Violence, and War.* Louisiana State University, 1982.

Cohen, E. A. *Citizens and Soldiers: The Dilemmas of Military Service.* Cornell University 1984.

Davis, J. W., Jr., and K. M. Dolbeare. *Little Groups of Neighbors: The Selective Service System.* Markham, 1968.

Franks, L. *Waiting Out a War.* Coward, McCann & Geoghegan, 1974.

Gaylin, W. *In the Service of Their Country: War Resisters in Prison.* Viking Press, 1970.

Gerhardt, J. M. *The Draft and Public Policy: Issues in Military Manpower Procurement.* Ohio State University, 1971.

Girdner, A., and A. Loftis. *The Great Betrayal; The Evacuation of the Japanese-Americans During World War II.* Macmillan, 1969.

Grodzins, M. *The Loyal and the Disloyal: Social Boundaries of Patriotism and Treason.* University of Chicago, 1956.

Irons, P. *Justice at War.* Oxford University, 1983.

Klaus, S., ed., *The Milligan Case.* Da Capo Press, 1970.

Little, R. W., ed. *Selective Service and American Society.* Sage Publications, 1969.

Lynd, A. *We Won't Go.* Beacon Press, 1968.

Marmion, H. A. *Selective Service: Conflict and Compromise.* Wiley, 1970.

McWilliams, C. *Prejudice: Japanese-Americans, Symbols of Racial Intolerance.* Little, Brown, 1944.

Sibley, M. Q., and P. E. Jacob. *Conscription of Conscience: The American State and the Conscientious Objector.* Cornell University, 1952.

Tenbroek, J. *Japanese-American Evacuation and Resettlement.* University of California, 1944.

————, et al. *Prejudice, War and the Constitution.* University of California, 1954.

Thomas, D. S. *The Salvage.* University of California, 1952.

————, and R. S. Nishimito. *The Spoilage,* University of California, 1946.

Wamsley, G. L. *Selective Service and a Changing America.* Merrill, 1969.

Weiner, F. B. *Civilians Under Military Justice: The British Practice Since 1689, Especially in North America.* University of Chicago, 1967.

Williams, R. N. *The New Exiles.* Liveright, 1971.

Willoughby, G. *Handbook for Conscientious Objectors.* Larchwood, 1964.

C. MILITARY PERSONNEL

Avine, A. *The Law of AWOL.* Oceana, 1957.

Aycock, W. B., and S. W. Wurfel. *Military Law Under the Uniform Code of Military Justice.* University of North Carolina, 1962.

————. *Women and the Military.* Brookings Institution, 1977.

Binkin, M., and S. J. Bach. *Blacks and the Military*. Brookings Institution, 1982.

Cortright, D. *Soldiers in Revolt: The American Military Today*. Doubleday, 1975.

DiMona, J. *Great Court-Martial Cases*. Grosset & Dunlap, 1972.

Edwards, M. O., and C. L. Decker. *The Serviceman and the Law*. Stackpole Press, 1951.

Everett, R. O. *Military Justice in the Armed Forces of the United States*. Military Service Publishing Co., 1956.

Finn, J., ed. *Conscience and Command: Justice and Discipline in the Military*. Viking Press, 1971.

Johnson, H., and G. Wilson. *Army in Anguish*. Pocket Books, 1971.

Moskos, C. C. *The American Enlisted Man: The Rank and File in Today's Military*. Sage Publications, 1970.

Motley, M. P. *The Invisible Soldier: The Experience of the Black Soldier, World War II*. Wayne State University, 1975.

Ulmer, S. S. *Military Justice and the Right to Counsel*. University of Kentucky, 1970.

Walker, D., ed. *Military Law*. Prentice-Hall, 1954.

West, L. C. *They Call It Justice: Command Influence and the Court-Martial System*. Viking Press, 1976.

VI. SEGREGATION/DESEGREGATION/INTEGRATION

(See also II, Philosophy of Civil Rights and Liberties; III.B., The Blacks.*)*

A. GENERAL

American Enterprise Institute. *Affirmative Action: The Answer to Discrimination?* AEI, 1976.

Ashmore, H. S. *Epitaph for Dixie*. Norton, 1957.

――――. *Hearts and Minds: The Anatomy of Racism from Roosevelt to Reagan*. McGraw-Hill, 1982.

――――. *The Other Side of Jordan: Negroes Outside the South*. Norton, 1960.

Balbus, I. D. *The Dialectics of Legal Repression: Black Rebels Before the American Criminal Courts*. Russell Sage Foundation, 1973.

Barnes, C. *Journey from Jim Crow: The Desegregation of Southern Transit*. Columbia University, 1983.

Benjamin, G. *Race Relations and the New York Commission on Human Rights*. Cornell University, 1974.

Berger, R. *Government by Judiciary: The Transformation of the Fourteenth Amendment*. Harvard University, 1975.

Black, E. *Southern Governors and Civil Rights: Racial Segregation As a Campaign Issue in the Second Reconstruction*. Harvard University, 1976.

Blaustein, A. P., and R. S. Zangrando. *Civil Rights and the American Negro: A Documentary History*. Trident, 1968.

Brink, W., and L. Harris. *Black and White: A Study of Racial Attitudes Today*. Simon and Schuster, 1967.

Brown, H. R. *Die, Nigger, Die!* Dial Press, 1969.

Buell, E. H., Jr., and R. A. Brisbin, Jr. *School Desegregation and Defended Neighborhoods: The Boston Controversy*. Lexington Books, 1982.

Burk, R. F. *The Eisenhower Administration and Black Civil Rights*. University of Tennessee, 1984.

Cable, G. W. *The Negro Question: A Selection of Writings on Civil Rights in the South*. Doubleday, 1890.

Carmichael, P. A. *The South and Segregation*. Public Affairs Press, 1966.

Carothers, L. A. *The Public Accommodations Law of 1964*. Smith College, 1968.

Chafe, W. H. *Civilities and Civil Rights: Greensboro, North Carolina, and the Black Struggle for Freedom*, Oxford University, 1981.

Clark, K. B. *Dark Ghetto: Dilemmas of Social Power.* Harper & Row, 1965.

Cohen, M., T. Nagel, and S. Scanlon, eds. *Equality and Preferential Treatment.* Princeton University, 1977.

Coles, R. *The Desegregation of Southern Schools: A Psychiatric Study.* Southern Regional Council and Anti-Defamation League, 1963.

Commager, H. A., ed. *The Struggle for Racial Equality.* Harper & Row, 1967.

Countryman, J., ed. *Discrimination and the Law.* University of Chicago, 1965.

Dabbs, J. M. *Who Speaks for the South?* Funk & Wagnalls, 1965.

Dalfiume, R. M. *Desegregation of the U.S. Armed Forces: Fighting on Two Fronts, 1939-1953.* University of Missouri, 1969.

Davis, A., Jr. *Racial Crisis in Public Education.* Anti-Defamation League, 1968.

Eastland, T., and W. J. Bennett. *Counting by Race: Equality from the Founding Fathers to Bakke and Weber.* Basic Books, 1979.

Ehrlich, W. *The Have No Rights: Dred Scott's Struggle for Freedom.* Greenwood Press, 1979.

Fehrenbacher, D. E. *The Dred Scott Case: Its Significance in American Law and Politics.* Oxford University, 1978.

Fortune Magazine. The Negro and the City. Anti-Defamation League, 1968.

Freedman, L., ed. *Southern Justice.* Pantheon Books, 1965.

Ginger, A. F., ed. *De Funis v. Odegaard, Records and Briefs.* Oceana, 1974.

Glazer, N. *Affirmative Discrimination.* Basic Books, 1976.

Goldman, A. H. *Justice and Reverse Discrimination.* Princeton University, 1979.

Graglia, L. A. *Disaster by Decree: The Supreme Court Decisions on Race and the Schools.* Cornell University, 1976.

Graham, H. D. *Crisis in Print: Desegregation and the Press in Tennessee.* Vanderbilt University, 1967.

Gross, B. R., ed. *Reverse Discriminatino.* Prometheus Books, 1977.

Handlin, O. *Fire-Bell in the Night: The Crisis in Civil Rights.* Little, Brown, 1964.

Hill, H., and J. Greenberg, *Citizen's Guide to De-Segregation.* Beacon Press, 1955.

Hoffman, N. J. *Mississippi Notebook.* David White, 1965.

Hopkins, V. C. *Dred Scott Case.* Atheneum, 1967.

Huie, W. B. *Three Lives for Mississippi.* World Council of Churches, 1965.

Jacobs, P. *Prelude to Riot.* Random House, 1967.

Johnson, C. S. *Patterns of Negro Segregation.* Harper, 1943.

Jones, A. J., Jr. *Law, Bureaucracy and Politics: The Implementation of Title VI of the Civil Rights Act of 1964.* University Press of America, 1982.

Kalodner, H. I., ed. *Limits of Justice: The Court's Role in Desegregation.* Ballinger, 1978.

Kotin, L., and W. F. Aikman. *Legal Foundations of Compulsory School Attendance.* Kennikat Press, 1980.

Kutler, S. I., ed. *The Dred Scott Decision: Law or Politics?* Houghton Mifflin, 1967.

————. *Judicial Power and Reconstruction Politics.* University of Chicago, 1968.

Latham, F. B. *The Dred Scott Decision, March 6, 1857.* Watts, 1857.

Leiserson, A., ed. *The American South in the 1960's.* Praeger, 1964.

Levin, B., and W. D. Hawley, eds. *The Courts, Social Science, and School Desegregation.* Winthrop, 1977.

Lincoln, C. E. *The Negro Pilgrimage in America.* Bantam Books, 1968.

Lockard, D. *Toward Equal Opportunity: A Study of State and Local Anti-Discrimination Laws.* Macmillan, 1968.

Loth, D., and H. Flemming. *Integration North and South.* Fund for the Republic, 1956.

Lubell, S. *White and Black: Test of a Nation.* Harper & Row, 1964.

MacIver, R. M., ed. *Discrimination and National Welfare.* Harper, 1949.

Mauney, C. P. *Evolving Equality: The Courts and Desegregation in Tennessee.* University of Tennessee, 1979.

Mendelson, W. *Discrimination.* Prentice-Hall, 1963.

Michael, W. E. *The Age of Error.* Vantage Press, 1957.

Mitchell, G. E., and W. H. Peace III. *The Angry Black South: Southern Negroes Tell Their Own Story.* Citadel Press, 1962.

Molotch, H. L. *Managed Integration: Dilemmas of Doing Good in the City.* University of California, 1973.

Morgan, C., Jr. *A Time to Speak.* Harper & Row, 1964.

Morris, W. *Yazoo: Integration in a Deep Southern Town.* Harper's Magazine Press, 1971.

Muse, B. *Ten Years of Prelude.* Random House (Vintage Books), 1964.

Nichols, L. *Breakthrough on the Color Front.* Random House, 1954.

Olsen, O. H., ed. *The Thui Disguise: Plessy v. Ferguson, a Documentary Presentation, 1864–1896.* Humanities Press, 1954.

O'Neill, Joseph E., ed. *The Breaking of the Wall: Aspects of Segregation.* Macmillan, 1961.

———, ed. *A Catholic Case Against Segregation.* Macmillan, 1961.

O'Neill, Robert M. *Discriminating Against Discrimination.* Indiana University, 1975.

Osofsky, G. *The Burden of Race: A Documentary History of Negro-White Relations in America.* Harper & Row, 1968.

Peters, W. *The Southern Temper.* Doubleday, 1959.

Pettigrew, T. F. *Epitaph for Jim Crow.* Anti-Defamation League, 1964.

———. *Racially Separate or Together.* Anti-Defamation League, 1969.

Roche, G. *The Balancing Act: Quota Hiring in Higher Education.* Open Court, 1974.

Romero, P., ed. *In Black America.* United Publishing, 1969.

Ross, J. M., and W. M. Berg. *"I Respectfully Disagree With the Judge's Order: The Boston Desegregation Controversy.* University Press of America, 1981.

Rossum, R. A. *Reverse Discrimination: The Constitutional Debate.* Dekker, 1980.

Silberman, C. E. *Crisis in Black and White.* Random House, 1964.

Silver, J. W. *Mississippi: The Closed Society.* Enl. ed. Harcourt, Brace & World, 1966.

Simkins, F. B. *The Everlasting South.* Louisiana State University, 1963.

Sindler, A. P., ed. *Change in the Contemporary South.* Duke University, 1964.

Southern Regional Council. *Intimidation, Reprisal and Violence in the South's Racial Crisis.* Southern Regional Council, 1959.

Stahl, D., F. B. Sussman, and N. J. Bloomfield. *The Community and Racial Crisis.* Practicing Law Institute, 1966.

Stampp, K. *The Peculiar Institution.* Knopf, 1963.

Stillman, R. J., II. *Integration of the Negro in the United States Armed Forces.* Praeger, 1968.

Stoff, S. *The Two-Way Street: Guideposts to Peaceful School Desegregation.* David-Hewart, 1967.

Suchman, E. A., J. P. Dean, and R. M. Williams, Jr. *Desegregation.* Anti-Defamation League, 1963.

Talmadge, H. E. *You and Segregation.* Dulcan, 1955.

Townsend, C. *Old Age: The Last Segregation.* Grossman, 1970.

Tucker, S. *Mississippi from Within.* Arco, 1965.

Tumin, N. M. *Desegregation: Readiness and Resistance.* Princeton University, 1959.

Tussman, J. *The Supreme Court on Racial Discrimination.* Oxford University, 1963.

U.S. *Enforcement: A Report on Equal Protection in the South.* Government Printing Office, 1965.

———. *With Liberty and Justice for All.* Government Printing Office, 1959.

Urban America, Inc., and the Urban Coalition. *One Year Later.* Praeger, 1969.

Vander Zander, J. W. *Race Relations in Transition: The Segregation Crisis in the South.* Random House, 1965.

Warren, R. P. *Segregation: The Inner Conflict in the South.* Random House, 1956.

Wasby, S. L., A. A. D'Amato, and R. Metrailer. *Desegregation from Brown to Alexander: An Exploration of Supreme Court Strategies.* Southern Illinois University, 1977.

Weinstein, A., and F. O. Gatell, eds. *The Segregation Era, 1863–1954.* Oxford University, 1970.

Wilhoit, F. M. *The Politics of Massive Resistance.* Braziller, 1973.

Wilkinson, J. H., III. *From Brown to Bakke.* Oxford University, 1979.

Williamson, J., comp. *The Origins of Segregation.* Heath, 1968.

Wirt, F. M. *Politics of Southern Equality: Law and Social Change in a Mississippi County.* Aldine-Atherton, 1972.

Woodward, C. V. *The Strange Career of Jim Crow.* 3d rev. ed. Oxford University, 1974.

Woofter, T. J. *Southern Race Progress: The Wavering Color Line.* Public Affairs Press, 1957.

Wolk, A. *The Presidency and Black Civil Rights: Eisenhower to Nixon.* Fairleigh Dickinson University, 1971.

Wolters, R. *The Burden of Brown: Thirty Years of School Desegregation.* University of Tennessee, 1984.

Yarbrough, T. E. *Judge Frank Johnson and Human Rights in Alabama.* University of Alabama, 1981.

Young, W. M. *Beyond Racism: Building an Open Society.* McGraw-Hill, 1969.

———. *To Be Equal.* McGraw-Hill, 1964.

Ziegler, B. M. *Desegregation and the Supreme Court.* Heath, 1953.

Zinn, H. *The Southern Mystique.* Knopf, 1965.

B. EDUCATION

Alexander, K., and K. F. Jordan. *Constitutional Reform of School Finance.* Lexington Books, 1973.

Anderson, M. *The Children of the South.* Farrar, Straus & Giroux, 1973.

Ashmore, H. S. *The Negro and the Schools.* Rev. ed. University of North Carolina, 1954.

Bailey, R. L. *Minority Admissions.* Lexington Books, 1978.

Barrett, R. H. *Integration at Ole Miss.* Quadrangle, 1965.

Bates, D. *The Long Shadow of Little Rock: A Memoir.* McKay, 1963.

Berman, D. M. *It Is So Ordered.* Norton, 1966.

Blaustein, A. P., and C. C. Ferguson, Jr. *Desegregation and the Law.* Random House (Vintage Books), 1962.

Blossom, V. *It Has Happened Here.* Harper, 1959.

Bolner, J., and R. Shalney. *Busing: The Political and Judicial Process.* Praeger, 1974.

Bork, R. H. *Constitutionality of the President's Busing Proposals.* American Enterprise Institute, 1972.

Boyle, S. P. *The Desegregated Heart.* Morrow, 1962.

Brady, T. P. *Black Monday.* Mississippi Association of Citizens' Councils, 1955.

Bresnick, D., S. Lachman, and M. Polner, *Black/White/Green/Red: The Politics of Education in Ethnic America.* Longman, 1958.

Brickman, W. W., and S. Lehrer. *The Countdown on Segregated Education.* Society for the Advancement of Education, 1960.

Brown, R. R. *Bigger than Little Rock.* Seabury Press, 1958.

Buchheimer, N., and A. Buchheimer. *Equality Through Integration.* Anti-Defamation League, 1969.

Campbell, E. A. *When a City Closes Its Schools.* University of North Carolina, 1960.

———, and T. F. Pettigrew. *Christiana in Racial Crisis: A Study of Little Rock's Ministry.* Public Affairs Press, 1959.

Carmichael, O., and W. James. *The Louisville Story.* Simon and Schuster, 1957.

Cataldo, E. F., M. W. Giles, and D. S. Gatlin. *School Desegregation Policy.* Heath, 1979.

Caughey, J., and L. Caughey. *School Segregation on Our Doorstep: The Los Angeles Story.* Quail. 1966.

Coles, R. *The Desegregation of Southern Schools: A Psychiatric Study.* Southern Regional Council and Anti-Defamation League, 1963.

Coons, J. E., S. Sugarman, and W. Clune. *Private Wealth and Public Education.* Harvard University, 1971.

Cottle, T. J. *Busing.* Beacon Press, 1976.

Cox, E. S. *The School Situation at Clinton.* Viking Press, 1957.

Crain, R. L. *The Politics of School Desegregation*. Aldine, 1968.

Daly, C. V., ed. *The Quality of Inequality: Urban and Suburban Public Schools*. University of Chicago, 1969.

Damerell, R. G. *Triumph in a White Suburb: The Dramatic Story of Teaneck, New Jersey*. Morrow, 1968.

Dean, J. P., and A. Rosen. *A Manual of Intergroup Relations*. University of Chicago, 1955.

Dentler, R. A., B. Mackler, and M. A. Warshauer, eds. *The Urban R's: Race Relations as the Problem in Urban Education*. Praeger, 1967.

Dobbs, F. M. *The Southern Heritage*. Knopf, 1958.

Dreyfuss, J., and C. Lawrence III. *The Bakke Case: The Politics of Inequality*. Harcourt Brace Jovanovich, 1979.

Duran, C. J. *A Moderate Among Extremists: Dwight D. Eisenhower and the School Desegregation Crisis*. Nelson-Hall, 1981.

Edwards, N. *The Courts and the Public Schools: The Legal Basis of School Organization and Administration*. University of Chicago, 1971.

Edwards, T. B., and F. M. Wirst, eds. *School Desegregation in the North: The Challenge and the Experience*. Chandler, 1971.

Eidenberg, E., and R. D. Morey. *An Act of Congress: The Legislative Process and the Making of Educational Policy*. Norton, 1969.

Faulkner, W., B. Mays, and C. Sims. *The Segregation Decisions: Three Views*. Southern Regional Council, 1956.

Fellman, D., ed. *The Supreme Court and Education*. Rev. ed. Columbia University, 1969.

Fleming, H. C., and J. Constable. *What's Happening in School Integration*. Public Affairs Committee, 1956.

Fletcher, J. L., Jr. *The Segregation Case and the Supreme Court*. Boston University, 1958.

Friedman, D. J. *White Militancy in Boston*. Lexington Books, 1972.

Fuchs, E. *Pickets at the Gates: The Challenge of Civil Rights in Urban Schools*. Free Press, 1966.

Gates, R. L. *The Making of Massive Resistance: Virginia; Politics of Public School Desegregation, 1954–1956*. University of North Carolina, 1964.

Giles, H. H. *The Integrated Classroom*. Basic Books, 1959.

Ginger, A. F., ed. *De Funis v. Odegaard: Records and Briefs*. Oceana, 1974.

Ginzberg, E. *The Negro Potential*. Columbia University, 1956.

Graglia, L. A. *Disaster by Decree: The Supreme Court Decisions on Race and the Schools*. Cornell University, 1976.

Green, D. R., and W. E. Guaerke. *If the Schools Are Closed*. Southern Regional Council, 1959.

Guthrie, J. W., et al. *Schools and Inequality*. MIT, 1974.

Gwaltney, F. I. *The Numbers of Our Days*. Random House, 1959.

Harlan, L. R. *Separate and Unequal*. University of North Carolina, 1958.

Harrison, B. *Education, Training and the Urban Ghetto*. University of Maryland, 1970.

Hill, R., and M. Feeley. *Affirmative School Integration: Efforts to Overcome De Facto Segregation in Urban Schools*. Sage Publications, 1969.

Hillson, J. *The Battle of Boston: Busing and the Struggle for School Desegregation*. Pathfinder Press, 1977.

Hogan, J. C. *The Schools, the Courts, and the Public Interest*. Lexington Books, 1974.

Holley, J. W. *Education and the Segregation Issue*. Frederick, 1955.

Hooker, C. P., ed. *The Courts and Education*. University of Chicago, 1978.

Hughes, L. W., W. M. Gordon, and L. W. Hillman. *Desegregating America's Schools*. Longman, 1980.

Humphrey, H. H., ed. *School Segregation: Documents and Commentaries*. Crowell, 1964.

Ivey, H., and J. Corey. *Action Patterns in School Desegregation: A Guidebook*. Phi Delta Kappa, 1959.

Jones, L. From Brown to Boston: Desegregation in Education. 1954–1974. Scarecrow Press, 1979.

Jones, L. G. E. Negro Schools in the Southern States. Oxford University, 1928.

Kalodner, H. I., and J. J. Fishman. Limits of Justice: The Court's Role in School Desegregation of Education Litigation. Ballinger, 1978.

Kilpatrick, J. J. The Southern Case for School Segregation. Crowell-Collier, 1962.

Kirp, D. L. Just Schools: The Idea of Racial Equality in American Education. University of California, 1982.

Kluger, R. Simple Justice: The History of Brown v. Board of Education and Black America's Struggle for Equality. Knopf, 1976.

Kurland, P. B., and G. Casper, eds. The Bakke Case: Legal Briefs and Oral Arguments. University Publications, 1979.

Lanoue, G. R., and B. L. R. Smith. The Politics of School Decentralization. Heath, 1972.

Lester, R. Antibias Regulation of Universities. Carnegie Foundation for the Advancement of Teaching, 1974.

Levin, B., and W. D. Hawley, eds. The Courts, Social Science, and School Desegregation. Transaction Books, 1977.

Levinson, F. H., and B. D. Wright, eds. School Desegregation: Shadow and Substance. University of Chicago, 1976.

Levy, L. W., and D. L. Jones. Jim Crow in Boston: The Origins of the "Separate But Equal" Doctrine. Da Capo Press, 1974.

Levy, F. Northern Schools and Civil Rights: The Racial Imbalance Act of Massachusetts. Markham, 1971.

Lord, W. The Past That Would Not Die. Harper & Row, 1965.

Mack, R. W., ed. Our Children's Burden: Studies of Desegregation in Nine American Communities. Random House, 1968.

Martin, J. B. The Deep South Says Never. Ballantine Books, 1957.

Maston, T. B. Segregation and Desegregation: A Christian Approach. Macmillan, 1959.

McCauley, P., and E. D. Bell, eds. Southern Schools: Progress and Problems. Southern Educational Reporting Service, 1959.

McCord, J. H., ed. With All Deliberate Speed. University of Illinois, 1969.

Metcalf, G. R. From Little Rock to Boston. Greenwood Press, 1983.

Miller, A. S. Racial Discrimination and Private Education. University of North Carolina, 1957.

Miller, L. The Petitioners: The Story of the Supreme Court of the United States and the Negro. Pantheon Books, 1966.

Mills, N., ed. The Great School Bus Controversy. Texas Christian University, 1973.

Muse, B. Virginia's Massive Resistance. Indiana University, 1961.

Orfield, G. Must We Bus? Segregated Schools and National Policy. Brookings Institution, 1978.

———. The Reconstruction of Southern Education: The Schools and the 1964 Civil Rights Act. Wiley, 1969.

Peltason, J. W. Fifty-Eight Lonely Men. Harcourt, Brace, 1961.

Peterson, P. E. School Politics, Chicago Style. University of Chicago, 1976.

Pierce, T. M., et al. White and Negro Schools in the South. Prentice-Hall, 1955.

Pincus, J. School Finance in Transition: The Courts and Educational Reform. Ballinger, 1974.

President's Commission for the Observance of Human Rights Year. Racism and American Education. Harper & Row, 1970.

Quint, H. H. Profile of Black and White: A Frank Portrait of South Carolina. Public Affairs Press, 1958.

Raffel, J. A. The Politics of School Desegregation: The Metropolitan Remedy in Delaware. Temple University, 1980.

Record, W. Little Rock, USA. Chandler, 1960.

Reutter, E. E. Schools and the Law. Oceana, 1965.

Roche, G. The Balancing Act: Quota Hiring in Higher Education. Open Court, 1974.

Rubin, L. *Busing and Backlash: White Against White in an Urban School District*. University of California, 1972.

St. John, N. *School Desegregation: Outcomes for Children*. Wiley, 1975.

Scott, J. I. E. *Negro Students and Their Colleges*. Meador, 1949.

Shoemaker, D., ed. *With All Deliberate Speed*. Harper, 1957.

Silverman, C. *The Little Rock Story*. University of Alabama, 1959.

Sims, W. E. *Political Education in Black and White: A Case Study*. University Press of America, 1976.

Sindler, A. P. *Bakke, De Funis, and Minority Admissions: The Quest for Equal Opportunity*. Longman, 1958.

Spurlock, C. *Education and the Supreme Court*. University of Illinois, 1955.

Stephan, W. G., and J. R. Feagin, eds. *School Segregation: Past, Present, and Future*. Plenum, 1980.

Sterling, D., and D. Gross. *Tender Warriors*. Hill & Wang, 1958.

Stoff, S. *The Two-Way Street: Guideposts to Peaceful School Desegregation*. David-Stewart, 1967.

Sullivan, N. V., et al. *Bound for Freedom: An Educator; Adventures in Prince Edward County*. Little, Brown, 1965.

Synnott, M. G. *The Half-Opened Door: Discrimination and Admissions at Harvard, Yale, and Princeton, 1900-1970*. Greenwood Press, 1979.

Swanson, B. E. *The Struggle for Equality*. Hobbs, Dorwin, 1966.

Taeuber, K. E., and A. F. Taeuber. *Negroes in Cities*. Aldine, 1965.

Tipton, J. H. *Community in Crisis: The Elimination of Segregation from a Public School System*. Columbia University Press, 1953.

Trillin, C. *An Education in Georgia*. Viking Press, 1964.

University of North Carolina. *When a City Closes Its Schools*. University of North Carolina Press, 1960.

Weinberg, M., ed. *Integrated Education*. Glencoe, 1968.

Wilkinson, J. H., III. *From Brown to Bakke*. Oxford University, 1979.

Williams, R. J., and M. W. Ryan, eds. *Schools in Transition: Community Experience in Desegregation*. Universtiy of North Carolina, 1954.

Wilson, R., ed. *Race and Equity in Higher Education*. Macmillan, 1982.

Wolf, E. P. *Trial and Error: The Detroit School Desegregation Case*. Wayne State University, 1981.

Wollenberg, C. M. *All Deliberate Speed: Segregation and Exclusion in California Schools, 1855-1975*. University of California, 1976.

Wolters, R. *The Burden of Brown: Thirty Years of School Desegregation*. University of Tennessee, 1984.

———. *The New Negro on Campus*. Princeton University, 1975.

Yarmolinsky, A., L. Liebman, and C. S. Schelling, eds. *Schooling in the City*. Harvard University, 1981.

C. HOUSING

Abrams, C. *Forbidden Neighbors: A Study of Prejudice in Housing*. Harper, 1955.

Babcock, R. F. *The Zoning Game: Municipal Practices and Policies*. University of Wisconsin, 1966.

Black, A. *Who's My Neighbor?* Public Affairs Committee, 1956.

Bradburn, N. M., S. Sudman, and G. L. Gockel. *Side by Side: Integrated Neighborhoods in America*. Quadrangle, 1971.

Braden, A. *The Wall Between*. Monthly Review Press, 1958.

California Commission on Race and Housing. *Where Shall We Live? Report of the Commission on Race and Housing*. University of California, 1958.

Casstevens, T. W. *Politics, Housing and Race Relations: California's Rumford Act and Proposition 14*. University of California, 1965.

Clark, K. B. *Dark Ghetto.* Harper & Row. 1965.
———. *Prejudice and Your Child.* Beacon Press, 1955.
Danielson, M. N. *The Politics of Exclusion.* Columbia University, 1976.
Deutsch, N. *Interracial Housing.* University of Minnesota, 1951.
Downs, A. *Opening Up the Suburbs: An Urban Strategy for America.* Yale University, 1974.
Eley, L. W., and T. W. Casstevens. *The Politics of Fair Housing Legislation: State and Local Case Studies.* Chandler, 1968.
Foley, E. P. *The Achieving Ghetto.* National Publishing Co., 1967.
Ford, W. S. *Interracial Public Housing in Border City.* Lexington Books, 1972.
Furstenberg, G. M. von, and A. R. Horowitz. *Patterns of Racial Discrimination.* Vol. 1, Housing. Lexington Books, 1976.
Glazer, N., and D. McEntire, eds. *Studies in Housing and Minority Groups.* University of California, 1961.
Grier, E., and G. Grier. *Equality and Beyond: Housing Segregation and the Goals of the Great Society.* Quadrangle, 1968.
———. *Privately Developed Interracial Housing: An Analysis of Experience.* University of California, 1961.
Hesslink, G. K. *Black Neighbors: Negroes in a Northern Rural Community.* Bobbs-Merrill, 1968.
Hirsch, A. R. *Making the Second Ghetto: Race and Housing in Chicago, 1940–1960.* Cambridge University, 1983.
Houseman, G. L. *The Right of Mobility.* Kennikat Press, 1979.
Johnson, C. S. *Patterns of Negro Segregation.* Harper, 1943.
Kain, J. F., and J. M. Quigley. *Housing Markets and Racial Discrimination.* Columbia University, 1969.
Kusmer, K. L. *A Ghetto Takes Shape: Black Cleveland, 1870–1930.* University of Illinois, 1976.
Laurenti, L. *Property Value and Race: Studies in Seven Cities.* University of California, 1960.
Lewis, H. D. *"I Might as Well Move to the Moon": A Case Study on Housing Discrimination and a Legal Manual.* Indiana University, 1974.
Long, H. H., and C. S. Johnson. *People v. Property: Race Restrictive Covenants in Housing.* Fisk University, 1947.
McIntire, D. *Residence and Race: Final and Comprehensive Report to the Commission on Race and Housing.* University of California, 1961.
Messner, S. D., ed. *Minority Groups and Housing: A Selected Bibliography, 1950–1967.* University of Connecticut, 1967.
Northwood, L. K., and E. A. E. Barth. *Urban Desegregations: Negro Pioneers and Their White Neighbors.* University of Washington, 1965.
Rabinowitz, F. F., and W. J. Siembieda. *Minorities in the Suburbs.* Heath, 1977.
Rabkin, C., and W. G. Grigsby. *The Demand for Housing in Racially Mixed Areas: A Study of Neighborhood Change.* University of California, 1961.
Rabkin, S. *A Landmark Decision of Segregation in Housing: Jones v. Mayer.* Anti-Defamation League, 1969.
Rainwater, L. *Behind Ghetto Walls: Black Family Life in a Federal Slum.* Aldine, 1970.
Rosen, H., and C. Rosen. *But Not Next Door.* Obolensky. 1962.
Schnare, A. B. *The Persistence of Racial Segregation in Housing.* Urban Institute Press, 1978.
Schroeder, O., Jr., and D. T. Smith, eds. *De Facto Segregation and Civil Rights.* Nein, 1963.
Thomas, N. C. *Rule 9: Politics, Administration, and Civil Rights.* Random House, 1966.
Vose, C. E. *Caucasians Only: The Supreme Court, the NAACP, and the Restrictive Covenant Cases.* University of California, 1959.
Warren, R. L., ed. *Politics and the Ghetto.* Aldine-Atherton, 1970.
Weaver, R. C. *The Negro Ghetto.* Harcourt, Brace, 1948.
Wheeler, K. *Peaceable Lane.* Simon and Schuster, 1960.
Wolman, H. *The Politics of Federal Housing.* Dodd, Mead, 1971.

D. EMPLOYMENT

Ashenfelter, O. C. *Racial Discrimination and Labor Markets*. University of Michigan, 1970.

Becker, Gary S. *The Economics of Discrimination*. Universtiy of Chicago, 1957.

Briggs, V. M., Jr., et al. *The Chicano Worker*. University of Texas, 1977.

Buffalo Law Review. *Toward Equal Opportunity in Employment: The Role of the State and Local Government*. Da Capo Press, 1971.

Bullock, R. *Merit Employment: Non-Discrimination in Industry*. Institute of Industrial Relations, Universtiy of California at Los Angeles. 1960.

Bureau of National Affairs. *The Equal Employment Opportunity Act*. BNA, 1973.

Cantor, M. *Black Labor in America*. Negro University Press, 1970.

Edwards, G. F. *The Negro Professional Class*. Free Press, 1959.

Ferman, L. A., J. L. Kornbluth, and J. A. Miller. *Negroes and Jobs: A Book of Readings*. University of Michigan, 1968.

Fisher, P. L., and R. L. Loewenstein. *Race and the News Media*. Praeger, 1967.

Furstenberg, G. M. von, and A. R. Horowitz. *Patterns of Racial Discrimination*. Vol. 2: *Employment*. Lexington Books, 1974.

Ginzberg, E. *The Negro Potential*. Columbia University, 1956.

Gould, W. B. *Black Workers in White Unions*. Cornell University, 1977.

Graves, W. B. *Fair Employment Practice Legislation in the U.S.: Federal-State-Municipal*. Library of Congress, 1951.

Greer, S. *Last Man In: Racial Access to Union Power*. Free Press, 1959.

Hill, H. *Black Labor and the American Legal System*. Bureau of National Affairs, 1977.

Hope, J., II. *Equality of Opportunity: A Union Approach to Fair Employment*. Public Affairs Press, 1956.

Hyman, J. D., and H. Schwartz. *Toward Equal Opportunity in Employment*. Da Capo Press, 1971.

Jacobson, J., ed. *The Negro and the American Labor Movement*. Doubleday, 1968.

Jacoway, E., and D. R. Colburn, ed. *Southern Businessmen and Desegregation*. Louisiana State University, 1980.

Kesselman, L. C. *The Social Politics of the FEPC: A Study in Reform Pressure Movement*. University of North Carolina, 1948.

Krislov, S. *The Negro in Federal Employment: The Quest for Equal Opportunity*. University of Minnesota, 1957.

Mandelbaum, David G. *Soldier Groups and Negro Soldiers*. University of California, 1952.

Marshall, R. *Employment Discrimination: The Impact of Legal Administrative Remedies*. Praeger, 1978.

———, and V. L. Christian, Jr. *Employment of Blacks in the South: A Perspective in the 1960's*. University of Texas, 1978.

Mobull, R. G. *Discrimination in the Labor Market*. University of Michigan, 1970.

Moon, B. *The High Cost of Prejudice*. Messner, 1947.

Nelson, D. D. *The Integration of the Negro into the U.S. Navy*. Farrar, Straus, 1951.

Norgren, P. H. *Employing the Negro in American Industry: A Study of Management Practices*. Industrial Relations Counselors, 1959.

Reich, M. *Racial Inequality: A Political-Economic Analysis*. Princeton University, 1981.

Reitzes, D. C. *Negroes and Medicine*. Harvard University, 1958.

Rosenbloom, D. H. *Federal Equal Employment Opportunity: Politics and Public Personnel Administration*. Praeger, 1977.

Ross, A., and H. Hill. *Employment, Race and Poverty*. Harcourt, Brace, 1967.

Ross, M. *All Manner of Men*. Reynal and Hitchcock, 1948.

Ruchames, L. *Race, Jobs, and Politics: The Story of F.E.P.C.* Columbia University, 1953.

Smith, H. A. *Freedom to Work*. Vantage Press, 1955.

Southall, Sara E. *Industry's Unfinished Business: Achieving Sound Industrial Relations and Fair Employment*. Twentieth Century Fund, 1966.

Sovern, M. I. *Legal Restraints on Racial Discrimination in Employment.* Twentieth Century Fund, 1966.

Takaki, R. *Violence in the Black Imagination.* Capricorn, 1975.

Wolkinson, B. W. *Blacks, Unions, and the EEOC: A Study of Administrative Futility.* Lexington Books, 1973.

E. TECHNIQUES OF THE BLACK CIVIL RIGHTS MOVEMENT

(The NAACP and other black associations, sit-ins, and other "ins"; the leaders of the general civil rights movement; activities; violence; responses.)

Aberbach, J. C., and J. L. Walker. *Race in the City.* Little, Brown, 1973.

Alinsky, S. *Rules for Radicals: A Pragmatic Primer for Realistic Radicals.* Random House, 1971.

Altshuler, A. *Community Control: The Black Demand for Participation in Large American Cities.* Bobbs-Merrill (Pegasus), 1970.

Bailey, H. A., Jr., ed. *Negro Politics in America.* Merrill, 1967.

Baldwin, J. *The Fire Next Time.* Dial Press, 1962.

Barbour, F. B. ed. *The Black Power Revolt.* Sargent, 1968.

Barker, L. J., and J. J. McCorry. *Black Americans and the Political System.* 2d ed. Winthrop, 1979.

Belfrage, S. *Freedom Summer.* Viking Press, 1965.

Boskin, J. *Urban Racial Violence in the Twentieth Century.* Glencoe, 1969.

Burns, W. H. *The Voices of Negro Protest in America.* Oxford University, 1963.

Button, J. W. *Black Violence: Political Impact of the 1960s Riots.* Princeton University, 1978.

Carmichael, S., and C. Hamilton. *Black Power: The Politics of Liberation in America.* Random House, (Vintage Books), 1967.

Chafe, W. H. *Civilities and Civil Rights: Greensboro, North Carolina, and the Black Struggle for Freedom.* Oxford University, 1980.

Clark, K. B., ed. *The Negro Protest.* Beacon Press, 1963.

Clarke, C. J. *These Rights They Seek.* Public Affairs Press, 1962.

Coffin, W. S., and E. E. Whitaker. *Law, Order and Civil Disobedience.* American Enterprise Institute, 1967.

Cohen, J., and W. S. Murphy. *Burn, Baby, Burn: The Los Angeles Race Riot, August, 1965.* Dutton, 1966.

Cole, L. A. *Blacks in Power: A Comparative Study of Black and White Elected Officials.* Princeton University, 1976

Cone, J. H. *Black Theology and Black Power.* Seabury Press, 1969.

Crain, R. L. *The Politics of School Desegregation.* Aldine, 1968.

Daly, C. U. *Urban Violence.* University of Chicago, 1969.

Dick, R. C. *Black Protest: Issues and Tactics.* Greenwood Press, 1974.

Ehle, N. *The Free Men.* Harper & Row, 1965.

Ellis, W. W. *White Ethnics and Black Power.* Aldine, 1969.

Elsinger, P. K. *The Politics of Displacement.* Academic Press, 1980.

Etzkowitz, H., and G. M. Schaflander. *Ghetto Crisis: Riots or Reconciliation.* Little, Brown, 1969.

Fisher, P. L., and R. L. Loewenstein. *Race and News Media.* Anti-Defamation League, 1967.

Foner, P. S. *The Black Panthers Speak.* Lippincott, 1970.

Garfinkel, H. *When Negroes March.* Free Press, 1959.

Gilbert, B. W. *Ten Blocks from the White House: Anatomy of the Washington Riots of 1968.* Praeger, 1968.

Greer, E., ed. *Black Liberation Politics: A Reader.* Allyn & Bacon, 1971.

Grimshaw, A. D. *Racial Violence in the United States.* Aldine, 1969.

Guerin, D. *Negroes on the March.* Weissman, 1956.

Hall, R. L. *Black Separatism in the United States.* American University, 1978.

Hamilton, C. V. The Politics of Civil Rights. Random House, 1967.

Hayden, T. Rebellion in Newark: Official Violence and Ghetto Response. Random House, 1967.

Holden, M., Jr. The Politics of the Black "Nation." Chandler, 1973.

Holloway, H. The Politics of the Southern Negro. Random House, 1969.

Howard, J. R., ed. Awakening Minorities. Aldine, 1970.

Hughes, L. Fight for Freedom: The Story of the NAACP. Norton, 1963.

Jack, R. L. History of the NAACP. Meador, 1943.

Jacobs, P. Prelude to Riot: A View of Urban American from the Bottom. Random House (Vintage Books), 1969.

Janowitz, M. The Social Control of Escalated Riots. University of Chicago, 1968.

Karnig, A. K., and S. Welch. Black Representation and Urban Policy. University of Chicago, 1981.

Killian, L. M. The Impossible Revolution: Black Power and the American Dream. Random House, 1968.

King, M. L., Jr. Strike Toward Freedom: The Montgomery Story. Harper, 1958.

———. Where Do We Go from Here? Chaos or Community? Harper & Row, 1967.

Knopf, T. A. Rumors, Race and Riots. Transaction Books, 1975.

Ladd, E. C., Jr. Negro Political Leadership in the South. Cornell University, 1961.

Lanoue, G., and B. Smith. The Politics of School Decentralization. Heath, 1973.

Lincoln, E. R. The Black Muslims in America. Beacon Press, 1961.

Lipsky, M., and D. J. Olson. Commission Politics: A Case Study of Riots. Transaction Books, 1976.

Locke, H. G. The Detroit Riots of 1967. Wayne State University, 1971.

Lomax, L. E. The Negro Revolt. Harper & Row, 1962.

McWorther, G., ed. The Political Sociology of the Negro: A Selective Review of the Literature. Anti-Defamation League, 1968.

Marx, G. Protest and Prejudice. Harper & Row, 1969.

Masotti, L. H., and D. R. Bowen, eds. Riots and Rebellion. Sage Publications, 1969.

Matthews, D. R., and J. W. Prothro. Negroes and the New Southern Politics. Harcourt, Brace & World, 1966.

Meier, A., ed. Black Experience II: The Transformation of Activism. Aldine, 1970.

———, and F. L. Broderick. Negro Protest Thought in the Twentieth Century. Bobbs-Merrill, 1966.

———, and E. M. Rudwick. CORE: A Study in the Civil Rights Movement, 1942-1968. Oxford University, 1973.

———. From Plantation to Ghetto. 3d ed. Hill & Wang, 1976.

Morris, M. D. The Black Political Experience in America. Harper & Row, 1975.

———. The Politics of Black America. Harper & Row, 1975.

Muse, B. The American Negro Revolutionary from Nonviolence to Black Power, 1963-1967. Indiana University, 1968.

Nelson, W. E., Jr., and P. J. Meranto. Electing Black Mayors: Political Action in the Black Community. Ohio State University, 1977.

Oates, S. B. The Fires of Jubilee: Nat Turner's Fierce Rebellion. New American Library, 1976.

Oppenheimer, M. The Urban Guerilla. Quadrangle, 1969.

Patterson, E. Black City Politics. Dodd, Mead, 1974.

Peck, J. Freedom Ride. Simon and Schuster, 1962.

Peeks, E. The Long Struggle for Black Power. Scribner, 1971.

Porter, B., and M. Dunn. The Miami Riot of 1960: Crossing the Bounds. Lexington Books, 1984.

Powledge, F. Black Power—White Resistance: Notes on the New Civil War. World, 1967.

Preston, M. B., L. J. Henderson, Jr., and P. Puryear, eds. The New Black Politics: The Search for Political Power. Longman, 1982.

Proudfoot, M. Diary of a Sit-In. University of North Carolina, 1962.

Raines, H. *My Soul Is Rested*. Bantam Books, 1978.

Record, W. *The NAACP and the Communist Party in Conflict*. Cornell University, 1964.

Reddick, L. D. *Crusader Without Violence*. Harper, 1959.

Rossi, P. H., ed. *Ghetto Revolts*. 2d ed. Transaction Books, 1973.

Rustin, B. *Strategies for Freedom: The Changing Patterns of Black Protest*. Columbia University, 1976.

Scott, J. *The Black Revolts: Racial Stratification in the U.S.A.* Transaction Books, 1976.

Sears, D., and J. B. McConahay. *The Politics of Violence: The New Urban Blacks and the Watts Riot*. Houghton Mifflin, 1973.

Shepherd, G. W., Jr., ed. *Racial Influences on American Foreign Policy*. Basic Books, 1970.

Stone, C. *Black Political Power in America*. Bobbs-Merrill, 1968.

Sutherland, E., ed. *Letters from Mississippi*. McGraw-Hill, 1965.

Tucker, S. *For Blacks Only*. Eerdmans, 1971.

Von Hoffman, N. *Mississippi Notebook*. David White, 1965.

Vose, C. E. *Caucasians Only: The Supreme Court, the NAACP, and the Restrictive Covenant Cases*. University of California, 1959.

Wagstaff, T. *Black Power: The Radical Response to White America*. Glencoe, 1968.

Wakefield, D. *Revolt in the South*. Grove Press, 1960.

Walker, J. L. *Sit-Ins in Atlanta: A Study of the Negro Revolt*. McGraw-Hill, 1964.

Waskow, I. *From Race-Riot to Sit-In: 1919 and the 1960's*. Doubleday, 1966.

Wilkinson, D. Y., ed. *Black Revolt: Strategies of Protest*. McCutchan, 1969.

Wilson, J. Q. *Negro Politics: The Search for Leadership*. University of Chicago, 1960.

Winter, S. B. *From Riot to Recovery: Newark After Ten Years*. University Press of America, 1979.

Wirt, F. W. *The Politics of Southern Equality*. Aldine, 1970.

Wright, E. *Memphis Politics: A Study in Racial Bloc-Voting*. McGraw-Hill, 1962.

Wright, N. Jr., *Black Power and Urban Unrest*. Hawthorn Books, 1967.

Wynn, D. W. *The Black Protest Movement*. Philosophical Library, 1974.

Zangrando, R. L. *The NAACP Crusade Against Lynching, 1909–1950*. Temple University, 1980.

Zinn, H. *Disobedience and Democracy: Nine Fallacies on Law and Order*. Random House, 1968.

———. *SNCC: The New Abolitionists*. Beacon Press, 1964.

VII. VOTING AND SUFFRAGE.

Aikin, C. *The Negro Votes*. Chandler, 1962.

Catt, C. C. Women Suffrage and Politics. Scribner, 1962.

———, and N. R. Shuler. *Women Suffrage and Politics: The Inner Story of the Suffrage Movement*. University of Washington, 1923.

Claude, R. *The Supreme Court and the Electoral Process*. Johns Hopkins University, 1970.

Elliott, W. E. T. *The Rise of Guardian Democracy: The Supreme Court's Role in Voting Rights Disputes, 1845–1969*. Harvard University, 1974.

Garrow, D. J. *Protest at Selma: Martin Luther King, Jr., and the Voting Rights Act of 1965*. Yale University, 1978.

Gillette, W. M. *The Right to Vote: Politics and the Passage of the Fifteenth Amendment*. Johns Hopkins University. 1965.

Grimes, A. P. *The Puritan Ethic and Woman Suffrage*. Oxford University, 1967.

Hamilton, C. V. *The Bench and the Ballot: Southern Federal Judges and Black Voters*. Oxford University, 1973.

Hine, D. C. *Black Victory: The Rise and Fall of the White Primary in Texas*. Kraus, 1979.

Karnig, A. K., and S. Welch. *Black Representation and Urban Policy*. University of Chicago, 1981.

Keech, W. R. *The Impact of Negro Voting: The Role of the Vote in the Quest for Equality*. Rand-McNally, 1968.

Key, V. O., Jr. *Southern Politics in State and Nation*. Knopf, 1949.

Kousser, J. M. *The Shaping of Southern Politics: Suffrage Restrictions, 1880–1910*. Yale University, 1973.

Kraditor, A. S. *The Ideas of the Women Suffrage Movement, 1890–1920*. Columbia University, 1963.

Lawson, S. F. *Black Ballots: Voting Rights in the South, 1944–1969*. Columbia University, 1976.

Lewinson, P. *Race, Class and Party: A History of Negro Suffrage and White Politics in the South*. Grossett & Dunlap, 1964.

Mathews, J. M. *Legislative and Judicial History of the Fifteenth Amendment*. Da Capo Press, 1971.

Mitchell, W. C. *Why Vote?* Markham, 1971.

Morgan, D. *Suffragists and Democrats*. Michigan State University, 1972.

Murray, R. K. *The 103rd Ballot: The Incredible Story of the Disastrous Democratic Convention of 1924*. Harper & Row, 1976.

Ogden, A. R. *The Poll Tax in the South*. University of Alabama, 1958.

Pomper, G. M. *Elections in America: Control and Influence in American Politics*. Dodd, Mead, 1968.

President's Committee on Civil Rights. *To Secure These Rights*. Government Printing Office, 1947.

Price, H. D. *The Negro in Southern Politics*. New York University, 1957.

Reitman, A., and R. B. Davidson. *The Election Process: Voting Laws and Procedures*. Oceana, 1972.

Smith, C. E. *Voting and Election Laws*. Oceana, 1960.

Strong, S. D. *Negroes, Ballots, and Judges*. University of Alabama, 1968.

Taper, B. *Gomillion Versus Lightfoot: The Tuskegee Gerrymander Case*. McGraw-Hill, 1962.

Washington Research Project. *The Shameful Blight: The Survival of Racial Discrimination in Voting in the South*. Washington Research Project, 1972.

Williamson, C. *American Suffrage from Property to Democracy, 1760–1860*. Princeton University, 1968.

VIII. EXPRESSION: SPEECH, PRESS, AND PETITION

Speech, subversion, conspiracy, civil disobedience, the press, radio, television, motion pictures, books, libel, petition.
(See also IV., Criminal Justice, Law, and Procedure; IX., Assembly and Association; XI., Academic Freedom and Responsibility; and especially XII., Morals, Obscenity, and Censorship.)

Alexander, J. *A Brief Narrative of the Case and Trial of John Peter Zenger*. Ed., S. N. Katz. Harvard University (Belknap Press), 1963.

American Enterprise Institute. *The Press and the Courts: Competing Principles*. AEI, 1978.

Anastaplo, G. *The Constitutionalist: Notes on the First Amendment*. Southern Methodist University, 1971.

Angoff, C. *The Book of Libel*. 2d ed. Barnes & Noble Books, 1966.

Archer, J. *Treason in America*. Hawthorn Books, 1971.

Arendt, H. *On Violence*. Harcourt, Brace & World, 1969.

Arens, R. *In Defense of Public Order*. Columbia University, 1961.

Arthur, W. A., and R. L. Crossman. *The Law of Newspapers*. McGraw-Hill, 1940.

Babb, L. L., ed. *Of the Press, by the Press, for the Press, and Others, Too*. Houghton Mifflin, 1976.

Barron, J. A. *Freedom of the Press for Whom: The Right of Access to Mass Media*. Indiana University, 1973.

Becker, C. L. *Freedom and Responsibility in the American Way of Life*, Knopf, 1945.

Bedau, H. A., ed. *Civil Disobedience: Theory and Practice*. Bobbs-Merrill (Pegasus), 1969.

Berns, W. *The First Amendment and the Future of American Democracy*. Basic Books, 1976.

———. *Freedom, Virtue, and the First Amendment*. Louisiana State University, 1957.

Blumer, H. and P. Houser. *Movies, Delinquency, and Crime*. Macmillan, 1933.

Bollan, W. *The Freedom of Speech and Writing upon Public Affairs Considered*. Da Capo Press, 1970.

Bosmajian, H., ed. *The Principles and Practice of Freedom of Speech*. 2d ed. Houghton Mifflin, 1983.

Brady, J. H. *Confusion Twice Confounded: The First Amendment and the Supreme Court, An Historical Study*. Seton Hall University, 1955.

Brindze, R. *Not to Be Broadcast: The Truth About the Radio*. Da Capo Press, 1970.

Brucker, H. *Freedom of Information*. Macmillan, 1949.

Buranelli, V., ed. *The Trial of Peter Zenger*. New York University, 1957.

Bury, J. B. *A History of Freedom of Thought*. Oxford University, 1952.

Bush, C. R., ed. *Free Press and Fair Trial*. University of Georgia, 1970.

Capaldi, N., ed. *Clear and Present Danger: The Free Speech Controversy*. Bobbs-Merrill (Pegasus), 1969.

Carter, C. A. *Media in the Courts*. National Center for State Courts, 1981.

Carter-Ruck, P. F. *Libel and Slander*. Fakr & Raber, 1972.

Carter, T. B., M. S. Franklin, & J. B. Wright. *The First Amendment and the Fourth Estate*. 3d ed. Foundation Press, 1985.

Case, R. D., ed. *The Press in Perspective*. Louisiana State University, 1963.

Castberg, F. *Freedom of Speech in the West*. Oceana, 1960.

Caughey, J. W. *In Clear and Present Danger: The Critical State of Our Freedoms*. University of Chicago, 1958.

Chafee, Z. *Free Speech in the United States*. Harvard University, 1941.

———. *Freedom of Speech*. Harcourt, 1920.

———. *Freedom of Speech and Press*. Harvard University, 1955.

———. *Government and Mass Communication: A Report from the Commission on Freedom of the Press*. Rev. ed. Doubleday (Anchor Books), 1965.

———. *The Inquiring Mind*. Harvard University, 1928; rpt. Da Capo Press, 1974.

———. *Thirty-Five Years with Freedom of Speech*. Harvard University, 1952.

Chandos, J., ed. *"To Deprave and Corrupt. . . ."* Souvenir Press, 1962.

Chener, W. L. *Freedom of the Press*. Harcourt, Brace, 1955.

Childress, J. F. *Civil Disobedience and Political Obligation: A Study in Christian Social Ethics*. Yale University, 1971.

Clark, D. G., and E. R. Hutchinson, eds. *Mass Media and the Law: Freedom and Restraint*. Wiley, 1970.

Clor, H. M., ed. *Civil Disorder and Violence: Essays on Causes and Cures*. Rand McNally, 1972.

———. *The Mass Media and Modern Democracy*. Rand McNally, 1974.

Clyde, W. *The Struggle for Freedom of the Press from Caxton to Cromwell*. Oxford University, 1934.

Coffin, W. S., Jr., and M. I. Leibman. *Civil Disobedience: Aid or Hindrance to Justice*. American Enterprise Institute, 1972.

Cogley, J. *Report on Blacklisting*. 2 vols. Fund for the Republic, 1956.

Cohen, C. *Civil Disobedience: Conscience, Tactics, and the Law*. Columbia University, 1971.

Commager, H. S. *Freedom, Loyalty, Dissent*. Oxford University, 1954.

Commission on Freedom of the Press. *American Radio: A Report on Broadcasting in the United States*. University of Chicago, 1947.

————. *A Free and Responsible Press: A General Report on Mass Communications*. University of Chicago, 1947.

————. *Freedom of the Movies: A Report on Self-Regulation from the Commission on Freedom of the Press*. Ed., Ruth A. Inglias, University of Chicago, 1947.

————. *Public Speaking to People: A Report on International Mass Communication*. University of Chicago, 1948.

Cooper, K. *The Right to Know: An Exposition of the Evils of News Suppression and Propaganda*. Farrar, Straus & Cudahy, 1956.

Cooper, T. *A Treatise on the Law of Libel and Liberty of the Press*. Hopkins, 1830,; rpt. Da Capo Press, 1970.

Cord, R. L. *Protest, Dissent and the Supreme Court*. Winthrop, 1971.

Cowen, Z. *Fair Trial v. a Free Press*. Center for the Study of Democratic Institutions, 1965.

Cox, A. *Freedom of Expression*. Harvard University, 1981.

Craig, Z. *The Banned Books of England and Other Stories*. George Allen, 1952.

Cross, H. L. *The People's Right to Know*. Columbia University, 1953.

Daniels, W. M., ed. *The Censorship of Books*. H. W. Wilson, 1954.

Dann, M. E., ed. *The Black Press, 1827-1890*. Capricorn, 1975.

Davis, D. B., ed. *The Fear of Conspiracy: Images of Un-American Subversion from the Revolution to the Present*. Cornell University, 1971.

Davila, A. *Libel Law and the Press*. International Press Institute, 1971.

Davis, J. C., ed. *When Men Revolt—and Why*. Free Press, 1970.

Dawson, S. A. *Freedom of the Press*. Columbia University, 1924.

Dean, J. *Hatred, Ridicule, or Contempt: A Book of Libel Cases*. Constable, 1953.

DeGrazia, E. *Censorship Landmarks*. Bowker, 1969.

Devol, K. S. *Mass Media and the Supreme Court*. 2d ed. Hastings House, 1976.

Dorsen, N., and S. Gillers. *None of Your Business: Government Secrecy in America*. Penguin Books, 1975.

Douglas, W. O. *Points of Rebellion*. Random House, 1970.

Downs, D. A. *Nazis in Skokie: Freedom, Communication, and the First Amendment*. Notre Dame University, 1985.

Downs, R. B., ed. *The First Freedom, Liberty, and Justice in the World of Books and Readings*. American Library Association, 1960.

Drinker, H. S. *Some Observation of the Freedoms of the First Amendment*. Boston University, 1957.

Eidenberg, E., and R. D. Morey. *An Act of Congress: The Legislative Process and the Making of Education Policy*. Norton, 1969.

Emerson, T. I. *The System of Freedom of Expression*. Random House, 1972.

————. *Toward a General Theory of the First Amendment*. Random House, 1967.

Ernst, M. L. *The First Freedom*. Macmillan, 1946; rpt. Da Capo Press, 1971.

"Father of Candor." *An Enquiry into the Doctrine, Lately Propagated, Concerning Libels, Warrants, and the Seizure of Papers*. Da Capo Press, 1970.

Facts on File, eds. *Government and the Media in Conflict*. Facts on File, 1974.

Farber, M. *Somebody Is Lying: The Story of Dr. X*. Doubleday, 1982.

Faulk, J. H. *Fear on Trial*. Simon and Schuster, 1964.

Fellman, D. *The Limits of Freedom*. Rutgers University, 1959.

Felsher, H., and M. Rosen. *The Press in the Jury Box*. Macmillan, 1966.

Fisher, P., and R. Lowenstein, eds. *Race and the News Media*. Anti-Defamation League, 1967.

Fliess, Peter J. *Freedom of the Press in the German Republic, 1918-1933*. Louisiana State University, 1955.

Forbath, P., and C. Winfrey. *The Adversaries: The President and the Press*. Regal Press, 1974.

Fortas, A. *Concerning Dissent and Civil Disobedience*. New American Library, 1968.

Franklin, M. A. *The Dynamics of American Law: The Legal Process and Freedom of Expression*. Foundation Press, 1968.

———. *The First Amendment and the Fourth Estate: Communications Law for Undergraduates*. 2d ed. Foundation Press, 1981.

Freeman, H. A., et al. *Civil Disobedience*. Center for the Study of Democratic Institutions, 1966.

Friedman, L. *The Wise Minority: An Argument for Draft Resistance and Civil Disobedience*. Dial Press, 1971.

Friendly, A., and R. L. Goldfarb. *Crime and Publicity: The Impact of News on the Administration of Justice*. Twentieth Century Fund, 1967.

Friendly, F. W. *Minnesota Rag: The Dramatic Story of the Landmark Supreme Court Case That Gave New Meaning for Freedom of the Press*. Random House, 1981.

Furneaux, P. *The Palladium of Conscience*. Da Capo Press, 1974.

Gerald, J. E. *News of Crime: Courts and Press in Conflict*. Greenwood Press, 1983.

———. *The Press and the Constitution, 1931–1947*. University of Minnesota, 1948.

Gill, J. *Tide Without Turning: Elijah P. Lovejoy and Freedom of the Press*. Starr King, 1958.

Gillett, C. R. *Banned Books*. 2 vols. Columbia University, 1932.

Gillmore, D. M. *Free Press and Fair Trial*. Public Affairs Press, 1966.

———, and J. Barron. *Mass Communication Law*. 2d ed. West, 1974.

Ginger, A. F., ed. *The Pentagon Papers Case Collection, Annotated Procedural Guide and Index*. Oceana, 1975.

Glessing, R. J. *The Underground Press in America*. Indiana University, 1971.

Goldfarb, R. L. *The Contempt Power*. Columbia University, 1963.

Goldwin, R. A., ed. *Civil Disobedience: Essays Old and New*. Rand McNally, 1969.

Goodman, W. *The Committee: The Extraordinary Career of the House Committee on Un-American Affairs*. Farrar, Straus & Giroux, 1968.

Graeber, D. A. *Crime News and the Public*. Praeger, 1980.

———. *Mass Media and American Politics*. Congressional Quarterly Press, 1980.

Grey, D. L. *The Supreme Court and the News Media*. Northwestern University, 1968.

Gurr, T. R. *Why Men Rebel*. Princeton University, 1970.

Hachten, W. A. *The Supreme Court on Freedom of the Press: Decisions and Dissents*. Iowa State University, 1968.

———. *The Supreme Court and the Press*. Public Affairs Press, 1965.

Haight, A. L. *Banned Books*. Bowker, 1956.

Haiman, F. S. *The First Freedoms: Speech, Press, Assembly*. American Civil Liberties Union, 1971.

———. *Freedom of Speech: Issues and Cases*. Random House, 1965.

———. *Speech and Law in a Free Society*. University of Chicago, 1981.

Haney, R. W. *Comstockery in America*. Houghton Mifflin, 1956.

Hay, G. *Two Essays on the Liberty of the Press*. Da Capo Press, 1970.

Helm, L. M., et al., eds. *Informing the People: A Public Affairs Handbook*. Longman, 1981.

Hemmer, J. J., Jr. *Communication Under Law*. Scarecrow Press, 1979.

Hentoff, N. *The First Freedom: The Tumultous History of Free Speech in America*. Dell (Delacorte Press), 1980.

Hocking, W. E. *Freedom of the Press: A Framework of Principle*. University of Chicago, 1945.

Hohenberg, J. *A Crisis for the American Press*. Columbia University, 1978.

———. *Free Press: Free People: The Best Cause*. Columbia University, 1971.

Hoyt, O. *Freedom of the News Media*. Seabury Press, 1973.

Hudon, E. G. *Freedom of Speech and Press in America*. Public Affairs Press, 1963.

Hughes, Frank. *Prejudice and the Press*. Devin-Adair, 1950.

Hyde, H. M. *Privacy and the Press*. Butterworth, 1947.

Hyman, A., and M. B. Johnson, eds. *Advertising and Free Speech.* Lexington Books, 1977.

Ickes, H. L. *Freedom of the Press Today.* Vanguard Press, 1941.

Inbau, F. E. *Free Press—Fair Trial.* Northwestern University, 1964; rpt. Da Capo Press, 1974.

Jennison, P. *Freedom to Read.* Public Affairs Pamphlets, 1965.

Johnson, G. W. *Peril and Promise: An Inquiry into Freedom of the Press.* Harper, 1958.

Kadish, M. R., and S. H. Kadish. *Discretion to Disobey: A Study of Lawful Departures from Legal Rules.* Stanford University, 1973.

Kahn, G. *Hollywood on Trial.* Boni and Gear, 1948.

Kalven, H., Jr. *The Negro and the First Amendment.* University of Chicago, 1965.

Kaplan, M. A. *Dissent and the State in Peace and War.* Dunellen, 1970.

Konvitz, M. R. *First Amendment Freedoms: Selected Cases on Freedom of Religion, Speech, Press, Assembly.* Cornell University, 1963.

——. *Fundamental Liberties of a Free People: Religion, Speech, Press, Assembly.* Cornell University, 1957.

Krislov, S. *The Supreme Court and Political Freedom.* Free Press, 1968.

Krueger, M., and F. Silvert. *Dissent Denied: The Democratic Response to Protest.* Elsevier, 1975.

Kurland, P. B., ed. *Free Speech and Association: The Supreme Court and the First Amendment.* University of Chicago, 1975.

Labunski, R. E. *The First Amendment Under Siege: The Politics of Broadcast Regulation.* Greenwood Press, 1981.

Lacy, D. *Freedom and Communication.* Illinois State University, 1961.

Ladenson, R. F. *A Philosophy of Free Expression and Its Constitutional Applications.* Rowman & Littlefield, 1982.

Landau, J. C., et al. *The Press and the Courts: Competing Principles.* American Enterprise Institute, 1978.

Lane, R., and J. J. Turner, J. *Riot, Race, and Tumult.* Greenwood Press, 1978.

Lawhorne, C. O. *Defamation and Public Officials.* Southern Illinois University, 1971.

Lawrence, J. S., ed. *Fair Use and Free Inquiry: Copyright Law and the News Media.* Ablex, 1980.

Levy, L. W. *Freedom of the Press from Zenger to Jefferson.* Bobbs-Merrill, 1966.

——. *Legacy of Suppression: Freedom of Speech and Press in Early American History.* Harvard University, 1960.

Lofton, J. *Justice and the Press.* Beacon Press, 1966.

——. *The Press as Guardian of the First Amendment.* University of South Carolina, 1980.

Luskin, J. *Lippman, Liberty and the Press.* University of Alabama, 1972.

McClennan, G. S. *Censorship in the United States.* H. W. Wilson, 1967.

McCoy, R. E. *Freedom of the Press: An Annotated Bibliography.* Southern Illinois University, 1968.

McKeon, R., et al. *The Freedom to Read.* Bowker, 1957.

McLuhan, M. *Understanding Media.* McGraw-Hill, 1964.

Medina, H. R. *Freedom of the Press and Fair Trial: Final Report with Recommendations.* Columbia University, 1967.

Meiklejohn, A. *Free Speech and Its Relation to Self-Government.* Harper. 1948.

——. *Political Freedom: The Constitutional Powers of the People.* Oxford University, 1960; rpt. 1965.

Miller, J. O. *Crisis in Freedom: The Alien and Sedition Acts.* Little Brown, 1951.

Miller, M. *The Judges and the Judged.* Doubleday, 1952.

Morloon, S. E., F. Merck, and F. Freidel. *Dissent in Three American Wars.* Harvard University, 1971.

Mott, F. L. *American Journalism.* Macmillan, 1950.

Murphy, J. G. *Civil Disobedience and Violence.* Wadsworth, 1971.

Murphy, P. L. *The Meaning of Freedom of Speech: First Amendment Freedoms from Wilson to FDR.* Greenwood Press, 1972.

Neier, A. *Defending My Enemy: American Nazis, the Skokie Case, and the Risks of Freedom*. Dutton, 1979.

Nelson, H. L., ed. *Freedom of the Press from Hamilton to the Warren Court*. Bobbs-Merrill, 1967.

———. *Libel in News of Congressional Investigating Committees*. University of Minnesota, 1961.

Nizer, L. *The Jury Returns*. Doubleday, 1966.

O'Brien, D. M. *The Public's Right to Know: The Supreme Court and the First Amendment*. Praeger, 1981.

O'Neil, R. M. *Free Speech: Responsible Communication Under the Law*. Bobbs-Merrill, 1972.

Owen, B. M. *Economics and Freedom of Expression: Media Structure and the First Amendment*. Ballinger, 1975.

Parks, S., ed. *Freedom of the Press: the Struggle for Copyright and the Development of the Laws of Libel*. Garland, 1980.

Patterson, G. *Free Speech and a Free Press*. Little, Brown, 1939.

Pell, E. *The Big Chill*. Beacon Press, 1984.

Pember, D. R. *Privacy and the Press: The Law, The Mass Media, and the First Amendment*. University of Washington, 1972.

Phelps, R. E. *Libel: Rights, Risks, Responsibilities*. MacMillan, 1966.

———, and E. D. Hamilton. *Libel*. Macmillan, 1967.

Randall, R. S. *Censorship of the Movies: The Social and Political Control of a Mass Medium*. University of Wisconsin, 1968.

Raymond, A. *The People's Right to Know: A Report on Government News Suppression*. American Civil Liberties Union, 1955.

Read, W. H. *America's Mass Media Merchants*. Johns Hopkins University, 1976.

Rolph, C. H., ed. *The Trial of Lady Chatterley*. Penguin Books, 1961.

Royal Commission on the Press. *Report of the Royal Commission on the Press, 1947–1949*. His Majesty's Stationery Office, 1949.

Rucker, B. W. *The First Freedom*. Southern Illinois University, 1968.

Salisbury, H. E. *Without Fear or Favor*. Times Books, 1980.

Schauer, F. *Free Speech: A Philosophical Inquiry*. Cambridge University, 1982.

Schmidt, R. C., Jr. *Freedom of the Press vs. Public Asccess*. Praeger, 1976.

Schroeder, T. *Constitutional Free Speech: Defined and Defended*. Da Capo Press, 1970.

———. *Free Speech for Radicals*. Da Capo Press, 1969.

Seldes, G. *Freedom of the Press*. Bobbs-Merrill, 1935.

———. *Never Tire of Protesting*. Stuart, 1968.

———. *The People Don't Know*. Gaer Association, 1949.

Shapiro, M. *Freedom of Speech: The Supreme Court and Judicial Review*. Prentice-Hall, 1966.

———. *The Pentagon Papers and the Courts*. Chandler, 1972.

Short, J. F., ed. *Collective Violence*. Aldine-Atherton, 1972.

Shuman, S. I., comp. *Law and Disorder: The Legitimacy of Direct Action as an Instrument of Social Policy*. Wayne State University, 1971.

Siebert, F. S. *Freedom of the Press in England, 1476–1776*. University of Illinois, 1952.

———. *The Rights and Privileges of the Press*. Appleton-Century. 1934.

Simmons, S. J. *The Fairness Doctrine and the Media*. University of California, 1978.

Simons, H., and J. Califano, eds. *The Media and the Law*. Praeger, 1976.

Singer, P. *Democracy and Disobedience*. Oxford University, 1973.

Smead, E. E. *Freedom of Speech by Radio and Television*. Public Affairs Press, 1947.

Smith, H. L. *Behind the Press in South Africa*. Stewart, 1947.

Smith, J. M. *Freedom of Speech by Radio and Television*. Public Affairs Press, 1958.

Sorel, G. *Reflections on Violence*. Collier, 1961.

Special Committee on Radio and Television of the Association of the Bar of the City of New York. *Radio, Television, and the Administration of Justice*. Columbia University, 1967.

Spring, S. *Risks and Rights in Publishing, Television, Radio, Motion Pictures, Advertising, and the Theatre*. Allen & Unwin, 1952.

Starr, I. *The Idea of Liberty: First Amendment Freedoms*. West, 1978.

Stevens, J. D. *Shaping the First Amendment*. Sage Publications, 1982.

Stiehm, J. *Nonviolent Power: Active and Passive Resistence in America*. Heath, 1972.

Straight, M. *Trial by Television and Other Encounters*. Rev. ed. Devon, 1979.

Sullivan, H. *Contempts by Publication*. Yale University, 1940.

———. *Trial by Newspaper*. Patriot, 1961.

Swayze, H. *Political Control of Literature in the U.S.S.R.: 1946-1959*. Howard University, 1962.

Taylor, T. *Two Studies in Constitutional Interpretation . . . and Fair Trial and Free Press*. Ohio State University, 1969.

Tedford, T. *Freedom of Speech*. Random House, 1985.

Thayer, F. *Legal Control of the Press*. Foundation Press, 1944.

Thomas, E. C. *The Law of Libel and Slander*. 3d ed. Oceana, 1973.

Thomson, J. *An Enquiry Concerning the Liberty and Licentiousness of the Press*. Da Capo Press, 1970.

Thoreau, H. D. *The Variorium Civil Disobedience*. Ed. Walter Harding. Rpt. Twayne, 1967.

Ungar, S. J. *The Papers and the Papers: An Account of the Legal and Political Battle over the Pentagon Papers*. Dutton, 1972.

University Publications of America. *The United States of America v. One Book Entitled Ulysses by James Joyce*. University Publications of America, 1985.

Van Alstyne, W. V. *Interpretations of the First Amendment*. Duke University, 1984.

Van Den Haag, E. *Political Violence and Civil Disobedience*. Harper & Row, 1972.

Van Gerpen, M. *Privileged Communication and the Press: The Citizen's Right to Know Versus the Law's Right to Confidential News Source Evidence*. Greenwood Press, 1979.

Von Der Mehden, E. B. *Comparative Political Violence*. Prentice-Hall, 1973.

Walzer, M. *Obligations: Essays on Disobedience, War, and Citizenship*. Harvard University, 1970.

Wasserstrom, W. *Civil Liberties and the Arts*. Syracuse University, 1964.

Whalen, C. W., Jr. *Your Right to Know*. Random House (Vintage Books), 1973.

White, F. *Camera in the Courtroom: A U.S. Survey*. Association for Education in Journalism, 1979.

White, L. *The American Radio*. University of Chicago, 1947.

Wicker, T. *On Press*. Viking Press, 1978.

Wiggins, J. R. *Freedom or Secrecy?* Oxford University, 1956.

Will, G. F., ed. *Press, Politics and Popular Government*. American Enterprise Institute, 1972.

Williams, F. *Press, Parliament and People*. Heinemann, 1946.

Williamson, E. G. *The American Student's Freedom of Expression*. University of Minnesota, 1966.

Wittenberg, P., ed. *Dangerous Words: A Guide to the Law of Libel*. Columbia University, 1960.

Wolff, R. P. *In Defense of Anarchism*. Harper & Row, 1970.

Worlman, T. *A Treatise Concerning Political Enquiry and the Liberty of the Press*. Da Capo Press, 1970.

Yankewich, L. R. *It's Libel or Contempt If You Print It*. Parker, 1950.

Young, A. F., ed. *Dissent: Explorations in the History of American Radicalism*. Northern Illinois University, 1968.

Zashin, E. M. *Civil Disobedience and Democracy*. Free Press, 1972.

Zinn, H. *Disobedience and Democracy*. Random House, 1968.

Zwiebach, B. *Civility and Disobedience*. Cambridge University, 1975.

IX. ASSEMBLY AND ASSOCIATION

(See also VIII, Expression: Speech, Press and Petition.)

Abernathy, G. The Right of Assembly and Association. 2d ed. University of South Carolina, 1981.

American Jewish Committee. Assault upon Freedom of Association. American Jewish Committee. 1957.

Fellman, D. The Constitutional Right of Association. University of Chicago, 1963.

Horn, R. A. Groups and the Constitution. AMS Press, 1971.

Mintz, B., with R. Spenser and J. R. Robinson. Assault upon Freedom of Association. American Jewish Committee, 1959.

Rice, C. E. Freedom of Association. New York University, 1962.

Robertson, D. B., ed. Voluntary Associations: A Study of Groups in Free Societies. Knox, 1966.

Smith, B. A Dangerous Freedom. Lippincott, 1954.

Wellington, H. H. Labor and the Legal Process. Yale University, 1918.

X. RELIGION

(See also V. Military Justice and Selective Service in Peace and War; VIII, Expression: Press, and Petition; XII, Morals, Obscenity, and Censorship.)

A. FREE EXERCISE

Allport, G. W. The Individual and His Religion. Macmillan, 1954.

Altfeld, E. M. The Jews' Struggle for Religious and Civil Liberty in Maryland. Johns Hopkins University, 1924.

Bainton, R. H. The Travail of Religious Liberty. Harper (Torchbooks), 1958.

Baltzell, E. D., Jr. Puritan Boston and Quaker Philadelphia. Free Press, 1979.

Bates, M. S. Religious Liberty: An Inquiry. Harper, 1945.

Beckford, J. A. The Trumpet of Prophecy: A Sociological Study of the Jehovah's Witnesses. Wiley, 1975.

Blackham, H. J. Religion in a Modern Society. Ungar, 1966.

Blackwell, V. V. O'er the Ramparts They Watched. Carlton, 1976.

Blakely, W. A. American State Papers and Related Docuements on Freedom in Religion. Religious Liberty Association, 1949.

Blau, J. L., ed. Cornerstones of Religious Freedom in America. Beacon Press, 1949.

Brady, H. Confusion Twice Confounded: The First Amendment and the Supreme Court. Seton Hall University, 1954.

Bromley, D. G., and A. D. Shufe, Jr. "Moonies" in America: Cult, Church, and Crusade. Sage Publications, 1979.

Broun, H. C., and G. Britt. Christians Only: A Study in Prejudice. Da Capo Press 1974.

Burstein, A. Law Concerning Religion in the United States. 2d ed. Oceana, 1966.

Cobb, S. H. The Rise of Religious Liberty in America. Johnson Reprint, 1975.

Cogley, J., ed. Religion in America: Original Essays on Religion in a Free Society. New American Library (Meridian Books), 1968.

Cohen, R. Sunday in the Sixties. Public Affairs Press, 1965.

Cook, B. B. "Sentencing the Unpatriotic." In The Quest for Social Justice, ed. R. M. Aderman. University of Wisconsin, 1983.

Cornell, J. The Conscientious Objector and the Law. John Day, 1943.

Damore, L. The "Crime" of Dorothy Sheridan. Arbor House, 1978.

Daum, A. Assault on the Bill of Rights: The Jewish Stake. Union of American Hebrew Congregations, 1982.

Davis, J. W., Jr., and K. M. Dolbeare. *Little Groups of Neighbors: The Selective Service System*. Markham, 1968.

Drinker, H. S. *Some Observations on the Freedoms of the First Amendment*. Boston University, 1957.

Dunn, W. K. *What Happened to Religious Education: The Decline of Religious Teaching in the Public Elementary School, 1776–1861*. Johns Hopkins University, 1958.

Educational Politics Commission. *Moral and Spiritual Values in the Public Schools*. National Education Association, 1951.

Fellman, D. *The Limits of Freedom*. Rutgers University, 1959.

Fenton, J. H. *The Catholic Vote*. Hauser, 1960.

Finn, J., ed. *A Conflict of Loyalties: The Case for Selective Conscientious Objection*. Bobbs-Merrill (Pegasus), 1968.

Harrison, E. G. *Visions of Glory: A History and a Memory of Jehovah's Witnesses*. Simon and Schuster, 1978.

Hartford, E. F. *Moral Values in Public Education: Lessons from the Kentucky Experience*. Harper, 1958.

Henry, V. *The Place of Religion in Public Schools: A Handbook to Guide Communities*. Harper, 1950.

Herberg, W. *Protestant-Catholic-Jew*. Rev. ed. Doubleday, 1960.

Hoekema, A. *The Four Major Cults: Christian Science, Jehovah's Witnesses, Mormonism, Seventh Day Adventists*. Erdmans, 1963.

Horan, D. J., and D. Mall, eds. *Death, Dying, and Euthanasia*. University Publications of America, 1976.

Horowitz, I. L., ed. *Science, Sin, and Scholarship: The Politics of Reverend Moon and the Unification Church*. MIT, 1979.

Hostetler, J. A. *The Amish Society*. Rev. ed. Johns Hopkins University, 1968.

Hudson, W. S. *Religion in America*. 2d ed. Scribner, 1973.

Johns, W. L. *Dateline Sunday, U.S.A.* Pacific Press Publishing Associaiton, 1967.

Keim, A. M. *Compulsory Education and the Amish: The Right Not to Be Modern*. Beacon Press, 1975.

Konvitz, M. R. *Religious Liberty and Conscience: A Constitutional Inquiry*. Viking Press, 1969.

Levy, L. W., ed. *Blasphemy in Massachusetts: Freedom of Conscience and the Abner Kneeland Case*. Da Capo Press, 1969.

Lincoln, C. E. *The Black Muslims in America*. Beacon Press, 1961.

Manwaring, D. R. *Render Unto Caesar: The Flag Salute Controversy*. University of Chicago, 1962.

Marnell, W. H. *The First Amendment: The History of Religious Freedom in America*. Doubleday, 1966.

———. *The First Amendment: Religious Freedom in America from Colonial Days to the School Prayer*. Doubleday (Anchor Books), 1966.

McCollum, V. *One Woman's Fight*. Rev. ed. Beacon Press, 1961.

McGrath, J. J., ed. *Church and State in American Law*. Bruce, 1962.

Mechling, J., ed. *Church, State and Public Policy: The New Shape of the Church-State Debate*. American Enterprise Institute, 1978.

Miller, G. T. *Religious Liberty in America: History and Prospect*. Westminster, 1976.

Miller, P. *Roger Williams*. Bobbs-Merrill, 1953.

Miller, W. L. *Religion and the Free Society*. Fund for the Republic, 1958.

Nelsen, H. M., and A. K. Nelsen. *Black Church in the Sixties*. University of Kentucky, 1975.

O'Brien F. W. *Justice Reed and the First Amendment: The Religion Clauses*. Georgetown University, 1958.

Pfeffer, L. *Religion, State, and the Burger Court*. Prometheus Press, 1985.

———. *Religious Freedom*. National Textbook, 1977.

Pike, E. R. *Jehovah's Witnesses*. Philosophical Library, 1954.

Polishook, I. H. *Roger Williams, John Cotton, and Religious Freedom.* Prentice-Hall, 1967.

Porter, E. S. *Conscience and the Court.* Prentice-Hall, 1962.

Quinlan, J. T., J. Quinlan, and P. Battelle, *Karen Ann: The Quinlans Tell Their Story.* Doubleday, 1977.

Quinlan, Karen, *In the Matter of: The Complete Legal Briefs, Court Proceedings, and Decision.* University Publications of America, 1975.

Raab, E., ed. *Religious Conflict in America: Studies of the Problem Beyond Bigotry.* Doubleday, 1964.

Rodgers, H. R., Jr. *Community Conflict, Public Opinion, and the Law: The Amish Dispute in Iowa.* Merrill, 1969.

Rowley, P. *New Gods in America.* McKay, 1971.

Russell, O. R. *Freedom to Die: Moral and Legal Aspects of Euthanasia.* Dell, 1976.

Rutherford, J. F. *Enemies.* Watchtower Society, 1937.

Spicer, G. W. *The Supreme Court and Fundamental Freedom.* Appleton-Century, 1959.

Shupe, A. D., Jr., and D. G. Bromley. *The New Vigilantes: Deprogrammers, Anti-Cultists, and the New Religions.* Sage Publications, 1980.

Sibley, M. Q. *The Obligation to Disobey: Conscience and the Law.* Council on Religion, 1970.

———, and P. E. Jacob. *Conscription of Conscience: The American State and the Conscientious Objector, 1940–1947.* Cornell University, 1952.

Starr, I. *The Idea of Liberty.* West, 1978.

Stevick, D. B. *Civil Disobedience and the Christian.* Seabury Press, 1969.

Stroup, H. *The Jehovah's Witnesses.* Columbia University, 1945.

Swancara, F. *Thomas Jefferson Versus Religious Oppression.* University Books, 1969.

Torpey, W. G. *Judicial Doctrines of Religious Rights in America.* University of North Carolina, 1948.

Trenchard, J., and T. Gordon. *Cato's Letters: Essays on Liberty, Civil and Religious.*, Rpt. Da Capo Press, 1971.

Walzer, M. *Just and Unjust Wars: A Moral Argument with Historical Illustrations.* Basic Books, 1977.

———. *Obligations.* Harvard University, 1970.

Wilson, B. *Religious Sects.* McGraw-Hill, 1970.

B. SEPARATION OF CHURCH AND STATE.

Abercrombie, C. L., III. *The Military Chaplain.* Sage Publications, 1977.

Acton, J. *Essays on Church and State.* Viking Press, 1953.

Adams, J. L. *The Growing Church Lobby in Washington.* Eerdmans, 1970.

Alley, R. S. *So Help Me God: Religion and the Presidency.* John Knox, 1972.

American Association of School Administrators. *Religion in the Public Schools.* AASA, 1964.

Antieau, C. J. *Freedom from Federal Establishment.* Bruce, 1964.

Arnold, O. C. *Religious Freedom on Trial.* Judson Press, 1978.

Bailey, S. K., and E. K. Mosher. *ESEA: The Office of Education Administers a Law.* Syracuse University, 1968.

Baker, J. T. *A Southern Baptist in the White House.* Westminster, 1977.

Balk, A. *The Religion Business.* John Knox, 1969.

Barker, Sir E. *Church, State and Education.* University of Michigan, 1957.

Barnes, R. P. *Under Orders: The Churches and Public Affairs.* Doubleday, 1961.

Barth, K. *Community, State, and Church.* Doubleday, 1960.

Bedsole, A. *The Supreme Court Decision on Bible Reading and Prayers: America's Black Letter Day.* Baker Book, 1967.

Benson, P. L., and D. L. Williams. *Religion on Capitol Hill: Myths and Realities.* Harper & Row, 1982.

Berman, H. J. *The Interaction of Law and Religion.* Abingdon Press, 1974.

Beth, L. P. *The American Theory of Church and State.* University of Florida, 1958.

Blanshard, P. *American Freedom and Catholic Power.* Beacon Press, 1958.

————. *Communism, Democracy and Catholic Power.* Beacon Press, 1951.

————. *God and Man in Washington.* Beacon Press, 1960.

————. *Religion and the Schools: The Great Controversy.* Beacon Press, 1963.

Blum, V. C. *Freedom of Choice in Education: Federal Aid for All Children.* Doubleday, 1965.

Boles, D. E. *The Bible, Religion, and the Public Schools.* 3d ed. Iowa State University, 1965.

————. *The Two Swords: Commentaries and Cases on Religion and Education.* Iowa State University, 1967.

Brady, J. H. *Confusion Twice Confounded: The First Amendment and the Supreme Court.* Seton Hall University, 1954.

Brickman, W. W., and S. Lehrer. *Religion, Government and Education.* Society for Advancement of Education, 1961.

Brown, N. C., ed. *The Study of Religion in the Public Schools: An Appraisal.* American Council on Education, 1958.

Buckley, T. E. *Church and State in Revolutionary Virginia, 1776–1787.* University of Virginia, 1977.

Butts, R. F. *The American Tradition in Religion and Education.* Beacon Press, 1950.

Byrnes, L. *Religion and Public Education.* Harper & Row, 1975.

Callahan, D. J., ed. *Federal Aid and Catholic Schools.* Helicon, 1964.

Cogdell, G. D. *What Price Parochaid?* Americans United for Separation of Church and State, 1970.

Cogley, J., ed. *Religion in America.* New American Library (Meridian Books), 1958.

Colombo, F. *God in America.* Columbia University, 1984.

Conway, F., and J. Siegelman. *Holy Terror.* Doubleday, 1982.

Cord, R. L. *Separation of Church and State: Historical Fact and Current Fiction.* Lambeth, 1982.

Corwin, E. S. *A Constitution of Power in a Secular State.* Michie, 1951.

Constanzo, John. *This Nation Under God: Church, State and Schools in America.* Herder and Herder, 1964.

Crosby, D. F. *God, Church and Flag: Senator Joseph R. McCarthy and the Catholic Church.* American University Press Service, 1978.

Dawson, J. M. *America's Way in Church, State, and Society.* Macmillan, 1953.

————. *Separate Church and State Now.* R. R. Smith, 1948.

Dierenfield, R. *Religion in American Public Schools.* Public Affairs Press, 1962.

Doerr, E. *The Conspiracy That Failed.* Americans United for Separation of Church and State, 1968.

Dolbeare, K. M., and P. E. Hammond. *The School Prayer Decisions: From Court Policy to Local Practice.* University of Chicago, 1971.

Douglas, W. O. *The Bible and the Schools.* Little, Brown, 1966.

Drinan, R. F. *Religion, the Courts, and Public Policy.* McGraw-Hill, 1963.

Drinker, H. S. *Some Observations on the Freedoms of the First Amendment.* Boston University, 1957.

Drovin, E. G. *The School Question: A Bibliography and Church-State Relationship in American Education, 1940–1960.* Catholic University, 1963.

Duker, O. *The Public Schools and Religion: The Legal Context.* Harper & Row, 1966.

Dulce, B., and E. J. Richter. *Religion and the Presidency.* Macmillan, 1962.

Dunn, W. K. *What Happened to Religious Education?* Johns Hopkins University, 1965.

Ebersole, L. *Church Lobbying in the Nation's Capitol.* Macmillan, 1962.

Edwards, N. *The Courts and the Public Schools.* University of Chicago, 1971.

Ehler, S. E., and J. B. Morral. *Church and State Through the Centuries.* Newman, 1954.

Eidenberg, E., and R. D. Morey. *An Act of Congress.* Norton, 1969.

Engel, D. E. *Religion in Public Education.* Paulist Press, 1974.

Erickson, D. A., ed. *Public Controls for Nonpublic Schools.* University of Chicago, 1969.

Fellman, D. *Religion in American Public Law.* Boston University, 1965.

————, ed. *The Supreme Court and Education.* Columbia University, 1960.

Fisher, W. E. *Politics, Poker and Piety: A Perspective on Cultural Religion in America.* Abingdon Press, 1972.

Frazier, E. F. *The Negro Church in America.* Schocken Books, 1969.

Freund, P. A., and R. Ulich. *Religion and the Public Schools.* Harvard University, 1965.

Frommer, A., ed. *The Bible and the Public Schools.* Liberal Press, 1963.

Fuchs, L. H. *John F. Kennedy and American Catholicism.* Meredith, 1967.

Gabel, R. J. *Public Funds for Church and Private Schools.* Catholic University, 1937.

Gellhorn, W., and R. K. Greenawalt. *The Sectarian College and the Public Purse: Fordham, A Case Study.* Oceana, 1970.

Georgetown University Institute for Church-State Law. *Freedom from Federal Establishment.* Bruce, 1964.

Gianella, D. A., ed. *Religion and the Public Order.* University of Chicago, 1964.

Goldstein, D. *Trial of Faith: Religion and Politics in Tocqueville's Thought.* Harcourt, Brace, 1975.

Gordis, R. *Religion and the Schools.* Fund for the Republic, 1959.

Greene, E. B. *Religion and the State: The Making and Testing of an American Tradition.* Cornell University, 1959.

Griffiths, W. E. *Religion, the Courts, and the Public Schools: A Century of Litigation.* Anderson, 1966.

Healey, R. M. *Jefferson on Religion in Public Education.* Yale University, 1962.

Heeley, A. V. *Why the Private School?* Harper, 1951.

Herzog, A. *The Church Trap.* Macmillan, 1969.

Hook, S. *Religion in a Free Society.* University of Nebraska, 1967.

Howard, A. E. D., J. W. Baker, and T. S. Derr. *Church, State, and Politics.* Roscoe Pound-American Trial Lawyers Foundation, 1982.

Howe, M. DeWolfe *Cases on Church and State in the United States.* Harvard University, 1952.

————. *The Garden and the Wilderness: Religion and Government in American Constitutional History.* University of Chicago, 1965.

James, C. F. *Documentary History of the Struggle for Religious Liberty in Virginia.* Da Costa, 1971.

Johnson, A. W., and F. Yost. *Separation of Church and State in the United States.* University of Minnesota, 1948.

Johnson, F. E., ed. *American Education and Religion: The Problem of Religion in the Schools.* Harper, 1952.

Johnson, R. M. *The Dynamics of Conscience.* Washington University, 1967.

Jorstad, E. *Evangelicals in the White House: The Cultural Maturation of Born-Again Christianity, 1960–1981.* Wiley, 1982.

Kallen, Horace M. *Secularism Is the Will of God: An Essay in the Social Philosophy of Democracy and Religion.* Twayne, 1954.

Kater, J. L., Jr. *Christians on the Right: The Moral Majority in Perspective.* Seabury Press, 1982.

Katz, W. G. *Religion and American Constitutions.* Northwestern University, 1964.

Kauper, P. G. *Civil Liberties and the Constitution.* University of Michigan, 1962.

————. *Religion and the Constitution.* Louisiana State University, 1964.

Kelly, D. M., ed. *Government Intervention in Religious Affairs.* Pilgrim Press, 1982.

————. *Why Churches Should Not Pay Taxes.* Harper & Row, 1977.

Kerwin, J. G. *Catholic Viewpoint on Church and State.* Hanover House, 1960.

Kilpatrick, J. J. *The Southern Case for School Segregation.* Crowell Collier, 1962.

Kommers, D. P., and M. J. Wahoske, eds. *Freedom and Education: Pierce v. Society of Sisters Reconsidered.* University of Notre Dame, 1978.

Krinsky, F. *The Politics of Religion in America.* Glencoe Press, 1968.

Kurland, P. B., ed. *Church and State: The Supreme Court and the First Amendment.* University of Chicago, 1975.

————. *Religion and the Law: Of Church and State and the Supreme Court*. Aldine, 1962.

Lanove, G. *Public Funds for Parochial Schools?* National Catholic Welfare Conference, USA, 1963.

Larson, M., and C. S. Lowell. *Praise the Lord for Tax Exemption*. Luce, 1969.

Laubach, J. H. *School Prayers: Congress, the Courts and the Public*. Public Affairs Press, 1969.

Lekachman, R., et al. *The Churches and the Public*. Center for the Study of Democratic Institutions, 1960.

Lenski, G. *The Religion Factor*. Doubleday, 1961.

Lo Bello, N. *The Vatican Empire*. Trident, 1969.

Loder, J. E. *Religion and the Public Schools*. Association Press, 1965.

Lowell, C. S. *The Great Church-State Fraud*. Luce, 1973.

Madden, W. *Religious Values and Secular Education*. Columbia University, 1950.

Malbin, M. J. *Religion and Politics: The Intentions of the Authors of the First Amendment*. American Enterprise Institute, 1978.

Manwaring, D. *Religion, Liberty and the State*. Bobbs-Merrill, 1971.

Manzullo, D. A. *Neither Sacred nor Profane: The Supreme Court and the Church*. Exposition Press, 1973.

Marty, M. E. *The New Shape of American Religion*. Harper & Row, 1958.

Mason, R. E. *Moral Values and Secular Education*. Columbia University, 1950.

Masters, N. A., R. H. Salisbury, and T. H. Eliot. *State Politics and the Public Schools*. Knopf, 1964.

McCarthy, M. M. *A Delicate Balance: Church, State, and the Schools*. Indiana University, 1984.

McCluskey, N. G. *Catholic Viewpoint on Education*. Hanover House, 1959.

McGaffney, E. McG., Jr. *Private Schools and the Public Good: Policy Alternatives for the Eighties*. University of Notre Dame, 1981.

McGill, R. *A Church, A School*. Abingdon Press, 1959.

McGrath, J. H., ed. *Church and State in American Law*. Bruce, 1962.

McMillan, R. C. *Religion in the Public Schools: An Introduction*. Mercer University, 1984.

Mechling, J., ed. *Church, State, and Public Policy: The New Shape of the Church-State Debate*. American Enterprise Institute, 1979.

Menendez, A. J. *Church-State Relations: An Annotated Bibliography*. Garland, 1976.

————. *Religion at the Polls*. Westminster Press, 1977.

Meranto, P. *The Politics of Federal Aid to Education in 1965: A Study in Political Innovation*. Syracuse University, 1967.

Michaelson, R. *Piety in the Public School*. Macmillan, 1970.

Miller, R. T., and R. B. Flowers. *Toward Benevolent Neutrality: Church, State, and the Supreme Court*. Markham, 1977.

Mitchell, B. *Law, Morality, and Religion in a Secular Society*. Oxford University, 1977.

Moehlman, C. *The Wall of Separation Between Church and State*. Beacon Press, 1951.

Morey, R. D. *An Act of Congress*. Norton, 1969.

Morgan, E. S., and Roger Williams. *The Church and the State*. Harcourt, Brace & World, 1967.

Morgan, R. E. *The Politics of Religious Conflict: Church and State in America*. 2d ed. University Press of America, 1980.

Muir, W. K. *Prayer in the Public Schools: Law and Attitude Change*. University of Chicago, 1967.

Nichols, R. F. *Religion and American Democracy*. Louisiana State University, 1959.

Northwestern University Law Review. *Constitutional Problems in Church-State Relations*. Da Capo Press, 1971.

Oaks, D. H., ed. *The Wall Between Church and State*. University of Chicago, 1963.

O'Brien, J. S. *The Supreme Court and the Religion-Education Controversy: A Tightrope to Entanglement*. Moore, 1974.

Odegaard, P. H. *Religion and Politics*. Oceana, 1960.

O'Hair, M. M. *Freedom Under Siege: The Impact of Organized Religion on Your Liberty and Your Pocketbook*. Tarcher, 1974.

O'Neill, J. M. *Catholicism and American Freedom*. Harper, 1952.

————. *Religion and Education Under the Constitution*. Harper, 1949.

Parsons, W. P. *The First Freedom: Considerations on Church and State in the United States*. McMullen, 1948.

Pfeffer, L. *Church, State and Freedom*. Rev. enl. ed. Beacon Press, 1967.

————. *Creeds in Competition*. Harper, 1959.

————. *God, Caesar, and Constitution: The Court as Referee of Church-State Confrontation*. Beacon Press, 1975.

Pike, J. A. *A Roman Catholic in the White House*. Doubleday, 1960.

Pines, B. Y. *Back to Basics*. Morrow, 1982.

Powell, T. *The School Bus Law: A Case Study in Education, Religion, and Politics*. Wesleyan University, 1960.

Pratt, J. W. *Religion, Politics, and Diversity: The Church-State Theme in New York History*. Cornell University, 1967.

Raab, E., ed. *Religious Conflict in America*. Doubleday (Anchor Books), 1964.

Rice, C. E. *The Supreme Court and Public Prayer: The Need for Restraint*. Fordham University, 1964.

Richter, E. J., and B. Dulce. *Religion and the Presidency*. Macmillan, 1962.

Robertson, D. B. *Should Churches Be Saved?* Westminster Press, 1969.

Robison, J. B. *The Case Against Parochaid*. American Civil Liberties Union, 1972.

Rock, J. *The Time Has Come*. Knopf, 1963.

St. John-Stevas, N. *Birth Control and Public Policy*. Center for the Study of Democratic Institutions, 1960.

Sanders, T. G. *Protestant Concepts of Church and State*. Holt, Rinehart and Winston, 1964.

Scalia, A. *Testimony on the Constitutionality of Tuition Tax Credits*. American Enterprise Institute, 1978.

Schultz, H. E. *Religious Education and the Public Schools*. University of California, 1955.

Shaver, E. L. *The Weekday Church School*. Pilgrim Press, 1956.

Shields, C. *Democracy and Catholicism in America*. McGraw-Hill, 1958.

Shupe, A., and W. A. Stacey, *Born Again Politics and the Moral Majority*. Mellen, 1982.

Silvert, K. H. *Churches and States: The Religious Institution and Modernization*. American University Field Staff, 1967.

Sizier, T. R., ed. *Religion and Public Education*. Houghton Mifflin, 1967.

Smith, E. A. *Church and State in Your Community*. Westminster Press, 1963.

————. *Religious Liberty in the United States: The Development of Church-State Thought Since the Revolutionary Era*. Fortress Press, 1972.

Sorauf, F. J. *The Wall of Separation: The Constitutional Politics of Church and State*. Princeton University, 1976.

Stallo, J. E., et al. *The Bible in the Public School*. Clarke, 1870.

Stedman, M. S., Jr. *Religion and Politics in America*. Harcourt, Brace & World, 1964.

Stokes, A. P. *Church and State in the United States*. 3 vols. Harper, 1950.

————, and L. Pfeffer. *Church and State in the United States*. Rev. ed. Harper & Row, 1964.

Sweet, W. W., ed. *Religion in Colonial America*. Scribner, 1942.

Swormley, J. M., Jr. *Religion, the State and the Schools*. Bobbs-Merrill (Pegasus), 1968.

Tarr, G. A. *Judicial Impact and State Supreme Courts: Establishment of Religion*. Heath, 1977.

Thayer, V. T. *The Attack upon the American Secular School*. Beacon Press, 1951.

————. *The Role of the School in American Society*. Dodd, Mead, 1966.

Tussman, J., ed. *The Supreme Court on Church and State*. Oxford University, 1962.

Umbret, L. *Render unto the People*. Abingdon Press, 1946.

Walter, E. A., ed. *Religion and the State University*. University of Michigan, 1958.

Ward, H. H. *Space-Age Sunday*. Macmillan, 1960.

Ward, L. R. *Federal Aid to Private Schools*. Newman, 1964.

———. *Religion in All the Schools*. Fides, 1960.

Weber, P. J., and D. A. Gilbert. *Private Churches and Public Money: Church-Government Fiscal Relations*. Greenwood Press, 1981.

Williams, R. *The Bloody Tenet of Persecution*. Hadden, 1848.

Wilson, J. F. *Church and State in American History*. Heath, 1965.

———. *Public Religion in American Culture*. Temple University, 1979.

Wolf, D. J. *Toward Consensus: Catholic-Protestant Interpretations of Church and State*. Doubleday, 1968.

Wood, J. E., Jr., ed. *Religion and Politics in the 1980's*. Baylor University, 1983.

———. *Religion, the State, and Education*. Baylor University, 1984.

World Council of Churches. *Church and State: Opening a New Ecumenical Discussion*. World Council of Churches, 1978.

Young, P. D. *God's Bullies: Power Politics and Religious Tyranny*. Holt, Rinehart and Winston, 1982.

Zabel, O. H. *God and Caesar in Nebraska: A Study of the Legal Relationship of Church and State, 1854–1954*. University of Nebraska, 1955.

XI. ACADEMIC FREEDOM AND RESPONSIBILITY

(See also VIII, Expression: Speech, Press, and Petition; XII, Morals, Obscenity, and Censorship.)

Alexander, K., and E. Solomon. *College and University Law*. Michie, 1972.

Baade, H. W., and R. O. Everett, eds. *Academic Freedom: The Scholar's Place in Modern Society*. Oceana, 1964.

Barth, A. *The Loyalty of Free Men*. New ed. Doubleday (Anchor Books), 1965.

Beale, H. K. *Are American Teachers Free?* Scribner, 1936.

Brubacher, K. *The Law and Higher Education*. Fairleigh Dickinson University, 1971.

Byse, C., and Joughin, L. *Tenure in American Higher Education*. Cornell University, 1959.

Caughey, J. W. *In Clear and Present Danger: The Critical State of Our Freedoms*. University of Chicago, 1960.

Chamberlain, J. *Freedom and Independence: The Hillsdale Story*. Hillsdale Press, 1979.

Chambers, M. M. *The Colleges and the Courts, 1946–1950: Judicial Decisions Regarding Higher Education in the U.S.* Columbia University, 1952.

———. *The Colleges and the Courts: The Developing Law of the Student and the College*. Interstate Press and Publishing, 1972.

Colton, D. L., and E. E. Graber. *Teacher Strikes and the Courts*. Lexington Books, 1982.

Countryman, V. *Un-American Activities in the State of Washington*. Cornell University, 1951.

Deese, J. *American Freedom and the Social Sciences*. Columbia University, 1975.

Douglas, W. O. *Freedom of the Mind*. Doubleday, 1964.

Earle, J., et al. *On Academic Freedom*. American Enterprise Institute, 1971.

Ehlers, H., and C. L. Gordon, eds. *Crucial Issues in Education*. Holt, 1959.

Fellman, D., ed. *The Supreme Court and Education*. Columbia University, 1960.

Finn, C. E., Jr. *Scholars, Dollars, and Bureaucrats*. Brookings Institutions, 1978.

Gardner, D. P. *The California Oath Controversy*. University of California, 1967.

Hofstadter, R., and W. P. Metzger. *The Development of Academic Freedom in the U.S.* Columbia University, 1955.

Holmes, G., ed. *Law and Discipline on Campus*. Institute of Continuing Legal Education, 1971.

Hook, S. *Academic Freedom and Academic Tenure*. Cowles, 1969.

———. *Heresy, Yes—Conspiracy, No!* Day, 1953.

————, P. Kurtz, and M. Todorovich, eds. *The University and the State.* Prometheus Books, 1979.

Hurlburd, D. *This Happened in Pasadena.* Macmillan, 1951.

Iversen, R. W. *The Communists and the Schools.* Harcourt, Brace, 1959.

Jones, H. M., ed. *Primer of Intellectual Freedom.* Harvard University, 1959.

Joughlin, L., ed. *Academic Freedom and Tenure: A Handbook for the AAUP.* University of Wisconsin, 1969.

Kahn, J. *The Threat to Academic Freedom.* Horizon Press, 1956.

Kemerer, F. R., and K. L. Deutsch. *Constitutional Rights and Student Life: Value Conflict in Law and Education.* West, 1979.

Kirk, R. *Academic Freedom: An Easy Definition.* Regnery, 1955.

Kruytbosch, C. E., and S. L. Messinger. *The State of the University: Authority and Change.* Sage Publication, 1970.

Ladd, E. C., Jr., and S. M. Lipset. *The Divided Academy: Professors and Politics.* Norton, 1976.

Lamont, C. *Freedom Is As Freedom Does: Civil Liberties Today.* Horizon Press, 1956.

Lester, R. A. *Antibias Regulation of Universities: Faculty Problems and Their Solutions.* McGraw-Hill, 1974.

Levine, H. *Political Issues Debated.* Prentice-Hall, 1982.

Lipset, S. M. *Student Politics.* Basic Books, 1967.

MacIver, R. M. *Academic Freedom in Our Time.* Columbia University, 1955.

Melby, E. O., and M. Puner. *Freedom and Public Education.* Praeger, 1953.

Metzger, W. P., ed. *The American Concept of Academic Freedom in Formation: A Collection of Essays and Reports.* Arno Press, 1977.

————, ed. *The Constitutional Status of Academic Tenure.* Arno Press, 1977.

————, ed. *Professors on Guard: The First AAUP Investigations.* Arno Press, 1977.

Metzger, W. P., and R. Hofstadter. *Academic Freedom in the United States.* Columbia University, 1955.

Metzger, W. P., et al. *Dimensions of Academic Freedom.* University of Illinois, 1968.

Miller, R. T., and R. B. Flowers. *Toward Benevolent Neutrality: Church, State, and the Supreme Court.* Baylor University, 1977.

Moos, M., and F. Roarke. *The Campus and the State.* Johns Hopkins University, 1959.

Morison, S. E. *Freedom in Contemporary Society.* Little, Brown, 1956.

Morris, A. *The Constitution and American Education.* West, 1974.

National Council of Teachers of English. *The Student's Right to Read.* National Council of Teachers of English, 1963.

Nelson, J., and G. Roberts, Jr. *The Censor and the Schools.* Little, Brown, 1963.

O'Hara, W., and J. Hill. *The Student/The College/The Law.* Teachers College, 1972.

Ratliff, R. C. *Constitutional Right of College Students: A Study in Case Law.* Scarecrow Press, 1972.

Reutter, E. E., Jr. *The School Administrator and Subversive Activities.* Columbia University, 1951.

Rose, A. M. *Libel and Academic Freedom.* University of Minnesota, 1968.

Rosenthal, A., ed. *Impurely Academic.* Transaction Books, 1979.

Steinberg, S. *The Academic Melting Pot.* Transaction Books, 1977.

Stewart, G. R. *The Year of the Oath: The Fight for Academic Freedom at the University of California.* Doubleday, 1950.

Summers, R. E., ed. *Freedom and Loyalty in Our Colleges.* Wilson, 1954.

Taylor, H. *On Education and Freedom.* Abelard-Schuman, 1954.

Van Doren, M. *Man's Right to Knowledge and the Free Use Thereof.* Columbia University, 1954.

Wallerstein, I., and P. Starr, eds. *The University Crisis Reader: Confrontation and Counterattack.* Random House (Vintage Books), 1971.

Walter, E. A., ed. *Religion and the State University.* University of Michigan, 1958.

Weber, P. J., and D. A. Gilbert. *Private Churches and Public Money: Church-Government Fiscal Relations.* Greenwood Press, 1979.

Whitfield, S. J. *Scott Nearing: Apostle of American Radicalism.* Columbia University, 1974.

Wilburn, J. R., ed. *Freedom, Order, and the University.* Pepperdine University, 1982.

Wilke, A. S., ed. *The Hidden Professorate: Credentialism, Professionalism, and the Tenure Crisis.* Greenwood Press, 1979.

Williams, M. F., ed. *Government in the Classroom.* Praeger, 1979.

Williamson, E. G., and J. L. Cowan. *The American Student's Freedom of Expression: A Research Appraisal.* University of Minnesota, 1966.

Wise, A. E. *Legislated Learning: The Bureaucratization of the American Classroom.* University of California, 1979.

Witmer, L., and Whitfield, S. *The Nearing Case.* Da Capo Press, 1974.

XII. MORALS, OBSCENITY AND CENSORSHIP

(See also II.D., Sex (Gender); IV.F., . . . Privacy; VIII, Expression: Speech, Press, and Petititon; X, Religion; XI, Academic Freedom and Responsibility.)

Barnett, W. *Sexual Freedom and the Constitution.* University of New Mexico, 1973.

Beman, L. *Selected Articles on Censorship of the Theater and Moving Pictures.* Wilson, 1961.

Blanshard, P. *The Right to Read: The Battle Against Censorship.* Beacon Press, 1955.

Boyer, P. S. *Purity in Print: The Nice Society's Movement and Book Censorship in America.* Scribner, 1968.

Brindze, R. *Not to Be Broadcast: The Truth About the Radio.* Da Capo Press, 1974.

Broun, H., and M. Leech. *Anthony Comstock, Roundsman of the Lord.* Boni, 1927.

Brucker, H. *Freedom of Information.* Macmillan, 1945.

Callahan, D. *Abortion: Law, Choice and Morality.* University of Michigan, 1966.

Carmen, I. H. *Movies, Censorship, and the Law.* University of Michigan, 1966.

Chafee, Z. *Government and Mass Communications.* University of Chicago, 1947.

Chandos, J., ed. *To Deprave and Corrupt.* Associated Press, 1963.

Clor, H. M., ed. *Censorship and Freedom of Expression: Essays on Obscenity and Law.* Rand McNally, 1971.

———. *Obscenity and Public Morality: Censorship in a Liberal Society.* University of Chicago, 1969.

Cogley, J. *Report on Blacklisting.* 2 vols. Fund for the Republic., 1956.

Commission on Freedom of the Press. *Mass Communication: A Report from the Commission of Freedom of the Press.* University of Chicago, 1947.

———. *People Speaking to People: A Report on International Mass Communication.* University of Chicago, 1948.

Craig, A. *The Banned Books of England and Other Countries.* Allen & Unwin, 1962.

———. *Suppressed Books: A History of the Conception of Literary Obscenity.* World, 1963.

Crowther, B. *Movies and Censorship.* Public Affairs Pamphlets, 1965.

Daniels, W. M., ed. *The Censorship of Books.* H. W. Wilson, 1954.

Davis, M. S. *Smut: Erotic Reality/Obscene Ideology.* University of Chicago, 1983.

De Grazia, E., and R. K. Newan. *Banned Films: Movies, Censors, and the First Amendment.* Bowker, 1983.

Dennett, M. W. *Birth Control Laws: Shall We Keep Them, Change Them, or Abolish Them?* Hitchcock, 1926.

Devlin, Sir P. *The Enforcement of Morals.* Oxford University, 1968.

Ernst, M. L., and A. Lindley. *The Censor Marches On.* Doubleday, Doran, 1940; rpt. Da Capo Press, 1971.

Ernst, M. L., and U. Schwartz. *Censorship: The Search for the Obscene.* Macmillan, 1964.

Ernst, M. L., and W. Seagle. *To The Pure: A Study of Obscenity and the Censor.* Viking Press, 1928.

Fellman, D. *The Censorship of Books.* Hauser, 1957.

Fiske, M. *Book Selection and Censorship.* University of California, 1959.

Ford, J. *Criminal Obscenity: A Plea for Its Suppression.* Revell, 1926.

Gagnon, J. H., ed. *The Sexual Scene.* 2d ed. Transaction Books, 1974.

Gardiner, R. C. *Catholic Viewpoints on Censorship.* Hanover House, 1957.

Gerber, A. B. *Sex, Pornography, and Justice.* Stuart, 1965.

Goldstein, M. J., et al. *Pornography and Sexual Deviance.* University of California, 1974.

Goode, E., and R. R. Troiden. *Sexual Deviance and Sexual Deviants.* Morrow, 1974.

Haight, A. L. *Banned Books.* Bowker, 1956.

Haney, R. W. *Comstockery in America: Patterns of Censorship and Control.* Beacon Press, 1960; rpt. Da Capo Press, 1974.

Hart, H. H., ed. *Censorship: For and Against.* Harvard University, 1971.

Hefley, J. *Textbooks on Trial.* Wheaton, 1976.

Hewitt, C. R. *Does Pornography Matter?* Routledge & Kegan Paul, 1961.

Hughes, D. A. *Perspectives on Pornography.* St. Martin's Press, 1970.

Hughes, G. *The Conscience of the Courts: Laws and Morals in American Life.* Doubleday, 1975.

Hutchinson, E. R. *Tropic of Cancer on Trial.* Grove Press, 1968.

Hyde, H. M. *A History of Pornography.* Farrar, Straus & Giroux, 1965.

Inglis, R. A. *Freedom of the Movies: A Report on Self-Regulation.* University of Chicago, 1947; rpt. Da Capo Press, 1974.

Jenkinson, E. *Censors in the Classroom.* Southern Illinois University, 1979.

Kauper, P. G. *Civil Liberties and the Constitution.* University of Michigan, 1962.

Kerr, W. *Criticism and Censorship.* Bruce, 1954.

Kilpatrick, J. J. *The Smut Peddlers.* Doubleday, 1960.

Kinsey, A. C., W. Pomeroy, and T. Martin. *Sexual Behavior in the Human Female.* Saunders, 1953.

————. *Sexual Behavior in the Human Male.* Saunders, 1948.

Knutson, D. C., ed. *Homosexuality and the Law.* Haworth Press, 1980.

Kronhause, E., and P. Kronhause. *Pornography and the Law.* Rev. ed. Ballantine Books, 1965.

Kuh, R. H. *Foolish Figleaves? Pornography in and out of Court.* Macmillan, 1967.

Kyle-Keith, R. *The High Price of Pornography.* Public Affairs Press, 1961.

Lewis, F. F. *Literature, Obscenity, and Law.* Southern Illinois University, 1976.

Lindesmith, A. R. *The Addict and the Law.* Indiana University, 1965.

Lockhart, W. B., chm. *The Report of the Commission of Obscenity and Pornography.* Government Printing Office, 1970.

MacMillan, K. *Censorship and Public Morality.* Lexington Books, 1983.

McCormick, J., and M. Macinnes, eds. *Versions of Censorship.* Doubleday, 1962.

McKeown, R., R. D. Merton, and W. Gellhorn. *The Freedom to Read: Perspective and Program.* Bowker, 1957.

Marcuse, L. *Obscene.* MacGibbon & Key, 1965.

Meiklejohn, D. *Freedom and the Public: Public and Private Morality in America.* Syracuse University, 1965.

Mock, J. R. *Censorship in 1917.* Princeton University, 1941; rpt. Da Capo Press, 1972.

Mueller, G. *Legal Regulation of Sexual Conduct.* Oceana, 1960.

Mumford, H., ed. *Primer of Intellectual Freedom.* Harvard University, 1949.

Murphy, The Rev. T. J. *Censorship: Government and Obscenity.* Helicon, 1963.

Nelson, J., and G. Roberts, Jr. *The Censor and the Schools.* Little, Brown, 1963.

Noonan, J. T. *The Morality of Abortion.* Harvard University, 1970.

Okudaira, Y. *Political Censorship in Japan: 1931–1945.* Institute of Legal Research, University of Pennsylvania, 1962.

Paul, J. C. N., and M. L. Schwartz. *Federal Censorship: Obscenity in the Mail.* Free Press, 1961.

Pilpel, H. F. *Obscenity and the Constitution.* Bowker, 1973.

Pivar, D. J. *Purity Crusade: Sexual Morality and Social Control.* Greenwood Press, 1973.

Polsky, N. *Hustlers, Beats and Others.* Aldine, 1967.

Putnam, G. H. *The Censorship of the Church of Rome.* Putnam, 1906.

Randall, R. S. *Censorship of the Movies: Social and Political Control of a Mass Medium.* University of Wisconsin, 1968.

Reitman, B. *Freedom on Trial: The Incredible Trial of Ralph Ginzburg.* Public Expression Council, 1966.

Rembar, C., *The End of Obscenity: The Trials of "Lady Chatterly," "Tropic of Cancer," and "Fanny Hill."* Random House, 1968.

Resnik, H. L. P., and M. E. Wolfgang, eds. *Sexual Behavior: Social, Clinical, and Legal Aspects.* Little, Brown, 1972.

Rist, R. C. *The Pornography Controversy.* Transaction Books, 1975.

Rolph, C. H., ed. *Does Pornography Matter?* Routledge & Kegan Paul, 1961.

————. *The Trial of Lady Chatterly.* Penguin Books, 1961.

St. John-Stevas, N. *Obscenity and the Law.* Secker & Warburg, 1956; rpt. Da Capo Press, 1974.

Sanger, M. *An Autobiography.* Norton, 1938.

Schroeder, T. *"Obscene" Literature and Constitutional Law.* Da Capo Press, 1972.

Schumach, M. *The Face on the Cutting Room Floor: The Story of Movie and Television Censorship.* Morrow, 1964; rpt. Da Capo, 1975.

Sharp, D. B., ed. *Commentaries on Obscenity.* Scarecrow Press, 1970.

Smead, E. E. *Freedom of Speech by Radio and Television.* Public Affairs Press, 1958.

Spring, S. *Risks and Rights in Publishing, Television, Radio, Motion Pictures, Advertising and the Theatre.* Allen & Unwin, 1952.

Stumpf, S. E. *Morality and the Law.* Vanderbilt University, 1968.

Summers, R. E. *Wartime Censorship of Press and Radio.* Wilson, 1942.

Sunderland, L. V. *Obscenity: The Court, the Congress, and the President's Commission.* American Enterprise Institute, 1974.

Thomas, J. L. *Lotteries, Frauds and Obscenity in the Mails.* Stephens, 1900.

Vidal, G. *The City and the Pillar.* Rev. ed. Dutton, 1965.

Wertham, F. *Seduction of the Innocent.* Rinehart, 1954.

Woods, L. B. *A Decade of Censorship.* Scarecrow Press, 1979.

XIII. IMMIGRATION, CITIZENSHIP, AND ALIENAGE

Alexander, N. *The Rights of Aliens Under the Federal Constitution.* Capitol, 1931.

Averbach, F. L. *Immigration Laws of the United States.* Bobbs-Merrill, 1961.

————. *The Immigration and Nationality Act.* Common Council for American Unity, 1952.

Bennett, M. T. *American Immigration Policies.* Public Affairs Press, 1964.

Bernard, W. S., ed. *American Immigration Policies.* Public Affairs Press, 1964.

Bouscaren, A. T. *The Security Aspects of Immigration Work.* Marquette University, 1959.

Bruce, J. C. *The Irony of Our Immigration Policy.* Random House, 1954.

Cable, J. L. *Loss of Citizenship: Denaturalization—The Alien in Wartime.* National Law Book, 1943.

Clark, J. P. *The Deportation of Aliens from the United States to Europe.* Columbia University, 1931.

Divine, R. A. *American Immigration Policy, 1924–1952.* Yale University, 1957.

Gettys, C. L. *The Law of Citizenship in the United States.* University of Chicago, 1934.

Glazer, N., ed. *Clamor at the Gates: The New American Immigration.* ICS Press, 1985.

Gordon, C., and H. Rosenfield. *Immigration Law and Procedure.* Banks, 1959.

Handlin, O. *Immigration as a Factor in American History.* Prentice-Hall, 1959.

————. *The Uprooted.* Little, Brown, 1951.

Hansen, M. L. *The Immigrant in American History.* Harvard University, 1940.

Hicks, J. D. *The American Nation.* Houghton Mifflin, 1959.

Higham, J. *Strangers in the Land: Patterns of American Nativism, 1860–1929*. Rutgers University, 1955.

Hull, E. *Without Justice for All: The Constitutional Rights of Aliens*. Greenwood Press, 1985.

Hutchinson, E. P. *Immigrants and Their Children, 1850–1950*. Wiley, 1956.

Jones, M. A. *American Immigration*. University of Chicago, 1960.

Kansas, S. *U.S. Immigration, Exclusion, Deportation, and Citizenship of the United States of America*. 2d ed. Bender, 1940.

Kent, D. P. *The Refugee Intellectual: The Americanization of the Immigrants of 1933–1941*. Columbia University, 1953.

Knauff, E. R. *The Ellen Knauff Story*. Norton, 1952; rpt. Da Capo Press, 1974.

Konvitz, M. R. *The Alien and Asiatics in American Law*. Cornell University, 1946.

———. *Civil Rights in Immigration*. Cornell University, 1953.

Kraus, M. *Immigration: The American Maxims from Pilgrims to Modern Refugees*. Van Nostrand, 1966.

Kritz, M. M., ed. *United States Immigration and Refugee Policy*. Lexington Books, 1983.

Lowenstein, E., ed. *The Alien and the Immigration Law*. Oceana, 1958.

Mutharika, A. P. *The Alien Under American Law*. Oceana, 1979.

Panunzio, C. M. *The Deportation Cases of 1919–1920*. Da Capo Press, 1970.

Post, L. F. *The Deportation Delirium of Nineteen-Twenty*. Kerr, 1923.

President's Commission of Immigration and Naturalization. *Whom We Shall Welcome*. Government Printing Office. 1953.

Rischin, M., ed. *Immigration and the American Tradition*. Bobbs-Merrill, 1976.

Schrieke, B. *Alien Americans*. Viking Press, 1936.

Schwartz, A. P. *The Open Society*. Clarion Books, 1969.

Sellen, H., ed. *Practice and Procedure Under the Immigration and Nationality Act*. New York University, 1954.

Solomon, B. ,. *Ancestors and Immigrants: A Changing New England Tradition*. Harvard University, 1956.

Silving, H. *Immigration and the United States*. Oceana, 1949.

Taiang, I. M. *The Question of Expatriation in America Prior to 1907*. Johns Hopkins University, 1942.

Tyler, P. *Immigration and the United States*. H. W. Wilson, 1956.

Van Vleck, W. C. *The Administrative Control of Aliens: A Study in Administrative Law and Procedure*. Commonwealth Fund, 1932

.Ziegler, B. M., ed. *Immigration: An American Dilemma*. Heath, 1953.

XIV. INTERNAL SECURITY: LOYALTY, SECURITY, THOUGHT CONTROL, CLASSIFIED DATA

A. GENERAL

Association of the Bar of the City of New York. *Equal Justice for the Accused*. Dodd, Mead, 1959.

———. *Report of the Special Committee on the Federal Loyalty-Security Program*. Da Capo Press, 1974.

Bates, E. S. *This Land of Liberty*. Da Capo Press, 1974.

Biddle, F. *The Fear of Freedom*. Doubleday, 1951.

Bontecou, E., ed. *The Federal Loyalty-Security Program*. Cornell University, 1953.

Brookings Institution. *Suggested Standards for Determining Un-American Activities*. Brookings Institution, 1945.

Chafee, Z. *Watchman, What of the Night*. Harvard University, 1942.

Chapin, B. *The American Law of Treason: Revolutionary and Early National Origin*. University of Washington, 1964.

Chase, H. W. *Security and Liberty: The Problem of Native Communists, 1947–1955*. Doubleday, 1955.

Coben, A. A. *Mitchell Palmer: Politician*. Columbia University, 1963.

Collins, F. L. *The F.B.I. in Peace and War*. Ace Books, 1943.

Commager, H. S. *Freedom, Loyalty, Dissent*. Oxford University, 1954.

Cook, T. I. *Democratic Rights Versus Communist Activity*. Doubleday, 1954.

Curti, M. *The Roots of American Loyalty*. Columbia University, 1946.

Davis, D. B. *The Fear of Conspiracy*. Cornell University, 1972.

Davis, J. *Character Assassination*. Philosophical Library, 1951.

Dowell, S. F. *A History of Criminal Syndicalism Legislation in the United States*. Johns Hopkins University, 1939.

Draper, T. *The Roots of American Communism*. Viking Press, 1957.

Gellhorn, W. *Security, Loyalty, and Science*. Cornell University, 1950.

Ginzberg, B. *Rededication to Freedom*. Simon and Schuster, 1959.

Goldbloom, M. *American Security and Freedom*. American Jewish Committee, 1955.

Grodzins, M. *The Loyal and the Disloyal: Social Boundaries of Patriotism and Treason*. University of Chicago, 1956.

Guttman, A., and B. M. Ziegler. *Communism, the Courts, and the Constitution*. Heath, 1964.

Harper, A. D. *The Politics of Loyalty: The White House and the Communist Issue, 1946–1952*. Greenwood Press, 1970.

Josephs, E. *The Character Assassins*. Reportorial Press, 1966.

Laswell, H. D. *National Security and Individual Freedom*. McGraw-Hill, 1950.

Miller, J. C. *Crisis in Freedom*. Little, Brown, 1951.

Mitchell, D. *1919: Red Mirage*. Macmillan, 1970.

Murphy, the Rev. T. J. *Censorship: Government and Obscenity*. Helicon, 1963.

Murray, R. K. *Red Scare: A Study in National Hysteria, 1919–1920*. University of Minnesota, 1955.

Navasky, V. S. *Naming Names*, Viking Press, 1980.

Peters, C., and T. Branch, eds. *Blowing the Whistle*. Praeger, 1977.

Peltason, J. *Constitutional Liberty and Seditious Activity*. Catt Memorial Fund, 1954.

Rankin, R. S., and W. R. Dallmayr. *Freedom and Emerging Powers in the Cold War*. Appleton-Century-Crofts, 1963.

Rourke, R. E. *Secrecy and Publicity: Dilemmas of Democracy*. Johns Hopkins University, 1961.

Rovere, R. H., and G. Brown, eds. *Loyalty and Security in a Democratic State*. Arno Press, 1977.

Schaar, J. H. *Loyalty to America: The Background and Consequences*. University of California at Los Angeles, 1957.

Schafer, S. *The Political Criminal: The Problems of Morality and Crime*. Free Press, 1974.

Schwartz, A. P. *The Open Society*. Simon and Schuster, 1968.

Seidman, J. *Communism in the United States: A Bibliography*. Cornell University, 1967.

Shapiro, M. *The Pentagon Papers and the Courts*. Chandler, 1973.

Shils, E. A. *The Torment of Secrecy: American Security Policies*. Free Press, 1956.

Summers, R. E. *Federal Information Controls in Peacetime*. H. W. Wilson, 1949.

Thayer, G. *The Farther Shores of Politics*. Simon and Schuster, 1952.

Wahlke, J. C. *Loyalty in a Democratic State*. Heath, 1952.

Weyl, N. *The Battle Against Disloyalty*. Crowell, 1951.

———. *Treason: The Story of Disloyalty and Betrayal in American History*. Public Affairs Press, 1950.

Wilson, H. H., and H. Glickman. *The Problem of Internal Security in Great Britain, 1948–1953*. Doubleday, 1954.

B. FEDERAL AND STATE STATUTES

Belknap, M. R. *Cold War Political Justice: The Smith Act, the Communist Party, and American Civil Liberties*. Greenwood Press, 1977.

Dowell, E. F. *A History of Criminal Syndicalism Legislation in the United States*. Johns Hopkins University, 1939; rpt. Da Capo Press, 1969.

Gellhorn, W., ed. *The States and the Subversion.* Cornell University, 1952.

Preston, W., Jr. *Aliens and Dissenters: Federal Suppression of Radicals, 1903–1933.* Harvard University, 1963.

Weinstein, S., and H. S. Brown, Jr. *Personnel Security Programs of the Federal Government.* Fund for the Republic, 1954.

C. GOVERNMENT EMPLOYMENT

Andrews, B., and P. Andrews. *A Tragedy of History: A Journalist's Confidential Role in the Hiss-Chambers Case.* McKay, 1963.

Brown, R. S., Jr. *Loyalty and Security: Employment Tests in the United States.* Yale University, 1958.

Caute, D. *The Great Fear: The Anti-Communist Purge Under Truman and Eisenhower.* Simon and Schuster, 1978.

Chambers, W. *Witness.* Random House, 1956.

Hiss, A. *In the Court of Public Opinion.* Knopf, 1957.

Hook, S. *The Paradoxes of Freedom.* University of California, 1962.

Lamont, C. *Freedom Is As Freedom Does: Civil Liberties Today.* Horizon Press, 1956.

Westin, A. *The Constitution and Loyalty Programs.* Catt Memorial Fund, 1954.

Yarmolinsky, A. *Case Studies in Personnel Security.* Bureau of National Affairs, 1955.

D. LEGISLATIVE AND RELATED INVESTIGATIONS

(General, McCarthyism, House Un-American Activities Committee, Alger Hiss, Executive Agencies.)

Alsop, J. W., Jr., and S. Alsop. *We Accuse: The Story of American Justice in the Case of Robert Oppenheimer.* Simon and Schuster, 1954.

Anderson, J., and R. W. May. *McCarthy: The Man, the Senator, the "Ism."* Beacon Press, 1952.

Andrews, B., and P. Andrews. *A Tragedy of History: A Journalist's Confidential Role in the Hiss-Chambers Case.* McKay, 1962.

———. *Washington Witch Hunt.* Random House, 1948.

Barrett, E. L., Jr. *The Tenney Committee: Legislative Investigation of Subversive Activities in California.* Cornell University, 1951.

Barth, A. *Government by Investigation.* Viking Press, 1955.

———. *The Loyalty of Free Men.* Rev. ed. Shoe String Press (Archon Books), 1965.

———. *When Congress Investigates Loyalty and Security in a Democracy.* Public Affairs Committee, 1956.

Bayley, E. R. *Joe McCarthy and the Press.* University of Wisconsin, 1981.

Beck, C. *Contempt of Congress: A Study of the Prosecutions Initiated by the Committee on Un-American Activities, 1945–1957.* Hauser, 1959.

Belfrage, C. *The American Inquisition, 1945–1960.* Bobbs-Merrill, 1973.

Bessie, A. *Inquisition in Eden.* Macmillan, 1965.

Buckley, W. F., Jr., and editors of the *National Review. The Committee and Its Critics.* Putnam, 1962.

———. and L. B. Bozell, *McCarthy and His Enemies.* Regnery, 1953.

Carr, R. K. *The Constitution and Congressional Investigation Committees.* Cornell University, 1954.

———. *The House Committee on Un-American Activities, 1945–1950.* Cornell University, 1952.

Chamberlain, L. H. *Loyalty and Legislative Action: A Survey of Activity by the New York State Legislature, 1919–1949.* Cornell University, 1951.

Chambers, W. *Witness.* Random House, 1956.

Cohn, R. *McCarthy.* New American Library, 1968.

Cook, F. J. *The Nightmare Decade: The Life and Times of Senator Joe McCarthy.* Random House, 1971.

———. *The Unfinished Story of Alger Hiss.* Morrow, 1958.

Cooke, A. *A Generation of Trial: U.S.A. v. Alger Hiss.* Knopf, 1950.

Cornell University Study. *The Tenney Committee: Study of Legislative Investigations of Subversive Activities in California.* Cornell University, 1962.

Countryman, V. *Un-American Activities in the State of Washington.* Cornell University, 1951.

Crosby, D. F. *God, Church, and Flag: Senator Joseph R. McCarthy and the Catholic Church, 1950–1957.* University of North Carolina, 1978.

De Antonio, E., and D. Talbot. *Point of Order: Documentary of the Army-McCarthy Hearings.* Norton, 1964.

Dimock, M. E. *Congressional Investigating Committees.* Johns Hopkins University, 1929.

Donner, F. J. *The Un-Americans.* Ballantine Books, 1961.

Eberling, E. J. *Congressional Investigations,* Columbia University, 1928.

Freeland, R. M. *The Truman Doctrine and the Origins of McCarthyism.* Knopf, 1971.

Fried, R. M. *Men Against McCarthy.* Columbia University, 1976.

Gellerman, W. *Martin Dies.* John Day, 1944.

Gillmor, D. *Fear the Accusor.* Abelard-Schuman, 1954.

Goldfarb, R. L. *The Contempt Power.* Columbia University, 1963.

Goodman, W. *The Committee: The Extraordinary Career of the House Committee on Un-American Activities.* Farrar, Straus & Giroux, 1968.

Gore, L. *Joe Must Go.* Messner, 1954.

Griffith, R. *The Politics of Fear: Joseph McCarthy and the Senate.* University of Kentucky, 1971.

Hamilton, J. *The Power to Probe: A Study of Congressional Investigations.* Random House, 1876.

Hellman, L. *Scoundrel Time.* Little, Brown, 1976.

Hiss, A. *In the Court of Public Opinion.* Knopf, 1957.

Hook, S. *Political Power and Personal Freedom: Critical Studies in Democracy, Communism, and Civil Rights.* Harper (Criterion), 1959.

Jaffe, J. F. *Crusade Against Radicalism: New York During the Red Scare, 1914–1924.* Kennikat Press, 1972.

Johnson, J. E. *Investigation Powers of Congress.* H. W. Wilson, 1951.

Jowitt, The Earl of. *The Strange Case of Alger Hiss.* Doubleday, 1953.

Kallen, H. M. *The Lamont Case: History of a Congressional Investigation.* Horizon Press, 1957.

Kemper, D. J. *Decade of Fear.* University of Missouri, 1965.

Lamb, E. *Trial by Battle.* Center for the Study of Democratic Institutions, 1964.

Lamont, C. *Freedom Is As Freedom Does: Civil Liberties Today.* Horizon Press, 1956.

Lattimore, O. *Ordeal by Slander.* Little, Brown, 1950.

McGeary, M. N. *The Development of Congressional Investigative Power.* Columbia University, 1940.

McWilliams, C. *Witch Hunt: The Revival of Heresy.* Little, Brown, 1950.

Matusow, H. *False Witness.* Cameron & Kahn, 1955.

Merson, M. *The Private Diary of a Public Servant.* Macmillan, 1955.

Navasky, V. S. *Naming Names.* Penguin Books, 1981.

Nelson, H. L. *Libel in News of Congressional Investigating Committees.* University of Minnesota, 1961.

Ogden, A. R. *The Dies Committee.* 2d ed. Catholic University, 1946.

Oshinsky, D. M. *A Conspiracy So Immense: The World of Joe McCarthy.* Free Press, 1983.

———. *Senator Joseph McCarthy and the American Labor Movement.* University of Missouri, 1975.

Oxnam, G. B. *I Protest: My Experience with the House Committee on Un-American Activities.* Harper, 1954.

Packer, H. L. *Ex-Communist Witnesses: Four Studies in Fact-Finding.* Stanford University, 1962.

Potter, C. E. *Days of Shame.* Coward-McCann, 1965.

Reeves, T. C. *The Life and Times of Joe McCarthy: A Biography.* Stein & Day, 1982.

Rogin, M. P. *The Intellectuals and McCarthy: The Radical Specter.* MIT, 1969.

Rorty, J., and M. Decter. *McCarthy and the Communists.* Beacon Press, 1954.

Rovere, R. *Senator Joe McCarthy.* Harcourt, Brace, 1959.

Schlesinger, A. M., Jr., and R. Bruns, eds. *Congress Investigates, 1792–1974.* Bowker, 1976.

Schrag, P. *Test of Loyalty: Daniel Ellsberg and the Rituals of Secret Government.* Simon and Schuster, 1972.

Seldes, G. *Witch Hunt.* Modern Age Books, 1940.

Sommerville, J. *The Communist Trials and the American Tradition: Expert Testimony on Force and Violence.* Cameron & Kahn, 1956.

Straight, M. *Trial by Television: The Army-McCarthy Hearings.* Beacon Press, 1954.

Tackwood, L. E., et al. *The Glass House Tapes.* Avon Books, 1974.

Taylor, T. *Grand Inquest: The Story of Congressional Investigations.* Simon and Schuster, 1955.

Thomas, L. *When Even Angels Wept: The Senator Joseph McCarthy Affair, A Story Without a Hero.* Morrow, 1973.

Thomas, N. *The Test of Freedom.* Norton, 1954.

Uphaux, W. *Commitment.* McGraw-Hill, 1964.

Warren, F. A. *Liberals and Communism: The "Red Decade" Revisited.* Indiana University, 1966.

Watkins, A. V. *Enough Rope.* University of Utah, 1970.

Weinstein, A. *Perjury: The Hiss-Chambers Case.* Knopf, 1978.

Wittenberg, P. *The Lamont Case: History of a Congressional Investigation.* Horizon Press, 1957.

E. THE COMMUNISTS

Almond, G. A. *The Appeals of Communism.* Princeton University, 1954.

Belknap, M. R. *Cold War Political Justice: The Smith Act, the Communist Party, and American Civil Liberties.* Greenwood Press, 1977.

Blanshard, P. *Communism, Democracy, and Catholic Power.* Beacon Press, 1951.

Bochenski, J. M., and G. Niemeyer. *Handbook on Communism.* Praeger, 1963.

Decter, M., ed. *The Profile of Communism: A Fact-by-Fact Primer.* Collier, 1962.

Dennis, E. *Ideas They Cannot Jail.* International Publishers, 1950.

Draper, T. *The Roots of American Communism.* Viking Press, 1957.

Eberling, E. J. *Congressional Investigations.* Columbia University, 1928.

Ernst, M. L., and D. Loth. *Report on the American Communist.* Holt, 1952.

Fund for the Republic. *Bibliography on the Communist Problem in the United States.* Fund for the Republic, 1955.

Gates, J. *The Story of an American Communist.* Nelson, 1958.

Guttmann, A., and B. Ziegler, eds. *Communism, the Courts, and the Constitution.* Heath, 1964.

Hoover, J. E. *Masters of Deceit.* Holt, 1958.

———. *A Study of Communism.* Holt, Rinehart and Winston, 1962.

Howe, I., and L. Coser. *The American Communist Party: A Critical History, 1919–1960.* Rev. ed. Praeger, 1962.

Hunit, R. N. G., ed. *Books on Communism.* Ampersand, 1959.

Iversen, R. W. *The Communists and the Schools.* Harcourt, Brace, 1959.

Johnson, J. E. *Should the Communist Party Be Outlawed?* Wilson, 1949.

Latham, E. *The Communist Controversy in Washington: From the New Deal to McCarthy.* Harvard University, 1966.

Miller, W. J., H. L. Roberts, and M. D. Shulman. *The Meaning of Communism.* Simon and Schuster, 1963.

Monnerot, J. *Sociology and Psychology of Communism.* Beacon Press, 1953.

Murray, R. K. *Red Scare.* McGraw-Hill, 1955.

Overstreet, H., and B. Overstreet. *What We Must Know About Communism.* Norton, 1958.

Palmer, E. E., ed. *The Communist Problems in America.* Crowell, 1951.

Record, W. *Race and Radicalism: The NAACP and the Communist Party in Conflict.* Cornell University, 1964.

Roy, R. L. *Communism and the Churches.* Harcourt, Brace, 1960.

Shannon, D. A. *The Decline of American Communism: A History of the Communist Party of the United States Since 1945.* Harcourt, Brace, 1959.

Sutherland, A. E. *Two Reference Volumes on Communism in the United States.* Harvard University, 1956.

Wechsler, J. A. *The Age of Suspicion.* Random House, 1953.

F. THE RIGHT WING

Alexander, C. C. *The Ku Klux Klan in the Southwest.* University of Kentucky, 1965.

Anti-Defamation League of B'Nai B'rith. *Extremism on the Right: A Handbook.* Anti-Defamation League, 1984.

Bell, D., ed. *The Radical Right.* Doubleday, 1963.

Bell, L. J. *In Hitler's Shadow: The Anatomy of American Nazism.* Kennikat Press, 1973.

Broyles, J. A. *The John Birch Society: Anatomy of a Protest.* Beacon Press, 1966.

Cain, E. *They'd Rather Be Right.* Macmillan, 1963.

Chalmer, D. M. *Hooded Americanism: The First Century of the Ku Klux Klan.* Doubleday, 1965.

Clabaugh, G. K. *Thunder on the Right: The Protestant Fundamentalists.* Nelson-Hall, 1974.

Crawford, A. *Thunder on the Right: The "New Right" and the Politics of Resentment.* Pantheon Books, 1979.

Diamond, S. A. *The Nazi Movement in the United States, 1924-1941.* Cornell University, 1974.

Ellsworth, R. E., and S. M. Harris. *American Right Wing.* University of Illinois, 1960.

Epstein, B. R., and A. Forster. *The Radical Right: Report on the John Birch Society and Its Allies.* Random House, 1967.

Ericson, E. L. *American Freedom and the Radical Right.* Ungar, 1982.

Fackre, G. *The Religious Right and the Christian Faith.* Eerdmans, 1982.

Forster, A., and B. R. Epstein. *Danger on the Right.* Random House, 1964.

Hapgood, N., ed. *Professional Patriots.* Boni, 1927.

Hill, S. S., and D. E. Owen. *The New Religious Political Right in America.* Abingdon Press, 1982.

Hofstadter, R. *The Paranoid Style: American Politics and Other Essays.* Knopf, 1965.

Jackson, K. T. *The Ku Klux Klan in the City.* Oxford University, 1967.

Janson, D., and B. Eisman. *The Far Right.* McGraw-Hill, 1963.

Lindbergh, C. A. *The Wartime Journals of Charles A. Lindbergh.* Harcourt Brace Jovanovich, 1970.

Lipset, S. M., and E. Raab. *The Politics of Unreason: Right-Wing Extremism in America, 1790-1977.* Rev. ed. University of Chicago, 1978.

Lowe, D. *KKK: The Invisible Empire.* Norton, 1967.

McEvoy, J., III. *Radicals or Conservatives: The Contemporary American Right.* Rand McNally, 1971.

McNall, S. G. *Career of a Radical Rightist.* Kennikat Press, 1973.

Maguire, D. C. *The New Subversives: Anti-Americanism of the Religious Right.* Crossroads Press, 1982.

New York Times, The, eds. *The Right Wing Individualist Tradition in America*. Arno Press, 1971.

Overstreet, H., and B. Overstreet. *The Strange Tactics of Extremism*. Norton, 1964.

Phillips, K. P. *Post-Conservative America*. Random House, 1982.

Randel, W. P. *The Ku Klux Klan: A Century of Infamy*. Chilton, 1965.

Redekopf, H. *The American Far Right: A Case Study of Billy James Hargis and Christian Crusade*. Eerdmans, 1968.

Rice, A. S. *The KKK in American Politics*. Public Affairs Press, 1962.

Rogger, H., and E. Weber. *The European Right: A Historical Profile*. University of California, 1966.

Rosenstone, R. A., ed. *Protest from the Right*. Glencoe, 1968.

Roy, R. L. *Apostles of Discord*. Beacon, 1953.

Schoenberger, R. A., ed. *The American Right Wing: Readings in Political Behavior*. Holt, Rinehart and Winston, 1969.

Sheinberg, M., and A. Kraditor. *Peddlers of Fear*. Public Affairs Press, 1966.

Sherwin, M. *The Extremists*. St. Martin's Press, 1953.

Steiner, G. *The Roots of the Right*. Harper & Row, 1971.

Thayer, G. *The Farther Shores of Politics*. Simon and Schuster, 1968.

Turner, W. W. *Power on the Right*. Ramparts Press, 1971.

Vetter, H. F. *Speak Out Against the New Right*. Beacon Press, 1982.

Walker, B. R. *The Christian Fright Peddlers*. Doubleday, 1964.

Welch, R. *Blue Book of the John Birch Society*. John Birch Society, 1958.

XV. FAMOUS CASES INVOLVING CIVIL RIGHTS AND LIBERTIES

A. SACCO-VANZETTI

Appel, P. P. *The Sacco-Vanzetti Case: A Transcript*. 6 vols. Holt, 1928–29.

Burlingham, C. C., and B. Flexner, eds. *The Sacco-Vanzetti Case: Transcript of the Trial of Nicola Sacco and Bartolomeo Vanzetti in the Courts of Massachusetts and Subsequent Proceedings, 1920–1927*. Holt, 1928. (See also the six-volume set published by Michael Glazier, Inc., 1978, with Introductory essay by W. O. Douglas.)

Bush, M. *Ben Shahn: The Passion of Sacco and Vanzetti*. Syracuse University, 1969.

Ehrmann, H. B. *The Case That Will Not Die*. Little, Brown, 1969.

———. *The Untried Case: The Sacco-Vanzetti Case and the Morelli Gang*. 2d ed. Vanguard Press, 1960.

Feliciani, A., and G. Jackson. *The Sacco-Vanzetti Case: Twenty Years Later*. Privately published, 1947.

Felix, D. *Protest: Sacco-Vanzetti and the Intellectuals*. Indiana University, 1965.

Feuerlicht, R. S. *Justice Crucified: The Story of Sacco and Vanzetti*. McGraw-Hill, 1977.

Frankel, O. K. *The Sacco-Vanzetti Case*. Knopf, 1931.

Frankfurter, F. *The Case of Sacco and Vanzetti: A Critical Analysis for Lawyers and Laymen*. Little, Brown, 1927; rpt. 1961, 1962.

Frankfurter, M. D., and G. Jackson, eds. *The Letters of Sacco and Vanzetti*. Octagon, 1928.

Jackson, B. *The Black Flag: A Look Back at the Strange Case of Nicola Sacco and Bartolomeo Vanzetti*. Routledge & Kegan Paul, 1980.

Joughin, L., and E. M. Morgan. *The Legacy of Sacco and Vanzetti*. Rev. ed. Princeton University, 1978.

Lyons, E. *The Life and Death of Sacco and Vanzetti*. Never, 1927; rpt. Da Capo Press, 1970.

Montgomery, R. H. *Sacco-Vanzetti: The Murder and the Myth*. Devin-Adair, 1960.

Musmanno, M. S. *After Twelve Years: The Sacco-Vanzetti Case*. Knopf, 1939.

Porter, K. A. *The Never-Ending Wrong*. Atlantic Monthly Press–Little, Brown, 1977.

Russell, F. *Tragedy in Dedham—The Story of the Sacco-Vanzetti Case*. McGraw-Hill, 1962.

Stark, L. *We Saw It Happen*. Simon and Schuster, 1939.

Valenti, M. *Question of Guilt*. Paperback Library, 1966.

B. LOEB-LEOPOLD

Darrow, C. S. *The Story of My Life*. Scribner, 1958.

Leopold, N. F. *Life Plus 99 Years*. Doubleday, 1958.

McKernan, M. *The Amazing Crime and Trial of Leopold and Loeb*. New American Library, 1958.

Weinberg, A. *Attorney for the Damned*. Simon and Schuster, 1957.

C. JOHN PETER ZENGER

Alexander, J. *A Brief Narrative of the Case and Trial of John Peter Zenger*. Ed., S. N. Katz. Harvard University (Belknap Press), 1964.

Buranelli, V., ed. *The Trial of Peter Zenger*. New York University, 1957.

Galt, T. *Peter Zenger's Fight for Freedom*. Crowell, 1951.

James, A. *A Brief Narrative of the Case and Trial of Peter Zenger, Printer of the New York Weekly Journal*. Rev. ed. Harvard University, 1963.

Levy, L. W., ed. *Freedom of the Press from Zenger to Jefferson*, Bobbs-Merrill, 1967.

Rutherford, L. *John Peter Zenger*. Peter Smith, 1904.

D. JOHN SCOPES: "THE MONKEY TRIAL"

Darrow, C. S. *The Story of My Life*. Scribner, 1958.

De Camp, L. S. *The Great Monkey Trial*. Doubleday, 1968.

Ginger, R. *Six Days or Forever: Tennessee v. John Thomas Scopes*. Houghton Mifflin, 1960.

Grebstein, S. H., ed. *Monkey Trial: The State of Tennessee v. John Thomas Scopes*. New American Library (Signet), 1960.

Scopes, J. T., and J. Presley. *Center of the Storm: Memoirs of John T. Scopes*. Holt, Rinehart and Winston, 1967.

Tompkins, J. R., ed. *John Scopes and Others: D-Day at Dayton, Reflections on the Scopes Trial*. Louisiana State University, 1965.

Weinberg, A. *Attorney for the Damned*. Simon and Schuster, 1957.

E. LEE HARVEY OSWALD, JACK RUBY, AND THE WARREN COMMISSION: J.F.K.'S ASSASSINATION

Anson, R. S. *"They've Killed the President!": The Search for the Murderers of John F. Kennedy*. Bantam Books, 1976.

Belli, M. M. *Dallas Justice: The Real Story of Jack Ruby and His Trial*. McKay, 1964.

Epstein, E. J. *Inquest: The Warren Commission and the Establishment of Truth*. Viking Press, 1967.

Facts on File, comps. *Three Assassinations: The Deaths of John and Robert Kennedy and Martin Luther King*. Facts on File, 1977.

Kaplan, J., and J. R. Walz. *The Trial of Jack Ruby*. Macmillan, 1965.

Lane, M. *A Citizen's Dissent: Mark Lane Replies*. Holt, Rinehart and Winston, 1968.

————. *Rush to Judgment: A Critique of the Warren Commission Inquiry*. Holt, Rinehart and Winston, 1966.

Lipton, D. S. *Best Evidence: Disguise and Deception in the Assassination of John F. Kennedy*. Macmillan, 1981.

McDonald, H. C. *Appointment in Dallas*. Zebra Books, 1976.

Meagher, S. *Accessories After the Fact: The Warren Commission, the Authorities, and the Report*. Bobbs-Merrill, 1968.

Newman, A. H. *The Assassination of John F. Kennedy: The Reason Why*. Potter, 1970.

Sauvage, L. *The Oswald Affair: An Examination of the Contradictions and Omissions of the Warren Report*. World, 1966.

Thompson, J. *Six Seconds in Dallas: A Micro Study of the Kennedy Assassination*. Random House, 1968.

Warren Commission. *Official Warren Commission Report on the Assassination of President John F. Kennedy*. Doubleday, 1964.

Wills, G., and O. Demaris. *Jack Ruby*. New American Library, 1968.

F. JAMES EARL RAY

Blair, C., Jr. *The Strange Case of James Earl Ray: The Man Who Murdered Martin Luther King, Jr.* Bantam Books, 1969.

Facts on File, comps. *Three Assassinations: The Deaths of John and Robert Kennedy and Martin Luther King*. Facts on File, 1977.

Frank, G. *An American Death: The True Story of the Assassination of Dr. Martin Luther King, Jr. and the Greatest Manhunt of Our Time*. Doubleday, 1972.

McMillan, G. *The Making of an Assassin: The Life of James Earl Ray*. Little, Brown, 1976.

G. "CHICAGO SEVEN"

Epstein, J. *The Great Conspiracy Trial: An Essay on Law, Liberty and the Constitution*. Random House, 1970.

Lukas, J. A. *The Barnyard Epithet and Other Obscenities: Notes on the Chicago Conspiracy Trial*. Harper & Row (Perennial), 1970.

Schultz, J. *Motion Denied: A New Report on the Chicago Conspiracy Trial*. Morrow, 1973.

H. OTHERS

Alibrandi, T., with F. H. Armani. *Privileged Information*. Dodd, Mead, 1984.

Bailey, F. L. *For the Defense*. Atheneum, 1975.

————, and H. Aronson. *The Defense Never Rests*. Stein & Day, 1971.

Bannan, J. F., and R. S. Bannan. *Law, Morality and Vietnam: The Peace Militants and the Courts*. Indiana University, 1974.

Becker, T. L. *Political Trials*. Bobbs-Merrill, 1971.

Belknap, M., ed. *American Political Trials*. Greenwood Press, 1981.

Berrigan, D. *The Trial of the Catonsville Nine*. Beacon Press, 1970.

Boskin, J., and F. Krinsky. *The Oppenheimer Affair: A Political Play in Three Acts*. Glencoe, 1968.

Cartwright, G. *Blood Will Tell: The Murder Trials of T. Cullen Davis*. Harcourt Brace Jovanovich, 1979.

Chalmers, A. K. *They Shall Be Free*. Doubleday, 1961.

Chessman, C. *Cell 2455 Death Row*. Prentice-Hall, 1954.

Cochran, M. *Texas v. Davis*. Bobbs-Merrill, 1981.

Conlin, J. *American Anti-War Movements*. Glencoe, 1968.

Cooke, A. *A Generation on Trial: U.S.A. vs. Alger Hiss*. Penguin Books, 1963.

Cornell, J. *The Trial of Ezra Pound*. John Day, 1966.

Davidson, I. D., and R. Gehman. *The Jury Is Still Out*. Harper, 1959.

Dewey, J., and H. M. Kallen, eds. *The Bertrand Russell Case*. Da Capo Press, 1972.

Dickler, G. *Man on Trial*. Dell (Delta Books), 1964.

Dinnerstein, L. *The Leo Frank Case*. Columbia University, 1968.

Donovan, J. B. *Strangers on a Bridge: The Case of Colonel Abel*. Atheneum, 1964.

Epstein, E. Z. *Notorious Divorces*. Stuart, 1977.

Fay, T. F., comp. and ed. *The Spiro Agnew Case: The Investigative and Legal Documents*. Glazier, 1978.

Fineberg, S. A. *The Rosenberg Case: Fact and Fiction*. Oceana, 1953.

Flynn, E. G. *The Alderson Story: My Life as a Political Prisoner*. International Publishers, 1963.

Foner, P. S. *The Case of Joe Hill*. International Publishers, 1965.

Franklin, C. *World Family Trials*. Taplinger, 1966.

Frost, R. H. *The Monkey Case*. Stanford University, 1969.

Furneaux, R. *Courtroom USA: 1*. Penguin Books, 1964.

————. *Courtroom USA: 2*. Penguin Books, 1964.

Gentry, K. *Frame-Up*. Norton, 1967.

Golden, H. *A Little Girl Is Dead*. World, 1965.

Gross, K. *The Alice Crimmins Case*. Knopf, 1975.

Grover, D. H. *Debaters and Dynamiters: The Story of the Haywood Trial*. Oregon State University, 1964.

Hays, A. G. *Trial by Prejudice*. Da Capo Press, 1971.

Hersey, J. *The Algiers Motel Incident*. Knopf, 1968.

Heymann, F. B., and W. H. Kenety. *The Murder Trial of Wilbur Jackson: A Homicide in the Family*. West, 1975.

Hopkins, E. J. *What Happened in the Mooney Case*. Da Capo Press, 1970.

Hopkins, V. C. *Dred Scott's Case*. Fordham University, 1951.

Huie, W. B. *Three Lives for Mississippi*. W. C. C. Books, 1965.

Hunt, H. P. *The Case of Thomas J. Mooney and Warren K. Billings*. Da Capo Press, 1971.

Kinoy, A. *Rights on Trial: The Odyssey of a People's Lawyer*. Harvard University, 1983.

Kirkwood, J. *American Grotesque: An Account of the Clay Shaw-Jim Garrison Affairs*. Simon and Schuster, 1970.

Kunstler, W. M. *The Case for Courage*. Morrow, 1962.

————. *The Minister and the Choir Singer: The Hall-Mills Murder Case*. Morrow, 1964.

Lustgarten, E. *The Murder and the Trial*. Scribner, 1958.

Marke, J. J. *Vignettes of Legal History*. Rothman, 1965.

Martin, C. H. *The Angelo Herndon Case and Southern Justice*. Louisiana State University, 1976.

Meeropol, M., and R. Meeropol. *We Are Your Sons: The Legacy of Ethel and Julius Rosenberg*. Houghton Mifflin, 1975.

Michael Glazier, Inc., comps. *Conspiracy Trials in America, 1919–1953*. Glazier, 1979.

Nelson, J., and R. J. Ostrow. *The F.B.I. and the Berrigans: The Makings of a Conspiracy*. Coward-McCann, 1972.

Nizer, L. *The Implosion Conspiracy*. Doubleday, 1973.

————. *My Life in Court*. Doubleday, 1961.

O'Brien, F. W. *Was Justice Done? Historic Trials on Review*. Rockford College, 1971.

Patterson, H., and E. Conrad. *Scottsboro Boy*. Doubleday, 1950.

Prettyman, E. B., Jr. *Death and the Supreme Court*. Avon Books, 1964.

Radosh, R., and J. Milton. *The Rosenberg File: A Search for the Truth*. Holt, Rinehart and Winston, 1983.

Raines, J. C., ed. *Conspiracy: The Implications of the Harrisburg Trial for the Democratic Tradition*. Harper & Row, 1974.

Reitman, B. *Freedom on Trial: The Incredible Trial of Ralph Ginzburg*. Public Expression Council, 1966.

Reston, J., Jr. *The Innocence of Joan Little*. Times Books, 1977.

Reynolds, Q. *Courtroom*. Farrar, Straus, 1950.

Rosenberg, C. E. *The Trial of the Assassin Guiteau: Psychiatry and Law in the Gilded Age*. University of Chicago, 1968.

Ruben, W. A. *The Mark Fein Case*. Dial Press, 1966.

Salter, K. W. *The Pentagon Papers Trial*. Justa, 1975.

————. *The Trial of Inez Garcia*. Justa, 1977.

Schneir, W., and M. Schneir. *Invitation to an Inquest*. Pantheon Books, 1983.

————. *Invitation to an Inquest: Reopening the Rosenberg "Atom Spy" Case*. Penguin Books, 1973.

Schrag, P. *Test of Loyalty: Daniel Ellsberg and the Rituals of Secret Government*. Simon and Schuster, 1974.

Shultz, J. *Motion Will Be Denied: A New Report on the Chicago Conspiracy*. Morrow, 1973.

Sharp, M. P. *Was Justice Done? The Rosenberg-Sobell Case*. Monthly Review Press, 1956.

Smith, J. C. *Alger Hiss: The True Story*. Penguin Books, 1977.

Stern, P. M. *The Oppenheimer Case: Security on Trial.* Harper & Row, 1969.

Tiger, E., ed. *In Re Alger Hiss.* Hill & Wang, 1979.

Villasenor, V. *Jury: The People vs. Juan Corona.* Little, Brown, 1976.

Weinstein, A. *The Hiss-Chambers Case.* Knopf, 1978.

Westin, A. F., and B. Mahoney. *The Trial of Martin Luther King.* Crowell, 1976.

Witmer, L. *The Nearing Case.* Da Capo Press, 1970.

Zerman, M. B. *Call the Final Witness: The People vs. Darrell R. Mathes as Seen by the Eleventh Juror.* Harper & Row, 1976.

Zimroth, P. *Perversions of Justice: The Prosecutions and Acquittal of the Panther 21.* Viking Press, 1974.

Indices

I
General Subject Index

II
Name Index

III
Court Case Index